International Directory of
COMPANY
HISTORIES

International Directory of
COMPANY HISTORIES

VOLUME 102

Editor

Tina Grant

ST. JAMES PRESS
A part of Gale, Cengage Learning

Detroit • New York • San Francisco • New Haven, Conn • Waterville, Maine • London

GALE
CENGAGE Learning

International Directory of Company
Histories, Volume 102
Tina Grant, Editor

Project Editor: Miranda H. Ferrara

Editorial: Virgil Burton, Donna Craft,
Louise Gagné, Peggy Geeseman, Julie
Gough, Linda Hall, Sonya Hill, Keith
Jones, Lynn Pearce, Holly Selden,
Justine Ventimiglia

Production Technology Specialist: Mike
Weaver

Imaging and Multimedia: John Watkins

Composition and Electronic Prepress: Gary
Leach, Evi Seoud

Manufacturing: Rhonda Dover

Product Manager: Jenai Mynatt

For product information and technology assistance, contact us at
Gale Customer Support, 1-800-877-4253.
For permission to use material from this text or product,
submit all requests online at **www.cengage.com/permissions.**
Further permissions questions can be emailed to
permissionrequest@cengage.com

Gale
27500 Drake Rd.
Farmington Hills, MI, 48331-3535

LIBRARY OF CONGRESS CATALOG NUMBER 89-190943
ISBN-13: 978-1-55862-636-2
ISBN-10: 1-55862-636-0

This title is also available as an e-book
ISBN-13: 978-1-55862-765-9   ISBN-10: 1-55862-765-0
Contact your Gale, a part of Cengage Learning sales representative for
ordering information.

BRITISH LIBRARY CATALOGUING IN PUBLICATION DATA
International directory of company histories, Vol. 102
Tina Grant
33.87409

Printed in the United States of America
1 2 3 4 5 6 7 13 12 11 10 09

Contents

Preface

The St. James Press series *The International Directory of Company Histories* (*IDCH*) is intended for reference use by students, business people, librarians, historians, economists, investors, job candidates, and others who seek to learn more about the historical development of the world's most important companies. To date, *IDCH* has covered more than 10,100 companies in 102 volumes.

INCLUSION CRITERIA

Most companies chosen for inclusion in *IDCH* have achieved a minimum of US$25 million in annual sales and are leading influences in their industries or geographical locations. Companies may be publicly held, private, or nonprofit. State-owned companies that are important in their industries and that may operate much like public or private companies also are included. Wholly owned subsidiaries and divisions are profiled if they meet the requirements for inclusion. Entries on companies that have had major changes since they were last profiled may be selected for updating.

The *IDCH* series highlights 25% private and nonprofit companies, and features updated entries on approximately 35 companies per volume.

ENTRY FORMAT

Each entry begins with the company's legal name; the address of its headquarters; its telephone, toll-free, and fax numbers; and its web site. A statement of public, private, state, or parent ownership follows. A company with a legal name in both English and the language of its headquarters country is listed by the English name, with the native-language name in parentheses.

The company's founding or earliest incorporation date, the number of employees, and the most recent available sales figures follow. Sales figures are given in local currencies with equivalents in U.S. dollars. For some private companies, sales figures are estimates and indicated by the abbreviation *est*. The entry lists the exchanges on which the company's stock is traded and its ticker symbol, as well as the company's NAICS codes.

Entries generally contain a *Company Perspectives* box which provides a short summary of the company's mission, goals, and ideals; a *Key Dates* box highlighting milestones in the company's history; lists of *Principal Subsidiaries*, *Principal Divisions*, *Principal Operating Units*, *Principal Competitors*; and articles for *Further Reading*.

American spelling is used throughout *IDCH*, and the word "billion" is used in its U.S. sense of one thousand million.

SOURCES

Entries have been compiled from publicly accessible sources both in print and on the Internet such as general and academic periodicals, books, and annual reports, as well as material supplied by the companies themselves.

CUMULATIVE INDEXES

IDCH contains three indexes: the **Cumulative Index to Companies**, which provides an alphabetical index to companies profiled in the *IDCH* series, the **Index to Industries**, which allows researchers to locate companies by their principal industry, and the **Geographic Index**, which lists companies alphabetically by the country of their headquarters. The indexes are cumulative and specific instructions for using them are found immediately preceding each index.

SPECIAL TO THIS VOLUME

This volume of *IDCH* contains the series' first entry on a Ukrainian company, the National Bank of Ukraine, based in Kiev.

SUGGESTIONS WELCOME

Comments and suggestions from users of *IDCH* on any aspect of the product as well as suggestions for companies to be included or updated are cordially invited. Please write:

The Editor
International Directory of Company Histories
St. James Press
Gale, Cengage Learning
27500 Drake Rd.
Farmington Hills, Michigan 48331-3535

St. James Press does not endorse any of the companies or products mentioned in this series. Companies appearing in the *International Directory of Company Histories* were selected without reference to their wishes and have in no way endorsed their entries.

Notes on Contributors

Gerald E. Brennan
Writer and musician based in Germany.

M. L. Cohen
Novelist, business writer, and researcher living in Paris.

Ed Dinger
Writer and editor based in Bronx, New York.

Heidi Feldman
Writer and editor based in California.

Paul R. Greenland
Illinois-based writer and researcher; author of three books and former senior editor of a national business magazine; contributor to *The Encyclopedia of Chicago History*, *The Encyclopedia of Religion*, and the *Encyclopedia of American Industries*.

Robert Halasz
Former editor in chief of *World Progress* and *Funk & Wagnalls New Encyclopedia Yearbook*; author, *The U.S. Marines* (Millbrook Press, 1993).

Evelyn Hauser
Researcher, writer and marketing specialist based in Germany.

Carrie Rothburd
Writer and editor specializing in corporate profiles, academic texts, and academic journal articles.

Christina M. Stansell
Writer and editor based in Louisville, Kentucky.

Frank Uhle
Ann Arbor-based writer; movie projectionist, disc jockey, and staff member of *Psychotronic Video* magazine.

Ellen D. Wernick
Florida&hphyen;based writer and editor.

A. Woodward
Wisconsin-based writer.

List of Abbreviations

¥ Japanese yen
£ United Kingdom pound
$ United States dollar

A

AB Aktiebolag (Finland, Sweden)
AB Oy Aktiebolag Osakeyhtiot (Finland)
A.E. Anonimos Eteria (Greece)
AED Emirati dirham
AG Aktiengesellschaft (Austria, Germany, Switzerland, Liechtenstein)
aG auf Gegenseitigkeit (Austria, Germany)
A.m.b.a. Andelsselskab med begraenset ansvar (Denmark)
A.O. Anonim Ortaklari/Ortakligi (Turkey)
ApS Amparteselskab (Denmark)
ARS Argentine peso
A.S. Anonim Sirketi (Turkey)
A/S Aksjeselskap (Norway)
A/S Aktieselskab (Denmark, Sweden)
Ay Avoinyhtio (Finland)
ATS Austrian shilling
AUD Australian dollar
ApS Amparteselskab (Denmark)
Ay Avoinyhtio (Finland)

B

B.A. Buttengewone Aansprakeiijkheid (Netherlands)
BEF Belgian franc

BHD Bahraini dinar
Bhd. Berhad (Malaysia, Brunei)
BND Brunei dollar
BRL Brazilian real
B.V. Besloten Vennootschap (Belgium, Netherlands)

C

C.A. Compania Anonima (Ecuador, Venezuela)
CAD Canadian dollar
C. de R.L. Compania de Responsabilidad Limitada (Spain)
CEO Chief Executive Officer
CFO Chief Financial Officer
CHF Swiss franc
Cia. Companhia (Brazil, Portugal)
Cia. Compania (Latin America [except Brazil], Spain)
Cia. Compagnia (Italy)
Cie. Compagnie (Belgium, France, Luxembourg, Netherlands)
CIO Chief Information Officer
CLP Chilean peso
CNY Chinese yuan
Co. Company
COO Chief Operating Officer
Coop. Cooperative
COP Colombian peso
Corp. Corporation
C. por A. Compania por Acciones (Dominican Republic)
CPT Cuideachta Phoibi Theoranta

(Republic of Ireland)
CRL Companhia a Responsabilidao Limitida (Portugal, Spain)
C.V. Commanditaire Vennootschap (Netherlands, Belgium)
CZK Czech koruna

D

D&B Dunn & Bradstreet
DEM German deutsche mark
Div. Division (United States)
DKK Danish krone
DZD Algerian dinar

E

EC Exempt Company (Arab countries)
Edms. Bpk. Eiendoms Beperk (South Africa)
EEK Estonian Kroon
eG eingetragene Genossenschaft (Germany)
EGMBH Eingetragene Genossenschaft mit beschraenkter Haftung (Austria, Germany)
EGP Egyptian pound
Ek For Ekonomisk Forening (Sweden)
EP Empresa Portuguesa (Portugal)
E.P.E. Etema Pemorismenis Evthynis (Greece)
ESOP Employee Stock Options and Ownership
ESP Spanish peseta

Et(s). Etablissement(s) (Belgium, France, Luxembourg)
eV eingetragener Verein (Germany)
EUR euro

F
FIM Finnish markka
FRF French franc

G
G.I.E. Groupement d'Interet Economique (France)
gGmbH gemeinnutzige Gesellschaft mit beschraenkter Haftung (Austria, Germany, Switzerland)
G.I.E. Groupement d'Interet Economique (France)
GmbH Gesellschaft mit beschraenkter Haftung (Austria, Germany, Switzerland)
GRD Greek drachma
GWA Gewerbte Amt (Austria, Germany)

H
HB Handelsbolag (Sweden)
HF Hlutafelag (Iceland)
HKD Hong Kong dollar
HUF Hungarian forint

I
IDR Indonesian rupiah
IEP Irish pound
ILS new Israeli shekel
Inc. Incorporated (United States, Canada)
INR Indian rupee
IPO Initial Public Offering
I/S Interesentselskap (Norway)
I/S Interessentselskab (Denmark)
ISK Icelandic krona
ITL Italian lira

J
JMD Jamaican dollar
JOD Jordanian dinar

K
KB Kommanditbolag (Sweden)
KES Kenyan schilling
Kft Korlatolt Felelossegu Tarsasag (Hungary)
KG Kommanditgesellschaft (Austria, Germany, Switzerland)

KGaA Kommanditgesellschaft auf Aktien (Austria, Germany, Switzerland)
KK Kabushiki Kaisha (Japan)
KPW North Korean won
KRW South Korean won
K/S Kommanditselskab (Denmark)
K/S Kommandittselskap (Norway)
KWD Kuwaiti dinar
Ky Kommandiitiyhtio (Finland)

L
LBO Leveraged Buyout
Lda. Limitada (Spain)
L.L.C. Limited Liability Company (Arab countries, Egypt, Greece, United States)
L.L.P. Limited Liability Partnership (United States)
L.P. Limited Partnership (Canada, South Africa, United Kingdom, United States)
Ltd. Limited
Ltda. Limitada (Brazil, Portugal)
Ltee. Limitee (Canada, France)
LUF Luxembourg franc

M
mbH mit beschraenkter Haftung (Austria, Germany)
Mij. Maatschappij (Netherlands)
MUR Mauritian rupee
MXN Mexican peso
MYR Malaysian ringgit

N
N.A. National Association (United States)
NGN Nigerian naira
NLG Netherlands guilder
NOK Norwegian krone
N.V. Naamloze Vennootschap (Belgium, Netherlands)
NZD New Zealand dollar

O
OAO Otkrytoe Aktsionernoe Obshchestve (Russia)
OHG Offene Handelsgesellschaft (Austria, Germany, Switzerland)
OMR Omani rial
OOO Obschestvo s Ogranichennoi Otvetstvennostiu (Russia)
OOUR Osnova Organizacija

Udruzenog Rada (Yugoslavia)
Oy Osakeyhtî (Finland)

P
P.C. Private Corp. (United States)
PEN Peruvian Nuevo Sol
PHP Philippine peso
PKR Pakistani rupee
P/L Part Lag (Norway)
PLC Public Limited Co. (United Kingdom, Ireland)
P.L.L.C. Professional Limited Liability Corporation (United States)
PLN Polish zloty
P.T. Perusahaan/Perseroan Terbatas (Indonesia)
PTE Portuguese escudo
Pte. Private (Singapore)
Pty. Proprietary (Australia, South Africa, United Kingdom)
Pvt. Private (India, Zimbabwe)
PVBA Personen Vennootschap met Beperkte Aansprakelijkheid (Belgium)
PYG Paraguay guarani

Q
QAR Qatar riyal

R
REIT Real Estate Investment Trust
RMB Chinese renminbi
Rt Reszvenytarsasag (Hungary)
RUB Russian ruble

S
S.A. Société Anonyme (Arab countries, Belgium, France, Jordan, Luxembourg, Switzerland)
S.A. Sociedad Anónima (Latin America [except Brazil], Spain, Mexico)
S.A. Sociedades Anônimas (Brazil, Portugal)
SAA Societe Anonyme Arabienne (Arab countries)
S.A.B. de C.V. Sociedad Anónima Bursátil de Capital Variable (Mexico)
S.A.C. Sociedad Anonima Comercial (Latin America [except Brazil])
S.A.C.I. Sociedad Anonima Comercial e Industrial (Latin America [except Brazil])

S.A.C.I.y.F. Sociedad Anonima Comercial e Industrial y Financiera (Latin America [except Brazil])

S.A. de C.V. Sociedad Anonima de Capital Variable (Mexico)

SAK Societe Anonyme Kuweitienne (Arab countries)

SAL Societe Anonyme Libanaise (Arab countries)

SAO Societe Anonyme Omanienne (Arab countries)

SAQ Societe Anonyme Qatarienne (Arab countries)

SAR Saudi riyal

S.A.R.L. Sociedade Anonima de Responsabilidade Limitada (Brazil, Portugal)

S.A.R.L. Société à Responsabilité Limitée (France, Belgium, Luxembourg)

S.A.S. Societá in Accomandita Semplice (Italy)

S.A.S. Societe Anonyme Syrienne (Arab countries)

S.C. Societe en Commandite (Belgium, France, Luxembourg)

S.C.A. Societe Cooperativa Agricole (France, Italy, Luxembourg)

S.C.I. Sociedad Cooperativa Ilimitada (Spain)

S.C.L. Sociedad Cooperativa Limitada (Spain)

S.C.R.L. Societe Cooperative a Responsabilite Limitee (Belgium)

Sdn. Bhd. Sendirian Berhad (Malaysia)

SEK Swedish krona

SGD Singapore dollar

S.L. Sociedad Limitada (Latin America [except Brazil], Portugal, Spain)

S/L Salgslag (Norway)

S.N.C. Société en Nom Collectif (France)

Soc. Sociedad (Latin America [except Brazil], Spain)

Soc. Sociedade (Brazil, Portugal)

Soc. Societa (Italy)

S.p.A. Società per Azioni (Italy)

Sp. z.o.o. Spółka z ograniczona odpowiedzialnoscia (Poland)

S.R.L. Sociedad de Responsabilidad Limitada (Spain, Mexico, Latin America [except Brazil])

S.R.L. Società a Responsabilità Limitata (Italy)

S.R.O. Spolecnost s Rucenim Omezenym (Czechoslovakia

S.S.K. Sherkate Sahami Khass (Iran)

Ste. Societe (France, Belgium, Luxembourg, Switzerland)

Ste. Cve. Societe Cooperative (Belgium)

S.V. Samemwerkende Vennootschap (Belgium)

S.Z.R.L. Societe Zairoise a Responsabilite Limitee (Zaire)

T

THB Thai baht

TND Tunisian dinar

TRL Turkish lira

TWD new Taiwan dollar

U

U.A. Uitgesloten Aansporakeiijkheid (Netherlands)

u.p.a. utan personligt ansvar (Sweden)

V

VAG Verein der Arbeitgeber (Austria, Germany)

VEB Venezuelan bolivar

VERTR Vertriebs (Austria, Germany)

VND Vietnamese dong

V.O.f. Vennootschap onder firma (Netherlands)

VVAG Versicherungsverein auf Gegenseitigkeit (Austria, Germany)

W–Z

WA Wettelika Aansprakalikhaed (Netherlands)

WLL With Limited Liability (Bahrain, Kuwait, Qatar, Saudi Arabia)

YK Yugen Kaisha (Japan)

ZAO Zakrytoe Aktsionernoe Obshchestve (Russia)

ZAR South African rand

ZMK Zambian kwacha

ZWD Zimbabwean dollar

Alliance Laundry
Holdings LLC

119 Shepard Street
Ripon, Wisconsin 54971
U.S.A.
Telephone: (920) 748-3121
Fax: (920) 748-4334
Web site: http://www.comlaundry.com

Private Company
Incorporated: 1908 as Barlow and Seelig Manufacturing
    Company
Employees: 1,650
Sales: $443.3 million (2007)
NAICS: 333312 Laundry Machinery and Equipment
    (Except Household-Type) Manufacturing; 335224
    Laundry Equipment, Household-Type, Manu-
    facturing

■ ■ ■

Alliance Commercial Laundry Holdings LLC is the parent company of Alliance Laundry Systems LLC, the leading manufacturer of commercial laundry equipment in the United States. The company, headquartered in Ripon, Wisconsin, was formerly known as Speed Queen. Speed Queen remains its most prominent brand of washers and dryers. Alliance Laundry also manufactures laundry equipment under the brand names Cissell, Huebsch, Ipso, and UniMac. Its products are found in laundromats, apartment buildings, college dormitories, and other commercial laundry operations.

Manufacturing is done at its large plant in Ripon. Alliance also owns a Belgian subsidiary, Laundry Systems Group NV, which operates two European manufacturing plants. Long a division of first McGraw-Edison and then Raytheon, Alliance Laundry was spun off as a private company in 1998. Since 2004 it has been owned by Teachers' Private Capital, a Toronto-based private-equity firm.

SMALL START IN THE UPPER MIDWEST

The company long known as Speed Queen got its start in 1908 when two business partners in the little town of Ripon, Wisconsin, bought some washing machines. Joseph Barlow had been a hardware dealer, and John Seelig had made his living selling tombstones. They went into business as Barlow and Seelig Manufacturing Company. Their initial venture was fueled with some hand-powered washers that they purchased from a manufacturer in Kansas City. Seelig had an aptitude for mechanics, and he was convinced that he could improve the design of the washers. So in 1908 Barlow and Seelig purchased the manufacturing rights to the washers for $2,000 and set up a tiny factory in a tin shop behind their hardware store.

The Kansas City appliance maker licensed the pair to sell only in Wisconsin and in Michigan's Upper Peninsula at first. The washers, which sold under the name White Cloud, were a big hit. So Barlow and Seelig purchased the patents to the machines from the Kansas City company. This allowed them to sell White Cloud without geographic limitations. They moved to bigger spaces several times during the next several years and continued to update and improve the design of the washing machines.

In 1911 the company introduced its first electric washers. It continued to make and sell hand-powered machines as well. In 1912 Barlow and Seelig broke ground on a new factory. The present-day manufacturing plant occupies the same site, although the facility has expanded many times.

Barlow and Seelig introduced many improvements to the washers. Business boomed through the 1920s. The brand name White Cloud gave way to The Big Three during those years. In 1927 Barlow and Seelig retired from the business they had founded. The next year the company introduced the brand name Speed Queen. This brand became so popular that the company was renamed Speed Queen in 1949.

WEATHERING THE GREAT DEPRESSION

In the meantime the Great Depression flattened many U.S. businesses and record numbers of people were unemployed. Ripon, Wisconsin, however, was one of the few bright spots during the dreary 1930s. While sales dropped sharply after 1929 for many businesses, Barlow and Seelig continued to expand. The company produced 18,000 washers a year in 1929, 1930, and 1931.

Sales continued to climb, hitting a record in 1936. By then the company was manufacturing 100,000 washers annually, a steep increase from the beginning of the decade. Speed Queen's maker competed with some 30 to 40 washer manufacturers in the United States. It had been somewhere near the bottom of the pack at the start of the Depression, but it was one of the top five manufacturers by the close of the decade.

During World War II the company was asked to convert its production to help the military. Barlow and Seelig ceased making washers between 1942 and 1946, instead turning out airplane parts and 20mm shells. The company resumed its former line of business in 1946, and also opened a new factory in nearby Omro, Wisconsin. Barlow and Seelig opened a third plant the next year, in Wautoma, Wisconsin.

UNDER THE SPEED QUEEN NAME

Barlow and Seelig had been famous for its Speed Queen brand since 1928. To acknowledge its principal product, the company changed its name to Speed Queen Corporation in 1949. Facilities expanded during the early postwar years. Speed Queen also began manufacturing clothes dryers. This was a natural companion for its washer line.

Speed Queen updated and expanded its Ripon plant several more times during the 1950s and 1960s. It brought out a line of paired automatic washers and dryers in 1953. In 1957 the company ventured into sales of commercial washers and dryers. This later became what Speed Queen was best known for. The company also made dry cleaning equipment beginning in the 1960s. A plant for dry cleaning machine manufacturing was opened in Juneau, Wisconsin, in 1965.

The company underwent a major management change in 1956 when it merged with the McGraw Electric Company. By the end of 1956 McGraw had itself merged with Thomas A. Edison, Inc. Speed Queen Corporation became the Speed Queen Division of McGraw-Edison Company. McGraw-Edison was a *Fortune* 500 company with interests in electrical power as well as electrical appliances. It had roughly 30 divisions and subsidiaries, as well as almost 60 manufacturing plants. McGraw-Edison had interests throughout North America, and by the early 1970s also had at least one manufacturing plant in Europe.

Speed Queen's expansion continued under McGraw-Edison. It added capacity, modernized its plants, and developed a wide distribution network. By the early 1970s Speed Queen laundry equipment was sold as far away as Tahiti, and the company had markets across Europe, as well as in Japan, Saudi Arabia, and South Africa. Speed Queen operated some 200 service centers in the United States and had sales offices in major cities across the country. The brand began advertising on television in 1971. Speed Queen was a household name, competing with laundry lines from Sears, General Electric, Westinghouse, and General Motors.

OWNERSHIP CHANGES AGAIN IN 1979

Although Speed Queen retained its name and its headquarters in Ripon, from 1956 to 1979 it was only one cog in a bigger conglomerate of electric power and appliance brands and companies. McGraw-Edison sold the Speed Queen division to another conglomerate, Raytheon, in 1979. Raytheon, based in Lexington, Massachusetts, had more disparate interests than McGraw-

KEY DATES

1908: Barlow and Seelig Manufacturing Company is founded.
1928: The company introduces the Speed Queen brand.
1949: Barlow and Seelig becomes the Speed Queen Corporation.
1956: Speed Queen is acquired by McGraw Electric, which becomes McGraw-Edison.
1979: McGraw-Edison sells the Speed Queen division to Raytheon.
1989: The Raytheon Appliance Group moves its headquarters to Amana, Iowa.
1998: Raytheon divests Speed Queen to a private-equity firm; the company's name is changed to Alliance Laundry.
2004: Teachers' Private Capital buys Alliance Laundry.

Edison. Its principal products included missiles, military aircraft, and military electronics.

Beginning in the 1960s, Raytheon had diversified into commercial products as well. It owned Amana, a major manufacturer of refrigerators, and had a host of other non-military interests. When Raytheon acquired Speed Queen, it combined the laundry appliance maker with Amana and with Caloric, a leading brand of stoves. These three formed Raytheon's appliance division.

Speed Queen's new owners continued to add to the Ripon manufacturing plant in the 1980s. Speed Queen also came out with new niche laundry equipment, such as small stacked washer and dryer units. Although it was innovative, Speed Queen did not deviate from its focus on laundry, which represented more than 20 percent of the total home appliance market. The laundry equipment market was still gradually expanding in the 1980s, so there was plenty of opportunity there without moving into other appliances.

Speed Queen was doing very well, with sales in the mid-1980s rising in double-digits, while the market as a whole grew only 1 percent to 5 percent. In its first five years with Raytheon, Speed Queen also doubled its share of the total laundry equipment market. Competitors Whirlpool and Maytag led the industry, but Speed Queen held an estimated 5 percent of the market by the mid-to-late 1980s.

DECADE OF CHANGE IN RAYTHEON'S APPLIANCE DIVISION

At its 80th anniversary in 1988 Speed Queen reiterated that laundry was its only line of business. That is, it had no plans to extend its brand into refrigerators and stoves, like its competitor General Electric. However, through Raytheon, Speed Queen was bound up with refrigerator-maker Amana and stove-maker Caloric, along with several other brands comprising Raytheon's appliance division. Raytheon began making changes to its appliance division in the late 1980s, and continued to make adjustments through the early 1990s. These would eventually affect Speed Queen's place in the appliance market.

In 1989, under new leadership for Raytheon's appliance group, the division headquarters moved from Lexington, Massachusetts, to Amana, Iowa. By this time the Amana name was associated with both the Amana refrigerator and the Radarange microwave oven. Caloric, which made stoves, had been considered something of a liability in that market. Raytheon closed Caloric's Topton, Pennsylvania, headquarters in the early 1990s, and some Caloric executives were let go. By 1993 sales and marketing of all of Raytheon's appliance brands had been consolidated in Amana.

Raytheon then took on the consolidation of service and distribution of its appliance brands. These changes did not come without snags. Yet Raytheon had high hopes for its appliance division. Sales of its military goods were falling, and the company aimed to make up the difference with significant growth in its commercial sectors. In 1992, Raytheon announced a goal of 60 percent growth in its appliance unit over the ensuing five years.

SET LOOSE IN 1998

Expectations established at the beginning of the decade changed considerably by the end of the 1990s. Raytheon decided to focus on its core business of military equipment, making two expensive acquisitions in the defense contracting industry. In 1997 Raytheon sold most of its appliance group to investment firm Goodman Holding for $550 million. Six months later Raytheon sold what was left of Speed Queen to another private investment firm. Bain Capital Inc. paid $358 million for Raytheon's commercial laundry business, which included Speed Queen's commercial lines and the brands Unimac and Huebsch. Because of a noncompete agreement with other members of Raytheon's appliance group, Speed Queen was to stay out of the home laundry market for five years.

The new commercial laundry equipment company took the name Alliance Laundry Systems LLC. It was run by former executives from Raytheon's appliance division and managers at its new parent, Bain Capital. The new company was the largest commercial laundry machine maker in the United States. Along with the large plant in Ripon, Alliance also operated plants in Marianna, Florida, and in Madisonville, Kentucky.

NEW OWNER IN 2004

The noncompete agreement expired in 2004, and Alliance Laundry announced that it would begin making washers and dryers for the residential market in the fall of that year. State assistance allowed it to add jobs at its plant in Ripon. The year 2004 was to be a turnaround year for the company. It embarked on plans to sell stock to the public, which would allow it to pay down debt and buy back some of the commercial laundry business still controlled by Raytheon.

However, instead of a traditional initial public offering (IPO), Alliance proposed a more complicated operation that had recently been approved by the Securities and Exchange Commission. This new kind of offering allowed a company to sell so-called income deposit securities, a mix of common stock and debt. The offering was to raise $375 million.

After about six months of negotiation, however, Alliance canceled its public offering. What happened instead was that another private-equity firm, Teachers' Private Capital, paid $450 million for Alliance. Teachers' was the private-equity branch of the Ontario Teachers' Pension Plan, which owned part or all of more than 100 companies, with total holdings of some $5.5 billion. Teachers' was interested in low-growth, high-cash-flow companies. It approached Alliance when other investors failed to appear interested in the nontraditional IPO.

Alliance announced a major expansion in Ripon in advance of the change of ownership. The next year it added another 250 jobs at the Ripon plant and closed down its factory in Marianna, Florida. It closed plants in Ohio and Kentucky, too, concentrating all its manufacturing in Wisconsin. By 2006, Alliance Laundry was the largest private employer in the town of Ripon. Revenue for 2006 reached $366 million, and sales were expected to grow. Alliance had about 40 percent of the commercial laundry business, making it far bigger than its nearest competitor.

STRATEGY FOR STEADY GROWTH

The company planned to make small acquisitions, and to count on a small but steady increase in the demand for commercial laundry equipment. Population growth in the low-to-middle income segment promised more need for coin-operated laundries. The middle of the first decade of the 2000s also saw the introduction of a new type of laundromat, one with additional services such as dry cleaning and tailoring, shipping and mailing, built on a much bigger format than older laundries. Alliance was also able to take advantage of the growing demand for energy-efficient equipment. It could promise customers significant savings on electricity and water by delivering modern, efficient machines.

Alliance Laundry also moved into European markets in 2007, with its purchase of a Belgian company known as Laundry System Group NV. The acquisition brought Alliance two manufacturing plants in Europe. Europe was Alliance's strongest market, made especially so by the weakness of the American dollar.

In the decade after leaving Raytheon, the former Speed Queen had become a revitalized company. Its focus was solely on laundry. It led the commercial laundry equipment market, holding onto the promise of slow growth in its domestic market, while venturing into higher growth markets abroad. After being a cog in two different large conglomerates, Alliance had resettled in its old headquarters in Ripon, Wisconsin. It had come back to its beginnings, but was nevertheless striking out in new directions, with new markets and innovative products.

A. Woodward

PRINCIPAL COMPETITORS

AB Electrolux; Whirlpool Corporation; Continental Girbau, Inc.

FURTHER READING

"Alliance Laundry Systems Completes Acquisition," *Business Wire*, May 5, 1998.

Barrett, Rick, "Coming Out of a Spin Cycle," *Milwaukee Journal Sentinel*, May 13, 2007.

———, "Ripon, Wis.-based Maker of Speed Queen Washers to Bring Machines Back," *Milwaukee Journal Sentinel*, October 16, 2004.

Beatty, Gerry, "More Consolidation at Raytheon," *HFD*, October 14, 1991, p. 150.

———, "Raytheon Hails Appliance Group," *HFD*, June 7, 1993, pp. 110, 122.

———, "Raytheon Still Making Changes," *HFD*, November 4, 1991, p. 119.

Beatty, Gerry, and David Jones, "Speed Queen Restructures Staff," *HFD*, March 12, 1990, p. 127.

"Company News: Raytheon in $358 Million Deal to Sell Laundry Business," *New York Times,* February 24, 1998.

Content, Thomas, "Speed Queen to Close Washer-Dryer Plant in Florida, Move Jobs to Ripon," *Milwaukee Journal Sentinel,* October 15, 2005.

———, "Wisconsin Washer, Dryer Maker Plans IPO to Raise $375 Million," *Milwaukee Journal Sentinel,* April 14, 2004.

DuPont, Ted, "Speed Queen Refines Strategy," *HFD,* October 10, 1988, p. 238.

———, "Speed Queen Remains Laundry Specialist," *HFD,* March 17, 1986, p. 78.

"Raytheon to Unload Commercial Laundry Enterprise," *HFN,* March 2, 1998, p. 42.

"Speed Queen Hears from Buyers," *Wisconsin Division of Economic Development Newsletter,* February 1971, pp. 1, 4.

"Speed Queen Marks 80 Years," *Oshkosh (Wisc.) Northwestern,* February 2, 1978.

Stevenson, Richard W., "Raytheon Is Looking Beyond the Pentagon," *New York Times,* February 20, 1991.

This Is a Speed Queen, Ripon, Wisc.: McGraw-Edison, 1972.

"Toronto Investors Buy Ripon, Wis., Maker of Speed Queen Washing Machines," *Milwaukee Journal Sentinel,* December 9, 2004.

AMAG Group

Utoquai 49
Zurich, CH-8008
Switzerland
Telephone: (41 44) 269-5353
Fax: (41 44) 269-5363
Web site: http://www.amag.ch

Private Company
Incorporated: 1945 as Neue AMAG Automobil- und
Motoren AG
Employees: 4,689 (2009)
Sales: CHF 4.2 billion ($4.4 billion) (2008)
NAICS: 441110 New Car Dealers; 441120 Used Car
Dealers; 532112 Passenger Car Leasing; 812930
Parking Lots and Garages

■ ■ ■

AMAG Group is Switzerland's number one new car
dealer. The group's main subsidiary, AMAG Automobil-
und Motoren AG, is the country's largest importer of
automobiles, based on contracts with European auto
manufacturers Volkswagen, Audi, SEAT, and Škoda.
Headquartered in Zurich, AMAG Automobil- und Motoren operates some 80 car dealerships throughout
Switzerland and has additional contracts with roughly
1,000 independent car dealers and automotive service
providers in the country. AMAG's used car sales
subsidiary, ROC AG, runs five so-called Occasion
Drive-Ins. AMAG's leasing arm AMAG Leasing AG offers financing to auto buyers. AMAG Service AG runs
six centrally located public parking garages in Zurich

and one in Bern and provides rental cars under a license
for the markets Switzerland and Liechtenstein with
Volkswagen-owned rental car company Europcar
International. AMAG Group is owned and controlled
through Careal Holding AG by company founder
Walter Haefner and his son Martin Haefner.

IMPORTING BRITISH AND
AMERICAN AUTOMOBILES AFTER
WORLD WAR II

In 1928 entrepreneur Jacques Tschudi founded AMAG
Automobil- und Motoren AG, a Chrysler car dealership
in Zurich, Switzerland. Tschudi sold the firm in 1939.
When the company went bankrupt in spring 1944,
entrepreneur Walter Haefner became a fiduciary. On
January 3, 1945, about three months before World War
II ended, Haefner founded a new company, Neue
AMAG Automobil- und Motoren AG. Only a few
months later, in August 1945, Haefner acquired his first
postwar customer, the English Standard Motor
Company.

After the import contract had been signed, the first
delivery of ten of Standard Motor's "Standard" sedans
arrived in Zurich in January 1946. Delivery in those
days meant that the new vehicles were driven across
Western Europe to Switzerland, where the snowed-in
roads often made for a challenging ride, and road accidents were not uncommon. In addition to the
Standard model, AMAG also imported a number of
Standard's sister brand Triumph, including sedans and
sports cars that were displayed in the company's spa-
cious showroom in Zurich's city center.

In late 1946 AMAG signed additional import contracts with American automakers for three U.S. brands: Chrysler, Plymouth, and Dodge. In the following years AMAG quickly expanded its network of dealerships and prospered as the demand for passenger cars rose rapidly in Switzerland. After only 14 months, the company proudly announced in April 1947 that the 1,000th Standard had been sold to an AMAG customer. The first American models which were featured in AMAG's showroom included Chrysler's "Windsor" and Plymouth's "Special De Luxe" model.

SUSTAINED SUCCESS WITH VOLKSWAGEN AND IN-HOUSE ASSEMBLY

On April 29, 1948, AMAG signed an import contract with Volkswagen—one of the most important milestones in the company's history. The partnership with the German auto manufacturer was the basis for AMAG's commercial success for many decades to come. In the eight months before the end of 1948 the company sold no less than 1,380 Volkswagen "Bugs." Swiss customers' initial skepticism regarding the unusual and compact design was soon overcome and the VW Bug became a bestseller, resulting in quickly rising sales figures for AMAG.

As the company's business volume expanded quickly during the late 1940s, AMAG made another important decision—to import components of passenger cars and assemble them in-house. In 1947 AMAG purchased the site of a former cement factory in Schinznach-Bad, a city about 20 miles northwest of Zurich, and set up an automobile assembly line there, along with a new office building that became the company's new headquarters. In 1949 AMAG's newly founded car assembly subsidiary Automontage Schinznach AG (ASAG) started assembling the first Plymouth and Standard sedans.

In 1954 AMAG sold the 10,000th VW Bug in Switzerland. In addition to the popular compact car, the

company also sold Volkswagen's compact transporters, minivan buses, and station wagons, which had been first introduced in the early 1950s and were very popular. During the 1950s AMAG also began to sell two more exclusive Volkswagen models developed and manufactured by Wilhelm Karmann, a German automotive manufacturing and engineering firm: the Volkswagen Bug convertible and the Karmann Ghia, a sassy two-seat sports car version of the Volkswagen Bug that was introduced as the "Volkswagen Bug in Sunday dress" in 1955.

The VW Karmann Ghia convertible was the only Volkswagen model assembled at AMAG's assembly plant in Schinznach-Bad, where Dodge and Plymouth vehicles from U.S. company Chrysler were also assembled. The elegant American designs were very popular in Switzerland and the carefully assembled and meticulously tested cars put out by "Montage Suisse," as ASAG's end products were marketed, earned a reputation for high solidity and craftsmanship.

A short-lived but nonetheless noteworthy AMAG project was the introduction of the so-called "ami-Roller" in 1949. Leaping on the popular trend for motor scooters, the company developed its own "pop version." Equipped with small wheels and a large gas tank, the moderately priced ami-Roller could drive 600 kilometers on one tank of gasoline and came in three bright colors—red, green, and blue. Between 1949 and 1952 AMAG sold about 4,500 ami-Rollers which were even exported to France and England. In 1953, however, the business was sold to a firm in England.

STAYING IN THE RACE WITH PORSCHE AND EXTENSIVE SERVICE NETWORK

Another historic step for AMAG was the import contract with German luxury car manufacturer Porsche that was sealed shortly after the 1951 Geneva Automobile Salon trade show. In the same year AMAG sold the first 78 of the legendary "Porsche 356" model in Switzerland. The company also began to combine Porsche's hard-earned image of building high-performance sports cars that are reliable and durable with AMAG's own marketing campaigns.

In the early 1950s AMAG's sales director, Hans Stanek, who was also a passionate driver, participated in several popular car races in Switzerland, on round tracks or on mountain roads, driving a racing car made by Porsche. In 1957, six years after the cooperation with Porsche had started, Stanek, by then AMAG's CEO, received the keys for the 1,000th imported sports car from CEO Ferdinand Porsche.

KEY DATES

1945: Walter Haefner founds Neue AMAG Automobil- und Motoren AG in Zurich.

1948: AMAG signs an import contract with Volkswagen.

1951: An import contract with German sports car manufacturer Porsche is sealed.

1957: AMAG's brand-new warehouse complex for spare parts opens in Buchs.

1965: A new distribution center in Birrfeld offers space for up to 8,000 imported vehicles.

1967: The company signs an import contract with Audi.

1980: AMAG's financing arm AMAG Leasing AG is founded.

1984: Spancar Automobile AG is set up to sell vehicles from Spanish automaker SEAT.

1989: AMAG imports the one millionth Volkswagen into Switzerland.

1992: AMAG's new subsidiary, Amoda Automobile AG, begins to sell Škoda vehicles.

1999: Spancar Automobile AG and Amoda Automobile AG are merged with AMAG.

2006: Porsche cancels the import contract with AMAG effective May 31, 2008.

Within a short time AMAG's network of company-managed and independent car dealerships in Switzerland had grown to about 30, most of them located centrally or at highly frequented routes at the outskirts or in the country's largest and most frequented cities, including Zurich, Geneva, Bern, Biel, and St. Gallen. One major highlight was a newly built complex on the edge of Zurich that combined a large showroom, a service station, and a then not-well-known gourmet restaurant called Mövenpick, allowing customers to watch their car being serviced while they had lunch. Along with opening new showrooms across the country, AMAG established a network of state-of-the-art service stations offering anything from gasoline and spare parts to testing, maintenance, and repair services.

Another important milestone in AMAG's history was the construction of a new warehouse complex for spare parts in the late 1950s. Until the end of 1956 AMAG had delivered spare parts to its associated dealerships from the company's warehouse in Schinznach-Bad. When AMAG ran out of space there, company management decided to invest in a large new central spare parts warehouse that was built on a new site in Buchs, about 20 miles east of Zurich. Equipped with the latest warehouse logistics, it became the largest and most modern warehouse of its kind in Switzerland.

FURTHER EXPANSION

AMAG continued to prosper beyond the postwar economic boom, mainly due to the unceasing popularity of Volkswagen and Porsche vehicles in Switzerland. At the same time, AMAG made some important strategic decisions that had a lasting impact on the company's market position. As motorization increased rapidly in Switzerland during the 1960s, AMAG replaced smaller branches with large sales and service centers that were better able to handle the growing business volume. As the VW Bugs arrived on new special transporters that carried eight at a time instead of two on one truck, AMAG soon needed to expand its storage space for newly arrived vehicles.

A brand-new parking space was built in Birrfeld near Schinznach-Bad, located at the crossroads of the North-South freeway and the one that went from east to west in Switzerland. The new facility, including one of the country's largest parking structures, provided room for up to 8,000 vehicles. At the same time AMAG expanded and modernized its central spare parts warehouse in Buchs in several steps during the 1960s. In 1972 the warehouse was given a second floor and an adjunct office building.

In the mid-1960s AMAG pioneered the "Drive-In" sales concept, popular in the United States, in Switzerland. Located at the highly traveled freeway connecting Zurich with Kloten airport, AMAG's "Occasions-Drive-In-Center" for used cars was the first of its kind in the whole country. A new chapter began for AMAG in 1967 when the company signed an import contract with German automaker Auto Union—better known as Audi—after Volkswagen had acquired the company three years earlier. After the merger of Auto Union with NSU Motorenwerke, another German car manufacturer acquired by Volkswagen in 1969, AMAG also started carrying NSU models in 1970. While Audi soon emerged as one of the top ten car brands in Switzerland, the production of NSU vehicles was discontinued in 1977.

After 24 years, in which more than 29,000 automobiles such as the Plymouth Valiant, Dodge Dart, De Soto, Studebaker, Barracuda, and VW Karmann-Ghia had been assembled in Schinznach-Bad, AMAG closed its "Montage Suisse" unit in 1972. During the 1970s the company continued to add large, modern sales and service units to its network that were run increasingly by independent franchisers. New AMAG franchise branches opened in fast-growing suburban areas and tourist centers such as Cham, Bachenbülach, Bellizona, Dulliken, Horgen, Jona, Kloten, Lausanne, Lucerne, Schaffhausen, and Volketswil.

CONTINUED SUCCESS WITH VOLKSWAGEN AND NEW VW AFFILIATES

AMAG's continued success in the 1980s was closely linked to the company's partnership with Volkswagen. After the 250,000th imported VW Bug in 1969 proved once again the unprecedented popularity of the legendary German car in Switzerland, the country's pioneering environmental laws, setting much stricter limits for exhaust and noise emissions in 1983, put a sudden end to AMAG's imports of the VW Bug. However, Volkswagen's success in the Alpine nation continued with the Golf model, which by 1975 had become the country's most popular, best-selling passenger car.

By 1978 the number of basic VW models had grown to five—Polo, Golf, Jetta, Scirocco, and Passat—all of which came in different variations in terms of engine performance, body design and interior, and equipment. The number of other vehicle models, including pickup trucks, transporters and minivans, had also grown significantly. In addition, a number of best-selling Audi and Porsche models contributed to AMAG's continuously increasing sales figures in the 1980s, which in 1985 amounted to over CHF 1.8 billion.

The year 1980 marked the end of an era for AMAG when the company discontinued the import of Chrysler automobiles. Four years later AMAG signed a new contract for the import of cars made by SEAT, after this Spanish auto manufacturer had signed an agreement with Volkswagen on cooperation, technical support, and licensing in 1982. In mid-1984 AMAG established a new subsidiary, SPANCAR Automobile AG, for importing and selling SEAT vehicles.

Another new subsidiary, AMODA Automobile AG, was founded in 1992 for the import of Škoda automobiles after Volkswagen had signed a cooperation agreement with the leading Czech car manufacturer in 1991. Headquartered in Zurich, AMODA began setting up separate Škoda sales outlets in the early 1992, such as in Lucerne and Bern. The same concept applied to the distribution of SEAT vehicles. In 1995, the year when AMAG celebrated its 50th anniversary, the company was by far Switzerland's number one auto importer.

NEW FACILITIES AND BUSINESS VENTURES

In 1980 AMAG's new leasing arm, AMAG Leasing AG, was founded with headquarters in Schinznach-Bad. During the 1980s and 1990s AMAG continued to expand its dealership network, it enlarged and modernized existing facilities, and added new ones to contain the company's continued growth. In spring 1988 AMAG's new training center in Schinznach-Bad opened its doors, where about 5,000 employees from auto centers servicing the brands sold by the company received instruction and practical training.

AMAG's central spare parts warehouse was also further expanded. The largest one of its kind in Switzerland, the facility housed roughly 130,000 different OEM parts and more than 20,000 accessories as well as tires and paint in 40,000 square meters. In 1993 AMAG introduced an express service for the Zurich metropolitan area that delivered spare parts and accessories to the region's VW, Audi, Porsche, SEAT, and Škoda dealers up to twice per day. By the mid-1990s the equivalent of about 270 railway cars of vehicles were being shipped to AMAG's 24 regional warehouses on average every month. In 1991 AMAG opened a state-of-the-art repair service center for commercial vehicles in Schinznach-Bad. Three years later, a new hall was added to AMAG's central parking facility in Birrfeld where about 70 employees tested and prepped up to 250 newly arrived vehicles per day.

In the late 1990s, as more global competitors entered the stagnating Swiss auto market, AMAG increasingly focused on marketing, offering new services to its customers, and launching additional ventures which supplemented the company's core business. One of those ventures was a 50-page merchandising mail-order catalog called "Amag-Boutique," offering anything from VW-key chains to Audi model cars and racetracks to Porsche Mountain bikes, which generated several million *Franken* in additional sales per year.

AMAG also offered its customers free technical testing services and an airport parking service in large Swiss cities. In addition, AMAG entered the rental car business when the company acquired a license from Volkswagen-owned rental car company Europcar International for Switzerland and Liechtenstein. Finally, the company invested in centrally located public parking garages in Zurich and one in Bern. The car rental and parking business was organized in a new subsidiary, AMAG Service AG. In 1999 Spancar Automobile AG and Amoda Automobile AG were merged with AMAG Automobil- und Motoren AG.

UNDER INCREASING PRESSURE AFTER THE TURN OF THE MILLENNIUM

At the dawn of the 21st century AMAG crossed the CHF 3 billion sales line for the first time. The company was still Switzerland's leading car dealer with a market share of roughly 20 percent. However, the company came under increasing pressure from competitors as well as from the automakers. Looking for additional revenues sources and for more control over the import business, some auto manufacturers set up their own dealership subsidiaries. One of them was Porsche. In 2007 the company founded a sales subsidiary in Switzerland and canceled the import contract with AMAG effective May 31, 2008.

On the other hand, AMAG was criticized by its main partners Volkswagen and Audi for decreasing sales of their makes, although they were still among the most popular in the country. The company felt ongoing pressure to modernize its showrooms, which would call for significant investments. These were challenging times for Martin Haefner, the company founder's son, who in 2005 took over the reins of AMAG from his 95-year-old father.

Evelyn Hauser

PRINCIPAL SUBSIDIARIES

AMAG Automobil- und Motoren AG; AMAG Leasing AG; AMAG Services AG; ROC AG.

PRINCIPAL COMPETITORS

Emil Frey AG; Opel Suisse S.A.; Renault Suisse S.A.; Belgische Alcopa Group; BMW (Schweiz) AG; Ford Motor Company (Switzerland) S.A.

FURTHER READING

"AMAG/2000-Umsatz uber 3 Mrd CHF, Marktanteil auf 20,5 von 20,6% gefallen," *AFX—Swiss,* January 19, 2001.

AMAG Gestern und heute, Schinznach-Bad, Switzerland: AMAG Automobil- und Motoren AG, 1995, 94 p.

"Amag steigert Umsatz um knapp 10% auf 3,5 Mrd CHF," *AFX–Swiss,* January 22, 2007.

"German Porsche to Set Up Swiss Sales Subsidiary," *Swiss Business Digest,* August 8, 2007.

Rehsche, Michael, "Marketing wird immer wichtiger," *Tages-Anzeiger,* October 8, 1998, p. 79.

Schneider, Heinz, "Kuenftig wird man noch mehr Auto fuers Geld erhalten," *SonntagsZeitung,* January 18, 1998, p. 85.

Tanda, Jean François, "Amag an den Karren gefahren," *SonntagsZeitung,* April 22, 2007, p. 64.

"UNP AMAG Automobil- und Motoren AG," *AFX–Swiss,* October 12, 2007.

American Nurses Association Inc.

—■—

8515 Georgia Avenue, Suite 400
Silver Spring, Maryland 20910-3492
U.S.A.
Telephone: (301) 628-5000
Toll Free: (800) 274-4262
Fax: (301) 628-5001
Web site: http://www.nursingworld.org

Private Association
Incorporated: 1901 as Nurses' Associated Alumnae
Employees: 225
Sales: $20.9 million (2007 est.)
NAICS: 813920 Professional Organizations

■ ■ ■

American Nurses Association Inc. (ANA) is a nonprofit professional organization representing about 2.9 million registered nurses through 54 constituent member associations, most of which are state organizations. The headquarters is located in Silver Spring, Maryland, in close proximity to Washington, D.C., where ANA lobbies Congress and regulatory agencies on healthcare matters affecting nurses and the general public. The organization also champions high standards in nursing, and advocates for the welfare of nurses in the workplace and the well-being of patients. A subsidiary, American Nurses Credentialing Center, the world's largest nurse credentialing organization, provides board certification for nurses, the fees for which provide the bulk (about 41 percent) of ANA's annual revenues. Certified nurses also

benefit, earning on average $9,000 a year more than their non-board certified counterparts.

ANA publishes three periodicals: *American Nurse,* the official publication of the organization; *American Nurse Today,* provided to ANA members at no cost; and *OJIN: The Online Journal of Issues in Nursing,* an online, peer-reviewed journal that covers nursing practice, research, education, and general healthcare issues. Another ANA unit also publishes books on nursing. The constituent member associations play a major role in directing the affairs of ANA through representation on the ANA House of Delegates, apportioned according to state membership counts. Most ANA members belong to the organization through their state member associations, although in some states nurses may join directly. In addition, registered nurses may join online as Individual Affiliates. ANA also has two Associate Organizational Members, United American Nurses and the Center for American Nurses, as well as 18 specialty associations that are recognized as organizational affiliate members.

CIVIL WAR HELPS ESTABLISH NURSING PROFESSION IN AMERICA

Prior to the Civil War, nursing was employment of the last resort in the United States, and inmates were often assigned the task in city hospitals. Thus, when the war began in 1861, there were few trained nurses available to care for the large volume of sick and wounded soldiers that were to come. In the North a corps of army nurses was created under the auspices of Dorothea

```
COMPANY PERSPECTIVES
                 ■

For more than 100 years ANA is the voice of nursing.
This voice is heard through policy development, lob-
bying, publications/newsletters, involvement and
partnerships with other organizations, and our pres-
ence on the Internet. ANA's work addresses the needs
of nurses in their professional settings as well as
patient care.
```

Lynde Dix. The importance of qualified nurses was then apparent, leading after the war to the establishment of nursing schools and the recognition of nursing as an actual occupation rather than a voluntary, charitable service. Aside from training, what was still necessary to make nursing a true profession was organization.

In the 1880s the first calls for an American nursing organization were made. In 1890, the *Trained Nurse,* the country's first nursing journal, published a proposed constitution for a national nurses' association. By this time there was an obvious need to standardize nursing education and nursing practices, as well as to find a way to promote the welfare of nurses, who were forced to work long hours at extremely low wages. A general meeting of nurses was held at the 1893 Chicago World's Fair, which hosted the International Congress of Charities, Correction, and Philanthropy. Out of this emerged the seeds for the American Society of Superintendents of Training Schools for Nurses, the purpose of which was to standardize training and promote the nursing profession.

The society held a convention in New York City in January 1894 and was formally established. One of its first acts was the organization of a national association of nurses. A committee then prepared the ground for an organization called the Nurses' Associated Alumnae of the United States and Canada, the predecessor to the ANA. The first meeting was held in February 1897 in Baltimore, Maryland. The constitution and bylaws were approved, officers were elected, and the first North American nurses' association was born. Serving as the first president was a Canadian-born nurse, Isabel Hampton Robb, a respected teacher and author. She also became one of the founders of the *American Journal of Nursing,* which would begin publishing in October 1900 under the ownership of a separate private company.

NEW NAME ADOPTED

In 1901 the association was incorporated in New York State, requiring that Canada be dropped from the name. The Nurses' Associated Alumnae then became a charter member of the International Council of Nurses in 1905, along with similar national organizations in Great Britain and Germany. Also during the early years of the 20th century, the National Association of Colored Graduate Nurses and the Nurses Corps of the U.S. Navy were established, both in 1908. A year later, the Nurses' Associated Alumnae worked with the American Red Cross to form the Red Cross Nursing Service.

The Nurses' Associated Alumnae changed its name to American Nurses Association in 1911. Since 1901, state nurses' associations had been established, and presidents of these state organizations, along with ANA officers, then created an Advisory Council. Also in 1911 ANA established a relief fund to assist nurses in financial need. A year later ANA participated in the creation of the National Organization for Public Health Nursing and became a member. In addition, it was accepted into membership of the National League of Nursing Education. On another front, ANA acquired the American Journal of Nursing Company, bringing its official publication in-house.

The relationship between ANA the state associations was modified in 1916, when individuals became members of the national organization through membership in their state associations. ANA bylaws were also amended to create the House of Delegates, which became ANA's governing body. In that same year, ANA was incorporated in the District of Columbia, an important step given that a main function of ANA was to lobby the federal government on behalf of nurses. A legislative section was organized in 1921.

ANA established a national headquarters in New York City in 1921, and in order to fund the operation, dues were increased from 15 cents to 50 cents per member. Two years later Agnes Deans became the first paid executive secretary at the national headquarters. Other developments during the 1920s included the appointment of the first special committee on ethical standards, which produced a tentative code of ethics that was adopted by ANA in 1926, and the appointment of the first field secretaries. Also during the decade membership was changed to require registered nurse status, and the ANA began the work of establishing standards for registries and private duty nursing.

GREAT DEPRESSION MODIFIES ANA'S ROLE

In 1930, the first full year of the Great Depression, ANA dissolved its national relief fund and instead

KEY DATES

1897: Nurses' Associated Alumnae of the United States and Canada holds its first meeting.

1901: Organization incorporated as Nurses' Associated Alumnae.

1911: American Nurses Association (ANA) name adopted.

1921: National headquarters established in New York City.

1952: Through consolidation of other associations, ANA becomes only membership association for professional nurses.

1968: ANA rescinds an 18-year-old policy that nurses would not strike during bargaining negotiations.

1973: American Academy of Nursing founded.

1992: ANA moves its national headquarters to the Washington, D.C., area.

1995: California Nurses Association disaffiliates from ANA.

1999: United American Nurses (UAN) formed as labor union arm.

2003: UAN becomes autonomous organization.

divided the remaining money among the state associations according to membership levels. Later in the decade ANA participated in the completion of a government survey of unemployed nurses, and helped states to fund employment for nurses on relief. During the 1930s, the association established employment standards for private duty nurses and nurses working in institutional settings, and championed eight-hour days, 48-hour workweeks, and vacations with pay for nurses. Also during the Depression years, male nurses for the first time were given the chance to become ANA members. In 1940 organized sections were created for male nurses as well as general staff nurses.

The first half of the 1940s was dominated by the events of World War II. ANA played a key role in the creation of the Nursing Council on National Defense. Renamed the National Nursing Council for War Service in 1942, it coordinated the activities of nurses on both national and local levels, and with the help of ANA conducted a study of nursing vacancies in U.S. hospitals. Through its state affiliates and local committees, ANA helped recruit nurses for military service. In 1944 ANA successfully lobbied Congress to grant commissioned rank to military nurses. A year later, as the war was coming to an end, ANA led a drive to collect uniforms and clothing for nurses in war-ravaged countries. The association also began studying what was to be done with 60,000 civilian nurses and 41,000 Army and Navy nurses during the postwar years.

In the second half of the 1940s, ANA moved on a number of fronts. It promoted an Economic Security Program that entailed improved working conditions and long-term economic security for nurses. ANA urged the state associations to become involved in collective bargaining for nurses. A public relations effort was launched to inform the public as well as nurses about developments in the nursing field. ANA called for the end of discrimination against minority groups, and in 1948 revised its bylaws to allow African American nurses denied admission to a state nurses' association to receive direct individual ANA membership. Progress was also made in the area of accreditation. In 1949 ANA joined with other national organizations to establish the National Nursing Accrediting Service, which issued its first list of accredited schools of nursing in October of that year.

During the postwar years, ANA and other national nurses' organizations began working toward consolidating their operations. In a preliminary step, ANA absorbed the activities of the National Association of Colored Graduate Nurses, which was dissolved in January 1951. A year later ANA became the sole national membership association for professional nurses, resulting in the closing of the National Organization for Public Health Nursing and the Association of Collegiate Schools of Nursing. ANA then established seven sections to represent various occupational groups of professional nurses. In 1954 it grew even larger, adding a new constituent association, the Virgin Islands Nurses' Association. A year later a charitable organization, the American Nurses' Foundation, was launched as a subsidiary, and by the end of the decade nurses living abroad were allowed to join ANA on an individual basis.

Strides were also made against discrimination; by 1954 only one state nurses' association had failed to amend its bylaws to ban discrimination. ANA promoted other progressive positions as well. In 1958 the House of Delegates declared an official position that healthcare was a right of all people and Congress should extend social security to include health insurance to beneficiaries of old age, survivors, and disability insurance. By the end of the 1950s, membership was approaching 200,000.

It was not until the end of 1962 that all state nurses' associations finally agreed to accept members regardless of race, color, or creed. Other developments also took place during this decade of turbulence and cultural change. In 1960 ANA issued a statement regarding nursing care standards in nursing homes and revised the Code for Professional Nurses. Later, the organization published policies and recommendations on health occupations supportive to nursing, and adopted a new code of ethics for practicing nurses. ANA's Legislative Department and the Washington office were combined in 1967 to create the Government Relations Department.

VIETNAM ERA STRIFE

In 1968 ANA rescinded an 18-year-old policy that nurses would not strike during bargaining negotiations, a change in approach that would become more important in the 1970s and beyond. In 1971 registered nurses at an Ames, Iowa, hospital, resigned en masse over the hospital's refusal to considered a number of noneconomic issues, including the establishment of a patient care committee, an orientation program for new staff members, a nursing care committee, and paid educational leave. ANA members grew even more militant following the 1974 amendment to the National Labor Relations Act that gave nurses working in the private sector the right to collective bargaining. Some state nurses' associations then dropped their own no-strike policies, leading to contentious labor negotiations and a growing number of work stoppages in certain areas, such as New York City. Moreover, nurses became a recruiting target of unions of teachers, municipal workers, retail clerks, and others looking to swell their ranks.

A large measure of this militant spirit was an outgrowth of the women's movement of the 1960s. In support of this effort, ANA in 1975 established a fund to promote the ratification of the Equal Rights Amendment. In other developments in the 1970s, ANA established the American Academy of Nursing in 1973 and a year later 26 ANA members were the first to be admitted. Also in 1974 the American Nurses' Foundation moved its office from New York City to Kansas City.

In 1980 ANA used its influence to persuade Congress to pass an amendment that prevented hospitals from using Medicare funds for anti-union activities. Much of the 1980s was devoted to lobbying Washington, such as the successful effort in 1985 to convince Congress to override a veto of a bill that created the National Center for Nursing Research at the National Institutes of Health. A number of challenges arose, however. Not only did ANA find itself pitted against the interests of other healthcare-related organiza-tions, such as the physicians' lobby, it had to contend with growing disenchantment within its own ranks that would continue into the 1990s.

In the meantime, ANA lobbied Washington in such areas as recruitment and retention programs to grow the number of nurses; creating opportunities serving Native Americans through the Indian Health Care Improvement Act of 1992; increasing funding for nursing programs in the Nurse Education Act in 1993; including nurses as a practitioner category able to certify the need for leave under the Family Medical Leave Act; including language in the North American Free Trade Agreement that would prevent Mexican or Canadian nurses from working in the United States without meeting state licensing criteria; the passage of health insurance portability legislation; the passage of the Minority Health Reauthorization Act; the introduction of the Patient Safety Act and other patients' rights legislation; and many other matters. Given the growing emphasis on lobbying efforts, it was not surprising that in 1992 the association moved its national headquarters to the Washington, D.C., area.

FACING CHALLENGES

Despite ANA's achievements, not everyone within the organization was pleased with the direction it had taken and what was perceived as an unwillingness to combat hospital "redesign," essentially a downsizing effort to cut costs. In 1995 the California Nurses Association (CNA) became the first state organization to disaffiliate itself from ANA. The militant San Francisco-based CNA contended that ANA had become too friendly with industry groups and that what was needed was a consumer-style watchdog and a single-payer healthcare system. As a result, CNA formed its own union, taking with it 10 percent of the membership and $1.8 million in annual dues.

ANA also had to contend with unions that continued to make attempts to sign nurses, competing with ANA state associations for the right to represent them. Because ANA was not part of the AFL-CIO it did not enjoy the courtesy normally extended to fellow members who usually refrained from raiding each other's memberships. To address this and other problems, the House of Delegates instituted a number of changes to ANA's bylaws. A national labor union, United American Nurses (UAN), was established to help constituent member associations in their collective bargaining efforts. It subsequently joined the AFL-CIO, bringing an end to the poaching of the ANA ranks. In addition, a task force was created to help the member associations in their workplace advocacy programs. To assist active duty military nurses, the Federal Nurses Association was formed as an ANA constituent. Policy-making was also streamlined.

Two more state associations, those of Massachusetts and Maine, elected to disaffiliate themselves from ANA in 2001. Massachusetts was by far a greater loss, taking with it 20,000 members and $1 million in annual dues. ANA initiated an even more extensive restructuring of its bylaws in 2003. New membership categories were created to provide new means for organizations and individuals to become part of ANA, thus creating a way for nurses in California, Massachusetts, and Maine to go around their disaffiliated state associations to join ANA. In addition, UAN and the workplace advocacy arm of ANA, Center for American Nurses, became autonomous organizations that retained links to ANA.

As the new century progressed, ANA continued its lobbying efforts, supporting legislation to address the problem of antibiotic-resistant diseases caused by the use of drugs in food-producing animals; the Medicare Prescription Drug Savings Act of 2005; the Safe Nursing and Patient Care Act; and other areas of concern. Also in 2006 ANA launched a new official journal, *American Nurse Today.* The organization continued to look for more ways to serve its constituents as well as to expand its ranks. In 2008 ANA added its 21st organizational affiliate, the Academy of Neonatal Nursing, thereby bringing another 315,000 nurses into its orbit.

Ed Dinger

PRINCIPAL SUBSIDIARIES

American Academy of Nursing; American Nurses Credentialing Center; American Nurses Foundation.

PRINCIPAL COMPETITORS

National Nurses Organizing Committee.

FURTHER READING

"ANA Delegates to Consider New Structure at June Meeting," *American Nurse,* May/June 2002, p. 10.

"ANA Reorganizes Structure to Better Meet Nurses' Needs," *American Nurse,* July/August 2003, p. 1.

Bellandi, Deanna, "Mass. Nurses Seek to Bolt ANA," *Modern Healthcare,* April 2, 2001, p. 22.

Flanagan, Lyndia, *One Strong Voice: The Story of the American Nurses' Association,* Kansas City, Mo.: Lowell Press, 1976.

Lumsdon, Kevin, "Faded Glory: Will Nursing Ever Be the Same?" *Hospitals & Health Networks,* December 5, 1995, p. 30.

Messina, Judith, "Nurses on Battlefield," *Crain's New York Business,* October 16, 2000, p. 1.

Moore, J. Duncan, Jr., "Breaking Apart: Some Nurses Depart ANA Affiliates for SEIU," *Modern Healthcare,* November 3, 1997, p. 24.

"Nursing Lobby Exerting Newfound Power in Washington," *Modern Healthcare,* December 4, 1987, p. 28.

Rauber, Chris, "Battles of State, National Nurses Groups Has Everyone Nursing a Grudge," *San Francisco Business Times,* October 6, 1995, p. 3.

Tomasson, Robert E., "Nurses' Growing Militancy Turns Strikes into Routine," *New York Times,* December 11, 1980.

Andrade Gutierrez S.A.

———————— ■ ————————

Avenida do Contorno 8123
Belo Horizonte, Minas Gerais 30110-910
Brazil
Telephone: (55 31) 3290-6699
Fax: (55 31) 3290-6636
Web site: http://www.andradegutierrez.com.br

Private Company
Founded: 1948
Employees: 16,701
Sales: BRL 7.89 billion ($4.68 billion) (2007)
NAICS: 236210 Industrial Building Construction;
237110 Water and Sewer Line and Related
Structures Construction; 237310 Highway, Street,
and Bridge Construction; 237990 Other Heavy and
Civil Engineering Construction; 517110 Wired
Telecommunications Carriers; 517212 Cellular and
Other Wireless Telecommunications; 531210 Of-
fices of Real Estate Agents and Brokers; 541512
Computer Systems Design Services; 551112 Offices
of Other Holding Companies

■ ■ ■

Andrade Gutierrez S.A., which often calls itself Grupo
AG, is the holding company for companies engaged in
heavy construction, civil engineering, public services
concessions, telecommunications, information technology, and real estate. Almost all its revenues derive, in
roughly equal proportions, from engineering and
construction, concessions, and telecommunications. As a
builder of such public works as roads and bridges, it

ranks as one of the largest in Brazil. Grupo AG's goal is
to be one of Brazil's five largest private companies by
2013.

HEAVY CONSTRUCTION COMPANY IN BRAZIL BEGINS BY BUILDING ROADS

Andrade Gutierrez was founded in 1948 in Belo Horizonte, the capital of the state of Minas Gerais, by Flávio
Gutierrez and the brothers Gabriel and Roberto
Andrade. The first office was Roberto's home. Starting
with one tractor, they dedicated themselves to building
roads. The company's first out-of-state assignment, in
1956, was roadwork on a highway between Belo Horizonte and Rio de Janeiro.

The same kind of projects occupied Andrade Gutierrez's attention during the 1960s. The firm participated
in the construction of Castelo Branco, the principal
highway between the city of São Paulo and the western
part of the state (also called São Paulo). It was Andrade
Gutierrez's first work in the state, Brazil's most prosperous and populous. In 1968 the company encountered
rain forest conditions for the first time when it started
construction on the road between Manaus, in the heart
of the Amazon river basin, and Porto Velho, near the
border with Bolivia.

In 1971 Andrade Gutierrez began work on the São
Paulo subway line. It subsequently was involved in the
construction of subways for the cities of Belo Horizone,
Brasília, Rio de Janeiro, and Salvador. In 1975 the
company began work on the Itaipu project, which
included the world's largest hydroelectric power plant.

Andrade Gutierrez began building the new Belo Horizonte airport in 1980 and completed the project in 1984. During this decade the company became engaged in activities, later abandoned, such as oil prospecting and drilling, tin mine exploration, and granite extraction. It also acquired Zagope SGPS Ltda., thereby entering engineering and construction in Portugal.

GOING ABROAD FOR WORK

Andrade Gutierrez's experience in the Amazon proved useful in the Republic of Congo (Brazzaville), where, in 1983, it won an $87 million contract to build an 83 mile highway through the jungle during the next four years. The deal included a promise to send a star soccer team to play the locals, and the subsequent match ended in a diplomatic tie. The workers included 500 pygmies who hacked a path through the vegetation. This was Andrade Gutierrez's first job abroad. The company, like other Brazilian contractors, was seeking business overseas because of cuts in spending for development projects within the country and delays in receiving payment from the federal and state government for work already completed.

By 1995 Andrade Gutierrez was earning as much as 40 percent of its revenues from contracts outside Brazil. Among the projects on which it worked during this decade were a new airport in Nassau, Bahamas (1990–95), an airport for Funchal, Portugal (1995–2001), and the Pereira-Dosquebradas viaduct in Colombia (1994–98). It also built roads in China and a hydroelectric plant in Chile.

EXPANDING AT HOME AND ABROAD

Andrade Gutierrez reached the $1 billion mark in annual sales in 1989. But big construction contracts in Brazil continued to be hard to come by, and as a result revenue dropped to as little as $700 million a year. Employment at AG fell from 22,000 in 1987 to less than 12,000 in 1995. Heavy construction still accounted for 80 percent of revenues, but the company began was looking to other sources of business.

Seeking income in public services, Andrade Gutierrez took stakes in Companhia de Saneamento do Estado do Paraná (Sanepar), the concessionaire for water and sewer services in the state of Paraná, and Companhia de Concessöes Rodoviários (CCR), which became the biggest company in its field by collecting tolls and managing highways that had been privatized by the Brazilian government. The first highway privatized was the Via Dutra, in 1995, linking São Paulo and Rio de Janeiro. It was turned over to Andrade Gutierrez and Camargo Corrêa S.A. under a 25-year concession. AG also won the concession to operate the bridge over Guanabara Bay linking Rio de Janeiro and Niterói.

The search for new revenue streams led Andrade Gutierrez into some unsuccessful ventures. Biotec, based on a system to turn organic waste into fertilizer in only five days, failed to gain traction. Also soon forgotten was AG's investment in Celma, a privatized company engaged in making airplane parts and repairing engines. The oil prospecting and drilling ventures were sold in 1996. The creation of a real estate arm resulted in big losses. Particularly costly were investments in an area for moving cargo in and out of the privatized port of Vitória, Espíritu Santo, and the construction of residential condominiums on the Atlantic coast near Rio de Janeiro.

One of Andrade Gutierrez's problems was that the construction and public services (or concessions) arms were working at cross purposes. The constructors wanted the biggest contracts possible for their work, while the concessions people, as managers, wanted to keep costs as low as possible. A restructuring effort, conducted with the aid of the McKinsey consulting firm, resulted in a document called AG 2000 that confirmed concessions as one of AG's priority areas.

AG TELECOM: 1994–2008

Andrade Gutierrez placed its biggest bet for growth on telecommunications, establishing AG Telecom in 1994 for ventures into telephony, telemessaging, fiber optic networks, data transmission, credit card management, and subscription television. Many of these activities were initiated on the expectation that the Brazilian government would privatize the nation's telecommunications system.

In 1998 Consortium Telemar, composed of six companies, including Grupo AG's construction subsidiary, purchased a fixed telephone line concession from the government for BRL 3.43 billion ($2.94 billion). Telemar soon controlled more fixed line telephones than any other Brazilian telecommunications

KEY DATES

1948: Andrade Gutierrez is founded in Belo Horizonte, Minas Gerais.

1956: The company receives its first assignment outside Minas Gerais.

1968: Andrade Gutierrez enters the Amazon rain forest on a road building assignment.

1971: The company begins work on the São Paulo subway line.

1975: Andrade Gutierrez joins in construction of the giant Itaipu hydroelectric project.

1984: The company completes construction of the new Belo Horizonte airport.

1989: Andrade Gutierrez's annual revenue passes $1 billion.

1995: The company has a role in managing Brazil's first privatized highway.

1997: Andrade Gutierrez takes a stake in Telemar, a telecommunications company.

2006: The concessions division buys a share of Light, S.A., Brazil's third largest energy company.

2008: Grupo AG's construction division is active in a dozen Latin American and African countries.

company. Not all these ventures were successful. Telemessaging, by means of pagers, lost $3 million in its three years of existence. AG Telecom also exited fiber optics, data transmission, and credit card management.

Telemar next purchased the Internet access arm of an online company and, in 2001, a license to provide wireless service in the same area where it was providing fixed lines. This service was expected to offer faster Internet connections than previously available. Named Oi ("Hi!"), the new mobile phone service began operating in 2002 and had two million subscribers within a year. Established in 2000 as a subsidiary of Telemar, Contax S.A. was, by the end of 2008, Brazil's major call center, with 71,000 employees and BRL 1.5 billion (about $850 million) in annual revenue.

By 2008 Telemar had become Oi Participações. The largest fixed line and fourth largest mobile phone operator in Brazil, Oi announced that year that it would purchase Brasil Telecom for $3.5 billion. With interests also in broadband and in subscription television, Oi would be one of the largest telecommunications companies in Latin America. AG Telecom, although

holding only a 10.3 percent stake in Oi, was considered one of its prime movers.

CONCESSIONS, CONSTRUCTION AND MORE: 2001–08

Construtora Andrade Gutierrez moved to São Paulo in 2001. The holding company remained in Belo Horizonte, however. Also that year, the International Finance Corporation, an arm of the World Bank, purchased a stake in the group's concessions subsidiary, Andrade Gutierrez Concessões. In 2006 this subsidiary acquired, with a joint partner, an 80 percent stake in Light, S.A., Brazil's third largest energy company. It subsequently sold half of its holding.

AG Concessões' holdings in 2007 included 17 percent of Companhia de Concessões Rodoviários (CCR), and 46 percent of Corporación Quiport S.A., which was operating the new Quito, Ecuador, airport. In 2008 CCR won a 30-year concession for the western part of the ring highway in metropolitan São Paulo. The concessions arm's subsidiary, Water Port S.A., also supplied the port of Santos with water.

Andrade Gutierrez's construction arm remained active in a number of countries. It built the Northeast Line aqueduct in the Dominican Republic (2002–04) and the new airport in Quito, Ecuador (2005–07), in which it became a shareholder in the terminal. It was constructing the Picachos Dam in the Mexican state of Sinaloa in 2007 and in that year won a contract to build a 36-story tower in Monterrey for the state government of Nuevo León. It was also planning, in 2008, to build a steel plant in Venezuela, and it was active in seven African countries. Operations in Europe, Africa, and Asia, which accounted for 54 percent of Construtora Andrade Gutierrez's foreign revenues in 2007, were being administered by Lisbon-based Zagope. Latin America accounted for the other 46 percent of the construction arm's overseas revenues.

In 2007 Construtora Andrade Gutierrez was engaged in a number of projects in Brazil. These included construction of a stretch of an Amazon gas pipeline; the southern part of the ring highway encircling metropolitan São Paulo; two hydroelectric power plants and one thermal plant; line four of the São Paulo metro; and a petrochemical cracking plant. By the end of 2008 Andrade Gutierrez's construction arm had built, in the company's 60 years, 23 hydroelectric dams and more than 20 roads, railways, ports, and airports.

Andrade Gutierrez was continuing to diversify its holdings during this period. The company took a half share in 2006 in Fundo AG Angra, a joint venture to grow sugarcane and convert it to ethanol in the state of Maranhão in the Amazon delta. Madeira Energia S.A.

was founded in 2007 to participate in hydroelectric and nuclear energy generation. Sérgio Andrade, son of Roberto Andrade, was chairman of the nine-member AG board. All nine were members of the Andrade and Gutierrez families. The board had veto power over any proposed project, and it was not inclined to make a commitment without studies that might last a year. Nevertheless, the company's president, Otávio Marques de Azevedo, estimated that, in the future, one-fifth of AG's revenues could come from new businesses.

Robert Halasz

PRINCIPAL SUBSIDIARIES

Andrade Gutierrez Concessões S.A. (77 percent); Andrade Gutierrez Telecommunicações Ltda.; Construtora Andrade Gutierrez S.A.

PRINCIPAL COMPETITORS

Camargo Corrêa S.A.; Odebrecht S.A.

FURTHER READING

"Ambitious Merger," *Business Latin America,* May 5, 2008, p. 4.

Foster, Angus, "Brazil M-way in Private Hands," *Financial Times,* October 31, 1995, p. 4.

Jardim, Lauro, "A Andrade Gutierrez está mudando de cara," *Exame,* September 13, 1995, pp. 38–40.

Lima, Samantha, "Com fôlego de iniciante," Exame, December 3, 2008, pp. 62–64.

Moffett, Matt, "Brazil to Award a Cellular Phone Business," *Wall Street Journal,* July 8, 1997, p. A10.

Netz, Clayton, "Concessão é o novo nome do jogo," *Exame,* August 28, 1996, pp. 44–45.

Ramos, Mivra, "Ganan brasilenas construcción de torre millonaria," *El Norte* (Monterrey, Mexico), June 27, 2007.

"Se a fartura acabou, cuide das finanças," Exame Melhores e Majores, August 1994, pp. 164, 166.

Whitley, Andrew, "Brazilian Company Wins 58m Congo Road Order," *Financial Times,* August 23, 1983, p. 2.

SCHLECKER

Anton Schlecker

―――――・―――――

Im Schleckerland
Ehingen, D-89579
Germany
Telephone: (49 7391) 584-0
Fax: (49 7391) 584-1256
Web site: http://www.schlecker.com

Private Company
Incorporated: 1975
Employees: 55,700
Sales: EUR 6.9 billion ($9.6 billion) (2007 est.)
NAICS: 446110 Pharmacies and Drug Stores

■ ■ ■

Anton Schlecker sees itself as Europe's leading drugstore chain with a total of over 14,155 outlets. In Germany the company leads the market with roughly 10,600 Schlecker drugstores, which can be found in almost all cities with 2,000 or more inhabitants. An additional 3,500 Schlecker stores can be found in other European countries, mainly in Austria and Spain, but also in France, Belgium, the Netherlands, Luxembourg, Denmark, Italy, Portugal, the Czech Republic, Poland, and Hungary. Schlecker stores feature manufacturers' brands, but also carry a growing range of items—from body care to cosmetics, baby food to pet food—under the main store brand, AS Schlecker. Additional high-quality body care products are sold under the WestLife brand for men, Rilanja for women, and Sanft for infants.

In addition to its tightly knit network of outlets, Schlecker offers some 100,000 items for sale at the company's online store. Orders can also be placed and picked up at any Schlecker outlet. The company's 30 modern logistics service centers supply all Schlecker stores in Europe. In 2008 Schlecker acquired Ihr Platz, Germany's fourth largest drugstore chain with about 700 stores. The company's personally liable sole proprietor and CEO is German billionaire Anton Schlecker, who also owns five department stores and several butcher stores in Bavaria and Baden-Württemberg.

MASTER BUTCHER BUILDS RETAIL EMPIRE

Even as a young man, Anton Schlecker made the headlines. At 21, he had passed the required tests and was hailed as the youngest master butcher of West Germany when he entered his father's business in 1965. Based in Ehingen, a Swabian city about 35 miles southwest of Nuremberg, the business consisted of a meat processing factory and 17 butcher stores which generated about DEM 7 million per year. However, soon after joining the family enterprise, Schlecker changed his focus from meat and sausages to cold cream and after shave, and set out on a journey that eventually made him one of the richest men in Germany. In the second half of the 1960s Schlecker set up Ehingen's first self-service department store at the outskirts of his hometown. After the new concept proved successful, Schlecker built similar stores in the Stuttgart region, including Schwäbisch-Gmünd, Geislingen, Neu-Ulm, and Göppingen, between 1972 and 1976.

COMPANY PERSPECTIVES

Schlecker is the market leader among discount drugstores in Germany. The tightly organized management under the leadership of Anton Schlecker makes possible swift decisions and their immediate realization. This competitive advantage by means of complete independence supports the company's expansion program which is to be continued decisively. ... Additional store openings in other countries are planned. The strategic goal is to penetrate and exploit domestic and foreign markets as much as possible.

When an amendment abolished the law that forbade drugstore owners to sell brand-name products below the manufacturer's recommended price in Germany in 1974, Schlecker sensed a promising new business opportunity in the form of discount drugstores. One year later, in 1975, Schlecker opened his first such store in Kirchheim unter Teck, about 15 miles southeast of Stuttgart. Starting with that first store, Anton Schlecker, together with his wife Christa, built a large retail empire within less than a decade. At first, they aimed at 50 stores altogether. However, in 1977, the number of Schlecker outlets surpassed the 100 mark. Then they aimed for a total of 500 stores; by 1984, the Schleckers opened their 1,000th discount drugstore.

Schlecker's business model was straightforward and simple: keep costs and prices as low as possible. To keep costs as low as possible, Schlecker located his stores in places where rents were relatively inexpensive—places such as smaller cities in rural areas, or less attractive neighborhoods in large cities. Where other retailers moved out, Schlecker moved in. The stores themselves were rather small and offered a very narrow range of only a few thousand products. The densely arranged shelves left just enough aisle space for one shopper, and rarely was there more than one salesperson working at a store at a time. To save costs, most stores were not even equipped with a telephone. The lower fixed costs allowed Schlecker to offer its often less-affluent clientele brand-name products at competitive prices and still make a profit. Schlecker also avoided paying interest on bank loans. Instead, he asked his suppliers for an extended payment grace period of 120 days to help finance his inventory.

In 1987 the Schleckers made the headlines again when kidnappers attacked the family in their Ehingen home just before Christmas, kidnapped their two teenage children, and demanded a ransom of DEM 18 million. Instead of calling the police, Anton Schlecker negotiated the price down to almost half the amount, which he then paid to the criminals. While his son and daughter were released right away, it took 11 years until the kidnappers were caught, prosecuted, and convicted.

EXPANDING BEYOND GERMANY

In the second half of the 1980s and in the early 1990s the number of new Schlecker stores continued to grow at a rapid pace. It was during that time period that Anton Schlecker began to expand his enterprise beyond Germany's borders. In 1987 the company started exporting its successful business model, at first by establishing a network of Schlecker outlets in Austria. Two years later, the first Schlecker stores were opened in the Netherlands, Spain, Belgium, and Luxembourg. After the fall of the Berlin Wall in November 1989, which marked the end of the existence of two separate German states, Schlecker quickly seized the opportunity and began to open new stores in eastern Germany.

Another major step was the takeover of the French Superdrug chain in 1991. By 1992 the number of Schlecker outlets abroad had grown to over 300 in Austria, more than 150 in the Netherlands, over 100 in Spain, and more than 50 in France. In 1994 there were more than 5,000 Schlecker stores in Europe, with the majority of them in Germany. The company's workforce had grown to over 18,500. Anton Schlecker was grossing more than DEM 4.5 billion a year. About 15 percent of the total was generated by the company's outlets outside of Germany. Schlecker's massive growth was financed exclusively out of the incoming cash flow, according to CEO Anton Schlecker.

However, the company's expansion abroad also posed a major challenge. Unlike in Schlecker's home market, where the company was able to purchase its merchandise at very low costs, buying the same products from the suppliers' foreign subsidiaries sometimes cost much more, due to national regulation, differences in established price levels, or manufacturers' pricing policies. While the company founder tried to negotiate better conditions with his suppliers, he also reportedly pressured them by "exporting" products he had purchased cheaply in Germany to his stores in the Netherlands or France.

Nonetheless, the company continued its international expansion before and after the turn of the millennium. In 1999 the first Schlecker drugstores opened in Italy. In 2004 Schlecker established its first stores in Denmark and Poland, followed by new store openings in Hungary and the Czech Republic in 2005.

KEY DATES

1967: Schlecker builds the first self-service department store in Ehingen.
1975: The first Schlecker drugstore opens in Kirchheim unter Teck.
1984: The company opens its 1,000th drugstore.
1987: Schlecker expands its drugstore network into Austria.
1989: The first Schlecker stores are opened in the Netherlands, Spain, Belgium, and Luxembourg.
1991: Schlecker takes over the French drugstore chain Superdrug.
1999: The first Schlecker outlets in Italy are opened.
2000: Online store Schlecker Home Shopping is launched.
2004: Schlecker opens new stores in Denmark and Poland.
2005: The company enters the market in the Czech Republic and Hungary.
2006: The first Schlecker outlets in Portugal are opened.
2008: German drugstore chain Ihr Platz is taken over.

One year later, the first Schlecker outlets were opened in Portugal. By that time there were 1,200 Schlecker stores in Austria and almost as many in Spain.

LABOR UNION CRITICISM RESULTS IN PROSECUTION

In the mid-1990s Anton Schlecker again made the headlines when some of the policies he implemented as cost-saving measures raised growing concerns among his employees, workers' rights activists, and the general public. In 1994, Germany's retail trade labor union, HBV, accused the company of paying employees less than the then-current hourly union pay scale, and of interfering with German labor law by blocking the formation of employee councils common in most large corporations. HBV also criticized the absence of telephones in the stores, which made Schlecker store clerks more likely to be victimized by robbers; and regular observations of employees' personal belongings by store managers to make sure that nothing was stolen, as reported by former Schlecker employees. Under increasing public pressure, Anton Schlecker promised to equip every store with a telephone, a safe, and an alarm within one year, and to allow the formation of employee councils.

HBV's claims that Schlecker knowingly underpaid hundreds of his employees stirred the interest of the office of the district attorney in Stuttgart. In February 1995, police searched Schlecker's headquarters and found incriminating documents that confirmed the company's alleged practice. In December 1995 Stuttgart's district attorney filed a lawsuit against Schlecker, his wife, and three top managers, claiming that in 1993 and 1994 they knowingly paid 805 female employees in the Baden-Württemberg district wages below the legally binding amount determined by the then-current general labor contract for retail trade workers. Instead of paying them fixed hourly wages, compensation was paid depending on the store's sales performance, which in most cases resulted in less than the legally mandated pay. Prosecutors also claimed that the accused had informed these employees that their pay was based on the collective labor agreement, although they knew that this was not true.

In the spring of 1998 Stuttgart's district attorney withdrew its initial fraud charges because of problems calculating the amount of damages caused by Schlecker's wage dumping practice. Instead, they filed a motion for an order of summary punishment against the Schleckers. Subsequently, Anton and Christa Schlecker were found guilty and sentenced by Stuttgart's municipal court to ten months on probation and a fine of DEM 2 million. In mid-2001 Schlecker signed a nationally binding agreement with the newly formed German service workers' labor union, Verdi, which recognized the existing union contract.

BUILDING AN INTERNET AND MAIL-ORDER ARM

In the spring of 2000 Schlecker launched its online store, Schlecker Home Shopping, at www.schlecker.com, starting out with about 2,000 items for sale. After spending roughly EUR 30 million on a state-of-the-art robotics-enhanced warehouse near the Ehingen headquarters for handling the additional online business, Schlecker continuously added new product lines to the store.

In the spring of 2002 the company made headlines again when Schlecker started selling cars over the Internet at prices between 12 and 24 percent below the manufacturer's sticker price. Under the arrangement, the cars had been registered by a car dealer for one day, the vehicles were regarded as used cars and therefore could be resold by Schlecker at a much lower price, although they were practically brand new. Schlecker immediately received legal threats from some of the car manufacturers and withdrew the offer for a few days. However, the extended media coverage of the company's spectacular sales promotion gave its online store a massive publicity boost.

Schlecker continued to offer cars at discounted prices online, and to add other products to his Internet store, including canned food, prepared meals, meat and fish delicacies, California wine, household items, toys, consumer electronics, mobile phone services, holiday vacations, and even lottery tickets. Again, Schlecker's strategy was straightforward and simple: to offer anything online that could be shipped to customers.

To give customers with no online access the opportunity to order products as well, the company launched Schlecker Bestellshop, a mail-order business. Twice a month Schlecker printed a new catalog called *Schlecker Bestellmagazin,* featuring bestsellers from the company's online store comprising a wide variety of products including home décor, jewelry, toys, kids' clothing, exclusive fragrances, books, and DVDs. Shoppers at Schlecker stores could place their orders in the store, by phone, or over the Internet, and pick them up at any Schlecker outlet if they wished.

By the later years of the first decade of the 21st century, Anton Schlecker's efforts to open up additional revenue streams through mail order and the Internet started to show encouraging results. The company reported growing sales in nontraditional product areas such as toys and electronics, and EUR 150 million in online sales annually. At the time, customers were able to choose from over 100,000 items for sale at the online store in cooperation with more than 150 manufacturers and other partner firms.

DECLINING PROFITS AND INCREASING COMPETITION CALL FOR STRATEGIC REORIENTATION

For more than 25 years, the history of Anton Schlecker had been a story of rapid growth and massive commercial success. However, in the early years of the 21st century the company's simple success formula showed clear signs of weakening performance. In Germany, average sales per store declined, as did the company's profits, due to increasing competitive pressure. To counter the trend of declining profit margins, Schlecker introduced a growing number of store brand products that yielded higher profits. In addition to the existing range of traditional drugstore items sold under the main store brand, AS Schlecker, the company introduced an additional range of high-quality body care products under

the WestLife brand for men, Rilanja for women, and Sanft for infants. As a result, the percentage of total sales generated by store brands climbed from about 9 percent in 1994 to roughly 15 percent ten years later.

In 2005, Schlecker's 30th anniversary year, the German press reported that, for the first time in its history, the company had closed several hundred loss-making outlets as a reaction to declining sales figures. To reverse the trend of shrinking revenues per outlet, the company streamlined product lines and introduced electronic payment via ATM cards to Schlecker stores. Schlecker nevertheless found itself in the midst of a dilemma. While the company's low costs did not allow an additional significant reduction, Schlecker was pushed by its immediate German competitors to fight increasingly fierce price wars. At the same time, the market leader's competitors were opening new stores at record speed and earning higher profits than Schlecker, which was losing ground in its core business areas of body care and detergents. The situation got even worse when a new competitor, German discount giant Lidl, entered Schlecker's core market segment by adding some 200 brand-name body and healthcare items to Lidl store shelves in 2005.

ACQUIRING A COMPETITOR

In the fall of 2007 Schlecker made headlines again when the company announced the takeover of Germany's fifth largest drugstore chain Ihr Platz, two years after that company had filed for bankruptcy and was then restructured by investors. The acquisition of the Osnabrück-based competitor with about 700 outlets and roughly 7,000 employees strengthened Schlecker's leading position in Germany, raising the company's market share to an estimated 44 percent. After the takeover, effective January 1, 2008, Schlecker decided to launch a two-brand strategy and let Ihr Platz remain a separate company. Since Ihr Platz outlets were much larger, carried at least twice as many products as Schlecker stores, and were often located in high-traffic areas, such as train stations, Anton Schlecker was planning to develop Ihr Platz into an upscale drugstore chain with a focus on wellness, beauty, and health-related products. In addition, Schlecker used the acquisition to accelerate the company's ongoing store optimization program. In 2008 the company began remodeling larger Schlecker stores into Ihr Platz outlets.

At the beginning of 2008 Schlecker announced a new five-point strategy for future growth to make up for declining sales in the company's core business. According to the plan, the company was going to focus on five business areas with a high growth potential, including the company's Internet and mail-order business, an online pharmacy, expanding Ihr Platz, further expansion abroad, and a new business division that focused on commercial customers such as clinics, elder homes, and hotels. At the time, Schlecker was still the largest German drugstore chain operator by far, running more stores and generating more sales than all of its largest competitors combined. Anton Schlecker was still the company's personally liable sole proprietor and CEO, remaining in the headlines as one of the world's wealthiest men on the *Forbes* list of billionaires. Together with his wife and their two children, son Lars and daughter Meike, both of whom had studied business administration at prestigious European business schools, Anton Schlecker was working hard toward realizing his vision of being the European market leader and, perhaps one day, even the largest drugstore company in the world.

Evelyn Hauser

PRINCIPAL COMPETITORS

dm-drogerie markt GmbH + Co. KG; Dirk Rossmann GmbH; Alliance Boots; Kruidvat Beheer BV; Matas A/S; amazon.com.

FURTHER READING

"Anklage gegen Anton Schlecker und Mitarbeiter erhoben," *Frankfurter Allgemeine Zeitung,* December 12, 1995, p. 21.

"Anton Schlecker wehrt sich gegen 'diffamierende HBV-Kampagne,'" *Frankfurter Allgemeine Zeitung,* December 16, 1994, p. 21.

"Austrian Trade Union Protests Against Schlecker," *Europe Intelligence Wire,* September 30, 2005.

Blau, John, "Online Drugstore Gives up Car Sales," *Network World,* May 6, 2002.

"Die Expansion geht weiter; Schlecker," *TextilWirtschaft,* J26, 1993, p. 14.

Fries, Tanja, and Bernd Biehl, "Schlecker startet Offensive mit Zusatzgeschäften," *Lebensmittel Zeitung,* J11, 2008, p. 6.

"Job Cuts Feared at Schlecker," *Europe Intelligence Wire,* October 26, 2004.

"Knueppeln, knausern, kontrollieren," *manager magazin online,* December 4, 2003.

Ossenberg, Heidi, "Kein Cent vergeudet—Schlecker-Chef wird 60," *dpa-AFX,* October 22, 2004.

"Schlecker Acquires Ihr Platz Drug Store Chain," *Cosmetics International,* February 22, 2008, p. 4.

"Schlecker Moves on German Drug Retailing," *Pharma Marketletter,* February 25, 2008.

"Schlecker Postpones OTC Sales," *Cosmetics International,* October 19, 2007, p. 3.

"Schlecker Targets German Drug Retail Market," *Financial Times,* October 10, 2007, p. 18.

"Schlecker to Cooperate with Vodafone," *Europe Intelligence Wire,* May 23, 2006.

"Schlecker verkauft Autos von Fiat, Ford und Smart per Internet," *Agence France Presse,* May 3, 2002.

"Schlecker wehrt sich gegen Vorwürfe," *Frankfurter Allgemeine Zeitung,* November 30, 1994, p. 22.

"Schlecker wird zur Kasse gebeten," *Lebensmittel Zeitung,* March 27, 1998, p. 28.

Arthur Lundgren Tecidos S.A.

Rua da Consolação 2411
São Paulo, São Paulo 01301-909
Brazil
Telephone: (55 11) 3150-8501
Fax: (55 11) 3150-8685
Web site: http://www.pernambucanas.com.br

Private Company
Founded: 1891 as Companhia de Tecidos Paulista
Employees: 17,194
Sales: $2.43 billion (2008 est.)
NAICS: 452111 Department Stores (Except Discount Department Stores); 551112 Offices of Other Holding Companies

■ ■ ■

Arthur Lundgren Tecidos S.A. is a holding company whose main property is the Casas Pernambucanas department store chain, Brazil's oldest retailer of this kind, with a full century in its line of business. The company also operates several other businesses, including a hotel and financial and real estate enterprises. Pernambucanas, with over 250 stores in seven Brazilian states, celebrated its 100th anniversary in 2008.

ORIGINS

Herman Theodor Lundgren came to Brazil from Sweden in the 1850s at the age of 20. He became a ship chandler, furnishing supplies for ships weighing anchor in Recife, Pernambuco, one of the Brazilian ports closest to Europe. He opened a gunpowder factory in Recife in 1865 and explosives warehouses in a dozen cities. In 1904 he turned to manufacturing cotton textiles in Paulista, west of Recife. He did so by purchasing Companhia de Tecidos Paulista, a small producer of sugar sacks that was in financial difficulty.

Lundgren died in 1907, leaving five children. Arthur took over management of the gunpowder factory and Frederico João the textile plant. What was first called Lojas Pernambucanas began as a simple stall or tent next to the Paulista factory in 1908. It offered fixed prices rather than haggling and could undercut competitors because, by selling the factory's wares directly, it avoided middlemen. A São Paulo branch opened in 1910. By 1920 there were dozens of these stores. They had different names: in northern Brazil, Lojas Paulista, and in the state of Ceará, farther north, A Pernambucana. From the state of Bahia south, the chain was called Casas Pernambucanas or simply Pernambucanas.

A second textile factory was established at Rio Tinto, Paraíba, in 1924. There the company had its own port, railway, water supplies, electricity, theater, and cinema. It sponsored churches and its own soccer team. The two plants provided 80 percent of the goods sold by the retail chain. A third textile factory opened in Santa Elisabeth, Minas Gerais, in the 1950s. By then the Lundgren family owned the largest such complex in South America.

Frederico João's bride died only three months after their wedding. After that he fathered 22 acknowledged children by 19 women, almost all of them workers at

KEY DATES

1904: Herman Theodor Lundgren founds a cotton textile plant in Recife, Pernambuco.
1908: The first Lundgren store begins as a stall or tent next to the factory.
1910: A branch of this store opens in São Paulo.
1924: The company establishes a second textile factory in Rio Tinto, Paraíba.
1975: The enterprise splits into four parts, which are quickly reduced to three.
1990: Two Lundgren companies remain, one in São Paulo, the other in Rio de Janeiro.
1997: The Rio de Janeiro company goes out of business.
2001: Internet commerce is introduced.
2008: The remaining São Paulo-based company celebrates the centenary of the chain.

the Paulista factory. The eventual suit by his offspring for a piece of the enterprise ultimately failed after occupying some 25 years—one of the longest judicial proceedings in the history of Brazil. Frederico João remained focused on business nevertheless. A controlling boss, he once slipped into the factory through a window to see if the employees were really working. He liked to sponsor and hire German and Italian veterans of World War I because they would work for lower wages than locals.

THRIVING AND GROWING

A manual of operations dating from the 1930s shows that Casas Pernambucanas spared few opportunities to publicize its wares. Advertising on radio was avoided because few of the chain's customers could afford receivers, and many of them, especially in rural areas, did not read newspapers, either. Posters on buses and trolley cars were considered more productive. Store managers were urged to advertise in circuses and cinemas and anywhere outdoors—on public walls, stall fronts and storefronts, even on boulders—where the chain could fix its image in the mind of consumers as the place to buy not only fabrics but also bedroom, kitchen, and bathroom wares.

In the chain's early days the location of new stores was often tied to available sea and river transport of the merchandise, but during the 1930s new Casas Pernambucanas units followed the coffee settlements that grew along the railroad lines extending westward into the

Brazilian interior. The retail chain numbered more than 400 stores in the 1940s.

For many Brazilians, the Casas Pernambucanas store was as integral a part of a small town as the local church, the post office, and the Banco do Brasil branch. Some of these localities had been settled by European immigrants, and for them the retail chain published catalogues in their native languages. For settlements too small to include a cinema, the company provided projectors and free movies—and filled the screen with its own ads. Eventually there may have been more than 1,000 stores—exceeding other retail networks—in municipalities scattered over the length of Brazil.

In the 1960s, Casas Pernambucanas, in order to sell winter clothing (although most of the country is tropical or subtropical), introduced a television commercial that became a classic. An animated character—a national icon still in use in the 21st century—was shown pounding on a door, accompanied by a jingle that began with the words, "Who's knocking? It's the cold!"

A DIVIDED THIRD GENERATION

Frederico João Lundgren died in 1946. Arthur, who then took over management of the stores and textile plants, died in 1967 or 1968, leaving the Lundgren enterprise to the next generation, with a triumvirate sharing control: Arthur's son Nilson for the factories, his brother Carlos in northeastern Brazil, and their cousin Frederico Axel in Rio de Janeiro. The former two stepped down in 1975, after a disagreement between Nilson and Erenita Helena Groschke Cavalcanti Lundgren, a cousin who was in charge of operations in São Paulo.

With half-ownership, Helena assumed command of Arthur Lundgren Tecidos S.A., the arm of the business operating in the state of São Paulo and states to the west and south. Under her leadership Casas Pernambucanas continued its movement—begun in the 1960s—into shopping centers. She established a number of larger stores called magazines and four large, high end department stores under the name Muricy.

The other branches of the business also went their separate ways, but in 1989 the remaining northern one, Lundgren Tecidos, which was losing money, fell into the hands of Lundgren Irmãos Tecidos S.A., which consisted of stores in the north and northeast, Rio de Janeiro, Minas Gerais, and Espírito Santo, the three textile plants, and the gunpowder factory. This company was owned by Nilson, Carlos, Frederico Axel, and Karl Herman Rüger, a Lundgren family in-law. Frederico Axel remained a principal shareholder in Arthur Lundgren Tecidos as well and was vice-chairman of its board.

During the 1970s, the São Paulo-based Casas Pernambucanas introduced home appliances in its stores, extended credit to its customers, and for the first time hired women to serve as sales clerks and in accounting and administration. The chain had already introduced ready-to-wear clothing, still something of a novelty since Brazilians were in the habit of buying fabrics to make clothing at home with sewing machines or to order them tailored to measure. In the 1980s it publicized itself by sponsoring motocross and other athletic events and by means of a balloon that traveled from city to city in the state of São Paulo.

The Rio-based company slowly followed the São Paulo-based company in modernizing its stores but did not introduce home appliances and home entertainment until 1990. Arthur Lundgren Tecidos began that decade with about 400 stores and 16,000 employees. Lundgren Irmãos Tecidos had 320 stores. Combined, they passed the $1 billion mark in sales for the first time in 1989 and held a 20 to 24 percent share of textile sales in Brazil.

Helena died in 1990 and was succeeded in her control of Arthur Lundgren Tecidos by her daughter Anita Louise Regina Harley. The São Paulo-based company survived and prospered during the decade. Arthur's children, however, squabbled over the allotment of shares in the Rio-based company. In what the business magazine *Exame* characterized as a scene out of a crime movie, Carlos threatened to kill his sister Selma, pointing a gun at her head. Although Lundgren Irmãos Tecidos was run by professional managers rather than Arthur's heirs, it could not meet its debts and went out of business in 1997.

CHANGE AND CONTINUITY

While Arthur Lundgren Tecidos survived the economic downturn of the late 1990s, six years of stagnant sales impelled it to close 160 stores and dismiss 6,000 workers, reducing the totals by late 2000 to 246 stores and 10,000 employees, respectively. The smaller locations were closed as Casas Pernambucanas aimed its sights at more affluent customers in larger cities and more prosperous areas. Even so, popular prices continued to prevail, since the chain's patrons ranged from lower middle class to working class. The average "ticket" was BRL 90 (about $45).

Credit was an important element. Casas Pernambucanas, which had introduced its own credit card in the 1990s, by this time had 2.2 million in circulation, and 70 percent of its sales were being made on credit. The chain had proprietary software for deciding which customers were creditworthy. Financing was ad-ministered by the company itself, and the amount in arrears was averaging only 2 percent of the total. Branch managers retained much latitude over individual store operations but were expected to show results. Management was concentrating on updating the chain's technology, since it did not even have a precise method to determine which products were selling briskly and which were languishing on the shelves. The Casas Pernambucanas customer could still buy fabrics and take them to a store tailor, equipped with tape measure and scissors, for conversion into clothing, but this accounted for less than 10 percent of the total business. The chain at this time ranked among the top seven national retailers in appliances, which included microwaves, television sets, and personal computers.

Casas Pernambucanas added cellular phones to the chain's merchandise in 2001, introduced Internet commerce that year, and launched the store's own shoe line in 2003. The following year Arthur Lundgren Tecidos opened a new distribution center for the chain in Barueri, São Paulo, and in 2005 it established a corporate "university" for its personnel. However, as late as 2002, the stores were losing money. Marketers considered Casas Pernambucanas still too closely tied to the past—to what one consultant called the era of *armarios,* exterior wardrobe closets—and in need of repositioning.

Marcelo Ferreira e Silva, formerly president of a supermarket chain, was hired in 2003 to be the retailer's director general, or chief operating officer. Charged with bringing fresh air to the enterprise, he introduced a computerized virtual store and added more products, including a shoe line. The number of company credit cards grew to more than 14 million. Under his direction Casas Pernambucanas also began to show more interest in presenting fashionable clothing.

LOOKING TO THE FUTURE

Casas Pernambucanas was profitable again by 2006. Although it was concentrating on raising productivity rather than expansion, by 2008 the number of stores had reached 277 in seven states. The holding company's sales grew 18 percent in 2007, with the department store chain accounting for three-quarters of the total. Its web site listed the following departments: electronics, information, film and photo, telephone and cellular, home appliances, white goods, hardware, health and beauty, lingerie, DVDs, games, toys, sports and leisure, watches, baby, kitchenware, bed, table, bath, rugs, and curtains.

To celebrate its 100th anniversary in late 2008, Casas Pernambucanas introduced a promotional campaign that included prizes, discount sales, and a commemorative book. However, the company did not relax its policy of refusing to make its executives available for interview by the press. Anita Harley maintained an office in the top floor of company headquarters, located above a Casas Pernambucanas store in downtown São Paulo, but she was rarely seen there or elsewhere, even by top executives. Nevertheless, it was said that no decision of any consequence was made without her knowledge and approval.

Anita Harley's reclusiveness only added to her allure, at least for journalists. A 2006 article in *Exame,* which included a rare photograph of the single, middle-aged woman, described her as tall, stout, and vaguely Teutonic, although her speech carried traces of Brazil's northeast, where she was born. Except for vacations at her home in her native Recife, she rarely left São Paulo, residing in three connected apartments in a hotel close to company headquarters. With the aid of one trusted executive—said to be the only person who could influence her—she normally conducted business from there by telephone, in a blunt and decisive manner. According to this article, Anita Harley inherited half-control of Arthur Lundgren Tecidos from her mother, but only until 2010, and held only about 30 percent of the shares, the same as Frederico Axel, her uncle. As a result the two alternated as chairman of the board, changing places every two years, with the other serving as vice-chairman. For continued control of the enterprise, Anita depended on the support of a group of nephews and nieces, shareholders who were represented on the board.

Because of the company's policy of silence, its plans for the future, including the succession, remained a mystery. Some 20 years or so earlier the Lundgrens had drawn up a list of norms for the more than 30 members of the fourth and fifth generations of the family who might want to work there. They would first have to gain experience somewhere else, and their fitness for promotion would be determined by a council composed of family members and veteran nonrelated executives. Anita Harley was known to have rejected offers by rival chains to buy the enterprise.

Robert Halasz

PRINCIPAL SUBSIDIARY

Pernambucanas Financiadora S.A.

PRINCIPAL COMPETITORS

Casas Bahia S.A.; Globex Utilidades S.A.; Lojas Americanas S.A.; Lojas Renner S.A.; Magazine Luiza S.A.

FURTHER READING

Alvim, Rosilene, *A Sedução da Cidade,* Rio de Janeiro: Graphia, 1997.

Barros, Guilherme, "A ex-rainha quer de volta seu trono," *Exame,* July 11, 1990, pp. 50–53.

Carvalho, Denise, "A discreta dama do varejo," *Exame,* August 2, 2006, pp. 58–59.

"Casas Pernambucanas, discreta e lucrativa," *Valor Econômico,* November 14, 2008.

"Con modelo antigo, Pernambucanas manterse no azul," *Valor Econômico,* March 17, 2006.

Furtado, José Maria, "A sobrevivente," *Exame,* November 1, 2001, pp. 62–64.

Góes, Raul de, *Un sueco emigra para o Nordeste,* Rio de Janeiro: Editora José Olympio, 1963.

"A herança que divide," *Exame,* March 18, 1992, p. 57.

Marcovitch, Jacques, *Pioneiros e empreendedores,* São Paulo: Editora Saraiva, 2007, vol. 3, pp. 29–62.

"Pioneira, rede de lojas Casas Pernambucanas faz 100 anos," *Folha de S. Paulo,* November 26, 2008.

Auntie Anne's, Inc.

48-50 West Chestnut Street, Suite 200
Lancaster, Pennsylvania 17603
U.S.A.
Telephone: (717) 435-1435
Fax: (717) 435-1436
Web site: http://www.auntieannes.com

Private Company
Incorporated: 1989
Employees: 190
Sales: $333.4 million (2008 est.)
NAICS: 722213 Snack and Nonalcoholic Beverage Bars

■ ■ ■

Auntie Anne's, Inc., is the world's largest hand-rolled soft pretzel franchiser, with more than 300 franchisees in over 980 locations. Auntie Anne's mixes, twists, bakes, and sells soft, warm pretzels as well as pretzel dogs and its signature lemonade. Operating in 20 countries, the company produces over 500,000 pretzels every two days, in full view of customers. Whether it is a seaweed-flavored pretzel in Singapore, a date pretzel in Saudi Arabia, or a Cinnamon Sugar Stix pretzel in Pennsylvania, Auntie Anne's guarantees the perfect pretzel.

ORIGINS

An Italian monk created the first pretzel sometime in the seventh century C.E. Twisting scraps of dough to resemble arms folded in prayer, he gave these *pretiolas*—little rewards—to his students. According to Anne Beiler, founder of Auntie Anne's, the holes in the pretzel represent the Holy Trinity. A thousand years later, immigrating Germans brought the pretzel to Pennsylvania. Anne Beiler grew up in the unique world of the Amish—an agrarian society of horse-drawn buggies and conservative religious tradition. Her hometown of Gap, Pennsylvania, had a population of just 2,000.

Beiler had an early introduction to the world of commerce, beginning at age 12, circa 1961, to bake pies and cakes for the family to sell. Three years later, she dropped out of school to work at a truck stop, handing her wages to her parents. This was the custom for many Amish girls, whose elders frowned on the secular influences of high schools. At 19, Anne married Jonas Beiler, who also had learned to bake as a youngster. The two then spent several years building churches in Pennsylvania and Texas.

Beiler had her first child at 22 and left the Amish Mennonite church at about the same time because she felt it was too strict. She said that she kept the faith and principles with which she was raised, however. Anne worked as a waitress and also stayed at home to rear two daughters, although she and Jonas would make time to take motorcycle rides together.

The Beilers moved back to Pennsylvania in 1987, where Jonas, an auto mechanic by trade, hoped to open a marriage and family counseling center for the Amish community in Lancaster County, who were reluctant to go to outsiders for help. To help raise money for this project, Anne took a part-time job managing a concession stand at a farmers market in Maryland, two hours

COMPANY PERSPECTIVES

The caring and goodness that go into every Auntie Anne's product are also the cornerstones of our relationships. For our loyal employees and valued franchisees, we offer our fullest support to help them grow and prosper. For our business associates, we promise devotion to the highest spiritual and ethical standards in all our business decisions and daily activities. For our customers, we pledge total consistency and excellence in products and services. For the communities we serve, we aspire to be a caring neighbor whose actions reflect reverence for traditional family values and Christian principles. Our profits will be invested to help others develop their greatest potential and to maintain our position as the innovative leader in the marketplace. We strive to make everything we do pay tribute to God who has entrusted us with this task.

away. It was there that she began rolling pretzels, which she noticed sold quickly and brought in a lot of profit. A 55-cent pretzel used only seven cents worth of ingredients, as *Forbes* later chronicled.

Within a year, she had rented her own 12-by-20-foot pretzel stand in Downingtown, Chester County, Pennsylvania, for $250 a month. She borrowed $6,000 from her in-laws to equip the stall. Beiler, who had 30 nieces and nephews, officially dubbed it "Auntie Anne's" when it opened in February 1988. The first items on the menu were pizza, stromboli, ice cream, and hand-rolled pretzels.

The first pretzels, based on a friend's recipe, were not hot sellers. In fact, according to *Forbes,* she was only bringing in $350 a weekend—barely enough to stay afloat. A bungled delivery of supplies led to a two-month period of pretzel experimentation. With a few extra ingredients suggested by husband Jonas, Anne Beiler came up with a softer, sweeter version. Pretzel sales quadrupled within a few months, and soon they were all she sold at her booth, rolling them in front of her customers in an entertaining presentation.

FROM FARMERS MARKETS TO FRANCHISES

After raising more capital, Beiler opened a second stand in Harrisburg, Pennsylvania, in July 1988. With a win-ning recipe and soon-to-be-famous name, the stage was set for franchising, which began in early 1989. She agreed to license the first franchise to her brother, Jake Smucker, who opened a shop in Middletown, Pennsylvania. The enterprise was very much a family affair. Auntie Anne had a sister making pretzel mix by hand. She did not give out the recipe to licensees, although an unauthorized version later appeared on the Internet. Another brother delivered it. Her husband and brother-in-law built the shops, and Anne's two daughters also helped.

Arrangements were quite informal at the beginning. Friends insisted on running their own stores, Beiler says; she simply asked for a percentage of monthly revenues in exchange for use of her name and recipe. A franchise fee between $2,500 and $5,000 was also paid. Beiler sold ten franchises in the first year, but the family had their hands full keeping openings on schedule; the system took in revenues of $1 million in 1990.

Beiler had seven siblings, and a younger brother, Carl Smucker, joined the company in August 1990 and recommended a six-month freeze on new franchises. When even he felt overwhelmed, he referred his sister to a franchising consultancy, which helped her devise a policy manual as well as a 100-page contract. To maintain brand integrity, the new agreement banned sales to supermarkets. In addition, the franchise fee increased substantially to $15,000. The consultant, David Hood, joined the staff as director of franchising in 1991 and eventually became company president.

With eight stores in 1989, the company added 42 stores in 1990, and 40 more by the end of 1991, for the most part in Pennsylvania, New York, and New Jersey. This string of success did not go unnoticed. *Inc.* magazine named Beiler "Entrepreneur of the Year" in 1992 and again in 1994, when the chain had 279 stores, all but 17 of them franchised. Income was $350,000 on revenues of $8 million. In 1994, needing cash to grow, the Beilers considered selling a stake to venture capitalists and going public. However, explained Anne in an article in *Inc.,* "Had we gone public, the pressure to perform financially would have been greater than our feelings about supporting our employees and franchisees." Deciding to stay private, the company reduced the number of company-owned stores and became more cost conscious.

In 1992, the free counseling center that Jonas Beiler had envisioned opened as the Family Information Center in Lancaster County, but the charitable giving did not end there. Among other groups, Beiler later became involved with the Angela Foundation, named after a daughter who died at 19 months. In all, Auntie Anne's gave $150,000 to charities in 1994, a largesse

KEY DATES

1988: Anne Beiler opens a booth selling fresh, hot pretzels at a Pennsylvania farmers market.
1990: Auntie Anne's reaches $1 million in revenues.
1992: The Beilers open a counseling center to help families in their local community.
1995: First international store opens in Jakarta.
2005: Samuel R. Beiler purchases company from founders.
2008: Corporate headquarters moves from Gap to Lancaster, Pennsylvania.

that frustrated loan officers. Auntie Anne herself was not beyond a few indulgences, however; she bought a white $36,000 Cadillac El Dorado. She and her husband also rode cross-country on motorcycles, visiting family-owned stores along the way.

GOING INTERNATIONAL

The Auntie Anne's phenomenon steadily worked its way through the malls of America in the mid-1990s. The chain had 344 stores at the end of 1995 and dwarfed competitors such as Pretzel Time and Gretel's Pretzels. Franchisees averaged $300,000 in revenues a year and the entire system took in more than $100 million in revenues. A far cry from Lancaster County, Auntie Anne's opened its first international location in Jakarta, Indonesia, where most people had never even heard of pretzels.

At the time, Auntie Anne's offered ten different types of pretzels and several sauces: caramel, sweet mustard, strawberry cream cheese, honey, marinara, and chocolate. Pretzel varieties included sour cream and onion, sesame seed, garlic, whole wheat, and caramel almond; they sold for about $1.25 each. For the sweet tooth, there were cinnamon sugar and Glazin' Raisin—two twisted answers to cinnamon buns. The smell of fresh-baked pretzels proved a powerful calling card; the company also offered free samples. In one case, it sent a pretzel cart dispensing them through a mall in Detroit. To get the name out, Auntie Anne's locations displayed brochures about nutrition facts, locations, and company history.

At the end of 1996, the chain had 408 stores. It continued to play up its Pennsylvania Dutch roots and boasted a considerable number of Amish operators, many of whom were related to each other, although some considered them relatively unsophisticated in

business. Beiler conceded in *Restaurant Business:* "It's very un-Amish, what I've done." Thanks to a congressional exemption, Amish franchisees did not have to pay Social Security taxes for their Amish employees. They also did not have to pay into the state workers' compensation fund.

Like bagels, the pretzel concept was catching on as a low-fat alternative to other mall snacks, such as pizza. Auntie Anne's largest competitor, Pretzelmaker, started in 1991, had 200 stores in 1997, and was developing a line of pretzel sandwiches. Gretel's Pretzels, which grew out of the pretzel business of Restaurant Systems, had just 15 stores. Mrs. Fields' Cookies, a master mall marketer, was test-marketing the "Pretzelwich" at a dozen of its 115 Hot Sam stores under the Pretzel Ovens name.

CONTINUED EXPANSION

In spite of all the interest in malls, only 5 percent of mall shoppers ever bought pretzels at the mall. Beiler took her case to the national media to try to reach more of them. Her unique woman's success story made for good copy. The campaign was aimed at women 25 to 54 years old—the bulk of mall shoppers. On the publicity tour, Beiler also offered advice for business owners: "To be successful in life, all you have to do is be a giver rather than a taker," as she was quoted in the *Patriot-News.* "Be a giver and life is full of surprises."

Auntie Anne's grew to 558 stores in 1998, although it accepted only ten out of 6,000 franchise applications that year. The company received 400 inquiries a month. In spite of its success, it remained a family business, with 30 of Anne Beiler's kinfolk working for the company, including a distant cousin, Sam Beiler, as chief operating officer. In all, it employed 100 employees at the home office and 35 in regional ones.

The company continued to open stores in enclosed malls, where sales remained strong. It had begun expanding, however, into train and plane terminals and outlet malls. It also dispatched a few trailer units to carnivals. Auntie Anne's introduced a new taste, the Parmesan Herb pretzel, in November 1998. A year later, it rolled out Auntie Anne's at Home Pretzel Kit in time for the Christmas season. The kits sold for about $10 and contained enough ingredients for ten Original or Cinnamon Sugar pretzels.

By 2000, the stores were selling ten varieties of pretzels, including Cinnamon Sugar and Jalapeño, as well as dipping sauces: three varieties of cream cheese; sweet mustard; marinara; caramel; cheese; and chocolate. Glazin' Raisin offered a low-fat alternative to cinnamon buns. In addition to lemonade, the stores served Dutch Ice, a frozen drink.

Auntie Anne's had nearly 600 locations around the world and was opening seven new ones every month at a cost to franchisees of about $150,000 to $250,000 each. The company reached into Thailand, Singapore, Indonesia, the Philippines, and Malaysia, and new stores were planned in Venezuela and Hong Kong. The Pretzel Japan Corporation opened the first Japanese store in Yokohama's new Mosaic Mall in March 2000. The following year, the company signed its first international agreements for franchises in the Middle East—in Saudi Arabia and the United Arab Emirates. Another agreement led to the opening of stores in South Korea. Sales in 2001 reached $217 million, a 4 percent increase over 2000.

ADVERTISING AND RE-BRANDING

In the early part of the decade, same-store sales grew soft as mall traffic slipped. Auntie Anne's began testing new advertising and promotional options to increase brand awareness and mall sales. In 2002, the company initiated new radio spots and began selling the at-home pretzel kits, gift certificates, and the illustrated book, *Auntie Anne, My Story*, through its web site. In 2003, it signed a seven-year agreement with the Philadelphia Eagles, making the chain the team's "preferred pretzel," and added television ads to its marketing portfolio. With the majority of its U.S. units located in shopping malls, the ten-second national spots continued the tagline from print and radio ads: "Auntie Anne's. The best reason to go to the mall."

Exploring expansion options, in 2004 the company opened a new bakery-café concept in Lancaster, Pennsylvania. The 30-seat Auntie Anne's Café offered breakfast, lunch, and dinner menus, including sandwiches served on pretzel rolls, salads, pizzas, and salads. Within a year, five cafés were in operation in Lancaster County. However, in 2006, the company closed four of them. Apparently, the Auntie Anne brand concept was so strong that customers coming to the restaurants wanted Auntie Anne's pretzels, not the items on the menu.

In April 2005, Jonas and Anne Beiler sold the company to Sam Beiler. Sam, a distant cousin, was one of the early franchisees, opening his first stand in 1989. He helped establish the company's regional structure and then moved to headquarters in 1997, where he concentrated on international expansion and overseeing the company-owned stores. He became president and CEO in 2001. Auntie Anne's led the soft-pretzel market segment, with 2004 sales of $247 million from 850 locations in 43 states and 12 foreign countries.

Some changes occurred under the new leadership. Most obvious was an 18-month-long re-branding process. Unveiled in August 2006, the new program included an updated logo with a contemporary font and a gold halo over a restyled pretzel and tagline "Perfect Pretzel." Posters and in-store packaging offered touches of humor, such as, "Spoiling dinner since 1988," and, "Almost too cute to eat. Almost." For employees, there were new uniforms, which they could customize, choosing to wear a ball cap, bandana, or skull cap, and long or short sleeves on bowling or camp shirts instead of the usual polo shirt.

Auntie Anne's continued its international expansion, moving into the United Kingdom and Ireland in 2006 and into Canada and China in 2008. That same year it moved its corporate headquarters from Gap to downtown Lancaster. Warehousing and fund-raising kit operations also moved into the city. The company continued to have record sales and, for the third year, was recognized as a World-Class Franchise by Fran Survey, the most prestigious rating in franchising. The company projected opening 94 new stores in 2009, including 42 in the United States and 52 internationally. Whether those goals would be reached would depend on the impact, domestically and globally, of the economic recession.

Frederick C. Ingram
Updated, Ellen D. Wernick

PRINCIPAL COMPETITORS

NexCen Brands Inc.; Wetzel's Pretzels LLC.

FURTHER READING

"Auntie Anne's Inks Deals for Three Countries," *Nation's Restaurant News,* July 9, 2001, p. 28.

"Auntie Anne's Offers Products on Enhanced Web Site," *Nation's Restaurant News,* December 9, 2002, p. 14.

"Auntie Anne's: Rolling Out Success One Pretzel at a Time," *Opportunities World,* March 2009.

"Auntie Anne's Signs Partnership Deal with Football's Eagles," *Nation's Restaurant News,* August 18, 2003, p. 18.

Ballon, Marc, "Pretzel Queen," *Forbes,* March 13, 1995, p. 112.

Beiler, Anne, *Twist of Faith: The Story of Anne Beiler, Founder of Auntie Anne's Pretzels,* Nashville, Tenn.: Thomas Nelson, 2008.

Bernstein, Charles, "Tandem Bikers," *Chain Leader,* November 2003, p. 100.

"Canada Now in a Twist over Auntie Anne's," *Canadian Corporate News,* June 30, 2008.

Carrera, Nora, "Business with Twist Draws Franchisors: Pretzel-maker Is the Second Largest Chain of Soft Pretzel Shops and Growing Fast," *Denver Rocky Mountain News,* March 17, 1997, p. 2B.

Cebrzynski, Gregg, "Restaurant Chains Say: Let the Buyer Be Aware," *Nation's Restaurant News,* March 23, 1998, p. 16.

———, "Snack Chains Boost Brand Awareness with Ads, Products," *Nation's Restaurant News,* August 5, 2002, p. 14.

———, "Two Firsts for Auntie Anne's: TV Spots, Kids Toy Promo," *Nation's Restaurant News,* February 3, 2003, p. 14.

Fisk, Holly Celeste, "Twist of Fate," *Entrepreneur,* July 1996, p. 207.

Hollister, Danielle C., "Founder of Auntie Anne's Pretzels Builds Franchise Operation," *Patriot-News,* April 5, 1998.

"In a Former Life: Anne Beiler," *Inc.,* September 2000, p. 107.

Jennings, Lisa, "Double-Digit Growth Sweetens 2nd-Tier Snack Brands' Results," *Nation's Restaurant News,* July 24, 2006, p. 88.

Kochak, Jacqueline, "A New Twist," *Restaurant Business,* September 15, 1998, pp. 80–81.

Kraybill, Donald, *Amish Enterprise: From Plows to Profits,* Baltimore, Md.: Johns Hopkins University, 1996.

Lion, Deborah, "Linda's Little Rewards," *Franchising World,* January/February 1996, p. 48.

Lisovicz, Susan, "Auntie Anne's CEO and Co-Founder," *Entrepreneurs Only,* CNNfn, October 13, 1999.

Mehegan, Sean, "The Modest Merchants," *Restaurant Business,* April 10, 1996, p. 57.

Mekeel, Tim, "Auntie Anne's Closes 4 of Its 5 Lancaster, Pa.–Area Restaurants," *Lancaster New Era,* October 10, 2006.

"A New Twist," *Restaurant Business,* June 15, 1997, pp. 71–75.

"Pretzels Plus," *Restaurants & Institutions,* February 1, 2004, p. 21.

Prewitt, Milford, "Auntie Anne's Promo Showcases Sweet Smell of Success," *Nation's Restaurant News,* February 27, 1995, p. 12.

Reinan, John, "Doing the Twist and It Goes Like This … ," *Tampa Bay Tribune,* Business and Finance Sec., April 16, 1999, p. 1.

Rohland, Pamela, "It's Twisted," *QSR Magazine,* March/April 1999.

Shepherd, Lauren, "Pretzel Time Name to Disappear," *Associated Press,* February 18, 2009.

"Soft Pretzel Maker Auntie Anne's to Open New Corporate HQ," *PR Newswire,* October 11, 2006.

Strauss, Karyn, "Breaking the Cookie-Cutter Image: Auntie Anne's Tests Interactive Units," *Nation's Restaurant News,* January 10, 2000, pp. 8, 72.

"Tempting the Tastebuds," *Business Franchise,* October 2006, p. 30.

Thierry, Lauren, and Bill Tucker, "Auntie Anne's CEO," *Entrepreneurs Only,* CNNfn, May 18, 1999.

Walkup, Carolyn, "Pretzel Players Put Twist on Menu Items; Segment Leader 'Anne's' Sold," *National Restaurant News,* January 17, 2005, p. 4.

"What Auntie Anne's Will Mean for the City," *Lancaster New Era,* October 12, 2006.

Back Bay Restaurant Group, Inc.

284 Newbury Street
Boston, Massachusetts 02115
U.S.A.
Telephone: (617) 536-2800
Toll Free: (800) 424-2753
Fax: (617) 236-4175
Web site: http://www.backbayrestaurantgroup.com

Private Company
Incorporated: 1983 as Westwood Restaurant Group
Employees: 8,000
Sales: $150.6 million (2007)
NAICS: 722110 Full-Service Restaurants

■ ■ ■

Back Bay Restaurant Group, Inc., owns and operates 34 full-service restaurants, primarily in Massachusetts but also in Connecticut, New York, New Jersey, New Hampshire, Rhode Island, Washington, D.C., and Florida. The company offers seven distinct restaurant concepts: Abe & Louie's (upscale steak house), Atlantic Fish (high-end seafood), Bouchée (French brasserie), Charley's (American), Coach Grill (upscale meat and seafood), Joe's American Bar and Grill (American), and Papa Razzi (Northern Italian). By using different restaurant concepts with similar menus, Back Bay is able to operate several locations in popular restaurant markets.

THE FIRST 20 YEARS

From the opening of his first restaurant, Boraschi's Café, in 1965, Charles Sarkis wanted to make dining out attractive and exciting, and he wanted to reach the young, upscale customer. "Our aim has always been to put out great food, quality service, and a great environment at a very reasonable check average," he explained in a 1991 *Restaurant Business* article.

By 1968 Sarkis had decided on the concept he thought would attract that clientele: American food served in a "saloon" setting. That year he opened the first Charley's Eating and Drinking Saloon on Newbury Street in Boston's Back Bay area. The restaurant was decorated with dark wood, etched glass, brass, and fabrics of burgundy and hunter green. The menu had five sandwiches, a salad, four entrees, two soups, and two appetizers. As he told Kevin Farrell in a 1988 article in *Restaurant Business,* "We did a lot of things first that are taken for granted now. In the late 1960s, we served shrimp by the piece. We prepped french fries from scratch. We put top-grade mustard on the tables. We offered gourmet hamburgers. And we had waiters introduce themselves to their customers using their first names." That practice was so important that a waiter who did not introduce himself stood to be disciplined.

Charley's became the flagship concept of The Westwood Group, Sarkis's company, but not the only one. In 1975 Sarkis introduced a Victorian-themed dining room, which he named J.C. Hillary's Ltd. He opened three that year: two in Boston (including Back Bay) and one in Dedham, Massachusetts, joining the Charley's in the region. This would become a Sarkis trademark, add-

COMPANY PERSPECTIVES

The company's philosophy is embedded in providing the perfect guest experience, its passion is over-the-top hospitality and its purpose is to have a positive impact on the people who choose to join their team. Back Bay measures success as real growth in sales and profit and has always believed that this is built in the six principles of excellence—Respect, Caring, Fairness, Quality, Fun and Leadership. With focus, passion and purpose in mind and excellence as their standard, Back Bay Restaurant Group has built a place of opportunity and success and created an enterprise that they celebrate and are proud to be part of, and that continues to endure and prosper.

ing an entirely new restaurant concept, not just opening another location.

In 1983 Sarkis expanded outside of his base, buying five restaurants in Florida and opening them as J.C. Hillary's locations. He also incorporated his restaurant business, naming it the Westwood Restaurant Group, Inc.

The next years were busy ones for Sarkis with updated menus and new restaurant concepts. In 1984 he opened Joe's American Bar & Grill in Back Bay, five blocks from the original Charley's on Newbury Street. This was an urban, upscale restaurant with a club atmosphere and a menu that featured grilled fish and meats, pasta, and seafood. It also offered a lighter menu in a separate dining room.

In 1985 The Famous Atlantic Fish Company debuted. This concept combined a bistro and raw bar and featured a wide variety of fresh seafood. Westwood Restaurant owned the restaurant's name and expansion rights, but Sarkis retained the original bistro separately, as he did with J.C. Hillary's. In 1986 Hillary's opened in Wayland, Massachusetts, a more formal, upscale version of J.C. Hillary's.

GROWING THE CONCEPTS

While business was doing well in New England, the company was having problems with its locations in Florida. Those five sites had never done as well as Westwood Restaurants expected them to, so the company put most of the restaurants up for sale. Despite that problem the company, with 19 restaurants, had annual sales in 1987 of $30 million. At the end of that year

Sarkis sold his privately held restaurant business to the Westwood Group, of which he was the majority shareholder. In addition to the restaurant business, the Westwood Group owned and operated Wonderland Dog Track, a greyhound racing facility in Massachusetts. The merger was viewed as a means of helping to infuse money into the track, which had seen its revenues fall.

By 1988 there were eight Charley's in Massachusetts, New Hampshire, and Connecticut. With seating for 108 people, the average per-person check was $10.50, and each unit averaged $3 million in volume a year. The menu had expanded over the years, and while it was still the narrowest among the five concepts, it included nine appetizers, four salads, 24 entrees, four hamburgers, deli sandwiches, individual pizzas, and a variety of desserts.

The three J.C. Hillary's locations remaining in the company had checks averaging $8 at lunch and $12 at dinner. The sole Hillary's unit was slightly more expensive, $8.50 for lunch and $15 in the evening. The prices were similar at the three Famous American Fish Company bistros. Meals at the two Joe's American Bar & Grill locations were the most expensive of the concepts, with lunches averaging $9 and dinners $17. Each of the units served liquor and had a bar, and all were open seven days a week for lunch and dinner. Four of the restaurants were within a five-block radius of each other in Boston's Back Bay. The others were located in regional shopping malls.

Despite the problems experienced in Florida, Sarkis was still interested in expanding beyond the New England region. He recognized he needed some help to do that, so he went outside the organization to hire people with experience operating larger chains. He also began developing a new dining concept in response to the growing demand for moderately priced, light, healthful Italian food.

INTRODUCING PAPA RAZZI

Papa Razzi, the company's Northern Italian bistro concept, was unveiled in Back Bay in November 1989, during the depths of Massachusetts' economic depression. As he had in building a new management team, Sarkis went outside the company to develop his new concept. The menu was more sophisticated than his previous ones had been and they required more skill in the kitchen. Along with veal chops, chicken dishes, and roast beef tenderloin, dinner customers could select pastas that ranged from spiral tubes with roasted eggplant, smoked mozzarella, tomatoes, basil, and Romano to hollow straws with Italian bacon, hot peppers, onions, and tomato sauce. There was also a special seafood pasta offered each day.

The restaurant also offered more than a dozen pizzas, which ranged in price from $6.75 to $10.95. Lunch customers could also order individual pizzas and Italian-style sandwiches with a salad. The restaurant was decorated in earth colors with marble and light wood accents. The first location featured a wood-burning pizza oven and a food display case, to emphasize the importance of food preparation at the restaurant. This was a shift from the earlier concepts, where the decorating emphasis had been on the dining room.

The concept was an immediate hit. Two more locations opened in Massachusetts by the end of 1991, and four more were added, including one outside New England in White Plains, New York, in 1992. The second Papa Razzi restaurant to open reached the original's $3 million plus annual sales level after being open for only three weeks. Papa Razzi locations tended to be larger than the Westwood's other restaurants, from 4,000 to 12,000 square feet, with seating for between 200 and 350 people. By the end of 1994 there were 13 units, with two located as far south as New Jersey.

Sarkis was not done introducing new concepts, however. In 1990 he renovated a Florida location and

reopened it as Rayz Riverside Café. Funkier and more casual than the other concepts, Rayz was decorated in a nautical/beach style, complete with menus shaped like suntanning reflectors. The menu included many of the dishes from the other restaurants, but also offered its own specialties: soft shell crabs in season, Maryland crab cakes, and rotisserie-grilled ribs and chicken. That November he opened the second Rayz in Cambridge, Massachusetts. At the end of 1990, the restaurant division had 21 units, with total annual sales of $50 million.

STRUCTURAL CHANGES

In April 1991 Sarkis reincorporated the Westwood Restaurant Group, Inc., as the Back Bay Restaurant Group, Inc., a wholly owned subsidiary of The Westwood Group. For the first time, Westwood began publicizing that its various restaurant brands had a common ownership. As Sarkis told *Restaurant Business,* "I used to think people might have negative associations if they saw us as a chain. But since 90 percent of our customers have a good experience, why shouldn't we want to let them know about our other restaurants?"

The concept of clustering the different concepts together had worked well in the Back Bay area, with the company reporting $15 million worth of business from its five different units there, compared to $5 million by a single-location competitor. Back Bay expected to follow that strategy as it expanded beyond New England.

In March 1992 Back Bay went public. The company, with 26 locations, ended the year with sales of $59.6 million and net income of $2.6 million.

Even as the company grew, Back Bay continued to stress its traditional standard of quality. Management trainees had to complete a ten-week course, during which they learned about the operations of the entire restaurant (kitchen, bar, and dining room) as well as food quality, customer service, employee relations, and issues related to liquor liability. The training made it relatively easy for managers to move among what the company was now calling its American concept restaurants or from one Papa Razzi location to another.

In 1993 Back Bay sold the remaining Florida property to the U.S. Department of Transportation for $4.7 million and formally separated from the Westwood Group. More units were opened, bringing the total number of locations by the end of the year to 31. Sales reached over $74 million, with profits of nearly $3.5 million. Nonetheless, trouble signs were developing. Average sales in the units had dropped slightly and same-store sales rose less than 1 percent compared with their revenues the year before.

The company continued to expand, reaching a peak of 37 restaurants at the end of 1994, with a total customer count of 5.3 million people. However, that growth and increased competition took their toll as profits fell 86 percent from 1993, even though sales were up 16 percent, to nearly $86 million. David Loeb, a restaurant analyst with The Chicago Corp. in Chicago, put it succinctly to Robin Lee Allen of *Nation's Restaurant News* in a 1995 article, "As someone at Shoney's said to me, 'In casual dining, the seats are growing faster than the fannies to fill them.'"

CHALLENGING TIMES

To attract customers, Back Bay initiated a Preferred Guest Program. Under the program, a customer received a $20 certificate good at any of the company's restaurants each time their account reflected $200 in food and drink purchases. The company also closed several older, underperforming sites and slowed its development plans. It did open new Joe's American Bar & Grill units in towns where a Papa Razzi already existed and, in February 1995, opened a Papa Razzi in Georgetown, in the District of Columbia.

Despite these efforts, same-store sales, particularly for the 17 Papa Razzi units, continued to drop during 1995 and by midyear the company was reporting a net loss. Back Bay countered by starting a summer radio campaign for Papa Razzi in the Boston area, a break with the company's traditional dependence on word-of-mouth publicity. The company also sent its Papa Razzi concept chef to Italy where he spent nine weeks studying regional cuisine.

In September the trattoria's five-year-old menu was expanded with the addition of dishes from southern Italy. The restaurants began using fresh pasta instead of dried, and new entrees ranged from a broiled veal chop served with linguine tossed with wild mushrooms in a Marsala wine sauce to whole-wheat pasta with sausage, Roma tomatoes, arugula, garlic, and fresh parsley. Olives, capers, and artichokes appeared in more dishes as well.

The total customer count increased 8 percent during the year, and the company had record sales of over $93 million. However, Back Bay and its 33 units operated at a $2.8 million loss for the year due to charges against closed restaurants and abandoned projects. Also in September, Sarkis was diagnosed with a brain tumor, which was eventually found to be benign.

REORGANIZING FOR RECOVERY

Company officers decided it was time to reorganize and strengthen the focus on operations: training, service, and product quality. Mark Hartzfeld was named executive vice-president and chief operating officer. The year did not begin well, as the Blizzard of 1996 dropped more than 100 inches of snow in Back Bay's major market. However, as the year passed, each fiscal quarter showed year-to-year earnings improvement. In September 1996 the company opened its first new restaurant in more than a year, a Joe's American Bar & Grill in Braintree, Massachusetts.

The financial picture improved during 1997 with the company reporting net income of just over one-half million dollars for the first six months, compared to a net loss for the period in 1996. In January 1997 Back Bay announced it had purchased the Cornucopia restaurant, located atop pilings in Boston Harbor. The company's eighth Joe's opened on the site in May, offering "American fare with a distinct seaside flair." That summer the last Rayz location closed, but customers could still get a taste of the sun as some of the concept's specialties were added to the menu of the nearby Papa Razzi.

A PRIVATE COMPANY AGAIN

Early in 1998 the company moved into Boston's high-end steak-house market, opening a 160-seat restaurant called Abe & Louie's on the site of Sarkis's first restaurant. Named after Sarkis's late father and one of his best friends, the new concept was immediately popular—Boston remembered the senior Sarkis, a well-known, convicted bookmaker and tax evader. Back Bay reported that net income for the year was up 55 percent to $2.69 million, on sales of $99.4 million. Customer counts were also up from 1997, to nearly 5.2 million.

Before 1998 ended, Sarkis and his management team formed a new company, SRC Holdings Inc., and began the process of taking Back Bay private. The nearly $40 million deal was settled in March 1999. "Restaurants are really not good public companies," Sarkis told *Nation's Restaurant News* in June 1999, continuing, "If you're off by one penny in earnings, Wall Street kills you."

One of its first actions as a private company was to convert several J.C. Hillary's locations to the extremely popular Joe's American Grill format. This resulted in sales increases of 30 percent to 90 percent at some of the renovated locations. The company also repositioned its Famous Atlantic Fish Co. as a high-end seafood restaurant and dropped the "famous" in the name. Finally, the company acquired The Red Coach Inn in Wayland, Massachusetts (which opened in 1935) and turned it into the Coach Grill, offering steaks and seafood in a casually elegant environment.

The company celebrated its 40th anniversary operating six successful concepts that specialized in steak and seafood, Italian and American style. Combined, the restaurants served a total of 6.5 million people a year. In 2005 an Abe & Louie's opened in Boca Raton, Florida, and company revenue reached $136.4 million, up from $133.2 million.

Sarkis still did not stop thinking about new options. In 2006 the company added a totally new concept to its portfolio, opening a French bistro in its Back Bay neighborhood. The two-story restaurant was named Bouchée, which means "mouthful" in French. It cost $5 million to construct and included a zinc bar and marble-topped tables on the first level and a more formal area upstairs.

In early 2009 the company introduced a new, contemporary design for Joe's American Bar & Grill. Costing $5 million to build, it offered a sushi bar, a retractable glass roof, and seating for 250, "It's what we call a Joe's of this year as opposed to a Joe's of 30 years ago," Sarkis told the *Boston Herald*.

This construction and renovation was financed through loans and a revolving fund, including a $40 million deal struck in 2008. Revenues rose in 2006 to $151.4 million, but sales growth slowed in 2007, totaling $150.6 million. As the consumer economy slowed, restaurants, especially full-service sites such as those of the Back Bay Restaurant Group, faced a challenging future.

Updated, Ellen D. Wernick

PRINCIPAL DIVISIONS

Abe & Louie's; Atlantic Fish; Bouchée; Charley's; Coach Grill; Joe's American Bar & Grill; Papa Razzi.

PRINCIPAL COMPETITORS

Legal Sea Foods; Applebee's Restaurants; Pizzeria Uno Restaurants.

FURTHER READING

Allen, Robin Lee, "At $40M, the Price Is Right for Back Bay to Go Private," *Nation's Restaurant News,* June 14, 1999, p. 4.

———, "Back Bay Back in Front with Reorganization, New Philosophy," *Nation's Restaurant News,* November 10, 1997, p.8.

———, "Back Bay Still Plagued by Competition, Operational Difficulties," *Nation's Restaurant News,* May 8, 1995, p. 11.

———, "Papa Razzi Adds Southern Touch to Menu," *Nation's Restaurant News* September 11, 1995, p. 7.

———, "Papa Razzi: Now That's Italian!" *Nation's Restaurant News,* May 16, 1994, p. 97.

Aronovich, Hanna, "Perfect Concepts: Developing Its Employees and Upholding High Standards, Back Bay Is Poised for Controlled Growth," *Food and Drink,* March–April 2005, pp. 98–99.

"Back Bay Acquires Cornucopia in Boston Harbor," *Nation's Restaurant News,* January 13, 1997, p. 2.

"Back Bay Restaurant Group Selects Flexible Lender, Signs First Deal with GE Capital Solutions," *Business Wire,* November 1, 2006.

Casper, Carol, "Rayz of Light in New England," *Restaurant Business,* December 10, 1991, p. 92.

"Charles Sarkis: 'Almost' Is Not an Option," *Boston Business Journal,* October 6, 2006.

"Company News; Back Bay Restaurant to Convert to Private Ownership," *New York Times,* December 4, 1998.

Farrell, Kevin, "Charles Sarkis's 'Front Door' Style," *Restaurant Business,* April 10, 1988, p. 130.

Fiedler, Terry G., "An Eat-and-Run Merger: Dog Track Owner Buys Restaurants to Nurture Profits," *New England Business,* April 6, 1987, p. 44.

Frumkin, Paul, "Boston's Back Bay Group Debuts French Brasserie Bouchee," *Nation's Restaurant News,* October 2, 2006, pp. 8–9.

———, "The Time They Are a Changin'—and Charles Sarkis Is Changing with Them," *Nation's Restaurant News,* December 2, 1991.

"GE Capital Solutions, Franchise Finance Completes $40 Million Deal with Back Bay Restaurant Group," *Business Wire,* March 18, 2008.

Grillo, Thomas, "Joe's to Take T.G.I. Friday's Former Space," *Boston Herald,* p. O17.

Grunwald, Michael, "Sarkis Blasts Critics," *Boston Globe,* December 18, 1993, p. 67.

Holland, Roberta, "Once Sizzling Steakhouses Cooled by Down Economy," *Boston Business Journal,* November 7, 2008. http://portland.bizjournals.com/boston/stories/2008/11/10/story3htm.

"New Stock Listings," *Wall Street Journal,* March 23, 1992, p. C4.

"Papa Razzi Parent Gets $33M Financing Package," *Nation's Restaurant News,* September 2, 2002, p. 88.

Schaffer, Mat, "Bouchee Brings Bit of Paris to Boston," *Boston Herald,* January 5, 207, p. E20.

"Second 100 Companies Ranked by U.S. Foodservice Revenues," *Nation's Restaurant News,* July 28, 2008, pp. 52–69.

Billing Services Group Ltd.

7411 John Smith Drive, Suite 1500
San Antonio, Texas 78229
U.S.A.
Telephone: (210) 949-7000
Toll Free: (888) 393-5854
Fax: (210) 949-7101
Web site: http://www.bsgclearing.com

Public Company
Incorporated: 1985 as U.S. Long Distance Corporation
Employees: 300
Sales: $180 million (2007)
Stock Exchanges: London
Ticker Symbol: BILL
NAICS: 518210 Data Processing, Hosting, and Related Services

■ ■ ■

Bermuda-based Billing Services Group Ltd. (BSG) is a leading player in the clearing and settlement industry. From its headquarters in San Antonio, Texas, BSG provides some 850 telecommunications, e-commerce, and digital media customers with a variety of advanced payment services on an outsourced basis. On behalf of its clients, BSG offers services such as billing, collection, and customer service.

In addition to operating through traditional payment channels such as credit cards, BSG offers a variety of alternative payment options, including its Bill2Phone and Bill2Phone Mobile services, which provide access to approximately 350 million customers via their phone bills.

U.S. LONG DISTANCE CORPORATION DEBUTS

Billing Services Group Ltd. was formed in 2003 when ABRY Partners, an equity firm specializing in media companies, acquired Avery Communications, as well as two companies (Billing Concepts and Enhanced Services Billing) that had originated with U.S. Long Distance Corporation. Through these three companies, BSG can trace its roots back to the mid-1980s.

Two of the companies that were part of the ABRY deal, Enhanced Services Billing and Billing Concepts, were established by U.S. Long Distance Corporation (USLD). That company was formed in 1985, in the Houston, Texas, garage of Parris H. "Butch" Holmes Jr., who used $50,000 to start a small pay-phone business. USLD experienced growth throughout the 1980s, and eventually became involved in the profitable billing industry. A business named Zero Plus Dialing became part of the USLD family in 1988, followed by US Billing in 1993 and Enhanced Services Billing the following year.

In 1996 USLD spun off its three billing-related concerns—Zero Plus Dialing, US Billing, and Enhanced Services Billing—to create a new publicly traded enterprise named Billing Information Concepts. At this time Butch Holmes served as chairman of both USLD and Billing Information Concepts. Growth continued in 1997 via the acquisition of billing services provider Computer Resources Management. That deal brought

COMPANY PERSPECTIVES

BSG manages diverse financial transactions for the nation's largest voice, data and IP communications companies with an extensive portfolio of clearinghouse services. We are uniquely able to reach hundreds of millions of end users, providing efficient and effective transaction processing solutions that authorize, collect and settle communications related charges on behalf of our customers.

the company an existing alliance with IBM, and enabled it to branch out beyond telecommunications and provide metered billing services for utility companies.

In mid-1997 Holmes resigned as USLD's chairman but continued to serve as the head of Billing Information Concepts, which changed its name to Billing Concepts Corp. in 1998. This change was followed by the acquisition of a billing services provider named Communications Software Consultants. By this time Billing Concepts was providing some 400 long-distance companies with billing services.

In September 1998 Billing Concepts shelled out $10 million for a 22 percent stake in Princeton Tele-Com Corporation. The privately held company, established by several Princeton University professors in 1983, specialized in the emerging area of electronic billing. A black mark against Billing Concepts occurred in early 1999, when a class-action lawsuit was filed against the company in U.S. District Court. The lawsuit alleged that Holmes and other company officials had inflated the price of Billing Concepts' stock by issuing misleading statements, allowing them to sell shares at an artificially high price. However, the company issued a statement arguing that the lawsuit had no merit.

NEW LEADERSHIP AND NEW DEALS FOR BILLING CONCEPTS

By early 1999 Billing Concepts' software and billing clearinghouse operations had achieved strong growth. In March, the company named a new president to head each division. Jacquelene Mitchell was named president and chief operating officer of clearinghouse division, while Kelly Simmons fulfilled the same role on the software side.

The following month plans were revealed to spin the two divisions off as separate publicly traded companies. The plan was for Holmes to serve as chair-

man of both companies, and as CEO of the software enterprise, which was named Aptis Inc. Billing Concepts President and Chief Operating Officer Alan Saltzman was to become CEO of Billing Concepts.

By August 1999 the divisional spinoff plans had been canceled. Saltzman resigned in September, and his departure was followed by that of Kelly Simmons in January 2000. Despite these setbacks Billing Concepts continued to grow, acquiring the Lubbock, Texas-based call center firm OSC in March. Formed in 1987, OSC had previously done business as Operator Service Co.

More leadership changes unfolded in July 2000. At that time Holmes named Michael Smith as Billing Solutions' president and chief operating officer. Blake Allen was chosen as president and CEO of the company's FI-Data arm, which provided the credit union industry with instant online loan approval services, and Teresa Sheridan was named president and chief operating officer of Aptis Software.

A major development occurred at Billing Concepts in September 2000. At that time the company agreed to sell three of its main divisions (OSC, Aptis Software, and LEC Billing) to Los Angeles-based Platinum Equity Holdings in a deal worth approximately $80 million. The deal with Platinum Equity—which was completed in October and included all but 15 of the company's 1,175 employees—was significant because it allowed Billing Concepts to concentrate on so-called new economy opportunities. At this time, the company turned its attention toward its FIData business.

In addition to FIData, Billing Concepts also was the lead investor in two other Internet-related companies. The first was Princeton eCom (formerly Princeton TeleCom Corporation), which claimed to have presented the first bill on the Internet. Additionally, Billing Concepts also was the leading investor in a business-to-business content delivery application service provider named COREintellect. Following the Platinum Equity deal, Billing Concepts adopted the name New Century Equity Holdings in 2001. That same year, the company sold its FIData business.

AVERY COMMUNICATIONS ORIGINS

Avery Communications Inc., the third company that was part of BSG's formation, originated in 1991, when it was established as a Texas-based telecommunications holding company. Developments at Avery during the early 1990s included its 1993 purchase of subsidiary Telco Group Inc.

KEY DATES

1985: Parris H. "Butch" Holmes Jr. forms a small pay-phone business named U.S. Long Distance Corp. (USLD) in his garage.

1988: USLD forms Zero Plus Dialing.

1991: Avery Communications Inc. is established as a Texas-based telecommunications holding company.

1993: US Billing becomes part of USLD.

1994: USLD forms Enhanced Services Billing.

1996: USLD spins off Zero Plus Dialing, US Billing, and Enhanced Services Billing to create a new publicly traded enterprise named Billing Information Concepts.

1998: Billing Information Concepts changes its name to Billing Concepts Corp.

2003: Boston-based equity fund ABRY Partners acquires Billing Concepts, Enhanced Services Billing, and Avery Communications, and combines the three companies into a new enterprise.

2004: ABRY merges its new business with ACI Billing Services Inc. and adopts the name Billing Services Group Ltd. (BSG).

2006: BSG combines what once had been EDS Interoperator Services GmbH with Billing Concepts to create a new operating subsidiary named BSG Clearing Solutions.

2007: Tampa-based Syniverse Holdings Inc. acquires BSG's wireless clearing and financial settlement operations in a cash deal worth $290 million.

During the mid-1990s, activity heated up as Avery formed two new businesses: Alternate Telephone and Communications Inc. and America Networks Commnet. In November 1994 Delaware-based Class Inc. acquired Avery Communications via a reverse merger, and operations continued under the retained Avery Communications name.

The company rounded out the first half of the decade by snapping up communications firm Bordercomm Inc., which was acquired by a newly formed Avery Communications subsidiary in August. Activity continued in 1996. In January Avery divested three businesses (American Networks Inc., Commnet Services Inc., and Telco Group Inc.) in exchange for ap-

proximately $496,500 of its own stock.

By mid-1997 Avery operated through two main subsidiaries. One of these concentrated on the installation and maintenance of microwave and telecommunications equipment. The other subsidiary, Hold Billing Services Ltd. (HBS), was focused on providing long-distance resellers and inter-exchange carriers with billing and collection services. At this time Patrick J. Haynes III served as Avery Communications' chairman, and its stock traded on the Electronic Bulletin Board under the symbol ATEX.

In early 1998 Avery Communications divested its Bordercomm and ATC operations in a deal that allowed it to acquire 419,000 shares of its own common stock. Sales for the year totaled $19.6 million, up from $11.6 million in 1997.

By early 1999, Mark Nielsen had been named as Avery Communications' president and CEO. In March of that year, the company announced plans to acquire Newport Beach, California-based Primal Systems Inc., a software company with expertise in the areas of customer relationship management, e-commerce, and electronic bill presentment and payment. The deal, which was in line with Avery's strategy to focus on Internet-related opportunities, was finalized in October.

AVERY BECOMES A PRIVATELY HELD COMPANY

Avery Communications ushered in the new millennium with plans to spin off HBS as a stand-alone company. However, the company changed its plans in the summer, and in August Avery's board voted to spin off Primal Solutions instead.

In mid-2000, Mark Nielsen resigned as Avery Communications' president and CEO. He was succeeded by Chairman Patrick Haynes. At this time, Rick Box served as the head of the company's HBS business.

A spike in the company's billing operations led to revenues of $36.5 million for the fiscal year ended December 31, 2000. This was an increase of 54 percent from revenues of $23.7 million in 1999.

The spinoff of Primal Solutions was completed in February 2001, at which time Avery also repurchased 1.75 million shares of its stock from New York-based Franklin Capital. Moving forward, Avery continued to serve as a holding company for HBS.

Other noteworthy developments in 2001 included subsidiary ACI Communications Inc.'s acquisition of assets from OAN Services Inc. in August, followed by ACI Billing Services Inc.'s acquisition of Qorus.com

Inc.'s assets in November. Avery capped off 2001 with a one-for-eight reverse stock split, as well as a new trading symbol (AVYC).

In early 2003 Avery Communications announced plans to transform itself into a privately held company. Following a one-for-five-thousand reverse stock split to reduce the number of its stockholders, this transformation was completed in July.

FORMATION OF THE BILLING SERVICES GROUP

In mid-December 2003 Boston-based ABRY Partners, one of North America's oldest and largest private-equity funds, acquired Billing Concepts, Enhanced Services Billing, and Avery Communications, and combined the three companies into a new enterprise. The deal resulted in the formation of a telecommunications billing and collections industry leader, led by former Avery Communications Chairman and CEO Patrick Haynes III, who retained the same positions at the new company.

ABRY quickly merged its new business with another enterprise, ACI Billing Services Inc., in January 2004, and adopted the name Billing Services Group (BSG). That year BSG's pro forma combined revenue totaled $141 million, down from $144 million in 2003.

Billing Concepts continued to function as a BSG subsidiary through 2005. Early the following year BSG combined what once had been EDS Interoperator Services GmbH with Billing Concepts to create a new operating subsidiary named BSG Clearing Solutions. The new name reflected the company's ability to clear data and financial transactions across many different communication platforms. Subsequently, a new web site, www.bsgclearing.com, was created to serve as one portal for its various solutions.

By 2006 BSG Clearing Solutions served approximately 570 communications companies throughout the world, and processed more than 15 billion transactions per year. In April that year Roland Josef Bopp was named CEO of BSG. He succeeded Patrick Haynes III, who remained with the organization as chairman. Chairman Patrick Heneghan was subsequently named vice-chairman.

Growth was such that by mid-2006, BSG Clearing Solutions' client base had grown to include 630 communications companies, for whom it processed some 20 billion transactions annually. At this time BSG Clearing Solutions furthered its growth by acquiring the third-party verification services unit of VoiceLog LLC in a cash deal worth approximately $15.63 million.

ROLLING OUT NEW PRODUCTS TO ENHANCE DIGITAL SECURITY

In April 2007 Tampa, Florida-based Syniverse Holdings Inc. announced plans to acquire BSG's wireless clearing and financial settlement operations in a cash deal worth $290 million. After BSG's shareholders okayed the deal, it was approved by the European Commission in December, following a five-month review process.

In the last half of the first decade of the 2000s BSG unveiled a number of new products. In October 2007 the company introduced Bill2Phone-Mobile, a service that allowed multimedia providers to send digital content such as games, stock updates, and videos to mobile phones, and then post the charges to subscribers' wireless phone bills.

In early 2008 BSG unveiled a risk management solution for prepaid gift cards. The verification service was targeted toward so-called card-not-present merchants (those who process gift card transactions electronically, as opposed to using the physical gift card at a cash register), who are especially susceptible to fraud. Midway through the year, the company rolled out its Bill2Phone-Mobile service, which allowed mobile phone users to accept collect calls.

In late 2008 BSG partnered with the billing and life-cycle management firm Aria Systems to roll out a new product that sought to help game publishers increase the safety and security of gambling transactions. BSG seemed to be prepared for continued success. From its origins in traditional telecommunications billing, the company had grown its service offerings to meet the needs of service providers and consumers in an era dominated by mobile and Internet-based communications.

Paul R. Greenland

PRINCIPAL SUBSIDIARIES

BSG Clearing Solutions.

PRINCIPAL COMPETITORS

Intec Telecom Systems plc; VeriSign Inc.; XIUS-bcgi.

FURTHER READING

"Abry Recaps Billing," *Daily Deal/The Deal,* April 14, 2005.

"Avery Unveils New Strategy and Recent Results," *PR Newswire,* June 15, 1999.

"Billing Concepts Completes Sale of Three Operating Divisions," *PR Newswire,* October 23, 2000.

"Billing Services Group Limited Announces New Name for Operating Companies, Global Expansion," *Business Wire,* January 9, 2006.

"European Commission Clears Acquisition of BSG by Syniverse Technologies," *Business Wire,* December 4, 2007.

"Primal Solutions, Inc. Completes Spin-Off from Parent Company, Avery Communications, Inc.," *PR Newswire,* February 13, 2001.

"USLD Founder Resigns as Chairman," *San Antonio Express-News,* June 3, 1997.

Blom Bank S.A.L.

—■—

PO Box 11-1912, Riad El-Solh
Beirut, 1107-2807
Lebanon
Telephone: (961 01) 743300
Fax: (961 01) 738946
Web site: http://www.blom.com.lb

Public Company
Incorporated: 1951 as Banque du Liban et d'Outre Mer
Employees: 2,216
Sales: $17.82 billion (2007)
Stock Exchanges: Beirut
Ticker Symbol: BLBD
NAICS: 522110 Commercial Banking

■ ■ ■

Blom Bank S.A.L. is Lebanon's largest bank and is also one of the most well-respected banks in the Middle East and North Africa. Founded in 1951 as Banque du Liban et d'Outre Mer, Blom has navigated decades of political and economic instability through conservative fiscal strategies, the diversification of its range of services, and a program of geographic expansion. Blom Bank operates 53 branches in Lebanon, and 40 more branches internationally, including 23 in Egypt, ten in Syria, and six in Jordan. The company also operates affiliated banks focused primarily on serving the Lebanese expatriate community in France, Switzerland, and Cyprus.

Since about 2005, Blom has extended its operations to include Qatar, Abu Dhabi, and Saudi Arabia. In ad-dition to its main banking operations, Blom controls Arope Insurance, a major full-service insurance group in Lebanon, and investment banking specialist Blominvest. Blom Bank is listed on the Beirut Stock Exchange, and posted total assets of nearly $18 billion, with pretax profits of $243 million, in 2007. The company is led by Saad Azhari, who serves as chairman and general manager of Blom Bank itself, while his father, Naaman Azhari, acts as chairman for the full Blom group of companies.

FOUNDING

Blom Bank was created by a group of four Beirut-based businessmen as Banque du Liban et d'Outre Mer (Blom) in 1951. The bank's name reflected the lasting French influence in Lebanon, which had been created under France's control in 1920 and had gained its independence in 1943. The post–World War II period represented a period of relative political and economic stability in Lebanon, which quickly gained stature as a leading cultural, tourism, and financial center in the Arab Middle East. Beirut became particularly known as a major hub for the region's banking industry, adopting Switzerland-styled banking secrecy policies.

Emile Boustany served as the bank's initial general manager. Blom revealed its international ambitions soon after its founding, with the establishment of its first overseas branch in Jeddah, Saudi Arabia, in 1952. In 1961, Boustany ceded the general manager's position to Naaman Azhari, a Syrian citizen, who was to play the major role in building the bank's operations over the

KEY DATES

1951: Four Beirut businessmen establish the Banque du Liban et d'Outre Mer (Blom).

1952: Blom establishes its first foreign branch office in Jeddah, Saudi Arabia.

1974: Blom founds Arope Insurance in partnership with SCOR, of France.

1976: Blom becomes partner in the founding of La Banque de l'Orient Arab et d'Outre Mer (Banorabe) in Paris.

1979: Banorabe becomes partner in Banque Banorient in Switzerland.

1982: Banorabe adds branches in Oman.

1994: Blom founds Banque d'Affaires du Liban et d'Outre Mer (later Blominvest Bank).

1996: Blom gains 100% control of Banorabe and Banorient (later Blom Bank France and Blom Bank Switzerland).

2001: Blom officially adopts the name Blom Bank S.A.L.; Blom opens first branch office in Syria.

2004: Blom becomes founding partner in Bank of Syria and Overseas, with a 39 percent stake.

2005: Blom acquires Misr Romanian Bank in Egypt for $100 million.

2008: Blom adds offices and branches in Abu Dhabi, Saudi Arabia, and Qatar.

next decades. By 1971, Azhari had taken over the chairmanship of the company as well. Three years later, Blom extended its range of financial services into the insurance sector, teaming up with France's SCOR to found Arope Insurance. In 1975 Blom entered Dubai, opening a branch there as well.

The outbreak of the Lebanese Civil War in 1975, which was to continue for the next decade and a half, caused a crisis in the country's banking industry. With large numbers of Lebanese fleeing the country, Blom responded with the creation of a new overseas bank. In 1976, Blom joined up with a group of Swiss and Arab investors to create La Banque de l'Orient Arab et d'Outre Mer, or Banorabe, in Paris. This bank focused especially on serving the interests of the growing Lebanese expatriate population. The success of that venture led the company to add operations in another center of the Lebanese diaspora, Geneva, Switzerland, with the creation of Banque Banorient in 1979.

BECOMING A LEBANESE BANKING LEADER

Closer to home, Blom marked further expansion, adding a branch in Sharjah, part of the United Arab Emirates, in 1978, and then opening a branch in Muscat, Oman, in 1982. The company also extended its European reach, establishing a branch in London in 1983. These expansion efforts were carried out through Blom's Banorabe affiliate. While 1983 marked the loss of the group's Jeddah office—which was taken over as part of the "Saudization" of the Saudi Arabian banking sector (a national plan to increase the number of Saudi nationals in jobs largely held by expatriate workers)—Blom's expansion had enabled it to claim the title of Lebanon's largest bank by the beginning of the 1980s.

The end of the Lebanese Civil War introduced a new period of political and economic stability in the country, which lasted into the middle of the first decade of the 21st century. Blom took advantage of the new calm to expand its domestic branch network to more than 40 branches at the dawn of the century, and to nearly 55 by 2009. In 1993, the bank established an offshore banking division in Limassol, Cyprus. The following year, Blom also created a dedicated investment banking unit, Banque d'Affaires du Liban et d'Outre Mer.

At the same time, Blom moved to consolidate its foreign affiliate operations. The first step in this process came in 1992, when Banque Banorabe took 100 percent control of Swiss-based Banque Banorient. Then, in 1996, Blom bought out its partners in Banorabe, gaining 100 percent of that bank as well. Naaman Azhari's leadership of the bank, which became the only Lebanese bank to achieve a BBB+ credit rating, brought him recognition as "The Best Banking Personality in the Arab World," as voted by the Association of Arab Banks in 1999. By then, Azhari had brought the next generation into the business, as one son, Samer Azhari, became general manager of both Blom Bank and Arope Insurance, and another son, Saad Azhari, became general manager of Banque d'Affaires du Liban et d'Outre Mer.

Blom celebrated its 50th anniversary in 2001 by formally adopting the name Blom Bank S.A.L. that year. The company also renamed its investment banking subsidiary that year, as Blominvest Bank. The streamlining of the company's brand was completed later in the decade, with the renaming of Banque Banorabe as Blom Bank France, and Banorient as Blom Bank (Switzerland) in 2006.

CONTINUED EXPANSION

Blom completed several more steps towards its goal of developing a pan-Arab presence. In 2000, the bank made preparations to enter Syria as that country relaxed its banking rules. By the end of the year, Blom had made its first move into that market, becoming the fourth foreign bank to receive a license to open branch offices in the country's seven free trade zones. Blom then opened its first branch office in the Damascus free trade zone in 2001. At the same time, Blom continued to lobby for the right to open a full-fledged bank in Syria. The group's efforts were rewarded in 2003 when Blom became the first foreign bank to receive a license to operate a private bank in Syria.

Backed by the International Finance Corporation (IFC), Blom established a new private bank, Bank of Syria and Overseas, in 2004. Blom's share of the new business stood at 39 percent, while the IFC took a 10 percent stake. The remaining shares were controlled by Syrian investors. Blom quickly built up a banking network in that country, and by the end of 2008 operated ten branches in Syria.

In the meantime, the company had also been exploring other horizons. The group entered the Jordanian market in 2004, opening a branch office in Amman that year. Soon after, the bank added branches in Haret Hreik and Aley, in Lebanon, as well. Blom had also been lobbying for permission to enter the Egyptian market at the dawn of the new century. When the Egyptian government refused to grant the bank a license outright, Blom instead looked for an acquisition to enable it to establish a presence in one of the largest of the Arabic-speaking markets.

Blom's opportunity came in 2005, when the Egyptian government launched the privatization of part of the country's state-owned banking holdings. Blom reached an agreement to acquire Banque Misr's 33 percent stake in Misr Romanian Bank, owned as a joint venture with two Romanian banks. As part of the purchase agreement, Blom also agreed to buy out the Romanian partners. By the end of 2005, Blom had gained control of nearly 97 percent of Misr Romanian. The purchase, which cost Blom nearly $100 million, gave Blom a network of eight banking branches in Egypt, as well as five branches in Romania serving the expatriate Arab community there.

Blom later increased its holding in Misr Romanian to 99 percent, and changed its name to Blom Bank Egypt. The company then launched an ambitious expansion of its Egyptian unit. Through 2007, Blom added five new Egyptian branches; by the end of the following year, Blom Bank Egypt had expanded again, to 23 branch offices.

PAN-ARAB BANKING LEADER FOR THE 21ST CENTURY

Blom continued its expansion elsewhere as well, adding new branches in Lebanon, and a fourth branch in Jordan, in the Wahadat district of Amman, in 2006. Blom also joined the trend toward providing Islamic banking services—which operated according to Islamic principles, most notably in their lending practices—by launching a new subsidiary, Blom Development Bank, in 2006. At the same time, Blom's flourishing insurance wing, by then more than 88 percent owned by Blom, joined its parent's international expansion. In 2006, Arope Insurance added its own Syrian subsidiary, Arope Syria, becoming the first private insurance company to enter that market.

Like the rest of Lebanon, Blom was hit hard by the brief war with Israel in August 2006 that saw the destruction of much of the country's infrastructure and plunged the country into a new period of political instability. As a result, Blom turned to its strategy to become a leading Pan-Arab bank for its next expansion moves. In 2007, the company announced its intention to apply for banking licenses in Algeria, Saudi Arabia, Qatar, and elsewhere.

Blom soon made good on its announcement, opening a representative office in Abu Dhabi in 2008, as well as launching a Saudi Arabian subsidiary of Blominvest that year. Backed by Blom's investment of some $40 million, Blominvest Saudi Arabia opened four branch offices in the country in that year. By the end of 2008, the bank had also received a license to operate in Qatar. Blom then established a subsidiary there, Blom Bank Qatar, raising its total international presence to 11 markets.

Blom retained its long-held title as Lebanon's leading bank, not only within the country, but also as the largest Lebanese bank operating internationally. As the first decade of the 21st century neared its end, Blom controlled nearly 30 percent of all Lebanese offshore assets, including nearly 34 percent of all offshore customer deposits. Meanwhile, as the rest of the world's banking community collapsed, dragging the world's economy into a severe recession, Blom enjoyed the advantages of the Lebanese Central Bank's highly conservative banking policies. As a result, Blom, like the rest of the Lebanese banking sector, had avoided taking on the toxic assets, especially the subprime mortgages, that had prompted the global banking meltdown. With a healthy asset portfolio of nearly $18 billion, Blom hoped to remain the Lebanese banking leading in the new century.

M. L. Cohen

PRINCIPAL SUBSIDIARIES

Arope Insurance S.A.L.; Arope Syria; Bank of Syria and Overseas S.A.L.; Blom Bank (Switzerland) S.A.; Blom Bank Egypt S.A.A.; Blom Bank France S.A.; Blom Bank Jordan; Blom Bank Qatar L.L.C.; Blom Development Bank S.A.L.; Blom Egypt Securities; Blominvest Bank S.A.L.; Blominvest Saudi Arabia.

PRINCIPAL COMPETITORS

Bank Audi SAL; Byblos Bank S.A.L.; BankMed S.A.L.; Fransabank SAL; Banque Libano-Francaise SAL; Bank of Beirut S.A.L.; Lebanese Canadian Bank S.A.L.; Credit Libanais S.A.L.; Societe Generale de Banque au Liban.

FURTHER READING

"Banks Post Record Profits, Look to Regional Expansion," *MEED Middle East Economic Digest,* February 10, 2006, p. 26.

"Blom Bank Egypt to Increase Capital to USD140m," *Global Banking News,* September 1, 2008.

"Blom Bank Set for Expansion," *MEED Middle East Economic Digest,* February 16, 2007, p. 36.

"Blom Opens First Branch in Syria," *MEED Middle East Economic Digest,* October 20, 2000, p. 10.

"Blom Set to Snap Up Misr Romanian Bank," *MEED Middle East Economic Digest,* December 2, 2005, p. 39.

"Central Banker of the Year—Middle East (Banque du Liban et d'Outre-Mer SAL)," *Banker,* January 1, 2009.

Gavin, James, "Business as Usual for Beirut," *MEED Middle East Economic Digest,* June 20, 2008, p. 46.

"Lebanon—Blom Bank," *Banker,* December 1, 2008.

Luxford, Kate, "Lebanese Bank Mergers Look Set for Revival," *Euromoney,* September 2005, p. 244.

Mirza, Adal, "Blom Bank: The Lebanese Institution's Twin Strategy of Acquisitions and Service Diversifications Is Aiding Expansion," *MEED Middle East Economic Digest,* September 26, 2008, p. 30.

Timewell, Stephen, "Activity on the Acquisition Trail—Lebanon's Top Two Banks Have Boosted Profits and Set Their Sights on Regional and Global Expansion, Despite Political Turmoil at Home," *Banker,* March 1, 2006.

Boenning & Scattergood Inc.

200 Barr Harbor Drive, Suite 300
West Conshohocken, Pennsylvania 19428-2979
U.S.A.
Telephone: (610) 832-1212
Toll Free: (800) 883-1212
Fax: (610) 832-1232
Web site: http://www.boenninginc.com

Private Company
Incorporated: 1916 as Henry D. Boenning & Co.
Employees: 91
Sales: $37.5 million (2007 est.)
NAICS: 522110 Commercial Banks

■ ■ ■

Boenning & Scattergood Inc. is the oldest independent investment firm in the Mid-Atlantic region, involved in both investment banking and private portfolio management. The Investment Banking unit provides a wide range of advisory and transaction services to corporate clients, including initial or secondary public offerings of stock; private placements of stock and recapitalizations; management buyouts; and mergers and acquisitions services, whether it be helping family business owners to sell their businesses, companies divesting or acquiring assets, or corporate mergers. The Equity Capital Markets group focuses on institutional clients, providing research on small to midsize companies and trading services, as well as acting as market maker for more than 200 NASDAQ-listed and over-the-counter securities.

In addition, the firm is involved in the public finance sector, crafting, underwriting, and distributing municipal bond issues for school districts, townships, and other public entities, mostly in the Mid-Atlantic region. Boenning & Scattergood's Private Client Group offers retail brokerage services, advising clients on the purchase of stock and equity securities, bonds and fixed income securities, mutual funds, exchange traded funds, and alternative investments. The unit also offers asset management services through 1914 Advisors, providing financial planning and portfolio management services to wealthy individuals, corporations, and institutions. In addition to its main office in West Conshohocken, Pennsylvania, the firm maintains branches in Ardmore, Berwyn, Lancaster, Langhorne, Pittsburgh, and Pottstown, Pennsylvania; Marmora, New Jersey; and New York City.

HENRY BOENNING FOUNDS FIRM

Boenning & Scattergood traces its history to 1914 and the establishment of Henry D. Boenning & Co. by Henry Dorr Boenning, Sr., in his hometown of Philadelphia, Pennsylvania. Born in 1889, the son of a noted Philadelphia physician, Boenning joined the Land Title & Trust Company of Philadelphia after graduating from Central High School in 1907. He clerked there while attending classes at the University of Pennsylvania until 1910 when he joined the firm of Stevens & Co. After two years Boenning joined banker Oscar R. Dare, and later became a partner. According to the 1920–22 edition of *Who's Who in Finance and Banking*, Boenning "started individually as Henry D. Boenning & Co.,

COMPANY PERSPECTIVES

Boenning and Scattergood is dedicated to exceeding the expectations of our clients by delivering financial solutions alongside our longstanding traditions of integrity, expertise and a commitment to client service.

bankers" in 1916. Boenning & Scattergood maintains 1914 as the firm's founding date, as reflected in the "1914 Advisors" name, but it is likely that 1914 marked the date that Boenning made partner with Dare's firm.

In September 1921 Boenning joined forces with another Philadelphia firm, Schibener & Co., both of which were dissolved to create a new partnership, Schibener, Boenning & Co. Schibener had been established earlier in 1921 when Charles F. Schibener, Daniel S. Blackman, and Arleigh P. Hess came together. Hess was the former manager of the sales and publicity departments of West & Co., while the other two had worked for Drexel & Co., the major Philadelphia banking house of the day.

Schibener served for 25 years as the private secretary of Edward T. Stotesbury, a major financier at the time. At the age of 17 in 1866 Stotesbury began to clerk for Anthony J. Drexel, senior partner of Drexel & Co. At the dawn of the 20th century Stotesbury became senior partner and the de facto leading Philadelphia financier as well as becoming a partner with affiliated J.P. Morgan & Co. in New York City. As Stotesbury's longtime private secretary, Schibener was well connected in both Philadelphia and New York financial circles, making him a valuable partner for Henry Boenning. By 1927, Schibener had left, and Henry Boenning was establishing a name for himself as a member of the Philadelphia Stock Exchange, where he served as treasurer. He was also an associated member of the New York Curb Exchange, later known as the American Stock Exchange.

HAROLD SCATTERGOOD JOINS FIRM

The Scattergood name became associated with Henry Boenning in 1935, when Harold Francis Scattergood, Sr., joined Schibener, Boenning & Co. as an equity trader. Born in Philadelphia in 1910, he was a 1929 graduate of St. Joseph's Preparatory School and then began his business career. At Schibener, Boenning the

young Scattergood quickly made his mark as a trader, especially adept at spotting overlooked investment opportunities. He paid particular attention to the public utility sector, hard hit during the years of the Great Depression. He spent countless hours attending bankruptcy proceedings for utility companies in the 1930s and early 1940s, and used his accumulated knowledge to make profitable investments in the sector and in the process earn a national reputation as a sage investor.

In June 1943 Henry Boenning died at the age of 53 following a lengthy illness. The loss of the firm's senior partner could have easily led to the demise of the firm, but Boenning's wife, Virginia, urged Scattergood to stay and help keep it in business. In July 1943 Boenning & Co. was reconfigured as a partnership, one of the partners being Henry D. Boenning, Jr., who was serving as a captain in the U.S. Army. Born in 1914, Boenning was a graduate of the University of Pennsylvania. He then attended Harvard Business School from 1935 to 1937 before joining the Army in 1939. He served through World War II, finally leaving the service in 1946 and joining Boenning & Co. A year later in 1947 a new partnership was formed and Harold Scattergood became senior partner. It was a decision that the younger Boenning readily agreed with, calling Scattergood the "glue that held everything together."

During the postwar years, Boenning & Co. continued to be a member of the New York Curb Exchange, which adopted the American Stock Exchange name in 1953, as well as what was then the Philadelphia Stock Exchange, which merged with the Baltimore Stock Exchange in 1949 and the Washington Stock Exchange in 1953 to become the Philadelphia Baltimore Washington (PBW) Stock Exchange. PBW also had associate membership agreements in Boston and Pittsburgh. Boenning was able to take advantage of its dual membership to establish reciprocal trading arrangements with Wall Street firms such as Merrill Lynch and Smith Barney to execute trades. Boenning maintained dual membership until the 1970s when it sold its seat on the American Stock Exchange, but it retained seats on PBW, which in 1976 reverted to the Philadelphia Stock Exchange name. Along the way, the firm encountered a problem with the American Stock Exchange, when in 1964 Henry Boenning, Jr., and another broker, John R. O'Connell, were found guilty of violating exchange rules earlier in the decade. In essence they allowed a nonmember broker to buy securities through the firm's seat and paid commissions to him. As a result, Boenning was fined $17,500 and the partners were suspended for six months.

NAME CHANGE

In 1970 Boenning & Co. was incorporated as Boenning & Scattergood Inc. In addition, Harold F. Scattergood, Jr., joined the firm after graduating from Marquette University. He began developing accounts of his own and attended the Executive Leadership Program at the Wharton School of Business at the University of Pennsylvania as he was being groomed to eventually succeed his father. That day came in November 1985 when at the age of 75 Harold Scattergood, Sr., died at his home. With his passing the link to the company's origins was effectively severed, and his son then led the firm into a new era, while Henry Boenning, Jr., remained as vice-president.

The younger Scattergood took over a boutique firm with about 55 retail brokers working out of five regional offices and assets of about $30 million. Eschewing the opportunity to be swallowed by a larger concern, Boenning & Scattergood Inc. remained content to be an independent regional brokerage firm serving a customer base that was also mostly regional, banking a good deal of its success on the ability to make good regional stock picks. While maintaining the emphasis on providing excellent service to clients and refraining from overreaching in what it had to offer, the firm under the guidance of Scattergood nevertheless expanded in its own way, mostly by strengthening the capabilities of

each department by hiring new talent. Thus, as the requirements of its retail, corporate, and institutional clients evolved, Boenning & Scattergood was ready to meet the challenge.

After years of making Center City Philadelphia its home, Boenning & Scattergood moved to the suburbs to West Conshohocken in 1991. Following an economic recovery in the early 1990s, the firm began a new expansion effort. In 1995 a municipal trading desk was opened, followed in 1999 by an Institutional Equity Trading unit. Along the way, some of the firm's employees decided to break away to focus on early stage investments in Philadelphia-area companies, especially those in the technology sector. In 1999 about a dozen of them established Emerging Growth Equities Ltd. with $2 million of their own money.

EXPANDING THROUGH ACQUISITIONS

Boenning and Scattergood grew at its own pace as it entered the new century. A Taxable Fixed Income Sales/Trading unit was added in 2000, followed a year later by a Derivative Strategy group. Also in 2001 the firm returned to investment banking by acquiring Berwind Financial LP, a division of Berwind Group, which represented the business interests of one of Philadelphia's most prominent Main Line families, who had made their fortune in the 1800s through railroads and coal. In the 1990s Berwind Financial had become involved in a number of leveraged acquisitions, and then as the economy began to struggle there were some setbacks. Clinipad Corp., a maker of sterile medical supplies, was closed in 2000, and in January 2001, the Classic Kitchen roll-up venture was forced to file for Chapter 11 bankruptcy protection. Believing that the competition in leveraged buyouts had become too steep, with too much money chasing too few deals, the Berwind family decided to exit the leveraged buyout field and sold Berwind Financial to Boenning & Scattergood. In addition to its buyout activities, Berwind Financial also provided merger and acquisition advice to Mid-Atlantic banks, a business that fit in well with Boenning & Scattergood.

Several Berwind executives came to Boenning & Scattergood, led by David P. Lazar, a specialist in mergers and acquisitions, management buyouts, and private placement of debt. His team quickly made their mark, in six months participating in four acquisitions, including the sale of Ohio-based United Lubricants Corp. to Quaker Chemical Co. of Conshohocken, Pennsylvania; the sale of a Wyomissing company, Construction Fasteners Inc., to a Swiss company; the sale of Second

National Bank of Masontown, Pennsylvania, to Parkvale Financial Corp. from the Pittsburgh area; and the sale of a Philadelphia meeting-management company, McGettigan Partners, to St. Louis-based Maritz Travel Co. Lazar's group was expanded further in the spring of 2002 with the hiring of three more investment bankers to focus on private-equity groups and middle market industrial companies, as well as closely held and privately held companies.

Later in 2002 Boenning & Scattergood expanded further, helping to better serve bank customers by acquiring another Philadelphia firm, F.J. Morrissey & Co., Inc., a specialty trading firm that served as market maker for more than 200 NASDAQ-listed and over-the-counter securities. Morrissey was established in Philadelphia by Frank J. Morrissey in 1937, and had been specializing in over-the-counter bank stocks for more than 65 years. As the decade progressed, Boenning & Scattergood launched a public finance practice in 2004, and 1914 Advisors was established in 2007 to serve the needs of high net worth individuals and corporate and institutional investors.

The firm's steady conservative business approach had served it well over the years, but in the aftermath of the mortgage lending crisis in 2008 that led to deep erosion in the stock market in 2009, that philosophy would be put to the test. There was every reason to suspect, however, that Boenning & Scattergood would find a way to navigate these difficult times, unlike larger, better-known firms that had fallen by the wayside.

Ed Dinger

PRINCIPAL DIVISIONS

1914 Advisors; Equity Capital Markets; Fixed Income; Investment Banking; Private Client Group; Public Finance.

PRINCIPAL COMPETITORS

Legg Mason, Inc.; Raymond James Financial, Inc.; Wachovia Securities, LLC.

FURTHER READING

Binzen, Peter, "A Venerable Firm Quietly Acquires an Investment Banking Team," *Philadelphia Inquirer,* April 8, 2002, p. D1.

Diamond, Jonathan, "Boenning & Scattergood: Stability in Volatile Market," *Philadelphia Business Journal,* October 6, 1986, p. 6B.

"Henry D. Boenning," *New York Times,* June 8, 1943.

"H.F. Scattergood, Stock Broker," *Philadelphia Inquirer,* November 25, 1985, p. B6.

Leonard, John William, *Who's Who in Finance and Banking,* New York: Who's Who in Finance, Incorporated, 1922.

Rottenberg, Carl, "Growing Emerging Growth," *Norristown (Pa.) Times Herald,* December 7, 2000.

BONGRAIN SA

Bongrain S.A.

42 rue Rieussec
Viroflay, 78220 Cedex
France
Telephone: (33 01) 34 58 63 00
Fax: (33 01) 30 24 03 83
Web site: http://www.bongrain.com

Public Company
Incorporated: 1919 as Fromagerie d'Illoud; 1970 as
   Bongrain-Gérard
Employees: 18,500
Sales: EUR 3.55 billion ($4.47 billion) (2008)
Stock Exchanges: Paris
Ticker Symbol: BH
NAICS: 311513 Cheese Manufacturing; 311512
   Creamery Butter Manufacturing

■ ■ ■

Bongrain SA manufactures cheese and dairy products
that are sold in nearly 125 countries around the world.
Using nearly three billion liters of milk each year, the
company manufactures a wide variety of cheeses, butters, and creams. Some of the company's brands include
Caprice des Dieux, Elle & Vire, Coeur de Lion, and
Saint Agur. The company's Alouette and Chavrie brands
can be found in grocery stores across the United States.
Bongrain holds leading market positions in the branded
cheese market in France, Germany, Spain, and many
central and eastern European countries.

ORIGINS

Bongrain was founded as a small family-run cheese-
making farm in 1919 in Illoud, a village in the Haute
Marne (Ardennes-Champagne) region of eastern France.
Jean-Noël Bongrain formed part of the second generation to operate the family business, together with his
older brother. However, after Bongrain's brother was
killed as a member of the Resistance during World War
II, the family company came entirely under the then 19-
year-old Jean-Noël Bongrain's leadership. Bongrain
quickly began to seek a new dimension for the small
Fromagerie d'Illoud, one that would break the mold of
the postwar French dairy industry, which was characterized chiefly by small or midsized independent
companies, each concentrating on regional varieties.
Among a single cheese variety, quality and other
characteristics, such as flavor and texture, could vary
widely, even when produced by the same company. The
idea of "nationally" branded cheeses was still barely
known—with Bel's La Vache Qui Rit forming one of
the few exceptions.

By the start of the 1950s, Bongrain, too, had begun
searching for his own unique cheese. Together with
employees, Bongrain spent some five years in research
and experimentation, perfecting a formula that would
provide not only a unique taste, but also the consistency
of quality needed to break out of the regional
boundaries. By the mid-1950s Bongrain had found his
cheese: a molded cheese, with a firm outer skin yet with
a soft, fresh-tasting center. Wedding modern production
methods with traditional French cheese-making
craftsmanship, Bongrain was able to provide the quality

COMPANY PERSPECTIVES

Bongrain aims to prepare and sell very high quality products and services which perfectly satisfy consumer expectations by being constantly innovative; to encourage the professional and social development of all the men and women working with and for the Group; to protect and grow the capital invested in our Group by preserving its independence and decision-making autonomy; to participate in the economic and social development of the countries where the Group is present and to serve the common good.

consistency needed to win over the French consumer, while maintaining an appealing flavor and texture.

Inventing the cheese was only part of the company's victory. Bongrain quickly proved himself an intuitive master of the art of marketing. Rather than package his new cheese in the common shape of the day (typically, round molds), Bongrain chose an oval form, instantly recognizable among the others. The cheese required a name as well, and Bongrain chose Caprice des Dieux ("caprice of the gods"). The cheese's label also was chosen carefully, although the original portrayal of Zeus and Poseidon would give way to a longer-lasting "angel" motif in the 1960s, while maintaining a tri-color scheme (blue for freshness, white for purity, red for passion) emulating the French flag.

A PERIOD OF GROWTH

The company proved equally adept at inventing marketing slogans to appeal to the French consumer, including the early "un amour de fromage." Bongrain also made ready use of radio and television and other advertising venues. With such techniques—unusual for the French cheese industry of the time—Bongrain sought to build the brand beyond simply another cheese variety. Caprice des Dieux proved a quick success, launching Bongrain on a national scale.

Bongrain soon began to look over the French border. By the end of the 1950s Caprice des Dieux had begun to captivate German consumers as well. In the following decade the company moved into other European markets, including Switzerland, Austria, Italy, and Spain. The company also established subsidiaries in each country to provide for distribution. In the 1960s Bongrain began to look for further domestic expansion opportunities. Growing demand for Caprice des Dieux

required the company to develop a more extensive supplier and production network. At the same time Bongrain sought to expand the company beyond its famous single product. During the 1960s the company established a steady supply of milk with a regional network of dairy producers.

The company also began buying other small cheese makers, for the time centered in the same region. The first wave of conglomeration in the food and dairy industries was already under way. Bongrain resisted this trend, instead operating its acquisitions as small-sized, "human-scale" subsidiaries linked to the regional dairy network. Production of the new acquisitions, however, was converted toward products supporting the company's plans to expand its portfolio of cheese varieties.

An early addition was Tartare, produced by the company's Fromarsac subsidiary in 1964. The new brand again displayed the company's care for packaging: Tartare became one of the first cheeses to be packaged in portions. In 1967 the company acquired Fromageries des Chaumes, launching the company into that cheese variety as well. This acquisition was followed the next year by that of Compagnie Fromagère de la Vallée de l'Ance. During the same period the company also had begun a similar policy in its foreign markets, acquiring a string of cheese producers in each country.

ACQUISITIONS CONTINUE

The 1970s would see Bongrain's company emerge as one of France's premier national cheese producers. In 1970 three major acquisitions, of Laiterie Centrale Krompholtz, Grand'Ouche, and especially Gérard, gave the company a new boost in size. In that year Fromagerie d'Illoud changed its name to Bongrain-Gérard. More French acquisitions followed, including those of the Laiterie de la Vallée du Dropt in 1971, Siclet in 1973, and Rambol in 1975, accompanied by the creation of another subsidiary, Société Savoyarde des Fromagers du Reblochon. Each acquisition would strengthen Bongrain's line of cheese varieties.

In the mid-1970s the company also began to look beyond Europe. In 1975 Bongrain entered South America, with the purchase of Polenghi in Brazil, the first of a series of Brazilian acquisitions that would establish Bongrain as that country's leading specialty cheese producer. The following year Bongrain made a move into the U.S. market with the takeover of Colombo. Bongrain was quick to adapt its technical and marketing strengths to the new market—and the taste buds of Americans—launching a line of successful products, including frozen yogurt, before branching out into other food products, including sauces.

KEY DATES

1919: Fromagerie d'Illoud is established.
1956: The Caprice des Dieux (Caprice of the Gods) cheese brand is launched.
1964: The Tartare brand hits store shelves.
1970: Laiterie Centrale Krompholtz, Grand'Ouche, and Gérard are acquired; Fromagerie d'Illoud changes its name to Bongrain-Gérard.
1975: The company enters the South American market.
1976: Bongrain begins U.S. expansion.
1980: The company adopts the Bongrain name and goes public.
1981: Australia's Lactos is acquired.
1992: Bongrain gains control of Compagnie Laitière Européenne.
2003: Angulo General Quesera S.L. and Edelweiss GmbH & Co. are acquired.
2006: Lactos is sold.
2007: Dutch dairy group Campina sells its Passendale cheese factory to Bongrain; the company's gastronomy division is sold.

By 1979 the company had firmly established itself as one of France's top cheese producers, as well as a leading specialty cheese maker worldwide. In that year the company reorganized, before going public the following year and adopting a new name, Bongrain. The company's plans for the 1980s continued its ambitious expansion. In 1980 the company set up new production facilities in Australia and New Zealand, complementing this development the following year with the acquisition of Australia's Lactos. These moves were made with an eye on positioning Bongrain to enter the rapidly developing Asian markets, anticipating the day when consumers in those countries might adopt more Western eating habits, including the consumption of cheese products.

Bongrain marked the 1980s with a long series of acquisitions, including Martinus in the Netherlands; Johnston, Kolb-Lena, and Real Fresh in the United States; Skandia and Campo Lindo in Brazil, and Horizons Laitiers in France. In 1989 alone, the company acquired nine companies, adding Italy's Ludovico and Faprena; Alta Dena in the United States; Hirz, of Switzerland; Millway Foods, of Great Britain; Aiuruoca, of Brazil; and three French concerns, La Cloche d'Or, La Fromagerie du Velay, and Fauquet.

Among the products launched by Bongrain were the successful P'tit Louis and Fol Epi cheeses. By this time, the company's annual sales neared FRF 6 billion.

During the same period the company also attempted to diversify, principally by the Bongrain family shareholding group, Soparind, through a separate company, IFM, which established a strong position in the prepared meat products market. The company met with more limited success as it attempted to enter the confectionery market; in the early 1990s the company would sell these activities to the foods giant BSN, later known as Danone. Together these activities, which remained private and separate from Bongrain SA, were estimated to contribute an additional FRF 6 billion in yearly sales.

OVERCOMING CHALLENGES

Bongrain started the 1990s with several new strategic moves, including the 1990 acquisition of Fromagerie Paul Renard and an alliance with the Union des Coopératives Bressor, which added that company's popular Bresse-Blue and Grièges brands. In 1992 rivals Bongrain and Besnier—itself continuing a long acquisition spree, including the acquisition of dairy producer Bridel, which had placed it as the country's leading dairy and cheese producer—went head-to-head for the control of the Union Laitière Normande (ULN). Bongrain won, taking a 10 percent share and operating control of the subsidiary, which was renamed Compagnie Laitière Européenne (CLE). CLE, however, would enter a difficult period, posting losses into the late 1990s.

Meanwhile, Bongrain was entering a new market: Eastern Europe. As these countries were opening up to foreign investment and establishing free markets with the end of Soviet dominance, Bongrain established positions in Hungary, with the acquisition of Veszpremtej, and in the Czech Republic, with the acquisition of Pribina, while also adding production facilities in Poland. The company also expanded its South American presence by moving into Chile and Uruguay in the mid-1990s. During this time the company embarked on an intensive capital investment program, designed to modernize its French production plants, including the building of new plants and the renovation of existing plants. The company's subsidiaries then were converted from single-product facilities to being capable of producing multiple cheese varieties.

The cost of these investments, coupled with a continuing recession, losses from the ULN, and pressure from elevated French milk prices, combined to put pressure on Bongrain. Revenues, which had risen to FRF

9.7 billion in 1992, fell to FRF 9.6 billion in 1993. Although the company's revenues would climb again in the mid-1990s, topping FRF 10.4 billion in 1996, its profitability was faltering, with net earnings dropping from FRF 366 million in 1994 to just FRF 300 million in 1996. In response—and as well as to ensure the company's succession, as Jean-Noêl Bongrain turned 72 years old—the company restructured its organization in September 1997. While sons Armand and Alex Bongrain took directorships in the company, actual operating leadership of the company fell to longtime family friend Bernard Lacan, former CEO for Nestlé subsidiary Findus.

FOCUS ON INTERNATIONAL EXPANSION

In 1998 Bongrain's difficulties appeared to be in the past as the company posted its results for the 1997 fiscal year. Sales had risen strongly to more than FRF 11 billion, and net earnings regained slightly to FRF 313 million. While certain of the company's markets remained under pressure, Bongrain was poised to continue its thrust to become an international cheese leader.

During the late 1990s, France's cheese industry was dominated by Bongrain, Besnier (whose named changed to Groupe Lactalis in 1999), and Bel, the country's top three cheese and dairy producers, together responsible for more than 50 percent of all cheeses sold in that country. Bongrain stood among the world leaders in cheese and dairy product sales, with an extensive international presence, including a strong position in the United States through its subsidiaries Zausner and Alta Dena and such brands as Real Fresh, which together provided some 16 percent of the company's annual sales. In South America, Bongrain had built a leading presence in Brazil and Argentina, with production facilities in Chile and Uruguay as well. Bongrain also continued to maintain a presence in the developing Asian countries.

Nevertheless, sales in Europe, especially France, continued to account for more than 80 percent of Bongrain's annual revenues, with France alone providing some 48 percent of revenues. Outside of France, Bongrain's principal European markets included Germany, which provided some 13 percent of sales, with Italy, Spain, and Portugal figuring among Bongrain's major European markets as well. With the mature French market—which counted more than 500 cheese specialties—providing limited opportunities for future growth, Bongrain continued to focus on international expansion in the late 1990s. The company made inroads in China and India in 1999.

MOVING INTO THE 21ST CENTURY

Bongrain entered the new millennium focused on growth as well as diversification. The company looked to industrial butter and animal feed operations to bolster its bottom line. During 2001, it formed a joint venture with Land O'Lakes, Inc., to produce sterile packaged cheese sauces in the United States. In 2003, Bongrain strengthened its position in Spain with the purchase of Angulo General Quesera S.L. Later that year it announced the purchase of Edelweiss GmbH & Co., a German manufacturer of the Bresso and Milkana brands.

Alex Bongrain took over as chairman when his father and founder Jean-Noêl Bongrain retired in 2004. The company and its domestic competitors were affected by several changes that year, including a reform in the Common Agricultural Policy that cut support prices for butter and milk powder as well as product subsidies. At the same time, a new agreement was formed in France that set new milk prices on a quarterly basis. These prices were based on several factors including changes in prices of international cheeses and differences in the average price of milk in Germany and France. Eastern European countries including Poland, Hungary, the Czech Republic, and Slovakia were admitted into the European Union that year. The price of milk increased dramatically in those countries, reaching levels found in Northern Europe.

Meanwhile, Bongrain put diversification on the back burner while continuing to bolster its cheese-related business. The company entered into a joint venture with Argentina-based Milkaut in 2006. One year later, the Dutch dairy group Campina sold its Passendale cheese factory to Bongrain. The company secured its position as the leading cheese maker in Belgium upon completion of the sale. Bongrain also teamed up with the Sodiaal Group to form a new subsidiary that would manufacture and market Camembert, Coulommiers, and Brie cheeses.

As part of its focus on core activities during this time, the company sold its gastronomy division and exited businesses related to veal calf farming. It also sold its Australian-based Lactos holdings, which accounted for less than 2 percent of overall sales. During 2007, the company was hit hard by the rising cost of milk and raw materials. The company saw the average price of milk rise from 7 to 56 percent in its operating countries during that year. Nevertheless, Bongrain's sales and profits remained steady. By focusing on its cheese and dairy products business and by developing new products, the company believed it was on track for success in the years to come.

M. L. Cohen
Updated, Christina M. Stansell

PRINCIPAL SUBSIDIARIES

Alliance Laitière Européenne; Compagnie Laitière Européenne (87.4%); Bongrain Europe; Bongrain International.

PRINCIPAL COMPETITORS

Fromageries Bel S.A.; Groupe Lactalis; Koninklijke FrieslandCampina N.V.

FURTHER READING

"Bongrain—Acquires New Cheese Brands," *Lebensmittel Zeitung LZ,* July 31, 2003.

"Le Bongrain nouveau est arrivé," *Le Figaro Economie,* September 29, 1997, p. 3.

"Bongrain-Sodiaal JV Approved," *Europolitics Agriculture,* October 26, 2007.

"Bongrain Targets 'Everyday' Cheese Buyers," *Just-Food,* May 15, 2007.

"Change of Generation at Bongrain," *Les Echos,* December 18, 2003.

Chirot, Françoise, "Bongrain: des profits sur un plateau," *Le Monde,* September 29, 1989, p. 29.

Denis, Anne, "Bongrain prépare la relève en modifiant ses statuts," *Les Echos,* September 9, 1997, p. 10.

———, "Bongrain reste confiant pour l'avenir malgré une rude année 1996," *Les Echos,* April 30, 1997, p. 15.

———, "Le groupe fromager Bongrain à la conquete de l'Amérique," *Les Echos,* April 26, 1995, p. 9.

"French Bongrain Confirms Takeover of Spanish Angulo General Quesera," *French News Digest,* February 24, 2003.

Jicquel, Jean-Luc, "Gros plan sur Bongrain," *RIA,* May 1997, p. 25.

"Land O'Lakes Inc.," *Food Institute Report,* December 18, 2000.

"Profits Up at Bongrain," *Les Echos,* March 13, 2008.

"Le resultat d'exploitation de Bongrain a augmenté de 22.9% en 1997," *Les Echos,* March 6, 1998, p. 12.

Sinchet-Lassabe, Ghislaine, "Bongrain maintient le cap," *Linéaires,* June 1997, p. 52.

Boulanger S.A.

BP 137, rue de la Haie Plouvier
Lesquin, F-59811
France
Telephone: (33 03) 20 49 46 46
Fax: (33 03) 20 49 47 27
Web site: http://www.boulanger.fr

Private Company
Founded: 1954
Employees: 5,500
Sales: EUR 1.5 billion ($1.9 billion) (2007 est.)
NAICS: 443112 Radio, Television, and Other Electronics Stores; 443111 Household Appliance Stores

■ ■ ■

Boulanger S.A. is one of France's top three home appliance and home electronics retail groups, along with Darty and Fnac. The company operates nearly 90 stores throughout France. Boulanger also operates two e-commerce web sites, and since 2008, its own 3D "island" in the "Second Life" online virtual community. In addition, Boulanger operates ten stores under the Destock'Boulanger name, selling demonstration models and remaindered products. Boulanger differentiates itself from its competitors by operating larger store formats. The company's largest stores, which at 4,000 square meters are also the largest home appliance and electronics stores in France, opened in Avignon and Toulon in 2008.

By operating larger stores than its competitors, Boulanger is also able to feature a wider range of products and brands. These include Boulanger's private label brands, including Essentiel B, a mid-range product line, and the discount Listo brand. In order to develop products for these brands, the company created a subsidiary, Sourcing et Création, in 2007. Also that year, Boulanger launched a service subsidiary, B Dom', which provides in-home installation, technical support, and other services. Boulanger is led by Thierry Mulliez, and is part of the Mulliez family's retail empire, which includes the Auchan, Decathlon, Leroy Merlin, Kiabi, and other retail chains. More than 95 percent of the company's employees own shares in the company. Boulanger's total annual revenues topped EUR 1.5 billion in 2007.

BROTHERLY BEGINNINGS

Boulanger began as a small shop opened by brothers Bernard and Gustave Boulanger in Lille in 1954. The shop featured radios built by Gustave Boulanger, while also offering repair services. Bernard tended to the retail side of the store's operations. When Gustave died at an early age, Bernard Boulanger continued on in business alone. The loss of his brother forced Boulanger to look elsewhere to stock the store shelves. Boulanger than began featuring brand-name appliances. Boulanger also expanded its range of appliances to include televisions, hi-fi equipment, and other appliances. At the same time, the store retained its early commitment to service, and became one of the first home appliance retailers in France to offer after-sales services.

The success of the Lille store led Boulanger to add a number of new stores throughout France's northern region during the 1960s and 1970s. Boulanger's stores grew in size to include a wide selection of home appliances and home electronics equipment. The company established a strong reputation for the quality of its services, notably for its well-trained and knowledgeable sales staff. By 1978, the company was ready to expand its operations to a national level. In that year, Boulanger opened its first store outside of the northern region, in Lyon. By 1982, Boulanger had opened its first store in Paris as well.

Boulanger's success attracted the attention of the Mulliez family, who had already established themselves among the leading names in the French retail sector. Like Boulanger, the Mulliez family had originated in France's Nord region, and from the late 1950s had built a retail empire based on a number of the country's leading chains, such as Auchan (supermarkets), Decathlon (sporting goods), Leroy Merlin (hardware), and Kiabi (clothing), among others. The family's holdings also grew to include a number of restaurant chains as well, most notably, Flunch.

EXPANDING WITH THE MULLIEZ FAMILY

In the early 1980s, the Mulliez group sought an entry into the fast-growing home appliance sector. Rather than develop their own chain, however, they approached Boulanger, then seeking capital for its further expansion. In 1983, Boulanger sold a minority stake in the company to the Association Familiale Mulliez, which oversaw the family's holdings. The partnership with the Mulliez group enabled Boulanger to expand its retail network to 11 stores by 1986. In that year, the Association Familiale Mulliez moved to take full control of Boulanger, which then became a part of the Auchan group. Boulanger then launched a still more aggressive expansion strategy, opening 15 stores over the next two years. By the end of 1989, the company's total network neared 40 stores.

This expansion came at a cost, however, as the company entered a long period of losses. Boulanger's financial situation was further exacerbated by the start of a recession in the early 1990s. As a result, the group halted its new store opening program. The company's difficulties encouraged Boulanger to launch a number of

new initiatives in the early 1990s. The company launched a new innovation in French retail when it began offering pricing guarantees to its customers. Under this program, Boulanger promised to reimburse its customers for the difference should a product's price drop within 30 days after its purchase.

The company also moved to restructure its logistics operations. In 1990, Boulanger inaugurated its national distribution center. The following year, the group put into place a central purchasing facility. These efforts played a role in allowing the company to become profitable once again by 1992. At that time, Boulanger's annual revenues reached FRF 2.1 billion (approximately $350 million).

In 1993, the company introduced another, if only symbolic, public relations effort. Amid the lingering effects of the recession, the growing influence of the large-scale supermarkets and hypermarkets on the French retail scene, and the early ravages of the outsourcing of manufacturing to low-wage markets in Asia and elsewhere, Boulanger teamed up with a number of major brand name manufacturers to launch a new "Made in France" initiative. For this, the company worked with suppliers to develop a line of seven products either manufactured or at least assembled in France. Boulanger then marketed the line with competitive pricing.

ATTEMPTING INTERNATIONAL EXPANSION

Boulanger took part in an overall Mulliez group initiative when shares in the company were offered to its employees for the first time in 1995. The response was enthusiastic; 80 percent of the company's employees were also shareholders. By 2001, that number had climbed to 95 percent. The move helped to reinforce employee commitment to the company, which gained a strong reputation for its highly trained sales staff. This reputation formed the basis of Boulanger's marketing effort into the 21st century, when the company launched a new campaign based on highly personalized customer service by its sales staff.

Competition remained intense in the French home appliance market in the 1990s, as market leader Darty expanded its chain to 200 stores, and other challengers, such as Conforama and But, expanded their home appliance sales. At the same time, the large-scale distribution channels had gained an increasing share of the market as well. Nonetheless, Boulanger continued to build its own network of stores, topping 70 stores at the dawn of the new century.

At the same time, the company began eyeing new frontiers. The fast-growing Spanish economy encouraged

KEY DATES

1954: Bernard and Gustave Boulanger open a store selling and repairing radios in Lille.

1978: Boulanger begins its national expansion, opening a store in Lyon.

1986: The Mulliez family acquires control of Boulanger and launches a new expansion of the chain.

1995: Boulanger allows its employees to become shareholders in the company.

1999: Boulanger launches a new store format, Destock'Boulanger.

2003: Boulanger launches a discount retail format, Electro Dépôt.

2005: The company launches its own private labels, Essentiel B and Listo, as well as its first e-commerce web site, Webdistrib.

2007: Boulanger launches e-commerce web site under the Boulanger name.

2008: Boulanger creates 3D "island" as part of "Second Life" online virtual community.

Boulanger to export its retail concept to that market. Boulanger opened its first two stores in Spain in 1998. Over the next decade, the company's Spanish network reached ten stores. Meanwhile, in France, Boulanger also responded to the growing pressure from the discount market. In 1999, the company opened the first store of a new retail format, called Destock'Boulanger. This store featured demonstration models and remaindered goods. The success of the initial store led the company to roll out a series of new stores, reaching ten by the end of the first decade of the 21st century.

Nevertheless, Boulanger's growth hit a speed bump at the beginning of the new century. Through the 1990s, the company appeared to have achieved both strong revenue growth and continued profitability. In the early years of the 21st century, however, the company's fortunes slipped again, in part due to a poorly executed transition to a new management software platform. While the group had continued to open new stores, the choice of some of the locations proved unprofitable. By 2003, the company appeared to have run out of steam.

NEW LEADER TO THE RESCUE

In that year, the Mulliez family called in Francis Cordelette, who had begun his career at Auchan in the

1970s, to take over as head of Boulanger. Cordelette quickly identified a number of factors hampering the company's growth. One of these was the company's failure to distinguish itself sufficiently from its competitors, particularly in its product offerings at the beginning of the new century. Rather than adopt competing companies' strategy of limiting their range of products, Boulanger instead took the opposite approach, expanding its store format and its range of products. To this end, Boulanger created a new department, which later became a subsidiary, called Sourcing et Création, which set out to develop new products for the company. This effort led to the creation of Boulanger's own private labels, Essentiel B for the mid-priced segment, and Listo for the discount range, in 2005. The company also created two new subsidiaries during this time: Electro Dépôt, which launched a new discount appliance retail format, and a wholesale business called SMS.

At the same time, Boulanger undertook a new expansion of its retail network, launching plans to open five or six new stores each year through the end of the decade. In support of this effort, the company also launched a new advertising campaign in 2005, emphasizing its personalized sales approach, under the tagline: Professionnel du Bien Choisir (Professionals of the Right Choice). This initiative was joined by the creation of a new services subsidiary, B Dom', which offered in-home installation, repairs, instruction, and related services.

By the end of 2008, the network of Boulanger stores neared 90 locations. In the second half of the decade, the company had also taken steps to explore new horizons. The group launched its first e-commerce web site in 2005, under the Webdistrib name. By 2007, the company had launched an e-commerce site under the Boulanger name as well, quickly ramping up its offering there to more than 10,000 products. In October 2008, Boulanger teamed up with IBM to become the first in France to create its own 3D "island" in the popular online community "Second Life," which allowed users to navigate through a virtual world. Back in the real world, Boulanger took steps to shed its money-losing Spanish operations. In September of that year, the company agreed to sell all ten of those stores to Portugal's Sonae for EUR 25 million.

With its focus then fixed on France, Boulanger continued in its effort to differentiate itself from its competitors. In 2008, the company developed a new, larger store format, boasting 4,000 square meters of selling space. The first two of the new format stores opened in Toulon and Avignon that year. The larger format enabled Boulanger to expand its product mix as well, as the company began selling complete kitchens and fittings. While the company braced itself for the slowdown in consumer spending amid the economic collapse at the end of the decade, Boulanger nonetheless appeared to have found a successful recipe for its future growth.

M. L. Cohen

PRINCIPAL DIVISIONS

B Dom'; SMS; Sourcing et Création.

PRINCIPAL COMPETITORS

PPR S.A.; Kingfisher plc; Fnac S.A.; Etablissements Darty et Fils S.A.S.; Quelle GmbH; Avenir Telecom S.A.

FURTHER READING

"Boulanger Dévoile Sa Nouvelle Signature à la Télévision," *LSA,* November 6, 2008.

"Boulanger Expands," *LSA,* October 3, 2002, p. 33.

"Boulanger Invests Euro 1.22 Mil in Latest Store," *EuropeIntelligence Wire,* October 9, 2002.

"Boulanger Prépare Deux Ouvertures en Août," *Distributique,* August 1, 2008.

"Boulanger Se Lance dans les Services à la Personne," *LSA,* December 15, 2006.

"Boulanger S'Engage pour L'Emploi avec Ses Fournisseurs," *Les Echos,* June 1993, p. 17.

Bray, Florence, "Boulanger: Tout pour l'Equipement de la Maison," *LSA,* January 18, 2007.

Henno, Jacques, "Boulanger Fait Ses Premiers Pas en 3D avec un Magasin Virtuel," *VNUnet.fr,* October 9, 2008.

"La Nouvelle Dimension de Boulanger," *LSA,* September 25, 2008.

"Le Portugais Sonae Rachète les Magasins Boulanger," *Points de Vente,* September 29, 2008.

Sauvage, Valerie, "Avec la Marque Essentiel B, Boulanger Sort Sa Griffe," *LaVoixEco.com,* July 22, 2008.

———, "Une Enseigne Qui En Connaît Un Rayon Depuis 50 Ans," *LaVoixEco.com,* July 22, 2008.

Visseyrias, Mathilde, "Boulanger Etoffe Son Réseau de Magasins," *Le Figaro,* August 21, 2008.

Brossard S.A.

BP 22, ZA Le Clos Mesnil
Le Neubo urg, F-27110
France
Telephone: (33 02) 32 35 58 15
Fax: (33 02) 32 35 68 67
Web site: http://www.brossard.fr

Public Company
Founded: 1817
Employees: 747
Sales: EUR 145 million ($182.8 million) (2008)
Stock Exchanges: Euronext Paris
Ticker Symbol: ALBRO
NAICS: 311412 Frozen Specialty Food Manufacturing;
    311211 Flour Milling; 311812 Commercial Bakeries; 311813 Frozen Bakery Product Manufacturing

∎ ∎ ∎

Brossard S.A. is one of France's leading producers of dough-based food specialties. The Le Neubourg-based company is present across the full spectrum of dough-based foods, including aperitifs, ready meals, pizzas, pastries, desserts, children's and family snacks, and cookies. Brossard controls two of France's best-known brands, Brossard and Savane, achieving recognition rates ranging from 89 percent to 98 percent, according to the category. The company also produces a range of Lenotre-branded products, as well as products under license for the Weight Watchers brand.

While Brossard may be known especially for its *boudoirs* (ladyfingers) and other cookies and packaged snack cakes, which generated more than 54 percent of its sales of EUR 145 million ($183 million) in 2008, the aperitifs segment, a culturally significant sector in France, is also a major revenue generator for the company, producing more than 18 percent of its sales. Brossard operates from four production sites, including its factory in Pithiviers, originally built in 1817, which is also its largest facility with nearly 7,700 square meters of production space. The other factories are located in Le Neubourg, Castelsarrasin, and Manosque. Brossard is listed on the Euronext Paris Stock Exchange and is controlled by Chairman and CEO Guy Schumacher.

PASTRY SHOP BEGINNINGS

Georges Brossard, a baker's son born in 1909, went into business on his own when he acquired a small pastry shop in Saint Jean d'Angely in the Charente-Maritime region of western France in 1931. By the following year, Brossard had decided to launch the industrial production of pastries, specializing in cookies and cakes. One specialty in particular became associated with the Brossard name: boudoirs, also known as ladyfingers, among other names. A French recipe created in the 15th century, the boudoir was an important ingredient for a number of France's favorite dessert recipes.

The postwar period witnessed a strong expansion of Brossard's company, particularly following Brossard's decision to invest in the construction of a new, modern factory in Saint Jean d'Angely in 1958. The new facility, one of the most modern in the country at the time, also permitted Brossard to expand its range of products. This led to the launch of the Savane brand in 1962. Featuring a line of packaged cakes and brownies, the Savane brand was among the first in France to incorporate preservatives. In this way, Brossard was able to ensure a long shelf life for its products. The Savane line quickly became a mainstay on the shelves of the rapidly increasing number of supermarkets making their appearance in the country at that time.

The growth of the supermarket sector represented a major opportunity for the company amid the booming French economy. The shift from a small grocery shop model to the large-format supermarket and even larger-format hypermarket stores stimulated demand for new generations of high margin packaged products. This demand provided not only an outlet for branded foods but also the potential for maximizing manufacturing capacity with production for the private-label, generic, and third-party channels.

At the same time, the rapid growth of a small number of major distribution groups, such as Carrefour, Auchan, LeClerc, and Intermarché, promised food manufacturers unprecedented access to the national market. Brossard recognized the need to align itself with a major partner in order to take full advantage of the new opportunities in the retail food sector. This led the company to agree to be acquired by U.S.-based baked-goods giant Pillsbury in 1968.

MERGER FOR GROWTH

Brossard was not Pillsbury's first entry into France, however. The U.S. company established a presence in the country in 1962, when it bought Gringoire, a company specialized in the production of biscuits and hard breads. Gringoire's history reached back to the tenth century, when an Armenian hermit by the name of Gregoire took up residence in a cave in Pithiviers, a village in the Gatine area not far from Niort. Gregoire began producing fruitcakes, using a mixture of honey and spices from a recipe from his native Armenia. Over the next centuries, Gregoire's fruitcakes and honey became closely associated with the region. The Gregoire name later became a brand in its own right, closely associated with another popular regional brand, Gringoire.

The origins of Gringoire began in the 16th century with a man named Provenchère, who produced patés and meat pies that he sold from a shop in Pithiviers. Provenchère's pastry products, which included lark patés, as well as patés based on quail, pheasant, hare, and partridge, among others, attracted the attention of King Charles IX, who named Provenchère as an official supplier to the Crown. The Provenchère family retained this position over the next centuries. By 1817, the family had founded their own factory in Pithiviers and trademarked both the Gringoire and Gregoire brands. By the dawn of the 20th century, the company had developed an expanded range of products, including patés and meat pies, vegetable and meat conserves, and petit fours and other pastry products.

In the new century, the company phased out the Gregoire brand in favor of the Gringoire brand and its "trumpeting hare" logo. By 1921, Gringoire had become the company's name. By this time, the company had narrowed its range of products, exiting the production of patés and conserves in exchange for a focus on the production of biscotti, a type of cookie.

Gringoire established itself as a major player in the French food markets in the post–World War II period. This came particularly following the company's launch of the first cellophane-wrapped biscotti in France in 1948. These were initially sold through the country's network of independent bakers. By the end of the 1950s, however, Gringoire too had begun developing products for distribution in the emerging supermarket sector.

Through the first half of the 1970s, Gringoire and Brossard operated as separate companies under the Pillsbury umbrella. The proximity of the two businesses to each other, however, soon led to a restructuring of Pillsbury's French operations. In 1976, Gringoire and Brossard were merged into a single company, Gringoire-Brossard.

MARKETING SUCCESS

The newly enlarged company launched a growth drive at the end of that decade, carrying out a number of acquisitions through the 1980s. Marketing played a major role in Gringoire-Brossard's success as well. The liberalization of France's television and radio broadcasting sector in the 1980s, which saw the creation of the country's first privately owned, commercial-based television channels, opened new advertising opportunities for the company. Gringoire-Brossard—still led by Georges Brossard—responded by introducing its own character-based advertising. "Papy Brossard" shortly became one of the icons of French television advertising during the decade, and helped to establish the Brossard brand as one of the best known in the country.

Brossard also began expanding its product range in the 1980s. The company launched production of its first frozen products in 1982, rolling out lines of both salty and sweet foods from a new factory in Castel Sarrasin, in the Tarn-et-Garonne region. With a total area of more than 11,000 square meters, and a total production area of nearly 7,000 square meters, the new factory almost doubled Brossard's existing manufacturing capacity. In 1987, the company formed a partnership with the noted Parisian restaurant and catering group Lenotre. Brossard then began producing and marketing a line of Lenotre's recipes under the Lenotre par Brossard brand.

Grand Metropolitan (Grand Met) acquired Pillsbury in 1989, taking over Gringoire-Brossard as well. Under Grand Met, Brossard maintained its steady growth. In 1990, for example, the company reinforced its frozen products offering after Grand Met acquired Belin Surgelés, a specialized producer of frozen cakes and snacks. Renamed as Brossard Surgelés, the new operation was formally merged into Brossard in 1994. By then, Brossard had completed a new expansion of its main Pithiviers production facility, which received ISO 9002 certification in 1993.

Starting in 1996, Brossard launched a reorganization of its food production, which included the launch of a new highly successful line, Savane Brownie. The following year, the company was acquired by the Sara Lee Corporation, then in the process of attempting to establish a European-wide presence. Under Sara Lee, Brossard once again streamlined its production. In 1999, the company agreed to sell its Saint Jean d'Angely factory, by then specialized in the production of boudoirs and other cookies. As part of that sale, Brossard agreed that it would not reenter the cookie segment, with the exception of boudoirs, for at least six years.

NEW OWNERS IN THE 21ST CENTURY

By the dawn of the 21st century, Sara Lee Corporation was forced to recognize that its ambitions to create a European-wide pastry and snack foods group faced a major obstacle, the extremely regional nature of European snack food and pastry preferences. At the same time, Brossard itself was struggling to maintain its momentum, and by the end of 2000 had slipped into the red, posting a loss of EUR 6 million ($5 million) by 2001. That year, Sara Lee decided to abandon the French food market, selling Brossard to a smaller group, Saveurs de France, for EUR 5 million.

Saveurs de France had been launched in 1986 by Guy Schumacher, who had previously worked for four years as part of Lenotre's management team. Schumacher had recognized the opportunity for developing a line of high-quality, frozen dough-based pastries and desserts, a sector that was largely under-exploited at the time. Based in Neubourg, Saveurs de France quickly rolled out a range of products spanning from the aperitifs segment to traditional cakes, supplying both the supermarket sector and the country's retail frozen foods specialists such as Thiriet.

Saveurs de France went public in 1997, listing its shares on the Paris Bourse's Nouveau Marché. The listing enabled Schumacher to launch a major expansion of the company's production capacity, which tripled in size by 1998. The company then sought to expand its range of products in order to establish itself as a prominent supplier to the private label channel. This led to a number of acquisitions, particularly of Pikiche, a company specialized in the production of frozen pizzas, and Sigal, a producer of doughnuts, in 1999. By the end of 2000, Saveurs de France's sales had risen from FRF 70 million (approximately $10 million) at the time of its public offering to more than FRF 300 million (approximately $55 million).

The acquisition of Brossard nearly quadrupled the size of Saveurs de France's annual revenues as the company emerged as a major national player in the dough-based foods segment. Following the acquisition, the company changed its name to Saveurs de France-Brossard SA. The company also created a new sales and marketing subsidiary, Brossard Distribution, coordinating the operations of the entire group.

The Brossard acquisition was nonetheless greeted with skepticism from the group's investors, who criticized the company for having paid too much for the money-losing Brossard. Soon after the merger, the company's share price plummeted. The group's difficulties with the stock market were compounded with its struggle to maintain its own revenue growth through the economic downturn at the beginning of the 21st century. Part of the company's troubles stemmed from a strategy of targeting the seasonal desserts market, which failed to deliver the momentum the group required.

RETURN TO COOKIE MAKING

Nonetheless, Schumacher continued to guide the integration of the group's newly expanded operations. By 2003, the company had adopted a new two-pronged strategy focusing on its strongest operations, those of pizza and frozen entrees. Saveurs de France-Brossard sought to expand its position in these markets, adding complementary lines of fresh pizzas and entrees, as well as developing a line of microwavable pastry products. The Brossard brand then became the group's engine, ultimately accounting for some 85 percent of the group's revenues.

This strategy enabled the group to cut its losses by 2004. The company's efforts were further rewarded as it gained the leading position in the French industrial pastry sector, surpassing perennial rival LU, owned by Danone, for the first time. The company also gained the leading place in its core "wood-burning oven cooked" pizza segment, taking more than 14 percent of that market. In 2005, Schumacher, whose control of the company had dropped to just 29 percent, launched a buyout offer to take 100 percent control of the company. The buyout was carried out through a new company, Tesc, set up in 2005, and was completed in 2006.

In 2007, the company, which had previously attempted to enter the Russian market, launching a production and marketing subsidiary there, decided to focus entirely on its growth in the French market. At home, the company appeared to have regained its momentum, rolling out a number of new product lines, including a high-end range marketed under the brand

"Un Recette de Lenotre" (A Lenotre Recipe) in celebration of the 20th anniversary of the two companies' partnership. That year also marked the end of the six-year moratorium as part of the sale of Gringoire, and in March 2007 the company announced its intention to launch a new line of Brossard-branded cookies.

This momentum led Schumacher to return to the stock market by the end of the year. Renamed Brossard S.A., the company then experienced a new surge in growth, with sales jumping by some 27 percent in the first half of 2008. With one of the best-known food brands in France, Brossard looked forward to continued growth in the future.

M. L. Cohen

PRINCIPAL SUBSIDIARIES

Brossard Distribution SAS; Friance SA; Savane Brossard SA; Saveurs de France Brossard SA; Sigal SAS.

PRINCIPAL COMPETITORS

Danone SA; Nestlé S.A.

FURTHER READING

"Brossard Investit le Rayon Biscuits avec 19 Références," *Les Marchés,* February 9, 2007.

Crosskey, Peter, "Baker Brossard Buoyed by Strong Q2," *just-food.com,* January 14, 2008.

———, "Brossard Posts FY Profit Amid Russia Exit," *just-food.com,* October 12, 2007.

"French Cake Firm Brossard Plans Return to Stock Market; Capacity Investments Expected," *FlexNews,* March 14, 2007.

Jones, Chris, "LeClerc in Delist Threat to 'Profiteering' Brands," *just-food.com,* January 17, 2008.

Santon, Jean, "A Saint-Jean d'Angély On Ne Boude Pas les Boudoirs," *L'Humanité,* February 9, 1999.

"Sara Lee to Unload Brossard," *Snack Food & Wholesale Bakery,* February 2001, p. 8.

"Saveurs de France-Brossard Déçoit et Chute en Bourse," *Les Echos,* March 25, 2003, p. 15.

"Saveurs de France Buys Brossard," *Les Echos,* January 17, 2001, p. 10.

"Saveurs de France Rachète les Biscuits Brossard Sara Lee," *L'Expansion,* January 16, 2001.

"Sur la Bonne Voie," *La Vie Financière,* September 3, 2004.

Todd, Stuart, "Brossard to Increase Capital, Eyes Biscuits Development," *just-food.com,* March 14, 2007.

Vermont

*Owned by Dairy Farmers
Since 1919*

Cabot Creamery
Cooperative, Inc.

1 Home Farm Way
Montpelier, Vermont 05602
U.S.A.
Telephone: (802) 563-2231
Toll Free: (888) 792-2268
Fax: (802) 563-2604
Web site: http://www.cabotcheese.com

Private Company
Incorporated: 1919 as Cabot Farmers Cooperative
   Creamery
Employees: 300
Sales: $400 million (2008 est.)
NAICS: 311513 Cheese Manufacturing

■ ■ ■

A subsidiary of Agri-Mark, Inc., Cabot Creamery Cooperative, Inc., is a farm dairy cooperative with about 400 members in upstate New York and New England. The Montpelier, Vermont-based company specializes in specialty cheddar cheeses, reduced-fat cheddars, and such flavored cheddars as Tuscan Hand-Rubbed Cheddar, Horseradish Cheddar, Habanero Cheddar, Chipotle Cheddar, Sun-Dried Tomato Basil Cheddar, and Chili-Lime Hand Rubbed Cheddar. Non-cheddar cheeses offered by Cabot include American Swiss, Monterey Jack, Colby Jack, Muenster, Fancy Blend Shredded Cheese, Pepper Jack, and Mozzarella. Cabot also produces butter, sour cream, plain and flavored yogurts, Greek-style yogurt, cottage cheese, a variety of dips, and whipped cream. In addition to its corporate offices, Cabot oper-

ates a 63,000-square-foot distribution center in Montpelier. Manufacturing is done at four plants, three located in Vermont and one in Massachusetts. At the facility in Cabot, Vermont, the company also maintains a retail sales outlet in the plant's visitors center. Products are also retailed at the Cabot Annex Store in Waterbury, Vermont.

ORIGINS

The art of cheesemaking, primarily cheddar, was brought to New England by the Puritans, but due to a number of factors it was not until the late 1800s that the dairy industry in Vermont took shape. Farmers had prospered from raising merino sheep, but as the West was settled and the breed was introduced in new locales the bottom fell out of wool prices, leading to a greater emphasis on diary farming in Vermont. Moreover, the expansion of the railroad system to distant states finally provided farmers access to such major markets as Montreal and Boston for less perishable products, such as cheese and butter. With the introduction of refrigerated cars around the beginning of the 20th century, Vermont dairy farmers would also be able to transport milk, cream, and yogurt as well. Initially farmers produced their own cheeses for sale, but the emergence of large-scale creameries and cheese factories put an end to this cottage industry, and farmers were forced to align themselves with larger, more efficient enterprises.

   In Cabot, Vermont, located about 20 miles northeast of Montpelier, a creamery was established by F.A. Messer in 1893. The town had been established in the 1780s and in the early 1800s it was known for producing whiskey from an abundant potato crop, and during the War of 1812, the locals were known to smuggle their wares into Montreal. Sheep then became an important industry but with the collapse of the wool market, farmers there as elsewhere in Vermont began to focus on dairy farming and soon were producing more milk than they could sell. Messer's Cabot Creamery used the excess milk of these local farmers to manufacture butter. It was not an especially profitable business for Messer, and in time he was no longer interested in running the creamery.

For Cabot-area dairy farmers the creamery remained an important outlet for their excess milk, and 94 of them joined forces in 1919 to buy the creamery and form a cooperative, the Cabot Farmers Cooperative Creamery. Each was levied $5 per cow, as well as a cord of wood for the creamery's boiler, in order to raise the $3,700 needed to buy out Messer. The creamery continued to produce butter, which was marketed under the Rosedale brand name, but was soon taking advantage of refrigeration, improved manufacturing techniques, and better distribution systems to ship fluid milk to bottlers across southern New England. In 1930 Cabot hired its first cheesemaker and began offering cheddar cheese for sale, followed by cottage cheese and sour cream.

BUILDING THE CABOT BRAND

Cabot enjoyed steady growth over the next three decades, and by 1960 the cooperative represented 600 farm families. The company continued to market its products under the Rosedale brand until the 1980s when the Cabot label was adopted and the company began to focus its marketing on the Cabot hometown name and the even stronger brand of Vermont itself. Playing a key role in this transformation was Chief Executive Officer Bill Davis. As a 24-year-old, Davis had joined Cabot in 1974 as a sales representative and marketing manager. Thus he was keenly aware of the importance of brand image and was responsible for replacing the non-specific Rosedale brand with the Cabot brand. He also placed an even greater commit-

ment on quality in order to build the Cabot brand.

One of Davis's first marketing efforts, taken in 1986, was the construction of a small visitors information center and gift shop in front of the plant. This facility was then put to good use in promoting the Cabot brand with the many tourists who visited the state. Establishing cheese-sampling stations at Vermont's ski resorts, starting with Jay Peak, Smugglers' Notch, and Killington in 1988, became a key way to increase brand awareness and drive traffic to the visitors center. "Skis and cheese became our mantra in the late 80s and early 90s," Cabot executive Roberta MacDonald told the *Times Argus* of Montpelier. During major tourist weekends, large displays were erected at the resorts at the end of the ski runs. "We used farmers and our employees to quite literally lob cheese hunks at tourists," MacDonald recalled in an interview with *Vermont Business Magazine*. Tossing cheese at potential customers became a standard ploy in the years to come.

When MacDonald began her marketing effort in 1988, Cabot was generating sales of $33 million, not enough to provide her with much of a marketing budget, thus forcing her to devote her resources to the ski slopes and craft shows where tourists could be found. In the meantime, the company invested in other areas to bolster its claims on quality. In 1987, for example, the company built New England's first onsite aging coolers and cutting/wrapping facilities. Product development was another major commitment. During that same year Cabot began construction on a new butter manufacturing plant in West Springfield, Massachusetts. Also in 1987 the company introduced a light cheddar cheese. Because the Food and Drug Administration had not established federal standards for light cheese it had to be marketed under another descriptive name, and the company chose Vitalite. Finally, in 1991 the low-calorie cheddar cheese could be marketed as light cheddar, which became a significant part of the company's growing sales.

AGRI-MARK ACQUIRES THE CO-OP

Finally, in the early 1990s MacDonald was able to budget some money for television advertising, albeit in a modest way. Along with the Vermont Ski Areas Association, Cabot began sponsoring the "This Week in Vermont" program, and would later be joined by Green Mountain Coffee Roasters. During its 10-second portion of a 30-second spot, Cabot urged people to visit its plant to "see where the taste of Cabot begins." Serving as the spokesperson was a farmer named John Malcolm, whose iconic look led to people tracking him down to see if he was an authentic farmer. Casting agents even

the 1990s the co-op began to reassess its business. It had the financial strength and marketing clout that Cabot lacked, but the smaller co-op possessed the retail brands that Agri-Mark could use to grow its value-added business to the benefit of its dairy farmer members. Thus, it acquired Cabot Farmers Cooperative Creamery, which then operated as an independent subsidiary under the Cabot Creamery Cooperative, Inc., name.

STEADY GROWTH INTO THE 21ST CENTURY

Agri-Mark used its deep pockets to grow Cabot. In 1994 a former Kraft plant in Middlebury, Vermont, was acquired and converted from Swiss cheese to cheddar cheese production. To obtain the required equipment, Agri-Mark also purchased a cheddar facility from Swiss Valley Farms in Iowa, and then had all of the equipment trucked to Middlebury. While this project cost about $12 million, the amount was half of what would have been spent to build a state-of-the-art cheddar plant from the ground up. The facility began producing cheese in July 1995. In the meantime, Bill Davis left Cabot in 1994 to buy and run Franklin County Cheese Company in Burlington, Vermont. He added several specialty food companies, resulting in the creation of a holding company, Waterbury Specialty Foods.

Agri-Mark also helped to finance a product development program at Cabot. In 1995 Cabot introduced several flavored cheddars, including tomato-basil, roasted onion and chive, garlic and dill, and five-peppercorn. A year later, Mediterranean with black olives and pimento and pesto cheddars were added as well. These new products helped to drive sales from $66 million in 1993 to more than $120 million by 1998, and $150 million by the start of the new century.

Cabot moved its headquarters and sales operations from Cabot to Montpelier in 2000. The co-op's new home was the former Conti-Tracey Reserve Center, a 4.3-acre site, leased from a Berlin, Vermont-based development and contracting company. In that same year, Cabot opened a $20 million whey protein processing plant in Middlebury, a state-of-the-art facility unique to the United States. Cabot's parent also invested in existing plants. The Cabot Creamery had its 30-year-old cheese vats replaced with newer, more efficient models. In 2003 Agri-Mark also used its coffers to add a sister company to Cabot, upstate New York-based McCadam Cheese, which had been in the cheddar cheesemaking business since the 1870s. The same marketing skills honed on Cabot were then applied to promoting the McCadam brand.

contacted Cabot to let them know of their roster of actors who could step in should the company look to cast a replacement.

Although successful in its efforts to produce high-quality products and establish its brand, Cabot was simply too small to adequately support that brand. For example, Cabot could not afford to pay the slotting fees charged by supermarkets to ensure the placement of Cabot cheese products on the shelves. In its efforts to develop Cabot into a national brand, the co-op took on more debt than it could handle. The financial situation became critical after it lost money in 1991, when Cabot not only had to contend with depressed milk prices but also attempted to reorganize both the co-op and the premiums paid to its member farmers. Cabot's primary lender, the Springfield Bank for Cooperatives, then demanded that the co-op reduce its debt load. Members were faced with the choice of selling the cheese plant or merging with a larger enterprise. In 1992 Cabot found a suitable partner in Agri-Mark, Inc., a major dairy cooperative in the Northeast, and in 1992 Agri-Mark acquired the smaller co-op, saving it from bankruptcy.

Agri-Mark grew out of the New England Milk Producers Association, established in Boston in 1916, representing dairy farmers throughout New England. The Agri-Mark name was adopted in 1980 with the acquisition of the Yankee Milk Producers business and H.P Hood processing plants. The focus of Agri-Mark was on the wholesale milk business, but by the start of

Agri-Mark did not neglect the needs of Cabot, however. In 2004 a new 62,000-square-foot warehouse was opened in Montpelier at the cost of $6 million, freeing up space in the manufacturing plant for further cheese packing to accommodate growing demand for the Cabot brand. Building on the popularity of its products, the co-op continued to unveil new offerings. Cabot Clothbound Cheddar was developed with a small family farm, Jasper Hill Farm, a product that was named "Best in Show" at the 23rd Annual Conference and Competition of the American Cheese Society in 2006. In late 2007 Cabot introduced a kosher-certified sharp cheddar. By this time sales were in the $400 million range, and there was every reason to expect that total to continue to grow steadily in the years to come.

Ed Dinger

PRINCIPAL COMPETITORS

Dairy Farmers of America, Inc.; Kraft Foods Inc.; Land O'Lakes, Inc.

FURTHER READING

Biemiller, Lawrence, "The State of Small Cheese," *Chronicle of Higher Education,* January 7, 2005.

Blackburn, Doug, "Still a Big Cheese," *Albany (N.Y.) Times Union,* February 20, 2004, p. 2.

Doeff, Gail, "Cabot: Vermont's Big Cheese," *Dairy Foods,* May 1996.

Feldman, Rachel, "Marketing Magic," *Montpelier-Barre (Vt.) Times Argus,* April 1, 2007.

Gorski, Donna, "The Home of White Cheddar," *Dairy Foods,* May 1994.

Hentcy, Kathleen, "Cabot Churns Its Way to the Top," *Vermont Business Magazine,* May 31, 1996.

Joy, Patrick, "Cabot Cheese Honored," *Montpelier-Barre (Vt.) Times Argus,* August 4, 2006.

Judge, Paul C., "From Country Boys to Big Cheese," *Fast Company,* December 2001, p. 38.

Marcel, Joyce, "The Connection Between Skis and Cheese," *Vermont Business Magazine,* September 1, 2000.

"NH, Vermont Dairy Farmers Approve Co-Op Merger," *New Hampshire Union Leader,* July 2, 1992, p. 21.

Smith, David W., "Cabot Honored for Its Marketing Efforts," *Montpelier-Barre (Vt.) Times Argus,* January 1, 2006.

Casella Waste Systems Inc.

---

25 Greens Hill Lane
Rutland, Vermont 05701
U.S.A.
Telephone: (802) 775-0325
Toll Free: (800) 227-3552
Fax: (802) 775-6198
Web site: http://www.casella.com

Public Company
Incorporated: 1975
Employees: 2,800
Sales: $579.5 million (2008)
Stock Exchanges: NASDAQ
Ticker Symbol: CWST
NAICS: 562111 Solid Waste Collection; 562212 Solid
   Waste Landfill

■ ■ ■

Based in Rutland, Vermont, Casella Waste Systems Inc. is a leading provider of both temporary and permanent solid waste collection and recycling services. In addition to providing residential service, the company serves a wide variety of commercial customers, including construction companies, electric utilities, hospitals, government agencies, manufacturing firms, and schools. Casella also ranks as one of the largest landfill operators in the northeastern United States. On an annual basis, the company oversees the disposal of approximately three million tons of solid waste. One example of Casella's efforts to dispose of waste responsibly is its Sustainable Environmental and Economic Development program.

The company employs various methods to obtain all possible resources from waste, such as the use of landfill gas collection systems that provide utilities with the energy needed to produce clean electricity. Through its GreenFiber joint venture with Louisiana-Pacific Corp., Casella transforms recycled paper into natural fiber insulation for the home improvement and construction markets. In addition, the company also converts organic waste such as wood, food, ash, and compost into renewable products for end uses such as landscaping and farm fertilization. These products are marketed by Casella's New England Organics business under the brand name earthlife.

FORMATIVE YEARS

Casella traces its roots back to 1975, when the company was established in Rutland, Vermont, as a one-truck enterprise. Early leadership was provided by John W. Casella, who was named chairman of Casella Waste Management Inc. in 1977. That year, the company established itself as a recycling pioneer by opening Vermont's first recycling center. From its humble beginning, the company devoted its formative years to gradually expanding operations throughout the state. By 1993, industry consolidation and growing levels of environmental regulation were among factors that prompted Casella to embark upon the acquisition path. That year, the company reincorporated in Delaware and became a holding company for a growing number of new subsidiaries. At that time, John Casella was named chairman, president, and CEO.

A formal strategy to acquire other solid waste industry players was developed and put into action midway through 1994. From May of that year through early 1998, Casella experienced astronomical growth. During this time period, the company had either acquired or secured long-term operating rights to 77 solid waste companies. Casella's strong growth during the late 1990s was marked by a number of key acquisitions. In 1997 the company completed a $4.9 million deal for the Teelon Group, which consisted of several waste collection businesses operating in the western region of New York State. Late that year, Casella also parted with $4.4 million in order to acquire South Portland, Maine-based Pine Tree Waste Inc. Around the same time, Casella merged with Winters Brothers Inc. and All Cycle Waste Inc.

Another significant event in 1997 occurred when the company's Casella T.I.R.E.S business received a $2.4 million contract from Maine's Department of Environmental Protection to clean up the largest tire dump in the state, which contained approximately 20 million tires. A special milestone was reached in October 1997, when Casella went public. The company rounded out the year by snapping up nine garbage haulers during the month of December.

EXPLOSIVE EXPANSION

By early 1998, Casella's footprint had expanded beyond Vermont to include northern Pennsylvania, upstate New York, New Hampshire, and Maine. The company's operations then included 33 transfer stations, 24 collection operations that served approximately 100,000 customers, and four landfills. Acquisitions continued at a blistering pace during the first half of 1998. That year, Casella acquired Angelica, New York-based Hyland Facility Associates Landfill. The deal resulted in the company's first landfill in its western region, where it also snapped up Allegheny County, New York-based Busy Bee Disposal Inc.

In Casella's central region, the company acquired a Lyndon, Vermont-based septic tank cleaning and liquid waste business named Johnson's Septic, and a Stowe, Vermont-based liquid waste management enterprise named Hartigan Co. A number of collection operations also were acquired in this region, including Bennington, Vermont-based Brian Pratt Co.; Corinth, Vermont-based J & N Rubbish Removal; Hardwick, Vermont-based JR's Trucking and Rubbish Removal; and Manchester, Vermont-based Bushee Trucking and Rubbish Removal. Expansion also occurred within the company's eastern region, where Pittsfield, Maine-based Bickford Enterprises Inc. became part of the Casella family.

Deals during the second half of 1998 included a merger with Hakes C & D Disposal Inc. in September. The following month, Casella combined its operations with Grasslands Inc.; Waste Stream Inc.; R.A. Bronson Inc.; BBC LLC; B&C Sanitation Corp.; North Country Trucking Inc.; Better Bedding Corp.; and NTC LLC. Finally, Casella merged with Northern Properties Corp. of Plattsburgh Inc. and Northern Sanitation Inc. in December. The company capped off the year with revenues of $118.1 million, up 48 percent from 1997 levels of $79.5 million.

Casella's revenues continued to soar in 1999, reaching $173.4 million. As the decade drew to a close, the company continued to expand its footprint by acquiring other companies. In April 1999 Casella merged with a number of other enterprises, including Portland C & D Landfill Inc.; Westfield Disposal Service Inc.; Blasdell Development Group Inc.; Natural Environmental Inc.; and Schultz Landfill Inc. Activity continued midway through the year, as Casella added Corning Community Disposal Inc. and Resource Waste Systems Inc.

Among all of the acquisitions that Casella made in 1999, one in particular was especially remarkable. At the beginning of the year, the company agreed to acquire Guttenberg, New Jersey-based recycling firm KTI Inc. The $338 million deal had the potential to significantly expand Casella's geographic footprint, because KTI had operations in 21 states, as well as Canada. Altogether, the company operated approximately 15 facilities that were organized within four divisions: commercial recycling, finished products, residential recycling, and waste-to-energy.

By April, the transaction was in jeopardy of falling apart because KTI had failed to meet certain terms of its agreement with Casella. However, by September the two companies had worked out an amended agreement, which called for Casella to acquire KTI for $104 million. Shareholders of both companies voted in favor

KEY DATES

1975: The company is established in Rutland, Vermont, as a one-truck enterprise.

1977: The business establishes Vermont's first recycling center.

1993: Casella reincorporates in Delaware and becomes a holding company for a growing number of new subsidiaries.

1997: The company goes public.

1999: Guttenberg, New Jersey-based KTI Inc. is acquired for $104 million, significantly expanding operations.

2001: John W. Casella is reelected chairman, and Chief Operating Officer James W. Bohlig is named president.

2008: Paul Larkin is named president and chief operating officer.

2009: The U.S. Environmental Protection Agency names Casella as the Landfill Methane Outreach Program's 2008 Industry Partner of the Year.

of the deal on December 8, and the deal was completed eight days later.

REFOCUSING

Casella began the new millennium on strong footing, securing $450 million in credit that could be used for continued acquisitions. Examples of activity in this area during 2000 included a deal with Allied Waste Industries for a Peabody, Massachusetts-based collection business; a collection operation and transfer station in Holliston, Massachusetts; and an Auburn, Massachusetts-based recycling facility and transfer station. In addition to the deal with Allied, the company also acquired a construction and demolition debris processing enterprise named Rochester Environmental Park, as well as a collection and transportation business named Alternate Energy Inc. that did business under the Giant Container banner.

Around the time of the KTI deal, Casella began identifying noncore assets that it could divest. This followed a strategy that called for a stronger focus on the company's traditional solid waste business. By April 2000, operations that brought in roughly $50 million had been earmarked for this purpose.

Several divestures occurred in 2001. Casella kicked off the year by selling its waste remediation and plastic

raw material distribution operations, which consisted of Annapolis, Maryland-based Manner Resins Inc. and Newington, New Hampshire-based Total Waste Management Inc. In March, Casella struck a deal with Energy National Inc. for the sale of its interest in Penobscot Energy Recovery Co. This was followed by the sale of a Telogia, Florida-based biomass incinerator, as well as a Cairo, Georgia-based wood-chipping operation, for $18 million. In September, Casella sold approximately 80 percent of its tire recycling assets to a private investor. The deal, which involved 15 recycling centers throughout the United States and Canada, generated $13 million for the company and pushed the total proceeds from its divestitures to $94 million.

On the acquisitions front, Casella struck several deals in 2001. In March the company secured full ownership in Maine Energy Recovery Co. Midway through the year, it arranged to acquire a 37.5 percent stake in New Heights Recovery and Power LLC from Oakhurst Company Inc. A number of leadership changes occurred in 2001 as well. John W. Casella was reelected chairman in June. In addition to that role, he continued to serve as CEO. Ross Pirasteh, who had been named chairman following the KTI deal, resigned. Additionally, Chief Operating Officer James W. Bohlig was named president.

RENEWABLE ENERGY EMPHASIS

In 2002 Casella began to focus more on the connection between municipal solid waste disposal and recycling. Early the following year, the company bolstered its operations in the northeastern United States by acquiring Scarborough, Maine-based William Goodman & Sons, which ranked as one of that state's largest independent recycling businesses. In addition, it snapped up the Hardwick Sanitary Landfill in Hardwick, Massachusetts.

Other deals in 2003 included a $4.2 million deal for the acquisition of the assets of All-Waste Services. In addition, Casella acquired Tyngsboro, Massachusetts-based Statewide Carting Inc. and paid out $5.3 million to acquire a stake in Evergreen National Indemnity Co. In September 2005, Blue Mountain Recycling LLC was acquired, resulting in the addition of processing facilities in both Montgomeryville and Philadelphia, Pennsylvania. The following month, the company's FCR Inc. subsidiary agreed to build a new recycling center in Hartford, Connecticut, in cooperation with the Connecticut Resources Recovery Authority, giving residents in 70 different towns and cities the ability to recycle additional materials, including oversized metal and plastic containers, as well as aerosol cans and recycled boxboard.

In 2006 Casella was focused on plans to expand capacity at its landfills. The company indicated that nearly one million tons of capacity would be added by 2011, resulting in roughly $24 million in additional earnings. Revenues reached $547 million in 2007, a 6.2 percent increase over the previous year. A slowdown in the construction market, as well as weak economic conditions in the northeast, had a negative impact on operations that year, leading to a $3 million net loss. Even still, Casella was able to expand its operations by acquiring 13 solid waste collection and recycling operations.

Casella began 2008 by naming James Bohlig as chief development officer and president of its renewables group. In addition, Paul Larkin was named president and chief operating officer. John Casella continued to provide leadership as chairman and CEO. In October of that year, the company's fourth gas-to-energy plant came online at its Angelica, New York-based Hyland landfill. By this time, the clean energy obtained from Casella's four landfills was enough to provide power for some 20,000 homes.

Casella began 2009 on a high note when the U.S. Environmental Protection Agency named it as the Landfill Methane Outreach Program's 2008 Industry Partner of the Year. The honor recognized the company for its efforts in the area of renewable energy projects. In a January 16, 2009, company news release, Chairman and CEO John Casella's comments reflected the company's philosophy and focus as it moved toward the second decade of the 21st century: "We believe that waste is no longer just a throw-away, but is instead a raw material for manufacturing new products and a resource for producing clean energy," he explained. From its roots as a one-truck operation during the mid-1970s, Casella had evolved into a leading regional solid waste and resource management operation with national aspirations.

Paul R. Greenland

PRINCIPAL SUBSIDIARIES

All Cycle Waste Inc.; Atlantic Coast Fibers Inc.; B. and C. Sanitation Corp.; Better Bedding Corp.; Blue Mountain Recycling LLC; Bristol Waste Management Inc.; C.V. Landfill Inc.; Casella Insurance Co.; Casella Major Account Services LLC; Casella Renewable Systems LLC; Casella RTG Investors Co. LLC; Casella Transportation Inc.; Casella Waste Management of Massachusetts Inc.; Casella Waste Management of New York Inc.; Casella Waste Management of Pennsylvania Inc.; Casella Waste Management Inc.; Casella Waste Services

of Ontario LLC; Casella Waste Systems Inc.; Chemung Landfill LLC; Colebrook Landfill LLC; Culchrome LLC; Corning Community Disposal Service Inc.; CWM All Waste LLC; Fairfield County Recycling LLC; FCR Camden LLC; FCR Florida LLC; FCR Greensboro LLC; FCR Greenville LLC; FCR Morris LLC; FCR Redemption LLC; FCR Tennessee LLC; FCR LLC; Forest Acquisitions Inc.; Green Mountain Glass LLC; Grasslands Inc.; GroundCo LLC; Hakes C & D Disposal Inc.; Hardwick Landfill Inc.; Hiram Hollow Regeneration Corp.; K-C International Ltd.; KTI Bio-Fuels Inc.; KTI Environmental Group Inc.; KTI New Jersey Fibers Inc.; KTI Operations Inc.; KTI Recycling of New England LLC; KTI Specialty Waste Services Inc.; KTI Inc.; Lewiston Landfill LLC; Maine Energy Recovery Company Limited Partnership; New England Landfill Solutions LLC; New England Waste Services of Massachusetts Inc.; New England Waste Services of Maine Inc.; New England Waste Services of New York Inc.; New England Waste Services of Vermont Inc.; New England Waste Services Inc.; Newbury Waste Management Inc.; NEWS of Worcester LLC; NEWSME Landfill Operations LLC; North Country Composting Services Inc.; North Country Environmental Services Inc.; North Country Trucking Inc.; Northern Sanitation Inc.; PERC Management Company LP; PERC Inc.; Pine Tree Waste Inc.; Portland C&D Site Inc.; R.A Bronson Inc.; Resource Recovery Systems LLC; Re-Source Transfer Services Inc.; ReSource Waste Systems Inc.; Rockingham Sand & Gravel LLC; Schultz Landfill Inc.; Southbridge Recycling & Disposal Park Inc.; Sunderland Waste Management Inc.; Templeton Landfill LLC; The Hyland Facility Associates; Total Waste Management Corp.; Trilogy Glass LLC; U.S. Fiber LLC; Waste-Stream Inc.; Westfield Disposal Service Inc; Winters Brothers Inc.

PRINCIPAL COMPETITORS

Covanta Holding Corporation; Entrx Corporation; TransCor Waste Services Inc.; Waste Connections Inc.

FURTHER READING

"Casella Acquires Goodman," *Official Board Markets,* April 5, 2003.

"Casella Waste Systems Completes KTI Transaction," *PR Newswire,* December 16, 1999.

"Casella Waste Systems Continues to Refocus on Core Business, Strengthen Balance Sheet; Acquires Additional Ownership Interest in Maine Energy; Sells Partial Interest in Penobscot Energy Recovery Company," *PR Newswire,* March 2, 2001.

"Casella Waste Systems Inc. Announces Fourth Quarter and Fiscal Year 1998 Financial Results; Company Reports

Fourth Quarter EPS of 10 Cents; Revenue Growth for Completed Fiscal Year Approaches 48 Percent," *PR Newswire,* June 23, 1998.

Johnson, Jim, "Casella Raises $13 Million, Sells 15 Tire Recycling Sites," *Waste News,* October 1, 2001.

———, "Northeast Expansion Plans; Casella Looks to 2011 to Complete Aggressive Landfill Strategy," *Waste News,* December 18, 2006.

Chelsea Ltd.

Stamford Bridge
Fulham Road
London, SW6 1HS
United Kingdom
Telephone: (44 207) 835 6000
Web site: http://www.chelseafc.com

Private Company
Founded: 1905 as Chelsea Football and Athletic Club
Employees: 160
Sales: £130 million ($188.22 million) (2008 est.)
NAICS: 711211 Sports Teams and Clubs

■ ■ ■

Chelsea Ltd. owns and operates Chelsea FC (Football Club), a team in the English Premier League, a national professional football (known as soccer in the United States) league. Located in London, Chelsea FC is one of the most popular, and at times, one of the most successful teams in English football. Chelsea FC also plays regularly in the Champions League. The club's home stadium is Stamford Bridge, which in addition to the stadium includes a hotel and shopping complex also operated by Chelsea Ltd. In addition to football, Chelsea Ltd. is also active in concession and parking operations, sports merchandising, hotel management, and real estate. The bulk of the firm's income is derived from gate receipts at games, licensed television broadcasts, and the sales of licensed Chelsea FC merchandise. Chelsea Ltd. is owned by Russian billionaire Roman Abramovich.

A SUCCESSFUL START IN LONDON

The Chelsea Football and Athletic Club was founded in 1905 by Gus Mears, a London entrepreneur. The team was formed specifically to play in Stamford Bridge, a stadium Mears had purchased the previous year. His original plan was to resell the stadium to the local Fulham team. Unable to come to an agreement with Fulham on the terms of the sale, however, Mears was persuaded to form a club of his own to play at the Bridge. In March 1905 he placed an announcement in the *Times* of London offering five thousand shares in the new club. They sold quickly. Mears applied for admission to the Football League, England's best football league at the time, and after a long meeting at London's Tavistock Hotel, reportedly lubricated by considerable amounts of alcohol provided by Mears, executives of the Football League approved the application. Mears settled on the name Chelsea after considering calling the club Kensington. Ironically Stamford Bridge is located in neither Chelsea nor Kensington, but in the district of Fulham and Hammersmith, whose name had distinctly working-class associations at the time.

The Blues, as the club became known after the color of their jerseys, played their first game at the Bridge against Liverpool in September 1905. The stadium helped Chelsea become a premier football attraction in the London area. It was well served by London public transportation lines, including bus, rail, and even steamship. Furthermore, as a result of improvements made by Mears, the stadium was soon one of the largest and most modern in English football. The Blues set an attendance record during their first season, when 67,000 fans witnessed a game against Manchester United at the Bridge in the spring of 1906. The team was so successful in its premier season that it was promoted to the Football League's First Division in the 1906–07 season. Encouraged, Mears began spending money to attract talented players—a practice that would become something of a Chelsea trademark over the decades—which helped make the team one of the most popular in England, at least with fans. Other teams, especially those in London, such as Arsenal, looked down on the Blues as "upstarts" and were none too disappointed when an injury-laden Chelsea team finished the 1909–10 season deep in the standings and had to return to the Second Division.

Chelsea, like other professional English football teams, continued their seasons following the start of World War I. Attendance dropped significantly, however. For example, a weekend game in November 1913 at Stamford Bridge drew 35,000 spectators; the same weekend in 1914, three months after the start of the war, attracted only 15,000, a 60 percent decline. Chelsea was able to boast of its first trip to the Football Association (FA) finals, the World Series of English football, in 1915, a game it lost. After the war, Chelsea's owners hoped to convert the Stamford Bridge venue into a national stadium that would regularly host various cup games of national significance. Although the FA finals were played there from 1920 through 1922, the FA's construction of Wembley Stadium put an end to those hopes.

A CONTROVERSIAL OWNER

Gus Mears died in 1912, and his brother J. T. Mears was running the club as the 1920s got under way. J. T. Mears was an owner surrounded by controversy. In the early 1920s allegations were made that Mears had misused club funds, in part by giving contracts to cronies rather than through open bids. The accusations

were serious enough that the FA launched an investigation and eventually issued a highly critical report. It called on Chelsea to expand its board to include directors from outside the Mears family, and stipulated that all further improvements to the Bridge were to be made under FA oversight, and that concessions contracts be awarded after open bidding had taken place.

In the later 1920s Mears introduced greyhound racing at the stadium. He may have been trying to expand the income potential of the stadium grounds, as Ken Bates would do 60 or more years later. Others speculate that members of the London underworld forced Mears to start racing. In any event, the dog races resulted in a major redesign of the stadium, including the addition of a gravel track for the dogs, a series of kennels, and a grandstand for race spectators. The improvements hurt Stamford Bridge as a football venue. The gravel track, in particular, greatly distanced the players on the field from the public in the stands and eliminated any intimacy the stadium had once had.

Chelsea returned to the First Division in 1932, where it would remain for the next 32 years. However, throughout the decade it never finished higher than eighth place. Nonetheless, Chelsea was a prosperous club. Player salaries were not high, but almost everything they needed was provided by the club. In 1935 J. T. Mears passed away, and the club went to his son, Joe Mears. However, his will specified that the Stamford Bridge stadium be put in a trust fund for his children. It was a split that would have fateful repercussions for Chelsea in the 1970s and 1980s.

INNOVATIONS AND SUCCESSES AFTER WORLD WAR II

First Division football was canceled in England for the duration of World War II. Chelsea played only unofficial regional games during that time. With the resumption of normal play in 1946, Chelsea once again began pouring its financial resources into player acquisition, especially of younger players, a policy that Chelsea would continue to favor into the 1970s. A significant innovation in the 1950s was the 1952 introduction of a magazine-style program for games that replaced the cards used previously. The appealing 16-page publication was the first of its kind in English football and included articles, statistics, profiles, and fans' letters. The media doubted it would last long. However, by the end of its first season of publication, Arsenal, one of Chelsea's biggest competitors, was planning a similar program of its own. A Chelsea high point of the 1950s was winning the First Division championship for the first time in club history. A decade would pass before the Blues won another cup of any kind.

KEY DATES

1904: Gus Mears purchases Stamford Bridge stadium.
1905: Chelsea Football Club (FC) is founded.
1912: Gus Mears dies.
1935: J. T. Mears dies.
1952: Magazine-style game program introduced.
1964: Chelsea FC makes tour of continental Europe.
1966: Joe Mears dies.
1982: Ken Bates purchases Chelsea FC.
1996: Chelsea FC goes public with listing on London Alternative Investment Market.
1997: Chelsea Megastore opens at Stamford Bridge.
2003: Roman Abramovich acquires Chelsea FC.

London of the 1960s was an "age of fur coats and diamonds" for Chelsea, in the words of club historian Rick Glanvill. Celebrities of all kinds were drawn to the club. Its players were paid generously. Average monthly salaries grew from £800 in the mid-1950s to £2,650 ten years later. The club also resumed spending large sums to get the best players. Between 1960 and 1971, Chelsea FC spent more on player acquisition than any other English team, £1.25 million. Chelsea went international in 1964 when it launched a tour of continental Europe and played against the French, German, Spanish, and Italian powerhouses, studying their tactics. They put the new knowledge to work upon their return to England, adopting the more subtle style of play that would characterize the club in the coming years.

The club embraced the media culture of the 1960s and was one of the first to outfit its stadium with permanent facilities for live TV broadcasts of games. It was also the first to install lights for night games. Stamford Bridge was, by this time, one of the worst stadiums in English football. Not only was it in dilapidated condition, it was a venue without a trace of intimacy, with the game taking place on the other side of the old greyhound track far from the spectators. There was again talk of transforming it into a national stadium to replace Wembley, but nothing came of it. However, a new grandstand was completed in time for the 1966–67 season.

RISE AND FALL

In 1966 Joe Mears passed away and responsibility for the club was given to his son Brian, who, despite his reputation as a chairman not particularly knowledgeable about football, presided over the most successful period to date in the Blues' history, winning the FA Cup in 1970, and the European Cup-Winners Cup in 1971. After the latter win, however, the club moved quickly into another period riddled by contention and debt. First, the Mears heirs who controlled the Stamford Bridge stadium trust decided the trust should be broken up and the stadium and land sold. After long negotiations in 1970, Chelsea FC agreed to purchase the facilities and land for £475,000 and to complete payments for the property no later than May 1974. At that time the club announced that it would build a new, state-of-the-art stadium on the Stamford Bridge grounds to replace the dilapidated existing facility, whose condition was so bad that authorities closed down the North Stand altogether for the danger to spectators. The redevelopment started in June 1972, but came to a halt after the completion of a single grandstand because of labor problems, inefficient management, the construction company's lack of experience in big stadium projects, rising costs, and delays.

The woeful state of Chelsea's finances was another major problem, and before long the club had defaulted on its payments for the stadium grounds. The construction, combined with the otherwise tight financial situation, also made it impossible for the Blues to sign talented players. Forced to rely on untested younger athletes, the club was relegated to the Second Division at the close of the 1974–75 season. It fought its way back to the First Division two seasons later only to be relegated again after the 1978–79 season, the worst in Chelsea's history, with only five wins and 27 losses. By 1977 the club was £4 million in debt and unable to complete the purchase of Stamford Bridge.

Furthermore, by the end of the 1970s the Blues had become synonymous with the ugly specter of hooliganism that had swept English football during the decade, to the point that Chelsea fans were for a time barred from attending away games. When the Tottenham Spurs returned 1,000 unsold tickets for the FA Cup quarterfinals against Chelsea at Stamford Bridge, its fans unwilling to risk the violence that they might encounter, club management knew it had to take steps to fight hooliganism and to improve the club's image. It issued a formal warning to its fans that in the future troublemakers would face lawsuits and fines imposed by the club. In the 1980s the club would work closely with hooligan ringleaders to reduce violence at games.

A NEW OWNER

On April 2, 1982, shackled with debt and no longer able to operate as a business, the Mears family sold

Chelsea FC to millionaire Ken Bates for £1 and the assumption of the club's debts. Bates immediately launched efforts to purchase the Stamford Bridge grounds. He was close to an agreement, when at the eleventh hour, the owner, Stamford Bridge Properties, sold the stadium and its grounds to a real estate development company, Marler Estates. It was soon clear that Marler intended eventually to tear down the stadium and replace it with upscale apartment buildings, hotels, and shops. After the Hammersmith and Fulham district council approved Marler's proposed project in June 1985, it seemed only a question of time until the Blues would be evicted from their historic pitch (field). Bates invoked a clause in the lease that prevented eviction until a new permanent home stadium had been found. He also bought shares in Marler Estates to fight from within, but the struggle dragged on. Finally in 1989 a frustrated Marler gave up and sold the property to a different developer.

A combination of events eventually rescued the club. First, a severe downturn in the English real estate market made redevelopment of the area much less profitable. Second, when the private Premier League was founded in 1992, the First Division teams were reorganized and left the Football League to join the Premiere League. When the Stamford Bridge owners sued the Chelsea Football and Athletic Club to force them out of the Stadium and won, it was ultimately for naught as all of Chelsea's assets had since been transferred to the new club, Chelsea Football Club, incorporated, for the Premier League. In 1993 the developer went bankrupt and Bates was able to reach an agreement with the company's debtors, in particular the Bank of Scotland, to ensure that Chelsea could continue to play at Stamford Bridge.

The battle had been costly for the club, however. Bates later calculated that he had spent almost £1 million on legal fees, money he was not able to spend on players or stadium improvements. Another source of expense for Bates was the Chelsea Village Limited Group, a company founded to pursue Bates's own redevelopment dreams at Stamford Bridge. They included a new 40,000-seat stadium, an adjoining 160-bedroom hotel, a landscaped garden village with 210 residences, plus underground parking lots, restaurants, an indoor sports arena, and the club's own railway station. Bates maintained these changes would make Chelsea the richest club in Europe.

GOING PUBLIC

Money, however, continued to present a major problem. As the 1990s continued, Chelsea found itself faced with

a dilemma: it could invest in stadium improvements, a critical outlay for a team which had one of the worst stadiums in European First Division football, or it could spend on player acquisition in a market that was growing increasingly expensive. By 1994 the team was receiving some £2 million per year from English football's broadcasting contract with British network BSkyB. Chelsea had also concluded a lucrative deal with the Coors Brewing Company for another £2 million. However, even with that additional income, Chelsea was still struggling. A chance ad placed by Bates in the *Financial Times* for potential investors in his Stamford Bridge development schemes drew a response from Matthew Harding, a Chelsea fan and the 89th richest person in Britain at that time. Harding put approximately £16.5 million of his own money into Chelsea and soon came to be seen as Bates's heir apparent.

With Harding's support, Chelsea was again able to bid for top-notch players, such as Ruud Gullit. To raise even more funds, Bates and Harding took Chelsea FC public in 1996, when it was listed on the London Alternative Investment Market. No new shares were issued; instead, Bates offered all but 28.55 percent of the shares he owned. Harding kept a 13.5 percent stake, with an understanding that he would be able later to increase his share to 25 percent. By the summer of 1996, however, the relationship between Bates and Harding was deteriorating, with Bates even refusing Harding admission to the directors' box at the stadium. The dispute ended abruptly with Harding's untimely death in a helicopter crash in October 1996.

In July 1997 Chelsea opened the 10,500-square-foot Chelsea Megastore, English football's largest sports paraphernalia store to date, at Stamford Bridge. The following November Bates opened a 160-bed luxury hotel on the stadium grounds. The new complex also included four restaurants, offices, and apartments. Despite all his efforts to modernize Stamford Bridge and to attract star players, success on the field continued to elude the Blues at the dawn of the 21st century. Despite massive outlays in player salaries, the team seemed unable to win any of the major English or European cups. The frustration was doubled for fans who not only had to endure their team's failure but also pay significantly higher ticket prices. Bates continued to attract investment, however, convincing Emirates Airlines to provide £24 million for a four-year sponsorship deal, just about enough to service the interest on Chelsea's outstanding debts, which by October 2001 had risen to £171 million.

CHANGING HANDS AGAIN

In 2003 Chelsea FC changed hands again when it was acquired, amid much controversy, by Roman Abramovich, reputedly the richest man in Russia and the 21st richest in the world at that time. In June 2003 Abramovich attended his first Champions League game. His reaction was immediate—he had to have a Champions League team of his own. He instructed advisers to draw up a short list of possibilities that included Manchester United, Tottenham, and Chelsea. Chelsea's London location tipped the balance in its favor. Before month's end, Abramovich had met with Chelsea lawyers, hammered out an agreement that gave Ken Bates more than £17 million and assumed all the club's outstanding debts, and taken over Chelsea FC. In all, Abramovich spent some £140 million to acquire the Blues. That was only the beginning, however. Within days of the acquisition's completion, Abramovich began reaching into his very deep pockets (he was said to be worth nearly £3.5 billion) to sign top-rank players such as Claude Makélélé, Geremi, Glen Johnson, Joe Cole, and Damien Duff.

Opinion on the takeover in England was mixed. Some reportedly resented a foreigner who could so decisively tip the balance of the Premier League. Others saw the spending spree as a threat to English football, although Ken Bates revealed shortly after the sale that Chelsea was approximately one year away from complete financial collapse. Still others questioned Abramovich's alleged ties (never verified) to Russian organized crime. Critics maintained that Abramovich damaged English football by putting such an emphasis on acquiring foreign stars, thus making it more difficult for young English players to have an impact on the game. Finally, Abramovich's critics accused him of short-term thinking, of wanting to win right away at any cost, perhaps even at the expense of building a solid team for the future. Others, however, countered that Abramovich's efforts not only improved Chelsea, they also led to a significant rise in the overall level of play in the English Premier League, breaking the traditional stranglehold of Manchester United and Arsenal. Advocates also said it was long overdue that foreign investors recognized the appeal of the English Premier League. Finally, they argued that Abramovich simply loved football and that could not be bad for the game.

Abramovich spent extravagantly. Between 2003 and 2008 he spent more than £409.5 million. Much was used to acquire players, but a good deal was also used to pay off Chelsea's crippling debt. Whatever else he did, Roman Abramovich ushered in the most successful period in Chelsea's history to date, during which the team won two Premier League titles, in 2005 and 2006;

two League Cups, in 2005 and 2007; and an FA Cup in 2007. In December 2006 Abramovich helped secure Chelsea FC's future with the establishment of a £500 million trust fund. The fund provided £50 million per year for ten years in the event of his death. The money was intended to provide funds for transferring players and for player salaries. In 2007, when Abramovich divorced his wife of 15 years, rumors circulated in English football circles that he would be selling Chelsea to free up cash for the settlement, expected to amount to some £5 billion. He stuck with the team, however. Chelsea announced that it expected to be completely debt free by 2010 and the world's largest football club by 2014. Whether these goals would be realized remained to be seen.

Gerald E. Brennan

PRINCIPAL SUBSIDIARIES

Chelsea Car Parks Ltd.; Chelsea Digital Media Ltd. (65%); Chelsea Football Club Ltd.; Chelsea Leisure Services Ltd.; The Hotel at Chelsea Ltd.; Chelsea FC Merchandising Ltd.; Chelsea FC plc; Stamford Bridge Securities Ltd.

PRINCIPAL COMPETITORS

Arsenal Football Club; Manchester United FC; Liverpool FC; Leeds United AFC; FC Bayern München; Real Madrid Club de Fútbol; Juventus FC; AC Milan.

FURTHER READING

Anderson, David, "What Did Roman Ever Do for Us?" *Mirror,* July 3, 2008, p. 68.

Brummer, Alex, "Ken Bates: Bluebeard of the Bridge," *Guardian,* February 16, 1998, p. 6.

Conn, David, "Fans Demand to Know Who Owns Chelsea," *Independent,* October 19, 2001, p. 27.

Draper, Rob, "Is this How ROMAN plans to rule the WORLD?" *Mail on Sunday* (London), January 16, 2005, p. 11.

Glanvill, Rick, *Chelsea FC: The Official Biography,* London: Headline, 2006.

Harding, Luke, "The Year Was 1980," *Guardian,* May 20, 2008, p. 24.

Harris, Harry, *Chelsea's Century,* London: Blake Publishing, 2005.

"Has the Whistle Gone on Roman's Game?" *South China Morning Post,* July 24, 2005, p. 13.

Hayes, Alex, "Tranquillity at Sea in Chelsea's Village," *Independent,* December 3, 2000, p. 5.

Hellier, David, "The Battle of Stamford Bridge," *Independent,* November 11, 1995, p. 28.

Hellier, David, and William Kay, "It's a Funny Old Business," *Independent,* November 13, 1994, p. 9.

Hughes, Ron, "Football Buccaneer Who Has Weathered Storms at the Bridge," *Times* (London), April 9, 1994.

Midgley, Dominic, and Chris Hutchins, *Abramovich: The Billionaire from Nowhere,* New York: HarperCollinsWillow, 2005.

Moore, Glenn, "The City Type Who Invested in His Dreams," *Independent,* September 23, 1995, p. 26.

Nisse, Jason, "Challenge to £8m Chelsea Transfer," *Mail on Sunday,* May 15, 1994, p. 71.

White, Clive, "Chelsea Join Jet Set with Pounds 24m Deal," *Independent,* January 26, 2001, p. 30.

Chocolat Frey AG

Bresteneggstrasse
Buchs/Aargau, 5033
Switzerland
Telephone: (41 0 62) 836 26 26
Fax: (41 0 62) 836 25 01
Web site: http://www.chocolatfrey.ch

Wholly Owned Subsidiary of Migros-Genossenschafts-Bund
Founded: 1887
Employees: 788
Sales: CHF 421 million ($398.81 million) (2008)
NAICS: 311320 Chocolate and Confectionery Manufacturing from Cacao Beans; 31134 Nonchocolate Confectionery Manufacturing

■ ■ ■

Chocolat Frey AG is a major producer of Swiss chocolate. Long the leading chocolate brand in Switzerland with a 38 percent market share (a standing bolstered by its association with parent company Migros-Genossenschafts-Bund, the operator of Switzerland's largest retail grocery chain), Chocolat Frey also exports its products worldwide under the Frey brand. The firm's product line includes approximately 2,400 items, and the company oversees production from raw cocoa beans through to the finished product at facilities in Buchs/Aargau, Switzerland. Frey is also notable as Switzerland's only chewing gum maker.

A NEW CHOCOLATE COMPANY IN SWITZERLAND

Chocolat Frey grew out of a company founded by brothers Max and Robert Frey in 1887. The impulse to specialize in chocolate came from Robert, whose career in business began at the chocolate maker S.A. de la Fabrique des Chocolats Amédée Kohler et fils in Lausanne, Switzerland. From there, he moved to Paris and took a job at Riccard & Greiss, a machine builder that, among other things, manufactured equipment for the production of chocolate. It was after he had become familiar with this type of machinery that Frey decided to go into chocolate making himself. He returned to Switzerland and in preparation took a job at a confectioner's where he further expanded his knowledge of the business.

In the meantime, his younger brother Max had been gaining business financial and administration skills at a company called Cramer-Frey in Zurich. From there he moved to a bank in Paris and finally to the overseas division of an import company in England. Max Frey eventually rejoined Cramer-Frey and was sent to work in Pernambuco, Brazil, where he almost certainly acquired firsthand familiarity with the cocoa trade. When Max returned to Europe, he joined forces with his brother and launched their chocolate company R. & M. Frey in Aarau, a small town in northwestern Switzerland. The two brothers' training meshed perfectly. Robert, with his extensive knowledge of chocolate making became the firm's technical director; Max, experienced in banking and trade, took over the business side of the company. About 12 years later, Paul Müller, a close friend of the Freys, joined the company's management to oversee its administration, and Max dedicated himself exclusively to the oversight of Frey's finances.

At first the Freys set up their production facilities at several locations in the Aarau region. However, as the firm began to grow, and its growth began almost at once, the Freys simultaneously expanded and centralized their operations, concentrating their works along a single stretch of highway in the town. They were fortunate to be located in Aarau; the city on the Aare River received one of Switzerland's first electrical power plants. Hence, practically from the very beginning, the Frey chocolate factory was powered by electricity and not by cumbersome and dirty coal-powered steam dynamos.

Frey chocolate quickly established itself in Switzerland as a product of quality. Their line of goods was a broad one in the early years, not limited exclusively to chocolate bars and cocoa, but, for a brief period, also including items such as soups and various health foods. As the product offering grew, so did demand for Frey chocolate. Robert Frey was continually preoccupied with introducing new goods, and soon he set his sights on the markets beyond the Swiss borders.

The legal form of the company evolved during its first 20 years of existence as well, reflecting its expansion. In 1900 it was transformed into a limited partnership called Kommanditgesellschaft R. & M. FREY & Co. Six years later, on January 1, 1906, the business form was altered once again by converting the firm into a share company with the stock split up between Robert and Max Frey and their de facto partner Paul Müller.

WARTIME OPPORTUNITIES AND DIFFICULTIES

In the summer of 1914 trade in most of Europe ground to a halt as a result of the outbreak of World War I. Although Swiss firms enjoyed a remarkable advantage (Switzerland retained neutral status and was able to

continue to trade in unhindered fashion with nations on both sides of the hostilities), demand for Frey chocolate products dropped precipitously immediately after the start of the war. Sales fell and workers' hours had to be cut drastically. Fortunately, the company was kept afloat by new domestic customers such as the Swiss military. Sales were also helped by the fact that during the war chocolate for the first time started to be seen as a basic foodstuff in Switzerland and not merely a luxury item. However, obtaining the raw materials necessary for the production of chocolate was a problem. By 1916 the company's annual sales had dropped to CHF 882,109. Exports did not cease altogether, although they were limited for the most part to France, Germany, and Sweden. In 1917 and 1918, the last two war years, the exports continued to decline, but demand in Switzerland boomed and the company's total sales nearly doubled to CHF 1.5 million.

The conclusion of the war did not mean a return to normality for Chocolat Frey. Demand for chocolate imports from Switzerland dropped tenfold in the first years of the 1920s, due in large part to weakened economies of the larger nations of Europe, in particular Germany, which had been strained to the breaking point by five years of war. In addition, Frey faced decreased demand in its domestic market where chocolate was slowly returning to its former status as a luxury product rather than a necessity.

Within just a few years, Chocolat Frey realized it was engaged in a battle for survival. It put emergency measures in place. Production was discontinued on weekends, then on other days as well. Workers were idled, although none were ever actually laid off. As the months dragged on the situation deteriorated. Things finally started turning around, albeit slowly, at the end of 1923, after the runaway inflation in Germany had ended. Nonetheless, it was a continuous struggle, and every chocolate maker in Switzerland was competing for the same domestic and foreign customers, usually in vain. The difficulties are reflected in the export figures for the entire Swiss chocolate industry from 1919 to 1937 when sales plummeted from CHF 106 million to only CHF 1.9 million. In addition, Frey, the maker of a premium product, was hurt by the introduction in the Swiss market of bargain chocolate brands made by the Migros company.

Another significant and positive occurrence of the 1920s was the entry of Robert Frey's son Robert Jr. into the business. Starting as an apprentice in 1921, after stints in both the production and administrative areas, he became one of the company's stockholders in 1927, taking over about one-third of his father's shares. The timing was fortunate. By the start of the 1930s both

KEY DATES

1887: Robert and Max Frey establish Kollektivfirma R. & M. Frey in Aarau.
1906: Company is reorganized as Aktiengesellschaft Chocolat Frey.
1933: Cofounder Max Frey dies.
1936: Robert Frey Jr. succeeds his father as technical director.
1950: Company is taken over by Migros-Genossenschafts-Bund.
1967: Production facility in Buchs, Switzerland, is established.
1974: Chewing gum is introduced to product line.
1994: Confiserie factory expansion is completed.
1997: "Chocolat Frey Goes International" campaign is launched.

founders' were in failing health. In 1932 Robert Frey Sr. turned over his position on the company board to his son, thus ensuring that the company remained a family enterprise for the foreseeable future. Max Frey died in 1933, and in 1936 Robert Frey Jr. succeeded his father as technical director of Chocolat Frey.

NEW PROBLEMS AND A NEW PARENT

World War II erupted at a time when the Swiss chocolate industry was in a period of serious crisis, with sales in the middle of a precipitous decline that had lasted nearly a decade and a half. Outside Switzerland, Europe was dividing once again into two enemy camps and heading into a war economy. Demand for chocolate, and hence sales, was driven even further below the levels of the late 1930s. In 1943 rationing of the raw materials needed for the manufacture of chocolate, including cocoa beans and sugar, was introduced, and the firm had to compensate by filling out its chocolate products with non-rationed goods, such as malt and almonds. To make matters even worse, many male workers were called up in the Swiss draft. They included most significantly Technical Director Robert Frey Jr. His absence left the firm leaderless as critical decisions could no longer be made at Frey board meetings.

By the time the war ended, the company and its leadership were in disarray, and Chocolat Frey found itself in a crisis situation unparalleled in its history. It was a deeply divided board that met for the first time

after the war in 1946. The serious situation led one member to recommend that the company close its doors for good, a proposal that was rejected. It was clear to both Robert Frey and Paul Müller, Frey's longtime business manager, however, that the relatively small firm would be hard pressed to survive the hard times on its own.

A brand-new set of postwar issues had developed, issues with which Chocolat Frey had to come to terms. Not all of them were necessarily bad. For example, demand for chocolate products was exploding in both Switzerland and foreign countries. However, meeting this demand put expensive demands on the firm. For example, to do so, it had to upgrade or replace its old or obsolete production equipment as well as expand its production facilities, which had remained essentially unaltered since the late 1920s. At the same time, qualified personnel had to be found and trained to work in the Frey chocolate factory.

Robert Frey realized that the only way his company could survive was with the assistance of a financially strong partner. In 1950 he found one: Migros-Genossenschafts-Bund, a group of companies that included a large chain of supermarkets in Switzerland, which itself had been engaged in chocolate making since 1930, when it introduced a line of low-priced chocolate in the Swiss market. In 1950 Migros acquired a 56 percent share in Chocolat Frey AG. The union was advantageous for both companies, bringing together the expertise of two established chocolate manufacturers. By the mid-1960s Frey was once again operating solidly. It moved into a new production facility in the Swiss town of Buchs in 1967. At the same time it was merged with Migros' other chocolate producer Jowa Schokoladefabrik. During this time Frey began expanding its line of products, adding hard candy and marzipan, and in 1974 at the request of its parent company Frey started producing chewing gum as well. Meanwhile the company's market share grew continuously, reaching CHF 169 million at the end of the 1970s.

EXPORT GROWTH AT THE END OF THE CENTURY

Chocolat Frey made significant advances in several areas during the 1980s. Sales continued to grow in Switzerland at least, and by 1982 the firm was the largest manufacturer of chocolate in the country. Around the same time it was decided to make a push to increase sales in foreign markets, in particular England, the United States, and Japan. By 1985 the strategy was showing its first signs of success. That year Frey reached an important milestone, recording sales of more than CHF 200 million for the first time in its history. The company took steps at the same time to expand and modernize its production.

A significant part of Frey's modernization efforts was the company's commitment to environmental protection. In 1982, in a joint project with its home canton of Aargau, Frey agreed to purchase *Fernwärme,* or "remote heat," from a nearby public trash incinerator. As a result, beginning in the mid-1980s Frey consumed virtually no heating oil. The firm received several citations for its advances in environmentally friendly manufacturing. At the end of the decade, a new factory expansion project, the so-called Confiserie Expansion, was launched to enable increased production of chewing gum that was to take place from 1991 to 1994.

From 1989 to 1990 foreign sales increased 15 percent and continued to grow in the 1990s. In 1997 the company launched a new campaign titled "Chocolat Frey Goes International," with the goal of strengthening export trade. In 1998 the firm had sales of CHF 285 million, of which exports accounted for about 12 percent. New moves included the introduction of new brands outside Switzerland, such as Swiss Delice and Swiss Frey. In 2001 the firm was producing about 1,300 various products, about 850 of which were for private Migros labels and some 50 for the export market. That year the Goes International project started bearing fruit, and by the end of 2002 exports had increased from 12.4 percent to 21.3 percent.

Since that time Frey chocolate products have been sold exclusively under the Frey brand in some 50 different countries worldwide. Chewing gum enjoyed a new boom as well, and in 2003 production was expanded to keep up with demand. As the decade ended exports had passed 32 percent of total sales, significantly surpassing the firm's original goal of 20 percent. After years of healthy two-digit growth, in 2008 Chocolat Frey found itself forced to contend with flattened growth in its chocolate division. Slight increases in the export market were canceled out by decreases in domestic sales. Chewing gum production, which by then had grown to include more than 100 products, had increased 17 percent and looking ahead, Chocolat Frey planned to build a fourth chewing gum production facility.

Gerald E. Brennan

PRINCIPAL COMPETITORS

The Hershey Company; Kraft Foods Deutschland GmbH; Nestlé S.A.; Alfred Ritter GmbH & Co. KG; Mars, Inc.; Stollwerck GmbH; Barry Callebaut GmbH; August Storck KG; Brandt Zwieback-Schokoladen GmbH + Co. KG.

FURTHER READING

Alstede, Heinz, "Heisser Sommer und neue Maerkte; Chocolat Frey liegt nach rasanter Exportsteigerung wieder im Plus," *Lebensmittel Zeitung,* May 21, 2004, p. 65.

Bender, Ralf, "Ausland wird starker," *Lebensmittel Zeitung,* May 23, 2008, p. 73.

———, "Fuehrende Position ausgebaut; Chocolat Frey mit guter Entwicklung bei Schokolade und Kaugummi," *Lebensmittel Zeitung,* May 26, 2006, p. 74.

———, "Gute Entwicklung bei Private Labels; Chocolat Frey kann im Export erneut zulegen," *Lebensmittel Zeitung,* May 23, 2003, p. 78.

———, "Leistung entscheidet; Kaugummisparte von Chocolat Frey ist stark exportorientiert," *Lebensmittel Zeitung,* May 10, 2002, p. 70.

———, "Mit individuellen Konzepten gegen Preisdruck," *Lebensmittel Zeitung,* May 23, 2003, p. 80.

———, "Vorteil der langen internationalen Erfahrung," *Lebensmittel Zeitung,* May 18, 2007, p. 62.

"Chocolat Frey: Sucht neue Märkte," *LZ.net,* January 25, 2005.

Chwallek, Andreas, "Export befluegelt Chocolat Frey AG," *Lebensmittel Zeitung,* March 10, 2006, p. 20.

"Gemeinsamer Auftritt für den Export," *Lebensmittel Zeitung,* May 18, 2007, p. 53.

Holland, Felix, "Gezielter Markenaufbau fuer das Ausland laeuft," *Lebensmittel Zeitung,* May 18, 2001, p. 70.

"Mit Handelsmarken in Europa praesent," *Lebensmittel Zeitung,* May 21, 1999, p. 54.

CKX, Inc.

650 Madison Avenue
New York, New York 10022-1029
U.S.A.
Telephone: (212) 838-3100
Fax: (212) 872-1473
Web site: http://ir.ckx.com

Public Company
Incorporated: 1984 as Sporting Life, Inc.
Employees: 619
Sales: $266.8 million (2007)
Stock Exchanges: NASDAQ
Ticker Symbol: CKXE
NAICS: 512110 Motion Picture and Video Production

■ ■ ■

CKX, Inc., is a New York City-based company that acquires, owns, develops, and commercializes entertainment content, including an 85 percent interest in the name, image, and likeness of singer Elvis Presley and an 80 percent interest in the similar rights to boxer Muhammad Ali. In addition, CKX owns 19 Entertainment Limited, the United Kingdom-based producer of the highly rated *American Idol* television program and versions of the *Idol* concept adapted to more than 100 countries. The subsidiary has also partnered with soccer player David Beckham and his wife Victoria, former member of the Spice Girls, to develop entertainment content. Another CKX acquisition is Morra, Brezner, Steinberg & Tenenbaum Entertainment Inc. (MBST), a full-service management firm that focuses on the

representation of comedic talent, including Robin Williams, Billy Crystal, and Woody Allen. MBST also serves as an adviser to Apple Corps, the holding company for the Beatles, and participates in film production, the firm's credits including *Arthur, Good Morning Vietnam,* and *Match Point.*

CKX is the latest venture of its chairman and chief executive officer, Robert F.X. Sillerman, a highly successful figure in the entertainment world who has a record of anticipating trends and a penchant for incorporating his initials in the names of his companies. What his initials stand for is a question he refuses to answer, although the record of his birth in the *New York Times* indicates he was born Robert Franklin Sillerman. His intention with CKX is wide ranging: to acquire interests in entertainment content and related assets of all types—including intellectual property like music, film, television, written works, and video games; fictional characters; names, images, and likenesses of famous people; and even corporate brands—and fully exploit these properties through all established and emerging media platforms.

ORIGINS IN RADIO

Robert Sillerman was born in New York City in 1948 and raised in the affluent Riverdale section of the Bronx, where he was educated at private schools. He grew up very familiar with the media industry. His father, Michael McKinley Sillerman, was a Baltimore-born graduate of the Peabody School of Music and after graduation, according to his *New York Times* obituary, helped "introduce European composers to American radio audiences." In 1940 he cofounded the Chicago-based Keystone Broadcasting System, serving as president from 1948 to 1952, after which he served two years as president of Television Programs of America, eventually leaving in 1959. The elder Sillerman worked briefly for National Telefilm Associates, but then went bankrupt when Robert Sillerman was 13. "I suppose if you were a psychiatrist you could say I wanted to do well, where my father had had a lack of success," Sillerman mused in a 2005 interview in *Fortune*.

Coming of age in the turbulent 1960s, Sillerman embraced both rock and roll and counterculture politics while displaying a talent for business. As a teen he started his own greeting card company, and while enrolled at Brandeis University he launched Youth Markets Consultants, Inc., to provide creative services, media buying, and sales advice to companies interested in marketing to the baby boom generation. After graduating magna cum laude in 1969 he continued to run the business until 1974, when he formed National Discount Marketers, Inc. Sillerman, like his father, was drawn to radio, however, and in 1978 he looked to invest in radio stations.

It was a time when many investors had concluded that radio had been superseded by television and would continue to become less relevant. What they failed to see was that radio was, in fact, continuing to grow. For Sillerman this misunderstanding simply meant properties could be had inexpensively. His plan was to acquire a slate of stations surrounding the highly valuable New York City market. Because he lacked both the capital and the experience in radio to raise the necessary funds, Sillerman needed a partner. He turned to one of New York City's most popular disc jockeys, Bruce Morrow, known on the air as "Cousin Brucie." Morrow was won over, later telling *Fortune*, "Bob can sell anything—it doesn't matter—he has that kind of head."

FROM RADIO TO LIVE
ENTERTAINMENT VENUES

The partnership yielded Sillerman-Morrow Broadcasting, and with Morrow on board Sillerman was able to raise $600,000 from a private investor and secure bank financing to acquire eight radio stations and one Atlanta

television station for $8.5 million over the next five years. More than just a name on the letterhead, Morrow used his radio experience to upgrade the station formats to increase audience share, while Sillerman leveraged his sales and marketing experience to improve advertising revenues and increase the value of the properties. When the Federal Communications Commission in 1985 relaxed the rules that limited ownership to seven AM stations and seven FM stations, Sillerman-Morrow cashed in, selling off their stations piecemeal for $50 million.

Still interested in radio, Sillerman took on a new partner, William Magee, Jr., a Barclays Bank broadcasting lender, to form Sillerman-Magee Communications Management, which by the end of the 1980s had acquired more than 50 radio stations and other media properties for about $1 billion. At the same time, Sillerman was working with the Bass family of Fort Worth, Texas, to assemble a stable of radio stations for a venture called Legacy Broadcasting. Sillerman sold most of his holdings shortly before the bottom fell out of the radio market, and a few years later he looked to take advantage of depressed prices. He formed SFX Broadcasting, Inc., in 1992 and took it public a year later. SFX owned about 70 stations by the time Sillerman sold SFX in 1997 for $2.1 billion, garnering a reported $219 million for himself.

Although extremely wealthy, Sillerman had no interest in retirement at the age of 40. Instead, as part of the SFX sale he spun off SFX Entertainment, Inc., as a separate entity and promptly acquired four major live entertainment production companies at a cost of $421 million. As a result he either owned or managed 39 major live entertainment venues in 21 of the country's top 50 cities. More acquisitions were to follow, creating such a powerhouse that the U.S Justice Department briefly looked into whether Sillerman was attempting to monopolize concert promotions. He then added sports branding companies, which formed the basis for SFX Sports Group, and created other units under the SFX label.

EMPHASIS ON EXPLOITING
CONTENT

In 2000 Sillerman sold the SFX behemoth for approximately $3 billion to Clear Channel Communications. He then failed in an attempt to acquire the Firm, a major Los Angeles-based artist-management company, and took several months off to undergo chemotherapy to treat tongue cancer. He returned to the limelight in late 2004 when he reached an agreement to acquire an 85 percent interest in Elvis Presley Enterprises, which controlled the singer's name

KEY DATES

1984: Sporting Life, Inc., is formed in Las Vegas.

1998: Sporting Life changes name to All-American SportPark, Inc.

2001: All-American SportPark is delisted by NAS-DAQ, renamed Sports Entertainment Enterprises.

2005: Robert F.X. Sillerman acquires Sports Entertainment Enterprises, renaming it CKX, Inc.; CKX acquires Elvis Presley image rights and 19 Entertainment.

2006: CKX acquires rights to Muhammad Ali image.

2008: Offer to take company private is withdrawn.

and likeness, as well as the Graceland museum, for $114 million. The deal was an opening salvo in Sillerman's attempt to exploit content in as many ways as possible. "Technology is breaking down the old lines of distribution," he explained to *Fortune*. "More and more content can go directly to consumers through cell phones, devices like iPods, and home video, which make content even more valuable."

To house the Presley property and complete the transaction, Sillerman acquired a shell corporation, Sports Entertainment Enterprises Inc., which in 2005 he would rename CKX, Inc., the C and K reportedly standing for "Content is King." Sports Entertainment Enterprises had been founded by Vaso Boreta in Las Vegas in 1974 as Las Vegas Discount Golf & Tennis, a retail sporting goods store that focused on golf and, to a lesser extent, tennis products. Ten years later Boreta formed a company called Sporting Life, Inc., to franchise the concept. The name was changed to St. Andrews Golf Corporation in 1988 and then to Saint Andrews Corporation in 1994. It was also in that year that Boreta's son, Ronald, began developing a multi-attraction, participatory amusement park in Las Vegas called All-American SportPark, a concept that he hoped to franchise around the world. Saint Andrews Corporation was taken public in 1994.

Opened in 1998, the amusement park featured a batting stadium with walls reminiscent of major league parks, a NASCAR go-track, and a driving range that included greens and sand traps. The parent company sold the franchising business in 1997 then changed its name the following year to All-American SportPark, Inc. The amusement park did not fare as well as expected,

however, and closed its doors in 2001. Later in the year, the company's stock, unable to maintain the minimum mandated price, was delisted by the NASDAQ. The name of the company was also changed to Sports Entertainment Enterprises.

Ronald Boreta received dozens of proposals from parties interested in acquiring the company, which could be used to tap the equities markets through a reverse merger—a faster, less-expensive way to take a company public. Boreta was introduced to Sillerman by a mutual friend, investment banker Jack Schneider of Allen & Co., and over the course of several months the two men worked out a deal in 2005 that allowed Sillerman to acquire 96 percent of Sports Entertainment Enterprises.

ACQUIRING RIGHTS TO VALUABLE ASSETS

In February 2005 Sillerman became chairman and CEO of what would then become CKX, Inc. On that same day the Elvis Presley deal was completed. Sillerman had been interested in owning a rock and roll property, and considered Presley along with the Beatles and the Rolling Stones to be the most desirable assets. Not only was Presley available, Elvis Presley Enterprises (EPE) was far from fully exploited. Presley left an estate in disarray when he died in 1977, having spent freely and lost control of his best-known songs. Five years later the estate was on the verge of bankruptcy, which led the family to open Presley's Memphis mansion, Graceland, to the public. In addition to running this venture, EPE added merchandising and licensing. A restaurant was also opened in Memphis under Presley's name, but failed in 2003, leading the Presley family to actively seek outside investors and perhaps fresh management, something that had been discussed for years but never acted upon.

When Sillerman entered the picture, he was once again in the right place at the right time. He met with Lisa Presley in New York in late 2004 and a deal was struck. In addition to the rights to the Elvis Presley name, image, likeness, and trademark, CKX received a 90-year lease on Graceland, royalty rights to 24 Presley movies, and publishing rights to 650 songs, albeit only a small portion of which were among the more valuable ones. Possible ways to exploit the brand included the opening of a Las Vegas casino with a Graceland theme, as well as Graceland-style properties around the world, and an upgrade of the Heartbreak Hotel located near Graceland, which could also be replicated in other locales.

Little more than a month after closing on the Presley deal, Sillerman struck again paying $196 million in cash and stock for a United Kingdom-based company, 19 Entertainment, founded by Simon Fuller, a music talent scout who discovered and managed top British acts and created the Spice Girls. He then conceived of a talent show concept with audience participation. The first incarnation, *Pop Idol*, debuted on Britain's ITV in 2001. Although it was a major hit, Fuller had trouble selling *Idol* in the United States. The Fox network took a chance on the idea and the resulting *American Idol* program became a smash hit and a veritable "cash cow." Fuller's company, 19 Entertainment, not only received a per episode fee from Fox, it took 10 percent of the recording revenues from the singing stars produced by the show, and franchised *Idol* around the world. To help finance the acquisition of 19 Entertainment and pay off loans to Bear Stearns, Sillerman made a public offering of CKX stock, raising $251 million.

ADDING MUHAMMAD ALI

CKX completed another deal in August 2005, acquiring the firm of Morra, Brezner, Steinberg & Tenenbaum Entertainment, Inc. (MBST), manager of comedic talent with a roster of 35 clients and producer of movies and television programming. Long-term employment agreements were also reached with the firm's principals, Larry Brezner, David Steinberg, and Steve Tenenbaum. A year later another property was brought into the fold: the name, image, likeness, and other rights of publicity of boxer Muhammad Ali, along with all existing license agreements. This business would operate under an entity called G.O.A.T. LLC, the initials standing for what Ali had regularly declared himself to be: the "Greatest of All Time." Ali and his wife retained a 20 percent stake in G.O.A.T. through the Ali Trust. CKX then licensed both Elvis Presley and Muhammad Ali to FX Luxury Realty, LLC, a Sillerman-controlled company, to develop themed real estate and attraction-based properties around the world.

The CKX properties generated $210.2 million in revenues in 2006, more than 70 percent of which came from 19 Entertainment. In general, Sillerman was interested in investing significantly to build the other properties but CKX investors balked at the idea, as demonstrated by a steady loss in value of the company's stock. In June 2007, Sillerman and Fuller made a bid to take CKX private in order to gain greater leverage in future plans by acquiring shares of the company's stock at $13.75 a share. The $1.33 billion offer languished, and as the economy took a significant turn for the worse in the autumn of 2008, Sillerman decided in November of that year to withdraw the offer.

According to filings made with the Securities and Exchange Commission, however, Sillerman and Fuller had not given up on taking CKX private. Rather, they were pursuing alternative financing options. In the meantime, the company enjoyed some notable successes, including the successful premiere of a new 19 Entertainment television program, *Superstars of Dance,* and the opening of the American Idol Experience show at Disney World. Given the track record of both Sillerman and Fuller, it was likely they would find a way to achieve their goal of taking CKX private and continuing to grow revenues well beyond the $266.8 million posted in 2007.

Ed Dinger

PRINCIPAL SUBSIDIARIES

19 Entertainment Limited; Elvis Presley Entertainment; G.O.A.T. LLC; Morra, Brezner, Steinberg & Tenenbaum Entertainment, Inc.

PRINCIPAL COMPETITORS

Brillstein Entertainment Partners, LLC; Carsey-Warner, LLC; Sony/ATV Music Publishing LLC.

FURTHER READING

Button, Graham, "Radio Waves," *Forbes,* July 22, 1991, p. 46.

Lieberman, David, "'American Idol' Parent to Go Private in $1.3B Deal," *USA Today,* June 4, 2007, p. B2.

———, "Master of the Fame Game," *USA Today,* October 17, 2006, p. B1.

———, "Media Magnate Acquires 'American Idol' Company," *USA Today,* March 21, 2005, p. B5.

McBride, Sarah, "CKX Punches Up $50 Million Deal for Ali Licensing," *Wall Street Journal,* April 12, 2006, p. A8.

"Michael McKinley Sillerman, 79, a Retired TV Program Executive," *New York Times,* April 14, 1979.

Petrozzello, Donna, "Robert F.X. Sillerman," *Broadcasting & Cable,* July 11, 1994, p. 69.

Rathbun, Elizabeth A., "SFX Expands into Concerts," *Broadcasting & Cable,* October 21, 1996, p. 24.

Serwer, Andy, "The Man Who Bought Elvis," *Fortune,* December 12, 2005, p. 80.

Sisario, Ben, "Music Industry Financier Buys 'American Idol,'" *New York Times,* March 19, 2005, p. B9.

Smith, Ethan, "CKX Buys 'American Idol' Firm," *Wall Street Journal,* March 21, 2005, p. B3.

———, "Elvis Is Star Attraction in Small Firm's Revival," *Wall Street Journal,* December 28, 2004, p. C3.

———, "Rights Owner of Elvis, 'Idol' Scuttle Plan to Go Private," *Wall Street Journal,* November 4, 2008, p. B1.

The Collins Companies Inc.

1618 Southwest First Avenue, Suite 500
Portland, Oregon 97201
U.S.A.
Telephone: (503) 227-1219
Toll Free: (800) 329-1219
Fax: (503) 227-5349
Web site: http://www.collinswood.com

Private Company
Incorporated: 1943 as Collins Pine Company
Employees: 395 (est.)
Sales: $192 (2007 est.)
NAICS: 321113 Sawmills

■ ■ ■

The Collins Companies Inc. sells hardwood and softwood lumber, hardwood veneer and veneer logs, particleboard, plywood, siding, and trim. Their materials are made from the trees they grow and harvest sustainably on 295,000 acres of timberlands. All three Collins forests in Pennsylvania, California, and Oregon, have been independently certified by Scientific Certification Systems (SCS) in accordance with the principles and criteria of the Forest Stewardship Council (FSC). The company prides itself on the fact that their materials come from bio-diverse, multilayered, canopied forests. Collins products bearing the CollinsWood trademark have been harvested sustainably and then manufactured by either Collins Pine in Chester, California; Kane Hardwoods in Kane, Pennsylvania; or Ostrander

Resources' in Lakeview, Oregon. Collins products are available internationally.

19TH-CENTURY ORIGINS

The history of Collins may be traced to the founder's father Truman Doud (T. D. or Teddy) Collins who was responsible for the family's interest in timber. In 1855, at age 24, Collins joined a five-man partnership and purchased an interest in 1,400 acres of timber and a steam mill near Whig Hill, Pennsylvania. Collins hailed from Cortlandville, New York, and worked on the Binghamton and Syracuse Railroad before becoming a laborer in the forests near Hickory, Pennsylvania. For a brief period in the early 1860s, Collins turned his attention to oil interests, purchasing land and a small oil refinery, but was ultimately unsuccessful. In 1867, after buying out his partners in Pennsylvania, Collins, his wife, and their one-year-old son Everell were living in Beaver Valley, Pennsylvania, where Collins was back in the lumber business. His men cut down the trees on his property, hauled them out by mule, oxen, or horses, and rafted them down creeks and rivers to mills.

Everell Stanton (E. S.) Collins grew up working in his father's mills and forests. At nine, he was packing shingles in his father's mill, and by age 18 he was running a mill. He had also patented a number of sawmill inventions. In 1887, he, his father, and his father's brother traveled to the Tia Juana Valley in Mexico to prospect for gold. Wanting to strike out on his own, E. S. Collins moved to California and bought 40 barren acres in Mexico. There he homesteaded, battling illness and exhaustion, until his concerned parents headed west to bring him home.

COMPANY PERSPECTIVES

■

At the Collins Companies, we believe that third party, independent certification of our forestland is the best way to protect the legacy of the total forest ecosystem—now and into the future. To achieve this, we have had to listen, learn, and change. We have. We also believe that integrating the principles of The Natural Step into our business operations will result in a sustainable society. Once more, it means we have had to listen, to learn, to change. And, again, we have. In some ways change is simple, in some ways it's complex. But if your principles demand that you work to create a healthy, viable Earth, in addition to a healthy, viable business, then you must risk change. You must be change.

On the way back to Pennsylvania, the Collinses stopped in Ostrander, Washington, where they visited with one of Teddy's friends in the timber business. When this friend fell ill in 1890, Teddy sent E. S. to Washington to supervise his sawmill, which was losing money. E. S. settled in, helped bill the mill and lumber trade there, and became a town leader. Between 1889 and 1905, he built a sawmill, a hotel, a church and parsonage, and a two-room school and community hall in Ostrander. He formed the Ostrander Railway & Timber Company in 1896, and the Silver Lake Railway & Lumber Company in 1903, a year after being elected to the Washington State Legislature. By 1914, when Teddy Collins died, Ostrander Railway and Timber company was a multimillion dollar business famous for its Douglas firs and for producing the longest timbers in the world.

CREATING A FAMILY BUSINESS

Following Teddy's death, E. S. returned to Pennsylvania to settle his father's affairs and oversee his various businesses and land holdings there, divesting some of them and putting others in charge of the rest. He then returned to Washington and continued to build on the lumber empire there through acquisitions. In 1924, for example, he bought the Milton Box Company of Glenwood, Washington, and renamed it Mt. Adams Pine Company. He also purchased the remaining shares of the Ostrander Railway & Timber Company, as well as the Silver Lake Railway Company in 1927. Also during the early 1920s, E. S. also closed the company's last family mill in Pennsylvania.

During the 1930s, E. S. Collins's two sons entered the family business; Alton Collins supervised operations in Ostrander, Washington, while Truman Collins went to work at the Mt. Adams Pine Company after graduation from a master's program at Harvard. By 1931, timber had become increasingly scarce around Glenwood, and Mt. Adams bought out the only other local mill in the area.

With help from his father, Truman Collins purchased the Grande Ronde Lumber Company and the Big Creek & Telocaset Railroad in Pondosa, Oregon, in 1931. In the mid-1930s, the Collinses saw the potential of truck logging addition, and in 1936, Truman formed the Ostrander Logging Company to start harvesting Douglas fir on the 37,320 acres of mostly virgin Douglas fir that Teddy and E. S. had purchased in 1914 in Clackamas County, Oregon. In 1937, E. S. formed the J. T. McDonald Logging Company with J. T. McDonald, who had overseen the Mt. Adam Box Company. In 1939, E. S., Truman Collins, McDonald, and others formed the Lakeview Logging Company, which operated continuously until 1945.

SUSTAINABILITY, EXPANSION, AND GROWTH

When Truman Collins took over the reins to the family's businesses upon E. S.'s death in 1940, he ushered in a new way of doing business. He envisioned ensuring a steady supply of timber through sustainable forestry; under his leadership, Collins' lumber companies began selectively harvesting trees. They also began to leave snags and downed logs on its woodlands, a practice that was at first practical but later proved environmentally sound.

Truman began his experiments in sustainable forestry on 67,800 untouched acres in the Sierra Nevada range near Chester, California, lands previously acquired by Teddy and partners. With George Flanagan, a Forest Service employee, and Wally Reed, who had experience in selective logging of high risk pines, the company set up a system of private roads, more than 500 one-acre, old-growth inventory plots, and a risk-rating system that allowed removal of individual trees that were not growing at a satisfactory rate. Using data gathered on each plot at ten-year intervals, Collins's foresters judged forest growth rates and planned for harvests that did not reduce the forest's overall board feet of wood. Out east, the Collins operations also instituted a management plan for second-growth forests in Pennsylvania, holding off harvesting there for the next 20 years.

By 1941, logs were being stockpiled in Chester Pond to start a sawmill for the company, which would

KEY DATES
■

1855: Teddy Collins purchases an interest in 1,400 acres of timber.

1896: Son E. S. Collins forms the Ostrander Railway & Timber Company.

1927: E. S. Collins buys the remaining shares of the Ostrander Railway & Timber Company.

1931: Truman Collins purchases the Grande Ronde Lumber Company and the Big Creek & Teloset Railroad.

1936: Truman Collins forms the Ostrander Logging Company.

1937: E. S. Collins forms the J. T. McDonald Logging Company.

1940: E. S. Collins dies; Truman Collins takes over as head of the company.

1942: Elmer Goudy becomes head of the company when Truman Collins joins the Naval Reserve.

1943: The company changes its name to Collins Pine Company.

1946: Collins Pine turns over the Grande Ronde Pine Company to a group of employees and liquidates the Ostrander Railway & Timber Company.

1947: The family founds the Collins Foundation.

1974: The new Collins Pine sawmill, later known as Kane Hardwood, is completed.

1990: The company's three forestry operations are consolidated.

1993: Collins Almanor Forest becomes the first privately owned industrial forestland in the United States to receive Forest Stewardship Council (FSC) certification for sustainable forestry.

1994: The Collins Pennsylvania Forest receives FSC certification.

1996: The Fremont Sawmill closes; the company opens Collins Products LLC.

1998: Lakeview Forest gains FSC certification.

2002: The Chester sawmill reopens after being upgraded.

2008: The Collins Upper Columbia Mill opens.

system, stepped in to head up logging operations when Collins left to serve in the Naval Reserve. After overseeing the change of the company's name to Collins Pine Company on January 19, 1943, Goudy presided over the opening of the sawmill in Chester later that year.

The 1940s also saw additional acquisitions and changes in Collins' operations. Collins purchased 13 miles of mainline railroad from the Red River Lumber Company to move its lumber from Chester to the nearest connection in Clear Creek, California. The railroad was incorporated as the Almanor Railroad Company and was wholly owned by Collins Pine. In 1944, the company acquired the Lakeview Lumber Company, which it renamed the Lakeview Sawmill Company in Lakeview, Oregon. The following year, it added the nearby Fremont Sawmill. In 1946 the company added the Wolf Creek tract of 17,000 acres in California, although it would not begin harvesting there until 1984. That same year, Collins opened the first of four Builder's Supply stores in northern California. Some divestitures during this time included the sale of the Grande Ronde Pine Company to a group of employees and the liquidation of the Ostrander Railway & Timber Company, the assets of which were sold to the Weyerhaeuser Company.

During this time the Collins family created several charitable foundations and trusts. Chief among these was The Collins Foundation, which Mary Laffey Collins, E. S.'s wife, and their adult children, Truman, Grace, and Alton, created in 1947 to "improve, enrich, and give greater expression to the religious, educational, cultural, and scientific endeavors in the state of Oregon and to assist in improving the quality of life in the state." As they explained in an April 1998 issue of the *Kane Republican:* "We are ... each of us ... a trustee of our time, our children, our businesses, our homes, and ... the land and freedoms that have been handed down to us by those who came before. Each of us has the responsibility to husband what has been given to him or her in trust, so that it will not have been diminished while in our care." The Collins Foundation initially gave grants of $5,000 for charitable, religious, educational, and scientific purposes. By the close of the century, its gifts had grown to total $5 million. Also, in 1956, the Collins Medical Trust began to support medical research and education in the state of Oregon.

Further afield, Truman Collins set the goal of establishing a presence for the company along the eastern seaboard. Toward that end, his initial land purchase was of approximately 10,000 acres from Wheeler & Dusenbury Company of Pennsylvania in 1950. Eventually, the company purchased 60,000 acres, including the Crary Farms in Sheffield, Pennsylvania.

become the Grande Ronde Pine Company. In 1942, Collins's brother-in-law Elmer Goudy, an attorney and the first state administrator of Oregon's public welfare

There it opened a Christmas tree operation. The company also purchased a share in Mull Drilling Company in 1955 and the following year acquired Harde's Lumber Company and almost 7,000 more acres of timberland in Pennsylvania.

NEW LEADERS AND A NEW COMPANY NAME

When, in 1964, Truman Collins died following a heart attack, Elmer Goudy, at age 63, became president of Collins Pine Company. That same year Maribeth Collins, Truman's wife, became chairman of the board of Collins Pine and head of The Collins Foundation. (She remained chairman until her retirement in 2005, when her daughter, Cheri Collins Smith, a graduate of the Wharton School of Business, replaced her.)

One of Goudy's first moves in 1965 was to sell Elk Lumber Company to Boise Cascade to pay the taxes on Truman's estate. He next purchased a sawmill in Paisley as a companion mill to the neighboring Lakeview, Oregon, Fremont Sawmill. Also, in keeping up with the company's East Coast operations, in 1966, he bought a small sawmill and timberlands in Lantz Corners, Pennsylvania. The Pennsylvania Christmas tree operation, however, was shuttered during this time.

Goudy retired in 1974, and his son, Alan Goudy, took over as president of Collins Pine. Alan had worked several summers in Chester, California, before graduating from Yale University with a master's degree in forestry and wood technology. He had overseen construction of the company's flakeboard plant in Chester around 1960 and had managed the plant until 1964. In 1974, he oversaw the building of the new Collins Pine sawmill, later known as Kane Hardwood, in Kane, Pennsylvania.

Alan Goudy was in charge of Collins Pine for only about eight years when he suffered a heart attack and opted to retire in early 1983. He was succeeded by Bob Lastofka, who, with experience running mills for Weyerhaeuser, became the first nonfamily chief executive of Collins Pine. The company was then facing several organizational challenges; the forests were in good shape, but the company's mills, which consisted of three separate operations (Kane Hardwood in Pennsylvania; Fremont Sawmill in Lakeview and Paisley, Oregon; and Collins Pine Company in Chester, Oregon) were losing money.

Lastofka first turned his attention to the Fremont Sawmill in Lakeview, Oregon. Fremont had an outdated mill and was competing for a dwindling supply of timber with Louisiana-Pacific, which also had a mill in Lakeview. It was clear there was room for only one large

softwood mill operation in Lakeview. In 1987 Fremont Sawmill made a successful bid for acquiring Louisiana-Pacific's Lakeview mill and its timberland in the surrounding area.

When Lastofka retired in 1989 James Quinn took over as president and chief executive officer of Collins Pine. Quinn had a degree in mechanical engineering from the University of Kansas and had been an engineering officer aboard naval ships before he went to work for paper manufacturer Crown Zellerbach. Quinn's first step in 1990 was to integrate the company's three separate operations. A new company, The Collins Companies Inc., was formed to oversee the newly integrated units.

CERTIFICATION, GROWTH, AND CONSERVATION

The company also elected to seek sustainable forestry certification by Scientific Certification Systems (SCS) in accordance with the principles and criteria of the Forest Stewardship Council (FSC). FSC is the only certifying body endorsed by major environmental organizations, such as the World Wildlife Fund, Greenpeace, Rainforest Alliance, National Wildlife Federation, and the Wilderness Society. In 1993 the Collins Almanor Forest in Chester, California, became the first privately owned forest in the United States to boast independent certification for assuring timber sustainability, forest system maintenance, and socioeconomic benefits to the local community. In 1994 the Collins Pennsylvania Forest gained certification followed in 1998 by the Collins Lakeview Forest.

Also under Quinn, the company instituted in its manufacturing and office facilities the principles of The Natural Step program of an international environmental organization by the same name dedicated to moving people and businesses toward cyclical resource-preserving methods. Collins adopted both The Natural Step and FSC principles companywide, instituting such measures as switching to recycled paper and to ceramic coffee cups, as well as using cooling towers to drop the temperature of its plants' wastewater and rerouting that water to landscaping. In the east, Kane Hardwood began working with the Fish and Game Commission to enhance habitat for ducks and other waterfowl in its Pennsylvania forests in the latter part of the 1990s. The company took some land out of production to provide undisturbed corridors for songbirds.

However, the company was still experiencing dwindling profits, partly in response to dips in lumber prices. Some operations were closed in response. Nevertheless, the company acquired Weyerhaeuser

Corporation's hardboard, siding, plywood, and particleboard plant in Klamath Falls, Oregon, in 1996. The new division was named Collins Products, LLC.

COMMITMENT TO SUSTAINABILITY AND COMMUNITY

By the time Eric Schooler, a veteran Oregon and Washington mill supervisor for Hampton Affiliates, became president in 2000, The Collins Companies were firmly committed to a course of forest stewardship to maintain, enhance, and improve forest health, and to increase the production of high-quality timber. Shortly after Schooler took charge, the sawmill in Chester shut down for a complete rebuild from December 2001 to September 2002. The Fremont Sawmill was next for renovations, and within six months, production had increased, lumber recovery was higher, and quality had improved. Schooler also expanded the company's hardwood division through the purchase of a mill in Richwood, West Virginia, in 2005 that had been in operation since 1901.

In the second half of the decade, The Collins Companies joined with GreenWood Resources to produce building materials from GreenWood's 35,000-acre tree farm in Boardman, Oregon. Collins began construction on a new mill, the Collins Upper Columbia Mill.

Still, as the first decade of the new century came to a close, The Collins Companies continued to face barriers to marketing its wood products as sustainably harvested. Despite growing arguments and consumer sentiment in favor of sustainable forestry, the lumber industry as a whole did not actively support certification, nor were consumers overwhelmingly willing to pay the higher costs of certified goods. In fact, because harvest levels were determined by forest growth rather than by mill requirements, only about 50 percent of the total number of logs processed by Collins came from company-owned timberlands; the rest Collins bought on the open market.

In response to these challenges, The Collins Companies' management made the decision to shift from a commodity market orientation toward higher-value specialty products and to use certification as a marketing tool. Collins would seek out or create outlets for the certified products it produced. As time went by, the company received more and more recognition for its sound, environmentally sustainable practices. As the company looked to a sustainable future for itself and its holdings, it strove to further increase recognition for its forestry practices and to move the forest products industry toward ever-greater reliance on sustainable methods of cultivation.

Carrie Rothburd

PRINCIPAL DIVISIONS

Kane Hardwood; Richwood Harwood; Chester Sawmill; Lakeview Sawmill; Collins Products LLC; Collins Builders Supply; Collins Upper Columbia Mill.

PRINCIPAL COMPETITORS

Georgia-Pacific Corporation; Weyerhaeuser Company.

FURTHER READING

"All Quiet in the Forest," *Crow's Forest Industry Journal,* August 1993.

Donnell, Rich, "Collins Companies Continues to Set Pace in Forest and Product Certification," *Panel World,* May 1999, p. 30.

"Kane Hardwood Division of Collins Pine Company," *Kane Republican,* April 30, 1998.

Sustainable Forestry Working Group, Oregon State University, 1998, p. 6-1.

Wojahn, Ellen, "They Say It Can't Be Done," *Oregon Business,* February 1998.

Cook Group Inc.

—■—

405 North Rogers Street
Bloomington, Indiana 47404-3739
U.S.A.
Telephone: (812) 339-2235
Toll Free: (800) 457-4500
Fax: (812) 339-3704
Web site: http://www.cookgroup.com

Private Company
Incorporated: 1963 as Cook Inc.
Employees: 9,000
Sales: $1.5 billion (2008 est.)
NAICS: 339112 Surgical and Medical Instrument
Manufacturing; 339113 Surgical Appliance and
Supplies Manufacturing

■ ■ ■

Cook Group Incorporated is a Bloomington, Indiana-based privately held company that in essence represents the business interests of billionaire William Alfred Cook. Medical manufacturing represents the bulk of the company's interests, including flagship subsidiary Cook Incorporated, a medical device manufacturer. Other medical device manufacturing subsidiaries include Cook Urological Incorporated, Cook Biotech Incorporated, Cook Endoscopy, and Cook Vascular Incorporated. Additional Cook companies supporting the device manufacturers are Sabin Corporation, providing plastic tubing and custom molded plastic parts, and K-Tube Corporation, a needle tubing manufacturer.

Affiliated companies include CFC, Inc., a real estate development company focusing on Bloomington and south central Indiana; Cook Aviation Inc., providing support services to Indiana's Monroe County Airport; Star Travel Services, Inc., a travel agency; Cook Family Health Center, a Bloomington-area managed healthcare provider; Grant Street Inn, a renovated historical landmark in Bloomington operating as a bed and breakfast; and French Lick Resort, a renovated resort located in the Hoosier National Forest, known for its mineral water springs.

SPARE BEDROOM ORIGINS

Born in Mattoon, Illinois, in 1931, company founder Bill Cook grew up in Canton, near Peoria, Illinois. After graduating from Northwestern University with a biology degree in preparation for studying medicine, he was drafted into the army, becoming an operating room technician whose regular task was to debride burn patients, victims of napalm and other war-related injuries. Debriding was a painful procedure, requiring affected skin to be repeatedly rubbed raw to prevent scabbing and eventual scarring. When his military stint was up, Cook was no longer interested in attending medical school. "I knew then that I didn't want to become a doctor," he recalled in his authorized biography. "I had an interest in medicine, but more in the mechanical parts of medicine."

With college roommate Brian Baldwin, Cook established Manufacturing Process Laboratories (MPL) in Chicago to produce hypodermic needles. He and his wife did not especially like the harsh Chicago winters,

COMPANY PERSPECTIVES

Since 1963, Cook has been a leader in developing health care devices that have improved lives around the world. With sales and marketing offices worldwide, we are at the forefront of medical research and product development in minimally invasive medical device technology for diagnostic and therapeutic procedures.

however, and in the early 1960s they began looking for a new place to live, finally settling on Bloomington, Indiana. Not only was the city well south of the state's "snow belt," it was relatively close to Cook's relatives in Illinois and his wife's family in Evansville, Indiana. Hence, he left MPL in 1963, relocated to Bloomington, and began searching for a new business idea. One of his cousins, Van Fucilla, told him of the revolutionary new "Seldinger technique," which used a needle, wire, and catheter to navigate the bloodstream and reach previously inaccessible parts of the body.

Selling his share of MPL, Cook then launched Cook Inc. for $1,500. In a spare bedroom, using a blowtorch he began producing handmade assemblies that included a catheter tube, needle, and guide wire. To clean the catheter, guide wires were dipped in acid kept in the couple's bathtub. Because of his cousin's tip, Cook was well positioned when later in the year Swedish radiologist Dr. Sven-Ivar Seldinger published an article describing his groundbreaking procedure. In late August 1963 Cook Inc. made its first sale: a pair of Seldinger Wire Guides at $3.50 each to the Illinois Masonic Hospital Association.

After outgrowing the apartment, and narrowly averting some potentially damaging accidents in the process, Bill Cook refurbished a dentist's office in 1964 to serve as a manufacturing plant, a space he shared with a real estate investment company. Shortly thereafter, Cook, taking advantage of his veterans benefits, bought a three-bedroom house and garage and had them converted into production facilities. Because the neighborhood, located just outside the Bloomington city limits, was already zoned for industry, Cook was able to construct other buildings on the two and one-half acre property as business dictated. At the time, most doctors made catheters and guides in their own laboratories, but they were gradually won over by the standardized, high-quality, and less-expensive product that Cook had to offer.

Along the way, Cook hired his first employee, Tom Osborne, the 17-year-old son of a local jeweler, to produce wire guides. A middling student, Osborne proved to be a naturally gifted inventor, much of whose work was born out of necessity. His first major contribution was the creation of a wire coiling machine that replaced a troublesome commercial coiler. Over the years, most of the patents that would come out of Cook Inc. bore Osborne's name.

PURSUING OTHER INTERESTS

Cook Inc. enjoyed strong growth in the late 1960s, annual sales increasing 600 percent from 1967 to 1969, growing from $132,000 to $922,000, as doctors realized that catheters and guides could be used to clear blocked arteries and for other surgical procedures. Development of stents—tubes used to open constricted blood vessels—as a new product line spurred business further in the 1970s. Bill Cook would also become a beneficiary of the products his company produced. In 1974 he suffered a heart attack and underwent bypass surgery. During his lengthy recovery, Cook and his wife began buying old properties and renovating them, leading to some of the real estate ventures of later years. When his health improved, Cook resumed his active leadership of the medical device company. In 1983 he again had heart problems, resulting in further bypass surgery. Rather than have a third bypass surgery, Cook would later make use of stents, although not his company's products, because by then he had divested that aspect of the company.

Bill Cook became involved in other medical-related businesses as the opportunity arose, not all of which were successful. In the early 1980s he bought a pacemaker company. Quickly realizing that he was out of his league, Cook sold the business. More successful was his move into injectables, a field he was familiar with from his days at MPL. Other ventures, like the renovation of historic properties, were purely due to his personal interests. An avid flyer since his days in college, Cook started a small charter airline, which proved to be more trouble than it was worth. Eventually Cook sold the fleet but kept Cook Aviation to serve as a refueling operation and provider of other support services to other carriers at Monroe County Airport.

Cook also indulged his interest in sports. In 1993 he spent $13 million to acquire a United Kingdom professional basketball team, the Manchester Giants. He was also given an opportunity to acquire an associated soccer club, Manchester United, for less than $25 million. Unfamiliar with English football, Cook passed on the opportunity. The team would go on to enjoy an extended run of success on its way to becoming one of

1963: Cook Inc. is founded by Bill Cook.
1993: Cook starts a Bloomington medical clinic, which will grow into the Cook Family Health Center.
2001: Cook Pharmaceutical Solutions is sold.
2003: Sale of Cook Inc. to Guidant Corporation is terminated.
2004: Cook Pharmica is founded.

the most valuable soccer clubs, and sports franchises, in the entire world, its eventual worth well in excess of $1 billion. As for the Manchester Giants, the basketball team won a championship in 2000, after which Cook sold the club.

GAYLE COOK KIDNAPPED

Although Cook became a very wealthy man, named to the *Forbes* list of the 400 richest people in America, he and his wife continued to live a modest life, content to remain in the house they bought in the 1960s. As they feared after the *Forbes* list was published, others took note of their worth as well. In March 1989 Cook's wife, Gayle, was abducted outside their home in the middle of the afternoon by a man named Arthur Curry, who demanded a ransom of $1.7 million. His plot was not especially well thought out, however; he had no plans beyond holding his victim in a van until his demands had been met. The Cooks, on the other hand, had already agreed that in the case of a kidnapping the one who was free would immediately call the Federal Bureau of Investigation (FBI), a step Bill Cook took as soon as he received the ransom demand and confirmed that it had not been a crank call. A day later the FBI traced one of Curry's calls to Cook, located the van, and arrested Curry without incident. Gayle Cook was freed, unharmed, after her 26-hour ordeal, and Curry was convicted of kidnapping and sentenced to 30 years in prison. The Cooks would be reluctant to be photographed after this incident, and reproductions of oil paintings of Bill Cook and his wife would become the only illustrations made available by the company.

Bill Cook's varied business interests continued in the 1990s. The Grant Street Inn renovation was completed in 1990, followed by the opening of the Bicycle Apartments in 1992, and the Lincoln Place condominiums and Showers Building renovation in 1993. Also in 1993, Cook started a Bloomington medi-

cal clinic, which would grow into the Cook Family Health Center. In 1997 he completed the West Baden Springs Hotel renovation.

CARL COOK RETURNS TO BLOOMINGTON

Following further heart problems, including suffering another heart attack on New Year's Day 1998, Bill Cook was advised to get his estate in order. Steps were then taken by the Cooks to transfer Cook Group stock to their son, Carl Cook, as well as to groom him to assume control of the myriad of family businesses. Born in 1962, Carl Cook had hardly been pampered growing up, even as his family became wealthy. His family's worth was not known either at Purdue University, where he graduated in 1984, or at the University of Iowa, where he earned a master's degree in business administration in 1987. Rather than go to work for his father in Bloomington, the young Cook spent a year working for the company in Europe, followed by a ten-year stint in Pittsburgh, Pennsylvania. Bill Cook, his health stabilized, continued to run things from Bloomington. It was not until completing a two-year stint at a Winston-Salem, North Carolina, plant that Carl Cook finally returned to Bloomington.

It was also through his son that Bill Cook developed a passion for drum and bugle corps. Carl had played for a Dubuque team, prompting the elder Cook in 1984 to begin investing in a new drum and bugle squad, sparing no expense. His Star of Indiana corps was provided with the best of instruments and uniforms and even had a mobile kitchen that fed them as they traveled around the country. In 1991 Star of Indiana won the world championship, but they were jeered by their rivals, who had to wash cars and hold countless fund-raisers in order to fund their operations. Mindful of the criticism, Bill Cook withdrew Star of Indiana from competition and instead used the members to create a show called "Blast!" Without plot or dialogue, "Blast!" toured widely as it was developed, ultimately making its debut on Broadway in 2001. While some reviewers were harsh, depicting the performance as little more than an energetic halftime show, "Blast!" nevertheless garnered the 2001 Tony award for "Best Theatrical Event." Afterward, the show would continue as a touring production.

COOK IN THE 21ST CENTURY

In August 2001 Bill Cook sold Cook Pharmaceutical Solutions, an injectable manufacturing concern, for $219 million. A year later he agreed to a much larger deal to sell Cook Inc. to Indianapolis-based Guidant Corporation, the former medical device division of Eli

Lilly and Company. Cook Inc. was in the final stages of U.S. Food and Drug Administration approval for a stent coated with anti-cancer drugs, which some trials indicated could help prevent the reblocking of an artery after balloon catheterization. Guidant ardently wooed Cook and he eventually agreed to relinquish Cook Inc. for $3 billion in stock. Poor clinical trials for the stent, however, caused Guidant to abandon the acquisition in January 2003. Far from disappointed, Bill Cook told the *Indianapolis Star,* "The best thing that happened was the deal didn't go through." A $50 million breakup fee also helped to alleviate any disappointment that he might have felt.

Following the aborted Guidant transaction Cook sold its imaging business for $250 million. With the funds realized from these events, Cook acquired a pair of company jets and in 2004 established a contract manufacturing operation for biopharmaceuticals called Cook Pharmica. Bill Cook continued to pursue nonmedical ventures as well. In 2005 he joined forces with Indianapolis real estate developer Bob Lauth to acquire a casino license, and together they began the $382 million French Lick Resort project, a renovation of the old West Baden Springs Hotel. The partners failed to see eye to eye, however; Lauth was unable to accept Cook's willingness to spend freely in order to make the renovation as complete as possible, including his desire to spend $600,000 for gold leaf in the hotel lobby. Other disputes resulted in the matter going to court.

Despite health concerns that troubled him for decades, Bill Cook remained in charge of his many business interests. His son Carl was also well versed in the different businesses and prepared to succeed his father. As a result, the continuity of Cook Group appeared to be secure for many years to come.

Ed Dinger

PRINCIPAL SUBSIDIARIES

Cook Inc.; Cook Urological Inc.; MED Institute, Inc.; Cook Biotech Inc.; Cook Endoscopy; Cook Pharmica; Cook Vascular Inc.

PRINCIPAL COMPETITORS

Boston Scientific Corporation; C.R. Bard, Inc.; Johnson & Johnson.

FURTHER READING

Hammel, Bob, *The Bill Cook Story: Ready Fire Aim!,* Bloomington: Indiana University Press, 2008.

Ketzenberger, John, "Crowning Achievement," *Indianapolis Star,* May 13, 2007, p. D1.

Merle, Renae, "What's a Billionaire to Do When He Gets Tired of the Stent Biz?" *Wall Street Journal,* April 19, 2001, p. A1.

Theobald, Bill, "Able to Maneuver," *Indianapolis Star,* May 3, 2004, p. C1.

Van der Dussen, Kurt, "Founder of Bloomington, Ind., Medical Firms Gives to Town as He Builds Company," *Bloomington Herald-Times,* July 31, 2002.

Wall, J. K., "Guidant and Cook Chart New Courses," *Indianapolis Star,* January 4, 2003, p. C1.

Wyman, Thomas P., "Eclecticism Defines Bill Cook," *Indianapolis Star,* July 31, 2002, p. C1.

Cosan Ltd.

■

Avenue Juscelino Kubitschek, 1726
São Paulo, São Paulo 04543-000
Brazil
Telephone: (55 11) 3897-9797
Fax: (55 11) 3897-9799
Web site: http://www.cosan.com.br

Public Company
Incorporated: 1936 as Copiagro S.A. Agro Pecuaria
Employees: 27,593
Sales: BRL 2.74 billion ($1.49 billion) (2008)
Stock Exchanges: New York
Ticker Symbol: CZZ
NAICS: 111930 Sugarcane Farming; 311311 Sugarcane
    Mills; 221122 Electric Power Distribution; 325188
    All Other Inorganic Chemical Manufacturing;
    447190 Other Gasoline Stations

■ ■ ■

Cosan Ltd. is the largest sugarcane producer and processor in the world. The cane, grown by the company on
land owned or leased in Brazil or purchased from other
Brazilian growers, is crushed in mills owned or leased by
the company and processed into refined sugar and ethanol, which is used in Brazil primarily as an additive to
gasoline. Cosan is the largest sugar producer in Brazil
and one of the three largest sugar producers in the
world. It is also the largest ethanol producer in Brazil
and the second largest in the world. Ethanol is produced
by fermenting the sugars from sugarcane juice and
molasses in tanks that also hold yeast. After the yeast is

separated, the remaining liquid is distilled to eliminate
water. Cosan employs sugarcane waste as fuel for its
plants and also sells it as fuel for plants that generate
electricity. It has also entered into consumer fuel
distribution by purchasing a large chain of service stations in Brazil.

THE COSTA PINTO SUGAR PLANTATION AND MILL

The growing of sugarcane in Brazil goes back to colonial
times, but the modernization that made the nation the
world's leading producer was due to the efforts in the
20th century of Italian immigrants to the state of São
Paulo, who principally occupied former coffee
plantations. Pedro Ometto was one such producer. He
founded the Costa Pinto mill in the city of Piracicaba in
1936, and then directed what became the Ometto
group until he died in 1966, sharing decision making
with his four brothers and a partner, Mário Dedini.
During the 1964–65 harvest the Costa Pinto plantation
mill took first place in Brazil in sugarcane and sugar
production by purchasing the production quota allot-
ments of smaller plantation-mills. After Ometto's death,
Dedini—proprietor of a group of 17 industrial
enterprises in his own right—left the business, and one
of the founder's seven children, his son Orlando, assumed the presidency.

One of Orlando Crisin Ometto's decisions, made in
1970, was to leave his position at Copersucar, a
cooperative founded in 1959 and by the early 1980s
representing more than 70 plants producing half the
sugar and 60 percent of the ethanol in São Paulo. Co-

COMPANY PERSPECTIVES

Cosan: Renewable energy for a better world.

persucar had great influence, then and later, on the federal government's policies in its field, especially the public body that bought sugar from the plants at a price independent of world commodity prices. The cooperative was the largest group in Latin America without foreign capital. However, Ometto reportedly found its leader, Jorge Wolney Atalla, unbearably dictatorial. At this time the Ometto group accounted for 12 percent of Brazil's sugar production and was the world's largest private exporter of sugar.

THE PLUNGE INTO ETHANOL PRODUCTION

A subsidized financing system was enacted in the early 1970s for the expansion and modernization of sugarcane plantations and sugar mills. After the Arab boycott of 1973–74 caused worldwide petroleum prices to quadruple, Brazil in 1975 initiated a program to develop alcohol (in the form of ethanol) from sugarcane as a fuel source and thus reduce the nation's dependence on imported oil. The waste matter, called bagasse, could be burned as fuel for the milling process, and any bagasse surplus could be used as fuel in generating electricity.

When world oil prices rose to over $40 a barrel in 1980, these efforts became more intense. The objective was to convert the nation's entire automobile fleet to pure alcohol models. The federal government promised to keep the price of ethanol 40 percent below that of gasoline, as well as offering other incentives for its use. Sugar producers, aided by huge government subsidies, began building hundreds of distilleries. Orlando Ometto, described by Warren Hoge of the *New York Times* as "the reigning 'sheikh' of the alcohol industry," was building the largest one in the world. In 1983 three-quarters of all new cars sold in Brazil were equipped with engines powered by pure alcohol. Ethanol was the main fuel used in more than 85 percent of the autos sold in Brazil between 1984 and 1989. By 1989 over 92 percent of new passenger cars sold were powered by alcohol.

Sugarcane production more than doubled between 1978 and 1982, and the area planted for the cane in São Paulo almost doubled, reaching 1.48 million hectares (3.66 million acres), with 82 million metric tons produced. Beginning in the mid 1980s, the Om-

etto family began to expand its operations by acquiring various mills in the state of São Paulo, including Usina Santa Helena and Usina São Francisco, which in 1986 became part of what was then Irmãos Franceschi Agricola Industrial e Comercial Ltda., Cosan's predecessor company. Usina Ipaussu was added in 1988.

Orlando Ometto died in 1988. He had always shared responsibility for the direction of the family enterprise with a brother-in-law, Celeo Silveira Mello, whose son Rubens had become vice-president of the group and saw himself as the natural successor. On Orlando's death, however, his son Sérgio challenged Rubens for leadership of the holding company's 20 enterprises. The struggle, sometime waged in Brazil's courts, did not end until 1993, when it was agreed that Sérgio would get control of 11 and Rubens the remaining nine. These companies were consolidated into three each, still under the same holding company, but without a president.

Sérgio's portion included Usina da Barra, then considered the largest sugar refinery in the world, and a tract in the state of Mato Grosso do Sul of almost 1,000 square miles of land, with 85,000 cattle. Rubens received direction of the Costa Pinto and Santa Bárbara properties, with their installations to produce sugar and alcohol, and among other holdings, an 84,000-acre irrigated tract in the state of Minas Gerais.

THE ETHANOL INDUSTRY STRUGGLES TO SURVIVE

In 1996 the company was granted a concession from the Brazilian government to build, develop, and operate a sugar-loading terminal in the port of Santos. In 1998 Usina Diamante and Usina da Serra became part of what would in 2000 become Cosan S.A. Indústria e Comércio, a merger of six Ometto-owned mills, with Rubens Ometto Silveira Mello as chairman of the board and chief executive officer.

By the late 1980s the sugarcane-to-ethanol program was falling victim to the law of unintended consequences. With an area the size of Denmark having been added to the planting of sugarcane, it was not easy for the government to provide the right subsidies, production quotas, and pricing structure to ensure production of the right amount of sugar and ethanol. Demand for sugar had leveled off, and the government was exporting it below production cost. However, cane producers were reluctant to convert the crop to ethanol because they regarded the price paid to them as too low. As a result, a shortage of the fuel developed, and motorists began to switch to cars with gasoline powered engines. So many motorists switched to gasoline that

KEY DATES

1936: Pedro Ometto opens the Costa Pinto sugar mill in Piracicaba, São Paulo.

1965: The plantation-mill reaches first place in Brazilian sugarcane and sugar production.

1970: The Ometto group accounts for 12 percent of Brazil's sugar production.

1993: The Ometto group consists of 20 enterprises, including the world's largest sugar refinery.

2000: Six Ometto-owned sugar plantation-mills are merged into Cosan.

2005: Cosan makes its initial public offering of stock on the São Paulo exchange.

2006: Cosan acquires Açucareira to become the largest sugar exporter in the world, with 16 mills.

2007: Cosan is reincorporated in Bermuda and sells stock on the New York Stock Exchange.

2008: Cosan purchases some 1,500 Esso branded service stations.

ethanol powered automobiles, although still one-third of the national fleet in 1995, were almost impossible to sell.

By this time ethanol production was no higher than it had been a decade earlier. Some 29 distilleries had closed by 1996. The ethanol industry was still struggling to survive in 1999, and many sugarcane planters had gone bankrupt. Sérgio Simões Ometto, president of the large Usina da Barra complex, told a *Financial Times* reporter that his enterprise was surviving only by converting cane to record amounts of sugar. The distillery tanks were corroding from deferred maintenance because Usina da Barra was selling ethanol below production cost, despite government efforts to prop up the price by such means as adding more of it to gasoline, which already consisted of 24 percent alcohol. Eventually a new generation of flex-fuel vehicles was produced with engines that could run on either gasoline or ethanol.

During this time the Ometto family was proprietor of Grupo Cosan/Bom Jesus, a consortium formed by five sugarcane-processing plants. This group expected to mill 8.5 metric tons of sugarcane in 1996, generating 550,000 tons of sugar and 300,000 tons of ethanol. Annual revenue was expected to be about $380 million, and some 3,000 workers were being employed by this group. Cosan was selling all the ethanol to a single distributor but had begun a joint venture with Shell

Brasil S.A. to provide the fuel directly to service stations.

Producing sugar was challenging as well, because world prices were at historically low levels. By 2001, however, plantation owners were feeling more positive because record production and exports were overcoming the effect of low prices. One consultant credited the removal of export restrictions and price controls for investment in new equipment and infrastructure. This, in turn, was said to have raised productivity and reduced costs.

GOING PUBLIC

The deregulation of the sugar industry that took place in 1999 paved the way for the consolidation of more than 300 mills owned by about 100 family companies, including the merger of the mills that formed Cosan in 2000. Cosan raised $403 million in 2005 by an initial public offering of 37 percent of the stock on the São Paulo Exchange. When the company acquired Açucareira Corona for $182 million in early 2006, it became the largest sugar exporter in the world to date, with 16 mills. Its revenues of $795 million in 2005 grew to $1.18 billion in 2006, of which sugar accounted for 60 percent; ethanol, 30 percent; and other projects, including energy generation, 10 percent. Cosan was then the second largest ethanol producer in the world.

Armed with $600 million in cash from the sale of stock and bonds, Cosan next went shopping for another sugar and ethanol producer, Vale do Rosário. However, this company fell instead into the hands of Santa Elisa, a rival that then, as Santelisa Vale S.A., became second in size to Cosan itself. The setback was particularly bitter to Cosan because Santa Elisa had on short notice unexpectedly secured emergency financing from Cosan's own bank, Banco Bradesco.

Another reverse resulted from Cosan's initial public offering on the New York Stock Exchange in 2007, after reorganizing itself as Cosan Limited, a Bermuda-based corporation. This offering established two classes of stock, which allowed chief executive Rubens Ometto Silveira Mello 90 percent of the voting power despite holding less than 4 percent of the Class A common stock being offered to the public. This offering, however, was received poorly, and Cosan raised only $1.05 billion from the U.S. offering and a Brazilian sequel, far less than the $2 billion it had sought. The value of the stock dropped 45 percent in the next three months as investors began to fear the prospect of a global recession. Cosan had a long term debt of BRL 2.19 billion ($1.29 billion).

By this time many financial observers were coming to the conclusion that investors, mostly private equity firms, had spent too much money in acquiring sugar- and ethanol-producing properties in São Paulo's Riberão Preto region. Cosan's executives decided that its money would be better spent modernizing its existing sugar mills and ethanol distilleries. However, in April 2008 the company moved in another direction, acquiring Exxon Mobil Corp.'s chain of 1,500 Esso branded service stations in 20 Brazilian states for $826 million and assumption of $198 million in debt. The transaction, which made Cosan Brazil's fifth largest fuel retailer, also included several distribution centers that were supplying fuel to airlines and industrial firms.

The chief executive of a rival firm said that Cosan was the first ethanol producer to expand downstream into distribution. Brazil's fuel distribution system, although in theory deregulated in 1993, continued to be based on terminals and service stations controlled by oil companies. Ethanol producers often had to ship their product hundreds of miles to distribution centers that then shipped it back large distances to filling stations.

A RETURN TO ETHANOL

Fiscal 2008 (the year ended April 30, 2008) was a boom year for Cosan's ethanol. Motorists rushed to buy the product as gasoline prices rose because of soaring world oil prices. Of the company's net sales, sugar accounted for 53 percent and ethanol for 41 percent. During the previous three years, sugar sales had outstripped ethanol by about a two-to-one margin.

By this time, Cosan's sugarcane crop was planted on about 572,000 hectares (1.41 million acres, or about 2,200 square miles, larger than the state of Delaware), of which the company owned 10 percent and leased 50 percent, buying the remainder of the crop from thousands of independent growers. Some of the leased land belonged to entities controlled by Rubens Ometto himself. The crop, comprising about 8 percent of Brazil's entire sugarcane production, was then sent to 18 mills, of which Cosan owned 16 and leased two, for crushing. Of the mills, 16 produced sugar and ethanol, while the other two produced only sugar. The da Barra mill had the world's largest crushing capacity at that time. Sugar for export accounted for 85 percent of the total.

Cosan accounted for about 7 percent of Brazil's ethanol production. The company was producing hydrous ethanol (51 percent of the total) for ethanol only and flex-fuel vehicles. Anhydrous ethanol was produced as an additive to gasoline and for industrial alcohol used by the chemical and petrochemical sectors. Cosan was selling ethanol mainly through gasoline distributors who were subsidiaries of such large oil companies as Petróleo Brasileiro S.A. (Petrobrás), Royal Dutch Shell, Exxon Mobil Corporation, and Chevron-Texaco Corp. They were required by law to distribute gasoline with an ethanol content ranging from 20 to 25 percent. Cosan's largest customer was Shell Brasil Ltda. Exports came to 11 percent of total net sales. Bagasse was produced from what remained of the sugarcane after separating water, sugar, and minerals from the cane. It was used as fuel in Cosan's plants, all of them self sufficient in energy.

Cosan planned to invest about $1.7 billion over the following five fiscal years (2009–13) to increase its processing capacity from 45 million to 65 million metric tons. The company was also building a complex in the state of Goiás consisting of sugarcane fields and mills for producing sugar and ethanol, at a cost of about $290 million. In addition, Cosan was also unveiling a $185 million real estate venture, called Projecto Radar, with money mostly raised from private investors. Radar would buy and develop farmland and lease it to agri-businesses, including Cosan itself, or sell it if the price was right.

Robert Halasz

PRINCIPAL SUBSIDIARY

Cosan S.A. Indústria e Comércio.

PRINCIPAL COMPETITORS

A.E. Staley Manufacturing Company; Archer Daniels Midland Company; Aventine Renewable Energy, Inc.; Cargill Inc.; Grupo Louis Dreyfus; Grupo Santelisa Vale; Sudzücker AG.

FURTHER READING

Barham, John, "Brazilian Sugar-Alcohol Strategy Turns Sour," *Financial Times,* June 21, 1989, p. 38.

———, "Sour Taste for Brazil's Sugar Growers," *Financial Times,* July 20, 1999, p. 34.

"Brazil Converts Its Sugar Surpluses into Fuel," *Financial Times,* November 9, 1983, p. 24.

Colitt, Raymond, "Sweet Smell of Success in Brazil," *Financial Times,* August 16, 2001, p. 30.

"Competing for Expansion," *LatinFinance,* March 2007.

Correa, Cristiane, "O Clã do Etanol," *Exame,* August 15, 2007, pp. 22–27.

Dawnay, Ivo, "Brazil's Alcohol Problem Leaves Headache," *Financial Times,* January 4, 1996, p. 46.

"Domestic M&A Transactions," *LatinFinance,* February 2008.

Duquette, Michel, *Grands Seigneurs et Multinationales,* Montreal: University of Montreal, 1989, pp. 54–55.

Edwards, John, "New Spirit for a Sagging Market," *Financial Times,* May 23, 1985, p. 38.

Hoge, Warren, "Brazil's Shift to Alcohol as Fuel," *New York Times,* October 13, 1980, pp. D1, D2.

McCurry, Patrick, "Sweet Source of Power," *Financial Times,* December 21, 1994, p. 9.

Miller, Ben, "Flipping Crops," *Latin Trade,* September 28, 2008.

O'Brien, Maria, "A Consolidated *Cosan* Hits the Highway," *LatinFinance,* June–July 2006, p. 18.

"Ontem Tapa, Hoje Afagos," *Exame,* December 22, 1993, 2pp. 52–53.

Regalado, Anthony, "Ethanol Maker Buys Exxon's Brazil Outlets," *Wall Street Journal,* April 25, 2008, p. B4.

Rumsey, John, and Sudip Roy, "All Roads Lead to Brazil," *LatinFinance,* September 2007.

Yoshizaki, Hugo T. Y., et al., "Decentralizing Ethanol Distribution in Southeastern Brazil," *Interfaces,* November/December 1996, pp. 24–34.

Detroit Media Partnership L.P.

615 West Lafayette Boulevard
Detroit, Michigan 48226-3124
U.S.A.
Telephone: (313) 222-6400
Web site: http://www.detroitmedia.com

95% Owned Subsidiary of Gannett Co., Inc.
Incorporated: 1989 as Detroit Newspaper Agency
Employees: 2,000
Sales: $185 million (2008 est.)
NAICS: 511110 Newspaper Publishers

■ ■ ■

The Detroit Media Partnership L.P. manages the business affairs of Detroit's daily newspapers, the *Detroit News* and *Detroit Free Press*. The two have independent editorial staffs but share business operations via a Joint Operating Agreement (JOA) that began in 1989. The company also produces various specialty publications and sells ads for the suburban papers of *Free Press* owner Gannett Co., Inc., which holds a 95 percent stake in the joint venture. The remainder is held by *News* owner MediaNews Group.

ORIGINS OF THE *DETROIT FREE PRESS:* 1831

The Detroit Media Partnership's two primary operating units, the *News* and *Free Press,* have a long and storied history. The *Free Press* traces its beginnings to May 5, 1831, when the first issue of the *Democratic Free Press*

and Michigan Intelligencer was published in Detroit by Sheldon McKnight. The paper was one of three then serving the town of 2,500, and began with a tiny staff and manually operated printing press. The paper moved to larger quarters in 1832 and shortened its name to the *Democratic Free Press.* When it became a daily three years later, its name was modified to the *Detroit Daily Free Press.*

The paper suffered several fires and changes of ownership during the early to mid-1800s, before coming under the wing of Wilbur F. Storey in 1853. He expanded the paper's coverage of national events with help from new technology such as the telegraph, while boosting local stories with an increase in staff. During his first year in control, Storey also made the *Free Press* the first paper in the country to publish a regular Sunday edition. Storey left in 1861, but the paper's growth continued under editor William E. Quinby, who added the first section targeted toward women in 1878, and in 1881 established a successful edition of the *Free Press* in London, England.

In 1906, with circulation standing at 40,000, a group of investors that included Detroit *Journal* owner E. D. Stair bought the *Free Press.* In 1913 the paper moved again to larger quarters, and in 1917 Stair bought controlling interest in the firm. Despite strong competition from the *Detroit News* and William Randolph Hearst's *Detroit Times,* circulation of the *Free Press* grew from 111,000 in 1917 to 201,000 in 1927. During this time the paper moved to a new, larger building on Lafayette Boulevard designed by legendary industrial architect Albert Kahn. In 1932 the *Free Press* won a

COMPANY PERSPECTIVES

Our single copy readers alone outnumber average quarter hour listeners to Detroit's Top 5 Radio stations during the morning drivetime peak.

prestigious Pulitzer Prize, the first of a number it would receive.

In May 1940, 81-year-old E. D. Stair sold the *Free Press* to John S. Knight, who owned several Ohio newspapers. In 1951 he named Lee Hills of the *Miami Herald* to the post of executive editor. Hills, who himself would win a Pulitzer Prize in 1956, increased *Free Press* circulation so that it finally overtook the *News*, although it was soon eclipsed when the latter bought Hearst's *Times* and took over its subscribers. Detroit was then a two-newspaper town, and the rivals dug in for a long and bitter fight for supremacy.

In 1964 both the *Free Press* and *News* suffered a 113-day strike by unionized pressmen, and in 1968 they were shut down for nine months in an even longer walkout. In 1974 Knight Newspapers, Inc., merged with Ridder Publications to form Knight-Ridder, Inc., giving the *Free Press* even stronger backing. Five years later the company invested $22.3 million to upgrade the paper's printing plant, but the battle with the *News* was still making it difficult to turn a profit.

DETROIT NEWS FOUNDED IN 1873

The *News* was founded on August 23, 1873, by James E. Scripps. Born in London, England, in 1835, Scripps had immigrated with his family to the United States and came of age on a farm in Illinois. His grandfather had been a newspaper publisher and his father a bookbinder, and after attending business college he worked as a reporter at the *Chicago Democratic Press* (published by a cousin) before moving to Detroit to edit the *Advertiser.* He became a partner in the *Advertiser* and helped merge it with the *Detroit Tribune* in 1862.

Scripps began formulating plans for a new paper for the workingman full of succinct, easy-to-read stories, priced at two cents (three cents less than the other local papers), but he was unable to persuade his partners to back it. In 1873 he left to found the *Evening News,* which would initially be printed at the *Free Press.* Within a year circulation was twice that of any other Detroit paper, and Scripps borrowed money from brother George and sister Ellen Scripps to build a print-

ing plant, also installing his siblings on the editorial board. In 1876 they founded an operating company called the Evening News Association.

In 1878 Scripps and several relatives lent money to younger half-brother Edward W. Scripps, who started the *Penny Press* in Cleveland. In 1880 the brothers cofounded the *St. Louis Evening Chronicle,* and in 1881 helped reorganize the *Cincinnati Penny Post.* The *Evening News* also bought the *Detroit Tribune* in 1891.

A long-simmering dispute with his relatives ended with James Scripps giving up his stakes in the other papers in exchange for controlling interest in the *Evening News* in 1903. He died in 1906 in Detroit, and control of the paper was left in trust for 30 years to his son, William, and sons-in-law George Booth and Edgar Whitcomb.

George Booth had in 1888 been made *Evening News* business manager, and then general manager in 1897. Born into a newspaper family in Canada, Booth himself would found a separate newspaper syndicate, Booth Newspapers, Inc., which over the next few decades established a chain of eight papers around the state of Michigan, including the *Grand Rapids Press* and *Bay City Times.*

NEWS ENTERS BROADCASTING IN 1920

In 1917 the *News* moved into its own Albert Kahn–designed building in downtown Detroit, and in 1920 the paper became one of the first in the United States to launch a radio station, WWJ, which would be operated from the *News* building. Both Booth and Scripps made many contributions to the cultural and educational growth of the Detroit area, with Scripps helping found the Detroit Institute of Arts and Booth creating the Cranbrook Foundation, which built several schools and a church on his estate north of Detroit. In 1929 George Booth retired as president of the *News* to oversee the Cranbrook Foundation, and James Scripps's 47-year-old son William E. Scripps took charge. In 1936 ownership of the firm passed to 48 Scripps heirs, according to James E. Scripps's will.

During the 1940s the Evening News Association created Michigan's first FM radio station, WWJ-FM, and its first television station, WWJ-TV. The latter became affiliated with the NBC network. In 1960 the firm bought the money-losing *Detroit Times* from the Hearst organization for $10 million and shuttered it, keeping the physical assets and subscribers. In 1963 Scripps descendant Peter Clark took charge of the *News* and worked to keep its subscription lead over the *Free Press,* then its only local rival. Like the *Free Press,* the firm suffered protracted strikes in 1964 and 1968.

KEY DATES

1831: First issue of the *Democratic Free Press and Michigan Intelligencer* published in Detroit by Sheldon McKnight.

1873: *Detroit News* founded by James E. Scripps.

1960: The *News* buys the money-losing *Detroit Times* from the Hearst organization for $10 million and shutters it.

1986: Gannett Co. buys Evening News Association for $717 million.

1989: Joint Operating Agreement (JOA) begins after appeals clear U.S. Supreme Court; Detroit Newspaper Agency (DNA) formed to run business operations of the two papers.

1995: Papers' six unions begin longest newspaper strike in U.S. history to date.

1997: Unions agree to return to work without contracts after 19 months.

2002: Specialty publishing unit Signature Media created.

2005: Gannett buys *Free Press* from Knight-Ridder; *News* sold to MediaNews Group; JOA restructured; Gannett takes control of Detroit Media Partnership L.P.

Seeking other sources of revenue in the face of tough competition at home, during the late 1960s and 1970s the Evening News Association expanded by purchasing small newspapers in New Jersey and California, including the daily *Palm Springs Desert Sun*. It also acquired TV stations in Tucson, Arizona; Mobile, Alabama; Austin, Texas; and Oklahoma City through subsidiary Universal Communications, which in 1978 swapped WWJ-TV for a CBS-affiliated station in Washington, D.C. By 1985 the firm had revenues of $310 million and a net profit of $13 million, with 3,600 employees.

JOINT OPERATING AGREEMENT IMPLEMENTED IN 1989

In 1970 the U.S. Congress passed the Newspaper Preservation Act, which created a narrow exception to antitrust laws for struggling papers called a Joint Operating Agreement (JOA), in which business operations would be combined but the papers would retain separate editorial staffs. It required approval of the U.S. attorney general, who had to be convinced that both papers could not continue to exist otherwise. Detroit

was one of a shrinking number of cities left with two dailies, and as losses mounted in the early 1980s the *Free Press* and *News* began examining the possibility of working together.

At this time the *Free Press* had weekday circulation of about 645,000, with the *News* topping it by 20,000. On Sunday, the *News* had an even larger lead of 107,000, selling 885,000 copies. The *News* published 62 percent of the area's print advertisements, in large part due to its wider dominance in outlying suburbs, and took in 70 percent of print ad revenues. Because of the intense competition between the papers, ad rates were approximately 25 percent below the U.S. average, and were often discounted even further by sales representatives.

Wall Street financial firm Bear Stearns estimated the annual losses of the *Free Press* at $9 million, and projected a profit of $20 million per year if a JOA was enacted. Losses at the *News* were similar, according to information leaked by an employee who was later fired, but were offset by the profits from the company's television stations. As rumors about the JOA grew, the Evening News Association's share price skyrocketed more than fivefold as several offers were tendered. The winning bidder was U.S. media giant Gannett Co., Inc., which bought the firm in early 1986 for $717 million.

Soon afterward, the owners of the two papers filed for a JOA, citing the *Free Press* as the one most likely to go under if it were not granted. The move was hotly contested by the papers' labor unions, as well as subscribers and local politicians, and after receiving approval from U.S. Attorney General Edwin Meese in 1987, it faced a round of appeals that ended in 1989 with a tie vote by the U.S. Supreme Court, which finally cleared the way for it to go forward, since in the event of a tie, the lower court's ruling stands. The papers would be allowed to share business operations and split profits for 100 years, while retaining editorial independence. It was the 22nd JOA granted to date, and the largest.

DETROIT NEWSPAPER AGENCY FOUNDED IN 1989

After final approval was granted, a new firm, the Detroit Newspaper Agency (DNA), was formed to manage the business operations of the two papers, with duties that included production, circulation, advertising, finances, human resources, and marketing. Gannett would have a three-to-two majority on the new firm's management committee, and its general counsel William J. Keating was named chief executive. The former U.S. congressman had also served as president of the *Cincinnati Enquirer*.

The *Free Press* and *News* would continue to publish weekday morning and afternoon editions, respectively, but would combine their Saturday and Sunday papers. As part of the agreement the *News* stopped printing a morning edition that had come to account for about a third of circulation, in exchange for providing the news, business, and sports sections of the Sunday joint edition and for Gannett taking a two-thirds majority on the board. Profits would be split according to a predetermined formula, with Gannett receiving 55 percent the first year and less as time went on.

Although the JOA had been seen as a sure way to return the papers to profitability, losses continued as ad space dropped when rates shot up to two or three times their heavily discounted levels, and readership fell in the wake of price increases. In 1989 the papers lost a total of $29 million.

Without its morning edition, circulation of the *News* suffered the most, dropping 28 percent by 1991. Circulation of the joint Sunday edition also fell 22 percent, to 1.2 million. The DNA sought to right things by cutting ad rates, working to improve the jumbled-looking Sunday paper, and cutting staffing with a series of layoffs and buyouts. The papers also added "zone editions" that featured regional stories for different markets, which were more attractive to local advertisers. By 1993 the *Free Press* was close to returning to profitability, while the *News* continued to record losses.

UNIONS WALK OUT IN JULY 1995

On July 13, 1995, contract negotiations with the papers' six unions reached an impasse and 2,500 employees walked off the job, initiating what would become the worst newspaper strike in U.S. history to date. The papers scrambled to publish a joint edition using members of management and staff recruited from other Gannett and Knight-Ridder papers, as well as locals willing to cross the picket lines.

As the months wore on the strikers founded a rival paper of their own as they continued to hold out hope for a settlement. One was not forthcoming, however, and in February 1997 the unions made an unconditional offer to return to their jobs without contracts, and the papers agreed to make a preferential hiring list for strikers, although they vowed to retain the replacement workers already in place. By this time daily circulation of the *News* had fallen to 240,000, and the *Free Press* to 366,000, with Sunday circulation just under 800,000. Prior to the strike, the *Free Press* had daily circulation of 532,000, and the *News* 354,000, with the combined Sunday paper topping 1.1 million. Estimates of money lost by the papers during the strike ranged from $140 million to $250 million.

In 1998 the *Free Press* moved its editorial offices into the *News* building on West Fort Street in downtown Detroit; printing operations had some time earlier been moved northward to suburban Sterling Heights. Circulation of both papers continued to slide, meanwhile, both from the lingering effects of the strike in the heavily pro-union area and other factors affecting the industry as a whole. Print newspaper readership was starting to feel the effects of the Internet, which offered free sources of information that were updated constantly. Ad revenues were also being hit hard by web sites such as craigslist.com and monster.com, which offered free or inexpensive ways to sell items, find jobs, and more. The two papers launched web sites, detnews.com and freep.com, but like many other print-based companies they found it difficult to adapt to the new business model and turn a profit.

In December 2000, some 1,982 days after it began, the last union contract was ratified, officially ending the longest strike in U.S. newspaper history to date. By 2003 relations had improved enough that the papers' unions approved new contracts by a three-to-one margin, although the number of employees then stood at just 1,500, down 1,000 from the prestrike total.

In 2002 the DNA launched a new unit called Signature Media to produce lifestyle magazine *Signature* for Detroit's affluent outlying suburbs. Other Signature publications would include *Strut,* a monthly women's magazine; *Vital,* a heath and fitness monthly; and a college guide. Signature also performed custom work for clients such as the Michigan Humane Society and Ann Arbor Art Fairs.

By this time the DNA had begun working with direct-marketer Advo, Inc., to produce inserts for smaller papers in Oakland and Macomb counties. The firm was also seeking ways to improve the online presence of the *News* and *Free Press,* linking with Gannett affiliates such as careerbuilder.com, homebuilder.com, and cars.com. The installation of a new $170 million printing press showed that the company still had faith in the long-term viability of print, however. In 2004 Gannett bought the Hometown Communications Network, Inc., which published a daily and numerous weekly newspapers and other publications in the Detroit suburbs and elsewhere. Their ad sales would be taken over by the DNA.

JOA RESTRUCTURED IN 2005

On August 3, 2005, a deal was announced in which Knight-Ridder would sell the *Free Press* to Gannett for $262 million, who would in turn sell the *News* to Denver-based MediaNews Group, Inc., as part of a six-paper realignment. The JOA was subsequently revamped and the managing body renamed Detroit Media Partnership L.P., headed by *Free Press* publisher David Hunke.

Gannett would become the main partner in the new firm, with a 95 percent stake. Minority partner MediaNews Group would not share in profits, but would receive annual payments starting at $5 million and then dropping to $1.9 million by 2012. The *News* would become a morning paper, and the JOA expiration date was amended from 2089 to 2025. Gannett would control the editorial budget at both papers, and the joint Sunday edition would be replaced by one produced solely by the *Free Press,* although the *News* could pay for a page of editorial content if it wished. The JOA could also be canceled after 2015 if there were three consecutive years of operating losses. Daily circulation of the *Free Press* at this time was 347,000, while the *News* had circulation of 219,000, and Sunday's joint edition numbered 683,000.

Circulation continued to decline as the Michigan economy felt the effects of the subprime crisis and the downturn in U.S. auto sales, and in the fall of 2007 the Detroit Media Partnership offered buyouts to 110 workers in an effort to cut staffing by 5 percent. Early the next year Gannett and partner Tribune Co. launched a nightlife-centered Metromix web site for Detroit, which would share ads and information with the "Play" section of the *Free Press.* By this time the Detroit Media Partnership's two flagship properties were being seen in print and online by 2.2 million readers weekly, or 59 percent of adults in the market.

On December 16, 2008, the Detroit Media Partnership announced several changes designed to meet advertiser and reader needs in a time when economics and the internet were impacting how people obtained information. The changes were intended to offer more robust digital delivery methods as well as the continued publication of the two daily newspapers. In the first quarter of 2009 the papers' digital information channels were expanded and included daily access to exact copies of each day's printed newspapers. Meanwhile, home delivery of the papers was changed to Thursdays, Fridays, and Sundays only, while printed copies were available at newsstands seven days per week.

Nearing the 20th year of joint operation, the Detroit Media Partnership L.P. was hoping that its new ownership structure and other operational changes would help it achieve sustained profitability. The challenges facing newspapers in the 21st century were many, but with the deep pockets of majority owner Gannett

Co., Inc., behind it, the firm appeared committed to take them on.

Frank Uhle

PRINCIPAL DIVISIONS

The *Detroit Free Press;* The *Detroit News;* Signature Media.

PRINCIPAL COMPETITORS

Advance Publications, Inc.; Journal Register Co.; The Washington Post Company; The E.W. Scripps Co.; CBS Corporation; Craigslist, Inc.; Monster Worldwide; eBay, Inc.

FURTHER READING

Burgher, Valerie, "Strike Hangover: DNA May Not Regain Old Life," *MediaWeek,* May 26, 1997, p. 14.

Collier, Joe Guy, "Buyouts Offered at *Free Press, Detroit News,*" *Knight-Ridder/Tribune Business News,* October 12, 2007.

Darlin, Damon, "Takeover Rumors Hit *Detroit News* Parent," *Wall Street Journal,* July 18, 1985, p. 6.

"Detroit Free Press History," http://www.freep.com/legacy/jobspage/club/fphist.htm, September 5, 2008.

Fitzgerald, Mark, "Detroit Shuffle Causes Some Key Changes in JOA," *Editor & Publisher,* November 2005, p. 10.

———, "Face-Off in Detroit," *Editor & Publisher,* July 22, 1995, p. 11.

Gargaro, Paul, "Laboring in Uncertainty," *Crain's Detroit Business,* February 24, 1997, p. 3.

———, "Report: Circulation Rises Slightly at *News, Free Press,*" *Crain's Detroit Business,* September 29, 1997, p. 3.

Gruley, Brian, *Paper Losses: A Modern Epic of Greed and Betrayal at America's Two Largest Newspaper Companies,* New York: Grove Press, 1993.

"James Edmund Scripps," *Dictionary of American Biography Base Set,* American Council of Learned Societies, 1928–36.

Levin, Doron P., "Gannett and Knight-Ridder Set Accord to Jointly Publish Two Detroit Papers," *Wall Street Journal,* April 15, 1986, p. 5.

Raphael, Steve, "Detroit Newspaper Agency in Last Tough Year for a While," *Crain's Detroit Business,* February 15, 1993, p. 3.

———, "DNA Has Hands Full," *Crain's Detroit Business,* April 2, 1990, p. 1.

Shea, Bill, "Web Sites to Tangle Over Young, Hip Detroiters," *Crain's Detroit Business,* March 17, 2008, p. 1.

Strupp, Joe, "Knight-Ridder, Gannett, MediaNews Strike Blockbuster Deal," *Editor & Publisher,* August 3, 2005.

EMCO Enterprises, Inc.

2121 East Walnut Street
Des Moines, Iowa 50317
U.S.A.
Telephone: (515) 265-6101
Fax: (515) 264-4210
Web site: http://www.emcodoors.com

Wholly Owned Subsidiary of Andersen Corporation
Incorporated: 1932 as Sam's House of 1,000,000 Parts
Employees: 900
Sales: $69.1 million (2008 est.)
NAICS: 332321 Metal Window and Door Manu-
facturing

■ ■ ■

EMCO Enterprises, Inc., is a wholly owned subsidiary
of Andersen Corporation, a major manufacturer of
windows and doors. EMCO specializes in easy-to-install
storm doors, screen doors, and accessories. The Forever
and EMCO brands are offered exclusively by big-box
retailer Home Depot, with whom EMCO has enjoyed a
long relationship. In addition, comparable EMCO-made
products bearing the Traditional label, as well as an
Economy series, are carried by Andersen's extensive
network of hardware stores, building supply companies,
lumberyards, home improvement centers, and other
retailers across the United States and Canada, and are
available online through www.stormdoors.com.

EMCO offers full-view doors with interchangeable
screens and glass panels and a range of self-storing
doors. The lower half of the self-storing doors are avail-

able with a "traditional" recessed-panel look or an
X-shaped "crossbuck" design. Upper half options include
a two-panel design with glass and screen panels that can
be stored within the doorframe; and glass panels that
operate independently behind insect screens to allow
ventilation from the top, bottom, or both. EMCO's
Economy series features windows and screens that snap
in and out of the doorframe. EMCO maintains its
corporate headquarters in Des Moines, Iowa, where
three manufacturing operations and a distribution center
are also maintained. Another plant and distribution
center located in Luray, Virginia, focuses on the lower
end of the product lines.

ORIGINS IN AUTO PARTS

EMCO was founded by Sam Engman, who was born
and raised in Russia. Around 1908, according to his son
Larry Engman, Sam immigrated to the United States,
his trip sponsored by a cousin who lived in Oskaloosa,
Iowa. Finding limited opportunity in Oskaloosa, Engman soon moved to Des Moines. There he put his
natural mechanical ability to work by salvaging usable
parts from wrecked automobiles. In time, he was able to
set himself up in business as Sam's Auto Parts. In 1932
he founded Sam's House of 1,000,000 Parts, considered
by EMCO to be its direct predecessor. While Engman
bought some parts from wholesalers, he mostly relied on
salvaged parts, which allowed him to stock such a wide
range of items that he gained a reputation as the best
source for hard-to-find auto parts.

Engman became involved in manufacturing in
1942. The United States had just entered World War II
and much of the country's industrial base had been

converted to the production of war materials. A Chicago friend of Engman, Nate Sherman, was having trouble finding the parts he needed to produce the mufflers and exhaust systems his International Parts Corporation manufactured. Sherman encouraged Engman to start a factory to supply him with muffler clamps and tailpipe hangers. Engman rented a nearby building in Des Moines, and with Sherman's help he bought the necessary equipment and began producing hangers and clamps. The relationship with Sherman would last for many years, well after Sherman established the well-known Midas muffler shop chain in the 1950s.

Engman had five sons whom he would start to bring into the business after the war, leading Sam's House of 1,000,000 Parts to be renamed S. Engman & Sons. The eldest, Milton, was the first to become involved in the company following his time in the Army Air Forces. He was followed by the next oldest, Gerald, after he completed his service in the Navy. By the time the next in line, Norman, was discharged from the service in 1955, the family decided that the business was no longer large enough to support four families, and Sam Engman began looking for a new product to produce.

DEVELOPING NEW PRODUCTS

In truth, Engman had been thinking for some time about a need for a product to manufacture during the winter months. Because most mufflers were bought in the warmer months when people were inclined to install them, the production of tailpipe hangers and muffler clamps was a seasonal business. Moreover, Engman, a generous man known to give car parts to any man in uniform for a simple promise to pay him back some day, was loathe to lay off his workers. Putting his inventive abilities to work, Engman devised a V-shaped table leg that was made out of the same wire rod that was used to produce the bolts in the muffler clamps. These table legs could then be attached to a piece of plywood, an old door, or other materials to create an inexpensive table. Norman was dispatched to Chicago to call on Ace Hardware, Montgomery Ward, and Spiegel,

and returned home with orders for a truckload of the table legs from each retailer.

S. Engman & Sons then became Engman Manufacturing Company, a name the family considered a little too unwieldy. Thus, the name was shortened to EMCO. The table leg business was conducted under the auspices of EMCO Specialty Products. Other products then followed, including wooden table legs, room dividers, and spindles for stair railings. The expansion in manufacturing allowed EMCO to absorb a fourth son, Stanley, and in 1959 the youngest, Larry, joined the family business.

Larry Engman made his first major contribution to EMCO in 1962 when he developed a new product line, decorative shutters. These were not functional shutters, but rather an inexpensive design feature for homeowners. They proved to be highly popular and were carried by Sears Roebuck, J.C. Penney, Montgomery Ward, and the hardware chains. In 1963, a year after the shutter made its debut, Sam Engman died, a victim of heart disease.

Larry Engman would also be responsible for the company's entry into the storm door business. In 1975 Engman paid his annual visit to New York City and had his customary "thank-you-for-your-business" lunch with John Kempf, the head buyer of building materials for the Penney's catalog, which by this time carried two or three pages of EMCO shutters. "I asked him, 'What can we do that's new and exciting together?'" Engman recalled in a 2009 interview. "Out of the blue he said, 'Plastic storm doors.'" At the time, storm doors were made out of wood, aluminum, or vinyl laminate, but no one was offering plastic storm doors.

INTRODUCING PLASTIC STORM DOORS

On his way back to Des Moines, Engman paid a visit to a design engineer he had worked with in the past, Walter Herbst, a principal of a small design firm, Herbst LaZar Bell Inc., which 50 years later emerged as the world's largest privately held product design consultancy. Herbst had helped EMCO in the design of table legs and spindles, and Engman knew that he had developed some expertise in plastics when a bowling craze swept Japan. During that time, large quantities of hardwood were diverted to Japan for new bowling alley construction, making it difficult to find wood, and Herbst was forced to design some products using plastic.

Engman envisioned a plastic storm door that had windows and screens that could be lowered into the doorframe. He asked Herbst if it was possible to develop such a product using plastic. The designer concurred

KEY DATES

1932: Sam Engman establishes Sam's House of 1,000,000 Parts in Des Moines, Iowa, to sell new and used auto parts.
1942: Engman begins manufacturing tailpipe hangers and muffler clamps.
1959: Sam's youngest son, Larry Engman, joins company.
1962: EMCO begins selling decorative shutters.
1977: Forever line of plastic storm doors is introduced.
1986: Larry Engman buys out brothers.
1996: Wood products division sold.
2000: Virginia plant opens.
2001: Larry Engman sells company to Andersen Corporation.

and agreed to take on the project. Two years later, in 1977, EMCO introduced the Forever line of high-end plastic storm doors featuring the patented store-in-door window and screen mechanism. The door retailed for around $179, about $100 higher than other storm doors on the market. It was Engman who insisted on the high price. "Everyone thought I was crazy," he recalled. "Even my family. But I said, 'Let's let the homeowner decide.'" Homeowners decided they liked the product and believed it was worth the price.

In the late 1970s the home centers were won over by the Forever door as well and began carrying the line. One of those home center chains was Handy Dan, which underwent a management shakeup following an ownership change in 1978. Three out-of-work former Handy Dan executives, Bernard Marcus, Arthur Blank, and Ronald Brill, established a new chain in Atlanta called Home Depot. EMCO would begin supplying the nascent chain when it operated just four Atlanta stores. The relationship deepened with time, and Home Depot became the largest customer of EMCO storm doors.

EMCO added to its Forever brand in the 1980s. The Forever View door was introduced in 1985, becoming the country's top-selling premium full-view storm door. A year later Larry Engman bought out his brothers, and under his leadership EMCO increased it sales of the Forever line, aided in large measure by national advertising, the only storm door manufacturer to do so. As a result, by the start of the 1990s, Forever was the most recognizable brand in its category.

ECONOMY LINE ADDED

More design advances were made in the 1990s. The SplineLoc insect screen retention system, which kept the screen intact while preventing it from being pulled out of the frame, was introduced in 1994. Three years later EMCO introduced UltraCore doors, relying on a composite material trademarked as ForeverTech. Storm doors had clearly become the core business for EMCO, and in 1996 the EmCo Wood Products division (which produced oak and hemlock spindles and stair parts in a plant located in Stanwood, Washington) was sold to Milwaukee, Wisconsin-based Design House Inc.

Through Home Depot, EMCO dominated the storm door market at the upscale end. Home Depot's policy was to carry products in three categories: Good, Better, and Best. While EMCO was well represented in the Better and Best categories, it had nothing to offer at the lowest level of the spectrum. In the late 1990s the company looked to address this gap and began scouting for a location in the United States where raw materials were readily available and labor was less expensive in order to produce a new door that could compete in the marketplace and still turn a profit. EMCO settled on Luray, Virginia, and in 2000 a plant opened there to produce an economy line of wood core doors, retailing between $59 and $69.

While EMCO was in the process of launching its Virginia operations, Larry Engman was contemplating an offer to sell the family business. In the late 1990s he was approached by Andersen Corporation, a large Minnesota window manufacturer. Andersen wanted to become involved in the storm door business as a natural complement to its window business. It could either start a storm door business from scratch or buy into the sector through the acquisition of an existing company with an established market share. EMCO held obvious appeal to Andersen.

ACQUISITION BY ANDERSEN

While the window market was highly fragmented, with Andersen leading the way with a share that was well under 10 percent, storm doors had few players. Home Depot, then carrying EMCO doors on an exclusive basis, controlled 40 percent of the market. Moreover, by acquiring EMCO, Andersen could increase its overall business with Home Depot in an efficient manner; the same trucks that brought EMCO doors to Home Depot stores could also carry Andersen windows. Selling the company was not an easy decision for Engman, however, and he held out for about two years. In the end, he decided the time had come for a change in lifestyle. He was also mindful of the history of heart disease in his family and wanted to fully enjoy the rest of his life. By the late 1980s he and his wife had begun living part of the year in California to avoid Iowa's harsh winters.

In 2001 Engman sold EMCO Enterprises to Andersen, EMCO became an independent subsidiary, and Engman retired as chairman and chief executive officer. His chief lieutenant of many years, J. Glasnapp, took over as president to run the operation for its new owners. Andersen wasted little time in expanding the operation, leading to the hiring of dozens of new workers in the three Des Moines plants. In 2002, to keep up with demand, EMCO invested more than $2 million in new equipment, machinery, and technology.

To remain competitive investments in technology became increasingly important. In 2004 EMCO hired Avatech Solutions, Inc., of Baltimore to serve as its design automation systems integrator. As a result of this relationship, EMCO was able to reduce the manufacture of parts from six to eight weeks to just three to five days. With the further financial backing of Andersen to keep operations current, and a well-earned reputation in

the market place, there was every reason to expect EMCO to enjoy success for years to come.

Ed Dinger

PRINCIPAL OPERATING UNITS

EMCO; Forever.

PRINCIPAL COMPETITORS

Columbia Windows & Doors; Larson Manufacturing Company, Inc.; Pella Corporation.

FURTHER READING

Bergstrom, Kathy, "EMCO Joins Andersen Fold," *Des Moines Register,* May 2, 2001, P. 1D.

Daykin, Tom, "Executives of Germantown, Wis., Home Improvement Supplier," *Milwaukee Journal,* January 12, 2001.

Joshi, Pradnya, "Design House Buys Firm's Wood Division," *Milwaukee Journal Sentinel,* November 5, 1996, p. 3.

Mathey, Anne, "EMCO Expands," *Des Moines Business Record,* December 31, 2001, p. 7.

Endress+Hauser $\boxed{\text{EH}}$

Endress+Hauser Holding
AG

—————■—————

Kägenstrasse 2
Reinach, 4153
Switzerland
Telephone: (41 61) 715 77 00
Fax: (41 61) 715 28 88
Web site: http://www.endress.com

Private Company
Founded: 1953
Employees: 7,855
Sales: $1.52 billion (2007)
NAICS: 333298 All Other Industrial Machinery Manufacturing; 334513 Instruments and Related Products Manufacturing for Measuring, Displaying, and Controlling Industrial Process Variables; 334514 Totalizing Fluid Meter and Counting Device Manufacturing; 334515 Instrument Manufacturing for Measuring and Testing Electricity and Electrical Signals; 334516 Analytical Laboratory Instrument Manufacturing; 334519 Other Measuring and Controlling Device Manufacturing; 541330 Engineering Services

■■■

Endress+Hauser Holding AG is a provider of sensors, instruments, systems, and services that measure level, flow, tank level, pressure, and temperature; conduct industrial liquid analysis; and register measurement data. Endress+Hauser measurement systems are used in manufacturing chemicals, petrochemicals, pharmaceuticals, and paper, as well as in food processing, water and waste water processing, mining, and many other industries. As a matter of principle, Endress+Hauser does not do business with defense-related industries. The company also offers specialized consulting services in areas such as production automation, logistics, asset management, marine automation, and fieldbus. Endress+Hauser provides a full program of in-house training for its customers. The firm is headquartered in Switzerland but also has a strong presence in southwestern Germany and neighboring France. Endress+Hauser is a private company fully owned by the Endress family.

A MEASUREMENT EQUIPMENT COMPANY IS BORN IN POSTWAR GERMANY

When Georg H. Endress, a 29-year-old Swiss engineer, returned to continental Europe in the early 1950s he brought with him an electronic level sensing device manufactured by the British company Fielden. His plan was to build and sell the apparatus, which was used to detect the level of fluids in tanks, in Germany, where such electronic sensors were as yet still unknown. At the same time he planned to develop and market his own line of measurement equipment. He found a partner in Ludwig Hauser, a 58-year-old German banker, who put up 800 marks of his own money together with 1,200 marks from his wife Luise and founded a company named L. Hauser KG to market the Fielden equipment.

Mrs. Hauser became the first business manager of the new firm—the L in its name stood for Luise—and

COMPANY PERSPECTIVES

The Credo of the Endress + Hauser Group: We learn from the customers we serve. We concentrate our resources on business we understand. We protect our status as an autonomous and independent corporation. We believe in autonomy and decentralization, but centralize a few core values. We encourage our employees to take responsibility for their actions. We manage by open communication, agree upon goals, and evaluate our success. We strive to set examples in the quality of our products and services. We seek motivated, committed and actively involved employees. We speak openly with each other. We handle information freely and responsibly. We wish to create an environment in which ideas and progress can be cultivated. We encourage our employees to be innovative. We recognize profitability as the driving force of our corporation.

they set up offices in a bedroom in their home in Lörrach in southern Germany, not far from the Swiss border. Meanwhile, Endress established his own company, G.H. Endress & Co, in Basel, Switzerland, to build the equipment, which would then be distributed by Hauser, who had established a licensing agreement with Fielden. By 1955 Ludwig Hauser had taken over management of their company from his wife. In 1957 Georg Endress became a partner in Hauser's firm, which changed its name to Endress + Hauser GmbH. Two years later the company was reorganized into Endress + Hauser GmbH & Co.

The company had grown in its brief existence. By 1955 it had net revenues of DEM 455,303; in 1957 they doubled to DEM 1.2 million. They would nearly double again in the next two years. One reason was that Georg Endress had begun almost immediately developing capacitive level measurement devices of his own design for which there was immediate demand. The first three, the Nivotester NC 5 and NC 6 along with the Silometer SM 3, went into production in 1957. Two improved models, the Nivotester NC 7 and the Silometer S 3, were launched in 1959.

Endress + Hauser enjoyed a significant advantage in it early years. It was the sole company in Europe manufacturing electronic level measurement equipment. As such it was able to set its prices as high as the market would bear without fear of being undercut by

competition. Also in Germany, where high-tech industries such as the chemical industry were rebuilding and modernizing, Endress + Hauser had a hungry market for its products.

GROWTH IN THE BOOM YEARS

By the end of the 1950s it was clear that Endress + Hauser could not afford to continue manufacturing in the makeshift building it had been using. A decision was made to move its 78 employees into a modern factory in the nearby town of Maulburg im Wiesenthal, a move that was completed in 1960. The first expansion did not stop with the new plant. Endress + Hauser also moved into foreign markets for the first time in 1960 when it opened a branch in the Dutch city of Amersfoort. Throughout the 1960s the firm opened additional branches in Switzerland, France, Belgium, Sweden, Austria, and Great Britain.

The significant technological breakthrough of the 1960s, the development of the transistor, was important for Endress + Hauser. Its early equipment had not only been large and unwieldy, it had also used electron tubes that wasted a great deal of heat and could send information over only a limited length of cable. Transistors eliminated those problems and made possible new devices in which the sensor and transformer were up to 80 meters apart. The first of these more flexible systems, the Nivotester NC 70, was introduced in 1964.

The company's client base continued to be primarily chemical enterprises. However, it started expanding into other business areas in the 1960s, including food industries such as breweries and coffee manufacturers, the petroleum industry, the nuclear industry, iron and steel foundries, trash collection companies, shipbuilders, paper manufacturers, and tire makers.

Each industry required specific types of sensors and as a result Endress + Hauser's product catalog expanded continuously until in mid-decade it contained some 600 various sensors. They included a range of new designs, including sensors using ultrasound and conductivity, which were introduced to great acclaim in 1965. In 1968 the firm introduced a device that used vibrations to detect levels in materials that were sticky, powdery, or fine-grained.

Demand for Endress + Hauser products grew steadily through the first half of the 1960s. Between 1961 and 1965 its sales increased from DEM 3.7 million to DEM 8.25 million. The unique and useful products were not the sole reason for this success. The company had always striven to provide a high level of

KEY DATES

1953: L. Hauser KG is founded in Lörrach, Germany.

1956: The first products developed in-house, Nivotester and Silometer, are launched.

1957: The company is renamed Endress + Hauser GmbH.

1959: Another reorganization changes the company name to Endress + Hauser GmbH & Co.

1960: Endress + Hauser's first foreign subsidiary is founded in Amersfoort, Netherlands.

1968: The first holding company, Mestra AG, is established in Basel, Switzerland.

1970: The company's first overseas branches are opened in Japan and the United States; Photo Print Electronic Co. (ppe) is founded.

1971: Cofounder Ludwig Hauser retires.

1975: Ludwig Hauser dies and the Endress family becomes sole owner of Endress + Hauser.

1985: The Maulburg plant adds pressure measurement to its activities.

1992: The company's first field bus measurement instruments are introduced.

1995: Georg H. Endress retires and son Klaus Endress becomes CEO.

1998: Sales top CHF1 billion; PatServe is founded to track E + H intellectual property rights.

2001: ppe is divested after significant losses are incurred in an attempt to enter mobile phone market.

2005: Innovative Technology IST in Wattwil, Switzerland, is acquired.

2007: PB Mesures and Pyrotemp Service Ltd. are acquired.

customer service to its clients. Its motto for the policy was *Erst dienen, dann verdienen*—"First serve, then earn." Special services included the custom development of specialty products for clients' individual requirements as well as Endress + Hauser educational courses offered for customers.

In 1968 Ludwig Hauser, then in his mid-70s, elected to step down as an active partner in the company. He sold his shares in Endress + Hauser and was replaced as partner by Georg Endress' wife Alice. In 1971 Hauser retired and left the management of the company's business completely.

GLOBAL ECONOMIC CRISES AND NEW COMPETITION

The German economy experienced the end of its famed postwar Wirtschaftwunder in 1967, when economic growth in the country ground to a near standstill. Nonetheless Endress + Hauser weathered the period better than many German companies. In 1968 it reported revenues of nearly DEM 13.3 million, which grew to DEM 24 million by 1970. Up to 1971 its growth rates were consistently between 30 and 40 percent annually. By then the firm had subsidiaries in most countries of Western Europe and more than 400 employees. It set its sights on new foreign markets, specifically Japan and the United States. In 1970 it achieved both goals, founding an American subsidiary, Endress + Hauser Inc., in Beverly, Massachusetts, and acquiring a holding in the Sakura Instrument Co. Ltd in Tokyo.

Business was going so well entering the 1970s that the firm started construction on a new 8,000-square-meter, four-story headquarters with a price tag of DEM 10 million. The structure was completed in 1973—just as the first worldwide oil crisis began, sending Germany into a recession. The economic crisis coincided unfortunately with other negative trends at Endress + Hauser. Competition within the measurement instruments market had been growing steadily as new firms, from the United States and Japan in particular, began bringing their own products to market, products often less expensive than those of Endress + Hauser.

For this reason E + H was forced to lower prices at a time when labor and other costs were climbing in Germany. In the depressed economy, orders fell at the same time, precisely after the firm had taken on sizable debt to build its headquarters. The end result was that the firm was thrown abruptly into its own private financial crisis.

Endress + Hauser had long realized that it had to diversify beyond level measurement products in order both to grow and to protect itself against fluctuations in the market for level measurement equipment. It had not completely implemented this diversification by the mid-1970s. At that time nearly 50 percent of revenues were still derived from level measurement products, and new competition from other manufacturers was gradually eating into that percentage.

By the end of the 1970s the company, although still essentially healthy, needed to address all these issues. It undertook to develop and introduce as a broad line of measurement and control technology as possible, to launch a cost optimization program, to reorganize its sales and service divisions, and to transform itself from an equipment manufacturer to a provider of a broad palette of customer solutions. It expanded in the 1970s as well, establishing new subsidiaries in Austria, Norway, Italy, Denmark and Finland. It founded a new American subsidiary, Ondyne Inc., a producer of humidity measurement technology, in Concord, California, and acquired Wiegel GmbH near Düsseldorf.

MICROELECTRONICS ENTER THE EQUATION

As the next decade began, Endress + Hauser was still perceived as a midsized specialty company. That changed in 1980 when the firm presented itself at international trade fairs as a group comprised of companies each with deep expertise in a particular area of measurement technology. E+H had cultivated this expertise through early cooperation with researchers at universities, an exception in mid-century among companies of its size. However, by 1982 it had 1,714 employees generating sales valued at CHF 184 million. The firm was taking part in a trend that saw southern Germany—the federal states of Bavaria and Baden-Württemberg—become the country's region with the highest growth rates.

The technological breakthrough of the decade was the development of microelectronics, which made possible significant developments in E+H measurement equipment. The firm embraced the new technology and as early as 1983 began bringing the results to market. They included humidity sensors in thin film technology and the Autozero 2000 magnetic-inductive flow meter, and the Liquiphant level limit switch. Microelectronics also made possible the introduction of new functions in established products, for example the ability to constantly monitor the operations of an entire measurement system.

The decade ended with the firm reporting the most successful year in its entire history with sales of more than CHF 535 million. Its global workforce had in the meantime exceeded 4,000, in part the result of new subsidiaries established in Brazil, South Africa, Singapore, and Hong Kong. The company reached a size in the 1980s that necessitated another reorganization that separated production completely from sales.

GLOBALIZATION AND A NEW GENERATION OF LEADERSHIP

As the 1980s drew to a close, Endress + Hauser once again had to tighten its belt. The company's finances were heavily burdened by the cost of new construction projects: a factory for the Flowtec subsidiary in France, a second facility for ppe in France, and a modern headquarters for the German administrative company.

However, for Endress + Hauser as for so many German companies, the beginning of the 1990s signaled new opportunities for revenue growth and foreign expansion.

The fall of the Berlin Wall in 1989 and the collapse of the Soviet Union just two years later opened vast new markets, both for sales and labor, in eastern Germany and in the nations of Eastern Europe and the former U.S.S.R. Thus the company was able to open new branches in Poland, Hungary, and the Czech Republic, as well as in Argentina, Mexico, Chile, Ireland, Portugal, Spain, and Australia. In eastern Germany, E+H established a factory in Saxony for the production of pH-electrodes.

The 1990s were also the period when European political and economic union became a reality. The establishment of the European Union in 1992 opened western European borders for the free flow of goods, services, and labor. The introduction of the euro as the currency common to most of Europe only intensified the impulse toward inter-country commerce in Europe. This was particularly important for Endress + Hauser, which had core administrative, sales, and production facilities scattered about the tri-national corner of Germany, France, and Switzerland. For example, the company by then had its headquarters in Reinach, Switzerland, its main production facility was located in Maulburg, and one of its most important subsidiaries, Flowtec, was split between Reinach and Cernay, France.

By the middle of the 1990s the sons of Georg H. Endress had assumed leading positions in the company. In 1995 the senior Endress, by then in his seventies, decided to retire from the day-to-day management of the company. His son Klaus became the new CEO, a position he continued to hold in 2009. The company flourished under the new leadership, recording the most successful year in its history in 1998, when its sales topped the CHF 1 billion mark for the first time.

PROBLEMS AND PROMISE OF A NEW MILLENNIUM

The start of the 2000s was a time of promise for the Endress + Hauser firm. In some 50 years time it had established itself as one of the premier sensor and measurement producers in the world. From the bedroom of a house in rural Germany, it had grown into a global conglomerate that employed a workforce of more than 6,000. Within a year new financial questions emerged, however. Its subsidiary ppe, a maker of circuitry, had made an ill-fated attempt to enter the market for cell phones. In 2001, just three years after the most successful year in company history, Endress + Hauser had to report a group loss of CHF

43.9 million. Ppe's failure was not unexpected and E+H reacted quickly. When a search for a buyer failed to turn up any offers, ppe started bankruptcy proceedings in December 2001.

As a result of the firm's rapid action, losses were contained, and in the following year Endress+Hauser reported a profit of about CHF 40 million on revenues of CHF 1.09 billion. The recovery was also helped by an expanding market share in its core business areas—devices to measure level, flow, pressure, and temperature. New construction continued in the first decade of the 2000s. A research and development center was completed at the end of the 1990s and expanded by 4,000 square meters in 2002. A year later a EUR 9.5 million administration building was started for E+H Maulburg, the largest subsidiary in the Endress+Hauser group.

In 2003 the firm made a leap into the Chinese market, with the establishment of a subsidiary in Suzhou. The company made a series of acquisitions in the latter half of the first decade of the 2000s. It acquired Innovative Technology IST in Wattwil, Switzerland, in 2005, and two years later PB Mesures, a French measurement engineering firm, and Pyrotemp Service Ltd.of Johannesburg, South Africa. Despite its size, Endress+Hauser remained committed to its status as a private, family-owned operation. In 2006 the Endress family partners drew up a charter for the company to protect that valued status.

Gerald E. Brennan

PRINCIPAL SUBSIDIARIES

Endress+Hauser Services AG; Endress+Hauser Finanz AG; Endress+Hauser Instruments International AG; Endress+Hauser Holding AG; Endress+Hauser Conducta Verwaltungs-GmbH; Endress+Hauser Gastec GmbH & Co.; Endress+Hauser Gastec GmbH & Co.; Endress+Hauser InfoServe Verwaltungs-GmbH; Endress+Hauser GmbH+Co. KG; Endress+Hauser Meßtechnik GmbH+Co KG; Endress+Hauser (Deutschland) AG+Co. KG; Endress+Hauser Logistik GmbH+Co. KG; Endress+Hauser Verwaltungs-GmbH; Endress+Hauser Consult AG; Endress+Hauser Instruments International AG; Endress+Hauser Czech s.r.o. (Czech Republic); Endress+Hauser Messtechnik GmbH+Co. KG (Germany); Endress+Hauser GmbH+Co. KG (Germany); Endress+Hauser Flowtec AG (Germany); Endress+Hauser A/S (Denmark); Endress+Hauser (India) Pvt. Ltd.; Endress+Hauser B.V. (Netherlands); Endress+Hauser (Pty.) Ltd (UK); Endress+Hauser Inc. (USA).

PRINCIPAL COMPETITORS

ABB Asea Brown Boveri Ltd.; GE Infrastructure Sensing UK; Mitsubishi Electric Corporation; Schneider Electric GmbH; Emerson Electric Co.; VEGA Grieshaber KG; Honeywell International Inc.; Invensys Group; SPX Corporation; Teledyne Isco Inc.; WIKA Alexander Wiegand GmbH & Co. KG.

FURTHER READING

"Endress-Gruppe mit weniger Gewinn," *Frankfurter Allgemeine Zeitung,* July 7, 1994, p. 17.
"Endress Hauser Hopes for RM16m Turnover," *New Straits Times* (Malaysia), July 17, 1999, p. 24.
"Evolution for Automation," *What's New in Industry,* July 20, 2005, p. 50.
"Fieldbus Community Is Bemused by Patents Fear," *Control and Instrumentation,* April 2000, p. 6.
"Georg Endress 70 Jahre," *Frankfurter Allgemeine Zeitung,* January 8, 1994, p. 14.
Piazza, Katrin, "Eine Kosten-Nutzen-Rechnung ist unmöglich das Geld ist aber gut angelegt," *HandelsZeitung,* November 23, 2005.
"Von der Pike auf zum Unternehmer," *HandelsZeitung,* April 22, 2004.

Essie Cosmetics, Ltd.

———————————■———————————

1919 37th Street
Astoria, New York 11105
U.S.A.
Telephone: (718) 726-5000
Fax: (718) 726-6780
Web site: http://www.essie.com

Private Company
Incorporated: 1981
Employees: 75
Sales: $150 million (2007 est.)
NAICS: 325620 Toilet Preparation Manufacturing

■ ■ ■

Based in Astoria, located in New York City's Queens borough, Essie Cosmetics, Ltd., is a privately held manufacturer of manicure preparations, best known for its nail polish sold to the salon and spa trade. The company offers more than 300 colors of nail polish, with new shades introduced every 90 days in collections of six. Aside from the trademarked square bottle with Essie embossed on the side, the nail polish is distinguished by whimsical names bestowed upon the shades by the company's founder and president, Esther Weingarten. The most famous is Ballet Slippers, but other names include Decadent Diva, Bags to Riches, Cloud Nine, Hard to Get, Pouf Daddy, Risky Business, Wicked, Wrapped in Rubies, and After Sex (labeled After Six in some markets). Essie nail polish has been worn by a wide range of famous women, from Madonna to Hillary Clinton.

Essie Cosmetics also offers nail treatments, including cuticle oil, ridge fillers, and glazes; nail solutions to build nail strength; and such nail accessories as files, pads, and toe separators. Other Essie product lines include the Smoothies brand of hand and body lotions; the Essie Spa line of oils, exfoliating scrubs, masques, and aroma-therapeutic crèmes; and lip gloss. Essie products are available to consumers at their local nail salon or full-service salon, or online through the company's web site. The products are carried by more than 55,000 salons and spas in nearly 100 countries around the world. Manufacturing is done at a company-owned plant in Astoria.

EARLY LOVE FOR NAIL POLISH

Essie Weingarten was raised in the Hollis Hills section of Queens in the 1950s and 1960s. Because of her father's death, she gained a good deal of practical business experience by helping her mother run the family business. She also developed a love for nail polish. As a reward for good behavior, starting at the age of 12 she was taken on Saturdays by her mother to the beauty parlor for a manicure. After high school Weingarten enrolled at New York's Fashion Institute of Technology to study fashion merchandising, while also working at Henri Bendel, a venerable Fifth Avenue boutique. After graduating in 1970 she went to work full-time as an assistant buyer, but left a year later when she was offered a job by a vendor who produced private-label panty hose. Weingarten stayed ten years, along the way gaining the confidence that she could successfully run her own business.

Weingarten decided she wanted to make and sell her own nail polish. Not only did she have a passion for the product, she knew that the salon market was dominated by one brand, Revlon. She did not like the choice of colors available, and she believed that many other women shared that opinion. Moreover, the salon polishes were numbered rather than named, making them hardly memorable to customers. Hence, she was convinced that there was an opening in the market for a high-quality, chip-resistant salon nail polish available in a wide variety of distinctive colors, bestowed with equally idiosyncratic names.

Weingarten began searching for a chemist who could make her concept into a reality. With little more to work with than the Yellow Pages, after much effort she finally met a chemist in 1980, Stanley Klinger, who was employed by a New Jersey manufacturing company. She provided him with items, the colors of which he was to match: fabrics, ribbons, a pincushion. About two months later he had a dozen shades of a chip-resistant nail polish to show her. She loved each one. By this time, Weingarten had quit her job. She had saved enough money to allow her to live for a year in the style to which she had grown accustomed and still have $10,000 to start Essie Cosmetics in 1981.

LAS VEGAS TRIP JUMP-STARTS ESSIE

Because of her limited budget Weingarten wanted to launch her new products where she could have the greatest impact at the lowest cost. She chose Las Vegas. At the time, manicures were not especially commonplace and were relatively expensive, limited mostly to women with disposable income. In Las Vegas there were a large number of women who not only made enough money to afford manicures, they always had to look beautiful. Not only showgirls, but also waitresses and even dealers had a vested interest in keeping their nails looking perfect. Weingarten flew to Las Vegas and traveled the length of the Strip, visiting the nail salon in

every hotel-casino, leaving samples of her initial line, 12 colors in three treatments, wherever she went. Of those 12 colors, five became lasting top sellers: Autumn Leaves, Baby's Breath, Black Cherry, Blanc, and Bordeaux.

When Weingarten returned from her trip, she found messages on her answering machine from Las Vegas salons wanting to place orders. Soon Weingarten also began receiving calls from salons around the country wanting to order the new nail polishes. What she had not realized about selecting Las Vegas as the site for her product launch was that people from all over the country vacationed there. Women who visited the hotel nail salons then returned home and asked their local salons to offer the new colors. Weingarten's timing to enter the market also proved to be fortuitous. Around 1983 she began noticing that nail salons were opening up across New York City, and soon nail salons were opening in all parts of the country. As a result, manicure prices began falling, and a wider group of women began to have their nails done on a regular basis, thus driving sales for Essie Cosmetics. Helping matters greatly was the recognition of Essie nail polish by fashion magazine editors and celebrities such as Cindy Crawford, Sharon Stone, and Madonna.

ENTERING FOREIGN MARKETS

In addition to domestic sales, Weingarten soon began developing foreign markets. In 1982 she was approached by someone who wanted to acquire a license to sell Essie nail polish in Japan. The products became an instant success and soon spread to Korea, then Singapore, followed by England, which became a base for Europe. The Continent proved to be a tough market to crack, especially Italy, much to the frustration of Weingarten, who twice each year made sales visits to Europe. Although very fashion conscious, most European women did not wear nail polish and paid scant attention to the state of their nails, finger or toe. It was not until the early 1990s that women there began to embrace nail polish and nail salons began cropping up in Europe.

Initially Essie nail polish was bottled in a standard container. It was not until Weingarten could prove that her sales justified the production of one million bottles per year that her manufacturer would create a mold just for her. After four years of strong sales growth, Weingarten was able to receive her own bottle. She designed a square bottle, one that nail salon technicians found easy to use. The shape also made it memorable, but because it offered no label, the bottle, and by extension the Essie product, was easy to mimic. A company called Dae Do International Ltd. did just that, forcing Essie Cosmetics

```
┌─────────────────────────────────────────────┐
│                                             │
│              KEY DATES                      │
│              ────■────                      │
│                                             │
│  1981:  Esther Weingarten starts Essie      │
│         Cosmetics to market nail polish.    │
│  1985:  Company introduces square bottle.   │
│  1988:  Lipstick introduced.                │
│  1993:  Company wins trademark fight over   │
│         bottle.                             │
│  2000:  Essie name embossed on side of      │
│         bottle.                             │
│  2004:  Ancillary manicure products         │
│         introduced.                         │
│  2008:  Esther Weingarten featured in new   │
│         print advertising campaign.         │
│                                             │
└─────────────────────────────────────────────┘
```

to go to court in 1992 to protect its business. A year later Essie was able to secure the rights to its signature square bottle.

Esther Weingarten in the mid-1980s added a partner, Max Sortino, when what began as a romantic interest turned into a business relationship as well. Sortino was an experienced businessman, but as the result of a divorce settlement, his ex-wife received their jointly held company. Although Weingarten was initially reluctant to mix business with her personal life, she soon came to realize that Sortino brought practical skills that allowed her to focus on the big picture, and the partnership flourished. Sortino was quick to realize that Weingarten's practice of selling directly to salons was not efficient and limited the company's growth potential. He urged her to make use of distributors, who could deploy legions of salespeople to promote Essie products. The company launched a second line of nail polish solely for distributors, sold under a different name, but what the market wanted was the Essie line. As a result, in the late 1980s the Essie salon business was turned over to distributors.

ADDING LIPSTICK

By the start of the 1990s the Essie brand was well entrenched, and with the trademark issue over the square bottle resolved, Essie Cosmetics prospered. In addition to nail polish, the company was also carrying a line of Essie lipstick, introduced in 1988. Salon customers had urged Essie to add lipstick to match the nail colors. Essie complied, but salons did not prove to be very good retailers. Department stores continued to dominate the lipstick trade, although Essie would still offer the product into the 21st century. The engine that drove the company remained nail polish, however. Weingarten kept the line fresh by continuously rolling out new colors and personally coining new names. In her Park Avenue apartment she kept a drawer that

contained ideas for new names that she jotted down when the inspiration struck. Like fashion designers, she also assembled the new nail colors into "collections," six new shades with fanciful names for every season. To stay current and scout for inspiration, she attended fashion shows to see what colors would be featured in the upcoming season, and she often worked in concert with designers in developing her collections.

Weingarten would also turn elsewhere for ideas. In the late 1990s, during a bull stock market, Weingarten realized that Essie sounded like the letters "S" and "E," the beginning of SEC (Securities and Exchange Commission) or the initials for "stock exchange." Moreover, when she visited the salon—for years Weingarten maintained a weekly appointment at an Upper East Side Manhattan salon—she overheard women talking about the stock market and other investments. As a result, she introduced a collection inspired by finance, with names such as Bonds Beige, Options Pink, Futures French, Munis Mauve, and T-Bills Putty.

NEW PRODUCT LINES FOR THE 21ST CENTURY

At the start of the new century, the company wanted to solidify the Essie brand and extend it to other products. In 2000 the signature square nail polish bottle was enhanced by having the Essie name embossed on the side. Pedicure products, as well as the Smoothie and Essie Spa lines of crèmes, hand and body lotions, and exfoliating scrubs were introduced. In 2004 the Essie name was applied to a five-item line of ancillary manicure products, including nail wipes impregnated with polish remover; lint-free pads for use with polish remover; a nail corrector, a tool for removing excess polish from the sides of nails; a cuticle pen to soften and moisturize nails; and a crystal nail file used to prevent the peeling and splitting of natural nails. In early 2006, lipstick was dropped in favor of a new lip gloss line.

Although Essie Cosmetics was expanding into new lines, nail polish remained at the heart of the company. Weingarten continued to roll out distinctive new collections for every season, six new colors four times a year. As ever, the lines were fun and quirky. The Cruise Collection introduced in 2005, for example, was created in alliance with The Cruise Lines International Association, designed with the pleasure of cruising as a theme and including such shades as Life Saver, Cruise Control, and Fun Ships.

Not only did the names of the Essie nail polish shades continue to receive attention and the products win industry awards, the woman who coined the fanciful names garnered recognition as well. In 2004 Esther Weingarten received the Cosmetic Executive Women Achiever Award. As her public profile increased, Weingarten was regularly interviewed by the press and also appeared on television. To exploit her image further and introduce her to a greater number of consumers, Essie Cosmetics unveiled a new print advertising campaign in the fall of 2008 anchored by Esther Weingarten. With business thriving around the world, there was every reason to believe that Essie Cosmetics would remain well entrenched in its niche market for years to come.

Ed Dinger

PRINCIPAL COMPETITORS

L'Oréal SA; OPI Products, Inc.; Orly International, Inc.

FURTHER READING

Eckler, Rebecca, "A Polished Look," *Saturday Post,* September 27, 2003.

"Essie: Nails and Nuances," *Global Cosmetic Industry,* July 2004, p. 11.

Naughton, Julie, "Essie Cosmetics to Launch New Nail Products Line," *WWD,* March 19, 2004, p. 6.

Prischak, Amanda, "They're Her Colors. The Rest of Us Just Wear Them," *New York Times,* June 22, 2008, p. CY5.

"Q&A: Liz Jones Spoke to Essie Weingarten, President & Founder, Essie Cosmetics, Ltd.," *Cosmetics International,* August 19, 2005, p. 8.

Exacompta Clairefontaine S.A.

———————————————— ■ ————————————————

19 rue de l'Abbaie
Etival Clairefontaine, F-88480
France
Telephone: (+33 03) 29 42 42 42
Fax: (+33 03) 29 42 42 00
Web site: http://www.exacomptaclairefontaine.fr

Public Company
Incorporated: 1904 as L. Nusse, E. Bodet et Cie
Employees: 3,364
Sales: EUR 546.18 million ($683 million) (2008)
Stock Exchanges: Euronext Paris
Ticker Symbols: 006416; EXAC
NAICS: 322121 Paper (Except Newsprint) Mills;
322233 Stationery, Tablet, and Related Product
Manufacturing; 323118 Blankbook, Loose-Leaf
Binder, and Device Manufacturing

■ ■ ■

Exacompta Clairefontaine S.A. is a leading producer of writing, printing, and copy paper; exercise books; notebook ledgers; office supplies; agendas and diaries; personal stationery; arts and crafts papers; and related items, such as calendars, writing pens, inks, and maps. Based in Etival-Clairefontaine, in France's Vosges region, Exacompta Clairefontaine also produces its own paper, operating three paper mills in France and a fourth in the Netherlands. The company operates through four primary divisions. Papeteries Clairefontaine, the oldest part of the company, oversees the group's paper production, including its main Etival-Clairefontaine mill and the group's other paper mills, as well as its Everbal paper recycling facility. This division also markets its paper, exercise books, and other products under the high-end Clairefontaine brand.

The Exacompta division oversees the group's production of office supply products, including folders, organizers, and storage products. Clairefontaine Rhodia distributes notepads, notebooks, drawing papers, wrapping papers, stamp and photo albums, and arts and crafts supplies. The last division, A.F.A. (Ateliers de Fabrication d'Agendas), produces agendas, calendars, maps, luxury stationery paper, and other items through subsidiaries including G. Lalo, Quo Vadis, A.B.I., and marine book publisher Interval Editions. The company also operates sales subsidiaries in Spain, the United States, the United Kingdom, Belgium, Ireland, Poland, and Morocco. Exacompta Clairefontaine is listed on the Euronext Paris stock exchange. More than 80 percent of the company remains controlled by the founding Bichelberger/Nusse family. Jean-Marie Nusse serves as the company's chief executive officer. In 2008, Exacompta Clairefontaine generated total revenues of EUR 546 million ($683 million).

FOUNDING A PAPER COMPANY

Exacompta Clairefontaine originated as a small paper mill founded by Jean-Baptiste Bichelberger in 1858. The mountainous Vosges region at that time was fast becoming a center of paper making in France, owing to its abundance of rivers, and later, to its vast forests. The Vosges region was also a major center of the French textiles industry—an important consideration since

COMPANY PERSPECTIVES

For many generations, our exercise books, school paper, ledgers, reams of copier paper, diaries, correspondence ranges or Fine Arts have become a true reference with students, professionals and the general public. Now, as in the past and in the future the paper with which these products are made is the main reason for their success. Our priority is to carefully define the best characteristics for each type of use and ensure constant quality from one production run to the next. All the paper manufactured on our four production sites receives the same careful attention to quality.

paper production remained based on cotton fiber until late in the 19th century. Bichelberger established his mill in the village of Etival-Clairefontaine. Over the next two decades, Bichelberger succeeded in establishing a thriving paper business under the Clairefontaine name.

Upon Bichelberger's death in 1877, his son Paul Bichelberger took over the direction of the paper mill. Joined by partner Émile Champon, Bichelberger converted the Clairefontaine mill to use wood pulp. The use of wood pulp as the raw material in paper production had been in development since the middle of the 19th century. With the perfection of the mechanical pulping process, particularly after 1885, wood pulp supplanted cotton fiber as the major raw material in paper production.

The large forests in the Vosges region then enabled the Clairefontaine mill to grow into a major producer of papers for the French market. A key factor in the company's success was the decision made by Bichelberger and Champon in 1877 to launch the production of envelope paper, followed by the fabrication of notebooks. The latter market had until then been dominated by the country's printing industry. With the institution of a mandatory free educational system in France, however, demand for notebooks grew strongly at the beginning of the 20th century.

The Nusse family name entered the business at the dawn of the century, as Louis Nusse, grandson of the company's founder, took over as head in 1904. Joining him was Étienne Bodet. The partners then gave the company the new name of L. Nusse, E. Bodet et Cie. Under the new generation, the company continued its strong growth; by the outbreak of World War I, the

company's payroll had grown to more than 1,100 employees. By then, the company had also gone public, having gained a listing in 1910 on the Nancy stock exchange as SA des Papeteries de Clairefontaine. World War I put a temporary halt to the company's growth, as the front came within five kilometers of the Clairefontaine paper mill. Nonetheless, the company's factory emerged unscathed from the war. Under the leadership of Leon Daridan, the Clairefontaine mill quickly resumed production.

CREATING A BRAND ICON

While Daridan headed the Clairefontaine operation, Charles Nusse, great-grandson of the company's founder, moved to Paris to found a new company. In 1928, Nusse founded Exacompta, which began printing and binding accounting ledgers from a small workshop. Nusse's insistence on creating a high-quality product enabled the company to grow rapidly through the next decade. Exacompta grew into a leading name for accounting ledgers, and under the subsidiary A.F.A. (which stood for Atelier de Fabrication d'Agendas), the company also began producing agendas and related office supply products. Nusse's operations were placed under the holding company, Etablissements Charles Nusse.

The outbreak of World War II once again brought an end to the Clairefontaine mill's growth. The new war brought even more dramatic consequences for the company, as large portions of the factory were destroyed. With the war's end, however, the company, still under the leadership of Leon Daridan, rebuilt its mill and resumed production.

The Clairefontaine mill's true success came after Charles Nusse took over as head and major shareholder of the company in 1950. Following the success of establishing the Exacompta brand, Nusse recognized the opportunity for similar success at Clairefontaine. The perfection of chemical wood pulp during the 20th century had enabled a major increase in total paper production, greatly lowering prices. This enabled the French school system to abandon the use of handheld slates in favor of the use of exercise books, featuring lined or grid paper.

Clairefontaine launched its own exercise book in 1951. Nusse again insisted on developing a high-quality product, and the company's exercise books featured a smooth, heavyweight paper, using violet inks. The company also varnished the cover, making it more resistant to wear. Accompanying the launch of the new exercise book was the creation of the Clairefontaine logo, designed by Nusse himself.

KEY DATES

1858: Jean-Baptiste Bichelberger founds a paper mill in Etival-Clairefontaine, France.

1877: Bichelberger's son Paul converts the Clairefontaine mill to use wood pulp; begins producing envelopes and exercise books.

1910: The company is listed on the Nancy stock exchange as SA des Papeteries de Clairefontaine.

1928: Charles Nusse, great-grandson of Bichelberger, founds A.F.A. (Atelier de Fabrication d'Agendas) in Paris; launches the Exacompta brand of accounting ledgers.

1950: Charles Nusse takes over as head of Clairefontaine.

1951: Clairefontaine launches its own exercise books.

1980: The company acquires a manufacturer of thermal paper rolls.

1996: The Nusse family's holdings are merged into a single company, Exacompta Clairefontaine SA.

1999: Exacompta Clairefontaine acquires Quo Vadis in Nantes.

2008: Exacompta Clairefontaine acquires Tollit & Harvey in the United Kingdom.

The Clairefontaine exercise book quickly became a bestseller in France, establishing the company's brand among the major paper companies in the country. Over the next decades, the Clairefontaine brand and logo grew into cultural icons, taking their place among the country's most famous brand names. By the time of Charles Nusse's death in 1971, the company had expanded the Clairefontaine range to include a variety of paper products.

MERGER CREATES EXACOMPTA CLAIREFONTAINE

Under the leadership of François Nusse at the time, Exacompta and Clairefontaine remained separate companies through the 1980s and into the 1990s, despite the common control over both companies by the Nusse family. The family's business focus remained largely on the paper industry throughout this period. In 1979, their holdings expanded with the acquisition of a paper distribution business, Bellegarde. The following year, the group moved into the production of thermal paper rolls

for fax and telex machines, buying Tourcoing-based Papyrus. The company abandoned thermal paper production in 1990, however.

The company invested in expanding its paper production into other areas instead. In 1990, for example, the company acquired Papeterie de Mandeure, based in the Doubs region, which specialized in the production of heavy papers. The group also expanded its distribution reach to include the fast-growing large-scale distribution sector. For this, the company formed a partnership with Reliure Sill, part of the Papeteries Sill distribution group. That partnership led to Clairefontaine's acquisition of Papeteries Sill in 1992.

The Nusse family had also begun to move toward combining their paper operations into a single company. As a first step in this process, Clairefontaine's listing was moved to the Paris Stock Exchange in 1987. The following year, Etablissement Charles Nusse, which until then had held a 49.5 percent stake in Clairefontaine, raised its shareholding to 61.5 percent. Then, in 1990, Etablissement Charles Nusse reached a cooperation agreement with Clairefontaine in order to develop a common management, marketing, and public relations strategy.

At the same time, the family continued to build out its range of holdings. For this, the group sought to expand both the range of its products and its geographical reach. The company fulfilled both objectives in 1992 when it acquired a stake in Germany's Brause & Cie. Founded in Iserlohn in 1850, Brause had become a noted manufacturer of pen nibs, before developing a focus on the production of hole punches, archive materials, and related office products. Brause also brought to the group its own distribution operations in Germany. Following the Brause acquisition, the group purchased another German company, Koehler GmbH, based in Altendorf. That company specialized in the production of stamp and photo albums.

In France, the Nusse family-owned group added its own paper recycling facility, Everbal, and a line of recycled paper products under that brand. That acquisition also strengthened the group's distribution operations, with the addition of Everbal's own distribution subsidiary, Rotopli. Rounding out the group's acquisitions into the middle of the 1990s was the addition of Sofac. That company operated under two subsidiaries, Calendriers Lavigne, a producer of calendars, and Editions Grafocarts, which produced city maps and marine navigation charts. These latest acquisitions followed the merger of the Nusse family's holdings into a single company, Exacompta Clairefontaine S.A., completed in 1996. The new company served as a holding company for the group's four primary operations, Clairefontaine, Exacompta, Papeteries Sill, and A.F.A.

FRENCH LEADER IN THE 21ST CENTURY

Exacompta Clairefontaine claimed one of the leading spots in the French paper industry, behind market leader Hamelin and its Oxford paper brand. Unlike Hamelin and most of its other competitors, Exacompta Clairefontaine maintained its position as an integrated paper company. Control over its own paper production enabled the company to maintain its high-quality standards. At the same time, faced with rising competition as the supermarket groups developed their own private label paper brands, Exacompta Clairefontaine launched its own lower priced brand, Calligraphe. Exacompta Clairefontaine developed operations as a supplier to the private label channel as well, a move that enabled the company to maximize its production capacity.

The company also completed several significant acquisitions. In 1997, the company purchased Papeteries Verilhac Frères. Founded in Lyon in 1932, that company was known especially for its Rhodia line of notepads and notebooks. Following its acquisition by Exacompta Clairefontaine, the company became known as Clairefontaine Rhodia. This purchase was followed by the 1998 takeover of Cartorel, based in Niort, France, which focused on the production of archival materials. Also in that year, Exacompta Clairefontaine acquired its first foreign paper production plant, with the purchase of Papierfabriek Schut BV in Holland. That purchase enabled Exacompta Clairefontaine to enter the market for art papers.

In 1999, the company rescued struggling Nantes-based Quo Vadis, a producer of high-end agendas that had built up its own international distribution operations. Under Exacompta Clairefontaine, Quo Vadis quickly returned to profitability by 2002, and expanded in 2003 with the acquisition of Raynard, based in La Guerche-de-Bretagne, a producer of advertising materials calendars, and public relations materials. Exacompta Clairefontaine also completed several new acquisitions, including Rolfax in 2000 and Claircell Classement in 2001.

A new generation took its place at the helm of the family-controlled company as Jean-Marie Nusse became the company's chief executive officer. A number of other members of the Nusse family were also active in the company, including Gilles Nusse, brother to Jean-Marie, who acted as head of Quo Vadis; and Guillaume Nusse, son of Jean-Marie Nusse, who joined the company around 2005.

Exacompta Clairefontaine continued to seek new growth opportunities in the second half of the decade. In 2008, for example, the company entered the U.K. market, buying Tollit & Harvey, a producer of classification materials and notebooks. By this time, Exacompta Clairefontaine had launched celebrations for its 150th anniversary. Exacompta Clairefontaine had become a leading player in the French and international paper industries.

M. L. Cohen

PRINCIPAL SUBSIDIARIES

Brause GmbH (Germany); Clairefontaine Rhodia Ltd. (UK); Clairefontaine Rhodia S.A.; Editions Quo Vadis; Ernst Stadelmann GmbH (Austria); Exaclair New York Inc. (USA); Exacompta SA; Koehler GmbH & Co. KG (Germany); Papeteries Verilhac Frères SA; Papeteries Clairefontaine S.A.; Papeteries Sill; Papierfabriek Schut BV.

PRINCIPAL COMPETITORS

Groupe Hamelin S.A.; International Paper Co.; Anglo American PLC; Kimberly-Clark Corporation; Stora Enso AB; Svenska Cellulosa AB; Weyerhaeuser Co.; UPM-Kymmene Corporation; Metsaeliitto Group; Financiere de l'Odet S.A.; Mondi PLC; Smurfit Kappa plc.

FURTHER READING

Ambrosi, Pascal, "Exacompta Clairefontaine Va Acquérir Tollit & Harvey," *L'Usine Nouvelle,* August 7, 2008.

———, "Exacompta-Clairefontaine se Recentre sur Son Coeur de Métier," *L'Usine Nouvelle,* March 19, 2003.

Béchaux, Stéphane, "Les Fabricans de Cahiers Ecrivent la GRH au Brouillon," *Liaisons Sociales Magazine,* September 1, 2008.

Beyer, Caroline, "Exacompta Clairefontaine: Le Papetier Fait Sa 150e Rentrée!" *Le Figaro,* October 6, 2008.

"Des Cahiers Verts pour la Rentrée," *Enviro2B,* September 3, 2008.

"Exacompta Clairefontaine: Chiffre d'Affaires en Hausse," *CercleFinance,* February 13, 2009.

Guilmard, Emmanuel, "Exacompta-Clairefontaine Rachète les Agendas Quo Vadis," *Les Echos,* March 18, 1999, p. 24.

———, "L'Imprimerie Bretonne Raynard Rachetée par Quo Vadis," *L'Usine Nouvelle,* March 17, 2003.

"Le Groupe Exacompta-Clairefontaine est le Leader sur Ce Marché," *Caractère,* February 6, 2007.

"Papeterie Clairefontaine 150 Ans de Petits Carreaux," *Le Republicain Lorraine,* June 14, 2008.

Renou, Fabien, "Oxford et Clairefontaine Quadrillent le Papier Français," *Journal du Net Economie,* September 9, 2007.

Van der Feer, Julien, "Le 'Papier Intelligent' la Conquête des Cahiers," *L'Expansion,* November 24, 2005.

Fishman & Tobin Inc.

625 Ridge Pike, Suite 320, Building E
Conshohocken, Pennsylvania 19428-1180
U.S.A.
Telephone: (610) 828-8400
Fax: (610) 828-4426
Web site: http://www.fishmantobin.com

Private Company
Incorporated: 1914
Employees: 2,500
Sales: Not Available
NAICS: 315224 Men's and Boys' Cut and Sew Trouser,
   Slack, and Jean Manufacturing

■ ■ ■

Based in Conshohocken, Pennsylvania, a suburb of Philadelphia, Fishman & Tobin Inc. (F&T) is a privately held children's apparel manufacturer, focusing on boys' dress wear and sportswear. To a lesser extent F&T sells young men's clothing and girls' apparel (through a Dockers licensing agreement). It is the top company in boys' dress wear and school uniforms, and is a major supplier of boys' apparel to such major retailers as J.C. Penney Co., Inc.; Sears, Roebuck & Co.; and Wal-Mart Stores, Inc. The company controls about 90 percent of the volume-priced boys' business. F&T manufactures under a host of licenses, ranging from clothing bearing the names of rappers Sean John and P Miller to well-known apparel brands, including Dockers, Izod, Liz Claiborne, Van Heusen, Nautica, Calvin Klein, Steve Harvey, and Arrow. The company maintains a showroom in New York City, where designing and licensing are also conducted. Over the years, F&T moved its manufacturing operations from Philadelphia to South Carolina, but all products are sourced overseas, primarily in the Dominican Republic and China. The company is owned and operated by the third generation of the Fishman and Tobin families.

ORIGINS

F&T was founded in 1914 when brothers-in-law Samuel Fishman and Louis Tobin opened a factory in South Philadelphia at Broad Street and Washington. In the beginning the company manufactured a wide variety of goods, including women's hats. It was not until the late 1920s that F&T became entrenched in children's apparel, finding success with boys' playwear, such as one-piece, short-legged garments sold through department stores like S.S. Kresge, the predecessor to the Kmart retailing chain. During the 1930s, in the midst of the Great Depression, F&T focused on value more than style, offering two-piece suits as well as "wash suits," made from materials that were washable in water and thus economical to maintain.

A second generation of the Fishman and Tobin families, Bernard Fishman, became involved in the business following World War II. A graduate of the Wharton School of Business of the University of Pennsylvania, the younger Fishman's tenure with F&T was delayed due to the war. It was not until 1945, after he had served in the Army in France, that he joined his father and uncle. It was Bernard Fishman who expanded F&T beyond boys' play clothing, establishing a boys' dress wear subsidiary called B&S Manufacturing that focused on private-label garments. The unit turned out suits and sport coats for department stores, including J.C. Penney and Sears. The "B" and "S" of the name stood for Bernard and Sylvan, the latter being Bernard's cousin, Sylvan M. Tobin, the son of Louis Tobin. Seven years younger than Bernard, Sylvan had joined the family business earlier in the 1950s. Bernard Fishman and Sylvan Tobin not only became business partners, they regarded one another as brothers, according to family members.

During the postwar era with its spike in population, the B&S dress wear business prospered and superseded the original playwear business, so that in the 1960s the unit dropped the B&S name and assumed the F&T banner. In order to remain competitive during this period, the company also began manufacturing in the southeastern United States, where labor was less expensive, opening a plant in Orangeburg, South Carolina, in 1964. It was the first in a series of moves around the world in search of less-expensive labor. In the 1970s F&T moved offshore, initially relocating manufacturing to Latin America, thus creating new complications to overcome—complying with quotas, duties, and other trade regulations. F&T continued to maintain a manufacturing operation in Philadelphia during this time, but eventually it became uncompetitive and would have to be closed.

THIRD GENERATION ENTERS THE BUSINESS

A third generation entered the ranks in the 1970s. A nephew of Sylvan Tobin, Jim Rosenfeld, was the first, joining F&T in 1975. Mark Fishman, the son of Bernard Fishman, followed him three years later after his graduation from Duke Law School. Like Samuel Fishman and Louis Tobin, and then Bernard Fishman and Sylvan Tobin, the newcomers who would one day lead

F&T maintained a close personal relationship, best friends since the age of 13. Mark Fishman would focus on the Pennsylvania operations, while Rosenfeld worked out of the New York sales office. When they became involved with the family business, F&T's customer base was limited to J.C. Penney and Sears. Under their initiative the company expanded to other department stores and channels, so that in time every major retailer was carrying F&T apparel.

The third generation also played an important role in keeping F&T timely. Realizing that boys' suits and sport coats were not as popular as they once had been, F&T began manufacturing twill pants. They proved successful, leading to an expansion into sportswear. In 1987 the company's dress clothing lines—the Jonathan Strong label for sizes four to seven, and the Public Notices line for sizes 8 to 20—introduced fleece wear, knit shirts, T-shirts, sweat suits, and other sportswear. All of the apparel was made offshore.

Boys' clothing had indeed changed a great deal since Samuel Fishman and Louis Tobin first began offering boys' playwear and wash suits. The days of sailor suits that came with pennywhistles were long forgotten, and the era of corduroy overalls was not far behind. Children had become more style conscious, largely influenced by television, a process accelerated by the advent of MTV in 1981; an increasing amount of advertising appealing to the younger demographic; and trips to the mall. Manufacturers such as F&T that had once made clothes that appealed to mothers then had to take into account the taste of the children as well.

Not only did children want to wear clothes similar to those worn by adults, they wanted these fashions sooner rather than later. "It used to take a year or two for styles to filter down from adults to children," Cheryl Miller, editor of trade publication *Kid Fashions,* told the *St. Louis Post-Dispatch,* in a 1989 interview. "Now it takes just a season." Stanley Kaye, director of the International Kids Fashion Show, a major New York trade show, added, "You can't design a line for Beaver Cleaver's mother and expect to stay in business." In effect, children made the buying decisions. Their mothers held veto power over price, but knew that buying something cheap that their children refused to wear was ultimately no bargain. At the same time, F&T along with other children's apparel manufacturers could not lose sight of the functional features that parents desired: wash and wear fabrics to eliminate the need for ironing, as well as durable fabrics, double-stitching, generous seams, elasticized waistbands, and turn-down hems.

In addition to fundamental changes in styling, the 1980s was a transitional period on a number of levels for F&T. In 1986 the original Philadelphia factory was finally closed, and during the course of the decade the bulk of the company's manufacturing was moved to its plants in the Dominican Republic. Moreover, in 1989 F&T opened its first operation in China, setting the stage for the eventual relocation of manufacturing to the Far East. Also of note during this time, Mark Fishman was named president of the company in 1989.

CELEBRITY LICENSING

F&T's move toward more fashionable clothing continued in the early 1990s, with the emphasis on producing clothes under the license of major apparel brands, including Izod, TFW Kidz, and Hank & Eddie. In 1998, F&T reached a licensing agreement with Liz Claiborne Inc. to produce a better casual line under the Claiborne Boys label for sizes 4 to 7 and 8 to 20, beginning in the fall of 1999. Other licenses acquired in the boys' line in the 1990s included Arrow, Van Heusen, and John Henry. In addition, F&T expanded into the young men's market. In the summer of 1999 the company added the licensing rights to the Z. Cavaricci label for both the young men's and boys' lines.

By the start of the new century, boys' and young men's fashion were heavily influenced by hip hop and rap artists, such as rapper-turned-entrepreneur Sean John "Puff Daddy" Combs. In the late 1990s the New York City–born Combs launched a young men's apparel company called Sean John. In May 2000 F&T secured an exclusive licensing agreement for boys' apparel sizes four to 20 that provided the company the right to design, produce, and distribute the apparel in the United States as well as Europe. Bloomingdale's, the first department store chain to carry the Sean John's men's collection, had urged Sean John to introduce a boys'

line, and Combs was inspired by his three young sons and the difficulty he had in finding clothes that suited their tastes.

Nevertheless, he was not interested in dressing them as young men, as reflected by the designs selected for the new Sean John Boys line. "It's a line for kids, not just adult clothes made smaller for kids," Combs told the *New York Post.* The approach of altering men's fashions to appeal to boys proved to be successful. The line generated an impressive $27 million in sales during its first year in distribution. "To go from nothing to that is a big deal in the kids' world," Jim Rosenfeld explained to the *Post.* Building on that start, F&T and Sean John added an infant and toddler line and began opening in-store shops at Macy's, Bloomingdale's, and other department stores.

F&T IN THE 21ST CENTURY

Success with Sean John Boys firmly established old guard F&T in the urban apparel field. In 2002 the company added another licensed boys' celebrity apparel line from rapper Master P, who joined forces with his son, 13-year-old Lil' Romeo, to form an urban-inspired apparel company under the P Miller brand. F&T handled both the boys' and young men's lines, which were athletic in inspiration in terms of styling (comfortable), color (bright), and materials (mesh, nylon, fleece, denim, and jersey). F&T would also add the boys' wear license for FUBU, another major urban street wear label.

By the dawn of the new century F&T manufactured its apparel in more than 20 countries in the Caribbean, Central America, and the Far East. Due to restrictions on the amount of cotton apparel China could export to the United States, F&T had to maintain a network of overseas operations. The company's office in China acquired cloth that was shipped to plants in El Salvador to be cut and sewn in order to receive easier access to the United States. In the early years of the 21st century an office was also opened in India to serve as a backup to the China operations. Wherever the clothing was finished, it was shipped to the United States through the Port of Miami. That destination would change after F&T decided in the fall of 2001 to open a new warehouse and distribution facility in an existing 283,000-square-foot warehouse in Orange Park, Florida. Because of its proximity to Jacksonville, Florida, shipments would then be made to the Jacksonville port. F&T had considered sites in Georgia, South Carolina, and elsewhere in Florida before settling on the Orange Park location.

F&T had not completely transformed itself into a fashion house for boys and young men in the new century, however. It still looked for steady, mundane, and far less glamorous lines of endeavor. Early in the decade a school uniform program with Izod was launched and quickly proved to be an excellent business, especially in mid- to late summer as students prepared to return to school. Despite such a short selling season, the school uniform program soon contributed about 20 percent of F&T's volume. That amount would grow even larger in the fall of 2008 after a licensing agreement was reached with the Dockers brand to produce a full range of tops, pants, outwear, and school uniforms for both boys and girls, sizes 4 to 20.

F&T looked for opportunities in menswear as well. In 2002 the company acquired a controlling interest in Kaikow Brothers LP, a men's and boys' slacks company. The deal brought with it the Gianfranco Ruffini license. In 2005 F&T then bought Jacob Siegel Co., a tailored coat and outerwear manufacturer. The Philadelphia-based company, founded in 1916, was owned by the Saft family, which shared a number of family connections to F&T. The merger had been considered for the past few years, with the Saft family looking to join forces with a company that was less seasonal than they.

The new century marked the end of an era as well. In 2006 Bernard Fishman, F&T's chairman, passed away in Florida at the age of 82. His cousin, partner, and close friend, Sylvan Tobin, was still living but not actively involved in F&T. The company they helped to grow for so many years faced fresh challenges, due in large measure to consolidation among the retail ranks that decreased the number of outlets among department and specialty stores. The school uniform business remained promising, and the company also hoped to expand in the men's area. Given that brand loyalties

began early in life, the company hoped that today's boys' wear customers might become tomorrow's menswear customer.

Ed Dinger

PRINCIPAL SUBSIDIARIES

Jacob Siegel LP.

PRINCIPAL COMPETITORS

Hickey-Freeman, Co., Inc.; J.A. Besner & Son Ltd; Peerless Clothing Inc.

FURTHER READING

Brubaker, Harold, "Worldly Thinking," *Philadelphia Inquirer,* June 13, 2004, p. E1.

Daniels, Earl, "Clothing Maker's New Warehouse to Bring About 200 Jobs to Clay County, Florida," *Florida Times-Union,* October 25, 2001.

Downey, Sally A., "Bernard Fishman, 82, Clothier," *Philadelphia Inquirer,* February 7, 2006, p. B7.

Gellers, Stan, "F&T Buys Stake in Jacob Siegel," *Daily News Record,* July 4, 2005, p. 9.

———, "Oh, Boys! With the Same Brands and Styles, This Younger Market Is Men's Wear in Training," *Daily News Record,* August 27, 2007, p. 140.

Gerson, Jill, "Pint-Size Kids Know What They Want," *St. Louis Post-Dispatch,* September 14, 1989, p. 15.

"Sean John Has Boys Stepping Up to (Fashion) Plate," *New York Post,* December 7, 2001, p. 48.

Sheinkopf, Evelyn, "Keeping It in the Family," *Daily News Record,* December 16, 2002, p. 24.

Ford Gum & Machine
Company, Inc.

---

18 Newton Avenue
Akron, New York 14001
U.S.A.
Telephone: (716) 542-4561
Fax: (716) 542-4610
Web site: http://www.fordgum.com

Private Company
Incorporated: 1934
Employees: 120
Sales: $23 million (2008 est.)
NAICS: 311340 Nonchocolate Confectionery Manu-
    facturing; 333311 Automatic Vending Machine
    Manufacturing; 454210 Vending Machine
    Operators

■ ■ ■

Ford Gum & Machine Company Inc., the leading gumball manufacturer in the United States, produces and
distributes its Ford brand gumballs and gum squares,
and Carousel brand gumball machines, in both classic
and modern designs, via product distributors, retails
outlets, and its web site. It sells packaged gum, hard
candy, and seasonal items under the brand names
Chunk-a-Chew, Yowser!! Bubble Gum Balls, and
Carousel. The company also is a private-label
manufacturer of confections and health-related products
for leading American brands. Ford Gum offers the vending industry nationwide a selection of machines, confections, and toys. It maintains headquarters in Akron,

New York, and bulk distribution centers in California
and Illinois.

ORIGINS

In 1913, 20-year-old Ford Mason, a roofing salesman in
upstate New York who was looking for off-season winter
work, embarked on a business venture when he borrowed the money to lease 102 chewing-gum vending
machines. Mason placed his machines in stores and
shops throughout western New York State, and he then
spent several years splitting his time between roofing in
the spring and summer and selling gumballs winter and
fall.

Mason eventually decided to focus on one line of
business. Quitting the roofing business and setting up
shop in the basement of his father's church, he hoped to
make a living as a gum salesman. However, gumball
machines at the time, a relatively new concept, were an
imperfect invention, operating unreliably and offering a
gum product that failed to excite the palate and lure
return customers. So the Reverend Mason, an ardent
supporter of his son's business venture, set to work to
improve the machine; in 1917, the Masons had their
first major breakthrough when the Reverend Mason
invented and patented the round gumball machine.

In 1934, Ford Mason founded Ford Gum &
Machine Co. and began to manufacture gum. The early
gumballs were coated with a coloring that rubbed off,
leaving the gumballs streaked, but the machines
nevertheless dispensed their product reliably, and the
gum, made with chiclé, was of a better quality than
previously available in machines.

Ford Gum & Machine had its second major breakthrough when it became the first gumball manufacturer to print its name on the product and to glaze its gum. The company invented the branding machine that could print the name Ford on each individual piece of gum. The name was printed in black on the uncoated gumball, and the gumball was then coated with color.

The company, led by Ford Mason, experienced steady growth for its first half century. Bubblegum proved, as Mason had predicted, to be a very stable, recession-proof business, and during the second half of the 1930s, the word "bubblegum" entered the English language and the American fancy. After establishing an exclusive distributor network of penny gumball machines affiliated with local and national charity organizations, such as Kiwanis, Lions Club and the Muscular Dystrophy Association, in the 1930s, the company's distributors placed more and more of its machines in stores throughout the United States. Store owners received a commission on Ford Gum's sales.

The number and style of Ford gumball machines increased, as did the variety of gumball shapes, sizes, and quantities dispensed. Company scientists in Ford Gum's laboratory invented new gum types, such as the hollow gumball, "to keep it at the same price through 50 years of inflation," explained George Stege, who became director of marketing at Ford Gum & Machine Co. in 1980. Along with other manufacturers, Ford Gum switched from chiclé as its gum base to its own manmade base. Ford's base was a mixture of 13 ingredients, which it mixed with sugar, corn syrup, and flavorings, measured from gallon-sized jugs.

CHANGES OF OWNERSHIP AND A NEW FOCUS ON GUM

In 1969 Mason sold his company to Automatic Service Company of Atlanta, Georgia, owner of several full-line vending companies and suppliers, for $1 million; he retired two years later. By 1985, there were 500,000

machines of 12 different machine types across the country and in Ontario, Canada, and Ford Gum & Machine was producing seven million pieces of gum per day. Yet the company's core product remained gum and not machines. "The vast majority of the business is products—gum," explained Stege in a 1985 *Business First* article, adding, "Machines are something we do to sell gum." There were 200 Ford Gum franchisers and a network of distributors at this time. Ford Gum also sold non-labeled gum to grocery stores for bulk sales and operated a small, over-the-counter business in Los Angeles, California.

Ford changed hands again in 1988, the year before Mason Ford died, when the Finnish company Huhtamaki Oy acquired it. Ford then became a division of Leaf Inc. of North America, a candy-maker subsidiary Huhtamaki Oy had purchased in 1987. By the end of the decade, Ford's 110 workers were producing close to eight million gumballs per day. Moreover, gum consumption was on the rise, according to the National Association of Chewing Gum Manufacturers. The advent of sugarless gums and gums that battled bad breath, as well as health-related gums—gums that served as tobacco substitutes and gums that fought plaque—drove gum sales from a $1.2 billion industry in 1989 to $1.3 billion in 1990.

Ford Gum had experimented with sugar-free gum and its not-so-popular root beer gum during the 1980s. In 1991, the company started to manufacture Xylifresh gum for Leaf. Although Ford Gum's operations were profitable under Huhtamaki Oy, in 1996, Huhtamaki Oy sold all of its holdings consolidated under Leaf to the Hershey Foods Corporation for $440 million. At the time Ford Gum had 100 employees, and about half of its business came from wholesale sales to bulk distributors in the United States, Canada, and Puerto Rico. The other half of its business came from private-label sales and production of specialty gum, such as a vitamin C gum for the health-food industry.

STEGE LEADS A MANAGEMENT BUYOUT IN 1997

Hershey, in turn, sold Ford Gum & Machine and Carousel in June 1997 to a management team led by George Stege, who became the company's president. Carousel had also been a division of Leaf, Inc., and its branded products, which included gum/snack machines and gumballs for in-home use, were incorporated into the new Ford Gum business. According to Stege, in an interview on the web site of his alma mater, the University of Buffalo, the buyout "significantly changed the face of the company. Before, we were a gum manufacturer that serviced the bulk vending industry

```
┌─────────────────────────────────────────────┐
│                                               │
│               KEY DATES                       │
│                   ■                           │
│  ─────────────────────────────────────────    │
│                                               │
│  1917:  Ford Mason founds Ford Vending Machine│
│         Company; his father, the Reverend     │
│         Mason, invents and patents the round  │
│         gumball machine.                      │
│  1934:  Mason begins manufacturing gum and    │
│         changes the name of the company to    │
│         Ford Gum & Machine Co.                │
│  1969:  Mason sells his company to Automatic  │
│         Service Company of Atlanta, Georgia.  │
│  1980:  George Stege joins Ford Gum & Machine │
│         as director of marketing.             │
│  1988:  Huhtamaki Oy of Finland purchases Ford│
│         Gum and makes it a division of Leaf   │
│         Inc.                                  │
│  1989:  Ford Mason dies.                      │
│  1996:  Huhtamaki Oy sells all of its holdings│
│         under Leaf to Hershey Foods           │
│         Corporation.                          │
│  1997:  Stege leads a management buyout of    │
│         Ford Gum; Stege becomes president of  │
│         the company.                          │
│  2003:  The company opens a new warehouse and │
│         distribution center in Illinois.      │
│                                               │
└─────────────────────────────────────────────┘
```

and we did some private label sales." The company unveiled a new corporate logo, redesigned its Carousel brand packaging, and began to focus on its private-label sales.

In the late 1990s, Ford Gum faced a new challenge as gum sales dropped. Adults consumed only about 40 percent of total gum dollars in the United States while making 75 percent of all gum purchases, so gum suppliers began to develop more products geared to adults. These included products to clean teeth, freshen breath, boost energy, and even purport to enhance one's love life. Ford Gum introduced its all-natural Ford Xtreme, a xylitol-based tablet gum, and Vitamin C Gum Balls, which it marketed to health-food stores and the health section of large grocery chains. It also signed a contract with Peelu USA, producer and distributor of natural oral health products, to distribute its gum.

In 1999, to appeal to the youth market, Carousel introduced a line of novelty candy and bubble gums that proved popular. A line of Lunch Box items included gum made to closely resemble bologna and hot dogs, while the Wallet line featured dollar bills, credit cards, and driver's licenses made of gum. Other products included gum jewels, fortune cookies and

briefcases. From 1998 to 2003, Ford Gum's retail business grew consistently.

Finally in 2000, retail sales of chewing gum began to increase again, the resurgence led by sugar-free, intensely flavored pellet gums. Revenues for gum manufacturers also increased due to the higher price points of the newer gums. Ford Gum, which had a growing number of value-added functional gums, extreme gums, and sugarless gums, saw the trend as "a reaction to changes in demographics as well as changes in healthy attitudes toward eating. … It's going to mean an increase in sugarless and expansion into extreme and value-added gum because that's where the market is going," according to Stege in the September 2000 *Professional Candy Buyer*.

Bubble gum also enjoyed renewed interest with buyers of all ages, sparked by the appearance of sugarless varieties. Carousel's line of novelty bubble gums performed well into the new century, as did Ford Gum's old staple, its gumballs in six flavors. By 2001, there were 500,000 Ford Gum machines around the country selling gumballs much larger than their predecessors, though hollow.

Competition was coming from a new segment, however. "The main competition is toys and charms," Stege explained in the *Hamilton Spectator* in 2001. He noted, "If you take a look at your typical rack, you see the machines with little capsules containing novelties." Candy manufacturers competing to capture kids' attention therefore had to come up with new novelty items rather than rely on branding alone. During the early 2000s, the company introduced a proliferation of Carousel-brand Easter, Christmas, Halloween, and Valentine-themed gums and candies, and novelty items, such as its fortune teller, baseball, and football-themed candies and gumball machines.

FOCUSING ON PRIVATE-LABEL SALES

From 2003 to 2008, Ford Gum also introduced more health-related, functional items, such as Cow Power Calcium Chewing Gum. As the low-carb craze took hold and sugar-free gums came to account for about two-thirds of the total gum market, the company also added sugar-free gumballs and sugar-free pomegranate/blueberry gum. Having opened a new warehouse and distribution center, which also housed to Ford Gum's sales and marketing offices, in Illinois, in 2003, the company was prepared to expand in each of its sales categories: private label, retail online, consumer online, and vending. Unlike Ford Mason, however, who had put most stock in bulk vending or retail sales, Stege intended to focus the company's growth in private-label sales.

Carrie Rothburd

PRINCIPAL DIVISIONS

Carousel.

PRINCIPAL COMPETITORS

Tootsie Roll Industries Inc.; Wm. Wrigley Jr. Company; Farley's & Sathers Candy Company Inc.; Chupa Chups SAU; Perfetti Van Mell USA Inc.; PEZ Candy Inc.

FURTHER READING

"Chewing Gum Bounces Back," *Professional Candy Buyer*, September 2000, p. 56.

Drury, Tracey Rosenthal, "Gum Producer Is Acquired by Hershey Foods," *Business First—Buffalo*, October 28, 1996, p. 9.

Loohauis, Jackie, "Chew on This a While: We Are Addicted to Colourful Globs of Rubbery Sugar," *Hamilton Spectator* (Ontario, Canada), April 14, 2001, p. K3.

Marzec, Michael, "Ford's the Cadillac of Gumball Makers," *Business First—Buffalo*, February 4, 1985, p. 1.

Schreiber, Cynthia, "The Gums of War," *Chicago Sun-Times*, March 24, 2003, p. 53.

Fuchs Petrolub AG

Friesenheimer Strasse 17
Mannheim, D-68169
Germany
Telephone: (49 621) 3802-0
Fax: (49 621) 3802-190
Web site: http://www.fuchs-oil.de

Public Company
Incorporated: 1981
Employees: 3,855
Sales: EUR 1.4 billion ($2 billion) (2008)
Stock Exchanges: Frankfurt am Main Stuttgart Zurich
Ticker Symbol: FPE
NAICS: 324191 Petroleum Lubricating Oil and Grease Manufacturing; 42272 Petroleum and Petroleum Products Wholesalers (Except Bulk Stations and Terminals); 325188 All Other Basic Organic Chemical Manufacturing; 325998 All Other Miscellaneous Chemical Product and Preparation Manufacturing

■ ■ ■

Fuchs Petrolub AG is one of the world's largest independent suppliers of lubricants. The company manufactures and markets several thousand different lubricants—oils, greases, metalworking fluids and related specialty products used in motor vehicles and in a broad variety of industries, such as mining, steel and metal processing, manufacturing, and the pharmaceutical industry. Based in Mannheim, Germany, Fuchs Petrolub operates about 50 subsidiaries around the globe and has

a strong foothold in Europe, North America, and Asia. The company is controlled by the Fuchs family and headed by CEO Stefan Fuchs, a grandson of company founder Rudolf Fuchs.

RESELLING BRANDED MOTOR OIL IS A COMMERCIAL SUCCESS

In 1931, 22-year-old merchant Rudolf Fuchs established his own import and sales company for lubricating oils for motor vehicles in Mannheim, Germany. The German economy at that time was in a deep recession, suffering the effects of the Great Depression in the United States, which brought in its wake a wave of bankruptcies and an army of six million unemployed workers. Fuchs, however, believed in his business. From having previously run the wholesale branch for lubricating oils of a Mannheim-based wholesale company, he had a thorough insight into this promising niche market.

Moreover, Fuchs was convinced that this was exactly the right time to enter this particular market. Mannheim, the city in which Daimler-Benz cofounder Carl Benz had driven his first *Motorwagen* in 1886, was a major center of industry and trade in Germany's Southwest, located around one of the country's main routes for the cross-country transportation of goods. In the early 1930s, most goods were still shipped to and from the city by train or by ship via the Rhine River, but also were shipped increasingly by truck. With motorization on the rise, Fuchs expected the demand for engine lubricants to grow significantly in the near future.

In spring 1931 Rudolf Fuchs and his fiancée, Irma Schmitt, who had finished an apprenticeship at the same company where Fuchs had worked, founded the business. The young entrepreneur rented a small space at the Mannheim slaughterhouse and bought his first batch of petroleum-based lubricating oil imported from Pennsylvania, reputedly the highest-quality engine oil available. He filled the "Guaranteed Pennsylvania Motor Oil" into smaller containers, resold them under his own brand name Penna Pura and delivered them to his first customers, shipping companies in Mannheim's harbor, by bicycle.

Fuchs's strategy to provide a high-quality product paid off quickly. The fact that Penna Pura kept the necessary maintenance on diesel engines relatively low and also slowed wear made it very popular among truck drivers. Soon the thriving business outgrew its workspace and was moved to a larger site. The first car replaced Fuchs's bicycle and helpers were hired to handle the growing business volume. While his wife Irma handled administration and shipping, Fuchs drove all across southern Germany to win new clients. Within only a few years Fuchs was selling his branded motor oil and about two dozen other specialty lubricants to shipping companies, farms, saw mills and brick makers in the Karlsruhe, Stuttgart, and Munich regions. Again, the business was moved to a larger site and the first delivery truck was purchased.

FROM TRADE TO MANUFACTURING IN 1936

The year 1936 marked a major milestone for the company. Using proven recipes, Rudolf Fuchs began to manufacture its own specialty transmission oils for the summers and winters. When in 1937 local agencies requested Fuchs move the operation out of the city center for security reasons (his goods were highly flammable), he purchased a new site in Mannheim's industrial harbor, where a brand-new factory was built that included oil mixing and filling facilities, a grease manufacturing facility, and a research lab. After the new factory was completed, the mass production of specialty lubricating oils from specifications by Fuchs started at the new company site in 1939.

In the meantime the enterprise continued to grow. The German economy began to recover after the National Socialist Party took power in 1933. However, all economic activity was soon put under Nazi control and directed at preparing the country for war. In the late 1930s the company became a major supplier of lubricants, such as water-soluble form oils and graphite lubricants, for the construction of the so-called Westwall, a gigantic defense installation along Germany's western border. By 1939 Rudolf Fuchs's enterprise was grossing almost one million reichsmark annually, with the majority stemming from automotive lubricants.

RESTRUCTURING THE PRODUCT PORTFOLIO DURING WARTIME

World War II started only a few days after the company was renamed Rudolf Fuchs Mineraloelwerk (Rudolf Fuchs Mineral Oil Factory). The war presented the company with a combination of challenges that threatened the existence of the enterprise. First, the company's main raw material, motor oils from Pennsylvania, was not available in Germany anymore and existing reserves were confiscated by the government. Also, most male employees, including Fuchs, were drafted into the military. Finally, Rudolf Fuchs's main clientele, shipping companies and transportation service providers, had to cut back their operations significantly and turn their fleets over to the military. Although Fuchs was freed from military duty and, as the appointed commissioner, controlled the allocation of technical lubricants in the Baden region, the rationed amount of oil his company received was rather modest.

During this time, Fuchs made the decision to expand his company's small line of specialty lubricants for industrial use. Despite the many problems he encountered, new production and testing facilities were installed and new products developed based on customer specifications. The belt transmission oil Renolit, which had been developed in-house, became a best-selling product. One important new customer was the metal processing industry which Rudolf Fuchs supplied with metalworking lubricants. As traditional raw materials became increasingly scarce, the company, in cooperation with Munich's Technical University, developed substitute products, such as emulsion lubricant substitutes.

By the early 1940s Rudolf Fuchs had greatly expanded its line of specialty lubricants, including lubricating and special greases such as Zinc greases for the furniture industry; machine, hydraulic, metalworking, and ship floor oils; different types of Vaseline, paraffin, ceresin, and wax; and specialty oils, including corrosion preventing oils, production and molding oils, and white oils for technical, pharmaceutical, and medical use. Rudolf Fuchs had become the largest independent supplier of specialty lubricants in southern Germany. Much of the company's workforce during this time consisted of forced labor from France and Russia. As Mannheim became the target of Allied bombing raids in 1943, administration was moved to the countryside while oil tanks were installed underground. One month before the city was occupied by the Allied forces in April 1945, Fuchs moved the remains of his enterprise, including staff and raw materials, to Walldürn in the Odenwald mountains.

GROWTH DURING POSTWAR RECONSTRUCTION

Fuchs found his company premises in relatively good shape when he and his sales director arrived in Mannheim on bicycles in spring 1945. In August of that year Fuchs received permission to resume business activities. With 26 employees and 2,000 containers of lubricants that he had hidden in the Odenwald and, therefore, saved from confiscation by the U.S. military, Fuchs began to rebuild his enterprise after the war.

While production facilities and administrative offices were being rebuilt in Mannheim, Fuchs continued to focus his efforts on selling specialty lubricants to industrial clients. Since the company's subsidiaries in Austria and Czechoslovakia had been lost as a result of the war, Fuchs and his growing sales staff targeted customers in the industrial centers of northern and western Germany, mainly companies involved in reconstruction such as saw mills, brick kilns, and cement and lime works.

After the currency reform of 1948 had ended government control of the market for petroleum and lubricants, Rudolf Fuchs began to take measures to revive the motor oil business. The company invested massively in advertising for Penna Pura at popular motor races and developed Penna Pura RC special oil for race car engines. To gain a foothold in the motor oil market for commercial vehicles, the company, in cooperation with vehicle manufacturers, developed a new HD-grade motor oil for diesel engines in 1949 that became an instant success in the booming commercial transportation industry.

With reconstruction moving into full gear and motorization picking up speed, Rudolf Fuchs entered the highly prosperous economic boom years of the 1950s. After two additional properties had been acquired at Mannheim industrial harbor, new production facilities and a brand-new factory were built there. In 1953, the company set up another plant in Hannover in close proximity to a large oil refinery that became one of the company's most important raw materials suppliers. Sales climbed continuously, year after year. To gain a cutting edge in the market, Rudolf Fuchs dedicated significant resources to new product development.

Among the most noteworthy results of the company's growing Research and Development (R&D) division were Ratak MEP, a water-soluble oil for metalworking applications; the corrosion-preventing lubricant Anticorit; and Penna Pura LD, a long-life diesel engine oil. By the end of the decade Rudolf Fuchs was one of West Germany's leading providers of mineral oil products. With production and sales subsidiaries in Mannheim, Duisburg, Hannover, Munich, and Nuremberg and about 340 employees on payroll, the company grossed DEM 15 million annually. The sudden death of company founder Rudolf Fuchs just before his 50th birthday in 1959 marked the end of the postwar reconstruction era.

NEW GEOGRAPHIC AND FINANCIAL MARKETS AFTER GENERATION CHANGE

The beginning of the 1960s marked a new era of massive international expansion for the company. Under the leadership of Rudolf Fuchs's son Manfred, who after finishing his degree in business administration took over as CEO at the age of 23 in 1963, the company set out to conquer the rest of the world marketplace. As early as in 1951 Rudolf Fuchs had shipped goods across Germany's border, beginning with exports to neighboring Austria and Switzerland. However, as the company established sales offices in most Western European countries as well as in Turkey during the 1960s, the export business soared. In 1968 Rudolf Fuchs set up its first two foreign subsidiaries in France and Spain. Two years later the company opened its first Asian sales office in Japan.

It soon became obvious that continued international growth required a new organizational structure and additional funds to finance it. Therefore, the company underwent a number of restructurings during the 1970s. In 1972 all domestic business was bundled together in Fuchs Mineraloelwerke GmbH. At the same time, Rudolf Fuchs KG, the limited partnership which was set up after the company founder's death, was transformed into the financial holding company Rudolf Fuchs GmbH & Co. Four years later, Fuchs Interoil GmbH was established as an organizational umbrella for the company's international subsidiaries. It was also in the mid-1970s when the Fuchs family shareholders began to open the company up to outside financial investors. The foundation of investment company Fuchs Beteiligungsgesellschaft for private and institutional investors in 1975 was the first step in that direction.

STRATEGIC FOCUS ON NICHE MARKETS AND GOING PUBLIC

The oil crises in 1973 and 1979 sent shock waves through the world economies, and the prices for mineral-oil-based products, including lubricants, skyrocketed. Rudolf Fuchs continued to prosper, but to defend its market position and independence against the

world's largest oil companies in an increasingly consolidating market, the Fuchs management kept its strategic focus on developing specialty lubricants for a broad variety of industrial uses (niche markets that seemed too small for the large players) and on achieving global market leadership in these niche markets.

In addition to establishing new subsidiaries in Western Europe the company also ventured into the Americas when Rudolf Fuchs set up a subsidiary in Brazil in 1973, followed by the foundation of Fuchs Oil Corporation in the United States five years later. Several measures during the same period further strengthened the company's market position in Germany, including the further expansion of production capacity in Mannheim and acquisitions of several Hamburg-based mineral oil product wholesalers and manufacturers. Rudolf Fuchs also acquired special lubricant and chemicals manufacturers in Western and Southern Germany, Switzerland and Spain.

By the end of the 1970s Rudolf Fuchs had become a group of roughly 30 companies with a workforce of 1,200 generating some DEM 40 million in annual sales. In the first half of the 1980s the company was again restructured to prepare for a public stock offering. After streamlining operations in France, Austria, and Spain, the public company Fuchs Petrolub AG was founded in Switzerland in 1981, to which consequently all of Rudolf Fuchs's international interests were transferred and in which the parent company had a majority vote. One year later the Swiss company's bearer shares were offered at the Zurich Stock Exchange. In 1984 Fuchs Beteiligungsgesellschaft KG was transformed into Fuchs Petrolub AG Oel+Chemie, a German public stock corporation. In the following year the company issued non-voting preference bearer shares in an initial public offering (IPO) which, from then on, were publicly traded on the stock exchanges in Frankfurt and Stuttgart.

INNOVATION-DRIVEN SPECIALIZATION AND GLOBALIZATION

The Fuchs Petrolub IPO in 1985 raised the necessary capital for the company's continued growth, driven by high investments in new-product development, acquisitions, and joint ventures around the globe. The company continuously increased its R&D capacity and continued to launch new specialty products, the foundation for becoming the global market leader in several niche markets. As environmental protection became increasingly important in product development, Fuchs Petrolub developed lubricants and functional fluids that were environmentally friendly, health-friendly, and easily disposable or even biodegradable and organic. The company launched environmentally safe oils for use in farm equipment and in chain saws as well as corrosion preventatives low in solvents and chlorine-free metalworking fluids. A major success was Titan GT1, synthetic low-friction, low-emission, and biodegradable motor oil with no mineral oil based fluids, polymers, or zinc compounds that measurably decreased fuel consumption at the same time.

The second pillar of Fuchs Petrolub's continuous growth during the 1980s and 1990s was massive international expansion by means of acquisitions and joint ventures in most regions of the world. In Western Europe the company took over Silkolene Lubricants and Century Oils in Britain in 1989 and 1991. After the disintegration of the communist Eastern Block, Fuchs Petrolub also expanded into Eastern Europe. By the mid-1990s Fuchs Petrolub had established production subsidiaries and joint ventures in the United States and Canada; Mexico, Brazil, and Argentina; South Africa, Australia, and New Zealand; Saudi Arabia and Lebanon; Malaysia, Singapore, Thailand, Taiwan, South Korea, India, and China; and Poland, the Czech Republic, Slovakia, and Croatia. In 1998 the company started a 50-50 joint venture with oil company DEA that transferred its lubricants division to Fuchs Mineraloelwerke, creating a unit with 780 employees generating EUR 230 million in sales. After DEA was taken over by Shell in 2002, the joint venture was discontinued. Fuchs Petrolub, however, took over most of DEA's lubricants activities which became Fuchs Europe Schmierstoffe. At the end of the 1990s the company began to streamline and synchronize its Eastern and Western European operations, closed down several factories and doubled production capacity at Mannheim headquarters. Fuchs Petrolub AG Oel + Chemie was transformed from a financial holding company into a management holding which also included a central purchasing department for the whole group. At the end of 1997 the German Fuchs Petrolub AG took over all shareholdings of the Swiss Fuchs Petrolub AG after the Swiss shareholders had exchanged their shares for the German parent company.

CONTINUED GLOBAL EXPANSION AND REORGANIZATION AFTER 2000

By 2000, Fuchs Petrolub had become the world's largest independent lubricants supplier grossing EUR 900 million annually. Global expansion continued in the new millennium with a special focus on the Asia-Pacific region and Eastern Europe—the most promising growth markets. The third family generation took over the reins in 2004 when Manfred Fuchs's son Stefan succeeded his father as CEO.

Between 1998 and 2007 Fuchs Petrolub's sales climbed by 70 percent, with the Asia-Pacific region and the Americas contributing more than one-third to total annual sales by the end of that period. The company had become a world market leader in several niche markets, including ecologically safe and biodegradable lubricants and metalworking fluids, metal working fluids in general, corrosion preventing agents, fire-resistant hydraulic fluids for underground mining, and sprayable adhesive lubricants for heavy open gear drives, It was also among the world's top suppliers of lubricating greases as well as of shock absorber oil to the European automotive industry.

Evelyn Hauser

PRINCIPAL SUBSIDIARIES

Fuchs Lubricants (UK) plc; Fuchs Lubritech (UK) Ltd.; Fuchs Lubrifiant France S.A.; Fuchs Belgium N.V.; Fuchs Oil Finland Oy; Motorex AG Langenthal (Switzerland); Fuchs Lubrificanti S.P.A. (Italy); Fuchs Lubricantes, S.A. (Spain); Fuchs Austria Schmiermittel Ges.M.B.H.; Fuchs Hellas S.A. (Greece); Opet Fuchs Madeni Yag Sanayi Ve Ticaret A. S. (Turkey); Fuchs Lubrificantes, Unip. Lda. (Portugal); Ooo Fuchs Oil (Russia); Fuchs Lubricants (China) Co. Ltd.; Fuchs Lubricants (India) Pvt. Ltd.; Fuchs Japan Ltd.; Fuchs Petrolube (Malaysia) Sdn. Bhd.; Fuchs Lubricants (Korea) Ltd.; Siam-Fuchs Lubricants Co. Ltd. (Thailand); Alhamrani-Fuchs Petroleum Saudi Arabia Limited; Fuchs Lubricants Iranian Co. (Pjs) (Iran); Fuchs Oil Middle East Ltd. (United Arab Emirates); Fuchs Petroleum S.A.R.L. (Lebanon); Fuchs Lubricants Co. (USA); Lubricantes Fuchs De Mexico, S.A. De C.V.; Fuchs Argentina S.A.; Fuchs Do Brasil S.A.; Fuchs Lubricants Canada Ltd.; Fuchs Oil Co. (Pl) Sp Z O.O. (Poland); Fuchs Oil Corp. (Cz) Spol. S.R.O. (Czech Republic); Jv Fuchs Mastyla Ukraina (Ukraine); Fuchs Oil Hungária Kft (Hungary); Fuchs Maziva D.O.O. (Croatia); Fuchs Oil Corp. (Sk) Spol. S.R.O. (Slovakia); Fuchs Lubricants (S.A.) (Pty.) Ltd. (South Africa); Fuchs Lubricants (Australasia) Pty. Ltd. (Australia).

PRINCIPAL COMPETITORS

Royal Dutch Shell plc; Exxon Mobil Corporation; Burmah Castrol plc.

FURTHER READING

"Acquisition Proves Painful Process for Lubes Supplier," *Petroleum Times*, March 13, 1992, p. 3.

"Alhamrani-Fuchs Marks 10th Anniversary of Plant," *Middle East Newsfile*, March 5, 1999.

"Century Bows to Bid," *Times*, April 20, 1991.

Cole, Robert, "German Company Takes over Silkolene," *Independent,* September 21, 1989, p. 29.

"DEA and Fuchs Co-operate in Lubricants," *Frankfurter Allgemeine Zeitung,* December 9, 1997, p. 29.

"Fuchs Buys Ohio Lube Maker," *Chemical Week,* May 15, 1996, p. 5.

"Fuchs Buys Parker Hannifin's Lubes," *Chemical Week,* February 11, 2004, p. 7.

"Fuchs Inaugurates Lubricant Plant in Bekasi," *Jakarta Post,* January 14, 2003.

"Fuchs Launches Pounds 35m Bid for Century Oils," *Guardian,* February 27, 1991.

Fuchs, Manfred, and Ulla Hofmann, *Fuchs 1931–2006: 75 Years of Excellence in Lubricants,* Mannheim: Fuchs Petrolub AG, 2006, 190 p.

"Germany's Fuchs Group Promises Additional Investments in Korea," *Korea Times,* June 16, 1999.

Knott, David, "Strategy to Survive Lubricants Turmoil," *Oil and Gas Journal,* July 5, 1999, p. 44.

"Pepperl und Fuchs Kft Projects Sales of HUF 1.5bn This Year," *MTI Econews,* April 4, 2001.

Siddiqi, Mazhar Hasan, "Nature-Friendly Lubricant in Saudi Market," *Moneyclips,* September 25, 1996.

Taib, Harris Iskandar, "Fuchs Banks on Quality," *New Straits Times* (Malaysia), May 23, 1999, p. 8.

"Two Oil-Based Plants Opened in Yanbu," *Moneyclips,* April 26, 1992.

Watcharapong, Thongrung, "Siam Tyre in Joint Venture with Fuchs," *Nation* (Thailand), November 11, 1997.

Geek Squad Inc.

7601 Penn Avenue South
Richfield, Minnesota 55423-3645
U.S.A.
Telephone: (612) 291-1000
Toll Free: (800) 433-5778
Fax: (612) 343-1095
Web site: http://www.geeksquad.com

Wholly Owned Subsidiary of Best Buy Co., Inc.
Incorporated: 1994
Employees: 12,000
Sales: $31.8 million (2007 est.)
NAICS: 541512 Computer Systems Design Services

■ ■ ■

A subsidiary of the Best Buy consumer electronics retail chain, Geek Squad Inc. is a computer repair service that has also expanded into serving other consumer technology needs. While Geek Squad handles repairs at Best Buy stores, they are best known for their in-home service and their unique appearance: white shirts, clip-on bow ties, badges, and black and white pseudo-police cars. Geek Squad charges a flat rate for computer repairs, including crashed hard drives, virus and spyware removal, home network set up, data backup and recovery, and hardware and software installation. In addition, Geek Squad installs home theater systems, provides gaming customization, offering iPod and MP3 services, and sets up and installs car and marine electronics. Geek Squad also caters to small businesses, installing audio and video systems, and providing

computer repairs and system upgrades, as well as network support. Beyond computers, Geek Squad repairs cameras and camcorders, and other small consumer electronics, as well as a host of appliances, including refrigerators, microwaves, washers, dryers, dishwashers, and ranges.

ORIGINS

A Chicago native, Robert Stephens, the founder of Geek Squad, was not a self-proclaimed technology "geek" in high school. Rather, he saw himself as a punk rocker, albeit one with an entrepreneurial spirit who became acquainted with computers at the age of eight. While growing up he learned several programming languages (including COBOL, FORTRAN, and Pascal) from classes he took at Great Lakes Naval Air Station. He put that knowledge to practical use as a teen when he began working at a mattress factory selling bedding. Frustrated with the six weeks it took for the front office to process his commission checks, Stephens decided to speed things up by creating a data base to keep track of his sales, thereby reducing his wait time to just two weeks. Other salespeople began paying to have him provide the same service for them. By the time he graduated from high school, Stephens had create an automated inventory scheduling and tracking system for the factory, and was being paid $30,000 a year to maintain it.

In 1989 Stephens took advantage of a scholarship to enroll at the Art Institute of Chicago, although he admitted that his decision was greatly influenced by the high ratio of females to males at art school. A year later he left to pursue a degree in computer science at the

COMPANY PERSPECTIVES

Geek Squad Agents and Installers are ready to take the hassle out of your technology woes. They have the know-how and skill to set up and install your computer, network, home theater solution and car audio, video and navigation systems.

University of Minnesota, and it was there with the help of a roommate that he found a night job repairing computers at the school's Human Factors Research Laboratory. He developed an excellent reputation as a reliable computer troubleshooter and people started hiring him to work on their office and home computers. Word of mouth eventually led to assignments with Cargill, Motorola, and other area corporations.

Three years after arriving at the University of Minnesota, Stephens had become the research lab's head engineer while growing a lucrative side business. Having lost interest in completing his degree, he decided to pursue a dream of starting a consulting company, preferably in a glamorous field. It was then he experienced an insight, as he related to the *New York Times* in a 2006 interview: "The World is dominated by plumbers and drywall contractors—the boring businesses. What if a creative person went into a boring business?"

CREATING A NAME AND A LOOK

In effect, Stephens decided to become a plumber for the personal computer world, formalizing what he was already doing on a freelance basis. His timing was perfect. The personal computer (PC) was becoming increasingly commonplace, but users were far from knowledgeable, often in need of help, and willing to pay for it. At first he thought of calling his business "Techno-Medic," illustrated by a logo featuring a runner clutching a wrench instead of a baton, but rejected the idea because he was afraid people might think he was a medical equipment repairman. Stephens also eschewed any name that included "computer repair," mindful that eventually he wanted to expand beyond PCs.

Because he wanted to suggest that the company was more than a one-man operation, he focused on the second part of the company name, turning to a thesaurus for help. After rejecting "associates" and "group," he embraced the word "squad," which led to an association with a police squad, in particular the 1960s *Dragnet* television series in which the detectives

were always dressed in suits and ties. As for the name of his squad, Stephens drew on the word "geek," often applied to computer and technology enthusiasts.

In short order, Stephens fleshed out a costume for himself and future members of the Geek Squad—black suit, black clip-on tie, fedora, and a badge—inspired by *Dragnet* and another 1960s television show, *Get Smart,* as well as films, *The Blues Brothers* and *Ghostbusters.* Also an old car buff, Stephens decided his "agents" should arrive in black-and-white painted "Geekmobiles," which were modified vintage cars or panel trucks. The first was a French-made car, a lime green 1958 Simca Aronde. In addition to the custom paint job, the car was adorned with a logo of the former art student's design. Looking for a "graphically pure" logo, Stephens settled on an oval with "Geek" in black script on an orange background in the top portion and "Squad" in white block letters on a black background below.

LAUNCHING GEEK SQUAD

The 23-year-old Stephens launched Geek Squad in the spring of 1994. Not only did he benefit from an established customer base and a rising demand for computer repair services, his Geek Squad persona and Geekmobile were eye catching and acted as a ready-made marketing campaign. Initially Stephens charged $25 an hour for his services, but soon moved to a flat fee, thus eliminating costly paperwork and the possible eventual problem of employee fraud. The flat fee would become a staple of the Geek Squad business model.

In the eight months of 1994 after starting Geek Squad, Stephens posted revenues of $45,000. That amount increased to $120,000 a year later, helped in large measure by a windfall of free publicity created by the Geek Squad name and trappings. An area business magazine first profiled the company in 1995. That article was faxed to *Newsweek,* which then cited Geek Squad in the Cyberscope Section in June 1995. Over the ensuing months more media attention was paid to Geek Squad, including features in the *Wall Street Journal, People,* various high-tech journals, and on television programs *Good Morning America* and *Extra.* Sales ballooned to $480,000 in 1996 and Geek Squad "special agents" numbered 14 employees.

Geek Squad continued to build its brand in the final years of the 1990s, becoming linked to a number of celebrity clients, primarily musicians such as the Rolling Stones, U2, Beck, and rapper/actor Ice Cube. The Geek Squad image had captured the public imagination to the extent that an idea was floated to produce a Disney movie based on the Geek Squad. While that did not come to fruition, an advice book did, *The Geek Squad*

KEY DATES

1994: Robert Stephens starts Geek Squad in Minneapolis.
1995: Local business magazine article leads to national exposure.
2000: Geek Squad and Best Buy launch pilot program.
2002: Best Buy acquires Geek Squad.
2007: European Geek Squad is established.
2008: Gaming services added.

Guide to Solving Any Computer Glitch, coauthored by Stephens and published by Simon and Schuster.

SELLING TO BEST BUY

By the early part of the 21st century, Geek Squad had expanded to Chicago, Los Angeles, and San Francisco. While the concept was ripe for nationwide expansion, Stephens was not interested in franchising Geek Squad, fearful that he would lose quality control. Instead he decided to align the business with a larger concern. In the fall of 2002 he sold Geek Squad to another Minneapolis-based company, consumer electronics retailer Best Buy Co. Inc., for a reported $3 million. It was a good fit for a number of reasons. The two enjoyed a long-term relationship. Starting out, one of Stephens's first customers was Best Buy, which hired Geek Squad to provide technical support when filming computer commercials. Over the years, a number of Best Buy employees, looking for a greater challenge, came to work for Geek Squad. In 2000 Best Buy and Geek Squad began forging a closer relationship through a pilot project at a Best Buy store in Ridgedale, Minnesota. The courtship culminated in the acquisition two years later.

For Geek Squad, still headed by Stephens, its new corporate parent provided immediate scale. In a matter of days, Geek Squad's 24-hour residential service was made available in 14 Best Buy stores, and plans were laid to roll out the service to all stores across North America, a process that would be completed two years later. For Best Buy, the addition of Geek Squad supplemented its successful in-store computer service and helped to differentiate the chain from such rivals as Circuit City, Sears, Wal-Mart, and warehouse clubs, as well as computer maker Dell, Amazon, and a plethora of other online retailers. Geek Squad also fit in perfectly with Best Buy's new "customer centricity" program and a greater emphasis on high-margin services to help offset increasingly low margins in consumer electronics. Moreover, Geek Squad complemented Best Buy's approach to advertising and marketing, targeting younger consumers and featuring hip commercials.

As Geek Squad was introduced to about 675 North American Best Buy stores in the ensuing months, the Geek Squad ranks swelled to include 5,500 "counter-intelligence agents," assigned to work the counters of their "precincts" in local Best Buy stores, many of them reassigned Best Buy employees; 820 "double agents," who primarily made house calls but also filled in at the stores; and a small group of "special agents," who worked on the complex networks of small businesses. In addition, Best Buy sought to leverage the Geek Squad brand by opening stand-alone computer repair stores, the first opening in Minneapolis in late 2003. More agents and stand-alone stores were to follow in the next two years. In addition to computer repairs, they would also be assigned to do home theater installations.

EUROPEAN EXPANSION

By the end of 2005 Geek Squad's staff approached 12,000 in number. A year later Geek Squad City, a 165,000-square-foot service depot, was established in Louisville, Kentucky. The depot centralized repair orders, the goal being to increase productivity, shorten repair times, and improve customer service. Geek Squad also opened a 24-hour computer support center in Fort Lauderdale, Florida, to allow agents to provide customer support by remotely connecting to and fixing problem computers. Also in 2006, Geek Squad turned its attention overseas, forging an alliance with the United Kingdom's Carphone Warehouse PLC through a 50-50 joint venture between Best Buy and the British retailer of mobile phones and service. European Geek Squad provided similar services as its American cousin in the United Kingdom and Europe starting in 2007.

Not all developments were positive for Geek Squad, however. In 2006 six underperforming stand-alone Geek Squad stores in Canada were closed. More troubling were charges that surfaced in 2007 that some Geek Squad employees copied files from customers' computers, including music files, personal photos, and pornography. Many of the allegations came from former Geek Squad employees. "Some agents," reported the *Minneapolis Star Tribune* in July 2007, "wonder whether the company expanded too quickly. Many of the new hires are college students who have little or no experience fixing computers, they say. Starting pay in many stores range from $10 to $12 an hour—not enough to retain quality technicians, some agents say." Moreover, they claimed that rather than take time to diagnose some computer problems, Geek Squad agents all too often resorted to a more expensive solution for the customer: a data backup and reinstallation of the operating system.

The conduct of Geek Squad agents became the subject of a court case in 2008. To help resolve some of the problems revealed during this episode, Geek Squad increased the number of remote audits of its computers to make sure the storage of any customer data was appropriate. Geek Squad agents were also forbidden to carry personal flash drives, so-called thumb drives, which could be used to quickly copy customer files. New hardware and software, moreover, limited the types of files agents could see while also permitting faster file scanning.

While implementing these precautions, Geek Squad continued to introduce new services. In late 2008 the company added a gaming set up service and parental control customization. Geek Squad Black Tie Protection was also introduced to provide service plans covering a variety of Best Buy products, including computers, televisions, and cameras. Although the Geek Squad's reputation was tarnished somewhat, in general the brand remained strong and there was every reason to believe the company would prosper as part of Best Buy, which itself looked to take advantage of a void in the marketplace created by the demise of its chief big-box rival, Circuit City.

Ed Dinger

PRINCIPAL COMPETITORS

CompUSA Inc.; Geeks on Call America, Inc.; Staples, Inc.

FURTHER READING

Carlson, Scott, "Best Buy Plans U.K. Geek Squad, Cell-Phone Store," *St. Paul Pioneer Press,* September 27, 2006.

Cruz, Sherri, "Best Buy and Geek Squad Join Forces," *Minneapolis (Minn.) Star Tribune,* October 25, 2002, p. 1D.

Darlin, Damon, "Never Mind the Clip-On Ties, Geek Squad Can Fix Your PC," *New York Times,* May 20, 2006, p. C1.

Foster, Lauren, "The March of the Geek Squad," *Financial Times,* November 24, 2004, p. 13.

Overfelt, Maggie, "These Guys Have a Cool Web Strategy," *FSB,* February 1, 2001, p. 49.

Seitz, Patrick, "Best Buy Looking Beyond Big Digital TV-Driven Growth," *Investor's Business Daily,* September 14, 2006, p. A4.

Serres, Chris, "Geeks Flex Muscles," *Minneapolis (Minn.) Star Tribune,* April 29, 2005, p. 1D.

———, "A Matter of Trust," *Minneapolis (Minn.) Star Tribune,* May 2, 2008, p. 1D.

———, "Some at Geek Squad Have Been Helping Themselves to Your Files," *Minneapolis (Minn.) Star Tribune,* July 22, 2007, p. 1A.

Spector, Robert, *Anytime, Anywhere,* Cambridge, Mass.: Perseus Publishing, 2002.

Youngblood, Dick, "Geek Squad Puts Fun into Computer Repair," *Minneapolis (Minn.) Star Tribune,* March 30, 1997, p. 3D.

The Go Daddy Group Inc.

—————■—————

14455 North Hayden Road, Suite 219
Scottsdale, Arizona 85260
U.S.A.
Telephone: (480) 505-8800
Fax: (480) 505-8844
Web site: http://www.godaddy.com

Private Company
Incorporated: 1997 as Jomax Technologies
Employees: 2,100
Sales: $163 million (2008 est.)
NAICS: 511210 Software Publishers; 541511 Custom
   Computer Programming Services

■ ■ ■

Domain names are the domain of The Go Daddy Group Inc. Based in Scottsdale, Arizona, the company is the largest domain name registrar in the world, with approximately 32 million domain names under management. On the Internet, every web site has a unique numeric address known as an Internet protocol (IP) address. A series of 11 or 12 numbers, IP addresses such as 123.456.78.910 would be cumbersome to use and remember. Instead, domain names—such as GoDaddy.com—are used to represent their numeric counterparts. Suffixes such as .com, .org, .gov, and .edu identify the type of individual or organization to which a domain name is assigned.

The flagship of The Go Daddy Group Inc. is its GoDaddy.com Inc. business. In addition, the company is comprised of a membership-based discount registrar called Blue Razor Domains, a private registration service called Domains by Proxy, a research and development business named Starfield Technologies, and the domain name reseller Wild West Domains Inc. Along with domain name registration, The Go Daddy Group also offers a range of other related services, including web site hosting, tools for developing web sites, e-commerce packages, and personalized e-mail.

FORMATIVE YEARS

The Go Daddy Group traces its origins to February 1997, when Bob Parsons, a former U.S. Marine, Vietnam veteran, and Purple Heart recipient, formed a company called Jomax Technologies, drawing its name from a road that he passed on his way to work. Prior to starting his own business, Parsons worked in a steel mill, earned an accounting degree from the University of Baltimore, and taught himself how to write software code after reading a book about the programming language BASIC. He established an Iowa-based software development company called Parsons Technology in 1984. Parsons Technology began succeeding in 1987, when Parsons and his wife, Martha, used a $50,000 loan to fund direct marketing efforts. *Inc.* ranked Parsons Technology as the nation's 11th fastest-growing privately held company in 1992. In 1994, Parsons Technology was sold to Intuit for $68.9 million, paving the way for the next endeavor for Parsons.

During its early years, Jomax offered custom web site development services. By 1999 the company was ready to roll out its first product, a do-it-yourself web site builder called WebSite Complete. In order to stand out among the many e-commerce companies that were then rushing to the market, Jomax decided that it needed a catchier name. On December 16, 2004, Parsons shared the story behind what transpired on his blog, BobParsons.me. "The one thing we knew for sure was that no one would remember a name like Jomax Technologies," he explained. "So we decided to dig in and try to come up with a better name. We worked for about a week and came up with nothing we liked. Then one day our new name literally fell out of the sky. Barbara Rechterman (my right hand person to this very day) and I were in my office. Someone said 'How about Big Daddy?' A quick check revealed that it was taken. Then I said 'How about Go Daddy?' And by golly, the name was available, so we bought it."

Parsons also explained how the company got its first logo. "I called a designer friend of mine, named Connie, who lives in Iowa and hired her to create a logo to go with our new name," he said. "Over the next few weeks she sent us a number of preliminary designs, none of which we liked. One night she and her little daughter were playing on her computer and drawing various images. She thought that one of the creations they drew that night was fun so she sent it to us. What Connie and her little girl drew that night we now know as 'The Go Daddy Guy' and after taking one look at it we knew that that would be our logo."

EARLY GROWTH

Moving forward as Go Daddy Software Inc., the company ushered in the new millennium by receiving accreditation from the Internet Corporation for Assigned Names and Numbers (ICANN)—a nonprofit organization that coordinates the Internet's naming system—to sell domain names. The company's strategy was to sell domain names at prices that were about 70 percent lower than those of its competitors, and then offer additional services. According to Go Daddy, GhettoJustice.com was the first domain name that it registered.

In 2001 operations were relocated to a new headquarters site in Scottsdale, Arizona. The following year, Go Daddy initiated a legal battle with competitor VeriSign, which had been sending domain name expiration notices to Go Daddy customers in an alleged attempt to steal their business. In June, a federal judge in Arizona ordered VeriSign to stop sending the notices.

It also was in 2002 that Go Daddy expanded its business offerings by establishing two new enterprises. These included a private domain registration business called Domains by Proxy Inc., as well as a registrar named Wild West Domains Inc. that allowed other parties to sell Go Daddy's services. On the heels of these new corporate additions, Go Daddy added a third business in 2003 named Blue Razor Domains. This new membership-based enterprise offered registrations at volume discounts. In addition, the company also established Secure Certificate Authority, as well as Starfield Technologies Inc., a research and development business complete with its own staff of software developers.

In order to make it easier for customers to pay for domain name registrations, Go Daddy began accepting online check payments for its products and services in August 2003. This distinguished the company among its competitors and allowed it to market to those without credit cards. Strategies such as this contributed to Go Daddy's status as the leading registrar of net new domains registered for three straight years, according to the firm Name Intelligence.

Heading into the middle of the decade, industry observers had taken notice of Go Daddy's explosive growth. In 2004 the company was named to the *Inc.* 500, ranking eighth on the publication's list of America's fastest growing privately held businesses. That year, the independent firm RegistrarStats named GoDaddy.com as the world's second largest domain name registrar. By this time GoDaddy.com and its sister companies had been organized under a parent company named The Go Daddy Group Inc. GoDaddy.com had almost four million domain names under registration, contributing to a grand total of 4.7 million domain names for the Go Daddy Group overall.

In September 2004, The Go Daddy Group acquired the information cataloging and searching software company Innerprise. The following month, the company announced that it had partnered with Sprint, Verizon, AT&T, SBC Laboratories, and MCI to establish Country Code 1 ENUM LLC. The purpose of the new business was to translate regular telephone numbers into domain names, thereby increasing the availability of such Internet-related services as e-mail, fax, and Internet-based telephony. By the year's end,

KEY DATES

1997: Bob Parsons forms Jomax Technologies.
1999: Jomax Technologies changes its name to Go Daddy Software Inc.
2000: Accreditation from the Internet Corporation for Assigned Names and Numbers is received, allowing the company to sell domain names.
2001: Operations are relocated to new headquarters site in Scottsdale, Arizona.
2004: The company ranks eighth on the *Inc.* 500.
2005: GoDaddy.com airs its first TV commercial during Super Bowl XXXIX; The Go Daddy Group surpasses Network Solutions as the world's top registrar.
2008: Customers total six million.

The Go Daddy Group was managing six million domain names for a base of two million customers.

FIRST TV COMMERCIAL DEBUTS

After establishing his own CEO blog in 2004 to discuss issues such as Super Bowl censorship, Bob Parsons exhibited his marketing savvy by creating GoDaddy.com's first TV commercial and debuting in during Super Bowl XXXIX in 2005. The risqué ad featuring adult film actress Candice Michelle was censored by Fox TV after its first airing. Publicity surrounding the incident resulted in an estimated $11.6 million worth of free media coverage, as well as a segment on the TV program *60 Minutes.*

Strong growth continued in the wake of the publicity stemming from GoDaddy.com's controversial Super Bowl commercial. In 2005 the number of domain names under management by The Go Daddy Group swelled to an industry leading ten million, and the company surpassed competitor Network Solutions as the world's top registrar in terms of new registrations and domains under management. The company's growth was especially remarkable considering the fact that it had risen to the top without acquiring any of its competitors.

With success came physical expansion. In addition to opening a third call center in Gilbert, Arizona, a new 270,000-square-foot facility was acquired in Phoenix, Arizona, for $9.5 million, paving the way for a new data center there. Other highlights during 2005 included accreditation to sell the .EU domain for organizations located within the European Community, as well as rapid growth within the company's secure certificate business. (Secure certificates are used to ensure secure online transactions, such as those between retailers and their customers.) In September, Go Daddy.com was named as the nation's largest shared hosting provider by the firm Netcraft Ltd. Specifically, this meant that among all of the web hosting companies in the United States, Go Daddy.com hosted the most sites.

Recognition continued late in the year, when Bob Parsons was honored with the Ed Denison Business Leader of the Year Award at the Arizona Governor's Celebration of Innovation Awards Dinner. The efforts made by Parsons to build a positive organizational culture reportedly contributed to The Go Daddy Group's success. One example of this was a focus on employee recognition. In 2005 alone, GoDaddy.com gave away $750,000 to its workers in the form of prizes, bonuses, and various rewards.

A major leadership change occurred in 2006, when Warren Adelman was named as company president, with Parsons remaining as CEO. That year, The Go Daddy Group saw its customer base swell to three million. As domain name registrations totaled 37,500 per day, the company saw its total domain names under management reach 14 million.

Growth and promotion seemed to go hand in hand as the attraction of new customers was aided by sponsorships and advertisements. For example, the company began sponsoring IndyCar driver Danica Patrick. It also unveiled another attention-getting Super Bowl commercial, of which it had to submit 14 versions before receiving network approval. The $2.4 million spot, once again featuring Candice Michelle, resulted in a 1,500 percent increase in traffic to GoDaddy.com's web site during the big game.

INDUSTRY LEADER

Positive developments continued in 2007. In addition to expanding its footprint to include operations in Denver, Colorado, and Tempe, Arizona, the company introduced a new subscription-based offering called the Discount Domain Club, which was targeted toward frequent domain name purchasers. More promotional activity also unfolded that year. In addition to unveiling another Super Bowl commercial, which the firm IAG Research dubbed the year's most-recalled television spot, the company became the broadcast sponsor of the Indy 500, via a deal with ABC. GoDaddy.com also expanded into the world of NASCAR and became a primary sponsor of Hendrick Motorsports, which included such well-known drivers as Dale Earnhardt, Jr., Ron Fellows, and Mark Martin.

The brand recognition generated by these and other promotional efforts helped drive The Go Daddy Group's customer base to the four million mark in 2007. These customers represented approximately 24 million domain names. Customer growth continued in 2008, when the company's client roster reached six million. By this time, The Go Daddy Group had also become the world's leading provider of new secure certificates.

GoDaddy.com continued its tradition of pushing the envelope during the Super Bowl in 2008. That year, the company had more of its prospective ads rejected by the Fox Network. Ultimately, it ran an ad called "Spot On," which pointed viewers to its web site where a variety of banned Super Bowl ads could be found. Other highlights in 2008 included the introduction of Microsoft Outlook mobile and group e-mail plans for small and midsized businesses, a visit to the company's headquarters by Prince Andrew, and the formation of a joint venture for the management of the domain name extension .ME.

Global economic conditions began to take a turn for the worse during 2008. By the year's end, many companies were implementing cutbacks and scaling back their workforces. However, The Go Daddy Group shelled out $2 million for its holiday party in celebration of a record year marked by a 40 percent rise in revenues. In addition, the company ramped up charitable donations, which totaled $1.65 million for the year, and continued to add new employees.

As the economy faltered, The Go Daddy Group continued to prosper. The company ushered in 2009 by advertising in the Super Bowl once again. However, this time it aired two different commercials. Beyond its advertisements, The Go Daddy Group continued its NASCAR sponsorship by teaming with Hendrick Motorsports and JR Motorsports. New offerings in early 2009 included an online mall named the Go Daddy Marketplace. In early 2009 The Go Daddy Group held a solid leadership position within the domain name sector. Three times bigger than its nearest competitor, the company claimed to have more than 33 million domain names under management. Based on its past performance, The Go Daddy Group seemed to be on course for continued success.

Paul R. Greenland

PRINCIPAL SUBSIDIARIES

Blue Razor Domains; Domains by Proxy; GoDaddy.com Inc.; Starfield Technologies; Wild West Domains Inc.

PRINCIPAL COMPETITORS

Network Solutions LLC; Register.com Inc.; United Internet AG.

FURTHER READING

"Go Daddy Defies Economic Trend—Planning Enormous Holiday Party!; Spending $2 Million to Honor Go Daddy Employees Who Delivered Record Year," *Business Wire*, December 9, 2008.

"GoDaddy.com Becomes World's Largest Domain Name Registrar," *PR Newswire US*, April 26, 2005.

"How Go Daddy Got Its Name, Its Logo (and What They Mean)," http://www.bobparsons.me, December 16, 2004.

Kasler, Dale, "Software Firm Marches to Its Own Beat," *Chicago Sun-Times*, May 28, 1995.

Sloan, Paul, "Who's Your Go Daddy?" *Business 2.0*, December 2006.

GoldToeMoretz, LLC

————— ■ —————

514 West 21st Street
Newton, North Carolina 28658
U.S.A.
Telephone: (828) 464-0751
Fax: (828) 465-4203
Web site: http://www.goldtoemoretz.com

Private Company
Incorporated: 1919 as Great American Knitting Mills
Employees: 2,500
Sales: $350 million (2007 est.)
NAICS: 315111 Sheer Hosiery Mills

■ ■ ■

Maintaining its corporate headquarters in Newton, North Carolina, GoldToeMoretz, LLC, is a major manufacturer of dress, casual, and athletic socks for men, women, and children. The company is the result of the 2006 merger of Gold Toe Brands and Moretz, Inc., and is best known for the Gold Toe brand, which since the 1930s has featured a distinctive gold-colored reinforced toe area. Other brands include Silver Toe, a step down from the Gold Toe line; the All Pro and Power Sox athletic sock lines; Auro socks for children; gt socks for women; and Gold Toe Gear socks for work and outdoor boots. Socks are also produced by license under the New Balance, Under Armour, Kathy Ireland, and Coleman labels.

Depending on intended use, a wide variety of special fibers in addition to cotton and wool blends are employed to produce the socks. They include stretch nylon for extra comfort; Coolmax and Duraspun, fabrics that allow for the release of moisture; Microsupreme, an acrylic fiber that provides a soft texture; filament rayon for increased strength and luster; Lycra Spandex, to provide support and retain shape; and Microfiber Nylon for a smooth and silky feel. GoldToeMoretz also offers support hose and slippers. Gold Toe brand products are primarily sold through department stores and sports specialty retailers, including Belk, Macy's, Dillard's, J.C. Penney, Bon Ton, Boscov's, Peebles, and Younkers.

GOLD TOE ORIGINS IN PENNSYLVANIA

The older of the two companies that combined to form GoldToeMoretz, LLC, Gold Toe Brands was established in 1919 as the Great American Knitting Mills in Bally, Pennsylvania. Details on this company's early history are sketchy. According to company information, Great American Knitting was founded by a pair of German immigrants. A *New York Times* obituary indicated that the men in question were Fritz Bendheim and his partner S. S. Stern. Bendheim was born around 1889 and came to the United States as a teenager; he was about 30 when Great American was formed following his service in the U.S. Army during World War I. Another source, the *Reading Eagle* of Reading, Pennsylvania, suggested that three German families had founded the company, but provided no further names. Regardless, Great American began manufacturing men's socks in Pennsylvania.

A decade after Great American was founded, the United States was thrust into the Great Depression in the wake of the stock market crash of 1929. Americans were then looking for hosiery that would be long lasting. Great American began reinforcing toes and heels by weaving in linen, and then in 1934, when the United States returned to the gold standard, the company decided to highlight this event by coloring the linen toe sections with gold thread. The highly distinctive look proved a brilliant stroke of branding, one that helped to drive sales without the need for extensive advertising. People would ask for the socks with the gold toe, and that description was eventually adopted as the brand name.

Stern died in 1941 and Bendheim replaced him as president of Great American. In 1952 the business was sold to Frank Bendheim (his relationship to Fritz Bendheim uncertain, but not likely his son) and two partners. Fritz Bendheim died three years later at the age of 66. The new owners took over a company that was not doing particularly well. It generated annual sales of $480,000, one-quarter of which came from the Gold Toe brand, sold through jobbers, intermediaries between wholesalers and retailers. The rest of Great American's revenues came from contract work for companies such as Munsingwear, Jockey, and Interwoven, and private label socks produced for Sears, J.C. Penney, and other retailers.

Frank Bendheim and his partners decided to focus on growing the more profitable Gold Toe brand, and began pursuing a strategy of forging exclusive distribution deals with the leading department store in every major city. To sweeten the deal, Great American also offered aggressive promotions. As a result, Great American was able to develop strong relationships with all of the top department stores in the United States, and Gold Toe became a very profitable sock brand. The power of the Gold Toe brand was demonstrated in 1964 when the Boston department store account, Filene's, decided to focus on its store brand. Great American responded by turning to the Jordan Marsh department store instead. Filene's customers were not happy about the change, complained bitterly, and soon Filene's reached an agreement to regain distribution rights to Gold Toe

socks. Boston then became a two-store town for Great American. In the mid-1970s, Bloomingdale's, the Manhattan account, moved into the Boston market as well and was allowed to carry Gold Toe socks. Bendheim and his team took note that the move to wide distribution did not hurt sales.

GREAT AMERICAN SOLD

In 1968 Bendheim and his partners sold Great American to Cluett, Peabody & Company, a conglomerate that owned such apparel brands as Arrow shirts, Duofold thermal underwear, and Van Raalte lingerie. Bendheim then ran Great American as a unit of this large parent company. In 1971 Great American began producing socks under the Arrow brand. Aside from the gold toe marking, the Arrow socks were identical to the Gold Toe socks, but they were sold by the Arrow shirt sales force, who were not very effective. In 1974 Great American took over the marketing of the line. A strategy similar to the one employed with Gold Toe was adopted, with Arrow socks offered on an exclusive basis to the number two department store in each market.

Gold Toe enjoyed its unique position in the highly fragmented sock industry, boasting by far the largest share of department store sales, but the market would begin to change in the late 1970s when Burlington Industries introduced a green stripe in the toes of its athletic socks and began putting some marketing muscle behind the trademark. Interwoven also began spending heavily on advertising, a significant departure in the way socks were promoted, to back the Sock Sense line of men's dress socks, hoping to capture some of the success enjoyed by a sister brand, No Nonsense panty hose. Because the socks were sold through supermarkets and drugstores, they did not have much effect on Gold Toe department store sales, but it was becoming increasingly clear that Great American needed to change.

Further complicating matters was the expansion of department store chains to the suburbs, which increasingly resulted in Gold Toe accounts overlapping in new markets and a breakdown in the policy of exclusivity. Moreover, in cities with larger populations a single department store could not dominate the market. Thus, Gold Toe was losing out on a great deal of potential sales because they simply were not available to a wide swath of consumers. By mid-1981 Great American began to consider dropping its policy of exclusivity, but there were obvious drawbacks to the change. The mills would not be able to increase volume while maintaining the same level of quality, the sales force would have to be expanded, and most importantly, relationships with the stores would be jeopardized. Great American would no longer be given preferential treatment by department

---

KEY DATES

1919: Great American Knitting Mills established.
1934: Gold Toe brand socks introduced.
1952: Founding families sell company.
1968: Cluett, Peabody & Company acquires company.
1983: Women's socks added.
1986: Boys' socks added.
1990: Bidermann Industries USA acquires Great American.
2002: Great American changes name to Gold Toe Brands.
2006: Gold Toe merges with Moretz, Inc.

stores, and the retailers that took on the Arrow brand, in many cases as a way to ingratiate themselves with Great American in hopes of one day gaining access to Gold Toe, would feel undercut. In the end Great American decided to open up distribution in 1982, but continued to limit the outlet for its products.

CHANGES IN OWNERSHIP AND LEADERSHIP

To grow sales further, Great American expanded its sport socks lines, a category that had enjoyed strong growth, and in 1983 it entered an entirely new segment of the market: women's socks. A line of boys' socks followed in 1986. Great American also launched the less expensive Silver Toe brand, carried by the Kmart retail chain. In the meantime, parent company Cluett, Peabody found itself the object of hostile takeover bids. In 1984 the company warded off the raiders by arranging a friendly merger with West Point–Pepperell Inc., which in turn, four years later, acquired another large textile company, J.P. Stevens & Company. The resulting West-Point Stevens then itself became a target for a hostile takeover, and responded by selling Cluett Peabody, including Great American, to Bidermann Industries USA, a subsidiary of Bidermann Group, a French apparel manufacturing concern. The deal closed in April 1990.

Serving as the head of Great American since the mid-1980s had been Don Linder, who stayed on after the change in ownership. When he died of a brain aneurysm in 1991, his longtime chief lieutenant, James Williams, succeeded him. A college athlete and chemistry major, Williams came to North Carolina to be a researcher for a pharmaceutical company, Upjohn,

but soon developed an interest in sales, becoming a sales manager at Upjohn before leaving to work as a stock broker and then joining Linder at Adams-Millis Hosiery Co.

After taking the helm at Great American, which at the time was generating nearly $100 million in annual sales, Williams continued the effort to widen distribution, adding J.C. Penney as a new retail partner. He also acquired the license to produce Esprit socks and hosiery for girls in 1991, and added a new product line, women's tights, in 1993. While Great American did well under his direction, the same could not be said for the parent company. In 1992 Bidermann restructured its U.S. operations, splitting into two groups, Bidermann Shirt Group and Bidermann Hosiery Group, with Williams taking over as president of the latter while retaining the presidency of Great American. The restructuring was intended to eliminate redundancies and help control costs. Although the hosiery group performed well, the shirt group struggled and lost money, and in July 1995 Bidermann was forced to file for Chapter 11 bankruptcy protection.

CORPORATE RESTRUCTURING

Under bankruptcy, Bidermann attempted to sell the hosiery unit to Renfro Corp., but the deal did not come to fruition. While still under Bidermann control, Great American received permission from bankruptcy court to produce hosiery under the Nautica label, and then in 1996 added the Joe Boxer hosiery license as well. Bidermann Industries was eventually restructured as Cluett American Group Inc., and by the end of the 1990s, with Great American leading the way, the company was profitable. Then on the rebound, in early 1999 it signed a letter of intent to acquire Newton, North Carolina-based Moretz Inc., a company that produced socks under the Moretz, Kathy Ireland, NASCAR, NFL Properties Inc., and Rawlings labels. The allure of the deal, Williams told the press, was that it would broaden Great American's mass market and sports specialty distribution efforts. Founded in 1946, Moretz generated about $45 million in annual sales. Three months after the letter of intent was signed, however, the deal was scuttled by mutual agreement. Both sides indicated a desire to revisit a consolidation, perhaps later in the year, but the union would have to be postponed even longer.

By the end of the 1990s, Great American was generating about $180 million in annual sales for Cluett American, three-quarters of which came from sales of Gold Toe branded products. As the company entered the new century it had to make the difficult decision to close the plant in Bally, Pennsylvania, bringing an end to the ties of Gold Toe to the Pennsylvania community. The plant, which had been in operation for more than 80 years, was no longer economically viable following the 1999 closure of its Pottstown dye works, an operation that lost its lease. The finishing work done in Bally was then transferred to a pair of Mexican plants, and other jobs were absorbed by the Burlington, North Carolina, plant.

NAME CHANGE TO GOLD TOE BRANDS INC.

Other changes were also in store. In the spring of 2002, Great American changed its name to Gold Toe Brands Inc., a move to further strengthen the Gold Toe brand and an effort to move into new retail channels. At the same time as the name change, the company introduced the Gold Toe Gear sports line, which it sold through major sporting goods retail chains, including Dick's Sporting Goods and Foot Locker. The move had been facilitated the previous year by the acquisition of assets from Ridgeview, Inc., a sports socks manufacturer that had lapsed into bankruptcy. Gold Toe also unveiled two more product lines, Auro and All Pro, which did not feature the gold toe, sold through Target stores. In 2003 two additional new products were added, Gold Toe ADC (All Day Comfort) and Gold Toe MAX, a high-performance sport sock. The products used engineered fibers that kept feet cool in hot temperatures and warm in cold temperatures.

Gold Toe Brands was looking to reposition itself as a marketing company, one that hoped to turn Gold Toe into a lifestyle brand rather than merely a sock brand. In keeping with this goal, the company developed new packaging and colorful marketing materials. For the first time in its history, Gold Toe launched a national ad campaign, making buys in such print properties as *USA Today* and *Sports Illustrated*. In 2004 Gold Toe increased its marketing budget to $4 million, five times what it spent only a few years earlier. That amount increased to $6 million in 2005 when the company launched an print campaign that played on the theme, "Seven steps along the golden path."

The merger between Gold Toe and Moretz finally became a reality in 2006. The deal was facilitated by The Blackstone Group, a private investment and advisory firm, which acquired Gold Toe and simultaneously merged it with Moretz. Senior management from both companies was retained, while Blackstone became majority owner of what was then known as GoldToeMoretz, LLC. John Moretz, the owner of the company his father had founded, was the second largest shareholder. He also became chief executive officer of the company, while Williams stayed on as president.

GoldToeMoretz continued the brand strategy begun by Gold Toe. In 2007 it signed football player Reggie Bush, a Heisman Trophy winner, to anchor a marketing campaign that included print ads and personal appearances on behalf of the Gold Toe dress sock line. On another front, the company established an online loyalty program for its Auro line of socks sold at Target. In order to maintain growth, the company also began to expand its international aspirations, needing to lower costs to become more competitive on a global basis. In 2008 plans were made to close a Burlington plant and move production to company facilities in Mexico and Asia. The U.S. operations would then focus more attention on product development and marketing. To help with the company's international push, John Moretz in September 2008 brought in a new president and chief operating officer, Stephen Lineberger, who had previously overseen the international business of Hanesbrands Inc. At the same time, it was announced that Jim Williams would retire at the end of the year following a transition period.

Ed Dinger

PRINCIPAL SUBSIDIARIES

Gold Toe Brands, Inc.; Moretz, Inc.

PRINCIPAL COMPETITORS

Hanesbrands Inc.; International Textile Group, Inc.; Renfro Corporation.

FURTHER READING

"Fritz Bendheim," *New York Times,* October 1, 1955.

"Gold Toe, Moretz to Merge Hosiery Businesses," *Textile World,* September/October 2006, p. 62.

Kletter, Melanie, "Changes Afoot at Gold Toe," *WWD,* February 4, 2002, p. 10.

Lebow, Joan, "Staying Ahead of the Competition No Easy Feat," *Daily News Record,* March 16, 1984, p. 8.

Lohrer, Robert, "Gold Toe's Golden Age," *Daily News Record,* June 4, 1999, p. 6.

Lucia, Tony, "North Carolina-based Sock Maker to Close Production Facility in Bally, Pa," *Reading (Pa.) Eagle,* October 31, 2001.

Marshall, Cheri T., "Great American Knitting Mills, Gold Toe Socks," Harvard Business School, 1984.

Papandrea, Roselee, "GoldToe Closing Plant," *Burlington (N.C.) Times-News,* January 8, 2008.

Russell, Thomas C., "No Mean Feet," *Business North Carolina,* July 2003, p. 26.

Tosczak, Mark, "Gold Toe Kicks Up Its Heels," *Greensboro (N. C.) News & Record,* June 29, 2003, p. E1.

Gonnella Baking Company

2006 West Erie Street
Chicago, Illinois 60612
U.S.A.
Telephone: (312) 733-2020
Toll Free: (800) 262-3442
Fax: (312) 733-7056
Web site: http://www.gonnella.com

Private Company
Incorporated: 1918
Employees: 400 (est.)
Sales: $100 million (2006 est.)
NAICS: 311812 Commercial Bakeries

■ ■ ■

Gonnella Baking Company is a leading Chicago bakery specializing in Italian and French style bread. Privately owned by the Gonnella family, the company sells frozen dough and fresh bread, rolls, breadsticks, and bread crumbs. The company's five facilities produce more than three million pounds of product each week.

EARLY YEARS

Gonnella Baking was established by Alessandro Gonnella in September 1886 in a small storefront on Chicago's De Koven Street. Gonnella, an immigrant from Barga, Italy, was a one-man operation initially. In addition to handling the daily tasks associated with running a small enterprise, each week he mixed dough, baked several hundred loaves of bread in a wood-

burning oven in the shop's basement, and delivered them to customers. After realizing some success, Gonnella was able to send for his wife, Marianna Marcucci, who traveled from Italy to join him in Chicago.

By 1890 the new business had grown to include two bakers and two horse-drawn delivery wagons. Six years later, growth prompted Gonnella Bakery to relocate to a larger facility at 540 North Sangamon Street. Family involvement in the bakery was strengthened in the early 1900s when Lawrence, Nicholas, and Luigi Marcucci (Alessandro's young brothers-in-law) came from Italy to join the business.

Prosperity continued during the early years of the 20th century. By this time, the company's horse-drawn wagons were making some 200 deliveries per day, according to the company. This growth led Gonnella Baking to construct a new plant in 1915. The facility, which was located on West Erie Street, became the company's corporate headquarters.

According to an article in the *Chicago Daily Tribune*, Alessandro, Lorenzo Marcucci, and Nicholas Marcucci incorporated the business in 1918, filing an application for incorporation with the Illinois secretary of state on January 14. The application listed Gonnella Baking's capital of $30,000.

STEADY GROWTH

Gonnella Baking embarked upon a path of steady growth during the 1920s and 1930s. The addition of new plants allowed the business to expand in such a way that, by the conclusion of World War II, commercial deliveries to restaurants and stores had become the company's staple, overtaking the home deliveries that had defined the business during its formative years.

Gonnella Baking celebrated its 75th anniversary in 1961. By this time, the company produced between 12 million and 15 million loaves of bread per year. Family involvement in the company remained strong, with Lawrence Marcucci serving as president, Nicholas Marcucci as treasurer, and Annunzio Gonnella, Alessandro's son, as secretary. In all, employment included several second- and third-generation members of the Gonnella and Marcucci families.

By 1968 Gonnella Baking was distributing its products in three states. That year the company selected a new agency to handle its advertising initiatives, moving its account from M.M. Fisher to Hurvis, Binzer & Churchill. At this time, Gonnella Baking was forming plans to use television advertising to market its baked goods.

A number of leadership changes took place at Gonnella Baking during the early 1970s. Secretary Annunzio Gonnella, who also was president of Chicago's Gold Cup Baking Co. and treasurer of Torino Baking Co., died in 1970. Two years later Lawrence Marcucci retired from the business, ending a 49-year term as company president and a 70-year career with the company. A new generation of Gonnella leadership was put in place.

CHALLENGES FOR A NEW GENERATION OF LEADERSHIP

In the early 1970s, a federal investigation began looking into antitrust and monopoly complaints regarding Chicago's Italian bakers. Part of the Sherman Antitrust Act established by Congress in 1890, antitrust laws were written "to protect trade and commerce against unlawful restraints and monopolies." The complaint against Gonnella was initially filed in October 1972 and was settled out of court in August 1974. In August 1973, the companies pleaded no contest to the government's criminal charges and were fined $100,000. The final judgment in 1974 decreed that Gonnella Baking, as well

as co-defendant Turano Baking Company, were not to "conspire to fix prices or restrain competition thru coercion or threats," according to the August 21, 1974, *Chicago Tribune*.

With the legal challenges past, Gonnella Baking moved into the future with new markets and products. The company began selling frozen bread dough to in-store bakeries. This segment of the company's business would eventually grow into a nationwide operation.

In 1979 cousins Michael and Lawrence Marcucci split from Gonnella Baking to start their own business, the Alpha Baking Company. The new enterprise competed with Gonnella Baking, and the new owners had their work cut out for them. By this time Gonnella Baking had evolved into one of the largest Italian bakeries in the world, producing some 750,000 loaves of hearth-baked bread per week from four plants in the Chicago area.

Gonnella Baking began the 1980s by acquiring a plant in the Chicago suburb of Schaumburg in 1980, in order to support the company's growing frozen dough business. In 1985, with Louis Marcucci at the helm of Gonnella Baking as chairman and president, the company could boast of profits of approximately $700,000 on annual sales of $26 million. The following year, Gonnella Baking built on its frozen dough business by marketing frozen loaves of bread to the restaurant industry. It also made plans to sell company-branded frozen dough and bread in supermarkets.

100 YEARS IN BUSINESS

Gonnella Baking celebrated its 100th anniversary in 1986. National Security Bank, which had a relationship with Gonnella Baking that dated back some 75 years, threw the company a party and presented Louis Marcucci with a bronzed loaf of Vienna bread. Also present was 90-year-old Fabio Conti, a relative of the Marcucci family who had begun working for the company driving a horse-drawn wagon in 1912 and still in 1986 continued to work in the business a few days a week.

The company entered the 1990s in hot competition with Berwyn, Illinois-based Turano Baking Company. The two companies, which had been rivals for many years, were focused on rolling out new products in an attempt to secure additional market share.

In 1990 Gonnella Baking introduced frozen garlic bread and garlic herb bread at such supermarkets as Jewel Food Stores and Dominick's Finer Foods Inc., following the introduction of frozen breadsticks two years before. By this time the company's annual sales totaled $32 million, about 33 percent of which was attributed

KEY DATES

1886: Gonnella Baking is established by Alessandro Gonnella in a small storefront on Chicago's De Koven Street.

1915: A new plant is built on West Erie Street that eventually becomes the company's headquarters.

1918: Gonnella Baking becomes an Illinois corporation, with capital of $30,000.

1970s: Frozen bread dough sales to in-store bakeries commence.

1986: Gonnella Baking celebrates its 100th anniversary.

2001: A Colonial Baking Co. plant in Aurora, Illinois, is acquired, adding a daily production capacity of 80,000 pounds when the facility opens in 2003.

2008: Company opens a new frozen product plant in Pennsylvania.

to frozen dough sales, a business that had grown to reach stores in 35 states. Gonnella Baking delivered its products with a fleet of 70 trucks.

Several leadership changes occurred in 1994. At that time, Robert A. Gonnella was named president, while the company appointed George F. Marcucci as treasurer and Roy Marcucci as secretary. By September of the following year, Gonnella Baking's sales were an estimated $41 million, more than half of which came from the sale of frozen dough. The company rounded out the mid-1990s with a new 1996 ad campaign titled "We bake to differ."

EXPANSION OF FACILITIES AND PRODUCT LINES

Gonnella Baking's product line continued to expand during the late 1990s. In 1998 the company added sliced breads, as well as hot dog and hamburger buns, to its product offerings. In 1999, Pewaukee, Wisconsin-based Briohn Building Corporation was selected to build a new office and distribution center for the company in Cudahy, Wisconsin. Another physical expansion effort took place in early 2001, when a former Colonial Baking plant in Aurora, Illinois, was acquired for approximately $1.5 million. Built on a ten-acre site, the 65,000-square-foot plant offered the possibility of future expansion.

The new Aurora facility, which opened its doors in 2003 and added a daily production capacity of 80,000 pounds, was the most expensive investment in the company's history, according to the March 6, 2003, issue of the *Chicago Daily Herald*. In addition to allowing for the production of 50 different kinds of sliced bread, the new plant helped the company to fulfill its role as the official hot dog bun supplier at Chicago's Wrigley Field baseball park and the new Miller Park stadium in Milwaukee. The deals, both of which were forged during the early 2000s, gave Gonnella Baking the ability to sell buns to some six million fans.

By 2003 the company also supplied buns to Chicago's United Center arena and a number of TGI Friday's restaurants. Gonnella Baking's family leadership had grown to span four generations and included President Lou Gonnella, Chief Financial Officer George Marcucci, Secretary Nick Marcucci, and Vice-President of Sales Paul Gonnella. In all, Gonnella or Marcucci family members comprised an estimated 10 percent of the company's 400-member workforce. Together, they contributed to an organization that recorded estimated sales of $90 million in 2003.

In addition to the new Aurora facility, Gonnella Baking by this time was operating three other Chicago-area plants, including the location in Schaumburg, Illinois (responsible for frozen dough and bread), its headquarters site in Chicago's West Town area (which produced French and Italian bread), and a facility for sliced bread and buns on the city's South Side, which was slated as a potential new location for research and development activities, following the relocation of sliced bread and bun production to Aurora.

In 2004 Gonnella Baking secured another major deal to supply its buns when it became the official hot dog bun supplier at Chicago's U.S. Cellular Field, home to the Chicago White Sox baseball team. After surviving the low-carbohydrate diet craze that swept the nation, by 2005 hot dog and hamburger buns had become Gonnella Baking's top category. However, the demand for healthier choices led the company to begin offering new products such as whole-grain breads. At this time, Gonnella Baking also began delivering bread directly to Jewel and Dominick's supermarkets, instead of shipping the bread to the supermarkets' warehouses. The new system improved freshness.

An important leadership change occurred in January 2006 when 58-year-old George F. Marcucci was promoted from corporate treasurer to president. However, Marcucci died in November of that year after a two-year struggle with cancer. Succeeding him was second cousin Nicholas Marcucci, who had begun working for the company on a part-time basis as a teenager some 30 years before.

By 2007 Gonnella Baking produced more than three million pounds of product weekly. That year, the company embarked upon its first major expansion effort outside of the Chicago area with the construction of a fifth plant in Hazelton, Pennsylvania. To support the growing size and complexity of its operation, AT&T Inc. was selected to provide local network and data services at all of the company's facilities. "We may be in a 90-year-old building, but now that we have global customers, it is time for us to have a sophisticated communications and data network system to help us better serve all of our customers, no matter how big or small," Vice-President of Sales and Marketing Thomas Marcucci explained in a June 5, 2007, *PR Newswire* release.

Family involvement at Gonnella Baking remained strong in 2008, with some 33 family members working for the business. While this was a point of pride, the scenario had always presented certain challenges. Commenting on this in the March 6, 2003, issue of the *Chicago Daily Herald,* then Vice-President of Sales Paul Gonnella said: "We all don't agree all the time. We all have different business philosophies. But in the end we know we've been blessed with an opportunity here." In the same article, Paul Gonnella described the advice he offered to family members when they first joined the business, which his grandfather had conveyed to him

years before. "Hopefully we'll be in the business another hundred years. This is a fantastic start, but you can't take it for granted."

Paul R. Greenland

PRINCIPAL COMPETITORS

Heinemann's Bakeries; Interstate Bakeries Corporation; Sara Lee Food & Beverage.

FURTHER READING

Cha, Tina, "Gonnella Baking Co. Broadens Its Horizons," *Chicago Daily Herald,* March 6, 2003.

Cleaver, Joanne, "Gonnella Reaches for Slice of Fresh-Frozen Bread," *Crain's Chicago Business,* March 24, 1986.

Crown, Judith, "Breaking with Bread: Rival Italian Bakers Seek Dough in Pasta, Frozen Food," *Crain's Chicago Business,* November 12, 1990, p. 19.

"Gonnella Baking Company Selects AT&T for Expanded Communications Network," *PR Newswire,* June 5, 2007.

Mikuys, Kim, "Gonnella Hits Home Run with Cubs," *Chicago Daily Herald,* April 13, 2000, p. 1.

"New Incorporations," *Chicago Daily Tribune,* January 15, 1918.

"A 75th Anniversary," *Chicago Daily Tribune,* September 29, 1961.

"2 Bread Firms Vow They Won't Fix Prices," *Chicago Tribune,* August 21, 1974.

Grendene S.A.

———————— ■ ————————

Avenue Pimentel Gomes 214 Expectativa
Sobral, Ceará 62040-050
Brazil
Telephone: (55 54) 2109-9000
Fax: (55 54) 2109-9998
Web site: http://www.grendene.com.br

Public Company
Incorporated: 1971
Employees: 23,290
Sales: BRL 1.53 billion ($784.62 million) (2007)
Stock Exchanges: São Paulo
Ticker Symbol: GRND
NAICS: 316211 Rubber and Plastics Footwear
    Manufacturing; 325211 Plastics Material and Resin
    Manufacturing

■ ■ ■

Grendene S.A., a Brazilian company, is one of the largest manufacturers of synthetic footwear in the world. It is the leading producer of sandals in the world and the leading world consumer of flexible PVC (polyvinyl chloride), of which it has 70 different formulations. The company owns exclusive proprietary technology for the production of footwear based on injected thermoplastic PVC and EVA (ethylene vinyl acetate) and has its own factory for the production of PVC. Grendene's main objective is to cover Brazil's nearly 400 million feet, but its footwear is also sold in more than 90 other countries. Its brand names include Grendha, Melissa, Ipanema, Ilhabela, Rider, and Grendene Kids.

PLASTIC COVERINGS FOR JUGS AND FEET

Grendene was founded in 1971 by twin brothers Alexandre and Pedro Grendene Bartelle. Their grandfather had decided to replace with plastic netting his company's product, a straw covering for the five-liter jugs of wine produced in the mountainous part of the state of Rio Grande do Sul. With three employees he and his grandsons began making the netting in Farroupilha, a small town that was to remain the site of a Grendene factory. In 1975, they started to make plastic parts for agricultural implements and machinery.

By 1977 the company was making plastic footwear parts such as soles and heels. It was the first to employ polyamide as the raw material for shoe components. "When we began to manufacture these, I realized it would be possible to manufacture the whole shoe," Pedro Grendene later told Julia Michaels for an *Advertising Age* article. In 1979 Grendene marketed its first successful shoe, under the brand name Melissa Aranha, by introducing Nuar, a plastic sole that was attached to cloth strips tied around the ankles.

This style, dating to ancient Rome, was still being employed by fishermen when Pedro observed them on the Riviera. "The product was new, suited to the Brazilian summer, sensual and innovative," he told Michaels, "and the marketing involved a level of advertising investment which, for a plastic shoe company, was unheard of at the time." An added bonus was the appearance of the Melissa-shod actress Sonia Braga—later to become an international film star—in the television serial drama

COMPANY PERSPECTIVES

To create products with a Brazilian profile, the inspiration sources are the streets, the eight thousand kilometers of white sand coastline, the tropical culture, and the needs and desires of millions of Brazilians. To create products with an international success, the inspiration sources are the world marketplace. Therefore the travel and the fashion research are unending.

Dancing Days. In 1980 Grendene opened another plant to manufacture its own molds for footwear production.

In 1983 Grendene began to hire famous shoe designers such as Jean-Paul Gaultier, Thierry Mugler, Jacqueline Jacobson, and Elisabeth De Seneville to create designs for the Melissa line. By the end of 1984, aided by incentives that had been extended to Brazilian exporters the previous decade, Grendene was exporting its footwear to 62 countries and had sued more than 40 companies around the world for stealing its designs. Producing 150,000 pairs per day, it claimed half of Brazil's market for plastic sandals. Some four million pairs were sold in the United States that year under the brand name Grendha, at an average price of $16 each.

Grendene unveiled its first line for girls in 1984, when it introduced the Melissinha line. Also that year, the company began to produce children's shoes under license for Disney and other companies marketing footwear featuring commercial characters such as Barbie. In 1986 Grendene introduced the Rider line for men, an after sports sandal. Company sales then came to more than $40 million a year. The twin brothers enjoyed their success to the full. They bought cattle ranches, hotels, and other businesses; drove racing cars; and made the rounds of their properties in two Lear jets and a Seneca propeller plane.

BIRTH AND DEVELOPMENT OF THE JELLY

By this time the Grendene brothers were onto something even bigger: the Cristal-brand transparent sandals that came to be known as "jellies." Introduced for the Brazilian summer beginning in October 1986, the sandals came in a variety of colors and four designer name versions, each under its own label and supported by its own advertising campaign. Two months later, Grendene added its Mutation Cristal line, basically the

same sandal but with its own larger distribution network and advertising campaign. For the Brazilian version of winter, the company was ready with a plastic boot that partly covered the jelly with patterned cloth and that also sported holes, fringes, and other decorative touches. Jellies later came under the Melissa brand.

In 1990 Grendene opened its first factory in poverty-plagued northeastern Brazil, where wages were considerably lower than in the relatively prosperous south. This plant in Fortaleza, Ceará, was joined in 1993 by another one in Sobral in the same state. Grendene also received tax benefits for locating in the northeast, which, in addition, was closer to international markets. In 1997 the company opened its third Ceará plant, which was dedicated to manufacturing EVA (ethylene vinyl acetate) footwear. By 2001 there were nine Grendene plants in Ceará. Although Brazil ranked third in the world in shoe production, lower costs were essential to footwear companies such as Grendene because of Chinese competition at the lower end of the market, both in Brazil and abroad.

Grendene formed an alliance in Brazil with Reebok International Ltd. in 1992 to produce the only Reebok shoes made in Latin America at the time. Four years later, Grendene signed an agreement with Reebok de México S.A. de C.V. to open a sneaker factory in the Mexican state of Guanajuato. Grendene took a majority stake in the venture, became proprietor of the plant and sold its production to Reebok, which in this way eliminated the 35 percent tariff it was paying to import its Asian-made sneakers into Mexico.

INTERNATIONAL SUCCESS

Jellies had a revival in the United States in the mid-1990s as part of a retro look championed by such fashion designers as Donna Karan, Patrick Cox, and Stephane Kelian. In 1995 the company introduced a high heeled style for Kelian, and the following year three different such styles for Cox. These jellies, under the Grendha label, were being supplied to U.S. retailers for about $13 a pair. Grendha was also the U.S. distributor for Grendene's unbranded jellies to U.S. chains such as Wal-Mart, Kmart, and Payless shoe stores. Grendene was also exporting plastic beach sandals to the United States as well as to Europe and other South American countries. When German supermodel Claudia Schiffer arrived in Rio de Janeiro in 1996 to pose in Melissa-brand jellies, she earned a reported $500,000 for three days during which she appeared in a fashion show, was photographed for a print advertisement, and was filmed for a television commercial.

Within Brazil, the company's Rider sports sandals were its most popular footwear. This product imitated

KEY DATES

1971: Grendene is founded as a plastic netting manufacturer.

1979: The company markets its first successful footwear product, a plastic sandal with the brand name Melissa.

1986: Grendene introduces Rider, an after sports sandal originally for men; the company also introduces its widely successful Cristal-brand transparent "jelly" sandal.

1990: Grendene opens the first of several plants in Brazil's poverty-stricken northeast.

2000: The company holds about four-fifths of the Brazilian market for plastic-injected sandals.

2001: Model Gisele Bündchen launches a new Grendene beach sandal, Ipanema.

2004: Grendene makes its initial public offering of stock, on the São Paulo exchange.

2007: Grendene is producing about one-sixth of the footwear made in Brazil.

features of Nike's air-injection sneakers, making Rider sandals lighter and more comfortable than similar footwear by competitors. Grendene's advertising agency, W/Brasil, was promoting Rider with the slogan, "Give your feet a holiday." Famous Brazilian soccer players, as well as tennis star Gustavo (Guga) Kuerten, endorsed the product.

Grendene was Brazil's major exporter of footwear in 2000, selling abroad about one-fifth of the 80 million pairs it produced. Some of these were for such recognized brands as Calvin Klein, Ralph Lauren, and Donna Karen. In Brazil it held about 80 percent of the market for plastic-injected sandals. The company was in the process of unveiling a new sandal with leather toes, featuring Sharon Stone in its advertising campaign. Nearly one-tenth of Grendene's revenues of $330 million in 2000 was devoted to marketing and $10 million to developing new products and technology.

GRENDENE IN THE 21ST CENTURY

In 2001, Grendene launched a new beach sandal, Ipanema, featuring Nordic blonde-tressed model Gisele Bündchen in what became an annual campaign. After she told the press that she wished to show more tattoos than the tiny star on her wrist, a new Grendene concept was born for 2006. In a television and film commercial,

according to Laurel Wentz of *Advertising Age,* "Gisele's nude body slowly becomes a canvas for the beauty of Brazil as delicate tattoos of toucans and butterflies and other flora and fauna spread along her curves to seductive music from the W/Brasil-produced CD Slow Motion Bossa Nova." Some 700,000 pairs were sold that year.

The 2007 campaign, devoted to publicizing indigenous culture and the need for environmental protection, found Bündchen in front of Madrid's Prado Museum in a feathered headdress, beaded necklace, and little else, in order to promote Ipanema sandals decorated by Xingu Indians. They were being sold in European department stores for about $30. About 700,000 pairs were sold in 2006.

Grendene had even bigger plans for the Melissa brand. Rival company São Paulo Alpargatas S.A. had earlier scored a sensational success with its plastic Havaiana thong sandal, or flip-flop. Adopted by Hollywood movie stars, the once-humble Havaiana even came in luxury versions, one of which was encrusted with Swarovski crystals, another with white gold. In 2005 Grendene launched similar Melissa flip-flops conceived by such internationally recognized designers and stylists as Karim Rashid, Judy Blame, Romero Britto, the Campana brothers, and Alexandre Herchcovitch. Some 200,000 pairs were sold in 2006, and by early 2007 these sandals could be found in about 500 points of sale outside Brazil for about $75 per pair. Within Brazil, the Melissa line was featuring two sandal-inspired pumps—one with a low heel, the other with a high wedge sole—by Herchcovitch.

Melissa-brand jellies were relaunched in the United States in 2006, and Grendene also offered jelly-style watches, handbags, earrings, and other accessories employing the company's proprietary technologies for injected thermoplastic and adding color to formed plastic items. By this time, the Melissa line included more than 20 other styles of shoes, plus a range of other accessories. Most of these were designed by Edson Matsuo, but twice a year guest designers such as Blame, Herchcovitch, Zaha Hadid, and Vivienne Westwood were being asked to create new styles for the line. Wholesale prices in the United States in 2007 ranged from $15.30 for the basic flip-flop to $200 for sandals covered with Swarovski crystals.

GOING PUBLIC

The Rider brand, by this time marketed for women as well as men, was available in more than 70 countries. Four sandal models with top straps were available in the United States in 2005 at suggested retail prices ranging from $20 to $35. The Mirage model for women was a thong sandal with a textured sole. Rider was also offering nine sneaker or running-shoe models in the United States at suggested retail prices ranging from $80 to $130. The company was also producing Grendene Kids, leader in its markets with about 30 lines in the children's market and licenses to produce brands such as Disney, Barbie, Hot Wheels, and Marvel. Ilhabela, a brand aimed at adolescent girls, was introduced in 2006.

In 2004 Grendene issued the first independent public offering of stock by a Brazilian footwear company. Some 17 percent of its shares were sold for a total of $187 million, but they failed to regain their initial value in the next few years. Company sales fell 12 percent in 2005 and did not reach the 2004 level again until 2007. Moreover, investors were disturbed by what one broker called a lack of transparency in communicating with investors. The number of Grendene shares held by public stockholders rose to 25 percent before the end of 2007, in keeping with a requirement of the São Paulo stock exchange.

Of Grendene's gross revenues of BRL 1.53 billion ($785 million) in 2007, Brazil accounted for 85 percent. Some 146 million pairs of footwear were produced, about 17 percent of Brazil's production and more than any other manufacturer. The company had 12 factories in five locations; the factory in Sobral consisted of seven units. Grendene also maintained a molding unit.

Grendene's competition included not only São Paulo Alpargatas, but also Vulcabrás S.A., whose chairman and chief executive officer was Pedro Grendene, vice-president and vice-chairman of Grendene. Twin brother Alexandre was chairman and chief executive officer of Grendene and vice-president and vice-chairman of Vulcabrás, which started out as a rubber company tied to Grendene but later entered into the manufacture and sale of footwear, sportswear, and other related items. Vulcabrás was Brazil's second largest athletic footwear manufacturer in 1992, when it introduced the Puma brand under license there. The company became independent under Pedro's direction in 1997.

Despite their identical genes, the two brothers maintained different lifestyles. Alexandre had seven children by seven women before marrying another woman in 2000, and he drove expensive sports cars, such as a Mercedes SLR that cost him almost a million dollars. Pedro led a much quieter life. Alexandre did not discourage speculation that Grendene and Vulcabrás might merge. In 2007 Alexandre owned about 40 percent of Grendene's stock, while Pedro owned about 20 percent.

Robert Halasz

PRINCIPAL SUBSIDIARIES

MHL Calçados Ltda.; Saddle Calzados S.A. (Argentina, 95%,); Saddle Corp. S.A. (Uruguay).

PRINCIPAL COMPETITORS

Calçados Azaléia S.A.; São Paulo Alpargatas S.A.; Vulcabrás S.A.

FURTHER READING

Carvalho, Denise, "Dois irmãos contra a China," *Exame,* August 1, 2007, pp. 60–61.

Duarte, Soraia, "El mundo a sus pies," *AméricaEconomía,* May 3, 2001, pp. 28–29.

Eveleigh, Robin, "Flip-flops Get to the Soul of the Nation," *Financial Times,* November 21, 1999, Weekend Supplement, p. 9.

Kepp, Michael, "Grendene Eyes New Expansion with IPO," *Footwear News,* November 8, 2004, p. 4.

———, "Jelly Jubilation," *Footwear News,* February 12, 1996, p. 52.

———, "Reebok Opens Path to Brazilian Sales," *Footwear News,* January 4, 1993, p. 8.

———, "Vulcabras Is Launching Puma Brand in Brazil," *Footwear News,* November 20, 1993, p. 24.

———, "Women in Rio Embracing Designer Plastic," *Footwear News,* August 26, 2004, p. 13.

Lima, Samantha, "O mercado não esqueceu," *Exame,* January 30, 2008, pp. 48–49.

McCurry, Patrick, "China Pinches Brazilian Shoe Exporters," *Financial Times,* December 13, 1994, p. 4.

Michaels, Julia, "Brazilian Marketer Tries to Stamp Out Imitations," *Advertising Age,* December 12, 1984, p. 18.

Naiditch, Suzana, "Nos passos das Havaianas," *Exame,* March 14, 2007, pp. 62–63.

Penteado, Claudia, "Grendene," *Advertising Age International,* December 1996, p. 14.

"Running with the 'After Sport' Craze," *Footwear Business,* November 2004, pp. 16–18, 20.

"Tendrá México fábrica Reebok," *El Norte* (Monterrey, Mexico), November 21, 1996, p. 5.

Wentz, Laurel, "Marketer: Grendene," *Advertising Age,* October 10, 2005, p. 12.

Williamson, Rusty, "Jellies Roll," *WWD,* October 4, 2007, p. 36S.

Groupe Ares S.A.

BP 390, 3-9 Ave. de Norvege
Courtaboeuf, F-91959 1 cedex
France
Telephone: (33 01) 69 86 60 00
Fax: (33 01) 69 28 19 18
Web site: http://www.ares.fr

Public Company
Incorporated: 1985 as GTI
Employees: 1,150
Sales: EUR 140 million ($175 million) (2008)
Stock Exchanges: Euronext Paris
Ticker Symbol: ARE
NAICS: 541512 Computer Systems Design Services;
    511210 Software Publishers

■ ■ ■

Groupe Ares S.A. is a French information technology (IT) company operating in three primary areas: IT services; Systems Integration Testing (SIT) services; and Business Management Support Solutions, focused particularly on the Arcole 3G software suite. Through its IT Services division, ARES provides IT architecture support and services, including data processing, backing, storage, tracking; systems resource optimization; consulting and software development and management services; and outsourcing services. The SIT division provides enterprise resource planning (ERP), building information management (BIM), and product lifecycle management (PLM) support, as well specialized systems integration services for the construction and industrial sectors.

The company's Software division is the exclusive provider of implementation and support services for the Arcole 3G business management software package. Ares was placed under bankruptcy protection in July 2008. It has trimmed down its operations, reducing its workforce from more than 2,000 to 1,150, and its annual revenues from a peak of nearly EUR 475 million to just EUR 140 million in 2009. Architect of this reorganization is Michael Berjamin, CEO and chairman. Groupe Ares is listed on the Euronext Paris Stock Exchange.

FOUNDING A FRENCH IT FLAGSHIP IN 1985

Maurice Bourlier counted among the pioneers of the French IT services sector. Born in 1946, Bourlier earned a master's degree in computer technology, and later earned a diploma from France's Institut National de Controle de Gestion as well. Bourlier's first job was for the Flammarion publishing house. In 1972, however, he joined Sincro, an earlier IT subsidiary of the Crédit Agricole bank. By 1976 Bourlier had risen to the post of adjunct to the managing director.

However, Bourlier's interest soon turned to entrepreneurship. In 1976 he launched his own company, called Seric, which became one of the first in France to specialize in providing software engineering and other information technology services. By the end of the decade, Bourlier had sold Seric to the fast-growing Anglo-French IT services group, SEMA. Bourlier remained with SEMA, taking the chief executive spot of several of that company's subsidiaries over the next five years.

COMPANY PERSPECTIVES

Over the years ARES has developed true mastery of and expertise in the various technological components of computer architecture. Our unique, cross-functional product line differentiates us and creates synergies for us. It emphasizes the readiness of the Group to combine value-added services with it as a regular matter. ARES has also developed an end-user approach which improves our understanding of customers' expectations, both technical and operating. In this way the Group demonstrates its ability to assist customers in choosing the solutions most suitable to their line of work and to provide a logically consistent information system. This technological expertise, recognized as it is by our customers and our partners, makes ARES the standard-setter in its market.

By the mid-1980s Bourlier sought his next entrepreneurial challenge. During the early years of Seric, Bourlier had built a relationship with one of the United States' fast-growing computing powerhouses, Hewlett-Packard (HP). When HP readied the launch of a new generation of servers, Bourlier became the first to receive a contract to distribute the servers for the French market. For this Bourlier founded a new company, GTI (for Groupement des Techniques Informatiques), which formed the basis of the Ares group. Over the next several years, GTI established itself as France's, and later Europe's, leading HP reseller.

Bourlier soon recognized the potential for developing operations beyond computer system reselling. In 1987 Bourlier merged GTI with Cogelog, a company founded in 1976 by Yann Cordell, creating Ares. Cogelog had been an early developer of "progiciels"— the French neologism, combining the French "professional" with "logiciel," designating software suites oriented toward the business applications sector. Cogelog's software suite had originally been developed for the UNIX platform. In 1988, however, Ares formed a partnership with Oracle, and redeveloped its software for that fast-growing platform. Ares then renamed its software package under the Arcole name—an anagram of Oracle. Arcole was also the site of a famous battle during the Napoleonic wars.

The launch of Arcole established Ares as a major force in the French computer and IT services sector, operating with the dual focus of software publishing and systems integration. The company began expanding its presence beyond the Paris region. For this, Ares launched a series of acquisitions, starting with Siris in 1988, LMC Informatique in 1989, and JPL Informatique in 1990.

Ares solidified its partnership with HP in 1990 when the two companies launched a partnership to develop systems integration services through the UNIX platform. In this way Ares established itself as a major player in the French market for open systems. Open systems—as opposed to the "closed" systems represented by Microsoft and Apple—allowed a degree of interoperability between various types of software across a common platform.

PUBLIC OFFERING IN 1999

Ares's systems integration operations took off in the early 1990s. By 1992 the company had begun receiving its first large-scale software development and systems integration contracts for the retailing sector, among others. By 1996 the company claimed the leadership position in the UNIX integration sector. The company also added a strong networking component, with the purchase of networks specialist Jistral in 1993. The company's sales at that time reached the equivalent of approximately EUR 63 million.

A partnership with IBM in 1995 provided Ares with an extension of its expertise into central systems implementation. That year Ares also completed the acquisition of CIGL and Nogema, further expanding its branch network. These acquisitions were followed by several more, including Altis in 1996 and Fininfor Micro in 1997. By the end of 1998 Ares revenues had risen to top EUR 250 million ($280 million).

Acquisitions also enabled the company to expand its range of services offered by its new business unit, Ares Global Services. Toward this end the company bought several new companies by 1999, including Sereti, a developer of time management software; PEC, which specialized in the integration of computer-aided design (CAD) systems; and GSR, a provider of web-based network installation and integration services. Fueling these acquisitions was the company's public offering which was completed in February 1999. Bourlier announced his intention to expand the company's network services operations from its current 12 percent of revenues to 25 percent of revenues by 2002. For this the company earmarked up to EUR 7.5 million for new acquisitions. These included Triade, an Internet specialist, in 2000, and Abridge and RCS in 2001.

At the same time Ares began building up a new operational pole, targeting the facilities management sector. For this Ares added another series of acquisitions,

KEY DATES

1985: Maurice Bourlier founds GTI in order to distribute Hewlett-Packard servers in France.
1987: Bourlier merges GTI with software developer Cogelog, forming Groupe Ares.
1999: Groupe Ares goes public, listing on the Euronext Paris Stock Exchange.
2004: With revenues falling, Bourlier names Jean-Jacques Salomon as company CEO.
2006: Salomon is replaced by Michael Berjamin, who also becomes company chairman.
2008: Ares is forced into bankruptcy protection and launches restructuring, selling off two-thirds of its operations.
2009: Ares announces it expects to emerge from bankruptcy protection by April 2009.

including Systex, LRI, and Editech in 2000. Other acquisitions made during this period helped fill out the group's existing services offerings. In 2000, for example, the company acquired CAD Atlantique, followed by the purchase of graphics engineering specialist Eurogis in 2001.

MARKET SLOWDOWN BRINGS TROUBLE

Ares's growth remained buoyant through most of the first half of the first decade of the 2000s. By the beginning of 2004 the company's sales had reached EUR 475 million. Yet acquisitions continued to fuel much of this growth, even as French IT market was undergoing a marked slowdown. This trend soon caught up with Ares as well. Having become accustomed to double-digit revenue growth through most of its history, Ares saw its expansion dip into the single digits. By the end of 2003 the company's revenues had advanced by just 2 percent over the previous year.

Part of the group's difficulties stemmed from the emergence of disagreement between Bourlier and other members of management, including Jean-Jacques Salomon, over the group's direction during a troubling period. Yet the more fundamental difficulty confronting the company was the evolution of the IT market itself, and especially the group's core computer systems distribution business. Into the first decade of the 2000s a growing number of computer makers, including Dell, IBM, and HP, had begun to bring their server and related distribution operations in-house. The result was sharp decreases in pricing—and consequent decreases in the margins available to resellers such as Ares. Forced to follow the manufacturers' pricing policies, Ares's own once-comfortable margins shrank to just a few euros per system.

In 2004 Bourlier agreed to step back from the group's management, turning over the CEO spot to Salomon. Bourlier nonetheless remained the group's largest shareholder. The company targeted a number of new efforts to restore its growth. One of these was an expansion beyond the French market, starting with a move into North Africa. This led the company to establish a partnership in Morocco in 2005. By 2007 the group had also added offices in Luxembourg and Belgium.

Within Ares itself, the company launched an effort to develop a more specialized software development and integration program. To this end, the company targeted specific sectors, including healthcare, industrial, and construction. Nonetheless. these efforts failed to produce the desired results. Company revenues began to slip for the first time in the company's history, dropping back to EUR 456 million at the end of 2005, and then to EUR 411 million by the end of 2006. Impatient, Bourlier, who remained the group's largest shareholder with a 23 percent stake, moved to replace Salomon with a new CEO, Michael Berjamin. By December 2006 Bourlier himself had stepped down from the company, turning over both the CEO and chairman roles to Berjamin.

BANKRUPTCY PROTECTION IN 2008

Berjamin brought more than 25 years of experience to Ares, including a stint as managing director of Transiciel before leading the integration of that operation after its acquisition by Cap Gemini. Berjamin moved to shed the group of its "commodity" distribution operations, where it achieved its lowest margins, in an effort to reduce the company's heavy reliance on its Architecture and Infrastructure division. Over the next two years Berjamin managed to reduce the division's share of revenues from nearly 74 percent to 68 percent. This effort came at a cost, however, as many of these operations were sold at a loss.

Ultimately these efforts proved to be too little too late as Ares faced the full force of the global economic downturn in 2008. At the beginning of that year the company attempted briefly to stem the collapse of its revenues with new acquisitions, including Adequat, Databail, and Selectis. Meanwhile the company's financial situation, already precarious, forced the company to lay off a number of its employees. By July 2008 Ares had been placed under bankruptcy protection.

Berjamin then announced the company's decision to take a new direction, reorienting itself fully as an IT services company. Toward this end the group sold the remainder of Architecture and Infrastructure operations—including Adequat and Databail—as well as its software developing business, including the Arcole software suite. The move eliminated some two-thirds of Ares revenues—dropping the company back to just EUR 140 million per year.

Ares focused its business around a core of providing software integration and support based on the Arcole software. At the end of 2008 the company entered into an exclusive agreement with De Gamma, the publishing group that had acquired Arcole from Ares, to provide software integration services for the software package. In February 2009 the two companies strengthened their partnership, as Ares became the first certified integration partner for Arcole Chronos, the software title's time management application. The CAD market remained another important market for the company, notably through its partnership with Autodesk, a leading publisher of CAD applications. A series of important contracts in late 2008 enabled Ares to claim the leading position as an Autodesk reseller and integrator in the French market.

By early 2009, despite the continuing harsh economic climate that had affected the whole of France's IT sector, Ares's restructuring appeared to be successful. In January of that year the company announced that it could emerge from bankruptcy protection by as early as April 2009. After more than 20 years as a French IT leader Ares had reinvented itself in hopes of brighter days in the future.

M. L. Cohen

PRINCIPAL SUBSIDIARIES

Ares Belgium; Ares Infogerance; Ares Luxembourg; Eurogis conseil; Infordi; S.A. Ares.

PRINCIPAL COMPETITORS

Cap Gemini S.A.; Accenture S.A.; Atos Origin S.A.; ALTEN S.A.; GFI Informatique S.A.; Bull S.A.S.; Altavia S.A.; Prodware S.A.; Devoteam S.A.; Cegid S.A.

FURTHER READING

Alessi, Fabrice, "Ares en crise: Jean-Jacques Salomon mis sur la touche," *Distributique,* July 1, 2006.

"Arès accélère sa mutation en SSII," *IT Manager,* July 4, 2006.

"Ares Builds Book for March 4 Debut on Second Marche," *Computergram International,* February 11, 1999.

"Ares: Où s'arrêtera la chute?" *IT Channel.info,* July 22, 2008.

Barathon, Didier, "Ares placé en observation par le Tribunal de Commerce pour 6 mois," *Reseaux-Telecoms.net,* July 22, 2008.

Bizouan, Angélique, "Jean-Jacques Salomon: 'Maurice Bourlier m'a chargé de faire évoluer le business model d'Ares,'" *Distributique,* June 8, 2006.

"Groupe Ares: Finalise l'acquisition d'Adequat et Databail," *L'Expansion,* February 5, 2008.

"Groupe Ares passe le pont d'Arcole," *IT Channel.info,* February 12, 2009.

"Maurice Bourlier: 'Les DSI sont très souvent mis en concurrence avec des prestataires extérieurs,'" *JDN Solutions,* February 12, 2005.

"Maurice Bourlier se retire," *01 Informatique,* December 15, 2006.

Groupe Dubreuil S.A.

BP 42, Actipôle 85
Belleville-sur-Vie, F-85170
France
Telephone: (33 02) 51 47 77 90
Fax: (33 02) 51 47 77 34
Web site: http://www.groupedubreuil.com

Private Company
Incorporated: 1924
Employees: 3,050
Sales: EUR 1.29 billion ($1.8 billion)(2008 est.)
NAICS: 441110 New Car Dealers; 424710 Petroleum
Bulk Stations and Terminals; 444130 Hardware
Stores; 444220 Nursery and Garden Centers;
445110 Supermarkets and Other Grocery (Except
Convenience) Stores; 481111 Scheduled Passenger
Air Transportation; 481211 Nonscheduled
Chartered Passenger Air Transportation; 551112
Offices of Other Holding Companies

■ ■ ■

Groupe Dubreuil S.A. is a holding company for a
diversified collection of businesses loosely focused
around a central core of distribution activities. The
company is the largest in its Vendée, France, department, and one of the top 20 companies in the larger
western region of France. Dubreuil's operations are
organized into several divisions: Automobile Distribution; Petroleum Products Distribution; Air Transport;
Construction and Lifting Equipment; Supermarkets;
Hardware Stores; and Renewable Energy. Automobile
distribution is the company's largest activity, representing 31 percent of its annual sales of EUR 1.3 billion
($1.8 billion) in 2008. This division includes the
company's network of Peugeot and Citroën automobile
concessions, as well as distribution of automobile parts,
through subsidiaries Opal and Oscar, which supply
automobile concessions, and control of 115 AD
automotive parts stores, which serve the professional
sector.

The Petroleum Products division, which generates
24 percent of sales, includes such businesses as Dubreuil
Carburants, a network of 60 service stations operating
under the Esso brand; Actigaz, a distributor of liquefied
natural gas; and Flamino, which distributes petroleum
products for home heating systems. The Air Transport
division operates as Air Caraïbes, the second largest
airline providing services to the French Caribbean and
other destinations. The division added 23 percent to the
group's sales in 2008. Dubreuil's retail holdings include
supermarket operations, with several SuperU locations,
and hardware stores under the Mr. Bricolage and Rural
Services names. Dubreuil's youngest division is its
Renewable Energy division, which includes several small
businesses involved in solar panel sales and installation
and solar power-based energy generation. Founded in
1924, Dubreuil remains a family-owned company, led
by Jean-Paul Dubreuil, son of the company's founder.

ORIGINS IN WHOLESALE BUSINESS

Henri Dubreuil came from a farming family based in
Chassenouil-du-Poitou, near La Roche sur Yon in

KEY DATES

1924: Henri Dubreuil takes over his cousin's wholesale grocery business in Roche sur Yon, France.
1950: Dubreuil launches the wholesale distribution of Esso petroleum products.
1966: Jean-Paul Dubreuil takes over as head of the company following the death of his father.
1975: Dubreuil launches Air Vendée, providing air service in the Vendée region.
1985: Dubreuil sells off most of its wholesale and retail food operations.
1991: Air Vendée launches flights between Nantes airport and Brussels, Amsterdam, and Geneva.
1992: Air Vendée expands to become Regional Airlines.
1994: Dubreuil acquires its first Peugeot automobile dealership.
1996: Regional Airlines goes public on the Paris Stock Exchange.
2000: Dubreuil sells its stake in Regional Airlines to Air France, founds Air Caraïbes.
2007: Dubreuil creates a new Renewable Energy division.

France's Vendée region. Dubreuil's own career interests turned to sales, however. In 1924, Dubreuil moved to La Roche sur Yon, where he took over a small wholesale business operated by his cousin, Gaston Moreau. Dubreuil initially served the local grocery community, delivering goods by cart. The addition of motor vehicles enabled him to reach a wider market as he extended his business to outlying villages. Dubreuil also sought to expand his company's range of goods, and in 1935 added the distribution of wine as well. In the years following World War II, Dubreuil recognized the opportunities offered by the fast-growing automotive sector.

In 1950, he added a new business delivering gasoline to local service stations. This new activity also formed the start of a long-lasting relationship with the Esso brand. Towards the end of the decade, Dubreuil was joined by his youngest son, Jean-Paul, who was born during World War II and had more or less grown up in the family business. Jean-Paul Dubreuil—who earned a pilot's license at the age of 16—initially went to study law at the University of Nantes. At the begin-

ning of the 1960s, however, Dubreuil left school to fulfill his military service in Algeria. Upon his return to France in 1964, Dubreuil decided to join his father's company, rather than return to school.

The younger Dubreuil recognized a growing trend in the grocery sector, as the first supermarkets appeared to challenge the traditional small grocer. The shift toward larger stores, and especially to large-scale distribution groups, was soon to have a major impact on the wholesale sector as well. The Dubreuil family had already begun to take steps to meet the transformation of the distribution industry. In 1961, the company joined the SPAR wholesale group, a move which permitted the company's own wholesale business to grow strongly through the first half of the decade.

Henri Dubreuil died in 1966, leaving Jean-Paul Dubreuil, then 22 years old, in charge of the company. Dubreuil soon convinced the company's bank to finance the construction of a new 4,200-square-meter warehouse facility near Nantes. The completion of this facility enabled Dubreuil to extend its wholesale business beyond the Vendée region.

TAKING FLIGHT IN 1975

The early 1970s marked the appearance of the first of the major supermarket groups in France, as well as the construction of the first hypermarkets—large-scale structures that combined a department store approach with full-service supermarkets. Dubreuil recognized that his wholesale operation needed to grow accordingly, and in 1971 he agreed to merge with two other SPAR wholesalers, creating OCEDIS. Just two years later, that company merged with another fast-growing wholesale group, Disco, creating OCEDISCO, based in Cholet.

Dubreuil then turned his interest to the retail side of the distribution sector. In 1974, he joined with his father-in-law, who operated his own wholesale business in Luçon, to convert that structure into a supermarket. For this, Dubreuil teamed up with Bravo, an association of independent supermarket operators, which later developed under the SuperU and HyperU banners. By 1975, Dubreuil had opened a second supermarket, in Sables d'Olonne, on the Vendée coast. Both stores were originally opened under the Bravo name. During the 1980s, the Luçon site adopted the hypermarket format, becoming HyperU, while the supermarket in Sables d'Olonne took on the SuperU name.

Dubreuil's interests expanded into other distribution sectors as well. In 1980, the company entered the retail hardware market, opening a store at a new shopping plaza in La Roche sur Yon. Once again, instead of attempting to develop his own branded store, Dubreuil joined with a larger group, Bricogite. Dubreuil's expanding retail operations provided an ever-growing flow of cash for the company's rapidly broadening range of interests. At the same time, Dubreuil began to spend increasing amounts of time traveling to the various locations of his growing business empire.

In 1975, Dubreuil put his pilot's license to work, and convinced a friend to join him in the purchase of an airplane, a small six-seat single engine plane. This allowed Dubreuil to found a new company, Air Vendée, to provide regional service to the area's business community. Before long, the company added a new twin-engine plane, increasing seating capacity. Dubreuil at first shared pilot duties for the young airline. By the end of the decade, however, the company had grown sufficiently to take on a dedicated pilot, as well as a mechanic. Air Vendée's move into regional prominence came especially after 1979, when the airline launched regular service flying between La Roche sur Yon and l'Ile d'Yeu. The addition enabled the company to serve both the resident island community, as well as the tourist market.

NEW DIRECTIONS

In the mid-1980s, Dubreuil moved to shift its focus away from the food sector. The group's new strategy came in response to the continuing rise of the large-scale distribution groups, which had not only succeeded in dominating the French grocery market, but had also placed the wholesale sector under increasing pressure. In 1985, Dubreuil sold most of its wholesale and retail food operations.

Instead, the company reinforced its operations in the automotive sector. The company continued to build up its service station business, ultimately overseeing a network of 60 service stations, while expanding its petroleum products wholesale distribution operations as well. This expansion was to continue through the 1990s. In 1999, for example, the company acquired Brétéché, a company that specialized in the distribution of domestic fuel and other petroleum products in the Brittany and Loire regions.

At the same time, Dubreuil moved to expand its air transport wing. Toward the end of the 1980s, the company, backed by the Nantes Chamber of Commerce, became determined to expand its air operations beyond the Vendée region. This led to the creation of new services, based at the Nantes Airport, in 1991. Starting with an 11-seat airplane, Air Vendée began offering flights linking Nantes with airports in Brussels, Amsterdam, and Geneva. The operation struggled at first, losing as much as FRF 1 million per year.

The outbreak of the Persian Gulf War that year provided a new opportunity for Dubreuil's air division. As the major airlines reduced their own flights, particularly in the smaller regional markets, Dubreuil saw an opportunity for creating a new airline. In 1992, Dubreuil joined with a number of other small operators, forming Regional Airlines.

Regional quickly stepped into the gap left by the major companies, offering flights between Lyon and Madrid, Lyon and Barcelona, Marseille and Madrid, and Marseille and Rome, among other destinations. By the mid-1990s, Regional's fleet had grown to 35 airplanes, including a number of Embraer jets for the company's longer flights. Regional's growth then led to a successful public offering on the Paris stock exchange in 1996. The Dubreuil company nonetheless retained control of Regional Airlines, and profited handsomely from the sale of that airline to Air France in 2000.

FOCUS ON AUTOMOBILES

Dubreuil's success in the air was matched with growth on the ground. In 1994, the company added a new distribution sector with the purchase of its first Peugeot automobile dealership, in Cholet. By 1996, the company had moved that business to a larger site in Cholet, while acquiring a second Peugeot dealership in La Rochelle. Over the next decade, the company continued to add new automobile concessions, including two Citroën dealerships in Luçon and Fontenay-le-Comte, in 2001. At the same time, the company built up its range of Peugeot sites, adding Cognac in 1998, Roche-sur-Yon and Bressuire in 2001, and Mans in 2004. Toward the end of the decade, the company operated a total of 16 dealerships.

The company's move into automobile distribution was accompanied by the addition of a new range of subsidiaries distributing automotive components and parts. In 2004, the company reached an agreement with Peugeot to create a central facility for its wholesale automotive parts and equipment operations. That site, called Opal, rapidly grew to include some 2,500 dealerships and garages among its clients.

The following year, Dubreuil extended its auto parts operations again, buying Auto Pièces Nantais (later renamed as Auto Pièces Atlantique), which operated five wholesale distribution centers for more than 80 retail auto parts stores operating under the AD banner. The addition of a sixth site enabled Dubreuil to extend its reach to 115 AD stores in the region. Dubreuil's automotive business grew in 2007 to include its Oscar used car platform. That facility, established next to the Opal operation, provided inspection and repair services for used vehicles acquired by and resold by Dubreuil's dealership network.

Distribution remained at the heart of other Dubreuil diversification moves during this period. The company entered the construction vehicle and equipment market in 1992, with the acquisition of M3. This business was soon extended with the opening of the group's first construction machinery rental agency, under the NewLoc banner, in La Rochelle in 2003.

FLYING HIGH IN THE 21ST CENTURY

Nevertheless, Dubreuil's most visible success came from its continued air travel interests. Even before the sale of Regional Airlines, Dubreuil had begun to invest elsewhere in the sector. In 1998, the company came across an opportunity to acquire a small and failing airline, Air Antilles, which provided inter-island transport in that French Caribbean possession. In 2000, Dubreuil added a second airline, Air Guadeloupe, and then merged the two together to form Air Caraïbes.

The new airline struggled against losses for its first three years, as Dubreuil and a new management team restructured its operations. An opportunity presented itself for Air Caraïbes in 2003, however, with the collapse of Air Liberté, which had previously been a major player in the region, with a flight linking the Antilles and Paris. Air Caraïbes rushed to take its place, and launched its own Antilles-Paris flight in 2004. Despite a price war launched by Air France in 2005, Air Caraïbes grew strongly. By 2008, the company had become profitable, boasting passenger totals of more than one million per year. In that year, the company added a fourth jet, and launched a new long-haul service linking French Guiana and Paris.

With Jean-Paul Dubreuil still at the helm of the company, Groupe Dubreuil showed no signs of slowing down at the end of the decade. Indeed, in 2007, the company turned its attention to the entirely new sector

of renewable energy. The company created a new division that year and began making a series of regional acquisitions. These included Solinvest, a company focused on solar-powered energy generation; and Solargie, providing solar panel sales and installation services. In 2008, the company acquired Volten, a wholesaler focused on the renewable energy market. With sales of nearly EUR 1.3 billion ($1.8 billion), Dubreuil looked forward to exploring new horizons in the future.

M. L. Cohen

PRINCIPAL SUBSIDIARIES

Air Caraïbes S.A.; Codimatra; M3 S.A.; Oscar SAS; Solargie SAS.

PRINCIPAL COMPETITORS

Air France S.A.; Carrefour S.A.; Casino S.A.; Feu Vert S.A.; Norauto S.A.

FURTHER READING

Bordet, Marie, "Jean-Paul Dubreuil: Un Pilotes aux Commandes d'Air Caraïbes," *Le Point,* January 8, 2009.

"Du Bocage aux Caraïbes," *Le Figaro,* October 31, 2008.

"Dubreuil Up in Air Caraïbes," *Les Echos,* April 12, 2000, p. 24.

Evina, Emmanuelle, "Jean-Paul Dubreuil Revendique Son Ame d'Epicier," *Points de Vente,* April 2, 2007.

"Jean-Paul Dubreuil, le PDG de la Compagnie Air Caraïbes Défie Air France aux Antilles," *Capital,* February 18, 2009.

Marty, Frédéric, "Dubreuil Offre un Oscar à Ses VO," *Le Journal de l'Automobile,* May 26, 2006.

Merrien, Tanguy, "Le Groupe Dubreuil Rachète AD à Nantes," *Le Journal de l'Automobile,* October 29, 2004.

Tallec, Isabelle, "L'Envol de la Grande Distribution," *L'Express,* January 25, 2007.

Vigoureux, Thierry, "Air Caraïbes Face à Air France en Guyane," *Le Figaro,* December 16, 2008.

Hikma Pharmaceuticals Ltd.

———————————■———————————

P.O. Box 182400
Amman, 11118
Jordan
Telephone: (962) 06 5802900
Fax: (962) 06 5817102
Web site: http://www.hikma.com

Public Company
Incorporated: 1978
Employees: 850
Sales: $448.8 million (2007)
Stock Exchanges: London
Ticker Symbol: HIK
NAICS: 325412 Pharmaceutical Preparation Manufacturing; 325411 Medicinal and Botanical Manufacturing

■ ■ ■

Hikma Pharmaceuticals Ltd. is Jordan's largest pharmaceuticals company and one of the largest in the Middle East–North Africa (MENA) region. Hikma also operates in the United States, through subsidiary West-Ward Pharmaceuticals, and Europe, with operations in Portugal and Germany. Hikma's business focuses on the manufacturing and distribution of branded generic, generic, and injectable pharmaceutical products. The company produces and markets more than 350 compounds in more than 725 dosages to nearly 50 countries. In the MENA region, the company focuses primarily on the branded generics market, including nearly 40 in-licensed products from major pharma-

ceuticals houses, as well as another 200 products under Hikma's own brand names. This Branded division generated nearly 45 percent of Hikma's $449 million in sales in 2007. Hikma's Generics division focuses on the U.S. market, with a portfolio of 44 non-branded solid generic pharmaceutical products. This division accounted for nearly 28 percent of group sales.

Hikma's Injectables division produces and distributes both branded and non-branded generic injectable products, including cephalosporin-based anti-infectives. The 2007 acquisition of two German companies, Ribosepharm and Thymoorgan, has also enabled the company to position itself in the market for injectable oncology products. The Injectables division, which generated 27 percent of the group's revenues, is also its most international, covering the MENA, U.S., and European markets. MENA remains the company's core market, with more than 51 percent of sales. The group's U.S. operations generate 32 percent, while Europe accounts for 17 percent. Hikma, which means "wisdom" in Arabic, is led by Said Darwazah, chief executive officer. His father, Samih Darwazah, who founded the company, remains the group's chairman. Younger son Mazen Darwazah serves as vice-chairman and CEO of the group's MENA operations. Hikma has been listed on the London Stock Exchange since 2005.

FOUNDING AN INDUSTRIAL PHARMACEUTICAL COMPANY IN 1978

A native of Jaffa, Samih Darwazah fled with his family to Amman, Jordan, following the Arab defeat by Israel

COMPANY PERSPECTIVES

Our strategy for growth is to build a strong and diverse product portfolio; to expand our geographic reach; to develop and leverage our global research and development capabilities and API sourcing strengths; and to continue to maintain the very high standards of our manufacturing capabilities.

in 1948. Then 18 years old, Darwazah went to Beirut, to study at the American University there. After earning a degree as a pharmacist, Darwazah traveled to Kuwait, where he found work as a dispensing pharmacist in a government hospital. In 1958, however, Darwazah decided to return to Jordan, where he opened his own pharmacy in Amman.

In the early 1960s Darwazah set his sights on new horizons. In 1963 he moved to the United States, winning a Fulbright Scholarship and earning a master's degree at the Saint Louis College of Pharmacy. Darwazah then took a job with Eli Lilly, becoming that company's regional marketing manager for the Middle East. Over the next 12 years Darwazah helped transform Eli Lilly into a major force in the MENA region's pharmaceuticals market.

In 1976, however, Darwazah, by then married with four children, once again decided to return to Jordan to establish his own pharmaceuticals company. As Darwazah told the *Jordan Times:* "I left a big job, a very big job ... my family wasn't happy for the change from a secure position to the uncertainties of the business world." By 1978 Darwazah had succeeded in raising $2 million in start-up capital, both from his own investments and from a number of other investors. Darwazah founded Hikma Pharmaceuticals that year, taking the Arabic word for wisdom for the company's name.

Industrial pharmaceutical production remained very limited in the MENA region at the time, with most companies focusing on pharmaceutical distribution. Darwazah, however, was determined to establish Hikma as a pharmaceuticals producer. As he told *Jordan Business:* "I chose to go into industry because I think an industrial venture is more beneficial to the country than just trading. It creates jobs, money, exports and foreign currency, and industry is a much more sustainable and long-term investment. You don't make money immediately, especially in pharmaceuticals."

Hikma's first factory was completed by the end of 1978. The company then launched production of its first—and only—product, Cefazolin, an anti-infective. As Darwazah predicted, the company's first year sales were modest, reaching just $100,000. Darwazah also recognized that the Jordanian market itself would be too small to support the company's growth objectives. Hikma quickly began developing a more regional focus, developing distribution operations to such markets as Lebanon and Syria.

By 1980 the company had also begun developing another key factor in its MENA region success. In that year, the company developed its first relationships with the global pharmaceuticals industry, receiving its first licenses to market branded generic products from the major groups under its own brand names. In this way, Hikma was able to avoid the need to run costly research and development programs into new compounds; instead, the company invested its efforts into the development of new dosage forms and sizes.

INTERNATIONAL FOCUS

Despite his years of experience in the region, Darwazah was soon confronted with the realities of doing business in the highly volatile Middle East region. In Lebanon, for example, already affected by the ongoing civil war, the company's fortunes fell dramatically following the Israeli takeover of the southern part of the country in 1982. The company's move into Iraq was similarly hampered by the outbreak of war between that country and Iran. Other markets, such as Syria and Sudan, banned the use of hard currency, forcing the company to accept goods, such marble, sesame seeds, and the like, in exchange for its pharmaceutical products.

The need to adapt its distribution efforts for the varying conditions in the MENA markets nonetheless provided a strong training ground for Hikma's future growth. By the end of the 1980s the company had begun to set its sights on expansion beyond the region. As Darwazah told *Jordan Business:* "I thus started to wonder why we were limiting ourselves to the Arabian market, and we decided to reach out to the American and European markets."

Eldest son Said Darwazah proved an important component in the company's international expansion. The younger Darwazah's business acumen had been put to the test while still studying for a degree in industrial engineering at Purdue University. After successfully negotiating the Middle East dealership for a local inline filler manufacturer, Said Darwazah was asked to spearhead Hikma's entry into the United States.

Darwazah's challenge was to acquire a U.S.-based pharmaceutical company for just $2 million. By 1991 Darwazah had located a prospect, in the form of New

```
┌─────────────────────────────────────────────────┐
│                                                   │
│              KEY DATES                            │
│                    ■                              │
│  ─────────────────────────────────────────────   │
│                                                   │
│  1978:  Samih Darwazah founds Hikma               │
│         Pharmaceuticals in order to produce       │
│         generic drugs for the Middle East–North   │
│         Africa (MENA) region.                     │
│  1991:  Hikma enters the U.S. market with the     │
│         acquisition of West-Ward Pharmaceuticals  │
│         in New Jersey.                             │
│  1996:  Hikma receives FDA approval for its       │
│         Jordanian manufacturing operations.       │
│  1997:  Hikma launches production at a new        │
│         factory for injectable pharmaceutical     │
│         products in Portugal.                     │
│  2005:  Hikma is listed on the London Stock       │
│         Exchange.                                 │
│  2007:  The company completes four acquisitions,  │
│         including Alkan (Egypt); Arab             │
│         Pharmaceutical Manufacturers (Jordan and  │
│         Saudi Arabia); Ribosepharm (Germany); and │
│         Thymoorgan (Germany).                     │
│                                                   │
└─────────────────────────────────────────────────┘
```

Jersey-based West-Ward Pharmaceuticals Corp., a manufacturer of non-branded generic drugs. The purchase of that struggling company quickly turned sour, however. Within weeks after the purchase, Hikma received a number of warning letters from the U.S. Food and Drug Administration (FDA) accusing the company of adulterating its drugs, and insisting on the use of two tamper-proof warning labels, instead of the single-label standard. The conflict with the FDA reached its peak after FDA officials requested that the company be shut down by the U.S. Attorney General's Office.

Hikma fought back, however, and ultimately reached an unprecedented out-of-court settlement, signing a consent decree that granted the FDA full monitoring and approval rights over the company's operations for a period of five years. Darwazah worked hard to bring West-Ward into compliance, while slashing the company's payroll in order to reduce its losses. The effort paid off, with the FDA acknowledging the company's compliance within six weeks. By the end of 1992 West-Ward's entire product line received FDA authorization and certification. By 1993 the FDA had withdrawn the consent decree, a first in FDA history.

STRETCHING TOO THIN

Backed by funding from its Jordanian parent, West-Ward gradually improved its balance sheet. By 1993 the

company had broken even, and by 1994 had begun to turn over a clear profit. By 1994 West-Ward had received full FDA compliance. Just two years later, Hikma itself became the first Arab pharmaceutical company to received full FDA approval for the U.S. market. This milestone proved essential for the company's development, as FDA approval helped pave the way for the company's entry into other markets. These included a move into the Eastern European market starting in 1992.

In 1995 Samih Darwazah was tapped by Jordan's new prime minister to join the new government's cabinet. Darwazah spent the next year as a minister to the Jordanian government, while Said Darwazah returned to Jordan to become Hikma's chief executive officer.

Hikma's expansion plans became still more ambitious in the mid-1990s. The company entered Saudi Arabia, forming the joint venture Jazeera Pharmaceutical Industries (JPI), with Hikma as the minority partner. The company also decided to establish manufacturing operations in Europe, launching construction of a factory for injectable pharmaceuticals in Portugal. That facility was completed in 1997. Back at home, the company also acquired a stake in a local chemical factory, in order to ensure part of its raw material supply.

The company financed this expansion by taking on debt—at a time when interest rates in the region had begun to soar, amid the economic turbulence that swept through most of the developing world in the late 1990s. At the same time the company's JPI operation hit a snag when the Saudi government failed to make good on a large sum of money it owed to Hikma. For more than two years Hikma hovered at the edge of bankruptcy.

ACHIEVING SUCCESS IN 21ST CENTURY

A turning point came toward the end of the 1990s when the company brought in new financial backing, selling a stake in the company to Citibank Venture Capital. The new partner also claimed seats on the board of directors, providing the company with a new level of professional management experience. The introduction of Citibank Venture Capital into the group's shareholding was also seen as a first step toward Hikma's future public listing.

The turn of the 21st century saw Hikma's health restored. The company had reason to celebrate after its Portugal plant received FDA approval in 2001. In that year the company launched the manufacturing of injectable powdered cephalosporin, a powerful antibiotic alternative to penicillin. Also that year, the company received approval to begin marketing its products in the United Kingdom for the first time.

By the early 2000s Hikma had built up two strong divisional poles. The group's largest enterprise was its branded generics business, which focused primarily on the MENA region. The group's non-branded generics operation, largely carried out through West-Ward in the United States, had also grown well. The success of operations in Portugal then encouraged the company to invest in a third direction: injectables, especially liquid injectables. This effort took off especially after 2003, as the company's production capacity for this category reached commercially viable levels.

The move into injectables and the necessity for future investment encouraged the company to seek new financial backing. By 2005, Said Darwazah, who completed his own tenure as Jordan's Minister of Public Health, had convinced his father of the need to take the family-owned company public. Hikma successfully listed its stock on the London Stock Exchange that year, raising nearly $125 million.

The public offering enabled the company to pay down part of its debt, while funding the expansion of its manufacturing capacity in both Jordan and Portugal. By 2006 the company had also bought full control of JPI in Saudi Arabia; JPI also gained FDA approval that year.

Hikma launched an acquisition drive, spending more than $300 million through 2007. The company first acquired Jordanian rival, Arab Pharmaceutical Manufacturers, with operations both in Jordan and in Saudi Arabia. Next, the company targeted an entry into the Egyptian market, the region's largest, with the purchase of Alkan, a generics manufacturer with sales of nearly $15 million, for $60.5 million.

Hikma also moved to boost its injectables operations, while at the same time targeting an expansion into the wider European market. This led the company to complete two acquisitions in Germany, of Ribosepharm GmbH, which specialized in generic injectable oncology drugs, and Thymoorgan GmbH, which focused on the contract manufacturing of injectable oncology products. In this way Hikma gained integrated operations in one of the fastest-growing drug markets in Europe.

The new acquisitions helped boost the company's sales to nearly $449 million in 2007, a gain of nearly 42 percent over the previous year, and nearly double its 2005 revenues. Said Darwazah promised still further growth for the company, forecasting a doubling of the company's revenues over the next four years. Hikma Pharmaceuticals had established itself as one of the MENA region's leading pharmaceuticals companies, and a growing force in the global market.

M. L. Cohen

PRINCIPAL SUBSIDIARIES

Al Jazeera Pharmaceutical Industries (Saudi Arabia); Arab Pharmaceutical Manufacturing Co.; Hikma Farmaceutica S.A (Portugal); Hikma Italia; Hikma Pharma SAE (Egypt); Hikma Pharmaceuticals Limited; Pharma Ixir Co. (Sudan; 51%); Ribosepharm GmbH (Germany); SARL Hikma Pharma Algeria; Thymoorgan GmbH Pharmazie & Co. KG (Germany); West-Ward Pharmaceuticals Corp. (USA).

PRINCIPAL COMPETITORS

Eagle Distilleries Co.; United Pharmaceutical Manufacturing Company Ltd.; Dar Al Dawa Development and Investment; Jordan Pharmaceuticals Manufacturing Company PLC; Veterinary and Agricultural Products Manufacturing Co.; Middle East Pharmaceutical and Chemical Industries and Medical Appliances; Jordan Industrial Resources Company Ltd.; Al Hayat for Pharmaceutical Industries.

FURTHER READING

Baharuddin, Zulkafly, "Samih Darwazah Confidently Positions Hikma International to Seize a Bigger Slice of the World Market," *Jordan Times*, March 30, 2000.

Blitz, Roger, "Branded Drugs Help Bolster Strong Growth at Hikma," *Financial Times*, July 14, 2006, p. 19.

Boles, Tracey, "Pharma Giant Hikma Is to List This Week," *Sunday Business*, October 30, 2005.

Darwazah, Samih T., *Building a Global Success: The Story of Samih Darwazah and the Rise of Hikma*, London: Hudson Books, 2005.

Davoudi, Salamander, "Buoyant Sales for Hikma," *Financial Times*, March 23, 2007, p. 21.

———, "Hikma Warns As Drug Price Competition Bites," *Financial Times*, January 19, 2007, p. 20.

Farrell, Sean, "Hikma Bids 80m for Jordanian Drug Maker," *Independent*, October 8, 2007, p. 44.

Hemming, Richard, "Hikma Getting over Its Generic Hiccup," *Investors Chronicle*, August 31, 2008.

"Hikma Buys German Oncology Company for $45 Million," *Jordan Times*, January 23, 2007.

"Hikma Foresees Strong Growth," *Jordan Times*, September 6, 2007.

"Hikma Has Lots of Eastern Promise," *Investors Chronicle*, March 18, 2008.

Mushtaq, Mubasshir, "Hikma's Innovation, R&D Leads to Global Expansion," *Dinar Standard,* July 13, 2008.

O'Doherty, John, "Brand Demand Bolsters Hikma," *Financial Times,* November 6, 2008.

"The Pinnacle of Triumph," *Jordan Business,* April 1, 2008.

"Samih Darwazah Named Ernst Young Middle East Entrepreneur of the Year 2007," *Albawaba.com,* February 24, 2008.

Urquhart, Lisa, "Hikma Gets on Acquisition Trail," *Financial Times,* March 30, 2006, p. 26.

Warwick-Ching, Lucy, "Injectables Help Give Hikma 16% Booster," *Financial Times,* September 6, 2007, p. 20.

Hilding Anders AB

Oestra Varvsgatan 4
Malmö, S-211 40
Sweden
Telephone: (46 040) 665 67 00
Fax: (46 040) 665 67 01
Web site: http://www.hildinganders.se

Private Company
Incorporated: 1939 as Hilding Anderssons Möbelfabrik
  AB
Employees: 5,351
Sales: SEK 7.06 billion ($1.1 billion) (2008)
NAICS: 337910 Mattress Manufacturing

■ ■ ■

Sweden-based Hilding Anders AB is the leading manufacturer of mattresses and beds in Europe, and one of the top bedding groups in the world. The company controls a portfolio of top European bedding brands, including its own Hilding Anders brand, as well as André Renault and Timbo in France, Eastborn in the Netherlands, Myer's and Dunlopillo in the United Kingdom, Slumberland in the United Kingdom; Jensen in Norway; Hespo in Croatia; Somilar in Spain; and Happy in Switzerland. In addition to producing mattresses, bed frames, and box springs under its own brands, Hilding Anders is also a major bedding manufacturer for the private-label market. Major clients include Ikea, Jysk, Conforama, and Beter Bed. Much of Hilding Anders' growth has come since the late 1990s, when the company launched an acquisition drive,

acquiring more than 20 bedding companies across Europe. Since 2006 Hilding Anders has also controlled 60 percent of Malysia-based Slumberland Asia Pacific, which operates factories in Malaysia, Thailand, China, and Indonesia. Hilding Anders operations include more than 30 subsidiaries, 21 factories, and sales in 28 European markets and 13 Asian markets. Led by CEO Anders Palsson, Hilding Anders is owned by the Candover investment group. In 2008, Hilding Anders posted revenues of SEK 7.06 billion ($1.1 billion).

A SWEDISH BEDDING COMPANY IN THE NINETIES

Hilding Anders was founded in 1939 by Hilding Andersson, who opened a furniture factory in Bjarnum Sweden. Originally known as Hilding Andersson Möbelfabrik, the company changed its name, to Hilding Anders Möbel, in 1961. In that year the company moved to a new factory in Hastveda. The Hilding Anders name became more closely associated with bedding in the early 1970s after the company patented its Polyspring mattress system in 1972.

The success of the Polyspring set the stage for the company's growth during the decade. By 1976 the company had won a major order to supply the interior furnishings for a large hotel in Russia. Even more important to the company's growth, however, was the creation of a partnership with a small but fast-growing new furniture retailer, Ikea. Hilding Anders would remain a major supplier of mattresses and boxsprings to the soon-to-be global home furnishings giant through the turn of the century. Nonetheless, Hilding Anders

Hilding Anders' strength is clearly manifested in the Group's brand portfolio. André Renault, Bico, Eastborn, Hilding, Jensen and Slumberland all represent brands in leading market positions. All together the Group owns strong brands in all price segments in Europe and Asia. Today Hilding Anders supplies a growing number of European retailers with beds in different product segments. These retailers include leading furniture chains and bed specialists such as IKEA, Jysk, Conforama, Beter Bed, Ilva and Dreams to name a few.

itself remained a small, largely locally focused company through the 1980s.

Leadership of the company was taken over by Bengt and Ann-Charlotte Adolfsson in 1987; they changed the company's name to Hilding Anders AB that year. The new owners led the company into a new era of growth as a specialized bedding manufacturer. Hilding Anders made its first acquisition in 1991, of Ekens Fabriker, another Swedish bed and mattress producer. The purchase more than doubled the group's annual revenues, to SEK 200 million (approximately $30 million).

In 1992 Hilding Anders expanded its private-label operations again as it teamed up with another fast-growing home furnishings retailer, Jysk, based in Denmark. That company was in the midst of its own international expansion drive, and the partnership with Hilding Anders came in support of Jysk's entry into Sweden. The company then strengthened its Swedish bed and mattress manufacturing presence through the purchase of Stjärnbädden AB.

INTERNATIONAL GROWTH AT THE TURN OF THE 21ST CENTURY

Hilding Anders' move into the bedding big leagues came at the end of the 1990s. In 1998 the Adolfssons sold 60 percent of the company to Swedish investment firm Atle AB (later part of Ratos). With this new injection of capital, the company launched a new phase in its growth—transforming the relatively small, Swedish-focused company into a European leader.

Acquisitions formed the core of Hilding Anders' growth strategy into the turn of the century. In 1998

the company made its first move outside of Sweden, buying Finland's Unituli Oy. This purchase helped raise the group's total sales to SEK 450 million by the end of that year. In the meantime, the company had been preparing an even larger expansion.

In November 1999 the company announced its plans to merge with rival Swedish bedding group Apax Intressenter, the holding company for Apax Industri. That company, majority control of which was also held by Atle, brought its own operations throughout the Scandinavian region. The merger of Apax into Hilding, which was completed in 1999, more than doubled Hilding Anders' total sales, to SEK 1 billion. As part of the merger, Nordic Capital, which had held shares in Apax, became part of Hilding Anders' shareholder group with a 32 percent stake.

Next Hilding Anders sought expansion beyond the Scandinavian region. This goal was achieved in 2001 when the company acquired Slumberland Holding AG, then the second largest mattress manufacturer in Europe. The addition of Slumberland boosted Hilding Anders itself into the European leadership. It also expanded the company's geographic reach, adding manufacturing and sales operations in the United Kingdom, Germany, France, Switzerland, the Netherlands, Austria, Hungary, the Czech Republic, and Poland.

Following that acquisition the company also purchased a 20 percent stake in Slumberland Asia Pacific Ltd., based in Malaysia, which held the rights to the Slumberland brand in the Asian Pacific region. In 2002, the group further expanded its U.K. operations with the acquisition of the rights to the Dunlopillo brand in the United Kingdom and Ireland. In the meantime Hilding Anders decided to exit the German operations where it owned Billerbeck, which had been part of Slumberland. In 2003 the company decided to sell that company because its focus of pillows and quilts did not fit with Hilding Anders' own focus on beds and mattresses.

NEW OWNERS AND NEW ACQUISITIONS IN 2003

Hilding Anders' expansion came in part as the company geared up for a public offering at the beginning of 2003. However in November of that year the group's shareholders reached an agreement instead to sell all of Hilding Anders' shares to the Bahrain-based investment vehicle Investcorp in a deal worth $495 million. Just a month earlier, Investcorp had sold off its holding in U.S.-based mattress leader Simmons, in a deal worth $1.1 billion. As part of the takeover by Investcorp, Bengt Adolfsson stepped down as Hilding Anders CEO, replaced by Anders Paulsson.

Hilding Anders continued its expansion strategy under its new owners. The company raised its French profile in 2004, adding Créations André Renault, one of France's leading bedding producers. That purchase followed the acquisition of Norway's Jensen Möbler, a company founded in 1947 with factories in Norway and Lithuania. Jensen was active throughout the Scandinavian region, as well as in England, Spain, and the Netherlands.

Next, the company targeted entry into the Balkans region. In 2005 the company added Croatia to its list of markets, taking over Hespo d.o.o. The purchase gave Hilding Anders the leading position in the Croatian market's bedding sector. The company later consolidated its Croatian presence, buying Zagreb-based bedding manufacturer Perfecta. Following that purchase, which also gave the company a chain of retail bedding stores, Hilding Anders gained a 55 percent share of the Croatian bedding market.

Hilding Anders found itself under new ownership, when Investcorp launched a streamlining of its portfolio, selling the company to British investment group Candover in 2006. While Paulsson remained the company's CEO, Hilding Anders' new owners allowed the group to shift its acquisition drive into high gear into the second half of the decade. The company launched a new string of acquisitions, starting with raising its stake in Slumberland Asia Pacific to 60 percent in 2006. Hilding

Anders then gained control of a company with manufacturing operations in Malaysia, China, Thailand, and Indonesia, a sales subsidiary in Singapore, and sales operations in 13 markets in the fast-developing region.

Europe nonetheless remained the company's primary market. In 2006, the group moved into Spain, acquiring that country's Somilar Group. Based in Valencia, Somilar not only gave Hilding Anders a national presence in Spain, it also added export operations into the Belgian, French, U.K., and other European markets.

CLAIMING THE EUROPEAN LEAD

Already present in the Czech Republic, through Slumberland Czeska, Hilding Anders moved to claim a leading position in that country's bedding market. Toward this end, in 2007 the company acquired Tropico, a Prague-based company with manufacturing operations in Slovakia as well.

The year 2007 proved pivotal for the group's acquisition strategy, as it completed a total of five major acquisitions that year. In addition to its Czech Republic and Croatian purchases, the company targeted the lead in the Netherlands' bedding market, buying that country's Eastborn. Soon after, the company turned to France, where it acquired bed frames specialist Timbo. The company then boosted its position in the United Kingdom, adding Myer's, one of the oldest and largest family-owned bedding manufacturers in the United Kingdom.

In 2008 Hilding Anders moved to fill a major gap in its European holdings. Into the second half of the decade, the group had begun preparing a reentry into Germany. This effort resulted in the creation of a new German subsidiary, Hilding Anders Deutschland GmbH. Through that subsidiary Hilding Anders began preparing the launch of new bedding models developed specifically for the Germany consumer market.

The move into Germany was shortly followed by an entry into Italy. This completed the company's coverage of the five largest European markets. For this expansion, the company reached an agreement to acquire Bedding Srl, based outside Treviso. By then, Hilding Anders had also reinforced its position in the Swiss market, where it acquired Happy AG, a family-owned bedding manufacturer founded in 1895. Together with the group's existing Swiss operations, which included the Bico brand, the addition of Happy positioned Hilding Anders as the leader in the Swiss bedding sector.

Hilding Anders' acquisition drive had enabled it maintain its strong growth, despite increasingly difficult economic conditions at the end of the decade. By 2008 the group's sales had risen past SEK 7 billion ($1.1 billion), multiplying its annual sales by some 15 times in just ten years. Through the second half of 2008 and into 2009, the company began taking steps to meet the slump in demand, launching a streamlining of its operations and carrying out a restructuring of its manufacturing operations in the United Kingdom and Switzerland. The Swedish group nonetheless looked forward to future growth as the leading European bedding specialist.

M. L. Cohen

PRINCIPAL SUBSIDIARIES

Bedding Srl (Italy); Créations André Renault SAS (France); Happy AG (Switzerland); Hilding Anders Deutschland GmbH; Hilding Anders UK Ltd.; Jensen Möbler A/S (Norway); Slumberland Asia Pacific Pty. (Malaysia); Somilar Group (Spain).

PRINCIPAL COMPETITORS

PinskDrev Industrial Woodworking Co.; Recticel S.A./ NV; Sime Singapore Ltd.; Remploy Ltd.; Beter Bed Holding N.V.; Ekornes ASA; Pikolin S.A.; Famco Holdings Ltd.; Compagnie Pikolin Recticel de Literie S.A.S.

FURTHER READING

"Happy Hilding Anders," *Cabinet Maker,* March 14, 2008, p. 5.

Harrington, Ben, "Investcorp Slim Down with an Autumn Clear-Out," *Daily Telegraph,* October 18, 2006.

"Hilding Anders Buys Myer's," *Cabinet Maker,* August 10, 2007, p. 3.

"Investcorp Puts Hilding Anders to Bed," *Acquisitions Monthly,* December 2003, p. 53.

"Slumberland Pour 100m Baht into Thai Operations," *Bangkok Post,* April 3, 2008.

Smith, Peter, "Slumberland Maker Sold for Euros 420m," *Financial Times,* November 25, 2003, p. 31.

"Steve Luddington: Time to Wake the Sleeping Giants," *Cabinet Maker,* December 3, 2004, p. 12.

ICON Health & Fitness, Inc.

---■---

1500 South 1000 West
Logan, Utah 84321
U.S.A.
Telephone: (435) 750-5000
Fax: (435) 750-0209
Web site: http://www.iconfitness.com

Private Company
Incorporated: 1977 as Weslo Design International, Inc.
Employees: 3,000
Sales: $852 million (2006 est.)
NAICS: 339920 Sporting and Athletic Goods Manufacturing

■ ■ ■

ICON Health & Fitness, Inc., is the world's largest manufacturer and marketer of fitness and exercise equipment. Sold under the brand names NordicTrack, ProForm, Weider, HealthRider, FreeMotion Fitness, Image, Weslo, Epic, Reebok, Gold's Gym, and iFIT, ICON products include treadmills, exercise bikes, elliptical trainers, strength training products, and various fitness accessories. ICON sells its products using branded web sites and through retailers including Sears, Wal-Mart, Kmart, Target, and Costco. The company also sells to commercial customers and has operations in Asia, Europe, Mexico, and Latin America.

ORIGINS AND PREDECESSOR FIRMS

In 1977 two college students started a small import business that would eventually become ICON Health &

Fitness. Longtime friends Scott Watterson and Gary Stevenson were majoring in business at Utah State University in Logan, Utah, when they and Bradley Sorenson incorporated Weslo Design International under Utah law. According to the company's incorporation papers, its original purpose was to "engage in wholesale and retail sales of clocks, furniture, marble, metals, insulation, and other raw materials and manufactured items, and to engage in export and import sales of such items, and to invest and make investments in real and personal property, and to engage in any business whatsoever." After graduating from Utah State, the founders expanded their product line by selling wood-burning stoves. To balance the seasonal sales of the stoves, they began selling trampolines and mini-trampolines, their entry into the exercise equipment field.

By 1983 the young company's annual sales had reached about $30 million, mostly from the sales of both kinds of trampolines and also exercise bicycles. At that point Stan Tuttleman, a Philadelphia businessman, bought 55 percent of Weslo, including all interests of Blaine Hancy, an early partner of Watterson and Stevenson. Under Tuttleman's ownership, Weslo continued to grow, reaching annual sales in 1988 of about $60 million. In 1988 Weider Health and Fitness acquired Weslo and ProForm and made them subsidiaries of the privately owned company founded by Ben and Joe Weider. Stevenson and Watterson continued to manage Weslo with stock options as an incentive. With new products such as motorized treadmills, Weslo's annual sales reached $202.4 million in 1991.

Our mission is to be the first in fitness with leading edge innovation; to provide long-term profitability for our customers, employees, and the company; to produce on-time, on-budget, quality products that exceed the consumer's expectations of function, form and value.

In 1993 the company began using television information commercials (infomercials) to sell its products. Cofounder Scott Watterson in ICON's January 1996 newsletter said, "Where we once marketed our products exclusively to the retail trade, the introduction of infomercials opened doors for our company to successfully reach the consumer directly." ICON's first major infomercial demonstrated the benefits of the Pro-Form Crosswalk treadmill. By January 1995 ICON's direct marketing program included print, broadcast, and direct-mail operations. Celebrities such as skater Peggy Fleming, baseball star George Brett, and NFL quarterbacks Roger Staubach and Steve Young eventually promoted ICON products in infomercials and various other formats.

THE FORMATION OF ICON HEALTH & FITNESS

Weider originally considered taking Weslo, Inc., and ProForm Fitness Products, Inc., public, but instead the owners decided to sell the two subsidiaries to Bain Capital, a Boston-based investment firm headed by Mitt Romney, who had ties to Utah through his membership in The Church of Jesus Christ of Latter-day Saints. Weider initially received $159.3 million in cash while keeping 25 percent ownership. In addition to Bain Capital, the new owners included founders Stevenson and Watterson and other executives. They incorporated ICON Health & Fitness, Inc., on November 14, 1994, by combining Weslo; ProForm; Legend Products, Inc.; and American Physical Therapy Inc., a Weider division. Watterson became ICON's chairman and CEO, while Stevenson served as president and chief operating officer.

Product innovations continued to fuel ICON's growth in the mid-1990s. For example, in 1995 the company introduced ProForm Crosswalk treadmills with a trademarked Space Saver feature that allowed home users to store the Crosswalk vertically. In 1996 ICON added 25,000 square feet of office space to its Logan, Utah, headquarters.

In 1996 ICON sold bonds to raise $82.5 million, most of which was used the following year to acquire HealthRider Corporation, a Salt Lake City company that sold a popular line of exercise equipment. Gary H. Smith and his wife, Helen, had in 1990 discovered the HealthRider machine designed by Doyle Lambert. After acquiring the patent rights, the Smiths incorporated ExerHealth Inc. in March 1991, with Gary Smith as the new company's president and CEO. In 1992 Exer-Health began using infomercials to sell its HealthRider, primarily to those at least 40 years old. The company added aeROBICRider and SportRider, two lower-priced versions of its original product, and added over 250 retail outlets in 33 states by 1996. In 1995 the firm began international sales using LaForza Limited to distribute its products in Europe. With the addition of HealthRider's annual sales of $250 million in 1995, ICON's sales in 1996 reached about $1 billion.

OVERCOMING CHALLENGES

In 1997 ICON acquired Hoggan Health Industries, a 20-year-old exercise equipment manufacturer. Unlike ICON, with its emphasis on home exercisers, Hoggan made equipment for institutional use in rehabilitation and fitness centers. ICON's annual sales were $836.2 million in fiscal 1997. That same year ICON faced two challenges. First, in June 1997 the Federal Trade Commission (FTC) charged ICON and three other fitness equipment companies with false advertising that exaggerated the fitness and weight-loss benefits of their machines. While denying any wrongdoing, ICON and the other companies admitted they could not back up any of their advertising claims. They all agreed not to make future claims without valid documentation. No fines or penalties were involved. The four companies settled quickly with the FTC to avoid expensive court actions.

Also in 1997 ICON voluntarily recalled 78,000 ProForm R930 Space Saver Riders after receiving reports of injuries due to the product's tendency to close into the upright storage position while being used. ICON cooperated in this recall with the Consumer Product Safety Commission, which worked with many other companies to prevent more injuries from similar products.

In the late 1990s NordicTrack, another leader in the exercise equipment industry, declared bankruptcy and then was purchased by ICON. Started in 1976 by Minnesota inventor Ed Pauls, NordicTrack had helped pioneer the fitness machine industry with its popular cross-country skiing device. In 1986 CML Group Inc. purchased NordicTrack, and sales continued to increase. From its peak sales of $477 million in 1993, Nordic-

1977: Weslo Design International, Inc., is founded.

1988: Weider Health and Fitness, Inc., purchases Weslo and ProForm.

1990: Weider acquires Image Inc.

1991: Weider acquires JumpKing Inc.

1992: Weider acquires Legend Sporting Goods.

1993: A direct consumer sales campaign is started using infomercials.

1994: ICON Health & Fitness, Inc., is created; Pro-Form is registered as an ISO 9001 manufacturer.

1995: ICON acquires Image, Inc., a Utah corporation.

1997: ICON acquires HealthRider Corporation and Hoggan Health Industries.

1998: ICON licenses Reebok home exercise equipment; CML Group Inc. announces in December its sale of bankrupt NordicTrack to ICON.

1999: ICON completes a major financial restructuring to reduce its heavy debt load.

2000: The company announces its agreement to acquire Ground Zero Design of Colorado Springs.

2001: FreeMotion Fitness Inc. is acquired; the company signs a licensing deal with Gold's Gym International.

2005: A new distribution center opens in Savannah, Georgia.

Track declined to $267 million in 1997. Facing stiff competition from makers of a variety of equipment, NordicTrack started 125 permanent retail mall stores and set up 100 temporary mall kiosks, instead of relying just on its usual infomercials and other forms of direct marketing. That "clumsy expansion was an invitation to disaster," said Jay Weiner in the December 14, 1998, *Business Week*. Faced with a saturated market, Nordic-Track filed for Chapter 11 bankruptcy in November 1998.

ICON Health & Fitness bid first to acquire Nordic-Track, and in December 1998 NordicTrack announced its intent to be acquired by ICON. The Utah company paid $12 million for the Chaska, Minnesota-based firm, which by that time had closed its retail stores. Although NordicTrack had declined as a business, its brand name remained popular. ICON used that reputation as it of-

fered new NordicTrack brand products. By 2000 NordicTrack treadmills, elliptical machines, recumbent bikes, and strength machines were available, some with small TV screens and Internet access.

LICENSING AGREEMENTS

In the late 1990s ICON began offering its products through licensing agreements with other firms. For example, in 1998 it signed an agreement with Reebok to produce home exercise equipment to be sold under the Reebok name. By 2000 it offered brand names Nordic-Track, ProForm, and HealthRider under various licensing agreements. Meanwhile, ICON in 1998 introduced its new ProForm Club Series of commercial treadmills, which surprised the fitness industry since ProForm previously was sold only to home consumers.

At the end of its fiscal year ending May 31, 1999, ICON Health & Fitness recorded total annual sales of $710 million, down about 5 percent from its 1998 total of $749 million. It also had a net loss in 1999 of $7.8 million compared to a 1998 net loss of $9.5 million. In fiscal 1999, "ICON chose to reduce its sales to longtime customers Service Merchandise, Venture Stores and Caldor, all of whom had credit problems," said ICON spokesperson Colleen Logan in a September 1, 1999, *Business Wire*. "That choice, although it reduced the Company's topline sales, helped protect its financial position."

Also in 1999 ICON introduced a web site for its recently acquired line of NordicTrack products. Cyber shoppers at www.nordictrack.com were invited to buy the company's products on a retail basis or through an online auction system. The interactive site also allowed people to type in personal data and then receive a health report with recommendations for better health.

By early 2000 ICON expanded its use of the Internet by introducing iFit.com, host to "the world's first Internet-controlled fitness equipment," according to a February 8, 2000, *Business Wire*. This new technology allowed exercisers to plug their equipment into their computers and then use the iFit.com web site to select various programs that could adjust speed, incline, resistance levels, or weight levels to get the best workout. The iFit.com technology received several awards in 2000, including a Best Value honor from the Good Housekeeping Institute and the Most Innovative Product designation from Sports Authority.

NEW PRODUCTS AND ACQUISITIONS

In 2000 ICON began designing and manufacturing eight models of scooters priced from $39 to $129.

ICON distributed its more expensive scooters through Sears and also Sports Authority, Dick's Sporting Goods, Oshman's, and other sporting goods stores. Scooters were first sold in early 1999 by other companies primarily to children, teenagers, and young adults. According to Huffy Vice-President Bill Smith in *Sporting Goods Business* on October 11, 2000, about 50,000 scooters were sold in 1999, but he expected at least five million would be sold by the end of 2000.

Groundbreaking was held in August 2000 for a new Texas industrial park that ICON would occupy. Located in Mesquite in the Dallas–Fort Worth area, the Skyline Business Park would accommodate ICON's plans for a 400,000-square-foot distribution facility. In December 2000 ICON announced it would not participate in the Super Show 2001 in Las Vegas. Described as the world's major trade show for sports equipment and fitness apparel, the Super Show had included ICON ever since it was first held in 1986. The show's general decline in the late 1990s and bad timing were two factors involved in ICON's decision, which was supported by spokespersons from both Sears and Dick's Sporting Goods.

ICON also acquired Ground Zero Design, a manufacturer of exercise equipment that had been founded in 1999. Based in Colorado Springs, Ground Zero planned to remain in Colorado Springs as an ICON division employing about 35 people. ICON purchased Ground Zero to help it enter the commercial market. "ICON dominates the consumer business; virtually everything you see at Sears or Sam's Club is ICON under various brand names," explained Roy Simonson, Ground Zero's cofounder in the *Colorado Springs Gazette-Telegraph*. "But they have no experience in the commercial market. They were looking for someone with fresh ideas already connected to the industry." Simonson designed what writer Steven Saint in the *Colorado Springs Gazette-Telegraph* called Ground Zero's "15-piece line of nontraditional training machines designed to follow the movement of the user's body rather than dictate a certain position or movement."

ICON IN THE 21ST CENTURY

At the start of the new millennium, ICON faced several challenges. It had to continue to find new customers, since most fitness machine owners would not consider purchasing a second fitness machine. Their customers were limited to middle or upper-class people or clubs that catered to such individuals. The good news was that the U.S. economy, although declining, remained basically healthy at the time, so many could afford to purchase their products. Many overweight Americans had much to gain from treadmills, the main fitness product sold in the United States, and other devices that ICON offered. The fitness equipment industry praised ICON's high-tech innovations, one of the company's obvious strengths.

ICON continued to look for ways to bolster revenues and profits. Its 2001 purchase of FreeMotion Fitness Inc. expanded its foothold in the commercial and specialty fitness markets. The company also signed a licensing agreement with Gold's Gym International, one the largest fitness chains in the world. The deal allowed ICON to manufacture and market a line of fitness equipment under the Gold's Gym brand name.

A July 2001 *Internet Wire* included comments made by ICON Chairman and CEO Scott Watterson: "Fitness industry sales and forecast for future growth are stronger than ever before, but yet there are millions of people still not working out." Watterson also claimed that a study published in the *Journal of Public Health* found that obesity was worse than drinking or smoking for a person's health. He went on to state, "Gold's Gym fitness equipment will be another excellent opportunity for people to get into fitness and improve their quality of life."

The U.S. economy began to weaken dramatically after the terrorist attacks against the United States on September 11, 2001, and continued to head toward what many analysts feared would be a recession. The fitness equipment market remained somewhat shielded from this decline. It grew from $3.7 billion in 2000 to $4.2 billion in early 2007. ICON failed to capitalize on this growth, however, and its profits began to fall. Accordingly, the company announced job cuts in 2007. It shuttered its Clearfield, Utah, manufacturing facility and moved most of its operations to its plant in Logan. In order to cut transportation costs, it also made changes in storage and shipping. It opened a new distribution center in Savannah, Georgia, in 2005.

During this period, ICON also remained focused on offering cutting edge products. For example, it released the NordicTrack Viewpoint 3000 treadmill in 2006. The new treadmill included a MP3 port, a built-in flat-screen television and sound system, and an iFit workout card that was designed to help a user plan workout routines and set weight-loss goals. While the U.S. economy continued to falter well into 2008, ICON not only focused on developing new products, but also worked diligently on controlling costs while attempting to shore up profits. With nearly 200 patents to its name and nine international locations, ICON remained the largest manufacturer and marketer of fitness equipment across the globe.

David M. Walden
Updated, Christina M. Stansell

PRINCIPAL COMPETITORS

Cybex International Inc.; Fitness Quest Inc.; Life Fitness.

FURTHER READING

Agoglia, John, "ICON Refinancing Is 'Critical' to Viability," *Sporting Goods Business*, October 11, 1999, p. 22.

————, "Reverse Order: ProForm Jumps from Home to Club," *Sporting Goods Business*, April 15, 1998, p. 16.

Boulton, Guy, "Shaping Up Business: ICON Health & Fitness Restructures to Shed Itself of Excessive Debt," *Salt Lake Tribune*, October 10, 1999, p. E1.

Cassidy, Hilary, "Will Scooters Keep Rolling Along?" *Sporting Goods Business*, October 11, 2000.

Cayton, Rodd, "Redlands Business Center Lands Fitness ICON," *Press-Enterprise*, July 17, 2007.

"Executive Focus: Gary H. Smith," *Deseret News*, June 6, 1993, p. M2.

"Fitness Industry Leader Releases TOP Brand Names for Licensing; ICON Health & Fitness Ready for Licensing Ventures," *Business Wire*, December 15, 2000.

"Fitness Leader Says No to the Super Show; ICON Health & Fitness Leaves Behind an Old Venue," *Business Wire*, December 15, 2000.

"Gold's Gym Announces Strategic Alliance to Market Fitness Equipment with ICON Health & Fitness," *Internet Wire*, July 25, 2001.

Grossman, Cathy Lynn, "Treadmill Sales Outpace Ski, Ab Machines," *USA Today*, November 23, 1998.

Hawthorne, Kate, "Pulling It All Together," *Marketeer*, May 1996.

"ICON Continues 21-Year Profit Streak; Receives Sears Order for 75,000 New Treadmills; Now Hiring for 250 Open Positions," *Business Wire*, September 1, 1999, p. 1.

"ICON Health & Fitness and iFit.com Awarded Retailer's Top Honors; Starting the Year Off Right, ICON and iFit.com Receive Major Awards in the First Quarter of 2000," *Business Wire*, May 22, 2000.

"ICON to Buy Ground Zero," *Salt Lake Tribune*, January 6, 2001, p. B4.

"iFit.com Works with Microsoft's Windows Media to Create World's First Internet Appliance for 'Body Surfing' the Web," *Business Wire*, February 8, 2000.

Knudson, Max B., "ProForm, Weslo Health-Equipment Firms Sign a Deal to Boost Their Fiscal Fitness," *Deseret News*, November 15, 1994, p. D7.

Kufahl, Pamela, and Jennipher Shaver, "Manufacturers Face Tough Economy," *Fitness Business Pro*, July 1, 2008.

Lee, Renee C., "Mesquite Development Groundbreaking Today ... ," *Fort Worth Star-Telegram*, August 24, 2000, p. 3.

"Logan's ICON Health Buys Hoggan Health," *Salt Lake Tribune*, February 19, 1997.

Lorenzi, Neal, "Consumer Product Safety Commission Product Recalls," *Professional Safety*, September 1997, p. 12.

McEvoy, Christopher, "FTC Cracks Down on Top Fitness Vendor," *Sporting Goods Business*, July 7, 1997, p. 42.

"NordicTrack Goes On-line; America's Number One Fitness Brand Launches High-Tech Outlet," *PR Newswire*, April 27, 1999, p. 1.

"NordicTrack Releases New Entertainment Treadmill," *ENP Newswire*, December 21, 2006.

Oberbeck, Steven, "Logan Exercise Equipment Manufacturer to Lay Off 250," *Salt Lake Tribune*, January 17, 2007.

Rebello, Joseph, "Bain Group to Buy Assets of Three Firms," *Wall Street Journal*, November 14, 1994, pp. A3, A6.

"Retail Entrepreneurs of the Year: Helen Smith, Gary Smith," *Chain Store Age*, December 1996, p. 94.

Retsky, Maxine Lans, "Exercise Good Judgment When Developing Your Advertising," *Marketing News*, August 18, 1997, p. 5.

Saint, Steven, "Maker of NordicTrack Buys Springs Firm," *Colorado Springs Gazette-Telegraph*, January 6, 2001, p. BUS1.

"Tailored for an LBO," *Mergers and Acquisitions*, November/December 1996, p. 26.

Villarosa, Linda, "A Fitness Industry, with Gadgets Galore," *New York Times*, April 25, 2000.

Walden, David M., "ICON Health & Fitness, Inc.," in *Centennial Utah: The Beehive State on the Eve of the Twenty-First Century*, by G. Wesley Johnson and Marian Ashby Johnson, pp. 134–35, Encino, Calif.: Cherbo Publishing Group, 1995.

Weiner, Jay, "How NordicTrack Lost Its Footing," *Business Week*, December 14, 1998, p. 138.

Integrity Media, Inc.

1000 Cody Road South
Mobile, Alabama 36695-3499
U.S.A.
Telephone: (251) 633-9000
Toll Free: (800) 533-6912
Fax: (251) 776-5134
Web site: http://www.integritymedia.com

Private Company
Incorporated: 1987 as Integrity Music Inc.
Employees: 218
Sales: $86 million (2007 est.)
NAICS: 334612 Prerecorded Compact Disc (Except
Software), Tape, and Record Reproducing

■ ■ ■

Integrity Media, Inc., is a privately held Mobile, Alabama-based communications company specializing in the production and distribution of Christian music, films, and other related ventures. Music is published under several labels: Integrity Music and Vertical Music, both based in Mobile, and INO Records, a Brentwood, Tennessee, operation. Genres include modern worship, praise and worship, urban/gospel, children's music, and "vertical music" (a style of worship music directed at God). Integrity Music has enjoyed notable success with the Songs 4 Worship compilation series co-branded with Time-Life Music. These titles are also available through the company's direct response division, Integrity Direct, which distributes Christian music, film, and digital products through direct mail as well as the Internet.

Together Integrity Music and INO enjoy a 13.5 percent share of the Christian music marketplace, making them the top independent labels in the field. Integrity also participates in the Spanish-language marketplace through Integrity en Espanol, which focuses on Latin Christian music.

Another Integrity Media venture is Worship-Kitchen, an online resource for worship leaders, offering music organizing tools, sheet music and chord charts, background tracks, and videos for use in worship services as well as training videos. The Integrity Live unit offers training to worship teams through seminars and workshops conducted across the country, covering such topics as songwriting, audio mixing, and worship space design, lighting, and production. Integrity Media also operates internationally through several subsidiaries: Integrity Media Asia Pte Ltd., Integrity Music Europe Ltd., Integrity Media Africa (Pty) Ltd., and Integrity International Group (covering Latin America). All told, Integrity products are sold in more than 160 countries.

COMPANY FOUNDED

Integrity Media grew out of Covenant Church of Mobile, founded in 1973 by Charles Simpson and a team of pastors. Simpson was an early leader of the Charismatic Renewal Movement and in 1969 helped to found *New Wine* magazine, which would become associated with Covenant Church in 1978. The publication was mailed to 100,000 homes in more than 100 nations and several years later was used to sell cassettes of recorded live praise services from Covenant Church. In 1985 a nonprofit company was established, Integrity

Communications, Inc., to market these tapes under the Hosanna label on a mail-order basis. The tapes proved to be far more popular than *New Wine,* which ceased publication in 1986. A year later *New Wine's* publisher, P. Michael Coleman, and Ed Lindquist acquired Integrity Communications from Charles Simpson Ministries, Inc., and created a for-profit direct-to-consumer music club called Integrity Music Inc., with Coleman serving as president and Simpson assuming a seat on the board of directors. Lindquist, serving as vice-president, left the company within a few years, but not before joining Coleman in 1988 to establish Worship International, Integrity's nonprofit ministry outreach.

Integrity found a ready market for its Hosanna tapes as well as other products, which would soon include children's songs, instrumental music, Scripture memory songs, and songbooks, as well as videos, such as Christian aerobic workouts. In 1988 a distribution agreement was reached with Sparrow Corporation, parent company of Sparrow Records, a California-based Christian record label that would relocate to Nashville in 1991. Working with Sparrow, Integrity did well in the praise and worship genre, but it also began to broaden its product lines to appeal to denominations beyond Charismatic churches. Integrity enjoyed a growth rate of about 25 percent, as revenues increased to $23.7 million in 1992, resulting in a net profit of $2.8 million. Outgrowing its facilities, Integrity was forced to use trailers for temporary quarters. Plans were approved in 1992 to construct an 18,000-square-foot building near its facilities. A year later Integrity acquired some facilities from Covenant Church, purchased other nearby property, and altered its plans to build a 30,000-square-foot office complex. Several months later another 15,000 square feet of space was added to the proposal.

GOING PUBLIC

After improving sales to $29.1 million and net income to $3.8 million in 1993, Integrity elected not to renew its distribution agreement with Sparrow after it expired on August 3, 1994. Instead, Coleman elected to use its own sales force to sell its products to Christian bookstores and general markets, such as Wal-Mart and Tower Records. Warehousing and fulfillment were handled by Belleville, Michigan-based Spring Arbor Distributors, which was very familiar with the Integrity line, having carried the products for several years. In addition to strong domestic growth, Integrity also built an international direct-to-church business through subsidiaries in Australia and the United Kingdom. The company also decided to branch out beyond concept products into the artist side of the music business, signing talent to its label.

To fund further growth, Integrity was taken public in July 1994. A few months later ground was finally broken on the company's new $4.2 million office complex. When the year came to an end, sales had increased to $34.8 million and net income totaled $2.8 million. Integrity stock, initially priced at $9 a share, increased in value to $13.50. All signs appeared hopeful for the fast-growing company, but in 1995 Integrity was introduced to the pitfalls that a public company could face. Results were disappointing in 1995. Although sales improved to $36.3 million, the company posted a net loss of more than $2 million. Well before that time, however, investors had punished the company, driving down the price of Integrity stock to $2.25 by mid-December after a third-quarter loss of more than $1 million.

Integrity's problems were many, including too much debt and too much spending, especially in marketing to support new product lines. There was also stiffer competition in the Christian music marketplace, as major music companies acquired the top independent Christian labels and Integrity discovered the difficulties involved in promoting individual artists. Investors were also disconcerted by Integrity's contributions to Worship International, which received $2.1 million from 1990 to July 1995. Moreover, in 1995 Integrity advanced Worship International $147,000 and donated $477,000. Integrity took steps to address its situation, including layoffs for 45 employees and a cut in salary for Coleman. While the exterior of the new office building was completed, interior work was postponed.

RETURN TO PROFITABILITY

Coleman and his executive team were forced to make adjustments and began seeking out market niches Integrity could fill while keeping costs balanced against revenues. As Integrity adapted to the new realities, difficult times continued in 1996, when revenues fell to $30.4 million and the company lost a further $3.5 million. There were some positive developments as well. A new financial arrangement was reached with an Austrian bank subsidiary, Creditanstalt Corporate Finance Inc. Costs were cut when Integrity eliminated ten sales positions and turned over the responsibilities to

```
┌─────────────────────────────────────────────┐
│                                               │
│              KEY DATES                        │
│                    ■                          │
│  ─────────────────────────────────────────    │
│                                               │
│  1985:  Nonprofit Integrity Communications,   │
│         Inc., formed to market mail-order     │
│         Christian music tapes.                │
│  1987:  For-profit direct-to-consumer music   │
│         club Integrity Music formed.          │
│  1994:  Company is taken public.              │
│  2000:  Integrity and Time-Life Music launch  │
│         Songs 4 Worship line.                 │
│  2002:  Integrity Music changes its name to   │
│         Integrity Media.                      │
│  2004:  Company is taken private.             │
│  2006:  Integrity Publishing sold.            │
│                                               │
└─────────────────────────────────────────────┘
```

Word Distribution, a move that also increased the company's retail market access.

Integrity returned to profitability in 1997, regaining lost ground on revenues, which improved to $32.4 million, resulting in a modest net gain of $642,000. Business continued to improve in the final years of the decade, with sales increasing to $38.8 million in 1998 and $45.6 million in 1999 and net income totaling $1.75 million and $1.4 million respectively. Indicative of Integrity's improving fortunes, five of its albums topped the 500,000 sales mark, certifying them as gold. In the video category, several Integrity titles were certified gold (sales of 250,000) and two *Just-for-Kids* videos reached the 500,000 sales level, garnering them platinum status. In addition, Integrity launched a new product, Integrity Notes, a direct-to-consumer greeting card line.

To build on its momentum, Integrity forged a partnership with Time-Life Music in 2000 to air commercials selling Christian music on network television. Integrity also created a concert series for broadcast on the PAX-TV Christian cable network. The company was not especially happy, however, about the lagging price of its stock, which by late 2000 was worth less than $2.40 a share. An investment banking firm was retained to review ways to improve shareholder value, a move that led to press speculation that a stock buyback plan was in the offing or that perhaps Coleman, who along with his family controlled about 70 percent of the stock, was considering taking the company private. For the year, sales increased to $51.8 million and net income to $1.7 million, some of the growth due to the successful launch of the Songs 4 Worship compilation line with Time-Life Music late in the year. The album series, backed by

extensive television advertising, continued to perform well in 2001, quickly becoming Time-Life's most successful continuity program. The first title in the series sold 1.8 million copies, and more than one million customers then signed up to receive additional monthly two-disc collections.

BOOK PUBLISHING UNIT FORMED

Integrity decided to break into the world of Christian book publishing in 2001. To head the venture, named Integrity Publishers, the company hired Byron Williamson, former president of Nelson/Word publishing group. He had also been president of Word Publishing before Nelson acquired the publishing firm. Williamson set up shop in Nashville and began assembling a staff in order to develop an initial list of 18 to 20 titles for release in the fall of 2002.

With the Songs 4 Worship line leading the way, accounting for sales of $24.5 million, Integrity grew revenues to $71 million and net income to $2.8 million in 2001. When sales for Songs 4 Worship dropped to $13.4 million a year later, however, Integrity experienced a decline in net sales to $66.3 million in 2002, and net income dipped to $2.2 million. Also in July 2002 Integrity Music changed its name to Integrity Media, which the company believed provided a better description of the far-flung enterprise. A few weeks later Integrity Publishing released its first list of 16 book titles. Sales were brisk to start, resulting in six titles making the Christian Booksellers Association bestseller list within six months and one title landing on the prestigious *New York Times* bestseller list. The publisher soon encountered difficult conditions, however, and sales fell off dramatically in 2003. Also in 2002, Integrity acquired M2 Communications and its M2.0 and INO music labels. The company was then renamed INO Records the following year.

INO contributed $7.6 million in partial-year revenues for its new parent in 2002, and in 2003 increased that amount to $12.8 million, a welcome improvement given that the Songs 4 Worship line continued to slip to $9 million in 2003. Integrity Publishers also provided $8.2 million in sales, helping Integrity Media to grow net sales to $74.3 million in 2003. Net income, on the other hand, dipped to $1.9 million. Exact sales figures were no longer available in 2004. In that year Coleman elected to take Integrity private. The price of the company's stock had shown some improvement, but the cost of complying with the new regulatory requirements of the Sarbanes-Oxley Act of 2002, in terms of both time and money, was not worth it to a small company such as Integrity. With a

$15 million infusion of cash from private equity firm Key Principal Partners, Coleman led a two-year management team effort that once again made Integrity a private company in July 2004.

Integrity became a private company in the full sense of the word. News of its successes and failures were less available to the world. Integrity Publishing apparently did not fare as well as Coleman had hoped, as evidenced by published reports that he offered the business to Nashville's Thomas Nelson Inc. in the summer of 2006. A sale was then concluded in September of that year. Nevertheless, Integrity remained eager for opportunities in other areas. In late 2006 it partnered with Sony BMG Music Entertainment to launch MWorship, a product that allowed users to text message prayers and perform other tasks. A year later the WorshipKitchen media download service for worship leaders was launched. At the same time, worship music, the longtime staple of Integrity Music, was evolving from a generic, unbranded form of church music into a genre populated by well-known leaders and acts. Worship music, as a result, began appearing on music charts, a trend that bode well for the future of Integrity Media.

Ed Dinger

PRINCIPAL SUBSIDIARIES

Integrity en Espanol; Integrity Music Inc.; INO Records; Media Asia Pte Ltd.; Integrity Music Europe Ltd.; Integrity Media Africa (Pty) Ltd.; Integrity International Group.

PRINCIPAL COMPETITORS

EMI Group Limited; Guideposts; Provident Music Group.

FURTHER READING

Chunn, Sherri, "Integrity Hits Some Sour Notes," *Mobile Register,* December 15, 1995, p. A1.

———, "Integrity Tunes Up with Refinancing," *Mobile Register,* August 25, 1996, p. F1.

———, "Integrity's Growth Continues," *Mobile Register,* November 22, 1994, p. B7.

Darden, Bob, "Integrity's Move to Spring Arbor Adds 20 Staffers," *Billboard,* April 2, 1994, p. 10.

Davidson, "Integrity Media Signs Acquisition Agreement," *Mobile Register,* March 3, 2004, p. B6.

Drobnic, Angie, "Integrity Stock Price Out of Tune?" *Mobile Register,* December 31, 2000, p. F1.

Holmes, "Integrity Music Grows," *Mobile Register,* March 12, 1994, p. D5.

Kiesling, Angie, "Williamson to Head New Publishing Entity," *Publishers Weekly,* July 2, 2001, p. 10.

Perry, "Covenant Church Has Experienced Great Growth," *Mobile Register,* May 20, 1995, p. B5.

Price, Deborah Evans, "Praise Be! Worship Music Jumps from the Church to the Charts," *Billboard,* October 11, 2008, p. 27.

Wilkinson, Kaija, "Integrity Media to Sell Publishing Arm to Nashville Firm," *Mobile Press-Register,* September 22, 2006, p. B7.

Williams, Roy L., "Integrity's Niche Marketing in Christian Music Pays Off," *Birmingham (Ala.) News,* January 9, 2000, p. 6H.

Jack B. Kelley, Inc.

— ■ —

801 South Fillmore Street, Suite 505
Amarillo, Texas 79121-1069
U.S.A.
Telephone: (806) 353-3553
Toll Free: (800) 225-5525
Fax: (806) 354-4999
Web site: http://www.jackbkelley.com

Private Company
Incorporated: 1969
Employees: 900
Sales: $176 million (2007)
NAICS: 484121 General Freight Trucking, Long-
   Distance, Truckload

■ ■ ■

A private company based in Amarillo, Texas, Jack B.
Kelley, Inc., (JBK) is a long-distance trucking company
operating throughout the continental United States as
well as parts of Canada and Alaska. JBK made its mark
with the transportation of helium and today transports a
variety of industrial gases and specialized chemicals,
including acetylene, argon, bromine, calcium bromide,
carbon dioxide, carbon monoxide, compressed air,
ethane, ethylene, hydrogen, hydrogen chloride,
hydrogen sulfide, methane, methyl alcohol natural gas,
nitrogen, nitrogen trifluoride, nitrous oxide, oxygen, and
zinc bromide. JBK maintains about 15 terminals in
more than a dozen states.

Through subsidiary City Machine & Welding, Inc.,
of Amarillo, JBK fabricates and compressed gas and

cryogenic liquid trailers. Another JBK subsidiary,
Specialty Trailer Leasing, leases trailers and storage
modules for compressed gases and cryogenic liquids on
both a short-term and long-term basis. Both of these
JBK operations are based in Amarillo with a branch in
La Porte, Texas. JBK's chief executive officer, Ken Kelley,
is the son of the founder, Jack B. Kelley.

FOUNDER, TEXAS BORN IN 1916

Jack Bryson Kelley was born near Whitesboro, Texas, in
November 1916. His father took a job with the state
highway department in 1925, resulting in the family
moving to Amarillo. Here Kelley displayed a willingness
to do hard work and an entrepreneurial spirit, selling ice
cream bars from his Radio Flyer wagon, maintaining a
newspaper route, and bagging groceries at a Piggly Wiggly store as a teen, in addition to other odd jobs. He
graduated from high school in 1935 in the midst of the
Great Depression.

Unable to find full-time employment, he worked as
a day laborer and continued to bag groceries on occasion until finally leaving town to work in a Colorado
mine. He later returned to Amarillo to work at a smelting operating tending the blast furnaces. A turning
point in his life came with the United States' entry into
World War II. Rather than wait to be drafted, in April
1942 Kelley enlisted in the U.S. Navy, serving for a
short time in the Pacific in the engine room of a landing
craft gunboat before receiving a stateside posting.

After his discharge from the Navy, the economy was
booming and Kelley was able to return home to find
work as a truck driver, his regular route stretching from

Amarillo to Colorado. One of his customers was a Pueblo, Colorado, toy balloon distributor who asked Kelley if he could acquire a cylinder of helium in Amarillo for him. Kelley knew nothing about the helium business or the importance of Amarillo to the industry, but he was about to learn something that would change his future.

Helium was found in natural gas deposits, mostly in the natural gas fields of southwest Wyoming and a stretch of land that spread from the Texas Panhandle into Kansas. Because helium was used to fill observation blimps during World War I, security of the helium sources had become a matter of national security. In the 1920s the government took control of production and zealously limited the distribution of the gas, which was dispensed by the United States Bureau of Mines in Amarillo. When Kelley naively attempted to buy a cylinder of helium for his customer, he soon learned that no private individual had a government contract to procure or transport helium.

KELLEY RECEIVES A HELIUM CONTRACT

Sensing a business opportunity, the entrepreneurial Kelley began the arduous and lengthy process of applying for a contract to buy and sell helium. With the help of a Bureau of Mines official, an ex-Marine, Fred Webster, who took a liking to his fellow veteran, Kelley was able to complete the application, which included a bond and deposit on the government-owned compressed gas cylinders. To make these payments, Kelley drew on his $500 discharge pay from the Navy. Thus, in early 1946 Jack Kelley received his helium contract, the only private citizen in the country to have one.

For the next few years selling and delivering helium was merely a side business, a way to make some extra money on his regular freight runs from Amarillo to Colorado. Always on the lookout for a way to make more money, Kelley pursued other business ventures as well. Recognizing the need for a truck stop along his regular route, he built the Hill Top Service Truck Stop near Springfield, Colorado, in 1951, relying on galvanized steel modular buildings manufactured by the Wonder Building Company.

Because no one in that area sold the buildings, Kelley became a Wonder Building franchisee; after opening his truck stop, he sold modular units to area farmers as low cost grain storage bins. As he became familiar with the business of his grain farmer customers, he recognized their need for reliable combines, the breakdown of which during harvesting season could prove to be a serious setback. Researching the combines on the market, he decided the best in the industry were the Gleaner-Baldwin models offered by Allis-Chalmers. He applied for the franchise for the Springfield area and started a Gleaner-Baldwin dealership that operated out of his truck stop.

While Kelley was assembling a small business empire in Colorado he continued his freight deliveries and the helium business grew. In time, he had so many balloon users, fairs, and carnivals ordering cylinders of helium from all parts of the country that he had to turn to other freight lines to make the deliveries. It became apparent that he needed to not only sell and arrange delivery of helium, but also he required the means to deliver large quantities of the gas himself.

Moreover, his customers were clamoring for ever growing quantities of helium, more than could be stored in the standard 242-cubic-foot cylinders. His research about compressed gas trailers took him to the Harrisburg Steel Company, which offered a trailer with 38 individual tubes, which could hold more than 64,000 cubic feet of helium. Kelley bought one of the trailers, which he would use in 1959 to deliver the helium needed to float the giant balloons of the Macy's Thanksgiving Day Parade in New York City.

NEW LEGISLATION COMPLICATES HELIUM BUSINESS

Devoting himself to the helium business, Kelley sold his Springfield interests. In 1961 he even began investing in oil and gas ventures in order to drill helium-producing wells, but the transport of the gas remained the focus of JBK. It was an endeavor that grew more challenging with the passage of the Helium Conservation Act of 1960, which further restricted helium ownership and its transport.

Kelley's main rivals in the delivery of helium came from the railroads. He was able to offer point-to-point delivery but needed to be able to haul even greater quantities. Furthermore, he had to win government ap-

KEY DATES

1946: Jack B. Kelley receives his first government helium contract.

1961: Kelley designs and builds a jumbo tube trailer to transport gases.

1969: Jack B. Kelley, Inc., is formed.

1980: Jack Kelley dies.

1986: Hawkeye Transport and W.S. Hatch Company are acquired.

1994: LNG Technologies USA, LLC, is formed.

2002: JBK Video Productions is sold.

proval to establish irregular truck routes in order to make deliveries throughout the country. It took three years to navigate the federal bureaucracy. This not only included winning over the Interstate Commerce Commission (ICC) but also the Department of Defense, the National Aeronautics and Space Administration, the National Oceanographic and Atmospheric Administration, and the National Science Foundation.

INNOVATION LEADS TO GOVERNMENT APPROVAL

In the meantime, Kelley studied the science of compressed gas enclosures and designed a jumbo tube trailer that was a major improvement over the basic concept of stacked tubes employed by Harrisburg Steel, overcoming problems that had defeated trained engineers. Because the maximum length of the trailer was defined, the only way to add volume was to increase the number of tubes and their individual size. Unfortunately, the additional tubes created forces that led to the trailers breaking apart on the road. Kelley's solution was a front-end tube connector that permitted the tubes to flex independently and eliminated the danger of the tubes twisting apart.

A major hurdle to building the trailer, however, was the need for 22-inch tubes to form the bottom row of the configuration. U.S. Steel was the only company capable of producing large-diameter steel tubing, but it manufactured tubes in only 18-inch and 24-inch diameters. Kelley had to navigate a corporate bureaucracy in order to place an order. In the end he had to guarantee a $100,000 payment in order to have the work begun.

In March 1961 Kelley's new jumbo tube trailer was finally completed at Amarillo's City Machine and Welding Shop, a future JBK subsidiary. The trailer would

prove to be a key element in the case Kelley made with the ICC in his bid for irregular truck routes, finally granted in October 1963.

SERVING THE SPACE INDUSTRY AND EXPANDING SERVICES

With the truck routes and new jumbo trailers, JBK enjoyed rapid growth. To better serve the aerospace industry, a helium transfer terminal was opened in San Diego for companies involved in the U.S. space program. The company also began to expand beyond helium transport. In 1968 a Louisiana chemical company dependent on carbon monoxide provided by a neighboring petrochemical plant contracted Kelley after its supplier was put out of commission by an explosion. The jumbo trailers were filled with carbon monoxide from a plant in Deer Park, Texas, and hauled to the Louisiana plant. Kelley's performance in this case promoted the company's name in the chemical and compressed gas industries, which soon led to the company handling other gases, including hydrogen, nitrogen, oxygen, methane, and ethylene.

Jack Kelley also began to study the science of cryogenics and how the use of super-cold materials could be use in material storage and transport. This effort led to the opening of a terminal and dedicated office to handle such shipments in La Porte, Texas. Another diversification move came in 1967 when Kelley acquired another trucking firm's authority to haul oil field equipment and pipe in Texas. Once again he displayed a flair for ingenuity, making use of four-wheel steerable dollies that were attached to the end of the long structures and driven by a second driver, allowing the loads to negotiate turns and rough terrain. This method opened up jobs to haul other oversized materials, such as pre-stressed 100-foot-long, 100,000-pound concrete construction beams.

JACK B. KELLEY, INC., IS FORMED

In July 1969 Jack B. Kelley, Inc., was formed to house Kelley's business ventures. Two years later he moved his operations to a 20-acre site in Amarillo, conveniently located near the Bureau of Mines' helium extraction plant. The following year, 1972, JBK opened a terminal in La Porte, followed by a branch in Magnolia, Arkansas, in 1976.

Ever since a childhood accident, Jack Kelley had never enjoyed the best of health, and twice as an adult he battled cancer. Nevertheless, he worked until the very end of life. When the end came in June 1980, Kelley completed a full day of work, sat down in an easy chair to watch the evening news on television, and dozed off. Due to heart failure he never awoke. His wife, Hazel, who had been heavily involved in his businesses from the very beginning, took over as JBK's chairperson, while their son Ken became president and CEO and daughter Sharon was named secretary-treasurer of the corporation.

Despite the loss of its founder, JBK continued to grow. Later in 1980 a terminal opened in Savannah, Georgia. A year after that a terminal opened in Seagraves, Texas, followed by terminals in Fontana, California, and Great Bend, Kansas, in 1983, and Dixon, California, in 1985. A year later JBK grew even larger through a pair of acquisitions: Hawkeyes Transport, an Iowa agricultural chemical carrier, and W.S. Hatch Company, a Utah-based large bulk-commodity carriers.

As a result of these expansions the following terminals in four states were added in 1986: Stanwood, Iowa; Rock Springs, Wyoming; Henderson, Nevada; and Woods Cross, Huntington, and Delta, Utah. Five more terminals opened in 1988: Theodore, Alabama; Austin, Nevada; and Phoenix, Clay Pool, and Tucson, Arizona. JBK closed the decade with the addition of a terminal in Wendover, Nevada. All told, by 1990 JBK maintained 23 terminals. Its fleet included more than 300 tractors and over 400 compressed gas tube trailers and more than 100 cryogenic trailers.

LNG TECHNOLOGIES FORMED

During the 1990s JBK continued to adapt to the times. In 1994 the company formed LNG Technologies USA, LLC, to become involved in vehicle-grade liquefied natural gas (LNG) for industrial use and as an alternative vehicle fuel. The company procured natural gas from the pipeline, liquefied it, and transported it to customers.

The business was expanded in 1995 with the acquisition of Austin, Texas-based TrenFuel, which maintained 11 vehicle CNG filling stations in Arizona, California, and Nevada. They were subsequently converted to LNG, laying the foundation for a nationwide LNG fueling infrastructure. The following year JBK became the first customer to accept delivery of a Kenworth truck with an LNG engine, another important step in the development of LNG as an important alternative fuel of the future.

By 2000 LNG Technologies emerged as the largest LNG wholesaler in the Western United States and

Mexico. The business was spun off from JBK, as were other ventures that were spawned by the trucking concern. The company's need for training videos led to the creation of JBK Video Productions, sold in 2002 to Synergy Communications Inc., which would continue to produce training programs for JBK.

Another spinoff was GTM Manufacturing, carrying on the visionary work Jack Kelley brought to the transportation of compressed gases. Building on where Kelley left off, GTM developed a lightweight container module designed to bundle tubes in groups of nine in a holding fixture that could fit inside a standardized shipping container or be hauled by rail or truck. Given the high cost of energy, the ability to transport low-cost natural gas to faraway places offered a great deal of promise. There was every reason to expect that in the new century the innovative spirit that had always been a part of JBK would continue to keep the company prosperous and lead to further promising spin-off ventures.

Ed Dinger

PRINCIPAL SUBSIDIARIES

City Machine & Welding, Inc.; Specialty Trailer Leasing.

PRINCIPAL COMPETITORS

Liquid Transport Corporation; McKenzie Tank Lines, Inc.; Superior Carriers Inc.

FURTHER READING

Foust-Peeples, Shanna, "Jack B. Kelley," *Amarillo Globe-News,* May 19, 2000.

"Hazel Kelley Wilson," *Amarillo Globe-News,* August 13, 2004.

McBride, Jim, "GTM Manufacturing Builds Compressed Gas Modules," *Amarillo Globe-News,* June 1, 2008.

Schwarz, George, "Semitrailers a Common Thread for Two City Companies," *Amarillo Globe-News,* December 19, 2005.

"Twenty-Four Karat: The Jack B. Kelley," Amarillo, Tex.: Sanders & Sanders, 1989, 126 p.

Weiner, Hollace, "Life, Legacy of Helium-Hauler Jack B. Kelley Is a Gas-Gas-Gas," *Fort Worth Star-Telegram,* February 13, 1994, p. 29.

Jordano's, Inc.

---

550 South Patterson Avenue
Santa Barbara, California 93111-2405
U.S.A.
Telephone: (805) 964-0611
Toll Free: (800) 325-2278
Fax: (805) 964-3821
Web site: http://www.jordanos.com

Private Company
Incorporated: 1928 as Jordano Brothers, Inc.
Employees: 540
Sales: $211 million (2008 est.)
NAICS: 424810 Beer and Ale Merchant Wholesalers

■ ■ ■

Jordano's, Inc., is a family-owned Santa Barbara, California-based company, its business divided between two divisions: Jordano's Foodservice and Pacific Beverage Company (PBC). The broad line foodservice unit covers nine Central and Southern California counties: Kern, Los Angeles, Orange, Riverside, San Bernardino, San Diego, San Luis Obispo, Santa Barbara, and Ventura. From its 155,000-square-foot, state-of-the-art warehouse distribution facility in Santa Barbara, Jordano's serves restaurants, hotels, casinos, cruise lines, schools, universities, heathcare facilities, government agencies, and other market segments. The company also maintains a marine and export department to accommodate offshore business. All told, Jordano's carries 10,000 different products, including fresh produce, fresh and frozen meat and seafood, dairy, frozen foods, dry

grocery, beverages, fine wines, non-foods, and equipment and supplies.

PBC is an Anheuser-Busch distributor and also carries Alliance Partners beers; a variety of craft beers, including offerings from Pyramid Brewing, Anchor Brewing, and Firestone Walker; and such imported beers as Heineken, Guinness, Carlsberg, and Labatt. Nonalcoholic beverages include Arizona iced teas and other beverages, Red Bull and other energy drinks, Jones Soda products, FRS fruit-flavored beverages, and water products from Nestlé Waters and Icelandic. PBC also distributes Ku Soju spirits and mixers and a handful of wines. PBC serves four California counties—Monterey, San Luis Obispo, Santa Barbara, and Venture—from distribution facilities located in Santa Margarita, Santa Maria, Santa Barbara, and Oxnard. Jordano's employees own about 22 percent of the company through an employee stock ownership plan.

JORDANO FAMILY IMMIGRATES TO AMERICA

The Jordanos came to the United States from a small town in northwestern Italy, Rivarolo Canavese, where the family name was known as Giordano. An in-law, Pietro Pomatto, was actually the first to make the journey in the 1880s at a time when his home country was enduring poor economic conditions and other difficulties. He settled in California, going to work at a ranch located north of Santa Barbara and saving his money to send for his pregnant sister and her husband, Giacomo Giordano. Because Giacomo had pledged to leave Italy only if his brothers Matteo and Giovanni

COMPANY PERSPECTIVES

The Mission of Jordano's Inc. is to be the premier marketer and supplier of food, beverages, and culinary equipment in the Santa Barbara, San Luis Obispo, and Ventura County area. We work to achieve this mission by building long-term relationships with the people who can make it a reality.

came as well, an arrangement was struck. The three Giordano brothers would make the trip first, and more money would be provided later to bring Pomatto's sister and baby after it was born. In this way the Giordanos set out for America. Soon, however, the brothers split up. Excited about prospects in Argentina, Giovanni headed to South America. The family never heard from him again. The remaining brothers landed at Ellis Island in New York Harbor and on the way to California, at the behest of a friend, stopped at Coal City, Illinois, to try coal mining. While Matteo would become a miner for the next three decades before returning to Italy after World War I, Giacomo quickly tired of the backbreaking work and continued on to Santa Barbara, arriving in 1888.

Changing his name to James, Giordano went to work for the Southern Pacific Railroad and saved enough money to send for his wife and son, Peter. He then became the manager of a dairy owned by a rancher named John Finley More. He would work for a related property, the More Ranch, for over 40 years. There his wife Annetta would give birth to a daughter and three more sons—Frank and twins, Dominic and John—before dying at the age of 37. It was Peter's inability to spell his last name in school that led to the creation of the Jordano name to replace Giordano. A teacher had simply spelled what she thought she had heard after asking Peter to pronounce his name.

Peter and his three brothers would become the founders of Jordano's, Inc. When he was just ten years old Peter began to learn the grocery business by going to work performing odd jobs during the summer at Cornwall and Son in Santa Barbara. Later, while attending Santa Barbara Business College, he worked nights doing the books at Cornwall Grocery. In 1908 his brothers John and Dominic became delivery boys at the store, and eventually the youngest brother, Frank, became a delivery boy as well. It was Dominic who first suggested the brothers start their own business together. They agreed and although there was no shortage of competi-

tion in Santa Barbara, they decided to open their own grocery store. In preparation John Jordano was dispatched in 1913 to Los Angeles to find work with area grocers in order to learn the latest practices in the field.

JORDANO BROTHERS OPEN FIRST GROCERY STORE

By 1915 the Jordano brothers were ready to launch their business. The oldest of the four was just 26 while the youngest, Frank, was just 16 and still attending business school. They cobbled together $2,500 in seed money, mostly through loans from friends and family. To hedge their bets, Peter kept his job at Cornwall's while the twins initially ran the family store, which was located at 706 State Street in Santa Barbara and opened its doors on March 1, 1915. The store did well, allowing Peter to quit Cornwall's and join his brothers full-time in 1916. The business was legally established as a partnership in 1919, and in 1928 was incorporated as Jordano Brothers, Inc.

The Jordanos were reportedly more forward thinking than many of their Santa Barbara competitors. Recognizing that Santa Barbara's business district was shifting to the north they began making plans to open a second store, one that would embrace an emerging trend in the grocery field: the cash-and-carry concept, which eliminated the problem of delinquent or nonpaying charge accounts. The new all-cash, walk-in-only uptown store opened in November 1918. Customers were not willing to give up the habit of phoning in their orders, however, and eventually the Jordano brothers had to cater to this demand.

Another visionary step taken by the Jordanos came in 1923, when they elected to close their two stores and relocate to a single expanded location well away from Santa Barbara's accepted State Street commercial district. Not only larger in size, the new store was modern in appearance. Because the rent was lower, the store could also offer lower prices than State Street grocers, and the Jordanos had no problem attracting customers to their new location. As a result, the store prospered, and the Jordanos continued to do well even during the Great Depression that followed the stock market crash of 1929.

After Peter Jordano died in 1931 from an infection following an injury sustained in an automobile accident, the family used the insurance money to open another store. Suited to the times, Store #2, as it was called, offered few embellishments and focused on low prices, becoming Santa Barbara's first self-service store. Store #3 was soon to follow, taking over a former Piggly Wiggly

```
┌─────────────────────────────────────────────────┐
│                                                 │
│              KEY DATES                          │
│                    ■                            │
│                                                 │
│  1915:  The four Jordano brothers open grocery store │
│         in Santa Barbara, California.           │
│  1928:  The grocery business is incorporated as Jor- │
│         dano Brothers, Inc.                     │
│  1933:  Jordano family begins selling alcoholic bever- │
│         ages through retail liquor stores following │
│         repeal of Prohibition.                  │
│  1948:  Institutional foods business Lloyd E. Cox, │
│         Inc., is acquired.                      │
│  1963:  Pacific Beverage Company (PBC) is formed │
│         to take over beer distribution.         │
│  1975:  Supermarkets are sold.                  │
│  1977:  Jordano's Foodservice is formed.        │
│  1987:  Wholesale liquor business is sold.      │
│  2003:  Jordano's Kitchen Supply is sold.       │
│                                                 │
└─────────────────────────────────────────────────┘
```

store in a fast-growing part of town in July 1935. A smaller fourth store then followed in 1938. Also during the 1930s a wholesale produce business was created to consolidate purchasing for the stores. In 1946 the family launched a wholesale meat division as well.

POSTWAR CHANGING OF THE GUARD

The Depression era also saw the second generation of Jordanos joining the family business. Dominic Jordano died in 1944 and the two remaining brothers began to decrease their involvement in the 1950s, leading to a group of four Jordano cousins gaining control: John Jordano, Jr., James Dominic Jordano, James Peter Jordano, and Peter C. Jordano. There would be a fifth store for the family to manage in 1951, one that at 7,600 square feet was larger than any grocery store Santa Barbara had seen and that was regarded as the city's first true supermarket. Another of the new large format stores, Store #6, followed in 1957. At the same time, outmoded Store #1 and Store #4 were closed. A year later ultramodern Store #7 opened, featuring the latest cash registers and checkout stands with conveyor belts.

The Jordano family ended the 1950s with the opening of Store #8, located on the edge of town, and the closing of Store #3, which would be replaced with larger Store #9 in 1961. Catering to a mostly Spanish-speaking community, this store would make the unusual decision at the time to seek bilingual employees. Also during the postwar era, the family added an institutional foods business, Lloyd E. Cox, Inc., a business acquired

in 1948. The name was changed in 1957 to Chef's Inc. and frozen foods were added to the mix. In 1961 the business became Chef's Vendor.

Jordano's expanded beyond the Santa Barbara market in the 1960s, opening supermarkets in new suburbs that were developed to house professors and staff members of the University of California–Santa Barbara, the campus of which was relocated to Goleta, California. Others stores were opened in San Luis Obispo as Jordano's took steps to grow into a regional, statewide supermarket chain. Through the acquisition of three Purity Markets stores in 1969, Jordano's added another San Luis Obispo location as well as units in Santa Maria and Paso Robles. By the start of the 1970s, the company was generating sales of $55 million. Early in the new decade, Store #17 opened in Carpinteria, a third Goleta location became Store #18, and Store #19 opened in Channel Islands.

PACIFIC BEVERAGE COMPANY FORMED

While the Jordano family was building a retail chain as well as running meat and produce wholesale operations, it was also laying the foundation for Pacific Beverage Company (PBC). In the beginning the grocery stores sold wine and beer, including Anheuser-Busch products, but with the coming of Prohibition in 1919 that business came to an end. With the repeal of Prohibition in 1933 the Jordanos resumed selling wine and beer through retail liquor stores. They also took advantage of their fleet of grocery delivery trucks to establish a wholesale liquor business to supply restaurants and other customers. A wholesale beer business would be added as well. Due to changes in the market, the family formed PBC in 1963 to take over the beer distribution operation. The liquor wholesale business was relegated to another subsidiary, Whole Beverage. Because of consolidation in the industry, Whole Beverage found it increasingly difficult to do business, and in 1987 the Jordanos elected to close the company and transfer its wine and imported beer lines to PBC.

As the 1970s progressed the Jordano family found it increasingly difficult to compete against the major supermarket chains. Jordano's supermarkets struggled to compete on price, margins were thin, and rapid expansion had taken its toll on the family's finances. By 1974 the Jordanos decided that they either had to declare bankruptcy or salvage what they could from the business. The second option was pursued, resulting in the 1975 sale of the remaining 13 supermarkets and the shutting down of the wholesale meat operation, leaving the family with PBC, the wholesale produce business, and Chef's Vendor, which was still a very profitable venture. Also that year the family sold Chef's Vendor and agreed not to compete in the institutional foodservice business for two years.

JORDANO'S FOODSERVICE ESTABLISHED

In 1977 the family under the leadership of Peter C. Jordano reentered the institutional food business under a new name, Jordano's Foodservice, building on what remained of the wholesale produce business of Jordano's Inc. Gradually the institutional business was rebuilt, helped in part by the 1979 acquisition of Devine Distribution and the opening of Jordano's Kitchen Supply in 1982 and Morganti Distribution in 1984. By 1985 Jordano's Inc. was generating $46 million in annual revenues from its foodservice and beverage units, a major improvement over the $19 million posted a decade earlier.

The employees of the Jordano's Inc. units gained a stake in the business through an employee stock ownership plan, and in the 1990s both of the company divisions enjoyed strong growth. As a member of the Pocahontas Foods U.S.A. Buying Group, Jordano's Foodservice emerged as the largest broad line supplier in its markets, with sales reaching $54 million by the end of the 1990s, an amount that would increase to $75 million in 2001. To keep pace with demand the unit upgraded its freezer and cooler capacity. Jordano's Kitchen Supply did not fare as well, however. In 2003 that segment was shuttered.

A year later Jordano's Foodservice was named National Food Service Distributor of the year by Pocahontas Foods. The division continued to thrive as the 21st century progressed, with annual sales approaching $100 million. To improve productivity and continue to keep up with demand, the division began employing a new warehouse management system at its Santa Barbara facility. Demand for beverage products, in the meantime, also outstripped PBC's abilities, resulting in a move to a new 125,000-square-foot distribution facility in Oxnard in the early years of the new century. Having made the successful transition from supermarket chain to foodservice and beverage distributor, Jordano's, Inc., appeared to be well placed to enjoy ongoing success in the years to come.

Ed Dinger

PRINCIPAL SUBSIDIARIES

Jordano's Foodservice; Pacific Beverage Company.

PRINCIPAL COMPETITORS

Liquid Investments Co., Inc.; SYSCO Food Services of Central California, Inc.; U.S. Foodservice, Inc.

FURTHER READING

de Garcia, Erin Graffy, *Remembering Jordanos,* Santa Barbara, Calif.: Kieran Publishing Company, 2004.

Hernandez, Raul, "Beverage Firm Hopes to Build Oxnard Facility," *Ventura County Star,* July 6, 2000, p. B1.

Moraga, Frank, "Several Firms Move to Larger Quarters in Ventura County," *Ventura County Star,* January 26, 2001.

Salkin, Stephanie, "Jordano's Targets $75 Million," *ID: The Information Source for Managers and DSRs,* June 2001, p. 24.

"Supplier Ends 90-Year Paper Chase," *Food Logistics,* April 15, 2006, p. 36.

KANEMATSU CORPORATION

Kanematsu Corporation

———■———

2-1, Shibaura 1-chome
Minato-ku
Tokyo, 105-8005
Japan
Telephone: (81 03) 5440-8111
Fax: (81 03) 5440-6500
Web site: http://www.kanematsu.co.jp

Public Company
Incorporated: 1967 as Kanematsu-Gosho Ltd.
Employees: 872
Sales: ¥1.24 trillion ($12.4 billion) (2008)
Stock Exchanges: Tokyo Osaka
Ticker Symbol: 79610
NAICS: 551112 Offices of Other Holding Companies

■ ■ ■

Kanematsu Corporation is a specialized trading company with six main operating segments: IT (Information Technology); Foods and Foodstuff; Iron and Steel; Plant and Machinery; Energy; and Life Science. Kanematsu originally operated as a *sogo shosha,* a general trading company conducting business in diversified import and export markets. Kanematsu was one of the nine largest trading companies in Japan. Like many of its peers, Kanematsu was forced to restructure in the late 1990s and early years of the new millennium as a result of the Asian economic crisis and the collapse of the bubble economy in Japan. The company, focused on specialized trading, has reorganized operations, shut-

tered and sold off unprofitable businesses, and reduced its overall subsidiary count to fewer than 130 entities.

EARLY HISTORY

F. Kanematsu & Co., Ltd., was established on August 15, 1889, by 44-year-old Fusajiro Kanematsu. With offices in Kobe, Japan, and a staff of seven persons, Kanematsu initially began trading operations in the Australian market. A branch office was set up the following year in Sydney, Australia, and the first shipment of 187 bales of Australian wool reached Japan. Trading operations expanded to include wheat, tallow, and other Australian products. In 1918 F. Kanematsu reorganized as a joint-stock company. As Japan's international trade grew dramatically during the early years of the 20th century, F. Kanematsu extended its operations into South Africa and South America. By 1936 it had opened U.S. branch offices in New York and in Seattle, Washington, and a subsidiary in New Zealand.

The Kanematsu Trading Corporation, a U.S. subsidiary, was formed in New York in 1941. Much of the trading operations of the company were curtailed during World War II, and as a trading company F. Kanematsu had little to do during the war. Expansion resumed after the war, with Kanematsu New York Inc. being formed in 1951. To adjust itself to postwar economic conditions, F. Kanematsu shifted from its traditional trade in textiles to other areas, including the overseas construction of papermaking plants. In 1961 the shares of F. Kanematsu were sold to the public and the company was listed on the Osaka Stock Exchange.

COMPANY PERSPECTIVES

We are more active than ever in expanding our businesses and strengthening our functions as a true business creator to achieve added value. Our target corporate image is to be: a company that never stops creating new businesses; a company with an established culture of ongoing reform and evolution; a company that steadfastly maintains a streamlined and highly efficient financial position; and a company that has built and operates a solid management system.

Yohei Kitagawa formed Kitagawa & Co. Ltd. in 1891 in Yokohama to engage in the import of cotton yarn. Offices subsequently were moved to Kobe and then to Osaka, where in 1905 the company was organized as The Gosho Co., Ltd.; it underwent a reorganization into a joint-stock company in 1917. Direct importing of cotton began from the United States in 1906 and from India in 1907. Crawford Gosho Co., Ltd., and Gosho Corporation, U.S. subsidiaries, were formed in 1912 and 1918, respectively. Until the beginning of World War II, Gosho continued its international trading operations, with cotton as its most important product. From 1935 to 1945, war years for Japan, Gosho withdrew from many international markets but continued to trade in raw materials. In 1943 it merged with Showa Cotton Co., Ltd., and Pacific Trading Co., Ltd. After World War II it began diversifying its business away from textiles. Gosho Trading Co., Ltd., was formed in Thailand in 1959.

1967 MERGER FORMS KANEMATSU-GOSHO

With the 1967 merger of the F. Kanematsu & Co. and The Gosho Co. into Kanematsu-Gosho Ltd., the surviving firm moved into the top ranks of Japanese trading companies. By 1968 the new company had changed its internal organization into the divisional structure that endured into the 21st century. The head office was moved to Tokyo in 1970. Shares of the company's stock were listed on the Tokyo and Nagoya stock exchanges in 1973. Sales for the fiscal year ended March 31, 1974, reached ¥1 trillion for the first time. Subsidiary companies were formed in Canada in 1972, France in 1973, and Hong Kong in 1975; an office was opened in Beijing in 1979. The oil price shocks of the 1970s caused difficulties for the company, as they did for

much of the Japanese economy. Structural improvements and several long-range plans restored profitability by the end of the 1980s.

As with all Japanese trading companies, Kanematsu-Gosho continued to seek new investment opportunities throughout the world. In 1986, for example, it filled an order with the People's Republic of China for ¥700 million worth of equipment for manufacturing semiconductors; in 1989 it took a 25 percent interest in a joint venture with Nishimbo Industries Inc. in constructing and operating the first cotton textile mill ever in California and also began participation in Kanebo Spinning Inc., a mill in Georgia. The company also became a player in world money markets when, in 1989, $130 million in dollar-denominated bonds with stock options were sold in the European financial market, and 25 million shares of new stock were issued at prevailing market prices. In 1990, convertible notes worth CHF 200 million were issued. Subsidiaries were formed in the United Kingdom in 1989, in Spain in 1990, and in Italy in 1991, with branch offices being opened in Bucharest, Warsaw, and Berlin in 1990. Also in 1990, Kanematsu-Gosho changed its name to Kanematsu Corporation. In 1991 the Kanematsu (Europe) Corporation was created and given general control over European operations.

As the structure of the world economy continued to evolve, general trading companies such as Kanematsu had to continue to develop new products to trade and new strategies for marketing those products. In particular, they had to adjust their offerings as the Japanese economy became less reliant on exports, with the domestic market becoming increasingly important for total sales. To keep abreast of these changes, in 1987 Kanematsu formed a research-and-development division to investigate new products. In 1990, it established a "Ladies Life and Living" team, an all-female marketing group with a responsibility for anticipating the product needs of women over the next decade.

The company shifted the emphasis of its operations during the 1980s by importing more products into Japan. In 1982 imports accounted for 24 percent of total sales, compared to 44 percent in 1991. Other categories of operations adjusted accordingly, with exports remaining 15 percent of total sales, domestic sales falling from 51 percent in 1982 to 27 percent in 1991, and overseas sales growing from 10 percent to 14 percent during that period.

OVERCOMING CHALLENGES

The bursting of the late 1980s Japanese economic bubble led to prolonged difficulties for Kanematsu in

KEY DATES

1889: F. Kanematsu & Co., Ltd., is established by 44-year-old Fusajiro Kanematsu.

1891: Yohei Kitagawa establishes Kitagawa & Co. Ltd.

1905: Kitagawa reorganizes as The Gosho Co., Ltd.

1941: The Kanematsu Trading Corporation, a U.S. subsidiary, is formed in New York.

1961: Shares of F. Kanematsu are sold to the public and the company lists on the Osaka Stock Exchange.

1967: Kanematsu-Gosho Ltd. is formed in the merger of F. Kanematsu & Co. and The Gosho Co.

1974: Sales reach ¥1 trillion for the first time.

1990: The company changes its name to Kanematsu Corp.

1999: Kanematsu announces a major restructuring plan in response to falling profits.

2007: The company sells a 55 percent stake in Kanematsu Textile Corp.

the 1990s. Nearly all of the *sogo shosha* had diversified aggressively into financial investments during the speculative bubble years, in large part because their traditional activity of marginally profitable commodity trading had been in a deep decline for years. In desperation the companies built large stock portfolios and became dependent on the revenues they could gain through arbitrage (or *zaiteku,* as it is known in Japan). Once the bubble burst, the *sogo shosha* were left with huge portfolios whose worth had plummeted; all of the trading companies were forced to eventually liquidate much of their stock holdings.

Unlike some of the larger trading companies, Kanematsu could not afford to quickly liquidate all of the bad investments it had made in the late 1980s; it had to do so gradually, writing some off in 1993 and 1994, and the rest in 1997, when the write-offs—and the liquidation of ten loss-making affiliates—led to an overall net loss of ¥27.53 billion ($221 million). This poor performance had followed net losses of ¥6.46 billion in 1994 and ¥15.2 billion in 1995. Kanematsu, like all of the *sogo shosha,* also felt a prolonged effect from its involvement in arbitrage in the form of damage to the company's financial credibility, leading to higher borrowing rates.

During the 1990s, with the Japanese economy in a lengthy recession, Kanematsu expanded aggressively in Asia, establishing numerous subsidiaries, affiliates, and joint ventures, particularly in China, Indonesia, Malaysia, Thailand, and Vietnam. By 1997 the company had 44 projects operational in China alone, where it established a Shanghai-based subsidiary in July 1996 to increase its internal trading activities within China. The following year Kanematsu created a Shanghai-based holding company to coordinate and support all of the company's operations in the burgeoning market that China had become.

MOVING INTO THE 21ST CENTURY

During this period Kanematsu also placed an increasing emphasis on such high-tech areas as electronics, communications, and information technologies. For example, in April 1996 Kanematsu established with a U.S. partner a U.S.-based joint venture called Extel Semiconductor Corp. to manufacture application-specific integrated circuit chips. In June 1996 Kanematsu acquired the Asia-Pacific operations of Memorex Telex N.V. for $25 million; Memorex Telex sold automatic tape libraries and network-related equipment and offered systems integration services. In December 1996 the company entered into a ¥1.8 billion contract to expand the rural telecommunications network of Nepal Telecommunications Corporation.

As another bubble burst with the outbreak of the Asian financial crisis in 1997, Kanematsu faced the possibility of a repeat of its difficulties stemming from the Japanese economic troubles of the late 1980s and early 1990s since it had grown rapidly in some of the most troubled economies: Indonesia, Korea, and Malaysia. Currency devaluations were cutting into demand in Southeast Asia by late 1997 and in turn hurting the profitability of most Japanese trading companies. Kanematsu was known for continually restructuring its activities to keep pace with world economic changes and it would have to do so again in order to survive this latest crisis threatening to undermine it.

Indeed, Kanematsu and its *sogo shosha* peers faced many challenges brought on by the Asian economic crisis, the bursting of the bubble economy, credit problems, and deflation. In response to these obstacles, Kanematsu ushered in a period of dramatic change. In May 1999, the company announced a major restructuring that included the removal of *sogo,* or general, from its name. The move signaled Kanematsu's focus on becoming a specialized trading company with core operations in electronics and semiconductors, food and foodstuffs, textiles, real estate, steel, and energy.

As part of its reorganization plan, Kanematsu announced it would cut the number of its subsidiaries from 229 to approximately 100. While unprofitable businesses were sold or shuttered, the company merged several of its key subsidiaries. Kanematsu Semiconductor Corp., Kanematsu Metals Ltd., and Kanematsu Electronic Trading joined together in 2001 to form Kanematsu Devices Corp. This new subsidiary became part of the company's IT division in 2003. Kanematsu also merged its machinery-related businesses together. Its chemical operations joined to form Kanematsu Chemicals Corp.

Kanematsu launched a new three-year business plan titled New KG200 in April 2004 that focused on reducing debt while pursuing new business opportunities in its food, IT, steel, and plants and machinery divisions. After completing that plan, a new three-year strategy was announced in 2007 under the name TeamKG120. Much like the previous plan, TeamKG210 was designed to shore up profits while strengthening core operations. As part of this strategy, the company sold a 55 percent stake in Kanematsu Textile Corp. in 2007. Kanematsu also expanded operations in New Delhi, India, and established a new machine tool subsidiary in Prague, Czech Republic. In addition, the company strengthened its foothold in IT markets in Suzhou and Wuxi, China.

By this time, Kanematsu's major divisions—made up of just under 130 subsidiaries—included IT, Foods and Foodstuff, Iron and Steel, Plant and Machinery, Energy, and Life Science. While economies in the United States and Europe faltered, growth in Chinese and Indian markets bode well for Kanematsu's fortunes. With profits rebounding in 2007 and 2008, Kanematsu's management believed it was poised for success in the years to come.

Donald R. Stabile
Updated, David E. Salamie; Christina M. Stansell

PRINCIPAL SUBSIDIARIES

Kanematsu Electronics Ltd.; Kanematsu Electronics Ltd.; Memorex Division; Nippon Office Systems Ltd.; Kanematsu Communications Ltd.; Kanematsu Aerospace Corporation; Kanematsu Global Technology Solutions; Kanematsu Food Corporation; Nippon Liquor Ltd.; Kanematsu Trading Corporation; Kyowa Steel Co., Ltd.; EiwaMetal Co., Ltd.; Kanematsu Hoplee Company Ltd.; Kanematsu KGK Corporation; Kanematsu Petroleum Corporation; Kanematsu Chemicals Corporation; Kanematsu Wellness Corporation; Kanematsu Textile Corporation; Kaneyo Co., Ltd.; P.T. Century Textile Industry; Shintoa Corporation; KIT Co., Ltd.; Central Express Ltd.; Kanematsu-NNK Corporation; Hokushin Co., Ltd.

PRINCIPAL COMPETITORS

Marubeni Corporation; Mitsui & Co. Ltd.; Sumitomo Corporation.

FURTHER READING

Hug, Dale, "Kanematsu Devices Corp. Absorbed into Group," *JCNN*, July 28, 2003.

Iwao, Ichiishi, "Sogo Shosha: Meeting New Challenges," *Journal of Japanese Trade & Industry*, January/February 1995, pp. 16–18.

"Japan: Kanematsu Corp. to Sell 55% Textile Share," *Just-Style*, March 6, 2007.

"Kanematsu's Prospects Improve on Restructuring," *Nikkei Weekly*, August 26, 2002.

KG Monthly: Special Issue, 100th Anniversary 1989, Tokyo: Kanematsu-Gosho Ltd., 1989.

"March of the Middlemen," *Economist*, September 24, 1988.

Rosario, Louise do, "Lose and Learn: Japan's Firms Pay Price of Financial Speculation," *Far Eastern Economic Review*, June 17, 1993, pp. 60–61.

"Sogo Shosha Changing to Weather Hard Times," *Daily Yomiuri*, December 21, 1999.

Terazono, Emiko, "Write-Offs to Put Kanematsu in ¥20bn Loss," *Financial Times*, September 6, 1996, p. 22.

"Top-Drawer Traders Talk—Kanematsu Corporation," *Japan Chemical Week*, January 18, 2001.

"Trading House Kanematsu Posts 12.4 bil. Yen Group Net Loss," *Japan Economic Newswire*, May 25, 2000.

Yonekawa, Shin'ichi, ed., *General Trading Companies: A Comparative and Historical Study*, Tokyo: United Nations University Press, 1990.

Yoshihara, Kunio, *Sogo Shosha: The Vanguard of the Japanese Economy*, Tokyo: Oxford University Press, 1982.

Young, Alexander, *The Sogo Shosha: Japan's Multinational Trading Companies*, Boulder, Colo.: Westview Press, 1979.

Keynote™

The Mobile & Internet Performance Authority™

Keynote Systems Inc.

777 Mariners Island Boulevard
San Mateo, California 94404
U.S.A.
Telephone: (650) 403-2400
Fax: (650) 403-5500
Web site: http://www.keynote.com

Public Company
Incorporated: 1995
Employees: 300
Sales: $76.9 million (2008)
Stock Exchanges: NASDAQ
Ticker Symbol: KEYN
NAICS: 561499 All Other Business Support Services

■ ■ ■

San Mateo, California-based Keynote Systems Inc. helps marketing and information technology (IT) companies improve their Internet presence and mobile communication systems through its on-demand test and measurement systems. These systems assess combinations of factors—language barriers, demographics, Internet connection methods (broadband or dial-up), and web browser/mobile device types in order to anticipate the performance of client web sites and applications. With approximately 2,800 customers (including American Express, Blue Cross/Blue Shield, Dell Computer, Caterpillar, Disney, eBay, Federal Express, UPS, and Verizon), Keynote operates in four main business lines: Customer Experience/UX Test and Measurement (end-user testing), Web Performance Test and Measurement,

Mobile Quality Test and Measurement, and VoIP (voice-over Internet protocol) and Streaming Test and Measurement.

FORMATIVE YEARS

The roots of Keynote Systems date back to June 15, 1995, when Jim Barrick and Andy Popell established the company in Redwood City, California, as a provider of software and consulting services. In November 1996 Keynote began beta testing its first web site performance measurement product, Keynote Perspective, which was slated for a January 1997 release. Specifically, the application allowed organizations to determine the amount of time users needed to log on to their web site. To offer a global perspective, the company had its software running at 96 points around the globe, 76 of which were located in the United States.

A flurry of events unfolded in 1997, at which time Jim Barrick served as Keynote's president and CEO. The company gained early credibility in April when its Keynote Business 40 Internet Performance Index— which measured the weekly average response time of leading web sites—was published in both *InfoWorld* and the *Wall Street Journal.* The company made its first sale at a trade show that month, securing $99 from PCOrder.com. In May, Keynote sold its first three-month subscription for $3,600, adding Inquiry.com as a customer.

Keynote rounded out 1997 with two major developments. In addition to coining its tagline, "The Internet Performance Authority," the company adopted new leadership when Umang Gupta was named chairman and CEO in December. Prior to joining Keynote, Gupta had served as CEO of the database firm Centura. Before that, he was general manager of Oracle Corp., where he helped pioneer the development of the personal computer database.

In an effort to woo would-be customers, Keynote kicked off 1998 by offering free web site performance appraisals. In addition, the company teamed up with MediaWays in order to offer its measurement services in Eastern and Continental Europe. In April of that year, Keynote secured its third round of equity funding, raising $4.7 million from Bessemer Venture Partners. At the end of 1998, Keynote relied upon 65 different automated measurement sites throughout the world. From these locations, download speeds for more than 1,800 web sites were measured every 15 minutes, resulting in more than 40,000 discrete measurements per week. It was around this time that the company unveiled its Keynote Perspective Full Page Component service, which was designed to measure web sites with continuously changing content, such as those providing news.

GOING PUBLIC

Progress kicked into high gear during the final year of the decade. In February 1999 Keynote established its Professional Services Division, the purpose of which was to help diagnose and solve web site–related reliability and performance problems for e-commerce companies. Building on the success of the company's first $500,000 month in March, Keynote secured $17 million in financing in April from a group of investors that included VeriSign and GE Capital.

By this time Keynote was performing more than ten million daily web site availability and performance measurements. Growth continued on the service front as the company rolled out a new service named Lifeline, which gauged the performance of small and midsized

e-commerce web sites. The new offering, co-branded with domain name provider Network Solutions Inc., cost $695 per year for each unique web address. As an incentive for prospective customers, a free web site performance assessment was offered.

Positive developments continued into the latter part of the year as the company's monthly sales swelled to $1 million in August. Keynote went public on September 24, 1999, selling four million shares of stock for $14 apiece. In 1999 the company recorded a net loss of $7.1 million, which was a sizable increase over the previous year's loss of $2.9 million. However, revenues soared 373 percent that year, reaching $7.3 million.

Keynote rounded out 1999 by bolstering its infrastructure to include 120 monitoring locations worldwide. At the time, measurements were performed using 220 computers at sites in Taipei, Tokyo, Sydney, Stockholm, Singapore, Seoul, Rio de Janeiro, Paris, Munich, Milan, Mexico City, Melbourne, London, Hong Kong, Geneva, Frankfurt, Brussels, and Amsterdam. In addition to expanding its infrastructure, Keynote also established a new headquarters facility in Paris.

Heading into the new millennium, Keynote served a base of nearly 520 customers, including IBM, Hewlett-Packard, Dell Computer, Charles Schwab, and Amazon.com. In addition, the company served several hundred other clients who received its measurement services through other providers.

After reincorporating in Delaware on March 31, 2000, Keynote's customer base surpassed the 1,000 mark on April 11, at which time Computer Associates, Subaru America, fusionOne, GetMusic.com, and eNutrition all became Keynote customers. The additions came on the heels of 94 percent customer growth in six months. Along with its new clients, Keynote bolstered its global reach even further to include approximately 500 computers that made some 24 million daily performance measurements.

In May 2000, the *San Francisco Chronicle* named Keynote to its list of the Bay Area's 50 fastest-growing public companies. That same month, the company agreed to acquire Velogic Inc. for approximately $50 million, leading to the introduction of the Keynote LoadPro service.

Rounding out a busy month, it also was in May that Keynote inked a deal to acquire Franklin Resources Inc.'s office complex in San Mateo, California, for about $80 million. Two months later, a $15 million cash deal was made for Digital Content L.L.C., allowing for the introduction of a service named Keynote Red Alert.

KEY DATES

1995: Jim Barrick and Andy Popell establish the company in Redwood City, California.
1997: The Keynote Business 40 Internet Performance Index is first published.
1999: Keynote goes public.
2000: Customers surpass the 1,000 mark.
2001: Keynote's common stock is added to the Russell 2000 Index.
2009: The company serves roughly 2,800 customers.

GROWTH THROUGH ACQUISITIONS

In January 2001, Keynote had about 27.9 million outstanding shares of common stock. At that time, the company announced plans to buy back as much as $50 million worth of its shares, some of which were earmarked for possible inclusion in employee benefit plans. The following month, *PC Magazine* named Keynote as one of the leading 100 Internet infrastructure companies, and as one of the five leading performance enhancement firms. By this time some 3,000 corporate IT departments were relying upon the company's service offerings.

Growth via acquisitions continued in 2001. Midway through the year, Keynote saw its common stock added to the Russell 2000 Index. Around the same time, the company snapped up Envive Corporation's MSP Division for $4 million, leading to the release of Keynote Test Perspective. The eventual rollout of Keynote Wireless Perspective was assured when OnDevice Corp. was acquired in October.

Keynote's product and service offerings continued to expand following further acquisitions throughout the early years of the new century. NetMechanic Inc. was acquired in May 2002, resulting in the addition of both Keynote WebIntegrity and Keynote NetMechanic. Finally, the company's Keynote WebEffective offering benefited from the acquisition of Enviz Inc. in a cash-and-stock deal that October.

The introduction of Keynote Streaming Perspective 3.0 followed the $567,000 acquisition of Streamcheck midway through 2003. Keynote capped off the year with the December acquisition of Xaffire Inc.'s Matrix-Net division. The $582,000 cash deal included Xaffire's Insight Service suite, which became Keynote Network Perspective.

More acquisitions unfolded during the middle years of the decade. The company ushered in 2004 by acquiring Mountain View, California-based NetRaker Corp. in April. The transaction bolstered Keynote's web analytics capabilities via the addition of two new products. Customer Experience Benchmark provided measurements of web site users' perceptions in a number of areas, while Research Manager combined web site usability studies with market research surveys. These new tools helped to further differentiate Keynote from its competitors. In addition, the NetRaker acquisition meant an additional $3 million in annual revenue.

In a deal worth roughly $1.9 million, Hudson Williams Corp. was purchased three months later, paving the way for Keynote's Web Performance Professional Services offering. Keynote concluded 2004 by acquiring San Mateo, California-based Vividence Corp. for about $20.57 million in September. The deal further strengthened Keynote's offerings in the customer experience management category and resulted in approximately $11 million in new annual revenue. In addition, Keynote gained Vividence's base of 130 customers, which included companies such as Williams-Sonoma Inc., FedEx Corp., and Citibank N.A.

EXPANDING INFRASTRUCTURE

In early 2005, Keynote acquired Hudson Williams Europe in a deal worth more than $260,000, further strengthening its Web Performance Professional Services. At the end of the year, Keynote finalized its 13th acquisition when it acquired Watchfire's GomezPro business unit, bolstering its capabilities in the customer experience management arena. Following the deal, GomezPro was renamed Keynote WebExcellence, with responsibility for the company's WebExcellence Analysis Service, as well as WebExcellence Scorecards.

By 2005 Keynote's services were used to monitor approximately 70 percent of the world's leading web sites, and the company counted more than half of the *Fortune* 100 among its customer base. Late in the year, the company was focused on ramping up its presence in the Asia-Pacific market. As part of this strategy, Jeff Kraatz was hired to serve as vice president and managing director for Asia-Pacific.

Compared to its earlier years, Keynote had significantly expanded its infrastructure by around 2005. By this time, a network of more than 1,600 computers in roughly 50 cities across the globe performed more than 16 million Internet performance measurements per day. Relying upon these measurements were some 13,000 individual users, as well as 2,300 IT and marketing departments.

Heading into the second half of the decade, Keynote bolstered its European presence when it spent $30.1 million to secure all outstanding shares of the German company Sigos, a company that produced mobile data network testing and monitoring systems. The deal benefited the company's SITE Test System and GlobalRoamer services. In order to better serve the growing population of people who used the popular BlackBerry mobile communication device, Keynote partnered with Fremont, California-based Zenprise, a developer of BlackBerry troubleshooting software, in October 2007. Specifically, Keynote planned to develop a network monitoring service to help Zenprise identify and resolve carrier, device, and infrastructure-related problems.

Keynote started 2008 off with another acquisition. In April, the company parted with roughly $3 million to buy the French software firm Zandan S.A. A noteworthy milestone was reached in September when the number of web site developers and IT professionals who had downloaded the company's Keynote Internet Testing Environment (KITE) reached the 1,000 mark. Specifically, KITE made it easier for companies to troubleshoot web application-related performance problems.

Progress continued during late 2008. In November, MobileVillage presented Keynote with a Gold Mobile Star Award for excellence in the Enterprise Software: Application Testing category. Expansion continued at this time, as the company's on-demand mobile test and measurement network grew to include Mexico City, Mexico; Madrid, Spain; Chennai, India; and Beijing, China.

By this time Keynote was billing itself in its literature as The Mobile and Internet Performance Authority. The company's ability to measure mobile performance had grown significantly, spanning some 200 mobile networks in about 70 different countries. Keynote served roughly 2,800 customers by early 2009, including leading companies such as Microsoft, Sprint, Disney, Dell, YouTube, and SonyEricsson. In order to perform its measurement services, the company relied upon some 2,500 computers and mobile devices that were positioned at 240 sites worldwide. Keynote found itself operating in a difficult economic climate in 2009.

However, based upon its record of growth and achievement, the company seemed well positioned for continued success during the 21st century's second decade.

Paul R. Greenland

PRINCIPAL SUBSIDIARIES

Keynote Canada; Keynote Europe Ltd. (UK); Keynote German Holding Company GmbH (Germany); Keynote German Management GmbH (Germany); Keynote SIGOS GmbH (Germany); Velogic Inc.; Vividence Corporation; Zandan S.A.

PRINCIPAL OPERATING UNITS

Customer Experience/UX Test and Measurement; Web Performance Test and Measurement; Mobile Quality Test and Measurement; VoIP and Streaming Test and Measurement.

PRINCIPAL COMPETITORS

Gomez Inc.; NetIQ Corporation; Omniture Inc.

FURTHER READING

Davey, Tom, "Apps Measure Web Access Time; Keynote's 'Agents' Mimic Real Log-ons," *PC Week,* November 4, 1996.

Joachim, David, "Web Analysis Service Keeps Rivals Honest," *InternetWeek,* September 29, 1997.

"Keynote Business 40 Internet Performance Index Debuts in the *Wall Street Journal* and in *InfoWorld;* Index Tracks Health of the Internet," *Business Wire,* April 10, 1997.

"Keynote Systems Named One of the 100 Top Internet Infrastructure Companies by *PC Magazine*," *Business Wire,* February 28, 2001.

"Keynote Systems Partners with Zenprise to Offer Customers Improved BlackBerry Network Support Services," *Business Wire,* October 22, 2007.

Walsh, Jeff, "Users Get Under Hood of Web Site Activity; Keynote Measures Service Levels," *InfoWorld,* November 11, 1996.

Knouse Foods Cooperative Inc.

———■———

800 Peach Glen Road
Peach Glen, Pennsylvania 17375
U.S.A.
Telephone: (717) 677-8181
Web site: http://www.knouse.com

Private Company
Incorporated: 1949
Employees: 1,200
Sales: $248.1 million (2007 est.)
NAICS: 111339 Noncitrus Fruit Farming

■ ■ ■

Knouse Foods Cooperative Inc. is a Peach Glen, Pennsylvania-based fruit growers' cooperative representing about 1,500 farmers in the Appalachian Mountains and parts of the Midwest. Best known for its apple products, the company owns several well-established retail brands, including Lucky Leaf, Musselman's, Apple Time, Speas Farm, and Lincoln. Products include applesauce, apple juice, apple butter, vinegar, and a wide variety of pie fillings. Specialty products include sliced apples, baked apples, apple rings, fried apples, cherries jubilee, and red tart pitted cherries. Knouse operates processing plants in Peach Glen, Chambersburg, Orrtanna, Biglerville, and Gardners, Pennsylvania; and Paw Paw, Michigan. Another plant maintained in Inwood, West Virginia, was slated for closure in 2008. Aside from its retail business, Knouse is also involved in the foodservice segment, providing products to restaurants, cafeterias, and healthcare facilities; developing custom-

ized products through its Industrial/Ingredient Division; and offering private-label and co-packing of sauces, juices, teas, other beverages, and nutraceuticals.

ORIGINS

The man behind the Knouse name was Milton E. Knouse. An orchard owner, in 1925 he bought a struggling apple processing plant in Peach Glen, Pennsylvania. The town was located in Adams County, best known for Gettysburg, site of the pivotal Civil War battle. The northern part of the county was especially well-suited for growing fruit, in particular apples, due to an annual average temperature of 54 degrees and an annual rainfall of 45 inches, reducing an orchard's vulnerability to frost damage or drought. As transportation improved, commercial orchards had become viable in the mid-1800s, leading to the emergence of a number of family fruit farms and processing plants in the area, including the Peach Glen facility Knouse acquired. He processed both the apples he grew and those of other farmers. He added a second applesauce processing plant in Chambersburg, Pennsylvania, and subsequently sold a stake in his holding company, Knouse Corporation, to National Fruit Company.

In 1948 National Fruit decided to sell its interests in Knouse Corp. A year later about 100 growers located in Pennsylvania, Maryland, Virginia, and West Virginia banded together to form a cooperative to market their apples, cherries, and peaches. They joined forces with Knouse, buying his processing plants in Peach Glen and Chambersburg, and installed him as chief executive officer of the new cooperative, which would also take his name, Knouse Foods Cooperative Inc. The company began operations in April 1949. Under Knouse's leadership it pursued a commitment to developing high-quality processing methods, in keeping with the excellent fruit that member-farmers provided to him. The plants turned out apple juice, applesauce, apple butters and jellies, and vinegar, and also processed cherries and produced tomato juice. He also took the important step of acquiring the Lucky Leaf brand, under which to market the co-op's products. After generating sales of $5 million in the first year, Knouse Foods acquired another plant, located in Orrtanna, Pennsylvania, to keep up with demand. That plant had been built by I. Z. Musselman, cousin of Christian Musselman, whose C.H. Musselman Company would one day contribute the Musselman's brand to the cooperative.

ACQUIRING THE MUSSELMAN'S LABEL

Even as he ran Knouse Foods, Milton Knouse remained a grower. In fact, during the 1950s he bought up farmland for his own benefit, accumulating 2,300 acres by 1957, when he sold his holdings to C.H. Musselman Company. He soon regretted that decision, and in 1958 he bought 600 acres in Adams County, followed in 1960 with the purchase of 800 acres in Franklin County, Pennsylvania. In 1966, he retired from Knouse Foods in order to focus on managing his orchards, known as M.E. Knouse Orchards, later taking the name Knouse Fruitlands Incorporated and retained by the Knouse family.

Replacing Milton Knouse as chief executive at Knouse Foods in June 1966 was Dean L. Carey. A native of Biglerville, Pennsylvania, he had started his career with the company at the beginning in 1949, serving as a cost accountant. Rising through the ranks, he was named general manager in 1963. It was under his guidance that Knouse Foods would grow into one of the country's major agricultural cooperatives and the Lucky Leaf brand would become well known to consumers.

In the early 1980s Carey oversaw a period of steady expansion at Knouse Foods. The Paw Paw, Michigan, plant was acquired in 1982, a move that opened up new markets for Lucky Leaf products. Two years later an even more significant acquisition was completed when Knouse acquired C.H. Musselman, picking up plants in Biglerville and Gardners, Pennsylvania, and Inwood, West Virginia, along with 6,000 acres of fruit farms. Perhaps of even greater importance was the addition of the venerable Musselman's label from Pet Milk Company.

Musselman's had been established in 1907 when John S. Musselman, Sr., and sons John S. Musselman, Jr., and Christian High Musselman acquired the Biglerville Canning Company, a small Pennsylvania operation that had been organized two years earlier as a growers' cooperative but had failed and was put up for sheriff's sale. The elder Musselman was experienced in the fruit packing business, having worked at a fruit canning plant in Lancaster, Pennsylvania. However, it was his 25-year-old son Christian and his wife Emma who became the driving force behind the new venture. They gave up their Lancaster County farm and moved to Biglerville. Four years later they bought out Christian's father and brother, and cofounded C.H. Musselman Company.

Following a successful first year in business they built a second canning plant in Gardners, Pennsylvania, which became operational in 1912. The Inwood, West Virginia, canning plant and vinegar distillery would follow in 1922, opening up new markets for Musselman. A preserves plant was added in Biglerville in 1928 to produce apple butters and jellies. Plants were later added in Paw Paw and St. Joseph, Michigan.

Upon the death of Christian Musselman in 1944, production manager John A. Hauser took over as president, but Emma Musselman remained very much involved, managing the Gardners plant and serving as vice-president until her death at the age of 86 in 1966. Under Hauser's leadership, the company acquired farmland, so that in the 1950s Musselman was operating 9,000 acres of farmland and orchards. By 1961 the company was generating more than $25 million in annual sales. In that year the Musselman family elected to sell the business to the Pet Milk in exchange for stock.

ADDING NEW PRODUCTS AND BRANDS

With the addition of the Musselman's label, Knouse was well established in the apple products sector. To keep pace with changing consumer tastes, the company looked to leverage its canning expertise to develop new products. In the 1980s customers began asking Knouse to consider mixing apples with other fruits. As a result, the Fruit'n Sauce product line was unveiled in 1987, offering flavors that combined apples with pieces of such fruit as apricot, cranberry, grapefruit, papaya, peach, pineapple, prune, raspberry, and strawberry. Not only were the products available in large jars and single-serve portions, they were suitable as a snack or dessert, and could be used as ice cream or pound cake toppings or served as a glaze. Greater production capacity resulting from the Musselman acquisition also allowed Knouse to begin co-packing for multi-material companies in 1989, offering sauces, juices, teas, beverages, nutraceuticals, and other products.

Knouse expanded further through acquisitions in the 1990s. The Apple Time brands of applesauce and apple juice were purchased from Santa Rosa, California-based Vacu-Dry Co. for $5 million. Established in 1933, Vacu-Dry produced dehydrated foods for commercial customers. In 1983 the company decided to add retail products and acquired Sebastopol Cooperative Cannery, which since 1949 had been selling apple sauce and apple juice under the Apple Time label. Although the Apple Time products Vacu-Dry inherited were of high quality and won numerous awards, the company encountered difficulties in its new, low-margin retail business, in particular the slotting fees that the supermarket chains charged in order to secure shelf space. After seven years of effort, Vacu-Dry elected to focus on its more profitable "low moisture" business and divested the Apple Time assets.

Knouse added further assets in 1993 with the acquisition of the Speas Farm and Lincoln juice lines from Sundor Brands Inc., a Procter & Gamble Company subsidiary. Speas Farm possessed a long heritage, founded in Kansas City in 1888 to produce vinegar. The company did not become involved in fruit juices until the 1970s, when it was acquired by the Pillsbury Company. Pillsbury then sold the label to Connecticut-based Sundor in 1988. The Lincoln label, on the other hand, was established in Massachusetts in 1950. The family business was sold to Seneca Foods, which in turn sold it to Lincoln. In addition to apple

and other fruit juices, the Lincoln label was applied to jellies and preserves, ice cream toppings, and syrups, enjoying success in New England markets. Speas Farm, in the meantime, had become a popular brand in the Midwest. The addition of the Speas Farm and Lincoln juice lines was strategically important to Knouse because consumers were loyal to regional brands and the company had experienced difficulty in gaining market share for Lucky Leaf and Musselman's in a number of markets. By acquiring these established brands, Knouse circumvented this problem.

OVERCOMING A TRAGEDY

The early 1990s also brought tragedy to Knouse Foods. In December 1993 a pair of maintenance workers at the Orrtanna apple-processing plant were killed in a refrigerated storage room, the result of an ammonia leak that was either caused by the procedure they followed, errors they committed, or through a combination of the two. In addition, another dozen people, including firemen responding to the scene, were also harmed and treated at local hospitals. The U.S. Occupational Safety and Health Administration investigated and in May 1994 fined Knouse $90,000 for several violations which the agency termed as "willful." Proud of its safety record and adamant that it had done no intentional wrong, the company objected strenuously to the use of the term "willful." Knouse appealed the matter, and in April 1995 a settlement was reached that lowered the fine to $70,000 and an alteration to the language of the finding. Moreover, Knouse did not have to admit to any wrongdoing.

Following a very successful tenure as Knouse chief executive, Dean Carey retired at the age of 74 in July 2000. He was replaced by Ken Guise, who also had a long association with the company. Guise joined Knouse in 1978 as an accountant and worked his way up through the ranks, serving as vice-president of marketing, assistant general manager, and vice-president/general manager before ascending to the top position in the organization. After taking charge, Guise led an effort to modernize the Lucky Leaf and Musselman's brands. For its part, Musselman's was well entrenched as the third largest brand in the apple products segment, trailing Mott's and private labels. A new director of marketing was hired, former Hershey executive Bob Fisher, and in 2003 a new advertising agency was named, Pittsburgh's Blattner Brunner.

Guise would have to make some difficult decisions in order to keep Knouse competitive. Because fewer apples were being produced in the West Virginia area, the land instead sold to developers, it was no longer economically viable to operate the Inwood processing plant. In the fall of 2008 Knouse announced that it would soon cease applesauce production there, although the warehousing, storage, and distribution operations would be maintained. While it was a bitter pill for employees and the Inwood community to swallow, it was a step that Guise and his management team believed the company had to take in order to continue to grow the business launched by Milton Knouse and grower-members 60 years earlier.

Ed Dinger

PRINCIPAL OPERATING UNITS

Apple Time; Lincoln; Lucky Leaf; Musselman's; Speas Farm.

PRINCIPAL COMPETITORS

Del Monte Foods Company; Motts LLP; Tree Top, Inc.

FURTHER READING

Bramson, Constance Y., "Apples Are at Core of New Fruit-Sauce Combination," *Patriot News,* September 2, 1987, p. C1.

Goulet, Neal G., "Food Firm Agrees to Pay Fine," *York (Pa.) Daily Record,* April 4, 1995, p. D5.

Jensen, Trevor, "Blattner Brunner Wins Knouse Foods," *Adweek,* September 15, 2003, p. 14.

Klaus, Mary, "Knouse Foods Wins Achievement Award," *Patriot News,* January 25, 1993, p. 6.

"Pet Milk Company Plans to Acquire C.H. Musselman," *New York Times,* May 19, 1961.

Roth, Jeffrey B., "Fruit Industry Has Rich History," *York Sunday News,* August 8, 2004, p. 5.

Sanger, Shari, "Former Knouse Foods Chief Was 'Caring,'" *Hanover (Pa.) Evening Sun,* March 8, 2005.

Thompson, Charles, "Adams Fruit Processor Acquires 2 Juice Brands," *Patriot News,* January 26, 1992, p. B3.

Korn/Ferry International

———————■———————

1900 Avenue of the Stars, Suite 2600
Los Angeles, California 90067-4507
U.S.A.
Telephone: (310) 552-1834
Fax: (310) 206-2600
Web site: http://www.kornferry.com

Public Company
Incorporated: 1969 as Korn/Ferry Enterprises
Employees: 2,584
Sales: $790.60 million (2008)
Stock Exchanges: New York
Ticker Symbol: KFY
NAICS: 541612 Human Resources and Executive
Search Consulting Services; 561310 Employment
Placement Agencies

■ ■ ■

Korn/Ferry International is the largest provider of retained executive recruitment in the world, and it also offers executive talent management solutions including outsourced and mid-level recruitment and leadership development solutions. The company operates more than 80 offices in 38 countries in the Americas, Asia/Pacific, Europe, the Middle East, and Africa. Its international client base includes large corporations, nonprofits, and other organizations. In 1998, it launched an Internet-based middle management recruitment service, Futurestep, in conjunction with the *Wall Street Journal*. The company, briefly public in the early 1970s, issued stock for a second time in 1999. Since the

early years of the 21st century, the company has diversified its services, focusing on retention and development in addition to recruitment.

BEGINNINGS

Korn/Ferry International was founded by a pair of restless partners at Peat Marwick Mitchell & Co. (later KPMG Worldwide). Lester Korn had earned his M.B.A. from UCLA in 1960 and had begun work on a Ph.D. at Harvard Business School when he left to join "Big 8" accounting firm Peat Marwick as a management consultant. In 1963 he was asked to run the company's executive search department on the West Coast and several years later was made a partner.

Richard Ferry, from Ohio, had earned a degree in accounting from Kent State University and had worked for several accounting firms, including one that he cofounded, before joining Peat Marwick in 1965. He, too, soon moved into the executive search field there, eventually succeeding Korn as West Coast search department manager. He became a partner in 1969. Despite the success of both men within the company, each found himself chafing at the constraints encountered in working for a large firm. In November 1969 they made the decision to form their own personnel consulting agency, Korn/Ferry Enterprises.

The initial scope of Korn/Ferry (the name was soon changed to Korn/Ferry International) included a range of personnel consulting services, only one facet of which was executive search. The two founders' strong backgrounds in this area and its relatively untapped market on the West Coast, however, led them to concentrate in it. The new partners started out sharing all the work, but over the next several years they hired additional employees, including several from Peat Marwick.

Korn/Ferry was put together in a more rigorously organized manner than the typical search firm of the era, which often worked as more of an "old boys' network" than a systematically run business. Lester Korn, the more public member of the team, took on the job of promoting the firm both to clients and to potential candidates. He hired public relations agencies to get the word out and also came up with the idea of performing surveys of executive vacancies for distribution to the media, which resulted in free publicity.

EARLY GROWTH

Richard Ferry, working more in the background, specialized in developing methods for running the company efficiently, which included using a research staff to handle many aspects of the search process, keeping careful records of time spent on each search, and creating a clear hierarchy of duties. Many other recruitment firms left the entire work load to a single person whose job included seeking out clients as well as tracking and "cold calling" prospective candidates. Ferry's systems parceled these tasks out to support staffers, leaving the senior members of the firm free to concentrate on keeping in touch with clients and conducting interviews of final candidates. An innovation during the company's first year was the creation of a specialty division dedicated to real estate.

The first several years of business were highly successful for Korn/Ferry, which soon opened offices in a number of cities, including New York, Houston, and Chicago. By its third year the company's annual revenues had risen to $1.8 million and its staff had grown to more than 40. Specialty divisions included petrochemicals/energy and financial services, in addition

to real estate. Expansion into Europe was accomplished in 1972 by a merger with the British search firm G.K. Dickinson Ltd., and the company also opened an office in Japan a few months later.

In 1972 the company's founders decided to take the firm public, selling ownership of a quarter of the business on the over-the-counter market for slightly less than a million dollars. Although highly profitable, and with annual sales growth of nearly 100 percent in 1973 and more than 40 percent in 1974, the stock value dropped from $8 to slightly more than $5. Finding that they were spending large amounts of their time dealing with the responsibilities of being publicly owned, Korn and Ferry decided to buy back the outstanding stock for $7 a share.

The company's growth continued at a rapid rate throughout the 1970s. The 1977 purchase of 49 percent of Latin American search firm Hazzard and Associates took Korn/Ferry south of the border, and the company expanded to Australia two years later with the acquisition of Guy Pease Associates. By the end of 1979, as it celebrated its tenth anniversary, Korn/Ferry had made partners of 59 of its senior recruiters. In 1980 the company was declared to be the number one search firm in the world by industry observer *Executive Recruiter News*.

CONTINUING SUCCESS

The early 1980s saw more strong years for the firm, and by 1985 Korn/Ferry boasted 106 partners, 11 specialty divisions, and revenues of an estimated $58 million. The company employed more than 400 and operated 36 offices worldwide. Income from overseas recruiting accounted for about a quarter of revenues, with a significant amount also derived from the financial services specialty. Korn/Ferry was performing 1,500 searches per year for executives earning salaries of more than $75,000. The firm's staff profited from its success, receiving performance-based bonuses that sometimes equaled 50 percent or more of their annual salaries.

The company had several high-profile success stories to its credit, including the recruiting of Peter Ueberroth to head the 1984 Olympic Committee and the placement of CEOs at corporations such as Storage Technology, Seafirst, and Nissan USA. It had also suffered embarrassment when a managing partner, David H. Charlson, resigned after it was discovered that he had padded his resume with a fictional M.B.A. degree from Stanford. Several other Korn/Ferry recruiters also left after they were found to be making exaggerated claims about their education.

KEY DATES

1969: Company is founded by Lester Korn and Richard Ferry.

1970: First specialty division is created for real estate recruiting.

1972: Company merges with G.K. Dickinson Ltd. of England; company makes initial public offering.

1974: Company returns to private ownership.

1977: Company acquires 49 percent of Hazzard and Associates, extends presence to Latin America.

1980: Korn/Ferry ranks as number one search firm, according to *Executive Recruiter News*.

1991: Founder Lester Korn leaves.

1993: Company purchases Carre Orban International of England.

1998: Company forms Futurestep online recruitment service.

1999: Company goes public for the second time.

2007: Korn/Ferry acquires the executive coaching firm LeaderSource.

2008: The company sets a new record for revenues.

The search business became increasingly competitive during these years, with clients seldom remaining loyal to a single firm and staging "shootouts" where competing recruiters made pitches to win a search. The financial rewards were great, however, as executive salaries spiraled upward and search firms' one-third commissions, based on the first of year salary, increased proportionately.

Revenues also were fed by a widespread erosion of employee loyalty and by the many companies that had poor internal systems for developing management talent. Although the majority of open positions were filled by the companies themselves, they were forced to rely on executive recruitment firms when internal candidates and advertising for applicants did not pan out. Executive recruiters, dubbed headhunters, were sometimes seen as shady operators who brazenly called unsuspecting employees to offer them positions at rival companies. The reality was that recruiters provided a necessary service, as they offered a discreet way for a company to entice needed staff away from competitors. Attention from recruiters became a sign of success for executives, who wondered what they were doing wrong if they did not regularly receive a certain number of calls from headhunters.

CHANGING TIMES

Korn/Ferry's business grew to an estimated $103.3 million in fiscal 1989, but the U.S. economy was leveling off and executive hiring, especially in the financial services area, began to decline. Revenues shrank to $97.3 million two years later, and the company reportedly trimmed its staff by 20 percent between 1990 and 1992. Korn/Ferry also took other steps to remain competitive, including reducing fees charged to clients, accelerating the pace of searching, and even guaranteeing its candidates' performance for up to a year from date of hire. Times were tough industrywide, and an estimated one-sixth of the 2,300 firms active in 1989 had closed their doors just three years later.

Founder Lester Korn, who had temporarily left the firm to serve as a representative to the United Nations in 1987 and 1988, departed for good in early 1991, and his ownership stake was purchased by Korn/Ferry's 140 partners. Richard Ferry added Korn's job of chairman to his own roles of president and CEO. With the economy on the mend in the early 1990s, the search business picked up and the company again began to look toward growth. In a move that greatly boosted its European presence, in 1993 Korn/Ferry purchased Carre Orban International of England for $20 million. The move paid off, as international recruiting soon became the company's largest growth area, amounting to half its revenues within four years. New offices were opened in such far-flung locales as Russia, India, and Asia.

By the mid-1990s the company also began pursuing a strategy of signing long-term agreements with major corporations. These recognized Korn/Ferry as the client's primary search firm, which helped reduce the dreaded "shootouts," but also limited the company's ability to recruit executives from its clients, which included AT&T, Johnson & Johnson, and General Electric. The deals typically guaranteed Korn/Ferry a minimum of $1 million a year in business, with the company promising lower fees and better service as part of the bargain. Korn/Ferry reported that it realized 20 percent of its revenues from such arrangements in 1995.

GOING ONLINE

In 1997, the company began to offer an Internet-based recruitment service in California, initially called Korn/Ferry: Careerlink. This targeted middle management executives and college graduates, an area in high demand in the late 1990s that Korn/Ferry had previously ignored. The trial run proved successful, and the company quickly moved to expand it nationally under a new name, Futurestep. The service, which was provided with assistance from the *Wall Street Journal* (which took no ownership stake), asked prospective candidates to register online. If they were being considered for a specific job, they would be interviewed later by a Korn/Ferry staffer. The number of people who chose to put their resumes online grew to more than 500,000 within the first 18 months. By 2000, the database was comprised of 800,000 job candidates.

Korn/Ferry went public again, issuing stock on the New York Stock Exchange in 1999. Following a disappointing start, by year's end Internet-dazzled investors had bid up the company's stock price significantly. Korn/Ferry later issued a "tracking stock" for subsidiary Futurestep, Inc. Following the public offering, the company began a round of acquisitions, purchasing Amrop International Australasia of Australia, Hofmann Herbold & Partner of Germany, and Crist Partners of Chicago. Cofounder Richard Ferry still held the title of chairman, with former COO Windle Priem filling the roles of president and CEO. He had replaced Michael Boxberger, who succeeded Ferry at those jobs in the mid-1990s.

Despite the general economic downturn, Korn/Ferry and its competitors did well in the late 1990s and 2000—a period dubbed the "halcyon days for headhunters" by a Korn/Ferry executive in the December 27, 2000, *New York Times*—resulting in the emergence of between 300 and 400 new firms in 1998 and 1999. According to the same issue of the *New York Times,* the executive recruiting industry grew in double digits annually between 1992 and 2000. At Korn/Ferry, fiscal revenues rose dramatically from $218 million in 1996 to $501 million in 2000, a record for the company that enabled it to regain its previous position as the nation's largest search firm. Revenues for the search industry as a whole grew a record (approximate) 30 percent in 2000, as cited in the March 11, 2002, *Business Week Online.*

In 2000, the company expanded business with seventeen offices in Europe and Asia by acquiring PA Consulting Group's executive search business. The company also acquired JobDirect, an online college recruitment company. In 2001, the company had over 100 offices in North America, Europe, Asia, and Latin America. That year, CEO Windle Priem retired and Korn/Ferry conducted a search for its own new chairman and chief executive. While Priem (as well as his predecessors at Korn/Ferry) was an inside hire, the company looked outside its ranks this time, hiring Paul C. Reilly of KPMG International. By hiring outside the company, Korn/Ferry leaders hoped they would acquire new strategies and ideas that would enable the company to succeed in its ongoing battle with competitor Heid-

rick & Struggles over which would be the biggest publicly traded headhunter.

WEATHERING DIFFICULTIES

The "halcyon days" darkened with a major slump for headhunters in 2001, as companies downsized their executive staffs, a trend that was exacerbated after the terrorist attacks against the United States on September 11, 2001. Executive searches fell 22 percent between the beginning of 2001 and September, and shares in Korn/Ferry's Futurestep recruiting site dropped dramatically to $16 in April 2002. For the first time in a decade, search firm revenues fell by an average of about 25 percent according to the March 11, 2002, *Business Week Online.*

Korn/Ferry dealt with the economic downturn by tightening its belt. The company had over-recruited during the dot-com bubble; Korn/Ferry CEO Paul Reilly eliminated 500 employees, or 20 percent of the company's workforce, and he instituted 10 percent executive pay cuts. The company also closed JobsDirect, its online college recruitment service.

The following year, Korn/Ferry sold $60 million in convertible bonds and stock to Friedman Fleischer & Lowe LLC in a private placement. The company's stock fell from $44 in 2000 to less than $7 in 2003. However, with rising job growth and analysts predicting mass retirement among the baby boomer generation, revenues were $476.4 million in 2005, and the company's stock returned to $23.18 in October 2006, with revenues that fiscal year of $615 million.

Having weathered the difficult years between 1998 and 2001 by cutting back, the company then boosted its revenues by diversifying its services to clients, re-imaging itself as both an executive search company and a "talent management" firm. In 2006, 20 percent of revenues were provided by side businesses that offered online tools for employee evaluation and recruitment. The company also added a new consulting business to advise its clients on compensation and benefits for top executives, in the wake of scandals in that area. To assist with its diversification, Korn/Ferry acquired the executive coaching firm LeaderSource in 2007 and in 2008 it acquired Lore International Institute, a provider of leadership development, executive education, and coaching services.

In 2007, Gary Burnison became Korn/Ferry's new CEO, having previously served the company as CFO and COO. Burnison continued to lead the company through a diversification process, offering more talent management services to its clients, and emphasizing the role of technology in supporting what the company called "bringing science into the art of search."

After a brief period of optimism, in 2008 the U.S. banking crisis sent recruitment firms scrambling for business once again as companies cut back on staff. Korn/Ferry's share prices dropped by 75 percent. As it did in 2001, Korn/Ferry responded by tightening its belt, announcing a 15 percent cut in its workforce to save $50 million a year.

Nevertheless, the company set a new record for revenues in 2008 at $791 million, a 21 percent increase over the previous year, and profits rose 12 percent over the previous year. All three of its business lines (Executive Recruitment, Futurestep, and Leadership Development Solutions) were profitable. The company was recognized with numerous awards for its new corporate image and the "Art & Science of Talent" campaign. The company's future would undoubtedly depend on U.S. economic recovery after the banking crisis. However, Korn/Ferry had weathered past financial storms and the company would likely make strategic decisions in order to secure its place as a leading global talent management firm in the years to come.

Frank Uhle
Updated, Heidi Feldman

PRINCIPAL SUBSIDIARIES

Lore International Institute; Executive Compensation Advisors, Inc.; Korn/Ferry International Futurestep, Inc.; Lominger Consulting, Inc.; LeaderSource Ltd.Inc.; Nihon Korn/Ferry International K.K. (Japan); Korn/Ferry International Pty Ltd. (Australia); Carre, Orban and Partners Ltd. (UK); Hoffmann, Herbold & Partners Beteiligungs GmbH (Germany); Korn/Ferry International S.A. (Argentina); Korn/Ferry International (Asia Pacific) Ltd. (Hong Kong).

PRINCIPAL COMPETITORS

Heidrick & Struggles International, Inc.; Russell Reynolds Associates, Inc.; Spencer Stuart Management Consultants N.V.; Egon Zehnder International.

FURTHER READING

Berry, Kate, "The Searcher: Paul Reilly Sold His Real Estate Development Firm to KPMG, Where He Rose to the Top Job, Then Jumped Ship to Lead Korn/Ferry," *Los Angeles Business Journal,* February 14, 2005, p. 19.

Bodovitz, Katherine, "Headhunters Face Off in Shootout As Search Industry Consolidates," *Crain's New York Business,* October 13, 1986, p. 17.

Breznick, Alan, "Korn/Ferry Searches for Profits," *Crain's New York Business,* December 7, 1992, p. 3.

Byrne, John A., *The Headhunters,* New York: Macmillan, 1986.

Eadie, Alison, "Masters of the Round-the-World Choose Headhunting," *Daily Telegraph London,* January 28, 1998, p. 65.

Finch, Camilla, "Recruiter Must Don Founder's Big Shoes," *Crain's New York Business,* May 11, 1992, p. 13.

Gabriel, Frederick, "Korn/Ferry Turns Clients into Partners with Deals," *Crain's New York Business,* July 29, 1996, p. 17.

Glater, Jonathan, "Management—Wanted: One C.E.O., Ready to Work; Long Boom and a Shortage of Top Executive Talent Fuel Growth of Recruiters," *New York Times,* December 27, 2000, p. 1.

Hagerty, Bob, and Joann S. Lublin, "Internet Putting Added Pressure on Headhunters," *Wall Street Journal,* February 14, 1997, p. A9D.

Helman, Christopher, "The Headless Headhunter," *Forbes,* April 30, 2001, p. 54.

"The Incredible Shrunken Headhunters," *Business Week Online,* March 11, 2002.

Montagu-Pollock, Matthew, "Headhunter Time," *Asiamoney,* October 2000, p. 21.

Newman, Morris, "Korn/Ferry International Founder Runs $64-Million Job Search Firm," *Los Angeles Business Journal,* February 22, 1988, p. 1.

Palazzo, Anthony, "Korn/Ferry Keeping Eye on Economy amid Cash Woes," *Los Angeles Business Journal,* December 10, 2001, p. 26.

Peltz, James F., "Stock Spotlight: Earnings, Economy Help Korn/Ferry Get Ahead," *Los Angeles Times,* January 18, 2000, p. C1.

Pettersson, Edvard, "Traditional Recruiter Tries New Scouting Techniques," *Los Angeles Business Journal,* October 23, 2000, p. 7.

Sarkisian, Nola L., "Korn/Ferry Now Flies High After Getting a Slow Start," *Los Angeles Business Journal,* October 11, 1999, p. 60.

Taub, Daniel, "Global Recruiting: Richard Ferry Helped Take Korn/Ferry International from Two-Man Office to World's No. 1 Executive Search Firm," *Los Angeles Business Journal,* December 16, 1996, p. 15.

Temes, Judy, "International Focus Pays Off at Korn/Ferry," *Crain's New York Business,* April 15, 1996, p. 16.

Vrana, Debora, "Executive Recruiter Korn/Ferry to Launch Long-Delayed IPO," *Los Angeles Times,* February 8, 1999, p. C1.

———, "Korn/Ferry IPO Gets Mixed Reviews," *Los Angeles Times,* August 24, 1998, p. D1.

Kwizda Holding GmbH

—————— ■ ——————

Dr. Karl Lueger-Ring 6
Vienna, A-1010
Austria
Telephone: (43 05) 99 77 10 0
Fax: (43 05) 99 77 10 260
Web site: http://www.kwizda.at

Private Company
Incorporated: 1853
Employees: 1,170
Sales: EUR 800 million ($1.17 billion) (2007)
NAICS: 325131 Inorganic Dye and Pigment Manufacturing; 325188 All Other Inorganic Chemical Manufacturing; 325412 Pharmaceutical Preparation Manufacturing

■ ■ ■

Kwizda Holding GmbH is one of Austria's largest privately owned pharmaceuticals companies. Kwizda operates through three primary companies. Kwizda Handel is Austria's second largest pharmaceutical wholesaler, distributing both Kwizda's own products as well as third-party pharmaceuticals, OTC medicines, herbs and herbal preparations, and other pharmacy and pharmaceutical supplies. The wholesale division also includes Mayrhofer Galenik, Mayrhofer Kräutergross-handel, and Apotronik, a specialist in hospital intravenous infusion systems. Kwizda Pharma oversees the group's preparation and production of branded and generic pharmaceuticals and OTC (over-the-counter) medicines. The group's drug products include prescription drugs such as Zanidip, Acentan, Mepril, Bisocor, and Doxapress, while its generics production includes amlodipin, famotidin, and ciprofloxacin.

The company's OTC list includes Adolorin, Kratalgin, Leaton, Sodexx, and Curol. Kwizda Agro focuses on the production of fertilizers and other products for the agricultural sector. Other members of the Kwizda group including Kwizda Kosmetik, a producer and distributor of cosmetics; garden supplies company Gartenhilfe GmbH; and roofing and sealing specialist Büsscher & Hoffmann. While Austria is the company's primary market, Kwizda operates subsidiaries in Germany, Italy, the Czech Republic, and Hungary. Founded in 1853 as a pharmacy, before becoming a noted supplier of veterinary products, Kwizda remains owned by the founding family and led by brothers and co-chief executive officers Richard and Johann Kwizda. Kwizda reported total sales of more than EUR 800 million ($1.17 million) in 2007.

PHARMACIST AND HORSE ENTHUSIAST IN 1853

Kwizda's origins lie in the middle of the 19th century and the beginnings of a modern medical industry in the Austria-Hungarian empire. In 1853 the young pharmacist Franz Johann Kwizda, then 26 years old, took over the "Apotheke zum Schwarzen Adler," in Korneuburg. That pharmacy had been in operation at least since the early 17th century.

Trained at the royal pharmacy in Vienna, Kwizda was also an avid horse enthusiast. This interest led Kwizda to specialize his own pharmaceutical focus in the development of veterinary preparations. Kwizda developed a number of animal feed supplements, for poultry and pigs, launching his own brand, Rössel-marke, soon after founding his pharmacy. Kwizda's research focus nonetheless remained on horses and led to the development of a "restitution fluid" that helped establish Kwizda's company among the leading pharmaceutical houses in Austria. By 1877 Kwizda had been named the official veterinary medicines supplier to the Habsburg Court. By then, too, Kwizda had begun shipping his restitution fluid and other veterinary products beyond the empire's borders.

Kwizda's sons joined him in the business, and by 1886 both Franz and Julius Kwizda had become shareholders in the business. Julius Kwizda emerged as the company's next leader, however, taking over from his father in 1888. Educated at the Vienna Pharmacy University, Julius Kwizda had spent several years working at the Court Pharmacies in Rome and Baden-Baden before joining the family business.

ADDING PHARMACEUTICALS IN THE 20TH CENTURY

Under Julius Kwizda, the pharmacy made the move into human pharmaceuticals. Kwizda also reinforced the company's export operations, while expanding the company's range of products. These efforts were crowned with the award of the Grand Prix medal at the Paris World Exhibition in 1900. The company had not abandoned the veterinary market, however. Among the group's products was a new system of straps that allowed tethered horses to graze. This was developed in conjunction with the Vienna Volunteer Fire Department.

The outbreak of World War I and the subsequent collapse of the Habsburg monarchy meant the end of an era for the Kwizda company as well. The breakup of the empire severely disrupted the company's operations, especially its former export operations. The rebuilding of the company's fortunes fell on the next generation, however, as Julius Kwizda passed away in the early 1920s. Taking his place in 1924 was son Richard Kwizda, who had studied at the Vienna University for Pharmacy and Chemistry before receiving his PhD from the University of Innsbruck.

Richard Kwizda became a major figure in Kwizda's history, expanding its sales by more than 600 times during his tenure. The company began working in partnership with the Austrian Pharmacy Association, launching a new preparation, "Rheumafluid Kwizda," in 1924. The company also began working with researchers at Austria's universities. This led the company to develop a number of new pharmaceutical products, including an analgesic, Adolorin, and a method for the large-scale production of a new sedative in the 1930s.

In 1924 Kwizda launched a new Department of Plant Protection in 1926. The unit, which later became known as Kwizda Agro, first focused on developing insecticides and other crop protection chemicals for the cereals and grains sector. In 1942 Kwizda Agro acquired its own estate in Sohnhof, where it set up an experimental farm.

In the meantime Kwizda had added another major branch of operations. In 1934 the company moved into the pharmaceutical wholesale business, establishing Kwizda Handel. That company later grew into Austria's second largest pharmaceutical wholesale house.

POSTWAR GROWTH

World War II brought about a new disruption to Kwizda's growth as many of the company's facilities were destroyed during the war. By the early 1950s Kwizda had largely completed the rebuilding of its operations and had relaunched its expansion. The group's postwar pharmaceuticals operations were boosted with the creation of a number of partnerships with leading global pharmaceutical groups, such as Eli Lilly and John Wyeth.

Kwizda's wholesale business enjoyed strong growth during the 1950s. At the same time the group also began building its own network of pharmacies in Austria. The company's Agro division also grew steadily, becoming the first to launch a hormone-based herbicide for cereals in 1953. This was followed by the release of Gesaprim, a riazine-based herbicide for corn crop protection in 1959.

During the 1950s the company also developed an interest in wood protection, founding a new subsidiary, Osterreichischen Holzschutzgesellschaft in 1954. Soon after, the company launched its Lignal brand of anti-parasite products. At the end of the decade, entry into wood protection led the company into another new direction. In 1959 the company acquired the roofing sealing specialist Busscher & Hoffmann, based in Enns.

Kwizda continued to focus on the Austrian market through most of the 1960s. Austria's small size,

KEY DATES

1853: Franz Johann Kwizda takes over the Zum Schwarzen Adler pharmacy in Korneuburg and begins producing veterinary products.

1888: Son Julius Kwizda takes over the company and launches production of human pharmaceuticals.

1926: Kwizda launches production of crop protection chemicals, under Richard Kwizda.

1934: Kwizda enters the pharmaceutical wholesale trade in Austria.

1954: Kwizda forms the wood protection subsidiary Osterreichischen Holzschutzgesellschaft.

1968: Kwizda establishes its first international subsidiary in Frankfurt.

1978: John and Richard Kwizda take over as the company's managing partners.

1990: Kwizda enters the Eastern Europe market with a subsidiary in Hungary.

1995: Kwizda enters the French market, setting up Vikem-Kwizda in Paris.

2002: Kwizda becomes the second largest pharmaceuticals wholesaler in Austria through the acquisition of Mayrhofer Pharmazeutika in Linz.

2005: Kwizda restructures as a holding company, Kwizda Holding GmbH.

2007: Kwizda enters Romania with the purchase of Agrovet Trade.

however, ultimately led the company to look beyond its borders. In 1968 Kwizda made its first move into the international market, establishing a subsidiary, Hormosan-Kwizda, in Frankfurt, Germany. The company's Agro division also posted a number of milestones during this period. In 1968, for example, the company became the first to launch a carboxin-based seed dressing agent that contained no mercury. Two years later the company introduced Betanal, a herbicide focused on the sugar beet sector.

Kwizda also began preparing the transition to the next generation. In 1969 brothers Richard and John Kwizda were named to the company's board of directors. Then, in 1978, the brothers took over as the company's managing partners. The pair would remain at the head of the family-owned company through the turn of the next century.

MODERNIZATION EFFORTS

Kwizda launched a modernization effort for its production and distribution operations during the 1980s. This included the construction of a new manufacturing plant for the Agro division in Leobendorf, near the group's Korneuburg headquarters, in 1982. The following year Kwizda established a new pharmaceutical production facility in Vienna, as well. The new factory allowed Kwizda to bring all of its pharmaceutical production under the same roof. The new Vienna facility also served as a logistics hub for the group's distribution operations. Later in the decade Kwizda also took steps to reorganize its wholesale operations. As part of this effort the company established new wholesale facilities in Vienna and Grodig in 1987.

The collapse of the Soviet Union and the end of the Communist era in Eastern Europe led to new opportunities for Kwizda. Austria's proximity to the newly opened markets in Central and Eastern Europe made these countries highly attractive expansion targets for the company. Kwizda moved quickly, setting up its first foreign subsidiary in the region in Budapest, Hungary, in 1990. By 1994 the company's Agro division had also entered Hungary, setting up Magyar Kwizda. Over the next decade Kwizda expanded further into the region, adding operations in Brno, Prague, Kraków, and Cluj, among other locations.

By then, too, the Agro division had increasingly begun to focus its operations around the pesticides market. In 1994, for example, Kwizda acquired the global rights to market Silmurin, a rodenticide developed by Sandoz. The company also extended its operations into the consumer market that year, with the purchase of Linz-based Gartenhilfe GmbH.

ACQUIRING SCALE IN THE 21ST CENTURY

Kwizda continued its strong growth through the late 1990s. The group's international expansion brought the company to Germany, where it established a new subsidiary, Kwizda Deutschland, in Frankfurt in 1994. The following year the company entered the French market, setting up Vikem-Kwizda in Paris as part of the group's Agro division. In 1998 Kwizda entered the Italian market, setting up a subsidiary in Bologna. Also that year, Kwizda reinforced its German presence, buying Munich-based Euflor, which was focused on the home gardening market. In 2004 Kwizda established a dedicated pharmaceuticals subsidiary in Munich, as well.

Acquisitions played an increasingly important role in Kwizda's growth into the new century. The company expanded its Agro operations through several purchases in the early 2000s. These included Sarea Saatguttechnik, a company established in 1929 that specialized in seed processing. The company then bought Gerhaus-based Agro Trial Center, a research and development facility established in 1986. Kwizda completed that purchase in 2001. The following year the company raised its French profile, with the purchase of France's LTI Tougon.

In Austria, Kwizda had completed its most significant acquisition to date. In 2002 the company agreed to buy one of its major rivals, Mayrhofer Pharmazeutika, based in Linz. The purchase not only strengthened Kwizda's pharmaceuticals production, but it also expanded its wholesale business, providing new access to the products from a range of both Austrian and international companies. The Mayrhofer purchase represented a significant increase in Kwizda's operations, as the company posted a revenue jump of more than 50 percent. Kwizda became the number two pharmacy wholesaler in Austria, behind Herba Chemosan.

Kwizda launched a restructuring of its operations in 2005. As part of that process, the company adopted a new holding company structure, changing its name to Kwizda Holding GmbH. The company then established its Agro division as a separate company, Kwizda Agro GmbH. Following the restructuring Kwiza's pharmaceutical operations, Kwizda Pharma GmbH, inaugurated a new production facility in Linz.

With its restructuring completed, Kwizda renewed its international expansion effort. In 2005, the company's Agro operation opened a new factory in France, in Val d'Ize. Kwizda also sought further growth in the Eastern European market. This led the company to Romania, where it bought Bucharest-based plant protection specialists Agrovet Trade in 2007. After more than 150 years Kwizda remained one of Austria's most vibrant family-owned businesses.

M. L. Cohen

PRINCIPAL SUBSIDIARIES

Büsscher & Hoffman GmbH; Gartenhilfe GmbH; Kwizda Agro GmbH; Kwizda Handel GmbH; Kwizda Kosmetik GmbH; Kwizda Pharma GmbH; Mayrhofer Kwizda GmbH.

PRINCIPAL COMPETITORS

Herba Chemosan GmbH.

FURTHER READING

Heinrich, Monika, "150 Jahre Kwizda: Der 'Schwarze Adler' Hob Ab," *OAZ Aktuell,* June 7, 2003.
"Kwizda Buys Mayrhofer," *Pharma Marketletter,* December 2, 2002.
"Kwizda Group Restructures," *Chemical Business NewsBase,* September 24, 2005.
"New Biosimilar Edges Toward Europe," *Pharmaceutical Technology Europe,* June 2008, p. 46.
"Sumitomo Pharmaceutical Allows French, Austrian Firms to Make Heart Drug," *Japan Economic Newswire,* September 9, 1987.

Lab Safety Supply, Inc.

401 South Wright Road
Janesville, Wisconsin 53546-8729
U.S.A.
Telephone: (608) 754-7160
Toll Free: (800) 356-0783
Fax: (608) 754-1806

Wholly Owned Subsidiary of W.W. Grainger Inc.
Incorporated: 1974
Sales: $147 million (2007 est.)
NAICS: 454113 Mail-Order Houses; 423840 Industrial
  Supplies Merchant Wholesalers

■ ■ ■

A subsidiary of W.W. Grainger, Lab Safety Supply, Inc., is a Janesville, Wisconsin-based mail-order catalog operation that carries more than 100,000 industrial and safety supplies, also available through the company's web site. Safety supplies include such items as eyewear, face masks, respirators, hard hats, air monitors, biosafety cleaning and waste disposal products, and protective clothing. Lab supplies and equipment products include scales, centrifuges, incubators, microscopes, autoclaves, fume extraction products, a full range of lab utensils, and plastic and glassware. Lab Safety also offers spill control supplies, material handling items, forestry and environmental equipment, facilities maintenance, and janitorial supplies. In addition, Lab Safety carries educational products, including training materials, displays, appropriate furniture, public safety products for law enforcement and other emergency responders, as well as signs, labels, and tapes.

The Lab Safety general catalog is regularly recognized in the mail-order industry for the depth of its product offerings and customer-friendly organization. In addition, the company offers targeted specialty catalogs, some of which are operated by subsidiaries, including Gempler's, focusing on the agricultural, horticultural, and grounds maintenance sectors; Ben Meadows Company, serving the forestry management and environmental markets; AW Direct, Inc., a supplier of towing, recovery, and service vehicle parts and accessories; Rand Materials Handling Equipment Co., a catalog operation for warehouse, storage, and packaging supplies; McFeely's Square Drive Screws, serving the woodworking industry with tools, hardware, and fasteners; Professional Equipment, catalog suppliers of testing equipment for builders, engineers, and others; Construction Book Express, Inc., offering educational materials to construction professionals and others; and Highsmith Inc., supplier of library furniture and supplies.

ORIGINS IN MOLECULAR MODELS

Lab Safety was founded in 1967 by Donald Hedberg and his wife, Geraldine Raisler Hedberg. In 1950 he graduated from Carthage College in Wisconsin with a degree in chemistry and began a career in teaching, serving as an instructor at the University of Illinois–Chicago for a decade. His wife graduated in 1951 from the University of Wisconsin–Stout with a degree in dietetics. They were living in Evanston, Illinois, raising three daughters in 1967 when he began designing molecular models for the school market. To direct market the models from their kitchen table, they formed a company called Science Related Materials Company. Business was steady enough that two years later they were able to move back to Wisconsin, establishing their company in Janesville, Wisconsin, about 50 miles west of Milwaukee.

The Hedbergs added laboratory safety supplies to their offerings in 1973, a move that had a dramatic effect on the company, so much so that a year later a subsidiary was incorporated as Lab Safety Supply, Inc. The first catalog was published in 1977, the same year that Lab Safety was spun off as an independent company. A modest black-and-white affair, the catalog was just 44 pages in length, a far cry from the catalogs that approached 2,000 pages two decades later. To keep pace with growing demand, caused in large measure by an ever growing number of federal health and safety regulations that needed to be met, the Hedbergs steadily added to the products they carried, resulting in the need for an ever-increasing warehouse.

By 1978, after three expansions, the Lab Safety facility was 140,000 square feet in size. Land was acquired on the outskirts of Janesville, and a new headquarters and distribution facility opened on the site in 1989. The Lab Safety catalog became larger, as well as more sophisticated, over the years. In 1986 it became a full-color publication, and in 1989 it was recognized by trade publication *Catalog Age,* which presented Lab Safety with its Gold Award for catalog excellence, the first of an unprecedented six consecutive Gold Awards. Lab Safety also took measures to improve customer service. In 1988 the company added a toll-free safety hotline, Safety TechLine, affording customers an opportunity to confer with safety experts on products as well as regulations and compliance.

W.W. GRAINGER, INC., ACQUIRES LAB SAFETY

Employing about 600 people, Lab Safety posted sales of more than $117 million in 1991. By this time the Hedbergs were in their 60s and one of their daughters, Peggy Stick, was serving as president. In order to allow

her parents to retire she looked for a buyer for the company and approached Skokie, Illinois-based W.W. Grainger, Inc., a giant distributor of industrial supplies. It was a good choice, given that Grainger lacked a catalog/direct marketing business. A deal was struck and in 1992 Grainger paid $160 million for Lab Safety. Stick stayed on to run the business, which became an independent subsidiary, on a three-year contract, and her parents indeed retired, devoting much of their time to a foundation they set up to donate millions of dollars to more than 100 charitable causes, while also serving on other foundation boards. After an extended battle with cancer, Geraldine Hedberg died at the age of 68 in 1998. Donald Hedberg subsequently remarried, the couple splitting their time between seasonal homes in Florida and Wisconsin.

Lab Safety's corporate parent was founded in Chicago in 1927 by William W. Grainger, an electrical engineer and motor designer, who became a wholesaler of electrical motors that he mostly marketed through a catalog under the *Motor Book* name. It was a market that enjoyed tremendous growth and Grainger expanded with it, establishing a national footprint by opening offices in Atlanta, Dallas, Philadelphia, and San Francisco by 1934, and ten more branches just three years later. Business was even better during the economic boom that followed World War II, so that by 1952 the company maintained 46 branches. Grainger became a manufacturer by acquiring Dayton Electric Manufacturing Company in 1966, and a few years later added electric motor maker McMillan Manufacturing.

In 1967 Grainger went public and in 1975 was listed on the New York Stock Exchange. The *Motor Book,* in the meantime, broadened its product offerings, so that in 1985 it was recast as the *Wholesale Net Price Catalog.* A year later the company began an effort to develop specialty distribution businesses, either as start-ups or through acquisition, including such niches as replacement parts, sanitary supplies, and general industrial products. In 1990 Grainger acquired Allied Safety, Inc., a distributor of protective clothing, respiratory systems, and other equipment for environmental cleanup projects or general workplace use. A year later Grainger added California-based Ball Industries, a commercial sanitary supply business. As a result, the chance to acquire well-established Lab Safety Supply was an opportunity Grainger eagerly embraced. In one stroke Grainger became the third largest company in the safety equipment sector.

CATALOG WINS PRAISE

Although ownership changed, Lab Safety remained a leader in its field, continuing to be recognized by its

KEY DATES

1967: Donald and Geraldine Hedberg begin selling molecular models for the school market in Evanston, Illinois.

1969: Hedbergs move to Janesville, Wisconsin.

1974: Lab Safety Supply, Inc., formed.

1977: First catalog published.

1992: W.W. Grainger, Inc., acquires Lab Safety.

1996: Lab Safety launches web site.

2001: Ben Meadows Company acquired.

2003: Gempler's acquired.

2005: AW Direct, Inc., acquired.

2008: Highsmith Inc. acquired.

peers for the breadth and organization of its catalog and the crispness of its copy, which adeptly avoided jargon. Moreover, the judges for *Catalog Age*'s Gold Award took note of Lab Safety's excellent customer service and toll-free numbers for phone orders, fax ordering, and Safety TechLine for product information and help with government regulation compliance. "The Lab Safety people really know their business," one judge commented in the 1992 deliberations. "They do everything right." Not only did the company's big book in Industrial Supplies continue to take home the Gold Award, Lab Safety's Signs, Labels & Tapes catalog also received a Silver Award in Business Specialty Products in the 1992 competition.

Even as the big book grew ever larger, judges remained impressed. "There's no doubt about it," one judged opined in 1993, "despite Lab Safety's size, the company is warm and personal." Another judge added, "If I were a safety professional receiving this catalog, I would order from it, I'd use it as a reference manual, I'd spec from it, I'd refer it to others in my field, I'd keep one in my supplier library, and I'd use it as a doorstop!" A year later, a judge suggested, "Let's just make a separate category for Lab Safety Supply. It's so good it's almost in a class by itself."

After Peggy Stick's contract expired, she was replaced as Lab Safety's president by Larry J. Loizzo in June 1996. Having joined the company in 1987, he was very familiar with its operations. Under his leadership, Lab Safety expanded beyond catalog sales in 1996 when it launched a web site to handle Internet sales, quickly establishing itself as the industry's largest online resource for safety supplies. Catalogs remained the backbone of the business, however. To better serve different market segments, the company produced specialty titles, which

numbered seven by 1998. A year later, as the company closed out the decade, the *General Catalog* neared 2,000 pages in length and the company offered through its family of catalogs and web site more than 65,000 products. At the start of the new century, the company offered customers another order option by creating a CD-ROM version.

BEN MEADOWS COMPANY ACQUIRED

With backing from its corporate parent, Lab Safety expanded its targeted specialty catalogs by way of acquisitions in the early years of the new century. The company in 2001 acquired Canton, Georgia-based Ben Meadows Company, a direct marketer of products for the forestry management and environmental markets, doing $20 million in annual sales from its catalog operation. Products included rain gear, coveralls, fire fighting clothes, eye wear, face shields, hats, first aid products, lumbering gear, fire fighting and rescue equipment, surveying equipment, hand and power tools, truck and all terrain vehicle accessories, and wildlife management products.

Another specialty catalog and Internet-sales acquisition followed in 2003 when Lab Safety purchased the Gempler's division of Belleville, Wisconsin-based Gempler's, Inc., which contained another catalog company, Duluth Trading Co., focusing on work wear. The mail-order operation generated more than $30 million in annual sales to the agricultural, horticultural, grounds maintenance, and contractor markets. Products included safety supplies, work wear and footwear, tractor and vehicle supplies, tires and supplies, shop and maintenance supplies, pest management products, and weed control products. The 20-year-old company had started out with a catalog selling tire repair supplies to farmers. In answer to requests from its customers, Gempler's began carrying protective equipment for mixing and loading chemicals, leading to a wide range of safety supplies and a widening group of customers, which soon came from the horticultural and grounds maintenance industries. Work wear was added in the mid-1990s, leading to the Duluth Trading Co. sideline.

Early in 2005 Lab Safety expanded further with the acquisition of Connecticut-based AW Direct, Inc., a direct marketer offering towing, recovery, and service vehicle parts and accessories. A year later, Pawtucket, Rhode Island-based Rand Materials Handling Equipment Co. was added to the fold. Founded in 1972, Rand was a catalog distributor of warehouse, storage, and packaging supplies, including material handling products, shelving and racking, and industrial storage supplies.

THREE MORE ACQUISITIONS COMPLETED

Three further acquisitions followed in 2007. First, Lab Safety acquired McFeely's Square Drive Screws, a direct marketer of specialty fasteners, hardware, and tools serving the professional woodworking industry. It was launched in 1978 by William J. McFeely III to sell domestic and exotic hardwoods, and following his death the company's focus shifted to woodworking tools and fasteners. Also in 2007 Lab Safety purchased Professional Equipment, a 20-year-old catalog operation that supplied tools and testing equipment to engineering, HVAC, and building professionals. In addition, Construction Book Express, Inc., was acquired. Established in 1998, the company served construction professionals, designers, architects, engineers, electricians, inspectors, educators, students, and building facility managers, providing them with educational materials on building and engineering codes, specifications, and exam-preparation guides.

In 2008 Lab Safety entered the library market, acquiring Highsmith Inc., a direct marketer of library furniture, equipment, and general supplies since 1956. Also included were Highsmith divisions providing educational materials for school children: Upstart, UpstartBooks, Library Sparks, and Edupress. While Lab Safety had expanded in a myriad of directions, the company had not performed up to the expectations of its parent company. In the fall of 2008 Grainger took steps to address the problem by electing to integrate Lab Safety's supply chain with that of Grainger in an effort to improve efficiencies. Lab Safety products would then be carried in all Grainger Industrial Supply warehouses across the country, leaving uncertain the future role of the Janesville distribution facility and its 950 employees.

Ed Dinger

PRINCIPAL SUBSIDIARIES

AW Direct, Inc.; Ben Meadows Company; McFeely's Square Drive Screws; Gempler's; Highsmith Inc.; Professional Equipment; Rand Materials Handling Equipment Co.

PRINCIPAL COMPETITORS

Industrial Distribution Group, Inc.; Turtle & Hughes Inc.; Wesco International, Inc.

FURTHER READING

"Gempler's Mail-Order Is Bought," *Wisconsin State Journal,* February 15, 2003, p. D10.

"Hedberg Dies," *Wisconsin State Journal,* April 28, 1998, p. 2B.

"Janesville Business to Expand," *Milwaukee Journal Sentinel,* November 26, 1994, p. D1.

"Lab Safety Is Almost Unbeatable," *Catalog Age,* September 1993, p. 140.

"Lab Safety Makes It Big Book Beautiful," *Catalog Age,* September 1994, p. 148.

"Lab Safety Spins Off a Winner," *Catalog Age,* September 1992, p. 134.

"Lab Safety Supply Buys Library Equipment Seller," *Wisconsin State Journal,* August 1, 2008, p. 33.

Leute, Jim, "Lab Safety, Grainger Combining Supply Lines," *Janesville Gazette,* November 20, 2008.

Miller, Paul, "W.W. Grainger Buying Lab Safety Supply," *Catalog Age,* May 1992, p. 12.

"Thumbs Up for Lab Safety Supply," *Catalog Age,* September 1994, p. 137.

Levi Strauss & Co.

1155 Battery Street
San Francisco, California 94111
U.S.A.
Telephone: (415) 501-6000
Fax: (415) 501-7112
Web site: http://www.levistrauss.com

Private Company
Incorporated: 1890
Employees: 11,400
Sales: $4.4 billion (2008 est.)
NAICS: 315224 Men's and Boys' Cut and Sew Trouser, Slack, and Jean Manufacturing; 315223 Men's and Boys' Cut and Sew Shirt (except Work Shirt) Manufacturing; 315221 Men's and Boys' Cut and Sew Underwear and Nightwear Manufacturing; 315232 Women's and Girls' Cut and Sew Blouse and Shirt Manufacturing; 315231 Women's and Girls' Cut and Sew Lingerie, Loungewear, and Nightwear Manufacturing

■ ■ ■

Levi Strauss & Co., one of the world's largest brand-name apparel marketers, gave the world blue jeans and grew enormously rich on this piece of U.S. culture. Indeed, around the world the name of the company's founder has grown to be synonymous with the pants he invented: Levi's. Levi Strauss markets apparel in more than 110 countries and works with contractors in 45 countries across the globe. The company's brands include Levi's, Docker's, and Signature by Levi Strauss & Co. Its products are sold in over 60,000 retail locations including 260 company-owned and 1,500 franchised stores. Levi Strauss is privately owned by descendants of the Levi Strauss family.

EARLY HISTORY

Levi Strauss, born in Bavaria in 1829, immigrated to the United States with his family in 1847 at the age of 18. In New York he was met by his two half-brothers, who had established a dry goods business. A year later, he was sent to Kentucky to live with relatives and walk the countryside peddling his brothers' goods. While Levi Strauss was still traveling the hills of the South, his older sister's husband, David Stern, established a dry goods store in San Francisco, California, in the wake of the 1849 California gold rush. The 1850 founding of this store marked the beginning of the company that would come to bear Levi Strauss's name. Three years later, Strauss made the arduous sea journey around Cape Horn to join his brother-in-law. San Francisco at the time was a booming frontier town, and the opportunity was ripe for a well-run business to flourish. Strauss and Stern set up their small store near the waterfront, where they could easily receive shipments of goods from the Strauss brothers back east.

Jeans, which would become the staple of the family business, were invented when Levi Strauss, noting the need for rugged pants for miners, had a tailor sew pants from some sturdy brown canvas he had brought with him on his journey. Once the supply of canvas was exhausted, Strauss turned to a thick fabric made in the French town of Nimes, known as *serge de Nimes,* which would be shortened to denim. The denim pants, dyed with indigo to make them blue, sold quickly, and the business of Levi Strauss & Co. expanded rapidly, moving three times to new and expanded quarters in the next 13 years. In 1866 the company moved to a luxurious new location on Battery Street, only to have the building cracked from roof to foundation in an earthquake two years later.

In 1872 the proprietors of Levi Strauss & Co. received a letter from Jacob Davis, a tailor in Nevada, offering them a half interest in the patent on a technique he had invented for strengthening the seams of pants by fastening them with rivets. In return, they would pay the cost of obtaining the patent. The cost was negligible, and Strauss and his brother-in-law quickly took the tailor up on his offer. The following year, the company was granted a patent on the use of rivets to secure pocket seams, and also on the double-arc stitching found on the back pockets of its pants.

At first the company had the pants sewn by tailors working individually at home, in the same way that the Strauss brothers in New York manufactured goods. Soon, however, the demand for the new pants became too great, despite the economic depression that had struck California in 1873, and the company collected its stitchers under one roof, in a small factory on Fremont Street, which was managed by Davis, the tailor from Nevada. Such remarkable success brought envious competitors, and Levi Strauss & Co. filed its first lawsuit for patent infringement against two other makers of riveted clothing in January 1874. On the second day of that month, David Stern, the founder of the original San Francisco concern, died. About two years later, Strauss's two oldest nephews, Jacob and Louis Stern, entered the firm with their uncle.

EXPANSION AND DISASTER

In 1877, in a climate of dire economic conditions, mobs attacked San Francisco's Chinatown, sacking and burning shops and homes in a three-day riot, as white men, unable to find work, took out their anger on the Chinese, who had been willing to work for lower wages.

In the wake of this event, Levi Strauss & Co. stopped hiring Chinese people as seamstresses, hoping that move would pacify its customers. Because this entailed paying higher wages, the company had to charge higher prices for its products and thus also find ways to deliver higher-quality goods.

In 1877 the Levi Strauss & Co. factory expanded, and the notable features of Levi's pants—the dark blue denim, the rivets, the stitching, the guarantee of quality—became further standardized. By 1879 the pants were selling for $1.46, and they were widely worn in the rough-and-tumble mines and ranches of the West. The firm also continued to sell other dry goods, chalking up sales of $2.4 million in 1880, and it prospered throughout the 1880s.

In 1886 the "Two Horse Brand" leather tag, showing a team of horses trying to pull apart a pair of pants, began to be sewn into the back of the company's "waist-high overalls," the term Levi Strauss preferred to "jeans." In 1890 the firm assigned its first lot numbers to its products, and the eventually infamous number "501" was assigned to the riveted pants. In that year as well, Levi Strauss & Co. was formally incorporated and 18,000 shares of stock in the company were issued to family members and employees. In September 1902 the patriarch of the company died. In his later years, Levi Strauss had entrusted the business largely to his four Stern nephews, who inherited the firm, in order to devote his energy to charitable and civic causes. Four years after Strauss's death the company endured another shock, when the Great San Francisco Earthquake and Fire of 1906 struck. Both the company's headquarters building on Battery Street and the factory on Fremont Street were destroyed. Along with the rest of the city, Levi Strauss & Co. rebuilt, but the ensuing years were difficult. In 1907 a financial panic, which started in New York and crept westward, caused a slowdown in business, and the company began to streamline the merchandise it sold, relying more and more on its own products. Overall, however, sales were flat, and the four Stern brothers had drifted into a pattern of hands-off management.

JEANS BECOME PRIMARY

In 1912 the company introduced its first innovative product in decades, Koveralls, playsuits for children designed by Simon Davis, the son of tailor Jacob Davis, who had followed his father into the business. Advertised widely, Koveralls became the first Levi Strauss & Co. product to be sold nationwide, helping the company to eventually break out of its regional market. The coming of World War I, and the boom in production for the war, had little or no impact on Levi Strauss

KEY DATES

1847: Levi Strauss immigrates to the United States with his family.
1853: Strauss and his brother-in-law set up a small shop in San Francisco.
1866: The company moves to a new location on Battery Street.
1872: Jacob Davis, a tailor in Nevada, offers Strauss a half interest in the patent on a technique he invented for strengthening the seams of pants by fastening them with rivets.
1873: The company is granted a patent on the use of rivets to secure pocket seams, and also on the double-arc stitching found on the back pockets of its pants.
1890: The later infamous number "501" is assigned to the riveted pants; Levi Strauss & Co. is formally incorporated.
1902: Levi Strauss dies; his four nephews take over the business.
1906: An earthquake and fire destroy the company's headquarters on Battery Street and the factory on Fremont Street.
1912: Koveralls are introduced and become the company's first nationally distributed product.
1935: Levi Strauss & Co. employees join the United Garment Workers union.
1936: The company adds the trademarked red "Levi's" tab to the back pocket of its pants.
1960: Preshrunk denim jeans are launched.
1971: Levi Strauss goes public.
1977: Levi Strauss & Co. is the largest clothing maker in the world.
1985: The company is taken private in a $1.45 billion leveraged buyout by the Haas family.
1986: Dockers pants make their debut.
2002: The Signature line is launched at Wal-Mart and Target stores.
2004: The company closes its last U.S. factory.
2008: Robert Haas leaves the company, marking the first time in company history that a non-family member leads the Levi Strauss board of directors.

& Co., since the company held no government contracts. Its riveted denim goods were sold only to the western laborers for whom they had originally been manufactured, and resale of eastern goods accounted for twice the sales of goods made at the San Francisco factory. Slowly, under the hands of the aging Stern brothers, who were resistant to change, Levi Strauss & Co.'s enterprise was losing ground.

In 1919 Sigmund Stern, who would take over the presidency of the company from his brother, Jacob, in 1921, brought aboard his son-in-law, Walter Haas, to give new blood to the leadership of Levi Strauss & Co. The Haas family, part of the Stern and Strauss clans by marriage, would continue to own the company well into the 1990s and beyond. Walter Haas had little background in the family business, but one of the first changes he made was to update the company's inefficient system of keeping financial records. Despite Haas's attempts at efficiency, the company was battered in the early 1920s by a steep drop in the cost of cotton, the primary raw material for its products, which allowed competitors from other parts of the nation to undercut its prices. Company profits fell one-third in 1920. In addition, Haas discovered that Levi Strauss & Co. was losing $1 on every dozen Koveralls sold. After a brief internal struggle, the price of Koveralls was adjusted, and steps to increase overall productivity, including the implementation of the assembly-line system, were taken.

The company began attaching belt loops to its basic denim pants in 1922 in addition to the traditional suspender buttons. Throughout the 1920s, Levi Strauss & Co. did business at a profit under the direction of Haas and his brother-in-law Daniel Koshland, a banker, whom he had brought into the firm to assist him. The firm found itself relying increasingly on the pants it manufactured, rather than the other dry goods it wholesaled, for the bulk of its profits. By 1929, 70 percent of the firm's profit was derived from its sale of jeans.

THE GREAT DEPRESSION AND WAR YEARS

With the stock market crash in 1929 and the subsequent Great Depression, Levi Strauss & Co. fell on hard times. The widespread unemployment that swept the country throughout the 1930s hit the manual laborers who bought the company's pants particularly hard. By 1930 the company's profits had vanished, and it posted a loss on sales that had fallen one-sixth. Unwilling to cut back production by firing workers, the company amassed a large backlog of unsold products, and then put its employees on a three-day workweek. By 1932 company sales had dropped to half their 1929 level. With the coming of the next year, however, unemployment peaked and sales of Levi's pants slowly began to pick up as the economy gradually improved.

In the economic turmoil of the 1930s, the growing U.S. union movement gained a new stronghold in San Francisco. Although workers in the Levi Strauss & Co. factory had not joined a union, organized labor's insistence that union workers wear union-made clothes sharply limited the company's sales in the heavily unionized San Francisco area. In 1935 Levi Strauss & Co. employees joined the United Garment Workers with management's acquiescence, thereby averting a strike and ending the virtual union boycott of Levi Strauss & Co.'s products.

The Depression and subsequent farm failures of the 1930s eventually worked in the company's favor, enabling it to break out of the relatively small market it had served since its inception. Western ranchers, unable to support themselves through agriculture, turned in the mid-1930s to tourism, inviting easterners to visit "dude ranches," where they were introduced to the cowboy's habitual garb, Levi's jeans. In addition, the advent and growth in popularity of Hollywood "western" movies further spread the word about Levi's jeans. In its advertising the company had always emphasized durability, but at this time it also stressed a certain western mystique. To capitalize on its growing brand identification, the company added the trademarked red "Levi's" tab to the back pocket of its pants in 1936, the first label to be placed on the outside of a piece of clothing. As demand increased, the vast stockpile of denim pants accumulated during the early years of the 1930s was depleted, and the factory returned to normal operation.

By 1939 the Levi Strauss & Co. blue denim "waist overall" had just begun to be popular outside the world of blue-collar workers. College students in California and Oregon adopted them as a fad, and slowly this humble item of clothing began to take on a status all its own. After the United States entered World War II, the government declared the jeans an essential commodity for the war effort, available only to defense workers. This restricted distribution made them an even more coveted item, and contributed, in the long run, to the brand's success. In the short run, however, wartime price restrictions cut into the company's profits.

TARGETING A BROADER MARKET

With the war's end, the company was well situated to prosper. Demographic shifts had brought a large number of potential new customers to the West Coast, and Levi Strauss & Co. operated five jeans factories, in a futile effort to keep up with demand. The immediate postwar years brought a significant production shortage, and the company instituted a strict program of allocation, favoring retailers that were longtime customers. By

1948 company profits for the first time topped $1 million on sales of four million pairs of pants.

In the booming postwar economy of the 1950s, Levi Strauss & Co. underwent the most significant transition in the company's history. Taking advantage of demographic trends, the company began to focus its marketing efforts on young people, members of the baby boom generation, who would wear its pants, then known colloquially as "Levi's," for play, not work. Targeting this new market involved widening the company's sales force to a truly nationwide scope, and shifting its emphasis from rural to more urban areas. As a sign of the company's future, Levi Strauss & Co. closed down its business wholesaling others' merchandise in the early 1950s.

In the 1950s Hollywood once again gave the company a large boost in its efforts to sell jeans to young people when actors such as Marlon Brando and James Dean appeared in *The Wild Ones* and *Rebel Without a Cause,* personifying youthful rebellion and wearing jeans. The pants were losing their status as a symbol of the rugged frontier and becoming instead a symbol of defiance toward the adult world. Levi's were on their way to becoming the uniform of an entire generation.

In 1954 the company branched out from denim to the sportswear business, launching "Lighter Blues," a line of casual slacks for men. The following year the company added jeans with zipper flies, as opposed to the traditional five-button fly, in an attempt to woo customers in the East, where the pants, relegated to department store bargain basements, lagged in popularity. By the end of the decade, Levi Strauss & Co. was selling 20 million pieces of clothing a year, half of them jeans. The company was growing fast, and profits were robust.

PRODUCT DEVELOPMENT
CONTINUES

In the late 1950s and early 1960s, Levi Strauss & Co. experimented with different products and lines of clothing in an effort to build on its reputation and diversify its offerings. In 1959 the company introduced "Orange, Lemon and Lime," pants in six bold colors, which were a short-lived hit. The following year, white Levi's were introduced, a duplicate of traditional jeans, but made in beige twill. Also in 1960, the company introduced preshrunk denim jeans, in an effort to overcome the objections of those customers who were uncomfortable with shrinking pants. In 1963 stretch denim and corduroy Levi's joined the fold.

In 1964, after an arduous and expensive process of development, Levi Strauss & Co. introduced Sta-Prest permanent-press pants. Although the product was an initial sales success, problems with the chemical process that created a crease resulted in a large number of defective pants, and it was only later that the pants were perfected. The following year, the company expanded its international division to cover Europe, relying on Europeans to manage company operations in their home countries.

Throughout the 1960s the company profited from movements in American society, such as campus rebellions and growth of the counterculture, in which jeans became a uniform. The company's growth was tremendous. New manufacturing facilities were added steadily, but demand for jeans still outstripped supply. In the mid-1960s, sales doubled in just three years to $152 million in 1966. That year, the company negotiated a $20 million loan to finance further expansion. Two years later, the company reorganized, establishing a division to produce and market women's clothing. By 1968 the company had grown to become one of the six largest clothing manufacturers in the United States, with sales nearing $200 million.

In 1971 Levi Strauss & Co.'s longstanding status as a wholly family- and employee-owned enterprise came to an end, when the company sold stock to the public for the first time. Denim jeans, Levi's in particular, had transcended the status of a mere product to become a worldwide social and cultural phenomenon, and the company could no longer raise enough capital privately to pay for needed expansion. The craze for jeans continued to grow, seemingly with no end in sight. The company coped with a constant shortage of denim. Levi Strauss & Co.'s existing, heavily centralized structure became inadequate, and operations were broken into four divisions: jeans, Levi's for women, boys' wear, and men's sportswear.

OVERCOMING CHALLENGES

The company's phenomenal growth caught up with it in 1973, when its European division found itself with huge supplies of jeans in an outmoded style—straight-legged, as opposed to flared, or bell-bottomed—with more of the same on order. The problem was the culmination of years of under-management, and cost the company $12 million as it tried to unload the overstock. For the first time since the Depression, Levi Strauss & Co. announced a losing quarter, and the company's stock price fell dramatically. The following year, European operations were reorganized, and the company moved its headquarters from the site it had occupied on Battery Street for 108 years to new quarters. Seven years later, the company would move again to Levi's Plaza, a newly built complex.

Despite the sobering demonstration in Europe of the company's fallibility, by 1974 sales of Levi Strauss & Co. products had reached $1 billion. The following year the company was once again reminded of the hazards of international business when it was revealed that Levi Strauss & Co. employees in international locations had bribed foreign officials on four separate occasions. When the incidents were discovered by the home office in San Francisco, the practice was immediately terminated. In addition, the company ran into trouble domestically in 1976 when the Federal Trade Commission accused it of price-fixing and restraint of trade because it prohibited retailers from discounting its products.

The company reached an agreement with the government in 1977 in which it did not admit wrongdoing, but gave up suggested pricing, retaining the freedom not to sell to certain retailers. In the next several years, the company settled several suits, brought in nine states, charging illegal price-setting practices. The 1970s also saw the formation of the company's community-affairs department, which was Levi Strauss & Co.'s philanthropic arm, and of community involvement teams, which were company-funded employee groups that participated in projects in communities in which Levi Strauss & Co. did business.

By 1977 Levi Strauss & Co. had become the largest clothing maker in the world. In addition to its original products, the company had grown through acquisitions, and also licensed its name to be used on other products, such as shoes and socks. Sales doubled in just four years, to hit $2 billion in 1979. Purchases such as Koracorp Industries Inc., a large maker of men's and women's sportswear, in 1979, and Santone Industries Inc., a menswear manufacturer, in 1981, prepared the ground for further growth.

A MAJOR RETRENCHING EFFORT

The company, by this time an industry behemoth, ran into difficulties in the early 1980s, however, as the demand for denim stabilized, and its profits flattened. Attempting to increase its distribution, the company reached agreements with several mass merchandisers, including J.C. Penney and Sears, to market its products. Nonetheless, earnings dropped nearly 25 percent in 1981, and the company undertook another reorganization, which included the elimination of one level of corporate management. Profits continued to plummet in 1982, and the company shut down nine plants, eliminating 2,000 jobs.

Levi Strauss & Co.'s fortunes made a short recovery in 1983, and the company planned a $40 million promotional tie-in with the 1984 Olympics to promote its relatively new active-wear division. Nevertheless, during the year of the Olympics, in which the firm dressed more than 60,000 participants in the games, profits were down again, and the company undertook a major retrenching, closing many factories and eliminating thousands of jobs. Faced with a demographic trend that showed the baby boomers outgrowing jeans, the company began heavy advertising campaigns, allied itself with designer Perry Ellis in an attempt to move into the high-fashion market, and continued its plans to retrench, as profits dropped by 50 percent.

In 1985, as Levi Strauss & Co. continued to restructure and cut back, the company was taken private in a leveraged buyout for $1.45 billion by the Haas family, descendants of its founders and longtime company leaders. Several other officers and directors also were members of the buyout group, Levi Strauss Associates Inc. The following year the company introduced a successful upscale men's pants line, Dockers, and, with increasing demand around the world for U.S. jeans, and with the addition of innovative finishes, such as bleaching or stonewashing, 1990 sales reached $4 billion.

The launch of the Dockers brand was one of the most successful in the history of the American apparel industry to date. The cotton pants appealed to older customers, whose expanding waistlines no longer fit into traditional jeans. Sales of Dockers alone came to $1 billion by 1994, and Dockers represented almost 30 percent of the company's domestic sales. However, this was only one part of the success of the newly private company. CEO Haas, along with Thomas Tusher, head of Levi's foreign operations, transformed the company's overseas markets. In the 1980s, Levi's had diversified its product in Europe into dozens of unrelated lines. Foreign operations accounted for only 23 percent of sales in 1984. Tusher and Haas moved to concentrate foreign sales on the classic "501" jeans, and positioned the pants as a high priced, prestige product. The company began selling its jeans at fashionable boutiques in Europe and Japan, at prices more than double the U.S. price. By 1992, foreign sales represented close to 40 percent of the company's revenues, and over 50 percent of profits.

UPS AND DOWNS

Levi Strauss also tried to upgrade the image of its pants in the United States, with great success. Levi Strauss spent $230 million on advertising in 1992, in a campaign to add glamour to its old standby. Levi's jeans, which were being sold at lower-end department stores such as J.C. Penney and Sears, began to appear in Macy's, with a considerably higher price tag. The company also began to open its own stand-alone jeans

boutiques. The flagship store in Manhattan opened across the street from Bloomingdale's in 1993. Standard "501" jeans there cost $47. Macy's charged $42, and J.C. Penney, $29.99. In Europe, the price could be over $80. The same pair of pants retailed at these drastically different prices depending on where it was bought. Under these circumstances, the company's profits soared. Earnings were $155 million on average in the 1980s. By 1990, earnings stood at $251 million, and the next year increased to $361 million. The next two years each also added a hundred million, until by 1995 the company earned over $700 million.

By 1996, Levi Strauss was virtually free of debt, and the company announced it would undertake a second leveraged buyout later in the year, to concentrate its stock in fewer hands. The company made plans to spend $90 million to open stand-alone Levi's stores, Dockers stores, and discount stores for both brands in the United States. Levi Strauss continued to expand its foreign markets, moving into Eastern Europe and expanding sales in India, for example. The company believed that the American market would continue to grow as well. The trend toward casual dress by office workers seemed to be increasing—according to one study, 90 percent of U.S. office workers were allowed to wear casual clothes to work on Friday by the mid-1990s. As jeans became more accepted in the white-collar world, the market for Levi's was expected to widen.

The company found itself in crisis mode once again, however, by the late 1990s. Consumer tastes had shifted, young shoppers were looking for new styles, and the company had failed to keep pace with changing fashion trends. Sales of Levi's pants fell 13 percent in 1998. With its market value falling and profits waning, the company was forced to shutter nearly 30 factories and cut over 16,000 jobs from 1997 to 1999. Philip Marineau was named president and CEO of Levi Strauss in 1999.

MOVING INTO THE 21ST CENTURY

Levi Strauss entered the new millennium on shaky ground. Its failure to adapt to new trends had left it in a precarious financial position. During 2003, the company posted a $502 million loss. "Levi's was the jean of the rock 'n' roll generation. We certainly haven't been the jean of the hip-hop generation," claimed CEO Marineau in a September 2004 *Herald-Sun* article. With sales down nearly 40 percent since 1996, the company was forced to shutter its last U.S. factory in early 2004. In 1990, the company had made nearly all of its merchandise on U.S. soil. By 2004, over 90 percent of Levi Strauss's products were manufactured abroad where

Levi Strauss & Co.

the cost of production was less than half of what it was in the United States.

The company made several moves in an attempt to bolster sales. During 2002, it launched its Signature line, which sold for $23 to $30 a pair at Wal-Mart and Target stores. The company put the Dockers brand up for sale in 2004 but took it off the market after failing to receive acceptable bids. John Anderson took the helm of Levi Strauss in 2006 when Marineau stepped down. Robert Haas left the company in 2008, marking the first time in company history that a non-family member—T. Gary Rogers—would lead the Levi Strauss board of directors.

Under new leadership, Levi Strauss began to focus on adding new items to its product arsenal, including tops, accessories, outerwear, underwear, and footwear. The company planned to revamp its Dockers brand and market it heavily in China and India. In addition, Levi Strauss set out to improve overall product quality, open new retail stores, and expand its footprint in the women's category of the industry. During 2008, nearly 72 percent of sales stemmed from its men's products while 42 percent of sales came from international operations. With the U.S. economy faltering, the company hoped to cash in on growing demand in China, India, and Russia, and eyed international growth as crucial to future profitability.

During 2008, Levi Strauss unveiled its "Live Unbuttoned" marketing campaign for its Levi's "501" brand. The campaign was the largest in the history of the "501" brand and touted the image of being free from inhibitions and convention. The company hoped to capture a new generation of Levi's wearers with the new campaign. While Levi Strauss remained the largest jeans company in the world, the company faced chal-

lenges in the years to come as it worked to attract new customers while shoring up sales and profits.

Elizabeth Rourke
Updated, A. Woodward; Christina M. Stansell

PRINCIPAL COMPETITORS

The Gap Inc.; V.F. Corporation; Wal-Mart Stores Inc.

FURTHER READING

"Client Profile—After All These Years, Is Levi's Washed Up?" *PR Week US,* December 6, 1999.

Cray, Ed, *Levi's: The "Shrink to Fit" Business That Stretched to Cover the Whole World,* Boston: Houghton Mifflin Company, 1978.

Everyone Knows His First Name, San Francisco: Levi Strauss & Co., 1985.

Lenzner, Robert, and Stephen S. Johnson, "A Few Yards of Denim and Five Copper Rivets," *Forbes,* February 26, 1996, pp. 82–87.

Liedtke, Michael, "Levi Strauss Founding Family Relinquishes Company Helm," *Hamilton Spectator* (Ontario), December 13, 2007.

Lipke, David, "Levi's Bets on Premium Positioning," *DNR,* April 14, 2008.

Mitchell, Russ, "Managing by Values," *Business Week,* August 1, 1994, pp. 46–52.

Munk, Nina, "The Levi Straddle," *Forbes,* January 17, 1994, pp. 44–45.

Ostrom, Mary Anne, "Faded Denim," *Herald-Sun,* September 18, 2004.

Teitelbaum, Richard S., "Companies to Watch," *Fortune,* February 8, 1993, p. 127.

Tucker, Ross, "Future Face of Levi's," *Women's Wear Daily,* April 9, 2008.

———, "Levi's Changing Guard: Marineau to Retire as CEO at End of '06," *Women's Wear Daily,* July 7, 2006.

Lewis-Goetz and Company, Inc.

———————————————— ■ ————————————————

650 Washington Road, Suite 210
Pittsburgh, Pennsylvania 15228
U.S.A.
Telephone: (412) 341-7100
Fax: (412) 341-7192
Web site: http://www.lewis-goetz.com

■ ■ ■

Private Company
Incorporated: 1935 as Boston Woven Hose & Rubber of Pittsburgh
Employees: 800
Sales: $250 million (2007)
NAICS: 423840 Industrial Supplies Merchant Wholesalers

■ ■ ■

Privately held Lewis-Goetz and Company, Inc., is a Pittsburgh, Pennsylvania-based distributor of industrial hose products, sealing products, and conveyor belt products, serving such industries as aggregate, agricultural, chemical, construction, food processing, oil and gas, mining, package handling, pharmaceuticals, power generation, pulp and paper/wood, and steel. Hose products include a wide variety of general industrial service hoses for air and water, chemicals, petroleum, and other purposes; stainless steel braided hose for special applications; smooth bore metal hose for use with dry bulk substances; hydraulic hose, made to accommodate a wide range of pressures and temperatures; and a large number of industry-specific hoses.

In addition, Lewis-Goetz offers couplings, fittings, nozzles, hose reels, and other accessories, as well as hose management services. Sealing products include metal gaskets, braided packing materials; rubbers, metal, fabric, and composite expansion joints; mechanical seals; hydraulic seals; oil seals; Teflon sheet and other sheet sealing products; and molded and extruded parts produced in all manner of shapes and size from an array of compound materials. Sealing products services include die cut and computer-operated gasket fabrication and cutting; inventory stocking programs; and training seminars. Aside from lightweight, heavyweight, and specialty conveyor belt products, Lewis-Goetz offers belt cleaners, pulleys, fasteners, repair kits, and other accessories, as well as belt installation and belt disposal, laser alignment, consulting, and other services. In addition to its two Pennsylvania operations, Lewis-Goetz maintains about 60 locations in more than 20 other states, and several provinces in Canada.

19TH-CENTURY ORIGINS

The seeds of Lewis-Goetz were planted in 1870 in Cambridge, Massachusetts, with the founding of Boston Woven Hose and Rubber Co. The company grew out of an invention of Lyman R. Blake, who a dozen years earlier made his mark by creating a machine to attach shoe uppers to soles. His new machine sewed rubber-coated canvas to produce hydraulic hose.

A retired army colonel, Theodore Ayrault Dodge, purchased this machine and began producing "Blake hose," a fire hose, to replace the riveted leather hoses that were in use at the time. Dodge soon pursued multi-ply-tubular fabric construction. After several years of effort he developed a robust fire hose that resulted in the 1880 establishment of the Boston Woven Hose Co. to manufacture the product, marketed under the Boston Bulldog logo. Business grew steadily and along the way other products were added, including gaskets, belting, packing, and mold-work. In 1894 bicycle tires were added.

In 1935 Ben Gooding Sr. established a Pittsburgh, Pennsylvania, branch of Boston Woven Hose, the ancestor of today's Lewis-Goetz. The small company served as a distributor of hose products to the area's steel and coal industries. In 1948 he opened another branch in Chicago. A few years later the company was renamed Gooding Rubber Company. When he retired in the 1950s the business was split between his sons: Robert Gooding took over the Chicago branch, while Ben Gooding Jr. ran the Pittsburgh operation.

ANDREW LEWIS AND DAVID GOETZ JOIN GOODING RUBBER: 1972

The Pittsburgh company began to move beyond serving the hose needs of the coal and steel industries in the late 1960s. To help facilitate the expansion, a branch office was opened in Beckley, West Virginia. The family-owned company also began to offer employees a chance to buy stock in the company. One of those employees was David R. Goetz, who would become the longtime chief executive officer and chairman of Lewis-Goetz.

A graduate of the University of Dayton, where he earned a degree in business administration, Goetz began his career in sales and marketing with The Goodyear Tire and Rubber Company, a major supplier to Gooding Rubber. One of his colleagues at Goodyear was

Andrew Lewis. In 1972 they were hired by Ben Gooding Jr. to establish a conveyor belt department.

In 1982 Goetz and Lewis acquired the business from Ben Gooding Jr., who then retired in April 1983. At the time annual sales were in the $10 million range, an improvement over the $4 million generated a decade earlier when they joined the company. In order to maintain this growth, however, they faced a host of challenges caused by difficult economic conditions. After taking stock of the company's sales force, the new owners discovered that there was a vast discrepancy in the amount of business for which individual salesmen were responsible. Although some salesmen were nudged into early retirement, the company actually grew the sales force despite a shrinking market for its products. New people were hired to relieve salespeople in the field of order-taking and other clerical tasks that kept them from their core responsibilities. In addition Gooding Rubber beefed up its service offerings with a new information technology system at its core that linked all of the company's locations.

GROWTH THROUGH ACQUISITIONS

Rather than simply weather the storm and wait for better economic conditions, the new management team sought to diversify and expand the business into new markets through acquisitions. In 1985 Richmond, Virginia-based Richmond Rubber Company was purchased, followed a year later by Rocky Mount, North Carolina-based Haynes, Inc. As a result, Gooding Rubber increased its purchasing power to make the company more competitive, as well as broadening the range of products it could offer.

After Gooding Rubber changed its name in 1989 to Gooding, Lewis, Goetz and Co., another acquisition was completed in 1991 when Cleveland, Ohio-based F.B. Wright Co. was brought into the fold. Later that year Pittsburgh's Shield Rubber Co. was also acquired, adding $20 million in sales and six distribution warehouses located in Pittsburgh and Erie, Pennsylvania, Baltimore, Cleveland, Chicago, and Clearwater, Florida. The consolidated company made its headquarters in Shield's former home office.

Thus, in a matter of months, Gooding essentially doubled in size, becoming a company with annual sales of $55 million, making it the largest distributor and fabricator of rubber hoses and conveyor belts in the United States. Unfortunately another downturn in the economy in the early 1990s led to a manufacturing slump that crippled business.

RECOVERY AND NEW GROWTH

Gooding changed its name to Lewis-Goetz and Company, Inc., and began rebuilding sales as the economy improved in the 1990s. With sales soon growing at a double-digit pace, the company by 1995 topped $60 million in annual sales. Helping to grow sales was the opening of a branch in Roanoke, Virginia, in 1995. A year later the company opened an eleventh branch in Ohio. Sales increased to $70.5 million to close the decade, but another manufacturing slump occurred in 2000. Having learned from previous experience, Lewis-Goetz was better positioned to deal with these conditions, quickly cutting expenses in order to maintain profits.

As business rebounded, Lewis-Goetz steadily improved sales to $101 million in 2005. That amount would more than double in 2006 with the acquisition of the Goodall Rubber Company from the Swedish firm, Trelleborg AB. The deal brought together two companies listed among the Big 50 industrial distributors by trade publication *Industrial Distribution:* Lewis-Goetz was ranked 46th and Goodall was ranked 43rd. The expanded Lewis-Goetz served customers from more than 50 locations.

GOODALL RUBBER THROUGH THE TRELLEBORG YEARS

Like Lewis-Goetz, the origins of Goodall Rubber reached back to the 1800s. The man behind the company name was Howard W. Goodall. When he was just 15 years old, in 1887, he quit school and took a job at Latta & Mulconroy Company, a Philadelphia, Pennsylvania-based rubber distributor. Possessing an inventive streak, Goodall began designing hose clamps and couplings, which soon became a profitable sideline for his employer.

In 1906 Goodall struck out on his own and, with former colleague William S. Feeny, founded the Goodall Rubber Company in Philadelphia. Five years later he opened a branch in New York City. Goodall also established the Knox Manufacturing Company to produce couplings and clamps, and in 1916 launched the Dixon Valve & Coupling Company in Philadelphia to serve the construction, mining, oil drilling, and railroad industries.

Due to health problems, he sold his interest in Goodall Rubber in 1924, although he continued to run Dixon Valve and eventually bought out his old employer, by that time named Mulconroy Company. Goodall remained active until 1951 when he became ill during a California sales trip and died a short time after his return home. The company that continued to bear his name carried on in the meantime, moving away from manufacturing to focus more on distribution as well as gaining a significant presence in Canada through acquisitions.

Trelleborg bought a stake in Goodall and in 1988 acquired 100 percent control. Trelleborg, named after the Swedish town where the company was founded in 1905, was a major European rubber manufacturer. After World War II the company made its mark by introducing the world's first snow tire, although ultimately the company would focus on the industrial rubber sector rather than tires.

It was also during this period that Trelleborg expanded internationally, adding dealers and agents to distribute its products throughout Europe, the United States, and the rest of the world. At the start of the 21st century, however, the company began looking to focus on its manufacturing operations. By the time Goodall was divested and acquired by Lewis-Goetz, Trelleborg was the third largest industrial rubber company in the world.

EQUITY FIRM ACQUIRES LEWIS-GOETZ

Although greatly enlarged through the addition of Goodall, Lewis-Goetz's appetite was far from satisfied. In July 2007 the company acquired Samson Industrial and its 15 locations. Based in Tulsa, Oklahoma, Samson was a distributor and fabricator of products specializing in fluid and material conveyance, fluid sealing, vibration and dampening, fastening, personal safety, and industrial tools.

Helping to finance the deal was the new parent of Lewis-Goetz, the Boston-based private equity firm of Audux Group LP, which acquired the company just prior to the Samson deal. Not only could Audux provide the funds needed for further growth, it also brought other attributes. "Their experience sourcing and integrating add-on acquisitions," David Goetz maintained in a press statement, "will be an important asset for us as we continue to grow our business." The Samson deal was especially important because it bolstered the position of Lewis-Goetz in the Gulf Coast and took the company into new markets in the Southeast.

At the start of 2008, David Goetz, on the verge of his 63rd birthday, stepped down as chief executive, turning over day-to-day control to company president Jeffrey T. Crane, while retaining the chairmanship. The 41-year-old Crane had 11 years of sales and marketing experience at Goodyear Tire and Rubber Co., and was also familiar with the Lewis-Goetz operation, having worked for the company for two years in the 1980s before earning a master's degree.

CONTINUED EXPANSION

Soon after assuming control, Crane was involved in a series of acquisitions. In late February 2008 most of the assets of Bellaire, Ohio-based Ja-Mar Conveyor and Components, a conveyor system install and service company, was acquired. The addition of Ja-Mar allowed Lewis-Goetz to continue to fill out its conveyor system offerings in pursuit of the ultimate goal of growing into a total conveyor system service provider.

In July 2008 Lewis-Goetz acquired the key assets of G&H Pumps and Compressors, Inc., a Shreveport, Louisiana-based company that provided pump repair and hydraulic services for trucks servicing the land-based oil and gas drilling market in Shreveport and the Texarkana area. Again, Lewis-Goetz was able to gain a foothold in a new market segment.

In the fall of 2008 Lewis-Goetz completed another acquisition, adding the Rubber Belting and Hose group of companies, mostly based in Kansas City: Rubber Belting & Hose, Mill & Elevator Supply, EBM Mill & Elevator Supply, and RBH Industrial Inc. As a result, Lewis-Goetz expanded its product lines to include material handling equipment serving the agricultural market, including grain conveyor belting and elevator belts and buckets. Moreover, the company gained a presence in the important agricultural markets of Kansas, Iowa, and Nebraska. With annual sales in the $250 million range,

Lewis-Goetz appeared to be well positioned to pursue further expansion in the years to come.

Ed Dinger

PRINCIPAL SUBSIDIARIES

Ja-Mar Conveyors & Components, Inc.; RBH Industrial Inc.; RBH/Mill & Elevator Supply; G&H Pumps and Compressors, Inc.; EBM Mill and Elevator Supply, Inc.

PRINCIPAL COMPETITORS

Applied Industrial Technologies, Inc.; Fenner PLC; Kaman Industrial Technologies Corporation.

FURTHER READING

"Belting Distributor Partners for Profit," *Industrial Distributor,* September 1997, p. 80.

Bonnanzio, John G. F., "Growing Beyond the Smokestacks," *Industrial Distribution,* March 1989, p. 39.

Cotter, Wes, and Karen Zapf, "Rubber Match," *Pittsburgh Business Times,* January 13, 1992, p. 1.

Gilman, Arthur, *The Cambridge of Eighteen Hundred and Ninety-Six,* Cambridge, Mass.: Riverside Press, 1896.

Griffiths, Kimberly, "Belting Out Sales," *Industrial Distribution,* September 2005, p. 38.

McCrea, Bridget, "Growing by Leaps and Bounds," *Industrial Distribution,* October 2001, p. H1.

Shaw, David, "Lewis-Goetz Buys Goodall Rubber from Trelleborg," *European Rubber Journal,* May 1, 2006, p. 9.

Tuttle, Al, "In Good Company," *Industrial Distribution,* April 2001, p. 62.

Liz Claiborne Inc.

—————— ■ ——————

1441 Broadway
New York, New York 10018-1805
U.S.A.
Telephone: (212) 354-4900
Fax: (212) 626-3416
Web site: http://www.lizclaiborneinc.com

Public Company
Incorporated: 1976
Employees: 15,000
Sales: $3.98 billion (2008)
Stock Exchanges: New York
Ticker Symbol: LIZ
NAICS: 315230 Women's and Girls' Cut and Sew Apparel Manufacturing; 315220 Men's and Boys' Cut and Sew Apparel Manufacturing; 315999 Other Apparel Accessories and Other Apparel Manufacturing; 316992 Women's Handbag and Purse Manufacturing

■ ■ ■

Liz Claiborne Inc. is one of America's leading apparel companies. A pioneer in making sportswear affordable for working women, the company designs women's and men's clothing, accessories, and fragrances under its various labels. It markets its global brands, such as Juicy Couture and Mexx, in company-owned retail boutiques, which generate about one-third of the company's revenue. On the wholesale side, its "partnered" brands, including Liz Claiborne New York, Monet, and Mac and Jac, can be found in department stores around the world. International sales generate just under one-third of the company's revenue.

FINDING A NICHE

Elisabeth "Liz" Claiborne was born in Brussels and raised in Europe and New Orleans. Her natural artistic flair led toward her goal of becoming a fashion designer. At age 20 she got her first break when she won a design contest sponsored by *Harper's Bazaar* magazine. Soon after that, she was employed as a sketcher and model in New York's garment district and worked her way through the ranks at several design firms. After serving for 16 years as the chief designer in Jonathan Logan's Youth Guild division, she realized that working women needed more wardrobe options. Unable to sell the concept of stylish, sporty, and affordable clothes for America's working women to her employer, Claiborne left the company and joined her husband, Arthur Ortenberg, and another partner, Leonard Boxer, to found Liz Claiborne Inc. in 1976. The three pooled $50,000 in savings and borrowed an additional $200,000 from friends and family to launch the company specializing in fashionable, functional, and affordable women's apparel. Shortly thereafter, Jerome Chazen joined the trio. The company showed a profit its first year and became the fastest-growing, most profitable U.S. apparel company in the 1980s.

Claiborne's timing was perfect; she began providing career clothes to women just as they started entering the workforce in record numbers. As Chazen stated in *Fortune,* "We knew we wanted to clothe women in the work force. We saw a niche where no pure player existed. What we didn't know was how many customers were out there." Clothes designers had not fully exploited one of the largest growing groups in America—women baby-boomers penetrating the labor market. Liz Claiborne ignored the traditional industry seasons of spring and fall, opting instead for six selling periods, including pre-spring, spring I, spring II, summer, fall, and holiday, to provide consumers with new styles every two months. These short cycles allowed more frequent updates of new styles and put clothes on the racks in the appropriate season. By adding cycles, stores cut their inventory costs and overseas suppliers were able to operate more efficiently with the two extra cycles filling their slack periods.

Additionally, Claiborne worked with retailers to change how clothes were displayed in their stores. To make it easier for shoppers to put together and purchase a complete outfit, she persuaded stores to place all her pieces—pants, skirts, shirts—in one department rather continue the practice of having separate departments for blouses, pants, and so forth. Liz Claiborne also made the decision not to field a traveling sales force. This determination, although disregarding conventional industry wisdom, stimulated the company's rapid growth. With virtually no overhead, Liz Claiborne was set for swift growth as sales skyrocketed.

INCREASED OFFERINGS

During the 1980s Liz Claiborne evolved from a basic sportswear business into a multifaceted fashion house. The company went public in 1981 at $19 per share, raising $6.1 million. The same year the company introduced a petite sportswear division, and added a dress division in 1982. When its research discovered that 70 percent of its women customers were also purchasing clothing for their husbands, it launched Claiborne, the company's expansion into men's clothing, in 1985. That year Claiborne also created the accessories division, which was formerly a licensee. Some components of this line included leather handbags, small leather goods, and bodywear. The company further expanded and introduced its signature scent in September 1986. The

cosmetics division began as a joint venture with Avon Cosmetics Ltd., and in 1988 the company gained full rights to the line.

In mid-1987, however, a slump hit the apparel business. Retail sales stalled in early 1988, inventories increased, and operating margins narrowed. In 1988, for the first time ever, Liz Claiborne's net earnings fell, by an estimated 11 percent, to $102 million. After years of 20 percent increases, sportswear sales increased only about 3 percent in 1988. Sales gains were becoming hard to achieve. Despite the slump, the company moved into the retail apparel business when it opened its first retail stores, offering the First Issue brand of casual women's sportswear. This break into apparel retailing was an expensive and highly risky proposition. Thirteen stores were launched in 1988 and the company showed that it could be successful in this type of diversification. In 1988 sales and marketing efforts also began in Canada. That year also marked an important milestone for Liz Claiborne Inc. After only ten years, the company was on *Fortune*'s list of the top 500 industrial companies. It was one of only two companies started by a woman to achieve that distinction. Also, as an 11-year-old enterprise, it was one of the youngest companies ever to make the cut.

Liz Claiborne was one of the first companies to test the concept of manufacturing overseas, beginning with an office in Hong Kong in 1976. The company did not own any factories, but made all of its merchandise through contracts with independent factories in 50 nations. The company reduced its reliance on Hong Kong, South Korea, and Taiwan in favor of countries such as Malaysia, China, and Sri Lanka, where labor was less expensive. Less than 10 percent of Liz Claiborne's products were made in the United States. There were drawbacks, though, to not owning the factories. To ensure that goods were produced to the high standards consumers expected, Liz Claiborne employed an overseas staff of almost 700 who regularly visited the factories.

STAND-ALONE RETAIL STORES

The company opened its first Liz Claiborne stores in 1989. These 18 stand-alone stores were placed in affluent suburban malls and served as laboratories for the company to test new designs and product presentations. They provided the company with immediate information regarding market trends through state-of-the-art bar coding and other electronic data interchange systems. Continuing to expand its offerings, Liz Claiborne focused on a long-overlooked group of consumers and introduced its Elisabeth division specializing in apparel for larger women. The line offered everything from career clothing and active wear to social occasion

KEY DATES

1976: Dress designer Liz Claiborne and partners establish the company.
1981: Company goes public.
1991: Company is listed on New York Stock Exchange.
1995: Paul R. Charron is named CEO.
1999: Company acquires Lucky Brand, Sigrid Olsen, and Laundry labels.
2003: Company acquires Juicy Couture brand.
2006: William L. McComb joins company as CEO; Kate Spade label is acquired.
2007: Liz Claiborne dies at age 78.
2008: Company sells Ellen Tracy, prAna, Sigrid Olsen, and Laundry labels.

dressing. The line was very well received and gained market leadership. Three Elisabeth stores were opened in 1989 serving the larger-sized consumer. In addition, the company operated 55 factory outlet stores that marketed unsold inventory from past seasons. Liz Claiborne positioned these outlets at a distance from the stores where its products were customarily sold.

In 1989 the Dana Buchman division was launched. This division specialized in a line of higher-priced women's career clothes created for the bridge market. Its prices spanned the difference between moderately priced ready-to-wear sportswear and designer creations.

In addition to the company stores, Liz Claiborne dominated the selling floors of major department stores—sometimes more than half the allotment for women's apparel. At the wholesale end, Liz Claiborne commanded extensive clout. The company had a rigid non-cancellation policy, meaning that if spring merchandise did not sell well in stores, retailers were still unable to cut summer orders. Nevertheless, Liz Claiborne generated what was known as strong "sell through." Its clothes were rarely marked down—only about 5 percent of its merchandise versus the industry norm of 15 percent. To reduce the risk of markdowns the company produced fewer goods than the level of demand forecast. Therefore, retailers got better profit margins and allowed Liz Claiborne more space on the floor. Nevertheless, because of limited space in department store floors, the company expanded abroad.

In January 1991 Liz Claiborne Inc. entered the United Kingdom and later that year it debuted in Spain. Liz Claiborne tailored its strategies when marketing its products outside the United States. In some United Kingdom stores, the company leased space and sold the product itself. In Japan, it marketed through a mail-order catalog, and in Singapore Liz Claiborne granted a retail license for the operation of Liz Claiborne stores. This strategy seemed to work well as international sales totaled $108.1 million in 1992, while six years earlier only $1.4 million of sales came from outside the United States.

NEW LABELS AND CHANGING DEMOGRAPHICS

A major challenge faced the company in 1989, when Liz Claiborne and Arthur Ortenberg announced they would resign from active management in order to pursue philanthropic interests. The status quo continued after the founders' departure as Jerry Chazen, the fourth original partner, was named chairman. A broad array of new products was introduced, including jewelry and sport shoes. Liz Claiborne further expanded its business to women's and men's optical frames, eyewear (fashion sunglasses and readers), and women's hosiery through licensing, and these revenues continued to climb.

Tailored suits for working women debuted in 1991. In May 1992 Liz Claiborne acquired three new labels from the bankrupt Russ Togs Inc. Crazy Horse casual wear was marketed in department and specialty stores. The Russ line offered updated career and casual apparel and was sold in moderate areas of department stores. The Villager line was offered in national and regional chain department stores and focused on career clothing and some casual wear. These and future acquisitions were expected to broaden the company's distribution and allow opportunities to expand clothing lines and create new products.

Such acquisitions were important because Liz Claiborne faced changing demographics. While the number of working women between the ages of 25 and 54 grew 43 percent in the 1980s, this would increase only about 25 percent during the 1990s. The company needed to become more visible in order to maintain market share. The combination of recession, increased competition in moderately priced sportswear, and the push into new markets led Liz Claiborne to seek a higher profile.

Liz Claiborne realized that cooperative advertising with retailers and its domination of department store floors was no longer enough. Instead, the company needed to solidify its fashion image and create a global corporate image. Advertising was critical if the company was to preserve strong relationships with consumers and retailers. Also, Liz Claiborne could not expect to gain a foothold in Europe with an unadvertised fashion brand.

Since floor space in Europe was much more limited, a company needed to advertise its image to get into the stores. Liz Claiborne did have an advantage in that the company stood for quality, value, and fit—exactly the standards of the Europeans and Japanese. In October 1991, the company launched its first print advertising campaign for apparel and accessories. The $6 million advertising campaign broke in the November 1991 issues of 15 consumer publications, including *HG, Vanity Fair,* and *Elle.*

FALLING SALES

Liz Claiborne was greatly concerned with listening to its customers. At the company's back-office operation in North Bergen, New Jersey, $10 million worth of IBM computers generated information on sales trends throughout the country. This automated inventory network allowed quick response to market demand. In addition to this network, Liz Claiborne employed about 150 specialists to solicit feedback from customers at stores around the country and 21 consultants who made sure that clothes and displays were arranged in stores according to company diagrams. Customer service telephones were staffed by 95 operators who fielded questions from retailers.

The company was noted for its well-organized management, distribution, and sales teams. In an industry where turmoil was a tradition, Liz Claiborne cultivated a strong team to run every aspect of the business. The company met industry challenges by following four guidelines it had instilled from its beginning: listen to consumers; create first-class products addressing their needs; price products with the consumer in mind; and always try to do more, and do it better. In 1992 *Fortune* once again named Liz Claiborne Inc. as one of the ten most admired corporations in America.

With $2.2 billion in sales and products in over 10,000 stores, Liz Claiborne was the largest women's apparel manufacturer in the world. However, the company's fortunes dramatically shifted in 1993. For the first time in the company's history, sales fell for the core Liz Claiborne Collection, Lizsport, and Lizwear lines. Net income fell 42 percent for the year. Some $300 million worth of merchandise went unsold. Business as usual was not working anymore. "That's too bad, because the old life was pretty good. In its heyday, Claiborne was regarded as the smartest, most efficient apparel outfit around," wrote Laura Zinn in a May 1994 *Business Week* article. "'When people were hired away from Claiborne, their new employers thought they were getting some magic,' says one ex-executive. Between 1985 and 1991, sales and net income almost quadrupled."

Critics said Liz Claiborne apparel had gone stale since the departure of the founder. Saks Fifth Avenue dropped the Claiborne core sportswear lines in 1993, and the new mass-market lines (Crazy Horse, Russ, and Villager) remained unprofitable. The company depended on just four department stores (Dillard's, May, Macy's, and Federated) for nearly half of its sales. Profits fell to $83 million in 1994 from a peak of $223 million in 1991.

NEW LEADERSHIP

Paul R. Charron, who moved from VF Corporation to Liz Claiborne in 1994 and was appointed CEO in 1995, led a restructuring drive. In 1995, 500 of the company's 8,000 employees were laid off and the unprofitable First Issue chain was closed. Charron then implemented a three-year program to cut expenses by $100 million, reduce excess inventory by 40 percent, and shorten production and delivery cycles by 25 percent. A major investment in technology helped the company improve clothing design and track sales more closely.

"Now Liz Claiborne is playing catch-up with a vengeance. The company, which has extremely deep pockets, and no debt, is marketing smartly cut silk suits and cocktail dresses as well as basic blue jeans and khaki pants," wrote Jill Jordan Sieder in a February 1996 *U.S. News & World Report* article. "'They're changing in all the right ways in a very tough environment,' explains Jennifer Black Groves, a retail analyst at Black & Co." With its image for fashion flair on the mend, Liz Claiborne rolled out a $25 million advertising campaign in early 1996. Print ads, supermodels, television commercials, and outdoor advertising dovetailed with an updated in-store marketing program. Charron, who was named chairman in May 1996, had also relaunched product lines, sold units to licensors, and added new products. For the first time since 1992, Liz Claiborne's largest unit, women's sportswear, registered sales increases on the year: up 10.8 percent to $1.23 billion. Dana Buchman's sales were boosted 38.5 percent to $188.7 million thanks to help from the Dana B. and Karan lines introduced in February 1996.

The announcement of a strategic licensing agreement with Donna Karan International Inc. in December 1997 marked the first time Liz Claiborne acted as a licensee rather than a licensor. The 15-year exclusive contract, under which Donna Karan would receive a minimum of $152 million in royalties, gave Liz Claiborne the right to source, distribute, and market DKNY Jeans and DKNY Active trademarks in the western hemisphere. Aided by cost reduction measures, operational improvements, and strong sales in core product areas, net sales for 1997 climbed to $2.41 billion and net income reached $185 million.

THE ACQUISITION ERA

The special markets division, formed in 1996 to encompass the moderate and value-priced brands, marked its first profitable quarter in 1998. The relaunched First Issue line was being sold exclusively in Sears, while the Crazy Horse label was offered by J.C. Penney. The division, which also housed Russ, Villager, and the newly acquired Emma James lines, benefited from Charron's experience with VF—the company moved from department store to a mass merchant focus during his tenure there. Liz Claiborne placed these popular priced products in Wal-Mart and Kmart and regional department stores such as Kohl's and Mervyn's. Special market sales were $104 million in 1997. With its DKNY licensing agreement in place, the company was banking on a variety of brands, from mass to bridge, to drive future growth. The company in 1998 was named one of the 50 best companies for Asians, African Americans, and Hispanics by *Fortune.* Nearly 41 percent of the 7,100 employees were minorities, and nearly 75 percent were women, with women comprising half the directors. However, just over 5 percent of senior executives were minorities.

Beginning in 1999, Charron moved aggressively with his acquisition strategy. Lucky Brand Jeans, Laundry by Shelli Segal (which became Laundry by Design), and Sigrid Olsen were all purchased in 1999. In 2000, the company bought fashion jeweler Monet Group and licensed a children's line called Liz Claiborne Kids to Baby Togs. Additional purchases included Mexx, the hip Dutch chain with over 800 stores around the world (2001), Ellen Tracy (2002), and Juicy Couture and Enyce (2003). In 2005, the company bought prAna sportswear and T-shirt maker C&C California, and in 2006, apparel lines Mac & Jac, Kensie, and Kensie Girl, along with handbag maker Kate Spade. The company also created new brands, such as Intuitions (2004) and Stamp 10, Tapemeasure, and Tint (2005).

During this period, the company signed agreements with various companies to manufacture items ranging from luggage to blankets to stationery to rugs. Net sales for 2006 reached $4.64 billion, up from 2007. However, net income declined $62 million from the previous year. At the end of 2006, Paul Charron retired from Liz Claiborne Inc.

CHANGE IN LEADERSHIP

In November 2006, William L. McComb joined Liz Claiborne as CEO. McComb, 45 at the time, came to the company from Johnson & Johnson, where he had been a group chairman. There, he was responsible for such brands as Tylenol and Motrin. McComb was faced with steep declines in the company's wholesale (department store) division and management of a huge array of labels as well as licensing agreements. In mid-2007, he announced a restructuring to create a new, more brand-focused organizational structure. This meant significant downsizing. By the end of 2007, the Emma James, Intuitions, JH Collectibles, and Tapemeasure brands had been sold, and 2008 saw the sale of Laundry by Design and C&C California, Ellen Tracy, and prAna, and the closing of Sigrid Olsen stores along with Mexx stores in Great Britain. As this was all happening, company founder Liz Claiborne died in 2007 at age 78.

Even as he was eliminating certain brands, McComb was trying to revive others. He hired Isaac Mizrahi to make the iconic Liz Claiborne label fashionable again. The company also developed new lines such as Liz & Co. for J.C. Penney and moved the Dana Buchman line to Kohl's department store. It entered new licensing agreements—with Donna Karan to create a new collection of men's sportswear and with Elizabeth Arden to make and distribute the Liz Claiborne fragrances globally. Not all McComb's efforts were successful, however. At the end of 2008, the company terminated its 50 percent partnership with the Narciso Rodriguez fashion house.

McComb's plan was to offer a smaller portfolio of labels organized into two segments. First were the so-called power brands: Juicy Couture, Kate Spade, Lucky Brand Jeans, and Mexx. These were primarily retail brands, selling in their own specialty and outlet stores. The emphasis on retail labels was critical. The consolidation of department stores, including Macy's, Claiborne's largest customer, led wholesale customers to concentrate on their own private brands. The other segment, the partnered brands, were department store based and included the Liz Claiborne brands, Monet jewelry brands, and licensed DKNY brands.

By 2009, McComb's restructuring was complete. Fourteen brands were gone and some 2,700 staff positions had been eliminated. During the first quarter, Mizrahi's first collection of Liz Claiborne New York appeared in department stores and the new Dana Buchman line appeared in Kohl's stores. The company extended its bank credit ability and signed an agreement with Li & Fung, the Hong Kong-based apparel export conglomerate, to be the exclusive buying agent for all its brands (except jewelry).

However, falling consumer spending at both the retail and wholesale levels was hitting Liz Claiborne as well as other clothes designers and retailers. Revenue for

2008 was down 10 percent from 2007 after adjusting for the closed businesses. Even its new retail stores and the increased revenue from its direct brands could not counter the losses from the department stores. The ultimate success of Liz Claiborne Inc. would depend on how well it handled the economic recession.

Carol Kieltyka
Updated, Kathleen Peippo; Ellen D. Wernick

PRINCIPAL OPERATING UNITS

Domestic-Based Direct Brands—Juicy Couture; Kate Spade; Lucky; International-Based Direct Brands—Mexx; Axcess; Claiborne; Concepts by Claiborne; Dana Buchman; Kensie; Liz & Co., Liz Claiborne; Mac & Jac; Marvella; Monet; Trifari; DKNY Jeans; DKNY Active; DKNY Men's.

PRINCIPAL COMPETITORS

Jones Apparel Group, Inc.; Polo Ralph Lauren Corporation; Benetton Group; Tommy Hilfiger Corporation; Columbia Sportswear Company; French Connection Group Plc; Gap, Inc.; Coach; Esprit; Guess.

FURTHER READING

Appelbaum, Cara, "Stepping Out," *Adweek's Marketing Week,* November 18, 1991, pp. 20–21.

Beckett, Whitney, "McComb's Revolution: Power Brands to Rule Leaner Liz Claiborne," *WWD,* July 12, 2007, p.1.

Birchall, Jonathan, "Liz Claiborne to Cut Brands and Focus on Retail Businesses," *Financial Times,* July 12, 2007, p. 25.

Chang, Michelle, "Liz Claiborne Inc.," *Analyst Report,* Morningstar.com, March 4, 2009.

Deveny, Kathleen, "Can Ms. Fashion Bounce Back?" *Business Week,* January 16, 1989, pp. 64–70.

D'Innocenzio, Anne, "Claiborne Tells Holders Good Times Ahead," *WWD,* May 15, 1998, pp. 2, 18.

Gannes, Stuart, "America's Fastest-Growing Companies," *Fortune,* May 23, 1988, pp. 28–40.

Hass, Nancy, "Like a Rock," *Financial World,* February 4, 1992, pp. 22–24.

Horyn, Cathy, "Can Liz Claiborne Get Its Groove Back?" *New York Times Magazine,* August 17, 2008, p. 250.

Kappner, Suzanne, "Liz Claiborne's Extreme Makeover," *Fortune,* December 8, 2008, p. 141.

Laurent, Lionel, "Liz Claiborne Brand Bumps Off Brit Stores," *Forbes.com,* February 27, 2008.

"Liz Claiborne Boss Plots Comeback Bid," *New York Post,* July 11, 2007, p. 34.

"Liz Claiborne Completes Strategic Review," *just-style.com,* March 18, 2008.

"Liz Claiborne, Inc.: Company Profile," http://www.datamonitor.com, September 22, 2008.

"Mexx, the Hip Euro-Styled Men's and Women's Apparel Chain Owned by Liz Claiborne, Has Opened Its First Store in the United States," *Chain Store Age,* November 2003, p. 18.

Rotenier, Nancy, "Niki and Me," *Forbes,* January 13, 1997, p. 96.

Ryan, Thomas J., "Dana Buchman Paces Claiborne Gains," *WWD,* April 2, 1997, p. 24.

———, "Karan's Jeanswear Royalties Put at $152M over 15 Years," *WWD,* April 1, 1998, p. 4.

Sellers, Patricia, "The Rag Trade's Reluctant Revolutionary," *Fortune,* January 5, 1987, pp. 36–38.

Sieder, Jill Jordan, "Liz Claiborne Gets Dressed for Success," *U.S. News & World Report,* February 26, 1996, pp. 55–56.

Vinzant, Carol, "Liz Claiborne: A Casual Success," *Fortune,* August 3, 1998, p. 106.

"A Vote of Confidence: Claiborne Board Backs CEO McComb's Strategy," *WWD,* February 21, 2008, p. 1.

Zinn, Laura, "Liz Claiborne Without Liz: Steady As She Goes," *Business Week,* September 17, 1990, pp. 70–74.

———, "A Sagging Bottom Line at Liz Claiborne," *Business Week,* May 16, 1994, pp. 56–57.

Long Island Power Authority

333 Earle Ovington Boulevard, Suite 403
Uniondale, New York 11553
U.S.A.
Telephone: (516) 222-7700
Fax: (516) 222-9137
Web site: http://www.lipower.org

State-Owned Company
Incorporated: 1986
Employees: 63
Sales: $21 million (2008 est.)
NAICS: 221121 Electric Bulk Power Transmission and
   Control; 221122 Electric Power Distribution

■ ■ ■

Long Island Power Authority (LIPA) operates as Long Island's primary electric service provider. The not-for-profit entity controlled by the New York State government owns the electric transmission and distribution network that supplies power to nearly 1.1 million customers on Long Island. In May 1998, LIPA took control of the transmission and distribution assets of Long Island Lighting Company (LILCO). With a history dating back to 1910, LILCO played an indispensable part in the economic growth of Long Island. At the same time, the investor-owned company was often embroiled in a succession of disputes over rate increases, environmental issues, and other concerns that buffeted its fortunes and threatened its stability. LILCO's plans to operate the Shoreham nuclear facility ended in

financial disaster that ultimately led to the creation of LIPA in 1986 and its takeover in 1998.

EARLY HISTORY

Long Island Lighting Company traces its genealogy back to the offices of E.L. Phillips and Company, located in 1910 on the 16th floor of a new skyscraper at 50 Church Street, New York City. Ellis Phillips, born in 1873 in western New York, held degrees in both mechanical and electrical engineering. He had worked for Westinghouse, Church & Kerr, one of the largest engineering and construction firms in the United States, and advanced to become head of design and construction for the company, but in 1904 he left to set up his own engineering consulting and contracting firm. Under the patronage of J. P. Morgan, Phillips also served the New York Stock Exchange as a utilities analyst.

As Phillips worked throughout New York, New Jersey, and Pennsylvania, he noticed many small electric light companies in need of more transmission lines and greater operational efficiency. Seizing an opportunity near his boyhood home, Phillips linked four communities together by forming the Genesee Valley Electric Company. Part of the capital for this endeavor was supplied by George W. Olmsted of the J.C. Curtis Leather Company in Ludlow, Pennsylvania. Olmsted and Phillips were business acquaintances, and as partners they soon sold Genesee to a larger adjacent company.

In similar fashion, the partners purchased small electric companies in Percy and Warsaw, New York, and sought to develop them into a larger enterprise. Over two decades they made many other acquisitions, creat-

COMPANY PERSPECTIVES

■

With the demand for electricity growing at a record-breaking pace, priorities at LIPA continue to focus on the customer—upgrading and enhancing the electric system, advancing energy efficiency, and developing and expanding alternative energy resources. LIPA is dedicated to improving the quality of life for everyone within its service territory.

ing the New York State Electric Corporation. Further growth transformed this firm into the Rochester Central Power Corporation. Simultaneously, Phillips and Olmsted sought similar opportunities on Long Island, where Clarence R. Dean, a supplier of generating equipment, became a valued source of information on many local electric companies.

On the last day of 1910, the Long Island Lighting Company (LILCO) was organized. The new company merged four small Suffolk County utilities: the Amityville Electric Light Company, the Islip Electric Light Company, the Northport Electric Light Company, and the Sayville Electric Company. On June 1, 1911, the New York Public Service Commission (PSC) allowed Long Island Lighting to begin to function. Five directors, including Phillips, Olmsted, and Dean, were authorized to issue $300,000 of common stock and sell $295,000 in bonds. Phillips became general manager at a salary of $200 per month. By the end of 1911, LILCO had grossed $70,000 serving 1,048 accounts. The company's business was conducted by four officers, four general office workers, and 34 other employees.

IMPROVEMENTS AND ACQUISITIONS

As revenues grew steadily, LILCO made rapid improvements to its system for generating and delivering electric power. New turbines were constructed and older ones relegated to standby or emergency status. In 1915 the company acquired the Babylon Electric Light Company. Two years later it added the Suffolk Gas & Electric Light Company and the South Shore Gas Company to its holdings. The company charter was amended in 1917 to provide coverage for all villages and towns in Suffolk County plus parts of adjacent Nassau County.

During World War I, LILCO made a special effort to supply electric service to the U.S. Army's Camp Upton in Yaphank. By the time of the arrival of the first

draftees in September 1917, the company had installed four transmission lines, a main distribution ring, and a substation to provide the new soldiers with the electrical comforts of the day.

In 1918 LILCO established a centralized billing service from an office in Bay Shore, and meter reading became a continuous task, with two readers working six days a week. Further acquisitions immediately followed the war; the Huntington Light & Power Company, the Huntington Gas Company, and the North Shore Electric Light & Power Company were all bought in 1919.

A major gas explosion at the Bay Shore works in 1919 interrupted service for three days. The accident pointed to the need for upgrading facilities, and improvements followed. Major acquisitions continued through the 1920s, as did projects to buy land and build gas works and power plants. The company set as its goal the accumulation of all its holdings into one company, simplifying rates, and standardizing operations, but also creating a monopoly. By 1925, with Long Island experiencing a real estate boom, LILCO was in a very favorable position. Loans were readily available, and 97 percent of all stockholders regularly attended meetings.

OVERCOMING PUBLIC OPPOSITION

Still, the public was not entirely satisfied with LILCO's performance. A group of consumers who had first organized to oppose a rate increase by the Long Island Railroad moved against LILCO in 1927. They presented a petition for a rate decrease to the Public Service Commission (PSC). The petition failed, but the PSC initiated comprehensive audits of LILCO and all other utilities in New York. Simultaneously, the state legislature established a committee to investigate the utility business.

Over the next decade, LILCO officers spent a good deal of time in hearings, confronting new regulations, and opposing rate cuts. In 1930 a series of hearings began that subjected the company to intense scrutiny. Nearly every aspect of LILCO's business was examined, including salaries, dividends, legal fees, contracts with E.L. Phillips and Company, and construction costs. In response to this negative publicity, the company inaugurated a community responsibility program in 1932. The company developed display models of its electric system, produced a movie about itself, and promoted tours of its facilities by school groups and clubs. Employees were encouraged to participate in a variety of activities such as cooking schools, light demonstrations, and an employee orchestra.

KEY DATES

∎

1910: The Long Island Lighting Company (LILCO) is organized by the merger of four small Suffolk County utilities.

1911: The New York Public Service Commission (PSC) allows LILCO to begin to function.

1917: The company charter is amended to provide coverage for all villages and towns in Suffolk County and parts of adjacent Nassau County.

1945: LILCO seeks permission from the Securities and Exchange Commission (SEC) and the PSC to effect a corporate reorganization by bringing most of its subsidiaries into a consolidated Long Island Lighting Company.

1950: The company gains final approval for its reorganization.

1965: President John J. Tuohy announces LILCO's intention to build a nuclear power plant on Long Island.

1986: Long Island Power Authority (LIPA) is created.

1989: LILCO sells the Shoreham facility to LIPA.

1994: The Shoreham facility is decommissioned.

1998: Reorganization results in LIPA falling under the auspices of KeySpan Energy Corporation.

2004: LIPA announces a new energy resource plan to secure an additional 1,000 megawatts by 2010.

2008: LIPA announces the possibility of additional rate hikes due to rising fuel costs.

In 1938 and 1944, hurricanes tested LILCO's ability to cope with severe natural disasters. On September 21, 1938, a hurricane, preceded by ten days of rain that softened the ground considerably, caused damage estimated at $500,000 to LILCO's equipment. Most service in Nassau County and 85 percent of service in Suffolk County was restored within four days. In September 1944 another hurricane knocked out 91 percent of LILCO's system. Most power was restored in about 12 days, aided considerably by LILCO's use of Nassau County's police radio network.

In the wake of this storm LILCO installed its own radio system. There were other changes in the 1940s, too. During World War II the company was forced to abandon its policy of not employing married women, as many single women resigned to marry men in military service. As restaurants closed during the war, the company also decided to open its own cafeterias. The first one, in the Mineola office, served lunch at cost. Ellis Phillips retired as chairman of the board in 1945. His position was not immediately filled, but Edward F. Barrett, later to serve as chairman, was named chief executive officer.

POSTWAR GROWTH

As World War II came to a close, LILCO's service area was still not much more than a conglomeration of small towns, large estates, and vacation retreats amid miles of farmland. Long Island's greatest period of growth, spurred by the migration of thousands of returning veterans and their new families to hundreds of bedroom communities such as Levittown, was just about to begin. LILCO positioned itself to meet this challenge by building new facilities, constructing new main lines, and establishing a connection to Consolidated Edison, its corporate neighbor to the west. All New York State power systems, in fact, were interconnected by 1948, a cooperative arrangement that played a key role in the great blackout of 1965.

In 1945 the company sought permission from the Securities and Exchange Commission (SEC) and the PSC to effect a corporate reorganization by bringing most of its subsidiaries into a consolidated Long Island Lighting Company. It was not until 1950, following many negotiations and preliminary decisions, that the reorganization gained final approval.

LILCO's managers continued to look ahead. In 1952 a 60-acre tract in Hicksville became the site of a new central headquarters housing facilities for system gas and electric controls, line crews, warehouses, repair shops, automotive maintenance, training classes, and later, administrative offices. The company also established an equity annuity plan to supplement the fixed benefits paid retirees since 1937. In 1953 the state granted LILCO a 3.5 percent rate increase, the first general electric rate boost in the company's history. At the close of 1954 LILCO joined Atomic Power Development Associates, composed of 43 companies looking for practical ways to use atomic materials to generate electricity.

While safe and inexpensive nuclear power remained a goal, the company continued to cope with other aspects of its business. Three hurricanes in 1954 caused severe damage and added $1.4 million to the year's operating expenses. In 1957 plans were made to purchase land in Northport for what would become the largest power station in the country. By 1959, when Ellis Phillips died at 85, LILCO's residential customers numbered more than half a million and annual revenues topped $100 million. Peak load electric use passed one million kilowatts in 1960, the same year that saw the number of customers using gas heat jump to six times what it had been just a decade before.

EXPANSION INTO NUCLEAR POWER LEADS TO CRISIS

President John J. Tuohy announced LILCO's intention to build a nuclear power plant on Long Island at a stockholders' meeting in April 1965. A year later the company bought 450 acres in the North Shore village of Shoreham for a 540-megawatt plant estimated to cost between $65 million and $75 million. A proposal to construct a second nuclear facility in Lloyd Harbor led to the creation of a citizens' group in opposition. Their study, completed in 1969, branded both plants uneconomical and unsafe.

The Lloyd Harbor proposal was withdrawn, but LILCO pressed on with Shoreham. In fact, when the demand for electricity increased in the summer of 1968 at twice the anticipated rate, the company redrew its plan and proposed an 820-megawatt plant. By September 1970, when federal construction permit hearings began before the Atomic Energy Commission, precursor of the Nuclear Regulatory Commission (NRC), citizen awareness of environmental hazards had grown considerably. In addition, the federal Environmental Policy Act of 1970 forced developers to guarantee that their projects would do no ecological harm.

The hearings set records for length and complexity. A total of 100 witnesses were heard in 70 sessions, 401 legal briefs were filed, and 20,000 pages of transcripts resulted. Three issues became paramount: the environmental impact of the plant's construction, safety measures in case of an accident, and the effects of radiation. The opposition also raised a new concern, how Long Island would be evacuated in the event of an emergency. The Atomic Energy Commission ruled that this issue need not be addressed until Shoreham applied for an operating license, and on April 12, 1973, the commission granted LILCO a construction permit.

Before construction began, however, the Organization of Petroleum Exporting Countries oil embargo drove petroleum prices skyward, and consumers conceded the need for alternative energy sources. LILCO had converted most of its plants from coal to oil in the 1960s and, due to the fast-rising price of oil, raised its rates 13 times in 12 years to offset rising costs. Every time rates were increased, however, demand dropped, and the company's fiscal woes deepened.

The price tag for completing the Shoreham plant, which ran well behind schedule, jumped to $1.2 billion by 1977. LILCO blamed most of the cost overruns on increased federal regulations, but outside studies pointed to poor supervision and abusive labor practices as well. The company took over design and construction responsibilities from an outside firm, but costs continued to rise.

The March 1979 accident at the Three Mile Island nuclear reactor in Pennsylvania delayed the NRC's consideration of an operating license for Shoreham. It also stimulated the anti-Shoreham faction and crystallized the debate around the evacuation issue. With the threat of a nuclear accident a demonstrated possibility, the fate of Shoreham was thrown into mainstream politics on Long Island and throughout New York State. Governor Hugh Carey and Nassau County Executive Francis T. Purcell continued to support the project, as did *The New York Times* and Long Island's *Newsday*. The estimated cost of completing the plant continued to rise, to $4.6 billion by 1986, an increase of more than $1 million per day between 1981 and 1986.

OPPOSITION CONTINUES

After Three Mile Island, the NRC required all nuclear plant operators to develop an evacuation plan in conjunction with local and state government. Suffolk County officials clashed with LILCO over virtually every aspect of the proposed plan, and eventually the county ended attempts to come to an agreement. One by one, county leaders dropped their support of the plant. County Executive Peter Cohalan, once in favor, changed his mind when he attempted to visit the plant site and found the gates locked. In February 1983 the county's legislature voted 15 to one that it believed Suffolk County could not safely be evacuated, a position bolstered by the support of Governor Mario Cuomo. In office only a month, he ordered state officials not to sanction any emergency response plan sponsored by LILCO.

The company's general financial health declined gravely during this crisis. Bond-rating agencies downgraded LILCO's bonds, and bankruptcy became a possibility. Critics accused the company of pushing ahead for an operating license for Shoreham simply to begin charging customers for the construction. Nevertheless, the plant neared completion. In August 1983, however, LILCO discovered cracks in the crankshafts of all three backup diesel generators, two of which would be needed to shut the plant down in an emergency. The following January, the company's directors voted to withhold payment of $26.2 million in county and local property taxes to protest opposition to the plant. With the crisis at its height, LILCO's president, Wilfred O. Uhl, retired, and its chairman, Charles Pierce, was replaced by board member William J. Catacosinos, a computer industry entrepreneur with little experience in utilities. Catacosinos commenced a massive austerity program, including cutting 1,000 jobs from a 5,900-member workforce, but stood by Shoreham resolutely.

The fight dragged on, and LILCO persisted against considerable opposition from government, the public, and the local business community. The company completed construction in 1984 without fanfare and repaired the generators, even installing a second backup set. The NRC in July 1985 approved operation at 5 percent of capacity, a low-level test prior to final licensing. LILCO's position got a sudden and unexpected boost when Peter Cohalan, fearful of financial ruin for Suffolk County, dropped his opposition in exchange for receipt of the company's back taxes.

The public rejected Cohalan's reversal and paid little heed as LILCO employees simulated a successful evacuation of the area within a ten-mile radius of the plant. Whatever credibility this drill might have engendered, however, had been lost in September 1985, when Hurricane Gloria knocked out electricity to 750,000 customers. LILCO took more than a week to restore power during which time Catacosinos absented himself from Long Island.

CREATING THE LONG ISLAND
POWER AUTHORITY

Support grew slowly in New York State for a bill to create the Long Island Power Authority (LIPA) to take over LILCO and close Shoreham. Some legislators backed the bill because of LILCO's increasingly high rates; others were convinced by the Soviet nuclear disaster at Chernobyl that nuclear power could never be safe. The bill passed the New York General Assembly on July 3, 1986, and Governor Cuomo signed it.

LILCO placed its hopes for survival as an investor-owned company with the NRC, which decided in 1987 to relax its rule that government had to participate in formulation of a disaster plan. A week later, the state PSC exerted its fiscal leverage for the first time. It denied LILCO's request for an $83 million rate hike and ordered the company and the state to end their deadlock.

After more than a year of intense negotiations, the disputing parties did just that. The PSC endorsed a wide-ranging settlement in April 1989, and LILCO stockholders approved it that June. Under its terms, Shoreham was fully licensed to operate, transferred to

LIPA for $1, and closed. LILCO was granted permission for a series of annual rate increases, targeted at 5 percent per year, for a ten-year period. The company also settled a lawsuit that Suffolk County had brought under the Racketeer Influenced and Corrupt Organizations Act, resumed dividend payments, and refinanced its long-term debt. The fuel rods were removed from Shoreham's reactor vessel in August 1989, and the plant stood idle. The cost of absorbing the Shoreham debt pushed LILCO's rates to the highest of any utility in the country.

LILCO seemed to recover some fiscal stability in the wake of the settlement. The price of its common stock rose, and it sold a $1.1 billion offering of debentures. Events in 1990, however, threw the company's future into doubt. Oil prices and inflation rose at rates higher than anticipated, threatening the adequacy of the proposed 5 percent annual rate increases. As the international situation in the Persian Gulf deteriorated in late 1990 and early 1991, LILCO requested rate hikes for the next three years with certain adjustments that would keep the 5 percent ceiling intact.

LIPA TAKES OVER LILCO

With the title of Shoreham officially transferred to LIPA in 1992, plans were set in motion to decommission the nuclear facility. In October 1994, Shoreham was officially shut down. That same month, Governor Cuomo announced that the state planned to buy out LILCO's distribution and transmission network with nearly $9 billion in LIPA bonds. New York State Senator George Pataki was elected governor in November of that year and immediately became involved in the state's plans regarding the LILCO takeover and also initiated a steep rate reduction strategy in an attempt to reduce rates by 20 percent by 2008.

Corporate reorganization ensued in the mid-1990s. During 1996, plans were announced to merge the remaining LILCO assets not involved in the LIPA deal with Brooklyn Union Gas Co., and Brooklyn Union changed its name to KeySpan Energy Corporation shortly thereafter. LILCO and KeySpan were then merged in May 1998 to form MarketSpan Corporation. The KeySpan subsidiary was tapped to manage LIPA's network until 2013. KeySpan eventually changed its name to National Grid in May 2008.

The chairman of LILCO at the time of the deal, Catacosinos, became chairman and CEO of MarketSpan. His tenure was short-lived, however, when the public was made aware that he received a $42 million severance package paid out by LILCO upon completion of its merger. Within just a few months,

Marketspan's stock lost $1 billion in value amid the negative publicity. Catacosinos was ousted in July 1998.

With their relationship off to a rocky start, LIPA and KeySpan Energy announced they had reached an agreement in December 1998 to put the Catacosinos scandal behind them. As part of the deal, KeySpan would pay for postage paid envelopes to be included in the bills for LIPA customers and LIPA would receive nearly $765,000 for costs related to legal fees in the investigation of compensation packages paid to Catacosinos and 24 other LILCO executives. In addition, Catacosinos was barred from any sort of involvement with KeySpan for 15 years. Many balked at this agreement, which included a private office, secretary, car, driver, and home security for Catacosinos for nearly two years in return for his agreement to end all involvement with KeySpan and related companies.

MOVING INTO THE 21ST CENTURY

As LIPA entered the new millennium its customers enjoyed lower prices. LILCO once had the highest rates of any electrical concern in the continental United States, but the LIPA takeover had succeeded in reducing electricity rates. With electricity demand soaring, LIPA was heavily focused at this time on securing resources to meet growing demand. During 2004 the company announced a new energy resource plan to secure an additional 1,000 megawatts of capacity by 2010. In addition, LIPA partnered with Neptune Regional Transmission System LLC to buy 660 megawatts of capacity by way of an undersea cable that was installed between Sayreville, New Jersey, and Levittown, New York. The agreement would allow LIPA to import the 660 megawatts from the Pennsylvania, New Jersey, and Maryland markets.

LIPA underwent a management change in 2007 when Chairman Richard M. Kessel was forced out by then Governor Eliot Spitzer. Spitzer named James L. Larocca chairman and Kevin S. Law president and CEO. Kessel was named president of New York Power Authority in 2008. Larocca left LIPA in December of that year and Howard E. Steinberg took the helm as acting chairman.

Higher fuel costs brought on in part by Hurricane Katrina forced LIPA to raise its rates by nearly 20 percent in 2005. With the price of oil and natural gas continuing to rise, the company was forced to implement additional rate increases. Governor David Paterson vetoed a bill in September 2008, which if passed, would have forced a review process by the New York State PSC on any LIPA rate increase over 2.5 percent. In December of that year, LIPA announced that it might have to raise rates by nearly 17 percent in the coming years.

Steven P. Gietschier
Updated, Christina M. Stansell

PRINCIPAL COMPETITORS

Consolidated Edison Inc.; National Grid USA; Power Authority of the State of New York.

FURTHER READING

Carolan, Matthew, and Raymond J. Keating, "The LIPA Lesson in Rearranging Risk," *Newsday,* August 11, 1998.

Carpenter, James W., *Lighting Long Island,* Hicksville, N.Y.: Long Island Lighting Co., n.d.

"Cuomo and LILCO Sign a New Accord to Shut Shoreham," *New York Times,* March 1, 1989.

Finn, Robert, "A Live Wire at the Top of LIPA," *New York Times,* July 30, 2006.

Freedman, Mitch, "The East End," *Newsday,* November 28, 1999.

Lambert, Bruce, "A Reversal of Fortune," *New York Times,* August 2, 1998.

Marks, Peter, "Shoreham: The History," *Newsday,* May 15, 1988.

Rather, John, "LIPA Beats the Heat but Barely," *New York Times,* August 8, 1999.

———, "Planning the Fate of a Nuclear Plant's Land," *New York Times,* January 4, 2009.

———, "Power Couple," *New York Times,* October 9, 2005.

Los Angeles Turf Club Inc.

---

285 West Huntington Drive
Arcadia, California 91007-3439
U.S.A.
Telephone: (626) 574-7223
Fax: (626) 446-1456
Web site: http://www.santaanita.com

*Wholly Owned Subsidiary of Magna Entertainment
Corporation*
Incorporated: 1933
Employees: 1,600
Sales: $328 million (2000 est.)
NAICS: 711212 Race Tracks

■ ■ ■

Doing business as Santa Anita Race Track, Los Angeles Turf Club Inc. is responsible for maintaining the facility and conducting the thoroughbred horseracing season at Santa Anita Park in Arcadia, California, which each season runs Wednesday through Sunday from December 26 through April 19. Santa Anita Park is the oldest racetrack in Southern California and known as one of the sport's greatest venues, home to such prestigious races as the Santa Anita Derby and the Santa Anita Handicap. The track also presents a fall racing season through the Oak Tree Racing Association, conducted from late September to early November. When Santa Anita has hosted the annual Breeders' Cup Championship, the event has been held during the fall season.

Santa Anita is owned by Magna Entertainment Corporation, the largest owner and operator of horse

tracks according to revenue. Other Magna-operated tracks include Golden Gate Fields, located in the San Francisco Bay Area; South Florida's Gulfstream Park; Laurel Park in the Washington, D.C., area; Lone Star Park at Grand Prairie near Dallas, Texas; The Meadows in Pittsburgh, Pennsylvania; Pimlico in Baltimore, Maryland; Portland Meadows in Oregon; Oklahoma's Remington Park; and Thistledown near Cleveland, Ohio. In addition, Magna owns and operates Magna Racino in Austria.

ORIGINS

The history of Santa Anita Park is linked to one of California's most colorful characters of the 19th century, E. J. "Lucky" Baldwin. Born in Ohio in 1828, Baldwin was a Wisconsin grocer when he decided in 1852 to move to the California gold fields that had opened up three years earlier. Rather than prospecting for gold, Baldwin began making his fortune through a brick making venture, which then provided the capital he needed to invest in mining stocks. Baldwin crawled through many miles of tunnels to inspect the mines he chose to invest in, yet the *San Francisco Chronicle* began calling him "Lucky" in his investments and the name stuck. He became a rich man, his wealth estimated to be $20 million. Known to be lucky in business, he was not especially lucky in love, albeit active. He was married four times and twice shot by women, including the sister of one woman suing him for breach of promise who grazed his head with a pistol shot in open court.

Baldwin became a prominent horseman in the United States, developing a string of thoroughbreds carrying his distinctive black and red Maltese cross silks that he raced in venues across the country. He also used some of his money in 1875 to acquire the 18,000-acre Rancho Santa Anita in Southern California, a dozen miles from Los Angeles. In 1903 he incorporated the town of Arcadia in the area and in 1907 opened a racetrack on his property. The history of the track would be brief, however. In February 1909 California enacted the Walker-Otis anti-racetrack gambling bill, bringing an end to gambling at racetracks in the state. Before the law went into effect the Santa Anita track closed. Moreover, the 81-year-old Baldwin died in March 1909 after a lengthy illness.

Racetrack gambling was reinstated in California in 1933. One of the first people to make an effort to build a new racetrack in the state was San Franciscan Charles "Doc" Strub, a former minor league baseball player, dentist, real estate investor, and horse racing buff. He formed a syndicate of financial backers, the St. Francis Jockey Club, receiving the first permit issued by the new California Horse Racing Board, but was unable to find a suitable track site in San Francisco when his efforts met stiff community resistance. He then turned his attention to Southern California and joined forces with a group of investors headed by comedy film producer Hal Roach, forming the Los Angeles Turf Club in 1933.

Roach's group wanted to build a track in Culver City, but in the midst of the Great Depression was unable to raise the $1 million required by the racing board in order to secure a license. Even the addition of Strub and his money was not enough to bring racing to Culver City. The chairman of the racing board, Carleton Burke, insisted that the Los Angeles Turf Club build on the site of Lucky Baldwin's former Santa Anita track. The land was available because Baldwin's daughter, Anita, was having difficulty paying the taxes.

SANTA ANITA PARK OPENS

With license in hand and a large parcel of land, initially 210 acres, purchased, the Los Angeles Turf Club under the leadership of Doc Strub began work on the new Santa Anita Park racetrack. Architect Gordon B. Kaufman was hired, and he produced an art deco design for what would be regarded as a jewel among racetracks.

Ground was broken in 1933, and on Christmas Day 1934 more than 30,000 people attended the first day of racing at the new park, including the likes of Al Jolson, Clark Gable, and Will Rogers.

After paying for the construction of Santa Anita, money was so tight that on opening day Strub had to borrow money in order to book the bets. Given the poor economy, it was not the best time to open a racetrack. In order to boost attendance that quickly fell off after opening day, Strub announced the creation of a race, the Santa Anita Handicap, offering a $100,000 prize, the world's richest purse at that time. What appeared to be sheer folly proved to a stroke of brilliant marketing. The free publicity the Santa Anita Handicap received put the track on the map, both for horsemen and spectators, more than repaying the investment in the prize money. The highest pedigree horses then raced and the wealthy and Hollywood celebrities filled the stands. It was at the Santa Anita Handicap in 1940 that Seabiscuit, the most popular horse of the Depression era, won his final start.

Santa Anita and Doc Strub were innovators on other fronts as well. The track was the first to have cameras positioned for photo finishes. The modern starting gates also made their debut at Santa Anita. After the start of World War II, the track was closed in 1942 and for the next two years Japanese Americans were interned on the site. Following the war Santa Anita reopened for racing and flourished once again. To provide European-style racing a downhill turf course was added in 1953.

ROBERT STRUB NAMED PRESIDENT

Doc Strub died in March 1958 at the age of 73. His son Robert P. Strub inherited a 21 percent stake in Los Angeles Turf Club. A Stanford University graduate, the younger Strub had been working at the track for years, working his way up through the organization, parking cars, selling admission tickets, and working in the mutuels money room. Two years after the death of his father, Strub faced off with board member Reese H. Taylor, the head of Union Oil Company, for control of the track. The matter came to a head in the spring of 1960 and the young Strub emerged victorious and was named president. Under his leadership, a major renovation of the facilities was completed in the 1960s, including an expanded grandstand and other seating options.

It was also in the 1960s that Oak Tree Racing Association became involved at Santa Anita. Three important men in California racing—Clement L. Hirsch, Louis R. Rowan, and Dr. Jack Robbins—formed

```
┌─────────────────────────────────────────────┐
│                                               │
│              KEY DATES                        │
│                   ■                           │
│                                               │
│  1933:  Los Angeles Turf Club Inc. is founded │
│         to build Santa Anita Park racetrack.  │
│  1934:  Santa Anita Park opens under Charles  │
│         "Doc" Strub's leadership.             │
│  1942:  Santa Anita Park closes and is used   │
│         as an internment camp for the next    │
│         two years.                            │
│  1958:  Doc Strub dies.                       │
│  1960:  Robert Strub assumes presidency.      │
│  1969:  Oak Tree Racing Association presents  │
│         first fall racing season.             │
│  1980:  Santa Anita Operating Co. becomes     │
│         parent company of Los Angeles Turf    │
│         Club.                                 │
│  1993:  Robert Strub dies.                    │
│  1997:  Meditrust Inc. acquires Santa Anita   │
│         Park.                                 │
│  1998:  Frank Stronach acquires the track.    │
│  2007:  Plans are approved for outdoor mall   │
│         project.                              │
│                                               │
└─────────────────────────────────────────────┘
```

Oak Tree in order to fill a gap in the Southern California racing calendar after Del Mar Racetrack eliminated its fall race. Oak Tree arranged to rent Santa Anita, presenting its first autumn race in 1969. The relationship between Santa Anita and Oak Tree would prove mutually beneficial and later allowed the track to participate in the prestigious and lucrative Breeders' Cup events held in the fall.

Santa Anita continued to thrive in the 1970s and into the 1980s, even as tracks located in other parts of the country began to struggle. New York, once a hotbed for horse racing, both thoroughbred and harness, saw a major decline in attendance due to the rise of off-track betting. The gambling outlet provided by casinos in nearby Atlantic City and tribal gaming in Connecticut would also take their toll, as would a state lottery.

NEW REALITIES IN RACING

The lottery came to California as well in 1985, but Strub had begun adjusting to the new realities despite Santa Anita holding the largest average daily attendance and average daily wagering of all thoroughbred tracks in the country. In 1980 the business was reorganized with the establishment of Santa Anita Operating Co., which then became the parent company for Los Angeles Turf Club. A real estate investment trust (REIT) was also created, and the Santa Anita companies began focusing on real estate development, such as opening a regional mall adjacent to the track. It also created a new revenue stream by allowing the simulcasting of races to Nevada casinos. Satellite wagering was added in 1987.

Unlike most previous down cycles in the economy when Santa Anita was able to carry on with little difficulty, the recession of the early 1990s proved different as the track experienced a sharp decline in track attendance and wagering. Much of the problem had been building for some time. The sport had not paid much attention to marketing, leading to a significant increase in the age of racing fans, disproportionately skewed toward men aged 45 to 64 years old. Simulcasting had been an industry attempt to improve revenues, allowing race fans to bet on races across the country, but the move only accelerated the drop in track attendance and did little to develop a new generation of race fans.

In 1993 Robert Strub died at the age of 74, succumbing to a degenerative neuromuscular condition known as Lou Gehrig's disease. He was replaced as chairman and chief executive officer of Los Angeles Turf Club by Stephen F. Keller, who had previously replaced him as CEO of Santa Anita Operating Co. and had been recruited two years earlier with the idea of succeeding Strub. Under Keller, Santa Anita continued to adjust to the new realities in racing. In late 1994, for example, an agreement was reached to make the track's race card available to the New York Off-Track Betting Corporation. He then had to contend with an unsolicited offer to buy Santa Anita Park that could have led to the closing of the track and the consolidation of all horse racing in Southern California at Hollywood Park. A competing offer of $383 million in 1997 from Meditrust Inc., a Massachusetts-based healthcare REIT, prevailed, however, and the track was saved.

FRANK STRONACH ACQUIRES SANTA ANITA

Meditrust quickly invested $7 million in renovations to upgrade Santa Anita, but less than a year after acquiring the track, the trust put it up for sale, due to changes in federal law that eliminated the tax advantages that had initially made the deal attractive. In December 1998 the Santa Anita companies were acquired by Frank Stronach, the owner of Magna International, a major Canadian auto parts company, and a prominent horse owner and breeder. Born in Austria, Stronach had immigrated to Canada in 1954 with less than $50 in his pockets and little facility with English. Although he had a background in tool and machine engineering, he began life in his new country washing dishes in a Toronto hospital.

Three years later in a Toronto garage Stronach started a tool and die company, Multimatic Investments

Limited, which soon began producing automotive components. In 1969 Stronach merged the company with Magna Electronics Corporation Limited to create Magna International. Along the way he began investing in racehorses, building up an impressive stable and winning many important races over the years. He paid $126 million for Santa Anita, laying the foundation for Magna Entertainment and the acquisition of further tracks across the country. In short order, Magna Entertainment would be vying with Churchill Downs Inc. as the leading racetrack companies.

After Stronach took over Santa Anita, the venerable track received some notable improvements, including the opening of a gourmet restaurant, the FrontRunner, which overlooked the finish line, an improved winner's circle, and a renovated apron area that was more fan-friendly. Nevertheless, as was the case with all racetracks, Santa Anita faced serious challenges as the new century dawned. It occupied a great deal of land in a highly populated part of the country, making it imperative that better use of the land be made year-round and not just during the racing seasons. Magna looked to take advantage of undeveloped land at Santa Anita Park to build a regional outdoor mall in partnership with developer Caruso Affiliated. After overcoming some problems the project eventually received approval in 2007 and the opening of the complex was slated for 2010.

The fortunes of the racing industry continued to decline, exacerbated by difficult economic conditions. Many of the Magna tracks were losing money and even Santa Anita was rumored to be on the block in 2008, but its prospects were decidedly better than most other racing venues. Longtime rival Hollywood Park founded itself in a difficult position, the land it occupied more valuable than the business the racetrack could provide. After a video gambling bill failed to pass the state legislature, eliminating the prospect of additional gaming revenues to be realized at the track, Hollywood Park's existence was not guaranteed after the 2008 racing season. Should the track be sold, razed, and the land developed, Santa Anita would likely benefit, at least in the short run, but the future of racing and Santa Anita Park nevertheless remained uncertain.

Ed Dinger

PRINCIPAL COMPETITORS
Hollywood Park.

FURTHER READING

Arrington, Debbie, "Is Racing Back on Track?" *Sacramento Bee,* December 27, 2008.

———, "Throughout State, Horse Racing Faces Uncertain Future," *Sacramento Bee,* August 12, 2007.

Bortstein, Larry, "Frank Stronach's Purchase of Santa Anita Puts One of the Most Prominent Thoroughbred Owners in the Saddle at the Track," *Orange County Register,* December 26, 1998, p. D1.

———, "Santa Anita Opens amid Big Concern," *Orange County Register,* December 26, 2008.

"Charles H. Strub of Santa Anita, 73," *New York Times,* March 29, 1958.

Christine, Bill, "Strub, 74, Resigns Post," *Los Angeles Times,* February 12, 1993, p. 9.

Harasta, Cathy, "Canadian Tycoon Races Ahead with Vision for Arcadia, Calif., Area," *Dallas Morning News,* October 20, 2002.

Hill, Gladwin, "Proxy Race Set for Santa Anita," *New York Times,* April 28, 1960.

Kumada, Mikio, "Track Owner Plans Vegas Makeover for Santa Anita," *Los Angeles Business Journal,* March 13, 2000, p. 12.

"Lucky Baldwin," *New York Times,* October 9, 1885.

"Lucky Baldwin Dies at the Age of 81," *New York Times,* March 2, 1909.

Milbert, Neil, "Racetrack Empires Building Up," *Chicago Tribune,* May 9, 2000.

Modesti, Kevin, "Santa Anita Executive Strub Dies," *Los Angeles Daily News,* May 6, 1993, p. S11.

Mullen, Liz, "Group Confirms It Might Close Santa Anita Track," *Los Angeles Business Journal,* October 28, 1996, p. 1.

Paris, Ellen, "Strub in the Stretch," *Forbes,* September 9, 1985, p. 80.

Rasmussen, Cecilia, "Gamble on Racetrack Paid Off," *Los Angeles Times,* December 20, 1998, p. 3.

York, Emily Bryson, "Hollywood Park Racing Nearing Its Finish Line," *Los Angeles Business Journal,* July 3, 2006, p. 1.

M·R·BEAL & COMPANY

M.R. Beal and Co.

———————■———————

110 Wall Street, Floor 6
New York, New York 10005-3827
U.S.A.
Telephone: (212) 983-3930
Toll Free: (800) 451-9702
Fax: (212) 983-4539
Web site: http://www.mrbeal.com

Private Company
Incorporated: 1988
Employees: 40
Sales: $307 million (2007 est.)
NAICS: 523110 Investment Banking and Securities
Dealing

■ ■ ■

M.R. Beal and Co. is a Wall Street investment banking firm with offices in Chicago, Dallas, and Sacramento. Originally formed to serve the municipal finance market, M.R. Beal has evolved into a multidimensional investment bank and is the oldest continuously operated minority-owned firm of its type in the United States. It is one of the country's top municipal bond underwriters, involved in all major sectors, including housing, school district, transportation, aviation, water, and general infrastructure. M.R. Beal also acts as financial adviser to municipalities regarding their capital needs. In addition, M.R. Beal provides corporate financing through equity underwriting, corporate debt, and corporate buybacks. The firm's institutional equity unit provides research on securities and trading services on listed and over-the-counter stocks as well as international issues through a broker-to-broker network. M.R. Beal also trades in fixed-income securities and municipal bonds. The firm's founder, Bernard B. Beal, serves as chairman and chief executive officer.

FOUNDER BRONX RAISED

Born around 1954, Bernard Beal was raised by his grandparents in New York City's South Bronx and later the Soundview section of the borough where his grandfather bought a house. Taking advantage of help provided by A Better Chance Foundation, which helped place children from low-income neighborhoods in some of the city's better public schools and area private schools, Beal attended high school at the Wooster School of Danbury, Connecticut. After graduating high school in 1972, Beal initially eschewed college in favor of investing his money in a share of a Jack in the Box restaurant in the Bronx. Working as a night manager at the store he was soon making enough money to afford his own apartment and a pair of motorcycles. He changed his mind about college when the restaurant was held up at gunpoint one evening and a bullet grazed his leg. He then enrolled at Carleton College in Northfield, Minnesota, where he further honed his entrepreneurial skills, starting a student café as well as running a record and tape business. After earning his undergraduate degree he was accepted to Stanford University's business school.

Upon graduating from Stanford with his master's of business administration degree in 1979, Beal returned to his hometown, taking a job on Wall Street with the E.F.

Hutton & Co. brokerage firm. He was given the choice to pursue the more glamorous corporate finance department or municipal bonds. Because of moral considerations, he opted for the latter, explaining to *Black Enterprise*, "It blended with my deep desire to do well and do good. I saw it as an opportunity to finance housing and healthcare." Focusing on housing and education finance, Beal worked his way through the ranks at Hutton, eventually serving as the head of the college and education group and establishing the housing group. During his final years with the firm he also gained experience in the corporate finance department. Along the way he earned a reputation as an innovative analyst, playing an important role in the creating of "put" bonds, which allowed holders to sell back bonds to the issuer, usually at par value, at specified dates before maturity, in effect sacrificing some yield for the sake of flexibility.

After Hutton was bought out by Shearson Lehman Brothers in 1988 in the wake of major losses the firm suffered in a stock market crash a few months earlier, Beal, who was a senior vice-president at Hutton, took stock of his position. Rather than start over further down the hierarchy of a new organization, he decided to strike out on his own and put into motion a business plan he had originally written during his Stanford days. Moreover, the time seemed right for an African American to start a municipal securities firm because affirmative action programs were being extended by a number of federal agencies and local governments, leading to the launch of a number of minority- and women-owned financial firms.

M.R. BEAL ESTABLISHED

In 1988 the 34-year-old Beal organized M.R. Beal as a limited partnership, the name of the firm drawing on the middle initials of his two children, Michael Manning and Erica Mae, and his wife, Valerie Rose. The *New York Times* speculated on why Beal did not use his own initials: "B.B.B. are not the best in an industry that likes things rated AAA." Seven associates joined Beal to establish the firm, each of similar age and Wall Street experience. They included Michael W. Geffrard,

formerly with James J. Lowrey & Co., who took over as managing director of finance advisory services; Diana L. Taylor, a Donaldson, Lufkin & Jenrette Securities Corporation senior vice-president, serving as managing director of investment banking; Hutton colleague Karen W. Valenstein, also a managing director of investment banking; and Robert S. L. Warendorf, another Hutton veteran, who took charge of syndicate and sales. In addition, Maxine C. Leftwich, former deputy program manager for Chicago's $180 million McCormick Place convention center expansion project, opened and headed a Chicago branch of the firm. M.R. Beal initially set up shop in Midtown Manhattan, in offices located on Fifth Avenue across from the main entrance to the main building of the New York Public Library at 42nd Street. The firm would later relocate farther south to the Wall Street district.

Beal told the *New York Times* at the time of the company's formation that he and his colleagues "saw an opportunity for a young aggressive creative firm that's well managed and maintaining its costs to succeed in the municipal finance sector." While the focus was on the municipal bond business, the new firm hedged its bets somewhat by also offering financial advisory work. M.R. Beal looked to take advantage of affirmative action and set-aside programs that brought minority-owned firms into bond underwriting, but it hardly faced a shortage of competition. Five years earlier, only a handful of such firms existed, but by this time about 20 minority-owned investment banking firms were vying for the same projects.

Any expectations Beal had that his former Hutton clients would automatically continue to do business with him were also disabused. Moreover, being included in a banking syndicate did not necessarily lead to a financial windfall. Other than the lead managers, most participants were fortunate to receive a modicum of bonds to sell, a problem that had been increasing as lead managers preferred to sell the bonds to institutions, who in turn sold them to their retail customers or packaged them for funds.

SEC CHANGES CAUSE TROUBLES

Nevertheless, the young firm was able to find its footing in a highly competitive field. In 1989 M.R. Beal became the financial adviser to East St. Louis, Illinois, the first financial company ever to manage a municipality on a daily basis. For the year the firm managed $7.5 billion in municipal issues. A new office was added in Los Angeles in 1990, and the firm, then numbering 23 associates, refined its management structure, with Beal turning over the presidency to Diana Taylor. He remained chairman and CEO.

```
┌─────────────────────────────────────────────┐
│                                             │
│            KEY DATES                        │
│                   ■                         │
│ ─────────────────────────────────────────── │
│ 1988:  Bernard Beal establishes M.R. Beal   │
│        and Co.                              │
│ 1990:  Los Angeles office opens.            │
│ 1994:  Securities and Exchange Commission   │
│        (SEC) probe is launched.             │
│ 2000:  Firm joins forces with money manager │
│        Shawn D. Baldwin to create Chicago-  │
│        based Capital Management Group        │
│        Advisors L.L.C.                      │
│ 2002:  Stanley Grayson named chief operating│
│        officer.                             │
│ 2006:  Dallas office opens.                 │
│                                             │
└─────────────────────────────────────────────┘
```

Helping to drive the business in the early 1990s was an access program instituted by the Federal National Mortgage Association (Fannie Mae) that named M.R. Beal as one of six minority investment banks that comprised the 48-member group that underwrote various residential securities. The firm also introduced some of its own funds in September 1990 aimed at institutional investors. Moreover, M.R. Beal began pursuing corporate finance business in 1992, leading to participation in about 15 securities offerings in the next decade, including the $10.62 billion initial public offering (IPO) of AT&T Wireless Group and the $3.23 billion IPO of Charter Communications, Inc. An asset management unit was also established around 1994.

Changes imposed by the Securities and Exchange Commission (SEC) in 1994 had an adverse impact on M. R. Beal. Municipal finance firms were then forbidden from making political contributions to officials in locales where they had business. As a result, municipal bond volume plummeted. Unlike older, larger firms that could simply shift their focus to different avenues, M.R. Beal and other minority firms found themselves with no alternatives and fighting over a much smaller market. To make matters worse, the SEC zealously investigated political contributions, a probe that devastated some black firms. M.R. Beal was caught up in the controversy as well when several publications reported that the firm was part of a group of minority investment banks that supposedly bribed a Wisconsin state senator in order to land bond underwriting contracts.

SURVIVING AND GROWING

Under a cloud of suspicion, M.R. Beal in October 1994 was removed from a new New York City bond underwriting syndicate at the behest of the city comptroller's office, which expressed concern about the Wisconsin investigation. The firm was never charged with any wrongdoing and was eventually reinstated to the syndicate, but the episode was a personal affront to Bernard Beal. "That was the worst experience of my career, and was quite insidious," he recalled in a 1998 interview with the *Bond Buyer*. "It's not something I took lightly; it was a cheap, unfair shot."

The controversy cost the firm three clients, Baltimore, Philadelphia, and the state of Oregon, and came close to putting it out of business. The saving grace was provided by the New York State comptroller's office, to which M.R. Beal made a concerted effort to provide all legal documents related to the case, including subpoenas, all part of a so-called truth packet. The decision by Comptroller Carl McCall, an African American, to stick by the firm likely saved M.R. Beal. The firm not only survived this difficult stretch, it reportedly learned some valuable lessons along the way, in particular the importance of communication in a crisis, both internally and externally. Employees as well as clients were kept abreast of M.R. Beal's involvement in the SEC investigation.

To grow its business, M.R. Beal in the fall of 1995 acquired Smith Mitchell Investment Group Inc., a women-owned, Seattle-based firm that underwrote bond issues east of Colorado. Around the same time, M.R. Beal elected to sell its asset management business, which after two years had grown the amount of money it had under management to $680 million. It was a venture that required a good deal of cash on hand, and in anticipation of a possible need for that cash, the firm sold the unit. It was a move Bernard Beal soon regretted, because the sector would enjoy strong growth in the years to come.

At the close of the 1990s M.R. Beal strengthened its corporate finance unit and improved its equity research capabilities. The firm regained a toehold in the asset management field in 2000, joining forces with money manager Shawn D. Baldwin to create a Chicago-based enterprise called Capital Management Group Advisors L.L.C., offering institutional investors a suite of investment products. M.R. Beal's primary role was to provide advice, while Baldwin ran the daily operations.

M.R. BEAL IN THE 21ST CENTURY

The new century brought an infusion of talent to the ranks of M.R. Beal. In the summer of 2002 the firm created a new position, chief operating officer, in order to lure Stanley E. Grayson while freeing up time for Bernard Beal to work on expanding the business. The 51-year-old Grayson was an experienced public finance banking executive with extensive government ties. He started his career in 1975 with Metropolitan Life Insurance Co. as a lawyer, and from 1984 to 1990 worked for the New York City mayor's office, eventually serving as deputy mayor for finance and economic development after stints in New York's Financial Services Corporation and the New York City Industrial Development Corporation. Grayson then spent six years in the public finance department of Goldman, Sachs & Co., and in 1996 joined Prudential Securities Inc. as a public finance banker. Two years later at Prudential he became the first African American to head the public finance department of a major Wall Street firm. In 2000, however, Prudential decided to exit the municipal bond underwriting business, and Grayson subsequently left.

Grayson was a good fit for M.R. Beal, which remained in the market for talent, much of which became available as Wall Street underwent a period of consolidation that resulted in a good deal of displaced executives. In 2006 the firm put an expansion program into effect that led to a hiring spree, primarily to improve new-issue and secondary sales and trading. In the summer of 2006 a municipal bond veteran, Karl Biggers, was hired to open a new office in Dallas to facilitate M.R. Beal's growth in the Southwest. A year later a pair of seasoned executive were added as well. James A. McGinley, a UBS Financial Services Inc. institutional trader, was hired to improve institutional sales, while Fernando Lopez, another UBS veteran, was named senior vice-president in charge of national underwriting. The following summer, in July 2008, John W. Jacobson and Mark J. Grimmig were recruited, both men named vice-presidents of institutional sales and trading. In November 2008, another veteran investment banker, Sean Boyea, a Morgan Stanley executive director in charge of the Los Angeles office, was lured away to run M.R. Beal's West Coast municipal bond operations.

The final months of 2008 brought a severe credit crunch to the financial sector, prompting M.R. Beal to adjust its strategy. The firm decided to return to the federal financing field. Once again, it also considered a return to the asset management business. M.R. Beal had survived some difficult times before, and there was every reason to expect that it would continue to find a way to remain viable in this challenging environment as well.

Ed Dinger

PRINCIPAL DIVISIONS

Investment Banking; Institutional Equity; Fixed Income Sales and Trading; Financial Advisory.

PRINCIPAL COMPETITORS

Blaylock & Partners, L.P.; Utendahl Capital Partners, L.P.; Williams Capital Group.

FURTHER READING

Achs, Nicole, "Big Fish in Finance," *American City & County,* April 1991, p. 66.

Albano, Christine, "M.R. Beal Names Biggers to Run Expansion from Dallas," *Bond Buyer,* August 17, 2006, p. 7.

"Beal Survives Tough Times," *Bond Buyer,* March 19, 1998, p. 32.

Cuff, Daniel F., "Ex-Shearson Aide Leads New Minority-Run Firm," *New York Times,* June 2, 1988, p. D5.

Dingle, Derek T., "M.R. Beal Has Become One of the Leading Black Investment Banks Through Innovation and Reinvention," *Black Enterprise,* June 2001, p. 220.

Gasparino, Charles, "New York Takes M.R. Beal Off Team Due to Federal Probe," *Bond Buyer,* January 26, 1995, p. 1.

McDonald, Michael, "A Veteran Gets Back in the Game: Stanley Grayson Named Beal COO," *Bond Buyer,* July 31, 2002, p. 1.

McKinney, Jeffrey, "Crisis & Opportunity," *Black Enterprise,* December 2008, p. 90.

Mysak, Joe, "Minority Firms See Mixed Success," *American Banker,* August 15, 1988.

O'Toole, Kathleen, "Blast Off Experts," *Stanford Business Magazine,* November 2004.

Tierney, John, "The Big City; Home Equity Is Where His Heart Is," *New York Times,* June 19, 2001.

Magna International Inc.

337 Magna Drive
Aurora, Ontario L4G 7K1
Canada
Telephone: (905) 726-2462
Fax: (905) 726-7164
Web site: http://www.magna.com

Public Company
Incorporated: 1969
Employees: 77,700
Sales: $26.07 billion (2007)
Stock Exchanges: New York Toronto
Ticker Symbols: MGA (NYSE); MG.A (Toronto)
NAICS: 336399 All Other Motor Vehicle Parts
    Manufacturing; 336370 Motor Vehicle Metal
    Stamping

■ ■ ■

Billing itself as the world's most diversified automotive supplier, Aurora, Ontario, Canada-based Magna International Inc. is a leading producer of automotive systems, assemblies, modules, and components. The company designs, engineers, tests, and manufactures systems devoted to automotive interiors; closure; electronics; exteriors; metal body and chassis; mirrors; power trains; roofs; and seating. In addition, Magna International also engineers and assembles complete vehicles. The company's operations consist of 86 facilities focusing on research and development or engineering, as well as 242 production centers. Toward the end of the first decade of the 21st century Magna

International served automotive original equipment manufacturers (OEMs) throughout Africa, Asia, Europe, North America, and South America with a workforce of 77,700 employees in 25 countries.

FORMATIVE YEARS

The origins of Magna International stretch back to 1957, when Frank Stronach, a native of Weiz, Austria, who had relocated to Canada three years earlier, started a one-man tool and die business called Multimatic Investments Ltd. Before establishing Multimatic, Stronach first worked as a dishwasher at a hospital in Kitchener, Ontario. Putting his tool and machine engineering skills to work, his new enterprise registered sales of $13,000 during its first year. In 1960 General Motors awarded Multimatic its first auto parts contract, calling upon the company to manufacture metal-stamped sun visor brackets.

In 1969 Multimatic Investments merged with Magna Electronics Corporation Ltd., a $4.4 million manufacturer of defense and industrial components that had begun trading on the Toronto Stock Exchange on December 20, 1962. An important development unfolded in 1971, at which time Stronach introduced a management philosophy called Fair Enterprise, which dictated the breakdown of profit sharing among various stakeholders, including workers, management, society, and investors. Sales totaled $6.8 million that year, and increased to $8.5 million in 1972.

On January 2, 1973, Magna Electronics adopted the name Magna International Inc. Sales swelled to $15.6 million that year and grew steadily throughout

COMPANY PERSPECTIVES

We are the most diversified automotive supplier in the world. We design, develop and manufacture automotive systems, assemblies, modules and components, and engineer and assemble complete vehicles, primarily for sale to original equipment manufacturers (OEMs) of cars and light trucks in our three geographic segments—North America, Europe, and Rest of World (primarily Asia, South America and Africa).

the early years of the decade, reaching $25.7 million in 1975. Sales at Magna international reached $35.9 million in 1976. That year, a significant focus on product diversification began, and the company organized specific divisions around groups of products. In addition, Magna International rolled out its Employee Equity Participation and Profit Sharing Program.

Sales continued to climb throughout the remainder of the decade, reaching $52.9 million in 1977, when a majority stake was acquired in Halifax, Nova Scotia-based Hermes Electronics Ltd. A three-for-one stock split was announced in 1978 as part of an effort to restructure the company's capital. Highlights that year included the formation of a joint venture to produce mufflers for the Volkswagen Beetle in Mexico, where a small muffler factory opened its doors. By this time Stronach was serving as chairman, and Helmut Hoffmann was president.

Magna International recorded sales of $83.8 million in 1978 and $108.3 million in 1979. The company rounded out the decade by entering the automotive plastics sector. Capital spending totaled $16 million, up from $15 million in 1978.

GROWTH AND PHYSICAL EXPANSION

After surviving a downturn in the automotive industry during the late 1970s, Magna International saw its sales increase slightly in 1980, reaching $119.9 million. By early 1981 the company was generating approximately 80 percent of its sales from the automotive industry. The remaining 20 percent was attributed to its defense operation, which was sold that year in order to focus solely on the automotive business.

During the early 1980s Magna International and its 12 subsidiaries employed a North American workforce

of approximately 4,000 people. By mid-1981 employees owned almost 33 percent of the company's stock. Sales reached $148 million in 1982, and climbed to $197.6 million the following year, at which time plans were under way for a new campus in Newmarket, Ontario. In 1983 Chairman Frank Stronach was supported at the senior leadership level by President and Chief Operating Officer Manfred Gingl.

In early 1984 Magna International announced plans to build a metal stamping plant in the United States. Located near Baltimore, Maryland, the purpose of the facility was to support a large General Motors minivan plant that was located nearby. Plans were finalized for another automotive parts stamping facility, in Milton, Ontario, in late 1985. That year, sales mushroomed to $451.1 million, up from $322.5 million in 1984.

Magna International's physical expansion continued into the 1980s and by 1987 Magna International had more than 80 plants located throughout North America. Other examples of new facilities included two factories in Nova Scotia, as well as a new plant in Bracebridge, Ontario.

Several noteworthy developments occurred in 1987. First, Magna International developed a concept vehicle named Torrero. In addition, the company's divisions were restructured into Automotive Systems Operating Groups. In order to supply engine and transmission components and systems, Magna International established the Tesma Group in 1988. The company's sales continued to skyrocket throughout the remainder of the decade. After reaching $653.3 million in 1986, sales climbed to $784.1 million in 1987 and $980 million in 1988. Magna International capped off the decade with sales of $1.2 billion.

INTERNATIONAL EXPANSION BEGINS

Magna International ushered in the 1990s with 125 plants located throughout North America, West Germany, and Austria. After selling a 50 percent stake in its four European manufacturing plants in January, the company's interest in DDM Plastics was sold the following month, followed by its stake in Lemmerz Industries midway through the year. Finally, Siemens Automotive acquired Magna International's MACI divisions in August 1990.

Sales were relatively flat during the early 1990s, inching up to $1.3 billion in 1991, $1.6 billion in 1992, and $1.9 billion in 1993. By December of that year preparations were under way to construct a new stamping plant in Moonville, South Carolina, in order to supply automotive body components for the first American-made BMWs.

KEY DATES

1957: Frank Stronach starts a one-man tool and die business called Multimatic Investments Ltd.

1960: General Motors awards Multimatic its first auto parts contract.

1969: Multimatic merges with Magna Electronics Corporation Ltd.

1973: Magna Electronics adopts the name Magna International Inc.

1989: Sales reach $1.2 billion.

1996: Stronach is inducted into the Canadian Business Hall of Fame.

1999: Magna International is named as the world's leading auto parts company by *Forbes* magazine.

2008: The company focuses heavily on emerging regions such as Eastern Europe and Asia.

2009: A new $108.7 million factory is planned in St. Petersburg, Russia.

Several noteworthy acquisitions occurred in 1994. In addition to parting with $52.7 million for a 60 percent stake in KS Automobile-Sicherheitstechnik GmbH, Magna International spent $14 million for 74 percent of Porsche Austria's Zipperle business. In December the company announced that it had been selected by one of the leading automotive manufacturers in the United States to build a custom vehicle, which would be rolled out during the latter part of the decade. Annual sales continued to climb, reaching $2.5 billion.

A number of important deals unfolded during the mid-1990s. During this time period Magna International acquired or increased its ownership of several companies and sold off others. For example, in 1995 the company spent $32.4 million for a 25.1 percent stake in Temic Bayern-Chemie Airbag GmbH. That same year, Magna International finalized the spinoff of its engine, transmission, and fuel systems arm, Tesma International Inc.

Founder Frank Stronach was inducted into the Canadian Business Hall of Fame in 1996. Several large deals unfolded that year. The $110 million acquisition of Marley Automotive Components Group occurred in April. Three months later, Magna International paid $28.9 million for the assets and operations of Pebra GmbH Paul Braun. A $135 million deal for the Farmington Hills, Michigan-based automotive seating systems

manufacturer Douglas & Lomason Co. followed in August.

Activity heated up considerably in December, at which time Magna International snapped up United Kingdom-based Caradon Rolinex plc for approximately $32 million. In addition, an 80 percent stake in both Temic Bayern-Chemie Airbag GmbH and MST Automotive GmbH Automobil-Sicherheitstechnik was sold to TRW Inc. for $418 million.

INTERNATIONAL EXPANSION CONTINUES

Magna International's sales soared to $5 billion in 1997, up from $3.8 billion the previous year. The company's Cosma business received what at the time was one of the largest contracts in industry history when it was chosen by General Motors to supply sport-utility vehicle and full-size pickup truck sub-frames. The deals that Magna International made in 1997 included the acquisition of Tricom Group Holdings Ltd. for $70.7 million and Georg Naher GmbH for $49.2 million. Following those transactions, the company snapped up YMOS Automotive Group for $145.2 million in cash during the latter part of the year.

In 1998 the University of Michigan presented its Entrepreneur of the Year Award to Frank Stronach. Some 40 years after starting his one-man tool and die business, Stronach had seen his enterprise grow into a company with 155 locations that were powered by a 49,000-member workforce. Magna International continued to expand the size of its corporate family throughout 1998. Early in the year, Rolta Morse S.p.A. was acquired for $42.9 million in cash. Around the same time, the company spent $25.5 million to acquire Paulisch GmbH & Co.

Midway through the year, TRIAM Automotive Inc. was obtained in a deal worth $77.3 million. Magna International then spent $380 million to acquire 94 percent of the automotive technology and engineering firm Steyr-Daimler-Puch AG, as well as a 50 percent stake in Steyr-Daimler-Puch Fahrzeugtechnik AG & Co. Full ownership of the former company was secured by the end of the year, for an additional $17 million. Magna International's sales climbed to $6 billion in 1998, at which time the company changed its fiscal year-end to December 31.

Several key developments marked the end of the 1990s. In 1999, what eventually became known as Magna Entertainment Corporation was formed, allowing the company to separate its automotive and non-automotive operations. Don Walker served as Magna International's CEO, and Frank Stronach continued to lead the company as chairman. That year, Magna International was named as the world's leading auto parts company by *Forbes* magazine. The company ended the decade with sales of $9.3 billion.

MAGNA INTERNATIONAL IN THE 21ST CENTURY

Magna International ushered in the new millennium by selling its 50 percent interest in Webasto Sunroofs Inc. to joint venture partner Webasto AG. In addition, Stronach received the Entrepreneur of the Year Lifetime Achievement Award from Ernst & Young. A new business named Magna Steyr was formed in March 2001 to develop concept and niche vehicles. That same year, Magna International also spun off its Intier Automotive Inc. business. Sales continue to climb, reaching $12.4 billion.

In 2002 Magna International acquired Chrysler's Austrian Eurostar factory in Graz, Austria, where 2,000 workers were engaged in production of the PT Cruiser and the Voyager minivan. Another major deal that year occurred in October, when the company spent $287 million to acquire Donnelly Corp., the automotive industry's second largest mirror supplier. Magna International furthered its global expansion in 2003, when it established a customer support center in Tokyo, Japan. Satellite offices also were planned in other areas of Japan, in order to better support business relationships with manufacturers such as Toyota.

In early 2004 Magna International's Tesma International business spent about $75 million to acquire Davis Industries. In September of that year, the company forged a deal to acquire DaimlerChrysler Corp.'s New Venture Gear Inc. business for about $431 million. Sales increased to $20.7 billion, up from $15.3 billion in 2003.

After taking several of its subsidiaries public during the previous decade, Magna International announced plans to make them private operations once again. In 2005, Intier Automotive Inc., Decoma International Inc., and Tesma International Inc. ceased trading as public companies.

Growth continued in 2006, when Magna International struck a $232 million deal to acquire CTS Fahrzeug-Dachsysteme GmbH from Porsche AG. During the latter part of the year, the company teamed up with Russia-based GAZ Group, a company owned by billionaire Oleg Deripaska, and forged a strategic alliance that would enable it to tap into the burgeoning Russian auto market.

Magna International's ties to Russia were strengthened in mid-2007, when Deripaska's Russian Machines

business agreed to acquire 20 million shares of the company for approximately $1.54 billion. The stock sale to Russian Machines was completed in September. Magna International used approximately $1.1 billion of the proceeds to buy back 11.9 million shares of its stock. The company rounded out 2007 with profits of $663 million on annual sales of $26.06 billion.

Growth continued into 2008, as Magna International moved forward with plans to construct 16 facilities in emerging regions such as Eastern Europe and Asia. In March, the company revealed plans for three new assembly plants in Mexico, which were expected to come online by 2010. In August, the acquisition of the Russian plastics components manufacturer Technoplast was announced.

Dire economic conditions were impacting industries worldwide by late 2008. In October, Oleg Deripaska divested his 20 percent stake in Magna International, which was provided to his creditors. Despite the difficult economic climate, Magna International continued to expand. Also in October, the company's Magna Electronics business acquired Rochester Hills, Michigan-based BluWav Systems, a developer of electric and energy-management systems for the hybrid vehicle market.

Heading into 2009, Magna International remained devoted to Russia's automotive industry. Despite difficult conditions there, the company announced plans to build a new factory in St. Petersburg. With construction costs estimated at $108.7 million, the facility was slated for completion in 2010, and was expected to come online in 2011.

Paul R. Greenland

PRINCIPAL SUBSIDIARIES

Cosma America Holdings Inc. (USA); Cosma International of America Inc. (USA); Decoma International Corp.; Decoma U.S. Holdings Inc. (USA); Intier Automotive Inc.; Intier Automotive of America Inc. (USA); Magna Automotive Holding AG (Austria); Magna Donnelly Corporation (USA); Magna International Automotive Holding AG (Austria); Magna International Investments S.A. (Luxembourg); Magna Powertrain AG & Co. KG (Austria); Magna Powertrain Inc.; Magna Powertrain USA Inc. (USA); Magna Steyr AG & Co. KG (Austria); Magna Steyr Fahrzeugtechnik AG & Co. KG (Austria); Magna Steyr Metalforming AG (Austria); Magna Structural Systems Inc.; Magna US Holding Inc. (USA); New Magna Investments S.A. (Belgium).

PRINCIPAL COMPETITORS

Dana Holding Corporation; Lear Corporation; Robert Bosch GmbH.

FURTHER READING

Cohn, Lynne M., "Magna Likes Nafta Opportunities in Mexico; Shareholders Told Exporting a Very Welcome Option," *American Metal Market,* December 7, 1993.

Keenan, Greg, "Magna Reverses Strategy, Plans to Take Parts Subsidiaries Private," *Globe & Mail* (Toronto, Canada), October 26, 2004.

Kryhul, Angela, and Lauri Giesen, "Magna Int'l Pumping Big Money into Building, Equipping New Plants," *American Metal Market,* May 12, 1986.

"Magna Increases Presence in Japan with New Center," *AsiaPulse News,* October 24, 2003.

"Market Perspective: Magna Plans Restructuring, Stock Split," *Globe & Mail* (Toronto, Canada), October 24, 1978.

"Russia: Magna Plans New Factories," *just-auto.com,* December 18, 2008.

Sherefkin, Robert, "Magna Says It Has Capability to Build Complete Vehicle," *Automotive News,* March 12, 2001.

MEDICINE SHOPPE INTERNATIONAL, INC.
a Cardinal Health company

Medicine Shoppe International, Inc.

——————————■——————————

1 Rider Trail Plaza Drive, Suite 300
Earth City, Missouri 63045-1313
U.S.A.
Telephone: (314) 993-6000
Toll Free: (800) 325-1397
Fax: (314) 872-5500
Web site: http://www.medshoppe.com

Wholly Owned Subsidiary of Cardinal Health Inc.
Incorporated: 1971
Employees: 400
Sales: $22.7 million (2008 est.)
NAICS: 533110 Owners and Lessors of Other Non-
　　Financial Assets

■ ■ ■

Maintaining its headquarters in the St. Louis suburb of Earth City, Missouri, Medicine Shoppe International, Inc. (MSI), is a subsidiary of Cardinal Health, Inc., franchising independent, community pharmacies under the Medicine Shoppe and Medicap Pharmacy banners. All told, the MSI chains include more than 850 stores in the United States and more than 400 pharmacies in other countries, including Canada, China, Japan, Indonesia, and in the Middle East. Unlike typical drugstore chains, Medicine Shoppe and Medicap Pharmacy shy away from typical front-of-store merchandise, focusing solely on pharmacy operations and services. As a result, the stores are much smaller than their major competitors. Some of the pharmacies also act as "Specialized Care Centers," focusing on

customized medications, suited for individual needs; specialized pharmacy offerings, including prescriptions to treat complex conditions, including HIV/AIDS, infertility, organ transplants, and cancer; immunizations and vaccines; diabetes screening, counseling, and treatment; and long term care, primarily serving the needs of people in nursing homes and assisted living facilities.

MEDICINE SHOPPE CONCEPT
CREATED

Medicine Shoppe took shape in the 1960s, developed by pharmacist Michael Busch. He was born in St. Louis in 1936, and after attending the University of Georgia, Busch completed his degree in pharmacy at St. Louis University in 1958. In the mid-1960s he opened a pharmacy in Belleville, Illinois, under the Medic Pharmacy name, followed by a second store a few years later. As would be the case with Medicine Shoppe, Busch's stores focused on the pharmacy, making a point not to carry chewing gum, candy, batteries, and other front-of-store merchandise. In his first radio ads, in fact, Busch billed Medic Pharmacy as the "non-drugstore." He came to believe there was an opening in the marketplace for a chain of such pharmacy-only stores, and in 1968 he began developing a business plan for Medicine Shoppe.

Busch's accountant, who helped with the financial projections used in the plan, introduced him to potential investors, and as a result Busch took on three partners. They were Joe Deutsch, who was involved in real estate, and two doctors, Mitchell Yanow and Ira Gall. Obstetricians and gynecologists, Yanow and Gall had established a joint practice in St. Louis in 1957. They would then form one of the state's first physician corporations. According to a 1985 article in *Forbes,* they "invested in a dozen drugstores as a tax shelter. The investment started making money and the doctors realized they had a concept on their hands. A consultant told them to franchise like everybody else in those days."

Busch's role was not mentioned in this rendition of the origins of Medicine Shoppe, although he would be in other news accounts over the years. Yanow died in 1998 and Gall in 2005. In a 2009 interview, Busch maintained that Yanow and Gall were investors who held seats on the board of directors but did not have day-to-day responsibilities, albeit Yanow served as chairman from 1970 until 1995. Busch, on the other hand, served as chief executive officer, and played the key role in the opening of the first 12 company-owned Medicine Shoppe stores in the first half of 1969. They were located in Peoria, Illinois; Nashville, Tennessee; and the Quad Cities of Moline and Rock Island, Illinois, and Bettendorf and Davenport, Iowa. Busch also insisted that it was his idea to franchise the Medicine Shoppe concept, he had sought out the consultant, and that he had to convince the board to pursue the idea. The first franchised store then opened in 1971, and the company changed its name to Medicine Shoppe International, Inc.

GOING PUBLIC

Busch served as CEO until 1974, when he left to pursue other business interests, giving up his career in pharmacy to become a serial entrepreneur. During his days as Medicine Shoppe's CEO, Busch had lectured widely about his business experience, appearing at such schools as the University of Iowa, Purdue University, Stanford University, and the University of Oklahoma. After leaving Medicine Shoppe, Busch started new businesses, including the Wharton Capital consulting firm, as well as running established concerns, including a tire

company, the non-food divisions of a grocery conglomerate, and the Naked Furniture franchise chain. He also continued to lecture to college audiences and business groups, often detailing the Medicine Shoppe success story.

In the same year that Busch left MSI, the Medicine Shoppe brand of nonprescription products was introduced. According to Busch, he was replaced as CEO by a man named Stan Burton. During his tenure, MSI in 1976 first began offering screening programs, starting with blood pressure checks. Following Burton's death, Jerome F. Sheldon became CEO in March 1980. Recruited the previous year, Sheldon was a law and business school graduate who had been an executive at TRW Inc.

In fiscal 1982 MSI topped the $100 million mark in annual sales for the first time in its history. On the strength of this performance, Sheldon took MSI public in 1983 at $12.50 a share, raising $11 million. The company put some of those funds to use fueling growth by offering financing to druggists looking to go into business for themselves. In fiscal 1984 sales reached $170 million and by early 1985 the number of franchised stores exceeded 500, located in 46 states, many of them the result of independent pharmacies converting to the Medicine Shoppe brand. To help the individual stores enjoy some of the benefits that came with being part of a chain, MSI in 1988 introduced Medicine Shoppe InterNet, Inc., a third-party marketing subsidiary that gave participating stores access to managed care plans. While still not embracing front-end merchandise, MSI did begin to focus on front-end sales by creating specialized departments to offer products to help customers with such conditions as diabetes and arthritis.

After ten years at the helm, Sheldon stepped down as CEO in May 1990. He was replaced by Chief Financial Officer David Abrahamson, who took over a chain of 835 stores, generating annual retail sales of more than $450 million, an amount that would grow to $516 million in fiscal 1990. For the previous ten years, in fact, MSI had enjoyed a 25 percent annual compound growth in earnings. Abrahamson had been with the company since 1985 when he was named CFO. In 1989 he added the title of senior vice-president of corporate services, adding marketing and human resources management responsibilities.

INTERNATIONAL EXPANSION

MSI aired its first national television commercials in 1991 to promote the Medicine Shoppe brand, part of a marketing campaign that had been in development for

KEY DATES

1969: First Medicine Shoppe stores open in Tennessee, Illinois, and Iowa.

1971: Company incorporates as Medicine Shoppe International, Inc. (MSI), and begins franchising.

1974: Founder Michael Busch steps downs as chief executive to pursue other business interests.

1983: Company is taken public.

1988: Medicine Shoppe InterNet, Inc., is introduced.

1991: International expansion effort begins.

1995: Cardinal Health, Inc., acquires Medicine Shoppe.

2003: Medicap Pharmacies Inc. is acquired.

several years. Aimed at women from 35 to 64 years of age, the ads played on the theme, "What a pharmacy is meant to be." The company also began looking at international expansion in 1991. A pair of agreements were reached, one with a Canadian investor group to open Medicine Shoppe stores in Canada, and another with Pro Healthcare International Co., Ltd., of Taiwan to serve as franchiser in the Republic of China and open stores in Taipei.

The early 1990s also brought new programs to help drive the business of franchisees. In 1992 a sampling promotion program targeting consumers over 50 years old was introduced under the Prime Time name, involving gift packs that included free sample products and coupons. In fiscal 1993 the Medicine Shoppe InterNet program strengthened its marketing efforts to grow franchisees' managed healthcare business. MSI also looked to open stores in nontraditional locations. In 1994, for example, it forged an agreement with Fiesta Mart Stores to add Medicine Shoppe pharmacies in several Houston, Texas–area grocery stores. Because Medicine Shoppe did not compete with supermarkets on health and beauty aids, focusing exclusively on prescriptions, its format was a natural fit for supermarkets looking to add a pharmacy for the convenience of their shoppers.

MSI continued to expand its international footprint in the mid-1990s. A master license agreement in Malaysia was signed, leading to the opening of 16 stores in that country and plans to expand into Singapore. By the fall of 1994 there were more than 80 Medicine Shoppe outlets operating outside the United States,

Taiwan the most represented country with 49 stores. At that same time the first units were also opened in Mexico. In the United States, MSI looked to bring more independent pharmacies into the fold with the introduction of the Conversion 2000 program in 1995, allowing independent pharmacies to join the Medicine Shoppe family for a modest initial investment of $2,000.

CARDINAL HEALTH ACQUIRES MEDICINE SHOPPE

In August 1991 MSI agreed to be sold to Cardinal Health, Inc., in a $348 million stock swap, a deal that would align one of the largest drug wholesalers in the United States with one of the largest retail pharmacy franchise operations. At the time, the Medicine Shoppe chain totaled 987 domestic franchised stores and 109 international units, resulting in systemwide sales of $923 million. For Cardinal, the deal was part of its transformation from a regional wholesaler to a major national pharmaceutical supplier. The acquisition was also a move that allowed Cardinal to grow beyond basic drug wholesaling, providing it with the ability to offer comprehensive prescription information services and value-added products through Medicine Shoppe's retail operations. Underlying this idea was the belief that the healthcare delivery system neglected to take advantage of the abilities of pharmacists. Abrahamson told the press, "We want to develop services and programs that more fully utilize the pharmacist's knowledge. These can be things as standard as monitoring drug compliance and delivering cognitive services." While MSI looked to make use of Cardinal's deep pockets to finance further growth, Cardinal hoped to take advantage of the retailer's deep drug utilization database.

After the transaction between MSI and Cardinal was completed in late 1995 (and Yanow stepped down as chairman after 25 years), MSI began advancing on a number of fronts. In 1996 a Disease Management Training Program was introduced, and the Medicine Shoppe Connect System began to be rolled out to stores. It connected them to corporate databases to provide help with a number of functions that would be added along the way, including accounting, purchasing, inventory management, prescription claims management, as well as help with disease management programs. The year 1996 was also noteworthy because for the first time systemwide sales surpassed the $1 billion mark, an amount that would increase to $1.22 billion a year later when the chain numbered 1,250 units.

MSI also eyed such new markets as Egypt, Europe, Japan, and Puerto Rico. In December 1998 MSI entered India with the opening of a franchise in Mumbai (Bombay). Also during the second half of the 1990s,

MSI forged fruitful relationships with other healthcare and pharmaceutical companies. In 1997 the company's Kansas and Missouri pharmacists worked with CIGNA HealthCare on a Disease Management Demonstration Project. At the end of the decade MSI launched targeted health event marketing programs in conjunction with pharmaceutical companies, such as the 1999 disease management pilot program initiated with Merck-Medco Managed Care to evaluate patients in Kentucky and Ohio with stomach conditions or gastrointestinal disorders and encourage them to pursue treatment.

MEDICINE SHOPPE IN THE 21ST CENTURY

Like his predecessor, Abrahamson resigned as CEO after serving ten years, in June 2000 turning over the reins to Thomas Slagle, the company's executive vice-president of franchise development. Slagle had come to MSI through Cardinal, where he had been a regional president. He took over a company that by year's end numbered 1,320 stores in 47 states and nine foreign countries, combining for retail sales of $1.89 billion. His tenure was brief, however. In August 2001 he was assigned to head another Cardinal subsidiary and Mark Parrish then oversaw MSI as chief executive of Cardinal's Pharmaceutical Distribution and Provider Services. Parrish named Bob Storch as MSI's president to take day-to-day responsibility but stepped in on a temporary basis after Storch resigned in October 2003. In early 2004 some stability returned to the top ranks when Terry Burnside was named president. Hired a short time before to be vice-president of marketing, Burnside had previously served as chief operating officer for Long's Drug, and also had experience with Bill's Drugs, McKesson Corp, and Alpha Beta Co.

Although Medicine Shoppe appeared to have been a good investment for Cardinal, there were rumors in 2003 that the wholesaler was on the verge of selling the business. Such speculation was put to rest later in the year, however, when Cardinal through MSI acquired Medicap Pharmacies Inc., a West Des Moines, Iowa-based pharmacy chain with 181 stores in 34 states, generating annual retail sales of $350 million. Medicap was founded in Des Moines in 1971 with a single retail store under the Medicine Chest name that would serve as a prototype for the Medicap chain. Franchising of the concept began in 1973. With the Medicap brand well established in its markets after 30 years, MSI elected to operate Medicap as a separate format with its own marketing group. Other operations, however, were integrated with MSI.

Systemwide retail sales were then in the $2.5 billion range, drawn from more than 1,400 stores. In the fall of 2007 the company began an international push, focusing on the Middle East, with stores opening in Dubai and the United Arab Emirates through a master franchise agreement signed with the Al Zahrawi Group in Dubai. While MSI continued to enjoy steady growth, changes took place at Cardinal in 2008, when plans were announced to cut 600 jobs and reorganize the business into two main segments. Once again, the press speculated that MSI might be put on the block, possibly fetching as much as $1 billion for Cardinal. During the early months of 2009 there were no indications that a sale of MSI was imminent, but in any event MSI continued to enjoy bright prospects for the future.

Ed Dinger

PRINCIPAL SUBSIDIARIES

Medicap Pharmacies Inc.

PRINCIPAL COMPETITORS

CVS Caremark Corporation; Rite Aid Corporation; Walgreen Co.

FURTHER READING

Brookman, Faye, "Medicine Shoppe Adopts a New Expansion Strategy," *Drug Topics,* June 3, 1991, p. 60.

"Cardinal Health Will Consolidate," *St. Louis Post-Dispatch,* July 9, 2008, p. C3.

"Expansion Continues at Medicine Shoppe," *Chain Drug Review,* April 20, 1992, p. 118.

Levy, Sandra, "Is Medicine Shoppe Sale in the Offing?" *Drug Topics,* June 16, 2003, p. 18.

———, "Medicine Shoppe to Acquire Medicap Pharmacies," *Drug Topics,* January 12, 2004, p. 76.

"Medicine Shoppe Airs First TV Ad Nationally," *Chain Drug Review,* November 18, 1991, p. 1.

"Medicine Shoppe Keeps 'Pushing the Envelope,'" *Chain Drug Review,* August 30, 2004, p. 87.

"Medicine Shoppe Retail Sales Thriving," *Drug Store News,* April 9, 1990, p. 95.

"MSI Helps Retail Pharmacists Take Control of Their Destiny," *Chain Drug Review,* April 23, 2001, p. 149.

"MSI Model Puts Focus on Personalized Patient Care," *Chain Drug Review,* November 10, 2008, p. 64.

Narisetti, Raju, "Cardinal Health Agrees to Buy Medicine Shoppe in Stock Swap," *Wall Street Journal,* August 29, 1995, p. B4.

Slutsker, Gary, "Attention, Druggists! Jerry Sheldon Puts Young Pharmacists in Business," *Forbes,* February 25, 1985, p. 90.

Stewart, Al, "Cardinal Agrees to Buy Medicine Shoppe," *Chain Drug Review,* September 11, 1995, p. 1.

Troy, Mike, "Cardinal, Medicine Shoppe Deal May Bode Well for Pharmacists, but Raises Questions," *Drug Store News,* September 18, 1995, p. 3.

————, "Medicine Shoppe Ties Success to Satisfied Customers," *Drug Store News,* May 1, 1995, p. 78.

The Merchants Company

1100 Edwards Street
Hattiesburg, Mississippi 39403
U.S.A.
Telephone: (601) 583-4351
Fax: (601) 582-5333
Web site: http://www.themerchantscompany.com

Private Company
Incorporated: 1904 as Fain Grocery Company
Employees: 420
Sales: $224.7 million (2007 est.)
NAICS: 722310 Food Service Contractors

■ ■ ■

Through its Merchants Foodservice division, The Merchants Company, based in Hattiesburg, Mississippi, is a leading foodservice distributor, operating in eight southeastern states. By sales volume, Merchants is one of the nation's leading distributors, ranking 19th among approximately 2,600 companies within its industry segment. The company is part of a member-owned purchasing and marketing cooperative named The Frosty Acres Brands Inc., which offers products under the Frosty Acres brand and many others.

The customer base for Merchants includes more than 5,000 hospitals, institutions, restaurants, and schools. Each week, Merchants delivers approximately 220,000 cases of food products, which are part of about 6,000 orders. The company handles this large volume efficiently via the use of technology, including computer systems that are used to communicate with its salespeople, customers, and vendors.

Merchants is owned by a family-owned holding company named Tatum Development Corp. The Tatums settled in south Mississippi in 1890, and family member W. S. F. Tatum was one of Hattiesburg's first mayors. The company found early success within the lumber industry, in which it operated until 1937, before becoming involved in natural gas distribution. Prior to obtaining full ownership of Merchants in 1988, the Tatums were part owners of the company.

FORMATIVE YEARS

The roots of Merchants can be traced to February 11, 1904, when the Fain Grocery Co. was formed in Hattiesburg, Mississippi, by a group of seven individuals. Operations were initially based in the former First Baptist Church, which was located near the railroad. With a small workforce of ten people and two horse-drawn wagons, the company embarked upon a steady pace of growth. Fain Grocery adopted a new name in 1907, three years after its formation, becoming The Merchants Grocery Co. That same year, construction began on a two-story brick warehouse on East Pine Street in Hattiesburg.

Merchants Grocery's new Hattiesburg warehouse, which cost roughly $30,000, was part of an aggressive physical expansion initiative. This involved the addition of a corn meal mill at that site in 1915, followed by a grain elevator and feed mill two years later. A steady stream of progress continued during the 1920s. Merchants ushered in the decade with a new

Hattiesburg-based cold storage facility in 1920, which was devoted to fresh fruit and vegetables. Three years later, in 1923, the company generated annual sales of $1 million for the first time.

Merchants erected a new Laurel, Mississippi-based feed manufacturing plant in 1924, and in 1927 the company began blending flour at that facility. In August 1926, Merchants held its first company picnic. Despite the summer weather, men in attendance wore long-sleeved shirts and neckties, while many women sported flapper-style hats. Another name change occurred in 1927, when The Merchants Grocery Co. abbreviated its nameplate, becoming The Merchants Co.

The supermarket industry began to evolve in the 1930s. At this time food distribution began to become more automated and streamlined at the wholesaler level. This was part of an effort to increase efficiency and reduce costs. At Merchants, this evolution took the form of a new Hattiesburg-based packinghouse, which was devoted to the sale of both fresh and frozen meat. During its first year, the operation generated sales of $295,000.

STEADY EXPANSION

Merchants continued to expand during the mid-1930s. In 1935, a feed mill was acquired in Gowdy, Mississippi. When that operation was destroyed by fire in 1945, it was replaced with a new grain elevator and feed mill. In 1946, an employee named Johnnie Mason joined the company as a warehouse worker, marking the beginning of a long career that finally ended with his retirement in 1992. During his tenure with Merchants, Mason benefited the company with his remarkable memory. Described as a human computer by one former colleague, Mason was known for committing much of the company's inventory, which included approximately 4,000 different items, to memory.

Merchants kicked off the 1950s by moving its grain operations to the town of Vicksburg, Mississippi, which afforded easy access to barges on the Mississippi River. Two years later, Ralston Purina acquired the Merchants plant in Jackson, Mississippi. Another noteworthy

development during the early 1950s was Merchants' formation of Central Packing Co. in 1951, which was made possible by the acquisition of a meat processing facility in the company's hometown of Hattiesburg.

An important personnel addition took place in 1956, when future CEO Donald W. Suber joined Merchants as a counter salesman in the town of Gulfport. After becoming acclimated with the company throughout the rest of the decade, Suber quickly climbed the company ladder. Merchants ended the 1950s by establishing an integrated poultry business in Hattiesburg named Forrest Farms, which it eventually sold. More change unfolded during the early 1960s, when the company's Central Packing Co. operation was replaced by a new operation named Pine Burr Packing Co. in 1961.

Donald Suber's career advancement was well under way by this time. In 1962, at the age of 26, he was named manager of Merchants' Gulfport warehouse. Six years later, his career took him to Hattiesburg, where he became general manager of the entire grocery division. Merchants continued to serve the grocery industry throughout the 1970s, and by 1979 Suber had been named the division's vice-president. While advancing his career, Suber had his finger on the pulse of the food industry. By the early 1980s it was clear to him that Merchants had to evolve in order to find continued success in the decades ahead. Specifically, the company needed to prepare itself for operations in a climate where small community grocery stores were being acquired by larger chains, and more people were eating out instead of preparing meals at home.

BEYOND GROCERIES

In 1982, Merchants decided to broaden its focus beyond the grocery trade and become a full-line foodservice distributor. The company's transformation was marked by a number of significant developments that year. In addition to shuttering its Pine Burr Packing Co. business, Merchants sold its grain elevators and streamlined its network of distribution centers from seven facilities to two. The company capped off the year with foodservice sales of about $10 million.

Midway through 1983, Merchants established its relationship with the food cooperative Frosty Acres. Donald Suber played a key role in developing the association between the two organizations, and would serve as chairman of Frosty Acres for 13 years. Donald Suber was named president of Merchants in 1987. Over the course of the next two decades, his impact on both the company and the community of Hattiesburg was substantial. This was due in part to his leadership skills.

In an article by Lynn Lofton, which appeared in the October 16, 2006, issue of the *Mississippi Business Journal,* Suber offered some insight into his leadership style. Explaining that he rose through the ranks "by the sweat of the brow," Suber said: "Everyone is a member of the 'Big M' family. I could call each employee by name until recently and I was involved with their lives. My approach has been different because I came through all facets of the company. I worked in the warehouse and on up when everything was done manually."

Progress continued at Merchants into the early 1990s. In 1992 the company entered the ranks of the nation's 50 leading broad-line food distributors for the first time, registering sales of $75.5 million. The following year, Merchants served a territory that spanned a 250-mile radius around the Mississippi towns of Hattiesburg and Jackson, and recorded sales of approximately $84 million. By this time, Donald Suber had assumed the additional role of chief operating officer.

CONTINUED GROWTH AND EXPANSION

Midway through 1993, Merchants was one of three distributors to receive a regional, two-year contract to serve Mississippi schools through a new state cooperative food procurement program, the largest statewide program of its kind nationwide to date. The deal meant an additional $15 million in annual revenue for Merchants.

Merchants continued on a path of progress heading into the mid-1990s. A new distribution center was acquired in 1994. By 1995, the company offered its customers some 6,000 different items, up from about 4,000 items in 1993. At this time, some 40 percent of Merchants' sales came from non-commercial customers, with the majority of that total coming from schools. In order to better serve the company's 8,000 accounts, Merchants began equipping some of its staff with laptop computers.

In March 1995, Merchants completed the expansion of its warehouse in Jackson, Mississippi, and transferred the operations of its Hattiesburg facility there. The Jackson site handled about 80 percent of Merchants' volume, with the remainder moving through the company's warehouse in Montgomery, Alabama. Merchants ended the year with sales of $93 million.

Major challenges for Merchants during the mid-1990s included competing with larger industry players like SYSCO Corp. In addition, the company worked hard to change the perception that it was a small-time grocery industry distributor. In fact, Merchants was able to offer anything its national competitors could through its membership in the Frosty Acres cooperative. Even so, the fact that Merchants was locally owned sometimes worked to its advantage, because smaller size meant greater flexibility.

Merchants' annual sales reached the $100 million mark in 1997, up more than 10 percent from the previous year due to growing business with multi-unit customers, especially fast-food restaurants. That year, a new development was the addition of fresh produce, milk, and dairy products to the company's product range.

REGIONAL LEADER IN THE 21ST CENTURY

Donald Suber was named president and CEO in 1998, and remained at the company's helm as it entered the new millennium. By 2001 Merchants had become the exclusive food supplier to all military bases in both Louisiana and Mississippi. In addition, the company also had restocked ships such as the USS *Cole,* USS *Iwo Jima,* USS *Yorktown,* USS *Ticonderoga,* USS *Grove,* USS *Gates,* and USS *Bulkeley.*

On the new customer front, Merchants furthered its expansion into the chain restaurant business in 2002. That year the company began serving customers such as Dairy Queen, TCBY, KFC, Bumpers, and others. In November, Merchants spent $8 million to acquire what once had been the Jitney Jungle Perishable Foods Warehouse in Jackson, Mississippi. Plans were made to expand the facility by 60,000 square feet, providing space for 50 new employees. The expansion was completed in mid-2003, resulting in a facility that spanned approximately 225,000 square feet.

In 2004 Merchants celebrated its 100th anniversary with a party at the Lake Terrace Convention Center. By this time, the company's workforce had grown to include 400 employees, and sales totaled approximately $200 million, up from about $150 million in 2003. The company served some 5,000 different customers with about 60 sales people and a fleet of 175 vehicles.

In early 2005, Executive Vice-President and Treasurer Andrew B. Mercier succeeded Donald Suber as president. At this time, Suber was named vice-chairman and CEO. Merchants' sales increased to about $250 million in 2005. Also that year, the company provided water, ice, and food to National Guard units, Red Cross workers, and military personnel during Hurricanes Katrina and Rita.

Donald Suber retired from Merchants in 2006, capping off a 50-year career with the company. Following his retirement, Mercier was named president and CEO. Mercier was at the company's helm when it pursued its first acquisition in November 2007, when it agreed to acquire the food service distribution business of Newberry, South Carolina-based Thomas & Howard Co. Inc. The deal strengthened Merchants' convenience store business, and made the company a stronger regional player in the Southeast.

By 2008 Merchants served a territory that spanned eight states in the Southeast. The company's base of approximately 5,000 customers received products from its locations in Jackson, Mississippi; Clanton, Alabama; and Newberry, South Carolina. Looking forward, Merchants appeared to be well positioned for continued growth.

Paul R. Greenland

PRINCIPAL COMPETITORS

Performance Food Group Co.; SYSCO Corporation; U.S. Foodservice Inc.

FURTHER READING

Gillette, Becky, "Tenacity, Timing Keys to Success for Tatum Development," *Mississippi Business Journal,* November 8, 1999.

Lofton, Lynn, "After 100 Years, Merchants Foodservice Still Changing," *Mississippi Business Journal,* October 16, 2006.

———, "Don Suber Completes 50-Year Career with Merchants," *Mississippi Business Journal,* October 16, 2006.

McNeill, George, "At Century Mark, Merchants Celebrates Number of Milestones," *Mississippi Business Journal,* October 25, 2004.

———, "The Merchants Company Closes In on 100-Year Milestone," *Mississippi Business Journal,* October 6, 2003.

Walters, Kevin, "Merchants on Sales High After 100 Years," *Associated Press State & Local Wire,* September 27, 2004.

Merial Ltd.

3239 Satellite Boulevard
Building 500
Duluth, Georgia 30096-4640
U.S.A.
Telephone: (678) 638-3000
Fax: (888) 637-4251
Web site: http://www.merial.com

Joint Venture of Merck & Co. and Sanofi-Aventis
Incorporated: 1997
Employees: 5,400
Sales: $2.6 billion (2008)
NAICS: 325412 Pharmaceutical Preparation Manufacturing; 325413 In-Vitro Diagnostic Substance Manufacturing; 325414 Biological Product (Except Diagnostic) Manufacturing

■ ■ ■

Merial Ltd. is the U.K.-registered, U.S.-based global leader in animal health care. Merial develops and produces pharmaceutical products, including medicines and vaccines, for pets, livestock, and wildlife. The company operations span the full range of animal diseases and conditions, and Merial's product portfolio includes anesthetic, antibiotic, antiparasitic, cardiovascular, gastrointestinal, and respiratory treatments. The company is also a leading developer and producer of animal vaccines, including vaccines for the prevention of avian flu, Marek's disease, and Newcastle disease. Merial's major branded products include top sellers such as Frontline, a tick and flea treatment for domestic pets; Heartgard, a heartworm preventive; Ivomec, an antiparasitic for cattle, sheep and swine; and Raboral, a rabies vaccine.

While the company's headquarters is in Duluth, Georgia, Merial operates at the global level, with sales reaching 150 countries backed by a network of more than 30 subsidiaries, including in the United Kingdom, France, Australia, New Zealand, Argentina, Germany, Taiwan, Japan, Thailand, Singapore, China, Russia, and Mexico. Together, the group's operations generated sales of $2.6 billion in 2008. Merial is a joint venture between Merck & Co. in the United States and Sanofi-Aventis in France. José Barella is the company's executive chairman.

NINETEENTH-CENTURY ORIGINS

Animal health played a prominent role in the development of the modern pharmaceuticals industry. In some instances, research in the animal health field provided a number of modern medicine's most important breakthroughs. Throughout most of the 20th century, the world's major pharmaceuticals companies were active in both the human and animal fields. Into the 21st century, however, the pharmaceuticals industry developed a more specialized business model, resulting in the creation of a number of companies focused wholly on animal health care. Among this new breed of company was Merial Ltd., created as a joint venture in 1997 through the merger of the animal health operations of France's Rhône-Poulenc (later Sanofi-Aventis) and Merck & Co., based in the United States.

Rhône-Poulenc's contribution to the merger was its Rhône Mérieux subsidiary. The Mérieux name had long been closely associated with the French pharmaceutical industry. In addition to providing the foundation for Rhône Mérieux, and then Merial, the Mérieux family was also at the origin of two other important French pharmaceutical players, bioMérieux and Sanofi Pasteur.

Marcel Mérieux was born in 1870 to a wealthy family involved in silk production. Mérieux initially studied as a chemist. In 1894, however, Mérieux was hired as an assistant to Émile Roux as part of the prestigious Pasteur Institute. Mérieux's interest turned to microbiology. Mérieux also adopted Pasteur's own attitude toward medicine, that there should be no barrier between human medicine and veterinary medicine. By 1896, Mérieux had founded his own laboratory, Institut Biologique Mérieux, in Lyon.

Mérieux initially turned his attention to the treatment of human diseases while his laboratory provided diagnostic services. In 1907, however, an inheritance from his mother enabled Mérieux to expand his research focus to include animals as well. That year Mérieux acquired a small property in Caluire, as well as a number of horses.

FIGHTING FOOT-AND-MOUTH DISEASE IN THE TWENTIES

World War I put an end to Mérieux's work, as he was drafted into the army, where he served as an ambulance driver. Decommissioned in 1917, Mérieux returned to Lyon to start again. Using an inheritance received from his father, Mérieux bought a 100-acre property in Marcy l'Étoile, outside of Lyon. This estate enabled Mérieux to increase his stable of horses and his production of tuberculin. The increase in production allowed Institut Mérieux to become primary supplier of tuberculin for the French government's mandatory testing for tuberculosis in schoolchildren, launched soon after the end of the war.

A major outbreak of foot-and-mouth disease in the Lyon region led to the lasting association of the Mérieux name and animal health. In 1926 Marcel Mérieux founded a new company, L'Etablissement Sérotherapique de la Fièvre Aphteuse (the French term for foot-and-mouth disease). As part of this effort Mérieux brought in a small herd of 12 infected cattle, which were placed in isolation on the property. This herd served as a factory, of sorts, for the company's production of an antitoxin. With production levels of some 400 liters per year, the company helped put an end to the foot-and-mouth disease outbreak. By then the small company had been joined by Mérieux's son Charles, who took over as its leader following his father's death in 1937.

The younger Mérieux helped transformed Institut Mérieux from a small Lyon laboratory into one of the world's major names in vaccine development. In the mid-1930s Mérieux developed its first foreign sales, after the Spanish and Argentinean governments authorized the import of the company's serums. Mérieux grew strongly through the decade. By 1935 the company was capable of producing 450,000 doses of serums and vaccines for veterinary use, as well as 15,000 doses of tuberculin per year.

As the French government prepared for World War II, however, the company's production turned toward anti-tetanus vaccines. In order to meet the demand the company began adding staff. By 1942, the company boasted more than 100 employees. While continuing to produce anti-tetanus vaccines and serums throughout the war, the company also supported the French Resistance by supplying serums for blood transfusions. Mérieux also produced protein-rich food supplements for children.

POSTWAR ANIMAL HEALTH SUCCESS

Following the war, and after a period in the United States, Charles Mérieux focused the company's research efforts on veterinary medicine. In 1947, the company created the Institut Français de la Fièvre Aphteuse (the French Foot-and-Mouth Institute). Mérieux then attacked the difficulty of producing the virus needed for vaccine. The traditional method used to harvest the virus required live animals. Cows were infected with the virus, then the virus was harvested from the pustules that formed on their skin. Instead, Mérieux succeeded in developing a synthetic culture capable of supporting the growth of the virus. In this way Mérieux succeeded in launching production of the serum on an industrial scale.

This success helped place Mérieux among the world's leading animal health companies. In the 1960s,

KEY DATES

1896: Marcel Mérieux founds the Institut Mérieux as a diagnostic laboratory in Lyon, France.

1926: Mérieux founds L'Etablissement Sérotherapique de la Fièvre Aphteuse to develop treatments and vaccines against foot-and-mouth disease.

1947: Mérieux focuses on animal health through a new subsidiary, Institut Français de la Fièvre Aphteuse.

1968: Rhône-Poulenc acquires majority control of Mérieux.

1983: Rhône-Poulenc merges all of its animal health operations into a new company, Rhône Mérieux.

1997: Rhône Mérieux and Merck Agvet merge to form Merial.

2009: Merial enters exclusive agreement for AviTech's ovo injection technology.

for example, when an outbreak of foot-and-mouth disease threatened livestock across Europe, Mérieux was able to launch a "vaccine barricade." The effort successfully stopped the spread of the epidemic. The experience enabled Mérieux to transfer its expertise to the human side as well. In 1974, for example, the company was instrumental in preventing a major meningitis epidemic in Brazil by inoculating more than 100 million people.

Charles Mérieux, who died at the age of 94 in 1991, was joined by sons Jean and Alain in the business. Alain Mérieux in particular became a new driving force in the French pharmaceuticals industry, founding a new company in 1963 that ultimately entered the 21st century as bioMérieux. By the end of the 1960s, Mérieux had grown into a global force in the production of vaccines, and Charles Mérieux had achieved recognition as one of the pioneers of preventive medicine.

Mérieux had by then become part of a larger group. In 1968 the Mérieux family agreed to sell 51 percent of the company's shares to Rhône-Poulenc, which by then had grown from Société Chimiques des Usines de Rhône to become one of France's largest companies. Rhône-Poulenc's own veterinary operations included the Institut de Sérothérapie de Toulouse, acquired in 1968, and the successful launch of a rabies vaccine based on deactivated virus, launched that year.

BECOMING RHÔNE MÉRIEUX IN 1983

Over the following decade Rhône-Poulenc continued to buy shares in Mérieux, tightening its control over the company. This led Rhône-Poulenc to move to consolidate all of its animal health holdings into a single company. In addition to Institut Mérieux and the Institut de Sérothérapie de Toulouse, Rhône-Poulenc's holdings at the time included two other companies, Specia and Roger Bellon. In 1984 these companies were merged with the animal health operations of Institut Mérieux, forming Rhône Mérieux. Mérieux's human medicine business was placed into a separate company, Pasteur Mérieux.

Like many of its counterparts in the animal health industry, Rhône Mérieux added a poultry genetics operation during the 1980s. The move was seen as offering strong potential for developing complementary businesses. In particular the companies hoped to develop synergies between the research and development activities of their animal health divisions, on the one hand, and their animal and seed genetics operations on the other. Rhône Mérieux's own subsidiaries grew to include the Institut de Selection Avicole.

Rhône-Poulenc acquired full control of Rhône Mérieux in 1994, signaling the exit of the founding Mérieux family from the company's shareholding. That year marked another major milestone for the company, with the launch of the Frontline parasiticide. Used for the treatment of fleas and ticks on domestic pets, Frontline quickly became a company bestseller and then one of the largest-selling products in the global animal health industry.

MERGING WITH MERCK AGVET IN 1997

The success of Frontline helped boost Rhône Mérieux to the number four position in the worldwide animal health market by 1996. The company could also lay claim to global leadership in the production of animal vaccines and serums. By then, however, Rhône Mérieux had become caught up in the growing global trend toward specialization in the pharmaceuticals industry. A factor behind this trend had been the increasing consolidation of the sector, which saw the creation of a number of large-scale, internationally operating groups.

Rhône-Poulenc, which emerged from the industry consolidation as Sanofi-Aventis in the middle of the first decade of the 2000s, sought to boost the stature of its own animal health operations. This led the company to reach a merger agreement with U.S.-based Merck & Co., which controlled Merck Agvet, then the second largest player in the animal health market. As part of the agreement, the two companies agreed to join their animal health and animal genetics operations into a new 50-50 joint venture, Merial Ltd. Merial opened a new corporate headquarters in London following the completion of the merger in 1997.

Merck Agvet provided a highly complementary business to that of Rhône Mérieux. The U.S. company's focus remained largely on the North American market, the industry's largest, in contrast to Rhône Mérieux's own commanding presence in the European market. Merck Agvet's focus on the animal health parasiticides segment also complemented Rhône Mérieux's core expertise in vaccine and pharmaceuticals.

Merck Agvet's own animal health operations stemmed from the parent company's origins at the turn of the 20th century with the production of animal disinfectants. In the 1930s Merck's discovery of Vitamin B12 added an important component to animal feed. In 1940 the company also pioneered the development of anti-coccidial compounds for the poultry industry. In the 1960s Merck added its Nicrazin and Amprol, two of the first veterinary products for birds, as well as a broad-spectrum antiparisitic, Thibenzole. In 1979 Merck created a dedicated animal health subsidiary, Merck Agvet. That company achieved its greatest success the following year, with the launch of ivermectin, a parasiticide that soon became the world's best-selling animal health compound.

GLOBAL LEADER IN THE 21ST CENTURY

By 2001 Merial had completed the integration of its parent companies' animal health operations. That year the company moved to consolidate its U.S. operations, opening a new headquarters in Duluth, Georgia. Because the North American market represented a significant part of Merial's overall revenues, the company soon transferred its global headquarters from the London office to the Georgia site.

While Frontline, which sold its one-billionth dose in 2008, and ivermectin remained bestsellers, Merial continued to seek new products in the new century. In 2003 the company acquired Qiagen NV's Pecura technology, which allowed Merial to begin development of a new family of drugs meant to reinforce animal immune systems. In 2005 the company received special authorization from the European Agency to launch a new vaccine, Circovac. The launch came amid an outbreak of porcine circovirus type 2 (PCV2) sweeping across France, Germany, the United Kingdom, Denmark, and Canada. By 2007 the company had received approval for the full launch of Circovac in Europe. That product received a new boost in 2009, as a number of studies revealed Circovac's positive impact on mortality rates, litter sizes, and other factors.

Merial also grew through partnerships and acquisitions. In 2003 the company formed a sales and marketing agreement with Elanco Animal Health in the United States. The agreement gave Elanco exclusive rights to market Merial's Ivomec branded line for swine. In 2007 Merial reinforced its presence in the New Zealand market, buying that country's Ancare. The following year the company formed a new alliance with Australia's Imugene, providing Merial with exclusive rights to that company's adenoviral vector technology. In 2009, Merial entered an agreement with AviTech LLC to become the exclusive distributor of that company's ovo injection systems technology, used for delivering vaccines directly into eggs.

By then Merial had completed a restructuring of its operations, which included a transition of its production network toward lean manufacturing techniques, as well as a reorganization of the group's regional operations. At the same time, Merial moved to exit the poultry genetics sector, selling off these operations, including Hubbard, in 2005.

The joint venture backing Merial also underwent its own changes, as Rhône-Poulenc merged with Hoechst to become Aventis in 2000, which was then absorbed by Sanofi-Synthelabo, becoming Sanofi-Aventis in 2004. However, the strength of the Merial operations meant that the joint venture remained quite solid, despite the changes in ownership. After more than 12 years, Merial remained one of the most successful joint ventures in the animal health industry.

M. L. Cohen

PRINCIPAL SUBSIDIARIES

Merial Animal Health Ltd. (UK); Merial Asia Pacific Pty. (Singapore); Merial Colombia S.A.; Merial Mexico S.A. de C.V.; Merial S.A.S. (France).

PRINCIPAL COMPETITORS

Bayer Animal Health AG; Novartis Animal Health; Janssen Pharmaceutica S.A./NV; Pfizer Animal Health Group, Inc.; Schering-Plough Corporation; Pharmacia & Upjohn, Inc.; IDEXX Laboratories, Inc.

FURTHER READING

"Additional Benefits of PCV2 Vaccine," *Farmers Guardian*, January 9, 2009, p. 30.

Cookson, Clive, "Animal Health Venture Highly Profitable," *Financial Times,* August 9, 2007, p. 2.

"De Marcel Mérieux au Biopole de Lyon," *Le Lettre Mensuel,* June 2008.

French, Liz, "Organizational Horsebower," *Health Executive,* February 2006, p. 31.

"Merck and Rhône-Poulenc in Joint Venture," *New York Times,* December 20, 1996.

"Merck Manual Celebrates 50 Years," *Feedstuffs,* March 28, 2005, p. 4.

"Merial Celebrates Decade in Animal Health," *DVM Newsmagazine,* September 2007, p. 24.

"Merial Defends World-Class Integrity," *Farmers Guardian,* August 10, 2007, p. 2.

"Merial, Elanco Form Strategic Alliance," *Feedstuffs,* November 24, 2003, p. 6.

"Merial Launches Circovac in EU," *Feedstuffs,* September 17, 2007, p. 17.

"Merial Ltd. Acquires the New Zealand Animal Health Products Company Ancare," *Agri Marketing,* November–December 2007, p. 11.

"Merial Moves into Stronger Position," *Agri Marketing,* September 2001, p. 70.

"Merial Opens New Headquarters," *Feedstuffs,* April 2, 2001, p. 7.

Rothnie, David, "Animal Pharm," *Acquisitions Monthly,* December 1998, p. 78.

Smith, Rod, "Aventis, Sanofi Merger Not Seen to Affect Merial," *Feedstuffs,* May 3, 2004, p. 6.

———, "Merial Sells Hubbard to Exit Poultry Genetics," *Feedstuffs,* April 4, 2005, p. 6.

Wright, Pearce, "Charles Mérieux: Virologist and Pioneer of Vaccine Production," *Guardian,* January 29, 2001.

Midway Games, Inc.

———■———

2704 West Roscoe Street
Chicago, Illinois 60618-5910
U.S.A.
Telephone: (773) 961-2222
Fax: (773) 961-1099
Web site: http://www.midway.com

Public Company
Incorporated: 1988
Employees: 900
Sales: $157.2 million (2007)
Stock Exchanges: New York
Ticker Symbol: MWY
NAICS: 334611 Prepackaged Software, Mass Reproducing; 511210 Games, Computer Software, Publishing; 339999 Coin-Operated Amusement Machines (Except Jukebox) Manufacturing

■ ■ ■

Midway Games, Inc., is a leading producer of video games. In the early years of its development Midway produced games exclusively for arcades and was the number one company in the coin-operated market. The company designed, published, and marketed games for coin-operated arcade machines until 2001, when it shifted to emphasize solely products for home video game consoles and personal computers. Until about the late 1990s, Midway published or distributed some of the most popular games in the industry, including its biggest success, the Mortal Kombat series, along with Cruis'n USA, NBA Jam, Defender, and PacMan.

Midway makes its home games in formats compatible for all the leading game models.

COMPANY ROOTS

In 1969 the Midway Manufacturing Company, a maker of amusement machines, was acquired by Bally, one of the nation's leading manufacturers of gaming pinball machines. In 1988 Bally's amusement game divisions were purchased for $8 million by its main competitor in the arcade game industry, WMS Industries of Chicago. That same year Midway Manufacturing Company was incorporated as a wholly owned subsidiary of WMS. Midway worked on some WMS pinball games, but the company primarily designed and produced video games for arcades.

Video games were going through a slump as the 1980s turned to the 1990s, but the entire industry revived abruptly when Midway introduced Mortal Kombat in 1992. The game achieved notoriety inside and outside the gamer community when it became known that secret codes had been programmed into the game: When activated, the codes changed Mortal Kombat from a run-of-the-mill kick-and-punch match between mutants into a bloody battle to the death at the conclusion of which the victor would rip the still-beating heart from his vanquished opponent's chest, or tear his hapless opponent's spine out and hold it triumphantly aloft, or blast his prostrate opponent to ashes.

The game unleashed a debate over the effect of violent video games on children, which continued throughout the 1990s. Nevertheless, the immense popularity of Mortal Kombat guaranteed that other games would compete to outdo it in both violence and realism. The game established Midway as a major force in the video game field and provided the company with the financial resources to develop new games and eventually expand beyond the arcade market.

In March 1994 Midway and Nintendo formed a 50-50 joint venture. Under its terms, Midway was to develop video games for new game machines being developed by Nintendo, among them the Nintendo 64, a home game console for which Midway agreed to develop a version of Cruis'n USA. The agreement gave the joint venture the distribution rights for home versions of any Cruis'n sequels developed for coin-operated machines. It also had first rights for negotiating distribution of the games Midway designed for Nintendo's next coin-operated system. The deal was an early step for Midway into the blossoming home video game market.

EXPANSION INTO THE HOME MARKET

Midway moved more decisively into the home market in April 1994 when it acquired three companies, Tradewest Inc., Tradewest International Inc., and the Leland Corporation, known collectively as Tradewest. Tradewest, located in Corsicana, Texas, designed and manufactured home video games. The initial price was $15 million with the remainder calculated as a percentage of future annual revenues. In June 1998 when Midway made the final payment, those additional costs had totaled $37 million. Tradewest retained its autonomy within Midway. Its 50-person staff formed the core of a new Midway subsidiary, which, like Tradewest, developed home video games. Midway's most profitable unit, Tradewest was eventually renamed Midway Home Entertainment.

Midway's decision to begin producing its own home video games followed the incredible success of the first two Mortal Kombat games. Those games, like all Midway's games at the time, were originally developed as arcade games. The home rights to Midway games were licensed to another game developer, Acclaim Entertainment, in 1989, a time of uncertainty in the home video game market. Acclaim sold five million copies of Mortal Kombat at a retail price of about $65 each.

Midway ended its licensing relationship with Acclaim in 1993. The marketing strategy it adopted when it began producing home video games was one Acclaim had pioneered with a great deal of success. Home games were released simultaneously in versions for all the popular home game systems. Midway Home Entertainment's staff was ideally suited for the strategy, because Tradewest had specialized in developing games for multiple platforms. The cross-platform strategy was extremely effective: It enabled the company to hit every potential market while a game was still popular; development, advertising, and promotional expenses could be spread out over more game units, lowering costs; and a successful arcade version operated as advertising for all home versions.

Midway's leadership in the arcade field gave it an additional advantage. Acclaim had established earlier that successful arcade games almost invariably went on to be successful home games. Acclaim's arcade sales thus functioned as market research, reducing the likelihood that a home game would not pay back its development costs. In September 1995, Midway released Mortal Kombat 3, the first home video game that it had developed in-house. Despite its release so late in the year, the game went on to be the nation's best-selling home video game in 1995, according to *TRSTS (Toy Retail Sales Tracking Service) Reports,* an industry magazine.

In March 1996, Midway purchased Atari Games from Time Warner. Midway paid $2 million up front for Atari, which had been experiencing problems since the early 1980s, and additional costs linked to the division's performance through 2000, with the total price paid estimated to have been $24 million in all. Midway obtained Atari's game development capability and its full library of classic video games such as Pac-Man and Centipede, as well as the right to use the Atari name on its coin-operated games. After the acquisition, the Atari division in Milpitas, California, remained an autonomous operation within Midway Games.

GOING PUBLIC

On September 13, 1996, Midway filed its intention with the Securities and Exchange Commission (SEC) to make an initial public offering of 5.1 million shares of common stock. Less than 15 percent of Midway com-

KEY DATES

1969: Bally acquires Midway Manufacturing Company.

1988: WMS Industries of Chicago acquires Bally's amusement game divisions, including Midway.

1992: Midway introduces Mortal Kombat.

1994: Midway forms joint venture with Nintendo.

1995: Midway enters home video game market with Mortal Kombat 3.

1996: Midway goes public.

2001: Midway leaves coin-operated sector to focus on home video market.

2004: Sumner Redstone announces plans to acquire Midway in Securities and Exchange Commission filing.

2005: Midway launches cross-promotional agreement with MTV.

2006: Sumner Redstone stops buying shares of Midway.

2008: Shari Redstone becomes president of Midway board of directors.

mon stock was being offered, with WMS Industries, Midway's parent company, continuing to hold approximately 33.4 million shares. The offering was greeted favorably by investors, because Midway seemed to be a strong presence in the video game market. Sales had increased to $245.4 million annually by June 1996, which represented fivefold growth since 1992. An important reason was the Mortal Kombat series, which accounted for 17 percent of Midway's sales in 1995 and 35 percent in 1996.

Midway's increasing involvement in home games was also a positive factor for investors. Midway Chairman Neil Nicastro told *Crain's Chicago Business,* "The home business provides superior earnings potential. It's so much bigger a market." Indeed, in 1996 there were 15,000 arcades in the United States, but 35 million homes with video games. Furthermore, the coin-operated business had begun to erode at a rate of 10 to 15 percent a year. By contrast, in 1994 home video games had accounted for 20 percent of Midway's total revenues, and by 1996 they made up 63 percent. In addition, Midway was the only American video game manufacturer that was strongly established in the arcade market, recognized as the testing ground for home games.

Investors had questions about Midway as well, wondering whether the untested company would be able to get home products out on schedule. Investors were also concerned as to how the added administrative, research and development, and marketing costs associated with the shift in focus to home video games would affect Midway's financial performance. Those costs had grown significantly. Between June 1995 and June 1996, the company's annual research and development outlays increased from $8.4 million to $32.5 million, while marketing costs jumped from $1.6 million to $22.8 million.

The offering was completed on October 29, 1996. The stock went for $20 a share and raised $108 million. According to *Crain's Chicago Business,* investor confidence in Midway was high, as indicated by the level of trading in the weeks immediately after the spinoff, and within two months the value of Midway stock was 15 percent higher. The company changed its name at the same time from Midway Manufacturing Company to Midway Games. All pinball operations handled by Midway for WMS were transferred to another subsidiary just prior to the public offering. Midway significantly boosted its outlay for research and development from $32.5 million in fiscal 1996 to $55.9 million in 1997.

STOCK DISCREPANCY SURFACES

Midway's fall 1996 home video line was marketed exclusively under its own trademark. Prior to that, its products had carried the Williams, Tradewest, Tengen, and Time Warner Interactive trademarks. Midway Games had a number of achievements during its 1996 fiscal year. It released five coin-operated games under its own name; it published eight new home games, including one of its most popular, Mortal Kombat 3; it released the Touchmaster, a coin-operated game platform with a touch screen; and Cruis'n USA won awards for innovation from various industry groups.

Three months after Midway's public offering, investors noted a strange discrepancy in the stock prices of Midway and its parent company, WMS. When Midway went public, WMS retained just over 86 percent of the total shares. Based on that figure, analysts calculated, each WMS share effectively owned 1.38 shares in Midway. At the mid-January 1997 price of $20 for a Midway share, every WMS share owned about $27.95 worth of Midway stock. WMS, however, was selling for only $23. The primary factor holding down the price of WMS shares, analysts reasoned, was the large percentage of Midway shares it held. That was Midway stock that was inaccessible to the market and investors could not arbitrage the difference in prices.

WMS Industries was itself uncertain how to deal with the problem. Keeping its Midway holdings would continue to depress its own value, but if WMS sold its Midway holdings it could end up paying 40 percent of the proceeds in taxes, and if it distributed the stock among its shareholders they could be liable for taxes. On August 11, 1997, WMS announced that it had decided on the latter course. Stockholders would receive the company's Midway stock on a pro-rata basis. The proposed spinoff hinged upon an Internal Revenue Service ruling over whether the deal would be tax free to WMS and its stockholders. The company hoped everything would be completed by early 1998. Thereafter, Midway would be listed as a "discontinued operation" on WMS's financial records.

Midway Games developed or licensed a broad line of games, including sports games such as Wayne Gretzky's 3D Hockey; racing games such as San Francisco Rush; and fighting games such as War Games and Mace. However, the most successful of all Midway's game titles to date was the Mortal Kombat line. Mortal Kombat ushered in boom times in the video game market, in particular for Midway Games. More than 15 million Mortal Kombat home games were sold. The game spawned a series of sequels, including versions 2, 3, and 4, Ultimate Mortal Kombat, Mortal Kombat Trilogy, and Mortal Kombat Mythologies: Sub Zero. By the beginning of 1998 Midway had earned a net $1 billion from all the Mortal Kombat arcade games. Mortal Kombat 3 sold 250,000 units and brought in $15 million during its first weekend on the market. In 1997, after other popular games appeared, the percentage was still 22 percent.

DEBATE OVER VIOLENCE CONTINUES

The debate about violent games was resumed after a series of schoolyard shootings in 1997 and 1998, after it was discovered that some of the boys involved in the shootings had played Mortal Kombat. Experts, however, were divided on the degree to which such games actually influenced violent behavior. What was important for game makers was the enthusiasm of video game players for carnage, and they began incorporating it into other games. Midway Games was no exception, producing Blitz, a no-holds-barred contest in which players maimed and dismembered opponents, and Bio Freaks, in which players could decapitate opponents.

In 1994 Midway licensed multimedia rights to Mortal Kombat to Threshold Entertainment, which turned the license into a property worth $3 billion. According to Threshold CEO Larry Kasanoff, Mortal Kombat became the fifth largest entertainment franchise in the world to date, ranking just after Batman and Star Trek. In all, there were over 100 licensed Mortal Kombat products on the market during this time. Threshold released two *Mortal Kombat* movies, the first of which made $100 million worldwide in 1995, and the second of which was the country's number one movie the weekend it opened in November 1997. Besides the movies, Threshold produced an animated TV series, a "Mortal Kombat" stage show at Radio city Music Hall, a "Mortal Kombat" CD-ROM, a "Home Mortal Kombat Special" on DIRECT TV, three soundtrack albums, one of which went platinum (one million copies sold), a live-action TV show, and one of the Internet's most popular web sites, mortalkombat. com.

In October 1997 the arcade version of Mortal Kombat 4 was released. The game, which the company dubbed "the final version" in press releases, was the first to use Midway's new Zeus chip. The chip was the key to a powerful new graphic system that enabled the game to process visual data about ten times faster than other systems, increasing the levels of realism proportionately. In 1998 Midway began promoting the Nintendo 64 version of Mortal Kombat 4 more aggressively than ever, weeks before the game was due to be released. A multimillion-dollar, music video-style television ad campaign coincided with the airing of the first *Mortal Kombat* movie on TBS, a film shown five times during May 1998. Midway also lowered the suggested retail price of Mortal Kombat 4 from $59.95 to $49.95.

COMMITMENT TO THE HOME MARKET

At the end of 1997, Midway announced that revenues had risen 13 percent to $73.7 million during its July–September 1997 quarter. During the same period, however, home game revenues fell from $47.6 million to $40.1 million, largely because the company had postponed the release of Top Gear Rally and Mace: The Dark Age until the end of September. Nevertheless, *TRSTS Reports* ranked Midway Games fourth among 62 video game companies in sales of 32- and 64-bit home video games for fiscal 1997, up from seventh place the previous year. The company released seven new arcade games and fifteen new home games. In 1997 Midway released more games for the new Nintendo 64 system than any company except Nintendo itself.

In February 1998 Midway broke with its previous marketing strategy and announced that the following summer it would release home versions of the game Bio Freaks before an arcade version appeared. According to a company spokesperson, Midway made the decision in response to high consumer demand for a new fighting game that took advantage of the graphic possibilities of the next generation game systems such as the Sony PlayStation and Nintendo 64. The company described the release as additional evidence of its commitment to the home market it was courting.

In March 1998 Midway expanded its product line into the market for personal computer games. It purchased back North American and Japanese distribution rights to Midway personal computer games that the company had granted to GT Interactive Software in 1995, a time when it was focusing its attention on the home console market. GT retained rights to distribute Midway personal computer games outside North America and Japan.

The Internal Revenue Service finally issued its ruling that the company's proposed spinoff would be tax free. On April 6, 1998, all Midway shares held by WMS were distributed among its shareholders. Each WMS share received 1.19773 Midway shares, and fractional shares were paid out in cash. Upon completion of the spinoff, Neil Nicastro resigned his positions as president, CEO, and chief operating officer of WMS to take over the chairmanship of Midway Games.

In the summer of 1998, total revenues grew by about 10 percent and the company expected its home video game revenues to double from the same quarter a year earlier, thanks to sales of games for the then new generation video consoles manufactured by Nintendo and Sony. Midway's arcade business continued to shrink, dropping by 25 percent compared to the previous year.

FINANCIAL CHALLENGES IN THE 21ST CENTURY

While Midway moved up from number five to number four in U.S. video game software unit sales for calendar 1999, the company went on to log a series of operating losses beginning in 2000. Midway's stock fell 71 percent in 2000, in part due to the lag in game purchasing caused by the impending introduction of the new generation of game playing technology. Investment analysts speculated that the company was ripe for acquisition.

In fact, the first decade of the 21st century buzzed with rumors that Viacom Chairman and CEO Sumner Redstone planned to acquire the company, enabling the company's stock price to remain high despite low sales performance. Redstone had begun gradually acquiring Midway stock in 1983, and by 2000 he owned 28 percent of Midway's shares, directly and through his holding company, National Amusements.

While analysts believed Midway would turn a corner after the release of new game technology, the company faltered when game arcades declined. In 2001, Midway phased out its declining coin-operated sector in favor of the more lucrative home video games market. However, the company continued to struggle. In fiscal 2001 the company ended the year with revenues that plummeted to $168.2 million (compared to $333.8 million in fiscal 2000). By fiscal 2003, the company's revenues had fallen even further to $93 million.

In 2003, David Zucker, previously with Disney and ESPN, took over as CEO. In 2004, the company finally had a profitable fourth quarter, the first since 2000. The 2004 fiscal year ended with a 74.7 percent increase in sales, and Midway moved up from number 16 to number 13 in unit sales by games publishers. By 2005, however, weak sales forced the company to lay off 8 percent of its workers. After this announcement, Midway stock prices plummeted from $23.26 to $9.91 in two months. Later, Zucker attracted public scrutiny that led to a class-action suit when it became apparent that he had sold 650,000 shares of Midway stock for $12.9 million immediately before the company announced its layoff and restructuring plans. In 2008, Zucker vacated his post as CEO.

THE ROLE OF SUMNER REDSTONE IN THE FUTURE OF MIDWAY

Perhaps the only reason the company remained afloat was the continued interest of Sumner Redstone. In 2004, Redstone, who had gradually acquired over 60 percent of the company's shares, announced in an SEC filing that he planned to acquire the low-performing company in order to infuse it with talent and grow it into an industry leader. Redstone persuaded the board of directors to cut membership from 11 to eight; pushed for the resignation of chairman Neil Nicastro; and placed his daughter, Shari Redstone, and Kenneth Cron on the board, with Cron serving as chairman. Redstone bought 1.25 million shares of stock from Nicastro, bringing his total ownership to about 72 percent. He hired an adviser to examine the possibility of taking the company private. In 2005, MTV (a division of Redstone's Viacom) entered into a cross-promotion agreement with Midway involving three video games.

In December 2006, with about 88 percent of the company's shares in hand, Redstone abruptly stopped buying shares of Midway. He moved his existing shares from National Amusements to the Sumco Company and he appointed his daughter, Shari Redstone, president. Ending a public family feud over what she saw as her father's wasted investment in Midway, Shari Redstone was elected president of Midway's board of directors in 2008, replacing Kenneth Cron. Industry analysts were uncertain as to whether the younger Redstone would seek a buyer for the company.

In 2008, Redstone's investment in Midway seemed squandered. In the November 3, 2008, *New York Times,* analyst Michael Pachter estimated that Redstone spent $500 to $700 million on Midway shares from 1983 to 2006 (in addition to substantial loans to keep Midway in business). By comparison, the company had lost $258.9 million in the period from fiscal 2005 to fiscal 2007 alone. When the U.S. financial crisis drove the price of stock in Viacom and CBS so low that it violated lending agreements, Redstone was forced to sell over $200 million in stock, threatening the sustainability of his media empire. Midway stood at a crossroads, and its long-deferred future course, it seemed, might finally be determined by Sumner and Shari Redstone.

Gerald Brennan
Updated, Heidi Feldman

PRINCIPAL SUBSIDIARIES

Midway Games GmbH; Midway Games SAS; Midway Amusement Games, LLC; Midway Games, Limited; Midway Home Entertainment, Inc.

PRINCIPAL COMPETITORS

Electronic Arts Inc.; Microsoft Corporation; Nintendo Co. Ltd.; Sony Corporation; Activision Blizzard Inc.; Konami Corporation; SCi Entertainment Group plc; Take-Two Interactive Software Inc.; Ubisoft Entertainment S.A.

FURTHER READING

Arango, Tim, "Struggles of a Game Maker Bog Down an Empire," *New York Times,* November 3, 2008, p. B1.

"Bally Zaps Its Video Games," *Time,* July 25, 1988.

Borden, Jeff, "Zapping Bad Guys Is Good Biz for Videogames Maker but Look Out! Rising Costs Could Whack Midway," *Crain's Chicago Business,* December 9, 1996.

"Charles H. Johnson & Associates Announces Filing of Securities Class Action Against Midway Games, Inc.," *PrimeZone Media Network,* August 2, 2007.

Chronis, George T., "Williams Buys Time Warner Interactive and Brings Back the Atari Brand Name," *Video Store Magazine,* April 7, 1996.

"A Creeping Takeover of Midway Games?" *Business Week,* November 13, 2000, p. 223.

Fabrikant, Geraldine, "If Following the Leader, Beware Quick Stops," *New York Times,* February 20, 2006, p. C1.

———, "Play Again, Mr. Redstone?" *New York Times,* November 27, 2006, p. C1.

Fritz, Ben, "Execs Give Midway a Closer Look," *Variety,* October 25, 2004, p. 8.

———, "Redstone Game for Midway Offer," *Daily Variety,* April 14, 2004, p. 5.

———, "Redstone Gets Back into the Game," *Variety,* January 7, 2008.

———, "Redstone to Buy Vidgamer," *Daily Variety,* April 29, 2004, p. 4.

———, "Sound Bites," *Variety,* March 24, 2008.

"Game Companies Post Upbeat Quarter," *Television Digest,* October 27, 1997.

Gaudiosi, John, "Midway Partnering with Hollywood," *Video Store,* August 17, 2003, p. 11.

Hein, Kenneth, "Midway Goes All the Way in '05 Back to Sales Surge: Videogame Maker Makes Its Play by Adding Marketing, Moxie," *Brandweek,* March 14, 2005, p. 21.

———, "Midway Puts More Muscle Behind Its Videogames: Ayzenberg Set to Break Ads Backing New NBA Ballers Title," *Adweek,* March 22, 2004, p. 17.

Henry, David, "WMS Stock Offers Bargain—For Brave," *USA Today,* January 1, 1997.

Horwitz, Jeremy, "Mortal Apathy?" *New York Times,* July 8, 2002, p. C4.

Levine, Robert, "MTV Finds a New Ally in Games," *New York Times,* June 27, 2005, p. C2.

McGarry, Mark J., "Short Cuts," *Newsday,* April 6, 1994.

"Midway Games Chairman Will Resign Next Week," *New York Times,* June 5, 2004.

"Midway Games Completes $42 Million Private Placement," *Business Wire,* May 22, 2001.

"Midway Games Completes Public Offering of 4,500,000 Shares of Common Stock," *Business Wire,* December 19, 2001.

"Midway Games Inc. Reports Fourth Quarter and Fiscal Year Results," *Business Wire,* September 5, 2001.

"Midway Games Moves Up to Fourth Position in 1999 U.S. Video Game Software Sales," *Business Wire,* February 1, 2000.

"Midway Legend No Longer in Coin-Op," *AB Europe,* July 2001, p. 9.

"Midway 'Re-Orienting not Shrinking' As More Jobs Go," *AB Europe,* July 2000, p. 5.

Morgenson, Gretchen, "Taking a Chance on Takeover Candidates," *New York Times,* October 1, 2000, p. BU1.

Mullman, Jeremy, "Stock Report: Bad News Doesn't Dent Midway," *Crain's Chicago Business,* August 15, 2005, p. 4.

"Redstone Considers Taking Midway Games Private," *New York Times,* June 9, 2004, p. C4.

Sasseen, Jane, "Midway's CEO Zucker's Safe Harbor; In Late 2005, the Executive Traded Almost 650,000 Shares of Company Stock, Just As It Began a Precipitous Decline. A Lucky Coincidence?" *Business Week Online,* November 1, 2006.

"Set to Mweove on Midway?" *Business Week,* November 15, 2004, p. 133.

"Technology Briefing Software: Midway Games Names Chairman," *New York Times,* June 15, 2004, p. C4.

"Technology Briefing Software: Midway Games Posts Profit," *New York Times,* March 1, 2005, p. C17.

"Technology Briefing Software: Midway to Raise $82.3 Million in Stock Offer," *New York Times,* April 14, 2004, p. C4.

"Unhappy Holidays for Vidgame Biz," *Variety,* December 26, 2005, p. 4.

Van de Mark, Donald, "Mortal Kombat: Interview with Larry Kasanoff, Threshold Entertainment," *Biz Buzz CNN,* November 20, 1997.

Mitsui Mining & Smelting Company, Ltd.

1-11-1 Osaki
Shinagawa-ku
Tokyo, 141-8584
Japan
Telephone: (81 03) 5437-8028
Fax: (81 03) 5437-8029
Web site: http://www.mitsui-kinzoku.co.jp

Public Company
Incorporated: 1950 as Kamioka Mining & Smelting Co.,
 Ltd.
Employees: 11,485
Sales: ¥595.46 billion ($5.94 billion) (2008)
Stock Exchanges: Tokyo Osaka Nagoya Sapporo Fukuoka
Ticker Symbol: 57060
NAICS: 212234 Copper Ore and Nickel Ore Mining;
 331521 Aluminum Die-Casting Foundries; 331411
 Primary Smelting and Refining of Copper

∎ ∎ ∎

Mitsui Mining & Smelting Company, Ltd. (MMS), also
known as Mitsui Kinzoku, is one of the world's largest
producers of zinc. The company smelts, refines, and
fabricates nonferrous metals including copper that are
used in high-tech industries. It also produces copper foil
and semiconductor packaging tapes, which are used in
the electronics industry, as well as automotive parts and
components and die-cast products used in a variety of
applications including automobiles and home
appliances. The company's operations are organized into
five business segments: Electronics Materials; Basic

Materials; Environmental Business; Parts Manufacturing
& Assembly; and Intermediate Materials.

EARLY HISTORY

MMS was created as Kamioka Mining & Smelting Co.,
Ltd., in 1950 when Mitsui Mining Company was forced
to dissolve by the Allied occupation forces in Japan.
Mitsui Mining was one of the oldest and most
important of the many affiliates of the Mitsui *zaibatsu*,
or conglomerate, its large coal mines having first been
acquired by the parent company in 1889. Mining of
coal and nonferrous metals quickly became one of the
three pillars of the vast Mitsui empire, along with banking and trade; and Mitsui Mining, which was founded
as a separate company in 1892, continued for many
years to occupy a central place in Mitsui's strategy. Able
at that time to exploit the labor of poorly paid women
and children, prison convicts, and often prisoners of
war, Mitsui Mining was not only extremely profitable
but also provided the steady income that allowed the
zaibatsu to diversify into other, riskier areas. The
company's bulwark was the mining of coal from its Miike mines on the island of Kyushu, but it soon acquired
a host of zinc, copper, lead, gold, and silver mines
around Japan. Its precious metals holdings were
especially important as a means of stabilizing income
during the often-wild price fluctuations of the industrial
metals, the value of gold tending at that time to remain
much more stable.

During Japan's frequent wars, Mitsui Mining also
reaped the benefits of increased demand for coal to fuel
ships and lead for the manufacture of bullets. When the

COMPANY PERSPECTIVES

We are committed to the basic principle of the manufacturing industry—to be the first to meet the needs of the market with safe, high-quality products delivered quickly—and we place this principle as the foundation of our management. We believe that the key to building a truly strong company and earning greater trust in this evolving environment is not to forget this basic principle. We are determined to achieve sustained growth by focusing on developing next-generation products that have world-class earnings capabilities and by focusing on businesses that best meet the needs of our customers.

Japanese began experimenting with chemical and bacteriological weaponry after World War I, Mitsui Chemical, a company carved out of Mitsui Mining, handled these. Mitsui Chemical also directed the reduction of coal into synthetic oil, critical to Japan's performance in World War II. During the later conflict, Mitsui Mining was the country's largest employer of Chinese and Korean prison laborers, whose treatment was reported to have been very poor.

Mitsui Mining was thus an integral part of Japan's war machine as well as remaining one of the key firms in the Mitsui group. As a result, when General Douglas MacArthur and the Allied occupation forces attempted to dismantle the monopolistic power of Japan's great *zaibatsu* at the conclusion of the war, Mitsui Mining was one of the dozen or so Mitsui affiliates singled out for special attention. The aim of the occupiers was both to weaken Japan's ability to wage war and to encourage Western-style democracy by fostering competition in each industry.

Mitsui Mining was felt to be doubly objectionable, having provided raw materials for the war effort and also ranking as Japan's leading producer of coal and nonferrous metals. Occupation authorities therefore ordered the company to be divided into two parts. Mitsui Mining Company was instructed to continue its coal production, based at the Miike mines, while Kamioka Mining & Smelting Company (KMS) was established to handle all other mining activities. In 1950 the two companies were legally separated and Mitsui Mining began its independent career in the new Japanese economy, one that was ostensibly free of the concentrated power formerly wielded by the *zaibatsu*.

POSTWAR DEVELOPMENT

The Allied disruption of the *zaibatsu* was successful in one respect, at least—the Mitsui family and the other leading Japanese industrialist families largely lost control of their conglomerates. The Allied reorganization of Japanese business groups was short-lived, with the anxiety of the United States over the potential spread of communism in Asia quickly overshadowing its concern with democracy in Japan. The United States wanted a strong, dependable Japan as its sentinel in the Far East, and it was evident that the tradition of cooperation and planning embodied in the *zaibatsu* concept was essential to Japan's past and future economic health, however poorly it satisfied Western ideas of free competition in the marketplace or at the ballot box. Serious anti-*zaibatsu* policies were dropped accordingly by the time of the creation of KMS, leaving the essential fabric of Japanese economic life unchanged and making it possible for the Mitsui companies slowly to reestablish their former network. One of the first manifestations of the reemergence of *zaibatsu* thus came in 1952, when Kamioka Mining & Smelting Co., Ltd., was renamed Mitsui Mining & Smelting Co., Ltd.

The new MMS had taken over from its parent company the largest and highest-quality zinc mine in Japan, and probably in the entire Eastern Hemisphere. The company's Kamioka works in Toyama Prefecture on the island of Honshu produced one-half of Japan's zinc in the early 1950s and continued to dominate the Japanese zinc market well into the year 2000. Another early success of MMS was in lead, of which it continued to provide one-third of Japan's requirements, down since the war but soon to increase again. The example of lead was typical in the history of MMS and Japan generally: in great demand during the war for bullet manufacturing, lead's value dropped practically to nothing in the chaotic, severely depressed postwar economy.

The phenomenal gains made by the Japanese economy during the next few decades, however, greatly expanded the number of peacetime uses for lead, chief among them the manufacture of batteries for automobiles and other end products. As Japan's auto industry slowly developed after the war, the demand for MMS's lead grew proportionately, fueled also by use of the metal in electric-wire sheathing and as a bearing material. MMS created a thriving business in lead by melting its bullets into batteries. A similar evolution could be traced in the example of precious metals, whose value as industrial catalysts and compounds grew tremendously after the war. MMS's gold and silver mines, although never large by world standards, thus continued to justify the expense of deeper exploration.

KEY DATES

1950: Kamioka Mining & Smelting Co., Ltd., is created.

1952: Kamioka Mining & Smelting is renamed Mitsui Mining & Smelting Co., Ltd. (MMS).

1968: Investigators determine that cadmium pollution from the Kamioka mines is causing a degenerative bone disease known as *itai-itai* or "ouch-ouch," among local residents.

1998: Mitsui Copper Foil (Hong Kong) Co. Ltd. is created.

2000: MMS teams up with Nippon Mining & Metals Co. Ltd. to create Pan Pacific Copper Co. Ltd.

2001: The company shutters its mining operations at the Kamioka Mine.

2002: Sumitomo Metal Mining Co. and MMS form MS Zinc Co. Ltd.

2006: The company begins zinc ore production at the Pallca Mine in Peru.

EXPANDING JAPANESE ECONOMY

Another important part of MMS's business in the early 1950s was the mining and smelting of copper. Because native deposits of copper had long been exhausted, MMS was forced to look overseas for its supplies and in 1953 began a long-term relationship with Marinduque Mining & Industrial Corporation of the Philippines, buying all of its copper production for the next 30 years. In the following years, the company made many similar deals with overseas firms, including a 1969 agreement with Utah Construction & Mining Company in British Columbia to smelt 60 percent of the copper mined in Utah. In the following year, MMS took advantage of the relative financial strength it enjoyed as a member of the Mitsui group by agreeing to participate in a loan package that would enable Freeport Sulphur Company, a U.S. firm, to build a copper mine and plant in Indonesia. For its share of the $20 million lent by a consortium of Japanese companies, MMS was entitled to buy a percentage of the copper concentrate produced by Freeport. By means of such financial networks, Japan gained access in the postwar period to the Asian raw materials it had tried unsuccessfully to take by force.

The tremendous expansion of the Japanese economy during the 1960s resulted in a proportionate surge in sales at MMS. The burgeoning Japanese auto industry bought not only lead for its batteries from MMS but also an increasing number of die-cast parts such as door latches. The manufacturing of such finished products marked a new era at MMS, which, like the rest of Japanese industry, began a slow shift from basic to value-added products in the face of increased price competition from other Asian industrial nations. Thus, just as Japan evolved from world domination in steel to that of shipbuilding and then to electronics, MMS began seeking ways to use its metal resources and experience in the manufacture of higher value-added products.

In 1981, for example, the company formed a joint venture in Tokyo with Mallinckrodt Incorporated to manufacture catalysts for the food processing, petrochemical, and synthetic fiber industries. Many catalysts made use of precious metals such as gold and platinum, which brought a greater return to refiners like MMS when sold in the form of complex industrial products rather than merely as ore. MMS continued its evolution from raw-material producer to manufacturer of material-based products, and the company clearly intended to proceed further in that direction during the late 1980s.

DEVELOPING MORE SOPHISTICATED GOODS

The Japanese postwar economic recovery resulted in a number of unwanted additions to Japanese life, including environmental pollution. The role of MMS as a smelter of metals led it into several entanglements in this area, the most notorious of which came to a head in 1968. For years the population living along the Jinsu River downstream from MMS's big Kamioka zinc mines had suffered from a variety of disorders, which the residents attributed to Kamioka's contaminated effluent. Japanese companies were traditionally uninterested in addressing such problems, and it was not until 1968 that investigators determined that cadmium pollution from the mines was causing a degenerative bone disease known as *itai-itai,* or "ouch-ouch," among local residents. A lawsuit was filed by 28 citizens on behalf of some 500 alleged victims of fatal or crippling *itai-itai* disease and, for the first time in Japanese history, the corporation was eventually found guilty and ordered to pay damages which in the aggregate amounted to approximately one year's net income.

Continued fluctuations in the price of raw materials in the 1970s and 1980s spurred MMS's desire to add more highly processed products to its mix of sales. While it remained one of the world's top zinc smelters, MMS also branched into the manufacturing of zinc alloys for precision casting, known in the trade as

ZAPREC; and into copper, which at 20 percent of sales was the company's most important metal. As a whole, the company still derived about 40 percent of its sales from base and precious metals in 1990, but was working hard to develop more processed metal products. This division, which contributed some 30 percent to corporate revenue, included an array of more sophisticated goods such as rolled copper products, including copper shingles with artificial patina and aluminum-oxide dispersion-strengthened copper.

MMS looked to the electronics field for a significant portion of its growth in the 1990s and beyond. Other products developed during the late 1980s and early 1990s were grouped under the new materials division. These included products made from high-purity metals such as tantalum and niobium, copper foil for laminates, and sputtering targets used in the application of very thin coats of metal. During 1990, the company adopted a new corporate logo and became known in Japan as Mitsui Kinzoku.

MMS did not entirely abandoned its traditional strengths, it continued to produce battery materials, for example, but the company clearly set its sights on joining the rest of Japan's manufacturers in the race to develop more complex and costly goods. The company was willing to entertain suggestions: the firm announced deals for the production of magnetic audiovisual materials, expanded copper-foil facilities, and the manufacture of artificial soil for Japan's crowded golf courses.

During the mid-1990s the company shuttered its lead refining business as part of a restructuring plan designed to shore up profits. It established two new subsidiaries in 1995 including Mitsui Siam Components Co. Ltd. and Mitsui-Huayang Automotive Components Co. Ltd. Mitsui Copper Foil (Hong Kong) Co. Ltd. was created in 1998. Company headquarters were moved to Osaki, Shinagawa-ku, Tokyo, in the following year.

MOVING INTO THE 21ST CENTURY

MMS faced increased competition and falling demand for zinc and electronics-related materials during the early years of the new millennium. In response to industry conditions, the company cut costs, revamped operations, and made several key joint ventures. MMS teamed up with Nippon Mining & Metals Co. Ltd. in 2000 to create Pan Pacific Copper Co. Ltd., which oversaw the copper activities of both companies. Two years later, it partnered with Sumitomo Metal Mining Co. to form MS Zinc Co. Ltd. In 2001, Mitsui Copper Foil (Guangdong) Co. Ltd. was created to produce electrodeposited copper foil in China. That same year, the company

shuttered its mining operations at the Kamioka Mine in an attempt to cut costs and improve profitability. During 2002, Mitsui Components Guangdong Co. Ltd. was established to produce automotive parts in China. It also acquired Ohi Seisakusho Co. Ltd. in 2003 to bolster its automotive components business.

In March 2006, the company began zinc ore production at the Pallca Mine in Peru. The company also continued to expand production of automotive components, opening new offices in Thailand and China. An automotive components subsidiary was also established in India in 2005. During this time period, MMS struggled to sustain consistent sales growth and profitability. In fiscal 2007, the company experienced losses in its semiconductor mounting materials business that included Tape Automated Bonding (TAB) tape and Chip On Film (COF) tape products. In addition, the price of zinc was lower than the company anticipated. Net income fell dramatically that year, from ¥31.3 billion recorded in the previous year to ¥7.8 billion in the fiscal year ending March 31, 2008.

For the first time since 1993, MMS anticipated it would post pretax losses in fiscal 2009. In January 2009, the company announced it would cut 4,000 employees and restructure operations in an attempt to increase revenue and shore up profits. MMS management, led by President and CEO Yoshihiko Takebayashi, was concerned about the company's financial situation but believed MMS stood well positioned for future growth. The global market for automobiles and electronics products, including LCD televisions and cellular phones, was expected to see steady growth in the coming years and MMS provided components to both of these industries.

Jonathan Martin
Updated, Christina M. Stansell

PRINCIPAL SUBSIDIARIES

Kamioka Mining & Smelting Co., Ltd; Hachinohe Smelting Co., Ltd.; Hikoshima Smelting Co., Ltd.; Okuaizu Geothermal Co., Ltd.; Taiwan Copper Foil Co., Ltd.; Mitsui Copper Foil (Malaysia) Sdn. Bhd.; MCS, Inc.; Mitsui Electronic Materials Co., Ltd.; Ohi Seisakusho Co., Ltd.; GECOM Corp.; Mitsui Siam Components Co., Ltd.; MESCO, Inc.; Mitsui Kinzoku Trading Co., Ltd.

PRINCIPAL COMPETITORS

Mitsubishi Materials Corp.; Sumitomo Metal Mining Co. Ltd.; Toho Zinc Co. Ltd.

FURTHER READING

"Japan's Mitsui Mining Lowers Profit Forecast, Cancels Dividend Plans," *Wall Street Journal,* January 28, 1994.

Klamann, Edmund, "Japanese Smelters Eager to Ratchet Up Capacity," *Reuters News,* August 12, 1996.

"Mitsui Kinzoku Seen Bracing for FY08 Pretax Loss," *Asia Pulse,* January 8, 2009.

"Mitsui Mining & Smelting to Cut 4 Thousand Workers/Late this September," *Japan Metal Daily,* January 21, 2009.

"Mitsui Mining, Nippon Mining to Launch Copper Project in Peru," *Kyodo News,* November 7, 2007.

"Nippon Mining, Mitsui Mining Form Joint Copper Sales Co.," *Dow Jones International News,* September 21, 2000.

Roberts, John G., *Mitsui: Three Centuries of Japanese Business,* New York: Weatherhill, 1989.

Yoshikawa, Miho, "Japan Fears Defeat in World Race for Resources," *Reuters News,* December 21, 2006.

MTI Enterprises Inc.

---

421 West 54th Street
New York, New York 10019
U.S.A.
Telephone: (212) 541-4684
Fax: (212) 397-4684
Web site: http://www.mtishows.com

Private Company
Incorporated: 1952 as Music Theatre International
Employees: 65
Sales: $38 million
NAICS: 533110 Owners and Lessors of Other Non-
    Financial Assets

■ ■ ■

MTI Enterprises Inc. is the holding company for Music Theatre International, a major licenser of Broadway, Off Broadway, and London's West End musicals and other theatrical productions. The New York City-based company controls the rights to more than 300 musicals and licenses more than 15,000 productions in the United States and Canada each year, catering to about 45,000 amateur and professional theatrical organizations, including high schools, colleges, and community theaters. MTI also uses subagents to license productions to more than 60 other countries. In addition to full-length productions, MTI offers abridged versions for productions by children. In an effort to develop a new audience for musical theater, the company offers The Broadway Junior Collection, a package that helps schools to mount classic musicals. MTI also offers the

MTI Concert Library, a collection of symphonic arrangements of full scores of Broadway shows as well as selected songs.

MTI has played a key role in keeping the work of many authors alive, and the secondary rights provide them and their families with a healthy income for many years. In some cases, musicals that were major Broadway disappointments, such as *Seussical: The Musical,* an adaptation of the works of Dr. Seuss, have gone on to become cash cows based on secondary rights. MTI is majority owned by Freddie Gershon, an entertainment lawyer with a rich background in popular music, musical theater, and film.

ORIGINS

Music Theatre International was founded in 1952 by orchestrator Don Walker, composer and lyricist Frank Loesser, and theatrical agent Allen B. Whitehead. Although MTI claims Loesser as its founder, according to his daughter Susan Loesser in a biography she wrote about her father, *A Most Remarkable Fella,* the idea for MTI originated with Walker. He was a versatile musical talent who started out orchestrating operettas, and soon branched out to arrangements for the popular big band Fred Waring's Pennsylvanians. Walker also became a Broadway mainstay and pioneer, his ability to transform the melodies of a composer into a complete orchestral instrumentation making him one of the first orchestrators to earn a continuous royalty from the shows he arranged.

The idea for MTI grew out of an assignment from Richard Rodgers of Rodgers and Hammerstein fame.

Rodgers was planning a revival of *Pal Joey* and asked Walker to reorchestrate some of the songs. The rights to the show were handled by Tams-Witmark Music Library. When Walker stopped by the office for the original orchestration he was surprised by the state of the materials he received. Complete numbers had been omitted by a careless staff. As a result, the people involved in the revival would have to reconstruct *Pal Joey*.

The situation inspired Walker with the idea for a licensing company that would focus on preserving the work of authors for posterity as well as licensing their secondary rights, a company he wanted to call Music Theatre. Because Rodgers and Hammerstein had three musicals about to go into subsidiary rights, *Oklahoma!*, *South Pacific*, and *Carousel*, Walker approached the pair about starting a new licensing agency using those shows as a foundation. Rodgers and Hammerstein were completely won over by Walker's pitch. They decided to start a licensing company with their shows as a base, Rodgers and Hammerstein Repertory, but without Walker.

Walker then knew that his idea was a good one, and believing there was room in the market for another musical licensing agency, he and his agent looked for another author who could supply source material. He had been talking to Frank Loesser about working together on what would become *The Most Happy Fella*, and he pitched the idea over the phone to Loesser in California. Loesser readily agreed to start the new busi-ness, Music Theatre International, as a subsidiary of his publishing company, Frank Music Corp.

MUSICAL THEATER BACKGROUND

Loesser was born in New York City in 1910. His father, a Prussian virtuoso pianist, provided Loesser with a strong musical background, but he proved to be a headstrong youth, refusing to speak German as his fam-ily desired and showing a predilection for music less sophisticated than that of his father. As a child he won third place in a citywide harmonic contest. Bored with college he flunked out of City College of New York in

his freshman year and tried his hand at a number of professions, including newspaper work and radio writing. He also wrote lyrics and slowly built a career that brought him in the mid-1930s to Hollywood, where he earned a living mostly writing the lyrics to novelty numbers. He served in the U.S. Army during World War II and crafted two of the most popular songs of the era, "They're Either Too Young or Too Old" and "Praise the Lord and Pass the Ammunition." He also began writing his own melodies during this period and after the war solidified his reputation as a composer-lyricist. In 1949 he won an Academy Award for his song "Baby, It's Cold Outside."

Loesser also expanded his ambition, turning his at-tention to the Broadway musical. He scored a hit with *Where's Charley?*, a show that would enjoy a two-year run, an impressive feat for the time. It was his next show, however, that established Loesser as one of the greats in musical theater history. In 1950 Loesser unveiled a musical based on the eccentric, wise-talking characters of Damon Runyon called *Guys and Dolls*, considered by many to be the greatest American musical of all time. Later Loesser would also pen *The Most Happy Fella*, and *How to Succeed in Business Without Re-ally Trying*.

The third MTI founder was Allen Whitehead, who was brought in to manage the agency. Born in North Carolina in 1919, Whitehead attended the University of South Carolina before leaving school in 1942 to enlist in the U.S. Navy during World War II. After his discharge in 1946, Whitehead was accepted to Yale Drama School but never enrolled. Instead, a temporary job in New York filling in for a theatrical agent launched his Broadway career. After teaming up with Loesser and Walker, Whitehead ran MTI as president, working out of the offices of a leading theatrical agent, Howard Hoyt. His clients provided six shows to supple-ment Loesser's *Where's Charley?* and *Guys and Dolls*. They included *Gentlemen Prefer Blondes, Call Me Madam*, and *High Button Shoes*. In 1960 Loesser formed Frank Productions, Inc., primarily to produce his own shows. Whitehead managed this business as well and served as Loesser's coproducer.

CHANGES IN OWNERSHIP

The three Loesser companies operated out of offices on West 57th Street in Manhattan during the 1950s and 1960s. MTI gained a solid reputation for preserving musical theater works as Walker had envisioned and its catalog grew steadily despite competition from Tams-Witmark and Rodgers and Hammerstein Repertory. Some of the early properties included *The Music Man, West Side Story*, and *A Funny Thing Happened on the Way to the Forum.* Aside from Broadway musicals, MTI enjoyed success with Off Broadway fare, most notably *The Fantasticks,* which opened in the 153-seat Sullivan Street Playhouse in May 1960. The original production would run for 42 years, making it the world's longest-running musical to date. Only a few years after the show debuted, MTI began licensing *The Fantasticks* to summer stock, community, and university theaters. It was also performed in dozens of countries.

Frank Loesser died in 1969 and for a time his wife Jo attempted to run her late husband's three businesses, but after a few years she dissolved Frank Productions and sold Frank Music and MTI. CBS Inc., holding company of the major television network, acquired MTI, which became part of the company's music publishing division, which in turn was part of the company's record group. It remained with CBS until 1986 when a new chief executive officer was installed at CBS, which was struggling at the time. The company's educational and professional publishing division was sold to Harcourt Brace Jovanovich Inc., and in a separate deal the music publishing division was carved out and sold to Charles Koppelman and Martin Bandier, the principal owners of Entertainment Co., a music publishing and production company.

MTI changed hands again in 1988 when Freddie Gershon acquired the company. Gershon was a man with a varied show business background. A native of New York City born in 1939, he trained as a child to be a classical musician at the Juilliard School of Music, studying there from 1948 to 1956. Instead of pursing a performance career, he earned a law degree from Columbia University in 1964 and became an entertainment attorney, representing a variety of clients before becoming counsel to The Robert Stigwood Group Ltd.

as well as chief operating officer. As such he was involved in the concert tours of such popular music artists as Eric Clapton, The Bee Gees, and Andy Gibb. He also represented the Broadway production and film of *Jesus Christ Superstar.*

CAMERON MACKINTOSH JOINS MTI

Well versed in marketing, Gershon looked to revitalize MTI and secondary licensing in general. "This has been a business where, for decades, people would be sent a catalogue and wait for the phone to ring," Gershon told *Back Stage.* To help him grow and market the company he took on a minority partner in 1991, producer Cameron Mackintosh, who had been enjoying success in transplanting West End musicals to Broadway, such as *Les Miserables* and *Miss Saigon.* The two men had been discussing the licensing of these two works and Mackintosh became enamored with the MTI catalog, leading to his investment in the company. A primary aim of Mackintosh was to expand MTI's international business by producing revivals of some of the catalog's musicals in the United Kingdom. He and Gershon also saw promise in Eastern Europe, where countries emerging from Communist rule were a ripe market for musical theater. MTI also looked to tap into the Japanese market, allying itself with TV Asahi to license American musicals in Japan for amateur and stock productions. Other efforts reflective of Gershon's emphasis on marketing included a video series of composers and directors discussing their works.

Over the years, the demographic of the Broadway audience had been skewing older, creating a need to interest a new generation in musical theater. In 1994 Gershon began developing what would become MTI's Broadway Junior Program, which helped to introduce theater, music, dance, and art to schoolchildren when it was launched in 1998. MTI-represented shows, such as *Annie, Guys and Dolls,* and *Fiddler on the Roof,* were adapted for performances by children and packaged to help in their mounting. In a matter of ten years more than 16,000 licensed Broadway Junior productions would be staged by elementary and middle schools in the United States and Canada. Studies commissioned by MTI revealed that the program in New York public schools helped students to develop not only performance skills but also confidence and a willingness to take chances as well. Moreover, the shows helped in growing school communities.

In revitalizing musical theater, MTI and Broadway found an important new ally in the Walt Disney Company. Not only did Disney help resurrect 42nd Street and stimulate ticket sales with the production of

Disney properties adapted into Broadway musicals, such as *Beauty and the Beast* and *The Lion King*, it used its cable television channel to stimulate interest in musicals geared toward young people and create new products for MTI to represent. In 2006 Disney broadcast *High School Musical*, a made-for-television film whose soundtrack was the number one release of the year. The show was quickly adapted for school and amateur productions and licensed through a partnership between MTI and Disney Theatrical Group.

NEW LENDING LIBRARY OPENS

Traditionally, MTI generated most of its revenues from professional productions, but in the 21st century the company became the beneficiary of a trend among high schools to mount increasingly more lavish productions, resulting in higher ticket prices and greater royalties for MTI and the authors it represented. There were also ancillary products to offer, such as MTI's RehearScore CD. Priced at $250, the disc included separate vocal and accompaniment lines allowing performers to use their personal computers to rehearse as much as they liked. There were also videos available to coach young actors in how to play particular parts. Schools also became more ambitious in the musicals they chose to mount, again benefiting MTI and its catalog that included *Les Miserables* and the works of Stephen Sondheim.

Demand for MTI material grew so much that the company outgrew its West Babylon, New York, lending library, leading to a move to a new facility in New Hartford, Connecticut, in 2007. The extra space would be needed following MTI's exclusive agreement with Disney to license all of its musicals. With sequels to *High School Musical* on the horizon, even more orders from high schools to keep MTI busy seemed likely. Interest in Broadway musicals also remained high. Pulitzer Prize–winning *Rent* was popular among high school students, but less so with school communities. Although the show had been modified to eliminate profane and sexually explicit lyrics and dialogue, some of its subject matter, namely homosexuality and AIDS, proved divisive in many communities around the country. At the very least, the controversy showed that musical theater remained vital in the United States and that MTI and the authors it represented could expect to enjoy continued success for many years to come.

Ed Dinger

PRINCIPAL SUBSIDIARIES

Music Theatre International.

PRINCIPAL COMPETITORS

Samuel French, Inc.; Tams-Witmark Music Library, Inc.; The Rodgers & Hammerstein Organization.

FURTHER READING

"Allen Whitehead Dies at 88," *Variety*, April 3, 2008.

Banach, Ken, "Music Theatre International Bringing 12 Jobs When It Relocates Warehouse," *Waterbury (Conn.) Republican-American*, March 6, 2007.

Bessman, Jim, "MTI Keeps Theater Young and Vibrant," *Billboard*, June 9, 2001, p. 58.

"CBS Selling Publishing Unit for $500 Million," *Associated Press*, October 24, 1986.

"Don Walker, 81, an Orchestrator of Broadway Musical Comedies," *New York Times*, September 13, 1989.

Fabrikant, Geraldine, "Harcourt to Pay CBS $500 Million for Unit," *New York Times*, October 25, 1986, p. 1.

Green, Jesse, "The Supersizing of the School Play," *New York Times*, May 8, 2005.

Healy, Patrick, "Tamer 'Rent' Is Too Wild for Some Schools," *New York Times*, February 20, 2009.

Loesser, Susan, *A Most Remarkable Fella: Frank Loesser and the Guys and Dolls in His Life*, New York: D.I. Fine, 1993.

McKinley, Jesse, "Far from the Spotlight, the True Powers of Broadway," *New York Times*, February 26, 2006.

Ramirez, Miriam, "High School Musical, How a Song and Dance Defined a Generation," *McAllen (Tex.) Monitor*, May 9, 2008.

Robertson, Campbell, "Stripped Down but Still Hatted, That Cat Is Back," *New York Times*, July 13, 2007.

Walsh, Thomas, "Mackintosh Gets Big Share of Musical Licenser," *Back Stage*, April 12, 1991, p. 3.

Mueller Sports Medicine, Inc.

1 Quench Drive
Prairie du Sac, Wisconsin 53578
U.S.A.
Telephone: (608) 643-8530
Fax: (608) 643-2568
Web site: http://www.muellersportsmed.com

Private Company
Incorporated: 1961 as Mueller Athletic Training Room
    Supplies
Employees: 100
Sales: $58.5 million (2007 est.)
NAICS: 325412 Pharmaceutical Preparations Manu-
    facturing

■ ■ ■

Family-owned Mueller Sports Medicine, Inc., is one of
the leading manufacturers and marketers of sports
medicine products, its founder, Curt Mueller, having essentially invented the category. The Prairie du Sac,
Wisconsin, company serves both retail and the team and
institutional segments of the sports medicine industry.
For the team and institutional market, Mueller's original
focus, the company offers protective gear; mouth guards;
bottles, carriers, and coolers; and such sports accessories
as ball cleaner, oral wedges to open the jaws of injured
athletes, and pine tar. Mueller also offers tape and taping supplies, elastic wraps, grip enhancers for a wide
variety of athletic endeavors, glare reducing grease sticks
and adhesive strips, flip-up sunglasses, abrasion control
and padding products, analgesics, cleaners and

disinfectants, wound care products and bandages, hot
and cold therapy products, and complete trainers' kits
and refill kits.

Mueller products are also carried by sporting goods
stores, including major retailers such as Dick's Sporting
Goods and Sports Authority. Moreover, the company
pioneered the sports medicine category in drug stores,
offering many of the products it provides to the team
and institutional market as well as items geared toward
weekend athletes, such as braces and supports. Mueller
also maintains distribution subsidiaries in Europe and
Japan, and does business in Central and South America.
Curt Mueller serves as the company's chief executive officer, while three of his children hold top management
positions.

FOUNDER: STAR HIGH SCHOOL ATHLETE

Company founder Curt Mueller was a star high school
athlete, earning 17 varsity letters in baseball, basketball,
football, golf, and track-and-field, as well as an excellent
student in his hometown of Prairie du Sac, Wisconsin.
In the mid-1950s he enrolled at the University of Wisconsin–Madison where as a walk-on he played power
forward on the basketball team while earning a degree
in pharmaceutical chemistry. After graduating in 1956
he went to work for Walgreens Drugstores in Chicago
before leaving in 1959 to join his father, Oliver, who
owned a pharmacy in Prairie du Sac.

While working for his father, Mueller soon
recognized a business opportunity. He noticed that high
school athletics programs being serviced by sporting

goods stores were receiving inferior training room supplies, hardly of the same quality a pharmacy would consider adequate. Hence, he conceived of the concept of "sports medicine" and the sale of pharmacy-quality goods to sports teams. In 1961 in the basement of his father's pharmacy, Mueller launched Mueller Athletic Training Room Supplies and began developing pharmaceutical grade products to serve the sporting goods, team, college, and professional markets. The products included athlete's foot treatments, a skin toughener spray, antibiotic ointment, antibacterial bar soap and presurgical foam spray, anesthetic lubricating ointment, and disinfectant. He also developed a salivary stimulant called Quench to eliminate "cotton mouth," available as a mist or mouthwash.

The early years were not without difficulties; Mueller struggled to persuade customers that sports medicine was not mere quackery, a perception that he had to overcome, especially as he sold his wares out of the trunk of his car. In the first year he generated sales of just $452. The quality of the products gradually created converts, however, and soon Mueller assembled a national sales force to reach both the team and retail markets. He also began looking overseas. In 1967 he began marketing his products around the world, printing catalogs in various languages to sell to countries in Europe and the Pacific Rim. In 1975 Mueller Sports Medicine became the first company of its kind to exhibit at the Spring and Autumn ISPO Trade Fairs.

QUENCH GUM INTRODUCED

New products under the Mueller name were added on a regular basis. In 1969 the company introduced an athletic shoe sole cleaner to prevent slipping. A year later the Medi-Kit was unveiled, featuring a tape tray designed to keep rolls free of damage. A colorless spray to curb bleeding was added in 1971, and in 1974 the company began marketing a product that would bring a good deal of exposure to the Mueller name: Quench Gum. Helping a great deal to promote the product was

the famed Harlem Globetrotters basketball team, whose members became early customers. Legendary Globetrotter Meadowlark Lemon even endorsed the product in print ads.

In 1979 Curt Mueller attempted to break into the chain drugstore market, developing a new line of sports braces and supports for this channel to replace the typical beige elastic products drugstores had carried for many years. "Mueller's message fell on deaf ears," according to *Chain Drug Review.* "A buyer from a local chain drugstore escorted him to the front door, pointed to a Herman's Sporting Goods store down the block, and said, 'Sports medicine, or whatever you call it, has a place in the sporting goods store, not the pharmacy.'"

Not one to be easily deterred, however, Mueller refused to be limited to the narrow retail outlet of sporting goods stores. In 1984 he introduced a full line of patented sport bracing products as well as the "Planogram Retail Sport Care" concept that laid out for retailers how and where the products should be displayed in order to merchandise the largest number of sports medicine products in the least amount of space. Mueller was then able to convince sporting goods stores to sell the company's products in the front of the store instead of relegating them to the back room. Mueller also began shrinking the packaging in order to maximize profits. In fact, the Mueller Sports Care displays were highly profitable, an attribute that earned greater commitment from sporting goods stores and won over drugstore chains. The program also included inventory controls, and retail clerks were better trained to sell the products through videos and seminars. With this success, Mueller was able to persuade Walgreens to add sports medicine departments in their midwestern stores.

INTERNATIONAL EXPANSION

In the meantime, Mueller Sports Medicine advanced on other fronts. Aside from the sport bracing line, the company brought to market a number of other products as well. Heel and lace pads were introduced in 1980, followed a year later by a newly formulated prewrap adherent pump spray, and a blood-clotting, spray-on bandage in 1982. The company then introduced a line of wound care products in 1983, including M-Lastic Tape and More Skin Dermal Pads. Colored prewrap products were added in 1985 under the Big Bold M-Wrap name.

In 1980 Mueller Japan was established in Tokyo to increase exports to the Far East. Mueller bolstered its position in the European sports medicine market with the creation of a factory sales force in 1986. A year later the Mueller Europe subsidiary established its

KEY DATES

1961: Curt Mueller establishes Mueller Athletic Training Room Supplies.
1967: International marketing of company products begins.
1974: Quench Gum is introduced.
1980: Mueller Japan is established in Tokyo.
1984: Planogram Retail Sport Care concept debuts.
1994: New 12-foot sports care department display is created.
2002: Curt Mueller is named to Sporting Goods Industry Hall of Fame.
2007: LifeCare for Her product line is introduced.

headquarters and opened a distribution center in Rotterdam, Netherlands. Later the operation would be relocated to Rijsenhout, near Amsterdam. In 1992 Mueller Canada and Mueller Australia were established to better serve those markets.

In the late 1980s Mueller developed the Magnum functional ACL knee brace, which included the patented Triaxial Hinge, allowing the brace to mirror the movement of the human knee, thus providing the company with entry to the orthopedic surgeon market. A doctor could fit an athlete with one of the new braces for about $1,000. The line received a boost when National Football League players began wearing the devices soon after they were introduced.

By the start of the 1990s the company was generating $10 million in annual sales, and while Quench Gum remained the best-known product, the line of knee and ankle braces made the primary contribution to the balance sheet. Meanwhile, Curt Mueller was searching in any number of directions to maintain growth, including among female athletes. The company introduced the Hot Stuff line of colorful knee supports, mostly targeting volleyball players. Athletic tape in school colors was also added to further tap into the high school and college team markets. Other products in the early 1990s included a non-sticky grip enhancer (Magic Grip Spray) in 1991. Two years later the company introduced wipes and sprays to check the possible spread of HIV/AIDS, and a number of other biohazard products to control blood-borne pathogens. Also in 1993 Mueller acquired Ohio-based Magnum Orthopedic and moved its production facilities to Prairie du Sac, where a new orthopedic laboratory was also built to allow the company to offer custom-made

knee braces. Mueller had been working with Magnum Orthopedic on a joint venture basis since the early 1980s, as it had with Analog Orthotics, which Mueller also brought into the fold in 1993.

EXPANDING THE PRODUCT LINE

Efforts to cut down the size of retail packaging reached a new level in 1994 when Mueller unveiled its 12-foot sports care department, which allowed more than 1,100 units to be merchandised in less than 20 square feet. According to a National Sporting Goods Association Business survey, the Mueller sports care display enjoyed an average gross profit margin of $300 per selling square foot compared to the industry average of $95.

The aging of baby boomers, along with their refusal to age without a struggle or give up their weekend sporting wars, helped to further spur sales for Mueller in the 1990s. To serve this market, Mueller developed a number of new products. In 1997 a line of one-size-fits-all neoprene products was introduced to support such areas as elbows, ankles, and wrists; as well as the Lite Brace, a one-hinged, one-size-fits-all ankle brace; and the Mueller Hinge 2100, a triple-hinged brace. The company also acquired the license to sell Aircast ankle support and elbow support braces, which relied on air cells to provide compression as needed. In addition, Mueller became the worldwide distributor of the Tuli Heel cup and related ankle brace and neoprene ankle supports, as well as the Cho Pat line of orthotic products, including a knee strap, knee braces, shin splints compression sleeves, Achilles tendon strap, and tennis elbow supports. At the same time, Mueller continued to develop its own products, including a taping kit suitable for a variety of uses other than sports, such as vacations and camping trips.

More one-size-fits-all products followed in the late 1990s. The Perfect Fit Ankle Brace made its debut in 1998. Using a lightweight material with an elastic heel, it fit comfortably inside the shoe, and Velcro closures provided a snug and adjustable fit. Mueller also introduced the Wonder Wrap, a nylon wrap with Velcro closures for the knee or ankle; a one-size-fits-all back brace; and an adjustable nose guard to protect users from suffering further damage to a broken nose.

MUELLER IN THE 21ST CENTURY

More one-size-fits-all products followed in the new century, including inexpensive triple-hinged knee braces; cold/hot therapy pads that could be cut to shape, microwaved or chilled; non-latex Soft Support Wrap, which was also waterproof and hypoallergenic; new ankle and knee supports using patented tension straps for an adjustable level of support; and a carpal tunnel Wrist Stabilizer that fit either the left or right wrist.

For his efforts in establishing the Sports Medicine category, Curt Mueller was inducted into the Sporting Goods Industry Hall of Fame in 2002, joining the likes of Alfred G. Spalding and Samuel Colt. Approaching 70 years of age, Mueller was far from ready to rest on his laurels. Instead, he and his children continued to look for ways to grow the company, developing new products as well as revitalizing favorites. For example, a reformulated Quench Gum offering extreme flavoring then in vogue was unveiled in 2002. New flavors were added in 2007 and sugar-free and aspartame-free varieties were introduced in 2008.

In the beginning the company had catered to high school boys, but the industry that Curt Mueller had done so much to develop had undergone a great deal of change over the years. Rather than an athletic trainer, his typical 21st century customer was a woman buying for herself and her family. It was not surprising, therefore, that in 2007 Mueller would introduce the LifeCare for Her line of ultralight, all-day supports for knees, ankles, elbows, and wrists. With a second generation of the Mueller family well seasoned in the sports medicine business, there was every reason to expect that the company would continue to adjust successfully to changing trends for many years to come.

Ed Dinger

PRINCIPAL DIVISIONS

Mueller Europe; Mueller Japan.

PRINCIPAL COMPETITORS

McDavid, Inc.; Russell Athletic; Trace Athletic Corporation.

FURTHER READING

Calandra, Bob, "Joint Effort," *Sporting Goods Business,* January 27, 1997, p. 36.

Firebaugh, Susan, "Bracing Times for Sport Medicine," *Milwaukee Journal,* October 21, 1990, p. 32.

Jacobson, Greg, "Milestone for Mueller," *MMR,* June 17, 2002, p. 121.

"Mueller Products Help People Stay Active," *Chain Drug Review,* July 2, 2001, p. 120.

"Mueller Pushes Envelope in Sports Medicine," *Chain Drug Review,* June 25, 2007, p. 139.

"Mueller Takes Sports Medicine to Baby Boomers," *Chain Drug Review,* June 6, 2005, p. 132.

"Mueller … the Sports Medicine Family," *Sporting Good Business,* August 1994, p. 46.

National Bank of Ukraine

9 Institutskaya Street
Kiev, 01601
Ukraine
Telephone: (38 044) 253 01 80
Fax: (38 044) 230 20 33
Web site: http://www.bank.gov.ua

State-Owned Company
Incorporated: 1991
Employees: 1,000
Total Assets: $43.23 billion (2007)
NAICS: 521110 Monetary Authorities-Central Banks

■ ■ ■

National Bank of Ukraine (NBU) is that country's central bank, charged with carrying out the fiscal and monetary policies of the Ukrainian government. NBU is responsible for minting and issuing the country's currency, the hryvnia; coordinating the country's gold and currency reserves; and establishing foreign exchange and interest rates. NBU also has oversight authority for the country's commercial banking system, enforcing banking legislation, coordinating electronic payment systems, and providing analysis, forecasting, and other information services. NBU participates in educational and training efforts, including the operation of a Banking University, in order to develop qualified personnel both for itself and for the Ukrainian banking sector as a whole. Although created in 1991, NBU's historic lack of independence from the Ukrainian government long hampered its ability to fulfill its functions as a central

bank. Since the passage of a new Banking Law in 2001, especially since the "Orange Revolution" of 2004, NBU has played an important role in stabilizing Ukraine's economy. Volodymyr Stelmakh was appointed NBU's president in 2004.

UKRAINIAN MONETARY HISTORY

Centuries of domination by its larger neighbors meant that Ukraine had never seen the development of a national banking system before the 20th century. The brief period of independence from 1917 to 1921 brought with it an early attempt to create a national Ukrainian currency. Following the proclamation of an independent Ukrainian People's Republic (UPR) in 1917, the new government declared the creation of a national currency, initially called the *karbovanets*. The government established a value for the new currency based on the gold standard. By December of that year the first 100 karbovanets banknote was placed into circulation.

The first counterfeit karbovanets quickly appeared in circulation as well. Faced with this situation the Ukrainian government rushed to replace the karbovanets with an entirely new currency, called the hryvnia. The new currency, which drew its name from a copper coin minted during an earlier phase in Ukrainian history, fulfilled a political purpose, underscoring the government's determination to form an independent state. Printed in Berlin, the first hryvnia banknotes, in denominations of two, 10, 100, 500, 1,000 and 2,000, were rushed into circulation in March 1918. At the same time the government issued coins, which took the name of kopiyka.

COMPANY PERSPECTIVES

According to the Constitution of Ukraine, the main function of the National Bank is to ensure the stability of Ukraine's monetary unit. To carry out its major function, the National Bank shall foster the stability of the banking system and within its competence, the price stability.

The struggle for control of Ukraine between the pro-Bolshevik UPR and the pro-European Ukrainian State led to a reissuing of a new series of karbovanets, and then again to the relaunch of the hryvnia. These efforts were for naught, however, as the newly emerging Soviet Union soon extended its control over Ukraine. By the early 1920s the first Soviet currency had been placed in circulation in Ukraine, which itself was absorbed into the Soviet Union. The collapse of the attempt to establish an independent nation also spelled the end to any hopes of establishing a national bank with its own national currency.

As part of the Soviet Union, Ukraine's banking sector was governed by regional branches of the U.S.S.R.'s four state-run banks, including the Gosbank, or State Bank, which served as the Soviet central bank. The National Bank of Ukraine (NBU) did not exist as such, but instead operated as the Ukraine branch of the Gosbank. This meant the Ukrainian branch had no authority to issue currency, perform regulatory functions, or otherwise steer Ukraine's financial and economic systems.

REFORMING THE SOVIET BANKING SYSTEM

Nonetheless, the Ukrainian component of the Gosbank provided a training ground of sorts for the development of the future NBU. Movements toward the reform of the region's banking sector took place in the 1980s, as the economic reform policies put into place by Soviet president Mikhail Gorbachev heralded the end of the centrally planned Communist economic system, and ultimately, the breakup of the Soviet Union itself.

The reform of the Soviet banking system in 1987 set into motion the first steps toward the creation of NBU. In that year, the Soviet government established a two-tier banking system based on the Western model. This involved the creation of a Central Bank, which did not engage in retail banking activities but instead acted as a regulatory agent overseeing a second tier of commercial banks. The four existing Soviet state banks were then reorganized into five commercial banks, Agroprombank, Promstrojbank, Zhilsotsbank, Sberbank, and Vneshtorgbank.

The arrival to power of Boris Yeltsin in 1991 brought an end to the Soviet Union. Ukraine then declared its independence, becoming the first member of the new Commonwealth of Independent States reorganization of most of the Soviet Union's former republics, including Russia. The new Verkhovna Rada, the Ukrainian parliament, quickly enacted legislation regarding the state's banking sector, passing the "Law On Banks and Banking" in March 1991.

The centerpiece of the new legislation involved the transformation of the former Ukraine branch of Gosbank into the country's central bank, National Bank of Ukraine, or NBU. Vladimir Matvienko was named as the bank's first president. Among NBU's first acts was to reorganize the Ukrainian operations of the five Soviet state banks. These were granted commercial banking licenses and were then renamed, becoming Oshchadbank, Prominvestbank, Ukrsotsbank, Ukraine, and Ukreximbank, respectively.

CENTRAL BANK FOR AN INDEPENDENT STATE

NBU launched an extremely liberal commercial licensing procedure, enabling a surge in new banks to appear in the country. By the end of 1991 there were 72 licensed banks in operation in Ukraine. By 1995 NBU had authorized the creation of more than 230 banks to operate in the extremely fragile Ukrainian economy.

Ukraine's economy remained highly intertwined with that of Russia's, as the country sought to transition from rubles to the creation of its own currency. Hampering the country's independent economic growth was the fact that large portions of the country's wealth remained tied up in Russia's Sberbank. So the country turned to the International Monetary Fund (IMF) and the World Bank, which pumped more than $10 billion into the country through the 1990s.

In 1992 NBU established a foreign currency exchange. The central bank then made a first step toward developing a national currency, launching the circulation of reusable coupons. By the end of the year, NBU had issued a non-cash currency, the karbovanetz, thereby exiting the group of countries still using the ruble as their currency. By the end of that year, NBU had also appointed a new president, Vadym Hetman.

Hetman was soon replaced, however, by a new and longer-lasting president, Viktor Yushchenko, who would

KEY DATES

1987: The Soviet Union creates a two-tier banking system with Gosbank (State Bank) serving as a central bank.

1991: Ukraine declares its independence and the Ukrainian branch of Gosbank becomes National Bank of Ukraine (NBU).

1994: NBU becomes responsible for the national mint.

1996: NBU launches Ukraine's national currency, the hryvnia.

2001: The new Law on Banks and Banking establishes NBU as an autonomous central bank independent of the Ukrainian government.

2008: The opposition party Yulia Tymoshenko Bloc introduces legislation to place NBU under government authority.

later become prime minister and then president of Ukraine. Yushchenko's banking career had begun during the Soviet era when he worked as an economist for the Russian Ulyanovsk branch of Gosbank. After becoming head of that branch Yushchenko was transferred to his native Ukraine, where he became the deputy director of Gosbank's Ukraine headquarters in 1985. By 1988 Yushchenko had been promoted to lead the Agroprombank in Ukraine.

One of Yushchenko's primary accomplishments during his leadership of NBU, which lasted until his appointment as prime minister in 1999, was the establishment of a true national currency. In 1994 NBU founded its own mint, including facilities for the printing of banknotes. By the following year NBU had released its first commemorative coin, marking the 50th anniversary of the end of World War II.

ON THE BRINK OF CHAOS

By 1996 NBU had readied the launch of the new Ukrainian currency, which it introduced that year as the hryvnia. In September 1996, NBU carried out a two-week transition period, replacing the karbovanets then in circulation. The launch of the hryvnia was hailed as an important step toward the stabilization of the increasingly chaotic Ukrainian economy.

Indeed, by the mid-1990s Ukraine's economy teetered on the brink of collapse as the country struggled to make the transition to a free market economy. As in Russia and other former Soviet republics, the country was beset by massive government corruption and political cronyism, which saw large parts of the country's industry and resources sold at a discounts amid an atmosphere of rampant political favoritism.

NBU's own ability to stabilize the economy was hampered by its lack of real power to carry out much need banking reforms. Although nominally autonomous, NBU in fact remained subject to the whims of the Ukrainian government, the monetary policies of which had been described as "irrational" and "perverse." As a result, through the first half of the 1990s the country was rocked by massive inflation (as high as 100 percent per month) while the exit from the ruble had more or less wiped out the savings of the entire country.

The government's insistence that NBU continue to issue credits both to the government and to the country's large commercial banks, most of which had been privatized and sold to the government's political cronies, only contributed to the coming collapse of the Ukrainian economy. Also, NBU later found itself accused of mishandling large swaths of the funds provided to Ukraine by the IMF. These included some $765 million in short-term loans, which were funneled to a number of commercial banks both in Ukraine and in Russia between 1996 and 1997.

This lack of stability gave rise to a powerful shadow economy. By the time of the economic collapse (sparked by Russia's own economic collapse in 1998) the black market was said to represent some 50 percent of all transactions in Ukraine. Nonetheless, NBU under Yushchenko was credited with having established a foundation for new growth in the country's economy. Tighter controls put into place under Yushchenko had, if nothing else, managed to end the period of hyperinflation in Ukraine, and established the hryvnia as a true national currency.

BECOMING A TRUE CENTRAL BANK IN THE 21ST CENTURY

Yushchenko's popularity rose among the exasperated Ukrainian population. This popularity led then-president and strongman Leonid Kuchma to name Yushchenko as the country's prime minister in 1999, in order to shore up Kuchma's own wavering power at the time. As prime minister Yushchenko pushed through a more strictly controlled monetary policy, which helped stimulate a new era of growth in Ukraine's economy.

Yushchenko's reform efforts ultimately resulted in the passage of new banking legislation in 2001 that finally established NBU as an autonomously operating body with the true powers of a central banking authority. NBU put a new board into place, led by Volodymyr Stelmakh.

These moves led to increasing friction between Yushchenko and the oligarchs that had gained control of much of Ukraine's financial and other industries under Kuchma. By 2001, Yushchenko was forced to step down as prime minister. This, however, set the stage for Yushchenko's new emergence as the leader of the so-called Orange Revolution, beating out Kuchma's handpicked successor, Viktor Yanukovych.

The new political landscape ushered in a period of relative economic calm in Ukraine. The prudent fiscal policies set in place by NBU helped ensure the stability of the hryvnia, and steady economic growth. By the middle of the decade, the country's gross domestic product registered gains of 7.4 percent and even more per year. In the meantime the political situation in Ukraine remained highly volatile. By 2006 with Yushchenko's government in crisis, Yanukovych was named prime minister.

Before long, NBU's autonomy had once again been called into question. In May 2008 the opposition led by the Yulia Tymoshenko Bloc introduced new legislation to place the central bank under government control. Later in the year, Ukraine became swept up in the global economic collapse. NBU once again found itself under pressure, amid the "freefall" in the hryvnia's value against the strengthening U.S. dollar. NBU, like its counterparts across the world, braced itself for a new period of financial and economic turmoil.

M. L. Cohen

PRINCIPAL SUBSIDIARIES

Banking University; Cherkassy Banking Institute; Kharkiv Banking Institute; Lviv Banking Institute; Ukrainian Banking Academy.

PRINCIPAL COMPETITORS

Oesterreichische Nationalbank; Narodowy Bank Polski; Ceska narodni banka; Banca Nationala a Romaniei; Magyar Nemzeti Bank; National Bank of Kazakhstan; Narodna banka Srbije; Bulgarian National Bank; Hrvatska narodna banka.

FURTHER READING

Kraus, James R., "U.S. Citizen in Key Post at Ukraine's Central Bank," *American Banker,* January 23, 1992.

Mellow, Craig, "A Ticking Clock in Kiev," *Institutional Investor International Edition,* June 2000, p. 11.

"National Bank of Ukraine to Punish Banks for Not Returning Client Deposits," *Russia & CIS Business and Financial Newswire,* October 24, 2008.

"National Bank of Ukraine Will Not Expand Support to Prominvestbank," *Russia & CIS Business and Financial Newswire,* October 23, 2008.

Rabij, Myron, "Ukraine Moves Towards International Banking Standards," *International Finance Law Review,* April 2001, p. 34.

Shen, Raphael, *Ukraine's Economic Reform,* Westport, Conn.: Praeger, 1996.

Trombly, Maria, "NASDAQ Lends Ukrainian Market Helping Hand," *Securities Industry News,* June 30, 2008.

Nature's Sunshine Products, Inc.

———— ■ ————

75 East 1700 South
Provo, Utah 84606
U.S.A.
Telephone: (801) 342-4300
Toll Free: (800) 223-8225
Fax: (801) 342-4305
Web site: http://www.naturessunshine.com

Public Company
Incorporated: 1972 as Hughes Development Corporation
Employees: 1,177
Sales: $366.6 million (2007)
Stock Exchanges: Over the Counter
Ticker Symbol: NATR
NAICS: 325411 Medicinal and Botanical Manufacturing; 325412 Pharmaceutical Preparation Manufacturing

■ ■ ■

Nature's Sunshine Products, Inc., is one of the largest manufacturers and marketers of nutritional and personal care products in the United States. The company's 718,500 independent distributors sell over 700 herbal products, vitamins and mineral supplements, personal care, nutritional drinks, and miscellaneous other products in over 30 countries across the globe. Accounting irregularities and subsequent investigations by the Securities and Exchange Commission and Department of Justice as well as an Internal Revenue Service audit have forced Nature's Sunshine to restate four years of financial reports. The company was delisted from the NASDAQ in 2006, and its stock remained in Pink Sheet status through 2008.

ORIGINS

The historical roots of the largest U.S. producer of encapsulated herbs stretch back to Provo, Utah, to the four-bedroom home of Eugene and Kristine Hughes and, specifically, to their kitchen table, which was the first manufacturing site for their fledgling business venture. It was a modest start, particularly given what the company later would become. Over the course of roughly two decades, Eugene and Kristine Hughes watched their enterprise develop into a $160 million per year business that eventually would employ, either on a part-time or full-time basis, more than a quarter million people. Nature's Sunshine's geographic presence expanded robustly as well, extending throughout the United States and into nine foreign countries. In just two decades, Nature's Sunshine would develop into a vast organization, recording growth on an exponential scale while enriching the founders, their original investors, and those who purchased stock in the company.

None of those fortunes would have been created without the misfortune suffered by Eugene Hughes and the helpful suggestion of a neighbor. In 1972 Eugene Hughes was suffering from a bleeding stomach ulcer. Neither Kristine, whose days were filled by raising seven children, nor Eugene, who was employed as a fourth-grade schoolteacher, were intent on launching an entrepreneurial career during the early 1970s. However, when a neighbor suggested a remedy for Eugene's ulcer, the seeds for Nature's Sunshine were planted.

Eugene, who developed his ulcer in the mid-1960s, had tried the conventional cures for stomach ulcers yet enjoyed little relief. He finally heeded his neighbor's advice and began swallowing spoonfuls of cayenne pepper; the neighbor had informed the couple that capsicum, which existed in abundant amounts in cayenne pepper, helped suppress the digestive acids that caused ulcers. For Eugene, the intimidating prospect of swallowing spicy red pepper powder to relieve the pain of an ulcer was exacerbated by its disagreeable taste, but he dutifully swallowed cayenne pepper and noticed an improvement in his condition.

Kristine Hughes then made her own suggestion, one that was nearly as integral to the formation of Nature's Sunshine as her neighbor's. To eliminate its unappealing taste, Kristine suggested the pepper powder be put in gelatin capsules. Those gelatin capsules were the couple's first products. Indeed, Eugene and Kristine Hughes spent their nights and weekends sitting at their kitchen table packing capsules full of red pepper. They persuaded the owner of a tiny local health food store in Provo to sell the capsules. For capital to launch their start-up business, the two put their persuasive powers to work once again to convince five of Eugene's six siblings to invest $150 each into Hughes Development Corporation (incorporated in 1972).

GROWTH AND EXPANSION

During the first decade of business, the foundation was established for the massive organization that would eventually hold a dominant place in the market for vitamins, minerals, and herbal supplements. Once the pursuit of health and fitness became a pervasive American trend, the business would enjoy accelerated growth, propelled by widespread consumer demand for salubrious, natural products. However, the founding couple also made pivotal moves that enabled their company to ride the crest of market demand for medicinal herbs and vitamins. Other natural products were added, such as chaparral for digestive problems, and goldenseal, which acted as a natural antibiotic, thus broadening the scope of the company's product line with each passing year.

In addition, salespeople, who sold the company's products door-to-door, were aggressively recruited and indoctrinated into an almost evangelical corporate culture that placed a premium on achieving sales records. These full-time and part-time independent sales representatives represented the backbone of the business. As their numbers grew, so did the geographic reach of the company. Enthusiasm for the company's products and effective sales techniques were imparted to aspirant salespeople at large sales conventions, where the engine that drove the company was fine-tuned.

As the company's success gained momentum, the business underwent several name changes before settling on the corporate title and brand name that would become familiar to hundreds of thousands of domestic and international customers during the late 1980s and 1990s. In 1973, one year after the business was founded, National Multi Corporation was organized as a holding company for Hughes Development Corporation. Two years later, Amtec Industries Incorporated was formed for the primary purpose of holding the stock of National Multi Corporation, and in 1982 the Nature's Sunshine Products, Inc., name was adopted.

Meanwhile, the company had been taken public in 1978, enabling others to share in the profits of the enterprise and generating an infusion of capital to sustain the company's expansion. In addition to a host of herbal supplements and other naturally medicinal products, water purifiers and personal care products were added to the ever-expanding roster of products, the aggregate demand for which pushed annual sales above $25 million by the end of the company's first decade of operation. Ten years of existence had resulted in ten years of success for the Hugheses and their thriving business, with annual sales increasing each year and the ranks of faithful and determined salespeople swelling annually.

OVERCOMING CHALLENGES IN 1985

The first blemish on Nature's Sunshine's record of growth occurred three years after the company celebrated its tenth anniversary. A new marketing incentive plan was announced that quickly hobbled previously unbridled growth, awakening management to the vagaries of the business world and the company's dependence on the their all-important sales force. A substantial portion of Nature's Sunshine's distributors, who comprised the core of the company's direct sales network, disliked the new compensation program and

KEY DATES

1972: Hughes Development Corporation is launched.

1973: National Multi Corporation is organized as a holding company for Hughes Development.

1975: Amtec Industries Incorporated is formed for the primary purpose of holding the stock of National Multi Corporation.

1978: The Hughes company is taken public.

1982: The Nature's Sunshine Products, Inc., name is adopted.

1989: Alan Kennedy is hired to run the rapidly growing company.

1991: Nature's Sunshine de Mexico is established.

1996: Kennedy is forced to resign.

2005: The company launches an internal investigation into its sales and commission activities in its foreign operations.

2006: The company's stock is delisted from the NASDAQ.

demonstrated their disfavor by cutting their ties to Nature's Sunshine and the nearly 200 products produced by the company. Once the exodus of distributors came to a halt, Kristine Hughes, who served as the company's chairwoman, and Eugene Hughes, the company's senior vice-president, found themselves without 28 percent of their distributors. Annual sales, for the first time in the company's history, declined in 1985, slipping from $33.3 million to $29.4 million, while earnings per share plummeted from 65 cents to 15 cents.

It was the first time Nature's Sunshine had recorded a decline in the number of distributors, an occurrence the Hugheses and the rest of the company's management did not want to see repeated. In mid-1985, Nature's Sunshine's compensation program was replaced with a more acceptable plan that halted the departure of distributors from the company's ranks. Management then began recruiting for additional distributors in earnest, hoping to replenish the company's sales force and invigorate sales. A bonus program for Nature's Sunshine distributors was reestablished and medical benefits were added to the list of perquisites offered to salespeople, enabling the company to score considerable success in attracting new and former distributors.

Nature's Sunshine's sales corps swelled 50 percent in the wake of 1985's losses, increasing to 25,000

distributors and roughly three times as many individual agents, while the number of products rose to more than 300 by the end of 1986. Buoyed by the increase in products and distributors, Nature's Sunshine's annual sales rebounded to $31 million in 1986 and to $38 million in 1987. Once the recovery was complete, Nature's Sunshine stood solidly positioned as the nation's largest producer of encapsulated herbs, occupying a coveted place in a market that was experiencing strong growth as increasing numbers of Americans sought alternative, natural ways of improving their health and fitness.

NEW LEADERSHIP

As the company exited the mid-1980s, there was justifiable cause for celebration. Its firm grasp on the U.S. market augured well for the company's future, but in international markets Nature's Sunshine was registering perhaps its most encouraging success. By the end of 1986, the company's foray into foreign markets had developed into a meaningful and burgeoning portion of its business, contributing 20 percent toward Nature's Sunshine's annual sales volume. Roughly half of the company's foreign sales were derived from Canada, while the balance was from customers in Australia and New Zealand, with a small sales network in Japan contributing to annual sales as well. In the years ahead, Nature's Sunshine would greatly increase its international presence, particularly in Latin America. Before such expansion occurred, however, the company needed to fix some problems at home, the resolution of which would invigorate the company's growth.

The company's annual sales continued to register successive gains after 1985's decline, jumping to $44.5 million in 1988 and to $52.1 million in 1989, while net income rose 56 percent in 1988, soaring to $3.3 million. Although the increase in net income pointed to an undoubtedly flourishing company, the 16 percent sales growth achieved in 1988 only mirrored the pace of growth recorded by the industry, which induced the Hugheses to begin looking for a way to accelerate their company's financial growth. The couple decided that Nature's Sunshine had grown too large to be operated as a family business and, instead, needed the experience of a professional direct-marketing leader. In 1989 they hired Alan Kennedy, the person who would invigorate Nature's Sunshine's growth.

In Kennedy the company gained a leader with a proven record of success. Kennedy had earned the reputation that would make him Nature's Sunshine's president in 1989 by helping Shaklee Corporation quadruple its sales during the late 1970s. Serving as Shaklee's chief marketing officer, Kennedy pushed the company toward the top tier of direct marketing companies to rank among giants such as Mary Kay Cosmetics and Amway. To be counted among these pioneering leaders in door-to-door sales was what the Hugheses hoped Kennedy could achieve for Nature's Sunshine. Kennedy knew, as they did, that the size of Nature's Sunshine's sales force directly dictated the magnitude of the company's sales volume, so he focused his initial efforts on recruiting additional salespeople.

In his first four years at Nature's Sunshine, Kennedy more than doubled the company's largely part-time sales army by boosting commissions paid to high production salespeople and creating a more inspirational atmosphere at sales conventions. Attendance at the company's sales meetings quadrupled as a consequence, and by the early 1990s more than 100,000 independent sales representatives were selling Nature's Sunshine products. Annual sales, which had begun to record ordinary increases before Kennedy's arrival, nearly tripled during his first four years of leadership, reaching $127 million in 1993, the bulk of which came from the company's strong presence in western and southern states.

FOCUSING ON FOREIGN MARKETS

As these gains in annual sales were being recorded, Kennedy also turned his attention to bolstering the company's involvement in foreign markets. A pivotal move in strengthening the company's international business was the establishment of a Mexican subsidiary, Nature's Sunshine de Mexico, in 1991. Once established in Mexico, the company moved into Central and South America, establishing operations in Costa Rica, Venezuela, Colombia, and Brazil, where the belief in medicinal herbs was considerably stronger than in the United States.

In late 1992, Nature's Sunshine sold its Australian and New Zealand marketing subsidiaries (Nature's Sunshine Products of Australia and Nature's Sunshine Products Ltd.) to local management, creating two independently owned and operated companies. A similar arrangement was made with Sunshine Scandinavia, AS, an independently owned-and-operated company located in Norway, as Nature's Sunshine built a small export network that also included China, the Philippines, and Hong Kong.

By 1993, annual sales had risen to $127 million, nearly 30 percent of which was derived from sales in foreign markets. Of the more than 350 products produced and sold by the company, 61 percent were herb-related products, while vitamins accounted for 23 percent. The balance of Nature's Sunshine's product mix consisted of homeopathic medicine, skin care products, and diet-related products.

In 1994, Kennedy continued to carve a deeper presence for Nature's Sunshine in foreign markets, forming a joint venture during the year with Tokyo Tanabe Company, a leading pharmaceutical company in Japan, to sell herbs and nutritional products. The market for vitamins, minerals, and herbal supplements by this time had grown dramatically since the Hugheses first entered the field in 1972. An estimated $4.6 billion was spent on vitamins, minerals, and herbal supplements in 1994, with the market for herbal supplements alone increasing 20 percent. With the bulk of its business dependent on herbal supplement sales, Nature's Sunshine stood poised for robust growth as it entered the mid-1990s and charted its plans for the future.

By the end of 1995, Nature's Sunshine was expected to announce sales of more than $200 million, as the 450 products sold by the company continued to meet widespread demand. The company was supported by its 291,000 independent sales representatives, who knocked on doors and presided over small groups in all 50 states and in nine foreign countries. With business growing briskly, particularly in Mexico and Latin America, Kennedy appeared to favor further international expansion.

His plans for the company came to a halt, however, when he was asked to resign in 1996. In a company statement published in a September 1996 article, Chairwoman Kristine Hughes commented, "Mr. Kennedy made significant contributions to Nature's Sunshine during his tenure, but it was the board's decision that a new management approach was needed." Daniel P. Howells eventually replaced the ousted Kennedy. Nature's Sunshine's appetite for international expansion did not appear to decrease under new leadership. To keep up with demand, the company opened a new $7 million manufacturing and warehouse facility in Spanish Fork, Utah, in 1998. It established its first Russian subsidiary the following year.

MOVING INTO THE 21ST CENTURY

The company continued to bolster its manufacturing capacity in the early years of the new millennium. Growth, foreign expansion, and product development remained at the forefront of the company's strategy. The firm gained a foothold in the Israeli market in 2000. During 2001, Nature's Sunshine secured exclusive rights to market a patented four-stage, ozone water purifier and also signed an agreement with HealtheTech Inc. to market their products through Nature's Sunshine distributors.

The company hit its first rough patch of the decade during 2002 when several of its international markets, including Venezuela, South Korea, Japan, and Brazil, experienced a decrease in sales volume. Nature's Sunshine saw a decline in sales and profits for the year. Howells resigned in 2003, leaving Douglas Faggioli, the company's chief operating officer, at the helm. Faggioli's job in the years to come would prove to be the most difficult of his career.

Problems surfaced in late 2005, when the company announced it had launched an internal investigation into its sales and commission activities within its foreign operations. Two months prior to the announcement, top executives, including Faggioli, sold over $2.9 million in stock. The company's auditor, KPMG LLP, claimed to find evidence that Faggioli and a board member knew about fraudulent actions but neglected to report them. When Nature's Sunshine failed to remove Faggioli and the accused board member, KPMG terminated its contract with the company. Faggioli stepped down in March 2006, but remained on the payroll. The company reinstated him in August of that year.

The company's internal investigation prompted an investigation by the Securities and Exchange Commission (SEC) and the U.S. Department of Justice as well as an Internal Revenue Service audit. These actions forced the company to restate its financial reports from 2002 to 2005. Its failure to meet SEC deadlines for financial reporting led to its delisting from the NAS-DAQ, which moved its stock to Pink Sheet status in 2006. Pink Sheet stocks were over-the-counter traded securities that failed to meet the standards required by major stock exchanges. Nature's Sunshine stock, which traded at a high of $23.24 in the fall of 2005, was valued at just over $10 per share in April 2006. By October 2008, its share price was as low as $4 per share.

According to SEC requirements, Nature's Sunshine would not be allowed to trade on a securities exchange until it became current in its financial reporting. As 2008 came to a close, the company's stock remained in Pink Sheet status. While Nature's Sunshine continued to operate as one of the largest manufacturers of nutritional and personal care products in the United States, its future success depended on its ability to overcome its accounting challenges.

Jeffrey L. Covell
Updated, Christina M. Stansell

PRINCIPAL SUBSIDIARIES

Nature's Sunshine Products Direct, Inc.; Nature's Sunshine Products of Canada, Ltd.; Nature's Sunshine Products de Mexico, S.A. de C.V.; Arrendadora Bonaventure, S.A. de C.V.; Nature's Sunshine Services, S.A. de C.V.; Nature's Sunshine Products de Colombia, S.A.; Nature's Sunshine Produtos Naturais Ltda.; Nature's Sunshine Produtos Naturais Ltda. (Brazil); Nature's Sunshine Marketing, Ltda. (Brazil); Nature's Sunshine, Japan Co., Ltd.; Nature's Sunshine Products N.S.P. de Venezuela, C.A.; Nature's Sunshine Products de Centroamérica; Nature's Sunshine Products de Panamá, S.A.; Nature's Sunshine Products de Guatemala, S.A.; Nature's Sunshine Products de El Salvador, S.A. de C.V.; Nature's Sunshine Products del Peru, S.A.; Nature's Sunshine Products del Ecuador, S.A.; Nature's Sunshine Products de Honduras, S.A.; Nature's Sunshine Products de Nicaragua, S.A.; Nature's Sunshine Products (Israel) Ltd.; Nature's Sunshine Products of Russia, Inc.; Nature's Sunshine Products Poland Sp. z.o.o.; Nature's Sunshine Products Dominicana, S.A.; Nature's Sunshine Products International Distribution B.V.; Nature's Sunshine Products International Holdings C.V.; NSP Casualty Insurance Company, Inc.; Consolidated Distribution Network, Inc.; Quality Nutrition International, Inc.; Synergy Worldwide Taiwan Inc.; Synergy Worldwide Inc.; Synergy Worldwide Marketing (Thailand) Ltd.; Synergy Worldwide Australia PTY Ltd.; Synergy Worldwide Korea Ltd.; Synergy Worldwide Japan K.K.; Synergy Worldwide (Singapore) PTE Ltd.; Synergy Worldwide Nutrition Israel Ltd.; Synergy Worldwide (Hong Kong) Ltd.; Synergy Worldwide Europe B.V.; PT Nature's Sunshine Products Indonesia; Synergy Worldwide Japan Ltd. (Y.K.); NATR Distribution (Malaysia) SDN. BHD.; Nature's Sunshine Products, Inc. (United Kingdom/Ireland).

PRINCIPAL COMPETITORS

Herbalife Ltd.; Nu Skin Enterprises Inc.; Shaklee Corp.

FURTHER READING

Beebe, Paul, "Nature's Sunshine to Make Its Case to SEC," *Salt Lake Tribune,* July 16, 2007.

Byrne, Harlan S., "Nature's Sunshine Products Inc.," *Barron's,* April 19, 1993, p. 45.

Carricaburu, Lisa, "Stormy Days for Nature's Sunshine," *Salt Lake Tribune,* September 18, 1996.

"Company Expects to Meet or Top Profit Estimates," *Wall Street Journal,* October 11, 1995, p. A4.

Fantin, Linda, "Nature's Sunshine in Bad Light," *Salt Lake Tribune,* April 5, 2006, p. C1.

Gilbert, Nick, "Nature's Sunshine: Hope for Hype," *Financial World,* October 10, 1995, p. 26.

"Healthy Trend," *Barron's,* May 18, 1987, p. 104.

Lewis, Kate Bohner, "Ulcers? Try Hot Pepper," *Forbes,* November 6, 1995, p. 242.

"Nature's Sunshine Products Plans to Increase Manufacturing Capacity As International Business Grows," *Business Wire,* March 2, 2000.

"Nature's Sunshine Products Reinstates CEO to Post," *Dow Jones Corporate Filings Alert,* August 24, 2006.

"Nature's Sunshine Under Scrutiny," *Deseret Morning News,* July 16, 2007.

Oberbeck, Steven, "Shareholders Face Dim Future," *Salt Lake Tribune,* November 9, 2007.

Slovak, Julianne, "Nature's Sunshine," *Fortune,* December 5, 1988, p. 140.

Stovall, Robert, "Lesser-Known Consumer Stocks," *Financial World,* July 22, 1986, p. 72.

Neckermann.de GmbH

Hanauer Landstrasse 360
Frankfurt am Main, D-60386
Germany
Telephone: (49 69) 404-4399
Fax: (49 69) 404-4440
Web site: http://www.neckermann.de

Private Company
Incorporated: 1950 as Neckermann Textil-Versand KG
Employees: 5,037 (2007)
Sales: EUR 1.4 billion ($1.9 billion) (2007)
NAICS: 454110 Electronic Shopping and Mail-Order Houses

■ ■ ■

Neckermann.de GmbH is one of Europe's largest electronic shopping and mail-order houses and the third largest mail-order company in Germany. With about 300,000 products for sale, from fashion to electronics and furniture, Neckermann generates more than half of its revenues via the Internet. Headquartered in Frankfurt am Main, the company has nine subsidiaries in other European countries, including Belgium and the Netherlands, Austria and Switzerland, Croatia, Slovakia and Slovenia, the Czech Republic, and Ukraine. Its German subsidiary, Happy Size Company Versandhandels GmbH, specializes in XL-fashion for women and men. Neckermann's three other German subsidiaries deal with customer service, management services, and logistics. American investment firm Sun Capital Partners holds a majority stake in the company which started out as a textiles mail-order house in postwar Germany.

HEAD START WITH TEXTILES VIA MAIL

The signs of destruction from World War II were still visible everywhere when the German entrepreneur Josef Neckermann, the son of a well-to-do coal merchant, founded his mail-order company, Neckermann Textil-Versand KG, in Frankfurt am Main in 1950. However, postwar reconstruction was getting underway and the introduction of a new currency in West Germany in 1948 had ended the era of black markets and scarcity. Life was slowly getting back to normal and Germans were ready to fill their closets with new clothes and their homes with new appliances. Neckermann's vision was to offer "luxury goods" at affordable prices, an idea that was not always easy to put into practice, but which became the foundation for the company's quick initial success.

On April 1, 1950, the same day the company was officially registered, Neckermann's first mail-order catalog, then still called a price list, was brought out. To make sure that it did not look like it was from a start-up company, the list with an initial print run of 100,000 received the issue number 120. On 12 pages it offered 133 different items, textile goods that were in high demand in every German household. There were a few spring dresses for the lady of the house and dress shirts for men; underwear and baby clothes; fabrics and wool; and aprons and household textiles.

Intuitively priced by the company founder according to his "gut feeling" of how much his customers would be willing to pay for them, the items quickly found a large clientele. In addition to his mail-order business Neckermann opened department stores in several western German cities, including Trier, Wurzburg, Hanau and Rosenheim. In the first year, Neckermann grossed ten million deutsche marks.

In 1951 Neckermann moved his enterprise into a large building near Frankfurt's Ostbahnhof train station which housed both a department store and the mail-order business. When it opened its doors for the first time on June 11, 1951, about 10,000 customers stormed into the store. Josef Neckermann wanted to offer his customers more than just textile goods. He envisioned a broad variety of products, similar to the traditional mail-order companies in England that offered their clientele in the countryside everything they needed, and to the large department stores in United States, such as Chicago-based Sears, Roebuck & Co. To promote his women's apparel, Neckermann held model fashion shows in every corner of the country.

"LUXURY GOODS" AT
AFFORDABLE PRICES

In 1953 Neckermann landed his first big coup, a competitively priced radio set that became an instant bestseller. However, it took the company founder awhile to find manufacturers who shared his idea that low prices made perfect business sense if there were just enough customers to buy the product. After many unsuccessful attempts, Neckermann found a small manufacturer in Bavaria who agreed to produce an attractive looking radio set with a high technical standard, which cost only about two-thirds of the usual market price. The 1953 catalog also contained other small electric devices as well as small pieces of furniture. At the end of the year, Neckermann reported a staggering DEM 100 million in sales.

While the business model remained the same, mass production, small profit margins and no middle-

men, Neckermann's product line, which was based on that model, continued to expand. When he landed his next bestseller in 1954, a TV set that also cost about 30 percent less than the competition's, Neckermann was suddenly confronted by a wave of hostility. Other manufacturers and retailers criticized the price buster's products. When that reduced Neckermann sales, they put out lower-priced models themselves.

When electric repair shops refused to fix Neckermann's products, Neckermann responded by setting up his own mobile technical service fleet. In 1954 the company also introduced a refrigerator with a cooling unit made in Luxembourg and a housing made in England that (despite the 20 percent in customs fees) was still less expensive than models from other German manufacturers.

Later in the decade Neckermann launched a line of furniture items suitable for mail order, including kitchen cabinets and benches, sofas, and coffee tables. Soon Neckermann's unconventional business approach stirred the interest of the media. The detailed reporting that followed, which included extensive discussions about the pros and cons of the company's products and pricing on radio talk shows, brought even more customers to Neckermann.

The company's next bestseller was a very affordable color TV set. By 1955 the Neckermann mail-order catalog was 200 pages thick and was published two times a year. The artistic drawings of the goods from the early days had been replaced by photos of the products, and the product descriptions of the early days, previously written by the company founder's wife, Annemarie, were done by professional copywriters.

MAKING THINGS POSSIBLE FOR
CUSTOMERS: RAPID EXPANSION

In 1960 a company slogan was introduced which reflected the philosophy of its founder: "Neckermann makes it possible." The slogan lasted for decades and ultimately became one of Germany's best-known claims by a company. Meanwhile the number of things made possible by Neckermann continued to grow. By the year the slogan was launched, Neckermann's line of furniture included more than 570 items, from plant stands to complete kitchens, including living room and bedroom ensembles. The catalog also contained washers and typewriters, bicycles and mopeds, and even coffee, liquor, and tobacco products.

Three years later Josef Neckermann surprised the competition with another idea. If furniture could be sold via mail-order catalog, why not homes? In 1963 a new subsidiary, Neckermann Eigenheim GmbH, was

KEY DATES

∎

1950: Entrepreneur Josef Neckermann establishes a mail-order company in Frankfurt am Main.

1953: Neckermann's reasonably priced radio set becomes an instant bestseller.

1960: The company slogan "Neckermann makes it possible" is introduced.

1968: Neckermann's first subsidiaries abroad are set up in France and the Netherlands.

1977: German department store company Karstadt AG acquires a majority share in Neckermann.

1989: Neckermann takes over Bavarian mail-order company Walz Group.

1994: The company acquires the Austrian mail-order house Kastner & Öhler.

1995: Neckermann launches its Internet presence, neckermann.de.

1996: The Danish mail-order company Bon'A Parte Postshop for textiles becomes a Neckermann subsidiary.

2006: A new name, neckermann.de, stresses the company's strategic focus on electronic commerce.

2008: American investment firm Sun Capital Partners acquires a majority stake in neckermann.de.

founded and began to sell prefabricated homes at competitive prices. A second new venture was launched in the same year. Neckermann targeted the awakening wanderlust of his customers and began offering holiday trips to popular travel destinations such as the Mediterranean—at competitive prices, of course. Two years later the travel business was organized in a newly established subsidiary, N-U-R Neckermann und Reisen GmbH.

In 1964 Neckermann entered the insurance business, for which an additional subsidiary, named "Neckura" Neckermann Versicherungs AG, was set up. To finance his new business ventures Josef Neckermann had transformed his company into a partnership limited by shares with his oldest son becoming the second personally liable partner. In the middle of the decade the company's new ventures combined grossed one billion deutsche marks for the first time.

Neckermann continued to make the headlines in the second half of the 1960s. When Neckermann offered to deliver frozen pig halves in special containers for much less than what his customers' local butchers

were charging in 1966, the others followed suit and lowered their prices. In the same year the Neckermann catalog contained a pastel mink coat for DEM 4,700 compared with the approximately DEM 6,000 it would cost at a store. By 1968 the Neckermann catalog contained more than 800 pages and the number of department stores in Germany had grown to 34, including one on Frankfurt's prominent shopping boulevard Zeil. In 1968 the company set up its first subsidiaries abroad, one in France and one in the Netherlands.

LOSS OF INDEPENDENCE AFTER FINANCIAL CRISIS

Although it made Neckermann very big in a very short time, the company founder's idea of compensating low margins with high volumes did not prove successful in the long run. While sales figures continued to increase, profit margins continued to decline during the 1960s and 1970s.

Around Neckermann's 25th anniversary year (during which the German economy was going through its second recession after World War II) the enterprise began to produce massive losses and its capital base shrank significantly. Only with financial support from the outside was Neckermann able to avoid bankruptcy. The support came from German department store company Karstadt AG, which acquired a majority share in Neckermann in 1977. However, the company founder and his son Peter had to give up control over the enterprise.

After Neckermann came under Karstadt's control, the company entered an era of slow recovery and organizational changes. Step by step, the enterprise was reduced to its original core business: selling products via mail-order catalog. The company's insurance arm "Neckura" Neckermann Versicherungs AG had been sold to Nationwide Mutual Insurance Company in 1975. Three years later Karstadt closed Neckermann's loss-making department stores and integrated the profitable ones into its own operations.

In 1981 Neckermann's tourism arm N-U-R was taken over completely by parent company Karstadt. One year later the company's subsidiary for prefabricated homes was sold to German construction company Hochtief. In 1984, when Karstadt's stake in Neckermann Versand AG had risen to 95 percent, the company was consolidated and integrated into the concern as a subsidiary. Under a new management team the company was downsized, cutting its workforce to roughly 10,000, about half of its former size.

After an attempt to reposition the company in the midpriced market segment failed, focusing on the low-

price segment finally proved successful. In 1987 Neckermann reported a profit for the first time in over a
decade. Five years later company founder Josef Neckermann passed away at age 79. Nevertheless, the strength
of the brand he had created carried his enterprise into
the new era of globalization and the Internet.

GROWTH THROUGH
ACQUISITIONS AND IMPROVED
CUSTOMER SERVICE

Beginning in 1989, Neckermann significantly expanded
its mail-order business through a number of acquisitions
in several niche markets. In that year the company took
over the southern German mail-order firm Versandhaus
Walz GmbH based in Bad Waldsee, Bavaria, which
specialized in products for infants. Two years later Neckermann bought Saalfrank Qualitätswerbeartikel GmbH,
a German mail-order house for promotional items based
in Schweinfurt. After the fall of the Berlin Wall in
November 1989 Neckermann also expanded its reach
into the new Eastern German states.

In 1994 the company acquired the Austrian mail-
order house Kastner & Öhler based in Graz, followed
by the takeover of the Danish mail-order company
Bon'A Parte Postshop for textile goods in 1996; the latter was mainly active in Scandinavia and the
Netherlands. In 1995 the company took over the
Austrian marketing firm Trend Produktvermarktungs
AG based in Vienna which focused on new mail-order
business in Poland, the Czech Republic, and Slovakia.
Two years later Neckermann acquired Krähe Versand
GmbH & Co. KG, a German mail-order company for
professional clothing. In 1997 the company also
launched Happy Size Company Versandhandels GmbH,
a new mail-order subsidiary specializing in XL-fashion
for women and men.

In 2000 Neckermann took over Fritz Berger AG, a
mail-order company for camping and outdoor
enthusiasts. One year later the company bought Hess
Natur-Textilien GmbH, a mail-order house specializing
in high-quality clothing and textile products made of
natural fibers. In 2003 Neckermann set up a new
subsidiary in Switzerland.

In addition to venturing into new geographic and
niche markets, Neckermann improved its own customer
service and internal logistics network. In 1989 the
company introduced its 24-hour express delivery service
for selected items, followed two years later by Neckermann's 24-7 telephone ordering service. In the first half
of the 1990s the company invested over DEM 100 million in a brand-new, state-of-the-art distribution center
that was built in Heideloh near Bitterfeld in Saxony-

Anhalt and opened in 1995. Neckermann's warehouse
facilities at Frankfurt headquarters were modernized as
well. In 1996 the company introduced one single
telephone number for phone orders and extended the
24-hour express delivery service to apparel and other
items.

STRATEGIC FOCUS ON THE
INTERNET AND
ORGANIZATIONAL CHANGE

The advent of the Internet as a new tool for commerce
in the mid-1990s opened up a brand-new sales channel
for Neckermann. In 1995 the company launched its Internet presence at www.neckermann.de. In the following
decade Neckermann continuously expanded and
improved its online store, which was increasingly geared
toward a younger clientele. By 2000 Neckermann's online store was grossing more than DEM 50 million in
annual sales. In 2006 the company was renamed
neckermann.de to stress its strategic focus on electronic
commerce. That year online sales exceeded the revenues
generated by catalog orders for the first time.

The ongoing consolidation in Germany's retail
landscape resulted in a series of organizational changes
for Neckermann. In 1999 Neckermann's parent
company merged with Germany's retail giant
Schickedanz Handelswerte GmbH & Co. KG, which
operated the country's number one mail-order house,
Quelle. Within the new KarstadtQuelle AG, Neckermann remained a separately operating business unit with
the exception of its logistics operations, which were
streamlined and synchronized with Quelle's.

To counteract the weak consumer spending climate
in Germany, new subsidiaries were set up in Eastern
Europe. However, when sales of KarstadtQuelle's two
mail-order subsidiaries dropped significantly in the
middle of the first decade of the 2000s, the company
decided to keep only one of the loss-producing ventures
(Quelle, the German market leader) and to groom
Neckermann for an initial public offering or to look for
potential buyers of the company.

According to *manager magazin*, there were about
one dozen possible buyers in 2007 that saw enough
promise in Neckermann to invest in the enterprise.
Finally, KarstadtQuelle, which by then had been
renamed Arcandor AG, sold a 51 percent stake in
neckermann.de to the American investment firm Sun
Capital Partners in March 2008. Neckermann's strategy
for getting back to profitability included significant cost
reductions by streamlining the product portfolio; cutting
back spending for advertising and personnel; the further
increase of the percentage of online sales and the

transformation of the company's online store into an online shopping mall with many shops, in cooperation with a variety of brand-name product manufacturers; and continued growth outside of Germany.

Evelyn Hauser

PRINCIPAL SUBSIDIARIES

Happy Size Company Versandhandels GmbH; Neckermann Logistik GmbH; Neckermann Contact Customer Service GmbH; Neckermann Management Service GmbH; Neckermann Switzerland; Neckermann Austria; Neckermann Belgium; Neckermann Netherlands; Neckermann Czech Republic; Neckermann Ukraine; Neckermann Croatia; Neckermann Slovakia; Neckermann Slovenia.

PRINCIPAL COMPETITORS

Quelle GmbH; Otto Group; amazon.de.

FURTHER READING

Die Kunst des Möglichen: Ein halbes Jahrhundert Neckermann. Frankfurt am Main, Germany: Neckermann Versand AG, 2000, 70 p.

Dunzenhöfer, Martin, "Mit Neckermann ist's unmöglich," *Börsen-Zeitung,* November 29, 2006, p. 9.

Giersberg, Georg, "Das Wetter, die Politik und der liebe Gott muessen mitspielen," *Frankfurter Allgemeine Zeitung,* March 31, 2000, p. 24.

————, "Ein kurzer Rausch und 30 Jahre Leiden," *Frankfurter Allgemeine Zeitung,* June 30, 2007, p. 18.

Heuer, Ina, "Eva und die Eckbank," *Berliner Morgenpost,* March 26, 2000, p. 5.

"Hintergrund: 'Neckermann macht's möglich': Mit zwölf Seiten fing es an," *DPA–AFX,* November 28, 2006.

"Investoren wollen Neckermann," *manager magazin online,* August 11, 2007.

"Karstadt trennt sich von Neckermann," *Hamburger Abendblatt,* November 29, 2006, p. 27.

Köhler, Manfred, "Neckermann machte vieles möglich," *Frankfurter Allgemeine Zeitung,* November 29, 2006, p. 47.

Meyer-Larsen, Werner, "Legenden des Wirtschaftswunders," *Spiegel,* May 17, 1999, p. 140.

"Schatten der Vergangenheit," *Hamburger Abendblatt,* December 19, 2001.

Vossen, Manfred, "Luxusgüter zu Gebrauchsartikeln; Neckermann feiert sein 50-jaehriges Jubilaeum," *Lebensmittel Zeitung,* April 7, 2000, p. 42.

The Newark Group, Inc.

20 Jackson Drive
Cranford, New Jersey 07016-3609
U.S.A.
Telephone: (908) 276-4000
Toll Free: (800) 777-7890
Fax: (908) 276-2888
Web site: http://www.newarkgroup.com

Private Company
Incorporated: 1912 as Newark Boxboard Company, Inc.
Employees: 3,166
Sales: $1.03 billion (2008 est.)
NAICS: 322130 Paperboard Mills

■ ■ ■

The Newark Group, Inc., is a private company based in Cranford, New Jersey, dedicated to the recycled paperboard business, its activities divided among three segments: Paperboard, Converted Products, and International. The Paperboard unit operates 11 recovered paper plants in North America under the Newark Recycled Fibers banner, relying on collected or purchased raw materials. The recovered paper is processed, baled, and supplied to the company's eight paperboard mills (Newark Paperboard Mills) or sold to other paperboard manufacturers. The recovered paper is mixed with water to create a stock that allows staples, wire, tape, and other contaminants to be removed. The water is then eliminated through the paperboard making process that includes a number of draining, pressing, and drying stages. The finished paperboard is generally palletized or wound into rolls and is used to make cardboard for consumer product packaging, folding cartons, industrial packaging, and high-strength grades for rigid boxes, tubes, and core products. The mills also produce the NewEx brand of graphicboard and the StressRelief brand of can separators.

Newark Group's Converted Products segment includes three units that convert paperboard. Newark Paperboard Products and its 17 plants turn out a variety of roll finishing materials, including cores, tubes, spools, roll wrap, and core plugs. Newark Solidboard Products turns recycled paperboard into laminated agricultural boxes under the Videpack brand, five-piece machine-erected agricultural boxes in the Packfort, and premium fish trays sold under the Tray Compact name. Newark Graphicboard Products and its five mills convert recycled paperboard into laminated book covers, board games, and jigsaw puzzles, as well as industrial packaging.

Newark Group's International segment consists of six converting plants in Spain, France, and Germany that manufacture laminated products, and graphicboard and solidboard packaging; and five converting plants in Spain, France, Germany, and the Netherlands. While not operating any recovered paper plants in Europe, Newark Group has a stake in three plants in Spain and Germany, which supply most of the raw material used by Newark's paperboard mills and converting plants on the Continent. Newark's founder Edward K. Mullen owns more than 79 percent of Newark's stock. His son, Chief Executive Officer Robert H. Mullen, owns 4.6 percent, while an employee stock ownership plan controls 16.2 percent.

COMPANY PERSPECTIVES

For over 80 years, we've been an industry leader in the collection of secondary fibers and the manufacturing and converting of 100% recycled paperboard.

ORIGINS

Edward Mullen was a student at Syracuse University when the United States entered World War II, resulting in an interruption in his education while he served as a pilot in the Army Air Forces for three years. He finally graduated in 1947, earning a degree in pulp and paper engineering from Syracuse. He then went to work for Richard Gair Company, a manufacturer of paperboard, folding cartons, and shipping containers. In 1952 he was named sales manager of the boxboard division. Mullen later joined Continental Can Company, serving as national paperboard sales manager. In 1958 he and three coinvestors acquired a stake in Newark Boxboard Company, Inc., a family-owned New Jersey business that he would then run and would later become the foundation for The Newark Group.

The McEwan family had established Newark Boxboard in 1912. The patriarch of the family, Robert B. McEwan, immigrated to the United States from Scotland, where he was born in Glasgow in 1828. The son of a paper maker, he came to America as a young man, settling in Bloomfield, New Jersey, and going to work for L.A. Brown, a manufacturer of air dried strawboard, similar to paperboard but made almost entirely from straw. After a stint in Connecticut, he returned to New Jersey, where in Caldwell in 1884 he and his seven sons began making paper under the name Robert McEwan & Sons, incorporated four years later as McEwan Brothers Company.

McEwan and sons Jesse L. and Richard W. developed a method to produce paperboard from recycled newspapers, naming the resulting product newsboard. The key to the method was keeping the paper stock extremely hot during the beating process while avoiding the introduction of any cold water, alkaline, or other bleaching agents. A patent was received by the McEwans in 1893. Their newsboard held a edge over the strawboard produced by western competitors because the McEwan operations were located close to most of the major folding box companies in the East, thus saving on transportation costs. At first the family licensed the technology rather than invest in large-scale production for themselves. It

was a plan that led to many patent infringement lawsuits and Robert McEwan's eventual decision to forgo licensing in favor of manufacturing, leading to the start of Newark Boxboard.

CREATING THE NEWARK GROUP

While heading Newark Boxboard, Edward Mullen helped develop paperboard structures for which he would share ten patents, leading him to cofound a separate company, Book Covers, Inc. (BCI), in 1962 to produce laminated paperboard used for book covers, loose-leaf binders, and game boards. While BCI remained an outside company, Mullen grew Newark Boxboard in the early 1970s, when the U.S. recycled paperboard industry underwent a period of consolidation including the closure of a large number of recycled paperboard mills. Newark Boxboard took advantage of conditions to acquire shuttered or neglected mills and then rebuild and modernize them. Mullen also acquired Newark's primary supplier of raw material, North Shore Recycled Fibers, a deal that not only ensured quality control of the mill feed but provided the company with other benefits of vertical integration. In 1976 Mullen engineered the merger of BCI with Newark Boxboard, as well as the acquisition of several mills from Continental Can, and purchased Newark Boxboard from its family owners to create The Newark Group.

The Newark Group pursued a decentralized business model, allowing a great deal of autonomy to the company's mill operations. BCI also continued to develop new products. In 1983 the company introduced FiberWrap, a wood replacement product for use in boxes that contained table grapes and other produce. Helping in the development of the product was a California company, Growers Packaging Co., which became part of The Newark Group in 1987 and continued to work with BCI in creating new packaging for grapes and tree fruit.

Other acquisitions were also completed in the 1980s. Southern Foam Products, a Dalton, Georgia, maker of fiber components that joined polyether and polyester foam with paperboard, was acquired. The company's foam lined products were used in protective packaging, photo albums, and sample books. In 1984 Newark swapped assets with Chicago-based Stone Container Corporation, exchanging a corrugating mill in Connecticut for boxboard mills in Franklin, Ohio, and Mobile, Alabama. In 1988 Newark acquired a Los Angeles recycled boxboard mill from Federal Paper Board Co., renaming the operation Newark Pacific Paperboard Corp. The following year, Newark Sierra Paperboard Corporation was created when Newark bought a Stockton, California, recycled paperboard mill

KEY DATES

1912: Newark Boxboard Company, Inc., is established by the McEwan family.
1958: Edward K. Mullen and three coinvestors acquire a stake in the company.
1962: Book Covers, Inc. (BCI), is founded.
1976: BCI merges with Newark Boxboard; Mullen and partners acquire Newark Boxboard to create The Newark Group.
1983: FiberWrap is introduced.
1995: Newark Paperboard Products Division is formed.
1999: European operations are added.
2003: Newark Boxboard plant is closed.
2004: Robert Mullen is named CEO.

from National Gypsum Co. Together these California mills added some 160,000 tons to Newark's production capacity.

During this time, the company also increased capacity by investing in a major expansion on a mill it owned in Mobile, Alabama. Acquired by Newark in the mid-1970s, Mobile Paperboard Corporation was the oldest paper mill in Alabama, established in 1918. In addition, other mills were acquired during this period, including Misco Paper Converters Inc., Cedartown Paperboard Co., and Paperboard Cores, Inc., bringing with them six more facilities in the Southeast. Thus, by early 1990, Newark was operating 11 recycled paperboard mills with a total capacity of 875,000 tons per year of paperboard, chipboard, laminated boards, tube and core stock, and other products. By the end of the year the company expanded further, acquiring another wastepaper recycler, Great Eastern Packing & Paper Stock Corp.

CHANGES IN LEADERSHIP

Edward Mullen's son, Robert H. Mullen, joined the company in the 1980s. A graduate of Upsala College, Mullen earned his master of business administration degree in finance and accounting from Columbia University Business School in 1984 and subsequently joined Newark. He started out as assistant superintendent of a paper machine in the Haverhill Paperboard Mill, a post he held until 1989. At that time he was named president of BCI and then added the responsibility of the Newark Paperboard Products Division in 1993. The younger Mullen then became chief

operating officer in 1996. Two years later his father stepped down as CEO, but instead of turning to his son, Edward Mullen tapped Fred G. von Zuben as his replacement. A 25-year veteran with the company, von Zuben started out in 1973 as a sales manager for BCI.

In 1995, as part of a branding effort, the companies acquired by the converting division over the years, including Misco Paper Converters, Paperboard Cores, Cedartown Paperboard, and Newark Fiber Products, then shared a common name: Newark Paperboard Products. More acquisitions followed in 1997. Yorktowne Paper Mills of Maine Inc. and its subsidiary, Mercer Paper Tube Corp., were acquired to add further mill capacity. All told, Newark received five tube and core plants and two recycled paperboard mills. Moreover, the deal greatly expanded the company's footprint in New England, which had been limited to a tube and core plant in Nashua, New Hampshire.

Newark was active on a number of fronts as the 1990s came to a close. In the spring of 1999 Newark acquired assets from Wisconsin-based Hayes Manufacturing Group Inc., including a converting facility in Neenah, Wisconsin, to provide a solidboard manufacturing capacity for the industrial packaging materials market. At the same time, Newark was turning its attention overseas, making its first major investment outside of the United States by acquiring Grupo San Andres in Spain, which included Papelera Catalana, Industrias San Andrews, and Bertaki as well as France's Atelier Des Landes. To manage its new European recycled paperboard business, Newark established an office in Barcelona.

Expansion efforts continued as the new century dawned. After considering the possibility of building a new mill in Ohio, the company opted instead to buy the existing Princeton Paper Mill in Fitchburg, Massachusetts, and invest $100 million in converting it into a paper recycling facility. The decision was heavily influenced by state support for the project that included $45.5 million in low interest state bonds and tax credits furnished by the state of Massachusetts. Moreover, the state helped Newark secure a reliable source of recyclable paper to feed the mill. Later in 2000 Newark added to its European operations, acquiring Fibor Packaging B.V., a Dutch maker of laminated solidboard and solidboard packaging. To close the year, Newark also added to its Canadian operations, acquiring the 49 percent interest it did not already own in Perma Tubes & Cores, Ltd., a paperboard mill in Richmond, British Columbia.

NEWARK BOXBOARD CLOSES

The early years of the new century were not an especially good time for the paper industry, which among other problems suffered from overcapacity, leading to the shutdown of mills across the country. Newark was not immune to these difficulties. In 2002 it shut down its Middleton, Ohio, paperboard mill, putting 50 people out of work. It was an older facility that was not efficient enough for current economic conditions. A year later Newark Boxboard was itself sacrificed, despite the historic significance to the company and the industry.

Robert Mullen took over as CEO in August 2004, and a year later was named chairman of the board as well, in both cases succeeding von Zuben. He took over a company that had to contend with the continuing problem of overcapacity in U.S. paper recycling along with the threat from Chinese imports. By the winter of 2005 Newark had shuttered five of its 18 mills, but even those moves were not enough to offset increasing energy and transportation costs as losses piled up. After turning a profit in fiscal 2003, Newark posted a net loss of $16.3 million on sales of $787.6 million in fiscal 2004, followed by a loss of $1.2 million on sales of $882.1 million in fiscal 2005. Despite cost-cutting efforts, Newark lost a further $16.3 million on sales of $852.4 million in fiscal 2006.

More restructuring followed. In early 2007 the company consolidated its Maine operations, relocating them from the South Gardiner plant to the more efficient Monmouth, Maine, plant. In fiscal 2007 Newark lost a further $4.2 million on sales of $923 million, and a year later recorded a net loss of $19.7 million, despite sales that topped the $1 billion mark due to price increases. A few months later Newark closed more plants, shutting down the Bennington Paperboard Mill in upstate New York and the Yorktown Paper Mills operation in Haverhill, Massachusetts. Given that the industry had been dealing with overcapacity for the past decade, it was uncertain when the shakeout in the industry would be completed and Newark could hope to return to profitability.

Ed Dinger

PRINCIPAL OPERATING UNITS

Paperboard; Converted Products; International.

PRINCIPAL COMPETITORS

Carustar Industries, Inc.; Rock-Tenn Company; Sonoco Products Company.

FURTHER READING

Deking, Noel, "Newark Group's 'Small' Companies Are Leaders in Recycled Board Market," *Pulp & Paper,* March 1990, p. 208.

Gnau, Thomas, "Middleton, Ohio, Paperboard Mill Shuts Down," *Middletown Journal,* October 22, 2002.

"Newark Companies Share Name," *Paperboard Packaging,* March 1, 1995, p. 9.

"Newark Group Closes Boxboard Mill," *Official Board Markets,* July 19, 2003, p. 13.

Rulison, Larry, "Paperboard Plant Closure to Leave 64 Jobless," *Albany (N.Y.) Times Union,* July 8, 2008, p. C1.

"Spanish Group Sold to Newark," *Paperboard Packaging,* March 1999, p. 16.

NIPPON MINING HOLDINGS, INC.

Nippon Mining Holdings Inc.

2-10-1, Toranomon 2-chome
Minato-ku
Tokyo, 105-0001
Japan
Telephone: (81 03) 5573-5170
Fax: (81 03) 5573-6784
Web site: http://www.shinnikko-hd.co.jp

Public Company
Incorporated: 2002
Employees: 10,316
Sales: ¥4.34 billion ($43.3 million) (2008)
Stock Exchanges: Tokyo Osaka Nagoya
Ticker Symbol: 5016
NAICS: 551112 Offices of Other Holding Companies

■ ■ ■

Nippon Mining Holdings Inc. operates in the petroleum and metals industries through its two major subsidiaries, Japan Energy Corporation and Nippon Mining & Metals Co. Ltd. Through its petroleum arm the company is involved in upstream and downstream operations including exploration and development, refining, and marketing of liquefied petroleum gas, lubricants, and petrochemicals. Its mining group oversees copper smelting and refining as well as other resource development, recycling, and various environmental services. The company announced plans to merge with Nippon Oil Corp. in 2008 to create the eighth largest oil company in the world based on sales.

EARLY HISTORY

The Kuhara Mining Company, predecessor of the Nippon Mining Co., Ltd., was established in 1905 by Fusanosuke Kuhara as a copper mining venture located in Hitachi village, later Hitachi City. As a result of rapid expansion, Kuhara decided to reorganize his enterprise into a joint stock company, with a capital of ¥10 million, in 1912.

Although the major business of the company was copper mining, Kuhara perceived that Japan had an energy supply problem, and he secretly began to look for opportunities for oil field development. In March 1914 the Nippon Oil Company located an abundant oil field, the Kurokawa well in Akita Prefecture, and the sudden oil price rise during World War I further stimulated Kuhara in his search for oil. He began to explore domestic oil fields after 1914, and built eight oil well development offices between 1916 and 1917. He also explored oil fields in northern Sakhalin, Borneo, Burma, and Malaya. In 1919 he entered into a joint venture with a Russian company to develop oil fields in northern Sakhalin. In 1921 this joint venture discovered a potentially rich oil field, but the Japanese Ministry of Foreign Affairs and other oil companies hoped to develop it as a national project. In 1919 the Ministry of Agriculture and Commerce established a joint stock company named Hokusin Kai, which later became Kita Karafuto (Northern Sakhalin) Oil Company. It was co-owned by Kuhara Mining, the Mitsui and Mitsubishi *zaibatsu*, Nippon Oil Company, and others.

During World War I, Kuhara Mining Company continuously expanded its business. However, after the war, economic conditions deteriorated and the company met financial difficulties. After 1920 Kuhara's business experienced losses and incurred a huge amount of debt. When Kuhara retired from the business and went into politics, his brother-in-law Yoshisuke Ayukawa took responsibility for the reconstruction of the company.

In March 1928 Ayukawa became president and in December he reorganized Kuhara Mining Company into a holding company, Nippon Sangyo (Industry) Co., Ltd. In April 1929 the mining and refinery division was separated and established as an independent company named the Nippon Mining Co., Ltd., with a capital of ¥50 million. Ayukawa then became chairman of the board and Masahiko Takeuchi became president.

After 1916 the company further explored the Akita oil field but failed to locate oil. In September 1933, however, a rich oil field, the Omonogawa oil well, was finally found. In 1936 and 1937 two further oil fields were found in Hokkaido. In 1934 a natural gas field was developed in the Tsutong area of Taiwan, where the company established natural gas and naphtha refining facilities.

In 1939 the company began to construct an integrated oil refinery plant to produce aviation gasoline at the request of the Japanese navy. However, construction stopped at the outbreak of the Pacific war in December 1941. In the late 1930s Nippon Kogyo acquired two oil refining companies and strengthened its oil refining division in the Akita area. In 1942, however, Teikoku Sekiyu (Empire Oil) Co. Ltd. was established as a state-owned company, and the Tsutong plants and the refining facilities of the Omono River oil wells were transferred to Teikoku Sekiyu.

POSTWAR GROWTH

In August 1945 the Pacific war of World War II ended, and Japan lost its former territories and occupied areas. Nippon Mining Co., Ltd., lost its foreign assets located in those areas, which had amounted to almost 40 percent of its total assets in 1943. After the war, the

company's major plants were Hitachi mining works and the Sagaseki refining facility, but production was down to almost nothing at the end of the latter half of 1945. By the end of 1946, production had recovered to one-third of the volume of wartime production, but the only active production facility was the Funagawa oil refinery. In 1946 the Funagawa refinery refined 56,483 kiloliters (kl) of crude oil and produced 53,794 kl of gasoline and other products.

In 1947 the Funagawa refinery converted from munitions manufacturing to civil use, and began to make solvent products and to diversify its product line. By 1951 the Funagawa refinery had lubrication oil production facilities, and established an integrated oil refinery system. Until June 1961 the Funagawa refinery was Nippon Kogyo's only active modern refinery facility.

The Allied powers had prohibited the rebuilding of oil refinery facilities on the Pacific coast of Japan, but lifted the prohibition in 1950. The Pacific coast of Japan became a good industrial location for the reduction of transportation costs and stimulation of import-export activities. As Nippon Mining had no refinery facilities on the Pacific coast, establishing a presence in this industrial zone became a strategic target for the company.

After 1955 the executives of the company realized that the Mizushima area in Okayama Prefecture would be an attractive site for a refinery complex. In 1958 the company started a feasibility study for the project. Construction began in July 1960, and the Mizushima complex began operation in June 1961. The Gulf Oil Corporation played an important role in the building of the Mizushima refinery complex, both in the supplying of finance and in the export of crude oil. In May 1960 secret transactions had been held in the Tokyo office of Gulf Oil Corporation; the agreement to a $15 million (¥5.4 billion) loan to build facilities and a ten-year contract for the import of a total of eight million barrels of crude oil were signed in September 1960.

LIBERALIZATION BEGINS

In June 1960 the Japanese government decided to liberalize crude oil imports (although processed oil imports to Japan, such as gasoline, were still restricted) and beginning in October 1962 carried out the liberalization in stages. However, to prevent overproduction and excess competition between oil refineries, the Ministry of International Trade and Industry (MITI) implemented the Oil Industry Law. By this law MITI maintained control of the Japanese-owned oil and petrochemical industries. In 1965 the Nippon Mining Co. established a joint sales company, Kyodo Oil

---

KEY DATES

■

1905: The Kuhara Mining Company, predecessor of the Nippon Mining Co., Ltd., is established by Fusanosuke Kuhara.

1912: Rapid expansion leads Kuhara to reorganize his enterprise into a joint stock company.

1928: The company is reorganized into a holding company named Nippon Sangyo (Industry) Co. Ltd.

1929: The mining and refinery division is separated and established as an independent company named the Nippon Mining Co., Ltd.

1961: The Mizushima oil refinery begins operations.

1965: Kyodo Oil Company Ltd. is established.

1979: Chita Oil Co. Ltd. is established.

1983: Chita Oil is fully integrated into Nippon Mining.

1992: Nippon Mining & Metals Co. Ltd. is created; Nippon Mining and Kyodo Oil Co. merge to form Nikko Kyodo Co. Ltd.

1993: Nikko Kyodo is renamed Japan Energy Corp.

1999: Japan Energy takes control of Kashima Oil Co. Ltd.

2002: Nippon Mining Holdings Inc. is established as a holding company.

2006: The operations of Nikko Metals, Nikko Materials, and Nippon Mining & Metals are consolidated under the Nippon Mining & Metals Co. name.

2008: Nippon Mining Holdings announces plans to merge with Nippon Oil Corp.

Company Ltd., with Asia Oil Company, Ltd., and Toa Oil Company Ltd., under the administrative guidance of MITI. The Nippon Mining stake was 34 percent, and those of Asia Oil Company and Toa Oil Company were 23 percent each, while the remaining 20 percent was owned by banks. A vice-president of Nippon Mining, Kazuo Hayashi, was appointed as president of Kyodo Oil Co., which united the oil tank yards and sales agencies of the three companies and went into operation in July 1966.

Kyodo Oil Company's market share was 10.9 percent, and the company held third position in the domestic market, after Nippon Oil Company in first place and Idemitsu Kosan in second. Nippon Mining dispatched 643 employees to Kyodo Oil Company to sustain sales activities temporarily, but by December 1966 almost all those dispatched had become permanent employees of Kyodo Oil Company. As a result of these arrangements, Nippon Mining's oil division became a de facto refinery division of Kyodo Oil Company. Thus a close relationship between Nippon Mining and Kyodo Oil Company was established.

Through the development of the Neurex processing system the company entered into the area of petrochemicals, launching a synthetic detergent product in November 1967. To further its diversification into petrochemicals, the company established Nikko Petrochemical Co. Ltd. in December 1967.

After the mid-1960s, the company built a petrochemical complex in Mizushima with Asahi Kasei Industry Company Ltd. In July 1968, Nippon Mining, with a stake of 20 percent, and Asahi Kasei, with a stake of 80 percent, jointly established Sanyo Petrochemical Company Ltd., with a capital of ¥750 million, to supply olefin gas to the complex. Sanyo Petrochemical Co. and Mitsubishi Kasei Industry Co. Ltd. established Mizushima Ethylene Co. Ltd., a 50-50 joint venture, to decompose naphtha. In November 1969 another jointly owned company, Sanyo Ethylene Co. Ltd., was established. Consequently, Nippon Mining's Mizushima refinery became the central raw material and energy supplier of the petrochemical complex.

The company also began to pursue backward integration into oil drilling. In December 1967 Nippon Mining Co., Maruzen Oil Co., and Daikyo Oil Co. jointly invested in offshore oil drilling in Abu Dhabi and established the jointly owned Abu Dhabi Oil Company Ltd. with equal stakes of 33.3 percent and capital of ¥600 million. By January 1971 there were four oil wells producing crude oil, and in May 1973 production reached a level of 40,000 barrels per day (b/d).

In September 1967 Nippon Mining established a joint venture company, the Petro-Coke Company Ltd., with Continental Oil Company of the United States and Sumitomo Shoji Co. Ltd., with a capital of ¥360 million. In 1969 this company began production of calcined petroleum cokes. As a result of expansion in the oil division, Nippon Mining began production at a lubricating oil factory in the Chiba Prefecture in May 1969.

RESPONDING TO CRISES

The two oil crises in 1973 and 1978 stimulated the reorganization of the Japanese petroleum industry including petrochemical production. In 1979 Nippon Mining acquired the Toa Kyoseki Company Ltd. from its parent companies, Chu Ito & Company and Toa Oil

Company. Toa Kyoseki Company was a relatively small refinery with a processing capacity of 100,000 b/d, established in 1973 under the guidance of MITI. It was in financial difficulties after the first oil crisis. Under the management of Nippon Mining, Toa Kyoseki changed its name to Chita Oil Co. Ltd., with a capital of ¥6 billion. Nippon Mining's stake was 61.67 percent, Kyodo Oil Company's stake was 33.3 percent, and Chu Ito & Company's stake was 5 percent. Chita Oil Co. contributed to the strengthening of the tie between Nippon Mining's oil division and the Kyodo Oil Company group. However, after the second oil crisis, with its unsettling influence on the business environment, Chita Oil Co. was fully integrated into Nippon Mining by permission of MITI, in July 1983.

After the second oil crisis the demand for petroleum declined, and the company restricted its crude oil refinery capacity at its three oil factories. As a result, Nippon Mining's crude oil refining capacity was 281,000 b/d in 1983 (with Mizushima producing 190,000, Funagawa 6,000, and Chita 85,000) a capacity almost unchanged until 1989.

In March 1985 Kyodo Oil group companies jointly established a research and development center for the development of oil products. In the following April, the management of the lubricating oil products research laboratory at Nippon Mining was transferred to the newly established Kyodo Oil group's research and development center.

In 1990 Nippon Mining Co., Ltd., was capitalized at ¥63.4 billion. To achieve further growth, the company promoted oil prospecting projects with Conoco and planned a full-scale launch into polypropylene and special resins. Although 55.6 percent of total sales came from the oil division in 1990, traditional divisions such as copper (15 percent of sales), metal products (7 percent), zinc (4 percent), gold (7 percent), and silver (1 percent) represented a large portion of total sales and profits, as did the new materials division (4 percent), and new ventures—including biochemicals (4 percent)—were expanding. During the early 1990s, the Nippon Mining Co. was one of the most successfully diversified companies in the mining and petroleum industry in Japan.

The company began to restructure operations in 1992. That year, Nippon Mining & Metals Co. Ltd. was created to oversee the metals businesses. In addition, Nippon Mining and Kyodo Oil Co. merged to form Nikko Kyodo Co. Ltd. The latter was renamed Japan Energy Corporation in 1993.

By the late 1990s, deregulation and intense competition forced many companies in Japan's petroleum industry to consolidate and merge. Japan Energy took control of Kashima Oil Co. Ltd. in 1999. Japan Energy also created Nikko Materials Co. Ltd. as a subsidiary to oversee its electronic materials operations. The company also launched a copper smelting and refining joint venture with a Korean firm.

MOVING INTO THE 21ST CENTURY

Japan Energy and Nippon Mining & Metals entered the new millennium on solid ground. Both companies remained profitable during this time period. In order to secure footing in their respective industries, the two firms announced plans in 2002 to form Nippon Mining Holdings Inc. as a holding company. An April 2002 *Japan Energy Scan* article reported the company's rationale for adopting this new organizational structure, claiming, "The deal will enable Japan Energy and Nippon Mining to efficiently use management resources and promptly cope with changes in the business climate while reinforcing their consolidated operations amid the growing globalization of the Japanese economy."

The company continued to restructure its business operations over the next few years. Nikko Metal Manufacturing Co. Ltd. was established in 2003 to oversee metal processing activities. Subsidiaries Nikko Metals, Nikko Materials, and Nippon Mining & Metals were then consolidated in 2006 under the Nippon Mining & Metals Co. name.

By this time, demand for petroleum products in Japan was falling, the price of crude oil was rising, and global economies were headed towards a recession. Japan Energy, responsible for the largest portion of Nippon Mining Holdings' net sales, aggressively pursued joint ventures to secure its position in the industry. As part of its plan to remain competitive while shoring up profits, the holding group announced plans to merge with Nippon Oil Corporation, Japan's largest integrated oil company, in December 2008.

The union of the two companies would create one of the top five largest manufacturing concerns in Japan and the eighth largest oil company in the world based on sales. Combined sales were forecast to be over ¥13 trillion and the new company would control 33 percent of Japan's gasoline market. The deal also fell in line with Japan's National Energy Strategy, which set forth initiatives to increase the country's ratio of oil developed and imported through domestic companies from 15 percent in 2008 to 40 percent by 2030.

Nippon Mining Holdings expected the merger to create an integrated energy, resources, and materials company capable of competing against large U.S. and European oil concerns in the global marketplace. The union was slated to take place in late 2009 with restructuring operations finalized in 2010. A new holding company was expected to be formed with three major business units overseeing oil refining and sales, oil field development, and metals.

Kenichi Yasumuro
Updated, Christina M. Stansell

PRINCIPAL SUBSIDIARIES

Japan Energy Corporation; Japan Energy Development Co., Ltd.; NMC Pearl River Mouth Oil Development Co., Ltd.; Southern Highlands Petroleum Co., Ltd.; Kashima Oil Co., Ltd.; Kashima Aromatics Co., Ltd.; JOMO-NET Co., Ltd.; JOMO Retail Service Co., Ltd.; J-Quest Co., Ltd.; Asia Shoji Co., Ltd.; JOMO Sun Energy Co., Ltd.; Japan Energy (Singapore) PTE. LTD.; Nikko Liquefied Gas Co., Ltd.; Kyo-Pro Co., Ltd.; JOMO-Pro Kanto Co., Ltd.; Petrocokes, Ltd.; Irvine Scientific Sales Co., Inc.; Nissho Shipping Co., Ltd.; Nippon Tanker Co., Ltd.; JOMO Enterprise Co., Ltd.; JOMO Support System Co., Ltd.; Abu Dhabi Oil Co., Ltd. (31.5%); United Petroleum Development Co., Ltd. (35%); Nippon Mining & Metals Co., Ltd.; Nippon Mining of Netherlands B.V.; Nippon LP Resources B.V.; Kasuga Mines Co., Ltd.; Japan Korea Joint Smelting Co., Ltd.; Pan Pacific Copper Co., Ltd.; Nikko Smelting & Refining Co., Ltd.; Hibi Kyodo Smelting Co., Ltd.; Pan Pacific Copper Taiwan Co., Ltd.; Pan Pacific Copper Shanghai Co., Ltd.; PPC Canada Enterprises Corp.; Minera Lumina Copper Chile S.A.; Compania Minera Quechua S.A.; Japan Copper Casting Co., Ltd.; Changzhou Jinyuan Copper Co., Ltd.; Kurobe Nikko Galva Co., Ltd.; Nikko Shoji Co., Ltd.; Nikko Metals Taiwan Co., Ltd.; Nikko Art & Craft Co., Ltd.; Nikko Environmental Services Co., Ltd.; Tomakomai Chemical Co., Ltd.; Nikko Tsuruga Recycle Co., Ltd.; Nikko Mikkaichi Recycle Co., Ltd.; Nikko Plant Saganoseki Co., Ltd.; Nippon Marine Co., Ltd.; Circum Pacific Navigation Co., Ltd.; Nikko Logistics Partners Co., Ltd.; Nissho Kou-un Co., Ltd.; Nikko Exploration and Development Co., Ltd.; Nikko Drilling Co., Ltd.; Nikko Metals Philippines, Inc.; Gould Electronics GmbH; Nikko Metals USA, Inc.; Nikko Metals Korea Co., Ltd.; Nikko Fuji Electronics Co., Ltd.; Nikko Fuji Electronics Dongguan Co., Ltd.; Nikko Coil Center Co., Ltd.; Nippon Precision Technology (Malaysia) Sdn. Bhd.; Nippon Mining Shanghai Co., Ltd.; Nippon Mining & Metals (Suzhou) Co., Ltd.; Nikko Fuji Precision (Wuxi) Co., Ltd.

PRINCIPAL DIVISIONS

Japan Energy Group; Nippon Metals & Mining Group.

PRINCIPAL COMPETITORS

Idemitsu Kosan Co., Ltd.; Nippon Oil Corporation; TonenGeneral Sekiyu K.K.

FURTHER READING

"Japan Energy, Nippon Mining to Form Joint Holding Firm," *Japan Energy Scan,* April 8, 2002.

Mizushima Seiyu sho 20-Nen no Ayumi, Tokyo: Nippon Kogyo K.K., 1984.

"New Nippon Mining & Metals to Seek Technological Synergy," *Japan Metal Bulletin,* March 28, 2006.

"Nikko Metal Manufacturing Starts Today," *Japan Metal Bulletin,* October 1, 2003, December 8, 2008.

"Nippon Mining Holdings to Complete Reorganization Oct. 1," *Japan Weekly Monitor,* August 4, 2003.

"Nippon Oil & Nippon Mining Merger Will Benefit," *Corporate Financing Week,* December 10, 2008.

"Nippon Oil, Nippon Mining to Merge," *Nikkei Weekly,* December 8, 2008.

Okabe, Akira, *Sangyo no Showa Shakai Shi, No.3 Sekiyu,* Tokyo: Nippon Keizai Hyoron Sha, 1986.

Rowley, Anthony, "Japan Aims to Be Major Oil and Gas Player," *Business Times Singapore,* January 12, 2009.

Toyo Keizai, ed., *Kaisha Shikiho (Quarterly Handbook of Japanese Public Companies),* Tokyo: Toyo Keizai Sha, 1950–90.

Yukashoken Hokokushyo Soran, Tokyo: Ministry of Finance Printing Division, 1983–89.

Nuqul Group of Companies

PO Box 154
Amman, 11118
Jordan
Telephone: (962 06) 4652688
Fax: (962 06) 4645669
Web site: http://www.nuqulgroup.com

Private Company
Incorporated: 1952
Employees: 5,000
Sales: $2.24 billion (2007 est.)
NAICS: 322291 Sanitary Paper Product Manufacturing;
551112 Offices of Other Holding Companies

■ ■ ■

The Nuqul Group of Companies is one of Jordan's leading conglomerates. The Amman-based company is comprised of nearly 30 subsidiaries operating across the Middle East. Nuqul's flagship is the Fine Hygienic Paper Co. Ltd., one of the Middle East region's leading producers of tissues, as well as toilet paper, kitchen towels, napkins, sanitary products, diapers, and other products, including drinking straws, stationery, wet wipes, and coasters. Fine operates manufacturing facilities in Jordan, Egypt, Lebanon, Dubai, Yemen, Sudan, Morocco, Saudi Arabia, and, since January 2009, Iran. Nuqul also owns and operates four paper mills, with two each in Jordan and in Egypt; a nonwoven textile facility, supporting the production of diapers and sanitary napkins; and two printing press subsidiaries in Jordan.

More diversified interests include a synthetic foam manufacturing unit; a subsidiary producing aluminum extrusions; ready-mix concrete supply; and the production of PVC pipes, fittings, and granules. Nuqul's combined revenues were estimated at nearly $2.25 billion in 2007. Founder Elia C. Nuqul remains the company's chairman of the board, and the Nuqul family retains full ownership of the company. Nonetheless, the family brought in professional management to head the group's operations around 2005, naming Nidal Eses and Salim Karadsheh as co-chief executive officers.

ORIGINS IN EXILE

Ramleh-born Elia Nuqul was studying as an engineering student at the University of Beirut when his family was forced to flee the Palestinian territories following the Arab defeat in the war against Israel in 1948. Nuqul left his studies to join his family, settling in Amman, Jordan. Having lost everything, Nuqul at first struggled to support his family through the early years of exile. Nonetheless, Nuqul became determined to build a future for himself and his family in Jordan.

By 1952, Nuqul, joined by his brothers, had founded a small trading company dealing primarily in foodstuffs and fast-moving consumer goods such as chewing gum, sugar, and grains. Nuqul also began importing tissue paper into Jordan. This market remained quite small at the time, due in large part to cultural differences from Western countries, where tissues and other hygienic papers had become household mainstays. Arabic restroom practices were based on the use of water rather than the West's reliance on paper, for example. Similarly, blowing one's nose into a tissue or handkerchief, a social imperative in the West, was seen as improper in much of the Middle East. Another reason for the traditionally low levels of tissue use in these markets might have been the relative lack of forests to supply the raw materials for paper production.

Nonetheless, the market for tissues grew strongly through the 1950s, in part because of the development of softer fibers. The region's high temperatures helped stimulate other uses for tissues, which could be used for wiping the perspiration from one's face and hands. By the late 1950s, Nuqul decided that the upsurge in tissue sales had become sufficient to support the company's extension into manufacturing. In 1958, the company founded Fine Hygienic Paper Co. Ltd. in order to produce tissues for the home market. Fine quickly established itself as the country's major tissue brand; Nuqul would later refer to his company as the "Kimberly-Clark of the Middle East." Over the next decade, the company expanded its range of paper products, adding such products as dinner napkins, toilet paper, and sanitary napkins.

DIVERSIFYING FOR GROWTH

The Arab loss to Israel during the 1967 Six-Day War resulted in the loss of a significant part of Nuqul's market, as the Palestinian territories came under Israeli control. At the same time, trade barriers established among the Arab countries made it difficult for the company to redirect its exports to these markets. As a

result, Nuqul developed a two-pronged strategy, based on the one hand on building a diversified, and increasingly integrated, network of companies in Jordan, and on the other by extending the group's manufacturing presence into other markets.

The company launched the first half of this strategy at the beginning of the 1970s, adding several new operations. These included Nuqul Engineering and Contracting Co., which grew into one of the country's leading suppliers of ready-mix concrete. Through this subsidiary, Nuqul built up its own fleet of concrete mixers and pumps, as well as its own cement batching facilities. Over the next decades, that company grew into a leading cement provider for the Jordanian market. In 1972, Nuqul added another new business, Arab Foam Factories Co. Ltd., which specialized in the production of synthetic foam used for the production of cushions and mattresses, as well as for household sponges and similar products.

That operation enabled the company to develop expertise in working with plastics, particularly polyurethane. This expertise enabled the company to move into new plastics areas later in the decade. In 1977, for example, the company founded United Group Plastics Co. That company specialized in the production of polyethylene bags and sandwich bags, as well as packaging and shrink-wrapping films.

Nuqul's first foreign expansion effort also came at the beginning of the 1970s. For this, Nuqul targeted the Lebanese market, setting up its first foreign subsidiary there in 1971. By the middle of the decade, the company captured a significant share of that country's tissue market. The company continued to grow there through the initial years of the Lebanese Civil War. However, in 1983, a bomb destroyed the company's operations there and the company was forced to abandon the Lebanese market. With the end of the civil war in 1990, Nuqul returned to Lebanon and succeeded in rebuilding the Fine brand as the top-selling tissue in that country.

REGIONAL EXPANSION

Nuqul's difficulties in Lebanon did not discourage the company from seeking further growth in the region. In 1985, the company targeted the Egyptian market, one of the largest in the Arabic-speaking region. The company launched construction of a tissue paper conversion plant at Al-Bardi, south of Cairo. Production at the new site began in 1990 and by the following year, Nuqul had expanded the facility into a full-fledged paper mill.

By this time, Nuqul had also entered the Yemen market, founding a subsidiary of Fine there in 1985.

KEY DATES

1952: Elia Nuqul and his brothers found a trading company in Amman, Jordan.

1958: Nuqul establishes its first manufacturing subsidiary, Fine Hygienic Paper, to produce tissues for the home market.

1971: The company establishes its first foreign subsidiary, in Lebanon.

1988: Nuqul creates Advanced Industries Co. (later Specialized Industries Co.) for the production of nonwoven fabrics for disposable diapers and related products.

1991: Nuqul commences operating a full-fledged paper mill in Egypt.

1992: Nuqul enters the printing sector, setting up Perfect Printing Press Co. in Jordan.

1995: Nuqul enters food production, creating Jordan-based Quality Food Co.

2007: Nuqul inaugurates its second paper mill in Jordan.

2009: Nuqul establishes manufacturing presence in Tehran, Iran.

That subsidiary then began construction of its own factory for the production of hygienic paper products. Production began at the facility in 1986, and by the beginning of the 21st century, Fine's Yemen plant had grown into one of that country's largest industrial operations.

Meanwhile, in Jordan, Nuqul was expanding its technologies in order to increase the integration of its existing operations. The company extended its plastics and packaging wing with the creation of Packaging Industries Co., which launched the production of printed, flexible packaging, such as shampoo bottles, toothpaste and pharmaceutical tubes, sanitary products, and the like. That company started operations in 1987.

In 1988, Nuqul also moved to extend its core paper-based hygienic business into the fast-growing market for disposable diapers and sanitary napkins. To this end, the company created another new subsidiary, Advanced Industries Co. (later Specialized Industries Co.), which became the first in the Middle East to produce nonwoven fabrics. With control of all of the major components for modern absorbent hygienic products, Nuqul established itself as a leader in the disposable diaper market in the Middle East. While much of Specialized Industries' production was devoted

to supplying Nuqul's own operations, the company also became a leading supplier to other diaper and sanitary napkins producers in the region.

Nuqul made further plans to expand its regional presence. The company targeted the United Arab Emirates, and the rapidly growing Dubai market in particular, establishing a new Fine Hygienic Paper subsidiary there in 1989. That company then launched construction of its own tissue converting plant, which became operational in 1991. By 1997, Nuqul had also established a trade subsidiary for the Palestinian territories. The new subsidiary distributed both the Fine brand range and products produced by Nuqul's other operations.

INTEGRATION

Through the 1990s, Nuqul continued to diversify its range of businesses, while nonetheless targeting the development of an integrated and/or interrelated network of companies. Toward this end, Nuqul entered the printing sector in 1992, setting up Perfect Printing Press Co. that year. The company established its press in Jordan, focusing on printing for packaging materials. The new company took over the Fine group's printing needs, while also providing printing services for the third-party sector. By the beginning of the 21st century, Perfect Printing had become the largest in Jordan.

Nuqul's success in the paper mill market in Egypt led the company to extend these operations into Jordan. In 1993, the company established the first of its Jordanian mills, setting up Al Keen Hygienic Paper Mill Co. The company then began construction of the mill, contracting for engineering and machinery from J.M. Voith AG. Production at the mill was launched in 1996, establishing Nuqul as the leading paper-based company in the Middle East.

At its United Group Plastics Co., Nuqul added new blow-molding capacity, enabling it to launch production of high-density polyethylene bottles, used for cooking oil and detergent, in 1993. Nuqul also targeted a further expansion of its industrial scope, setting up Modern Aluminum Industries Co. (MODAL) in 1994. This subsidiary launched construction of a factory for the production of extruded aluminum products, such as architectural profiles.

Nuqul's diversification effort also led it into food production, with the creation of Jordan-based Quality Food Co. in 1995. That company began producing canned meats, and then sausages and other chilled meats, under the Unium brand name, beginning in 1997. Other diversified additions to the Nuqul group at the dawn of the new century included the creation of an engineering subsidiary; the launch of production of printing cylinders and plates; and the creation of a subsidiary producing PVC pipes.

LEADING JORDANIAN CONGLOMERATE IN THE 21ST CENTURY

The booming demand for disposable absorbent products including diapers as well as the rapidly developing market for adult incontinence products throughout the Middle East region encouraged Nuqul to increase its own capacity. In 1998, the company carried out a $40 million expansion of its Specialized Industries operation, adding a second facility in Sahab. The new plant boosted the company's capacity to 7,500 tons per year. By the beginning of the new century, exports accounted for the largest part of this subsidiary's operations, with more than 85 percent of its production shipping outside of Jordan.

Other Nuqul businesses also expanded at the end of the 1990s. These included Packing Industries Co., which in 1998 extended its own facility to a total annual capacity of 2,400 tons. The following year, Nuqul boosted its paper range, setting up a new subsidiary, Quality Printing Press Company. That company expanded the company's range with the manufacturing of various types of paper, including photocopy and printing paper, as well as rolls for fax machines, cash registers, and the like.

While Nuqul's diversified operations had grown strongly, its Fine hygienic paper operations remained the group's flagship. In 2000, the company expanded its Dubai operations, which reached a total production area of 15,000 square meters. Nuqul also introduced Fine into the Sudanese market, creating its subsidiary there in 2005. Also in that year, Nuqul carried out a major expansion and modernization of its Specialized Industries operation, positioning itself as the leading supplier of disposable hygienic products for the region. The company continued to extend its reach throughout the Persian Gulf region, and particularly into Iran, where it established a manufacturing subsidiary in Tehran at the beginning of 2009.

Nuqul also took steps to increase its own paper production. The company added a second mill in Egypt in Al-Sindian in 2005. This was shortly followed by the inauguration of a second mill in Jordan, at Al-Snobar, in 2007. By then, Nuqul had established itself as Jordan's leading conglomerate, with sales estimated at nearly $2.5 billion. Founder Elia Nuqul, who published his biography in 2008, remained the company's chairman. Nonetheless, Nuqul had recognized the need to bring in professional management to ensure the future success of

his company. In 2004, Nuqul brought in Nidal Eses and Salim Karadsheh to serve as the company's co-chief executive officers.

M. L. Cohen

PRINCIPAL SUBSIDIARIES

Al-Bardi Paper Mill Co. S.A.E. (Egypt); Al-Keena Hygienic Paper Mill Co. Ltd. (Jordan); Fine Hygienic Paper Company Ltd.; Fine Hygienic Paper F.Z.E. (Dubai); Modern Aluminum Industries Co. Ltd. (Jordan); Nuqul Brothers Co. Ltd. (Lebanon); Packaging Industries Co. Ltd. (Jordan); Quality Food Co. Ltd. (Jordan); Quality Plastic Industries Co. Ltd. (Jordan); United Group Plastics Co. Ltd. (Jordan).

PRINCIPAL COMPETITORS

Flexible Packaging (Proprietary) Ltd.; Pyramids Paper Mills S.A.E. Flora; Arab Paper and Hygienic Products Company S.A.E./CARMEN; Sano Bruno's Enterprises Ltd.; Gulf Paper Manufacturing Company KSC.

FURTHER READING

"Elia Nuqul, Chairman of Nuqul Group Launches His Biography Entitled 'A Promise Fulfilled,'" *albawaba.com*, December 23, 2008.

"Fine Grows by 21pc," *TradeArabia*, January 14, 2009.

"Fine Looks Back on a Year Filled with Achievements, and Anticipates More to Come in 2007," *Middle East*, January 22, 2007.

"Fine Posts over 20 Percent Growth in 2008," *albawaba.com*, January 13, 2009.

Habboush, Mahmoud, "Specialised Industries Company Opens New $40m Non-woven Fabric Plant," *Jordan Times*, June 7, 2006.

"Jordanian Industrial Giant Signs with Scala," *Asia Africa Intelligence Wire*, September 22, 2003.

"Nuqul Group Partners with Hikmat Road Safety for Better Roads," *albawaba.com*, July 13, 2008.

"Nuqul Group Sets an Example for the Arab Excellence Awards," *albawaba.com*, January 26, 2009.

"Nuqul Group Vows to Continue Investment Trend," *Asia Africa Intelligence Wire*, June 10, 2003.

"Nuqul Leasing Provides Aramex with a Fleet of Over 50 Vehicles," *albawaba.com*, August 3, 2008.

"Nuqul Ventures International," *albawaba.com*, September 15, 2008.

O'Brien, Hugh, "Nuqul Moves Ahead at Impressive Pace," *Perini Journal*, October 2006.

"Paper Money," *ArabianBusiness.com*, February 10, 2009.

Wheatcroft, Andrew, and Christina Z. Hawatmeh, *A Promise Fulfilled—Elia Costandi Nuqul and His Business Odyssey*, New York: I.B. Tauris Publishers, 2008.

1-800-FLOWERS.COM, Inc.

1 Old Country Road
Carle Place, New York 11514-1801
U.S.A.
Telephone: (516) 237-6000
Toll Free: (800) FLOWERS
Fax: (516) 237-6060
Web site: http://www.1800flowers.com

Public Company
Incorporated: 1987
Employees: 4,000
Sales: $912.6 million (2007)
Stock Exchanges: NASDAQ
Ticker Symbol: FLWS
NAICS: 453110 Florists

■ ■ ■

Headquartered in Carle Place, New York, 1-800-FLOWERS.COM, Inc., is the world's largest florist. Recognized for the quality of its flowers and customer service, the company guarantees the freshness of its floral arrangements for one week. As a leading integrated marketer, the company maintains 100 franchised and company-owned retail stores, a Bloom-Net network of approximately 9,000 florists across America, a web site (www.1800flowers.com), and other interactive services through electronic retail partners including America Online, Microsoft Network (MSN), and Yahoo!. A phone order system is also available 24 hours a day, seven days a week. The company's retail outlets, designed to resemble European flower shops, are located in such major markets as New York, Los Angeles, Chicago, San Francisco, San Diego, San Antonio, and Phoenix.

JAMES MCCANN: SOCIAL WORKER TURNED FLORIST

James McCann transformed 1-800-FLOWERS.COM from a small struggling business into a successful international operation. As a young man living with his family in Queens, New York, McCann had initially hoped to become a police officer and studied at John Jay College of Criminal Justice in New York in the 1970s. He eventually became a social worker, however, accepting a job as the administrator of a youth home in Rockaway, New York.

Finding that he needed to supplement his income from social work, he also went into business for himself in 1976, purchasing Flora Plenty, a small flower shop, using $10,000 that friends and relatives had lent him. "In the early days," McCann explained in *Forbes,* "you have no choice; you have all of your net worth in the business. I was running a cash business with a cigar-box mentality. I would never be able to give a bank a financial statement, because I had no clue. But I knew that if I wanted to build an enterprise with some legacy value, I had to make the leap into the legitimate world, doing everything the way you're supposed to."

McCann's little shop grew into a 14-store chain earning about $50,000 a year by the 1980s. McCann then made Flora Plenty a C corporation and put himself on the payroll. Using his real estate and stock market assets—as well as mortgaging his home several times—

COMPANY PERSPECTIVES

For more than 30 years, 1-800-FLOWERS.COM Inc.—"Your Florist of Choice"—has been providing customers around the world with the freshest flowers and finest selection of plants, gift baskets, gourmet foods, confections and plush stuffed animals perfect for every occasion. 1-800-FLOWERS.COM offers the best of both worlds: exquisite, florist-designed arrangements individually created by some of the world's top floral artists and hand-delivered the same day, and spectacular flowers shipped overnight "Fresh from Our Growers." Customers can "call, click or come in" to shop 1-800-FLOWERS.COM twenty four hours a day, 7 days a week at 1-800-356-9377 or www. 1800flowers.com. Sales and Service Specialists are available 24/7, and fast and reliable delivery is offered same day, any day. As always, 100 percent satisfaction and freshness are guaranteed. The 1-800-FLOWERS. COM collection of brands also includes home decor and children's gifts; gourmet gifts including popcorn and specialty treats; exceptional cookies and baked gifts; premium chocolates and confections; gourmet foods; wine gifts; gift baskets; and the BloomNet international floral wire service which provides quality products and diverse services to a select network of florists.

McCann acquired 1-800-FLOWERS in 1987. Headquartered in Dallas, Texas, 1-800-FLOWERS was then struggling financially, losing about $400,000 monthly.

McCann paid $7 million for the poorly managed 1-800-FLOWERS, and then spent another $9 million covering the company's debts and liquidating assets. Nevertheless, McCann was able to turn the company around, largely by marketing flower delivery through telephone orders. At first, 1-800-FLOWERS used FTD, a florist delivery cooperative with thousands of members, including McCann's company. Thus, 1-800-FLOWERS retained a 20 percent fee from each order placed through FTD.

In 1993, however, FTD launched a floral phone service of its own, and McCann positioned 1-800-FLOWERS to compete directly with FTD. Using previously untapped toll-free telephone technology, McCann capitalized on consumers' needs for convenience and competitive pricing. McCann offered his customers a seven-day freshness guarantee, as well as a 100 percent satisfaction guarantee. He also established a Frequent Flowers Club for repeat customers. While FTD's service lost approximately $13 million during this time, 1-800-FLOWERS had achieved $100 million in annual sales by 1993.

THE BUSINESS TAKES ROOT

Over time, McCann contracted new affiliates and established telecenters throughout the United States. As technological advancements permitted, he also became active in electronic retailing. In 1992, 1-800-FLOWERS launched its first online store site on CompuServe's Electronic Mall. Eventually the company joined with a strategic Internet development partner, Fry Multimedia of Ann Arbor, Michigan, to create a site driven by Microsoft Site Server Commerce. By the end of 1997, 10 percent of the company's annual sales came from interactive marketing, about $30 million, and *PC Magazine* recognized the company's web site as one of the top 100 web sites of the year.

In October 1994, 1-800-FLOWERS purchased the Conroy's Flowers franchise system, established in 1961 and headquartered in Long Beach, California. One of the larger retail floral chains in the western United States and with the most stores in the 1-800-FLOWERS retail system, Conroy's Flowers played an important role in the company's success. For example, *Entrepreneur Magazine* named Conroy's/1-800-FLOWERS the best floral franchiser in its 1996 listing of top 500 franchisers.

In August 1995, 1-800-FLOWERS established a toll-free telephone number for its customers around the world. In cooperation with AT&T's USADirect 800 service, the florist provided customers in more than 130 countries with the technology to purchase flowers and gifts for friends and relatives in the United States without paying international and in some cases local telephone charges. By using AT&T Language Line operators, 1-800-FLOWERS communicated with customers in more than 20 languages, a great convenience for customers traveling abroad, business professionals, and military personnel stationed overseas.

THE 1995 DOCUMERCIAL

During the 1995–96 holiday season, 1-800-FLOWERS initiated its first documercial. A combined infomercial and documentary, The Fresh Flower Half Hour appeared in three large markets in early morning and late night time slots. On December 4, 1995, as part of the company's $30 million marketing plan, 1-800-

KEY DATES

1987: James McCann acquires 1-800-FLOWERS.
1992: 1-800-FLOWERS launches its first online store.
1995: 1-800-FLOWERS establishes a toll-free telephone number for its customers around the world.
1997: 1-800-FLOWERS introduces an enhanced version of its BloomLink system to network online with its franchisees.
1999: The company goes public and changes its name to 1-800-FLOWERS.COM.
2007: The company launches 1-800flowers.mobi for mobile phone users.

FLOWERS launched the half-hour television program covering the operations of the company, floral care, and home decorating. Appearing for the Christmas holiday buying season, The Fresh Flower Half Hour aired on network affiliates in New York, Phoenix, and San Antonio markets before national broadcasting.

Entertaining and informative, the half-hour program profiled the business activities of 1-800-FLOWERS, including coverage of its Floraversity training program and procedures for handling and caring for flowers. The Fresh Flower Half Hour also featured home decorating advice and four two-minute direct response opportunities to purchase a holiday flower tree arrangement.

Sales for the 1995–96 Christmas season broke records for the company. Although retail sales nationally had been uneven or disappointing for many retailers, 1-800-FLOWERS saw its sales grow 39 percent over the previous year's. The company also enjoyed strong sales during the Valentine's Day holiday in 1996, accumulating an increase of 32 percent above sales for 1995.

Among the reasons for the increased sales were population and consumer attitude shifts. Industry observers noted that aging baby boomers were becoming more accepting of sending flowers as gifts, and more women, in particular, were buying flowers as gifts for others. While in the past most flower purchasers were men, busier lifestyles demanded more convenient forms of gift giving just when sending flowers became easier. Conveniently, 1-800-FLOWERS offered its customers service by telephone, via interactive media, or in person at one of the 150 company-owned/franchised retail stores throughout the United States.

The company's sales from Mother's Day—the highest volume sales day in the floral industry—increased 31 percent from 1995 to 1996. Sales and order volumes for this holiday, traditionally about 16 percent of the company's annual revenue, swelled in all of the company's marketing platforms. Telephone calls broke the million mark, setting a record for the company, and interactive sales increased 314 percent over the same time for the preceding year. December 1996 online sales exceeded those of the previous year by three times, and web site sales increased tenfold.

INTERACTIVE MARKETING

By 1997, 1-800-FLOWERS conducted about 10 percent of its business through interactive marketing online. The company expected its share of the online market to grow as additional convenience-conscious customers became more familiar with new technologies. Thus, the florist developed a system of online gift reminders to save customers the embarrassment of forgetting a birthday or anniversary. Based on this program's success, 1-800-FLOWERS also started mailing reminder postcards—about 100,000 monthly in 1997.

To compete more effectively in the interactive market, 1-800-FLOWERS contracted with Network Computer, Inc., a subsidiary of Oracle Corporation, to install 2,000 of the company's computers—connected to an NC Enterprise Server—at 1-800-FLOWERS establishments in April 1997. The first corporate client to adopt Larry Ellison's Oracle-backed Java computing system in place of a mainframe terminal environment, 1-800-FLOWERS then operated seven telecenters throughout the nation.

Within a few months, 1-800-FLOWERS announced a new four-year agreement with America Online. As that service's exclusive online florist, the company anticipated more than $250 million in sales from this arrangement. The florist also redesigned its award-winning web site, the fifth revision of the site in three years, to facilitate holiday shopping in November 1997. Changes to the site included a one-click-to-product process that simplified shopping online. Specifically, this streamlined process allowed customers to order merchandise from the web site's home page; in the past, online shoppers needed to browse through several pages before placing an order. The new system offered web site visitors faster service and greater convenience in an effort to turn more browsers into buyers.

In addition, the web site included an updated look and expanded content. For example, the site featured a new registration area, an expanded floral reference and how-to area, a retail store locator, and information on the company's franchising efforts.

In December 1997, 1-800-FLOWERS introduced an enhanced version of its BloomLink system to network online with its franchisees. BloomLink initially served as a vehicle for order processing, but partnering with AT&T, 1-800-FLOWERS transformed it into a web-based communications system that offered basic ordering capabilities, a home page on the web for individual florists, online training programs, e-mail and chat groups, and wholesale purchase opportunities with farms worldwide. As a comprehensive, open architecture system, BloomLink allowed florists to interact with other communication networks or point-of-sales systems with software provided by 1-800-FLOWERS at no charge.

December 1997 sales through the internet reached a record-setting $4 million, about 10 percent of the company's total holiday sales. Customers placed approximately 80,000 orders through the company's web site and through online services such as America Online, the Microsoft Network, and CompuServe. In all, Internet sales rose 150 percent from the preceding year, with men representing two-thirds of the online buyers.

With nine million customers nationwide in 1997, 1-800-FLOWERS neared sales of $300 million. The increased growth in sales (about 25 percent since 1996) prompted 1-800-FLOWERS to open new stores in New Hyde Park, Selden, West Babylon, Bay Ridge, and Brooklyn, New York, and on Manhattan's East Side.

ENTERING THE CATALOG MARKET AND GOING PUBLIC

In 1998, the company was the world's largest florist, with over 150 company-owned and franchised stores plus Internet sales, and it boasted over 10 percent annual sales growth. Of sales, 65 percent were earned on the phone, 25 percent in stores, and 10 percent via the Internet. That year, the company became the first to sell goods to mobile phone users using wireless technology, with an option linked to personal calendars to press a button and order flowers via a dedicated wireless-only number at 1-800-FLOWERS.

In 1998, 1-800-FLOWERS entered the catalog market with the purchase of an 80 percent interest in Plow & Hearth, a home-and-garden products marketer. Plow & Hearth founder Peter Rice continued to administer the 18-year-old company as a subsidiary of the florist.

Also in 1998, 1-800-FLOWERS added a new management level. Owing to its consistent growth and

expansion over the years, the company appointed four employees to serve as vice-presidents: Donna Iucolano, director of interactive services; Bill Shea, company treasurer; Tom Hartnett, director of store operations; and Vinnie McVeigh, director of worldwide call center operations. Previously, Chris McCann, brother of Jim McCann, held the only vice-president position, and he became a senior vice-president at the time of the new appointments.

The company went public in August 1999, and, based on the increasing role of Internet sales in its business, appended ".com" to its name. Jim McCann, who had won much recognition for his work at the company, being named Direct Marketer of the Year, Retailer of the Year, and Entrepreneur of the Year, hoped to triple the company's size. As he told *Long Island Business News:* "We just want to get bigger and better at what we do at a pace we could handle."

GROWTH AND DIVERSIFICATION

The beginning of the 21st century was good for 1-800-FLOWERS.COM. Between 2000 and 2007, total net revenues increased 240 percent, steadily soaring from $379.5 million to $912.6 million. However, the company lost money for several years after going public, achieving its first profitable quarter in 2001.

To increase profitability, the company added several product lines with higher margins to its basic flower business, including gardening products, through an agreement with America Online (1999); a Specialty Boutique area, including fine jewelry, collectibles, and gifts (2000); natural toys through its acquisition of The Children's Group, including Hearthsong and Magic Cabin Dolls (2001); food gifts and gift baskets through its acquisition of The Popcorn Factory (2002); cookies and baked gift items through the purchase of Cheryl & Company (2005); and candy through the acquisition of Fannie May Confection Brands, Inc. (2006).

Exemplifying the company's increasingly diverse product lines, in 2001 it sold 2.5 million roses, 50,000 boxes of chocolate, and 20,000 plush toys. Online revenues accounted for 35.5 percent of total net revenues, and non-floral gifts made up 55.7 percent of total combined online and telephonic revenues. By 2002, non-floral gifts comprised 62.1 percent of total combined online and telephonic revenues.

The company also developed an Operational Excellence program to examine ways to build revenue and decrease costs. In 2004, this program catalyzed the makeover of the company's catalog and its distribution methods, resulting in an 89 percent increase in sales.

In order to enhance its core product, flowers, the company sought to set itself apart from its competitors by offering the work of celebrity floral designers. The company began offering floral designs by Jane Packer—whose list of famous clients included the British royal family, Giorgio Armani, Givenchy, Dustin Hoffman, and Kate Moss—in 2005; and Preston Bailey—who boasted a client list including Donald Trump, Oprah Winfrey, Liza Minnelli, Joan Rivers, and Catherine Zeta Jones—in 2006.

The company also continued to explore ways to link its marketing efforts to consumer technology, offering convenient purchasing to customers of its electronic retail partners. For example, in 2000, AOLbyPhone enabled AOL members to enter a shopping area, hear information about 1-800-FLOWERS.COM products, and say "connect me" to transfer to a sales specialist. In 2007, the company launched 1-800flowers.mobi, an Internet site for mobile phone users, and it linked its rewards program to Facebook.

A major challenge facing online florists was how to accommodate the huge increases in business during peak times (Mother's Day, Valentine's Day, and Christmas) without hiring more staff than needed at other times of the year. In 2007, with about 75 percent of its sales conducted through the World Wide Web, the company launched a new Internet system that balanced order loads across three geographically dispersed web systems, hosted by AT&T. The company also formed a mutually beneficial and innovative partnership with Choice Hotels, whereby Choice agents handled flower sales at peak times, and, in return, 1-800-FLOWERS.COM agents helped Choice book hotel rooms in the busy summer months.

AWARDS AND ACCOLADES

The public took notice of 1-800-FLOWERS.COM's achievements in the 21st century, and the company received several awards. In 2001, the Long Island Web Developers Guild selected the company for top honors in its first annual Web Awards of Long Island, and *Forbes* honored the company's web site in its "Best of the Web" list. The company also earned the New Media Diamond Award in the CRM Grand Prix for customer service, and it received a number of Best of Long Island awards for e-commerce. In 2002, the company's main web site was named best in the gifting category in a study by the Direct Marketing Association. In 2006, 1-800-FLOWERS.COM was named Global Call Center of the Year by the International Customer Management Institute in the large call center category. That year, the company also received a Network World's Enterprise All-Star Award for its use of the Securify system, which assisted with security monitoring and controls. In 2008,

the company was named the Laureate Honoree by Computerworld Honors Program.

Despite 1-800-FLOWERS.COM's seeming success, the company's stock prices ebbed and flowed in the early years of the new century. Stock prices rose to $17.40 in January 2002, but fell to $7.11 in September of that year. By February 2006, stock had fallen to $6.30 a share. However, most analysts attributed these fluctuations to changes in the broader market rather than to the performance of 1-800-FLOWERS.COM. Firmly rooted in an increasingly electronic consumer world, the world's largest florist seemed likely to continue along a stable path to success.

Charity Anne Dorgan
Updated, Heidi Feldman

PRINCIPAL SUBSIDIARIES

Teleway; Plow & Hearth; 1-800-FLOWERS RETAIL Inc.; The Children's Group; The Popcorn Factory; Cheryl & Company; Fannie May Confection Brands, Inc.

PRINCIPAL COMPETITORS

FTD.Com; Harry & David Holdings, Inc.; Teleflora.

FURTHER READING

Bartlett, Michael, "Revenues, Net Income Bloom for 1800Flowers.com," *Newsbytes,* January 23, 2002.

Campbell, Tricia, "The Drama of Selling," *Sales & Marketing Management,* December 1997, p. 92.

Del Franco, Mark, "1-800-Flowers Blooms After Redo," *Catalog Age,* January 1, 2005.

"Exhibiting Flower Power; 2: 1-800-flowers.com Inc.," *Crain's New York Business,* November 26, 2001, p. 18.

"Flowers.Com to Buy Maker of Baked Gift Items," *New York Times,* March 12, 2005, p. C4.

Gabriel, Frederick, "Millionaires of Silicon Alley: Jim McCann," *Crain's New York Business,* November 29, 1999, p. 46.

Hein, Kenneth, "Willie Nelson Gets Picked to Pick for 1-800-Flowers," *Brandweek,* January 21, 2002, p. 5.

Hickey, Kathleen, "Always in Bloom: 1-800-FLOWERS.COM Fulfills Orders Nationwide, Overseas Through Extranet System Linking Florists," *Traffic World,* November 25, 2002, p. 17.

"In Online Odyssey, 1-800-FLOWERS Lands on Microsoft's Plaza Mall," *Interactive Marketing News,* November 15, 1996.

Johnson, Stephen S., "Flower Power," *Forbes,* July 4, 1994, p. 144.

Markus, Stuart, "1-800-Flowers.com Wins Award for Customer Service," *Long Island Business News,* July 6, 2001, p. 12A.

Martorana, Jamie, "New Management Team Blooming at 1-800-FLOWERS," *Long Island Business News,* July 27, 1998, p. 9A.

McCann, Jim, "Building Relationships On-Line Is True Promise of Interactive Marketing," *Marketing News,* October 27, 1997, p. 10.

————, *Stop and Sell the Roses,* New York: Ballantine Books, 1998.

McCune, Jenny C., "On the Train Gang," *Management Review,* October 1994, p. 57.

McKenna, Patrick, "Ellison's Network Computers Heading to 1-800-Flowers," *Newsbytes,* April 7, 1997.

Miller, Paul, "Flowering Hearth: 1-800-FLOWERS Buys 80 Percent of Plow & Hearth," *Catalog Age,* May 1998, p. 5.

Moiduddin, Abed, "War of the Roses; The Online Flower Powerhouses Are Going Head-to-Head This Valentine's Day. Here's Why 1-800-Flowers May Deserve a Closer Look from Investors," *Business Week Online,* February 14, 2006.

Oberndorf, Shannon, "Flower Power Half Hour," *Catalog Age,* March 1996, p. 28.

"1-800-Flowers.com," *Research,* December 2004, p. 66.

"1-800-Flowers.com Acquires Toy Company," *Long Island Business News,* June 15, 2001, p. 21A.

"1-800-Flowers.com Tops Web Awards," *Long Island Business News,* March 23, 2001, p. 11A.

"Online: 1-800-FLOWERS," *Report on Electronic Commerce,* January 14, 1997.

Pellet, Jennifer, and George Schira, "This Bud's for You," *Chief Executive* (U.S.), March 1997, p. 24.

"The Popcorn Factory Sold to 1-800-Flowers.com," *Catalog Age,* June 1, 2002.

"Ringing Up Sales with Cable," *Mediaweek,* March 27, 1995, p. S30.

Warshaw, Michael, "Invest in Yourself; Get Professional Help and Diversify Your Fortune, Says the Owner of Industry Giant 1-800-FLOWERS," *Success,* April 1997, pp. 27–28.

Patrick Cudahy Inc.

———————■———————

3500 East Barnard Avenue
Cudahy, Wisconsin 53110
U.S.A.
Telephone: (414) 744-2000
Toll Free: (800) 386-6900
Fax: (414) 744-4213
Web site: http://www.patrickcudahy.com

Wholly Owned Subsidiary of Smithfield Foods, Inc.
Incorporated: 1888 as Cudahy Brothers
Employees: 1,100
Sales: $499 million (2008 est.)
NAICS: 311612 Meat Processed from Carcasses;
5441990 All Other Professional, Scientific, and
Technical Services

■ ■ ■

Patrick Cudahy Inc. is one of the leading pork process-ing and packaging companies in the United States. Patrick Cudahy produces a full line of ham, bacon, and sausage; a line of deli meats including Italian sausage and salami; and sausage, bacon, ham, pepperoni, and sliced meats for the foodservice industry. The company offers an array of meat products aimed at the Hispanic market under the La Abuelita brand, and pepperoni and deli meats under the Pavone brand. The company's fats and oils division also produces a variety of lard and shortening products. Cudahy has a long history in the Midwest, where it was once a principal hog slaughterer. The company moved from slaughtering to processing after emerging from a long strike and bankruptcy in the

late 1980s. Founded in 1888, Patrick Cudahy Inc. changed hands several times and has been a subsidiary of Virginia-based Smithfield Foods, Inc., since 1984.

A HARDWORKING IMMIGRANT

Patrick Cudahy Inc. is named for its founder, who was born in Ireland in 1849. His family immigrated to the United States when he was only a few months old, and Patrick grew up in Milwaukee, Wisconsin. He had his first job in the meatpacking field when he was only 13 years old. He was employed as a "carrying boy" in the meatpacking firm Edward Roddis. Before the era of refrigeration, meatpacking was a wintertime business, so in the summer months, young Patrick gained experience working in gardens and nurseries. At the age of 17, he apprenticed to a stonecutter, but at some point he returned to meatpacking. By the time he was 25, he had been promoted to superintendent of the packing plant Plankinton and Armour. Cudahy was reportedly a savvy performer and oversaw Plankinton's change of product line from barrel pork to cured meat. The company's owner was impressed with his acumen, and sold him a one-sixteenth interest in the business in 1874.

Within another ten years, Patrick Cudahy had risen to become owner Plankinton's junior partner. When Plankinton retired in 1888, he sold his interest in the firm to Cudahy and his brother John. John had a financial interest in the company but was not active in management. However, the company acknowledged his contribution, taking the name Cudahy Brothers. The new company grew rapidly. Its main business was sup-plying cured pork to Europe. By 1892, Cudahy Brothers had made inroads across the United States and Canada, and sold its pork in major cities in England, Ireland, Germany, and Scandinavia.

Patrick Cudahy and his brother had bought out the interest of John Plankinton and renamed the company. However, after the elder Plankinton's death in 1891, Plankinton's son began interfering in the business, preventing Cudahy from making needed improvements to the plant. Cudahy decided to build new facilities, and in fact a new town, two miles outside of Milwaukee. The area had been known as Buckthorn, but it soon became the thriving town of Cudahy, Wisconsin. Cudahy quickly had its own rail line and streetcar system. Its hotels, parks, and schools were built on streets bearing the names of Patrick Cudahy's many friends in the meatpacking industry.

Cudahy began building the town just as financial disaster struck in what became known as the Panic of 1893. Brother John lost a fortune, and Milwaukee banks became wary of lending to Patrick. A business acquaintance introduced Cudahy to bankers in Boston, and with a substantial loan, Cudahy was able to keep his business afloat. The effects of the Panic of 1893 lasted for some five years, but Cudahy weathered the rough times. The company advertised for workers in foreign-language newspapers in major American cities. The town of Cudahy became a magnet for immigrants from Eastern and Central Europe. Workers were able to buy cottages from the company, paying for them with modest deductions from their paychecks. Cudahy built an impressive five-story factory, and then set up branch businesses in Milwaukee, elsewhere in Wisconsin, and in Illinois and Michigan. By the mid-1920s, Cudahy Brothers ran 85 retail meat outlets in these three states.

CHANGES IN LEADERSHIP

Patrick Cudahy died in 1919. His son Michael became president, a post he held until 1960. Michael had been vice-president for ten years, and had grown up in the business, so he had plenty of experience. His tenure was marked by some difficulties right at the outset. When he succeeded his father in 1919, the American Federation of Labor attempted to organize the nonunion workers at the Cudahy plant. This action led to a three-month strike. It ended without the union gaining recognition.

While the company was roiled with labor difficulties, it had to adapt to a major shift in markets. During founder Patrick Cudahy's era, the company had done significant business exporting pork products to Europe, but a trade battle between the United States and European manufacturers led to new tariffs. When the United States enacted a new tariff to protect itself from European businesses, Great Britain struck back with legislation that gave trade preference to its colonies and former colonies and to South America. As a result, Cudahy Brothers lost its British market. The company retrenched in the 1920s, developing products for its domestic market.

In 1928, Cudahy opened a new division, producing vacuum-cooked meats. The next year, it also began producing ox tongue and pork tongue, and dried beef. During the years of the Great Depression, Cudahy managed to keep afloat. The company had no debt, and it even invested in new equipment. Cudahy installed a low-temperature freezer called a sharp freezer in 1930, said to be the first of its type in the meatpacking industry. The war years brought a boom, and in the 1940s the company sold meat under as many as 79 different labels. It also sold cheese, butter, oils, and lard, and had a business in specialty meats in Mexico.

The 1940s had been boom years for Cudahy, but rising costs in the 1950s put a damper on profits. Still under the leadership of Michael Cudahy, the company ventured into some new product lines. It began packing salami for several domestic producers, and in 1954, it introduced its own line of hot dogs. Around this time, the company introduced its tagline, "smoked with sweet apple wood." In 1957, the company changed its name from Cudahy Brothers Co. to Patrick Cudahy Inc.

Michael Cudahy stepped down from leadership of the company in 1961. He was succeeded by his son Richard. Like his father before him, Richard became president during a particularly difficult time, and had to immediately prove his management skills. The company was not profitable at that time, as the meatpacking industry as a whole endured a painful recession. Richard Cudahy had to negotiate with the company's union, the Packinghouse Workers, and agreed to fund workers' pensions. He was also able to get increased worker productivity, helping the bottom line considerably. The company also made inroads into new markets, phasing

KEY DATES

1874: Patrick Cudahy buys part interest in meat-packing business.

1888: Patrick and brother John take over company, found Cudahy Brothers.

1919: Patrick's son Michael becomes president.

1957: Name changed to Patrick Cudahy Inc.

1961: Third generation takes over.

1971: Bluebird, Inc., buys company.

1980: Cudahy and parent company acquired by Northern Foods of England.

1984: Cudahy sold to Smithfield Foods.

1987: Two-year labor strike begins.

1997: Company completes multimillion-dollar upgrade.

2005: Hispanic meat producer 814 Americas acquired.

out beef products and increasing sales and distribution in the growing Chicago area. Cudahy began producing a line of pepperoni under the Rosso brand, and this did well as demand for pizza grew.

NEW OWNERSHIP

By 1970, Patrick Cudahy Inc. was making record profits. However, its facilities were outdated and this stymied further growth, so top management reached the decision to find a buyer. In 1971, a Philadelphia company, Bluebird, Inc., agreed to buy Cudahy for $5 million. Bluebird was experienced in the packing industry, and owned a major Chicago meat processor, Agar. Bluebird burgeoned during the 1970s, and its sales by the end of the decade were rising sharply, to over $124 million.

Sales at Cudahy were about $90 million annually during the 1970s. The company added new product lines and invested in new equipment. It worked on producing meat from hogs closer to its Wisconsin plant, to reduce its logistical costs. Cudahy improved its sausage and bacon production and added to its existing canned meats product line. The company also made efficient use of the hogs it slaughtered. It had markets for hog bristles and manure, as well as for every cut of meat. The company's workforce doubled over the 1970s, from 500 to 1,000. Bluebird, the parent company, had invested in much new machinery, and was prepared to make new additions.

In 1980, Patrick Cudahy Inc. asked the city of Cudahy to raise a bond of $5 million so the company could invest in more improvements. While the city council was mulling over the bond issue, parent company Bluebird was sold to a British firm, Northern Foods of England. The price for Bluebird was $72 million. Northern Foods was a huge company, with sales of $840 million and some 16,000 people in its employ. The new ownership, however, seemed to do little to change things at Cudahy.

The city came through with a modified bond issue, and the company made significant improvements and additions to its plant. It was still in the midst of major renovations in 1983 when Northern management announced that it was selling Patrick Cudahy. The meat industry was again in somewhat of a slump, and Northern preferred to cut Cudahy loose. A Philadelphia businessman stepped forward to buy the company for $30 million. However, this deal fell apart at the last minute, and Cudahy remained in Northern's hands for another year and a half. Then in December 1984, Smithfield Foods, a renowned ham processor in Smithfield, Virginia, came forward with an offer of $29 million, and Cudahy changed hands again.

BITTER STRIKE LASTS TWO YEARS

Alan Anderson, who had been Cudahy's president for five years in the 1970s, returned in 1984 to run the company again under Smithfield. In 1986, he handed the job to a handpicked successor, Roger Kapella. Kapella had more than 25 years of experience in meat-packing, and he was prepared to see the company through changing market conditions. One difficulty with Cudahy was that its labor practices were not competitive when compared to firms that had started up in the previous two decades. Cudahy was paying about $9 an hour to its unionized workers, while other companies were paying several dollars an hour less.

Cudahy management asked the union to take a pay cut in order to keep the company in good financial shape. The union refused, and in January 1987 Cudahy workers went on strike. The strike continued for 28 months, with dire costs to both sides. The union believed that the company was not bargaining in good faith and that it wanted to force a strike in order to bring the union down. The union appealed to the National Labor Relations Board and won on these grounds. However, Cudahy appealed the board's ruling and was eventually triumphant. Meanwhile Cudahy posted a loss for fiscal 1987, and the parent company too lost profits. By December 1987, Cudahy had closed its slaughterhouse, laid off 70 percent of its workers, and filed for bankruptcy.

The strike ended in April 1989, and Cudahy emerged from bankruptcy later that year. In early 1990, Cudahy's workers approved a new contract that set their wages at around $7.50 an hour. Both sides had made concessions. One of the workers quoted in a March 1, 1990, story in the *Richmond (Virginia) Times-Dispatch* on the new contract claimed, "No one really won." Both the company and the industry had changed a lot, and 1990 marked a new beginning. Cudahy was by this time a meat processor rather than a slaughterhouse or meatpacker.

NEW VIGOR AFTER STRIKE

With its grueling labor dispute behind it, Cudahy made significant changes to bring it through the 1990s and into the next century. The company came out with new products such as reduced-fat meats that fit with current consumer needs. It made new labels for its products, updating its look. In 1993, Cudahy made a significant renovation to its main cutting floor. Then in 1995, the company spent $13 million to build a new wing on its century-old plant. This was the biggest upgrade the company had made since it moved to Cudahy. In a gesture toward overcoming the company's troubled past, the groundbreaking was done by Wisconsin's governor, Cudahy's president, eight union stewards, and six employees. The new wing was finished in 1997, ten years after the strike began.

Cudahy then had increased capacity for sausage and cured meats, precooked meats, and sliced meats. It also had more refrigerated warehouse space and an updated shipping department. Cudahy had a long history, but in the late 1990s it was as modern as it could be. Controls were computerized, workers' jobs had been realigned to reduce physical strain, and an advanced laboratory checked for quality, moisture, nutritional content, and the like. The company's workforce had fallen to below 300 a decade earlier. After all the improvements, Cudahy employed about 900 people. Both Cudahy and parent Smithfield reported gains in revenue and profit for fiscal 1998. The company seemed on a firm path by the end of the decade.

CONTINUED EXPANSION IN THE 21ST CENTURY

Patrick Cudahy continued to add to and improve its plants in the early years of the new century. By 2001, the company employed some 1,160 people in Cudahy. That year it announced another expansion, expected to

cost about $20 million and to add another 300 jobs. Sales in 2002 were estimated at more than $200 million. In 2003, the company announced plans to renovate an abandoned meat processing plant in nearby Iowa, adding more than 100 jobs in that state.

Roger Kapella, who had been president since 1986, shortly after the Smithfield takeover, stepped down in 2004. He was succeeded by William G. Otis. Otis had been senior vice-president, and had some 25 years of experience in the meatpacking industry. One significant development that followed the change in leadership was Cudahy's acquisition of a New Jersey-based company, 814 Americas, that specialized in meats for the Hispanic market. Cudahy had a fast-growing line of meats for the Hispanic market, which it marketed under the La Abuelita label. In 2005 it paid an undisclosed amount for 814 Americas, buying it from its Spanish parent, Campofrio Alimentacion S.A. La Abuelita had been a stellar performer for Cudahy, and demographic trends suggested Hispanic foods would continue to be a growth area, so this acquisition seemed to be a good fit.

The food industry as a whole was roiled by rising prices in the new century. Cudahy's parent Smithfield Foods had experienced a troubling drop in income as well as stock price by mid-2008. As corn prices rose, pork became more expensive, and Smithfield saw its income fall as much as 94 percent in the fourth quarter of 2008. Its stock price too dropped drastically. In early 2009, Smithfield announced that it was selling 5 percent of its stock to China's largest agricultural trading company, Cofco. As a subsidiary company, Patrick Cudahy did not need to announce revenue and profits, and so it was hard to tell how its parent's troubles impacted the Wisconsin company. In any case, Cudahy had faced many crises in its long history, going all the way back to the Panic of 1893. The company had weathered economic downturns, sudden shifts in markets, changing labor conditions, and new customer needs. The company seemed prepared for whatever circumstances the ensuing decades would bring.

A. Woodward

PRINCIPAL DIVISIONS

Retail Products; Deli Products; Foodservice Products; Refined Fats and Oils.

PRINCIPAL COMPETITORS

Fred Usinger, Inc.; Johnsonville Sausage, LLC; Klement Sausage Co., Inc.

FURTHER READING

Becker, Mary, and Del Hauenstein, *A Journey Through the Past, Present and Future: Patrick Cudahy Since 1888*, Cudahy,

Wisc: Patrick Cudahy Inc., 1990.

Celebrating 110 Years of Goodness: 1888–1998, Cudahy, Wisc.: Patrick Cudahy Inc., 1998.

Clayton, Chris, "Cudahy Plant to Add 140 Jobs," *Omaha World-Herald,* August 17, 2005, p. D1.

"Cudahy Inc. Union Votes for Contract," *Richmond (Va.) Times-Dispatch,* March 1, 1990, p. 23.

Daykin, Tom, "Low Hog Prices Hurt Farmers, Help Processors," *Milwaukee Journal Sentinel,* December 18, 1998, p. 1.

———, "Patrick Cudahy to Add 300 Jobs in Expansion," *Milwaukee Journal Sentinel,* June 9, 2001, p. D1.

Gallagher, Kathleen, "Patrick Cudahy Buys Hispanic Sausage Maker," *Milwaukee Journal Sentinel,* March 22, 2005, p. 1.

Lynch, Kevin, "Union Strike Relived in 'The Line,'" *Wisconsin State Journal,* September 19, 1996, p. 4.

"Meatpacking Plant Lays Off 700 Workers," *Richmond (Va.) Times-Dispatch,* December 4, 1987, p. 12.

"Patrick Cudahy Picks New President," *Milwaukee Journal Sentinel,* May 22, 2004, p. D3.

Pradnya, Joshi, "Patrick Cudahy Plans $11 Million Expansion," *Milwaukee Journal Sentinel,* July 17, 1995, p. D6.

"Strike Caused Losses for Patrick Cudahy," *Richmond (Va.) Times-Dispatch,* June 8, 1987, p. B5.

Walzer, Philip, "Smithfield Shares Sink As Credit Rating, Stock Are Downgraded," *Norfolk Virginian-Pilot,* June 27, 2008.

Petry Media Corporation

3 East 54th Street, 18th Floor
New York, New York 10022-3108
U.S.A.
Telephone: (212) 230-5900
Fax: (212) 230-5876
Web site: http://www.petrymedia.com

Private Company
Incorporated: 1995
Employees: 400
Sales: $909 million (2002 est.)
NAICS: 541810 Advertising Agencies

■ ■ ■

Petry Media Corporation is a New York City-based holding company that specializes in representing local television stations. Petry provides administrative support and advisory services through its four operating divisions: Petry Television, Blair Television, Petry International, and PMC Direct Response. Petry Television and Blair Television represent local television stations, collecting an inventory of 30-second spots that can then be sold to national advertisers. Between them they have more than 300 client television stations. Beyond ad sales, the divisions offer marketing services, including research, programming, creative services, and information services. They also specialize in political and advocacy group advertising, and through Digerati iSales Petry sells national advertising for the web sites of their local television station clients.

Petry International provides the same basic spot market services as Petry Television and Blair Television but to international broadcast networks and multicultural media properties based in the United States, appealing to advertisers looking to reach more of a global audience. PMC Direct Response focuses on direct response television (DRTV), selling station time to producers of 30-minute "infomercials" and shorter formats. In addition to its New York headquarters, Petry Media maintains 20 branch offices in key media markets across the United States. Petry Media is owned by management and the New York investment firm Patriarch Partners, LLC.

DEPRESSION-ERA ROOTS

The seeds for both Petry Television and Blair Television were planted in the 1930s when the two companies were devoted to the radio industry. Born in the late 1890s, Edward Petry was a radio industry pioneer, the first, in early 1932, to start a representation business to help local radio stations in major cities sell spot ads. Before that time, only sponsors had brokers and they were able to pit stations against one another to receive the lowest possible price.

The idea behind Edward Petry & Co., Inc., was to represent a single station in a market, selling its time to the ad agencies that represented the sponsors. Thus, top stations could leverage their position to sell advertising time at higher prices, either through spot ads or program sponsorship, to companies seeking national and regional exposure. Petry's first client was Hubbard Broadcasting, whose KSTP radio station in Minneapolis–St. Paul, Minnesota, was the first station to be solely funded by ad revenues. The idea of station representation caught on slowly, but by the end of the 1930s the concept was well entrenched.

Edward Petry solidified his reputation as a forward thinker in the 1940s when he turned his attention to the next mass medium that was beginning to emerge, television. In 1941, when only a handful of consumers owned televisions, Petry sold the first spot ad, a 20-second commercial for the Bulova Watch Company that cost $9 to air. Television spot sales would prove to be a perfect companion to Petry's main radio representation business, but after World War II television assumed increasing importance. In 1971 Edward Petry & Co. decided to focus entirely on television station representation and sold the radio side of the business. In the meantime, the company's founder retired in 1964 and died at the age of 73 in June 1970.

JOHN BLAIR & COMPANY FORMED

The man behind Blair Television was John Portwood Blair, born in Chicago in 1900. After graduating from the University of Wisconsin in 1921 he joined the *Chicago American* newspaper in the sales department. He then moved to Detroit to become the local manager for *General Outdoor Advertising,* followed by a stint with the J. Walter Thompson advertising agency. Deciding to start his own business, Blair borrowed money from his life insurance policy and established a partnership that would become John Blair & Company in 1935. Taking advantage of the opportunity opened up by Petry, Blair became a radio station representative and starting in Chicago quickly opened offices across the country. Also like Petry, Blair recognized the importance of television, and in 1948 formed Blair Television to focus on selling spot ads for local television stations, the first national sales representation organization in the field.

Blair retired in 1966, and lived until 1983, dying at the age of 83. Following his departure, Jack W. Fritz, taking over as chief executive in 1972 after 19 years with Blair Television, drove the firm's growth and

moved into new areas. Diversification became necessary because for a time in the 1960s and 1970s the major broadcast groups tried to do without representatives such as Petry and Blair and handle spot sales to national advertisers themselves. The effort would be abandoned for the most part, but not before some of the smaller rep firms went out of business, leaving more spot sales opportunities for the likes of Blair and Petry. Under Fritz, Blair used its graphics unit, which had focused on such areas as catalogs and annual reports, to pursue the newspaper-insert coupon business after one of its printing customers that was involved in the niche went bankrupt. The result was John Blair Marketing. Fritz also took Blair into radio and television station ownership.

BLAIR SUFFERS FROM 1984 DECISION

In 1983 Blair generated $414 million in sales, netting $18 million. While the business was successful, Fritz wanted to grow it even larger, and in 1984 embarked on an ill-fated attempt to achieve that goal. Taking the advice of consulting firm Arthur D. Little, he paid $36 million to acquire Advo-Systems Inc., the largest U.S. distributor of coupon circulars through the mail, for $36 million, followed by an investment of another $100 million in an attempt to rapidly expand the business. What the consultants did not count on, however, was that local newspapers and other coupon vendors responded to the threat from Advo by slashing rates in order to keep their advertisers. Not only did Advo have to follow suit in market after market, it had to contend with a postage increase that further hurt margins. As a consequence, Blair began to hemorrhage money, and in November 1985 initiated a restructuring effort organized by Salomon Brothers Inc. that included the sale of assets.

In early 1986 the freestanding newspaper-insert coupon operation was sold, followed by the American Printings & Lithographers printing unit, which was sold to its management team. At the same time, Blair became the target of a hostile takeover bid from Mac-Fadden Holdings Inc. To thwart MacFadden, Blair agreed to sell a controlling interest to Reliance Capital Group in 1986, clearing the way for the sale of Advo, followed by the sale of Blair's radio and television stations and other assets and leading to the spin off of the television rep business under the Blair Communications banner.

Petry and Blair came together in 1995 when Petry Media was formed to acquire Blair Television for approximately $25 million, bringing together the second- and third-highest billing television rep firms. Combined

KEY DATES

1932: Edward Petry & Company formed.
1935: John Blair & Company established.
1941: Petry sells first television spot ad.
1948: Blair Television becomes first television national sales representation organization in the field.
1995: Petry Television and Blair Television brought together under Petry Media.
2003: Patriarch Partners acquires majority stake.
2009: Company announces plan to combine Petry Television and Blair Television under the Petry brand.

they represented 250 stations, accounting for $1.8 billion of the $8 billion spot TV ad market, with Petry Television accounting for $1 billion of that amount. The two companies carried on as separate operations, relying on their own management and sales teams, although some back-office operations were shared. In this way, by maintaining so-called firewalls to keep business dealings ethical, Petry Media could represent more than one television station in a market through their two brands.

INDUSTRY CONSOLIDATION

In addition to its core television rep business, Petry Media expanded on other fronts in the latter half of the 1990s, turning its attention to the emergence of new media. Realtime, an interactive media sales representation company, was acquired in February 1996 to form the Petry Interactive division. Realtime brought with it offices in San Francisco and New York, and subsequent branches were added in Chicago and Los Angeles. Realtime also provided some diversity, an important consideration given the consolidation under way among television ownership groups, especially the stations owned and operated by the broadcast networks. Some of these larger entities began creating their own spot sales divisions, thus cutting out station reps like Petry and Blair.

In 1996, one of Petry largest clients was Fox TV, representing the spot ads of Fox's five largest owned-and-operated (O&O) stations, located in New York, Boston, Philadelphia, Chicago, and Los Angeles. Fox was considering a move to take sales in-house in the wake of its acquisition of New World Communications and its ten stations. In anticipation, Petry in 1996 sought diversity and another revenue stream while

supplementing its service offerings to the TV stations it represented by acquiring majority control of Indenet Inc., a provider of support services to the television advertising industry. In addition to television stations, the three-year-old Los Angeles company served broadcast networks, cable programmers, syndicators, and advertisers, offering a software and hardware management system to schedule TV spots and keep track of traffic and ad billings.

Consolidation of television station ownership adversely impacted Petry in another way as well, making the need for additional revenue streams increasingly important. One of Petry's clients, Hubbard Broadcasting, swapped a Tampa, Florida, television station for a pair of stations owned by Paramount Stations Group in Rochester and Albany, New York, and New Mexico. In order to take on Hubbard's new Albany station, Petry had to give up representation of an Albany station owned by Freedom Broadcasting, which then elected to switch the business of four other stations from Petry to another station rep firm. Petry also lost client stations in Atlanta, Pittsburgh, Washington, and Miami when network owner NBC decided to take sales in-house.

In February 1997 Petry secured a new Fox contract, which included 12 Fox-owned stations and the ten former New World Communications stations. As part of the deal Petry also acquired New World Television Sales, an in-house rep firm that became known as Fox Television Sales. The combination of Petry Television, Blair Television, and Fox Television Sales made Petry Media the largest television station rep with about $2.5 billion in annual billings.

BID TO SELL COMPANY FAILS

Upheaval in the station rep business continued in the late 1990s. Radio broadcaster Chancellor Media Corporation acquired Katz Media Corporation, the third largest station rep firm with $1.7 billion in annual billings, in 1997. A year later Chancellor set its sights on Petry. An agreement was reached to buy Petry for $150 million. Petry was then to be combined with Katz to decrease the number of television rep firms to just two. The transaction was held up, however, as Chancellor failed in its attempt to merge with Clear Channel Communications. In an effort to reassure Wall Street, Chancellor promised to focus on its core radio business and in 1999 scuttled the acquisition of Petry as well as a much larger deal for LIN Television Corp. LIN then considered a possible acquisition of Petry, and that deal also failed to reach fruition when the two parties were unable to agree on terms.

Still independent as it entered the new century, Petry took steps to consolidate its operations. In 2000 the company renewed its lease on a midtown Manhattan office building, adding 36,000 square feet in order to bring the three station rep firms to the same address. The idea that Petry Television, Blair Television, and Fox Television Sales could maintain the firewalls that separated them had become less important in time. What had started out as a sharing of accounting and other back-office functions had since evolved into the merging of the programming departments. Coming together under a single roof, therefore, was hardly a momentous development. What was more important was finding ways to save money to offset a decline in commission rates for national spot advertising. Commissions that had been 15 percent a decade earlier were less than 10 percent, and in the case of large clients could be as low as 6 percent.

PETRY IN THE 21ST CENTURY

The early years of the new century were difficult for Petry, which had taken on too much debt and began to default on its loans. Around the start of 2003, Patriarch Partners, LLC, bought up the bad loans to acquire a controlling stake in Petry and then tried to improve the company in an effort to sell it and take a profit. In 2004 Clear Channel appeared interested but nothing came of those talks. To tap into new revenue sources, Petry in 2005 established Petry International to take advantage of the globalization of the media, followed by Digerati iSales to sell advertising for television station web sites.

However, the new businesses did not bring in enough revenue to offset worsening economic conditions and the loss of major clients as well as key executives. In the spring of 2008, Gannett Broadcasting took its $400 million in spot billings to rival TeleRap, a Cox Communications unit, resulting in layoffs at Petry. For some time consideration had been given to combining Blair Television and Petry Television, to create a single brand, and in 2009 the company announced that the time had come for Blair to be merged into Petry to create a more efficient operation. Going forward Petry hoped to build its rep business by adding more cable networks. It also held out high hopes for Digerati iSales and Petry International, especially an initiative in China. Leading the company was Alexander "Sandy" Brown, installed as chief executive officer in February 2009. The media veteran told *TVNewsday* that he was determined to win back former clients, adding, "You better believe that I'm going to be knocking on their doors to ask them to come back. We're going to be aggressive in that

area. Petry's been around for a long time and it's not going anywhere."

Ed Dinger

PRINCIPAL SUBSIDIARIES

Horizon Media, Inc.; Katz Media Group, Inc.; National Cable Communications LLC.

PRINCIPAL DIVISIONS

Blair Television; Petry Television; Petry International; PMC Direct Response.

PRINCIPAL COMPETITORS

Katz Media Group Inc.; Horizon Media Inc.

FURTHER READING

Behar, Richard, "Modern Romances," *Forbes,* June 2, 1986, p. 44.

Cohen, Laurie P., "Steinberg Firm Agrees to Buy John Blair & Co.," *Wall Street Journal,* June 4, 1986, p. 1.

"Don't Count Petry Media Out Just Yet," *TVNewsday,* July 29, 2008.

"Edward Petry, 73, Founded Broadcast Sales Agency," *New York Times,* June 16, 1970.

Freeman, Michael, "Petry Bags Fox O&O Sales," *Mediaweek,* February 3, 1997, p. 6.

———, "Petry Protects Its Flank," *Mediaweek,* October 14, 1996, p. 6.

———, "Rep Firms Playing Musical Chairs," *Mediaweek,* December 9, 1996, p. 26.

McClellan, Steve, "Consolidation Hits Ad Reps, Too," *Broadcasting & Cable,* November 6, 2000, p. 38.

———, "Fox Deal Makes Petry Largest Rep," *Broadcasting & Cable,* February 3, 1997, p. 8.

———, "Petry Buying Blair, Cox Buying MMT," *Broadcasting & Cable,* September 18, 1995, p. 11.

"Reposition Petry in Troubled Times," *TVNewsday,* February 10, 2009.

Rogan, Helen, "John Blair Is an Unlikely Takeover Prospect, but That Hasn't Stemmed a Flood of Rumors," *Wall Street Journal,* November 6, 1985, p. 1.

Sherrid, Pamela, "One of a Kind (John Blair & Co.)," *Forbes,* December 6, 1982, p. 162.

Sterling, Christopher H., and John Michael Kittross, *Stay Tuned: A History of American Broadcasting,* third edition, Philadelphia, Pa.: Lawrence Erbaum Associates, 2002.

Waggoner, Walter H., "John P. Blair, Founder and Honorary Chairman Emeritus of John Blair & Co., Dies," *New York Times,* May 27, 1983, p. 7.

Phillips Lytle LLP

———■———

1 HSBC Center, Suite 3400
Buffalo, New York 14203-2834
U.S.A.
Telephone: (716) 847-8400
Fax: (716) 852-6100
Web stie: http://www.phillipslytle.com

Private Company
Incorporated: 1834
Employees: 465
Sales: $192 million (2008 est.)
NAICS: 541110 Offices of Lawyers

■ ■ ■

Phillips Lytle LLP is one of the largest and oldest legal firms based in Buffalo, New York. The partnership also maintains branch offices elsewhere in the state, including New York City, Albany, Garden City, Rochester, and two locations in Chautauqua. Altogether the firm employs 170 attorneys, of which 87 are partners. Phillips Lytle divides its 45 practice areas into five main groups: Commercial, Corporate, Family Wealth Planning, Labor and Employment, and Litigation. The firm serves a wide range of business clients, from family-run and middle-market companies to *Fortune* 500 and multinational corporations. Its roster of clients includes Archer Daniels Midland Company, AT&T, BlueCross BlueShield of Western New York, Citibank, Coach, Emerson Electric, Ford Motor Credit Company, National Fuel, and Rich Products Corporation. Phillips Lytle is also in the DuPont Primary Law Firm network, a

relationship that began in 1944. In order to serve clients on an international basis, Phillips Lytle belongs to an international affiliation of corporate law firms located around the world.

ORIGINS

Phillips Lytle was founded in Buffalo in 1834 by Orsamus Holmes Marshall. His Connecticut-born father, Dr. John Ellis Marshall, was one of the early inhabitants of the Village of Buffalo laid out in 1804. Buffalo experienced slow growth until the War of 1812 when it became a military outpost, an event that brought Dr. Marshall to Buffalo in his capacity as surgeon to the Second Regiment of the New York State Militia. When Buffalo was threatened by the British army, he sent his pregnant wife to live with relatives in Franklin, Connecticut, where in February 1813 she gave birth to a son they named Orsamus. Removal to the east proved to be a wise decision. Later in the year the British and their Native American allies captured Buffalo, burning it almost entirely to the ground and sending many of its citizens to Montreal as prisoners. After the war, in 1815, Dr. Marshall moved his family to Buffalo and helped rebuild the community, which then became the county seat.

Orsamus Marshall cobbled together an education in the frontier community of Buffalo, attending school in the homes of a number of teachers before being sent at the age of 12 to the Polytechnic School at Chittenango, New York; a year later he entered a military school. He enrolled at Union College in Schenectady, New York, at the age of 16 and two years later graduated, returned to Buffalo, and began reading law in the office of Austin &

Barker. In the spring of 1833 Marshall traveled east to enter Yale College for a course of law lectures. The following year he was admitted to the practice of law in New York State and began his legal career, thus laying the foundation for Phillips Lytle.

MARINE MIDLAND BANK RELATIONSHIP BEGINS

Marshall had a number of law partners in the early years of his career, starting with William A. Mosely. After that partnership was dissolved Marshall worked with Horatio J. Stow, and when Stow became the local recorder, Marshall entered into a partnership with Nathan K. Hall that lasted until Hall was named first judge of the county in 1841. Marshall then practiced alone for several years before taking Alexander W. Harvey as a partner. A major turning point in the firm's history, one that would resonate deep into the next century, was the firm's work in starting the Marine Trust Company in 1850 to finance the growing Great Lakes shipping trade. As the trust spread throughout New York State it changed its name to Marine Midland Bank (eventually becoming HSBC Bank USA). The relationship established the firm as a commercial law firm and as the bank grew so too did the firm, which on the strength of its relationship with Marine Midland secured other major clients.

According to Phillips Lytle materials, Marshall retired from Marshall & Harvey in 1862, the same year that Lyman K. Bass joined the firm, resulting in a name change to Harvey & Bass. A different story was told by the *History of the City of Buffalo* published in 1884 and the *Memorial and Family History of Erie County New York* published in 1908. These sources indicated that Harvey "removed to New York in 1863" and that Marshall took his son, Charles De Angelis Marshall, into

partnership after the latter was admitted to the bar in 1864, the resulting firm known as O.H. & C.D. Marshall. The elder Marshall, both sources maintained, retired from the active practice of law in 1867. He devoted the rest of his life to the writing of history, gaining a reputation as a historian of the Native American tribes of western New York, having over the years befriended many chiefs, including Red Jacket, the Seneca chief who became a famous spokesman and negotiator for Native Americans. Marshall died in July 1884.

GROVER CLEVELAND JOINS FIRM

After his father's retirement, Charles Marshall took Spencer Clinton as a partner, creating the firm of Marshall & Clinton. Other partners would come and go, leading to a bevy of firm names, but Phillips Lytle would branch off from the partnership formed by Alexander Harvey and Lyman Bass rather than Orsamus Marshall and his son. Bass took George Gorham as partner in 1867, and then in 1872 formed a partnership with Wilson S. Bissell, creating Bass & Bissell. Two years later they accepted as partner Grover Cleveland, resulting in Bass, Cleveland & Bissell.

Cleveland was a close friend of Bass who was not only a well-established lawyer but also a man with political ambitions, as was Bass. In fact, Bass defeated Cleveland to become district attorney for Erie County in 1865 when the two men were roommates. Over time, however, Cleveland's political career would overshadow that of his friend. Cleveland was elected mayor of Buffalo in 1881 and two years later became governor of New York State. In 1884 he was elected president of the United States, and in 1892 became the first person to be elected president for a second term after being out of office.

Due to poor health, Bass left the law firm in 1877 to live in Colorado Springs, Colorado, but then found himself practicing law again at the behest of a railroad, eventually earning accolades as a railroad lawyer when he won a major case before the U.S. Supreme Court. Following the departure of Bass, Cleveland became the lead attorney of the Buffalo firm until his political career took precedence and he left the firm after becoming governor. As a result the firm was reorganized as Bissell, Sicard & Goodyear, with Bissell himself earning a reputation as a prominent railroad lawyer.

As president, Cleveland named William Bissell to serve as his postmaster general from 1893 to 1895. Bissell had declined an offer to serve in Cleveland's first administration, explaining to the *New York Times,* "I do not want it to be said that any of Mr. Cleveland's

KEY DATES

◼

1834: Orsamus H. Marshall founds firm in Buffalo, New York.

1850: Association with Marine Trust Company (later Marine Midland Bank and eventually HSBC Bank USA) begins.

1867: Marshall retires from the active practice of law.

1874: Future U.S. President Grover Cleveland joins firm.

1928: George F. Phillips joins firm.

1944: DuPont becomes client.

1946: William E. Lytle joins firm.

1982: Rochester firm acquired.

1994: Fredonia office added through merger.

2003: Firm assumes Phillips Lytle LLP name.

2006: Albany firm acquired to launch Capital and Innovation practice group.

2009: The firm celebrates its 175th anniversary.

personal friends are office seekers." After his stint as postmaster general, Bissell returned to Buffalo to resume the practice of law with partners Martin Carey and James McCormick Mitchell. They were joined in 1897 by Walter P. Cooke, Bissell's former clerk, to create the firm of Bissell, Carey & Cooke. Cooke would go on to become chairman of the Marine Trust Company while Mitchell became an authority on tax and constitutional issues.

GEORGE PHILLIPS JOINS FIRM

More prominent people joined the firm In the early decades of the 20th century. In 1906, at the behest of Walter Cooke, Daniel J. Kenefick, former State Supreme Court justice (a post attained when he was just 35) and former Erie County district attorney, partnered with Cooke and Mitchell to establish Kenefick, Cooke & Mitchell. Five years later the deputy attorney general of New York State, Edward H. Letchworth, resigned his position to join the firm. Another person of note in Buffalo, Colonel Christopher Baldy, joined the firm in 1921. The man who would one day supply half of the Phillips Lytle name, George F. Phillips, joined the firm in 1928.

The foundation of the modern-day practice of Phillips Lytle was established in 1929 when the firm was reorganized as Kenefick, Cooke, Mitchell, Bass & Letchworth. Two years later Cooke, a man who had also

brought luster to the firm, died. Aside from serving as Marine's chairman, Cooke had been president of the New York State Bar Association, and after World War I he served at The Hague as president of the Arbitration Tribunal and went to France as the U.S. representative to the reparations committee. For his service overseas he was made an officer of the Legion of Honor by the French government, and received similar honors from Italy, Belgium, and Germany.

The 1940s were a period of transition for the firm. It began representing DuPont in 1944, handling a variety of corporate, regulatory, litigation, and bankruptcy concerns for the chemical giant. During the postwar era the firm also experienced a major changing of the guard in the partnership ranks. James Mitchell passed away in 1948 at the age of 75, followed a year later by 86-year-old Kenefick. By this time fresh talent had been incorporated. Daniel G. Yorkey joined the firm in 1945, and the next year 41-year-old William E. Lytle became a partner, providing Phillips Lytle with the second half of its name. Raised in Geneva, New York, Lytle graduated from Harvard Law School in 1929 and began practicing law in New York City. In 1934 he moved to Buffalo to take a position at Kenefick, Cooke. In 1948 former U.S. Attorney Robert M. Hitchcock also joined the firm. Two years later he and the firm became caught up in Senator Joseph McCarthy's probe into Communist penetration in the State Department.

While working for the Department of Justice, Hitchcock in 1945 prosecuted a case involving the unlawful possession of papers by people connected to *Amerasia,* a New York magazine of Far Eastern affairs. The original charges of espionage had to be dropped because some evidence had been illegally obtained. McCarthy deemed the affair "operation whitewash," leading to Hitchcock being called to testify before a Senate subcommittee regarding the circumstances of his joining Kenefick, Cooke. McCarthy and other critics noted that one of the people cleared in the Amerasia case was coeditor Louise Mitchell, niece of James Mitchell. Hitchcock testified that there was "not the slightest connection between the Amerasia case and my association with my present firm." He insisted that Lyman Bass had been responsible for bringing him into the firm and that he did not meet James Mitchell until after an employment agreement had already been reached. Like so many of the charges McCarthy made during his time in the national spotlight, they consisted of few facts and a wealth of innuendo.

LYTLE MAKES PARTNER

Due to the loss of Cooke and Mitchell, the firm was recast in 1950, although Kenefick's name was retained, becoming Kenefick, Bass, Letchworth, Baldy & Phillips. Lytle made senior partner in 1959 and a year later Walter J. Mahoney, the former majority leader of the New York State Senate, was added as partner, leading to another reorganization. For the first time the Lytle name was included as the firm became known as Phillips, Mahoney, Lytle, Yorkey & Letchworth. Five years later Mahoney was named a State Supreme Court justice, leading to the firm being renamed Phillips, Lytle, Yorkey, Letchworth, Hitchcock & Blaine. Just two years later, in 1967, the firm's name was shuffled again after John F. Huber, Jr., joined as partner, leading to the coining of Phillips, Lytle, Hitchcock, Blaine and Huber LLP. This name would remain unchanged for nearly four decades, despite the deaths of Phillips in 1971, Hitchcock in 1981, and Lytle in 1989.

The 1970s were a time of expansion for the firm. During that time the firm represented Occidental Petroleum in the litigation connected to the Love Canal incident, the Niagara Falls, New York, neighborhood where thousands of pounds of toxic waste from Hooker Chemical (an Occidental subsidiary) were found buried beneath a school. The community suffered an unusual level of miscarriages, birth defects, and other health problems. The firm's representation of Occidental laid the foundation for a nationally recognized environmental law group. Also during this period, the firm expanded through merger, combining in 1978 with Cadwell & Sharpe to establish an office in Chautauqua.

Leading the firm for the final two decades of the 20th century was Robert M. Greene, who took over as chief executive officer and managing partner in 1981. Greene thrived in the role and gained some attention for a booklet he penned for the American Bar Association called *Managing Partner 101: A Primer on Firm Leadership*. It was under his leadership that Phillips Lytle enjoyed steady expansion. In 1982 it added a Rochester office by merging with Sullivan, Johnson, Peters, Burns, Adams and Mullen. In that same year the firm also opened its New York City office.

CONTINUED EXPANSION IN THE 21ST CENTURY

In 1994 an office was added in Fredonia through a merger with Collesano, Sommer & Eades. In the meantime, the firm cast off an operation, in 1991 spinning off its workers' compensation practice into a separate firm. Because of an increase in workplace accident litigation, the firm wanted to avoid a potential conflict of interest and the chance it might be defending more than one company in a particular case. Given the choice between workers' compensation business and turning away corporate business, the firm elected to give

up the workers' compensation practice. Also of note in the 1990s, the firm's relationship with DuPont deepened. Not satisfied using more than 350 law firms around the country, DuPont began a three-and-a-half-year process in 1992 to reduce that number into a select network of Primary Law Firms, one of which became Phillips Lytle.

Phillips Lytle continued to grow in the 21st century. Another Buffalo firm was absorbed in 2000, 82-year-old Albrecht, Maguire, Heffern & Gregg, bringing with it an expertise in franchise law and not-for-profits. To better serve its downstate clients, the firm opened a Long Island office in Garden City in 2002, focusing on commercial banking and public finance. In 2003 an office was also opened in Albany, and after 22 years as CEO and another 14 years as managing partner, Greene stepped down in order to focus on expanding the firm's healthcare practice and free up time for his community activities. It was also in 2003 that the firm shortened its name to Phillips Lytle LLP.

Without Greene, the firm continued to expand. The Albany office added a Capital and Innovation practice group in 2006 with the acquisition of Honen & Wood P.C., a move that brought six attorneys: three partners and three associates. The purpose of the new practice was essentially to bring together inventors and investors. In 2009 the firm celebrated its 175th anniversary. The economy was enduring a difficult time, leading Buffalo's largest law firm, Hodgson Russ LLP, to lay off some employees. Phillips Lytle, on the other hand, extended offers to a number of new attorneys to join the firm in the fall. Because of the diversity of its practice groups, Phillips Lytle was able to move lawyers to areas where work was plentiful and did not anticipate the need for layoffs in the near future.

Ed Dinger

PRINCIPAL OPERATING UNITS

Commercial; Corporate; Family Wealth Planning; Labor and Employment; Litigation.

PRINCIPAL COMPETITORS

Bond Schoeneck & King LLP; Hodgson Russ LLP; Nixon Peabody LLP.

FURTHER READING

Chandler, Matt, "Law Firm Layoffs," *Buffalo Business First*, February 3, 2009.

———, "Phillips Lytle Gears Up for 175th Year," *Buffalo Business First*, January 21, 2009.

"Daniel J. Kenefick, a Retired Jurist," *New York Times,* December 27, 1949.

Epstein, Jonathan D., "In Business for Going on 200 Years," *America's Intelligence Wire,* March 1, 2009.

"J. M. Mitchell Dies; Headed State Bar," *New York Times,* October 15, 1948.

Memorial and Family History of Erie County New York, Buffalo, N.Y.: Genealogical Publishing Company, 1908.

Robinson, David, "Greene Stepping Down at Phillips Lytle," *Buffalo News,* March 26, 2003, p. B7.

Smith, H. Perry, *History of the City of Buffalo and Erie County,* Syracuse, N.Y.: D. Mason & Co., 1884.

Sokolowski, Jodi, "Phillips Lytle Adds 6 from Albany Firm," *Buffalo Business First,* January 27, 2006.

———, "Phillips Lytle Forms Capital, Innovation Group," *Buffalo Business First,* July 14, 2006.

White, William S., "Data Held Faulty In Amerasia Case," *New York Times,* May 27, 1950.

"William E. Lytle Dies; Was Partner with Buffalo's Biggest Law Firm," *Buffalo News,* March 25, 1989.

"Wilson Shannon Bissell," *New York Times,* March 5, 1893.

Premiere Radio Networks, Inc.

15260 Ventura Boulevard, 4th Floor
Sherman Oaks, California 91403-5307
U.S.A.
Telephone: (818) 377-5300
Fax: (818) 377-5333
Web site: http://www.premiereradio.com

Wholly Owned Subsidiary of Clear Channel Communications, Inc.
Incorporated: 1987
Employees: 700
Sales: $140 million (2007 est.)
NAICS: 515111 Radio Networks

■ ■ ■

A subsidiary of radio giant Clear Channel Communications, Inc., Sherman Oaks, California-based Premiere Radio Networks, Inc., syndicates a wide variety of satellite-delivered radio programs and services. Entertainment programs include the popular-song countdown shows of Casey Kasem, Ryan Seacrest, and others; the Steve Harvey Morning Show; and the Blair Garner Show for the late-night slot. Premiere's stable of talk show hosts include Rush Limbaugh, Sean Hannity, Glenn Beck, and Dr. Laura Schlessinger. Sports talk hosts include Bob Costas and Jim Rome. Premiere syndicates FOX Sports Radio and the FOX Sports Actuality & Update Service, providing subscribers with play-by-play audio clips and interviews as well as sports updates programming. Premiere also offers a wide range of prep, research, and production services, such as music

libraries in a variety genres; audio clips of celebrity interviews, television programs, movies, sound effects, and parodies; jingle libraries; the Hazardous Comedy Network and its parody songs and topical contributions; and the Invasion Production Library of production music, special effects, and other materials needed for radio station imaging. All told, Premiere syndicates about 90 radio programs to more than 5,000 radio stations, reaching nearly 200 million listeners each week. In addition to its Sherman Oaks headquarters, the company maintains 13 other offices in the United States, including Atlanta, Boston, Chicago, Dallas, Detroit, and New York.

ON THE ROAD TO SYNDICATION

Premiere Radio was founded in 1987 by Stephen C. Lehman and Timothy M. Kelly, both on-air personalities at KIIS-AM and FM in Los Angeles. Lehman graduated magna cum laude with a degree in communications from the University of Nevada, Las Vegas, where he was a student disc jockey. He held a variety of jobs in the radio business, including a stint as national sales manager for Innerview Radio Networks, and two years involved in building radio networks for independent radio syndications. He also worked as a radio personality, joining KIIS in 1984 and working afternoons from ten to two.

To make use of his spare time and knowledge of radio syndication, Lehman began developing his own programming, as Stephen Lehman Productions, that could be sold to other stations. He began with 90-second comedy shows, including a comedic soap opera, which was picked up by about 25 stations. He then developed *National Lampoon's True Facts,* reporting unusual but true news items.

The show caught the attention of Mutual Broadcasting, which picked up the show. After Mutual was acquired by Westwood One, Lehman decided to take back his show and handle sales himself. Finding the task more difficult than he expected, however, and hardly able to cover expenses, Lehman was in need of more programming to offer. For this he turned to fellow KIIS disc jockey Tim Kelly.

TIM KELLY, A RADIO CHILDHOOD

The son of a radio personality, Tim Kelly had grown up in the radio business. As a teenager he went to work for a Buffalo radio station, mostly running errands. When a disc jockey failed to show up for work one day, the 16-year-old was thrust on the air for three hours. He did well and was encouraged by the station's program director to think about making a career as a disc jockey. Taking the suggestion to heart, Kelly did become an on-air personality and programmer, becoming a radio vagabond, working at stations in San Antonio, Denver, Boston, Washington, and Chicago, before joining KIIS in Los Angeles.

While working as a station programmer in Boston in the mid-1970s Kelly was regularly approached about carrying Casey Kasem's "American Top 40" weekend countdown show, but he resisted because the style of the program clashed with the station's full-week programming and did not always match up in terms of "stop sets," regular locations for advertising and promotions.

While working in Los Angeles at KIIS-FM, a top 40 format station, he often hosted the "Hot 30" countdown, which inspired him to create a Top 40 program that provided artist drop-ins and scripts, including lead-ins and post-song commentary, which lo-

cal stations could use with their own on-air personalities and adjust to fit their stop sets. Kelley called it the *Plain Rap Countdown,* the name later changing to *Plain Wrap Countdown.* It filled a programming need for many stations, and before long around 300 stations signed up for the service.

Lehman and Kelly recognized the benefits of teaming up, and with each contributing $15,000 in capital, along with their respective shows, they launched a syndication company. They also had a "premiere" credit card, used primarily to cover their bar tabs, and decided to apply the word to the name of their new company, resulting in Premiere Radio Networks. Kelly explained in a 2008 interview with *Inside Radio,* "We thought it was a good word [since] we were 'premiering' a new network."

COWORKERS GROW A COMPANY TOGETHER

Premiere Radio was incorporated and launched in January 1987. The underlying concept of the syndicator, in keeping with the genesis of *Plain Wrap,* was to offer generic programming to radio stations, allowing them to retain their own identities. "We produced stuff that would make them sound great and enhance their local programming. We didn't care about getting [on-air credit]," Lehman told the *Los Angeles Daily News,* continuing, "Our intent was to make the little radio station the hero and not the big network."

Kelley focused on script production as executive vice-president of programming while Lehman concentrated on sales as chief executive officer. Other founding partners of Premiere included Edward A. Mann, another KIIS veteran, who served as the head of marketing; Kraig T. Kitchin, executive vice-president of sales, who would become the longtime president and chief operating officer of the company; and Louise Palanker, a writer-producer-performer who served as vice-president of the creative end of the business.

In addition to *Plain Wrap* and *National Lampoon's True Facts,* Premiere initially offered *The Cla'ence All My Children Update.* By the end of the company's first year about 250 stations carried Premiere programming, allowing Lehman to quit KIIS and concentrate on running the business full time. In exchange for its programming, Premiere received advertising time from the stations, which it then sold to national advertisers.

This arrangement proved popular with radio stations, and Premiere enjoyed strong growth. Revenues reached $7.2 million in fiscal 1990, and increased to $9.6 million in fiscal 1991, resulting in net earnings of $878,000. With more than 1,400 stations carrying its

KEY DATES

1987: Coworkers Stephen Lehman and Timothy Kelly launch a radio syndication network and name it Premiere Radio Networks.
1992: The company is taken public.
1997: Jacor Communications acquires Premiere.
1999: Clear Channel Communications acquires Jacor.
2000: FOX Sports Radio Network is established.
2008: Rush Limbaugh renews his contract.

14 syndicated programs, Premiere netted $1.2 million on sales of $10.1 million in fiscal 1992, making it the fifth largest radio programming syndicator.

GOING PUBLIC IN 1992

In 1991 Premiere added a research element to the business, acquiring Mediabase, a company that monitored music on radio stations in major markets for a variety of research purposes. In 1992 Premiere was taken public, raising funds that the company earmarked to expand programming and build a wired programming market as well as to acquire radio stations. In November 1992 the company acquired a Denver radio station for $3.55 million to serve as the flagship station for the wired program.

Another acquisition followed in late 1993 when Premiere bought nine programs from Olympia Networks, including five sports programs, three comedies, and a country music show. A few months later, the company sold the sports programs for $2.7 million to Major Networks Inc., reporting a pretax gain of $1.7 million. At the same time Premiere continued to act as the exclusive network sales rep for the sports programs as part of a separate agreement reached with Major Networks.

Other acquisitions followed in the mid-1990s. A jingle house and radio music production company, Broadcast Results Group, was acquired in 1995 for $2.75 million. A year later Premiere paid $1.2 million to acquire a second jingle house, Philadelphia Music Works, as well as $8.5 million for comedy syndicator Cutler Productions, which brought with it six comedy and music shows syndicated to 700 stations across the country.

Premiere also looked to become involved in Internet broadcasting. In August 1995 Premiere unveiled

premrad.com. Developed by new employee Eric Canale, the site was among the first to stream audio content. The following year, Premiere invested $4 million in Internet broadcast provider AudioNet, part of an agreement in which Premiere provided marketing services and sales representation to AudioNet. For its part, AudioNet agreed to advertise on stations affiliated with Premiere and include Premiere's online content on its web site.

News Corp. acquired a stake in Premiere in 1995 through Archon Communication, an investment company controlled by Michael Milken. Two years later, in April 1997, complete control of Premiere was acquired by Cincinnati-based Jacor Communications for $190 million. Founded in 1979 by Georgia native Terry Jacobs, a former insurance executive, Jacor had started out by acquiring small radio stations and moved into larger markets. It fell into financial difficulty in the early 1990s and was restructured by real estate mogul Sam Zell. His deep pockets allowed Jacor to become a major player in radio ownership after the rules were changed by the Telecommunications Act of 1996. It also began acquiring national programming, picking up some syndicated shows.

In March 1997 Jacor made headlines with its acquired syndicator EFM Media Management, best known for producing the top-rated Rush Limbaugh show. Less than a month later Premiere was brought into the fold as well, transforming Jacor into a giant in the programming content field. For Premiere, the deal allowed it to continue its aggressive growth strategy. Lehman stayed on as Premiere's CEO for a short time and then left to pursue other media ventures, while Kelly and some of the other founding partners remained for several more years.

DR. LAURA PROGRAM IS ACQUIRED IN 1997

With the financial heft of its new corporate parent, Premiere was able to continue its pattern of growth. Later in 1997 it acquired the *Dr. Laura Program,* an advice program hosted by Dr. Laura Schlessinger. Early in 1998 Premiere added Hot Mix Radio Network Inc., syndicator of seven programs carried by 150 stations. Premiere became part of an even larger organization in 1999 when Jacor Communications was acquired by Clear Channel Communications, Inc., a fast-growing media company with international interests, in a $4 billion deal.

As part of the Clear Channel family, Premiere possessed even greater fiscal resources as it continued to expand. MJI Broadcasting Inc., a provider of radio-focused Internet and interactive media services, was acquired in November 1999. A year later Clear Channel acquired AMFM Inc. and integrated AMFM Radio Network into Premiere's operations. Also in 2000 Premiere joined forces with FOX Sports to create FOX Sports Radio Network. A few months later, Premiere restructured its operations to focus on FOX Sports Radio Network, canceling 20 programs and services.

Adjustments to the lineup were a regular part of the business. In 2002 the company canceled 15 radio shows, including *Rockline,* a long-running program with a 20-year tenure. In 2002 Premiere launched *The Suzie Orman Show,* but before the year was out the financial advice program was canceled. Ryan Seacrest's *Live from the Lounge* program, an artist showcase, was canceled less than two years after its debut, while at the same time Seacrest's drive-time radio show was retained and *American Top 40 with Ryan Seacrest* became a worldwide success.

EXPANDING WITH NEW TALENT AND BRANDS

New shows were also added on a regular basis. *The Glenn Beck Program,* featuring politically conservative talker Glenn Beck, was added in 2001. The distribution rights to the *Delilah* radio program were acquired in 2004, and the Fox News Radio Network was unveiled in 2005. Bob Costas debuted a two-hour weekend talk show, *Costas on the Radio,* in 2006. A year later, *The Keith Sweat Hotel* and *Dawson McAllister Live* were nationally syndicated. In 2008 *The Jesus Christ Show* began national syndication, and another conservative talk show host, Sean Hannity, entered into a long-term co-syndication agreement with Premiere.

Premiere had to contend with some backlash due to the controversial nature of some of its talk show hosts. In 2000 Laura Schlessinger faced an advertising boycott from gay and lesbian groups following remarks she made that they found offensive. The king of talk radio, Rush Limbaugh, encountered his own controversies as well, including a bid to serve as a football commentator on ESPN that came to quick end following remarks about a black quarterback.

In 2003 Limbaugh entered a rehabilitation program to combat a prescription drug problem. During his absence, Premiere struggled to find guests hosts that could adequately fill in for him. In 2006 Limbaugh mimicked and mocked the Parkinson disease symptoms of Michael J. Fox, who had made an ad supporting political candidates who supported embryonic stem cell research. Stoking outrage was Limbaugh's trademark,

however, and such controversies did little to diminish his standing with his loyal audience. In 2008, 20 years after he began his syndicated radio career, Limbaugh renewed his agreement with Premiere.

Premiere stayed abreast of changing trends in the media just as it kept pace with audience tastes. In 2003 the company began offering radio stations data on the popularity of songs drawn from information provided by P2P file sharing networks. In 2008 Premiere launched the *iTunes Download,* a Top-30 show based on what people were buying from Apple's iTunes. Premiere followed the market in other ways as well. In 2007 it struck a deal with Goldmark Intermedia to take its programs and services to India and that country's fast-growing commercial radio market. This kind of nimbleness promised to keep Premiere as one of the world's top radio syndicators for years to come.

Ed Dinger

PRINCIPAL DIVISIONS

Talk Programs; Entertainment Programs; Sports; Prep, Research, Imaging & Production.

PRINCIPAL COMPETITORS

ABC Radio Network, Inc.; Sirius XM Radio Inc.; Westwood One, Inc.

FURTHER READING

Barron, David, "Fox, Premiere Plan Sports Radio Network," *Houston Chronicle,* March 15, 2000, p. 10.

Gubernick, Lisa, "Generic Radio," *Forbes,* July 20, 1992, p. 80.

Kinosian, Mike, "The Timmer's Latest Pick to Click," *Inside Radio,* November 3, 2008.

Oppelaar, Justin, "Premiere Cuts 15 Radio Shows," *Daily Variety,* November 6, 2002, p. 5.

Petrozzello, Donna, "Jacor in a Rush," *Broadcasting & Cable,* March 24, 1997, p. 51.

Reece, Doug, "Jacor Purchases Premiere," *Billboard,* April 19, 1997, p. 8.

"Rush Limbaugh Renews with Premiere Radio and Clear Channel," *Entertainment Close-Up,* July 7, 2008.

Slovak, Julianne, "Premiere Radio Networks," *Fortune,* May 22, 1989, p. 144.

Sword, Doug, "Jacobs Masterminds Jacor's Expansion," *Cincinnati Business Courier,* September 8, 1986, p. 1.

Wilcox, Gregory J., "Making Waves in Radio," *Los Angeles Daily News,* June 28, 1993, p. B1.

Prodware S.A.

——————•——————

45 quai de la Seine
Paris, F-75019
France
Telephone: (33 01) 55 26 11 11
Fax: (33 01) 55 45 15 39
Web site: http://www.prodware.fr

Public Company
Incorporated: 1989
Employees: 877
Sales: EUR 94.6 million ($118 million) (2008)
Stock Exchanges: Euronext Paris
Ticker Symbol: ALPROD
NAICS: 541512 Computer Systems Design Services

■ ■ ■

Prodware S.A. is one of France's leading and fastest-growing providers of information technology (IT) services and integration software to the small and medium business sector. Prodware operates in four primary business areas. The largest, Enterprise Resource Planning (ERP) and Customer Relationship Management (CRM) Solutions, accounts for more than half of the group's sales. This division is one of the leading providers of Microsoft Dynamics support services in France. Other divisions include Networks, Security, and Telecom, which accounts for 28 percent of revenues; Business Intelligence Development, adding 11 percent of revenues; and Prodware Business Solutions, which adds 10 percent to group sales.

These operations enable Prodware to position itself as a full-scale vertical solutions provider, covering the products of the three major business management software systems, Sage, Microsoft, and Divalto. Since 2008, Prodware has also been only one of a dozen Microsoft Global Partners, receiving marketing and sales support from the software giant. Prodware has fueled its strong growth in France through a long series of acquisitions, including C2A, Winit SA, and Anelia (formerly part of IBM), Maulde Technologies. The company's operations include 21 branches in France, as well as operations in Tunisia, Morocco, Israel, Romania, Luxembourg, and Belgium. In 2008, the company's total revenues grew to more than EUR 96 million ($118 million). Led by Philippe Bouaziz, founder, president, and chairman, Prodware is listed on the Euronext Paris Stock Exchange.

FOUNDING A SOFTWARE INTEGRATOR

Prodware was founded in Paris by a group of friends and schoolmates led by Philippe Bouaziz in 1989. From the start, the company targeted the development and integration of software for the business sector, focusing on three key areas: engineering, networks, and software development. Much of the company's early operations involved establishing computer networks, as well as client-specific software engineering services.

Bouaziz had long held an interest in the burgeoning computer sciences, and had been admitted into the prestigious Institut d'Informatique d'Enterprises, the first in France to address the specific software and

COMPANY PERSPECTIVES

Strong and controlled growth. In the past few years Prodware has combined strong organic growth with successful external growth. This external growth has allowed us to increase our installed base, extend our French national coverage and expand our growing international presence. We have also been able to, through the mutualisation of our internal resources, increase the return on our infrastructure investments.

Prodware thus intends to continue its policy of successful integration, a policy that, through our intensive customer focus has allowed us to accompany our customer's development through our "Up-sell" and "Cross Sell" strategies.

computer engineering needs of the business sector. Bouaziz graduated from the school in 1988, and then took a job with Texas Instruments Europe in their Research, Development, and Support Department, before becoming manager of technical operations. At the same time, Bouaziz continued his studies, earning a doctorate at the Université Pierre et Marie Curie in Paris. Bouaziz also published a number of research papers dealing with software development and computer languages. During this period, Bouaziz also served as a consultant for a number of businesses, including working with a publisher of financial management software.

By 1995 Prodwar, and the French IT market, had grown sufficiently for Bouaziz to begin focusing his efforts on the company's expansion. Into the late 1990s, Prodware began developing its national expansion strategy. For this, the company chose to target the country's small and medium-sized business (SMB) sector, notably companies ranging from ten to 2,000 employees. This vast market (France counted more than 100,000 businesses in this size range at the dawn of the 21st century) provided strong potential for Prodware's growth. Targeting this market also allowed Prodware to avoid head-to-head competition with its larger competitors, such as Cap Gemini, Atos, and Bull, which focused on the market for larger and multinational companies.

Prodware also adapted its offerings to the rapid changes in the IT world. The company set its sights on developing integrated multi-pronged services solutions, with a focus on the ERP (enterprise resource planning) and CRM (customer relationship management) markets.

At the same time the company also sought to expand its networking expertise, particularly in the highly sensitive security sector. Software engineering remained a part of the group's services package as well. By the middle of the first decade of the new century, Prodware had also added Business Intelligence as a fourth component.

ACQUIRING A NATIONAL NETWORK

Prodware's ambitions were to expand its operations to a national level. Acquisitions and partnerships therefore formed a major part of its strategy at the end of the 20th century. Among the group's first purchases, both in 1999, were those of two Paris-based companies, Codix-on-Line, an Internet services provider; and Affip, a distributor of Sage software. Also that year, the company formed partnerships with two other Sage distributors, Sybel and Saari, both of which would be acquired by Sage. At the same time, the company formed a partnership with Navision, an ERP specialist soon to be acquired by the Microsoft Corporation. In this way, Prodware became an important partner for two of the major business management software providers.

In 2001, Prodware bought LGSF, then the largest supplier of Sage software for the French SMB market. That purchase also enabled the company to develop a new industrialized process model for its future operations. By the end of that year, Prodware had expanded its client base to more than 2,000 across France. The company had also begun to build a network of regional offices. The first of these opened for the Rhône-Alpes region in 2001; this was followed by a West Atlantic office in 2002. In 2003, the company added three more regional offices, in Nord-Pas-de-Calais; Languedoc-Roussillon; and Provence-Alpes-Côte d'Azur.

Meanwhile, Prodware continued its acquisition drive. In 2002, the company reinforced its presence in the midsized business market, acquiring Sillage, which distributed Sage products in the Paris-Île-de-France region. The company also took over Thesia, a distributor of both Sage and Navision products. This acquisition not only reinforced the group's Paris presence, but also provided its first international clientele. By the end of that year, Prodware's revenues had grown to EUR 12 million.

Under Bouaziz's direction, Prodware remained a company driven by research and development. In 2003, however, Bouaziz brought in a new chief executive, Alain Conrard, who reoriented the company toward a strategy driven by a sales and marketing model. Conrard quickly led the company through several new

KEY DATES

1989: Prodware is founded to offer business software development and integration services to the Paris market.

1999: Prodware launches strategy of expansion through acquisition, buying Codix-on-Line and Affip, among others.

2001: Prodware acquires LGSF and becomes leading supplier of Sage software to the small and medium-sized business market in France.

2006: Prodware goes public, listing its shares on the Alternext board of the Euronext Paris Stock Exchange.

2007: Prodware begins international expansion strategy, buying Winit in Belgium.

2008: Prodware is named a Microsoft Global Partner.

acquisitions. These included Lyon-based Adeo, as well as Ivelem, in Sophia-Antipolis, both Sage distributors. Another opportunity came when rival GFI Informatique decided to focus its own business on Sage rival Adonix. In August 2003, GFI agreed to transfer its Sage operations, including 150 clients, to Prodware.

Prodware continued to build its regional network as well. The company added the southwest region through its purchase of Datasoft, based in Toulouse. That company also brought Prodware a stake in its first international subsidiary, in Tunisia. By the end of 2003 Prodware had also added operations in the French northeastern region, buying Mulhouse-based Infosoft.

PUBLIC OFFERING

Toward the middle of the decade, Prodware was adding to its range of products as part of its strategy of becoming a fully integrated solutions provider for the SMB segment of the IT market. The company entered into a partnership agreement with Interlogiciel, publisher of ERP software specifically for the SMB sector. The company also developed its expertise in the other leading management software packages, such as Divalto and Microsoft Dynamics Ax. Also, starting in 2004, the company began targeting gaps in its regional coverage for Sage applications, acquiring a number of small businesses. This led the company into Nantes and Lille that year.

By this time, Prodware had also begun developing a number of other marketing initiatives. In 2004, for example, the company rolled out its Naviloc program, allowing smaller companies to lease its software packages on a monthly basis. The company also launched a new marketing strategy targeting specific business sectors with specialized packages. This effort took off in 2005, with the purchase of SMI, which focused on the building and construction industry.

By the end of 2005, Prodware had added five new offices, including regional offices in Isère and Centre, as well as in Nancy, Perpignan, and Bourgoin-Jallieu. At the same time, Prodware began gearing up for an accelerated expansion drive as it sought to reach critical mass in the French market. As part of this strategy, the company went public in 2006, listing its shares on the Euronext Paris Stock Exchange's Alternext board. By then, the company's sales had topped EUR 27 million per year. The company also boasted coverage of 85 percent of France, and counted more than 5,200 clients.

The public offering enabled the company to step up its acquisition drive. By the end of 2006, the company had completed several new acquisitions, including Groupe Sylviance, with offices in La Rochelle, Bordeaux, and Le Cid; Edic, publisher of the Cormag and Cordis software packages; Tecso, including its software unit M2I, focused on the wine and leasing markets; and Interface Data, which added another 2,200 clients to Prodware's portfolio, as well as 95 employees and revenues of EUR 10 million.

Toward the end of 2006, Prodware once again adjusted its operational model. The company launched a restructuring of its operations, transitioning from its former regional focus to its new position as a full-scale vertically integrated IT solutions provider. As part of this effort, the company also moved to transfer part of its operations to the nearshore market, launching new subsidiaries in Israel, Tunisia, and Maurice Island.

TARGETING THE INTERNATIONAL MARKET

The year 2007 marked the completion of Prodware's domestic expansion strategy. By the end of that year, the company had completed several new acquisitions, expanding not only its geographic network, but also its range of specialized services. The purchase of Maulde Technologies, for example, allowed the company to claim the French leadership position in the market for management software developed specifically for catalogues, both paper-based and online. Another acquisition, of Anelia, a subsidiary of IBM France, helped consolidate Prodware's presence in the French southwest, while also boosting Prodware's operations in the SAP All-in-One and PCI Sage X3 platforms.

By then, Prodware had also completed its most significant acquisition to date, buying C2A, a major player in the northern France market for the Microsoft Dynamics platform. The addition of C2A added another EUR 25 million to Prodware's revenues, which neared EUR 70 million by the end of 2007. Prodware had succeeded not only in becoming the leading player in the SMB market in France, but also in positioning itself for its next development phase to become an international player. The addition of C2A also brought the company into the Romanian market.

Prodware targeted the French-speaking market for its initial international expansion. This led the company to Belgium, where it acquired Winit, a specialist in Microsoft-based ERP applications and particularly the Dynamics AX platform. Winit also gave Prodware an entry into the Luxembourg market.

Prodware's strengthening relationship with Microsoft brought the company into Morocco in February 2008, as the two companies formed a partnership to market Dynamics in that country. Just one month later, Prodware achieved a new boost to its international profile when it became one of less than a dozen Microsoft Global Partners, placing the company alongside such major players as Accenture and Cap Gemini.

With this new distinction, Prodware set its sights on a wider expansion of its international presence. Prodware announced its plan to develop a presence in the West African market, starting with the Ivory Coast. The company's ambitions, however, ranged farther still, as Philippe Bouaziz announced plans to expand the company's reach into Eastern Europe, the Middle East, China, and the United States.

Despite the global financial crisis, Prodware maintained its steady revenue growth into 2009, posting a rise in revenues to nearly EUR 95 million ($118 million) for the 2008 year. While the company's focus remained on its foreign expansion, Prodware also continued to explore new product areas. In January 2009, for example, the company announced its intention to incorporate Sustainable Development criteria into its integration services. Prodware itself looked forward to sustained growth into the next decade.

M. L. Cohen

PRINCIPAL SUBSIDIARIES

ABCRM; Anelia; BTS; C2A; C2A Luxembourg; C2A Roumanie; Datasoft Tunisie; Maulde Technologies; N2A SI; Ordosoftware; Prodware Israel; Prodware Tunisie; Winit SA; Winit SAS.

PRINCIPAL COMPETITORS

Cap Gemini S.A.; Accenture SA; Atos Origin S.A.; ALTEN S.A.; GFI Informatique S.A.; Bull S.A.S.; Altavia S.A.; Devoteam S.A.; Cegid S.A.

FURTHER READING

Alessi, Fabrice, "Prodware Intégrera le Développement Durable dans Ses Applications," *Distributique,* January 26, 2009.

Barathon, Didier, "Prodware Devient Partenaire Global de Microsoft," *Distributique,* March 10, 2008.

Bizouarn, Angélique, "Prodware Rachète le Groupe Sylviance," *Distributique,* March 29, 2006.

Launay, Bertrand, "Prodware Recoit le Soutien de Microsoft," *L'Expansion,* March 7, 2008.

"L'Éditeur de Progriciel Prodware Grossit de Moitié," *01 Informatique,* April 20, 2007.

"Prodware: Acquisition de Anelia, une Filiale d'IBM," *L'Expansion,* October 1, 2007.

"Prodware: Acquisition de la Société Belge Winit," *L'Expansion,* September 19, 2007.

"Prodware Acquisition de la Société Maulde Technologies," *L'Expansion,* November 16, 2007.

"Prodware Consolide Son Développement International," *Décision Distributique,* December 17, 2006.

"Prodware: L'AGE Approuve la Fusion de C2A," *L'Expansion,* November 8, 2007.

"Prodware s'Offre une Filiale d'IBM," *01 Informatique,* October 5, 2007.

"Prodware Vise une Croissance Régulière de sa Rentabilité," *AGEFI,* May 6, 2008.

Waché, Olivier, "Prodware Réorganise Ses Activités," *Décision Distribution,* October 16, 2006.

Pyramid Breweries Inc.

———————■———————

91 South Royal Brougham Way
Seattle, Washington 98134
U.S.A.
Telephone: (206) 682-8322
Fax: (206) 682-8420
Web site: http://www.pyramidbrew.com

Wholly Owned Subsidiary of Independent Brewers United Inc.
Incorporated: 1984 as Hart Brewing, Inc.
Employees: 502
Sales: $47.7 million (2007)
NAICS: 31212 Breweries; 312111 Soft Drink Manufacturing

■ ■ ■

Pyramid Breweries, Inc., is a craft brewer of specialty beers under the Pyramid and MacTarnahan's labels. Pyramid brews its beers at two breweries in Seattle, Washington, and Berkeley, California, both of which include attached alehouses with restaurants. During 2007, the company sold over 200,000 barrels of beer and nearly 45,000 barrels of soda products. The company also sells its beverages through a network of independent distributors in 38 states. Independent Brewers United Inc., the parent company of Magic Hat Brewing Company & Performing Arts Center Inc., acquired Pyramid in 2008.

1984–85: A TALE OF TWO BREWERIES

Pyramid Breweries was formed by the union of two small craft breweries, or microbreweries, in the state of Washington. The first, Hart Brewing, Inc., was established in 1984 in the small western Washington logging town of Kalama by Beth Hartwell and her husband. Hart's inaugural beer, Pyramid Pale Ale, was one of the first microbrews to be produced in America.

The second of the breweries was The Thomas Kemper Brewery, of Bainbridge Island, just across Puget Sound from Seattle. The Thomas Kemper Brewery was formed in 1985 by two friends, Andy Thomas and Will Kemper, who both had degrees in chemical engineering. Their operation was a small one, housed in the men's basements. Despite its size, however, the brewery's full-bodied, German-style lagers managed to attract a local following. Just a year after starting the brewing operation, Thomas and Kemper moved into a new facility, just outside the town of Poulsbo on the Washington coast.

In 1986, while The Thomas Kemper Brewery settled into its new home in Poulsbo, Hart Brewing introduced its second beer, Pyramid Wheaten Ale. The Wheaten Ale was the first year-round wheat beer produced in America since Prohibition. Three years later, in 1989, the Hartwells sold their growing brewery to five Seattle investors.

While 1989 brought a change in ownership for Hart, the year marked the beginning of an annual tradition for Thomas Kemper: that year, the brewery held its first Oktoberfest. Held at the brewing facility, this promotional event was designed to introduce the Thomas Kemper beers to area residents and visitors. Although the Oktoberfest celebration started out on a small scale, it rapidly gained popularity, soon drawing thousands of visitors to the small town.

At one of these Oktoberfests Thomas Kemper's brewers introduced a new beverage that would eventually evolve into its own product line. Wanting to offer non-drinkers and children their own special beverage, the brewery created a batch of hand-crafted root beer. The root beer was an enormous hit; by some accounts, the soda actually outsold the beer. A year later, encouraged by the root beer success, Thomas and Kemper formed the Thomas Kemper Soda Company to develop and market a line of premium beverages that were more flavorful than the average soda.

1992: JOINING FORCES

In 1992, with Hart Brewing and Thomas Kemper both picking up steam, the two breweries merged. Under the terms of the deal, Hart acquired the Thomas Kemper Brewery, but not the Thomas Kemper Soda Company, which remained as a stand-alone business under Thomas's and Kemper's ownership. Hart then made a second significant step toward expansion, moving into a newly built, 11,000-square-foot facility in Kalama and leaving behind its original home on the town's Main Street.

The Hart-Thomas Kemper merger came at an important time for the breweries; both were on the verge of introducing significant new products. In 1993 Thomas Kemper introduced a German-inspired raspberry wheat beer called Weizen Berry. Weizen Berry was an immediate success, soon becoming the most popular fruit beer in the Northwest. Also introduced in 1993, Hart's new Hefeweizen, a full-flavored, unfiltered wheat beer, became an instant favorite with beer lovers in the region.

By the middle of the 1990s the two breweries were thriving. Hart Brewing had become the fourth largest craft brewer in the United States. Thomas Kemper was likewise showing amazing growth, with 1995 year-end

sales up 100 percent over 1994 sales. The Thomas Kemper brand was one of the top three brands in the state. Encouraged by skyrocketing sales and increasing consumer demand for microbrews, in March 1995 Hart opened a second brewery in downtown Seattle. This facility, which was located near the city's Kingdome football and baseball stadium, had a 250-seat adjoining alehouse.

GOING PUBLIC, EXPANDING GEOGRAPHICALLY

In late 1995 Hart went public, selling two million shares of its stock and netting $34.2 million. The company used proceeds from its initial public offering to expand its production capacity in both the Seattle and Kalama breweries. By the end of 1996 the Kalama facility's annual capacity had been extended to 95,000 barrels from its original 10,000-barrel output. The Seattle brewery's capacity had increased from 40,000 to 98,000 barrels. With the higher production ability in the Seattle brewery, Hart decided to close the original Thomas Kemper facility in Poulsbo and move its operations to Seattle.

Throughout the 1990s Hart's sales had grown exponentially. By the beginning of 1996 the company's annual revenues had climbed to $25.3 million, up from just $2.9 million three years earlier. Its three best-selling brands were Pyramid Hefeweizen, Pyramid Apricot Ale, and the original Pyramid Pale Ale. Because the Pyramid line made up the bulk of the company's sales and reputation, in 1996 Hart Brewing, Inc., changed its name to Pyramid Breweries, Inc. It continued, however, to market its Thomas Kemper products under the Thomas Kemper name.

At the end of 1996, although it had shown tremendous revenue growth, Pyramid was still very much a regional brewer; the majority of its improved sales had come from an increased market share in the states of Oregon and Washington. In early 1997, however, the company moved to broaden its geographic presence, opening a new brewery and alehouse in Berkeley, California, its first operation outside Washington. The new facility was in a renovated warehouse within walking distance of the University of California at Berkeley campus. It consisted of 122,000 square feet, a 260-seat alehouse/restaurant and an annual production capacity of 80,000 barrels. The large size of the facility offered much potential for expansion; Pyramid estimated that it could ultimately extend the brewery's production capacity to 200,000 barrels, if warranted.

KEY DATES

1984: Hart Brewing, Inc., is formed in Kalama, Washington.

1985: Andy Thomas and Will Kemper form The Thomas Kemper Brewery.

1989: Hart Brewing is acquired by Seattle investors.

1991: Thomas and Kemper form The Thomas Kemper Soda Company.

1992: Hart Brewing acquires The Thomas Kemper Brewery.

1995: Hart opens a new brewery and alehouse in Seattle and makes an initial public offering.

1996: Hart changes its name to Pyramid Breweries, Inc.

1997: Pyramid acquires The Thomas Kemper Soda Company, closes down the original Thomas Kemper brewery, and opens a new brewery and alehouse in Berkeley, California.

1999: Martin Kelly becomes Pyramid's president and CEO.

2002: The company opens an alehouse in Walnut Creek, California.

2004: Portland Brewing Company is acquired.

2008: Independent Brewers United Inc. acquires Pyramid.

CHALLENGES TO THE GROWTH STRATEGY

The Berkeley brewery was to be a first step in a long-term growth strategy. Pyramid planned to develop an entire network of similar breweries in various high-traffic regional markets across the country. The company also planned to achieve greater geographic penetration by aggressively expanding its distribution network. In 1996 it kicked off this initiative, adding 20 new states to its distribution territory. By the end of the year the company's products were available in a total of 31 states. Sales in Washington, Oregon, and California still accounted for more than 80 percent of total revenues, however.

Pyramid also diversified its product line in 1997, purchasing The Thomas Kemper Soda Company, which had been left out of the 1992 merger. The acquisition added two premium sodas—root beer and cream soda—to the Thomas Kemper brand. It also provided the small soda company with capital needed to grow. Within a year of having been acquired by Pyramid,

Thomas Kemper Soda had introduced two new beverages: Orange Cream Soda and Black Cherry Soda.

Despite the company's efforts to expand, 1996 and 1997 were challenging years for Pyramid. The craft, or microbrew, market had grown extremely rapidly, with small, independent breweries springing into existence at a breathtaking pace. This proliferation of craft brewers, both in the Pacific Northwest and across the nation, led to greatly heightened competition for Pyramid in all of its markets.

To make matters worse, the growing consumer interest in microbrews during the early 1990s had enticed virtually all of the major domestic brewers into the fray; such industry giants as Anheuser-Busch, Miller Brewing, and others had introduced full-flavored, European-style beers to compete with the microbrews. Many had also formed alliances with or made investments in specific craft brewers. Competition from these national brewers was particularly damaging to Pyramid; with their much greater financial resources, influence, and distribution networks, the national companies were able to drive down product prices and reduce distribution options for the smaller breweries.

Pyramid's finances began to show the effects of the adverse market conditions in 1996. Sales flattened, increasing only 2 percent over 1995, and net income plummeted. The company took steps to trim overhead and boost profits in 1997, closing down its Kalama, Washington, brewery and redistributing production between its Seattle and Berkeley facilities. Sales for that year improved by 13.6 percent, but Pyramid still ended up with a $2.1 million net loss at year-end.

ATTEMPTING A TURNAROUND

The company spent part of 1998 rethinking and refocusing both its growth strategy and its marketing efforts. It suspended its earlier strategy of building a chain of breweries in various locations, deciding instead to focus efforts on its existing Northwest/West Coast markets. It also initiated a new marketing campaign, themed "Have a good beer," and introduced new product packaging and promotional materials for both its Pyramid and Thomas Kemper lines.

However, 1998 financial results were no more promising than 1997's had been. Sales decreased by 7.2 percent, and Pyramid again posted a net loss. In July the investment firm of Sugar Mountain Capital, LLC, purchased a 19.5 percent stake in the flagging company. As part of the acquisition, Sugar Mountain's managing partner, Kurt Dammeier, joined Pyramid's board of directors. The company also brought in two new top-level executives: Gary McGrath and Martin Kelly. McGrath, formerly employed by Miller Brewing

Company, became Pyramid's new vice-president of sales in November 1999. Kelly, a former executive of both Miller Brewing and Coca-Cola, became the company's chief operating officer. Both men were beverage industry veterans of more than 15 years, and it was hoped that their expertise would be pivotal in the company's turnaround.

At the end of 1999, Kelly was promoted to CEO and president, replacing the company's president of more than seven years, George Hancock. At the same time, Dammeier, who had become the company's largest shareholder, became chairman of the board of directors. Meanwhile, Pyramid continued to falter. Although 1999 sales showed a slight improvement, the company posted a net loss of $4.4 million for the year. Shortly after assuming his new position, Kelly announced a reorganization of executive management and called for a strategic review of operations. As part of the reorganization two new top-level positions were created: director of brewery operations and director of corporate operations. Both positions reported directly to Kelly and were filled by existing Pyramid employees.

Kelly also announced the company's first quarterly cash dividend and authorized a stock buyback of up to $2 million in shares. "Paying a cash dividend, in addition to our stock repurchase program, reflects our confidence in Pyramid's future prospects," he explained in a February 24, 2000, press release, adding "These actions also reflect our commitment to improve returns for Pyramid shareholders."

As Pyramid continued its efforts to reverse the downward trend of the late 1990s, it pinned part of its hopes on its alehouse operations. This segment of the company was perhaps the most promising, posting a 16 percent revenue gain in 1999. "We feel that our Alehouse Division has substantial opportunity to add value to the company, both by improving existing operations and achieving unit growth through acquisitions or new developments," Kelly said in a February 2, 2000, press release. Another potential area of growth for Pyramid lay in its soda subsidiary. Wholesale soda shipments increased 11 percent in 1999, in marked contrast to beer shipments, which increased only 2 percent.

MOVING INTO THE NEW MILLENNIUM

With the craft beer industry experiencing significant growth during the early years of the new millennium, Pyramid revamped its strategy and focused on growing its specialty craft beers business. It continued to introduce new beers, including the Broken Rake Amber Ale, Curve Ball Kolsch, and Coastline Pilsner. Pyramid also opened a new alehouse in Walnut Creek,

California, in 2002. Two years later the company acquired the Portland Brewing Company, adding the MacTarnahan beer labels to its fold. CEO Kelly left the company that year and company director George Hancock temporarily took over day-to-day operations. After a series of management changes, Scott Barnum took over as CEO in 2006.

Sales of Pyramid's flagship brand, Hefeweizen, were strong at this time and revenues in 2006 reached $54.3 million, an increase of 7 percent over the previous year. Nevertheless, the company continued to struggle with profits. During 2005 Pyramid posted a loss of $1.1 million. An audit of the company's tax filings lead to a 2006 payout of $700,000 to the federal Alcohol and Tobacco Tax and Trade Bureau. The company's net loss climbed to $1.6 million that year. During 2007 the company sold the Thomas Kemper Soda brand to The Kemper Company. The $3.1 million deal included a five-year supply contract in which Pyramid would continue to manufacture Thomas Kemper soda products.

Meanwhile, the beer industry was undergoing a period of consolidation brought on by high commodity prices, intense competition, and a slowing economy. Amid takeover speculation Pyramid management maintained they would not sell out, but instead look for strategic acquisitions. This outlook changed, however, when the company failed to produce the profits necessary to fuel growth. Independent Brewers United Inc. (IBU), the parent company of Vermont-based Magic Hat Brewing Company & Performing Arts Center Inc., made a play for Pyramid in April 2008. The $35 million deal was finalized in August of that year with IBU paying $2.75 per share and assuming approximately $9.8 million in debt. Kelly, who served as president and CEO of Magic Hat, once again found himself at the helm of Pyramid.

As an IBU subsidiary, Pyramid believed it was well-positioned for growth and expansion, especially in the eastern portion of the United States. During 2008 the craft brew industry experienced a 5 percent increase in shipment volume, growing at a steady pace compared with the domestic and imported beer segments. Pyramid Breweries was among the top ten craft brewing companies in the United States and hoped to strengthen its position in the coming years.

Shawna Brynildssen
Updated, Christina M. Stansell

PRINCIPAL COMPETITORS

The Boston Beer Company Inc.; Craft Brewers Alliance Inc.; MillerCoors LLC.

FURTHER READING

Brevetti, Francine, "Pyramid Celebrating, Looking to Expand," *Oakland (Calif.) Tribune,* April 26, 2007.

Goodison, Donna, "Brewing Up Business," *Boston Herald,* February 23, 2009.

Levisohn, Ben, "Trouble Brewing for Craft Beer Makers," *BusinessWeek.com,* July 7, 2008.

"Magic Hat Completes Pyramid Breweries Takeover," *Just-Drinks,* August 5, 2008.

Marcial, Gene G., "Microbrews—Without the Froth," *Business Week,* March 16, 1998, p. 96.

"Pyramid Alehouse Opens in Walnut Creek," *Modern Brewery Age,* May 6, 2002.

"Pyramid Breweries Inc. Declares Regular Quarterly Cash Dividend," *Business Wire,* February 24, 2000.

"Pyramid Breweries Inc.," *Seattle Post-Intelligencer,* December 20, 1999, Bus. Sec.

"Pyramid Chairman and CEO Steps Down," *Just-Drinks,* February 27, 2004.

"Pyramid Completes Portland Acquisition," *Modern Brewery Age,* August 9, 2004.

"Pyramid, Redhook Indicate Recovery in Craft-Beer Market," *Seattle Post-Intelligencer,* August 6, 1999.

Richman, Dan, "Pyramid Breweries Inc. Agrees to Be Taken Over," *Seattle Post-Intelligencer,* April 30, 2008.

"Tax Bill Hits Pyramid Breweries in 2006," *Just-Drinks,* March 12, 2007.

Redcats S.A.

110 rue de Blanche-maille
Roubaix, F-59100
France
Telephone: (33 01) 56 92 98 00
Fax: (33 01) 56 92 98 01
Web site: http://www.redcats.com

Wholly Owned Subsidiary of PPR S.A.
Incorporated: 1922 as Filatures de la Redoute
Employees: 20,031
Sales: EUR 3.69 billion ($4.63 billion) (2008)
NAICS: 454113 Mail-Order Houses; 551112 Offices of
 Other Holding Companies

■ ■ ■

Redcats S.A. is one of the world's leading home-shopping companies. The Roubaix, France-based company, part of the PPR group, controls 14 catalog, online, and retail brands across 30 countries. The company, which operates 60 e-commerce web sites, boasts an active client base of more than 29 million customers, generating nearly EUR 3.7 billion ($4.7 billion) in revenues in 2008. The group's French operations, which continue to produce more than 48 percent of the group's total sales, are led by its La Redoute flagship. Other French home-shopping brands include Vertbaudet, La Maison de Valérie, Somewhere, Cyrillus, and Daxon.

The company's next largest market is the United States, which accounted for nearly 30 percent of the company's sales. In the United States, Redcats focuses primarily on the plus-size market, through Woman Within (formerly Lane Bryant); Roamans, and its Intimate Promise lingerie offshoot; Jessica London; the Avenue chain of nearly 500 retail stores; and the men's catalog KingSize. The company also owns The Sportsman's Guide and the Golf Warehouse, and has branched out into home furnishings through Brylane Home. The Scandinavian market is the group's third major market, generating nearly 9 percent of sales through the flagship Ellos, as well as Josefssons, La Redoute, and others. Other Redcats markets include Austria; the Benelux countries of Belgium, the Netherlands, and Luxembourg; Canada; Croatia; Germany; Greece; Italy; Portugal; Switzerland; Spain; Saudi Arabia; and the United Kingdom; primarily through online versions of the La Redoute brand. Jean-Michel Noir was named Redcats' CEO in February 2009.

FOUNDING A YARN COMPANY IN 1831

For much of its history, Redcats was known as La Redoute, which remained one of the most well-known brands in France into the 21st century. La Redoute's origins began in the 1830s when Joseph Pollet, son of a local farmer, moved to the town of Roubaix, a center of the French wool and textiles industries. Pollet had already been involved in the textile trade, producing cotton linen starting in 1831. Following his move to Roubaix in 1837 Pollet set up a workshop producing wool yarn, becoming one of the first to use a newly invented mechanical comb.

COMPANY PERSPECTIVES

Redcats Group, a way of being. The six attitudes form the basis of the PPR spirit. They express Redcats Group' management style and serve as guidelines for behaviour. Conveyed through example from management, they need to be shared and upheld by all: succeeding together; speaking honestly; having a sense of time; looking ahead; taking ambition to the highest level; mastering complexity.

Pollet himself proved something of an inventor, and over the years he patented a number of improvements to the yarn production method. The business prospered, building a reputation both for the high-quality and low prices of its yarns. Pollet's son Charles took over the family business and launched its first expansion. In 1873 the company built a new factory on a street known as La Redoute—possibly the site of a former redoubt, or exterior fortification, set up to protect the main fortified city in ancient times. The company then became known as La Filature de la Redoute.

The Pollet family business remained prosperous through the turn of the century. The company struggled through World War I, and especially in the difficult economic climate in the immediate postwar years, which saw the collapse of much of the Roubaix region's textiles industry. Following a string of order cancellations, by 1922 the Pollet yarn factory was near bankruptcy as well.

HOME SHOPPING INNOVATION IN 1922

In order to raise cash and to reduce the company's stocks, Pollet placed a small classified advertisement in the local newspaper. Titled simply "Pour Tricoter" ("For Knitting"), the advertisement announced the sale of the company's goods at discounted prices. Potential customers were able place their orders directly at the factory for delivery at their homes. The advertisement was a success, marking the beginning of the French home shopping industry. In response to the advertisement's success, the company developed its first catalog in 1924. Called Filatures de la Redoute, the catalog originally featured only its yarns. The company also began publishing a number of albums devoted to knitting and crochet, and in 1925 launched its own magazine, *Pénélopé, Travaux de Laine et Mode,* distributed free to its customers.

The remarkable success of the mail-order business enabled the Pollet company to return to growth through the 1920s. By the end of the decade the company counted more than 600,000 direct-mail customers. Recognizing the potential to expand its sales beyond yarn, in 1928 the company published a new 16-page knitwear catalog. The new catalog featured just 40 items, and illustrations remained hand-drawn.

Filatures de La Redoute soon launched an expansion of its product range. In 1931 the company added a new catalog dedicated to "special fantasy hosiery." The company's primary catalog grew correspondingly. La Redoute innovated again with the introduction of the first black-and-white photographs in 1933. In 1935 the company added the "Usage Redoute" label. Items labeled as such were guaranteed by the company for quality and wear.

MAIL-ORDER FOCUS IN THE POSTWAR ERA

World War II put a temporary end to the company's growth. In 1939 the company was forced to stop publishing its catalog. Continuing paper shortages following the war delayed the return of the company's mail-order operations until the end of the 1940s. The first issue of the new Redoute catalog appeared in 1949 and featured 32 pages.

Filatures de La Redoute responded to the fast-growing French economy in the postwar period by expanding its product range beyond knitwear for the first time. In the 1950s the company, which continued to design most of its own garments, launched new lines featuring newly developing synthetic fibers, such as Tergal (polyester) and nylon. As part of its service offering, the company began promising 48-hour deliveries in 1954. The company also launched its first color catalog in 1959.

By then the company had also made its first move toward its transformation into a mail-order department store. In 1956 the company introduced a new catalog, called Ventac, featuring a range of home furnishing and leisure goods. This catalog later merged into the main catalog, which grew to more than 46,000 items at the beginning of the 1960s. In keeping with its multicategory focus the company changed its name to La Redoute à Roubaix in 1963. That same year the company shut down its manufacturing operations in order to focus fully on its fast-growing mail-order operations. La Redoute then went public the following year, listing its shares on the Paris stock exchange. The Pollet family nonetheless remained the company's majority shareholders.

KEY DATES
■

1837: Joseph Pollet establishes a yarn-spinning business in Roubaix, France.

1873: Son Charles Pollet constructs a yarn factory on Roubaix's La Redoute street.

1922: La Filatures de La Redoute places its first advertisement for mail-order sales.

1928: Launch of the first La Filatures de La Redoute catalog to sell finished knitwear.

1964: The company goes public as La Redoute.

1986: La Redoute agrees to merge with Le Printemps, which gains majority control in 1988.

1992: Groupe Pinault acquires Le Printemps, then buys out Pollet family's stake in La Redoute, forming Pinault-Printemps-Redoute (PPR).

2000: Following acquisition of U.S.-based Brylane, the La Redoute mail-order division is renamed as Redcats.

2007: Redcats reinforces its U.S. presence through purchase of the Avenue retail store network.

2008: La Redoute in France announces decision to phase out its catalog stores.

MODERNIZATION EFFORTS

During the 1960s, La Redoute teamed up with the era's recording and film stars, who were often featured modeling the group's clothing designs in its catalogs. In 1966 the company formed a new partnership with *Elle* magazine, highlighting items selected by the famed French fashion magazine in the company's catalog. At the end of the 1960s, La Redoute also launched its first designer collaboration, teaming up with Emmanuelle Khanh, who designed 32 garments for the company's 1969 catalog.

The company continued to modernize its service operations as well. In 1966 La Redoute opened the first of a national chain of catalog stores. The retail shops enabled customers to try on certain items, receive assistance from sales personnel, and to place and pick up orders at the store. The company added its own call center in 1969, allowing customers to place order by telephone for the first time. The following year La Redoute founded a financial services subsidiary, Finaref, and then launched its Kangarou revolving credit card. In 1973 the company also updated its catalog, with all items illustrated by color photographs.

A long strike by French postal workers encouraged La Redoute to break new ground in its logistics effort.

In 1974 the company launched its own fleet of delivery vehicles. The company also added a new type of shop, the "Rendez-vous Catalog" store, which were connected to the company's warehouses by computer. The success of the company's logistics effort backed the launch of the company's "Delivery in 48 hours or your money back" promise, introduced in 1984. That promise was later shortened to just 24 hours.

ACQUISITION BY PPR

By the 1980s La Redoute had established itself as France's leading mail-order company. The company turned its attention toward expanding both its range of catalogs and its international presence. In 1983 La Redoute made its first acquisition, of Movitex, a company originally established in the late 1940s marketing underwear for seniors. That company had created its own catalog business, Daxon, in 1974, featuring ready-to-wear clothing.

La Redoute followed up that acquisition with a move into children's clothing, buying Cyrillus, a catalog launched in 1977, in 1984. The following year, the company made its first foreign moves, launching La Redoute catalogs adapted to the Belgium, Luxembourg, and Portuguese markets.

The group's French catalog offering in the meantime adapted to the growing trend toward branded and designer fashions. In 1985 La Redoute began selling items from such "youth" brands as Levis, Bensimon, and Et Vous. The group also began developing a designer line. Over the years this line has featured the works of such noted designers as Marithé and François Girbaud and Anne-Marie Beretta. The success of the design range later led the company to launch its "Guest of the Season" haute couture line, starting with Marc Aubidet in 1992. That line was to feature such names as Issey Miyaké, Karl Lagerfeld, Yves Saint Laurent, Sonia Rykiel, and Jean-Paul Gaultier.

By this time La Redoute had become the cornerstone of one of France's largest fortunes. This process started in 1986 when La Redoute reached a merger agreement with French department store group Le Printemps. Le Printemps initially acquired a minority stake in La Redoute, but by 1988 had acquired more than 50 percent of the catalog company.

As part of a larger group, La Redoute launched a new expansion effort, buying Switzerland-based children's clothing catalog specialist Vertbaudet in 1988. Also that year, the company acquired a 25 percent stake in Empire Stores, one of the leading mail-order clothing companies in the United Kingdom. The company's stake in Empire rose to nearly 99 percent by 1991. That year La Redoute also took over another small but growing French home furnishings catalog, La Maison de Valérie. Other acquisitions by the company included Vestro, Italy's second largest mail-order group, and Prénatal, a retail chain with 325 stores in Italy, Portugal, Spain, Austria, and Germany.

MORE INTERNATIONAL EXPANSION

In 1992 Groupe Pinault, originally founded by François Pinault as a timber trading company in the 1960s, launched a takeover bid for the Printemps group. Pinault-Printemps, as the company's new name became, soon moved to gain full control of La Redoute, buying out the remaining shares held by the Pollet family in 1994. Pinault's company then took on the name of Pinault-Printemps-Redoute, before becoming PPR at the end of the decade. By then PPR had begun its transformation into one of France's largest conglomerates, with a particularly strong presence in the luxury goods market.

La Redoute nonetheless remained an important pillar of the PPR group. The group began its transition to online sales in 1995, launching its first e-commerce capable web site that year. The move to Internet-based sales also enabled the company to shorten its delivery times in France to just 24 hours.

The international market became the scene of La Redoute's strongest growth into the next century. Backed by its new parent, the company targeted a number of new acquisitions, starting with the purchase of Swedish and Scandinavian home shopping leader Ellos Gruppen in 1997. Two years later La Redoute entered the U.S. market, buying that country's Brylane in 1999. Brylane controlled such catalogs as Lane Bryant, Roaman's, Lerner, Bridgewater, and KingSize, with a strong focus on the plus-size market. The purchase of Brylane allowed the company to roll out a La Redoute edition for the U.S. market in that year.

TRANSFORMING INTO REDCATS

With nine brands in its portfolio, and operations already spanning nearly 20 countries, the company moved to distinguish between the company itself and its flagship La Redoute catalog. This led to the company's change of name, to Redcats, in 2000. The new, English-based name—a contraction of "Redoute" and "catalog"—reinforced the company's international focus. The group's U.S. subsidiary later changed its name from Brylane to Redcats USA.

Redcats continued to reinforce its international presence through the first decade of the 2000s. In 2004,

for example, the company added a second Scandinavian operation, buying Jotex, which specialized in mail-order textiles. In the United States the group began to expand its operations beyond the plus-size clothing market, launching Brylane Home in 2002, then acquiring the Sportsman's Guide and The Golf Warehouse in 2006. Nonetheless, the plus-size market—in a country where fully two-thirds of people were overweight—retained the group's primary focus. In 2007 the company reinforced its presence in this segment with the purchase of the 500-store Avenue retail chain.

While the group's retail operations in the United States were expanding, in France the company continued the transition of its La Redoute and other home shopping brands to a focus on online sales. This effort came as part of an effort to shore up the group's slipping revenues, which had begun to slip at the end of the first decade of the 2000s, as the company's online sales failed to take up the slack of its falling mail-order business. As part of an effort to relaunch La Redoute's sales growth, the company announced its intention to close more than 80 of its French catalog stores over the next four years. In February 2009 parent company PPR appointed Jean-Michel Noir, formerly with the Vivarte Group, as chairman and CEO. Noir prepared to lead Redcats into the post-mail-order era, and maintain the company's stature as one of the world's leading home-shopping groups.

M. L. Cohen

PRINCIPAL SUBSIDIARIES

Redcats (UK) plc; Redcats A.S.; Redcats Oy (Finland); Redcats USA L.P.

PRINCIPAL COMPETITORS

CVS Caremark Corporation; Target Corporation; Royal Ahold N.V.; Sears, Roebuck and Co.; Artemis S.A.; Macy's Inc.; J.C. Penney Company Inc.; H and M Hennes and Mauritz AB; Limited Brands Inc.; Home Retail Group PLC; QVC Inc.; 3 Suisses International S.A.

FURTHER READING

"Au Service de Ces Dames," *Strategies Magazine,* January 23, 1998.

Berman, Phyllis, "That's Redcat, Not Redneck," *Forbes,* March 24, 2008, p. 138.

Debouté, Alexandre, and Marie Maudieu, "La Redoute Rafraîchit Son Look," *Stratégies Magazine,* March 13, 2008.

Franco, Mark Del, "Redcats' New Brand Within," *Multichannel Merchant,* March 1, 2007.

"La Redoute to Close 81 Sites in Relaunch Plan," *just-style.com,* October 21, 2008.

"Le Developpement de So Redoute Suspendu," *Europe Intelligence Wire,* October 13, 2008.

Lillo, Andrea, "Brylane Boss Has Close Company Ties," *Home Textiles Today,* December 1, 2003, p. 8.

"PPR Appoints Noir as Redcats Boss," *just-style.com,* February 11, 2009.

"Redcats Completes United Retail Tender Offer," *just-style.com,* November 1, 2007.

Tierney, Jim, "Redcats USA Prefers Plus Sizes," *Multichannel Merchant,* March 1, 2008.

Weisman, Katherine, "French Twist: Redoute Hits U.S.," *WWD,* May 10, 1999, p. 10.

Williamson, Rusty, "PPR's Redcats USA Targets Trendy-Minded Customers," *WWD,* May 24, 2007, p. 8.

Ripley Corp S.A.

—■—

Huérfanos 1052
Santiago,
Chile
Telephone: (56 2) 694-1000
Fax: (56 2) 694-1855
Web site: http://www.ripley.cl

Public Company
Founded: 1964
Employees: Not Available
Sales: CLP 940.96 billion ($1.89 billion) (2007)
Stock Exchanges: Santiago
Ticker Symbol: RIPLEY
NAICS: 452111 Department Stores (Except Discount Department Stores); 522110 Commercial Banks; 522210 Credit Card Issuing; 524121 Direct Property and Casualty Insurance Carriers; 531120 Lessors of Nonresidential Buildings; 561510 Travel Agencies

■ ■ ■

Ripley Corp S.A. is one of the largest retail companies in Chile and Peru. Its main line of business is the sale of clothing, accessories, and home furnishings through different department store formats, but it also sells a broader range of merchandise, including big ticket items such as computers and major home appliances. The company has also created banks in both Chile and Peru to provide credit and other financial services to its customers. In addition, Ripley participates in the ownership of malls and other businesses associated with retail,

such as insurance. In Chile, Ripley ranks in the top three among department store chains in size. It is the only major retailer in Chile that does not have a presence in supermarkets or home centers.

FOUNDING AND EARLY YEARS

Ripley was founded by Marcelo and Alberto Calderón Crispín in Santiago, the capital of Chile and its largest city. The two brothers dropped out of school in 1955, selling trousers under the name American Pants. They began manufacturing pants in 1962 under the name Johnson's, and added men's clothing and accessories such as shirts and ties. Moving into retail in order to sell the merchandise they were producing was the next step, and Ripley was opened in 1964 for this purpose.

The Calderón brothers gave their enterprises English language names in the belief that such names were good for business. The Ripley name came from a tie store that they liked on Broadway in New York. The next two stores were originally named Harry (for Clint Eastwood's Dirty Harry) and Bond (for James Bond) before they also assumed the Ripley name. Lázaro Calderón Volchinsky, director general of Ripley, recalled the early days of the retail chain in a 2007 article appearing in the newspaper *El Mercurio.* He began visiting the stores with his father, Alberto, as a child, and at the age of 15 started working there during summer vacations. During this period, in the first half of the 1980s, there were still only three stores and no more than 150 employees. However, the company had introduced its own credit card in 1976.

KEY DATES

■

1964: Marcelo and Alberto Calderón found Ripley, a clothing store.

1976: The company introduces its own credit card for its customers.

1985: The company opens its first department store, Ripley San Diego.

1986: Ripley opens its first store outside Santiago, in Concepción.

1988: The retail chain places a store in a shopping mall for the first time.

1993: Store opening in the Parque Arauco mall makes Ripley a major national chain.

1997: Ripley enters Peru, where it becomes a leading retailer.

2000: The retail chain enters Santiago's high end Alto Las Condes mall.

2002: Ripley opens its own bank.

2005: Ripley goes public on the Santiago Stock Exchange.

2006: Ripley establishes its own television channel.

2007: Ripley and a partner pledge to build stores and commercial centers in Mexico.

Ripley opened its first department store, Ripley San Diego, in 1985. The following year the retailer launched its first store outside Santiago, in Concepción, and in 1988 it entered a shopping mall for the first time, in Santiago's Panorámico. However, Ripley did not become a major national chain until it opened a store in Santiago's Parque Arauco shopping mall in 1993. Parque Arauco was one of several major commercial centers to have made an appearance in Chile during this time. The stores located there based their business to a considerable degree on extending credit to their customers, including installment payments. The anchor tenants were usually department stores.

Among the department store chains, Ripley was directed at the lower-end consumer at this time. Some 60 to 70 percent of its sales occurred during promotional sales events. Some 70 percent of purchases were made with Ripley's own credit card, 10 percent with third-party credit, and 20 percent with cash. Annual revenue was about $300 million.

Ripley's success in this market was followed by a change of image and strong brand repositioning as it aimed at attracting a more affluent consumer. The number of its credit cards passed a million in 1999. In 2000 the retail chain opened its flagship store in Santiago's high-end Ripley Alto Las Condes mall and also made its wares available on the Internet for the first time. That year the company also established Ripley Insurance Brokers, and in 2002 it founded Banco Ripley. Ancillary businesses, particularly in the area of financial services, were making a significant contribution to the bottom line, and the company also established Ripley Travel around this time. The company had also entered Peru in 1997.

GOING PUBLIC

Ripley ranked fifth among Chilean retailers in its market sector in 2003, when it had 21 stores. However, by the end of 2004 the company had passed Almacenes Paris to become Chile's second largest department store chain, trailing only Falabella and occupying 28 percent of its market sector. The company's assets were valued at about $1 billion. Ripley entered Santiago's stock market in 2005, garnering $215 million by the sale of 15 percent of the stock. The Calderón brothers retained 81 percent of the shares.

There were 29 points of sale in Chile at this time, of which 14 were in Santiago. Ripley's ambition was to put a store in all eight major malls in the Santiago area, and by the end of 2007 the chain was in seven of them. One of these opened in Portal La Dehesa in 2006, where the chain, which had hired a multinational team of designers, introduced red as its signature color in answer to Falabella's green and Paris's sky blue. Going upscale, it raised its prices by an average of 10 percent, not by increasing prices on existing articles but by adding merchandise of higher quality. Ripley also opened offices in Hong Kong in order to have better control of its prices and raise the quality of its products.

Ripley was finding that it no longer had a price advantage in clothing, especially because supermarkets and hypermarkets carried their own clothing lines. The company was expanding further into fashion, having signed exclusive agreements with brands such as Pepe Jeans, Oakley, Quicksilver, Cacharel, North Face, Marquis, Regatta, and Tatienne. Interviewed for *El Mercurio,* a Ripley executive said, "A consumer that buys by price has minimal loyalty to the brand, but the customer that begins to buy by brand and aggregate value, this is where loyalty is generated, and that customer remains one over time." Higher-end customers also provided a larger profit margin and more revenue per square meter of space.

Ripley established its own television channel in 2006, broadcasting ten hours per day. It focused on beauty, fitness, and home, promoting products by means of contracted "faces" such as supermodel Cindy Crawford.

Ripley's revenues grew to about $1.5 billion in 2006, although its share of the Chilean department store market dropped to 25 percent. The company earmarked $120 million for six more stores in Chile, three more in Peru, and a new distribution center, plus $70 million more for a mall to be built in Concepción. Ripley's goal was to increase by one-fifth its total of 273,000 square meters of selling space, and its emphasis was on growth outside Santiago—both abroad and in provincial Chilean cities such as Calera, Los Andes, Puerto Montt, Quilpué, and Valdivia. In 2007 Ripley exercised an option to buy a 22.5 percent stake in the shopping centers being built in three other Chilean towns.

LOOKING OUTSIDE CHILE

A significant share of Ripley's revenues was coming from financial services, which had grown 17 percent in Chile and 31 percent in Peru during 2006. Banco Ripley, which had 41 branches, was the second most profitable retail bank in Chile during the year. In 2007 the company opened a Banco Ripley in Peru, where the chain had become one of the nation's leading retailers, accounting for about one-fourth of company sales. There were nine stores, seven under the Ripley name and two lower-end stores under a format called Max. All were in the Lima area, where in 2007 Ripley held more than half of the market.

In addition, the company in 2007 launched a joint venture with Mall Plaza and rival Falabella to construct commercial centers in Peru, beginning with shopping malls in three provincial Peruvian cities at a cost of $138 million. Ripley took a 40 percent stake in the enterprise, which was named Inversiones Corporativas Alfa.

Believing that the Chilean market was becoming saturated, Ripley was also planning to move into a third country in 2008, and it was assembling a treasury of almost $500 million for this purpose. In December 2007 the company announced a joint venture with Grupo Bal, S.A. de C.V., owner of the high-end Mexican department store chain El Palacio de Hierro. The two pledged to invest $400 million over four years in constructing not only stores and commercial centers in Mexico but also divisions of financial services and real estate. Grupo Bal was to provide 52.5 percent of the capital and Ripley the remaining 47.5 percent.

To explain the implications of this transaction, Lázaro Calderón granted an interview—the first ever accorded by his family to a newspaper—to Chile's most prestigious daily, *El Mercurio.* Ripley's director general said that the venture would be aimed at Mexico's middle class—the largest in Spanish-speaking America—by means of a new chain doing business under a name not yet determined. He saw the possibility of extending its scope to the United States, Central America, and the Caribbean in the future.

SURVIVING TROUBLED TIMES

Calderón also told his *El Comercio* interviewers that Ripley's plan for 2007 and 2008 called for investments in Chile and Peru worth $440 million for new stores, the new distribution center, and technology. In Peru, the company was planning to open 20 Banco Ripley branches by the end of the first quarter of 2009. Five new stores were to open in Chile, but the number was later cut to three.

In Chile, the company was seeking to recover from a difficult 2007, in which profits fell about three-quarters, principally because of poor performance in financial services. Andrés Roccatagliata, the new director general for Ripley Chile, announced that the company would save money by combining its three distribution centers in one place and bolstering its purchasing office in Hong Kong.

Ripley had 39 stores in Chile and ten in Peru in 2008. More than seven million company credit cards had been issued by the end of 2007. Peru accounted for one-quarter of sales in that year, and financial services also accounted for one-quarter of sales. In addition to clothing, Ripley's departments included computers, home entertainment components such as television sets, DVDs and CDs, home appliances such as washing machines, other electronics goods, kitchen appliances and items, bedroom items, furniture, sporting goods, toys, health and beauty items, merchandise for babies and pets, and gifts and entertainment.

The seven-member governing board of Ripley was chaired by Lázaro Calderón and included his brothers Andrés and Michel. Their uncle Marcelo, the sole proprietor of Johnson's, S.A.—by this time also a retail chain—appeared to come under financial strain following the world economic crisis manifested in late 2008. In order to make payments to his suppliers, Marcelo Calderón sold half his shares in Ripley to Alberto in early 2009 for perhaps the equivalent of $160 million.

Robert Halasz

PRINCIPAL SUBSIDIARIES

Ripley Chile S.A.; Ripley Financiero S.A.; Ripley Internacional S.A.; Ripley Retail Ltda.; Ripley Retail II Ltda. (70%).

PRINCIPAL COMPETITORS

Empresas Almacenas Paris S.A.; S.A.C.I. Falabella.

FURTHER READING

Ascencio, Alejandro, "Solamente Palacio?" *Expansión,* June 23–July 6, 2008, pp. 162, 164, 166.

"Banco Ripley apuesta por tecnología y más sucursales," *El Mercurio de Chile,* January 29, 2007.

Burgos, Sandra, "Mr. Ripley," *Capital,* June 27–July 10, 2008, pp. 33–36.

Chevarria León, Fernando, "Ripley llegará a las principales ciudades," *El Comercio del Perú,* August 4, 2007.

Derosas, Francisco, "Multitiendas en guerra por marcas exclusivas," *El Mercurio de Chile,* September 5, 2006.

Derosas, Francisco, and Azucena González, "Ésta ha sido una de las decisions más relevantes en la historia de Ripley," *El Mercurio de Chile,* December 9, 2007.

Derosas, Francisco, and Daniel Zunino, "Ripley abre las puertas de su tienda 'estrella' y revela sus planes," *El Mercurio de Chile,* October 28, 2006.

"Marcelo Calderón debutará en la bolsa," *Gestión,* December 2004, p. 10.

"Marcelo Calderon habría evaluado desprenderse de todas such acciones en Ripley," *El Mercurio de Chile,* December 25, 2008.

"Parti mi relación con Ripley como a los seis años," *El Mercurio de Chile,* December 9, 2007.

Pérez R., Soledad, "Ripley muestra los dientes," *Capital,* April 6–19, 2007, pp. 52–56.

"This Latin Tiger Is Friendly," *Chain Store Age,* April 1996, Latin American supplement, p. 13.

Rocky Brands, Inc.

39 East Canal Street
Nelsonville, Ohio 45764
U.S.A.
Telephone: (740) 753-1951
Fax: (740) 753-4024
Web site: http://www.rockyboots.com

Public Company
Incorporated: 1932 as The William Brooks Shoe Company
Employees: 1,600
Sales: $275.3 million (2007)
Stock Exchanges: NASDAQ
Ticker Symbol: RCKY
NAICS: 316213 Men's Footwear (Except Athletic) Manufacturing; 316214 Women's Footwear (Except Athletic) Manufacturing; 316219 Other Footwear Manufacturing

∎ ∎ ∎

Rocky Brands, Inc., formerly known as Rocky Shoes & Boots, Inc., designs, manufactures, and markets premium-quality men's and women's footwear under the brand names of Rocky Outdoor Gear, Georgia Boot, Durango, Lehigh, and Dickies. The company's product line ranges from hunting, hiking, and Western-styled boots to footwear used by the U.S. Military Special Forces. Rocky Brands' products are sold in over 10,000 retail locations in the United States and Canada including sporting good stores, outdoor retailers, independent shoe retailers, hardware stores, uniform stores, and other specialty retailers. The company's products can also be found in catalogs, on web sites, and in the Rocky Factory Outlet store in Ohio. The company closed its continental U.S. manufacturing facility in Nelsonville, Ohio, in 2001.

THE WILLIAM BROOKS SHOE COMPANY, 1932–59

In 1932 William Brooks founded The William Brooks Shoe Company in Nelsonville, Ohio, about 60 miles southeast of Columbus, joined by his brother F. M. "Mike" Brooks. Both men had lost their jobs during the Great Depression when Godman Shoe Co. of Columbus went bankrupt. In 1937 Mike's 17-year-old son, John W. Brooks, joined the company, taking a break only to serve four years in the U.S. Army during World War II. The two brothers ran the business until the mid-1950s when they had a falling out. Bill, the original founder, bought out Mike, and the two never spoke again.

THE IRVING DREW SHOE CO., 1959–74

In 1959, convinced that the U.S. shoe industry was going under, Bill began looking for a buyer for the business. Mike's son, John, offered to buy it, but his uncle refused, saying he was doing him a favor, and pointing to the hundreds of other domestic shoe companies, and the first imports, which were a lot less expensive, starting to come from Japan. Bill sold the business to The Irving Drew Shoe Co., a women's-shoe company, headquartered in Lancaster, Ohio, and John remained in the company as an employee.

For 25 years ownership was out of the Brooks family. John remained on through the entire Irving Drew ownership period, eventually rising to plant manager. Eventually, Irving Drew began to struggle as offshore shoe manufacturing boomed and competitors lowered their margins and, concurrently, their prices. After losing money for three years running, The Irving Drew Shoe Co. announced its closing in 1974. John, realizing that his dream of owning his own company might finally come to fruition, with five children to raise and a modest salary, put a meager $500 of his own money into the venture, and borrowed $640,000 from various banks to purchase the company, worth about $1.3 million, from Irving Drew.

JOHN W. BROOKS AND THE RETURN OF THE WILLIAM BROOKS SHOE CO., 1975

After the purchase in 1975 John formed John W. Brooks, Inc., as an Ohio corporation, reacquired the operating assets of the original company, and moved the principal executive offices back to Nelsonville, renaming the company The William Brooks Shoe Co. in honor of his uncle. Then he called his son Mike, who was working in a tannery in Milwaukee, Wisconsin.

Mike had left college early and gone to Milan, Italy, where he spent a year studying shoe design at the well-known Ars Satoria trade school. He had already spent time in the shoe business, working at U.S. Shoe Corp. and at two leather tanning companies. Against John's worry that the business might not work out, Mike quit his job the very next day, taking a huge pay cut, and moved his family back to Nelsonville. There, Mike found disaster—no bank financing, aging machinery, three years of losses, the plant in disarray, morale at an all-time low because of layoffs, meager raises, and workers' medical insurance in a bad state.

Mike turned things around quickly, designing a new pair of hiking boots, and going out on the road to sell them. He worked to speed up production and ease the company's cash needs and spent time roaming the factory floor, attempting to buoy the spirits of a demoralized workforce. Then the cavalry arrived. Dave Fraedrich, hired by John right out of college, came aboard as a financial guru and Bob Hollenbaugh, a childhood friend of Mike, became manager of shipping, personnel, and purchasing. The three became a triad and worked together, plotting company strategies over beer in the evenings.

The father-and-son team quarreled about the way to run their business. Mike began to think about taking the company public right away, because the company was always highly leveraged and never had enough capital to do anything properly. But John, a bitter survivor of the Great Depression and the stock market crash of the 1930s, refused to expand, wanting to keep control of the company in the family. The two were at an impasse for nearly a year and a half. Their options were: sell a piece of the business to raise funds, continue running the company undercapitalized, or sell it outright. In the meantime, business continued as best it could under the strain.

MOVING FORWARD INSTEAD OF DYING

In 1975 the United States was emerging from the worst downturn since the 1930s. Imports, from steel to semiconductors, flooded into the U.S. market. The Midwest was hit hard, with so many manufacturing facilities closed down that it was named the Rustbelt. Likewise, the shoe industry went from its plateau of the 1950s into a steep dive. In 1970 imported shoes accounted for 30 percent of the market. By 1980 imports had climbed to 50 percent and were still going up. During those ten years, over 300 domestic shoe plants shut their doors for good.

The Brooks Company's regular customers, Sears and J.C. Penney, bought nearly 80 percent of the company's output. The company was bringing in nearly $8 million a year, but could not continue to run things the way they were. Plummeting import prices were killing the U.S. shoemaker, salaries were dropping, the plant was decrepit, the machinery was failing, and something had to be done.

In 1979, during a meeting in Chicago with a buyer for Sears, Mike finally realized the battle was being lost. He had asked for a 50 cent per pair increase in the purchase price. The buyer balked and asked to speak with John. John drove out with Mike the following week, 400 miles, since he hated to fly, and the meeting degenerated from the start. John, worried about losing the account, waffled on the price; Mike stuck to his story. Sears agreed to the price increase, but only until it could find a less expensive alternative, probably a Korean shoemaker.

KEY DATES

1932: William and Mike Brooks establish the William Brooks Shoe Co.
1959: The company is sold to The Irving Drew Shoe Co.
1975: John Brooks purchases the company.
1977: The first Rocky branded boot is produced.
1983: The company begins marketing "occupational" shoes, such as those worn by police officers and mail carriers, under the Rocky brand.
1987: A factory is established in the Dominican Republic.
1988: A second offshore facility opens in Puerto Rico.
1992: The company adopts the Rocky Shoes & Boots name.
1993: Rocky Shoes goes public.
2001: The company closes its Nelsonville factory.
2005: EJ Footwear Group is acquired.
2006: The company changes its name to Rocky Brands Inc.

As the company struggled in the early 1980s, the shoe market itself saw new life. Numerous upstart companies entered the fray; others began to prosper. Distinctive products with brand names and premium prices became the rage. Shoes were sold through new retail channels, not just the old shoe stores and department stores. Advertising costs soared. "Athletic" shoes became a new rage. Nike led in athletic shoes; Timberland led in boots. However, old-time manufacturers in the Midwest and elsewhere in the United States kept going under, and another 300 manufacturers closed up shop. The only way for a traditional shoe company to survive was to rethink everything from manufacturing to sales and distribution.

When Mike created his new red-laced hiking boots to sell to Sears in the mid-1970s, he called them "Rocky," thinking it sounded strong and bold and All-American. He had a new box designed, with a picture of a bighorn sheep on it, put the boots in it, and put Bob Hollenbaugh out on the streets to sell them. Approaching independent dealers in Ohio and the surrounding areas, Hollenbaugh made sales at margins far higher than Sears would give.

In 1983 the company began marketing "occupational" shoes, such as those worn by police officers and mail carriers, under the Rocky brand. This opened up new markets and new distribution methods. Mike was also watching Timberland. He knew he had to reinvent the wheel, by making a new and distinctive product and then selling it through the path of least resistance. The company also had to broaden and deepen its line past just the four Rocky boots it was then offering.

REBUILDING THE COMPANY, ONE PRODUCT AT A TIME

Shoe by shoe, the company slowly continued to gain strength. In 1984 the company introduced the Rocky Stalkers boots. In 1987 Five Star Enterprises Ltd., a Cayman Islands corporation, was formed by John and Mike, two other executive officers of the company, and Eric M. Beraza, a retired executive officer of the company, to produce shoe and boot uppers at a manufacturing facility located in La Vega, Dominican Republic. The following year Lifestyle Footwear, Inc., a Delaware corporation, was established as a subsidiary of Rocky Co. and commenced operations at a manufacturing facility in Aquadilla, Puerto Rico. Also that year, the company released its Rocky Cornstalkers boots.

A strategic victory was created by Hollenbaugh as he beat the bushes out on the road, lining up hundreds of reps, meeting hundreds of buyers, creating a distribution network unparalleled by any other U.S. shoemaker. Hunting and sporting goods stores, mostly in the Midwest, carried the "Made in the USA"-labeled, waterproof boots, and were willing to pay a bit more for them. Hollenbaugh developed catalogs, learned the advertising industry, and spearheaded campaigns in outdoor magazines. Sales rose as the company, in 1988, reached $20 million in annual revenue.

The following year, Mike created a new line of products that could hold its own against Korean and Taiwanese imports when he found Gore-Tex, a patented membrane that allowed moisture escape, but kept water droplets out, created by W.L. Gore & Associates. Taking a chance on the new technology, Mike quickly created Gore-Tex boots, which everyone loved. No other companies could duplicate them without serious money being put into the project, because Gore & Associates asked for all footwear customers to fork over a $25,000 licensing fee. Other manufacturers became furious; Mike Brooks, however, loved it and showed up the next day with a $25,000 check and a bottle of champagne to share with CEO Bob Gore, knowing his investment in the latter company had paid off.

In August 1991 John walked into Mike's office and said he was retiring, and walked out, leaving $11.25 million in debt to Mike and his four siblings and their spouses. He gave up his controlling interest in the family business and divided it equally among Mike and his two brothers and two sisters, all of whom worked for the company, retaining a small interest in the Dominican plant. It cleared the way for Mike to take the company public. That year, as he struggled to do so, total sales reached $29.8 million, with a net income of $577,000. Total sales for 1992 climbed to $32.5 million, with net sales nearly tripling over the previous year, to $1.6 million.

BECOMING ROCKY SHOES & BOOTS

In February 1993 Mike Brooks did manage to take the company public, spending nearly three-quarters of a million dollars in the process, changing the name to Rocky Shoes & Boots and initiating the company's initial public offering. Selling approximately 1.9 million shares at $10 apiece on the NASDAQ under the symbol RCKY, and bringing in nearly $14 million, the company was able to help pay off its debt and add a bit of working capital. The five family members, along with three longtime employees, retained a 47 percent interest in the company, and John cashed in his interest shortly thereafter, remaining with the company as a semiretired employee. Net income for 1993 nearly reached $1.8 million on net sales of $41.2 million.

In 1994 the company released the "4 Way Stop" line of occupational shoes designed for foodservice workers, who often encounter wet, slippery conditions, featuring an exclusive "downspout" design sole that causes liquid to flow through the sole and out the sides, increasing traction and exceeding the U.S. government's standards for slip-resistance by a factor of two. In August of that year the company opened a 25,000-square-foot building in Nelsonville, Ohio, adjacent to the company's manufacturing facilities, which included 12,500 square feet of office space and a 12,500-square-foot factory outlet store, to replace a 3,000-square-foot one. Opened in September, the expanded outlet sold first-quality, irregular, and closeout Rocky footwear and accessories, as well as footwear and apparel from other manufacturers.

Other achievements that year included the company investing $2.7 million in new equipment and changeover to modular manufacturing. Six lines of boots were added to the Rocky Safari series of lightweight hiking boots. The company achieved records that year, with net sales increasing 28 percent to $52.9 million, and sales of Rocky rugged outdoor footwear increasing 42

percent to $28.7 million. Net income for 1994 repeated at just above $1.8 million.

ADDING CLOTHING TO THE ROCKY LINE

In January 1995 both Rocky Shoes and competitor Wolverine World Wide entered the apparel business, launching workwear lines of clothing. The company also signed a licensing agent, The Kravetz Group, to help it market and license its products. The company also introduced the Rocky Professionals line of occupational shoes, with dress-shoe-styling designed for safety forces and general occupational markets. This line featured waterproof leather uppers, lightweight soles and materials, slip-resistant polyurethane-injected soles, breathable linings, and superior lateral stability.

The retail market for shoes struggled in 1995 and footwear stocks dipped. Rocky attributed a fourth-quarter 1995 sales drop to a decrease in hand-sewn casual shoe sales for a private-label customer, among other things. Retail sales from the factory outlet store were approximately $2.7 million, making up some 7.6 percent of net sales for the year. In fiscal 1995, the company ended the year with $60.2 million in total revenue, with net income dropping slightly to $1.4 million.

John W. Brooks, the consummate shoemaker, passed away in February 1996, ending a nearly 60-year career in the shoe industry. His company continued as three new styles were introduced by mid-1996, including Snow Stalkers, Sidewinders, and Tuff Terrainers. The company also changed the end of its fiscal year from June 30 to December 31. Total revenue for 1996 reached $73.2 million, with a net income of $2.8 million. During the first quarter of 1997, sales were especially strong in the Outdoor and Handsewn categories.

In January 1998 the company installed a System 21–style enterprise resource planning (ERP) system from JBA International, as part of an effort to improve the company's reporting and tracking capabilities. Also early that year, the company discontinued the sale of footwear uppers to a private-label customer. By June the company, with its Nelsonville, Ohio-based facility employing some 250 people, was one of the last remaining U.S. footwear companies with a domestic production plant. In August, the company announced it would repurchase up to 300,000 shares of stock in the following year. In September, Hurricane Georges affected the company's manufacturing facilities in Puerto Rico and the Dominican Republic when production was interrupted for approximately one week, and Hurricane

Mitch hammered Puerto Rico, the Caribbean, and Central America again. Still the company expected to post new record income and sales that year, and hoped to continue on into the 21st century as a venerable leader in the U.S. shoe industry.

MOVING INTO THE 21ST CENTURY

The cost of producing footwear in the United States was high in the early years of the 2000s, forcing Rocky Shoes to cut 110 jobs from its Nelsonville facility in 2000. At the time, over 97 percent of shoes sold in the U.S. were imports. The company soon made the decision to shutter plant altogether. The last pair of Ohio-made Rocky boots were packaged and shipped on November 21, 2001. Mike Brooks commented on the trend to produce overseas in a November 2001 *Columbus Dispatch* article claiming, "You either change, or you die."

Intent on growing its business, Rocky Shoes looked for ways to expand its footprint. During 2001, the company secured a government contract to produce military boots. It also acquired Gates-Mills Inc., an outdoor and dress glove manufacturer. The company moved into the Western footwear market that year, adding Western-styled boots as well as apparel to its product line.

Perhaps its boldest move came in 2004 when it announced plans to acquire EJ Footwear Group, which would double the size of the company. The deal, worth over $87.7 million in cash and another $10 million in Rocky Shoes stock, was sealed in early 2005. During 2006, the company adopted the Rocky Brands Inc. name to reflect its growing portfolio of brands which included Rocky Outdoor Gear, Georgia Boot, Durango, Lehigh, and Dickies.

Rocky Brands faced increased competition as the U.S. economy faltered and consumer spending slowed. In an attempt to shore up profits and cut costs, the company consolidated its distribution operations. Meanwhile, it pursued slow and steady international growth in European markets. On the home front, it signed a new licensing deal with Haas Outdoors Inc. to produce and market the Mossy Oak line of hunting and casual footwear and expanded its licensing agreement with Williamson-Dickie to manufacture and market the Dickies brand of footwear through 2010. The company also secured military contracts in 2007 and 2008 to produce footwear for the U.S. Army as well as U.S. Military Special Forces.

While profits were down in 2007, sales increased slightly over the previous year by 4.5 percent. The retail environment in the United States remained weak but Rocky Brands management was optimistic about its success in the years to come. "We've made great progress. I'm proud of what we've built," chairman and CEO Brooks claimed in an April 2007 *Footwear News* article. He continued, "It's hard work, and it probably always will be."

Daryl F. Mallett
Updated, Christina M. Stansell

PRINCIPAL COMPETITORS

Red Wing Shoe Company Inc.; The Timberland Company; Wolverine World Wide Inc.

FURTHER READING

Berg, Susan M., "Made in the USA," *Business First—Columbus,* June 12, 1998, p. 39.

Derby, Meredith, "Paper Trail," *Footwear News,* April 30, 2007.

Newman, Eric, "A Foreign Affair," *Footwear News,* April 30, 2007.

Price, Rita, "Rocky Shoes Closing One More," *Columbus Dispatch,* November 22, 2001.

"Rocky 1932–2007," *Footwear News,* April 30, 2007.

"Rocky Shoes & Boots Buys EJ Footwear," *Sporting Goods Business,* January 1, 2005.

"Rocky Shoes & Boots Inc.," *New York Times,* October 6, 1997.

"Rocky Shoes & Boots Inc.," *Wall Street Journal,* May 13, 1998.

"Rocky Shoes Has Rights Plan," *Wall Street Journal,* November 12, 1997.

Rudolph, Ron, Bob Woodward, and Eric Perlman, "Foot Retrofit," *Snow Country,* Spring 1995, p. 20.

"Rugged Footwear Brands Step into Apparel Business," *Sporting Goods Business,* January 1, 1995, p. 26.

Sammon, Lindsay E., "Branding Muscle," *Footwear News,* April 30, 2007.

Shook, Carrie, "R. G. Barry Loses Steam," *Business First—Columbus,* December 12, 1994, p. 24.

———, "Rocky Shoes & Boots Climbs," *Business First—Columbus,* September 25, 1995, p. 20.

———, "Rocky Shoes & Boots Makes Gain," *Business First—Columbus,* October 16, 1995, p. 22.

"Taking Stock," *Business First—Columbus,* December 6, 1996, p. 34.

"Taking the ERP Trail," *Computerworld,* January 12, 1998, p. 39.

"US: Dickies and Rocky Brands Extend License Deal," *Just-Style,* April 14, 2008.

"US: Rocky Announces Name Change," *Just-Style,* May 25, 2006.

Walter, Rebecca, "Rocky Shoes IPO Strained Family Ties," *Business First—Columbus,* December 12, 1994, p. 1.

———, "When the Baby Is the Family Business," *Business First—Columbus,* December 5, 1994, p. 1.

SAFRAN

---■---

2, boulevard du General Martial-Valin
Paris, 75724 Cedex 15
France
Telephone: (33 01) 40 60 80 80
Fax: (33 01) 40 60 81 02
Web site: http://www.safran-group.com/

Public Company
Incorporated: 1924 as Société d'Applications Générales
  de l'Electricité et de la Mécanique
Employees: 57,000
Sales: EUR 10.33 billion ($14.56 billion) (2008 est.)
Stock Exchanges: Euronext Paris
Ticker Symbol: SAF
NAICS: 336412 Aircraft Engine and Engine Parts
  Manufacturing; 541710 Research and Development
  in the Physical, Engineering, and Life Sciences

■ ■ ■

SAFRAN, created by the 2005 merger of Snecma and
SAGEM, operates in the aerospace propulsion, aircraft
equipment, and defense security industries. Based in
Paris, France, the company oversees approximately 100
companies that provide engines for commercial and
military aircraft; jet engines for missiles; landing gear
and braking systems for commercial and military
airplanes and helicopters; navigation and guidance
equipment; avionics systems; and unmanned aerial
vehicles. The creation of SAFRAN, which means "rud-
der blade" in French, was thought to be orchestrated in

part by then Finance Minister Nicolas Sarkozy, who
later became France's 23rd president.

HISTORY OF SNECMA

France has produced its share of aviation pioneers. No
less important than the airframe designers and the pilots
were the people who produced engines powerful enough
and light enough for powered flight to finally take wing.
The technology for the first airplane engines was
developed at the same time as early automotive engines.
A steam engine powered an early flight attempt by Clé-
ment Ader in 1890. Internal combustion engines
provided a better power-to-weight ratio, yet most of the
early engines sold to aircraft designers were derived from
those found in automobiles.

In 1906 Santos Dumont made the first gasoline-
powered flight in Europe using a V8 Antoinette engine
producing up to 50 horsepower. Anzani, the Renault
brothers, and other firms produced workable engines.
According to Snecma's official history, the first airplane
motor to be considered a true worldwide success was the
50 horsepower Omega, a seven-cylinder rotary engine
produced by Gnome. The famed aviator Henri Farman
flew a Voisin aircraft powered by an Omega engine to
set a 1909 distance and endurance record (180
kilometers in 3 hours and 15 minutes).

Snecma traces its origins to the Société des Moteurs
Gnome, founded in 1905 by Louis Seguin. In 1915 this
firm merged with the Société des Moteurs Le Rhône,
founded three years earlier by Louis Verdet, to form
Gnome & Rhône. While Gnome continued to produce
rotary engines in the 50 to 100 horsepower range,

COMPANY PERSPECTIVES

■

SAFRAN's corporate strategy will be focused on the following fundamental objectives. We will consolidate or develop our leadership positions in all of our businesses, by: continuous research & development initiatives to ensure the technological independence of the new group and sustain our high-level expertise; applying these high-tech competencies to products and systems intended for markets offering a profitable growth outlook; controlling the entire life cycle of these products, from design to support; consolidating current partnerships; remaining open to other partnerships, if they are compatible with our current programs; winning, alone or in partnership, significant shares of all new major programs, whether in aerospace, defense/security or telecommunications; deepening our ties with customers by starting up operations in selected locations; continuing to develop prime contracting capability for large-scale aerospace systems, to give our customers a comprehensive, unified offering; and continuing to examine all favorable external growth opportunities.

Rhône refined its fixed-cylinder engines to produce 200 horsepower. However, both these lines of engines were being outclassed in terms of reliability, economy, or power by several contemporary engine manufacturers.

Nevertheless, the merged companies were quite successful commercially, thanks to licensed production in Great Britain, Russia, the United States, Sweden, Germany, and Japan, as well as joint ventures in Italy and elsewhere.

RETOOLING BETWEEN THE WARS

A number of factors hit Gnome & Rhône (G&R) hard after World War I. A huge tax burden was levied based on the firm's previous international success. At the same time, a mass of war surplus engines glutted the market. Unlike its other domestic rivals, Gnome & Rhône lacked experience in areas apart from aero engines, a market glutted by thousands of surplus motors. A variety of schemes, from making sewing machines to engines for farm tractors or cars, all failed.

In constant francs, the company's sales in 1921 were almost half those of 1913, although the factories were five times larger, noted one scholar in the journal

Entreprise et Histoire. That year the legendary company reduced its employment from 6,500 workers to 1,200.

Production of motorcycles under the G&R was one area that produced quite satisfactory results in the marketplace; in fact these machines gained a devoted following. In 1922 the English firm Bristol licensed to G&R the right to produce its powerful air-cooled radial engines producing up to 450 horsepower, as well as the freedom to sell them anywhere in the world except for the United States and the territories of the British Empire. With the support of its banks, G&R was able to retool its workshops to build engines, including the new Jupiter introduced in 1923. At the time, G&R had also taken a significant holding in a French-Romanian airline, which helped establish its engines in Eastern Europe.

ERA OF NEW GROWTH

Between 1924 and 1928, sales increased more than sixfold. At the same time, the air, sea, and land branches of the French military were deciding that their outdated equipment was in need of replacement, resulting in another blossoming market at home. Expanding commercial fleets produced still more demand. The radial Jupiter engines earned a reputation for being simple to run and easy to fix, even if in-line and V8 engines made by Hispano-Suiza and Lorraine-Dietrich were more powerful.

A novel program instituted in 1924 allowed the lease of the engines for a given number of flight-hours, which relieved designers and manufacturers of some of the financial strain associated with bringing out new models of aircraft. The popular Jupiter engine was subsequently licensed for production in several European countries as well as the Soviet Union and Japan.

G&R introduced its K family of engines in 1928. In terms of power, this series culminated in the 750 horsepower 14K licensed to a Soviet factory for eventual use in Antonov transports. G&R's designers evolved L, M, and N families of engines by 1939; one of the latter achieved 1,150 horsepower.

Air power would play a determining role during World War II, and G&R engines had a significant part to play. The Soviet Union's Molotov factory was producing 300 licensed G&R engines a month in 1940 for use in biplanes and Sukhoi fighters. In Japan Mitsui illegally copied the 850 horsepower 14K engine, producing the "Suizei" powerplant found in the Mitsubishi Zeroes that attacked Pearl Harbor. During the Nazi occupation of France G&R became a subsidiary of BMW. Emmanuel Chadeau wrote in *Entreprises et Histoire* that

KEY DATES

1905: Société des Moteurs Gnome is founded.

1915: Gnome merges with Société des Moteurs Le Rhône.

1922: G&R begins producing Bristol radial engines under license.

1924: Marcel Môme creates the Société d'Applications Générales de l'Electricité et de la Mécanique (SAGEM).

1945: Snecma is created.

1959: Snecma begins producing Pratt & Whitney engines under license.

1968: Snecma acquires control of Hispano-Suiza.

1971: Snecma enters into a longstanding partnership with General Electric.

1985: Snecma merges with rocket engine producer SEP.

1994: The Messier-Bugatti landing gear unit merges with Dowty of Britain.

2000: Labinal and Hurel-Dubois are acquired.

2001: The French government plans, then postpones Snecma privatization.

2004: The government sells a 35 percent stake in Snecma in an initial public offering.

2005: Snecma and SAGEM merge to form SAFRAN.

2008: The SAGEM Communications business is sold.

G&R thereby influenced 16 manufacturers in 14 countries during the war; this offshore production nearly equaled G&R's own output of 8,000 motors a year—together accounting for a quarter of the worldwide market.

SNECMA CREATED IN 1945

The high share price that G&R commanded prevented it from being nationalized before the war. However, this was not the case after the Liberation. SNECMA, la Société nationale d'étude et de construction de moteurs d'aviation, was thus created on May 29, 1945. The company was an amalgamation of diverse design bureaus and workshops; it inherited a workforce of 10,000 mostly part-time employees.

Along with G&R, Snecma was given some of the factories of the Société des moteurs et automobiles Lorraine, formerly Lorraine-Dietrich, which had been nationalized as La Société nationale des moteurs and had been relegated to making parts for tanks. Some of Snecma's other facilities had been devoted to the production of German Junkers engines by the thousands during the Nazi occupation. G&R also owned a factory of the Aéroplanes Voisin firm, which had gone bankrupt in 1938.

Unfortunately, the British government preferred to grant licenses for the newly acquired jet engine technology to rival Hispano-Suiza in the immediate postwar period. During these years Snecma suffered many of the same disadvantages as G&R had immediately after World War I. It was not until 1950, wrote Chadeau, that budgetary crisis forced a restructuring that closed unproductive plants and reequipped modern ones to give the firm some hope of a future.

Given their apparent importance in the future of military aviation, jet engines were the prime focus of Snecma's development in the 1950s. However, the company did not abandon propeller-driven aircraft. In 1951 the firm acquired a license from the Bristol firm to produce the 2,080 horsepower Hercules engine for use in Noratlas military transports; nearly 1,400 of these were produced by 1964.

NEW GENERATION OF MILITARY ENGINE DESIGN

The creation of jet engines in the World War II propelled planes allowed a huge leap in aircraft performance. However, in the period immediately after the war, the devastated nations of Europe were unable to match American and Soviet research into jet engine design until the middle of the 1950s. A group of 120 former BMW engineers were assembled in the French controlled sector of Germany in 1946 and integrated into the Snecma team in France in 1950. From their efforts sprang the ATAR series of military engines, the first of which was created in 1948. Their first test of an engine equipped with afterburner came in 1953. The SO-4050 Vautour was the first plane powered by these engines; other better-known fighters included the Mystère and Super-Mystère, and Mirage III, IV, and V. Planes powered by these engines set several speed records and enjoyed a lively export trade.

Meanwhile, Hispano-Suiza had been producing jet engines under license from Rolls-Royce, including the famous Tay engine, which it began building in 1954. The next year, it introduced its own turbojet, known as the Verdon, which was installed in Mystère IV aircraft.

Another French firm, Turboméca, was making quite low-powered jet engines, although in 1960 it began producing the Adour engine for the Jaguar fighter in cooperation with Rolls-Royce. Turboméca also produced engines for turboprops and, most notably turbine-driven helicopters, which it supplied to a variety of French and foreign firms. Another firm, Microtubo, was launched in 1961 to produce small turbojets.

While Hispano-Suiza and Turboméca were signing deals with Rolls-Royce, in November 1959 Snecma entered a contract to produce Pratt & Whitney's popular JT8-D engine in France. The JT8-D powered several American military jets as well as the DC-8 and Boeing 707 airliners. Snecma signed an agreement with Bristol Engines in November 1962 to develop the Olympus engines for the Concorde supersonic transport.

In 1968 Snecma took control over Hispano-Suiza, which included the mechanical engineering firm Bugatti, the landing gear manufacturer Messier, and the engine maker Berthiez. All of these were at the edge of ruin.

REVITALIZATION

Several initiatives would result in Snecma recapturing a leading place among aircraft engine makers by the end of the 1970s. Even though only a few examples of the Concorde would be produced, Snecma gained considerable experience and prestige through its participation. In 1969 the firm had begun development of its M56 engine, which would first appear on the market in 1976. An even more far-reaching program was launched in 1971 with General Electric, which was eager to break Pratt & Whitney's domination of the U.S. market.

Under this agreement Snecma was to produce 20 percent of GE-s type CF6 engines (CF meaning "commercial fan"), which were destined for use in several Boeing airliners. In addition they would also be used in the first planes made by Airbus Industrie, the new European consortium created to challenge U.S. control of the industry. A second contract provided for the joint production of the CFM 56 engine. The CFM International joint venture was formally created in 1974. Snecma expanded its role in the CFM program after the CF6 engine was chosen for both the Airbus A310 and Boeing 767. In late 1980 Snecma and GE began planning a new $30 million plant in France to accommodate its production.

The French government mandated the merger of the Société Europénne de Propulsion (SEP) with Snecma in 1984. SEP produced rocket engines used in the Ariane space program and was merged with Snecma due to concerns it could not meet increasing production demands. By 1985 Snecma was taking a half share of CFM contracts, including a $2.7 billion order for 137 engines to reequip the U.S. Air Force's aerial refueling fleet.

CONSOLIDATION AND CHANGE

The unprecedented airline industry downturn recession in the early 1990s resulted in consolidation among suppliers. In early 1994 Snecma merged its Messier-Bugatti landing gear subsidiary with Dowty, owned by the United Kingdom's TI Group. Messier-Bugatti was effectively privatized for the merger. However, the two cultures of the merged parties clashed; TI Group exited the Messier-Dowty joint venture by the end of 1997.

In the mid-1990s Snecma's engine business encountered its first civil market downturn ever, according to CEO Gerard Renon. It lost $100 million on sales of $1.8 billion in 1993. Workforce cuts and other measures were taken to increase productivity and shorten production cycles. Employment was reduced from 14,000 in late 1990 to 11,500 in December 1996. A unique four-way alliance between Snecma, GE, Pratt & Whitney, and MTU to develop a small jet engine fell apart in September 1994. Meanwhile, CFM's market share of engines for larger jets approached 70 percent.

When Jean-Paul Bechat became Snecma's new head in the summer of 1996, following the brief reign of Bernard Dufour, he stated the company was close to bankruptcy and full of conflict. However, within a year things were closer to normal—operating profit rose 70 percent, to FRF 440 million in 1996. After losing FRF 280 million in 1996, Snecma posted a net profit of FRF 750 million ($122 million) for 1997. Exports accounted for about 70 percent of turnover, with more than three-quarters of these coming from the civil sector.

NEW DIVISION MEETS GROWING MARKET NEED

As the life span of jet engines increased, scheduled maintenance became a more important source of business. A new division, Snecma Services, was created in January 1997, to offer support services for landing systems and engines. By 1999 it had sales of $400 million and 2,000 employees. The Snecma group as a whole reported revenues of $5.3 billion for 1999. That year, CFM International celebrated the delivery of its 10,000th engine; the joint venture was widely held to be the most successful Europe-U.S. collaboration ever.

Snecma was converted into a holding company in January 2000. Snecma Moteurs was created to consolidate its air and space propulsion operations. Later in the year, Snecma acquired Labinal group for $1.1 billion but sold its automotive businesses. Part of Labinal's holdings included Turbomeca, which produced nearly $1 billion worth of turbine engines for helicopters and fixed-wing military planes. Snecma also acquired the British engine nacelle/thrust reverser manufacturer

Hurel-Dubois in 2000, which it soon consolidated with Hispano-Suiza to form Hurel-Hispano.

Between 1995 and 2000, sales rose 100 percent, reaching FRF 36.9 billion (EUR 5.65 billion), mostly on the strength of acquisitions. Exports accounted for most of the increase, while rapidly growing commercial sales accounted for 84 percent of the total.

PLANS FOR PRIVATIZING ARE POSTPONED

Plans to privatize Snecma were developed throughout 2001. A merger of Snecma's ballistic propulsion activities with those of rocket engine and munitions manufacturer SNPE, was also under consideration. The French government planned to sell a quarter of Snecma in an initial public offering if market conditions were favorable, hoping to garner EUR 1.5 billion from the sale. These plans were put on hold after the September 11 terrorist attacks against the United States produced a downturn in the markets. The EUR 500 million SNPE merger, dubbed the Herakles project, had begun to fall apart over the question of leadership.

During the year, Snecma entered a joint venture with Rolls-Royce to produce engines for the next generation of European military aircraft. It had also tapped low-cost, quality Russian engineering talent from NPO Saturn to develop a new engine for regional jets. A collaboration between Snecma and FiatAvio (Italy), ITP (Spain), MTU Aero Engines (Germany), Rolls-Royce, and Techspace Aero (Belgium) was developing a turboprop engine for the Airbus A400M military transport. Meanwhile, Snecma Services entered a maintenance, repair, and overhaul venture with Sabena Technics.

HISTORY OF SAGEM

Marcel Môme created the Société d'Applications Générales de l'Electricité et de la Mécanique (SAGEM) in Paris in 1924. Formed initially to produce tools and other equipment for French tire maker Michelin, Môme, who remained at the head of the company until 1962, soon turned to the defense industry. After the end of World War II, the company became still more closely involved in the country's defense and aeronautics industries. The company continued its defense focus through the leadership of its second president, Robert Labarre, who took over the lead of the company from Môme and remained in place until 1987.

Although SAGEM remained primarily a defense contractor, the company also branched out into the telecommunications sector, perfecting a line of telex

machine products to become the world's second largest manufacturer in the category. SAGEM's emphasis on research and development enabled it quickly to capture the world leadership in the next generation of screen-based telex machines, which appeared in the early 1980s. By then, however, a new type of communications product was appearing on the market, threatening SAGEM's position.

FACSIMILE TECHNOLOGY EMERGES AS A MARKET-SHAPING FORCE

The arrival of the first facsimile machines, a technology developed in Japan, promised a new means of communication—and the end of the dominance of the costlier telex machine. The facsimile machine, although still mostly confined to businesses, promised to become a household appliance by the early 1990s. Caught by surprise, most of the European electronics community, including heavyweights such as Alcatel and Siemens, found itself outpaced by such Asian rivals as Matsushita, Samsung, and Canon.

Rather than attempt to enter the head-to-head competition for the facsimile market, yet eager to save the market position built up through its telex sales, SAGEM took an approach different from that of its larger European competitors. Instead of risking its own resources on developing the technology to produce its own facsimile machines, particularly given the high cost of developing first-generation technology, SAGEM entered a distribution agreement with Japan's Murata, in which the French company took over the marketing of two of Murata's low-end and mid-level facsimile (fax) machines in Europe. The agreement also called for SAGEM to adapt the fax machines to the various specifications of the European market—an area in which the company's long leadership of the telex machine market had given it ample experience.

By the mid-1980s the competition to produce the first generation of fax machines had exhausted many of SAGEM's would-be competitors. SAGEM, which had used its Murata distribution deal as a stepping-stone to developing and perfecting its own fax machine technology, now prepared to enter the fray. By then the company was also boasting new management, as Pierre Faurre, leading a management buyout of the company in 1985, prepared to take over the reins from Robert Labarre.

Faurre would be credited with reshaping SAGEM into one of France's and Europe's leading high-technology specialists. Graduating at the top of his class at the elite French university Polytechnique, Faurre had earned a Ph.D. at Stanford University before joining the prestigious Corps des Mines in 1967. At the same time, Faurre joined in establishing the French Research Institute of Computer Science and Automation (IN-RIA), while serving as a technical consultant for SAGEM. Faurre formally joined SAGEM in 1972, first as the company's general secretary, then as its general manager in 1983.

HIGH-TECHNOLOGY LEADER

Faurre had immediately grasped the importance of the new fax machines and the need for SAGEM to compete in this new arena—particularly as it threatened to render the telex all but obsolete. At the same time, the emerging political climate, as the Soviet Union introduced new liberties—and prepared to collapse by decade's end—spelled the end of the era of huge defense budgets, placing SAGEM in the position of seeing the collapse of its primary market as well.

In 1987, after Faurre was named chairman and CEO of the company, SAGEM entered the battle for the fax machine manufacturing market. During the company's distribution agreement with Murata, its own research and development component, which comprised nearly one-third of its workforce, had not only allowed the company to catch up to its competitors, but also to surpass them with cutting-edge innovations. As such, the first SAGEM fax machine was also the smallest to feature the A4 format size. SAGEM continued to post innovations in the category, adding screen menus to its fax machines in 1988.

In 1989 the company helped to revolutionize the fax machine market when it introduced the first machine capable of printing on standard paper, instead of the expensive thermal paper used by earlier machines. The company also saw rising sales, topping the FRF 10 billion mark in 1990, with communications products taking a growing share against the company's defense sector revenues.

The new machine helped boost SAGEM to the ranks of the world's leading fax machine manufacturers—and enabled the company to capture the European leadership early in the 1990s. The company also extended its product range, which allowed it to end its distribution agreement with Murata. SAGEM's experience in the European market gave it a competitive edge against its Japanese competitors, who tended to introduce standard models that then had to be adapted to each of the various country-specific norms then in place throughout the Continent. SAGEM was able instead to produce its models for each specific market, which placed the company's machines in high demand

among such third parties as France Telecom, British Telecom, Telefax, Impronta, Alcatel, and Siemens. By the early 1990s less than one-third of SAGEM's production actually bore the company's own name.

CREATING A NEW MARKET FOR FAX TECHNOLOGY

In 1991 SAGEM helped again to revolutionize the fax machine market when it launched the first machines destined to be sold not to corporations, but to individual consumers. The new generation of machines, sold in department stores, also became a significant part of a growing movement toward home offices, even before the appearance of widespread Internet access. The movement into the consumer market encouraged the company to strengthen its mass production facilities, as SAGEM began building a manufacturing network into such countries as Germany, Brazil, Spain, the United States, and the Czech Republic by the end of the decade.

By controlling almost the totality of its production—from the design to production of components—SAGEM had given itself a strong high-technology foundation. The company's excellence in communications technologies was to stand it in good stead as the years leading up to the 21st century quickly proved to be the inauguration of a new era in communication. The perfection of mobile telephony to the new digital television technologies and the debut of the so-called Net economy, as well as the refinement of electronic automotive and other systems, all represented potential bonanzas for SAGEM. By the mid-1990s SAGEM had developed a reputation as a highly successful high-tech niche player, with communications products ranging from its fax machines, credit card readers, and digital set-top boxes.

The company entered the automotive market in the mid-1990s. Adapting its technology to automotive control systems and other automotive components enabled the company quickly to place itself among the top ranks of European automobile electronics suppliers. The company also started an acquisition drive to expand its technology reach, buying Souriau Diagnostique, a maker of engine controls, and Eyquem, which manufactured more than 75 million spark plugs per year. Meanwhile, the company made a foray into televisions, purchasing Kasui. In addition, SAGEM was making a mark in the race to provide digital set-top boxes and decoders for satellite television, especially in the United States, providing decoders for the Echostar system.

GROWING ON THE STRENGTH OF COMMUNICATIONS TECHNOLOGY

By the mid-1990s SAGEM's revenues had climbed to more than FRF 15 billion. The company had easily weathered the extended economic crisis as well, posting steady increases in net profits, which neared FRF 550 million in 1995. The company's international sales also were taking an increasingly prominent place in SA-GEM's balance sheet, reaching one-third of total sales. By then, too, the company's communications products had outpaced, in large part, its defense sector activity, which accounted for only 22 percent of its sales. SA-GEM's automotive branch, launched in the mid-1990s, quickly grew to match the size of the company's defense division. However, communications products continued to provide the fuel for the company's growth.

The company had placed itself, meanwhile, in prime position to reap the benefits of the coming explosion in the mobile telephone market. Although the mobile telephones at first were restricted for the most part to a corporate market, the definition of a European-wide GSM (Global System for Mobile communications) mobile telephony standard, the deregulation of Europe's telephone markets, and the introduction of competition, as former national telephone monopolies were shattered, helped introduce the mobile telephone to the mass market. Beginning in 1997, with the appearance of affordable mobile telephones and consumer-oriented subscription plans, sales of mobile telephones skyrocketed. SAGEM quickly became one of the world's leading manufacturers of GSM telephones, and the undisputed French leader, with some 50 percent of the market.

BENEFITING FROM THE NET-BASED ECONOMY

Even as SAGEM's fortunes soared with the mobile telephone booming, it also was reaping the rewards of strong investment in Internet and networking technologies, as the world's economies began a shift toward the Net-based economy. At the same time, SAGEM benefited as France and other countries stepped up their levels of defense spending, replacing aging equipment with new, cutting-edge systems. By 1999 the company sales leaped more than 19 percent from the year before, topping FRF 22.3 billion. SAGEM also was eminently profitable, with net profits nearing the FRF 1 billion mark. In that year the company helped boost its defense division with the acquisition of defense technology company SFIM, formerly held by French investment bank Paribas and nuclear powerhouse Framatome.

In 2000 SAGEM hoped to improve on its already strong performance, forecasting rises in revenues of as much as 30 percent. After turning around the money-losing SFIM operation, that subsidiary and others were consolidated as operating divisions of SAGEM. The company was optimistic about the adoption of the next-generation WAP (wireless access protocol) telephones. The rollout of that technology, however, did not meet with the anticipated acceptance by mid-2000. Nonetheless, the convergence of the Internet with the mobile telephone seemed a near certainty as the new century got under way. SAGEM's position at the technology center promised strong growth for the future.

CREATING SAFRAN

During the early years of the 2000s many industries, including those related to communications and aerospace, underwent periods of transformation and consolidation. Snecma and SAGEM decided to join forces in a deal which was announced in October 2004. Until earlier that year, the French government retained 97 percent ownership in Snecma. Its plans for partial privatization set forth in early 2001 had remained on hold due to a continued downturn in the aviation industry. Nevertheless, the government went ahead with its initial public offering, selling a 35 percent stake in the company and raising nearly $1.74 billion from the sale.

The merger, thought to be partially orchestrated by then Finance Minister Nicolas Sarkozy, was met with criticism. A November 2004 *Flight International* article commented on the doubt surrounding the deal claiming: "France's financial community has certainly reacted with skepticism to the merger of Snecma and Sagem, viewing it, not as a logical consolidation of two highly regarded technology companies, but as an opportunistic attempt by the French government to create another industrial superhero spanning aircraft engines and hardware, defense electronics and mobile phones, as well as to cash in on the sale of a billion euros of its Snecma shares." The French government responded to the criticism, denying reports that it had proposed the merger.

The deal reached fruition in 2005 and created the world's 14th largest defense company with revenues slated to reach $14 billion. Dubbed SAFRAN—the French word for "rudder"—the merged companies believed the union created a global powerhouse that would benefit from complementary product lines. SAF-RAN's creation, however, failed to yield quick results. In fact, net income fell 60 percent in 2006 and the company's management team was in turmoil after several executive members resigned. When the dust settled on management changes, Jean-Paul Herteman was left at the helm.

Herteman quickly set forth a new business plan focused on SAFRAN's core aerospace, defense, and security activities. The company sold its SAGEM Communications arm to The Gores Group in early 2008 for approximately $560.9 million. It also set plans in motion to jettison its mobile phones business. With net income on the rise in 2007, it appeared as though SAFRAN's strategy was sound. During 2008 the company purchased SDU, a leading European supplier of secure identification documents, and Printrak, Motorola's U.S.-based biometrics business. In addition the company's lucrative partnership with General Electric was renewed until 2040. While only time would tell if the creation of SAFRAN would pay off in the long run, the company's management team was confident it was on track for success in the years to come.

Frederick C. Ingram; M. L. Cohen
Updated, Christina M. Stansell

PRINCIPAL SUBSIDIARIES

Snecma S.A.; SAGEM S.A.

PRINCIPAL DIVISIONS

Aerospace Propulsion; Aircraft Equipment; Defense Security.

PRINCIPAL COMPETITORS

The Boeing Company; GE Aviation; Rolls-Royce Corporation.

FURTHER READING

Boyer, Michael, "CFM International Flying High," *Cincinnati Enquirer*, January 23, 1995, p. D1.

———, "French Partnership Lifts GE; Venture's Health Appears Robust," *Cincinnati Enquirer*, March 13, 2001, p. B5.

Burt, Tim, "Two Months to Light on the Right Logo: Tim Burt on the Marriage of Landing Gear Makers Dowty and Messier," *Financial Times*, Companies & Finance Sec., August 13, 1996, p. 18.

Chadeau, Emmanuel, "Contraintes technologiques et stratégies internationales: le moteur d'aviation, 1920–1970," *Entreprises et Histoire*, April 1992, pp. 61–78.

Cox, Bob, "Grand Prairie Copter Firm Sold; Turbomeca's French Parent Company Is Bought," *Fort Worth Star-Telegram*, May 6, 2000, p. 2.

Edgecliffe-Johnson, Andrew, "TI Ends French Aerospace Link-Up; Three-Year-Old Venture Halted by £207m Disposal,"

Financial Times, Companies & Markets Sec., December 11, 1997, p. 23.

"Flourishing Snecma Shrugs Off State-Ownership Stereotype," *Interavia*, May 1999, p. 30.

Gallard, Philippe, "Comment SAGEM a conquis le fax Europen," *Le Nouvel Economiste*, November 25, 1994, p. 66.

"General Electric, Snecma Plan New Plant in France," *Aviation Week & Space Technology*, November 3, 1980, p. 218.

"Herakles: un enjeu capital pour Snecma," *Le Figaro*, September 11, 2001.

Jacquier, Jean-Francois, "SAGEM, l'empire des niches," *L'Expansion*, June 11, 1995, p. 62.

Jasper, Chris, "SNECMA Services Seeks Partner to Expand On-Wing Engine Repairs," *Flight International*, October 17, 2000, p. 30.

Lamm, Patrick, Philippe Escande, and Vincent Collen, "Interview: Le president de SAGEM, Pierre Faurre," *Les Echos*, January 11, 2000, p. 16.

———, "Premiere World Orders Digital TV Decoders from SAGEM," *European Report*, September 2, 2000.

———, "SAGEM Embellishing European Market Position," *Wireless Today*, October 15, 1999.

Macrae, Duncan, "Restructured Snecma Flying Out of Turbulence," *Interavia*, July/August 1997, p. 21.

Macrae, Duncan, and Antony Angrand, "Snecma Enjoys View from the Top," *Interavia*, February 2001, pp. 10–12.

Mallet, Victor, "France to Sell Off a Quarter of Snecma," *Financial Times*, Companies & Finance International, June 25, 2001, p. 24.

———, "Snecma to Delay Listing While Markets Suffer," *Financial Times*, Companies & Finance International, September 18, 2001, p. 32.

Marsh, David, "Snecma Takes Half Share in $2.7 Billion US Air Force Order," *Financial Times*, January 17, 1985.

Morrison, Murdo, "Searching for Synergies at Safran," *Flight International*, June 14, 2005.

———, "A Very French Affair," *Flight International*, November 9, 2004.

Norris, Guy, "Overhauls Bolster a Strong Market," *Financial Times*, Survey—Aerospace, June 18, 2001, p. 9.

"Reversing the Flow," *Flight International*, January 26, 1994.

Rothman, Andrea, "Safran Returning to Its Aviation Roots," *International Herald Tribune*, November 9, 2007.

"Safran at Peace; Looks Abroad for Growth," *Forecast International Defense Intelligence Newsletters*, November 5, 2008.

"SEP Modifying Programs After Merger," *Aviation Week & Space Technology*, August 13, 1984, p. 81.

Shifrin, Carole A., "TI Group, Snecma Combine Landing Gear Businesses," *Aviation Week & Space Technology*, March 14, 1994, p. 28.

Skapinker, Michael, "French Inherit Dowty Spirit," *Financial Times*, Companies & Finance Sec., December 12, 1997, p. 26.

"Snecma Awaits Recovery for Privatization," *Forecast International,* November 10, 2003.

"Snecma Prepares for Privatization," *Aviation Week & Space Technology,* January 1, 2001, p. 43.

"Snecma Seeks Larger Role in Engine Project," *Aviation Week & Space Technology,* January 25, 1982, p. 36.

"Snecma Set for More Consolidation," *Interavia,* July/August 2001, pp. 28–29.

"Snecma Sets Recovery Plan for CFM56 Engine Production," *Aviation Week & Space Technology,* May 30, 1988, p. 27.

Sparaco, Pierre, "Snecma Program to Cut Engine Operating Costs," *Aviation Week & Space Technology,* April 8, 1996, p. 58.

———, "Snecma Sabena Joint Venture Seeks Engine MRO Growth," *Aviation Week & Space Technology,* May 21, 2001, pp. 70–71.

———, "Snecma Seeks Efficiency Gains to Counter Declining Sales," *Aviation Week & Space Technology,* May 16, 1994, p. 35.

———, "Snecma Services Completes Extensive Restructuring," *Aviation Week & Space Technology,* April 2, 2001, pp. 98–99.

Sutton, Oliver, "Snecma Chief Looks to Future, and Partner?" *Interavia,* July/August 1999, p. 22.

Taverna, Michael A., and Pierra Sparaco, "Is Bigger Better?" *Aviation Week & Space Technology,* November 8, 2004.

Taverna, Michael A., "Snecma Pins Growth on New Service Set-Up," *Aviation Week & Space Technology,* March 29, 1999, pp. 81f.

———, "Snecma, Russian Partners Plan Regional Airliner Engine," *Aviation Week & Space Technology,* October 4, 2001, p. 69.

———, "Turbomeca Buy Gives Snecma a Foothold in the Turboshaft Market," *Aviation Week & Space Technology,* September 4, 2000, p. 41.

Schincariol Participações e Representações S.A.

Avenue Primo Schincariol 2222/2300
Itu, São Paulo 13312-900
Brazil
Telephone: (55 11) 4022-9500
Fax: (55 11) 4022-9555
Web site: http://www.schincariol.com.br

Private Company
Founded: 1939
Employees: 8,500
Sales: $2.67 billion (2007 est.)
NAICS: 312111 Soft Drink Manufacturing; 312120
    Breweries

■ ■ ■

Schincariol Participações e Representações S.A. is an increasingly endangered species in the 21st century: a large, family owned beverage producer not in the hands of a multinational giant. Although Schincariol turns out a range of soft drinks, it is best known for its David vs. Goliath struggle in Brazil, which ranks fourth among nations in beer consumption, against InBev S.A., the Belgium-based world's largest beer producer. Although a relatively young brewer, Schincariol has carved out a significant share of this large market. The group operates through several companies, not all of them engaged in beverages.

BASEMENT ORIGINS

Pietro Schincariol was an Italian who arrived in Brazil around 1900 with his father and brother. They had little

money but much experience in the production of wine and distilled beverages. Pietro and his wife—also an Italian immigrant—had children, who by the 1930s, were grown and living in various parts of the state of São Paulo. Son Primo Schincariol and his wife moved to Itu in 1938 and with only BRL 8,000 ($667) opened a business in the basement of their home, producing a tutti-frutti flavored soda that they named Itubáina in honor of the town. They also produced a cocoa liquor, cognac, anisette, and quinine-treated wine. These beverages were distributed in bottles washed by hand and delivered to local merchants by donkey.

In the 1960s Schincariol transformed itself from a family business—although by then one of significant size—to a corporation. During this period the family purchased modern equipment to speed production. They rented land in Itu in 1964 and erected a plant with a few manual and semiautomatic machines. The facility functioned with about 30 employees. Its products were sold door-to-door, still only in Itu. José Nelson Schincariol and his brother Gilberto, although still youths, were emerging as the future leaders of the enterprise.

In 1977, the Schincariols signed a ten-year agreement with the Antarctica brewery, which undertook to bottle their soda. When the agreement expired, however, they rejected a proposed 20-year pact that would have ended their role as producers of soft drinks. Instead, they decided not only to resume bottling and distributing their product but also to make beer—an old dream of Primo's that was fulfilled in 1989 with the introduction of the Pilsen-style brew named Schincariol. Some

COMPANY PERSPECTIVES

To transform the Schincariol brands into market leaders so that they are seen as a synonym of quality and excellence in products and services. To generate satisfactory income levels for distribution networks within national and uniform standards, permitting self-sustainability and continuous reinvestment in the business. To consolidate an entrepreneurial culture of the Schincariol Group with its employees, clients, suppliers and partners that is based on the belief and example of the Schincariol family with its determination to grow through hard work, faith and the pride of being Brazilian.

50,000 to 100,000 crates of beer were produced each month.

In 1997 mineral water was added to the Schincariol line. Before the century ended, Schincariol beverages were available not only in Brazil but in numerous countries abroad. In 2002 the company introduced a beer named Primus in honor of its founder. Nova Schin, launched the following year, despite its higher price achieved remarkable success, which was attributed to its smooth flavor and award winning advertising campaign. Also introduced that year was another beer, Glacial. Between 1998 and 2004 Schincariol nearly doubled its share of the Brazilian beer market. Its revenues nearly tripled between 1997 and 2003, a period in which it built five factories beyond its home base in São Paulo.

FACING CHALLENGES

Schincariol was also expanding in other beverages. Skinka, an energy fruit drink, was introduced in 2002. Schin citrus drinks and tonic water and Tuca soft drinks were added the following year. Schin Cola Citrus made its debut in 2004, when the company also added N52, a beer with tequila and lemon flavors that the company called the first "aromatized" beer in Brazil. In 2005 Schincariol partnered with the Cartoon Network in presenting a new line of soft drinks, Mini Schin, aimed for the children's market.

Expansion took a toll, however. Schincariol invested large sums to build its five new plants in areas where competition for beer drinkers was less intense than in the state of São Paulo. Two more plants opened in 2004. To launch Nova Schin, a beer priced 70 percent higher than Schincariol but of better quality—and still lower in price than the competition—the company spent about $50 million in advertising and marketing costs, plus an additional $70 million or so over the next two years during a media blitz that repeated continuously a simple—and in the end, persuasive—slogan: *Experimenta!* (Try It!). Nevertheless, Companhia de Bebidas de Américas (AmBev), owner of the Brahma, Antarctica, and Skol brands, still held at least two-thirds of the market. Schincariol suffered an operating loss in 2000, another one in 2001, and a much larger one in 2002.

José Nelson Schincariol, the company president, was murdered two weeks before the introduction of Nova Schin, shot three times as he was parking his car in the garage of his home. The crime, never solved, was attributed to an unsuccessful attempt at robbery. Nelson, as he was called, was not easy to replace; a workaholic, he had devoted his life to the business, never taking a vacation. His death initially placed the firm under a hastily formed directorate of veteran executives who had previously reported to him. Among them were his sons, Alexandre and Adriano, his brother Gilberto, and nephews Gilberto, Jr., and José Augusto.

It was Adriano who, although only 27, emerged as chief executive of Schincariol. He had started in the sales department when only 17 and had passed by stages through all the other areas and was director of marketing at the time of his father's death. In that position he was waging a costly and increasingly bitter war against AmBev, which stole Nova Schin's chief spokesperson, pop singer Zeca Pagodinho, and then featured him promoting Brahma in its own television commercials—even before the singer's contract with Schincariol had expired. Adriano claimed that his company was frozen out of nearly one-fifth of the bars, shops, and restaurants in São Paulo because of exclusive contracts with AmBev. Furthermore, AmBev had no scruples about launching a price war to undercut rivals.

LEGAL TROUBLES

By mid-2004, however, all the cost and effort had proved worthwhile. Schincariol had passed Cervejarias Kaiser Brasil S.A. to become Brazil's second largest beer company, and Adriano Schincariol claimed that his company's sales had climbed 50 percent in only four months. The enterprise's subsidiary in northeastern Brazil had risen to number one in its sector. Schincariol also told a reporter that two-thirds of the heavy debt the enterprise had taken on was in the form of low cost loans from BNDES, Brazil's government-owned development bank.

However, AmBev—which merged with InterBrew S.A. in 2004 to form InBev, the world's leading

KEY DATES ▪

1939: Primo Schincariol and his wife begin producing homemade beverages in Itu, São Paulo.

1964: The Schincariols rent land in Itu to build a factory for their enterprise.

1977: The Schincariols sign a ten-year bottling agreement with the Antarctica brewery.

1989: Schincariol introduces its first beer, a Pilsen-style brew.

1997: Mineral water is added to the Schincariol line.

2003: José Nelson Schincariol, company president, is murdered while parking his car in the garage of his home; introduction of Nova Schin solidifies Schincariol's position among beer producers.

2004: Schincariol is Brazil's second largest brewery.

2005: Schincariol's facilities are raided and its executives arrested for tax fraud and other charges.

2007: Schincariol purchases two premium beers aimed at a more profitable segment of the market.

brewery—was not finished playing hardball. After Brazilian officials found Schincariol's beers being sold at reduced prices on the border with Argentina and Paraguay, AmBev accused its rival of raising money for its expansion by evading taxes. In 2005 federal police raided Schincariol's offices and breweries, arresting more than 70 people in 12 states, including Adriano and other senior executives in what was named Operação Cevada (Operation Barley). The police accused Schincariol and some of its distributors of underreporting sales, illegal purchases of raw materials, and submitting false tax returns in order to cheat the government.

As a result of the tax imbroglio, the development bank placed curbs on Schincariol's borrowing for a time. Even so, the company continued to make new acquisitions. In 2006 it purchased Baden Baden, produced by the artisanal microbrewery Campos do Jordão in São Paulo, and Conny Indústria e Comércio de Sucos e Refrigerantes Ltda., a soft drink producer in the state of Alagoas. Its sales rose 18 percent during the year, with beer accounting for 71 percent of the total.

In early 2007 Schincariol hired Fernando Terni, president of Nokia Corporation's Brazilian subsidiary, to be its chief executive officer. Terni first assembled a new team of executives, a task, in spite of attractive salaries

offered, not made easy by the company's equivocal reputation. He even had trouble recruiting outsiders for the board of directors. Next, he cleaned up the practices that had led to the tax scandal. Finally, he decided to reduce Schincariol's dependence on Nova Schin. During 2007 the company invested over BRL 250 million (about $132 million) to purchase two additional beers: Devassa (from Rio de Janeiro-based Cerveja Devassa) and Nobel (from Bebidas Igarassu). These were premium beers aimed at a more profitable segment of the market. Young & Rubicam, Inc.'s, Brazilian subsidiary and W/Brasil were hired to promote the new brands.

EXPANDING DISTRIBUTION AND MARKET SHARE

Terni also took measures to shore up Schincariol's shaky distribution system. The enterprise was losing shelf space both in areas where it had long been strong, such as the interior of the state of São Paulo, and in areas where it had always had problems establishing a presence, such as Rio de Janeiro and west-central Brazil. Schincariol increased the number of its own distribution centers from 8 to 42, the majority of them in southeastern Brazil. Other distributors were replaced, especially in the northeast, where Schincariol was strongest and where it opened another brewery at the beginning of 2008.

Schincariol held 13.6 percent of Brazil's beer market at the end of 2007. It sought in 2008 to shore up its weakness in Rio de Janeiro—where its share of the market was only 1.5 percent—by purchasing from AmBev the Cintra brand, which also had a presence in the states of Espirito Santo, Minas Gerais, and the interior of São Paulo. Also during the year the company bought Eisenbahn, an artisanal beer made in Blumenau, Santa Catarina. These acquisitions brought to eight the number of beer companies controlled by Schincariol and to 14 the number of its plants. The artisanal beers that Schincariol had acquired were to be featured in 22 bars to be opened by the end of 2008 and 100 by 2012. Ninety of these were expected to be franchised operations, with the others wholly owned and operated by Schincariol.

Schincariol had a significant presence in other beverages. The company had been producing the soft drinks Iturbina and Magã since 1954. Schincariol mineral water, from seven springs, was available with or without carbonation and also with lemon. Frothos, introduced in 2007, was a new line of fruit drinks and came in grape, orange, mango, passion fruit, guava, and peach flavors. A diet version was also available in grape, peach, mango, and passion fruit. Also new was Skinka, a fruit drink line for children in purple and red and also in citrus flavored yellow and green. A line of Schin soft drinks called *refrigerantes* was offered in guaraná, cola, orange, and lemon flavors, with the former two also available in a diet version. The company was also producing Schin tonic water.

Many observers saw Schincariol as the next South American brewery to inevitably be swallowed up in the hectic competition between the world's major beer producers. The chief suitor was said to be the world's second largest brewer, SABMiller plc, which reportedly had taken itself out of the running, but only temporarily, because of the tax scandal. Adriano Schincariol denied any interest in selling the company and said all its actions were intended to keep the enterprise under family control.

Robert Halasz

PRINCIPAL SUBSIDIARIES

Cia. de Bebidas do Rio de Janeiro; Primo Schincariol Indústria e Comércio de Cervejas e Refrigerantes do Nordeste S.A.; Schincariol Indústria e Comércio de Cervejas e Refrigerantes do Norte-Nordeste S.A.; Schincariol Indústria e Comércio de Cervejas e Refrigerantes S.A.; Primo Schincariol Indústria e Refrigerantes do Nordeste S.A.; Schincariol Participações e Repreentações S.A.

PRINCIPAL COMPETITORS

Cervejerias Kaiser Brasil S.A.; Companhia de Bebidas das Américas.

FURTHER READING

Almeida, Gilberto, "Entre a Tragédia e o Sucesso," *Exame Melhores e Maiores,* July 2004, pp. 200, 202.

Benson, Todd, "Brazil: No. 2 Brewery Raided in Tax Inquiry," *New York Times,* June 16, 2005, p. C4.

Caetano, José Roberto, "Tempo de Experimentar," *Exame,* October 15, 2003, pp. 50–52.

Euromonitor International, "Analysis: Schincariol Back on Track and Attracting Attention," http://www.just-drinks.com, March 21, 2007.

Onaga, Marcelo, "Agora Começa a Fase Dois," *Exame,* December 19, 2007, pp. 68–70.

Samor, Geraldo, "Battle Brews in Brazil's Beer Market," *Wall Street Journal,* September 29, 2004, p. B2B.

———, "Brewers' Brawl Breaks Out in Brazil," *Wall Street Journal,* April 19, 2004, p. B6.

Walsh, Andrea, "Molson's Brazil Suds Sales Go Flat," *Toronto Star,* July 4, 2004, p. C3.

Scolari's Food and Drug Company

255 South McCarran Boulevard
Sparks, Nevada 89431-5809
U.S.A.
Telephone: (775) 331-7700
Toll Free: (800) 439-0635
Fax: (775) 331-2860
Web site: http://www.scolaristores.com

Private Company
Incorporated: 1982 as Scolari's Warehouse Markets
Employees: 1,400
Sales: $300 million (2007 est.)
NAICS: 445110 Supermarkets and Other Grocery (except Convenience) Stores

■ ■ ■

Based in Sparks, Nevada, Scolari's Food and Drug Company is the largest privately held supermarket chain in northern Nevada with 12 stores, including six in Reno, and single stores in Fernley, Gardnerville, Sparks, Sun Valley, Tonopah, and Yerington. The family-owned company also operates four stores in California's Central Coast area in Paso Robles, Pismo Beach, San Luis Obispo, and Santa Barbara. Nine of the Nevada units are superstores, featuring several specialty departments, including pharmacies, bakery/delis, video rentals, and floral. In addition, the Scolari family operates two Reno stores and one in Carson City under the Sak 'N Save banner and franchises a Save-A-Lot store in Las Vegas. Subsidiary Bavarian Wholesale Grocery supplies the stores from its Sparks warehouse.

Scolari's Food and Drug is run by brothers Joey and Jerry Scolari, who share the chief executive role. Their father, Joseph Scolari, is chairman of the board. Although the Scolaris are known as hands-on owners, paying regular visits to their chain of stores, they also delegate a great deal of authority to store managers and employees to better serve the needs of their customers, a policy that provides an edge against much larger competitors, which may not be able to adapt as quickly to changing market conditions. The Scolari stores are also very active in their communities. The company's Friendship Fund helps nonprofit organizations to raise money by allowing shoppers to designate 1 percent of their shopping orders to individual charities.

FAMILY OPENS FIRST GROCERY STORE

Although Scolari's operations are the result of a 1982 acquisition of an existing supermarket chain, the company dates its origins to 1947 when Joseph Scolari and his father opened a grocery store in the town of Orcutt in California's Central Coast region. Scolari lived nearby and his sons, Joey and Jerry, grew up helping out in the store. "We were Dad's best help," Joey Scolari told *Supermarket News* in 2004. "Whether it was unloading trucks or sweeping floors, we did it all. It was hard work." The elder Scolari opened more stores and his sons, in time, assumed management positions. Joey elected to leave the family business to enroll in college and try a different career. He returned, however, managing and turning around an underperforming store, and then working at the corporate level, serving as the chain's liquor buyer.

Joseph Scolari's chain grew at an increased rate in the 1970s, helped in part by the acquisitions of Jordanos stores. Like the Scolaris, the Jordano family operated a chain of 13 independent supermarkets, but finding it increasingly difficult to compete against the larger chains, the Jordanos elected to sell their stores, eventually transforming the remaining operations into a successful broad-line foodservice and beverage distribution company. By 1979 Joseph Scolari owned a chain of 11 supermarkets and was ready to cash in on a lifetime of effort. He offered to sell the business to his two sons, but in the end the family decided the best option was to sell the stores to Lucky Stores Inc., which bought the Scolari supermarkets in 1979 and converted them to the Lucky banner.

As part of the sale, the Scolari family signed a limited noncompete agreement that barred them from the supermarket business for a time. As a result, the Scolari brothers began developing shopping centers and tried their hand at the convenience store sector, but as soon as possible they returned to the supermarket business. They bought a Mayfair Market in Hanford, California, in 1980, followed later in the year by the purchase of the family's old Orcutt store.

REBUILDING AS SCOLARI'S WAREHOUSE MARKETS

The crucial step in rebuilding the Scolari chain came in 1982 when they heard that a man named Don Baldwin was looking to sell his struggling operation that included 12 Warehouse Markets and two Reno Shop 'N Kart stores. Not only was the company deep in debt, operating expenses were far too high for the operation to be profitable. Nevertheless, the Scolari family believed the acquisition was a risk worth taking. Joseph Scolari became chairman of the company, known as Scolari's Warehouse Markets, but remained in California to run a small chain of supermarkets that for the time being were housed under a different corporation, allowing his sons,

both in their mid- to late 20s at the time, to run the Nevada business on a day-to-day basis.

The elder Scolari was, however, always available to dispense advice. Aside from the practical, Joseph Scolari also instilled a strong sense of business ethics. Jim Minor, whose advertising agency worked with the family, recalled in a 2003 interview with the *Reno Gazette-Journal* a time when Scolari scolded a consultant who urged the family to "attack" the competition. "We are in awe of our competition," Scolari insisted. "We respect them." Rather than attack the competition, he preferred to learn from them.

The Scolaris nevertheless faced a daunting task in turning around the Warehouse Markets stores. To get expenses in line with margins, they had to lower their labor costs, resulting in job cuts, a move that initially hurt their popularity with workers. To manage the enterprise, Joey and Jerry Scolari divided their responsibilities while sharing major power equally. Although they alternated the presidency each year, they made key decisions together, meeting frequently to address immediate issues as well as to formulate long-range plans. On a daily basis Joey assumed responsibility for grocery products, frozen products, and warehouse operations, while his younger brother focused on perishables.

SOUTH RENO SUPERSTORE OPENS

As part of the turnaround effort, the company began shifting away from the warehouse format, based on volume buying and low pricing, instead converting the units into conventional stores and superstores while adding the Scolari name. Some of the older stores were also shut down while others were remodeled. The company's precarious financial situation was soon stabilized and after two years Scolari's Warehouse Markets was profitable. The family could then turn its attention to opening new stores to replace the units that had been closed. This effort in the 1980s culminated in June 1987 with the opening of a South Reno superstore, which represented a major departure from all of the others stores in the market. "This store," Joey Scolari told *Progressive Grocer* at the time, "is the culmination of all the ideas we had about what a supermarket should be."

Outside, the store featured Spanish mission-style architecture and its pink façade offered an upscale look that was in marked contrast with every other area supermarket. Inside, the store offered 38,000 square feet of selling space but felt much smaller because of a small frontage dictated by the design of the shopping center, whose developer wanted to include a number of small shops in the front of the center. Thus, the supermarket spread out from its entrance, offering ample space for a

KEY DATES

■

1947: Joseph Scolari opens grocery store in Orcutt, California.
1979: Scolari sells 11-store chain to Lucky Stores Inc.
1982: Scolari's sons, Joey and Jerry, acquire 12 Warehouse Markets in Nevada.
1987: First superstore opens.
1988: Friendship Fund established.
1991: Company name changed to Scolari's Food and Drug Company.
1998: Two California stores sold.
2005: Food Club private-label line adopted.
2008: Sexual harassment charges settled.

deli, bakery, hand-dipped ice cream section, floral shop, seafood/meat department, a wine and liquor area, video rental and camera bar, pharmacy, and at the front of the store a bank of 20 slot machines—obligatory in the Reno market.

The store was ahead of its time in other ways as well. It included a computer-controlled refrigeration and energy management system, to take better care of items as well as to lower utility bills. Despite being twice as large as some of its other stores and running twice as many refrigerators and freezers, the new store consumed about the same amount of energy. It was also one of the first area stores equipped with EFT (electronic funds transfer) technology.

NAME CHANGE

Despite a grocery war in Reno that forced the company to slash prices and led to layoffs to contain costs, Scolari's Warehouse Markets was generating $170 million by the start of the 1990s. The chain at this stage consisted of 16 stores in northern Nevada, ranging in size from 17,000 square feet to 50,000 square feet. The company began phasing out the Warehouse Market name and focusing on the superstore category. Given this approach, the company changed its name in 1991 to Scolari's Food and Drug Company. A major part of the chain's plan for continued growth was the revamping of its bakery departments, one area that was hardly in the vanguard of its supermarket operations and had failed to keep up with the times. Part of the problem was the cuts to management staff that resulted from the price wars that lingered into the 1990s. To redress that shortcoming, in July 1990 the Scolari brothers hired a

new bakery adviser to replace the one they had previously let go. Lori Gunther, who had held a similar post in Salt Lake City with Smith's Food and Drug, was brought on and began updating the bakeries and delis, including equipment as well as product offerings.

Because many of its customers were dual-income families with limited time to shop, and many others were elderly, Scolari's introduced a home shopping and delivery service in the early 1990s that permitted customers to call or fax orders, which were then packed by employees at four of the stores serving as fulfillment centers. In essence, the new service was little more than the normal service provided by every grocer at the beginning of the 20th century, when telephone orders and neighborhood delivery boys were the norm, but nearly 100 years later the concept seemed like a novelty.

Also to drive the business in the new decade, Scolari's stepped up its community involvement efforts. Having established the Friendship Fund in 1988 to help support charitable organizations, in 1991 the chain promoted a recycling initiative by cosponsoring full-page ads in the *Reno Gazette-Journal* asking consumers to "Step on It" and do a better job of preparing aluminum cans and plastic products for recycling. The Reno stores also began working with a hospital to provide blood pressure checks and cholesterol screening, along with the dissemination of nutritional and other health information.

TWO CALIFORNIA STORES SOLD

In the mid-1990s the six family-owned California stores were folded into Scolari's Food and Drug. By 1998 the 22-store chain generated annual sales of $300 million, a significant portion of which came from the retail pharmacies and sale of over-the-counter products. This business was so important to Scolari's that it joined the National Association of Chain Drug Stores. Early in 1998 the company trimmed its portfolio, selling two of the stores, located in Hanford and Corcoran in the southern San Joaquin Valley, because they were not a good fit with the four other stores in the Central Coast area.

Scolari's Nevada holdings were cut further in the new century, eventually reduced to a dozen. Nevertheless, the chain remained the largest independent in northern Nevada and held its own against much larger chains. Part of Scolari's success came from empowering local store managers to make many decisions on their own, from ordering special products for their market to choosing which charities to fund. "If you let (employees) do what comes naturally," Joey Scolari told the *Reno Gazette-Journal* in 2003, "They are going to take care of the customer. That's the kind of people we are trying to hire and cultivate and have in our company." Store managers also delegated authority to people below them, and as a result Scolari's was quicker than larger rivals to adapt to changes in local markets.

In recognition of a half-century of contributions to the Central Coast grocery business the Scolari family— Joseph, Joey, and Jerry—were inducted as a group into the California Grocers Association Educational Foundation Hall of Achievement in 2003. Theirs was a highly competitive business, however, and what was achieved in the past offered no guarantee of success in the future. In addition to competition from publicly owned chains such as Albertsons, Smith's Food and Drug, Safeway, and Super Kmart, Scolari's by 2005 had to contend with Boise, Idaho-based WinCo Foods Inc. and its massive warehouse stores encroaching on the territory. Even more of a threat was Wal-Mart, which placed an ever-increasing role on grocery store operations and was making a concerted push in northern Nevada, opening several of its supercenters there. As part of an effort to better compete on price in this challenging environment, Scolari's built up its private-label product offerings in 2005 by adding several lines offers by Topco Associates, including the Food Club grocery line, Top Crest household products line, and Paws, a high-end pet food line.

FACING CHALLENGES

Another competitive edge Scolari's possessed was its solid reputation for food safety. In 2006 it became one of the first supermarket chains to receive NSF Food Safety & Quality Certification for food safety and quality. To receive the certification all of Scolari's stores participated in the "Shop Fresh" program of NSF International, a nonprofit public health and safety company that had been in operation for more than 60 years. The arduous program required that a certified food manager be on duty for every shift, and that food safety and sanitation audits and microbial monitoring be conducted monthly and meet NSF certification standards. Scolari's also looked to take advantage of technology to maintain its reputation for customer service and a shopper-friendly atmosphere in its stores. In late 2007 the company hired Revionics, a retail advanced pricing system developer, to serve as a technology partner in a price and promotion optimization program intended to attract and retain loyal customers.

Scolari's received some adverse publicity in 2008 when it had to contend with sexual harassment claims filed by 19 female employees, several of them teenagers. The U.S. Equal Employment Opportunity Commission charged that senior Scolari officers across multiple stores in the Reno area had engaged in lewd and inappropriate conduct and that Scolari's management, when faced with complaints, had done nothing to stop the unlawful conduct. In September 2008 the company agreed to pay $425,000 to the 19 women in order to settle the matter. Nevertheless, the company denied the claims, maintaining that it chose to settle the suit because a trial would be "too disruptive to the many Scolari's associates scheduled to testify."

Due to the effects of a faltering economy, Scolari's had to adjust to conditions in 2009. A hiring freeze was imposed and plans to expand were put on hold. For years Scolari's territory had experienced strong population growth and grocers were eager to open stores near the new housing developments. With the bursting of the housing bubble, however, every supermarket chain adopted a wait-and-see attitude. The fight was then over existing customers, a battle fought by providing excellent customer service. Even more important in times of economic crisis, the emphasis was on price. As a result, Scolari's held weekly meetings to review the food advertisements of the competition and craft a response. The times posed a challenge, but that was hardly new for a family involved in the grocery business for more than 60 years. "Someone once said, 'There's always a wolf at your door,'" Joey Scolari told the *Reno Gazette-Journal*. "So what you do this week is only as good as this week. We plan around that."

Ed Dinger

PRINCIPAL SUBSIDIARIES

Bavarian Wholesale Grocery.

PRINCIPAL COMPETITORS

Ralph's Grocery Company; Safeway Inc.; Wal-Mart Stores, Inc.

FURTHER READING

Bath, Alison, "A Family Affair," *Reno Gazette-Journal,* March 2, 2003, p. 1E.

Donegan, Priscilla, "Scolari's Big Payoff," *Progressive Grocer,* April 1988, p. 130.

Gattuso, Greg, "One Family's Survival," *Supermarket News,* November 24, 2004, p. 15.

Moses, Lucia, "Scolari's Switches to Topco Brands," *Supermarket News,* May 2, 2005, p. 133.

O'Driscoll, Bill, "Contact Gives Scolari's an Edge," *Reno Gazette-Journal,* February 18, 2009.

Riell, Howard, "At Scolari's, New Superstore Format Means Deli/Bakery Update," *Supermarket Business,* March 1991, p. 69.

"Scolari's Honored for Dedication to Food Safety, Quality," *Reno Gazette-Journal,* July 21, 2006, p. 1G.

Shell Vacations LLC

---

40 Skokie Boulevard, Suite 350
Northbrook, Illinois 60062-4600
U.S.A.
Telephone: (847) 564-4600
Fax: (847) 564-0703
Web site: http://www.shellvacationsonline.com

Private Company
Incorporated: 1963 as Shell Development Corporation
Employees: 2,246
Sales: $440.2 million (2007 est.)
NAICS: 531210 Offices of Real Estate Agents and
   Brokers

■ ■ ■

Shell Vacations LLC is a timeshare company based in the Chicago area. Through Shell Vacations Club, the company operates 23 resorts located in Arizona, California, Canada, Hawaii, Mexico, Nevada, New Hampshire, Oregon, Texas, and Wisconsin. The club's 120,000 owners and members are able to book time at the different resorts on a points basis. By purchasing a points package, members are in reality purchasing a real estate interest in a Home Club, where members are given priority. Each resort and unit type is awarded a points value, depending on location, time of year, and type of accommodation. Club points, awarded annually, are then redeemed by members as they see fit. Points can also be banked for the following year, borrowed from the next year, and even shared with other club members. Extra points can also be purchased if needed,

and unused points can be redeemed for accommodations outside of the Shell system, for air travel, cruises, spa treatments, whitewater rafting and other activities, and merchandise.

People with deeded weeks at any of the Shell resorts can convert their interest to membership in the club, established in 1999. Nevertheless, club members are still levied annual maintenance fees, as well as annual club fees, to cover the cost of the reservation system and exchange services, and members who bank points or take advantage of other options are subject to transaction fees. Serving as Shell's chairman and chief executive officer is cofounder Sheldon Harvey Ginsburg.

ORIGINS

Shell was cofounded by Sheldon Harvey Ginsburg, an accountant, and real estate lawyer Perry James Snyderman. The older of the two, Snyderman was born in Chicago in 1932, the son of a men's clothing store owner. He earned a degree in economics from Bradley University in 1954, followed by a law degree from De-Paul University Law School four years later, his postgraduate education interrupted by a stint in the Army when he was drafted at the end of the Korean War. Snyderman then went to work for a Chicago law firm, Rudnick & Wolfe, and began practicing real estate law.

Also born in Chicago, albeit six years later, Ginsburg was the eldest son of small business owners. His mother ran a women's clothing store while his father owned the Airway Fountain and Tobacco Store in downtown Chicago, a business he sold when Ginsburg

COMPANY PERSPECTIVES

Our Mission is to be the acknowledged provider of select branded leisure and vacation products and services by constantly refining an innovative, flexible, and quality points-based vacation club in a corporate culture that always places our employees, customers, owners and members at the heart of every activity. With our mission comes a powerful commitment that we make to every owner and member of Shell Vacations Club. Nothing matters more to us than their satisfaction—so we will do everything possible to make their membership rewarding in every way. Our commitment covers every aspect of membership, from the quality of our resorts, to the expertise of SVC Member Services Representatives, to the strategic business partners we choose. This is the spirit that has guided us to date, and that will continue to set us apart.

was 15 to begin selling real estate. Ginsburg graduated with a degree in commerce from DePaul University in 1959 and a year later became a certified public accountant. He went to work for the Chicago accounting firm of Beckerman, Terrell and Co. for two years before starting his own practice.

Ginsburg and Snyderman shared a tenuous family connection: Ginsburg's wife at the time was a distant cousin of Snyderman. The two men met for the first time at a family holiday party in 1962 and soon the accountant and attorney began referring business to one another and made some investments together. They also learned something about the hospitality industry. Ginsburg's first client, Max Stein, was the owner of three summer resorts in Elkhart Lake, Wisconsin, which catered to vacationers in the same way the Catskill resorts did for New Yorkers. When Stein tired of managing his Pine Point Resort, he asked if Ginsburg was interested in the post. Ginsburg enlisted Snyderman and a cousin, and together they spent Thursday through Sunday each week of the summer managing the resort and learning the business.

In 1963 Ginsburg and Snyderman deepened their business relationship when they became involved in real estate syndication. Moreover, Ginsburg became the accountant for Rudnick & Wolfe, and Snyderman served as the attorney for the accounting firm. Their first project, developed with a mutual client, was a Chicago building that included a pair of retail stores and ten apartments. Next, they bought a parking garage, demolished it, and on the site built a 68-unit apartment building, Surrey House. To announce the project they sent out a press release, which included Ginsburg's name. After some local papers printed the notice, Ginsburg was contacted by the Illinois Society for Certified Public Accountants and told that he was in effect advertising himself through the press release, a breach in ethics that could cost him his CPA license. To rectify the situation Ginsburg was told to form a "shell organization." Ginsburg complied, creating a company playfully called Shell Development Corporation, which would later change its name to Shell Group and one day become Shell Vacations LLC.

ENTERING THE TIMESHARE INDUSTRY

Through Shell Development, Ginsburg and Snyderman developed a variety of residential, commercial and retail, and office complexes. They became involved in the timeshare industry in 1978 when they acquired the Vistana Resort in Orlando, Florida, home of Disney World. With 98 condominiums and a 150-acre site capable of further development, Vistana had been foreclosed by First Wisconsin Real Estate Investment Trust and abandoned for almost three years. The partners paid a visit to find an unfinished property, including a hole where a swimming pool was to be installed, and what had been constructed was shoddy in both design and execution. Nevertheless, after Ginsburg and Snyderman took stock of the market, in particular Disney's rentals, they decided to buy the property. Backed by Continental Illinois National Bank and Trust Co., with whom they had done business, they hired a construction firm to complete Vistana and also hired someone to initiate condominium sales and manage the property, which opened in July 1978.

Only after the acquisition of Vistana did Ginsburg and Snyderman become aware of timesharing. They and some of Vistana's staff learned more at an American Land Development Association meeting, and in July 1980 Vistana began selling timeshare unit-weeks in a dozen of Vistana's condominiums. Shell Group sold Vistana at the end of 1986 to General Development Corporation for $33.7 million and the assumption of debt and agreed not to participate in the Florida timesharing business for a stipulated period.

Shell Group was involved in a host of development projects across the country aside from timeshare properties in the 1980s. Locked out of Florida, Shell Group decided to pursue timeshare projects elsewhere. An outside company brought to them a Hawaii property,

KEY DATES

1963: Perry Snyderman and Sheldon Ginsburg create Shell Development Corporation to engage in real estate development.

1978: Shell acquires Vistana Resort in Orlando, Florida.

1980: Vistana begins selling timeshare unit-weeks in a dozen condominiums.

1986: Vistana is sold; Shell agrees not to participate in the Florida timeshare business for a stipulated period.

1997: Shell Group merges with Grand Vacations Company, creating Shell Vacations LLC.

1999: Shell Vacations Club is launched.

2002: Ginsburg and others buy out Snyderman.

2004: Shell introduces a program franchising its points.

2008: Shell introduces the real-time satisfaction Market Metrix survey system.

Kona Coast Resort, originally a 14-acre, 68-unit property. Other Hawaii interests followed in the early 1990s. Shell Group acquired condominium inventory in Lawai Beach Resort and Pono Kai Resort, and acquired most of the units of Waikola Village. The company acquired Orange Tree Golf and Conference Center in Scottsdale, Arizona, a resort brought to Shell's attention by Ginsburg's son, Howard, a University of Arizona student who worked in the resort's marketing program. Timeshare projects were also developed in California. In addition, Shell Group participated in some joint ventures in the late 1980s, including Shell/Remic International, a California company that supported a wide variety of resort projects with planning, marketing, and sales services. Another joint venture, Shell Winners Circle, invested in Winners Circle Resorts International, Inc., from 1988 to 1994.

SHELL MERGES WITH GRAND VACATIONS

By 1995 Shell Group emerged as the fifth largest vacation interval ownership company, with properties in Arizona, California, Florida, Hawaii, and Canada. A year later the timeshare industry experienced a period of consolidation, and early in 1997 Shell Group followed suit by merging with Grand Vacations Company, the resulting company taking the name of Shell Vacations LLC. It was a deal that did not bring with it any

properties. Rather, Grand Vacations offered a wealth of expertise, in particular that of Edward H. McMullen, Sr., a major player in the vacation ownership industry since 1977 when he founded the American Resorts Group of Companies.

McMullen's company was responsible for a number of innovations in the vacation ownership field, and in 1984 he merged American resorts with Marriott Corporation to create the first international vacation ownership company. After leaving Marriott Ownership Resorts, Inc., in 1991, McMullen formed a joint venture with Hilton Grand Vacations Company, which he ran as managing director until selling his interest to Hilton Hotels Corp. in June 1996. Six months later he and three associates joined forces with Shell Group to create Shell Vacations. In essence, Shell Group added McMullen's name, while McMullen gained access to Shell's ready capital.

McMullen served as managing director for Shell Vacations until August 2000, when he sold his interest and pursued other opportunities. During his brief tenure with Shell, the company added properties in San Francisco, Arizona, and Hawaii, and opened a new national telemarketing center. Moreover, in 1999 Shell introduced Shell Vacations Club to pursue the new points format in vacation ownership, providing owners with a great deal more flexibility and access to a range of resort destinations. The move also helped to drive revenues, which grew fourfold from 1999 to 2002, increasing from $42 million to more than $160 million. A year later sales topped $190 million.

Two years after McMullen left, 70-year-old Perry Snyderman was also ready to leave the business. In June 2002 Ginsburg and his family, along with senior executives, bought out the cofounder's interest in the 13 resorts that comprised Shell Vacations. Despite the loss of his longtime partner, Ginsburg continued to grow Shell. The company looked for new properties in Hawaii, especially on the island of Maui. Shell also invested in the Little Sweden resort in Wisconsin and acquired its first Las Vegas property, the Desert Rose Resort, purchased in January 2004.

INNOVATIONS AND IMPROVEMENTS

In addition to adding new resorts, Shell looked to further increase vacation ownership flexibility and expand its membership. In 2004 the company introduced a program that franchised its points system to outside resort owners, who could participate in the club network without giving up control of their operations. Franchisees received help in marketing, interactive sales, property management, accounting, and regulatory compliance, as well as referrals to financing sources. The first franchisee, signed in 2005, was a San Antonio resort, Salado Creek, developed by Canadian investors, who were especially in need of help with U.S. regulatory issues. Later in the year, a New Hampshire resort, Crotched Mountain Resort & Spa, became the second franchisee, helping Shell to extend its reach to New England, a goal for several years.

Shell also looked to help its owner-members by testing a program to help them sell their units, thus addressing one of the greatest shortcomings of vacation interval ownership: resales. In 2005 the company began offering the affinity program created by Value Guaranteed Vacations Inc. (VGV Inc.), called VGV Club, providing a ready buyer to a timeshare owner wanting to sell. Club members also had the right after ten years of ownership to sell their timeshare to VGV Inc. for an amount equal to the original purchase price. To help ensure that the guest experience was of the highest quality, as well as to improve employee engagement, Shell in 2008 introduced a real-time satisfaction Market Metrix survey system. The program helped management to more quickly identify and resolve problems, resulting in a rapid increase in customer satisfaction results.

While programs and amenities were appreciated, what mattered most to members were the properties themselves. In 2006 Shell opened a pair of Napa Valley, California, resorts: The Meritage Resort and Vino Bello Resort. The addition of these properties helped to drive Shell's revenues to $440.2 million in 2007. A year later two more Florida properties were added to Shell's resort portfolio: The Boulevard in Miami's South Beach and Tierra del Sol in the Orlando area. Moreover, Shell upgraded several of its properties, including the Desert Rose, a former budget suite motel in Las Vegas that received a design award in 2005 for its interior conversion. Renovations in 2006 included the Whistler resort in British Columbia, Canada; the Peacock Suites in Anaheim; and the Donatello and the Inn at the Opera in San Francisco. A year later a major renovation was completed at the Kona Coast Resort in Hawaii. While far from the largest timeshare company, Shell Vacations was well positioned to continue its steady long-term growth.

Ed Dinger

PRINCIPAL SUBSIDIARIES

Shell Vacations Club, L.P.; Shell Vacations Hospitality.

PRINCIPAL COMPETITORS

Hilton Grand Vacations Company, LLC; Marriott Vacation Club International; Wyndham Vacation Ownership.

FURTHER READING

Evans, Michelle, "Buying a Little Piece of Paradise," *Crain's Chicago Business,* April 16, 2007, p. 26.

Jefferson, Steve, "Healthy Hawaii Sales Lure Another Time-Share Company," *Pacific Business News,* November 1, 2002.

Leposky, Rosalie E., "Sheldon H. Ginsburg & Perry J. Snyderman—Shell Vacations Club," *Resort Trades,* February 1998.

———, "Sheldon H. Ginsburg & Perry J. Snyderman—The Men," *Resort Trades,* February 1998.

"Shell Launches Vegas Sales Drive," *Lodging Hospitality,* February 2004, p. 26.

"Shell Vacations Launches Franchise Unit," *Lodging Hospitality,* May 15, 2004, p. 32.

Skousen, Sandi M., "Time-Share Merger Creates Marketing Powerhouse," *Pacific Business News,* January 10, 1997.

Sonnenschein Nath and Rosenthal LLP

233 South Wacker Drive, Suite 7800
Chicago, Illinois 60606-6404
U.S.A.
Telephone: (312) 876-8000
Toll Free: (888) 858-6429
Fax: (312) 876-7934
Web site: http://www.sonnenschein.com

Private Company
Incorporated: 1906 as Sonnenschein Berkson & Blumenthal
Employees: 1,576
Sales: $478 million (2007 est.)
NAICS: 541110 Offices of Lawyers

■ ■ ■

With headquarters in Chicago's Sears Tower, Sonnenschein Nath & Rosenthal LLP is one of the nation's leading law firms, with 15 offices throughout the United States and Europe. The firm's staff of approximately 800 attorneys offers counsel in a wide range of legal disciplines, including antitrust, competition and marketing; bankruptcy; corporate; employee benefits and executive compensation; environmental; healthcare; insurance; international; Internet, communications and data protection; labor and employment; litigation; media and entertainment; public law and policy strategies; real estate; taxation; and venture capital/emerging growth companies. Sonnenschein counts many of the world's leading companies among its customer base, including ABN AMRO/LaSalle Bank, Allstate, Citi-

group, the City of Chicago, General Electric, S.C. Johnson & Son Inc., McDonald's, NBC Universal, Sara Lee, Sears, Sony, and Sprint Nextel.

FORMATIVE YEARS

Sonnenschein's roots date back to early 20th-century Chicago, where the law firm was established on April 1, 1906, by Edward Sonnenschein, Maurice Berkson, and Isadore Blumenthal. Offices were initially located in the city's old Stock Exchange Building. Born in Chicago in 1881, Sonnenschein graduated from the University of Michigan in 1904, the same year he was admitted to the bar. During his career, he became a recognized authority in the field of real estate law. Edward Sonnenschein's brother, Hugo, became part of the firm in 1907. Like his brother, Hugo attended the University of Michigan, where he graduated with honors in 1905. While Edward specialized in real estate law, Hugo focused on corporate law.

The firm's formative years were marked by a number of name changes, the first of which occurred in 1909. That year, the departure of Isadore Blumenthal resulted in the new name of Sonnenschein Berkson & Sonnenschein. Another name change occurred in 1910, at which time the name Sonnenschein Berkson & Fishell was adopted. When Fishell left the firm in 1917, the name was changed to Sonnenschein Berkson & Lautman. The following year, the name Sonnenschein Berkson Lautman & Levinson was adopted.

Leading up to the 1920s, a wide variety of individuals and companies became Sonnenschein clients. These included sisters Minnie and Ada Everleigh, who operated Chicago's famous Everleigh Club bordello. In addition to adding new clients, the firm added a handful of new attorneys during the 1920s, beginning with a University of Chicago Law School graduate named Bernard Nath in 1921. Nath, who became a partner in 1928, went on to represent many leading commercial real estate firms in Chicago, including Arthur Rubloff, L. J. Sheridan, and Draper and Kramer. He served as chairman of the national executive committee of the National Commission of the Anti-Defamation League during the 1930s, during a period of rampant anti-Semitism.

Following the addition of Nath, Harvard Law School graduate and World War I veteran Sam Rosenthal joined the firm in 1926. After working as a general practitioner, Rosenthal would go on to become an expert in the area of corporate law, as well as trusts and estates. In addition to handling several high-profile Chicago real estate deals during the Roaring Twenties, Sonnenschein also relocated its offices to the Chicago Temple Building in 1923, which at the time was the tallest structure in the city.

The stock market crash of 1929 and the following Great Depression spelled new opportunity for Sonnenschein. The firm, which generated about half of its work from real estate law, found itself in a growth position. New attorneys were hired to handle foreclosures and other real estate–related work.

A PERIOD OF GROWTH

Sonnenschein ushered in the 1930s with another name change, becoming Sonnenschein Berkson Lautman Levinson & Morse in 1931. The following year, the firm was chosen to represent a new insurance company named Allstate, which had been established by Sears. By the mid-1930s, growth had allowed Sonnenschein to become Chicago's second largest law firm. During this time, however, a tragic loss occurred when Edward Sonnenschein died at the age of 54, following an operation at the Michael Reese Hospital.

In addition to the loss of Edward Sonnenschein, downswings in commercial and residential construction presented another challenge for the firm during the last half of the 1930s. Following this difficult period, Sonnenschein employed a mere 22 attorneys by the early 1940s. Brighter times were ahead following World War II. In 1945 Sonnenschein began to find significant business in the corporate sector. Among the firm's clients was railroad car manufacturer GATX. Interstate Vending was another leading corporate client that came on board as the firm headed into the 1950s.

Sonnenschein was involved in a variety of significant real estate developments during the 1950s. In addition to projects involving shopping centers, the firm was involved in major housing developments such as Lake Meadow in 1952, as well as Prairie Shores in 1957. These racially integrated developments would have a major impact on the city of Chicago. The firm withstood another loss in 1956. After suffering a cerebral hemorrhage while vacationing in Pebble Beach, California, Hugo Sonnenschein died on September 1 at the age of 73.

Changes continued during the latter part of the decade. In 1957 another name change occurred when the firm was reconstituted as Sonnenschein Lautman Levinson Rieser Carlin & Nath. Sonnenschein ushered in the 1960s by working with Arthur Rubloff to develop a neighborhood called Carl Sandburg Village on the city's Near North Side. In 1963, the firm once again modified its nameplate, becoming Sonnenschein Levinson Carlin Nath & Rosenthal. Two years later, Sonnenschein relocated its offices from the Chicago Temple Building, from which it had operated for approximately 40 years, to The Brunswick Building. Another major development occurred in 1966, when McDonald's became a Sonnenschein client.

BIG DEALS

The 1970s were marked by strong growth at Sonnenschein. In addition to adding many attorneys to its staff, the firm was involved in a number of high profile deals. For example, in 1972 Sonnenschein was involved in the sale of the Chicago and North Western Railroad to the railroad's employees. At the time, the deal was one of the largest of its kind in U.S. history. The following year, another name change occurred. Following the death of David Levinson, the firm was reconstituted as Sonnenschein Carlin Nath & Rosenthal. Following the new name came new offices, when Sonnenschein relocated to Chicago's famous Sears Tower in 1975.

Sonnenschein was involved in several high-profile deals with McDonald's owner Ray Kroc during the mid-

KEY DATES

1906: Edward Sonnenschein, Maurice Berkson, and Isadore Blumenthal establish law firm in Chicago.

1921: Bernard Nath joins the firm.

1923: Offices move to the Chicago Temple Building.

1926: Sam Rosenthal joins the firm.

1965: The firm relocates to The Brunswick Building.

1975: Sonnenschein moves its offices to Chicago's Sears Tower.

1985: Harold Shapiro becomes the firm's first chairman.

1990: The name Sonnenschein Nath & Rosenthal is adopted.

2003: The firm revises its name to Sonnenschein Nath & Rosenthal LLP.

2006: Sonnenschein celebrates its 100th anniversary.

1970s. The firm represented Kroc when he acquired the San Diego Padres in 1974, and again two years later when he bought a World Hockey League team called the San Diego Mariners.

Another important milestone during the mid-1970s occurred when Sonnenschein welcomed its first female partner. Jean Allard—who had worked as vice-president of business and finance at the University of Chicago, served as the University of Chicago Law School's assistant dean, and provided occasional advice to the White House—was eventually named as the most powerful woman in Chicago by the *Chicago Tribune.* By 1979 Sonnenschein's staff of attorneys had swelled to 100, doubled from a decade before.

In addition to serving corporate clients in the United States, Sonnenschein had its eye on the international scene during the early 1980s. This was evident by the establishment of a new firm named Sonnenschein Walter & Conston in 1981. A venture with the New York law firm of Walter, Conston, Schurtman & Gumpel, the new enterprise was based in Chicago and focused on providing legal services to American clients in Europe, as well as European clients in the Midwestern United States.

In 1985 the firm helped represent McDonald's in a class-action lawsuit filed by some of its franchisees. The lawsuit claimed that the requirement that McDonald's outlets sell only Coca-Cola products violated antitrust

laws, and represented a hardship because it forced franchisees to buy cola syrup at higher than normal prices. After a decade of legal wrangling, the case was finally dismissed by the U.S. District Court, which found no wrongdoing on McDonald's part.

A major leadership change occurred in 1985, when Sonnenschein named partner Harold Shapiro as its first chairman. That same year, the firm established an office in New York, followed by an office in Washington, D.C., in 1986. It also was in 1986 that a Harvard Law School graduate named Scott Turow joined Sonnenschein. Prior to coming on board, he had written a legal thriller titled *Presumed Innocent,* which went on to become a best-selling novel as well as a movie starring actor Harrison Ford. Sonnenschein rounded out the 1980s by establishing a new West Coast office in San Francisco.

RAPID CHANGES

The 1990s began with a flurry of changes. After operating under the same name since 1973, the firm once again revised its name in 1990, becoming Sonnenschein Nath & Rosenthal. The firm continued its growth on the West Coast by opening a new office in Los Angeles in 1990. That same year, a location also was established in St. Louis, Missouri. Another leadership change unfolded when Don Lubin was named as Sonnenschein's chairman in 1991. He was at the helm when the firm handled several major cases, including the $2.4 billion initial public offering of Allstate in 1993, which was considered the largest in U.S. history to date.

A new office was established in Kansas City, Missouri, in 1994, initially beginning with three attorneys who had been with the firm Spencer Fane Britt & Browne. That year, Sonnenschein bid farewell to partner Sam Rosenthal, who passed away at the age of 95. Another connection to the firm's early years was lost two years later, when Bernard Nath died in September 1996. Two months previously, he had celebrated 75 years of service with Sonnenschein. In the midst of continued growth, Don Lubin passed the chairman's torch to Duane Quani in 1997. By the end of the decade, Sonnenschein had become one of the largest law firms in the United States, with a staff of approximately 500 attorneys, 200 of whom worked in Chicago. On the international front, the firm decided to close its London office in 1999 when the operation proved unprofitable.

Sonnenschein, with a name taken from the German word for sunshine, kicked off the new millennium with a new brand strategy. The company's new identity focused on that word, de-emphasizing the Nath and

Rosenthal names, and included a new logo that appeared on the firm's stationery, business cards, and web site. Strong growth continued during the early years of the new century. In 2000 the firm added new attorneys in a number of areas, including intellectual property and technology, corporate litigation, international trade, and bankruptcy.

SONNENSCHEIN IN THE 21ST CENTURY

At this time Sonnenschein's attorneys were involved in a number of high-profile deals, including an antitrust case between client Sun Microsystems and Microsoft that resulted in a $2 billion settlement for Sun. In 2001 the firm also represented Mediacom Communications Corp. in its $2.1 billion cash acquisition of cable systems from AT&T Broadband. Sonnenschein opened a new office in West Palm Beach, Florida, that year, followed by a location in Short Hills, New Jersey, in 2002, when the firm also acquired the New York-based law firm Rubin-Baum LLP. That resulted in the addition of approximately 50 new lawyers. In 2003 the firm revised its name to Sonnenschein Nath & Rosenthal LLP.

In 2005, Harold Shapiro, who served as the firm's first chairman, passed away. However, that year the firm also celebrated the development of the Legacy Charter School. Located in an underserved West Side Chicago neighborhood, Sonnenschein invested $1 million to develop the school. In 2006 Sonnenschein celebrated its 100th anniversary. Midway through the year, the company established a presence in Brussels after acquiring two hotel and hospitality lawyers from the firm Squire Sanders & Dempsey. By this time, Sonnenschein had grown to include some 800 lawyers in nine offices throughout the United States.

In 2007 plans were under way to reestablish a presence in London, following an eight-year absence. By this time Elliott Portnoy had been named chairman. Dif-

ficult economic conditions were having a major impact on the corporate and real estate sectors by 2008. These events caused Sonnenschein to begin laying off employees nationwide. In May, the firm terminated 37 attorneys, as well as 87 support staff and secretaries. By late August, the firm had stopped hiring new attorneys.

Difficult economic conditions continued in 2009. However, following a century of growth and development, Sonnenschein seemed well prepared to ride out the storm.

Paul R. Greenland

PRINCIPAL COMPETITORS

Mayer Brown; Sidley Austin LLP; Skadden, Arps, Slate, Meagher & Flom LLP.

FURTHER READING

"Bernard Nath, 97; Lawyer Advised Real Estate Firms," *Chicago Sun-Times,* September 21, 1996.

"E. Sonnenschein, Lawyer, Is Dead After Operation," *Chicago Daily Tribune,* December 9, 1935.

King, Suzanne, "Sonnenschein Marketing Takes Brand New Approach," *Kansas City Business Journal,* March 24, 2000.

Knoblauch, Mary, "The Most Powerful Women in Chicago," *Chicago Tribune,* January 11, 1976.

"Samuel R. Rosenthal, 95, Senior Law Partner," *Chicago Sun-Times,* November 7, 1994.

Shear, Jeff, "A Lawyer Courts Best-Sellerdom," *New York Times,* June 7, 1987.

"Sonnenschein, Lawyer, Civic Leader, Dies," *Chicago Daily Tribune,* September 3, 1956.

Strobel, Lee, "2 Law Firms Form 3d, Woo Europe Clients," *Chicago Tribune,* October 16, 1981.

Thomas, Mike, "King of Legal Thrillers Too Chicago to Hold Court," *Chicago Sun-Times,* November 10, 2002.

Southern Progress
Corporation

———————■———————

2100 Lakeshore Drive
Birmingham, Alabama 35209
U.S.A.
Telephone: (205) 445-6000
Toll Free: (800) 366-4712
Fax: (205) 445-5936
Web site: http://www.southernprogress.com

Wholly Owned Subsidiary of Time, Inc./Time Warner, Inc.
Incorporated: 1886 as *Progressive Farmer*
Employees: 1,000
Sales: $1 billion (2008 est.)
NAICS: 511120 Periodical Publishers; 511130 Book
   Publishers; 519130 Internet Publishing and
   Broadcasting and Web Search Portals; 454390
   Other Direct Selling Establishments

■ ■ ■

Southern Progress Corporation publishes popular lifestyle magazines *Sunset, Coastal Living, Cooking Light, Health, Southern Accents,* as well as its flagship title *Southern Living.* The Time, Inc./Time Warner subsidiary also produces books via its Oxmoor House imprint, operates web sites such as MyRecipes.com and MyHomeIdeas.com through SPC Digital, and runs a home party sales unit called Southern Living at HOME.

BEGINNINGS

The origins of Southern Progress date to 1886, when Colonel Leonidas L. Polk founded the *Progressive Farmer* in North Carolina. Born on a farm in 1837, Polk was elected to the state legislature in 1860 and commissioned a colonel after being named to head the state militia. He enlisted in the North Carolina Regiment to fight for the Confederacy in the Civil War and was reelected to the legislature in 1864. After the war's end Polk resumed farming, founded the town of Polkton, and started the weekly *Ansonian* newspaper. In 1877 he was named North Carolina's first commissioner of agriculture, but he resigned three years later, frustrated with the lack of legislative support, and began working for the *Raleigh News* as a reporter.

In 1886 Polk founded a weekly journal called the *Progressive Farmer* to advocate for improvements such as the creation of a state agricultural college, which was subsequently established. In addition to its political and practical content, the publication reached out to other members of farm families with poetry, recipes, and humor. In 1889 Polk was elected president of the two-million-member National Farmers Alliance and Industrial Union, for which *Progressive Farmer* would serve as the voice. Popular with both the former Confederate and Union soldiers in its ranks, Polk was considered a likely U.S. presidential candidate, but he died suddenly in 1892 of a bladder hemorrhage.

After his death John L. Ramsey was named editor of the *Progressive Farmer,* and in 1899 the 18-year-old Clarence Poe took the job. In 1903 Poe and three partners bought the publication for $7,500, and under their Agricultural Publishing Company they continued to expand, boosting circulation from 5,000 to 36,000 by 1909. After a merger with the Mississippi-based *Southern Farm Gazette,* the company's headquarters were

COMPANY PERSPECTIVES

Southern Progress Corporation has a rich heritage of excellence and integrity in the publishing industry, dating back to 1886. Over the years, Southern Progress has established itself as one of the largest lifestyle publishers in the country. In addition to nationally recognized magazines, the company has been successful in extending its magazine brands to include books and a direct-selling operation.

moved in 1911 from Raleigh to Birmingham, Alabama, roughly halfway between the two locations. At this time the firm was also renamed Progressive Farmer Company.

During the 1910s and 1920s the firm continued to acquire smaller publications such as *Southern Ruralist,* and by the early 1930s, when five regional editions were offered, circulation had risen to nearly 1.4 million. *Progressive Farmer* was at that time the leading Southern farm periodical.

By 1952 the magazine carried more than 750,000 lines of advertising, which accounted for $5.5 million in revenues, and a decade later circulation peaked at more than 1.4 million. By this time the number of family farms was falling, however, as increasing numbers of Southerners moved to urban areas and the influence of large agribusiness began to take hold. Seeing its future prospects dimming, the company's management began looking for new ways to grow.

SOUTHERN LIVING LAUNCHED IN 1966

The concept for a new magazine was suggested by advertising manager Emory Cunningham, a former Auburn University journalism student and World War II pilot who had begun working as a *Progressive Farmer* sales representative in 1948. Noting both the growing urbanization of the South and its increasingly negative portrayal in the media, he proposed a new "lifestyle" monthly called *Southern Living.* After a column of that name began appearing in *Progressive Farmer* in 1963, a spinoff magazine was launched in February 1966.

The new publication eschewed an overt editorial stance, instead offering readers a gently uplifting connection to their rural Southern roots via upbeat articles on culture, gardening, food, home design, and travel. Starting with circulation of 250,000, the 25-cent magazine was turning a profit within 18 months,

unusually fast for the industry. Growth continued steadily, in part due to enhancements based on the style of popular West Coast-themed *Sunset.* Within a decade *Southern Living* had more than 1.3 million subscribers and was twice as profitable as established national titles including *Playboy.*

In 1968 Emory Cunningham was named publisher and president of the company, which also during that time created a new book division called Oxmoor House. This division's stock-in-trade would be titles drawn from popular *Southern Living* subjects such as cooking, home design, gardening, and travel. In its first decade the unit published more than 100 books, expanding in 1974 into art titles with *Jericho: The South Beheld.* Backed with a huge direct-mail ad campaign, the firm sold more than 150,000 copies of the book of sentimental paintings and text.

In 1970 the company had also added another new venture, *Creative Ideas for Living,* a craft magazine targeted at women. Unlike *Southern Living,* whose primary audience lived in eight states, the *Creative Ideas* publication would appear on newsstands around the country.

In 1981 the Progressive Farmer Co. changed its name to Southern Progress Corporation, reflecting the success of *Southern Living,* which was the most popular magazine of its type in the United States. It boasted 120 or more pages of ads each month, and its subscribers (who accounted for the bulk of sales) had a significantly higher median income than regional or national averages and were more likely to own a home and travel. The company's revenues were growing at a rate of 16 percent a year and reached $165 million in 1984, with profits estimated at nearly a quarter of that total. Southern Progress at this time employed 550.

SALE TO TIME IN 1985

In early 1985 Time, Inc., which had been courting the firm for over a decade, bought it for $480 million, the largest amount paid up to that time for a magazine company. The money would go to some 200 heirs of the four families that had bought it in 1903. This was also the first instance of Time adding an outside title to its stable of periodicals that included *Time, Life, People, Fortune,* and *Sports Illustrated.* Circulation of *Southern Living* at that time stood at 2.3 million, with *Creative Ideas for Living* selling 735,000 copies and *Progressive Farmer* 573,000 annually. Under the new ownership Emory Cunningham and his staff would remain in charge of the company, which continued to be headquartered in Birmingham, and Cunningham was named a vice-president of Time, Inc.

KEY DATES
■

1886: Colonel Leonidas L. Polk founds the *Progressive Farmer* in North Carolina.

1930s: Following acquisitions of smaller journals, circulation nears 1.4 million.

1966: New monthly magazine *Southern Living* debuts and quickly becomes a success.

1970: Nationally distributed women's magazine *Creative Ideas for Living* is introduced.

1985: Southern Progress Corp. is sold to Time, Inc., for $480 million.

1987: *Cooking Light* debuts.

1988: *Creative Ideas for Living* is sold for $7.5 million; *Travel South* is acquired.

1990: Time buys *Sunset* magazine and adds it to Southern Progress portfolio.

1996: *Weight Watchers* magazine purchased from H.J. Heinz Co.

1997: *Coastal Living* debuts.

2004: *Cottage Living* is introduced.

2007: *Progressive Farmer* is sold to DTN.

In September 1985 the first issue of a new upscale sister magazine, *Southern Living Classics,* hit newsstands, and a month later Southern Progress bought the W.R.C. Smith Publishing Co. of Atlanta, publisher of the glossy bimonthly home and garden publication *Southern Accents* and smaller *Sports Merchandiser* magazine. The 80-year-old W.R.C. Smith firm had launched *Southern Accents* in 1977, and its 200,000 subscribers increased to 225,000 when *Southern Living Classics* was folded into it.

In March 1987 Southern Progress launched the bimonthly *Cooking Light, the Magazine of Food and Fitness,* which focused on low-calorie recipes and tips for healthy living. It had grown out of a popular column of that title in *Southern Living* and a series of cookbooks published by Oxmoor House. In the summer, 66-year-old Emory Cunningham stepped down as CEO of the firm, although he would remain board chairman. The chief executive role was subsequently filled by company president Don Logan.

In April 1988 Southern Progress sold *Creative Ideas for Living* to PSC Publications for $7.5 million, and in August it acquired *Southern Travel* from the New York Times Co. The quarterly 210,000-circulation magazine subsequently reverted to its original name of *Travel South* and later evolved into the quarterly *Travel Guide.*

Early the next year the firm also bought a 70 percent stake in the three-year-old arts and culture-focused *Southern* magazine, which had circulation of 275,000. Its headquarters were moved from Little Rock, Arkansas, to Birmingham, where it was redesigned and named *Southpoint.* Publication was suspended in June 1990, however, after it failed to meet the company's advertising and circulation objectives.

SUNSET ACQUIRED IN 1990

In 1990 Time, Inc., bought popular lifestyle magazine and *Southern Living* inspiration *Sunset* and placed it under the Southern Progress umbrella, although it would remain editorially independent. Launched in 1898, *Sunset* had been created by the Sunset Limited railroad, which was trying to boost interest in the state of California to sell land that it owned there. In the late 1880s and early 1900s, the state was regarded unfavorably in the greater United States, and the publication tried to improve this image with upbeat articles about its attributes.

After it was purchased by a group of employees in 1914, *Sunset* sought a national presence and began to feature prominent writers such as Mark Twain and Sinclair Lewis. In 1929 it was acquired by Lawrence Lane, who subsequently changed it to resemble the popular *Better Homes and Gardens,* with lush photographs and articles on cooking, home décor, gardening, and travel. The company also established a book publishing division that would churn out hundreds of gardening, decorating, and cooking titles. It was subsequently combined with Oxmoor House.

In 1992 Don Logan was named president of Time, Inc. (then itself a unit of the merged Time Warner Inc.), and the Southern Progress CEO job was handed to senior vice-president Jim Nelson, who was himself bumped up to a Time executive post two years later and replaced by Southern Progress Vice-President Tom Angelillo. In 1994 the firm introduced a *Southern Living* Visa card, which offered users discounts on the magazine and related products.

In the spring of 1996 the company bought North American rights to *Weight Watchers* magazine from the H.J. Heinz Co., which would retain weight-loss center operator Weight Watchers International and the Weight Watchers Food Co. The offices of the one million–circulation monthly would be moved from New York to Birmingham. *Cooking Light* publisher Jeff Ward was placed in charge of the new acquisition, which he switched to a bimonthly while seeking to boost ad pages. Several spinoffs, including a cookbook and personal planner, were added as well. In late 1996 the firm also launched its first web site, Southern Living Online.

In April 1997 Southern Progress introduced *Coastal Living,* a retooled version of the recently purchased *Coastal Home.* The glossy bimonthly targeted people who lived or vacationed near the ocean, and featured articles on homes, travel, and entertaining. In December 1998 the company also bought the U.K. edition of *Weight Watchers* from Heinz.

HEALTH BECOMES PART OF SOUTHERN PROGRESS IN 1999

In 1999 Time shifted a magazine it had purchased in 1994, *Health,* into the Southern Progress portfolio. Founded in California in 1987 as *Hippocrates,* this magazine had launched a spinoff called *In Health* that became simply *Health* after Time bought the rights to the shorter name. The women's wellness magazine's operations were later moved from San Francisco to Birmingham.

In early 2000 Southern Progress sold *Weight Watchers* to Artal Luxembourg S.A., which had purchased Weight Watchers International from Heinz. With the dot-com boom in full flower, in May the company bought a stake in online craft vendor Craftopia.com and in November launched *hotdots,* a bimonthly magazine targeted at women who shopped online. It hit newsstands just as the Internet-fueled NASDAQ was beginning to tumble, however, and after a second issue was quietly shut down.

The company's ultimate parent, Time Warner, merged with America Online in late 2000, and in January 2001 it was announced that 200 jobs would be cut from its Birmingham workforce of 1,200 as part of a corporate restructuring. In January the firm also introduced Southern Living at HOME, a home party sales unit that offered a range of garden, kitchen, and food products. For 2001 Southern Progress had estimated revenues of $625 million and an operating profit of $170 million, making it one of the most profitable units in the Time stable. Approximately one-third of revenues came from the publication of books and other items by Oxmoor House.

Southern Progress's success and profitability were enhanced by marketing programs such as an annual "Idea House" built by many of its magazines, which was largely paid for by a featured builder and various advertisers. The latter were happy to receive attention in editorial space, and the firm's costs were reduced, although after receiving a letter of reprimand from the American Society of Magazine Editors in 1997, the use of such underwriting was made more transparent. The

company had always maintained a close relationship with its advertisers, however, notifying them in advance about stories relevant to their operations, for example. Other marketing efforts included *Southern Living*'s sponsorship of an annual flower show at Walt Disney's Epcot Center, a touring demonstration van operated by *Cooking Light,* and Oxmoor House's ongoing use of direct mail to sell books and other products.

COTTAGE LIVING DEBUTS IN 2004

In the fall of 2004 the firm introduced a new title called *Cottage Living,* which would be published nine times per year. The upscale lifestyle publication, which had been several years in development, was targeted toward women. It received the second-biggest launch in Time, Inc., history, and the initial printing of 500,000 grew to 650,000 by its third issue. During the year *Sunset* was also redesigned to give it a cleaner, more modern look that would appeal to younger readers. It had circulation of more than 1.4 million. In August 2005, 200,000 copies of a youth-oriented *Sunset* spinoff, *Living 101,* appeared on newsstands, although it was not picked up for serial publication.

In January 2007 Southern Progress sold its original magazine, the *Progressive Farmer,* to Nebraska-based agricultural information provider DTN. In May a new web site called MyRecipes.com was launched, which would feature 25,000 recipes from *Cooking Light, Sunset, Southern Living,* and other Southern Progress and Time magazines such as *Real Simple,* as well as original videos and other content. It would be operated by a new division called SPC Digital, which later added other spinoff sites such as MyHomeIdeas.com.

For 2007 Southern Progress's magazines had advertising revenues of $663 million, led by *Southern Living* with $206 million and *Coastal Living* with $143 million. Although still profitable, the rates of ad and revenue growth were slightly lower than figures for the industry as a whole.

The March 2008 issue of *Southern Living* featured the title's first full redesign since its founding. It would include a special Healthy Living section, as well as a new column called Get Inspired. The magazine's median reader age had crept upward to 50, and the changes were made in a bid to attract younger readers. *Southern Progress* continued to be the firm's flagship title, with circulation of 2.8 million.

In the fall of 2008 Time, Inc., announced it would cut several dozen jobs in Birmingham, and soon afterward a number of top Southern Progress executives, including CEO Tom Angelillo and the editor of *Coastal Living,* departed. In November production of *Cottage*

Living was suspended. Former company head and Time CEO Don Logan had left the parent firm in 2005, and with Time's new management team having no direct ties to Southern Progress, rumors began circulating that it might be sold or largely run from New York.

Nearly one-and-a-quarter centuries after its founding, Southern Progress Corporation had built up a strong portfolio of magazines and books. Although the publishing industry was struggling in the face of a economic downturns and the shift to digital formats, established brands such as *Southern Living* and *Sunset* remained profitable and appeared capable of weathering future storms.

Frank Uhle

PRINCIPAL SUBSIDIARIES

Oxmoor House; SPC Digital; Southern Living at HOME; SPConnect; Sunset Publishing Corporation; Sunset Custom Media Solutions.

PRINCIPAL COMPETITORS

Meredith Corporation; Hearst Magazines; The Condé Nast Publications; Lagardere Active; Martha Stewart Living Omnimedia, Inc.; Rodale, Inc.

FURTHER READING

Barmash, Isadore, "*Cooking Light* to Make Its Debut in March," *New York Times*, August 7, 1986.

Bater, Jeff, "Publishers Settle Charges over Book Club Marketing," *Dow Jones News Service*, November 7, 2002.

Bennett, Elizabeth, "*Southern Living:* Publisher Cunningham Credits a Simple Concept for Making His Magazine a Success," *Washington Post*, July 7, 1978.

Blyth, Myrna, "Cozying Up with a New Glossy," *New York Sun*, August 19, 2004.

Fine, Jon, "*Hotdots* Shopping Mag to Get $5 Million Launch," *Advertising Age*, August 28, 2000, p. 11.

Goolrick, Chester, "One Way to Succeed in Sun Belt Is Simply to Sing Its Praises," *Wall Street Journal*, November 23, 1981, p. 1.

Landro, Laura, "Time Inc. to Buy a Publisher for $480 Million," *Wall Street Journal*, February 22, 1985.

Lee, Elizabeth, "Big-Name Newcomer Gets Overwhelming Welcome," *Atlanta Journal-Constitution*, September 6, 2001, p. BE12.

Levine, Rob, "The Cunningham Empire," *Atlanta Journal-Constitution*, April 27, 1986, p. H4.

"Magazine Publisher Eliminating 200 Jobs in Birmingham," *Associated Press Newswires*, January 25, 2001.

Morgan, Richard, "Southern Progress: Bewkes' Next Focus?" *Daily Deal*, May 9, 2008.

Moses, Lucia, "*Southern Living* Plots Redesign; Aims for Ads," *Mediaweek*, October 15, 2007.

Reed, Roy, "Birmingham Publisher Propelled by Regionalism," *New York Times*, September 7, 1976, p. 38.

Riley, Sam G., and Gary Selnow, *Regional Interest Magazines of the United States*, Westport, Conn.: Greenwood, 1991.

Rose, Matthew, "Fruitful Union: Wedding 'Church' and 'State' Works at Time Inc. Unit," *Wall Street Journal*, October 1, 2002, p. A1.

"Southern Progress Bakes MyRecipes.com," *Mediaweek*, May 21, 2007.

"Time Inc. Closes *Cottage Living* Magazine," *Associated Press Newswires*, November 19, 2008.

Tomberlin, Michael, "Southern Progress Cuts More Jobs in Birmingham Metro Area," *Birmingham News*, November 22, 2008.

Waldrop, Judith W., "Affluent *Southern Living*," *American Demographics*, October 1, 1986.

Whitman, Janet, "Time Inc. Unit to Launch *Cottage Living* Magazine," *Dow Jones News Service*, November 7, 2003.

Wollenberg, Skip, "Time Warner Unit Suspends Publication of *Southpoint* Magazine," *Associated Press Newswires*, May 15, 1990.

Sumitomo Corporation

8-11 Harumi, 1-chome
Chuo-ku
Tokyo, 100-8610
Japan
Telephone: (81 03) 5166-5000
Fax: (81 03) 5166-6203
Web site: http://www.sumitomocorp.co.jp

Public Company
Incorporated: 1919 as Osaka Hokko Kaisha Ltd.
Employees: 65,494
Sales: ¥3.67 trillion ($37.3 billion) (2007 est.)
Stock Exchanges: Tokyo
Ticker Symbol: 8053
NAICS: 421510 Metals Service Centers and Offices; 421520 Coal and Other Mineral and Ore Wholesalers; 421830 Industrial Machinery and Equipment Wholesalers; 422690 Other Chemical and Allied Products Wholesalers; 422720 Petroleum and Petroleum Products Wholesalers (Except Bulk Stations and Terminals)

■ ■ ■

With interests in products from metals and chemicals to textiles and consumer goods, Sumitomo Corporation is characterized as a *sogo shosha,* or general trading company. The company oversees a network of nearly 150 offices and approximately 800 subsidiaries and affiliated companies. Sumitomo is organized into eight business units: Metal Products; Transportation & Construction Systems; Infrastructure; Media, Network, & Lifestyle Retail; Chemical & Electronics; Mineral Resources & Energy; General Products & Real Estate; and Financial & Logistics.

During 2007, operations in Japan accounted for 37 percent of overall profits, the Asia/China region shored up 21 percent, The Americas accounted for 18 percent, and business in Europe brought in 11 percent of total profits. The company has roots as a Japanese *keiretsu,* a family of businesses linked through Japanese history and tradition, as well as cross-shareholdings and interlocking directorates. This scheme historically provided Sumitomo affiliates with common and well-known brand names, access to credit, and protection from hostile takeovers.

16TH-CENTURY ORIGINS

The "spiritual pillar" of the Sumitomo Corporation was Masatomo Sumitomo, the first head of the family and founder of the business. He was born just north of Kyoto in 1585 and became a Buddhist priest. At the age of 45 he opened a small medicine and book shop called the Fujiya. There he established a set of highly moralistic principles for conducting business which were passed down through subsequent generations to form the basis for the modern Sumitomo company charter.

Since Masatomo's marriage had produced no sons, his brother-in-law Riemon Soga was adopted into the family. Masatomo and Riemon were also related by a common lineage to the noble Heike family. When Masatomo died in 1652, Riemon Soga became head of the House of Sumitomo.

As a young man, Riemon worked as an apprentice

in a copper refinery. In 1590, at 18, he opened his own shop in Kyoto called the Izumiya, literally the "Fountainhead Shop." For the company's logo he adopted the *igeta,* the ancient character for "well frame." Twentieth-century annual reports noted that the character "symbolizes the fresh, sparkling water gushing from a fountainhead, which forms a mighty river and finally flows into the vast ocean." The *igeta* would become a metaphor for Sumitomo's own growth over the ensuing centuries.

Japanese refineries at this time lacked the technology to remove small, naturally occurring quantities of gold and silver from copper. These precious metals were sold to foreign traders as copper and were later extracted overseas at a great profit. Riemon Soga, however, learned about a refining procedure used by the foreigners (who were called *nanban-jin,* or "southern barbarians") which involved adding lead to molten copper and smelting with charcoal to remove silver from copper, and later lead from silver. This method, known as *nanban-buki,* made Riemon and the Izumiya very successful. Contrary to what may have been expected of an entrepreneur, Soga unselfishly instructed his competitors in the *nanban-buki* method.

17TH-CENTURY DEVELOPMENTS

When Riemon Soga died in 1636, the Izumiya passed to his second son, Chubei. His first son, Tomomochi, married Masatomo's daughter and was adopted by the Sumitomo family. He established a separate copper refinery and crafting shop that was also named Izumiya.

At the age of 16 Tomomochi moved his business from Kyoto to Osaka, which was recovering from damage incurred during a war between Tokugawa and Toyotomi armies. Tomomochi's competitors welcomed him to Osaka in a demonstration of their gratitude to his father. The Izumiya expanded quickly and later absorbed both the Fujiya and the original Izumiya operated by his

brother. By the time of Tomomochi's death in 1662, the Izumiya in Osaka had become the center of the Japanese copper industry.

With Tomomochi's death, his fifth son, Tomonobu, became the third head of the Sumitomo family at the age of 15. In 1680 he gained permission from the Tokugawa Shogunate to rehabilitate the Yoshioka Copper Mine, which had been worked to exhaustion over a period of centuries. Shortly after Sumitomo commenced revitalization of the Yoshioka mine in 1684, it was discovered that Tomonobu's younger brother Tomosada had committed several serious errors in the management of the family brokerage house, which subsequently was forced to liquidate. This placed the entire family enterprise in jeopardy.

The following year Tomonobu, who was a partner in the brokerage operation, was obliged to resign all his company posts at the age of only 38. He was succeeded as head of the family by his 15-year-old son Tomoyoshi. The Izumiya endured several more years of hardship, but eventually recovered. In the meantime, restoration of the Yoshioka site continued.

MINING TWO SIDES OF ONE MOUNTAIN

In June 1690 the manager of the Yoshioka mine, Jyuemon Tamuke, was approached by a man from the island of Shikoku who quite unexpectedly confided in Jyuemon that he had discovered a promising rock formation on the side of the mountain opposite the Tatsukawa Copper Mine, where he was employed as a miner. An expedition was ordered to investigate the area. The results immediately convinced the Sumitomo family to apply to the Shogunate for permission to mine the site, called Besshi. A permit was granted the following May, and digging commenced in December. Despite a fire in 1694 that claimed the lives of 133 people, Besshi was ambitiously developed and over the next one hundred years produced more copper than any other mine.

The Besshi and Tatsukawa mines continued to operate on both faces of the same mountain but were prevented from coordinating their operations because the Shogunate was opposed to giving one family control over such a large natural resource. In 1749 representatives from both mines convinced the government that the failing Tatsukawa mine could remain viable only if it was placed under Sumitomo management. By 1762 Tatsukawa was again faced with closure unless its operations were fully integrated with Besshi. That year the government permitted the Sumitomo family to purchase the mine.

During the next century the Sumitomo family remained involved in a variety of business activities. The

KEY DATES

1585: Masatomo Sumitomo is born.

1919: Osaka Hokko Kaisha Ltd. is established.

1945: The company is reorganized at a general trading company; adopts the Nihon Kensetsu Sangyo Kaisha, Ltd., name.

1952: The company officially changes its name to Sumitomo Shoji Kaisha Ltd.

1978: The company adopts the English version of its name—Sumitomo Corporation.

1995: Jupiter Telecommunications Co. Ltd. is established.

2001: The company reorganizes; headquarters are moved to Chuo-ku, Tokyo.

2007: Sumitomo Corporation Vietnam Ltd. Co. is created; record earnings are posted for the fifth consecutive year.

primary trade, around which all other ventures revolved, was copper production. While the Sumitomos' wealth increased, no innovations were made in the smelting process, and no real business acumen was displayed. The Besshi mine became a liability, dependent on government subsidies. In 1867 the family business was renamed Sumitomo Honten (head office) and designated as the central office for all Sumitomo activities.

During 1865 armed forces of the Choshu clan initiated a military campaign against the Tokugawa government, with whom the Sumitomo family had cultivated close ties. Despite its relationship with the Tokugawa Shogunate, the Besshi subsidies were suspended and the Sumitomo family was ordered to remit substantial amounts of money in war taxes to help fund government counteroffensives. Three years later the Choshu were joined by the Tosa and Satsuma clans, and together they succeeded in overthrowing the Shogunate and restoring the Meiji emperor.

INNOVATION UNDER THE LEADERSHIP OF SAIHEI HIROSE

In the process, the Besshi mine was sealed by Tosa forces and the Sumitomo copper warehouses at Osaka were occupied by the Satsuma. Saihei Hirose, who had just been appointed general manager of the Besshi mine, met with the leader of the Tosa forces, Ganyemon Kawada (later president of the Bank of Japan). He persuaded Kawada to evacuate the Sumitomo properties

after convincing him that the family unwillingly supported the Shogunate.

Still, the company was in very poor financial condition. The defeated warlords of the Shogunate defaulted on loans from the Sumitomo financial office, and the currencies it held greatly decreased in value. In addition, the Besshi mine had degenerated to the point where it was nearly unworkable. At this point there was strong pressure from within the family to sell the mine.

Hirose was determined to rehabilitate the Besshi mine. He secured new sources of food for the employees, constructed new housing, and even established a day care center. After he settled an ownership dispute with the government, Hirose proceeded with the modernization of the mine. Hirose managed to obtain numerous loans that required him to mortgage most of the family's property. In 1873 he hired a French engineer named Louis Larroque to prepare a study on Besshi with recommendations for its modernization. Hirose did not extend Larroque's two-year contract, but instead sent two of his own employees to Europe to study French methods of mining and metallurgy.

Hirose introduced a number of technological innovations to Japanese mining in 1880, including the use of dynamite and jackhammers. He purchased a steam-powered ship and train engine, and incorporated the substitution of coke for charcoal in the smelting process. He established his own sales and supply branches, including an export office. Large areas of woodland were purchased for lumber, and a machine manufacturing and repair shop was established. The productivity of the Besshi mine rose quickly; annual copper production increased from 420 tons in 1868 to over 1800 tons in 1888.

Saihei Hirose was regarded as the most important figure in Sumitomo's modern history. In addition to being given credit for saving the family enterprise, he successfully asserted the independence of the business from the government and contributed greatly to the development and growth of Osaka. He retired in 1894 and died 20 years later at the age of 86.

Hirose was replaced by his nephew, Teigo Iba, who continued to emphasize the modernization of Besshi, but also advocated the diversification of the Sumitomo family enterprise. Iba formalized the family banking operations in 1895 when he established the Sumitomo Bank.

A PERIOD OF CHANGE AND EXPANSION: 1920–30

Iba stepped down in 1904, proclaiming that only younger, more dynamic managers possessed the imagination and courage to implement new strategies and take risks. He was succeeded by Asaya Suzuki, who led the company until his death in 1922. In 1919, Osaka Hokko Kaisha Ltd. was established to oversee a land reclamation project in Osaka Bay. During Suzuki's tenure Sumitomo was reorganized as a limited partnership, and renamed Sumitomo So-Honten in 1921. Suzuki also reemphasized Masatomo's founding precepts of moralistic and trustworthy conduct. He was remembered as a highly principled manager who expected nothing less than strict adherence to ethical business practices.

Between 1922 and 1930 two more men served briefly as the top executive, Kinkichi Nakata and Kanchiki Yukawa. During their leadership Sumitomo branched out into several more fields with the creation of new subsidiaries. By this time Sumitomo had grown to become one of Japan's largest industrial concerns. It was one of the country's few but powerful *zaibatsu*, or "money cliques," which emerged after the Meiji Restoration. Unlike the other *zaibatsu*, Mitsui, Mitsubishi, and Furukawa, Sumitomo did not become involved in the purchase of high-growth "model" industries which were established by the Meiji government and later turned over to private enterprise. Sumitomo's prominence had been gained purely on the virtues of its existing operations.

In 1930 Sumitomo appointed Masatune Ogura to serve as director general. He supervised the company's incorporation as Sumitomo Honsha (trading company), Ltd., in 1937. Yet his 11 years as chief executive were complicated by right-wing nationalists operating within the military. They gained influence in Japanese politics through intimidation and assassination and openly attacked the *zaibatsu* for their preoccupation with self-interest and "lack of sympathy" for the masses. However, of the *zaibatsu*, Sumitomo was spared most often from militarist terrorism. Whatever his political beliefs, Ogura was drafted into the militarist government in 1941 to serve as a cabinet minister.

Later that year Japan began a full-scale war of conquest in Asia aimed at establishing a regional economic order centered around Japan. For Sumitomo's new chairman, Shunnosuke Furuta, it was an extremely difficult period. He was required to make special efforts in order to keep the company's various divisions together; the unusual circumstances of war had forced Sumitomo's subsidiaries to adopt a more autonomous, presidential form of management. Additionally, the company and its 200,000 employees were not fully prepared for the wartime mobilization.

WARTIME DISRUPTION AND POSTWAR REORGANIZATION

Japan's fortunes in World War II began to change during 1942. Within the year American bombers were within range of targets on the Japanese mainland. Since Sumitomo was a large industrial concern, and therefore essential to the Japanese military, its factories were exposed to frequent bombings. When the war ended in August of 1945, virtually all of Japan's industrial capability had been destroyed.

Japan was placed under the administration of a military occupation authority called SCAP, an acronym for the Supreme Commander of Allied Powers. SCAP imposed a variety of American-style commercial laws, including an antimonopoly law, which mandated the complete dissolution of all *zaibatsu*. Despite strong criticism from some quarters, Shunnosuke Furuta complied with the edict and supervised the breakup of the Sumitomo Honsha, or parent company, into several fully independent firms, all of which were forbidden to use the *igeta* logo.

In the following months thousands of Japanese citizens, including Sumitomo employees who were posted overseas, returned to Japan. It was extremely demoralizing for those who had been fortunate enough to avoid areas of battle. Furuta worked very hard to ensure that all his employees could remain employed and healthy. The Honsha was reorganized in November 1945. Furuta made the difficult decision to set the company on a new course of business. Under its new name, the Nihon Kensetsu Sangyo Kaisha, Ltd., was established as a general trading company, or *sogo shosha*.

In the years following World War II, particularly during the Korean War, the restrictive commercial laws were gradually relaxed. The former Sumitomo companies began to establish affiliations through the Sumitomo Bank and limited cross-ownership of stock. The *igeta* came back into use and a monthly meeting, the Hakusui-kai, or "White Water Club," was established so that the individual heads of the affiliated Sumitomo companies could coordinate business strategies. This did not, however, mark the reformation of the *zaibatsu*, which had a more disciplined, autocratic management style.

GROWTH AS A TRADING HOUSE

On June 1, 1952, the company officially changed its name to Sumitomo Shoji Kaisha, literally the "Sumitomo Commercial Affairs Company." It became the trading house for the various Sumitomo affiliated companies at a time when Japan was experiencing a period of phenomenal economic growth. As Japan grew in economic importance, Sumitomo Shoji established a number of foreign offices. Products handled by the company soon included iron and steel, non-ferrous metals, electrical and industrial equipment, chemicals, textiles, fuel, agricultural and marine products, and real estate. Sales transactions rose from $254 million in 1955 to $2.3 billion in 1965, then to over $26 billion in 1975, and reached nearly $74 billion by 1985. The company adopted the Sumitomo Corporation name in 1978.

The *keiretsu* organizational scheme emerged from this phenomenal growth, which was accompanied by an accumulation of debt. Majority holdings of virtually all affiliates were maintained within the *keiretsu,* thereby preventing hostile takeovers when share prices of a given member slipped dangerously low. If, for instance, Sumitomo Heavy Industries was in danger of being purchased by a competitor, the affiliated Sumitomo companies would collectively refuse to sell their controlling interest.

Sumitomo's fortunes, as well as the Japanese economy, declined in the late 1980s and early 1990s. Falling demand in Sumitomo's all-important metals and chemicals sectors combined with a "strong-yen recession" to precipitate steady revenue shortfalls—from ¥20 trillion in 1991 to ¥17 trillion in 1994. After four years of sector-leading profits, Sumitomo Bank fell to second place among the world's leaders. Its difficulties included bad loans to affiliate Itoman and to the former Soviet Union that culminated in the 1990 resignation of the bank's chairman.

In spite of such setbacks the group was able to invest in several promising new ventures in the early 1990s. Media investments captured the most attention, especially a joint cable television venture in 1995 with America's Tele-Communications, Inc., which created Jupiter Telecommunications Co. Ltd. Other new enterprises included: a chain of Western-style drugstores called TomoD's; marketing of such American clothing brands as Eddie Bauer and Gotcha; creation of a digital communications system in Russia; filmmaking; and environmentally friendly products.

Sumitomo's business interests in the early to mid-1990s focused on metals (about 38 percent of annual revenues), machinery (about 31 percent of annual revenues), and chemicals and fuels (about 15 percent of annual sales). Other interests extended to motor vehicles (under the Mazda and Nissan labels), media, real estate, insurance, textiles, and foodstuffs. Although such massive business concerns typically developed reputations for being impersonal, Sumitomo historically showed concern for the well-being of employees and customers. In 1994, Sumitomo Corporation President Tomiichi Ak-

iyama's letter to shareholders reemphasized that consideration: "Valuing our customers' trust above all, and with foresight, flexibility, and an entrepreneurial spirit, we will deal with the changing times." The Sumitomo companies adhered closely to basic principles of conduct in which harmony and patriotism were emphasized.

The latter half of the 1990s proved to be challenging for Sumitomo and the other large trading houses in Japan due to the Asian economic crisis, the bursting of the bubble economy, credit problems, and deflation. Japan's faltering economy forced Sumitomo to seek joint ventures as well as international expansion to remain profitable.

MOVING INTO THE NEW MILLENNIUM

Sumitomo spent the early years of the new millennium restructuring its operations. During 2001 the company adopted an organizational structure which included the creation of six corporate groups, nine business units, and 28 business divisions. Later that year the company's headquarters were moved to Chuo-ku, Tokyo. Sumitomo continued to revamp its operations over the next several years in order to shore up profits and its strategy paid off. An April 2005 *Wall Street Journal* article commented on the restructuring seen at most trading companies in Japan: Yuka Hayashi wrote that Japan's *sogo shoshas,* "have transformed themselves into modern-day merchant banks, investing in ventures from Australia to Chile. They are crucial suppliers of capital, a sort of private-equity industry in themselves, although they often provide services, from financing to consulting, to go along with their investments. They are among the fastest-growing and most profitable concerns traded on Tokyo's stock exchange."

With earnings on the rise, Sumitomo found itself in a position to expand its business while shedding unprofitable units. The company moved into Abu Dhabi by acquiring a 20 percent interest in Shuweihat CMS International Power Company. It also expanded its Indonesian and Peruvian copper mining operations, moved into the nickel and cobalt mining industry in Madagascar, and expanded its investment in coal mining operations in Australia, and in its gold mining business in Alaska. During 2007 Sumitomo Corporation Vietnam Ltd. Co. was established to oversee operations in industrial zone construction, investment, steel, distribution, and logistics. Sumitomo acquired the remaining interest in the home-shopping Jupiter Shop Channel the following year.

Sumitomo's net income increased steadily from fiscal 2003. While the sharp downturn in the U.S.

economy in 2008 began to take its toll in several of the company's business groups, strong growth in Europe and China offset the declines. During fiscal 2008 some of the company's business segments experienced profit growth while other divisions fell victim to the slowing global economy. Nevertheless, Sumitomo management—led by president and CEO Susumo Kato—was confident the company was on track for success in the years to come.

Updated, April Dougal Gasbarre, Christina M. Stansell

PRINCIPAL SUBSIDIARIES

Sumitomo Corporation Hokkaido Co. Ltd.; Sumitomo Corporation Kyushu Co. Ltd.; Sumitomo Corporation Tohoku Co. Ltd.; Sumitomo Corporation Vietnam Ltd. Co.

PRINCIPAL OPERATING UNITS

Metal Products; Infrastructure; Chemical & Electronics; General Products & Real Estate; Corporate Group; Chubu Regional; Transportation & Construction Systems; Media, Network & Lifestyle Retail; Mineral Resources & Energy; Financial & Logistics; Kansai Regional.

PRINCIPAL COMPETITORS

ITOCHU Corporation; Mitsubishi Corporation; Mitsui & Co. Ltd.

FURTHER READING

Caryl, Christian, and Akiko Kashiwagi, "Back in the Black; Japan's Once-Powerful Trading Firms Have Revived, Thanks to the Commodities Boom," *Newsweek,* May 8, 2006.

Hayashi, Yuka, "New Tricks for Japan's Old Dogs," *Wall Street Journal,* April 7, 2005.

"Japanese Trading Companies: Captive and Content," *Economist,* December 6, 2008.

"The Mighty Keiretsu," *Industry Week,* January 20, 1992, pp. 52–54.

Neff, Robert, "For Bankrupt Companies, Happiness Is a Warm Keiretsu," *Business Week,* October 26, 1992, pp. 48–49.

"Sumitomo Corp., TCI Set Up CATV Joint Firm," *Jiji Press English News Service,* January 18, 1995.

"Vietnam: Sumitomo Corporation Debuts in Vietnam," *Thai News Service,* November 13, 2007.

Young, Alexander, *The Soga Shosha: Japan's Multinational Trading Company,* Boulder, Colo.: Westview Press, 1979.

Sunkist

Sunkist Growers, Inc.

———————————■———————————

14130 Riverside Drive
Sherman Oaks, California 91423-2313
U.S.A.
Telephone: (818) 986-4800
Fax: (818) 379-7405
Web site: http://www.sunkist.com

Member-Owned Cooperative
Incorporated: 1893 as the Southern California Fruit
    Growers Exchange
Employees: 500 (est.)
Sales: $993.6 million (2007 est.)
NAICS: 424480 Fresh Fruit and Vegetable Merchant
    Wholesalers; 424420 Packaged Frozen Food
    Merchant Wholesalers; 424490 Other Grocery and
    Related Product Merchant Wholesalers; 533110
    Owners and Lessors of Other Non-Financial Assets;
    541690 Other Scientific and Technical Consulting
    Services; 541870 Advertising Material Distribution
    Services

■ ■ ■

Sunkist Growers, Inc., is a not-for-profit organization
operated for the California and Arizona citrus growers
who compose its membership. In the first decade of the
21st century, Sunkist's membership comprised over
6,000 citrus farmers, 17 district exchanges, and approximately 34 local associations (packinghouses). The
cooperative markets oranges, lemons, grapefruit, and
tangerines in the United States and abroad, using its
"less-than-perfect" fruit to produce processed citrus

products such as juices, peels, and oils for use in food
products. Owned and controlled by its member-growers,
the only individuals eligible to sit on its board of directors, Sunkist markets the world-recognized Sunkist
brand name and coordinates the timing of the harvest
and release of its members' fruit to achieve superior
prices. The majority of the member-growers farm 40
acres or less. Through licensing agreements, Sunkist's
name is used on products including fruit juices, sodas,
snacks, vitamins, and culinary ingredients around the
world. In 2007, Sunkist marketed over 600 products in
more than 50 countries on five continents.

ORIGINS IN THE 19TH CENTURY

Sunkist's formation in the late 19th century was a function of the burgeoning growth recorded by California's
citrus industry during the period. The larger the young
industry became, the greater the need for a cooperative
of Sunkist's ilk. Commercial citrus production began in
the region roughly a half-century before the birth of
Sunkist, when the first commercial orchard took root in
1840. From this starting point, a series of events spurred
growth, transforming that single orchard situated in
what would later become downtown Los Angeles into a
thriving industry and an integral component of the
state's economy. The forces that promoted the growth of
the citrus industry provided the reason for Sunkist's
creation.

The first significant event occurred in 1848, when
the beginning of California's gold rush lured prodigious
waves of fortune seekers into the region. As the state's
population increased exponentially, its ability to meet

COMPANY PERSPECTIVES

We are a leading international citrus supplier, but you might be surprised to know that we don't own a single citrus grove. And although we're a billion dollar a year organization, you can't buy stock—because there isn't any. Why? Because Sunkist is a cooperative—a not-for-profit company. Our 6,000 members, all California and Arizona citrus growers, have joined forces to produce the high-quality Sunkist fruit you've come to know and love. Sunkist is one of the 10 largest marketing cooperatives in America and the largest marketing cooperative in the world's fruit and vegetable industry.

the food demands of its new residents was stretched beyond capacity. Vitamin-rich fruits and vegetables were in short supply, causing many of the new Californians to develop scurvy. Citrus production was increased as a response, but an even greater boon to the fledgling citrus industry occurred 20 years later when the transcontinental railroad was completed in 1870. Within ten years of the first rail shipment, the volume of California citrus moving east had grown to more than 2,000 rail cars annually. In another five years the volume had doubled. California citrus had become big business.

At roughly the same time that the eastward and westward rail lines reached their meeting point in Promontory, Utah, the first seedless, navel oranges arrived in California. Two parent trees were shipped from Brazil to Southern California by American missionaries and planted in Riverside in 1873, marking the introduction of what would prove to be a highly prized variety of orange into a rapidly expanding market. Finally, the opening of the Atchison, Topeka, and Santa Fe railroad in 1885, which connected Los Angeles to the rest of the country, provided the last significant factor propelling the growth of the citrus industry before Sunkist's debut as a cooperative.

As the 1880s gave way to the 1890s, "a veritable boom in orange planting" was under way, according to an early Sunkist historian. The industry was growing by leaps and bounds, measured in part by the dramatic increase in citrus planting activity. Between 1880 and 1893 California's citrus acreage increased from 3,000 to more than 40,000, underscoring the heightened demand for oranges and lemons. As the revenue generated from citrus production escalated, however, there was one sector of the industry excluded from sharing in the riches.

The growers were watching others get rich from the citrus they grew, and as the 1890s began, they found what little power they had quickly slipping away. Collective action was the response, and Sunkist emerged as the lasting answer.

ORGANIZING GROWERS: THE SOUTHERN CALIFORNIA FRUIT GROWERS EXCHANGE

The orange growers began to watch their share of the citrus revenue dwindle when production exceeded the local market demand. With local markets glutted, the orange growers realized their survival depended on shipping their fruit to distant markets, but this realization was far easier to apprehend than it was to put into action. Amid the packinghouse owners, distributors, agents, and speculators—the "middlemen" of the citrus trade—the growers ranked a distant last in terms of exercising any control over the industry. They were independent, small-scale farmers presiding over modest groves of 5, 10, or 15 acres, without the organization and training to distribute their produce effectively.

The growers' weak bargaining position worsened in 1891 when agents decided they would no longer buy fruit F.O.B., or freight-on-board, a purchase term meaning the buyer pays the transportation charges and assumes all risk of damage and delay in transit not caused by the shipper. Instead, the agents declared they would handle the citrus only on consignment, a decision that shifted the risk from distributor to the scattered ranks of independent citrus growers. Forced either to accept the offers of local speculators or consign their fruit to commission agents in the East, the California citrus growers were cornered into an untenable position. Successive years of widespread financial losses—the "Red Ink" years—followed during the early 1890s, forcing the growers to marshal their forces and organize against a system they believed was unjust.

A number of attempts to band growers together occurred before the commission houses refused to purchase fruit F.O.B., with the first attempt taking place in 1885 when The Orange Growers Protective Union of Southern California was formed. Other attempts at collective action followed during the ensuing years, but all failed for one reason or another. Their brief existences, however, did lay the foundation for the one cooperative organization that would endure, the Southern California Fruit Growers Exchange, Sunkist's predecessor.

Formed in 1893, the Exchange was organized as a federated structure, member-owned and operated, comprising regional marketing cooperatives, known as district exchanges. During its first season, the Exchange

KEY DATES

1893: The Southern California Fruit Growers Exchange is founded.

1905: The company extends its purview to encompass the entire state and changes its name to California Fruit Growers Exchange.

1907: The company launches a timber supply company.

1909: The Sunkist trademark is registered.

1914: The cooperative's product division is founded with a small marmalade factory.

1926: The Sunkist trademark is used on fresh oranges for the first time.

1951: The Sunkist trademark is branded on frozen concentrates and other canned citrus juices.

1952: The company changes its name to Sunkist Growers.

1974: The cooperative licenses its name to the Ben Myerson Candy Co., Inc.

1977: Sales pass the $500,000 mark.

1988: The cooperative forms a new subsidiary, Sunkist Real Estate, Inc.

1990: Sales reach $1 billion.

1998: A freeze devastates the citrus industry, with damaging results that persist for two years.

2001: Sunkist enters into an agreement with Texas grapefruit growers to supplement its California and Arizona fruits.

2004: Sunkist Fun Fruit, intended for school food-service, debuts.

2007: The company introduces new products aimed at an increasingly health-conscious market.

represented 80 percent of the orange growers of Southern California and shipped 6,000 of the 7,000 carloads of produce shipped by all of the state's growers. By regulating shipments and directing the fruit where demand was the highest, the Exchange made an immediate impact on the financial well-being of its member-growers, quickly erasing the painful memory of the "Red Ink" years.

EXPANSION IN CALIFORNIA

By the end of the first season growers realized an average net price of roughly $1 per box of oranges, a return that far exceeded what many would have earned without the Exchange's existence. It was the common belief that without the Exchange, growers would have fallen short of earning $0.25 per box, the realization of which prompted many nonmembers to seriously consider joining the Exchange's ranks. By the end of the nineteenth century the cooperative was firmly established as the indispensable ally of the formerly powerless orange growers in Southern California. There were 1,700 members from 75 local packing associations and 12 district exchanges working together, bringing in $3.7 million in sales.

As the Exchange prospered and expanded in Southern California, others noted the superior return member-growers were earning from their groves, namely, those growers working the land to the north. In California's San Joaquin Valley citrus growers were suffering from many of the same problems that had plagued their counterparts in the south. By 1905, after more than a decade of watching the southern growers prosper under the beneficent control of the Exchange, the northern growers clamored to join the Exchange. In response, the Exchange extended its purview to encompass the entire state.

With the addition of member-growers in the north, the Exchange changed its name to reflect its broader geographic base, adopting the California Fruit Growers Exchange as its new corporate title, and stood solidly positioned as one of the most promising cooperative organizations in North America. Although the Exchange on paper owned very little (the furniture in its Los Angeles office representing its only asset), there was a powerful force operating behind what appeared to be a barren corporate shell. The cooperative owned no citrus groves or property, it held no financial interest in packinghouses, district exchanges, or other local property, yet it represented 45 percent of California's citrus industry through its 5,000 grower-members. In all, the cooperative governed more than 14,000 carloads of citrus when it adopted its new name, with sales returns eclipsing $7 million.

BIRTH OF THE SUNKIST NAME

Geographic expansion was followed by diversification, something the cooperative would do with vigor following World War II. Its first meaningful step in this direction occurred in 1907, when the Exchange formed its own timber supply company. Unable to secure a steady supply of reasonably priced wood for packing crates, the cooperative created the Fruit Growers Supply Company, which set the precedent for the Exchange's synergistic approach to the business of agriculture in later years.

The inaugural year of the Fruit Growers Supply Company also marked the Exchange's first foray into advertising. In 1907 the cooperative launched a major advertising campaign—reportedly the first time a perishable food product was advertised—that introduced the use of the Sunkist brand name. The Sunkist trademark, registered in 1909, became one of the most effective marketing tools for the cooperative from this point forward, on its way toward becoming one of the most recognizable trademarks in the world.

Over the course of the next two decades the Exchange grew into a formidable force, its highlight achievements punctuating the progress of a cooperative with far-reaching capabilities. In 1914 the cooperative's product division was founded with a small marmalade factory, followed by entries into the production of citrus byproducts and the production of orange juice. Advertising became more sophisticated as the years passed, emphasizing the health and nutrition advantages inherent in citrus consumption, and the cooperative bolstered its membership rolls, becoming the unrivaled representative of growers throughout California.

By the end of the 1920s the Exchange comprised more than 13,000 citrus fruit growers who produced more than 75 percent of the California citrus crop. Geographic expansion had carried the Exchange's membership ranks into neighboring Arizona, where the cooperative could look forward to providing its marketing and distributing services to untapped citrus-growing regions. In California, the cooperative had won over a considerable majority of the state's citrus producers. In 1932, amid the torturous economic environment of the Great Depression, three out of every four citrus growers in California were members of the Exchange.

THE GREAT DEPRESSION AND POSTWAR PERIOD

The economic collapse of the 1930s sent shock waves throughout the United States, creating a maelstrom of economic turmoil. Citrus growers were not excluded from the pervasive financial panic sweeping the nation. By 1933 citrus prices had dropped to or below the cost of production, making profit an impossibility. However, instead of retreating and slowing its shipments, the Exchange continued to offer normal volumes throughout the Great Depression. The cooperative extended additional credit, reasoning that there was nothing to be gained by curtailing its activities. "It seemed better to take the risk," explained a Sunkist official at the time, "than permit the fruit to remain, and probably waste, in California, for sales lost with a perishable commodity are never regained."

Careful management carried the cooperative through the difficult 1930s, and by its 50th anniversary

in 1943, the frenetic activity of world war had vanquished any remnants of economic ruin. Midway through World War II, Sunkist was as robust an organization as it ever had been. Within the cooperative there were 200 local packinghouses feeding into 25 local district exchanges, packing more than 37 million boxes of oranges, lemons, and grapefruit. During the economic boom period of the 1950s and 1960s, growth, diversification, integration, and the modernizing and streamlining of operations became the key words describing a corporate world fast on the move. Sunkist, from 1945 forward, began to take on a new shape, broadening and expanding to compete effectively in the new world surrounding it.

One of the most important developments during the postwar period was increasing the awareness and regard for the Sunkist brand name in the minds of consumers. Toward this end, the cooperative registered a marketing triumph, effectively removing the cooperative from the business of commodity selling, in which the winners and losers were determined by whoever priced their products the lowest. As recognition and respect for the Sunkist brand increased through sophisticated advertising efforts, consumers demonstrated their willingness to pay more for a Sunkist orange than for the non-Sunkist variety.

The cooperative had first successfully stamped the Sunkist trademark on fresh oranges in 1926 and in 1951 began branding its trademark on frozen concentrates and other canned citrus juices. In 1952 the cooperative made the ultimate acknowledgment of the importance of the Sunkist name by changing its own name from the California Fruit Growers Exchange to Sunkist Growers, forever allying the cooperative and its member-growers with the ubiquitous brand.

Another decisive postwar move was the cooperative's penetration of foreign markets, particularly its foray into Japan. At first, however, the cooperative's biggest foreign market was in Europe, where nearly eight million cartons of fruit were shipped annually during the early 1960s. By the late 1960s Sunkist was shipping more than 12 million cartons abroad annually, while at home the company controlled roughly 80 percent of the citrus crop in the Far West.

UPS AND DOWNS

The energy crisis of the early and mid-1970s severely hobbled Sunkist's burgeoning export business, as the costs of shipping fruit overseas tripled, but overall the 1970s were years of robust growth. In 1974 the cooperative licensed its name to the Ben Myerson Candy Co., Inc., which began producing fruit jellied pectin made from Sunkist's citrus byproducts. Three years later an agreement was reached with General Cinema Corporation to market citrus-flavored carbonated drinks bearing the Sunkist trademark, as the cooperative sought to realize the full financial benefits of its esteemed brand.

Because of these and other efforts, sales swelled 50 percent between 1973 and 1979, eclipsing the $500,000 mark in 1977. By this point there were 6,500 ranches signed on as Sunkist members in California and Arizona, with the groves ranging in size from five acres to as much as 10,000 acres. Expansion overseas had led to the establishment of three foreign subsidiaries, and the company's domestic efforts were supported by 37 fresh fruit sales offices scattered throughout the country.

Sales reached their next milestone of $1 billion in 1990, following a decade that saw the number of member-growers decrease while the average size of member farms increased. The decline in membership had begun during the 1960s, when there were nearly 15,000 member-growers, but the decline had become more precipitous as the cooperative entered the 1980s.

By 1983 membership was down to 5,000 and its share of the Far West citrus crop had fallen from nearly 80 percent to 56 percent, as the encroachment of commercial firms into the western citrus industry altered the face of citrus farming. Sunkist officials realized that the cooperative's survival depended on maintaining a large volume base and that any further erosion of the cooperative's membership rolls would cause decided injury to the 90-year-old organization. To gain new members, membership requirements were eased during the decade, overhead costs were reduced, and in 1988 the cooperative formed a new subsidiary, Sunkist Real Estate, Inc. Through Sunkist Real Estate, members received real estate, financial, and investment services, as well as short-term financing. Gradually, the cooperative's membership rose.

WEATHERING STORMS

Although the 1990s began with the longest, coldest freeze in California's history to date, most of the decade was positive for the cooperative. After three decades of investment, export business accounted for roughly a third of the cooperative's sales volume during the decade, which represented a considerable amount of overseas business considering that annual revenue eclipsed $1 billion during the 1990s. In 1997, revenues reached $1.075 billion, with payments to members at an all-time record of $867 million and 86 million cartons of fresh citrus sales. By the end of the decade, as the cooperative settled into its second century of operation, there were 6,500 citrus farmers in California and

Arizona who counted themselves as Sunkist growers.

Nevertheless, in the late 1990s, Sunkist encountered several obstacles. One challenge resulted from the end of artificial quotas that had regulated citrus production since the New Deal era. The quotas had bolstered Sunkist's authority in the field, enabling the company to maintain high prices and establish what the October 5, 1998, *Forbes* called a "cartel-like market discipline." When the federal law that imposed the quotas was changed in 1994, the price of Sunkist membership lost its value for some growers.

At the same time, Sunkist faced competition in the late 1990s from Argentina's formidable citrus industry and Spain's easy-to-peel and inexpensive Clementine oranges. To make matters worse, a freeze in 1998 devastated the industry, damaging the quality, taste, size, and price of fruit for two years.

At this juncture, after Sunkist President Russell Hanlin retired, the cooperative hired Vincent Lupinacci (formerly of Pepsi, Sara Lee, and Six Flags amusement parks) as its new president. Under Lupinacci, Sunkist began marketing imported Argentinean lemons. Lupinacci lasted only two and a half years in his position, resigning suddenly in 2000.

STRATEGIES FOR A GLOBAL MARKET

Lupinacci left the company at a very difficult time, with rising global competition from European and South American growers of citrus and other crops, along with increasing retail consolidation and the emergence of a variety of new produce products. After a five-month national search, Sunkist hired Jeffrey D. Gargiulo, CEO of Gargiulo Inc., a major U.S. producer of fresh fruits and vegetables, as its new president, a position he would occupy until 2005. Indicating the difficult conditions for the industry as a whole, Sunkist revenues in 2000 had fallen to $847 million (from $1.1 billion a decade earlier); nevertheless, the company was Number 18 on the *Business Journal* list.

Gargiulo, an international trade specialist, restructured the company, reorganizing several divisions, redesigning sales and marketing strategies to leverage Sunkist's brand name, reducing the size of the board of directors and recruiting new expertise, increasing overseas licensing, and introducing new fruit products that responded to market demand. In 2001, Sunkist supplemented its California and Arizona fruits when it entered into an agreement with Texas grapefruit growers, and the company began to look at other growing options outside the United States. In fiscal 2001, the company's revenues increased for the first time in two years, jumping to $993 million (an 11 percent increase over the previous year). Payments to growers also increased 10 percent.

In 2003, Sunkist made plans to provide a line of the increasingly popular precut fruits. Sunkist Fun Fruit, intended for school foodservice, debuted in 2004. The company also began importing fruit from Australia, South Africa, and Argentina in the summer months (foreign sourcing during times when citrus was out-of-season in California and Arizona helped the company respond to the global demand from retailers for year-round citrus). When citrus supplies exceeded demand in 2003, Sunkist began licensing strawberries. Sunkist revenues fell for the second year in a row in 2003, decreasing 2.3 percent to $941 million. However, in 2004 revenues increased to $975 million while prices for navel and Valencia oranges rose, reflecting heightened buyer confidence in the quality of the fruit.

In 2006, Sunkist revenues soared to $1.1 billion, the highest in the company's history to date. Then, after an excellent start to the growing season, a freeze in 2007 dramatically reduced crop supplies. By this time experienced in freeze-management strategies, Sunkist growers harvested and packed as much fruit as they could upon learning of the oncoming freeze, and, as a result, impact was minimized and the year was relatively successful. Sunkist began the consolidation of its Citrus Juice & Oils operations, launching what would become the largest world-class processing facility for citrus byproducts on the West Coast of the United States. The company also introduced two new products aimed at an increasingly health-conscious market: Sunkist Naturals (100 percent juices and smoothies) and Premium Sweet (jarred fruit packed in juice).

Having weathered the storms of over 100 years in business, Sunkist's decades of leadership in the U.S. citrus industry pointed to a similarly influential role in the years ahead. Perhaps the cooperative's greatest strength was its name, a brand imprinted on the minds of consumers that promised to endure.

Jeffrey L. Covell
Updated, Heidi Feldman

PRINCIPAL SUBSIDIARIES

Fruit Growers Supply Company; Sunkist Real Estate, Inc.

PRINCIPAL COMPETITORS

Chiquita Brands; Dole Foods; Tropicana.

FURTHER READING

Cline Harry, "Citrus Freeze Disheartening After Strong Sunkist '06 Season," *Western Farm Press (Online Exclusive)*, February 23, 2007.

"Fixed/Variable Produce—Citrus," *Progressive Grocer*, November 15, 2006, p. 97.

Lubove, Seth, "Rebellion in the Orange Groves," *Forbes*, October 5, 1998, p. 76.

Martinez, Carlos, "After More than a Century, Sunkist Has Learned to Adapt," *San Fernando Valley Business Journal*, June 23, 2003, p. 25.

McLain, Jim, "Sunkist Growers Get Good Reports at Meeting in Ventura County, Calif.," *Ventura County Star*, February 11, 2002.

———, "Wal-Mart Executive Delivers Warning to Sunkist Citrus Growers," *Knight-Ridder/Tribune Business News*, February 19, 2004.

Merlo, Catherine, *Heritage of Gold: The First 100 Years of Sunkist Growers, Inc.*, Sherman Oaks, Calif.: Sunkist Growers, Inc.

Paris, Ellen, "Sunset in the Groves?" *Forbes*, March 23, 1987, p. 35.

Pollock, Dennis, "Sunkist Growers Cheer Bumper Crop, Higher Prices," *Knight-Ridder/Tribune Business News*, February 17, 2005.

Pondel, Evan, "U.S.-Based Fruit Companies Face Falling Prices," *Daily News*, November 29, 2001.

Rodriguez, Robert, "Sunkist Revenue Falls Again," *Fresno Bee*, February 19, 2004, p. C1.

Saltzman, Darrell, "Staying Alive—Privately," *Los Angeles Business Journal*, October 29, 2001, p. 1.

Smith, Claire, "New Global Strategy: Year-Round Citrus Demand Has Sunkist Tapping Foreign Market Supplies," *Rural Cooperatives*, September–October 2003, p. 4.

Steinberg, Jim, "Resignation Leaves Sunkist Seeking Leader," *Knight-Ridder/Tribune Business News*, November 28, 2000.

"Sunkist Bursting Out All Over," *Supermarket News*, February 9, 1998, p. 12.

"Sunkist Growers and Taylor Farms Create Joint Venture," *Western Farm Press (Online Exclusive)*, March 15, 2006.

"Sunkist Growers Coop to Buy Foreign Fruit," *Kiplinger Agricultural Letter*, September 19, 2003.

"Sunkist Reports Record Year for California Citrus Sales," *Knight-Ridder/Tribune Business News*, February 11, 1998, p. 2.

Syntax-Brillian
Corporation

■

1600 North Desert Drive
Tempe, Arizona 85281-1230
U.S.A.
Telephone: (602) 389-8888
Fax: (602) 389-8801
Web site: http://www.syntaxbrillian.com

Delisted Public Company
Incorporated: 1986 as Three-Five Systems, Inc.
Employees: 293 (2007)
Sales: $697.6 million (2007)
NAICS: 334310 Audio and Video Equipment Manufacturing

■ ■ ■

Syntax-Brillian Corporation is a public company based in Tempe, Arizona, best known for the Olevia value-priced brand of high-definition televisions (HDTVs). Once flying high from the sale of HDTVs to mass retailers such as Sears, Target, Kmart, and Circuit City, Syntax crashed in 2008, leading to bankruptcy and a delisting of its stock from the NASDAQ. Ensuing shareholder lawsuits have hampered management's efforts to sell the Olevia assets to a former vendor. Brillian did succeed, however, in divesting its digital camera subsidiary, Vivitar Corporation.

ORIGINS AS THREE-FIVE SYSTEMS

Syntax-Brillian Corporation was formed in 2005 through the merger of Brillian Corporation and Syntax Groups Corporation. The older of the two was Brillian, which began as a division of Phoenix, Arizona-based Three-Five Systems, Inc. (TFS). In turn, TFS was established in 1986 when National Semiconductor Corp. spun off its money-losing optoelectronic components division in a leveraged buyout to private investors. The "Three-Five" name referred to the periodic table groups and the elements needed to make semiconductors.

TFS's management did not perform well, and just a year later one of the initial investors, David Buchanan, was hired to run the struggling company. The ex-Marine was well suited to the task. He held an undergraduate and master's degree in electrical engineering from the University of Iowa, and from 1958 to 1967 worked for a number of top electronics companies, including General Dynamics, Sperry Flight Systems, and General Electric Computer Department in Phoenix. He was also familiar with the plight of start-ups, having founded Peripherals Inc., maker of disk-testing equipment, in 1967, and Talos Systems Inc., which produced digitizers for the computer graphics industry. He sold both, and in the 1980s became a private venture capital investor. After becoming chief executive of TFS, he devoted all of his time to growing the Phoenix company.

TFS designed and produced products that used LCD (liquid crystal display) and LED (light-emitting diode) technology, from digital displays on clocks, calculators, and other products, to remote control devices. The company enjoyed modest growth, increasing sales from $8.4 million in 1987 to $10.8 million in 1989, having turned profitable in 1988. In 1990, to expand the business further, Buchanan engineered a merger with Electronic Research Associates Inc. (ERA), a publicly traded Connecticut-based optoelectronics products company. TFS received a majority interest in the new company and applied the Three-Five name to ERA to become a NASDAQ-listed company. Becoming a public company was a secondary benefit, however. Buchanan was more interested in acquiring ERA's technology, in particular a keyboard-integrated product, as well as expanding its operations and customer base.

GROWING WITH THE COMMUNICATIONS TECHNOLOGY BOOM

Buchanan focused on LCD technology, establishing the United States' largest LCD laboratory, although to keep down labor costs product assembly was done in the Philippines. Where TFS made its mark in the mid-1900s was with cellular telephone displays, signing a major deal with Motorola. TFS enjoyed a meteoric rise, increasing profits tenfold and twice making the list of the *Forbes* 200 Best Small Companies. The company's stock reached $50 a share in 1994, split two-for-one, and was again soon valued at $50 a share.

Buchanan recognized that TFS was overly dependent on Motorola and began to build up the company's infrastructure in order to diversify, but before any progress could be made, Motorola made changes to its product line in early 1996 and slashed the number of TFS panels it would need. As a result, revenues dropped from $92 million to $61 million, the company reported a net loss, and the price of its stock plummeted to less than $9 a share.

Fortunately for TFS it had little debt and was able to absorb the loss of Motorola's business, which continued to provide about one-third of revenues. Smaller customers helped to make up the difference, and Buchanan began investing in the development of microdisplays and a proprietary technology, liquid crystal intense display (LCID).

In 1998 TFS became involved in the miniature liquid-crystal-on-silicon (LCOS) display technology used in cellular phones and other mobile devices by acquiring the right to use backpanels and optics developed by a Palo Alto, California start-up, Siliscape Inc. A year later

TFS acquired assets from its former corporate parent when National Semiconductor sold its microdisplay operations, including additional LCOS technology.

As the new century unfolded and cellular phones using the new LCD panels soared in number, TFS again became overly dependent on Motorola, which accounted for 80 percent of the company's $160.7 million in sales in 2000, when net income totaled $14.8 million. An economic downturn then had an adverse impact on the company, resulting in a drop in sales to $119.1 million in 2001 and a net loss of $17.8 million. In addition to cellular phone display panels, TFS applied its technology to multimedia projectors and high-definition television sets. In early 2002 it added near-to-eye technology through the acquisition of assets from Zight Corp. of Boulder, Colorado.

BRILLIAN CORPORATION FORMED: 2003

In 2003 TFS decided to specialize in electronics manufacturing services. It packaged its microdisplay division as an entity called Brillian Corporation, which was spun off as a stock distribution in September of that year. TFS pursued its new business model, but did not fare well and filed for bankruptcy protection in September 2005. The following year the company was liquidated.

Brillian, in the meantime, established headquarters in Tempe, Arizona, and maintained a Personal Display Systems Group in Boulder. Serving as president and chief executive officer was Vincent F. Sollitto, Jr., who possessed more than 30 years of experience in the electronics field, including a seven-year stint as CEO of Photon Dynamics, Inc., where he was involved in increasing yields for flat-panel-display manufacturers. Under his leadership, Brillian looked to apply its different display technologies to the production of HDTVs, portable business projectors, headsets for video gaming, and head-mounted displays used by the military.

Brillian had hoped to sell its LCOS chip to TV manufacturers, but found limited interest, primarily because of the uncertainty surrounding a start-up provider. Soon after being spun off, Brillian announced instead that it would use the LCOS technology to develop 720- and 1,080-pixel rear-projection HDTVs. In May 2004 the company's new rear-projection HDTV, a 65-inch model, was unveiled, receiving positive reviews. Less expensive than other flat-panel televisions using LCD or plasma technology, the Brillian LCOS set was still pricey for most consumers, retailing between $7,000 and $9,000.

Brillian was not alone in producing rear-projection television using LCOS, and other rear-project methods were also available, most notably digital light processor (DLP) technology championed by Texas Instruments, which possessed a critical head start in the market. Brillian had a deal to supply Sears with a quantity of 65-inch LCOS TVs in 2004, but it was unable to secure the light engines it needed and the purchase fell through. The light engine, which included the chips and optics, was the guts of the television, accounting for 70 percent of the cost. Brillian decided to take light engine production in-house. To help in making this shift, the company agreed in the summer of 2005 to merge with a maker of LCD HDTVs, Syntax Groups Corporation of City of Industry, California.

SYNTAX SPUN OFF: 2004

Syntax was formed in March 2004 by Lasertech Computer Distributor Inc. Established in 1994 Lasertech was a national distributor of computers, software, mainboards, and peripherals such as CD-ROM drives and sound cards. With James Li serving as CEO, Syntax introduced a line of competitively price LCD HDTVs (20-inch, 27-inch, and 30-inch) under the Olevia label soon after becoming an independent company. Olevia HDTVs quickly made their mark in the North American market, becoming the fastest-growing LCD TV in a matter of months, carried by such retailers as Target and Staples, and online through Amazon.com and Target.com. Larger models, including a LCOS rear-projection TV, were soon to follow.

Also in 2004 Syntax began marketing Olevia LCD TVs in Asian markets. To maintain growth of the Olevia brand, Syntax considered making an initial public offering that it hoped would net $15 million. The company was also open to a reverse merger. In July 2004 Syntax elected to merge with Brillian; the deal was completed later in the year. Although Syntax shareholders received 70 percent of the merged company, Sollitto was retained as chairman and CEO.

The reasons for the Syntax-Brillian merger were manifold. From the perspective of Brillian, the deal helped financially. A round of funding had brought $10 million to Brillian, but it was only enough money to keep the company in business until the merger was completed. Brillian also looked to make Syntax a customer for the light engines it was going to produce for itself, thereby keeping its manufacturing facility busy and lowering unit costs. By merging with Brillian, Syntax obtained an inexpensive way to go public, making it easier to tap the equity markets in the United States and overseas. The company also looked to take advantage of Brillian's research and development capabilities and manufacturing assets.

Syntax, in turn, possessed marketing assets that could benefit Brillian. By bringing together Syntax's Olevia value-priced brand with Brillian's higher-end LCOS sets, Sollitto was hopeful of creating a full-service HDTV company, one that could offer small bedroom LCD sets as well as large living room LCOS sets. The Olevia brand provided entry into the retail space while the higher-end Brillian products took the company into the space controlled by the Customer Electronic Design & Installation Association.

POST-MERGER SUCCESSES

Syntax-Brillian enjoyed some initial success, driven primarily by the sale of Olevia LCD TVs. In fiscal 2006, ending June 30 of that year, the company posted revenues of nearly $193 million. To support growth the company in October 2006 opened a 50,000-square-foot high-definition, flat-panel manufacturing plant in Ontario, California, the first on its kind in the United States. By assembling the larger Olevia sets at home instead of in Taiwan, the company saved on shipping costs and import taxes, and could maintain better control on quality.

While the company enjoyed success in the LCD market, the LCOS TV market remained problematic. Although the company produced a superior product, it faced stiff competition from the likes of Sony and had no choice but to greatly lower costs. In an effort to achieve that end, Syntax-Brillian in 2006 formed a joint venture with China South Industries Group, a state-owned conglomerate, to produce the light engines, which had been made in Arizona at a cost disadvantage.

Another major development in 2006 was the $26 million stock acquisition of Vivitar Corporation, a California manufacturer of photography equipment and optics. Established in Hollywood in 1938 by a pair of German immigrants, Max Ponder and John Best, the company was originally known as Ponder and Best, a photographic distribution company. It was not until the 1970s that it commissioned the manufacture of lenses under the Vivitar name. A wide range of cameras, flashes, binoculars, projectors, and camera accessories were to follow.

The addition of the Vivitar brand brought product diversity to Syntax-Brillian and the company's established retail distribution channels opened up Europe and other markets and retail channels to Olevia HDTVs. Moreover, the companies possessed complementary digital imaging technologies. The deal also paved the way for an investment by Vivitar's primary contract manufacturer, Premier Image Technology Corporation, which along with TCV Group, Olevia's primary supplier of plastic injection molded parts, agreed in late 2006 to pay $10 million for a stake in Syntax-Brillian.

CONDITIONS DETERIORATE IN 2007

Syntax-Brillian reached a high-water mark in fiscal 2007, when sales approached $700 million and the company posted net earnings of $29.8 million. Soon after the fiscal year closed, however, conditions began to deteriorate rapidly, as credit tightening in Asia adversely impacted the supply-chain partners of Syntax-Brillian. After the company failed to meet revenue forecasts, investors punished the stock, leading to cascading changes.

The chief financial officer left, followed by a change at the top, with Sollitto stepping down as CEO in favor of James Li in the beginning of October 2007. Two weeks later Syntax-Brillian announced that it planned to sell or close its Tempe operations, part of a 120-day review to improve cash flow and the company's standing with Wall Street. In April 2008 the company announced several changes, including a new manufacturing agreement with Compal Electronics for Olevia HDTVs, a streamlining of the companies retail and online partners, and staff cuts that were expected to reduce overhead costs by 20 percent.

Syntax-Brillian was unable to stem the tide, however. In June 2008 Li left the company to "address personal issues," and an interim CEO, Greg Rayburn, took over as CEO. A month later the company filed for Chapter 11 bankruptcy protection. Vivitar was not included in the filing, but on the same day, management announced that the subsidiary would be put up for sale outside the bankruptcy proceedings. In August 2008 Vivitar was sold to Sakar International Inc. In the meantime, the NASDAQ began proceedings to delist Syntax-Brillian stock, and TVC Group formed Olevia

International Group LLC, which arranged to acquire the Olevia HDTV assets by assuming $60 million of Syntax-Brillian's debt.

The Olevia deal did not sit well with angry stockholders, however. Many of them petitioned the bankruptcy court to delay the transaction pending an investigation into possible conflicts of interest. The matter lingered into the fall of 2008. In March 2009 while the U.S. bankruptcy court was considering Syntax-Brillian's bankruptcy plan, an investigation was launched by federal agencies on the suspicion of fraud in some of the company's dealings with vendors overseas. Still, the Olevia brand remained in the marketplace. A Blu-Ray high-definition DVD player was unveiled in early October 2008. Whether Olevia LCD TVs would return as part of Syntax-Brillian or under the auspices of Olevia International remained very much an unanswered question.

Ed Dinger

PRINCIPAL COMPETITORS

LG Group; Samsung Electronics Co.; Vizo, Inc.

FURTHER READING

Barrett, William P., "Another Match, Please," *Forbes*, September 8, 1997, p. 130.

Clark, Don, "Brillian's TV Is Crisp, but Will Consumers See It?" *Wall Street Journal*, September 23, 2004, p. B4.

Darlin, Damon, "The No-Name Brand Behind the Latest Flat-Panel Price War," *New York Times*, February 12, 2007, p. C1.

Felt, Kevin, "A Clear Picture," *San Gabriel Valley Tribune*, October 14, 2004.

Iritani, Evelyn, "Maker of HDTVs Aims for Big Time," *Los Angeles Times*, September 3, 2006, p. C1.

Johnson, Andrew, "Syntax-Brillian Files for Chapter 11 amid Suits, Climbing Debt," *Arizona Republic*, July 9, 2008, p. D1.

———, "Syntax-Brillian Shareholders: Don't Sell Assets," *Arizona Republic*, July 31, 2008, p. D1.

Luebke, Cathy, "Vote Scheduled for this Month on Three-Five Systems Merger," *Business Journal—Serving Phoenix & the Valley of the Sun*, April 9, 1990, p. 5.

Rudnick, Michael, "Syntax/Brillian Now in the Picture," *HFN*, July 25, 2005, p. 6.

"Syntax to Acquire LCOS Maker Brillian," *Extreme Tech.com*, July 13, 2005.

Taylor, Ed, "HDTV Maker Hopes to Redefine Business," *Mesa (Ariz.) Tribune*, October 23, 2007.

———, "High Definition TV Maker Brillian Completes Merger with Syntax Groups," *Mesa (Ariz.) Tribune*, December 2, 2005.

———, "Tempe, Ariz.-Based High-Tech Displays Producer Sets Date for Spinoff," *Mesa (Ariz.) Tribune,* August 28, 2003.

———, "Tempe, Ariz.-based Three-Five Systems Spin-Off Unveils New High Definition TV," *Mesa (Ariz.) Tribune,* May 14, 2004.

Temple-Inland

Temple-Inland Inc.

———————— ∎ ————————

1300 Mopac Expressway South
Austin, Texas 78746
U.S.A.
Telephone: (512) 434-5800
Fax: (512) 434-3750
Web site: http://www.templeinland.com

Public Company
Incorporated: 1983
Employees: 12,000
Sales: $3.92 billion (2007)
Stock Exchanges: New York
Ticker Symbol: TIN
NAICS: 322130 Paperboard Mills; 322211 Corrugated
and Solid Fiber Box Manufacturing; 321113
Sawmills; 321211 Hardwood Veneer and Plywood
Manufacturing; 321212 Softwood Veneer and
Plywood Manufacturing; 321219 Reconstituted
Wood Product Manufacturing

■ ■ ■

Temple-Inland Inc. manufacturers corrugated packaging
and building products. The company produces over 3.6
million tons of boxes each year, securing its position as
the third largest producer of corrugated packaging in
North America. Temple-Inland also manufacturers
lumber, gypsum, particleboard, medium-density
fiberboard (MDF), and fiberboard. The company
launched a major restructuring effort in 2006, which
culminated in the spinoff of its financial services arm,
Guaranty Financial Group Inc., and its real estate busi-

ness, Forestar Real Estate Group Inc. Temple-Inland also
sold its timberland assets in October 2007.

TEXAS ORIGINS

What would become Temple-Inland Inc. began in 1893,
when Thomas Louis Latane Temple, Sr., founded
Southern Pine Lumber Company on 7,000 acres of East
Texas, Angelina County, timberland. Temple built the
town of Diboll around his company, and by 1894 the
first sawmill was operating, cutting 50,000 board feet of
old growth timber each day. During the next few years,
Southern Pine Lumber Company continued to expand
its operations in Diboll. In 1903 the company built its
second sawmill and in 1907 created a hardwood mill. In
1910 Temple Lumber Company was formed and
established operations in Hemphill and Pineland, both
in Sabine County, Texas.

In 1934 Thomas Temple died, leaving his son
Arthur with 200,000 acres of land and a company that
was $2 billion in debt. Three years later the Hemphill
sawmill was destroyed by fire, and Temple Lumber
Company operations moved to a smaller mill in
Pineland. Recovery was on the way, however. During
these early years and through the housing boom following World War II, Southern Pine Lumber primarily
produced basic lumber products, both hardwood and
pine, for the construction and furniture industries. By
the 1950s technology offered new directions and opportunity for growth. Southern Pine Lumber Company
began converting chips, sawdust, and shavings into
panel products. In subsequent years, the company
pioneered the production of southern pine plywood,

COMPANY PERSPECTIVES

■

At Temple-Inland, our mission "to be the best" drives everything we do. What does it mean to be the best? It means an unsurpassed customer commitment—delivering the highest-value products and services and continually exceeding expectations. It means building the best team—from the executive offices to the plant floor—and giving them the right tools, environment and opportunities to thrive. Being the best means driving efficiency in everything we do—continually finding new ways to lower our costs and maximize our resources. It also means being the best corporate citizens, investing in our communities and always maintaining our integrity. Execution is key to winning. It takes everyone, every day, pulling in the same direction and focused on what matters—driving value. We will be best through our excellence in execution and our commitment to creating superior and sustainable shareholder value.

particleboard, gypsum wallboard, and other building materials.

Credit for substantial growth in the 1950s was due to the aggressive leadership of the grandson of Thomas Temple, Arthur Temple, who took over in 1951. Under his direction, the company used technological advances in the forest industry to expand the company's production and reduce its debt. In 1954 Southern Pine Lumber built a new plant in Diboll for fiberboard production, using wood waste and whole pine chips to make asphalt-coated insulation sheathing. Southern Pine Lumber of Diboll and Temple Lumber of Pineland merged in 1956, taking Southern Pine Lumber's name.

In 1962 Southern Pine Lumber purchased the controlling interest in Lumbermen's Investment Corporation of Austin, Texas, a mortgage banking and real estate development company that became a wholly owned subsidiary in the early 1970s. In 1963 gypsum wallboard production began with the purchase of Texas Gypsum, of Dallas, that also became a wholly owned subsidiary of the company. That same year, Southern Pine Lumber set up a joint venture with United States Plywood Corporation to build a $3 million plywood-sheathing plant at Diboll. The plant, supplied with raw material from 400,000 acres of Southern Pine Lumber's timberland, was designed for producing plywood for sheathing, rock decking, subflooring, and industrial uses.

After several successful years of operating the plant as a joint venture, the company bought out United States Plywood.

In 1963 Southern Pine Lumber Company changed its name to Temple Industries, Inc., and built a pilot plant in Pineland to make particleboard from sawdust and shavings. After 70 years of business, the company's land holdings had grown to more than 450,000 acres. In 1964 Temple Industries expanded into financial services, including mortgage banking and insurance. In 1966 the company built a stud mill at Pineland. In 1969 it rebuilt the Diboll sawmill a year after it was destroyed by fire and, also that year, acquired two beverage-case plants in Chattanooga, Tennessee, and Dallas. Two new wholly owned subsidiaries joined Temple Industries in 1969: Sabine Investment Company of Texas, Inc., was formed, and Temple Associates, Inc., was acquired.

CONTINUED GROWTH AND OWNERSHIP CHANGE

The 1970s were even more significant for the company, beginning with the production of medium-density siding and the expansion of the fiberboard operation. Temple Industries formed Creative Homes, Inc., in Diboll, to build mobile and modular homes. In 1971 the company built a new particleboard plant in Diboll, and in 1972 acquired AFCO Industries, Inc., manufacturer of do-it-yourself consumer products. That same year Temple's West Memphis, Tennessee, gypsum operation began production.

The decade, however, was defined by the events of 1973, when Time Inc. acquired Temple Industries and merged it with its Eastex Pulp and Paper Company subsidiary to form Temple-Eastex Incorporated. Eastex Pulp and Paper had been founded in the early 1950s by Time and Houston Oil Company, as East Texas Pulp and Paper. Houston Oil's 670,000 acres of southern pine and hardwood provided raw material for the new paper mill, opened at Evadale, Texas, in 1954. Time had purchased Houston Oil's 50 percent ownership in 1956, thus acquiring the 670,000 acres of timberland.

When Time created Temple-Eastex, magazines were providing only about one-fourth of Time's sales, and Time officials decided to expand the company's more profitable forest products business. Both companies were looking to diversify, and Time's underperforming stock made it vulnerable to takeover. Temple met with Eastex president R. M. (Mike) Buckley, and the arrangements were made. Time bought Temple Industries for stock, and the Temples became Time's largest outside shareholders.

KEY DATES

1893: Southern Pine Lumber Company is founded in Texas.

1910: Temple Lumber Company is founded.

1956: Temple Lumber and Southern Pine merge; the new company retains the Southern Pine Lumber Company name.

1963: Southern Pine is renamed Temple Industries, Inc.

1973: Time Inc. acquires Temple Industries and merges it with Eastex Pulp and Paper Company to form Temple-Eastex Incorporated.

1978: Time Inc. purchases Inland Container Corporation.

1983: Time divests its forest products companies and creates a separate company, Temple-Inland Inc., made up of Temple-Eastex Incorporated, Inland Container Corporation, and several other operations.

1988: Temple-Eastex changes its name to Temple-Inland Forest Products Corporation; financial services operations are expanded with the purchase of three Texas savings and loans; the three combine to form Guaranty Federal Savings Bank.

1992: Subsidiaries Kilgore Federal Savings and Loan Association and Guaranty Federal Savings Bank merge to form Guaranty Federal Bank, F.S.B.

2000: Gaylord Container Corp. is acquired; company headquarters move to Austin.

2007: The company spins off Guaranty Financial Group and Forestar Real Estate Group; the timberland assets are sold.

Temple-Eastex produced lumber and other building materials, in addition to paperboard used for household paper products. In 1974 Temple-Eastex opened a new particleboard plant in Thomson, Georgia, and a new plywood plant in Pineland, Texas. In 1975 the stud mill at Pineland was automated, and all operations except plywood and studs were phased out. That same year Temple-Eastex installed an innovative process for bleaching of pulp, required for white paper products, in the Evadale mill, as part of an expansion in kraft pulp capacity. The $55 million Temple-Eastex expansion boosted Evadale production by 17 percent. The company stayed busy during the late 1970s with openings, closings, purchases, and moves. A wood molasses plant was built in Diboll in 1977 to use the wood sugars found in the wastewater from fiber products. The following year a $100 million capital improvement was begun at Evadale to further enhance operations there. In 1978 Arthur Temple became vice-chairman of Time and served in that position until 1983. In 1979 Temple-Eastex moved into new corporate offices in Diboll, while the nearby plywood operation was closed permanently.

GOING SOLO

The 1980s started off smoothly with some improvements at the Diboll mill. In 1980 a plastic-foam operation was put on line to manufacture urethane for rigid foam insulation, and the company's newest and largest wood-fired boiler began operation. A new chip mill and log processing operation was constructed in 1982 in Pineland to supply chips to Evadale, plywood and stud logs to Pineland, and fuel for all other operations. In 1982, however, the company was fined $40,000 by the Texas Air Control Board for violating state particulate rate and opacity standards. In addition to the fine, the Evadale kraft pulp and paper mill was required to install two electrostatic precipitators.

In 1983, ten years after acquiring Temple Industries, Time decided to spin off the company's forest products operations into a separate company, again as an anti-takeover measure. Time distributed 90 percent of the common stock in the newly formed company, Temple-Inland Inc., to its shareholders. Time also agreed to sell the balance of its holdings within five years after the spinoff.

Temple-Inland, which was then comprised of Temple-Eastex, Inland Container Corporation, and several other operations, offered a wide range of products, including plywood, fiberboard, lumber, particleboard, gypsum, rigid foam board, and wall paneling. The building products division operated five retail stores in Texas and one in Louisiana. Temple-Inland also had successful financial services operations, offering mortgage banking, real estate development, and insurance. The company's heaviest volume, however, came from its container and containerboard segment, which accounted for 59 percent of the company's earnings in 1989. This segment ranked fifth in containerboard production in the United States and third among the country's 800 corrugated box producers in 1990.

Inland Container Corporation, a fully integrated packaging company, made corrugated boxes and other containers at its six paper mills. The company got its start in 1918 when Herman C. Krannert started Anderson Box Company in Anderson, Indiana, to make ventilated corrugated boxes for the shipment of chickens. By 1925 he moved to Indianapolis, Indiana, and opened the first Inland Box Company plant the following year. The company acquired a second plant in Middletown, Ohio, in 1929, and in 1930 was reincorporated as Inland Container Corporation. By 1946 Inland Container had grown into a multi-plant box maker but was relying entirely on outside sources for its paper supply. Later that year, through a joint venture with The Mead Corporation, Georgia Kraft Company, half of which was owned by Inland Container, was formed, and construction of a new linerboard mill was begun at Macon, Georgia. Georgia Kraft owned approximately one million acres of timberland in Georgia and Alabama and operated three linerboard mills with five machines, as well as plywood and lumber mills.

AGGRESSIVE GROWTH STANCE

In 1958 Inland Container acquired a majority of the outstanding stock of General Box Corporation, which, when combined with shares previously held, gave Inland Container more than 50 percent control of that company. This acquisition led to an antitrust charge in 1960 by the Federal Trade Commission against Inland Container for its purchase of shares of General Box's Louisville, Kentucky, plant. Inland Container was ordered to sell the corrugated shipping container plant that it had acquired from General Box.

In the late 1960s, Inland Container further integrated its operations with construction of a corrugating medium mill in Tennessee, which began operations in 1970. In 1978 Time paid $272 million to buy Inland Container. Other operating divisions of Inland Container marketed packaging materials for the agricultural, horticultural, and poultry industries, and manufactured and marketed paper and reinforced box tapes.

Following the 1983 spinoff, Temple-Inland incorporated Inland Container and Temple-Eastex. Temple-Inland adopted the same aggressive stance as its subsidiaries had in previous years. The Temple family was still in control of the company, although it had been expanded, diversified, and modernized since Thomas Temple began operations in 1894. During its first year of business, the subsidiary Temple-Eastex purchased Elmendorf Board of Claremont, New Hampshire, a manufacturer of oriented strand board. The next year, the company acquired National Fidelity Life Insurance Company of Kansas for $28 million with

an eye to expanding its financial services group. In December 1987 Temple-Inland Financial Services acquired Kilgore Federal Savings and Loan Association in Texas for $10 million.

In 1986 Temple-Inland purchased a linerboard mill, three box manufacturing plants, a short line railroad, and approximately 260,000 acres of timberland in east Texas and Louisiana at a cost of about $220 million, from Owens-Illinois, a Toledo, Ohio-based packaging company. The mill, in Orange, Texas, greatly increased the company's capacity for production of linerboard. The mill and timberland were also valuable because of their proximity to Temple-Inland's other facilities. That same year, Temple-Eastex announced construction of a $30 million wood-converting facility in Buna, Texas. The facility was intended as a high-tech sawmill and low-cost residue provider to paper mills in the Texas cities of Evadale and Orange.

EXPANDING FINANCIAL SERVICES

In 1988 Temple-Eastex Incorporated changed its name to Temple-Inland Forest Products Corporation. That same year Georgia Kraft Company was dissolved and its assets divided between Temple-Inland and Mead. Temple-Inland acquired the Rome, Georgia, linerboard mills, a sawmill in Rome, and more than 400,000 acres of timberland.

The big news of 1988, however, was the purchase of three insolvent Texas savings and loans. Temple-Inland, along with Trammell Crow and Mason Best Company, bought Delta Savings Association of Texas, in Alvin; Guaranty Federal Savings & Loan Association of Dallas; and First Federal Savings & Loan Association of Austin. The three institutions were combined into one, Guaranty Federal Savings Bank, operating in Dallas, of which Temple-Inland had an 80 percent interest. Temple-Inland's initial outlay was $75 million, and the company committed to contribute another $50 million by January 1991. Temple-Inland was hoping for future payoffs. Purchase of the institutions was a low-risk investment that complemented the company's plans for growth in its financial services group.

In 1989 Temple-Inland was deemed "the most undervalued paper stock on the Big Board" by *Business Week,* May 22, 1989. The company was described as having superb leadership but stock that failed to reflect Temple-Inland's rapid growth. The following year, Temple-Inland sold its Great American Reserve Insurance Company, using the $10 million profit from the sale to bolster Guaranty Federal's capital to expand its home mortgage lending and consumer banking services.

Also in 1990, the company started a new sawmill in De-Quincy, Louisiana, which produced chips for the Evadale and Orange mills, as well as 100 million board feet of lumber annually. In 1991 the company expanded and upgraded its recycled linerboard mill in Ontario, California.

Demand for paper products was consistent during the late 1980s and early 1990s, and the demand for linerboard for corrugated boxes continued to increase. Containers and containerboard sales accounted for more than one-half of the company's profits. The smaller, but highly profitable bleached pulp and paperboard division had seen a rise in demand. This division was one of the company's strongest segments, with bleached paperboard being used for many products, including paper cups and paper plates.

FOCUS ON NEW TECHNOLOGY

In 1991 Arthur Temple, Jr., retired, and Clifford Grum was appointed chairman and CEO. Grum was the first chairman with no ties to the Temple family. Grum announced that Temple-Inland would focus on new technology, including synthetic paper products such as heat-resistant microwave containers, in the 1990s. He predicted that synthetic paper would play an increasingly important role in the future of the industry. Temple-Inland sought to expand its paper operations, and the company acquired Rand-Whitney Packaging in 1994. The following year the company's Latin America presence grew with the opening of a box plant in Chile and a corrugated container sheet facility in Mexico.

Temple-Inland's financial services division grew steadily through the early 1990s, aided by a string of strategic acquisitions. In 1991 the company purchased Capitol Mortgage Bankers, Inc., and the following year its subsidiaries, Guaranty Federal Savings Bank and Kilgore Federal Savings and Loan Association, merged its operations and formed Guaranty Federal Bank, F.S.B. Guaranty acquired the First Saving Bank of San Antonio in 1994 for about $42 million.

Paper market conditions worsened in the late 1990s, and worldwide demand declined, spurring Temple-Inland to restructure its paper products division in 1998. Operating earnings for the paper group were $113 million in 1996, but in 1997 they dropped to a loss of $39 million. Despite poor market conditions, Temple-Inland began operating two new corrugated packaging facilities in 1997, one in Ohio and the other in Mexico. Also that year the company sold the operating assets of Temple-Inland Food Service Corporation, a subsidiary, and closed a box plant in Pennsylvania.

RESTRUCTURING TO BECOME MORE COMPETITIVE

In 1998 the paper group opted for a more decentralized structure in the hope of becoming more competitive. The company set a goal of increasing its paper division earnings by $150 million, despite a continued dreary outlook for paper markets. Temple-Inland closed corrugated packaging facilities in Newark, California, because they were considered noncompetitive and outdated, and sold the Rexford Paper Company, determined to be a non-core asset. Paperboard production was curbed to balance inventory levels. Temple-Inland also added new plants in 1998, with two new sheet plants, located in Tennessee and Virginia, beginning operations. In 1998 operating earnings fared better than 1997, reaching $32.5 million. The improvement was attributed to an increase in the average prices for corrugated packaging and paperboard; box prices fell 19 percent in 1996, dropped an average of 11 percent in 1997, and improved in 1998, with box prices averaging 7 percent higher than 1997 prices.

In 1999 Temple-Inland and Caraustar Industries, Inc., entered into an agreement to form Premier Boxboard Limited LLC, which would operate a Temple-Inland-owned mill in Indiana. Plans to convert the containerboard mill to one able to produce lightweight gypsum facing paper commenced immediately. The company also sold its bleached paperboard facility in Evadale, Texas, to Westvaco Corp. that year.

The building products group enjoyed growth and profitability in the late 1990s despite tumbling lumber markets. Although average lumber prices fell 10 percent in 1998, increases in U.S. housing starts and the strong U.S. economy deflected losses. In addition, Temple-Inland began to diversify and moved more aggressively into the composite panel market to provide alternatives to traditional lumber. In 1996, as part of a joint venture with Caraustar, Temple-Inland purchased a wallboard facility and a gypsum quarry in Texas. Under the terms of the agreement of the joint venture, named Standard Gypsum L.L.C., Temple-Inland agreed to manage and operate the two facilities, while Caraustar would provide gypsum paperboard supplies.

COMMITMENT TO CONTINUING GROWTH

To meet increasing demand for medium-density fiberboard (MDF) and offset declines in lumber prices in the late 1990s, Temple-Inland acquired two MDF plants from MacMillan Bloedel Limited for about $106 million in 1998. The plants, located in Pennsylvania and Ontario, Canada, complemented the company's particleboard operations, as many particleboard customers also used MDF. Temple-Inland continued to strengthen its gypsum wallboard and fiber-cement operations to facilitate rapidly growing construction markets, completing a fiber-cement plant in Texas and progressing with the construction of a gypsum wallboard plant in Tennessee during 1998. Temple-Inland also streamlined its building products operations by implementing modernization plans; the company renovated its Diboll, Texas, mill, modernized its Buna, Texas, sawmill, and converted its Pineland, Texas, sawmill to manufacture lumber rather than plywood.

Temple-Inland's financial services division achieved record earnings in the late 1990s and continued its growth strategy. In 1997 Temple-Inland bought California Financial Holding Company, the parent company of Stockton Savings Bank F.S.B. of Stockton, California. Two years later the company acquired HF Bancorp, Inc., the parent company of Hemet Federal Savings and Loan Association, for $120 million. The purchase greatly expanded Guaranty Federal Bank's geographic reach and strengthened its operations in the Southern California region.

Although mortgage loan rates were at record lows in the late 1990s, the low rates resulted in high numbers of new mortgage originations. To capitalize on the highly active mortgage market, Temple-Inland acquired Western Cities Mortgage Corporation for $11.5 million in 1996, and a year later the company purchased Knutson Mortgage Corporation for approximately $14.6 million. Temple-Inland's mortgage operations, which served primarily single-family home buyers through 78 offices, saw production volumes nearly double from 1997 to 1998.

Despite uncertain market conditions, Temple-Inland remained committed to improving operations and revenues. The company planned to take advantage of promising markets, such as the MDF and gypsum wallboard segments, and to divest of non-strategic operations. With a diverse offering of paper and building products, access to more than two million acres of timberland, and financial services that included more than 135 Guaranty Federal Bank branches in Texas and California, Temple-Inland seemed prepared to head into the 21st century.

CHANGES IN THE 21ST CENTURY

Temple-Inland entered the new millennium intent on growth. During 2000, the company purchased Gaylord Container Corp., securing its position as a leading producer of corrugated packaging in North America. It also acquired Chesapeake Packaging Co. and Elgin Cor-

rugated Box Co. that year. At the same time, company headquarters moved from Diboll to Austin, Texas.

Increased competition and harsh market conditions forced the company to revamp its strategy in order to shore up profits. As part of its efforts, Temple-Inland launched Project TIP—Transformation, Innovation, and Performance—in 2003. This initiative was set in place to control costs while streamlining operations and set the stage for major changes in the years to come.

During 2006 Temple-Inland created Forestar Real Estate Group to oversee the real estate operations of its forest products and its financial services businesses. While economic conditions in the United States continued to weaken, the company set plans in motion to separate its businesses. At the same time, Temple-Inland was under pressure from corporate raider Carl Icahn, who purchased a 6.7 percent stake in the company in January 2007. Icahn demanded that the company break apart to increase shareholder value and threatened a proxy fight that would remove several board members. A November 2007 *Wall Street Journal* article explained the rationale, claiming, "The idea behind the breakup, as is usually the case, is that the pieces are supposed to be worth more than the whole."

Temple-Inland placated Icahn and in 2007 announced that it planned to spin off its Forestar Real Estate Group and its Guaranty Financial Group. In addition, the company also sold 1.55 million acres of timberland in a $2.4 billion deal to Campbell Group Inc. Temple-Inland used the proceeds from the sale to pay down nearly $700 million in debt. CEO Kenneth Jastrow stepped down after the spinoffs were complete, leaving Doyle R. Simons at the helm.

When the dust settled on the company's restructuring efforts, Temple-Inland's operating structure was significantly different. Formerly a conglomerate with varied holdings, the new Temple-Inland was focused on corrugated packaging and building products. Under the leadership of Simons, the company planned to move forward and expand its business in the years to come. Whether it would be able to maximize profits while separated from its real estate and financial businesses, however, remained to be seen.

Leslie C. Halpern
Updated, Mariko Fujinaka; Christina M. Stansell

PRINCIPAL SUBSIDIARIES

TIN Inc.; Corporate Commercial Realty, Inc.; Del-Tin Fiber L.L.C. (50%); GCC Southeastern Corporation; Gaylord Container de Mexico, S.A. de C.V.; El Morro

Corrugated Box Corporation; El Morro Corrugated Box Corporation; Harima M.I.D, Inc. (25%); Inland International Holding Company CLS, S.A. de C.V.; Crockett Baja, S.A. de C.V.; Inland Corrugados de Mexico, S.A. de C.V.; Grupo Inland, S.A. de C.V.; Inland Corrugados de Monterrey, S.A. de C.V.; IM Servicios, S.A. de C.V.; Inland Paper Company, Inc.; Midwest Sheets Company, LLC; Premier Boxboard L.L.C. (50%); Sabine River & Northern Railroad Company; Schiffenhaus California, LLC (25%); Scotch Investment Company; Sunbelt Insurance Company; Templar Essex Inc.; Temple Associates, Inc.; Temple-Inland Forest Products International Inc.; 507789 N.B. Ltd.; Temple-Inland Resource Company; Temple-Inland Funding Corporation; Texas South-Eastern Railroad Company; TIN Land Financing LLC; TIN Timber Financing LLC.

PRINCIPAL COMPETITORS

International Paper Company; Weyerhaeuser Company; American Gypsum Company.

FURTHER READING

Antosh, Nelson, "Temple-Inland Agrees to Buy California Thrift," *Houston Chronicle,* December 10, 1996, p. 2.

Chipello, Christopher J., "All-Star Analysts 1999 Survey: Paper & Forest Products," *Wall Street Journal,* June 29, 1999, p. R12.

Chronology of Temple-Inland Operations, Diboll, Tex.: Temple-Inland, 1990.

Greenberg, Herb, "MarketWatch Weekend Investor: Temple-Inland Deal: Not as Smart?" *Wall Street Journal,* November 17, 2007.

Jennings, Diane, "Emotional Investment: E. Texas Town Finds Century-Old Ties to Lumber Giant Are Slowly Eroding," *Dallas Morning News,* May 12, 1996, p. A1.

A Proud Tradition, Diboll, Tex.: Temple-Inland, 1984.

Rockwell, Lilly, "Temple-Inland Sells Timberland for $2.4 Billion," *Austin American-Statesman,* August 7, 2007.

———, "Uncertain Outlook for Temple-Inland After Split into Three Firms," *Austin American-Statesman,* January 6, 2008.

"Temple-Inland Urged to Hire Consultant," *Dallas Morning News,* March 27, 1999, p. F3.

"Temple Raises Offer to Debtholders of Gaylord," *Wall Street Journal,* December 5, 2001.

"Westvaco to Acquire Paperboard Facility," *Wall Street Journal,* October 5, 1999, p. B13.

Zehr, Dan, "Temple-Inland Chief Executive to Depart After Seeing Company Through Spinoffs," *Austin American-Statesman,* April 3, 2007.

Tenedora Nemak, S.A. de C.V.

────────■────────

Libramiento Arco Vial km. 3.8
Villa de García, Nuevo León
Mexico
Telephone: (52 81) 8748-5200
Fax: (52 81) 8746-5226
Web site: http://www.nemak.com

Wholly Owned Subsidiary of Alfa, S.A.B. de C.V.
Founded: 1979
Employees: 14,885
Sales: MXN 32.91 billion ($2.95 billion) (2008)
NAICS: 331521 Aluminum Die-Castings; 551112 Offices of Other Holding Companies

■ ■ ■

Tenedora Nemak, S.A. de C.V., is the holding company for the world's leading producer of aluminum cylinder heads and engine blocks for automotive engines. These products account for about 90 percent of the company's revenues, but the company also manufactures aluminum transmission parts for motor vehicles. Nemak's customers include almost all the world's automakers, but primary ones are General Motors Corp., Ford Motor Co., Chrysler LLC, Hyundai Motor Co., Nissan Motor Co., Porsche AG, and Volkswagen AG. The company's rapid growth is a point of pride in Mexico because it exemplifies success on the basis of high technology rather than cheap labor or access to nonrenewable resources. It is a subsidiary of Alfa, S.A.B. de C.V., one of Mexico's largest conglomerates.

LEARNING TO MAKE ALUMINUM CYLINDER HEADS: 1979–90

Grupo Industrial Alfa, S.A. de C.V. (later simply Alfa, S.A. de C.V.) an industrial conglomerate that at the time was the largest in Mexico, created Nemak in 1979 to produce aluminum cylinder heads for motor vehicles. Based in Monterrey, Alfa was present in 39 industrial sectors and had so many companies (143) under its corporate umbrella that as one historian observed, its holdings appeared to be the contents of that city's yellow pages. The company's debt-fueled expansion ended when the economic crisis of the early 1980s drove it into insolvency, but Nemak, which at the time was merely a subsidiary of a subsidiary named Versax, S.A. de C.V., survived. (Versax, which held other unrelated businesses, was dissolved in 2006.)

Despite the chaos within Alfa, Nemak was a well designed and well run company. According to *Auto World,* "In the early days of Mexican manufacturing competitiveness set over a conception of low wages, low skills, and low value added production, Nemak challenged the maquiladora model from its very birth ... the firm was from the beginning bred with a cocktail of heavy capital investments, vanguard technology, and high level experienced management."

Nemak secured investment from Ford Motor Company in 1981. Its original product was aluminum cylinder heads, which needed to be manufactured using complex casting methods to ensure maximal engine efficiency. In 1982 the company purchased technology for manufacturing from Alutek but switched to Teksid S.p.A. two years later. This company was a subsidiary of

---

COMPANY PERSPECTIVES

■

Nemak is a company committed to satisfy the needs of the global automotive industry by manufacturing high tech aluminum components. We aim to be a leading company in technology, cost, quality and response time. We look for an integral development for our personnel and our suppliers and we recognize our responsibility to the environment. As a consequence of the above, we aim to have a leading participation in the global automotive market and to maximize the profitability of our shareholder's net worth.

---

the Italian automaker Fiat S.p.A. For many years Ford and Teksid each held a one-fifth stake in Nemak. Auto parts accounted for 8 percent of Alfa's sales in 1987 and included aluminum cylinder heads for Ford, which was a vital customer for Nemak in its early years.

The Teksid connection was especially important to Nemak in its early years as its own engineers and technicians learned to understand the nature of the cylinder head casting process. A research and development unit established in 1990 conducted a series of trials intended to produce cylinder heads that could meet more exacting specifications for automotive engines and both reduce waste in the manufacturing process and in the amount of energy required for manufacture. The staff also developed modeling software that would help produce new castings more rapidly than in the past.

CYLINDER HEADS PLUS ENGINE BLOCKS: 1995–96

By 1995 Nemak was one of the two largest suppliers of aluminum cylinder head castings in North America that was not controlled by a U.S.-based automaker. The other was Teksid. That year the company acquired North and South American rights to a casting process regarded as the preliminary step in establishing a casting facility for aluminum engine blocks. (The engine block houses the cylinders—the piston chambers in the engine—and their components; the cylinder head, along with the head gasket, seals the cylinders.)

This accord, struck with Comalco Ltd., an Australian company, provided for the use of a process known as low pressure precision sand technology to make the castings for the blocks in Comalco's pilot production facility in Lewisport, Kentucky. At the time

fewer than 10 percent of the world's new automobiles were being made with aluminum monoblocks. By 1998, however, Ford would contract Nemak to make such blocks for the North American versions of the new I-4 and I-5 engines it was developing. General Motors Corp. followed suit by hiring the company to produce blocks for a new V-8 engine.

By mid-1996 Nemak was the leading producer of engine cylinder heads in North America, with a capacity of 3.5 million heads per year. The company had opened a second plant for this purpose and was producing 13 models for 8 automotive plants in Mexico, the United States, and Canada, which were tied more closely economically by the recently enacted North American Free Trade Agreement. Exports represented 97 percent of the total. A contract had been signed to make aluminum cylinder heads for engines being used in Chrysler Corporation's Jeep Truck models.

Nemak held one-quarter of the market for cylinder heads in North America in 1995 and reached sales of $140 million the following year. In 1996 the company obtained a nine-year, $65 million credit line from the World Bank's International Finance Corporation and a group of foreign banks, and a $25 million long term credit line from foreign banks led by Union Bank of Switzerland (later UBS AG).

MORE PLANTS, MORE CLIENTS: 1997–99

By 1997 Alfa felt confident enough of Nemak's future to end its partnership with Teksid, which sold its stake in the enterprise back to Versax. The company was opening its third plant and was producing all the aluminum cylinder heads made in Mexico with the exception of those for Nissan Motor Company and Volkswagen AG, which were being made by these two companies themselves for their Mexican automotive plants. Before the year was over Nemak began exporting to Europe for the first time, sending aluminum cylinder heads to Opel-Vauxhall plants in England. It had also begun producing aluminum engine blocks for General Motors' Corvette models. Sales soared to $200 million in 1997.

During 1998 Nemak initiated operations at its fourth and fifth plants. The latter was constructed, at a cost of $75 million, to build aluminum cylinder heads and monoblocks for Ford. Nemak also began exporting aluminum cylinder heads to Opel in Austria. Ford, General Motors, and Chrysler were the customers for about 90 percent of the company's production, in roughly equal proportions, while Renault, Vauxhall, and Opel accounted for the remaining 10 percent. The

KEY DATES

1979: Nemak is founded by Grupo Industrial Alfa.

1981: Ford Motor Company takes a minority stake in the fledgling enterprise.

1987: Nemak's aluminum cylinder heads account for 8 percent of Alfa's sales.

1995: Nemak acquires, from Australian company Comalco Ltd., the rights to a casting process for aluminum engine blocks.

2000: The company buys two Ford plants in Canada for casting aluminum engine parts.

2002: Nemak opens its first European factory, in the Czech Republic.

2007: Nemak purchases 18 castings plants from three different companies.

2008: Nemak makes about one-fourth of all cylinder heads and engine blocks in the world.

company also opened a technology center in 1998.

Nemak manufactured more than 5 million cylinder heads, or roughly one-tenth of the world total, in 1999, second only to Teksid. Its sales rose to about $325 million that year.

Of the company's 2,500 employees, almost all based in and around Monterrey, 570 were managers and technicians, and almost 400 had degrees in engineering. Among its technical achievements was an excellent recycling operation, according to many automotive materials engineers. In 2000 *American Metal Market* reported that, "Those who have seen its equipment and operations in Mexico, and the airy high domed roofs that characterize its plants, have expressed their admiration and respect for the company."

WORLDWIDE MANUFACTURER: 2000–07

In 2000 Ford sold Nemak its two largest aluminum engine parts casting plants, both of them in Canada's province of Ontario. The facility in Windsor produced blocks, while the one in Essex focused on casting heads and pistons. Meanwhile, the existing Nemak plants were busy turning out parts for other engines including cylinder head castings for DaimlerChrysler AG's new V-6 truck engines and front drive V-6 automobile engines, and blocks for the latter; blocks for a General Motors V-8 passenger car engine; and heads for a DaimlerChrysler V-8 engine to be produced in Mexico.

The collapse of the technology stock bubble in the United States in 2000 led to a recession that resulted in a temporary lull in Nemak's expansion. However, in 2002 the company opened its first plant in Europe, a $45 million facility in Most, Czech Republic. This factory's production of aluminum heads was reserved entirely for General Motors V-6 engines. Nemak was lured to the Central European country by an attractive package of incentives, including ten years free of a certain tax, a $6,500 annual contribution by the government for each person employed, and 30 hectares (75 acres), serviced by gas, light, and water links for only $10,000. The Czech Republic also offered lower priced labor and energy than Mexico. Nemak, in 2005, acquired Rautenbach AG, a German company producing high tech aluminum components in Germany and Slovakia.

With Alfa's sale of its shares in the steel company Hylsamex, S.A. de C.V. in 2005, the conglomerate collected about $1 billion in cash. Armed with some of this money, Nemak—now a direct subsidiary of Alfa and the conglomerate's second largest enterprise—purchased, in 2007, the four automotive castings plants of Norsk Hydro ASA for $544 million. These factories had turned out six million engine heads the previous year and had estimated revenue of $640 million that year.

Nemak followed up this acquisition by purchasing a number of plants of TK Aluminum Ltd. for $485 million and allotting nearly 7 percent of its shares to TK Aluminum at a future date. (Alfa had raised its stake in Nemak to 85 percent in 2004 and 93 percent in 2007.) TK Aluminum was the parent of Teksid Aluminum S.à. r.l., S.C.A., which was the successor to Teksid, S.p.A. Soon after, Nemak purchased Castech S.A., which was making aluminum automotive components in Mexico for Grupo Industrial Saltillo, S.A. de C.V., for $72 million in cash and the assumption of $64 million in debt.

THE FUTURE

With these acquisitions the company had more than doubled its annual sales. It was now the world leader in aluminum monoblocks and heads for engines, with 21 percent of the market. The acquisitions had also added high pressure die casting and Rotacast to its technology assets. The former was used in the production of small size engine blocks and the latter for diesel engine parts. The acquired plants were integrated with those already being operated by Nemak in Mexico, Canada, the Czech Republic, Germany, and Slovakia.

In May 2008 Nemak had 27 plants, of which ten were in Mexico, three each in the United States and Germany, two in Canada, and one each in Argentina, Austria, Brazil, China, the Czech Republic, Hungary,

Poland, Slovakia, and Sweden. During the summer Alfa sold two more steel plants and used the money to buy aluminum plants from Fiat and Norsk Hydro for $1.2 billion.

The company's share of the world market for aluminum heads and blocks had grown to about one-quarter of the total. There was room for expansion, given that 60 percent of the engine monoblocks of automobiles made in the United States were of cast iron rather than aluminum, and the latter was considered a superior material for engine efficiency. Nemak's revenues from cylinder heads were about twice those from engine blocks.

Only one market remained for Nemak to exploit—Asia, which then accounted for only 1 percent of company sales, compared to 57 percent in North America and 35 percent in Europe, Africa, and Australia. The company was selling auto parts to India Motor Parts & Accessories Limited and Nissan and was trying to persuade Toyota Motor Corporation to stop making its own heads and blocks and buy Nemak's instead. The company had two plants in China with a minority partner, Shanghai Automotive Industry Corporation—China's largest automaker—but these facilities accounted for less than 2 percent of Nemak's world capacity.

Nemak held an important technological advantage, according to an article in the Mexican business magazine *Expansión,* in which the author claimed that the company turned out its products in one-third less time than its closest competitors, therefore enabling its customers to offer new models more rapidly.

As 2008 ended Nemak faced the same economic pressures as other companies caught in the throes of the world financial crisis. Normally the company closed its nine Mexican plants for a week during the Christmas season, but this time it extended the closing for a second week. The Essex plant was to shut down for good at the beginning of 2009. World sales had dropped about 10 percent. Nevertheless, Nemak increased its consolidated revenues, which included acquisitions, in 2008. Exports—that is, sales outside of Mexico—accounted for 94 percent of revenue.

Robert Halasz

PRINCIPAL SUBSIDIARIES

Exportadora Nemak, S.A. de C.V.; Nemak S.A.; Nemak Aluminio de México, S.A. de C.V.; Nemak Czech Republic, S.r.o. (Czech Republic); Nemak Exterior, S.L. (Spain); Nemak of Canada Co. (Canada); Nemak Nanjing Aluminum Foundry Co., Ltd. (China; 70%); Nemak Slovakia, S.r.o. (Slovakia).

PRINCIPAL COMPETITORS

Honsel International Technologies S.A.; Montupet S.A.

FURTHER READING

Black, Thomas, "El gran motor regio," *Expansión,* June 23–July 6, 2008, pp. 352–53.

Downey, Stephen, "Global Buying Spree Started in 2005," *Automotive News,* June 2, 2008, p. 30.

"Ford Seen Giving Nemak Control of Casting Plants," *American Metal Market,* April 18, 2000, pp. 1, 16.

"Iron and Aluminum Casting in Monterrey," *Auto World,* January 2005, Mexico Report supplement, pp. 16–18.

Lerner, Matthew, "Meanwhile Nemak Goes on a $1-Billion Buying Binge," *American Metal Market,* February 2008, p. 49.

Marsh, Peter, "The Art of Being Good in Parts," *Financial Times,* March 1, 2000, p. 14.

"Nemak Sets the Pace in Aluminum Parts Casting," *American Metal Market,* May 15, 2000, p. 7.

Sánchez Novoa, César, "Arranca Nemak en Europa," *Reforma,* October 7, 2003, p. 7.

———, "Controla Alfa 80% de Nemak," *El Norte,* March 11, 1997, p. 1.

———, "Crecen ventas de Nemak 33%," *El Norte,* January 9, 1998, p. 5.

———, "Estrenará Nemak quinta nave industrial," *El Norte,* October 17, 1998, p. 9.

———, "Fija Nemak su mirada en el mercado asiático," *El Norte,* August 24, 2007, p. 8.

———, "Obtiene Nemak crédito," *El Norte,* June 26, 1996, p. 26.

———, "Pararán 9 plantas de Nemak," *El Norte,* December 19, 2008, p. 1.

———, "Revoluciona Alfa area de autopartes," *Palabra,* March 16, 2007, p. 14.

Wrigley, Al, "Nemak Revs up for Aluminum Engine Block Race," *American Metal Market,* May 25, 1995, p. 12.

Tergal Industries S.A.S.

Rue Jules Vercruysse
BP 1
Gauchy, 02430
France
Telephone: (33 03) 23 64 44 51
Fax: (33 03) 23 64 44 60
Web site: http://www.tergal-fibres.com

Private Company
Incorporated: 1995 as Tergal Fibres
Employees: 130
Sales: EUR 130 million ($181.9 million) (2007 est.)
NAICS: 325222 Noncellulosic Organic Fiber
    Manufacturing

■ ■ ■

Tergal Industries S.A.S. is fighting to remain France's last producer of PET (polyethylene terephthalate) resins and polyester fibers. The company, based in Gauchy in the L'Aisne region, produces more than 65,000 metric tons of PET and more than 35,000 tons of polyester fiber, and generates revenues of more than EUR 130 million ($180 million) per year. However, Tergal is dwarfed by its major global competitors, which include DuPont, Montedison, and Trevira. The company's PET resins production, for example, represents just 2 percent of the total European market. As a result, Tergal positions itself as a niche player for the development and production of specialty products.

This strategy has led the company to develop a number of innovative products, including its Reseko

branded recycled food-quality PET resin, and LacPET (light active compound polyethylene terephthalate), used especially for long-life milk bottles. Tergal, formed through a management buyout of Rhone-Poulenc's French PET operation in the late 1990s, has been hit hard by the global economic turmoil, and particularly by fluctuations in its raw materials prices. The company has managed to fight off bankruptcy, however, and in January 2009 the company won a court battle against its creditors to continue its operations. Tergal is led by Chief Executive Officer Alain Escat.

ORIGINS

Tergal's origins can be traced to the beginnings of the development of artificial fibers. Viscose was among the first of the modern fibers that were to revolutionize the textiles industry especially, but other industries as well, including packaging. This fiber, based on a solution of cellulose xanthate, was developed at the end of the 19th century by French scientist Hilaire de Chardonnet. It was not until 1902, however, that a method for manufacturing the material was invented by three scientists in England. They received a patent on the method. The first use of viscose, which as its name suggested remained in a viscous state, was as a fabric liner.

Initially viscose was highly brittle in its hardened state, and so was unsuitable for manufacturing solid objects. This problem was soon solved, however, and by 1904 manufacturers had developed means of spinning viscose into thread for use as a textile fiber. Viscose represented something of a revolution in the textiles industry, especially in the creation of undergarments.

COMPANY PERSPECTIVES

◼

Know-how backing innovation. Tergal Industries has developed acknowledged know-how in the synthesis of PET for Fibre and Packaging applications. Thanks to our R&D department, innovation is at the core of our strategy; from recycled PET resin to high-tech fibres through LacPET, a light barrier PET resin, we aim to meet today's demands.

Viscose allowed producers to develop far lighter fabrics for use in stockings and other undergarments, which had traditionally been made of wool and cotton. By the 1920s, viscose had largely replaced these materials as the material of choice for stockings. Manufacturers had in the meantime developed other uses for viscose fibers, particular as a liner for clothing, home furnishing fabrics, towels and tablecloths, sponges, and even as the inner lining for early pneumatic tires. Viscose provided the basis for another important invention, cellophane, developed by the Bernheim brothers.

France played a leading role in the development of viscose fiber through the 1920s, led by the Comptoir des Textiles Artificiels, an association of French viscose manufacturers. Further development of viscose fibers led to the creation of a new fabric type, rayon, which became a hugely popular textile material for the next several decades.

The demand for viscose in the post–World War I era led a pair of businessmen, Émile Chatin and Joseph Gillet, to establish a new cellulose-based rayon manufacturing company in 1921. Called Compagnie Nouvelle des Applications de la Cellulose (CNAC), the company launched construction of its factory that year. For this, CNAC chose the town of Gauchy, located near Saint Quentin in L'Aisne, northeast of Paris. That area was already a major textiles region in France, with a well-developed transportation infrastructure. The region was also close to the major coal producers to the north; this proximity was necessary, given the fuel-intensive nature of viscose production.

Gauchy and the surrounding region had been devastated by World War I. Indeed, the site chosen for the factory had itself been situated at the front of the trench war for a long period and still bore the scars. Construction of the factory was completed in 1923, and Chatin's son-in-law, Rigollot, became the company's first managing director. Because of the lack of French manpower following the war, the company turned to immigrants from Eastern Europe, particularly Hungary and Poland. CNAC's initial interest turned to the production of a new type of thread, developed in conjunction with the Bernheim brothers, called Celta. This product, which featured a hollow thread, enabled the production of fabrics very similar to natural fabrics.

SURVIVING WORLD WAR II

CNAC struggled through much of its first decade in implementing Celta production, however, which required a more delicate manufacturing process than the more common Cidena thread. In order to maintain its financial viability, CNAC added a second line for the production of Cidena in 1935. Cidena was used especially by the hat making industry. In 1938, CNAC introduced a third production line for the production of fibranne. This was a new fabric type, similar to rayon, which imitated the feel of linen. Fibranne also marked a turning point in the viscose textile market. In 1938, scientists had developed a means of synthesizing cellulose; fibranne then became the first fully manmade fabric. Fibranne proved essential to CNAC's survival during the German occupation of France during World War II. Due to the lack of raw materials, particularly natural cellulose, the company focused wholly on its fibranne production for the duration. The company's new managing director, who took over in 1941, also succeeded in getting the factory classified as "V Betrieb," which provided it with some guarantees for its continuing operations. Nonetheless, the company suffered the loss of a signification proportion of its workers, many of whom were taken to Germany as part of the Nazi forced labor program. Others died in the German camps.

The Gauchy factory emerged from the war unscathed by the bombs that had destroyed much of France's industrial infrastructure. The company quickly ramped up its production again, particularly for fibranne and Cidena. The company's workforce, which had neared 1,000 before the war, was around 700 at this time.

Demand for the group's textile fibers remained high through the 1950s. However, the company was soon to be confronted with the appearance of new manmade fiber types that quickly captured the global textiles industry. The rapid development of the petroleum industry and the related rise of the petrochemicals sector had led scientists to develop an extraordinary range of applications for components of the fossil fuel. As early as 1929, the research of Wallace Carothers had touched upon the potential of combining ethylene glycol with terephthalic acid. It was not until 1941, however, that two British scientists, John Whinfield and James Dickson, patented the substance resulting from this

KEY DATES

1921: Compagnie Nouvelle des Applications de la Cellulose (CNAC) is founded in Gauchy to produce viscose fiber.

1972: The Gauchy factory is acquired by Rhône-Poulenc.

1978: The Gauchy site becomes home to all of Rhône-Poulenc's polyester fiber production.

1985: Rhône-Poulenc launches production of PET (polyethylene terephthalate) resin for packaging film.

1995: The Gauchy business changes its name to Tergal Fibres.

1996: The company, working with Danone, becomes the first to introduce a PET-based bottle for drinking water.

1998: Tergal Fibres becomes an independent company through a management buyout.

2006: Tergal Fibres changes its name to Tergal Industries.

2009: Tergal fights off bankruptcy proceedings by winning a six-month reprieve against its creditors.

combination. The new polyester material was called polyethylene terephthalate, or PET.

SHIFTING TO POLYESTER

Whinfield and Dickson, working with the inventors W. K. Birtwhistle and C. G. Ritchie, then produced the first polyester fiber. The new fiber, introduced in 1941 and initially manufactured by British chemicals giant Imperial Chemical Industries (ICI), was given the name of terylene. U.S.-based DuPont, which had been focusing its own fiber developments on nylon, bought the rights to work with terylene in 1945. By 1950, DuPont had succeeded in adapting its nylon technology to the new material, creating the second polyester fiber, Dacron. Just two years later, DuPont introduced a new PET-based material, mylar film. In France, meanwhile, that country's chemicals and pharmaceuticals giant Rhône-Poulenc had acquired its own license from ICI. In 1954, the company launched its own polyester fiber, called Tergal.

The growing market for inexpensive polyester textiles quickly outpaced the viscose industry. By the early 1970s, much of France's viscose industry had

begun to disappear. CNAC itself disappeared, after Rhône-Poulenc acquired the Gauchy factory in 1972. At first the new management maintained the site's existing viscose-based production, while constructing a new—modern and highly automated—polyester plant next to the original factory. By 1976, however, Rhône-Poulenc had shut down the original Gauchy factory. Two years later, the site became the home of all of Rhône-Poulenc's polyester fiber production.

While Rhône-Poulenc later expanded its polyester fiber business into a global operation, with subsidiaries in Brazil, the United Kingdom, and elsewhere, the Gauchy site remained one of its largest polyester facilities and the only such site in France. In 1985, the French operation expanded its business, launching production of PET resins used for the production of film and other packaging materials. PET resins grew into a major part of the Gauchy plant's operations. By 1992, the facility had achieved ISO 9001 certification.

Rhône-Poulenc, which had been nationalized in the early 1980s and then re-privatized in the early 1990s, began to restructure its operations ahead of a future concentration as a pharmaceuticals business. In 1995, the company created a new Fibres and Polymers business unit, which took over operation of the Gauchy factory. At that time, the Gauchy business changed its name, becoming Tergal Fibres.

BECOMING INDEPENDENT

Tergal Fibres by then faced an increasingly competitive market, as Asian markets began to build up their own industrial production of polyester fibers and fabrics. By the late 1990s, Tergal found itself struggling to compete against the lower-priced Asian producers. In response, Tergal invested strongly in research and development. This effort enabled the company to achieve a number of significant breakthroughs over the next several years. In 1996 the company became the first in the industry to introduce a discontinuous polyester microfiber, called Filifine by the company.

Tergal's work in the packaging sector also led it to another success at mid-decade. In 1996, the company, working with Danone, became the first to introduce a PET-based bottle for drinking water. This development represented something of a revolution for the drinking water industry. The PET bottles were much lighter than earlier plastic bottles, helping to slash transportation costs. At the same time, PET bottles were more resistant, decreasing breakage. PET bottles were also easily collapsible when empty, occupying less area in landfills.

Tergal continued to invest through the late 1990s. In 1998, for example, the company expanded its factory with solid-state post-condensation technology. At the same time, the company had begun preparing for its independence. In 1998, Rhône-Poulenc, which was preparing to merge with Germany's Hoescht to become Rhodia, announced its intention to sell off all of its polyester resins and films operations worldwide. Tergal's turn came in October 1998, through a management buyout backed by Financiere Natexis, EPF Partners, and ABN Amro. As part of the buyout, Tergal was taken over by Compagnie Europeene de Polyester (CEP), a holding company created for the purpose.

The new Tergal was soon hit by the collapse in polyester prices resulting from the economic crisis that swept through much of Asia at the end of the 1990s. As a result, the company's revenues in its first year of business as an independent company dropped by about 11 percent, down to EUR 69 million by the end of 1999. Tergal remained optimistic, however, at the dawn of the 21st century, in part because its strong research and development effort provided it with a pipeline of some 14 new products in development. Tergal also launched an investment to expand its production capacity at the beginning of the new century, spending more than $10 million to expand the Gauchy facility by the end of 2000.

FIGHTING FOR SURVIVAL

By 2003, Tergal had succeeded in boosting its total PET resin production capacity to more than 65,000 metric tons per year. In that year, the company's research and development effort paid off, with the launch of production of a new recycled polyester resin, called Reseko. That product soon earned approval as a food-grade product. The company launched production of Reseko on a commercial scale in 2005.

By then, Tergal had debuted another innovative PET-based product. The introduction of LacPET (light active compound polyethylene terephthalate) represented a major breakthrough for the European dairy community. The new resin, which incorporated titanium dioxide in the production process, permitted the production of PET bottles providing single-layer ultraviolet-barrier protection. This made the bottles suitable for use as packaging for long shelf life UHT (ultra-high-temperature) milk, the most common milk product in much of Europe. LacPET was first approved for use in Spain, and by 2006 had been launched by Groupe Leche Pascuale there.

Tergal, which changed its name to Tergal Industries in 2006, launched LacPET on the French market in 2007. The new bottle type was quickly adopted by most of the country's leading milk packagers. Despite the suc-

cess of its new product, which helped boost the company's sales past EUR 100 million, and then to EUR 130 million ($180 million) by 2008, Tergal Industries found itself struggling for survival toward the end of the decade.

Tergal had nearly been driven to bankruptcy in 2006, in part because its major supplier changed its payment policies from a 60-day delay to a 30-day delay. Hit hard by the surge in oil prices—as the price soared to an unprecedented peak of nearly $150 per barrel in the summer of 2008—Tergal found itself in a delicate position. With the price of its raw materials rising, Tergal was under more pressure than ever from the fast-growing and lower-margin Asian markets. Tergal managed to fight off bankruptcy, in part by streamlining its workforce.

The launch of LacPET in France in 2007 provided the company with new hope, but the global economic collapse of 2008 hit the company hard. By the end of 2008, the company once again struggled to remain afloat. The company's major shareholders announced their intention to force Tergal into bankruptcy and sell off the company's assets. Tergal fought back, however, ultimately winning a six-month reprieve from the courts. By January 2009, Tergal won a new six-month reprieve. By then, the drop in global oil prices had caused a significant drop in Tergal's own raw materials prices. At the same time, the rapid acceptance of Lac-PET provided Tergal with hope for further revenue growth. As the last PET producer in France, Tergal hoped to continue a manufacturing tradition that spanned more than 85 years.

M. L. Cohen

PRINCIPAL COMPETITORS

Montedison Spa; Trevira GmbH; Kosa Inc.; DuPont Inc.; Alpek; Teijin KK.

FURTHER READING

Deltour, Florence, "Tergal: Encore Six Mois de Sursis," *L'Aisne Nouvelle,* January 26, 2009.

"La Cession de Tergal Industries: Dernier Espoir," *L'Aisne Nouvelle,* August 4, 2008.

"Le Directeur Explique Pourquoi Tergal Va Mal," *L'Aisne Nouvelle,* September 17, 2008.

Michel, Maurice-Charles, "L'Usine de Gaucy, la Cellulose," *Les Années Viscose,* First Semester, 2002.

"Rhodia Cède Tergal Fibres, Sa Dernière Grosse Activité de Polyester en Europe," *Les Echos,* September 29, 1998, p. 10.

"Tergal Fibres Innove dans les Résines PET pour Bouteilles," *Plastiques Magazine,* June 4, 2004.

"Tergal Fibres Lance une Innovation," *Journal du Net,* February 1, 2007.

"Tergal Fibres Souhaite Doubler Sa Taille," *Les Echos,* December 7, 1999, p. 14.

"Un Nouveau Délai pour Tergal Fibres," *L'Union,* January 24, 2009.

Young, Ian, "Rhodia Exits Polyester in Europe," *Chemical Week,* October 7, 1998, p. 17.

Trigano S.A.

100 rue Petit
Paris, F-75185 Cedex 19
France
Telephone: (33 01) 44 52 16 20
Fax: (33 01) 44 52 16 21
Web site: http://www.trigano.fr

Public Company
Incorporated: 1945
Employees: 4,100
Sales: EUR 875.5 million ($1.1 billion) (2008)
Stock Exchanges: Euronext Paris
Ticker Symbol: TRI
NAICS: 336213 Motor Home Manufacturing; 336214
Travel Trailer and Camper Manufacturing

■ ■ ■

Trigano S.A. is Europe's leading manufacturer of recreational vehicles, including camping cars, caravans, mobile homes, and other leisure vehicles. The company controls more than 20 brand names, including Chaussan, Caravelair, Challenger, Sterkemann, Trigano, Autostar, Euro Mobil, and Camping Profi. The company is also active in the Leisure Accessories market, producing trailers, camping equipment, and garden equipment and furnishings, including playground equipment and swimming pools, under brands including Trigano, Plisson, Sorel, Erka, Amca, and Rulquin. Trigano's Recreational Vehicle division is by far its largest, accounting for more than 88 percent of group sales of EUR 875.5 million ($1.1 billion) in 2008. Within this category, the

company's Camping-cars production remains its largest, generating 68.5 percent of total group sales. Paris-headquartered Trigano claims a 22.1 percent share of the total European recreational vehicle (RV) market, ahead of longtime rival Hymer in Germany. The company is especially active in the French, Belgian, Italian, German, Spanish, and U.K. markets. Trigano is led by CEO, chairman, and majority shareholder François Feuillet. The company is listed on the Euronext Paris Stock Exchange.

FROM CAMPING TENT SALES TO CARAVANS

The Trigano name's long association with France's vacation and leisure sector stemmed from the opening of a small canvas workshop set up in 1935 by Edgard Trigano, whose Jewish family had immigrated to France earlier in the century. Father Raymond Trigano owned a grocery in Montreuil-sous-Bois. Edgard was the eldest of six; his younger brothers included Gilbert and André.

The creation of the Trigano tent company soon received an important boost. The arrival of the socialist Popular Front government to power brought a revolution in the French leisure sector. In 1936 the government passed legislation providing for paid vacation leave for all of France's workers. With more people able to afford to take vacation than ever before, demand for the Triganos' tents soared. World War II soon put an end to the festivities, however, as the Trigano family were forced into hiding from the Nazi occupational forces. Gilbert Trigano traveled south, where he joined the Communist Resistance.

In 1945, as the war ended, Raymond and André Trigano formed a new business, Etablissements Trigano, which specialized in camping supplies and sports equipment. Gilbert Trigano, then working as a journalist for *l'Humanité,* joined the company soon after. The Triganos initially traded in U.S. army surplus goods left behind by the departing American forces. In 1950 Gilbert Trigano was approached by a friend, Gerard Blitz, a Belgian diamond merchant then in the process of conceiving a new type of vacation village. Trigano agreed to supply Blitz with tents from the family business. Instead of taking a down-payment, Trigano instead received a share of Blitz's company—which became known as Club Mediterrannée. By 1953 Gilbert Trigano had become a full partner with Blitz, and the following year left his family's business to build Club Med into a vacation empire.

The success of Club Med, and the fast-growing French vacation market in general, encouraged Etablissements Trigano to invest more aggressively in the camping sector, particularly in its tent operations. The company began developing its own tent designs, and in 1956 opened its own tent manufacturing plant. The company quickly established the Trigano name as a leader in the French camping tent sector.

Trigano followed the evolution of the French vacation and leisure sector through the 1960s. The economic boom that marked the French postwar period saw a move from camping to more upscale vacation accommodations. A particularly fast-growing segment was the RV market, as increasing numbers of French vacationers took to the road in camping cars, caravans, tent trailers, and the like. In 1971, Trigano, under the leadership of André Trigano, decided to enter this market as well, buying SNIAS, a producer of caravans under the Caravelair brand name, with a factory in Trignac, in the Loire Atlantique region.

That purchase quickly turned sour for the Trigano family. After several years of struggling financially, the company at last agreed to be acquired by government-owned Crédit Lyonnais in 1974. André Trigano then left the company to found a new business under his own name, which specialized in tourism and travel services. In the meantime the Trigano company's new management made the decision to close the Trignac factory in favor of a new and larger production facility in Tournon, in the Ardeche region, which would launch production in 1976. By the end of 1974 Trigano's new management completed its first acquisition, of rival caravan-maker Sterckemann, based in Seclin, in the north of France.

NEW OWNERS IN 1987

The late 1970s were difficult years for the RV sector. Hit hard by the sudden rise in fuel prices stemming from the Arab oil embargo earlier in the decade, the sector suffered from the long economic downturn that lasted into the early 1980s. Trigano's owner, Crédit Lyonnaise, brought in new management to lead the company in 1980, under François Feuillet. Among Feuillet's early decisions was to lead the company into the production of motorized camping cars in 1984. By 1985 Trigano had launched its own brand of camping car, under the Challenger name.

That year Trigano also launched a line of camping car accessories, under the name Euro-Accessoires. The company also began producing caravans under subcontract from another well-known French brand, Chausson. However, Feuillet had increasingly come into conflict with Crédit Lyonnais, which disagreed with Feuillet's strategy for the company. The dispute ultimately led to a buyout; Feuillet and partner Robert Bernard purchased Trigano from Crédit Lyonnais in 1987. Each acquired a 50 percent share of the company.

Soon after this, Trigano exited its original business as a distributor of camping goods and equipment to focus entirely on its growing RV operations. These included an exclusive license to distribute a line of Electrolux-branded accessories for RVs. In 1987 the company also shut down its Seclin factory, transferring the manufacture of the Sterckemann line to the Tournon site.

Trigano then launched a new, acquisition-driven growth strategy that enabled the company to capture the French market leadership and established the company as one of Europe's top RV specialists. The company's first new acquisition came in 1988 with the purchase of Raclet, which specialized in the production of camping equipment and RV accessories. This was followed by another camping equipment group, Jamet, in 1990.

The year 1990 also marked Trigano's emergence into the French top ranks with the takeover of the Chausson brand. Also that year Robert Bernard decided to exit the company, selling a 38 percent stake to a

KEY DATES

1935: Edgard Trigano opens a workshop producing canvas tents and tarpaulins.

1945: Father Raymond Trigano launches Etablissements Trigano with sons Gilbert and André in order to sell camping and sports equipment.

1950: Gilbert Trigano agrees to supply tents to Club Med, before joining that company.

1956: Trigano launches production of tents under its own name.

1971: Trigano enters the recreational vehicle sector through purchase of the Caravelaire brand.

1974: Credit Lyonnais acquires control of Trigano.

1987: François Feuillet and Robert Bernard acquire Trigano from Credit Lyonnais and launch Trigano's expansion-through-acquisition strategy.

1998: Trigano goes public.

1999: The company completes its first international acquisition, of Caravans International in Italy.

2005: Trigano enters the German market with its purchase of Euro Mobil.

group of investors. Trigano itself acquired 10 percent of Bernard's stake, while Feuillet bought an additional 2 percent of the company, giving him majority control.

PUBLIC OFFERING IN 1998

Trigano filled out its RV offering in 1991 with the purchase of the Palace brand of mobile home. This product line was chiefly distributed to campsite operators and thus remained a small part of Trigano's overall operations. Trigano also added a new subsidiary in 1991, Trois Soleils, which specialized in caravan rentals. The following year, the company added another business segment, with the purchase of AMCA Noval, a French producer of garden equipment and recreational trailers. This segment grew again with the purchase of Aliza (garden equipment) in 1994, IBI (trailers) in 1995, and Artix (garden equipment) in 1996. Trigano also added the Plisson camping equipment brand in 1994.

Other acquisitions completed through the late 1990s included Autostar RVs in 1998. The company also completed the purchases of two producers of RV accessories, Clairval and Maitre Equipement in 1999.

Trigano went public in 1998 in order to allow its investors to cash out their holdings. The company then changed its name to Trigano S.A. The public offering also provided the company with the capital to launch its next expansion phase. For the new century, the company targeted an entry into the wider European market, in order to establish itself as a true European leader. The company's first move outside of France came in September 1999, when the company bought Italy's Caravans International and its RV brand, Auto-Trail. The purchase also gave the company a second major production facility.

Trigano returned to Italy in June 2001, buying that country's motor caravan producer, ARCA. In France, Trigano purchased another motor caravan company, Caravanes La Mancelle, at the end of that same year. At the same time, the company boosted its RV furnishings portfolio with the acquisition of Arts et Bois, a specialist in that market.

In 2002 Trigano targeted entry into two important European RV markets—the United Kingdom and Spain. For the former, the company acquired Riddiough, a manufacturer of RV accessories. In Spain the group added its own motor caravans brand, Benimar-Ocarsa.

EXPANSION BEFORE BRACING FOR A ROUGH RIDE

By 2005 Trigano had succeeded in gaining leading positions in a number of markets, including France, Italy, the United Kingdom, and Spain and Portugal. The largest RV markets in Europe, however, lay to the north, including Germany—home of Trigano's largest rival, Hymer—and the Scandinavian markets. In 2005 Trigano made its move into the German market, buying that country's Euro-Mobil. The purchase helped raise Trigano's overall market share in Germany, giving it two brands, Euro Mobil and Karmann Mobil, as well as an RV accessories unit, Camping-Profi.

In 2006 Trigano completed another, smaller purchase of U.K.-based RV accessories group Grove Products, rounding out an acquisition drive that spanned nearly two decades. The company also looked back on an unbroken record of double-digit revenue growth, gaining an average of 15 percent per year. By the end of 2008 the company's sales had grown from just over EUR 300 million in 1999 to more than EUR 875 million ($1.1 billion).

That year Trigano found itself mired in the free-falling economy as the world slipped into a new economic crisis. Sales slowed as customers adopted a "wait and see" attitude toward new purchases. The market was also affected by soaring oil prices, which reached unprecedented levels in the summer of 2008. Trigano, meanwhile, was further hit by flooding that destroyed more than 400 RVs at its Tournon factory in September of that year. While the company managed to return to production there just three weeks later, the market for RVs dried up at the end of the year.

Trigano was forced to respond to the difficult financial circumstances by cutting more than 500 temporary jobs. The company also placed its factory on standstill during most of December and January. By February 2009 the company had instituted a series of part-time layoffs, reducing employees' work by one day per week. Fortunately Trigano had earlier begun preparing itself and its dealer network for the downturn: while a number of its competitors sought to maintain sales by offering buying incentives, Trigano instead chose to reduce its production as sales slowed in 2008. In this way the company avoided burdening its dealer network with unsold stock. Trigano braced itself for a rough ride as the new recession was expected to last at least through 2009. With more than half a century as one of France's leading names in camping and caravaning, Trigano looked forward to smoother roads ahead.

M. L. Cohen

PRINCIPAL SUBSIDIARIES

Arca Camper (Italy; 88.6%); Auto Trail VR Ltd (UK); Autostar S.A.; Benimar-Ocarsa S.A. (Spain); Camping-Cars Chausson; Camping-Profi GmbH (Germany); Caravanes La Mancelle; Delwyn Enterprises Ltd (UK); Deutsche Reisemobil Vermietungs GmbH (Germany);

E.T. Riddiough Ltd (United Kingdom; 94%); Eura Mobil GmbH (Germany); European Motorhomes GmbH (Germany); Karmann-Mobil Vertriebs GmbH (Germany); Sorelpol (Poland); Terres Neuves (Tunisia); Trigano Belgium; Trigano BV (Netherlands; 75%).

PRINCIPAL COMPETITORS

Hymer AG; Knaus Tabbert Group GmbH; Dethleffs GmbH and Company KG; Swift Group Ltd.; Pilote S.A.; Robert Bosch Sp. z.o.o.; Willerby Holiday Homes Ltd.; Elnagh S.p.A.; Keenwork Ltd.

FURTHER READING

Charbonnier, Robin, "Du Chômage Partiel Jusqu'à Fin Avril à Trigano VDL," *Le Dauphine Liberé,* February 10, 2009.

———, "Trigano VDL et Inoplast Auront-ils des Aides de l'Etat?" *Le Dauphine Liberé,* February 10, 2009.

Fauconnier, Flore, "Le Camping ... et les Camping-Cars, C'est Trigano," *Journal du Net,* July 26, 2006.

"Trigano (Camping Cars) Va Réduire Ses Capacités de Production," *Agence France Presse,* November 26, 2008.

"Trigano Confiant dans le Marché Européen des Loisirs de Plein Air," *Les Echos,* December 10, 2003, p. 22.

"Trigano: Une Affair Qui Roule," *La Vie Financière,* September 2, 2005.

"Trigano: Vise un 1 MdE de Chiffre d'Affaires Annuel," *Cercle-Finance,* March 26, 2008.

"Trois Semaines Après, l'Entreprise Trigano (Camping Cars) Rédemarre Enfin," *Le Dauphine Liberé,* September 29, 2008.

Voisin, Christophe, "Trigano: Une Année à Oublier," *Boursier. com,* September 23, 2008.

Turbomeca S.A.

Avenue Joseph Szydlowski
Bordes, F-64511 Cedex
France
Telephone: (33 05) 59 12 50 00
Fax: (33 05) 59 53 15 12
Web site: http://www.turbomeca.fr

Wholly Owned Subsidiary of Safran S.A.
Incorporated: 1938
Employees: 6,107
Sales: EUR 990 million ($1.45 billion) (2007 est.)
NAICS: 336412 Aircraft Engine and Engine Parts
    Manufacturing

■ ■ ■

Turbomeca S.A. is the world's leading manufacturer of gas turbines for helicopters. The Bordes, France-based company, which pioneered the development of gas turbines in the early 1950s, has produced more than 50,000 engines over the decades, racking up more than 88 million operating hours. In 2008, the company produced more than 1,300 motors, primarily for the light and medium helicopter segments. More than 15,000 of Turbomeca's turbines are in operation around the world—the company's engines provide up to 40 years of service. As a result, maintenance and repairs account for a significant portion of the company's revenues, which topped EUR 990 million ($1.45 billion) in 2007. In addition to helicopter engines, Turbomeca also produces jet aircraft engines, largely through its participation in the longstanding Adour

engine joint venture with Rolls-Royce. The Adour engine is used to power trainer aircraft and light combat aircraft, and has been deployed by more than 22 air forces around the world.

Turbomeca operates through a network of factories and sales and repair facilities in France, the United Kingdom, Germany, the United States, Canada, Brazil, Uruguay, South Africa, India, Singapore, Japan, Australia, and China. The company also operates a subsidiary, Microturbo, based in Toulouse, France. Microturbo is one of the world's leading developers of turbines for missiles and target drones, and also produces starting systems, auxiliary power units, and related aircraft components. Turbomeca itself is part of the Safran Group of companies, formed through the merger of Sagem and SNECMA (Société Nationale d'Étude et de Construction de Moteurs d'Aviation) in 2005. Pierre Fabre is Turbomeca's chief executive officer and chairman.

ESTABLISHING A FRENCH PISTON PRODUCER

Turbomeca was founded in 1938 by Joseph Szydlowski. Born in Chelm, then part of czarist Russia, to a well-known Jewish family (Szydlowski's older brother became one of the founders of the kibbutz movement in Israel), Szydlowski was conscripted into the Russian army during World War I. Szydlowski, just 18 at the start of the war, was captured by the Germans and imprisoned in East Prussia. Following the outbreak of the Russian Revolution, however, Szydlowski decided to remain in Germany, where he soon distinguished himself as an

KEY DATES

1938: Joseph Szydlowski founds Turbomeca to produce aircraft pistons and engines.

1948: Turbomeca becomes the first company to develop a gas turbine for helicopters.

1965: The company forms a joint venture with Rolls-Royce to provide engines for Jaguar aircraft.

1980: Turbomeca opens a subsidiary in the United States.

1989: Following Szydlowski's death, Groupe Labinal takes control of Turbomeca.

2000: SNECMA (Société Nationale d'Étude et de Construction de Moteurs d'Aviation) acquires full control of Turbomeca.

2005: SNECMA merges with Sagem to become Safran.

2008: Turbomeca announces a plan to open its first manufacturing plant in the United States.

engineer and inventor. Szydlowski's interest turned to the fast-developing automotive engine sector. By 1920, Szydlowski had received his first patent.

Over the next decade, Szydlowski married and had two children while building a career as an engineering consultant for a number of prominent German manufacturers, notably Krupp and Gagenau. Szydlowski's work at German aircraft giant Junkers, however, was to have the greatest impact on his future career. At Junkers, Szydlowski participated in the development of aircraft engines and components, particularly compressors, and established himself as one of the top engineers in the field.

The rise of Nazism and the growing anti-semitism in Germany in the late 1920s forced Szydlowski and his family to leave Germany. Szydlowski was invited to France by the then air force minister, who asked Szydlowski to work on the development of a diesel aircraft engine. Szydlowski joined the Salmson company, based outside of Paris, and began working with a noted physicist, André Planiol, on the diesel engine and corresponding piston.

The team's diesel design failed to provide the required power. On the other hand, the group successfully completed the piston design, and in 1936 received its first order to fit out a new series of military aircraft built by Hispano-Suiza. By 1938, Szydlowski and Planiol had launched their own company—Tur-

bomeca—to produce the pistons. The company's first production site was initially based at the Salmson works in Boulogne-Billancourt. The outbreak of World War II in 1939, however, brought the company a major new order for compressors. This led Turbomeca to set up its own factory, in Mézières-sur-Seine.

The French defeat the following year forced the company to flee the Paris region. Turbomeca set up new temporary quarters at Saint Pé de Bigorre in 1940, where it launched production of aircraft compressors for the Free French and Allied forces. By 1941, the company had begun acquiring land for its permanent site, in Bordes, at the base of the Pyrenees Mountains, transferring its production there by the end of the year. Following the German invasion of the southern part of France, however, Joseph Szydlowski moved to Switzerland, where he remained for the rest of the war. Turbomeca's Bordes factory was then stripped of its equipment by the Germans.

POSTWAR GAS TURBINE PIONEER

Szydlowski returned to France in September 1944 and reoutfitted the Bordes factory. The company continued to produce pistons, ultimately supplying more than 3,000 to Hispano-Suiza. However, with the appearance of the first jet engines during the war, Szydlowski recognized that the future for piston-based engines in the aircraft industry had dimmed considerably. Szydlowski then turned Turbomeca's operations toward developing expertise in turbine engines. At the end of 1945, the company founded a new engineering office at Bregens, working with a team of German engineers from Daimler Benz as part of a government contract to develop a large-scale turbine. That project proved unfeasible, however, and the French air ministry abandoned the project in 1946.

The Bregens office was then moved to Turbomeca's Bordes site. Instead of pursuing the development of large-scale turbines—a market already covered by larger rival SNECMA—Turbomeca decided to focus on small and midsized designs. This led the company to begin adapting the jet turbine for a new category—helicopters. While the first helicopter had flown in 1907, helicopters remained limited by their reliance on traditional internal combustion engine designs into the postwar period.

However, in 1948 Turbomeca made history by successfully testing the world's first gas turbine for a helicopter, the TT782. The company gave the engine the name Orédon, after the name of a lake in the Pyrenees Mountains, establishing a company tradition in which all of its products were named after lakes, mountains, or other landmarks of the Pyrenees region.

Turbomeca continued developing its turbine design, and by 1951 the world's first successful turbine-powered helicopter, the S01120-Ariel III (built by the predecessor to Eurocopter), completed its test flight. Turbomeca went from success to success through that decade. The company introduced its Artouste turbine in the early 1950s, which became the powerhouse behind the Alouette helicopter introduced in 1955 and firmly established Turbomeca among the world's leading producers of turbines for helicopters.

Turbomeca also developed its turbine technology for other aircraft. Turbomeca debuted the Marboré turbine for the Fouga Magister in 1952, establishing itself as a major producer of turbines for light military aircraft and drones. By 1959, Turbomeca had launched a new generation of turbine, the Marboré VI, which became one of its top-selling products. Turbomeca itself produced more than 5,000 of these turbines, while Teledyne in the United States built another 10,000 under license, notably for the Cessna T37.

FORMING PARTNERSHIPS

By the 1960s, the company had positioned itself among the top French aerospace players. This status was underscored when the French and British militaries backed a series of partnerships for the development and construction of a number of new aircraft designs. Turbomeca was tapped to join two projects. The first, launched in 1965, called for the outfitting of the Puma aircraft with Turbomeca's Turmo engine. The second became a partnership with Rolls-Royce, which began developing the Jaguar aircraft, based on Turbomeca's Adour engine design. As part of this effort, Turbomeca established a new factory in Tarnos in 1965. The first Jaguars appeared in 1968. Turbomeca's collaboration with Rolls-Royce was highly successful; indeed, the partnership lasted into the next century, becoming the longest-lasting aircraft partnership in the industry. In January 2008, the two companies announced that they had agreed to extend the partnership for another 30 years.

During the 1970s, Turbomeca joined another successful partnership, teaming up with SNECMA and the Germany companies MTU and KHD to develop the Larzac engine for the Alphajet. That aircraft was launched in 1973, and the Larzac series of engines became one of Turbomeca's core product families, with new generations remaining in production into the next century.

Turbomeca's operations in helicopter turbines continued to prove successful as well. The company's Alouette turbines, then in their third generation, were chosen to outfit the Lama helicopter. In 1972, a Lama SA-315 established a new altitude record for helicopters, flying past 12,400 meters (40,800 feet). That record was to remain unbroken into the next century. The company also developed a new generation of its original Arriel turboshaft, which became another major success.

Turbomeca's operations remained focused on France through most of the 1970s. In 1977, however, the company established its first foreign subsidiary, Turbomeca do Brasil. This was followed by an entry into the United States, where the company established Turbomeca Engine Corporation in Dallas in 1980. That company then opened its own assembly and maintenance plant for Turbomeca's strong-selling Arriel engine in the United States. The Arriel family grew to include the Arriel 1S, which by 1986 powered the Sikorsky S76A helicopter, among others.

EMPHASIS ON DIVERSIFYING

By this time, Turbomeca had begun an effort to diversify its production, in part in response to a slowdown in aircraft orders in the early 1980s. One direction the company took was to develop the production of auxiliary power units for aircraft. The company also began investigating ways to convert its aircraft-based turbine expertise for land and marine uses. Among the group's products developed during this time was the Makila, an industrial and marine turbine, in partnership with Volvo Aero Engines and Ulstein Turbines as part of the Euréka project.

In 1987, Szydlowski, who had continued to own full control of the company, decided to bring in a new shareholder. Szydlowski agreed to sell an initial 45 percent stake to Labinal that year. The move came just ahead of Szydlowski's death in 1988 at the age of 92. By then, Szydlowski had been recognized as one of France's greatest industrialists of the 20th century and Turbomeca had become a leading player in the global aerospace industry. Szydlowski's daughter, Sonia Meton, took over as the company's CEO, a position she held until her accidental death in 1996. In the meantime, Labinal acquired full control of Turbomeca in 1989. As part of that transaction, however, the Szydlowski family, through its holding company Sopartech, gained majority ownership of Labinal.

Under Sonia Meton's leadership Turbomeca focused on developing its export operations, maintaining its production base in France. As part of this effort, the company began establishing an international network of sales subsidiaries. By the end of the decade, under the leadership of Jean-Bernard Cocheteux, the company had launched operations in the United Kingdom, Germany, and Japan, as well as a subsidiary in Australia for the Australasian region, another in Uruguay covering South America, and a third in Singapore, for the Asian Pacific region.

Nonetheless, the first half of the 1990s was a difficult period for the company. The end of the Cold War had led to a sharp drop in defense spending. Meanwhile, the recession at the beginning of the decade—which lingered into the middle of the decade in much of Europe—placed further pressure on the company. As a result, Turbomeca was forced to shed jobs. By 1995, the company's payroll had dropped from a high of 4,500 to just 3,500.

At the same time, the company's focus turned increasingly to its helicopter turbine operations. These were boosted by the successful launch of the Tiger helicopter, based on Turbomeca's MTR390 engines, in 1991, followed by the launch of the NH90 helicopter, which incorporated Turbomeca's RTM322 engine, in 1995. While the company continued to develop aircraft engines, notably through its partnership with Rolls-Royce, by the dawn of the new century helicopters had become the company's largest revenue generator.

NEW PARENTS IN THE 21ST CENTURY

In 2000, Turbomeca agreed to be acquired by its larger French defense and aerospace rival, SNECMA. The purchase also brought Turbomeca a new subsidiary, Microturbo, specialized in the production of engines for missiles and target drones. The following year, the company brought in a new CEO, Emeric d'Arcimoles. The new management reoriented the company's operations from its longstanding technical focus to a more market-oriented approach. Part of the impetus behind this change was that the largest share of Turbomeca's sales and profits at this time came from its repair and maintenance services. With its engines rated for life spans as long as 40 years, the group recognized that its service component represented a major part of its future growth. Accordingly, the company began expanding its international network of subsidiaries to include their own repair and maintenance facilities.

Turbomeca also developed a new range of partnerships. In 2003 in South Africa, for example, the company joined with state-owned Denel to found the Turbomeca Africa joint venture, with Turbomeca holding 51 percent. The following year, the company entered India, launching a joint venture with Hindustan Aeronautics Limited (HAL). That partnership was formed as part of a contract from the Indian government for more than 600 engines, including 318 Ardiden

engines to be incorporated into the new Dhruv helicopter. That helicopter took its first test flight in 2007 and completed its first full flight in January 2009.

Turbomeca had also begun expanding its operational base. The company entered the Chinese market, signing a cooperation agreement—and gaining a partial manufacturing license—with that country's AVIC II in 2005. Turbomeca then established its own subsidiary in Beijing. In the United States, Turbomeca completed an $11 million expansion of its Texas repair and service facility in 2006. Then, in 2008, the company announced plans to establish its first manufacturing plant in the United States, in North Carolina. Also that year, Turbomeca announced plans to spend EUR 10 million to open a second Brazilian assembly and maintenance facility.

Turbomeca by this time found itself under a new parent company, Safran, formed through the 2005 merger of SNECMA with Sagem. Turbomeca then became Safran's specialized producer of light to midweight turbines, both for helicopters and other light aircraft. Taking the lead of the company, which achieved revenues of EUR 900 million in 2007, was Pierre Fabre, who was named the company's CEO and chairman in 2008. In early 2009, Fabre announced that Turbomeca's future development program would be focusing much of its research and development spending on developing new "green" technologies to reduce its engines' fuel consumption and pollution emissions. After more than 70 years, Turbomeca continued to fly high in the global helicopter engine market.

M. L. Cohen

PRINCIPAL SUBSIDIARIES

Beijing Turbomeca Changkong (China); CGTM SA; Microturbo SA; Turbomeca Africa Pty (South Africa); Turbomeca Asia-Pacific (Singapore); Turbomeca Beijing Helicopter Engines Trading Co. Ltd. (China); Turbomeca Canada Inc.; Turbomeca do Brasil Spa; Turbomeca Japan KK; Turbomeca Manufacturing Inc. (USA); Turbomeca Turbochargers Industrial India Ltd. (India); Turbomeca UK Ltd.; Turbomeca USA Inc.

PRINCIPAL COMPETITORS

Bell Helicopter Textron Inc.; Fiat S.p.A.; United Technologies Corp.; Volvo Group; GE Aircraft Engines; Rolls-Royce Group PLC; Ishikawajima-Harima Heavy Industries Company Ltd.

FURTHER READING

Chalmers, Robyn, "Turbomeca Seen Boosting SA's Position in Aerospace Arena," *Africa News Service*, May 6, 2002.

Condom, Pierre, "Cruising Through the Crisis," *Interavia Business & Technology,* May 2002, p. 9.

Cox, Bob, "Engine Firm Eyes Expansion," *Fort Worth Star-Telegram,* October 25, 2006.

———, "French-Owned Turbomeca Ships Helicopter Engines Made in Texas," *Fort Worth-Star Telegram,* July 15, 2003.

Decôme, Guy, *Joseph Szydlowski et Son Temps,* Paris: Conseil Imprim, 1999.

"French Major Turbomeca Opens Subsidiary Here," *Business Line,* December 11, 2005.

Noetinger, J., "Joseph Szydlowski: Tout pour le Turbine," *Air & Cosmos,* June 12, 1982.

Oliver, Julia, "Aeronautics Firm to Build Plant," *Charlotte-Observer,* April 22, 2007.

"Rolls-Royce Wins Order for 68 More Turbomeca Engines from Australian Government," *Europe Intelligence Wire,* March 20, 2007.

"Turbomeca Annonce le Succès du Premier Vol de Dhruv de HAL," *Le Revenu,* February 12, 2009.

"Turbomeca Invests in Helicopter Parts and Maintenance in Rio," *America's Intelligence Wire,* July 30, 2008.

"Turbo-Powered UK Operation," *News,* April 29, 2008.

Weisberger, Harry, "Turbomeca Says 'Green' Is the Color of Success," *AINonline,* February 23, 2009.

Urban Engineers, Inc.

—————— ∎ ——————

530 Walnut Street
Philadelphia, Pennsylvania 19106-3603
U.S.A.
Telephone: (215) 922-8080
Fax: (215) 922-8082
Web site: http://www.urbanengineers.com

Private Company
Incorporated: 1960
Employees: 350
Sales: $40 million (2008 est.)
NAICS: 541330 Engineering Services

∎ ∎ ∎

Maintaining its headquarters in Philadelphia, Pennsylvania, Urban Engineers, Inc., is an engineering and construction management company serving the northeastern United States. Branch offices are located in Connecticut; New York City; New Jersey; Delaware; Maryland; and Pennsylvania. Urban divides its practice among six groups. The Transportation group includes highway and street projects, bridges, public transportation systems, airports, and ports; Facilities and Building Systems provides structural engineering, site development, and mechanical, electrical, plumbing, and fire protection design services. The Construction Services unit includes cost estimating, scheduling, management, testing, and claims litigation support.

Site and environmental assessments, remedial and groundwater investigations, permit and regulatory compliance, lead paint and asbestos management, and water and wastewater engineering all funder the auspices of the Environmental Services unit. Planning/GIS (geographic information systems), provides transit and transportation planning as well as land use and environmental planning. Finally, Program Management services offers consulting help, oversight, construction cost compliance, or the shepherding of an entire construction project from planning to activation. Urban is primarily owned by President Edward M. D'Alba and Executive Vice-President Joseph P. McAtee. Employees also own about 40 percent of the company, an amount that grows each year.

EARLY FOCUS ON HIGHWAY DESIGN

Urban Engineers was founded in Philadelphia in August 1960 by its longtime president, Robert C. Olson and two partners. Born in the Bronx, New York, Olson earned a degree in engineering from Yale University and also served as a Marine Corps captain during World War II. Prior to his move to Philadelphia he worked on a number of major New York City–area projects, including the Brooklyn-Queens Connecting Highway and the Cross-Bronx Expressway. Urban and its initial workforce of seven worked out of a row house and focused mostly on highway design. As a result, the firm was heavily dependent on federal, state, and local funding, which because of its uncertain nature resulted in volatile earnings in the early days. Because Pennsylvania's state highway funds were tied to the number of gallons of gasoline sold, for example, Urban suffered during the Arab oil embargo of the early 1970s. With high prices,

COMPANY PERSPECTIVES

We will strive to be our clients' first choice through planning, engineering and management excellence.

people bought less gasoline, resulting in cutbacks in highway funding.

Early on, Urban quickly realized that if it were to secure work beyond Philadelphia, it would have to open branch offices. The first office, established in the mid-1960s, was across the river in Camden, New Jersey. The company worked with the city's major employers, Campbell Soup and RCA, on initiatives related to the Greater Camden Movement, an urban redevelopment effort. Although none of the projects ever progressed beyond the drawing board, Urban used the experience to secure a number of New Jersey contracts over the years, involving the Camden Waterfront, RCA's production test centers, and in the 1980s the design of a New Jersey Turnpike section in southern New Jersey.

Other branch offices opened as well, including one in Erie, Pennsylvania, which was followed by an office in Buffalo, New York. The firm also dabbled in international projects, including infrastructure work in Nigeria. In the 1970s Urban was hired by the shah of Iran to design a private casino, a project never completed due to a revolution that toppled the secular shah and installed a religious regime headed by the Ayatollah Khomeini.

REACHING A TURNING POINT

By the mid-1970s Urban was still a modest engineering firm, its growth stifled by a reputation as just a highway design shop. A turning point was reached in 1975, one that Olson told the *Philadelphia Inquirer* was a make-or-break opportunity for the firm, when it won the five-year prime design contract for the Center City Commuter Tunnel in Philadelphia, which linked the city's Reading and Penn Central rail lines. Urban had done some preliminary design work on the tunnel in 1965, but the project was postponed and not revived until Mayor Frank Rizzo pushed it through and helped Urban secure the contract.

In addition Urban and two other firms—the local offices of Kansas City, Missouri-based Howard Needles Tammen & Bergendoff and New York's Parsons Brinckerhoff Inc.—formed a $22.3 million joint venture to provide construction management services for six years,

from 1978 when construction began until November 1984 when the 1.7-mile tunnel opened. "The tunnel kept hundreds of our engineers busy full time," Olson told the *Inquirer*. "It was just an unbelievable job. We had to move underground utilities—gas, water, electric, sewer pipes—and even the underpinnings of the Reading Terminal building." The complexity of the project and the coordination needed to ensure it was completed on time and on budget was what made it such a key experience for Urban. Any serious problems would have had an adverse impact on the reputation of Urban. Instead, the tunnel project proved to be a shining moment for the aspiring firm.

As the prime design contractor, Urban earned $3.5 million in fees and another $6 million for its share of the construction management contract. Additionally, the project led to other tunnel contracts around the country and three national awards for design and construction. Moreover, it paved the way for more work in the construction management field. In 1984 Urban received two Philadelphia-area contracts from the Pennsylvania Department of Transportation (PennDot), which recognized that Urban had gained expertise that could be put to good use. One of the new contracts was to manage the construction of the Schuylkill Expressway and another to design two sections of Interstate 476. In 1985 awarded Urban and another firm a contract to manage the construction of the Vine Street Expressway in downtown Philadelphia. Other Philadelphia projects in which Urban participated included the design of the Airport High-Speed Line, construction management of the Market-Frankford rail line, construction management at the Civic Center, and a variety of structural renovations to area buildings, including the Temple University campus.

CHANGES IN OWNERSHIP

Urban was sold in 1990 and Olson retired. Three years later Edward D'Alba and Joseph McAtee became the principal owners. A graduate of Drexel University in Philadelphia with a degree in civil engineering, McAtee joined Urban in 1967. Raised in Yonkers, New York, D'Alba was the son of an engineer. He earned a bachelor of science degree in civil engineering from the Worcester Polytechnic Institute in Massachusetts in 1973. A year later he moved from Cleveland to Philadelphia in order to enroll in graduate school at the University of Pennsylvania and to work toward a master of science degree in civil and urban engineering. He also joined Urban as a project engineer.

Another reason for D'Alba's move to Philadelphia was his love for the Schuylkill River and a passion for the sport of rowing. In his acceptance speech upon win-

KEY DATES

1960: Company founded by Robert C. Olson and partners.
1975: Firm awarded Center City Commuter Tunnel design contract.
1978: Urban and joint venture partner win contract to manage construction of tunnel project.
1990: Olson retires.
1993: Edward D'Alba and Joseph McAtee become principal owners.
2000: Firm receives ISO 9001 certification.
2004: Pennsylvania Turnpike Commission awards Urban four contracts.
2006: Warrendale, Pennsylvania, office opens.

ning Engineer of the Year in the Delaware Valley in 2002, D'Alba recalled, "My journey to this podium began 40 years ago, when as a child of ten, I made my first visit to the Delaware Valley to visit an engineering company. It was a startup organization that had risen from the ashes of a bankrupt company. It was the beginning of Urban Engineers." While he said he understood little of what he saw in the small engineers' office, his impression of the river and the waterworks, of the rowers and the mansions that lined the water, left a lasting mark. "That trip, and those experiences of place, sparked a dream that I hoped some day to live."

D'Alba received his master of science degree in 1977. He then worked his way up through the Urban ranks until he assumed the presidency, all the while making time to row on the Schuylkill every day at six in the morning as a member of the Undine Barge Club. Under new leadership Urban in the 1990s continued to build on the reputation established during Olson's term and enjoyed steady growth. Sales reached $28 million in 1997 and by the end of the decade that number reached $33 million. These were hardly staggering amounts, especially in light of the revenues generated by the megafirms in the industry. D'Alba expressed no interest in that kind of expansion. Instead, the focus was on serving clients and generating repeat business. In Philadelphia the firm was well respected and it continued to land important assignments, such as the Kvaerner Philadelphia Shipyard in the late 1990s, the National Constitution Center in the late 1990s and early part of the new century, and the new sports facilities, a new baseball park and football stadium in South Philadelphia, in the early years of the 21st century. The firm was well aware, however, that in new markets it

had little chance of winning major contracts when competing against the large firms. Instead, Urban was willing to accept the small jobs that held no interest for the competition. After a few more assignments of this nature, a level of trust was established, and Urban's ability to land a larger project was greatly increased.

WINNING NEW AND REPEAT BUSINESS

Another selling point for Urban as it entered the new century and celebrated its 40th anniversary was receiving ISO 9001 certification, making it one of only a handful of consulting engineering firms in the country to have the quality of its services recognized in this manner. For this and other reasons, Urban received a steady flow of new contracts. In 2000 it won a contract to provide engineering services to the Philadelphia Regional Port Authority as the city sought to expand its international shipping capabilities. PennDot selected Urban to provide construction management services for a Route 309 Expressway Reconstruction Project in Montgomery County, Pennsylvania. Also in 2000, Urban was able to use its expertise in rail to find work on the Panama Canal designing crossover assemblies in the renovation of the tow tracks used by the locomotives to help ships navigate the canal locks.

Repeat business continued as the decade progressed. In 2004 the firm was selected by the Philadelphia Regional Port Authority to design security improvements at the marine terminals. Also in 2004, the Pennsylvania Turnpike Commission awarded Urban contracts to provide project management services for the design development of four turnpike roadway reconstruction projects and preliminary work on the widening and reconstruction of the Northeast Extension of the Pennsylvania Turnpike.

In that same year the South Jersey Transportation Planning Organization hired Urban to conduct a planning study of the Route 130/49 corridor; Cape May County contracted the firm to study ways to ease seasonal traffic congestion; and in the northern part of the state the New Jersey Sports and Exposition Authority hired Urban to provide construction management services for the Meadowlands Railroad and Roadway Improvement Project. In 2005 the firm landed work with another repeat client, the Philadelphia International Airport, to extend runways. Elsewhere, Urban was hired to design roadway improvements in Cape May County; help Stamford, Connecticut, ease traffic congestion; provide construction inspection for highway and bridge projects in Delaware; and the Buffalo office was contracted to conduct similar work for a section of the New York Thruway.

SURVIVING THE RECESSION

More highway work was taken on in 2006 when PennDot hired Urban to provide construction management on a 6.3-mile section of U.S. 202 in Chester County, Pennsylvania, and another contract to help in the modernization of the U.S. 422 River Crossing. The Pennsylvania Turnpike Commission also awarded Urban a major contract to manage the construction of an interchange that would directly link the turnpike to Interstate 95, making this major highway continuous throughout the Mid-Atlantic region. Meanwhile, PennDot's counterpart in Connecticut awarded the firm a contract to inspect the construction of several bridges.

To improve its chances of securing more work in western Pennsylvania as well as neighboring sections of Ohio and West Virginia, Urban opened an office in Warrendale, Pennsylvania, in 2006. Public transportation and airport projects followed in 2007, when the firm was awarded a contract by New Jersey Transit to manage the Metropark Station Platform Reconstruction Project, and fast-growing Bradley International Airport in Hartford, Connecticut, hired Urban to design a new passenger terminal complex.

To better serve its New Jersey clients, Urban relocated to a larger facility in Cherry Hill, New Jersey, near Philadelphia, in 2008. The Buffalo office was also reorganized to better serve that region. To keep pace with the firm's growing business about three dozen new engineers, planners, and other personnel were added to the various offices during the year. In all likelihood more new hires were to follow. Urban had always benefited from times of recession, when the government invested in public works projects, all of which needed to be designed and the construction managed. As the U.S. economy faltered, a new administration in Washington came into office and passed a massive stimulus bill that included infrastructure projects that would likely keep Urban Engineers busy for years to come.

Ed Dinger

PRINCIPAL OPERATING UNITS

Transportation; Facilities and Building Systems; Construction Services; Environmental Services; Planning/GIS; Program Management.

PRINCIPAL COMPETITORS

Parsons Brinckerhoff Inc.; Genesis Engineers Inc; Granary Associates.

FURTHER READING

Bivens, Terry, "Engineering-Service Firms Adapting, Thriving," *Philadelphia Inquirer,* October 20, 1986, p. C1.
————, "A Firm That's Paved Many a Way for Phila," *Philadelphia Inquirer,* March 24, 1986, p. C1.
Geiger, Mia, "Sculling New Heights," *Philadelphia Business Journal,* September 22, 2000, p. 31.
"Robert C. Olson Headed Own Engineering Company," *Portland (Me.) Press Herald,* January 18, 1997, p. 9B.

Van de Velde

Van de Velde S.A./NV

Lageweg 4
Schellebelle, B-9260
Belgium
Telephone: (32 09) 365 21 00
Fax: (32 09) 365 21 70
Web site: http://www.vandevelde.eu

Public Company
Incorporated: 1919
Employees: 1,530
Sales: EUR 133 million ($166 million) (2008)
Stock Exchanges: Euronext Brussels
Ticker Symbol: VAN
NAICS: 315231 Women's and Girls' Cut and Sew
    Lingerie, Loungewear, and Nightwear Manu-
    facturing

■ ■ ■

Van de Velde S.A./N.V. is one of Europe's top three designers, producers and distributors of luxury lingerie, and the leader in the Benelux (Belgium, Netherlands, Luxembourg) market. The Schellebelle, Belgium-based company operates through three core brands. Marie Jo is the company's flagship brand, representing the "haute lingerie" category. Marie Jo is the leading lingerie brand in the Benelux market and one of the top three luxury lingerie brands across most of Western Europe. The Marie Jo brand family also includes Marie Jo L'Aventure, marketed toward a more youthful clientele; and Marie Jo Intense, launched in 2008 as a line of luxury sports lingerie. Together, the Marie Jo brand fam-

ily accounts for approximately 57 percent of Van de Velde's total revenues, which topped EUR 133 million ($166 million) in 2008.

Van de Velde also controls the PrimaDonna lingerie brand, originally launched in Germany in 1865, and one of the few lingerie brands that accommodate larger-size women. In 2008, Van de Velde acquired Eurocorset, based in Spain, and its Andres Sarda brand, one of the leaders in the Spanish premium lingerie segment. Most of Van de Velde's manufacturing is carried out overseas, primarily in Tunisia and China, including through publicly listed, Hong Kong-based Top Form International, in which Van de Velde holds a 23.3 percent stake. In the United States, Van de Velde has a 49 percent stake in Intimacy, a small-but-growing luxury lingerie retail chain. Van de Velde itself is listed on the Euronext Brussels Stock Exchange; the founding Van de Velde family maintains majority control of the company, with nearly 60 percent of shares. Lucas Laureys, a member of the family, is the company's chairman. Ignace Van Doorselaere is chief executive officer, and the first non-family member to lead the company.

FROM CORSET MAKER TO LINGERIE PIONEER

Van de Velde stemmed from a small corset-making workshop opened by the husband and wife team of Achiel and Margaretha Van de Velde in the town of Schellebelle, in Belgium, in 1919. Before long, the Van de Velde name became closely connected with high-end and high-quality figure-correcting undergarments.

COMPANY PERSPECTIVES

Our mission is to shape the body and mind of women. The company's attention is exclusively focused on offering women the best fitting, most fashionable products as part of a high-quality, exceptionally wide collection of luxury lingerie. This is only possible through stores that invest in themselves and their consumer service with an attractive interior design, a friendly welcome and optimal assistance demanded of good fitting fashionable lingerie. We have to be a sufficiently important partner for the specialist retailer on every market we trade on. In geographical terms we are mainly focused on Europe and North America.

The end of World War II introduced new opportunities for the company, which included the Van de Velde's son William. The advent of new textile types, especially manmade fibers, introduced new possibilities in lingerie design. The Van de Veldes responded by introducing their own bra, panty, and other lingerie designs using the new materials.

The success of the new fabrics and new types of lingerie quickly relegated the more bulky and often uncomfortable corset design to the past. By 1949 William Van de Velde, joined by his wife, Livine van der Wee, made the decision to focus the company's production solely on the more modern lingerie types. That year the company launched something of a revolution in the European lingerie industry: the production of matching bra and panty sets.

William Van de Velde was joined by his sister Gaby and her husband Raoul Laureys, and over the next two decades the company grew steadily, becoming a major supplier of high-quality lingerie to the Belgian market. The company also began developing its first export sales, starting with the neighboring Netherlands market. By the end of the 1970s international sales accounted for some 39 percent of the group's total revenues.

By then the third generation of Van de Veldes had begun taking over the company's operations. The three leaders of that generation were Karel and Harman van de Velde and Lucas Laureys. Each played an important role in building Van de Velde into its later position as a European luxury lingerie leader. While Karel Van de Velde became head of the company's design department, his brother Herman created an internationally focused organizational structure for the company. Their activities were complemented by the marketing and sales strategy developed by Lucas Laureys.

A major feature of this strategy was the launch of the company's own branded lingerie line, originally called Marie Jolie, in 1981. Before long, the company had shortened the brand's name to Marie Jo. The new brand was also one of the first to market packaged lingerie sets.

INTERNATIONAL GROWTH

Van de Velde's timing showed foresight as the bohemian—and often braless—fashion culture of the 1970s evolved into an intensely brand-conscious, and soon luxury-oriented and designer label-dominated consumer market. The creation of the Marie Jo brand enabled the company to position itself as a leader in the Benelux market's luxury lingerie sector. During the 1980s the company launched the highly popular "Tulle" line, launching the trend toward transparent lingerie. By the 1990s, Van de Velde's market program had enabled the brand to achieve commanding recognition rates—in Belgium, for example, the company claimed a recognition rate of 100 percent.

Van de Velde's rising sales soon outstripped capacity at its main Schellebelle factory. Instead of expanding that facility, the company became one of the first in the sector to develop a delocalized production model, relying on workers outside Belgium for some of its garment construction. This effort was launched in 1986 when the company began outsourcing the most labor-intensive step in its production (the stitching, or assembly, of its garments) to subcontractors in France. That country remained a significant source for Van de Velde's production through the mid-1990s, when it continued to represent 24 percent of the group's total assembly operations.

In the 1980s Van de Velde also became one of the first in the West to begin working with Asian manufacturers, turning to Hong Kong-based Top Form International. That company, which was founded in 1966 to produce undergarments for the U.S. market, eventually grew into one of the world largest brassiere manufacturers.

Van de Velde sought a stronger entry into the larger German market at the beginning of the 1990s. This led the company to complete the acquisition of the PrimaDonna brand from PrimaDonna Wilhelm Meyer-Jischen in 1990. PrimaDonna traced its own history back to 1865, and had built up a strong position in the German market as a producer of lingerie for larger women. Following the acquisition, Van de Velde moved

KEY DATES

1919: Achiel and Margaretha Van de Velde open a corset-making shop in Schellebelle, Belgium.

1949: Van de Velde abandons corsets and specializes in the production of lingerie.

1981: The company launches its own luxury lingerie brand, Marie Jo.

1991: Van de Velde acquires the PrimaDonna brand in Germany.

1997: Van de Velde goes public, listing on the Euronext Brussels exchange.

2002: The company launches its own Marie Jo retail store format.

2007: Van de Velde acquires a 49.99% stake in U.S.-based lingerie retailer Intimacy.

2008: Van de Velde acquires Eurocorset in Spain and its Andres Sarda brand.

to position the PrimaDonna brand toward a more upscale market. At the same time, the company expanded the brand's range of sizes. In this way, Van de Velde became one of only a few luxury lingerie groups able to market specifically for the larger woman.

PUBLIC OFFERING IN 1997

The acquisition of PrimaDonna also encouraged the company to take a new step forward in its delocalized production strategy. PrimaDonna continued to be manufactured in Germany, where high labor rates made it difficult for the brand to compete. At the same time, the collapse of the Soviet bloc had opened new manufacturing opportunities in Eastern Europe. In 1992, therefore, Van de Velde decided to establish its own production facilities in Szekszárd, Hungary. That facility grew to employ more than 350 workers and by the middle of 1996 accounted for 13 percent of Van de Velde's production.

Van de Velde continued to shift its production outside of Belgium through the 1990s. In 1996, the company opened its own factory in Tunisia, which had become a major source of textiles production for the European market. In this way, Van de Velde targeted a reduction of its Schellebelle factory's share of the group's production to just 15 percent by the turn of the century. The creation of the Tunisian subsidiary at the same time enabled the company to transfer the bulk of its subcontracting operations outside of France—by the

turn of the century, that country represented less than 1 percent of Van de Velde's total production.

Van de Velde went public in 1997, placing nearly 40 percent of its shares on the Euronext Brussels stock exchange. By then, the third generation of the Van de Velde family had begun to approach retirement, and while there were more than 20 members in the family's fourth generation, none had entered the company's operations. The public offering prepared the way for Van de Velde to make the transition from family-operated company to a professionally managed, family-controlled business.

The success of the Marie Jo brand, and the addition of PrimaDonna as a second brand, had enabled Van de Velde to achieve strong growth over the past years. From sales of just BEF 164 million in 1981, Van de Velde had grown to an internationally operating company producing sales of more than BEF 1.8 billion at the time of its public offering. Much of this growth came from the company's successful effort to build its international sales. By the time of its public offering, exports accounted for 77 percent of Van de Velde's total revenues. Germany by then had become the group's single largest market, generating 35 percent of its revenues.

NEW BRANDS FOR THE 21ST CENTURY

The group's success in managing its brands encouraged the company to launch a new brand for the late 1990s. As the demographic for the company's core Marie Jo brand began to age, the company recognized the opportunity to extend its reach into a more youthful and youth-oriented market, which favored minimalist lingerie styles. This led to the launch of the Marie Jo L'Aventure line in 1997. The brand was quickly successfully, and soon was responsible for generating some 15 percent of the group's total revenues.

In the first decade of the 2000s Van de Velde moved to strengthen its relationship with Top Form International. By then, the Hong Kong-based company, which completed its own public offering in 1991, had grown to account for some 54 percent of Van de Velde's production. Acquiring a significant stake in Top Form—Van de Velde bought out the 21.58 percent stake held by one of Top Form's founders—was also seen as a means of protecting Van de Velde's own interests, giving the Belgian company a voice in Top Form's future strategy. Following the share purchase, Van de Velde joined with Top Form to create a new holding company Guliano Pty Ltd. That company, held at 49.99 percent by Van de Velde, then acquired a 43.62 percent stake in Top Form.

Van de Velde also sought further expansion for its flagship Marie Jo brand. In 2001, the company launched a new luxury label, Marie Jo l'Exclusive, targeting the ultra high end of the lingerie market. At the same time, Van de Velde began preparing its entry into its own branded retail operations.

Traditionally, Van de Velde's sales had come through a large network of small-scale, independent retail shops. While this channel remained an important one for the company, and included more than 4,800 stores through the end of the 1990s, Van de Velde had been forced to confront a growing trend in the lingerie market. Through the 1990s and into the first decade of the 2000s, a growing number of mass retailers, represented on the one hand by department stores such as H&M and Zara, and on the other by the large supermarket and hypermarket groups, had gained an increasing share of the overall lingerie market. While these channels typically focused on the low- to mid-range lingerie segments, Van de Velde nonetheless felt the pressure as the independent sector was forced to respond.

In 2002 Van de Velde joined a number of its major competitors in launching its own retail format. For this, the company established a subsidiary, Osedis, which oversaw the development of the Marie Jo retail store format. The first two Marie Jo shops opened by the end of that year; by 2006 the company had opened a total of 11 stores. Most of these stores were located in mid-sized French and German towns, in order to avoid direct competition with the larger department store groups.

Growth at Van de Velde's retail operation remained slow, however, in part because the company sought to avoid competing with its independent retailer customers. Starting in 2007 the company closed four of the Marie Jo shops. In an effort to breathe new life into the retail business, the company debuted a new concept, "Lingerie Styling," providing shoppers with a more personalized approach to lingerie fitting.

The lingerie styling concept soon led Van de Velde to the United States, where it joined forces with one of its larger customers there, the small-but-growing Intimacy lingerie chain set up in the early 1990s by Susan Nethero. Van de Velde and Nethero formed a strategic alliance, with Van de Velde acquiring a 49.99 percent stake in the Intimacy chain. The new partners then announced their intention to expand the Intimacy chain to as many as 25 shops by 2012. By the end of 2008, the chain had doubled in size, with six stores in operation.

Van de Velde in the meantime had expanded its own operations. In 2008 the company launched a new extension of the Marie Jo brand, a line of sports bras and related lingerie under the Marie Jo Intense name. Also that year Van de Velde acquired Spain's Eurocorset, a company founded in 1961, which had launched its own luxury lingerie line, Andres Sarda, in the mid-1980s. The acquisition cost the company nearly EUR 14 million but added some EUR 13 million in revenues—allowing the company to post a slight revenue gain despite the economic collapse that year. Under CEO Ignace Van Doorselaere, who, in 2004, became the first non-family member to lead the company, Van de Velde hoped to weather the economic crisis and maintain its status as one of Europe's leading luxury lingerie producers.

M. L. Cohen

PRINCIPAL SUBSIDIARIES

Guliano HK Limited (Hong Kong); Guliano Pte Ltd (Singapore); Intimacy Inc. (United States; 49%); Societe de Confection de Kondar S.A.R.L.; Van de Velde Finland Oy (Finland); Van de Velde France S.A.R.L.; Van de Velde Gebroeders Verwaltungs Gmbh (Germany); Van de Velde Gmbh & Co. (Germany); Van de Velde Iberica Rd. (Spain); Van de Velde Italy SRL; Van de Velde Marie Jo SA (Luxembourg); Van de Velde Mode BV (Netherlands); Van de Velde North America (USA); Van de Velde Retail Inc. (USA); Van de Velde Termelo Es Kereskedelmi Kft (Hungary); Van de Velde Tunesie S.A.R.L.; Van de Velde U.K. Ltd.

PRINCIPAL COMPETITORS

Industria de Diseno Textil S.A.; Liz Claiborne Inc.; Triumph International Vertriebsgesellschaft AG; Etablissements Robert Gonfreville; Warnaco Group Inc.; Fruit of the Loom Inc.; Cortefiel S.A.; Etam Developpement S.C.A.; Mango S.L.; Damartex S.A.; BTX Group A/S; Dim S.A.S.

FURTHER READING

"Lingerieproducent Van de Velde Herschikt Productie," *Het Nieuwsblad,* January 1, 2009.

"Van de Velde Acquires Lingerie Brand Andres Sarda," *Tendersinfo,* June 22, 2008.

"Van de Velde Increases Top Form Stake," *just-style.com,* August 19, 2008.

"Van de Velde Invests in Intimacy," *just-style.com,* March 29, 2007.

"Van de Velde Produceert Enkel Nog 'Schone Lingerie,'" *Het Nieuwsblad,* December 2, 2003.

"Van de Velde Slikt Omzetdaling,"*De Streekkrant,* January 8, 2009.

"Van de Velde to Shut Down Plant in Hungary," *Hungarian News Agency MTI,* January 7, 2009.

Weale, Natasha, "Northern Delights," *Sunday Mail,* April 21, 2002, p. 3.

Wheeler, Caroline, "Brum the Breast of British," *Sunday Mercury,* April 28, 2002, p. 11.

"Winst Van de Velde met 8% Gedaald," *Express.be,* February 17, 2009.

Weather Shield
Manufacturing, Inc.

───────────●───────────

One Weather Shield Plaza
Medford, Wisconsin 54451
U.S.A.
Telephone: (715) 748-2100
Fax: (715) 748-6999
Web site: http://www.weathershield.com

Private Company
Incorporated: 1958 as Weather Shield Aluminum
 Products, Inc.
Employees: 4,000
Sales: $375 million (2007 est.)
NAICS: 321918 Other Millwork (Including Flooring);
 332321 Metal Window and Door Manufacturing

■ ■ ■

Weather Shield Manufacturing, Inc., is a privately held, Medford, Wisconsin-based maker of high-quality, impact-resistant windows, patio doors, and entry doors. Product lines include the Collections upscale line of southwestern-style wood windows and doors; the premium Legacy line of wood and aluminum windows and doors; the signature Weather Shield line of all wood or aluminum-clad wood windows and doors; LifeGuard windows and doors engineered to withstand severe coastal weather and meet necessary building codes in those areas; the low maintenance ProShield line of vinyl-clad wood windows and doors; the Visions line of vinyl

windows and doors; Custom Shield windows and doors designed to fit within existing frames; and the HR175 line of energy-efficient windows suitable for historic renovations.

Weather Shield also offers tilt sash replacement kits to restore existing windows, as well as entrance doors available in heights as tall as ten feet with a variety of panel styles and wood finishes, as well as glass and leaded decorative glass. Patio doors come hinged, sliding, or telescoping. In addition to its Medford site, Weather Shield maintains manufacturing facilities in Ladysmith, Greenwood, and Park Falls, Wisconsin, and Logan, Utah. Trucking subsidiary Weather Shield Transportation Limited delivers the items across the country. Weather Shield is owned and managed by the Schield family.

ORIGINS

The Schield family first became involved in the manufacture of windows and doors in 1953 when Edward "Lee" Schield, using $300 in seed money, began handcrafting aluminum windows and doors in a rented Medford garage. He did well enough that two years later his brother David joined him and together they formed a partnership, initially operating out of the attic of a funeral home. Later in 1955 they acquired the Medford Cooperative Creamery building and converted it into the company's first true factory and hired the plant's first manager. A year later, business was strong enough to necessitate the hiring of the first full-time salesman and office manager. In 1958 the business was incorporated as Weather Shield Aluminum Products, Inc., with Lee Schield serving as president.

Weather Shield expanded further in the 1960s. At the start of the decade, the company added wood windows to its inventory, relying on parts supplied by a local firm, Harvey Millwork Company. A year later strong sales justified the purchase of the company's first tractor-trailer delivery truck. The company surpassed the $1 million level in sales by 1967. That same year it dropped aluminum from its name to become Weather Shield Manufacturing, Inc., a name more appropriate for a company that in the 1960s was expanding its product offerings to include vinyl-clad wood windows as well as casements and awnings, which led to the printing of Weather Shield's first architectural products catalog. The company was also gaining a reputation as an innovator. In 1968 it introduced the industry's first triple-glazed windows. A year later it unveiled a new insulated steel door.

Weather Shield began growing more vertically integrated. In 1966 an insulated glassmaking company, 4-S Glass, was created. Weather Shield Vinyl Industries was launched in 1969 to produce vinyl window and door components, including weather stripping and jamb liners. Harvey Millwork was then acquired in 1970, and a year later the operation was strengthened by the acquisition of a Wausau, Wisconsin, millwork company and its newer equipment, which was transferred to the Medford operation. The following year Harvey Millwork, 4-S Glass, and Vinyl Industries were merged into Weather Shield, becoming separate divisions. In 1973 Great Lakes Millwork of Ladysmith, Wisconsin, was acquired as well. When Weather Shield was reorganized in 1975, Great Lakes became the Ladysmith Division, while Harvey Millwork was designated the Millwork Division, 4-S Glass became the Glass Division, and Weather Shield Vinyl Products served as the Vinyl Division. In addition, operations were maintained in Colorado, Indiana, Michigan, North Dakota, and Pennsylvania by the end of the decade.

ADDING TRANSPORTATION AND SERVICE

To keep up with demand for its products, Weather Shield began assembling a delivery fleet of trucks by leasing a dozen tractors and 24 trailers in 1972. Five years later it evolved into the owner-operator freight enterprise, Weather Shield Transportation Limited. To improve the service side of the business, Weather Shield in 1975 began hiring a network of servicemen who resided in the areas they covered. By 1977 the company was producing more than 375,000 windows and doors, leading that year to a $2 million expansion program. By the end of the decade Weather Shield enjoyed the third largest market share in window sales in the United States.

Also of note in the 1970s, a second generation of the Schield family became involved in the business, as Lee Schield's sons Kevin, Mark, and Brian took summer plant jobs. In 1979 Mark and Kevin joined Weather Shield on a full-time basis, the former becoming a sales coordinator and the latter taking a manufacturing position. Two years later Kevin Schield was dispatched to Rapid City, South Dakota, to manage a distribution facility, and in 1985 Mark Schield moved to Harrisburg, Pennsylvania, to manage another distribution facility.

To better serve the western part of the United States, Weather Shield in 1980 bought an existing 57,000-square-foot plant in Logan, Utah, which was converted to produce windows and doors. Two years later a 100,000-square-foot addition to the plant was completed after a major fire destroyed a portion of the plant, which was put out of commission for about three months. Also at the start of the 1980s, the door manufacturing operations of the Ladysmith Division were supplemented by the acquisition of a former Needlecraft plant in the community. In 1987 a new division was formed to manufacture a line of replacement windows, branded two years later as Custom Shield. It was also in 1987 that the company's dealer-direct sales model was changed to builder-direct, leading to the closing of the distribution facilities other than the Logan, Utah, location. Mark and Kevin Schield returned to Wisconsin and in 1991 were named vice-presidents of the company.

Weather Shield entered the 1990s a fast-growing company. To keep pace with its expansion, the company in 1991 acquired the former headquarters of Tombstone Pizza and its 20.7-acre site. The five-year-old 61,000-square-foot facility was one of the largest office buildings in northwestern Wisconsin. The property had become available following the acquisition of Tombstone by Kraft Foods.

KEY DATES

1958: Weather Shield Aluminum Products, Inc., is formed.

1966: 4-S Glass is established; company name is changed to Weather Shield Manufacturing, Inc.

1975: Weather Shield is reorganized to include several new divisions.

1977: Weather Shield Transportation Ltd. is formed.

1980: Logan, Utah, facility is acquired and converted to produce windows and doors.

1987: Transition to builder-direct sales model begins.

1991: Company acquires former headquarters and site of Tombstone Pizza.

1992: Visions 2000 vinyl line is launched.

1995: ProShield line of vinyl-clad wood windows and doors is introduced.

2001: Park Falls, Wisconsin, plant opens; sister company, Peachtree Doors and Windows, Inc., is acquired.

2006: Company opens research and development laboratory and testing facility.

INTRODUCING NEW LINES

While still very much devoted to wood products—in 1991 the company began offering interior cherry wood units—Weather Shield had to adapt to higher wood prices due to scarcity caused by environmental concerns, as well as stricter standards for energy conservation that could not be met by aluminum windows. As a result a new vinyl line of windows and doors, marketed under the Visions 2000 banner, was introduced in 1992, and a plant was opened in Greenwood, Wisconsin, to assemble the products. In addition, Visions 2000 provided Weather Shield with an entry into the lower-priced market for new single family and multifamily home construction and remodeling projects. The company also took steps to improve productivity and customer satisfaction by adopting a Total Quality Management program.

Weather Shield's vinyl products proved extremely popular, leading to another product launch. In 1995 the company unveiled the ProShield line of vinyl-clad wood windows and doors. To manufacture both the Visions 2000 and ProShield product lines, the Logan plant was upgraded in 1995. Weather Shield extended its product offerings in other directions as well. The upscale HR175

replacement window line, the Custom Wood Interiors Collection, and the Legacy Series line of premium double-hung and casement windows were introduced in 1998. A year later American Fir was added as an option to the Custom Wood Interiors Collection. In the meantime, the company added a number of window glazing options, including Simulated Divided Lite and True Divided Lite, as well as making insulated Low E2 glazing—ThermoGold, featuring actual gold particles—standard in all product lines. In 2000 Weather Shield upgraded its severe weather products by adding laminated glass options offered by Solutia Corporation.

With sales surging, due in large part to robust home construction, Weather Shield opened a new 400,000-square-foot plant in Park Falls, Wisconsin, in 2001 to manufacture entry and patio doors. In that same year, the company introduced a newly designed line of French patio doors, followed up in 2004 with a new telescoping patio door system, featuring as many as six sliding panels. The extra production capacity of the Park Falls plant was also needed following the 2001 agreement signed with Kaycan Ltd., a vinyl and aluminum siding manufacturer, to distribute the Weather Shield product lines throughout Canada, where Kaycan enjoyed a major presence.

In addition to growing Weather Shield, the Schield family added a sister company in 2001, acquiring Peachtree Doors and Windows, Inc. Based in Mosinee, Wisconsin, Peachtree was credited in 1959 with designing the industry's first airtight aluminum sliding glass patio door. The Schield family opted to keep Peachtree and Weather Shield separate businesses, although there was some overlap in administrative and executive functions.

EMPHASIS ON RESEARCH AND DEVELOPMENT AND TESTING

Weather Shield continued to develop and introduce other new products in the early years of the new millennium. A new entry door systems program became available in 2004, including steel and fiberglass entry doors. A year later the LifeGuard line of insulated impact-resistant windows and doors was introduced, designed to meet exacting building codes in coastal regions. Demand for such products had been growing due to a greater frequency of destructive hurricanes in areas other than the traditional Florida market. By this time, the market extended from New York to Texas. In a matter of two years, the business grew almost fourfold. Weather Shield depended on outside testing laboratories located as far away as Pennsylvania in the development and certification of these impact resistant products, a time-consuming and expensive process.

To expedite development and certification, the company in 2006 opened its own 10,800-square-foot research and development laboratory and testing facility, including an air cannon that could mimic the effects of a hurricane by hurling an eight-foot two-by-four board at windows and doors at 35 miles per hour. The facility could also test windows and doors geared toward colder climes such as Wisconsin, determining air and water infiltration as well as structural performance. The company estimated that the onsite facility allowed it to save four to six weeks on development and certification, thus allowing it to take advantage of peak product demand during times of severe weather while saving money on certification testing.

Weather Shield credited the work ethic of Wisconsin employees as a major factor in its success. The Schield family indicated no desire to transfer manufacturing elsewhere in the country, yet it needed skilled workers in order to remain competitive. To help in this regard, the state issued a $42,000 grant in 2006 to provide training to more than 300 employees at five Weather Shield plants in Wisconsin through Northcentral Technical College. Another key to ongoing success was developing products that met the needs of customers. In response to requests from architects, builders, and owners of luxury homes, Weather Shield in 2006 introduced the Collections line of ultra high-end wood windows and doors with a southwestern flair. Enhancements to existing lines followed as well, but as new home construction dropped in 2008, exacerbated by tightening credit, demand for windows and doors fell as the entire housing market was forced to retrench. To cope with these adverse conditions, the company was forced to lay off workers. Weather Shield hoped to call back its workers as soon as possible, but as the economy worsened, the time frame was uncertain.

Ed Dinger

PRINCIPAL SUBSIDIARIES

Weather Shield Transportation Ltd.

PRINCIPAL COMPETITORS

Andersen Corporation; JELD-WEN, Inc.; Pella Corporation.

FURTHER READING

Bednarek, David I., "Here's Looking at You," *Milwaukee Journal,* November 17, 1991, p. 1.

———, "Medford Company Buys Building from Tombstone," *Milwaukee Journal,* October 28, 1991, p. 8.

"Business Hopes Grant Keeps Jobs in State," *Marshfield News-Herald,* August 23, 2006, p. 1A.

Multer, Mark, "Window and Door Maker Builds New Research, Testing Facility in Medford," *Mansfield News-Herald,* November 28, 2006, p. 1A.

Savage, Mark, "Medford, Wis.-based Door Maker to Build Plant in River Falls," *Milwaukee Journal Sentinel,* May 17, 2000.

"Weather Shield Is Ready to Meet New Energy Regulations," *Professional Builder and Remodeler,* January 15, 1992, p. 298.

"Weather Shield Unveils Cuts," *Eau Claire (Wisc.) Leader-Telegram,* February 12, 2008.

William Morris Agency, Inc.

———————————————— ■ ————————————————

1 William Morris Place
Beverly Hills, California 90212
U.S.A.
Telephone: (310) 859-4000
Fax: (310) 859-4462
Web site: http://www.wma.com

Private Company
Incorporated: 1898 as William Morris, Vaudeville Agent
Employees: 600
Sales: $300 million (2008 est.)
NAICS: 711410 Agents and Managers for Artists, Athletes, Entertainers, and Other Public Figures

■ ■ ■

With more than 110 years under its belt, the William Morris Agency, Inc. (WMA), is America's oldest and largest talent brokerage. Over the decades, the agency established and nurtured the careers of some of the entertainment industry's brightest stars. The Morris stable has included vaudevillians George Burns and Gracie Allen, movie industry pioneers Al Jolson and Charlie Chaplin, trailblazing television personalities like Milton Berle, rock-and-roll king Elvis Presley, and scores of celebrities in between. WMA has operations in every aspect of the entertainment industry, including motion pictures, television, music, Broadway and theatrical touring, book publishing, commercial endorsements, sports marketing, corporate consulting, digital media, and video games. The company's client list in 2008 was impressive—it represented both the National Hockey

League and the National Football League, along with well-known movie stars such as Mel Gibson, Denzel Washington, and Steven Martin, just to name a few.

LATE 19TH-CENTURY FOUNDATIONS

The William Morris Agency's roots stretch back to New York City in 1882. That was when nine-year-old Zelman Moses and his family immigrated from Germany to the United States. The boy soon Anglicized his name to William Morris and quit school to clerk at a local grocery. Although he held a good-paying office job throughout his teen years, an economic crisis brought his first career in publishing to an end in the 1890s.

Morris went to work as a clerk for a top stage impresario in 1893 and had soon earned himself a partnership in the business. When the owner died, however, his wife rescinded the partnership. Morris started his own company, William Morris, Vaudeville Agent, in 1898, establishing his monogram ("W" and "M" interwoven as four "Xs") as a trademark that would stand for decades to come. In exchange for finding venues for vaudeville acts, he kept a portion—usually 10 percent—of the entertainers' pay. Filling a void left by his former partner, Morris quickly established himself as an agent with great connections and an eye for talent.

In the first two decades of the 20th century, Morris assembled a collection of widely known acts headlined by the likes of Scottish bagpiper and comic Harry Lauder, Oklahoman Will Rogers, and Charlie Chaplin. When the owner of a chain of theaters tried to blackball Morris and his clients, the agent formed his own confederation of theaters. Although Morris would continue to battle power-hungry theater owners through the 1920s, his control over popular talent always gave him the upper hand.

Morris's link to the performers helped to protect his livelihood despite changes in the entertainment industry. For example, when movies and radio began to deflate the power of the vaudeville theaters in the late 1920s, Morris took his acts to the new media. Many of his vaudevillians, including Amos 'n' Andy, Martha Raye, and George Burns and Gracie Allen, became radio stars. Others such as Charlie Chaplin and the Marx Brothers made the transition to film. The venue mattered little to Morris beyond finding a suitable fit, for no matter where his stars appeared, he received 10 percent of their pay.

William Morris cheated death on a number of occasions. He was struck with tuberculosis in 1902, but after taking Dr. Trudeau's Adirondack Mountain rest cure, he returned to work in 1905. He and his wife were set to take the *Titanic*'s ill-fated maiden voyage in 1912, but canceled the trip so that he could clear up a theater booking snafu. He was supposed to sail on the *Lusitania* in May 1915, but was still in New York when it was sunk by the Germans. In fact, Morris lived long enough to see his agency establish offices in London, Chicago, and Los Angeles. After retiring in 1930, he died in 1932 while playing pinochle with friends at the Friars Club.

THE GREAT DEPRESSION AND WORLD WAR II

Son William Morris, Jr., became the de jure head of the agency, but it was Abe Lastfogel who truly filled the senior Morris's shoes. Lastfogel, who like the senior Morris was a Jewish immigrant, had joined the talent brokerage in 1912 at the age of 14. Morris, Jr., continued to concentrate on the Los Angeles outpost, which he had headed since 1930, while Lastfogel guided the New York headquarters. By the time of the death of Morris, Sr., the Great Depression had begun to take its toll on the agency; it lost a combined total of $45,000 in 1931 and 1932.

WMA found an unlikely savior in Mae West, who went on to become the top grosser at the box office in the 1930s. After its initial dip, entertainment proved a Depression-hardy industry. Over the course of the decade, revenues multiplied from about $500,000 to $15 million as the agency's client roster grew to number in the hundreds. While big-name film and radio deals contributed two-thirds of this turnover, the other third came from lesser known departments, including vaudeville, nightclub, and literary management. Not only did the agency represent well-established stars but it also nurtured what it called "the stars of the future." As a William Morris Agency advertisement once stressed, "Our Small Act of Today Is Our Big Act of Tomorrow." In 1938 the agency moved its West Coast office to posh Beverly Hills. Its early real estate purchases throughout the area would become a major source of wealth in the decades to come.

For WMA's contribution to the Allied effort during World War II, Abe Lastfogel organized USO shows featuring more than 7,000 entertainers, including such luminaries as Bing Crosby, Dinah Shore, Marlene Dietrich, James Stewart, Clark Gable, and Humphrey Bogart.

EXPANSION INTO TELEVISION

In the postwar era Morris's roster included Mickey Rooney, Laurence Olivier, Danny Kaye, Vivien Leigh, Katharine Hepburn, and Rita Hayworth. The agency also discovered and launched Marilyn Monroe in her career. Morris merged with the Berg-Allenberg Agency in 1949, bringing in such Hollywood luminaries as Clark Gable, Judy Garland, Frank Capra, Edward G. Robinson, and Robert Mitchum. It also branched into television during this period. According to Frank Rose, author of a 1995 history of the agency: "In the early years the talent agencies essentially produced the shows, even lining up guests, taking care of all sorts of details." In fact, Morris agents were responsible for packaging such immensely popular productions as *The Milton Berle Show, Texaco Star Theater,* and *Your Show of Shows. Make Room for Daddy,* starring Danny Thomas, was another Morris vehicle of the 1950s.

When Bill Morris, Jr., retired from the agency in 1952, Abe Lastfogel became de facto head of William Morris. During the decade, the group represented Elvis Presley and revived Frank Sinatra's career. The agency also sparked the quiz show craze with the 1955 launch

```
┌─────────────────────────────────────────────────┐
│                                                   │
│                  KEY DATES                        │
│                      ■                            │
│                                                   │
│  1898:  William Morris establishes his company as │
│         William Morris, Vaudeville Agent.         │
│  1912:  Abe Lastfogel joins the company at the    │
│         age of 14.                                │
│  1932:  Morris dies; Lastfogel and Morris, Jr.,   │
│         head up the company.                      │
│  1949:  Morris merges with the Berg-Allenberg     │
│         Agency.                                   │
│  1955:  The agency sparks the quiz show craze     │
│         with the launch of *The $64,000 Question.*│
│  1975:  Rowland Perkins, Bill Haber, Mike         │
│         Rosenfeld, Mike Ovitz, and Ron Meyer      │
│         leave William Morris Agency (WMA) to      │
│         form Creative Artists Agency.             │
│  1991:  Jerry Katzman is named president.         │
│  1992:  The company acquires Triad Artists Inc.   │
│  1999:  Jim Wiatt joins the company.              │
│  2000:  The Writers Shop is acquired.             │
│  2002:  Premier Talent Agency is purchased.       │
│  2003:  The company opens an office in Miami      │
│         Beach, Florida.                           │
│  2004:  Operations begin in Shanghai, China.      │
│  2007:  Agent Ed Limato joins WMA, bringing with  │
│         him an impressive client list.            │
│                                                   │
└─────────────────────────────────────────────────┘
```

of *The $64,000 Question.* Other agents booked comedy and variety acts to the nightclubs and casinos springing up in Las Vegas. These venues continued to serve as "feeders" to the film and television operations, seeking out new talent and molding it into the next generation of movie and TV stars.

Film stars of the 1960s on the Morris roster included Anne Bancroft, Carol Channing, Katharine Hepburn, Jack Lemmon, Sophia Loren, Walter Matthau, Kim Novak, Natalie Wood, Spencer Tracy, Gregory Peck, and Barbra Streisand. The agency also expanded into the music industry during this time, representing such diverse acts as folk artists Paul Simon and Art Garfunkel, British rockers the Rolling Stones, Motown divas the Supremes, and teen idols the Beach Boys.

Nevertheless, it was television that became William Morris's biggest moneymaker in the 1960s, contributing around 60 percent of revenues or more than $7 million by the end of the decade. According to a 1989 article in *Forbes* magazine, "In the mid-1960s Morris was the

undisputed kingpin of the television business, with some 9 hours on network prime time."

When Abe Lastfogel retired in 1969, he divided up all of the agency's voting stock among its key executives and employees. He was succeeded by attorney/accountant Nat Lefkowitz. At that time, WMA was bringing in an estimated $12 million annually, and it boasted hundreds of employees at offices in New York, Chicago, Beverly Hills, London, Paris, Munich, Rome, and Madrid.

FRACTURE AND DECLINE

Although the transition from Lastfogel to Lefkowitz appeared to have been a smooth transfer of power, WMA was fraught with internal strife. While the agency's corps of young, eager talent brokers multiplied, positions at the top remained filled by sexagenarians. Only Phil Weltman, a high-ranking executive in the television division, was in favor of grooming a cadre of younger men for top positions. Weltman's ideas were anathema to the Morris corporate culture, which prized long-term loyalty and rewarded it with promotions, but only after decades of service. The agency was becoming a training ground for other Hollywood professions; music industry executive David Geffen, television producer Aaron Spelling, and television executive Barry Diller all got their starts in the Morris mailroom.

When Lefkowitz unceremoniously fired Weltman in 1975, several of Weltman's young apprentices saw the writing on the wall. That year Rowland Perkins, Bill Haber, Mike Rosenfeld, Mike Ovitz, and Ron Meyer left to form Creative Artists Agency (CAA). The new agency and other defectors soon lured away more than a dozen major clients, including Barbra Streisand, Robert Redford, Brian De Palma, Goldie Hawn, Mel Gibson, Michelle Pfeiffer, Kevin Costner, Jane Fonda, Alan Alda, and Chevy Chase.

Back at Morris, Lefkowitz was moved up to the newly established—and empty—post of co-chairman, a title shared with octogenarian Abe Lastfogel. Lefkowitz was succeeded as president by Sammy Weisbord, who had joined the agency in 1931 at the age of 19 as Lastfogel's assistant and had risen through the ranks of the television division. December 1980 brought another management reorganization. While Weisbord remained president, the two aging past presidents were dubbed "cochairmen emeriti" and the board expanded to include seven new members—the first newcomers since the early 1950s. It was not exactly an influx of new blood, however; not one director was under the age of 50. Weisbord went into semiretirement in 1984 and was succeeded by Lee Stevens, who guided the company until his death in February 1989. At that time, Norman Brokaw ascended to the top management position.

The frequent management upheavals of the 1980s did not do much to burnish WMA's dulled reputation. Before long, it had become the butt of an oft-quoted joke: "How do you commit the perfect murder? Kill your wife and go to work for WMA. They'll never find you." Trade publications such as *Los Angeles Magazine* and *Variety* sounded the agency's death knell with headlines like "Whither William Morris?" and "R.I.P.?"

The obituaries for WMA were premature, however. While the business did rely heavily on past glories and the residuals they generated, it retained several big stars, including Bill Cosby, Clint Eastwood, Jack Lemmon, Tim Robbins, Uma Thurman, Tom Hanks, and John Malkovich. Moreover, estimated revenues had doubled from $30 million in 1984 to more than $60 million by the end of the decade, when the company represented about 2,000 clients.

SIGNS OF LIFE

In January 1991 three senior agents left WMA for a rival, taking with them a mix of well-established and up-and-coming stars including James Spader, Gérard Depardieu, Andie MacDowell, Anjelica Huston, Tim Robbins, Julia Roberts, and Anne Bancroft. Former head of television Jerry Katzman ascended to the presidency of WMA in 1991 with a mandate from the company to breathe new life into the agency. In 1992, he executed what *Variety* characterized as "one of the first bold moves in a long time by the huge firm that was once the undisputed industry leader." The acquisition of Triad Artists Inc. brought Morris 50 agents, along with action-film star Bruce Willis and the alternative music group Red Hot Chili Peppers. The acquisition of the Jim Halsey Co. boosted the agency's penetration of the reinvigorated country music industry, and the purchase of Charles Dorris and Associates made Morris a leader in the growing field of contemporary Christian music.

Morris may have gotten its biggest break in 1995, when CAA Chairman Michael Ovitz—who since his departure from Morris in 1975 had become known as perhaps the most powerful man in Hollywood—left the agency he founded to join the Walt Disney Company. In the wake of this upheaval, Morris picked up Whoopi Goldberg and re-signed Sylvester Stallone.

Jerry Katzman advanced to the post of vice-chairman in April 1997 and Arnold Rifkin, director of the film division, added the day-to-day management of the agency to his list of responsibilities. At that time the Morris roster included teen brother act Hanson, clothing designer Tommy Hilfiger, Asian action-film star

Jackie Chan, supermodel Cindy Crawford, and Olympic ice skater Oksana Baiul.

At 100 years old in 1998, the agency appeared to be returning to life. James A. Wiatt, former cochairman of competitor International Creative Management, joined WMA as president in 1999. He brought with him clients including Eddie Murphy as well as several well-known and respected directors. He made quick changes to the agency's business structure, cutting ten agents from its Los Angeles and New York offices.

MOVING INTO THE 21ST CENTURY

Under Wiatt's leadership, WMA spent the early years of the new millennium expanding its business, both domestically and abroad. It acquired The Writers Shop in 2000, adding new writing talent to its growing pool of authors and novelists. Two years later, it bought Premier Talent Agency, adding names such as Roger Waters, The Who, Keith Richards, Tom Petty and the Heartbreakers, the Pretenders, and Sinead O'Connor to its client list.

WMA also strengthened its presence in the United States by opening a new office in Miami Beach, Florida, in 2003. One year later it moved into China and opened its first Asian office in Shanghai. Operations in London were bolstered in 2007 and new offices were opened in London's famous Centre Point Tower.

WMA underwent changes in management in late 2004 when the head of its television operations, Sam Haskell, and several other executives left the company. The move eventually left Wiatt to assume the chairmanship along with his CEO duties, while Norman Brokaw remained chairman emeritus and David Wirtschafter became president.

During 2006 WMA added the National Hockey League to its growing list of corporate clients, which by this time included the National Football League, Anheuser-Busch, General Motors, Harrah's Entertainment, and Hilton Hotels. WMA also scored a coup when agent Ed Limato joined the company's ranks in 2007. He brought with him well-known actors including Mel Gibson, Denzel Washington, Steve Martin, and Richard Gere.

By 2008, WMA claimed to be the largest and most diversified talent and literary agency in the world. With activities in every aspect of the entertainment industry, an impressive and growing client list, and well-earned industry respect, the 110-year-old company was thriving and appeared to be well positioned for success in the years to come.

April D. Gasbarre
Updated, Christina M. Stansell

PRINCIPAL COMPETITORS

Creative Artists Agency Inc.; IMG; International Creative Management Inc.

FURTHER READING

Baker, John F., "WMA to Acquire Writers Shop," *Publishers Weekly,* January 15, 2001.

Barnes, Brooks, "Top Talent Agent Joins William Morris," *New York Times,* August 17, 2007.

Bart, Peter, "Whither William Morris?" *Variety,* October 19, 1992, pp. 5–6.

Bernstein, Amy, and Frank Rose, "They Made Mae West a Star," *U.S. News & World Report,* August 7, 1995, p. 51.

Block, Alex Ben, "William Morris Power Play," *Television Week,* December 20, 2004.

Gubernick, Lisa, "Backs to the Future," *Forbes,* April 15, 1991, p. 10.

———, "Living Off the Past," *Forbes,* June 12, 1989, pp. 48–52.

Kit, Zorianna, and Dana Harris, "Out of Commission at WMA," *Hollywood Reporter,* September 30, 1999.

"The National Hockey League Teams with the William Morris Agency to Expand Brand Presence in Entertainment Community," *Business Wire,* February 1, 2006.

Ressner, Jeffrey, "R.I.P?" *Los Angeles Magazine,* May 1991, pp. A61–A69.

Rose, Frank, *The Agency: William Morris and the Hidden History of Show Business,* New York: HarperBusiness, 1995.

———, "The Case of the Ankling Agents," *Premiere,* August 1991, pp. 54–61.

"The 10%ers Solution," *Time,* November 2, 1992, p. 19.

Waddell, Ray, "William Morris Agency Acquires Premier Talent," *Billboard,* March 16, 2002.

———, "William Morris Agency Buys Dorris and Associates," *Amusement Business,* April 5, 1993, p. 6.

WSI Corporation

400 Minuteman Road
Andover, Massachusetts 01810-1093
U.S.A.
Telephone: (978) 983-6300
Fax: (978) 983-6400
Web site: http://www.wsi.com

Private Company
Incorporated: 1978 as Weather Services International
Employees: 220
Sales: $42 million (2008 est.)
NAICS: 518210 Data Processing, Hosting, and Related
Services; 541990 All Other Professional, Scientific,
and Technical Services

∎ ∎ ∎

With headquarters in Andover, Massachusetts, and international operations in Birmingham, England, WSI Corporation is a leading provider of weather forecast data. The company is owned by an investment group that includes NBC Universal, Bain Capital, and The Blackstone Group. Relying upon its proprietary technology and a workforce of 220 people—some 40 percent of whom are meteorologists—WSI provides forecasts to a variety of markets, including the aviation, energy trading, media, and utility sectors. The company claims to operate the largest commercial meteorological database in the world, which draws information from a number of sources, including the U.S. National Weather Service and the U.S. military, as well as a number of

international agencies, world governments, and commercial vendors.

WSI provides local, national, and global weather forecasts, as well as travel information, to consumers via its Intellicast service, which operates the web site www.intellicast.com. On the corporate side, WSI counts companies such as CNN, Bloomberg Television, NBC, and FOX among its media customers. In addition, the company also serves aviation industry clients such as the Federal Aviation Administration, American Airlines, Delta, FedEx, and the National Aeronautics and Space Administration (NASA). WSI rounds out its client roster with leading energy traders such as Morgan Stanley, Goldman Sachs, and Constellation Energy.

FORMATIVE YEARS

The origins of WSI date back to 1978, when the company was established as Weather Services International. One year after its formation, the company made its mark by providing election-related graphics for on-air use during the mayoral election in Boston. The 1980s were filled with many firsts for WSI. According to the company, dial-up modems were first used to provide aviation briefings in 1980. In 1982 WSI began providing services to a newly formed entity called The Weather Channel. That same year, the company provided its first satellite image to Boston-based television station WBZ.

In 1984 WSI introduced a new service called SKItalk, which provided reports on skiing weather conditions at ski areas throughout the country. In addition to individual users, the service also was marketed to television and radio stations. Another new service introduced in 1984 was WSI FAXbrief, which provided DIFAX (digital facsimile) charts from the National Weather Service by telephone.

In recognition of its status as the leading aviation weather service, WSI received the first of many PRASE awards from *Professional Pilot Magazine* in 1985. Using data obtained from models, the company also began providing visualizations of forecasted satellite graphics that year. By 1987 WSI employed a workforce of 65 people. The company's customer base included approximately 250 television stations, as well as aviation centers and agricultural firms, which relied upon WSI for graphical weather data. At this time, headquarters were located in Bedford, Massachusetts. In addition, the company also operated a data center in Reading, Massachusetts. It also was in 1987 that WSI made plans to build its first network management center, as part of a larger effort to revamp its corporate information technology network.

More pioneering developments unfolded during the late 1980s, beginning with WSI NOWrad in 1988, which allowed the company to introduce the first mosaic radar visualization graphics. The following year, WSI NOWrad was used to depict hurricane structure for television viewers. The company capped off the decade with another PRASE award from *Professional Pilot Magazine* in 1989. This marked the fifth consecutive year that WSI received the award for being the top aviation weather service.

Progress continued during the 1990s. WSI ushered in the decade by adding CNN to its customer base. By 1990, the number of meteorologists and forecasters using its NOWrad radar system had reached the 600 mark. The company claimed that the system offered 25 times the definition and clarity of competing systems. NOWrad worked by drawing information from multiple radar site computers throughout the nation. With the help of special computer software, WSI produced physical representations of the data and superimposed them onto maps, thereby creating a "mosaic" view of the weather in a given area. Around that same time, WSI

introduced a service called NOWsat, which synchronized the radar-based images provided by NOWrad with satellite images. This allowed meteorologists and forecasters to show visual representations of both precipitation and clouds.

OWNERSHIP CHANGES

In mid-1991, WSI's parent company, a Reading, Massachusetts-based applied information technology firm named The Analytic Sciences Corporation (TASC), agreed to merge with Primark in a deal worth $166.6 million. With a workforce of 1,800 people, TASC had been founded in 1966 by Dr. Arthur Gelb and Harry B. Silverman, who remained with the firm following the deal, which was completed in August. WSI continued to operate as a subsidiary of TASC Inc., which in turn became a wholly owned subsidiary of Primark.

By 1992 WSI was led by President Mark Gildersleeve. That year, the company began using the Polar Orbiter Earth Satellites to provide global satellite images. In addition, WSI became the first company to partner with the National Weather Service (NWS) to offer Next Generation Weather Radar (NEXRAD) images. In February 1992, the company achieved pioneer status when it transmitted real-time NEXRAD radar imagery to NBC's WRC-TV station in Washington, D.C. NEXRAD was a program developed by the NWS, the Department of Defense, and the Federal Aviation Administration. Relying upon 137 Doppler Radar Sites throughout the United States, NEXRAD sought to use the latest technology to improve weather forecasting and the detection of severe weather. With a goal of providing value-added products to both private and government sector clients, WSI served as an official NEXRAD Information Dissemination Service provider.

In 1995 WSI rolled out a consumer-focused web site called Intellicast.com. In August of that year, the company partnered with NBC News and became the main source of local and world weather information for the Microsoft Network (MSN). Another ownership change occurred during the late 1990s. In December 1997, Primark Corp. forged an agreement to sell TASC Inc., including WSI, to defense contractor Litton Industries Inc. in a cash deal worth $432 million.

LEADING PROVIDER WORLDWIDE

In 1998 the company unveiled an Internet-based aviation briefing service for commercial aviation pilots, which was the first of its kind. That November, the company introduced an interactive, 8,000-square-foot traveling museum exhibit called Powers of Nature,

KEY DATES

1978: The company is established as Weather Services International.

1991: WSI's parent company, Reading, Massachusetts-based The Analytic Sciences Corp. (TASC), agrees to merge with Primark Corp. in a deal worth $166.6 million.

1997: Primark agrees to sell TASC, including WSI, to defense contractor Litton Industries Inc. in a cash deal worth $432 million.

2000: Norfolk, Virginia-based Landmark Communications Inc. agrees to acquire WSI from Litton Industries for $120 million in cash.

2007: WSI acquires weather radar manufacturer Enterprise Electronics Corp.

2008: Landmark Communications agrees to sell The Weather Channel Companies, including WSI, to an investment group consisting of NBC Universal, Bain Capital, and The Blackstone Group.

which it developed in partnership with the Franklin Institute Science Museum in Philadelphia. It also was in late 1998 that WSI announced that it had forged an agreement with Time Warner Cable to develop a 24-hour cable television station devoted to providing local weather forecasts, using data from the company's Weather by Intellicast service.

By the late 1990s WSI had evolved into one of the leading weather data, imagery, and forecast service providers worldwide. In addition to serving television and radio markets—including *NBC News Today*, where on-air personality Al Roker used the company's WEATHERproducer product to deliver eye-catching forecasts—WSI counted government agencies, aviation firms, utilities, and agricultural businesses among its customer base. WSI rounded out the 1990s by establishing an agreement with the Tel Aviv, Israel-based holding company Almedia to supply media and aviation markets in the Middle East and portions of Europe with new weather technology. In addition, the company won another PRASE Award in 1999—its fifth of the decade—from *Professional Pilot Magazine*.

WSI ushered in the new millennium with another ownership change. This time, Norfolk, Virginia-based Landmark Communications Inc., which owned The Weather Channel, agreed to acquire WSI from Litton Industries for $120 million in cash. The Weather Chan-

nel and WSI enjoyed a customer relationship dating back many years. At this time WSI continued under the leadership of President Mark Gildersleeve, who had served in that capacity for nine years. The company's WeatherProducer product was used by approximately 300 television stations throughout North America, including CNN. In September 2000, CNN signed a five-year contract extension with WSI, allowing it to use weather data and graphics for its CNN, CNN Headline News, and CNN International channels.

PRODUCT AND SERVICE DEVELOPMENT

The early years of the new century were marked by a series of new product and service introductions at WSI. In addition to a video-animated forecasting tool called Skycast, which allowed forecasters to visually depict what weather conditions might look like if viewers were looking out of their windows, in 2001 the company introduced a new 24-hour weather channel named WeatherNow for Time Warner Cable. A 24-hour Spanish language television news and weather channel also was unveiled that year in partnership with Time Warner Cable.

That same year, a weather/flight tracking and flight planning data source called Pilotbrief Vector Dispatch was introduced for the regional airline market. In addition, the company also added a comparative forecasting tool for energy traders to its Energycast PowerTrader service. In early 2002, WSI struck a deal with the company ViGYAN for the purchase of real-time, in-flight technology called Pilot Weather Advisor, which delivered weather information to pilots in the cockpit.

Another new service was introduced in mid-2003, at which time WSI introduced Energycast Alert!, which enabled energy transmission and distribution companies to forecast weather-related power outages. Later that year, a service called WSI Pilotbrief Pro was unveiled, giving professional pilots a single workspace where they could obtain integrated airspace, weather, and navigation information. Another highlight that year occurred when *R&D Magazine* named the company's WSI In-Flight datalink product as one of the Top 100 innovations in technology.

Accomplishments and new product/service introductions continued during the middle of the decade. WSI received Associate Member of the Year honors from the Aircraft Electronics Association in 2004. Early the following year, the company introduced a free newsletter for natural gas and power traders. In addition, a commercial weather service called NowNet was introduced, which relied upon a network of weather sensors and cameras to deliver local forecasts from specific locations, such as airports.

In 2006 a new WSI InFlight system was introduced that allowed the company to provide aviation weather information for aircraft via Sirius Satellite Radio. Midway through the year, WSI began offering polar forecasts specific to the Arctic Circle, which airlines relied upon to make decisions regarding flights between the Far East and North America. Around the same time, NASA ordered 18 of WSI's InFlight systems for use on astronaut trainer/proficiency aircraft at the Johnson Space Center. The company rounded out 2006 by introducing a new automated operational decision support tool for airports called WSI Hubcast.

INDUSTRY LEADER

By the start of 2007, WSI served more than half of the broadcasters and cable networks in the United States through the provision of weather-related graphics and data services. Midway through that year, WSI teamed with Pitney Bowes MapInfo in order to integrate real-time weather forecast information into the latter company's location intelligence applications. Specifically, these tools were used by insurance companies, reinsurers, and other parties to evaluate weather-related risks—such as floods or hurricanes—associated with given geographic areas.

It also was in mid-2007 that WSI received another PRASE award from *Professional Pilot Magazine.* This was the ninth consecutive year WSI received the award. Another major development unfolded in July, when WSI acquired weather radar manufacturer Enterprise Electronics Corporation.

The next few years were characterized by a continuous stream of new product and service introductions. For example, in April 2008 WSI announced the introduction of its WSI LiveCat Forecast service, which helped to predict both the intensity and path of tropical storms and hurricanes as far as ten days in advance. Several months later, the company unveiled WSI Tropical MarketFirst, which provided energy traders with advanced knowledge of volatile tropical forecasts. In October 2008, WSI PilotBrief Mobile was introduced, providing pilots with access to the company's aviation weather and hazard products on their mobile devices.

WSI changed hands once again in July 2008. At that time, Landmark Communications agreed to sell The Weather Channel Companies, including WSI, to an investment group consisting of NBC Universal, Bain Capital, and The Blackstone Group. Following the deal, WSI continued to roll out new offerings in 2009. WSI WindCast came online in February, providing the energy market with wind power and wind speed forecasts for wind farms. A new offering for the reinsurance market was introduced that same month. Called WSI PreCat Forecast Europe, the tool focused on predicting both the number and location of European windstorms in a given season. Finally, WSI LiveCat Forecast Pacific also was introduced in February 2009, providing longer-term predictions regarding the intensity and path of storms in eastern Asia.

Despite difficult economic conditions, the forecast for WSI seemed promising as the company headed toward the second decade of the 21st century. Over the course of more than 25 years, the company had developed a solid position of leadership within the weather industry.

Paul R. Greenland

PRINCIPAL COMPETITORS

AccuWeather Inc.; Meteorlogix LLC; Weather Central Inc.; Weather Metrics Inc.; Weather Watch Inc.

FURTHER READING

Dujardin, Peter, "Hampton, Va., Aerospace Research Firm Finds Buyer for Weather-Data System," *Knight-Ridder/Tribune Business News,* April 18, 2002.

Glater, Jonathan, "Analytic Sciences Accepts Offer from Primark of $165 Million," *Boston Globe,* July 10, 1991.

Korzeniowski, Paul, "Users Views; Small Firm Goes in Big for Net Control," *Network World,* April 13, 1987.

"Primark's TASC Unit to be Acquired by Litton Industries Inc.; Primark to Focus on Information Content for the Financial Industry," *PR Newswire,* December 8, 1997.

"Weather Service Finds Buyer," *Times Union,* February 9, 2000.

"WSI Acquires Pilot Weather Advisor," *PR Newswire,* April 8, 2002.

"WSI Announces Acquisition of Enterprise Electronics Corporation," *Business Wire,* July 24, 2007.

Zain

Shuwaikh, Airport Road
Kuwait P.O. Box: 22244
Safat, 13083
Kuwait
Telephone: (965) 464-4444
Fax: (965) 483-7755
Web site: http://www.zain.com

Public Company
Incorporated: 1983 as Mobile Telecommunications
 Company (MTC)
Employees: 12,700
Sales: $5.91 billion (2007)
Stock Exchanges: Kuwait
Ticker Symbol: MTC
NAICS: 517212 Cellular and Other Wireless Telecom-
 munications

■ ■ ■

Zain is one of the largest and fastest-growing mobile telecommunications providers in the Middle East and Africa. The Kuwait-based company, formerly known as Mobile Telecommunications Company (MTC) until a rebranding exercise was completed in 2008, is focused on the goal of joining the global telecom top ten. Launched in 2003, Zain's expansion strategy—called "3x3x3"—has brought it into more than 22 countries, with a total population base of nearly 550 million people. The company's own subscriber base has swelled from just 600,000 to more than 56 million at the beginning of 2009. Zain serves these markets through what it

calls the first borderless network in the telecommunications industry, dubbed One Network.

Major markets for Zain outside of Kuwait include Iraq, Saudi Arabia, Jordan, Bahrain, and Sudan. Zain's major presence in Africa, especially the sub-Saharan region, stems from its acquisition of Celtel International (since rebranded as Zain), which operates in Kenya, Nigeria, Uganda, Zambia, Chad, Gabon, and since December 2008, Ghana, among other markets. In early 2009, the company also entered the Palestinian territories, signing a partnership agreement with Paltel there. Zain is listed on the Kuwait Stock Exchange. The state-owned Kuwaiti Investment Authority controls 25 percent of the company, while Al Kharafi & Sons, Kuwait's leading conglomerate, holds a 12 percent stake. Zain Saudi Arabia and Zain Zambia are also listed on their countries' respective stock exchanges. CEO Saad al Barrak has led the company since the early years of the 21st century.

MIDDLE EAST MOBILE PIONEER

Zain built a 20-year history as a pioneering mobile telecommunications company in the Middle East region before launching its international expansion strategy in the early years of the 21st century. The company originated as Mobile Telecommunications Company (MTC), established as part of a Kuwaiti government initiative to introduce mobile telecommunications to the Middle East in 1983. MTC adopted the TACS (Total Access Communication System) standard in development in the United Kingdom as a variant of the U.S.-developed AMPS (Advanced Mobile Phone Service)

COMPANY PERSPECTIVES

Mission to lead. Ultimately, our mission can be distilled down to this: to cement Zain as a leading global mobile operator that provides professional, world-class mobile and data services to all our customers, wherever they are, worldwide. And we aim to achieve this by exceeding our customers' expectations, rewarding our employees, and providing returns beyond reasonable expectations for our shareholders. Our aim is to define what it means to be "world class." World-class telecommunications services. This is our business, and innovation is how we achieve success.

standard. By 1986, MTC had become the first in the Middle East to base its network on the newly extended TACS standard, which became known as ETACS.

These early analog cellular networks remained rather limited. Sound quality was often poor, while handsets were of necessity quite large and cumbersome. The early analog systems were also highly prone to "cloning," a means of hacking phone numbers for use in unauthorized handsets. By the early 1980s, members of the European community recognized the need to develop a new internationally acceptable digital cellular platform. Work on that effort, initially under the auspices of the Groupe Speciale Mobile, led to the launch of GSM (Global System for Mobile communications) in 1990. The first GSM network was launched in Finland in 1991.

The superiority of the new standard enabled the international GSM network to grow rapidly, and by 1993 more than one million GSM subscriber lines had been opened. MTC recognized the advantages of switching to the new standard as well, and by 1994 the company became one of the first in the Middle East region to roll out a GSM-based network. MTC, which retained the monopoly over mobile telecommunications in the domestic market, grew rapidly in Kuwait, quickly extending its total subscriber base to 600,000.

MTC initially operated solely on a subscriber basis. However, in 1999 the company recognized the potential for adding prepaid mobile phone services, becoming the first in the region to do so. Prepaid services were to provide the engine for the growth of the mobile telecommunications sector in the Middle East as well as Africa and other developing areas, where low income

rates remained a high barrier for both fixed line and mobile telecommunications penetration.

MTC faced a threat at home at the end of the 1990s, as the Kuwaiti government decided to open the mobile telecommunications market to competition. By 1999, the government had sold two new licenses for the Kuwaiti market, to a new company, National Mobile Telecommunications Company (NMTC, more widely known under its Wataniya brand), and to Saudi Telecom. In preparation for the loss of its monopoly, MTC went public, listing its shares on the Kuwaiti Stock Exchange in 1999. The Kuwaiti market was officially opened to competition in 2000.

ESTABLISHING A REGIONAL PRESENCE

The Kuwaiti government continued to sell off its stake in MTC, reducing its holding to 49 percent by 2000 and to 25 percent by 2001. The company's large free float enabled it to attract strong investor interest, such as from the Al Kharafi family, one of Kuwait's leading families, and their company, the Al Kharafi & Sons conglomerate. MTC also attracted interest from within the mobile telecommunications industry, particularly as the largest players were jockeying for position among the global leadership. In 2002, MTC agreed to enter a cobranding agreement with Vodafone, relaunching the Kuwaiti network as MTC Vodafone.

MTC had also begun to develop its own international ambitions. In 2002, the company brought in a new CEO, Saad al Barrak. Soon after, MTC launched a new nine-year strategy dubbed "3x3x3." This plan called for a three-pronged expansion program. The first three-year phase was to establish MTC as a major player in the Middle East region by 2005. The next three-year phase targeted the group's international expansion, with completion of this objective slated for 2008. The following three years were then to be devoted to raising MTC into the ranks of the top ten global players by 2011.

The group's ambitions were impressive, particularly in light of its status in 2002. With just 691,000 customers, and revenues of only $571 million in 2002, MTC was still a very small participant in the international mobile telecommunications market. Nevertheless, al Barrak and MTC quickly proved equal to their ambitions.

In January 2003, MTC unveiled an agreement to pay $424 million to acquire 91.5 percent of the leading mobile telephone services provider in Jordan, Fastlink. That company, originally known as Jordan Mobile Telephone Services Company Ltd., had been the first to

ing a subscriber base of nearly 3.2 million, and total revenues of more than $1.3 billion.

BECOMING AN INTERNATIONAL OPERATOR

MTC then set out to enact the second phase of the 3x3x3 strategy, seeking out international expansion opportunities. The group's opportunity came in 2005, when it agreed to pay $3.36 billion to acquire Celtel Africa. While some observers criticized MTC for paying too high a price for the Netherlands-registered company, the Celtel acquisition instantly allowed MTC to position itself as a major force in the sub-Saharan Africa market. MTC then boasted of a presence in 15 African markets, including Kenya, Zambia, both Congos, Gabon, Sierra Leone, Ghana, Chad, Uganda, Malawi, Tanzania, Niger, Madagascar, Chad, and Burkina Faso.

MTC quickly moved to expand Celtel's reach, buying up majority control in Madacom, the leading mobile operation in Madagascar, at the end of 2005. In 2006, the company gained full control over Sudan's Mobitel, paying $1.3 billion for that business. By May of that year, MTC added one of Africa's largest markets, Nigeria, through the $1 billion acquisition of a 65 percent stake in that country's mobile leader, Vmobile. The move added another five million customers to MTC's total subscriber base, which topped 27 million by the end of 2006.

The company in the meantime had resumed its role as innovator as well. In May 2006, the company's Bahrain network became the first in the region to launch the new 3.5G standard. Soon after, MTC launched something of a telecommunications marketing revolution when it launched its One Network, described by the company as the first-ever borderless network. The service, initially limited to the group's operations in Tanzania, Kenya, and Uganda, allowed its users there to call in any of the One Network markets at the local rate, with no roaming charges, while receiving incoming calls for free. By 2007, the company had extended One Network service to include the African west coast markets, before rolling out the service to its operations across the entire continent.

SETTING SIGHTS ON BECOMING A GLOBAL LEADER

In 2007, MTC prepared to launch the next phase of its 3x3x3 strategy, as it set its sights on building itself into a global leader. The company continued to fill in its regional offerings. In 2007, for example, the company led an investment consortium that bid more than $6

KEY DATES

1983: Mobile Telecommunications Company (MTC) is established to launch a mobile telephone network in Kuwait.

1994: MTC rolls out GSM (Global System for Mobile communications) network in Kuwait.

1999: MTC goes public as Kuwait prepares to open mobile telecommunications market to competition.

2002: MTC launches its 3x3x3 expansion strategy.

2003: MTC acquires Fastlink in Jordan to kick off its expansion through acquisition strategy.

2005: MTC enters Africa through acquisition of Celtel.

2007: MTC changes its name to Zain and begins rebranding its mobile operations.

2008: Celtel network in Africa is rebranded under the Zain name.

2009: Zain expects to achieve revenues of more than $10 billion.

---

introduce mobile services in Jordan, launching its GSM-based network in 1994. By the time of its acquisition, Fastlink boasted a subscriber base of more than 2.2 million. MTC subsequently raised its stake in Fastlink to 96.5 percent.

Soon after the Fastlink purchase, MTC moved into Bahrain, acquiring that market's second mobile telecommunications license. The entry into Bahrain allowed MTC to again play the role of pioneer, as it became one of the first in the Middle East to introduce a high-speed 3G mobile network. The company launched its Bahrain operations under the MTC Vodafone brand that year.

By then, the company had also gained a license to enter the Iraqi market, as that country began to rebuild its infrastructure following the U.S. invasion in 2003. MTC announced its intention to launch mobile services in Iraq under the MTC Atheer brand. The company's license in Iraq initially covered only the country's central region. By the end of 2004, MTC had added another Middle East market as well, reaching agreement to take over the management of a mobile telephone license for the Lebanese market. MTC launched its Lebanese service as MTC Touch.

By the end of 2004, MTC had made strong progress in completing the first phase of the 3x3x3 strategy. The company had by this time established itself as a major contender in the Middle East region, boast-

billion to acquire the third mobile telephone license in Saudi Arabia. The company launched its commercial services there in 2008. MTC also stepped up its presence in the Iraqi market in 2007, winning its bid to acquire one of three licenses to operate on a national basis in that country. By the end of the year, MTC had also acquired its chief rival in Iraq, the Iraqna mobile group, a subsidiary of Egypt's Orascom Telecom. MTC paid $1.2 billion for Iraqna, becoming the largest mobile services group in Iraq.

MTC's rapid expansion—and future ambitions—also led it to break away from Vodafone in the second half of the decade. The companies agreed to drop their cobranding relationship, while maintaining a technical partnership. This move allowed MTC to begin developing its rebranding strategy. In September 2007, the company announced its intention to change its name to Zain, and to rebrand its operations in Kuwait, Bahrain, Jordan, and Sudan under the Zain brand. The successful rollout soon led Zain to extend its new brand deeper across its operations. In January 2008, the group's Iraqi business took on the Zain name. By August 2008, the company had rolled out the Zain brand across its African network, replacing the Celtel name.

Zain had also continued to expand its One Network coverage in Africa, adding the service to six more countries toward the end of 2007. The move expanded One Network service across 12 countries, potentially reaching almost half of the total population of Africa. The success of the One Network concept encouraged Zain to introduce it separately to the Middle East region in 2008, initially with service in Bahrain, Iraq, Jordan, and Sudan. Following the rebranding of Celtel, Zain combined the two networks to form a single One Network, spanning 15 countries across two continents, with a total potential population of more than 450 million.

By 2009, Zain had largely completed the second phase of its 3x3x3 strategy, having expanded its customer base to more than 56 million across 22 countries. The latest entries into the group's network included Ghana, based on the group's acquisition of a 75 percent stake in Western Telesystems in 2007, which launched operations in December 2008. In January 2009, the company reached a partnership agreement with Paltel, allowing Zain to enter the Palestinian territories as well. Zain expected to acquire a majority stake in Paltel as early as March 2009.

As Zain's revenues were expected to top $10 billion by the end of 2009, a number of industry observers had begun to see the company as a potential candidate for takeover by one of its still larger international rivals. Zain, however, indicated its intention to remain independent and to fight off any takeover attempt. In the meantime, the company began weighing its options for the implementation of the "global" phase of its 3x3x3 strategy.

M. L. Cohen

PRINCIPAL SUBSIDIARIES

Atheer Telecom Iraq Ltd.; Celtel International B.V (Netherlands); Mada Leletisalat LLC (Saudi Arabia; 50%); Mobile Telecommunications Company International B.V. (Netherlands); Mobile Telecommunications Company Lebanon (MTC) S.A.R.L; Pella Investment Company (Jordan; 96.516%); Sudanese Mobile Telephone Company Limited; Western Telesystems Limited Ghana; Zain Saudi Arabia (25%); Zain Zambia.

PRINCIPAL COMPETITORS

CELSYS Ltd.; Etisalat; Tanzania Telecommunications Company Ltd.; Maroc Telecom S.A.; Saudi Arabia Telecom; Qtel; Orascom Telecom Holding S.A.E.; Telecom Egypt; National Mobile Telecommunications Company KSC.

FURTHER READING

"Aiming High," *Total Telecom Magazine*, March 1, 2008.

"A Brand New Zain," *New African*, October 2008, p. 66.

Hadfield, Will, "Baghdad Levies Fines on Two of Three Mobile Operators," *MEED Middle East Economic Digest*, January 23, 2009, p. 14.

———, "Busy Lines of Engagement," *MEED Middle East Economic Digest*, September 28, 2007, p. 27.

"In a Hurry for Growth," *Global Telecoms Business*, March–April 2006, p. 26.

James, Ed, "The Regional Force Be with You," *MEED Middle East Economic Digest*, October 7, 2005, p. 48.

"Kenya's Zain Phone Firm Launches Money Transfer Service," *BBC Monitoring International*, February 17, 2009.

Melly, Paul, "Zain: The Launch of the Kuwaiti Telecoms Operator's Saudi Operation Is the Latest Step in Its Expansion Strategy," *MEED Middle East Economic Digest*, November 21, 2008, p. 34.

Mullen, Jethro, "Zain Looking for Deals Despite Tough Climate," *Zawya Dow Jones Newswires*, February 17, 2009.

"Paltel Agrees to Partnership with Zain," *Telecompaper Africa/ Asia*, February 12, 2009.

"Rebranded Zain Plans to End Middle East Roaming Charges," *Global Telecoms Business*, January–February 2008.

Versi, Anver, "How Do You Rebrand an Icon?" *African Business,* October 2008, p. 42.

Williams, Stephen, "The Zain Gain," *Middle East,* October 2008, p. 46.

"Zain Still Has Eyes on Foreign Expansion," *Total Telecom Online,* July 4, 2008.

Ziment Group Inc.

———◼———

825 3rd Avenue, 28th Floor
New York, New York 10022
U.S.A.
Telephone: (212) 647-7200
Fax: (212) 647-7659
Web site: http://www.zimentgroup.com

Subsidiary of Kantar Group
Incorporated: 1976 as Ziment Associates Inc.
Employees: 350
Sales: $229.8 million (2007 est.)
NAICS: 541910 Marketing Research and Public
Opinion Polling

◼ ◼ ◼

New York City-based Ziment Group Inc. is comprised of several global marketing research companies serving the pharmaceutical and healthcare industries. The flagship unit, known simply as Ziment, is a full-service marketing research firm catering to the needs of pharmaceutical, biotech, and medical device companies around the world by employing a set of proprietary practices the company bills as "From Compound to Profit." Information is drawn from panels of more than 350,000 patients and 200,000 physicians and healthcare professionals in the United States and Europe. Offices are located in about 15 U.S. cities as well as the United Kingdom, France, Germany, and Spain.

Another Ziment Group company is Consumer Health Sciences, providing insights on patients and other healthcare consumers through a database resulting from the annual self-reported National Health and Wellness Survey of patients in the United States, Europe, and Asia. Other more specific surveys are conducted in over 75 therapeutic categories. The imap (Integrated Marketing and Promotions) Research unit focuses on market research for pharmaceutical companies. Another subsidiary, All Global Ltd., is a data collection agency using telephone, Internet, and field service to aid marketing researchers in the healthcare and pharmaceutical fields. Offices are maintained in New York, Barcelona, and London. Finally, All Global Viewing operates a facility in London, England, with several studios that can be used to conduct focus groups and view them in operation. The company also offers video streaming, catering, moderators, office facilities, and courier services. Ziment Group is a subsidiary of London, England-based WPP Group plc, one of the world's largest media and communications services conglomerates.

COMPANY FOUNDED IN NEW YORK CITY

The flagship unit of Ziment Group was founded as Ziment Associates Inc. in New York City in 1976 by Larry Ziment. Born in New York City in 1927, the son of immigrants from Russia and Poland, Ziment served in the U.S. Army at the end of World War II and then used his G.I. Bill benefits to attend New York University. After receiving a degree in psychology, he stayed at the school to earn a master's degree in math and pursue a doctorate, although he never completed that degree. In 1952 he went to work at the market research firm of Alfred Politz, Inc.

The head of that firm, Alfred Politz, was a German-born theoretical physicist who came to market research by writing short stories, which led to success in journalism, and a position as advertising director of a German publishing company. After starting a marketing consulting firm in Germany in the 1930s, Politz fled Nazi Germany, making his way to New York City in 1937. Taking a job at the Roper Opinion Research Company, he began to develop theories on the proper way to conduct random sampling surveys. His innovative sampling techniques became the backbone of the advertising media research company he then founded. Thus, Larry Ziment found himself in an ideal place to learn marketing research from a pioneer in the field, and to conduct projects with such forward-thinking corporations as Pillsbury and General Cigar.

With 24 years of experience, Ziment was then ready to start his own firm to apply cutting-edge survey techniques to his own roster of clients and redress what he perceived as the fundamental flaws in the practice of market research consulting at the time. The data collection process, he believed, was not stringent enough, leading to unreliable information that did not allow for sound marketing decisions. Ziment's goal was to follow exact sampling standards to present clients with data they could actually use in making effective—and ultimately profitable—marketing decisions.

The company, then known as Ziment Associates, was very much a one-man boutique operation in the early days, as Larry Ziment used the contacts he had developed over the years to land strategic market research projects from consumer package, financial services, and healthcare companies. Growing up, his son Howard helped his father with the business. At age 12 he was tabulating survey responses. By 14 he was writing questions, and a year later he was conducting his own surveys. The younger Ziment then earned a marketing degree from Georgetown University in 1986

and went to work at Saatchi and Saatchi Compton Advertising. After his father died in August 1986, he returned to the family business to run it with his mother and sister. It was under the leadership of Howard Ziment that the company grew into a major concern.

NEW FOCUS

An important step in the development of Ziment Group was taken in 1988 when the Ziment family took stock of the business. Realizing that packaged goods was a mature business offering limited growth opportunities, the Ziments decided to focus on the healthcare and pharmaceutical industries, as well as telecommunications, while continuing to service some long-term packaged goods clients, including a major beer company. The Ziments correctly understood that as pharmaceutical companies increased their direct appeals to consumers, they would be in need of usable market research. Howard Ziment initially experienced some difficulty in pitching the firm's services to pharmaceutical firms, which did not see a need for such research, but they would often call back a few months later, by then understanding why market research was important, and engage Ziment.

In 1990 Ziment Group began taking on international research projects through The Research Alliance, a global coalition of marketing research firms. Through this network Ziment Group was able to partner with other full-service independent market research firms to gather data overseas while continuing to administer the project and provide analysis from New York. In 1991 Ziment Group reached an important milestone when for the first time in its history it topped the $1 million mark in annual revenues.

In the 1990s Ziment Group continued to grow its healthcare and pharmaceutical business as well as its telecommunications business. The first office outside of New York City was opened in 1995. Two years later revenues exceeded $10 million, and in 1999 the company was for the first time named to the coveted list of the top 50 U.S. research organizations compiled by Honomichi for *Marketing News,* published by the American Marketing Association.

Ziment Group further solidified its reputation in 2000 when it established the largest panel of physicians in the United States. Because it was online as WebSurveyMD.com, the panel was instantly available for research queries. As Howard Ziment explained to the press, "Physicians are difficult to access and interview, but with more than 85% now online an Internet-based approach is both time-efficient and cost-effective."

```
┌─────────────────────────────────────────┐
│                                         │
│            KEY DATES                    │
│                 ■                       │
│  ─────────────────────────────────      │
│  1976: Larry Ziment founds Ziment       │
│        Associates in New York City to   │
│        conduct market research.         │
│  1986: Howard Ziment joins company.     │
│  1988: Firm focuses on pharmaceutical   │
│        and health-care industries.      │
│  1995: First office outside of New York │
│        City opens.                      │
│  2001: WPP Group plc acquires Ziment    │
│        Group.                           │
│  2002: First office in Europe opens.    │
│  2004: The imap (Integrated Marketing   │
│        and Promotions) Research unit is │
│        established.                     │
│  2005: Consumer Health Sciences         │
│        acquired.                        │
│  2007: All Global Ltd. acquired.        │
│                                         │
└─────────────────────────────────────────┘
```

Moreover, online surveying techniques had been refined, so they were just as reliable, if not more so, than telephone and mail surveys, and enjoyed a higher response rate. Ziment Group was then able to forge an alliance with Salu, Inc., a company that provided a full-service Internet business hub to physicians according to specialty via its Salu.net portal. WebSurveyMD.com became available through Salu.net, making it easier for physicians to participate in online surveys. Not only were the physicians able to have an impact on policy and other developments in their specialties, but they also were paid a stipend for their participation.

Later in 2000 Ziment Group used WebSurveyMD.com in another partnership with InfoScriber Corporation, which was creating the country's first online physician network to study the decision-making process employed by physicians in prescribing drugs, with the resulting database used in marketing decisions by pharmaceutical and healthcare companies. The co-marketing agreement with InfoScriber and Ziment Group brought together data collected by InfoScriber and WebSurveyMD.com to provide pharmaceutical companies with valuable insights about the marketplace.

COMPANY SOLD TO WPP GROUP

In 2000 Ziment Group generated about $18.8 million in annual revenues from five operating units spread across a dozen U.S. offices. To fulfill the company's global aspirations, however, it needed a partner in the quickly consolidating media landscape. In May 2001 Howard Ziment reached an agreement to sell the company to the Kantar Group, part of communications services giant WPP Group plc. WPP had begun to take shape only 15 years earlier when British-born Harvard

Business School graduate and advertising executive Martin Sorrell took a manufacturing company called Wire and Plastics Products plc, renamed it WPP Group plc, and began adding marketing services to the mix through a number of United Kingdom acquisitions. He soon turned his attention to the United States and acquired general advertising agencies as well. In short order, WPP acquired Ogilvy Group and Saatchi & Saatchi, Sorrell's former employer. In 1995 WPP formed the Kantar Group to hold the research businesses it had accumulated along the way. In 2000 WPP acquired the marketing concern Young & Rubicam Inc. for $4.7 million, the largest transaction in advertising history to date.

The acquisition of Ziment Group, a few months after the Young & Rubicam deal, caused hardly a ripple by comparison, but it was significant nonetheless for Kantar, which itself had grown into a $1 billion per year enterprise. It also forwarded WPP's strategy of establishing leadership positions in fast-growing sectors, in this case healthcare and pharmaceuticals. Kantar's chief executive officer, David Jenkins, told the press that Ziment Group was expected to help grow the company's global brands while forming the basis of a new global healthcare practice: "We believe that through Ziment, our healthcare research business can mirror the success of sister companies like Common Health, the largest healthcare advertising agency in the world." From the perspective of Ziment, becoming part of Kantar and the WPP family allowed the research firm to better serve its clients on the world stage. "By combining Ziment's healthcare market knowledge with Kantar's global research infrastructure that spans across 80 offices in 56 countries," Howard Ziment commented in a prepared statement, "we will truly be able to fulfill this promise."

FIRST EUROPEAN OFFICE OPENS

Howard Ziment remained chief executive officer of Ziment Group, but the backing of its new corporate parent soon became apparent. To take its international business to the next level, the company hired Mark Nissenfeld to serve as chief operating officer of the Ziment International division. Nissenfeld came with eight years of experience in heading the Global Healthcare practice at a major international healthcare marketing research consulting firm. In 2002 Ziment opened its first office in Europe, located in London, England. Offices in France and Germany followed in 2004. In the meantime, following the sale to Kantar, Ziment Group phased out its telecommunications business, which over the years had evolved into a high-technology niche. It had enjoyed steady growth in the 1990s, but the healthcare and pharmaceutical side of the business had become so successful that the telecommunications work was overshadowed. The legacy packaged goods clients were phased out as well.

While international expansion was clearly a priority for Ziment Group, the firm did not lose focus on its core competency, innovative techniques to produce useful decision-making information. In 2004 it unveiled TAGZ, a method using a proprietary algorithm that helped pharmaceutical marketers conducting segmentation research to include a wider range of physicians, even those who had not been involved in the initial qualifying round, in order to develop larger, more useful target lists of physicians who were likely to be responsive to the marketing of certain products. TAGZ was positioned as a far less expensive, and just as accurate, alternative to the qualifying tests that segmentation normally required. In 2005 Ziment Group introduced demand calibration, a way of using an algorithm to handicap the traditional problem of pharmaceutical market research in which physicians inflated how much they planned to prescribe a new product and patients exaggerated their intention of requesting the product from their doctors. The Ziment approach was a significant improvement over the rule of thumb previously employed by the industry, which was to divide by two or even three to arrive at a result.

INTERNAL AND EXTERNAL GROWTH

Ziment Group expanded its operations internally in 2004 with the launch of a new division, imap (Integrated Marketing and Promotions) Research, to specialize in the conducting of multi-client studies for pharmaceutical and healthcare clients. Rather than typical custom-designed market tracking research, imap's multi-client approach allowed multiple companies to share the expense of research projects as well as the mutual benefits of better understanding the therapeutic marketplaces in which their products competed. In 2005 Ziment Group enjoyed a measure of external growth when it added Princeton, New Jersey-based Consumer Health Sciences, which had been part of WPP's purchase of Grey Global Group and was then carved off to become part of Ziment Group. The flagship offering of the new unit was the National Health and Wellness Survey, conducted annually with 45,000 adult participants in the United States and 20,000 Europeans, and covering a wide range of healthcare topics. It was an especially valuable tool because the data extended back to 1998, making the pool of information extremely useful to clients, who could take advantage of it to cut the time and costs of custom research.

Ziment Group grew further in January 2007 with the acquisition of All Global Ltd., a London data collection company that used telephone, Internet, and field services to conduct healthcare and pharmaceutical marketing research. In addition, the All Global Viewing unit provided viewing studios where focus groups could be held. All Global would later subsume the operations of Ziment Group's New York-based WebSurveyResearch operations.

Ziment Group underwent significant changes in the top management ranks in November 2006. Howard Ziment turned over the CEO post to Lynnette Cooke and became chairman. Cooke had been with Ziment Group since 1997, when she opened the company's midwest office. She held a number of positions in the firm, including CEO of Ziment Custom, the firm's primary marketing research and consulting division, the job she held before succeeding Ziment. Cooke continued to serve as CEO of Ziment Custom until February 2008, when she turned over the reins to John Tapper, the unit's chief operating officer. Later in 2008 Ziment Custom became simply Ziment, part of an effort to streamline and reinvigorate the image of the flagship unit, which in the previous five years had enjoyed explosive growth. There was every reason to believe that it and Ziment Group would continue to thrive as part of the WPP family for years to come.

Ed Dinger

PRINCIPAL SUBSIDIARIES

All Global Ltd.; All Global Viewing; Consumer Health Sciences; imap Research; Ziment.

PRINCIPAL COMPETITORS

GfK Aktiengesellschaft; Ipsos SA; Marketing Research Services, Inc.

FURTHER READING

Elliott, Stuart, "Acquisitions by 2 Agencies," *New York Times,* May 20, 2001.

"New Market Research Tool by Ziment Will Radically Change How Pharmaceutical Companies Sell Prescription Drugs to Physicians," *Business Wire,* March 9, 2004.

"WPP Group PLC Acquisition," *Regulatory News Service,* May 9, 2001.

"Ziment Announces Demand Calibration," *Business Wire,* May 6, 2004.

"Ziment Changes Corporate Identity," *PrimeZone Media Network,* June 5, 2008.

"The Ziment Group Acquires Consumer Health Sciences," *Business Wire*, April 18, 2005.

"The Ziment Group Announces New Roles for Senior Management," *Business Wire*, November 15, 2006.

"Ziment Group Announces Organization of New Division," *Business Wire*, November 4, 2004.

"Ziment Markets Forecasting Tool," *Medical Marketing & Media*, June 2004.

Cumulative Index to Companies

American Campus Communities, Inc., 85 1–5
American Can Co. *see* Primerica Corp.
The American Cancer Society, 24 23–25
American Capital Strategies, Ltd., 91 21–24
American Cast Iron Pipe Company, 50 17–20
American Civil Liberties Union (ACLU), 60 28–31
American Classic Voyages Company, 27 34–37
American Coin Merchandising, Inc., 28 15–17; 74 13–16 (upd.)
American Colloid Co., 13 32–35 *see* AMCOL International Corp.
American Commercial Lines Inc., 99 31–34
American Cotton Growers Association *see* Plains Cotton Cooperative Association.
American Crystal Sugar Company, 11 13–15; 32 29–33 (upd.)
American Cyanamid, I 300–02; 8 24–26 (upd.)
American Eagle Outfitters, Inc., 24 26–28; 55 21–24 (upd.)
American Ecology Corporation, 77 36–39
American Electric Power Company, V 546–49; 45 17–21 (upd.)
American Express Company, II 395–99; 10 59–64 (upd.); 38 42–48 (upd.)
American Family Corporation, III 187–89 *see also* AFLAC Inc.
American Financial Group Inc., III 190–92; 48 6–10 (upd.)
American Foods Group, 43 23–27
American Furniture Company, Inc., 21 32–34
American General Corporation, III 193–94; 10 65–67 (upd.); 46 20–23 (upd.)
American General Finance Corp., 11 16–17
American Girl, Inc., 69 16–19 (upd)
American Golf Corporation, 45 22–24
American Gramaphone LLC, 52 18–20
American Greetings Corporation, 7 23–25; 22 33–36 (upd.); 59 34–39 (upd.)
American Healthways, Inc., 65 40–42
American Home Mortgage Holdings, Inc., 46 24–26
American Home Products, I 622–24; 10 68–70 (upd.) *see also* Wyeth.
American Homestar Corporation, 18 26–29; 41 17–20 (upd.)
American Institute of Certified Public Accountants (AICPA), 44 27–30
American International Group, Inc., III 195–98; 15 15–19 (upd.); 47 13–19 (upd.)
American Italian Pasta Company, 27 38–40; 76 18–21 (upd.)
American Kennel Club, Inc., 74 17–19
American Lawyer Media Holdings, Inc., 32 34–37
American Library Association, 86 15–19

American Licorice Company, 86 20–23
American Locker Group Incorporated, 34 19–21
American Lung Association, 48 11–14
American Machine and Metals *see* AMETEK, Inc.
American Maize-Products Co., 14 17–20
American Management Association, 76 22–25
American Management Systems, Inc., 11 18–20
American Media, Inc., 27 41–44; 82 10–15 (upd.)
American Medical Association, 39 15–18
American Medical International, Inc., III 73–75
American Medical Response, Inc., 39 19–22
American Metals Corporation *see* Reliance Steel & Aluminum Co.
American Modern Insurance Group *see* The Midland Co.
American Motors Corp., I 135–37 *see also* DaimlerChrysler AG.
América Móvil, S.A. de C.V., 80 5–8
American MSI Corporation *see* Moldflow Corp.
American National Insurance Company, 8 27–29; 27 45–48 (upd.)
American Nurses Association Inc., 102 11–15
American Olean Tile Company *see* Armstrong Holdings, Inc.
American Oriental Bioengineering Inc., 93 45–48
American Pad & Paper Company, 20 18–21
American Pfauter *see* Gleason Corp.
American Pharmaceutical Partners, Inc., 69 20–22
American Pop Corn Company, 59 40–43
American Power Conversion Corporation, 24 29–31; 67 18–20 (upd.)
American Premier Underwriters, Inc., 10 71–74
American President Companies Ltd., 6 353–55 *see also* APL Ltd.
American Printing House for the Blind, 26 13–15
American Re Corporation, 10 75–77; 35 34–37 (upd.)
American Red Cross, 40 26–29
American Reprographics Company, 75 24–26
American Residential Mortgage Corporation, 8 30–31
American Restaurant Partners, L.P., 93 49–52
American Retirement Corporation, 42 9–12 *see also* Brookdale Senior Living.
American Rice, Inc., 33 30–33
American Rug Craftsmen *see* Mohawk Industries, Inc.

American Safety Razor Company, 20 22–24
American Savings Bank *see* Hawaiian Electric Industries, Inc.
American Science & Engineering, Inc., 81 22–25
American Seating Company, 78 7–11
American Skiing Company, 28 18–21
American Society for the Prevention of Cruelty to Animals (ASPCA), 68 19–22
The American Society of Composers, Authors and Publishers (ASCAP), 29 21–24
American Software Inc., 22 214; 25 20–22
American Standard Companies Inc., III 663–65; 30 46–50 (upd.)
American States Water Company, 46 27–30
American Steamship Company *see* GATX.
American Stores Company, II 604–06; 22 37–40 (upd.) *see also* Albertson's, Inc.
American Superconductor Corporation, 97 32–36
American Technical Ceramics Corp., 67 21–23
American Telephone and Telegraph Company *see* AT&T.
American Tobacco Co. *see* B.A.T. Industries PLC.; Fortune Brands, Inc.
American Tourister, Inc., 16 19–21 *see also* Samsonite Corp.
American Tower Corporation, 33 34–38
American Vanguard Corporation, 47 20–22
American Water Works Company, Inc., 6 443–45; 38 49–52 (upd.)
American Woodmark Corporation, 31 13–16
American Yearbook Company *see* Jostens, Inc.
AmeriCares Foundation, Inc., 87 23–28
Amerigon Incorporated, 97 37–40
AMERIGROUP Corporation, 69 23–26
Amerihost Properties, Inc., 30 51–53
AmeriSource Health Corporation, 37 9–11 (upd.)
AmerisourceBergen Corporation, 64 22–28 (upd.)
Ameristar Casinos, Inc., 33 39–42; 69 27–31 (upd.)
Ameritech Corporation, V 265–68; 18 30–34 (upd.) *see also* AT&T Corp.
Ameritrade Holding Corporation, 34 27–30
Ameriwood Industries International Corp., 17 15–17 *see also* Dorel Industries Inc.
Amerock Corporation, 53 37–40
Ameron International Corporation, 67 24–26
Amersham PLC, 50 21–25
Ames Department Stores, Inc., 9 20–22; 30 54–57 (upd.)
AMETEK, Inc., 9 23–25

Boral Limited, III 672–74; 43 72–76 (upd.)

Borden, Inc., II 470–73; 22 91–96 (upd.)

Borders Group, Inc., 15 61–62; 43 77–79 (upd.)

Borealis AG, 94 83–86

Borg-Warner Automotive, Inc., 14 63–66; 32 93–97 (upd.)

Borg-Warner Corporation, III 438–41 *see also* Burns International.

BorgWarner Inc., 85 38–44 (upd.)

Borland International, Inc., 9 80–82

Boron, LePore & Associates, Inc., 45 43–45

Bosch *see* Robert Bosch GmbH.

Boscov's Department Store, Inc., 31 68–70

Bose Corporation, 13 108–10; 36 98–101 (upd.)

Boss Holdings, Inc., 97 78–81

Boston Acoustics, Inc., 22 97–99

The Boston Beer Company, Inc., 18 70–73; 50 111–15 (upd.)

Boston Celtics Limited Partnership, 14 67–69

Boston Chicken, Inc., 12 42–44 *see also* Boston Market Corp.

The Boston Consulting Group, 58 32–35

Boston Edison Company, 12 45–47

Boston Market Corporation, 48 64–67 (upd.)

Boston Pizza International Inc., 88 33–38

Boston Professional Hockey Association Inc., 39 61–63

Boston Properties, Inc., 22 100–02

Boston Scientific Corporation, 37 37–40; 77 58–63 (upd.)

The Boston Symphony Orchestra Inc., 93 95–99

Bou-Matic, 62 42–44

Boulanger S.A., 102 57–60

Bourbon *see* Groupe Bourbon S.A.

Bourbon Corporation, 82 49-52

Bouygues S.A., I 562–64; 24 77–80 (upd.); 97 82–87 (upd.)

Bovis *see* Peninsular and Oriental Steam Navigation Company (Bovis Division)

Bowater PLC, IV 257–59

Bowlin Travel Centers, Inc., 99 71–75

Bowne & Co., Inc., 23 61–64; 79 74–80 (upd.)

Bowthorpe plc, 33 70–72

The Boy Scouts of America, 34 66–69

Boyd Bros. Transportation Inc., 39 64–66

Boyd Coffee Company, 53 73–75

Boyd Gaming Corporation, 43 80–82

The Boyds Collection, Ltd., 29 71–73

Boyne USA Resorts, 71 65–68

Boys & Girls Clubs of America, 69 73–75

Bozell Worldwide Inc., 25 89–91

Bozzuto's, Inc., 13 111–12

BP p.l.c., 45 46–56 (upd.)

BPB plc, 83 46-49

Braathens ASA, 47 60–62

Brach's Confections, Inc., 15 63–65; 74 43–46 (upd.)

Bradford & Bingley PLC, 65 77–80

Bradlees Discount Department Store Company, 12 48–50

Bradley Air Services Ltd., 56 38–40

Brady Corporation, 78 50–55 (upd.)

Brake Bros plc, 45 57–59

Bramalea Ltd., 9 83–85

Brambles Industries Limited, 42 47–50

Brammer PLC, 77 64–67

The Branch Group, Inc., 72 43–45

BrandPartners Group, Inc., 58 36–38

Brannock Device Company, 48 68–70

Brascan Corporation, 67 71–73

Brasfield & Gorrie LLC, 87 72–75

Brasil Telecom Participaçoes S.A., 57 67–70

Brass Eagle Inc., 34 70–72

Brauerei Beck & Co., 9 86–87; 33 73–76 (upd.)

Braun GmbH, 51 55–58

Brazil Fast Food Corporation, 74 47–49

Brazos Sportswear, Inc., 23 65–67

Breeze-Eastern Corporation, 95 67–70

Bremer Financial Corp., 45 60–63

Brenntag Holding GmbH & Co. KG, 8 68–69; 23 68–70 (upd.); 101 85–90 (upd.)

Brescia Group *see* Grupo Brescia.

Briazz, Inc., 53 76–79

The Brickman Group, Ltd., 87 76–79

Bricorama S.A., 68 62–64

Bridgeport Machines, Inc., 17 52–54

Bridgestone Corporation, V 234–35; 21 72–75 (upd.); 59 87–92 (upd.)

Bridgford Foods Corporation, 27 71–73

Briggs & Stratton Corporation, 8 70–73; 27 74–78 (upd.)

Brigham Exploration Company, 75 72–74

Brigham's Inc., 72 46–48

Bright Horizons Family Solutions, Inc., 31 71–73

Brightpoint, Inc., 18 74–77

Brillstein-Grey Entertainment, 80 41–45

The Brink's Company, 58 39–43 (upd.)

Brinker International, Inc., 10 176–78; 38 100–03 (upd.); 75 75–79 (upd.)

BRIO AB, 24 81–83

Brioche Pasquier S.A., 58 44–46

Brioni Roman Style S.p.A., 67 74–76

BRISA Auto-estradas de Portugal S.A., 64 55–58

Bristol Farms, 101 91–95

Bristol Hotel Company, 23 71–73

Bristol-Myers Squibb Company, III 17–19; 9 88–91 (upd.); 37 41–45 (upd.)

Bristow Helicopters Ltd., 70 26–28

Britannia Soft Drinks Ltd. (Britvic), 71 69–71

Britannica.com *see* Encyclopaedia Britannica, Inc.

Brite Voice Systems, Inc., 20 75–78

British Aerospace plc, I 50–53; 24 84–90 (upd.)

British Airways plc, I 92–95; 14 70–74 (upd.); 43 83–88 (upd.)

British American Tobacco PLC, 50 116–19 (upd.)

British-Borneo Oil & Gas PLC, 34 73–75

British Broadcasting Corporation Ltd., 7 52–55; 21 76–79 (upd.); 89 111–17 (upd.)

British Coal Corporation, IV 38–40

British Columbia Telephone Company, 6 309–11

British Energy Plc, 49 65–68 *see also* British Nuclear Fuels PLC.

The British Film Institute, 80 46–50

British Gas plc, V 559–63 *see also* Centrica plc.

British Land Plc, 54 38–41

British Midland plc, 38 104–06

The British Museum, 71 72–74

British Nuclear Fuels PLC, 6 451–54

British Oxygen Co *see* BOC Group.

The British Petroleum Company plc, IV 378–80; 7 56–59 (upd.); 21 80–84 (upd.) *see also* BP p.l.c.

British Railways Board, V 421–24

British Sky Broadcasting Group plc, 20 79–81; 60 66–69 (upd.)

British Steel plc, IV 41–43; 19 62–65 (upd.)

British Sugar plc, 84 25–29

British Telecommunications plc, V 279–82; 15 66–70 (upd.) *see also* BT Group plc.

The British United Provident Association Limited, 79 81–84

British Vita plc, 9 92–93; 33 77–79 (upd.)

British World Airlines Ltd., 18 78–80

Britvic Soft Drinks Limited *see* Britannia Soft Drinks Ltd. (Britvic)

Broadcast Music Inc., 23 74–77; 90 74–79 (upd.)

Broadcom Corporation, 34 76–79; 90 80–85 (upd.)

The Broadmoor Hotel, 30 82–85

Broadwing Corporation, 70 29–32

Brobeck, Phleger & Harrison, LLP, 31 74–76

Brockhaus *see* Bibliographisches Institut & F.A. Brockhaus AG.

Brodart Company, 84 30–33

Broder Bros. Co., 38 107–09

Broderbund Software, Inc., 13 113–16; 29 74–78 (upd.)

Broken Hill Proprietary Company Ltd., IV 44–47; 22 103–08 (upd.) *see also* BHP Billiton.

Bronco Drilling Company, Inc., 89 118–21

Bronco Wine Company, 101 96–99

Bronner Brothers Inc., 92 29–32

Bronner Display & Sign Advertising, Inc., 82 53-57

Brookdale Senior Living, 91 69–73

Brooke Group Ltd., 15 71–73 *see also* Vector Group Ltd.

The Daiei, Inc., V 39–40; 17 123–25
(upd.); 41 113–16 (upd.)

Daihatsu Motor Company, Ltd., 7
110–12; 21 162–64 (upd.)

Daiichikosho Company Ltd., 86
101–04

Daikin Industries, Ltd., III 460–61

Daiko Advertising Inc., 79 132–35

Daily Journal Corporation, 101 152–55

Daily Mail and General Trust plc, 19
118–20

The Daimaru, Inc., V 41–42; 42
98–100 (upd.)

Daimler-Benz Aerospace AG, 16 150–52

Daimler-Benz AG, I 149–51; 15 140–44
(upd.)

DaimlerChrysler AG, 34 128–37 (upd.);
64 100–07 (upd.)

Dain Rauscher Corporation, 35 138–41
(upd.)

Daio Paper Corporation, IV 266–67; 84
86–89 (upd.)

Dairy Crest Group plc, 32 131–33

Dairy Farm International Holdings
Ltd., 97 125–28

Dairy Farmers of America, Inc., 94
143–46

Dairy Mart Convenience Stores, Inc., 7
113–15; 25 124–27 (upd.) *see also*
Alimentation Couche-Tard Inc.

Dairy Queen *see* International Dairy
Queen, Inc.

Dairyland Healthcare Solutions, 73
99–101

Daishowa Paper Manufacturing Co.,
Ltd., IV 268–70; 57 100–03 (upd.)

Daisy Outdoor Products Inc., 58 85–88

Daisytek International Corporation, 18
128–30

Daiwa Bank, Ltd., II 276–77; 39
109–11 (upd.)

Daiwa Securities Company, Limited, II
405–06

Daiwa Securities Group Inc., 55 115–18
(upd.)

Daktronics, Inc., 32 134–37

Dal-Tile International Inc., 22 169–71

Dale and Thomas Popcorn LLC, 100
131–34

Dale Carnegie & Associates Inc., 28
85–87; 78 78–82 (upd.)

Dalgety PLC, II 499–500 *see also* PIC
International Group PLC

Dalhoff Larsen & Horneman A/S, 96
95–99

Dalian Shide Group, 91 136–39

Dalkia Holding, 66 68–70

Dallah Albaraka Group, 72 83–86

Dallas Cowboys Football Club, Ltd., 33
122–25

Dallas Semiconductor Corporation, 13
191–93; 31 143–46 (upd.)

Dalli-Werke GmbH & Co. KG, 86
105–10

Dallis Coffee, Inc., 86 111–14

Damark International, Inc., 18 131–34
see also Provell Inc.

Damartex S.A., 98 84–87

Dames & Moore, Inc., 25 128–31 *see
also* URS Corp.

Dan River Inc., 35 142–46; 86 115–20
(upd.)

Dana Holding Corporation, I 152–53;
10 264–66 (upd.); 99 127–134 (upd.)

Danaher Corporation, 7 116–17; 77
129–33 (upd.)

Danaos Corporation, 91 140–43

Daniel Measurement and Control, Inc.,
16 153–55; 74 96–99 (upd.)

Daniel Thwaites Plc, 95 122–25

Danisco A/S, 44 134–37

Dannon Co., Inc., 14 149–51

Danone Group *see* Groupe Danone.

Danske Bank Aktieselskab, 50 148–51

Danskin, Inc., 12 93–95; 62 88–92
(upd.)

Danzas Group, V 441–43; 40 136–39
(upd.)

D'Arcy Masius Benton & Bowles, Inc.,
6 20–22; 32 138–43 (upd.)

Darden Restaurants, Inc., 16 156–58;
44 138–42 (upd.)

Darigold, Inc., 9 159–61

Darling International Inc., 85 81–84

Dart Group PLC, 16 159–62; 77
134–37 (upd.)

Darty S.A., 27 118–20

DASA *see* Daimler-Benz Aerospace AG.

Dassault-Breguet *see* Avions Marcel
Dassault-Breguet Aviation.

Dassault Systèmes S.A., 25 132–34 *see
also* Groupe Dassault Aviation SA.

Data Broadcasting Corporation, 31
147–50

Data General Corporation, 8 137–40 *see
also* EMC Corp.

Datapoint Corporation, 11 67–70

Datascope Corporation, 39 112–14

Datek Online Holdings Corp., 32
144–46

Dauphin Deposit Corporation, 14
152–54

Dave & Buster's, Inc., 33 126–29

The Davey Tree Expert Company, 11
71–73

The David and Lucile Packard
Foundation, 41 117–19

The David J. Joseph Company, 14
155–56; 76 128–30 (upd.)

David Jones Ltd., 60 100–02

David's Bridal, Inc., 33 130–32

Davide Campari-Milano S.p.A., 57
104–06

Davis Polk & Wardwell, 36 151–54

Davis Service Group PLC, 45 139–41

DaVita Inc., 73 102–05

DAW Technologies, Inc., 25 135–37

Dawn Food Products, Inc., 17 126–28

Dawson Holdings PLC, 43 132–34

Day & Zimmermann Inc., 9 162–64; 31
151–55 (upd.)

Day International, Inc., 84 90–93

Day Runner, Inc., 14 157–58; 41
120–23 (upd.)

Dayton Hudson Corporation, V 43–44;
18 135–37 (upd.) *see also* Target Corp.

DB *see* Deutsche Bundesbahn.

dba Luftfahrtgesellschaft mbH, 76
131–33

DC Comics Inc., 25 138–41; 98 88–94
(upd.)

DC Shoes, Inc., 60 103–05

DCN S.A., 75 125–27

DDB Worldwide Communications, 14
159–61 *see also* Omnicom Group Inc.

DDi Corp., 7 118–20; 97 129–32
(upd.)

De Beers Consolidated Mines Limited /
De Beers Centenary AG, IV 64–68; 7
121–26 (upd.); 28 88–94 (upd.)

De Dietrich & Cie., 31 156–59

De La Rue plc, 10 267–69; 34 138–43
(upd.); 46 251

Dean & DeLuca, Inc., 36 155–57

Dean Foods Company, 7 127–29; 21
165–68 (upd.); 73 106–15 (upd.)

Dean Witter, Discover & Co., 12 96–98
see also Morgan Stanley Dean Witter &
Co.

Dearborn Mid-West Conveyor
Company, 56 78–80

Death Row Records, 27 121–23 *see also*
Tha Row Records.

Deb Shops, Inc., 16 163–65; 76 134–37
(upd.)

Debeka Krankenversicherungsverein auf
Gegenseitigkeit, 72 87–90

Debenhams plc, 28 95–97; 101 156–60
(upd.)

Debevoise & Plimpton, 39 115–17

DEC *see* Digital Equipment Corp.

Deceuninck N.V., 84 94–97

Dechert, 43 135–38

Deckers Outdoor Corporation, 22
172–74; 98 95–98 (upd.)

Decora Industries, Inc., 31 160–62

Decorator Industries Inc., 68 101–04

DeCrane Aircraft Holdings Inc., 36
158–60

DeepTech International Inc., 21 169–71

Deere & Company, III 462–64; 21
172–76 (upd.); 42 101–06 (upd.)

Defiance, Inc., 22 175–78

Degussa-Hüls AG, IV 69–72; 32 147–53
(upd.)

DeKalb Genetics Corporation, 17
129–31 *see also* Monsanto Co.

Del Laboratories, Inc., 28 98–100

Del Monte Foods Company, 7 130–32;
23 163–66 (upd.)

Del Taco, Inc., 58 89–92

Del Webb Corporation, 14 162–64 *see
also* Pulte Homes, Inc.

Delachaux S.A., 76 138–40

Delaware North Companies Inc., 7
133–36; 96 100–05 (upd.)

Delco Electronics Corporation *see* GM
Hughes Electronics Corp.

Delhaize "Le Lion" S.A., 44 143–46

Deli Universal NV, 66 71–74

dELiA*s Inc., 29 141–44

Delicato Vineyards, Inc., 50 152–55

Dell Computer Corporation, 9 165–66;
31 163–66 (upd.); 63 122–26 (upd.)

G

Harry London Candies, Inc., 70 110–12

Harry N. Abrams, Inc., 58 152–55

Harry Winston Inc., 45 184–87

Harry's Farmers Market Inc., 23 263–66 *see also* Whole Foods Market, Inc.

Harry's Fresh Foods *see* The Harris Soup Company (Harry's Fresh Foods)

Harsco Corporation, 8 245–47 *see also* United Defense Industries, Inc.

Harte-Hanks Communications, Inc., 17 220–22; 63 186–89 (upd.)

Hartmann Inc., 96 172–76

Hartmarx Corporation, 8 248–50; 32 246–50 (upd.)

The Hartstone Group plc, 14 224–26

The Hartz Mountain Corporation, 12 230–32; 46 220–23 (upd.)

Harvey Norman Holdings Ltd., 56 153–55

Harveys Casino Resorts, 27 199–201 *see also* Harrah's Entertainment, Inc.

Harza Engineering Company, 14 227–28

Hasbro, Inc., III 504–06; 16 264–68 (upd.); 43 229–34 (upd.)

Haskel International, Inc., 59 218–20

Hastings Entertainment, Inc., 29 229–31

Hastings Manufacturing Company, 56 156–58

Hauser, Inc., 46 224–27

Havas, SA, 10 345–48; 33 178–82 (upd.) *see also* Vivendi Universal Publishing

Haverty Furniture Companies, Inc., 31 246–49

Hawaiian Airlines Inc., 22 251–53 (upd.) *see also* HAL Inc.

Hawaiian Electric Industries, Inc., 9 274–77

Hawaiian Holdings, Inc., 96 177–81 (upd.)

Hawk Corporation, 59 221–23

Hawker Siddeley Group Public Limited Company, III 507–10

Hawkeye Holdings LLC, 86 246–49

Hawkins Chemical, Inc., 16 269–72

Haworth Inc., 8 251–52; 39 205–08 (upd.)

Hay Group Holdings, Inc., 100 210–14

Hay House, Inc., 93 241–45

Hayel Saeed Anam Group of Cos., 92 158–61

Hayes Corporation, 24 210–14

Hayes Lemmerz International, Inc., 27 202–04

Haynes International, Inc., 88 163–66

Haynes Publishing Group P.L.C., 71 169–71

Hays plc, 27 205–07; 78 149–53 (upd.)

Hazelden Foundation, 28 176–79

Hazlewood Foods plc, 32 251–53

HBO *see* Home Box Office Inc.

HCA—The Healthcare Company, 35 215–18 (upd.)

HCI Direct, Inc., 55 196–98

HDI (Haftpflichtverband der Deutschen Industrie Versicherung auf Gegenseitigkeit V.a.G.), 53 159–63

HDOS Enterprises, 72 167–69

HDR Inc., 48 203–05

Head N.V., 55 199–201

Headlam Group plc, 95 170–73

Headwaters Incorporated, 56 159–62

Headway Corporate Resources, Inc., 40 236–38

Health Care & Retirement Corporation, 22 254–56

Health Communications, Inc., 72 170–73

Health Management Associates, Inc., 56 163–65

Health O Meter Products Inc., 14 229–31

Health Risk Management, Inc., 24 215–17

Health Systems International, Inc., 11 174–76

HealthExtras, Inc., 75 185–87

HealthMarkets, Inc., 88 167–72 (upd.)

HealthSouth Corporation, 14 232–34; 33 183–86 (upd.)

Healthtex, Inc., 17 223–25 *see also* VF Corp.

The Hearst Corporation, IV 625–27; 19 201–04 (upd.); 46 228–32 (upd.)

Heartland Express, Inc., 18 225–27

The Heat Group, 53 164–66

Hechinger Company, 12 233–36

Hecla Mining Company, 20 293–96

Heekin Can Inc., 13 254–56 *see also* Ball Corp.

Heelys, Inc., 87 213–216

Heery International, Inc., 58 156–59

HEICO Corporation, 30 236–38

Heidelberger Druckmaschinen AG, 40 239–41

Heidelberger Zement AG, 31 250–53

Heidrick & Struggles International, Inc., 28 180–82

Heijmans N.V., 66 176–78

Heileman Brewing Co *see* G. Heileman Brewing Co.

Heilig-Meyers Company, 14 235–37; 40 242–46 (upd.)

Heineken N.V., I 256–58; 13 257–59 (upd.); 34 200–04 (upd.); 90 230–36 (upd.)

Heinrich Deichmann-Schuhe GmbH & Co. KG, 88 173–77

Heinz Co *see* H.J. Heinz Co.

Helen of Troy Corporation, 18 228–30

Helene Curtis Industries, Inc., 8 253–54; 28 183–85 (upd.) *see also* Unilever PLC.

Helix Energy Solutions Group, Inc., 81 173–77

Hella KGaA Hueck & Co., 66 179–83

Hellenic Petroleum SA, 64 175–77

Heller, Ehrman, White & McAuliffe, 41 200–02

Helly Hansen ASA, 25 205–07

Helmerich & Payne, Inc., 18 231–33

Helmsley Enterprises, Inc., 9 278–80; 39 209–12 (upd.)

Helzberg Diamonds, 40 247–49

Hemisphere GPS Inc., 99 210–213

Hemlo Gold Mines Inc., 9 281–82 *see also* Newmont Mining Corp.

Henderson Land Development Company Ltd., 70 113–15

Hendrick Motorsports, Inc., 89 250–53

Henkel KGaA, III 31–34; 34 205–10 (upd.); 95 174–83 (upd.)

Henkel Manco Inc., 22 257–59

The Henley Group, Inc., III 511–12

Hennes & Mauritz AB, 29 232–34 *see also* H&M Hennes & Mauritz AB

Henry Boot plc, 76 175–77

Henry Crown and Company, 91 233–36

Henry Dreyfuss Associates LLC, 88 178–82

Henry Ford Health System, 84 183–187

Henry Modell & Company Inc., 32 263–65

Henry Schein, Inc., 31 254–56; 70 116–19 (upd.)

Hensel Phelps Construction Company, 72 174–77

Hensley & Company, 64 178–80

HEPCO *see* Hokkaido Electric Power Company Inc.

Her Majesty's Stationery Office, 7 215–18

Heraeus Holding GmbH, IV 98–100; 54 159–63 (upd.)

Herald Media, Inc., 91 237–41

Herbalife Ltd., 17 226–29; 41 203–06 (upd.); 92 162–67 (upd.)

Hercules Inc., I 343–45; 22 260–63 (upd.); 66 184–88 (upd.)

Hercules Technology Growth Capital, Inc., 87 217–220

Herley Industries, Inc., 33 187–89

Herman Goelitz, Inc., 28 186–88 *see also* Jelly Belly Candy Co.

Herman Goldner Company, Inc., 100 215–18

Herman Miller, Inc., 8 255–57; 77 180–86 (upd.)

Hermès International S.A., 14 238–40; 34 211–14 (upd.)

Hero Group, 100 219–24

Héroux-Devtek Inc., 69 205–07

Herr Foods Inc., 84 188–191

Herradura *see* Grupo Industrial Herradura, S.A. de C.V.

Herschend Family Entertainment Corporation, 73 173–76

Hershey Foods Corporation, II 510–12; 15 219–22 (upd.); 51 156–60 (upd.)

Herstal *see* Groupe Herstal S.A.

Hertie Waren- und Kaufhaus GmbH, V 72–74

The Hertz Corporation, 9 283–85; 33 190–93 (upd.); 101 240–45 (upd.)

Heska Corporation, 39 213–16

Heublein Inc., I 259–61

Heuer *see* TAG Heuer International SA.

Heuliez *see* Groupe Henri Heuliez S.A.

Majesco Entertainment Company, 85 225–29

The Major Automotive Companies, Inc., 45 260–62

Make-A-Wish Foundation of America, 97 262–65

Makhteshim-Agan Industries Ltd., 85 230–34

Makita Corporation, 22 333–35; 59 270–73 (upd.)

Malayan Banking Berhad, 72 215–18

Malaysian Airline System Berhad, 6 100–02; 29 300–03 (upd.); 97 266–71 (upd.)

Malcolm Pirnie, Inc., 42 242–44

Malden Mills Industries, Inc., 16 351–53 *see also* Polartec LLC.

Malév Plc, 24 310–12

Mallinckrodt Group Inc., 19 251–53

Malt-O-Meal Company, 22 336–38; 63 249–53 (upd.)

Mammoet Transport B.V., 26 278–80

Mammoth Mountain Ski Area, 101 322–25

Man Aktiengesellschaft, III 561–63

MAN Roland Druckmaschinen AG, 94 294–98

Management and Training Corporation, 28 253–56

Manatron, Inc., 86 260–63

Manchester United Football Club plc, 30 296–98

Mandalay Resort Group, 32 322–26 (upd.)

Mandom Corporation, 82 205–08

Manhattan Associates, Inc., 67 243–45

Manhattan Group, LLC, 80 228–31

Manheim, 88 244–48

Manila Electric Company (Meralco), 56 214–16

Manischewitz Company *see* B. Manischewitz Co.

Manitoba Telecom Services, Inc., 61 184–87

Manitou BF S.A., 27 294–96

The Manitowoc Company, Inc., 18 318–21; 59 274–79 (upd.)

Mannatech Inc., 33 282–85

Mannesmann AG, III 564–67; 14 326–29 (upd.); 38 296–301 (upd.) *see also* Vodafone Group PLC.

Mannheim Steamroller *see* American Gramophone LLC.

Manning Selvage & Lee (MS&L), 76 252–54

MannKind Corporation, 87 300–303

Manor Care, Inc., 6 187–90; 25 306–10 (upd.)

Manpower Inc., 9 326–27; 30 299–302 (upd.); 73 215–18 (upd.)

ManTech International Corporation, 97 272–75

Manufactured Home Communities, Inc., 22 339–41

Manufacturers Hanover Corporation, II 312–14 *see also* Chemical Bank.

Manulife Financial Corporation, 85 235–38

Manutan International S.A., 72 219–21

Manville Corporation, III 706–09; 7 291–95 (upd.) *see also* Johns Manville Corp.

MAPCO Inc., IV 458–59

MAPICS, Inc., 55 256–58

Maple Grove Farms of Vermont, 88 249–52

Maple Leaf Foods Inc., 41 249–53

Maple Leaf Sports & Entertainment Ltd., 61 188–90

Maples Industries, Inc., 83 260-263

Marble Slab Creamery, Inc., 87 304–307

March of Dimes, 31 322–25

Marchesi Antinori SRL, 42 245–48

Marchex, Inc., 72 222–24

marchFIRST, Inc., 34 261–64

Marco Business Products, Inc., 75 244–46

Marco's Franchising LLC, 86 264–67

Marcolin S.p.A., 61 191–94

Marconi plc, 33 286–90 (upd.)

Marcopolo S.A., 79 247–50

The Marcus Corporation, 21 359–63

Marelli *see* Magneti Marelli Holding SpA.

Marfin Popular Bank plc, 92 222–26

Margarete Steiff GmbH, 23 334–37

Marie Brizard et Roger International S.A.S., 22 342–44; 97 276–80 (upd.)

Marie Callender's Restaurant & Bakery, Inc., 28 257–59

Mariella Burani Fashion Group, 92 227–30

Marine Products Corporation, 75 247–49

MarineMax, Inc., 30 303–05

Mariner Energy, Inc., 101 326–29

Marion Laboratories Inc., I 648–49

Marion Merrell Dow, Inc., 9 328–29 (upd.)

Marionnaud Parfumeries SA, 51 233–35

Marisa Christina, Inc., 15 290–92

Maritz Inc., 38 302–05

Mark IV Industries, Inc., 7 296–98; 28 260–64 (upd.)

Mark T. Wendell Tea Company, 94 299–302

The Mark Travel Corporation, 80 232–35

Märklin Holding GmbH, 70 163–66

Marks and Spencer p.l.c., V 124–26; 24 313–17 (upd.); 85 239–47 (upd.)

Marks Brothers Jewelers, Inc., 24 318–20 *see also* Whitehall Jewellers, Inc.

Marlin Business Services Corp., 89 317–19

The Marmon Group, Inc., IV 135–38; 16 354–57 (upd.); 70 167–72 (upd.)

Marquette Electronics, Inc., 13 326–28

Marriott International, Inc., III 102–03; 21 364–67 (upd.); 83 264-270 (upd.)

Mars, Incorporated, 7 299–301; 40 302–05 (upd.)

Mars Petcare US Inc., 96 269–72

Marsh & McLennan Companies, Inc., III 282–84; 45 263–67 (upd.)

Marsh Supermarkets, Inc., 17 300–02; 76 255–58 (upd.)

Marshall & Ilsley Corporation, 56 217–20

Marshall Amplification plc, 62 239–42

Marshall Field's, 63 254–63 *see also* Target Corp.

Marshalls Incorporated, 13 329–31

Martek Biosciences Corporation, 65 218–20

Martell and Company S.A., 82 213–16

Marten Transport, Ltd., 84 243–246

Martha Stewart Living Omnimedia, Inc., 24 321–23; 73 219–22 (upd.)

Martignetti Companies, 84 247–250

Martin-Baker Aircraft Company Limited, 61 195–97

Martin Franchises, Inc., 80 236–39

Martin Guitar Company *see* C.F. Martin & Co., Inc.

Martin Industries, Inc., 44 274–77

Martin Marietta Corporation, I 67–69 *see also* Lockheed Martin Corp.

Martin's Super Markets, Inc., 101 330–33

MartinLogan, Ltd., 85 248–51

Martini & Rossi SpA, 63 264–66

Martz Group, 56 221–23

Marubeni Corporation, I 492–95; 24 324–27 (upd.)

Maruha Group Inc., 75 250–53 (upd.)

Marui Company Ltd., V 127; 62 243–45 (upd.)

Maruzen Co., Limited, 18 322–24

Marvel Entertainment, Inc., 10 400–02; 78 212–19 (upd.)

Marvin Lumber & Cedar Company, 22 345–47

Mary Kay Inc., 9 330–32; 30 306–09 (upd.); 84 251–256 (upd.)

Maryland & Virginia Milk Producers Cooperative Association, Inc., 80 240–43

Maryville Data Systems Inc., 96 273–76

Marzotto S.p.A., 20 356–58; 67 246–49 (upd.)

The Maschhoffs, Inc., 82 217–20

Masco Corporation, III 568–71; 20 359–63 (upd.); 39 263–68 (upd.)

Maserati *see* Officine Alfieri Maserati S.p.A.

Mashantucket Pequot Gaming Enterprise Inc., 35 282–85

Masland Corporation, 17 303–05 *see also* Lear Corp.

Masonite International Corporation, 63 267–69

Massachusetts Mutual Life Insurance Company, III 285–87; 53 210–13 (upd.)

Massey Energy Company, 57 236–38

MasTec, Inc., 55 259–63 (upd.)

Mastellone Hermanos S.A., 101 334–37

Master Lock Company, 45 268–71

MasterBrand Cabinets, Inc., 71 216–18

MasterCard Worldwide, 9 333–35; 96 277–81 (upd.)

Owens & Minor, Inc., 16 398–401; 68 282–85 (upd.)
Owens Corning, III 720–23; 20 413–17 (upd.); 98 285–91 (upd.)
Owens-Illinois, Inc., I 609–11; 26 350–53 (upd.); 85 311–18 (upd.)
Owosso Corporation, 29 366–68
Oxfam GB, 87 359–362
Oxford Health Plans, Inc., 16 402–04
Oxford Industries, Inc., 8 406–08; 84 290–296 (upd.)

P

P&C Foods Inc., 8 409–11
P & F Industries, Inc., 45 327–29
P&G see Procter & Gamble Co.
P.C. Richard & Son Corp., 23 372–74
P.F. Chang's China Bistro, Inc., 37 297–99; 86 317–21 (upd.)
P.H. Glatfelter Company, 8 412–14; 30 349–52 (upd.); 83 291–297 (upd.)
P.W. Minor and Son, Inc., 100 321–24
PACCAR Inc., I 185–86; 26 354–56 (upd.)
Pacer International, Inc., 54 274–76
Pacer Technology, 40 347–49
Pacific Basin Shipping Ltd., 86 322–26
Pacific Clay Products Inc., 88 292–95
Pacific Coast Building Products, Inc., 94 338–41
Pacific Coast Feather Company, 67 294–96
Pacific Coast Restaurants, Inc., 90 318–21
Pacific Dunlop Limited, 10 444–46 see also Ansell Ltd.
Pacific Enterprises, V 682–84 see also Sempra Energy.
Pacific Ethanol, Inc., 81 269–72
Pacific Gas and Electric Company, V 685–87 see also PG&E Corp.
Pacific Internet Limited, 87 363–366
Pacific Mutual Holding Company, 98 292–96
Pacific Sunwear of California, Inc., 28 343–45; 47 425
Pacific Telecom, Inc., 6 325–28
Pacific Telesis Group, V 318–20 see also SBC Communications.
PacifiCare Health Systems, Inc., 11 378–80
PacifiCorp, Inc., V 688–90; 26 357–60 (upd.)
Packaging Corporation of America, 12 376–78; 51 282–85 (upd.)
Packard Bell Electronics, Inc., 13 387–89
Packeteer, Inc., 81 273–76
Paddock Publications, Inc., 53 263–65
Paddy Power plc, 98 297–300
PagesJaunes Groupe SA, 79 306–09
Paging Network Inc., 11 381–83
Pagnossin S.p.A., 73 248–50
PaineWebber Group Inc., II 444–46; 22 404–07 (upd.) see also UBS AG.
Pakistan International Airlines Corporation, 46 323–26

Pakistan State Oil Company Ltd., 81 277–80
PAL see Philippine Airlines, Inc.
Palace Sports & Entertainment, Inc., 97 320–25
Palfinger AG, 100 325–28
PALIC see Pan-American Life Insurance Co.
Pall Corporation, 9 396–98; 72 263–66 (upd.)
Palm Harbor Homes, Inc., 39 316–18
Palm, Inc., 36 355–57; 75 310–14 (upd.)
Palm Management Corporation, 71 265–68
Palmer & Cay, Inc., 69 285–87
Palmer Candy Company, 80 277–81
Palmer Co. see R. M. Palmer Co.
Paloma Industries Ltd., 71 269–71
Palomar Medical Technologies, Inc., 22 408–10
Pamida Holdings Corporation, 15 341–43
The Pampered Chef Ltd., 18 406–08; 78 292–96 (upd.)
Pamplin Corp. see R.B. Pamplin Corp.
Pan-American Life Insurance Company, 48 311–13
Pan American World Airways, Inc., I 115–16; 12 379–81 (upd.)
Panalpina World Transport (Holding) Ltd., 47 286–88
Panamerican Beverages, Inc., 47 289–91; 54 74
PanAmSat Corporation, 46 327–29
Panattoni Development Company, Inc., 99 327–330
Panavision Inc., 24 372–74
Pancho's Mexican Buffet, Inc., 46 330–32
Panda Restaurant Group, Inc., 35 327–29; 97 326–30 (upd.)
Panera Bread Company, 44 327–29
Panhandle Eastern Corporation, V 691–92 see also CMS Energy Corp.
Pantone Inc., 53 266–69
The Pantry, Inc., 36 358–60
Panzani, 84 297–300
Papa Gino's Holdings Corporation, Inc., 86 327–30
Papa John's International, Inc., 15 344–46; 71 272–76 (upd.)
Papa Murphy's International, Inc., 54 277–79
Papeteries de Lancey, 23 366–68
Papetti's Hygrade Egg Products, Inc., 39 319–21
Pappas Restaurants, Inc., 76 302–04
Par Pharmaceutical Companies, Inc., 65 286–88
The Paradies Shops, Inc., 88 296–99
Paradise Music & Entertainment, Inc., 42 271–74
Paradores de Turismo de Espana S.A., 73 251–53
Parallel Petroleum Corporation, 101 400–03

Parametric Technology Corp., 16 405–07
Paramount Pictures Corporation, II 154–56; 94 342–47 (upd.)
Paramount Resources Ltd., 87 367–370
PAREXEL International Corporation, 84 301–304
Parfums Givenchy S.A., 100 329–32
Paribas see BNP Paribas Group.
Paris Corporation, 22 411–13
Parisian, Inc., 14 374–76 see also Belk, Inc.
Park Corp., 22 414–16
Park-Ohio Holdings Corp., 17 371–73; 85 319–23 (upd.)
Parker Drilling Company, 28 346–48
Parker-Hannifin Corporation, III 601–03; 24 375–78 (upd.); 99 331–337 (upd.)
Parlex Corporation, 61 279–81
Parmalat Finanziaria SpA, 50 343–46
Parque Arauco S.A., 72 267–69
Parras see Compañia Industrial de Parras, S.A. de C.V. (CIPSA).
Parsons Brinckerhoff, Inc., 34 333–36
The Parsons Corporation, 8 415–17; 56 263–67 (upd.)
PartnerRe Ltd., 83 298–301
Partouche SA see Groupe Partouche SA.
Party City Corporation, 54 280–82
Pathé SA, 29 369–71 see also Chargeurs International.
Pathmark Stores, Inc., 23 369–71; 101 404–08 (upd.)
Patina Oil & Gas Corporation, 24 379–81
Patrick Cudahy Inc., 102 321–25
Patrick Industries, Inc., 30 342–45
Patriot Transportation Holding, Inc., 91 371–74
Patterson Dental Co., 19 289–91
Patterson-UTI Energy, Inc., 55 293–95
Patton Boggs LLP, 71 277–79
Paul Harris Stores, Inc., 18 409–12
Paul, Hastings, Janofsky & Walker LLP, 27 357–59
Paul Mueller Company, 65 289–91
Paul Reed Smith Guitar Company, 89 345–48
The Paul Revere Corporation, 12 382–83
Paul-Son Gaming Corporation, 66 249–51
Paul, Weiss, Rifkind, Wharton & Garrison, 47 292–94
Paulaner Brauerei GmbH & Co. KG, 35 330–33
Paxson Communications Corporation, 33 322–26
Pay 'N Pak Stores, Inc., 9 399–401
Paychex, Inc., 15 347–49; 46 333–36 (upd.)
Payless Cashways, Inc., 11 384–86; 44 330–33 (upd.)
Payless ShoeSource, Inc., 18 413–15; 69 288–92 (upd.)
PayPal Inc., 58 266–69
PBL see Publishing and Broadcasting Ltd.

Provident Bankshares Corporation, 85 340–43

Provident Life and Accident Insurance Company of America, III 331–33 *see also* UnumProvident Corp.

Providian Financial Corporation, 52 284–90 (upd.)

Provigo Inc., II 651–53; 51 301–04 (upd.)

Provimi S.A., 80 292–95

Prudential Financial Inc., III 337–41; 30 360–64 (upd.); 82 292–98 (upd.)

Prudential plc, III 334–36; 48 325–29 (upd.)

PSA Peugeot Citroen S.A., 28 370–74 (upd.); 54 126

PSF *see* Premium Standard Farms, Inc.

PSI Resources, 6 555–57

Psion PLC, 45 346–49

Psychemedics Corporation, 89 358–61

Psychiatric Solutions, Inc., 68 297–300

PT Astra International Tbk, 56 283–86

PT Bank Buana Indonesia Tbk, 60 240–42

PT Indosat Tbk, 93 354–57

PTT Public Company Ltd., 56 287–90

Pubco Corporation, 17 383–85

Public Service Company of Colorado, 6 558–60

Public Service Company of New Hampshire, 21 408–12; 55 313–18 (upd.)

Public Service Company of New Mexico, 6 561–64 *see also* PNM Resources Inc.

Public Service Enterprise Group Inc., V 701–03; 44 360–63 (upd.)

Public Storage, Inc., 21 52 291–93

Publicis Groupe, 19 329–32; 77 346–50 (upd.)

Publishers Clearing House, 23 393–95; 64 313–16 (upd.)

Publishers Group, Inc., 35 357–59

Publishing and Broadcasting Limited, 54 299–302

Publix Super Markets Inc., 7 440–42; 31 371–74 (upd.)

Puck Lazaroff Inc. *see* The Wolfgang Puck Food Company, Inc.

Pueblo Xtra International, Inc., 47 311–13

Puerto Rico Electric Power Authority, 47 314–16

Puget Sound Energy Inc., 6 565–67; 50 365–68 (upd.)

Puig Beauty and Fashion Group S.L., 60 243–46

Pulaski Furniture Corporation, 33 349–52; 80 296–99 (upd.)

Pulitzer Inc., 15 375–77; 58 280–83 (upd.)

Pulsar Internacional S.A., 21 413–15

Pulte Homes, Inc., 8 436–38; 42 291–94 (upd.)

Puma AG Rudolf Dassler Sport, 35 360–63

Pumpkin Masters, Inc., 48 330–32

Punch International N.V., 66 258–60

Punch Taverns plc, 70 240–42

Puratos S.A./NV, 92 315–18

Pure World, Inc., 72 285–87

Purina Mills, Inc., 32 376–79

Puritan-Bennett Corporation, 13 419–21

Purolator Products Company, 21 416–18; 74 253–56 (upd.)

Putt-Putt Golf Courses of America, Inc., 23 396–98

PVC Container Corporation, 67 312–14

PW Eagle, Inc., 48 333–36

PWA Group, IV 323–25 *see also* Svenska Cellulosa.

Pyramid Breweries Inc., 33 353–55; 102 343–47 (upd.)

Pyramid Companies, 54 303–05

PZ Cussons plc, 72 288–90

Q

Q.E.P. Co., Inc., 65 292–94

Qantas Airways Ltd., 6 109–13; 24 396–401 (upd.); 68 301–07 (upd.)

Qatar Airways Company Q.C.S.C., 87 404–407

Qatar National Bank SAQ, 87 408–411

Qatar Petroleum, IV 524–26; 98 324–28 (upd.)

Qatar Telecom QSA, 87 412–415

Qdoba Restaurant Corporation, 93 358–62

Qiagen N.V., 39 333–35

QLT Inc., 71 291–94

QRS Music Technologies, Inc., 95 349–53

QSC Audio Products, Inc., 56 291–93

QSS Group, Inc., 100 358–61

Quad/Graphics, Inc., 19 333–36

Quaker Chemical Corp., 91 388–91

Quaker Fabric Corp., 19 337–39

Quaker Foods North America, II 558–60; 12 409–12 (upd.); 34 363–67 (upd.); 73 268–73 (upd.)

Quaker State Corporation, 7 443–45; 21 419–22 (upd.) *see also* Pennzoil-Quaker State Co.

QUALCOMM Incorporated, 20 438–41; 47 317–21 (upd.)

Quality Chekd Dairies, Inc., 48 337–39

Quality Dining, Inc., 18 437–40

Quality Food Centers, Inc., 17 386–88 *see also* Kroger Co.

Quality Systems, Inc., 81 328–31

Quanex Corporation, 13 422–24; 62 286–89 (upd.)

Quanta Computer Inc., 47 322–24

Quanta Services, Inc., 79 338–41

Quantum Chemical Corporation, 8 439–41

Quantum Corporation, 10 458–59; 62 290–93 (upd.)

Quark, Inc., 36 375–79

Québec Hydro-Electric Commission *see* Hydro-Québec.

Quebecor Inc., 12 412–14; 47 325–28 (upd.)

Quelle Group, V 165–67 *see also* Karstadt Quelle AG.

Quest Diagnostics Inc., 26 390–92

Questar Corporation, 6 568–70; 26 386–89 (upd.)

The Quick & Reilly Group, Inc., 20 442–44

Quick Restaurants S.A., 94 357–60

Quicken Loans, Inc., 93 363–67

Quidel Corporation, 80 300–03

The Quigley Corporation, 62 294–97

Quiksilver, Inc., 18 441–43; 79 342–47 (upd.)

QuikTrip Corporation, 36 380–83

Quill Corporation, 28 375–77

Quilmes Industrial (QUINSA) S.A., 67 315–17

Quinn Emanuel Urquhart Oliver & Hedges, LLP, 99 350–353

Quintiles Transnational Corporation, 21 423–25; 68 308–12 (upd.)

Quixote Corporation, 15 378–80

The Quizno's Corporation, 42 295–98

Quovadx Inc., 70 243–46

QVC Inc., 9 428–29; 58 284–87 (upd.)

Qwest Communications International, Inc., 37 312–17

R

R&B, Inc., 51 305–07

R.B. Pamplin Corp., 45 350–52

R.C. Bigelow, Inc., 49 334–36

R.C. Willey Home Furnishings, 72 291–93

R.G. Barry Corp., 17 389–91; 44 364–67 (upd.)

R. Griggs Group Limited, 23 399–402; 31 413–14

R.H. Macy & Co., Inc., V 168–70; 8 442–45 (upd.); 30 379–83 (upd.) *see also* Macy's, Inc.

R.J. Reynolds Tobacco Holdings, Inc., 30 384–87 (upd.)

R. M. Palmer Co., 89 362–64

R.P. Scherer Corporation, I 678–80 *see also* Cardinal Health, Inc.

R.R. Bowker LLC, 100 362–66

R.R. Donnelley & Sons Company, IV 660–62; 38 368–71 (upd.)

Rabobank Group, 26 419; 33 356–58

RAC *see* Roy Anderson Corp.

Racal-Datacom Inc., 11 408–10

Racal Electronics PLC, II 83–84 *see also* Thales S.A.

Racing Champions Corporation, 37 318–20

Rack Room Shoes, Inc., 84 314–317

Radeberger Gruppe AG, 75 332–35

Radian Group Inc., 42 299–301 *see also* Onex Corp.

Radiation Therapy Services, Inc., 85 344–47

Radio Flyer Inc., 34 368–70

Radio One, Inc., 67 318–21

RadioShack Corporation, 36 384–88 (upd.); 101 416–23 (upd.)

Radius Inc., 16 417–19

RAE Systems Inc., 83 311–314

RAG AG, 35 364–67; 60 247–51 (upd.)

Rag Shops, Inc., 30 365–67

Research in Motion Ltd., 54 310–14
Research Triangle Institute, 83 322-325
Réseau Ferré de France, 66 266–68
Reser's Fine Foods, Inc., 81 337–40
Resorts International, Inc., 12 418–20
Resource America, Inc., 42 311–14
Resources Connection, Inc., 81 341–44
Response Oncology, Inc., 27 385–87
Restaurant Associates Corporation, 66
  269–72
Restaurants Unlimited, Inc., 13 435–37
Restoration Hardware, Inc., 30 376–78;
  96 347–51 (upd.)
Retail Ventures, Inc., 82 299–03 (upd.)
Retractable Technologies, Inc., 99
  366–369
Reuters Group PLC, IV 668–70; 22
  450–53 (upd.); 63 323–27 (upd.)
Revco D.S., Inc., V 171–73 *see also* CVS
  Corp.
Revell-Monogram Inc., 16 427–29
Revere Electric Supply Company, 96
  352–55
Revere Ware Corporation, 22 454–56
Revlon Inc., III 54–57; 17 400–04
  (upd.); 64 330–35 (upd.)
Rewards Network Inc., 70 271–75
  (upd.)
REX Stores Corp., 10 468–69
Rexam PLC, 32 380–85 (upd.); 85
  353–61 (upd.)
Rexel, Inc., 15 384–87
Rexnord Corporation, 21 429–32; 76
  315–19 (upd.)
The Reynolds and Reynolds Company,
  50 376–79
Reynolds Metals Company, IV 186–88;
  19 346–48 (upd.) *see also* Alcoa Inc.
RF Micro Devices, Inc., 43 311–13
RFC Franchising LLC, 68 317–19
RFF *see* Réseau Ferré de France.
RGI *see* Rockefeller Group International.
Rheinmetall AG, 9 443–46; 97 343–49
  (upd.)
RHI AG, 53 283–86
Rhino Entertainment Company, 18
  457–60; 70 276–80 (upd.)
RHM *see* Ranks Hovis McDougall.
Rhodes Inc., 23 412–14
Rhodia SA, 38 378–80
Rhône-Poulenc S.A., I 388–90; 10
  470–72 (upd.)
Rica Foods, Inc., 41 328–30
Ricardo plc, 90 352–56
Rich Products Corporation, 7 448–49;
  38 381–84 (upd.); 93 368–74 (upd.)
The Richards Group, Inc., 58 300–02
Richardson Electronics, Ltd., 17 405–07
Richardson Industries, Inc., 62 298–301
Richfood Holdings, Inc., 7 450–51; *see
  also* Supervalu Inc.
Richton International Corporation, 39
  344–46
Richtree Inc., 63 328–30
Richwood Building Products, Inc. *see* Ply
  Gem Industries Inc.
Rickenbacker International Corp., 91
  408–12

Ricoh Company, Ltd., III 159–61; 36
  389–93 (upd.)
Ricola Ltd., 62 302–04
Riddell Sports Inc., 22 457–59; 23 449
Ride, Inc., 22 460–63
Ridley Corporation Ltd., 62 305–07
Riedel Tiroler Glashuette GmbH, 99
  370–373
The Riese Organization, 38 385–88
Rieter Holding AG, 42 315–17
Riggs National Corporation, 13 438–40
Right Management Consultants, Inc.,
  42 318–21
Riklis Family Corp., 9 447–50
Rimage Corp., 89 369–72
Rinascente S.p.A., 71 308–10
Rinker Group Ltd., 65 298–301
Rio Tinto plc, 19 349–53 (upd.) 50
  380–85 (upd.)
Ripley Corp S.A., 102 353–56
Ripley Entertainment, Inc., 74 273–76
Riser Foods, Inc., 9 451–54 *see also*
  Giant Eagle, Inc.
Ritchie Bros. Auctioneers Inc., 41
  331–34
Rite Aid Corporation, V 174–76; 19
  354–57 (upd.); 63 331–37 (upd.)
Ritter Sport *see* Alfred Ritter GmbH &
  Co. KG.
Ritter's Frozen Custard *see* RFC
  Franchising LLC.
Ritz Camera Centers, 34 375–77
The Ritz-Carlton Hotel Company,
  L.L.C., 9 455–57; 29 403–06 (upd.);
  71 311–16 (upd.)
Ritz-Craft Corporation of Pennsylvania
  Inc., 94 365–68
Riunione Adriatica di Sicurtà SpA, III
  345–48
Riva Fire *see* Gruppo Riva Fire SpA.
The Rival Company, 19 358–60
River Oaks Furniture, Inc., 43 314–16
River Ranch Fresh Foods LLC, 88
  322–25
Riverbed Technology, Inc., 101 428–31
Riverwood International Corporation,
  11 420–23; 48 340–44 (upd.) *see also*
  Graphic Packaging Holding Co.
Riviana Foods, 27 388–91
Riviera Holdings Corporation, 75
  340–43
Riviera Tool Company, 89 373–76
RJR Nabisco Holdings Corp., V 408–10
  see also R.J Reynolds Tobacco Holdings
  Inc., Nabisco Brands, Inc.; R.J.
  Reynolds Industries, Inc.
RM Auctions, Inc., 88 326–29
RMC Group p.l.c., III 737–40; 34
  378–83 (upd.)
RMH Teleservices, Inc., 42 322–24
Roadhouse Grill, Inc., 22 464–66
Roadmaster Industries, Inc., 16 430–33
Roadway Express, Inc., V 502–03; 25
  395–98 (upd.)
Roanoke Electric Steel Corporation, 45
  368–70
Robbins & Myers Inc., 15 388–90
Roberds Inc., 19 361–63

Robert Bosch GmbH, I 392–93; 16
  434–37 (upd.); 43 317–21 (upd.)
Robert Half International Inc., 18
  461–63; 70 281–84 (upd.)
Robert Mondavi Corporation, 15
  391–94; 50 386–90 (upd.)
Robert Talbott Inc., 88 330–33
Robert W. Baird & Co. Incorporated,
  67 328–30
Robert Wood Johnson Foundation, 35
  375–78
Robertet SA, 39 347–49
Roberts Pharmaceutical Corporation, 16
  438–40
Robertson-Ceco Corporation, 19
  364–66
Robins, Kaplan, Miller & Ciresi L.L.P.,
  89 377–81
Robinson Helicopter Company, 51
  315–17
ROC *see* Royal Olympic Cruise Lines Inc.
Rocawear Apparel LLC, 77 355–58
Roche Biomedical Laboratories, Inc., 11
  424–26 *see also* Laboratory Corporation
  of America Holdings.
Roche Bioscience, 14 403–06 (upd.)
Rochester Gas And Electric
  Corporation, 6 571–73
Rochester Telephone Corporation, 6
  332–34
Röchling Gruppe, 94 369–74
Rock Bottom Restaurants, Inc., 25
  399–401; 68 320–23 (upd.)
Rock-It Cargo USA, Inc., 86 339–42
Rock of Ages Corporation, 37 329–32
Rock-Tenn Company, 13 441–43; 59
  347–51 (upd.)
The Rockefeller Foundation, 34 384–87
Rockefeller Group International Inc., 58
  303–06
Rockford Corporation, 43 322–25
Rockford Products Corporation, 55
  323–25
RockShox, Inc., 26 412–14
Rockwell Automation, 43 326–31
  (upd.)
Rockwell International Corporation, I
  78–80; 11 427–30 (upd.)
Rockwell Medical Technologies, Inc., 88
  334–37
Rocky Brands, Inc., 26 415–18; 102
  357–62 (upd.)
Rocky Mountain Chocolate Factory,
  Inc., 73 280–82
Rodale, Inc., 23 415–17; 47 336–39
  (upd.)
Rodamco N.V., 26 419–21
Rodda Paint Company, 98 329–32
Rodriguez Group S.A., 90 357–60
ROFIN-SINAR Technologies Inc, 81
  345–48
Rogers Communications Inc., 30
  388–92 (upd.) *see also* Maclean Hunter
  Publishing Ltd.
Rogers Corporation, 61 310–13; 80
  313–17 (upd.)
Rohde & Schwarz GmbH & Co. KG,
  39 350–53

Valley Proteins, Inc., 91 500–03
ValleyCrest Companies, 81 411–14 (upd.)
Vallourec SA, 54 391–94
Valmet Oy, III 647–49 *see also* Metso Corp.
Valmont Industries, Inc., 19 469–72
Valora Holding AG, 98 425–28
Valorem S.A., 88 427–30
Valores Industriales S.A., 19 473–75
The Valspar Corporation, 8 552–54; 32 483–86 (upd.); 77 462–68 (upd.)
Value City Department Stores, Inc., 38 473–75 *see also* Retail Ventures, Inc.
Value Line, Inc., 16 506–08; 73 358–61 (upd.)
Value Merchants Inc., 13 541–43
ValueClick, Inc., 49 432–34
ValueVision International, Inc., 22 534–36
Valve Corporation, 101 483–86
Van Camp Seafood Company, Inc., 7 556–57 *see also* Chicken of the Sea International.
Van de Velde S.A./NV, 102 439–43
Van Hool S.A./NV, 96 442–45
Van Houtte Inc., 39 409–11
Van Lanschot NV, 79 456–59
Van Leer N.V. *see* Royal Packaging Industries Van Leer N.V.; Greif Inc.
Van's Aircraft, Inc., 65 349–51
Vance Publishing Corporation, 64 398–401
Vanderbilt University Medical Center, 99 474–477
The Vanguard Group, Inc., 14 530–32; 34 486–89 (upd.)
Vanguard Health Systems Inc., 70 338–40
Vans, Inc., 16 509–11; 47 423–26 (upd.)
Vapores *see* Compañia Sud Americana de Vapores S.A.
Varco International, Inc., 42 418–20
Vari-Lite International, Inc., 35 434–36
Varian Associates Inc., 12 504–06
Varian, Inc., 48 407–11 (upd.)
Variety Wholesalers, Inc., 73 362–64
Variflex, Inc., 51 391–93
VARIG S.A. (Viação Aérea Rio-Grandense), 6 133–35; 29 494–97 (upd.)
Varity Corporation, III 650–52 *see also* AGCO Corp.
Varlen Corporation, 16 512–14
Varsity Brands, Inc., 15 516–18; 94 436–40 (upd.)
Varta AG, 23 495–99
VASCO Data Security International, Inc., 79 460–63
Vastar Resources, Inc., 24 524–26
Vattenfall AB, 57 395–98
Vauxhall Motors Limited, 73 365–69
VBA - Bloemenveiling Aalsmeer, 88 431–34
VCA Antech, Inc., 58 353–55
Veba A.G., I 542–43; 15 519–21 (upd.) *see also* E.On AG.

Vebego International BV, 49 435–37
VECO International, Inc., 7 558–59 *see also* CH2M Hill Ltd.
Vector Aerospace Corporation, 97 441–44
Vector Group Ltd., 35 437–40 (upd.)
Vectren Corporation, 98 429–36 (upd.)
Vedior NV, 35 441–43
Veeco Instruments Inc., 32 487–90
Veidekke ASA, 98 437–40
Veit Companies, 43 440–42; 92 398–402 (upd.)
Velcro Industries N.V., 19 476–78; 72 361–64 (upd.)
Velocity Express Corporation, 49 438–41; 94 441–46 (upd.)
Velux A/S, 86 412–15
Venator Group Inc., 35 444–49 (upd.) *see also* Foot Locker Inc.
Vencor, Inc., 16 515–17
Vendex International N.V., 13 544–46 *see also* Koninklijke Vendex KBB N.V. (Royal Vendex KBB N.V.).
Vendôme Luxury Group plc, 27 487–89
Venetian Casino Resort, LLC, 47 427–29
Ventana Medical Systems, Inc., 75 392–94
Ventura Foods LLC, 90 420–23
Venture Stores Inc., 12 507–09
VeraSun Energy Corporation, 87 447–450
Verbatim Corporation, 14 533–35; 74 371–74 (upd.)
Vereinigte Elektrizitätswerke Westfalen AG, IV V 744–47
Veridian Corporation, 54 395–97
VeriFone, Inc., 18 541–44; 76 368–71 (upd.)
Verint Systems Inc., 73 370–72
VeriSign, Inc., 47 430–34
Veritas Software Corporation, 45 427–31
Verity Inc., 68 388–91
Verizon Communications Inc., 43 443–49 (upd.); 78 432–40 (upd.)
Verlagsgruppe Georg von Holtzbrinck GmbH, 35 450–53
Verlagsgruppe Weltbild GmbH, 98 441–46
Vermeer Manufacturing Company, 17 507–10
The Vermont Country Store, 93 478–82
Vermont Pure Holdings, Ltd., 51 394–96
The Vermont Teddy Bear Co., Inc., 36 500–02
Versace *see* Gianni Versace SpA.
Vertex Pharmaceuticals Incorporated, 83 440–443
Vertis Communications, 84 418–421
Vertrue Inc., 77 469–72
Vestas Wind Systems A/S, 73 373–75
Vestey Group Ltd., 95 433–37
Veuve Clicquot Ponsardin SCS, 98 447–51
VEW AG, 39 412–15

VF Corporation, V 390–92; 17 511–14 (upd.); 54 398–404 (upd.)
VHA Inc., 53 345–47
Viacom Inc., 7 560–62; 23 500–03 (upd.); 67 367–71 (upd.) *see also* Paramount Pictures Corp.
Viad Corp., 73 376–78
Viag AG, IV 229–32 *see also* E.On AG.
ViaSat, Inc., 54 405–08
Viasoft Inc., 27 490–93; 59 27
VIASYS Healthcare, Inc., 52 389–91
Viasystems Group, Inc., 67 372–74
Viatech Continental Can Company, Inc., 25 512–15 (upd.)
Vicat S.A., 70 341–43
Vickers plc, 27 494–97
Vicon Industries, Inc., 44 440–42
VICORP Restaurants, Inc., 12 510–12; 48 412–15 (upd.)
Victor Company of Japan, Limited, II 118–19; 26 511–13 (upd.); 83 444–449 (upd.)
Victoria Coach Station Ltd. *see* London Regional Transport.
Victoria Group, III 399–401; 44 443–46 (upd.)
Victorinox AG, 21 515–17; 74 375–78 (upd.)
Vicunha Têxtil S.A., 78 441–44
Victory Refrigeration, Inc., 82 403–06
Videojet Technologies, Inc., 90 424–27
Vidrala S.A., 67 375–77
Viel & Cie, 76 372–74
Vienna Sausage Manufacturing Co., 14 536–37
Viessmann Werke GmbH & Co., 37 411–14
Viewpoint International, Inc., 66 354–56
ViewSonic Corporation, 72 365–67
Viking Office Products, Inc., 10 544–46 *see also* Office Depot, Inc.
Viking Range Corporation, 66 357–59
Viking Yacht Company, 96 446–49
Village Roadshow Ltd., 58 356–59
Village Super Market, Inc., 7 563–64
Village Voice Media, Inc., 38 476–79
Villeroy & Boch AG, 37 415–18
Vilmorin Clause et Cie, 70 344–46
AO VimpelCom, 48 416–19
Vin & Spirit AB, 31 458–61 *see also* V&S Vin & Sprit AB.
Viña Concha y Toro S.A., 45 432–34
Vinci, 27 54; 43 450–52; 49 44
Vincor International Inc., 50 518–21
Vinmonopolet A/S, 100 434–37
Vinson & Elkins L.L.P., 30 481–83
Vintage Petroleum, Inc., 42 421–23
Vinton Studios, 63 420–22
Vion Food Group NV, 85 438–41
Virbac Corporation, 74 379–81
Virco Manufacturing Corporation, 17 515–17
Virgin Group Ltd., 12 513–15; 32 491–96 (upd.); 89 479–86 (upd.)
Virginia Dare Extract Company, Inc., 94 447–50
Viridian Group plc, 64 402–04

Zoom Technologies, Inc., 18 569–71; 53
    379–82 (upd.)
Zoran Corporation, 77 489–92
The Zubair Corporation L.L.C., 96
    468–72

Zuffa L.L.C., 89 503–07
Zumiez, Inc., 77 493–96
Zumtobel AG, 50 544–48
Zurich Financial Services, III 410–12;
    42 448–53 (upd.); 93 502–10 (upd.)

Zygo Corporation, 42 454–57
Zytec Corporation, 19 513–15 *see also*
    Artesyn Technologies Inc.

Index to Industries

Aerospace

Offshore Logistics, Inc., 37
Pakistan International Airlines
 Corporation, 46
Pan American World Airways, Inc., I; 12
 (upd.)
Panalpina World Transport (Holding)
 Ltd., 47
People Express Airlines, Inc., I
Petroleum Helicopters, Inc., 35
PHI, Inc., 80 (upd.)
Philippine Airlines, Inc., 6; 23 (upd.)
Pinnacle Airlines Corp., 73
Preussag AG, 42 (upd.)
Qantas Airways Ltd., 6; 24 (upd.); 68
 (upd.)
Qatar Airways Company Q.C.S.C., 87
Reno Air Inc., 23
Royal Brunei Airlines Sdn Bhd, 99
Royal Nepal Airline Corporation, 41
Ryanair Holdings plc, 35
SAA (Pty) Ltd., 28
Sabena S.A./N.V., 33
The SAS Group, 34 (upd.)
Saudi Arabian Airlines, 6; 27 (upd.)
Scandinavian Airlines System, I
Singapore Airlines Limited, 6; 27 (upd.);
 83 (upd.)
SkyWest, Inc., 25
Société d'Exploitation AOM Air Liberté
 SA (AirLib), 53
Société Luxembourgeoise de Navigation
 Aérienne S.A., 64
Société Tunisienne de l'Air-Tunisair, 49
Southwest Airlines Co., 6; 24 (upd.); 71
 (upd.)
Spirit Airlines, Inc., 31
Sterling European Airlines A/S, 70
Sun Country Airlines, 30
Swiss Air Transport Company, Ltd., I
Swiss International Air Lines Ltd., 48
TAM Linhas Aéreas S.A., 68
TAME (Transportes Aéreos Militares
 Ecuatorianos), 100
TAP—Air Portugal Transportes Aéreos
 Portugueses S.A., 46
TAROM S.A., 64
Texas Air Corporation, I
Thai Airways International Public
 Company Limited, 6; 27 (upd.)
Tower Air, Inc., 28
Trans World Airlines, Inc., I; 12 (upd.);
 35 (upd.)
TransBrasil S/A Linhas Aéreas, 31
Transportes Aereos Portugueses, S.A., 6
Turkish Airlines Inc. (Türk Hava Yollari
 A.O.), 72
TV Guide, Inc., 43 (upd.)
UAL Corporation, 34 (upd.)
United Airlines, I; 6 (upd.)
US Airways Group, Inc., I; 6 (upd.); 28
 (upd.); 52 (upd.)
VARIG S.A. (Viação Aérea
 Rio-Grandense), 6; 29 (upd.)
Virgin Group Ltd., 12; 32 (upd.); 89
 (upd.)
Volga-Dnepr Group, 82
Vueling Airlines S.A., 97
WestJet Airlines Ltd., 38

Uzbekistan Airways National Air
 Company, 99

Automotive

AB Volvo, I; 7 (upd.); 26 (upd.); 67
 (upd.)
Accubuilt, Inc., 74
Adam Opel AG, 7; 21 (upd.); 61 (upd.)
ADESA, Inc., 71
Advance Auto Parts, Inc., 57
Aftermarket Technology Corp., 83
Aisin Seiki Co., Ltd., 48 (upd.)
Alamo Rent A Car, Inc., 6; 24 (upd.); 84
 (upd.)
Alfa Romeo, 13; 36 (upd.)
Alvis Plc, 47
America's Car-Mart, Inc., 64
American Motors Corporation, I
Amerigon Incorporated, 97
Applied Power Inc., 32 (upd.)
Arnold Clark Automobiles Ltd., 60
ArvinMeritor, Inc., 8; 54 (upd.)
Asbury Automotive Group Inc., 60
ASC, Inc., 55
Autobacs Seven Company Ltd., 76
Autocam Corporation, 51
Autoliv, Inc., 65
Automobiles Citroen, 7
Automobili Lamborghini Holding S.p.A.,
 13; 34 (upd.); 91 (upd.)
AutoNation, Inc., 50
AutoTrader.com, L.L.C., 91
AVTOVAZ Joint Stock Company, 65
Bajaj Auto Limited, 39
Bayerische Motoren Werke AG, I; 11
 (upd.); 38 (upd.)
Belron International Ltd., 76
Bendix Corporation, I
Blue Bird Corporation, 35
Bombardier Inc., 42 (upd.)
BorgWarner Inc., 14; 32 (upd.); 85 (upd.)
The Budd Company, 8
Bugatti Automobiles S.A.S., 94
Canadian Tire Corporation, Limited, 71
 (upd.)
CarMax, Inc., 55
CARQUEST Corporation, 29
Caterpillar Inc., 63 (upd.)
Checker Motors Corp., 89
China Automotive Systems Inc., 87
Chrysler Corporation, I; 11 (upd.)
Commercial Vehicle Group, Inc., 81
CNH Global N.V., 38 (upd.); 99 (upd.)
Consorcio G Grupo Dina, S.A. de C.V.,
 36
Crown Equipment Corporation, 15; 93
 (upd.)
CSK Auto Corporation, 38
Cummins Engine Company, Inc., I; 12
 (upd.); 40 (upd.)
Custom Chrome, Inc., 16
Daihatsu Motor Company, Ltd., 7; 21
 (upd.)
Daimler-Benz A.G., I; 15 (upd.)
DaimlerChrysler AG, 34 (upd.); 64 (upd.)
Dana Holding Corporation, I; 10 (upd.);
 99 (upd.)
Danaher Corporation, 77 (upd.)

Deere & Company, 42 (upd.)
Delphi Automotive Systems Corporation,
 45
D'Ieteren S.A./NV, 98
Directed Electronics, Inc., 87
Discount Tire Company Inc., 84
Don Massey Cadillac, Inc., 37
Donaldson Company, Inc., 49 (upd.)
Douglas & Lomason Company, 16
Dräxlmaier Group, 90
DriveTime Automotive Group Inc., 68
 (upd.)
Ducati Motor Holding SpA, 30; 86 (upd.)
Eaton Corporation, I; 10 (upd.); 67
 (upd.)
Echlin Inc., I; 11 (upd.)
Edelbrock Corporation, 37
Faurecia S.A., 70
Federal-Mogul Corporation, I; 10 (upd.);
 26 (upd.)
Ferrara Fire Apparatus, Inc., 84
Ferrari S.p.A., 13; 36 (upd.)
Fiat SpA, I; 11 (upd.); 50 (upd.)
FinishMaster, Inc., 24
Force Protection Inc., 95
Ford Motor Company, I; 11 (upd.); 36
 (upd.); 64 (upd.)
Ford Motor Company, S.A. de C.V., 20
Fruehauf Corporation, I
General Motors Corporation, I; 10 (upd.);
 36 (upd.); 64 (upd.)
Gentex Corporation, 26
Genuine Parts Company, 9; 45 (upd.)
GKN plc, III; 38 (upd.); 89 (upd.)
Group 1 Automotive, Inc., 52
Groupe Henri Heuliez S.A., 100
Grupo Ficosa International, 90
Guardian Industries Corp., 87
Harley-Davidson Inc., 7; 25 (upd.)
Hastings Manufacturing Company, 56
Hayes Lemmerz International, Inc., 27
Hendrick Motorsports, Inc., 89
The Hertz Corporation, 9; 33 (upd.); 101
 (upd.)
Hino Motors, Ltd., 7; 21 (upd.)
Holden Ltd., 62
Holley Performance Products Inc., 52
Hometown Auto Retailers, Inc., 44
Honda Motor Company Limited (Honda
 Giken Kogyo Kabushiki Kaisha), I; 10
 (upd.); 29 (upd.); 96 (upd.)
Hyundai Group, III; 7 (upd.); 56 (upd.)
Insurance Auto Auctions, Inc., 23
Isuzu Motors, Ltd., 9; 23 (upd.); 57
 (upd.)
INTERMET Corporation, 77 (upd.)
Jardine Cycle & Carriage Ltd., 73
Kawasaki Heavy Industries, Ltd., 63
 (upd.)
Kelsey-Hayes Group of Companies, 7; 27
 (upd.)
Key Safety Systems, Inc., 63
Kia Motors Corporation, 12; 29 (upd.)
Kolbenschmidt Pierburg AG, 97
Kwik-Fit Holdings plc, 54
Lazy Days RV Center, Inc., 69
Lear Corporation, 71 (upd.)
Lear Seating Corporation, 16

Beverages

Conglomerates

Containers

Drugs & Pharmaceuticals

Hauser, Inc., 46
Heska Corporation, 39
Hexal AG, 69
Hikma Pharmaceuticals Ltd., 102
Hospira, Inc., 71
Huntingdon Life Sciences Group plc, 42
ICN Pharmaceuticals, Inc., 52
Immucor, Inc., 81
Integrated BioPharma, Inc., 83
IVAX Corporation, 55 (upd.)
Janssen Pharmaceutica N.V., 80
Johnson & Johnson, III; 8 (upd.)
Jones Medical Industries, Inc., 24
The Judge Group, Inc., 51
King Pharmaceuticals, Inc., 54
Kinray Inc., 85
Kos Pharmaceuticals, Inc., 63
Kyowa Hakko Kogyo Co., Ltd., 48 (upd.)
Laboratoires Arkopharma S.A., 75
Laboratoires Pierre Fabre S.A., 100
Leiner Health Products Inc., 34
Ligand Pharmaceuticals Incorporated, 47
MannKind Corporation, 87
Marion Merrell Dow, Inc., I; 9 (upd.)
Matrixx Initiatives, Inc., 74
McKesson Corporation, 12; 47 (upd.)
Medicis Pharmaceutical Corporation, 59
MedImmune, Inc., 35
Merck & Co., Inc., I; 11 (upd.); 34
    (upd.); 95 (upd.)
Merial Ltd., 102
Merz Group, 81
Miles Laboratories, I
Millennium Pharmaceuticals, Inc., 47
Monsanto Company, 29 (upd.), 77 (upd.)
Moore Medical Corp., 17
Murdock Madaus Schwabe, 26
Mylan Laboratories Inc., I; 20 (upd.); 59
    (upd.)
Myriad Genetics, Inc., 95
Nadro S.A. de C.V., 86
Nastech Pharmaceutical Company Inc., 79
National Patent Development
    Corporation, 13
Natrol, Inc., 49
Natural Alternatives International, Inc., 49
Nektar Therapeutics, 91
Novartis AG, 39 (upd.)
Noven Pharmaceuticals, Inc., 55
Novo Nordisk A/S, I; 61 (upd.)
Obagi Medical Products, Inc., 95
Omnicare, Inc., 49
Omrix Biopharmaceuticals, Inc., 95
Par Pharmaceutical Companies, Inc., 65
PDL BioPharma, Inc., 90
Perrigo Company, 59 (upd.)
Pfizer Inc., I; 9 (upd.); 38 (upd.); 79
    (upd.)
Pharmacia & Upjohn Inc., I; 25 (upd.)
Pharmion Corporation, 91
PLIVA d.d., 70
PolyMedica Corporation, 77
POZEN Inc., 81
QLT Inc., 71
The Quigley Corporation, 62
Quintiles Transnational Corporation, 21
R.P. Scherer, I
Ranbaxy Laboratories Ltd., 70

ratiopharm Group, 84
Reckitt Benckiser plc, II; 42 (upd.); 91
    (upd.)
Roberts Pharmaceutical Corporation, 16
Roche Bioscience, 14 (upd.)
Rorer Group, I
Roussel Uclaf, I; 8 (upd.)
Salix Pharmaceuticals, Ltd., 93
Sandoz Ltd., I
Sankyo Company, Ltd., I; 56 (upd.)
The Sanofi-Synthélabo Group, I; 49
    (upd.)
Schering AG, I; 50 (upd.)
Schering-Plough Corporation, I; 14
    (upd.); 49 (upd.); 99 (upd.)
Sepracor Inc., 45
Serono S.A., 47
Shionogi & Co., Ltd., III; 17 (upd.); 98
    (upd.)
Sigma-Aldrich Corporation, I; 36 (upd.);
    93 (upd.)
SmithKline Beecham plc, I; 32 (upd.)
Solvay S.A., 61 (upd.)
Squibb Corporation, I
Sterling Drug, Inc., I
Stiefel Laboratories, Inc., 90
Sun Pharmaceutical Industries Ltd., 57
The Sunrider Corporation, 26
Syntex Corporation, I
Takeda Chemical Industries, Ltd., I
Taro Pharmaceutical Industries Ltd., 65
Teva Pharmaceutical Industries Ltd., 22;
    54 (upd.)
UCB Pharma SA, 98
The Upjohn Company, I; 8 (upd.)
Vertex Pharmaceuticals Incorporated, 83
Virbac Corporation, 74
Vitalink Pharmacy Services, Inc., 15
Warner Chilcott Limited, 85
Warner-Lambert Co., I; 10 (upd.)
Watson Pharmaceuticals Inc., 16; 56
    (upd.)
The Wellcome Foundation Ltd., I
Zentiva N.V./Zentiva, a.s., 99
Zila, Inc., 46

Electrical & Electronics

ABB ASEA Brown Boveri Ltd., II; 22
    (upd.)
ABB Ltd., 65 (upd.)
Acer Incorporated, 16; 73 (upd.)
Acuson Corporation, 10; 36 (upd.)
ADC Telecommunications, Inc., 30 (upd.)
Adtran Inc., 22
Advanced Micro Devices, Inc., 6; 30
    (upd.); 99 (upd.)
Advanced Technology Laboratories, Inc., 9
Agere Systems Inc., 61
Agilent Technologies Inc., 38; 93 (upd.)
Agilysys Inc., 76 (upd.)
Aiwa Co., Ltd., 30
AKG Acoustics GmbH, 62
Akzo Nobel N.V., 13; 41 (upd.)
Alienware Corporation, 81
Alliant Techsystems Inc., 30 (upd.); 77
    (upd.)
AlliedSignal Inc., 22 (upd.)
Alpine Electronics, Inc., 13

Alps Electric Co., Ltd., II
Altera Corporation, 18; 43 (upd.)
Altron Incorporated, 20
Amdahl Corporation, 40 (upd.)
American Power Conversion Corporation,
    24; 67 (upd.)
American Superconductor Corporation,
    97
American Technical Ceramics Corp., 67
Amerigon Incorporated, 97
Amkor Technology, Inc., 69
AMP Incorporated, II; 14 (upd.)
Amphenol Corporation, 40
Amstrad plc, 48 (upd.)
Analog Devices, Inc., 10
Analogic Corporation, 23
Anam Group, 23
Anaren Microwave, Inc., 33
Andrew Corporation, 10; 32 (upd.)
Anixter International, Inc., 88
Anritsu Corporation, 68
Apex Digital, Inc., 63
Apple Computer, Inc., 36 (upd.); 77
    (upd.)
Applied Power Inc., 32 (upd.)
Applied Signal Technology, Inc., 87
Argon ST, Inc., 81
Arotech Corporation, 93
ARRIS Group, Inc., 89
Arrow Electronics, Inc., 10; 50 (upd.)
Ascend Communications, Inc., 24
Astronics Corporation, 35
Atari Corporation, 9; 23 (upd.); 66 (upd.)
ATI Technologies Inc., 79
Atmel Corporation, 17
ATMI, Inc., 93
AU Optronics Corporation, 67
Audiovox Corporation, 34; 90 (upd.)
Ault Incorporated, 34
Autodesk, Inc., 10; 89 (upd.)
Avnet, Inc., 9
AVX Corporation, 67
Axcelis Technologies, Inc., 95
Axsys Technologies, Inc., 93
Ballard Power Systems Inc., 73
Bang & Olufsen Holding A/S, 37; 86
    (upd.)
Barco NV, 44
Bell Microproducts Inc., 69
Benchmark Electronics, Inc., 40
Bicoastal Corporation, II
Black Box Corporation, 20; 96 (upd.)
Blonder Tongue Laboratories, Inc., 48
Blue Coat Systems, Inc., 83
BMC Industries, Inc., 59 (upd.)
Bogen Communications International,
    Inc., 62
Bose Corporation, 13; 36 (upd.)
Boston Acoustics, Inc., 22
Bowthorpe plc, 33
Braun GmbH, 51
Broadcom Corporation, 34; 90 (upd.)
Bull S.A., 43 (upd.)
Burr-Brown Corporation, 19
BVR Systems (1998) Ltd., 93
C-COR.net Corp., 38
Cabletron Systems, Inc., 10
Cadence Design Systems, Inc., 48 (upd.)

Medis Technologies Ltd., 77
Merix Corporation, 36; 75 (upd.)
Methode Electronics, Inc., 13
Midway Games, Inc., 25; 102 (upd.)
Mitel Corporation, 18
MITRE Corporation, 26
Mitsubishi Electric Corporation, II; 44 (upd.)
Molex Incorporated, 54 (upd.)
Monster Cable Products, Inc., 69
Motorola, Inc., II; 11 (upd.); 34 (upd.); 93 (upd.)
N.F. Smith & Associates LP, 70
Nam Tai Electronics, Inc., 61
National Instruments Corporation, 22
National Presto Industries, Inc., 16; 43 (upd.)
National Semiconductor Corporation, II; 26 (upd.); 69 (upd.)
NEC Corporation, II; 21 (upd.); 57 (upd.)
Network Equipment Technologies Inc., 92
Nexans SA, 54
Nintendo Co., Ltd., 28 (upd.)
Nokia Corporation, II; 17 (upd.); 38 (upd.); 77 (upd.)
Nortel Networks Corporation, 36 (upd.)
Northrop Grumman Corporation, 45 (upd.)
Oak Technology, Inc., 22
Océ N.V., 24; 91 (upd.)
Oki Electric Industry Company, Limited, II
Omnicell, Inc., 89
Omron Corporation, II; 28 (upd.)
OPTEK Technology Inc., 98
Orbotech Ltd., 75
Otari Inc., 89
Otter Tail Power Company, 18
Palm, Inc., 36; 75 (upd.)
Palomar Medical Technologies, Inc., 22
Parlex Corporation, 61
The Peak Technologies Group, Inc., 14
Peavey Electronics Corporation, 16
Philips Electronics N.V., II; 13 (upd.)
Philips Electronics North America Corp., 13
Pioneer Electronic Corporation, 28 (upd.)
Pioneer-Standard Electronics Inc., 19
Pitney Bowes Inc., 47 (upd.)
Pittway Corporation, 9
Pixelworks, Inc., 69
Planar Systems, Inc., 61
The Plessey Company, PLC, II
Plexus Corporation, 35; 80 (upd.)
Polk Audio, Inc., 34
Polaroid Corporation, III; 7 (upd.); 28 (upd.); 93 (upd.)
Potter & Brumfield Inc., 11
Premier Industrial Corporation, 9
Protection One, Inc., 32
Quanta Computer Inc., 47; 79 (upd.)
Racal Electronics PLC, II
RadioShack Corporation, 36 (upd.); 101 (upd.)
Radius Inc., 16
RAE Systems Inc., 83
Ramtron International Corporation, 89

Raychem Corporation, 8
Rayovac Corporation, 13
Raytheon Company, II; 11 (upd.); 38 (upd.)
RCA Corporation, II
Read-Rite Corp., 10
Redback Networks, Inc., 92
Reliance Electric Company, 9
Research in Motion Ltd., 54
Rexel, Inc., 15
Richardson Electronics, Ltd., 17
Ricoh Company, Ltd., 36 (upd.)
Rimage Corp., 89
The Rival Company, 19
Rockford Corporation, 43
Rogers Corporation, 61
S&C Electric Company, 15
SAGEM S.A., 37
St. Louis Music, Inc., 48
Sam Ash Music Corporation, 30
Samsung Electronics Co., Ltd., 14; 41 (upd.)
SANYO Electric Co., Ltd., II; 36 (upd.); 95 (upd.)
Sarnoff Corporation, 57
ScanSource, Inc., 29; 74 (upd.)
Schneider S.A., II; 18 (upd.)
SCI Systems, Inc., 9
Scientific-Atlanta, Inc., 45 (upd.)
Scitex Corporation Ltd., 24
Seagate Technology, Inc., 34 (upd.)
SEGA Corporation, 73
Semitool, Inc., 79 (upd.)
Semtech Corporation, 32
Sennheiser Electronic GmbH & Co. KG, 66
Sensormatic Electronics Corp., 11
Sensory Science Corporation, 37
SGI, 29 (upd.)
Sharp Corporation, II; 12 (upd.); 40 (upd.)
Sheldahl Inc., 23
Shure Inc., 60
Siemens AG, II; 14 (upd.); 57 (upd.)
Silicon Graphics Incorporated, 9
Siltronic AG, 90
SL Industries, Inc., 77
SMART Modular Technologies, Inc., 86
Smiths Industries PLC, 25
Solectron Corporation, 12; 48 (upd.)
Sony Corporation, II; 12 (upd.); 40 (upd.)
Spansion Inc., 80
Spectrum Control, Inc., 67
SPX Corporation, 47 (upd.)
Square D, 90
Sterling Electronics Corp., 18
STMicroelectronics NV, 52
Strix Ltd., 51
Stuart C. Irby Company, 58
Sumitomo Electric Industries, Ltd., II
Sun Microsystems, Inc., 7; 30 (upd.); 91 (upd.)
Sunbeam-Oster Co., Inc., 9
SunPower Corporation, 91
Suntech Power Holdings Company Ltd., 89
Synaptics Incorporated, 95

Syneron Medical Ltd., 91
SYNNEX Corporation, 73
Synopsys, Inc., 11; 69 (upd.)
Syntax-Brillian Corporation, 102
Sypris Solutions, Inc., 85
SyQuest Technology, Inc., 18
Tandy Corporation, II; 12 (upd.)
Tatung Co., 23
TDK Corporation, II; 17 (upd.); 49 (upd.)
TEAC Corporation 78
Tech-Sym Corporation, 18
Technitrol, Inc., 29
Tektronix, Inc., 8
Teledyne Technologies Inc., 62 (upd.)
Telxon Corporation, 10
Teradyne, Inc., 11; 98 (upd.)
Texas Instruments Inc., II; 11 (upd.); 46 (upd.)
Thales S.A., 42
Thomas & Betts Corporation, 11; 54 (upd.)
THOMSON multimedia S.A., II; 42 (upd.)
THQ, Inc., 92 (upd.)
The Titan Corporation, 36
TomTom N.V., 81
Tops Appliance City, Inc., 17
Toromont Industries, Ltd., 21
Trans-Lux Corporation, 51
Trimble Navigation Limited, 40
TriQuint Semiconductor, Inc., 63
Tweeter Home Entertainment Group, Inc., 30
Ultimate Electronics, Inc., 69 (upd.)
Ultrak Inc., 24
Uniden Corporation, 98
United Microelectronics Corporation, 98
Universal Electronics Inc., 39
Universal Security Instruments, Inc., 96
Varian Associates Inc., 12
Veeco Instruments Inc., 32
VIASYS Healthcare, Inc., 52
Viasystems Group, Inc., 67
Vicon Industries, Inc., 44
Victor Company of Japan, Limited, II; 26 (upd.); 83 (upd.)
Vishay Intertechnology, Inc., 21; 80 (upd.)
Vitesse Semiconductor Corporation, 32
Vitro Corp., 10
Vizio, Inc., 100
VLSI Technology, Inc., 16
VTech Holdings Ltd., 77
Wells-Gardner Electronics Corporation, 43
Westinghouse Electric Corporation, II; 12 (upd.)
Winbond Electronics Corporation, 74
Wincor Nixdorf Holding GmbH, 69 (upd.)
Wyle Electronics, 14
Xantrex Technology Inc., 97
Xerox Corporation, III; 6 (upd.); 26 (upd.); 69 (upd.)
Yageo Corporation, 16; 98 (upd.)
York Research Corporation, 35
Zenith Data Systems, Inc., 10

Engineering & Management Services

Entertainment & Leisure

Financial Services: Banks

Financial Services: Excluding Banks

Food Products

Food Services & Retailers

Shoney's, Inc., 7; 23 (upd.)
ShowBiz Pizza Time, Inc., 13
Skyline Chili, Inc., 62
Smart & Final, Inc., 16
Smith's Food & Drug Centers, Inc., 8; 57 (upd.)
Sobeys Inc., 80
Sodexho SA, 29; 91 (upd.)
Somerfield plc, 47 (upd.)
Sonic Corporation, 14; 37 (upd.)
Souper Salad, Inc., 98
Southeast Frozen Foods Company, L.P., 99
The Southland Corporation, II; 7 (upd.)
Spaghetti Warehouse, Inc., 25
SPAR Handels AG, 35
Spartan Stores Inc., 8
Starbucks Corporation, 13; 34 (upd.); 77 (upd.)
Stater Bros. Holdings Inc., 64
The Steak n Shake Company, 41; 96 (upd.)
Steinberg Incorporated, II
Stew Leonard's, 56
The Stop & Shop Supermarket Company, II; 68 (upd.)
Subway, 32
Super Food Services, Inc., 15
Supermarkets General Holdings Corporation, II
Supervalu Inc., II; 18 (upd.); 50 (upd.)
SWH Corporation, 70
SYSCO Corporation, II; 24 (upd.); 75 (upd.)
Taco Bell Corporation, 7; 21 (upd.); 74 (upd.)
Taco Cabana, Inc., 23; 72 (upd.)
Taco John's International, Inc., 15; 63 (upd.)
TCBY Systems LLC, 17; 98 (upd.)
Tchibo GmbH, 82
TelePizza S.A., 33
Tesco PLC, II
Texas Roadhouse, Inc., 69
Thomas & Howard Company, Inc., 90
Timber Lodge Steakhouse, Inc., 73
Tops Markets LLC, 60
Total Entertainment Restaurant Corporation, 46
Toupargel-Agrigel S.A., 76
Trader Joe's Company, 13; 50 (upd.)
Travel Ports of America, Inc., 17
Tree of Life, Inc., 29
Triarc Companies, Inc., 34 (upd.)
Tubby's, Inc., 53
Tully's Coffee Corporation, 51
Tumbleweed, Inc., 33; 80 (upd.)
TW Services, Inc., II
Ukrop's Super Markets Inc., 39; 101 (upd.)
Unified Grocers, Inc., 93
Unique Casual Restaurants, Inc., 27
United Dairy Farmers, Inc., 74
United Natural Foods, Inc., 32; 76 (upd.)
Uno Restaurant Holdings Corporation, 18; 70 (upd.)
Uwajimaya, Inc., 60
Vail Resorts, Inc., 43 (upd.)

Valora Holding AG, 98
VICORP Restaurants, Inc., 12; 48 (upd.)
Victory Refrigeration, Inc., 82
Village Super Market, Inc., 7
The Vons Companies, Incorporated, 7; 28 (upd.)
W. H. Braum, Inc., 80
Waffle House Inc., 14; 60 (upd.)
Wahoo's Fish Taco, 96
Wakefern Food Corporation, 33
Waldbaum, Inc., 19
Wall Street Deli, Inc., 33
Wawa Inc., 17; 78 (upd.)
Wegmans Food Markets, Inc., 9; 41 (upd.)
Weis Markets, Inc., 15
Wendy's International, Inc., 8; 23 (upd.); 47 (upd.)
The WesterN SizzliN Corporation, 60
Wetterau Incorporated, II
Whitbread PLC, I; 20 (upd.); 52 (upd.); 97 (upd.)
White Castle Management Company, 12; 36 (upd.); 85 (upd.)
White Rose, Inc., 24
Whittard of Chelsea Plc, 61
Whole Foods Market, Inc., 50 (upd.)
Wild Oats Markets, Inc., 19; 41 (upd.)
Willow Run Foods, Inc., 100
Winchell's Donut Houses Operating Company, L.P., 60
WinCo Foods Inc., 60
Winn-Dixie Stores, Inc., II; 21 (upd.); 59 (upd.)
Wm. Morrison Supermarkets PLC, 38
Wolfgang Puck Worldwide, Inc., 26; 70 (upd.)
Worldwide Restaurant Concepts, Inc., 47
Yoshinoya D & C Company Ltd., 88
Young & Co.'s Brewery, P.L.C., 38
Yucaipa Cos., 17
Yum! Brands Inc., 58
Zingerman's Community of Businesses, 68

Health & Personal Care Products

Abaxis, Inc., 83
Abbott Laboratories, I; 11 (upd.); 40 (upd.); 93 (upd.)
Accuray Incorporated, 95
Advanced Medical Optics, Inc., 79
Advanced Neuromodulation Systems, Inc., 73
Akorn, Inc., 32
ALARIS Medical Systems, Inc., 65
Alberto-Culver Company, 8; 36 (upd.); 91 (upd.)
Alco Health Services Corporation, III
Alès Groupe, 81
Allergan, Inc., 10; 30 (upd.); 77 (upd.)
American Oriental Bioengineering Inc., 93
American Safety Razor Company, 20
American Stores Company, 22 (upd.)
Amway Corporation, III; 13 (upd.)
AngioDynamics, Inc., 81
ArthroCare Corporation, 73
Artsana SpA, 92

Ascendia Brands, Inc., 97
Atkins Nutritionals, Inc., 58
Aveda Corporation, 24
Avon Products, Inc., III; 19 (upd.); 46 (upd.)
Bally Total Fitness Holding Corp., 25
Bare Escentuals, Inc., 91
Bausch & Lomb Inc., 7; 25 (upd.); 96 (upd.)
Baxter International Inc., I; 10 (upd.)
BeautiControl Cosmetics, Inc., 21
Becton, Dickinson and Company, I; 11 (upd.); 36 (upd.); 101 (upd.)
Beiersdorf AG, 29
Big B, Inc., 17
Bindley Western Industries, Inc., 9
Biolase Technology, Inc., 87
Biomet, Inc., 10; 93 (upd.)
BioScrip Inc., 98
Biosite Incorporated, 73
Block Drug Company, Inc., 8; 27 (upd.)
The Body Shop International plc, 53 (upd.)
Boiron S.A., 73
Bolton Group B.V., 86
The Boots Company PLC, 24 (upd.)
Boston Scientific Corporation, 77 (upd.)
Bristol-Myers Squibb Company, III; 9 (upd.)
Bronner Brothers Inc., 92
C.R. Bard Inc., 9
Candela Corporation, 48
Cantel Medical Corporation, 80
Cardinal Health, Inc., 18; 50 (upd.)
Carl Zeiss AG, III; 34 (upd.); 91 (upd.)
Carson, Inc., 31
Carter-Wallace, Inc., 8
Caswell-Massey Co. Ltd., 51
CCA Industries, Inc., 53
Chattem, Inc., 17; 88 (upd.)
Chesebrough-Pond's USA, Inc., 8
Chindex International, Inc., 101
Chronimed, Inc., 26
Church & Dwight Co., Inc., 68 (upd.)
Cintas Corporation, 51 (upd.)
The Clorox Company, III; 22 (upd.); 81 (upd.)
CNS, Inc., 20
Colgate-Palmolive Company, III; 14 (upd.); 35 (upd.)
Combe Inc., 72
Conair Corp., 17
CONMED Corporation, 87
Connetics Corporation, 70
Cordis Corp., 19
Cosmair, Inc., 8
Cosmolab Inc., 96
Coty, Inc., 36
Covidien Ltd., 91
Cybex International, Inc., 49
Cytyc Corporation, 69
Dade Behring Holdings Inc., 71
Dalli-Werke GmbH & Co. KG, 86
Datascope Corporation, 39
Del Laboratories, Inc., 28
Deltec, Inc., 56
Dentsply International Inc., 10
DEP Corporation, 20

Health Care Services

Hotels

Information Technology

586

VASCO Data Security International, Inc., 79
Verbatim Corporation, 14
Veridian Corporation, 54
VeriFone Holdings, Inc., 18; 76 (upd.)
Verint Systems Inc., 73
VeriSign, Inc., 47
Veritas Software Corporation, 45
Verity Inc., 68
Viasoft Inc., 27
Vital Images, Inc., 85
VMware, Inc., 90
Volt Information Sciences Inc., 26
Wanadoo S.A., 75
Wang Laboratories, Inc., III; 6 (upd.)
Weather Central Inc., 100
WebMD Corporation, 65
WebEx Communications, Inc., 81
West Group, 34 (upd.)
Westcon Group, Inc., 67
Western Digital Corporation, 25; 92 (upd.)
Wikimedia Foundation, Inc., 91
Wind River Systems, Inc., 37
Wipro Limited, 43
Witness Systems, Inc., 87
Wolters Kluwer NV, 33 (upd.)
WordPerfect Corporation, 10
WSI Corporation, 102
Wyse Technology, Inc., 15
Xerox Corporation, III; 6 (upd.); 26 (upd.); 69 (upd.)
Xilinx, Inc., 16; 82 (upd.)
Yahoo! Inc., 27; 70 (upd.)
YouTube, Inc., 90
Zanett, Inc., 92
Zapata Corporation, 25
Ziff Davis Media Inc., 36 (upd.)
Zilog, Inc., 15

Insurance

AEGON N.V., III; 50 (upd.)
Aetna Inc., III; 21 (upd.); 63 (upd.)
AFLAC Incorporated, 10 (upd.); 38 (upd.)
Alexander & Alexander Services Inc., 10
Alfa Corporation, 60
Alleanza Assicurazioni S.p.A., 65
Alleghany Corporation, 10
Allianz AG, III; 15 (upd.); 57 (upd.)
Allmerica Financial Corporation, 63
The Allstate Corporation, 10; 27 (upd.)
AMB Generali Holding AG, 51
American Family Corporation, III
American Financial Group Inc., III; 48 (upd.)
American General Corporation, III; 10 (upd.); 46 (upd.)
American International Group, Inc., III; 15 (upd.); 47 (upd.)
American National Insurance Company, 8; 27 (upd.)
American Premier Underwriters, Inc., 10
American Re Corporation, 10; 35 (upd.)
N.V. AMEV, III
AOK-Bundesverband (Federation of the AOK) 78
Aon Corporation, III; 45 (upd.)

Arthur J. Gallagher & Co., 73
Assicurazioni Generali SpA, III; 15 (upd.)
Assurances Générales de France, 63
Assured Guaranty Ltd., 93
Atlantic American Corporation, 44
Aviva PLC, 50 (upd.)
Axa, III
AXA Colonia Konzern AG, 27; 49 (upd.)
B.A.T. Industries PLC, 22 (upd.)
Baldwin & Lyons, Inc., 51
Bâloise-Holding, 40
Benfield Greig Group plc, 53
Berkshire Hathaway Inc., III; 18 (upd.); 42 (upd.); 89 (upd.)
Blue Cross and Blue Shield Association, 10
British United Provident Association Limited (BUPAL), 79
Brown & Brown, Inc., 41
Business Men's Assurance Company of America, 14
Capital Holding Corporation, III
Catholic Order of Foresters, 24; 97 (upd.)
China Life Insurance Company Limited, 65
ChoicePoint Inc., 65
The Chubb Corporation, III; 14 (upd.); 37 (upd.)
CIGNA Corporation, III; 22 (upd.); 45 (upd.)
Cincinnati Financial Corporation, 16; 44 (upd.)
CNA Financial Corporation, III; 38 (upd.)
Commercial Union PLC, III
Connecticut Mutual Life Insurance Company, III
Conseco Inc., 10; 33 (upd.)
The Continental Corporation, III
Crawford & Company, 87
Debeka Krankenversicherungsverein auf Gegenseitigkeit, 72
The Doctors' Company, 55
Empire Blue Cross and Blue Shield, III
Enbridge Inc., 43
Endurance Specialty Holdings Ltd., 85
Engle Homes, Inc., 46
The Equitable Life Assurance Society of the United States Fireman's Fund Insurance Company, III
ERGO Versicherungsgruppe AG, 44
Erie Indemnity Company, 35
Fairfax Financial Holdings Limited, 57
Farm Family Holdings, Inc., 39
Farmers Insurance Group of Companies, 25
Federal Deposit Insurance Corporation, 93
Fidelity National Financial Inc., 54
The First American Corporation, 52
First Executive Corporation, III
Foundation Health Corporation, 12
Gainsco, Inc., 22
GEICO Corporation, 10; 40 (upd.)
General Accident PLC, III
General Re Corporation, III; 24 (upd.)
Gerling-Konzern Versicherungs-Beteiligungs-Aktiengesellschaft, 51

GraceKennedy Ltd., 92
Great-West Lifeco Inc., III
Groupama S.A., 76
Gryphon Holdings, Inc., 21
Guardian Financial Services, 64 (upd.)
Guardian Royal Exchange Plc, 11
Harleysville Group Inc., 37
HDI (Haftpflichtverband der Deutschen Industrie Versicherung auf Gegenseitigkeit V.a.G.), 53
HealthExtras, Inc., 75
HealthMarkets, Inc., 88 (upd.)
Hilb, Rogal & Hobbs Company, 77
The Home Insurance Company, III
Horace Mann Educators Corporation, 22; 90 (upd.)
Household International, Inc., 21 (upd.)
Hub International Limited, 89
HUK-Coburg, 58
Humana Inc., III; 24 (upd.); 101 (upd.)
Irish Life & Permanent Plc, 59
Jackson National Life Insurance Company, 8
Jefferson-Pilot Corporation, 11; 29 (upd.)
John Hancock Financial Services, Inc., III; 42 (upd.)
Johnson & Higgins, 14
Kaiser Foundation Health Plan, Inc., 53
Kemper Corporation, III; 15 (upd.)
LandAmerica Financial Group, Inc., 85
Legal & General Group Plc, III; 24 (upd.); 101 (upd.)
The Liberty Corporation, 22
Liberty Mutual Holding Company, 59
LifeWise Health Plan of Oregon, Inc., 90
Lincoln National Corporation, III; 25 (upd.)
Lloyd's, 74 (upd.)
Lloyd's of London, III; 22 (upd.)
The Loewen Group Inc., 40 (upd.)
Lutheran Brotherhood, 31
Manulife Financial Corporation, 85
Marsh & McLennan Companies, Inc., III; 45 (upd.)
Massachusetts Mutual Life Insurance Company, III; 53 (upd.)
MBIA Inc., 73
The Meiji Mutual Life Insurance Company, III
Mercury General Corporation, 25
Metropolitan Life Insurance Company, III; 52 (upd.)
MGIC Investment Corp., 52
The Midland Company, 65
Millea Holdings Inc., 64 (upd.)
Mitsui Marine and Fire Insurance Company, Limited, III
Mitsui Mutual Life Insurance Company, III; 39 (upd.)
Modern Woodmen of America, 66
Munich Re (Münchener Rückversicherungs-Gesellschaft Aktiengesellschaft in München), III; 46 (upd.)
The Mutual Benefit Life Insurance Company, III
The Mutual Life Insurance Company of New York, III

Legal Services

Manufacturing

Panavision Inc., 24
Park Corp., 22
Park-Ohio Holdings Corp., 17; 85 (upd.)
Parker-Hannifin Corporation, III; 24
   (upd.); 99 (upd.)
Parlex Corporation, 61
Patrick Industries, Inc., 30
Paul Mueller Company, 65
Pearl Corporation 78
Pechiney SA, IV; 45 (upd.)
Peg Perego SpA, 88
Pelican Products, Inc., 86
Pelikan Holding AG, 92
Pella Corporation, 12; 39 (upd.); 89
   (upd.)
Penn Engineering & Manufacturing
   Corp., 28
Pennington Seed Inc., 98
Pentair, Inc., 7; 26 (upd.); 81 (upd.)
Pentax Corporation 78
Pentech International, Inc., 29
PerkinElmer Inc. 7; 78 (upd.)
Peterson American Corporation, 55
Phillips-Van Heusen Corporation, 24
Phoenix AG, 68
Phoenix Mecano AG, 61
Photo-Me International Plc, 83
Physio-Control International Corp., 18
Picanol N.V., 96
Pilkington Group Limited, III; 34 (upd.);
   87 (upd.)
Pilot Pen Corporation of America, 82
Pinguely-Haulotte SA, 51
Pioneer Electronic Corporation, III
Pirelli & C. S.p.A., 75 (upd.)
Piscines Desjoyaux S.A., 84
Pitney Bowes, Inc., 19
Pittway Corporation, 33 (upd.)
Planar Systems, Inc., 61
PlayCore, Inc., 27
Playmates Toys, 23
Playskool, Inc., 25
Pleasant Company, 27
Pliant Corporation, 98
Ply Gem Industries Inc., 12
Pochet SA, 55
Polaris Industries Inc., 12; 35 (upd.); 77
   (upd.)
Polaroid Corporation, III; 7 (upd.); 28
   (upd.); 93 (upd.)
The Porcelain and Fine China Companies
   Ltd., 69
Portmeirion Group plc, 88
Pou Chen Corporation, 81
PPG Industries, Inc., III; 22 (upd.); 81
   (upd.)
Prada Holding B.V., 45
Pranda Jewelry plc, 70
Praxair, Inc., 48 (upd.)
Precision Castparts Corp., 15
Premark International, Inc., III
Pressman Toy Corporation, 56
Presstek, Inc., 33
Price Pfister, Inc., 70
Prince Sports Group, Inc., 15
Printpack, Inc., 68
Printronix, Inc., 18
Puig Beauty and Fashion Group S.L., 60

Pulaski Furniture Corporation, 33; 80
   (upd.)
Pumpkin Masters, Inc., 48
Punch International N.V., 66
Pure World, Inc., 72
Puritan-Bennett Corporation, 13
Purolator Products Company, 21; 74
   (upd.)
PVC Container Corporation, 67
PW Eagle, Inc., 48
Q.E.P. Co., Inc., 65
QRS Music Technologies, Inc., 95
QSC Audio Products, Inc., 56
Quixote Corporation, 15 '
R. Griggs Group Limited, 23
Racing Champions Corporation, 37
Radio Flyer Inc., 34
Rain Bird Corporation, 84
Raleigh UK Ltd., 65
Rapala-Normark Group, Ltd., 30
RathGibson Inc., 90
Raven Industries, Inc., 33
Raychem Corporation, 8
Rayovac Corporation, 39 (upd.)
Raytech Corporation, 61
Recovery Engineering, Inc., 25
Red Spot Paint & Varnish Company, 55
Red Wing Pottery Sales, Inc., 52
Red Wing Shoe Company, Inc., 9; 30
   (upd.); 83 (upd.)
Reed & Barton Corporation, 67
Regal-Beloit Corporation, 18; 97 (upd.)
Reichhold Chemicals, Inc., 10
Remington Arms Company, Inc., 12; 40
   (upd.)
Remington Products Company, L.L.C., 42
RENK AG, 37
Renner Herrmann S.A., 79
REpower Systems AG, 101
Revell-Monogram Inc., 16
Revere Ware Corporation, 22
Revlon Inc., 64 (upd.)
Rexam PLC, 32 (upd.); 85 (upd.)
Rexnord Corporation, 21; 76 (upd.)
RF Micro Devices, Inc., 43
Rheinmetall AG, 9; 97 (upd.)
RHI AG, 53
Richardson Industries, Inc., 62
Rickenbacker International Corp., 91
Riddell Sports Inc., 22
Riedel Tiroler Glashuette GmbH, 99
Rieter Holding AG, 42
River Oaks Furniture, Inc., 43
Riviera Tool Company, 89
RMC Group p.l.c., 34 (upd.)
Roadmaster Industries, Inc., 16
Robbins & Myers Inc., 15
Robertson-Ceco Corporation, 19
Rock-Tenn Company, 59 (upd.)
Rockford Products Corporation, 55
RockShox, Inc., 26
Rockwell Automation, I; 11 (upd.); 43
   (upd.)
Rockwell Medical Technologies, Inc., 88
Rodda Paint Company, 98
Rodriguez Group S.A., 90
ROFIN-SINAR Technologies Inc., 81
Rogers Corporation, 61

Rohde & Schwarz GmbH & Co. KG, 39
Rohm and Haas Company, 77 (upd.)
ROHN Industries, Inc., 22
Rohr Incorporated, 9
Roland Corporation, 38
Rollerblade, Inc., 15; 34 (upd.)
Rolls-Royce Group PLC, 67 (upd.)
Ronson PLC, 49
Roper Industries, Inc., 15; 50 (upd.)
Rose Art Industries, 58
Roseburg Forest Products Company, 58
Rotork plc, 46
Royal Appliance Manufacturing Company,
   15
Royal Canin S.A., 39
Royal Doulton plc, 14; 38 (upd.)
Royal Group Technologies Limited, 73
RPC Group PLC, 81
RPM International Inc., 8; 36 (upd.); 91
   (upd.)
RTI Biologics, Inc., 96
Rubbermaid Incorporated, III
Russ Berrie and Company, Inc., 12; 82
   (upd.)
Rusty, Inc., 95
S.C. Johnson & Son, Inc., III; 28 (upd.);
   89 (upd.)
Sabaté Diosos SA, 48
Safe Flight Instrument Corporation, 71
Safeskin Corporation, 18
Safety Components International, Inc., 63
Safilo SpA, 54
SAFRAN, 102 (upd.)
St. Jude Medical, Inc., 11; 43 (upd.); 97
   (upd.)
Salant Corporation, 12; 51 (upd.)
Salton, Inc., 30; 88 (upd.)
Salzgitter AG, IV; 101 (upd.)
Samick Musical Instruments Co., Ltd., 56
Samsonite Corporation, 13; 43 (upd.)
Samuel Cabot Inc., 53
Sandvik AB, 32 (upd.); 77 (upd.)
Sanford L.P., 82
Sanitec Corporation, 51
SANLUIS Corporación, S.A.B. de C.V.,
   95
Sanrio Company, Ltd., 38
SANYO Electric Co., Ltd., II; 36 (upd.);
   95 (upd.)
Sapa AB, 84
Sara Lee Corporation, II; 15 (upd.); 54
   (upd.); 99 (upd.)
Sauder Woodworking Company, 12; 35
   (upd.)
Sauer-Danfoss Inc., 61
Sawtek Inc., 43 (upd.)
Schindler Holding AG, 29
Schlage Lock Company, 82
Schlumberger Limited, III
School-Tech, Inc., 62
Schott Corporation, 53
Scotsman Industries, Inc., 20
Scott Fetzer Company, 12; 80 (upd.)
The Scotts Company, 22
Scovill Fasteners Inc., 24
Sea Ray Boats Inc., 96
SeaChange International, Inc., 79
Sealed Air Corporation, 14; 57 (upd.)

True Temper Sports, Inc., 95
TRUMPF GmbH + Co. KG, 86
TRW Automotive Holdings Corp., 75
(upd.)
Tubos de Acero de Mexico, S.A.
(TAMSA), 41
Tultex Corporation, 13
Tupperware Corporation, 28
TurboChef Technologies, Inc., 83
Turbomeca S.A., 102
Turtle Wax, Inc., 15; 93 (upd.)
TVI Corporation, 99
Twin Disc, Inc., 21
II-VI Incorporated, 69
Ty Inc., 33; 86 (upd.)
Tyco International Ltd., III; 28 (upd.)
Tyco Toys, Inc., 12
U.S. Robotics Corporation, 9; 66 (upd.)
Ube Industries, Ltd., 38 (upd.)
Ultralife Batteries, Inc., 58
ULVAC, Inc., 80
United Defense Industries, Inc., 30; 66
(upd.)
United Dominion Industries Limited, 8;
16 (upd.)
United Industrial Corporation, 37
United States Filter Corporation, 20
United States Pipe and Foundry
Company, 62
Unitika Ltd., 53 (upd.)
Unitog Co., 19
Universal Manufacturing Company, 88
Ushio Inc., 91
Usinas Siderúrgicas de Minas Gerais S.A.,
77
Utah Medical Products, Inc., 36
UTStarcom, Inc., 77
VA TECH ELIN EBG GmbH, 49
Vaillant GmbH, 44
Valley National Gases, Inc., 85
Vallourec SA, 54
Valmet Corporation (Valmet Oy), III
Valmont Industries, Inc., 19
The Valspar Corporation, 8
Vari-Lite International, Inc., 35
Varian, Inc., 48 (upd.)
Variflex, Inc., 51
Varity Corporation, III
Varlen Corporation, 16
Varta AG, 23
Velcro Industries N.V., 19; 72 (upd.)
Velux A/S, 86
Ventana Medical Systems, Inc., 75
Verbatim Corporation, 74 (upd.)
Vermeer Manufacturing Company, 17
Vestas Wind Systems A/S, 73
Viasystems Group, Inc., 67
Vickers plc, 27
Victor Company of Japan, Limited, II; 26
(upd.); 83 (upd.)
Victorinox AG, 21; 74 (upd.)
Videojet Technologies, Inc., 90
Vidrala S.A., 67
Viessmann Werke GmbH & Co., 37
ViewSonic Corporation, 72
Viking Range Corporation, 66
Viking Yacht Company, 96
Villeroy & Boch AG, 37

Virco Manufacturing Corporation, 17
Viscofan S.A., 70
Viskase Companies, Inc., 55
Vita Plus Corporation, 60
Vitro Corporativo S.A. de C.V., 34
voestalpine AG, 57 (upd.)
Vorwerk & Co., 27
Vosper Thornycroft Holding plc, 41
Vossloh AG, 53
VTech Holdings Ltd., 77
W.A. Whitney Company, 53
W.C. Bradley Co., 69
W.H. Brady Co., 17
W.L. Gore & Associates, Inc., 14; 60
(upd.)
W.W. Grainger, Inc., 26 (upd.); 68 (upd.)
Wabash National Corp., 13
Wabtec Corporation, 40
Wacker Construction Equipment AG, 95
Wahl Clipper Corporation, 86
Walbro Corporation, 13
Walter Industries, Inc., 72 (upd.)
Wärtsilä Corporation, 100
Washington Scientific Industries, Inc., 17
Wassall Plc, 18
Waterford Wedgwood plc, 12; 34 (upd.)
Water Pik Technologies, Inc., 34; 83
(upd.)
Waters Corporation, 43
Watts Industries, Inc., 19
Watts of Lydney Group Ltd., 71
WD-40 Company, 18
We-No-Nah Canoe, Inc., 98
Weather Shield Manufacturing, Inc., 102
Webasto Roof Systems Inc., 97
Weber-Stephen Products Co., 40
Weeres Industries Corporation, 52
Weg S.A. 78
The Weir Group PLC, 85
Welbilt Corp., 19
Wellman, Inc., 8; 52 (upd.)
Weru Aktiengesellschaft, 18
West Bend Co., 14
Westell Technologies, Inc., 57
Westerbeke Corporation, 60
Western Digital Corporation, 25; 92
(upd.)
Wheaton Science Products, 60 (upd.)
Wheeling-Pittsburgh Corporation, 58
(upd.)
Whirlpool Corporation, III; 12 (upd.); 59
(upd.)
White Consolidated Industries Inc., 13
Wilbert, Inc., 56
Wilkinson Sword Ltd., 60
William L. Bonnell Company, Inc., 66
William Zinsser & Company, Inc., 58
Williamson-Dickie Manufacturing
Company, 45 (upd.)
Wilson Sporting Goods Company, 24; 84
(upd.)
Wilton Products, Inc., 97
Wincor Nixdorf Holding GmbH, 69
(upd.)
Windmere Corporation, 16
Winegard Company, 56
Winnebago Industries, Inc., 7; 27 (upd.);
96 (upd.)

WinsLoew Furniture, Inc., 21
The Wiremold Company, 81
WMS Industries, Inc., 15; 53 (upd.)
Wolverine Tube Inc., 23
Wood-Mode, Inc., 23
Woodcraft Industries Inc., 61
Woodward Governor Company, 13; 49
(upd.)
Wright Medical Group, Inc., 61
Württembergische Metallwarenfabrik AG
(WMF), 60
Wyant Corporation, 30
Wyman-Gordon Company, 14
Wynn's International, Inc., 33
X-Rite, Inc., 48
Xerox Corporation, III; 6 (upd.); 26
(upd.); 69 (upd.)
Yamaha Corporation, III; 16 (upd.); 40
(upd.); 99 (upd.)
The Yokohama Rubber Company,
Limited, V; 19 (upd.); 91 (upd.)
The York Group, Inc., 50
York International Corp., 13
Young Innovations, Inc., 44
Zapf Creation AG, 95
Zebra Technologies Corporation, 53
(upd.)
ZERO Corporation, 17; 88 (upd.)
ZiLOG, Inc., 72 (upd.)
Zindart Ltd., 60
Zippo Manufacturing Company, 18; 71
(upd.)
Zodiac S.A., 36
Zygo Corporation, 42

Materials

AK Steel Holding Corporation, 19
American Biltrite Inc., 16
American Colloid Co., 13
American Standard Inc., III
Ameriwood Industries International Corp.,
17
Anhui Conch Cement Company Limited,
99
Apasco S.A. de C.V., 51
Apogee Enterprises, Inc., 8
Asahi Glass Company, Limited, III
Asbury Carbons, Inc., 68
Bairnco Corporation, 28
Bayou Steel Corporation, 31
Berry Plastics Group Inc., 21; 98 (upd.)
Blessings Corp., 19
Blue Circle Industries PLC, III
Bodycote International PLC, 63
Boral Limited, III
British Vita PLC, 9
Brush Engineered Materials Inc., 67
Bryce Corporation, 100
California Steel Industries, Inc., 67
Callanan Industries, Inc., 60
Cameron & Barkley Company, 28
Carborundum Company, 15
Carl Zeiss AG, III; 34 (upd.); 91 (upd.)
Carlisle Companies Inc., 8; 82 (upd.)
Carter Holt Harvey Ltd., 70
Cementos Argos S.A., 91
Cemex SA de CV, 20
Century Aluminum Company, 52

Mining & Metals

Paper & Forestry

Personal Services

Petroleum

Real Estate

Retail & Wholesale

Textiles & Apparel

Illinois Central Corporation, 11
International Shipholding Corporation, Inc., 27
J.B. Hunt Transport Services Inc., 12
J Lauritzen A/S, 90
Jack B. Kelley, Inc., 102
John Menzies plc, 39
Kansas City Southern Industries, Inc., 6; 26 (upd.)
The Kansas City Southern Railway Company, 92
Kawasaki Kisen Kaisha, Ltd., V; 56 (upd.)
Keio Corporation, V; 96 (upd.)
Keolis SA, 51
Kinki Nippon Railway Company Ltd., V
Kirby Corporation, 18; 66 (upd.)
Knight Transportation, Inc., 64
Koninklijke Nedlloyd Groep N.V., 6
Kuehne & Nagel International AG, V; 53 (upd.)
La Poste, V; 47 (upd.)
Laidlaw International, Inc., 80
Landstar System, Inc., 63
Leaseway Transportation Corp., 12
Loma Negra C.I.A.S.A., 95
London Regional Transport, 6
The Long Island Rail Road Company, 68
Lynden Incorporated, 91
Maine Central Railroad Company, 16
Mammoet Transport B.V., 26
Marten Transport, Ltd., 84
Martz Group, 56
Mayflower Group Inc., 6
Mercury Air Group, Inc., 20
The Mersey Docks and Harbour Company, 30
Metropolitan Transportation Authority, 35
Miller Industries, Inc., 26
Mitsui O.S.K. Lines Ltd., V; 96 (upd.)
Moran Towing Corporation, Inc., 15
The Morgan Group, Inc., 46
Morris Travel Services L.L.C., 26
Motor Cargo Industries, Inc., 35
National Car Rental System, Inc., 10
National Express Group PLC, 50
National Railroad Passenger Corporation (Amtrak), 22; 66 (upd.)
Neptune Orient Lines Limited, 47
NFC plc, 6
Nippon Express Company, Ltd., V; 64 (upd.)
Nippon Yusen Kabushiki Kaisha (NYK), V; 72 (upd.)
Norfolk Southern Corporation, V; 29 (upd.); 75 (upd.)
Oak Harbor Freight Lines, Inc., 53
Ocean Group plc, 6
Odakyu Electric Railway Co., Ltd., V; 68 (upd.)
Odfjell SE, 101
Odyssey Marine Exploration, Inc., 91
Oglebay Norton Company, 17
Old Dominion Freight Line, Inc., 57
OMI Corporation, 59
The Oppenheimer Group, 76
Oshkosh Corporation, 7; 98 (upd.)
Österreichische Bundesbahnen GmbH, 6
OTR Express, Inc., 25

Overnite Corporation, 14; 58 (upd.)
Overseas Shipholding Group, Inc., 11
Pacer International, Inc., 54
Pacific Basin Shipping Ltd., 86
Patriot Transportation Holding, Inc., 91
The Peninsular and Oriental Steam Navigation Company, V; 38 (upd.)
Penske Corporation, V; 19 (upd.); 84 (upd.)
PHH Arval, V; 53 (upd.)
Pilot Air Freight Corp., 67
Plantation Pipe Line Company, 68
Polar Air Cargo Inc., 60
The Port Authority of New York and New Jersey, 48
Port Imperial Ferry Corporation, 70
Post Office Group, V
Preston Corporation, 6
RailTex, Inc., 20
Railtrack Group PLC, 50
REpower Systems AG, 101
Réseau Ferré de France, 66
Roadway Express, Inc., V; 25 (upd.)
Rock-It Cargo USA, Inc., 86
Royal Olympic Cruise Lines Inc., 52
Royal Vopak NV, 41
Russian Railways Joint Stock Co., 93
Ryder System, Inc., V; 24 (upd.)
Saia, Inc., 98
Santa Fe Pacific Corporation, V
Schenker-Rhenus AG, 6
Schneider National, Inc., 36; 77 (upd.)
Seaboard Corporation, 36; 85 (upd.)
SEACOR Holdings Inc., 83
Securicor Plc, 45
Seibu Railway Company Ltd., V; 74 (upd.)
Seino Transportation Company, Ltd., 6
Simon Transportation Services Inc., 27
Smithway Motor Xpress Corporation, 39
Société Nationale des Chemins de Fer Français, V; 57 (upd.)
Société Norbert Dentressangle S.A., 67
Southern Pacific Transportation Company, V
Spee-Dee Delivery Service, Inc., 93
Stagecoach Holdings plc, 30
Stelmar Shipping Ltd., 52
Stevedoring Services of America Inc., 28
Stinnes AG, 8; 59 (upd.)
Stolt-Nielsen S.A., 42
Sunoco, Inc., 28 (upd.); 83 (upd.)
Swift Transportation Co., Inc., 42
The Swiss Federal Railways (Schweizerische Bundesbahnen), V
Swissport International Ltd., 70
Teekay Shipping Corporation, 25; 82 (upd.)
Tibbett & Britten Group plc, 32
Tidewater Inc., 11; 37 (upd.)
TNT Freightways Corporation, 14
TNT Post Group N.V., V; 27 (upd.); 30 (upd.)
Tobu Railway Company Ltd., 6; 98 (upd.)
Tokyu Corporation, V
Totem Resources Corporation, 9
TPG N.V., 64 (upd.)

Trailer Bridge, Inc., 41
Transnet Ltd., 6
Transport Corporation of America, Inc., 49
Trico Marine Services, Inc., 89
Tsakos Energy Navigation Ltd., 91
TTX Company, 6; 66 (upd.)
U.S. Delivery Systems, Inc., 22
Union Pacific Corporation, V; 28 (upd.); 79 (upd.)
United Parcel Service of America Inc., V; 17 (upd.)
United Parcel Service, Inc., 63
United Road Services, Inc., 69
United States Postal Service, 14; 34 (upd.)
US 1 Industries, Inc., 89
USA Truck, Inc., 42
Velocity Express Corporation, 49
Werner Enterprises, Inc., 26
Wheels Inc., 96
Wincanton plc, 52
Wisconsin Central Transportation Corporation, 24
Wright Express Corporation, 80
Yamato Transport Co. Ltd., V; 49 (upd.)
Yellow Corporation, 14; 45 (upd.)
Yellow Freight System, Inc. of Delaware, V
YRC Worldwide Inc., 90 (upd.)

Utilities

AES Corporation, 10; 13 (upd.); 53 (upd.)
Aggreko Plc, 45
Air & Water Technologies Corporation, 6
Alberta Energy Company Ltd., 16; 43 (upd.)
Allegheny Energy, Inc., V; 38 (upd.)
Ameren Corporation, 60 (upd.)
American Electric Power Company, Inc., V; 45 (upd.)
American States Water Company, 46
American Water Works Company, Inc., 6; 38 (upd.)
Aquarion Company, 84
Aquila, Inc., 50 (upd.)
Arkla, Inc., V
Associated Natural Gas Corporation, 11
Atlanta Gas Light Company, 6; 23 (upd.)
Atlantic Energy, Inc., 6
Atmos Energy Corporation, 43
Avista Corporation, 69 (upd.)
Baltimore Gas and Electric Company, V; 25 (upd.)
Bay State Gas Company, 38
Bayernwerk AG, V; 23 (upd.)
Berlinwasser Holding AG, 90
Bewag AG, 39
Big Rivers Electric Corporation, 11
Black Hills Corporation, 20
Bonneville Power Administration, 50
Boston Edison Company, 12
Bouygues S.A., I; 24 (upd.); 97 (upd.)
British Energy Plc, 49
British Gas plc, V
British Nuclear Fuels plc, 6
Brooklyn Union Gas, 6
California Water Service Group, 79

Waste Services

Geographic Index

Ghana

Greece

Jamaica

Japan

United States

National Audubon Society, 26
National Auto Credit, Inc., 16
The National Bank of South Carolina, 76
National Beverage Corporation, 26; 88
  (upd.)
National Broadcasting Company, Inc., II;
  6 (upd.); 28 (upd.)
National Can Corporation, I
National Car Rental System, Inc., 10
National City Corporation, 15; 97 (upd.)
National Collegiate Athletic Association,
  96
National Convenience Stores
  Incorporated, 7
National Discount Brokers Group, Inc.,
  28
National Distillers and Chemical
  Corporation, I
National Educational Music Co. Ltd., 47
National Envelope Corporation, 32
National Equipment Services, Inc., 57
National Financial Partners Corp., 65
National Football League, 29
National Frozen Foods Corporation, 94
National Fuel Gas Company, 6; 95 (upd.)
National Geographic Society, 9; 30 (upd.);
  79 (upd.)
National Grape Cooperative Association,
  Inc., 20
National Grid USA, 51 (upd.)
National Gypsum Company, 10
National Health Laboratories
  Incorporated, 11
National Heritage Academies, Inc., 60
National Hockey League, 35
National Home Centers, Inc., 44
National Instruments Corporation, 22
National Intergroup, Inc., V
National Jewish Health, 101
National Journal Group Inc., 67
National Media Corporation, 27
National Medical Enterprises, Inc., III
National Medical Health Card Systems,
  Inc. 79
National Oilwell, Inc., 54
National Organization for Women, Inc.,
  55
National Patent Development
  Corporation, 13
National Picture & Frame Company, 24
National Presto Industries, Inc., 16; 43
  (upd.)
National Public Radio, Inc., 19; 47 (upd.)
National R.V. Holdings, Inc., 32
National Railroad Passenger Corporation
  (Amtrak), 22; 66 (upd.)
National Record Mart, Inc., 29
National Research Corporation, 87
National Rifle Association of America, 37
National Sanitary Supply Co., 16
National Semiconductor Corporation, II;
  VI, 26 (upd.); 69 (upd.)
National Service Industries, Inc., 11; 54
  (upd.)
National Standard Co., 13
National Starch and Chemical Company,
  49
National Steel Corporation, 12

National TechTeam, Inc., 41
National Thoroughbred Racing
  Association, 58
National Weather Service, 91
National Wine & Spirits, Inc., 49
NationsBank Corporation, 10
Natrol, Inc., 49
Natural Alternatives International, Inc., 49
Natural Ovens Bakery, Inc., 72
Natural Selection Foods, 54
Natural Wonders Inc., 14
Naturally Fresh, Inc., 88
The Nature Conservancy, 28
Nature's Sunshine Products, Inc., 15; 102
  (upd.)
Naumes, Inc., 81
Nautica Enterprises, Inc., 18; 44 (upd.)
Navarre Corporation, 24
Navigant Consulting, Inc., 93
Navigant International, Inc., 47
The Navigators Group, Inc., 92
Navistar International Corporation, I; 10
  (upd.)
NAVTEQ Corporation, 69
Navy Exchange Service Command, 31
Navy Federal Credit Union, 33
NBD Bancorp, Inc., 11
NBGS International, Inc., 73
NBTY, Inc., 31
NCH Corporation, 8
NCI Building Systems, Inc., 88
NCL Corporation 79
NCNB Corporation, II
NCO Group, Inc., 42
NCR Corporation, III; 6 (upd.); 30
  (upd.); 90 (upd.)
Nebraska Book Company, Inc., 65
Nebraska Furniture Mart, Inc., 94
Nebraska Public Power District, 29
Neenah Foundry Company, 68
Neff Corp., 32
NeighborCare, Inc., 67 (upd.)
The Neiman Marcus Group, Inc., 12; 49
  (upd.)
Nektar Therapeutics, 91
Neogen Corporation, 94
NERCO, Inc., 7
NetCracker Technology Corporation, 98
Netezza Corporation, 69
Netflix, Inc., 58
NETGEAR, Inc., 81
NetIQ Corporation 79
NetJets Inc., 96 (upd.)
Netscape Communications Corporation,
  15; 35 (upd.)
Network Appliance, Inc., 58
Network Associates, Inc., 25
Network Equipment Technologies Inc., 92
The Newark Group, Inc., 102
Neuberger Berman Inc., 57
NeuStar, Inc., 81
Neutrogena Corporation, 17
Nevada Bell Telephone Company, 14
Nevada Power Company, 11
Nevamar Company, 82
New Balance Athletic Shoe, Inc., 25; 68
  (upd.)
New Belgium Brewing Company, Inc., 68

New Brunswick Scientific Co., Inc., 45
New Chapter Inc., 96
New Dana Perfumes Company, 37
New England Business Service Inc., 18;
  78 (upd.)
New England Confectionery Co., 15
New England Electric System, V
New England Mutual Life Insurance
  Company, III
New Jersey Devils, 84
New Jersey Manufacturers Insurance
  Company, 96
New Jersey Resources Corporation, 54
New Line Cinema, Inc., 47
New Orleans Saints LP, 58
The New Piper Aircraft, Inc., 44
New Plan Realty Trust, 11
New Seasons Market, 75
New Street Capital Inc., 8
New Times, Inc., 45
New Valley Corporation, 17
New World Pasta Company, 53
New World Restaurant Group, Inc., 44
New York City Health and Hospitals
  Corporation, 60
New York City Off-Track Betting
  Corporation, 51
New York Community Bancorp Inc. 78
New York Daily News, 32
New York Health Care, Inc., 72
New York Life Insurance Company, III;
  45 (upd.)
New York Restaurant Group, Inc., 32
New York Shakespeare Festival
  Management, 93
New York State Electric and Gas, 6
New York Stock Exchange, Inc., 9; 39
  (upd.)
The New York Times Company, IV; 19
  (upd.); 61 (upd.)
Neways Inc. 78
Newcor, Inc., 40
Newell Rubbermaid Inc., 9; 52 (upd.)
Newfield Exploration Company, 65
Newhall Land and Farming Company, 14
Newly Weds Foods, Inc., 74
Newman's Own, Inc., 37
Newmont Mining Corporation, 7; 94
  (upd.)
Newpark Resources, Inc., 63
Newport Corporation, 71
Newport News Shipbuilding Inc., 13; 38
  (upd.)
News America Publishing Inc., 12
NewYork-Presbyterian Hospital, 59
Nexstar Broadcasting Group, Inc., 73
Nextel Communications, Inc., 10; 27
  (upd.)
NFL Films, 75
NFO Worldwide, Inc., 24
NGC Corporation, 18
Niagara Corporation, 28
Niagara Mohawk Holdings Inc., V; 45
  (upd.)
Nichols Research Corporation, 18
Nicklaus Companies, 45
Nicole Miller, 98
Nicor Inc., 6; 86 (upd.)

Value Line, Inc., 16; 73 (upd.)
Value Merchants Inc., 13
ValueClick, Inc., 49
ValueVision International, Inc., 22
Valve Corporation, 101
Van Camp Seafood Company, Inc., 7
Van's Aircraft, Inc., 65
Vance Publishing Corporation, 64
Vanderbilt University Medical Center, 99
The Vanguard Group, Inc., 14; 34 (upd.)
Vanguard Health Systems Inc., 70
Vans, Inc., 16; 47 (upd.)
Varco International, Inc., 42
Vari-Lite International, Inc., 35
Varian, Inc., 12; 48 (upd.)
Variety Wholesalers, Inc., 73
Variflex, Inc., 51
Varlen Corporation, 16
Varsity Spirit Corp., 15
VASCO Data Security International, Inc.
  79
Vastar Resources, Inc., 24
VCA Antech, Inc., 58
VECO International, Inc., 7
Vector Group Ltd., 35 (upd.)
Vectren Corporation, 98 (upd.)
Veeco Instruments Inc., 32
Veit Companies, 43; 92 (upd.)
Velocity Express Corporation, 49; 94
  (upd.)
Venator Group Inc., 35 (upd.)
Vencor, Inc., 16
Venetian Casino Resort, LLC, 47
Ventana Medical Systems, Inc., 75
Ventura Foods LLC, 90
Venture Stores Inc., 12
VeraSun Energy Corporation, 87
Verbatim Corporation, 14; 74 (upd.)
Veridian Corporation, 54
VeriFone Holdings, Inc., 18; 76 (upd.)
Verint Systems Inc., 73
VeriSign, Inc., 47
Veritas Software Corporation, 45
Verity Inc., 68
Verizon Communications, 43 (upd.); 78
  (upd.)
Vermeer Manufacturing Company, 17
The Vermont Country Store, 93
Vermont Pure Holdings, Ltd., 51
The Vermont Teddy Bear Co., Inc., 36
Vertex Pharmaceuticals Incorporated, 83
Vertis Communications, 84
Vertrue Inc., 77
VF Corporation, V; 17 (upd.); 54 (upd.)
VHA Inc., 53
Viacom Inc., 7; 23 (upd.); 67 (upd.)
Viad Corp., 73
ViaSat, Inc., 54
Viasoft Inc., 27
VIASYS Healthcare, Inc., 52
Viasystems Group, Inc., 67
Viatech Continental Can Company, Inc.,
  25 (upd.)
Vicon Industries, Inc., 44
VICORP Restaurants, Inc., 12; 48 (upd.)
Victory Refrigeration, Inc., 82
Videojet Technologies, Inc., 90
Vienna Sausage Manufacturing Co., 14

Viewpoint International, Inc., 66
ViewSonic Corporation, 72
Viking Office Products, Inc., 10
Viking Range Corporation, 66
Viking Yacht Company, 96
Village Super Market, Inc., 7
Village Voice Media, Inc., 38
Vinson & Elkins L.L.P., 30
Vintage Petroleum, Inc., 42
Vinton Studios, 63
Virbac Corporation, 74
Virco Manufacturing Corporation, 17
Virginia Dare Extract Company, Inc., 94
Visa International, 9; 26 (upd.)
Vishay Intertechnology, Inc., 21; 80
  (upd.)
Vision Service Plan Inc., 77
Viskase Companies, Inc., 55
Vista Bakery, Inc., 56
Vista Chemical Company, I
Vistana, Inc., 22
VISX, Incorporated, 30
Vita Food Products Inc., 99
Vita Plus Corporation, 60
Vital Images, Inc., 85
Vitalink Pharmacy Services, Inc., 15
Vitamin Shoppe Industries, Inc., 60
Vitesse Semiconductor Corporation, 32
Vitro Corp., 10
Vivra, Inc., 18
Vizio, Inc., 100
Vlasic Foods International Inc., 25
VLSI Technology, Inc., 16
VMware, Inc., 90
Volcom, Inc., 77
Volkert and Associates, Inc., 98
Volt Information Sciences Inc., 26
Volunteers of America, Inc., 66
Von Maur Inc., 64
Vonage Holdings Corp., 81
The Vons Companies, Incorporated, 7; 28
  (upd.)
Vornado Realty Trust, 20
Vought Aircraft Industries, Inc., 49
Vulcan Materials Company, 7; 52 (upd.)
W. Atlee Burpee & Co., 27
W.A. Whitney Company, 53
W.B Doner & Co., 56
W.B. Mason Company, 98
W.C. Bradley Co., 69
W. H. Braum, Inc., 80
W.H. Brady Co., 17
W.L. Gore & Associates, Inc., 14; 60
  (upd.)
W.P. Carey & Co. LLC, 49
W.R. Berkley Corporation, 15; 74 (upd.)
W.R. Grace & Company, I; 50 (upd.)
W.W. Grainger, Inc., V; 26 (upd.); 68
  (upd.)
W.W. Norton & Company, Inc., 28
Waban Inc., 13
Wabash National Corp., 13
Wabtec Corporation, 40
Wachovia Bank of Georgia, N.A., 16
Wachovia Bank of South Carolina, N.A.,
  16
Wachovia Corporation, 12; 46 (upd.)
Wachtell, Lipton, Rosen & Katz, 47

The Wackenhut Corporation, 14; 63
  (upd.)
Waddell & Reed, Inc., 22
Waffle House Inc., 14; 60 (upd.)
Wagers Inc. (Idaho Candy Company), 86
Waggener Edstrom, 42
Wah Chang, 82
Wahl Clipper Corporation, 86
Wahoo's Fish Taco, 96
Wakefern Food Corporation, 33
Wal-Mart Stores, Inc., V; 8 (upd.); 26
  (upd.); 63 (upd.)
Walbridge Aldinger Co., 38
Walbro Corporation, 13
Waldbaum, Inc., 19
Waldenbooks, 17; 86 (upd.)
Walgreen Co., V; 20 (upd.); 65 (upd.)
Walker Manufacturing Company, 19
Wall Drug Store, Inc., 40
Wall Street Deli, Inc., 33
Wallace Computer Services, Inc., 36
Walsworth Publishing Co. 78
The Walt Disney Company, II; 6 (upd.);
  30 (upd.); 63 (upd.)
Walter Industries, Inc., II; 22 (upd.); 72
  (upd.)
Walton Monroe Mills, Inc., 8
Wang Laboratories, Inc., III; 6 (upd.)
The Warnaco Group Inc., 12; 46 (upd.)
Warner Communications Inc., II
Warner Music Group Corporation, 90
  (upd.)
Warner-Lambert Co., I; 10 (upd.)
Warners' Stellian Inc., 67
Warrantech Corporation, 53
Warrell Corporation, 68
Warwick Valley Telephone Company, 55
The Washington Companies, 33
Washington Federal, Inc., 17
Washington Football, Inc., 35
Washington Gas Light Company, 19
Washington Mutual, Inc., 17; 93 (upd.)
Washington National Corporation, 12
Washington Natural Gas Company, 9
The Washington Post Company, IV; 20
  (upd.)
Washington Scientific Industries, Inc., 17
Washington Water Power Company, 6
Waste Connections, Inc., 46
Waste Holdings, Inc., 41
Waste Management, Inc., V
Water Pik Technologies, Inc., 34; 83
  (upd.)
Waterhouse Investor Services, Inc., 18
Waters Corporation, 43
Watkins-Johnson Company, 15
Watsco Inc., 52
Watson Pharmaceuticals Inc., 16; 56
  (upd.)
Watson Wyatt Worldwide, 42
Watts Industries, Inc., 19
Wausau-Mosinee Paper Corporation, 60
  (upd.)
Waverly, Inc., 16
Wawa Inc., 17; 78 (upd.)
WAXIE Sanitary Supply, 100
Waxman Industries, Inc., 9
WD-40 Company, 18; 87 (upd.)